January 31 – February 4, 2015
Austin, TX, USA

**Association for
Computing Machinery**

Advancing Computing as a Science & Profession

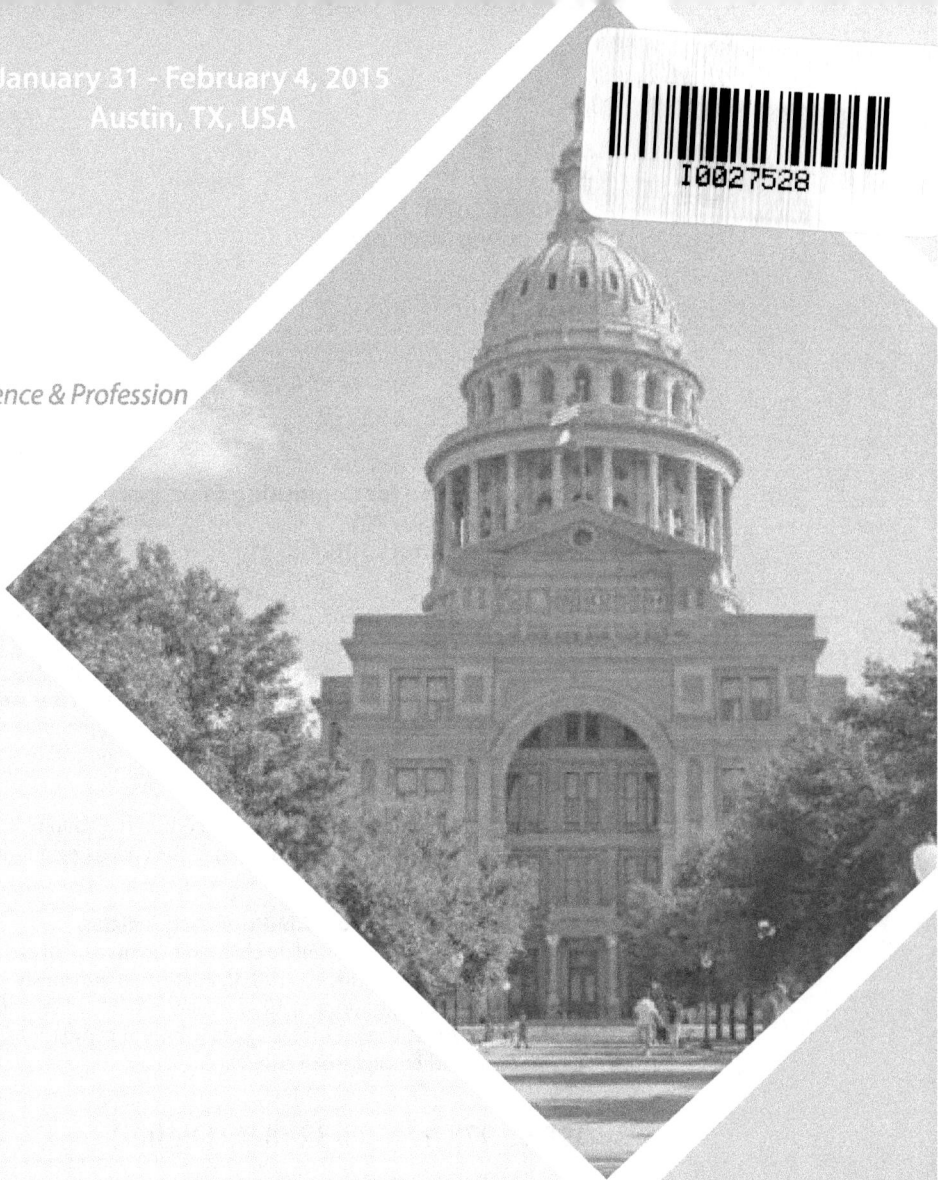

ICPE'15

Proceedings of the 6th ACM/SPEC International Conference on
Performance Engineering

Sponsored by:
ACM SIGSOFT, ACM SIGMETRICS and SPEC

Supported by:
Oracle Labs

**Association for
Computing Machinery**

Advancing Computing as a Science & Profession

The Association for Computing Machinery
2 Penn Plaza, Suite 701
New York, New York 10121-0701

Notice to Past Authors of ACM-Published Articles

ISBN: 978-1-4503-3248-4 (Digital)

ISBN: 978-1-4503-3508-9 (Print)

Additional copies may be ordered prepaid from:

ACM Order Department
PO Box 30777
New York, NY 10087-0777, USA

Phone: 1-800-342-6626 (USA and Canada)
+1-212-626-0500 (Global)
Fax: +1-212-944-1318
E-mail: acmhelp@acm.org
Hours of Operation: 8:30 am – 4:30 pm ET

Printed in the USA

Letter from the General Chairs

Dear Conference Participants:

It is our pleasure to welcome you to Austin and to the Joint ACM/SPEC International Conference on Performance Engineering, ICPE 2015. ICPE is a merger of ACM's Workshop on Software and Performance (WOSP) and SPEC's International Performance Evaluation Workshop (SIPEW).

The focus of WOSP is in the intersection of software and performance, rather than one discipline in isolation. Since its inception in 1998, WOSP has brought together software engineers, developers, performance analysts and software performance engineers who are addressing the challenges of increasing system complexity, rapidly evolving software technologies, short time to market, incomplete documentation, and less-than-adequate methods, models and tools for developing, modeling, and measuring scalable, high-performance software.

SIPEW, which is part of the SPEC Benchmark Workshop Series, was established by the Standard Performance Evaluation Corporation (SPEC) with the goal to bridge the gap between theory and practice in the field of system performance evaluation, by offering a forum for sharing ideas and experiences between industry and academia. The workshop provides a platform for researchers and industry practitioners to share and present their experiences, discuss challenges, and report state-of-the-art and in-progress research in all aspects of performance evaluation including both hardware and software issues.

The ACM/SPEC International Conference on Performance Engineering (ICPE) brings together the WOSP and SIPEW communities building on their common interests and complementary nature. ACM's membership consists of individuals from academia, industry, and government worldwide. SPEC's membership consists of industrial organizations, universities and research institutes. We are continuing to bridge the two communities to build on each other's experience, energy, and expertise.

This year we have continued the tracks that have worked well in the past: the research track, an explicit industrial applications and experience track with a separate program committee, a work-in-progress and vision track, and demos and posters. We have also expanded the pre-conference Workshops and Tutorials.

Overall, 56 submissions were received in the main research and industrial tracks and there were over 116 submissions in all the tracks. The accepted papers cover a range of different topics in performance engineering with a good balance between theoretical and practical contributions from both industry and academia.

We would like to thank Catalina Lladó, Kai Sachs, and Herb Schwetman for chairing the research and industrial program committees; William Knottenbelt and Yaomin Chen for the demos and posters; Catia Trubiani for the tutorials; Marin Litoiu and J. Nelson Amaral for the workshops; and Zhibin Yu for trying to organize a new Ph.D. Workshop. We are grateful to these chairs and the many reviewers for putting together an excellent conference program. We would also like to thank all the other Chairs for their excellent assistance in organizing all the other aspects of the conference: Simona Bernardi - publications, Anoush Najarian - finance, Amy Spellmann and Andre van Hoorn - publicity and web site management, Ram Krishnan - registration, Andre Bondi and Paul Gratz - awards, and Nasr Ullah - local organization. Everyone brought a level of excellency and commitment to their job. We appreciate their hard work and commitment to making ICPE a success. Thanks also to Dianne Rice from SPEC for providing administrative support, as well as to Diana Brantuas, April Mosqus, Stephanie Sabal, Adrienne Griscti and others at ACM Headquarters for their continuous support. Special thanks also to Lisa Tolles from the Sheridan Proceedings Service for processing the papers in a timely manner. Finally, we would like to acknowledge the support and guidance of the ICPE Steering Committee.

Last but not least, we thank our sponsors SPEC, ACM SIGMETRICS and ACM SIGSOFT, and our generous corporate supporter Oracle.

On behalf of the organizing committee, we welcome you to Austin. Thank you for joining us and we look forward to a mutually rewarding experience.

Lizy K. John
ICPE 2015 General Co-Chair (SPEC)
UT Austin, USA

Connie U. Smith
ICPE 2015 General Co-Chair (ACM)
L&S Computer Technology, Inc., USA

Program Chairs' Welcome

This year is the 6th International Conference on Performance Engineering - ICPE'15, which grew out of the ACM Workshop on Software Performance (WOSP since 1998) and the SPEC International Performance Engineering Workshop (SIPEW since 2008), taking place in Austin. It is a great pleasure for us to offer an outstanding technical program, which we believe is reflecting the idea behind the ICPE - integrating theory and practice in the field of performance engineering.

Overall, we received 116 submissions across all tracks. The main research track attracted 56 submissions, each paper was reviewed by at least four reviewers and we finally accepted 15 high-quality submissions as full papers and three as short papers. The Industry and Experience Track received 18 submissions, of which 7 were selected for inclusion in the program. Further, the program committee selected 9 submissions for the Vision/Work-in-Progress track. Six tutorials and a poster & demo exhibition are completing the program. As in previous years, we decided to group the submissions according their topics, not the track they were submitted to. We believe that the exchange between industry and academia is fostered by presenting research and industry submissions together in the same session.

The program covers all traditional ICPE topics such as software performance engineering and benchmarking with a good balance between theoretical and practical contributions. Additionally, we saw an increasing number of submissions discussing how to apply performance engineering techniques in the context of big data, cloud and Internet of things. We are very proud to have two excellent keynote speakers as part of our program:

- Todd Austin, from University of Michingan, USA, talking about *Bridging the Moore's Law Performance Gap with Innovation Scaling*

and

- Adrian Cockcroft, from Battery Ventures, USA, talking about *Cloud Native Cost Optimization*.

There are three co-located workshops extending the program – the 4th International Workshop on Large-Scale Testing (LT 2015), the 1st Workshop on Performance Analysis of Big data Systems (PABS) and the 1st Workshop on Challenges in Performance Methods for Software Development (WOSP-C 2015).

We are confident that the program will provide you with many new ideas and encourage the discussion and exchange between the participants.

Kai Sachs
ICPE 2015 Program Co-Chair
SAP SE, Germany

Catalina M. Lladó
ICPE 2015 Program Co-Chair
University of the Balearic Islands, Spain

Herb Schwetman
ICPE 2015 Industrial Chair
Oracle Labs, USA

Table of Contents

Session: Performance and Power

Session: Web Performance

Session: Benchmarks and Empirical Studies - Workloads, Scenarios and Implementations

Session: Performance Modelling and Prediction II

Session: Tutorials

Workshop Summaries

Author Index

ICPE 2015 Conference Organization

General Chairs: Lizy K. John *(UT Austin, USA)*
Connie U. Smith *(L&S Computer Technology, Inc., USA)*

Program Chairs: Kai Sachs *(SAP SE, Germany)*
Catalina M. Lladó *(University of the Balearic Islands, Spain)*

Industrial Chair: Herb Schwetman *(Oracle Labs, USA)*

Tutorial Chair: Catia Trubiani *(Gran Sasso Science Institute, Italy)*

Demos and Posters Chairs: William Knottenbelt *(Imperial College, UK)*
Yao-Min Chen *(Oracle, USA)*

PhD Workshop Chair: Zhibin Yu *(Chinese Academy of Sciences, China)*

Workshop Chairs: J. Nelson Amaral *(University of Alberta, Canada)*
Marin Litoiu *(York University, Canada)*

Publication Chair: Simona Bernardi *(Centro Universitario de la Defensa, AGM, Spain)*

Finance Chair: Anoush Najarian *(Mathworks, USA)*

Publicity Chairs: Amy Spellmann *(The 451 Group, USA)*
Andre van Hoorn *(University of Stuttgart, Germany)*

Registration Chair: Ram Krishnan *(University of Texas at San Antonio, USA)*

Award Chairs: Andre B. Bondi *(Siemens Corporate Research, USA)*
Paul V. Gratz *(Texas A&M University, USA)*

Local Organization Chair: Nasr Ullah *(Samsung, USA)*

Web Chair: Andre van Hoorn *(University of Stuttgart, Germany)*

Steering Committee Chairs: Andre B. Bondi *(Siemens Corporate Research, USA)*
Samuel Kounev *(University of Würzburg, Germany)*

Steering Committee: J. Nelson Amaral *(University of Alberta, Canada)*
Vittorio Cortellessa *(Università di L'Aquila, Italy)*
Klaus-Dieter Lange *(Hewlett-Packard Company, USA)*
Raffaela Mirandola *(Politecnico di Milano, Italy)*
Meikel Poess *(Oracle Corporation, USA)*
Jerry Rolia *(HP Labs, UK)*
Kai Sachs *(SAP SE, Germany)*
Bran Selic *(ObjecTime Limited, Canada)*

ICPE 2015 Sponsor & Supporters

Sponsors:

SIG**S**OFT
SPECIAL INTEREST GROUP ON   SOFTWARE ENGINEERING

ACM SIGMETRICS
special interest group on performance evaluation

spec
Research

Corporate Support: Oracle Labs

Bridging the Moore's Law Performance Gap with Innovation Scaling

[Keynote Talk]

Todd Austin
University of Michigan
2260 Hayward Avenue
Ann Arbor (USA)
austin@umich.edu

ABSTRACT

The end of Dennard scaling and the tyranny of Ahmdal's law have created significant barriers to system scaling, leading to a gap between today's system performance and where Moore's law predicted it should be.

I believe the solution to this problem is to scale innovation. Finding better solutions to improve system performance and efficiency, and doing this more quickly than previously possible could address the growing performance gap.

In this talk, I will highlight a number of simple (and not so simple) ideas to address this challenge.

Categories and Subject Descriptors

B.8 [**Performance and Reliability**]: Miscellaneous; C.1 [**Processor Architectures**]: General; C.4 [**Performance of Systems**]: Performance attributes

General Terms

Computer Architecture, Performance

Keywords

System Performance, System Efficiency, System Scaling

Short Bio

Todd Austin is a Professor of Electrical Engineering and Computer Science at the University of Michigan in Ann Arbor.

His research interests include computer architecture, robust and secure system design, hardware and software verification, and performance analysis tools and techniques.

Currently Todd is director of C-FAR, the Center for Future Architectures Research, a multi-university SRC/ DARPA funded center that is seeking technologies to scale the performance and efficiency of future computing systems.

Prior to joining academia, Todd was a Senior Computer Architect in Intel's Microcomputer Research Labs, a product-oriented research laboratory in Hillsboro, Oregon. Todd is the first to take credit (but the last to accept blame) for creating the SimpleScalar Tool Set, a popular collection of computer architecture performance analysis tools. Todd is co-author (with Andrew Tanenbaum) of the undergraduate computer architecture textbook, "Structured Computer Architecture, 6th Ed".

In addition to his work in academia, Todd is founder and President of SimpleScalar LLC and co-founder of InTempo Design LLC. In 2002, Todd was a Sloan Research Fellow, and in 2007 he received the ACM Maurice Wilkes Award for "innovative contributions in Computer Architecture including the SimpleScalar Toolkit and the DIVA and Razor architectures". Todd received his PhD in Computer Science from the University of Wisconsin in 1996.

ICPE'15, Jan. 31–Feb. 4, 2015, Austin, Texas, USA.
ACM 978-1-4503-3248-4/15/01.
http://dx.doi.org/10.1145/2668930.2693196 .

Reducing Task Completion Time in Mobile Offloading Systems through Online Adaptive Local Restart

Qiushi Wang
Department of Mathematics and Computer Science
Freie Universität Berlin
Takustr.9, Berlin, Germany
qiushi.wang@fu-berlin.de

Katinka Wolter
Department of Mathematics and Computer Science
Freie Universität Berlin
Takustr.9, Berlin, Germany
katinka.wolter@fu-berlin.de

ABSTRACT

Offloading is an advanced technique to improve the performance of mobile devices. In a mobile offloading system, heavy computations are migrated from resource constrained mobile devices to powerful cloud servers through a wireless network connection. The unreliable wireless network often disturbs system operation. Task completion can be delayed or interrupted by congestion or packet loss in the network. To deal with this problem the offloaded jobs can be locally restarted and completed in the mobile device itself.

In this paper, we propose a dynamic scheme to determine whether and when to locally restart a task. First, we design an experiment to explore the impact of packet loss and delay in unreliable networks on the completion time of an offloading task. Then, we mathematically derive the prerequisites for local restart and selection of the optimal timeout. The analysis result confirms that local restart is beneficial when the distribution of task completion time has high variance. Further, a dynamic local restart scheme is proposed for mobile applications. This scheme keeps track of the variance of the probability density function of the distribution of task completion time. This is done using a dynamic histogram, which collects and updates data at run time. The efficiency of the local restart scheme is confirmed by experimental results. The experiment shows that local restart at the right time achieves better performance than always offloading.

Categories and Subject Descriptors

C.4 [**Performance of Systems**]: Fault tolerance; D.2.8 [**Software Engineering**]: Metrics—*performance measures*

General Terms

Performance, Reliability

Keywords

Mobile Offloading; Restart; Unreliable Network; Dynamic Histogram

1. INTRODUCTION

In recent years, a large number of applications have been developed for mobile devices. Obviously, many of these colourful applications have added convenience to our lives. For example, tourists will never worry about getting lost in an unfamiliar city, various navigation applications can provide the precise route information about any destination a tourist may want to visit. However, although the invention of more advanced mobile devices has improved their computational capability, the implementation of compute intensive applications is still limited by the constraint of the mobile device hardware, for example the long time operation of microchips cannot be sustained by low capacity batteries. Moreover, this constraint is not merely a temporary technological deficiency but is intrinsic to mobility [32]. The trend in development of mobile device architectures and batteries shows the difficulty to overcome this constraint in the near future. Therefore, the concept of offloading to the Cloud is employed to handle performance problems [14]. By migrating heavy computation to resourceful cloud servers, mobile devices can overcome the limitation of deficient resources. Repeated offloading can be necessary in image recognition, where an image search can be split into several section, that need repeated offloading. Another scenario where offloading can be applied is online game, for instance, playing chess with a computer opponent who is in Cloud.

The smooth offloading of computation from mobile devices to cloud servers depends on a fast and stable network connection, which guarantees seamless communication. With wireless networks such as WiFi, 3G or LTE, this seems in principle possible. Unfortunately, the quality of a network is not constant across space and time. Consequently, the execution of the offloading task may suffer from long delays or even failures in the network. In addition, using wireless connectivity demands high energy[6]. The limited battery capacity cannot support the mobile device to wait an unpredictable time for the network to recover, which may take very long.

As introduced in [44], if the offloading task needs an unknown time to migrate computation through the unreliable network connection, re-executing and completing the computations locally by the mobile device can save both time and energy. This re-execution mechanism is a type of restart. When the offloading task fails, the mobile device may retry offloading or restart the task using the resources in the local mobile device instead of those in the Cloud. In this paper we only consider local execution after a restart. The key problem behind restart is when to launch it. There clearly exists a tradeoff between the cost of local or remote retry and waiting for the offloading to succeed. In [44], a static method is proposed to find the optimal timeout when to restart locally by analysing the system performance using stochastic models. It has been shown through simulation that the optimal timeout changes when the quality of the network deteriorates. In this paper we confirm those previous simulation results by analysing experimental data and dynamically adapt the optimal restart time at run time in order to account for the variation of the network quality.

We have to solve several problems: First, the quality of the network must be assessed, second, the variation of the network quality must be monitored based on which then an estimate of the optimal restart timeout is computed. We assume that the system performance is positively correlated with the network quality, and use the task completion time as a metric to evaluate system performance. Although the energy consumption is also very important to evaluate performance, as introduced in [6, 11, 26], we are not able to easily determine energy usage and fall back to task completion time. We state that for our purposes there is a sufficiently strong correlation between energy consumption and task run time. To monitor the variation in network quality we dynamically build a histogram of the task completion time which provides a good and timely estimate of its distribution. We propose a method to periodically update the histogram.

The main contributions of this paper are 1) we experimentally confirm the impact of network quality on mobile offloading decisions, 2) we mathematically derive conditions for applying local restart and the optimal timeout based on a greedy method, and 3) we propose a dynamic online scheme to determine whether and when to launch a local restart.

The remainder of this paper is organized as follows: In Section 2 we briefly recapitulate the background on related concepts of mobile offloading, the restart algorithm and dynamic histogram generation. In Section 3 we introduce an experiment to study the impact of packet loss and delay on the task completion time. The experimental results confirm the need for local restart. Next, in Section 4 we describe the mathematical derivation of a condition which is used to determine whether and when to launch a local restart. The dynamic local restart scheme itself is introduced in Section 5. Its efficiency is illustrated using experiments. Finally, conclusions are in Section 6.

2. BACKGROUND AND RELATED WORK

Mobile offloading as a concept has been around for more than a decade. Thin clients using a remote infrastructure for compute-intensive tasks have already been seen as a method for addressing the challenges of distribution and mobility as in pervasive computing [33]. Powerful distributed systems as in Cloud computing aim at turning computing as utility into reality [8]. Recently, mobile offloading has been developed as to merge Cloud computing and mobile computing. Research in offloading methods can be divided into three main directions [14]: client-server communication, virtual machine migration and mobile agents.

We will now discuss related work in all three areas.

1. Client-server communication: communication can be supported by pre-installation of the application in both the mobile client and the server. In this case one can benefit from existing stable protocols for process communication between mobile and surrogate devices. This is the basis for the systems in [15, 4, 23, 19, 12, 20].

2. Virtual machine migration: offloading can be implemented as the migration of the complete virtual machine executing the application. The most fascinating property of this method is that no code is changed for offloading of a program. The memory image of a mobile client is copied and transferred to the destination server without interrupting or stopping any execution on the client. Although this method has clear advantages as it avoids having two versions of a program, it requires a high volume of transferred data [7, 11, 18, 34].

3. Mobile agents: Scavenger [21] introduces a framework that partitions and distributes heavy jobs to mobile surrogates in the vicinity rather than to cloud servers. Offloading to more than one surrogate is the merit of this framework.

Few of the above approaches tackle the problem of when to offload and which communication partner to choose. In [2] the authors design a Markov decision process to find the optimal aging control policies, which decide when to connect to the server and which network link to use.

All offloading systems mentioned so far may suffer under poor network condition and the application of well-designed fault-tolerance methods is in place. Restart is a simple and popular recovery scheme to mitigate network failures. It can be very effective for certain types of failures and its performance has been widely studied. Markov chain models and Laplace transforms have been developed to analyse the performance of restart for improving the expected task completion time [3, 27, 35, 22, 5]. These analyses strongly support the efficiency of restart if the best restart timeout is known. Their implementation in an online algorithm for practical application is not straight forward. A fast method based on iteration theory to identify the optimal restart time is presented in [25]. The algorithm is improved in [41, 40, 42]. It is tailored for Internet applications in [30].

The restart algorithm mentioned above relies on the probability density function *pdf* of the task completion time. In pratice, a density function is approximated by the corresponding histogram. Since the distribution of the completion time in a real-time system keeps changing with the operation, a dynamic method to adapt the histogram is required. In [13] the bucket width is adjusted when the number of samples in some buckets satisfy a given criterion. Histogram data can be stored in a structure called Q-digest which is a binary tree [36]. This allows to quickly find quantiles of the data set using a post-order traversal on the tree. In [16] the data stream is compressed by wavelet transform into a sketch. The quantile query is answered by estimating the original data with the sketch. All these methods can be used to set up the histogram for the restart algorithm. We do not evaluate the different algorithms in this paper. We use a width-fixed histogram and propose a cost-effective method to update the histogram at run time.

3. OFFLOADING OVER AN UNRELIABLE NETWORK

In order to observe and analyse the impact of an unreliable network connection on the mobile offloading system we design an experiment. Using the experiment we show that the performance changes in the system under changing network quality. We assume that the task completion time consists of the remote execution time and the data transmission time. Generally, the execution time is assumed constant for a given task and device and delays are added by data transfer. In particular, we assume that the task completion time on the mobile device and on the cloud server can be different, but both will be more or less constant for identical tasks at different times. The offloading completion time varies greatly because data transmission times are not the same. The impact of heavy load on the system is not considered in this paper. From experimental results these assumptions seem reasonable.

In the remainder of this section we first introduce our mobile offloading system and the sample application which we use here for demonstration purposes. Then we experimentally demonstrate how system performance varies over the day due to changing load in our wireless network over the day. The task completion time is described by fitting a distribution to selected subsets of the data. This shows that the variance in the task completion time distribution increases significantly for certain subsets of the data.

3.1 Experiment Configuration

Offloading can be beneficial if two conditions hold. First, the task must consist of heavy computation requirement and, second, a small amount of data must be transmitted between the mobile device and the server. An application which meets both requirements is Optical Character Recognition (OCR), but there are many more. OCR is a method to recognise the characters on a binary image with optional polygonal text regions. Generally, the recognition algorithm consists of three steps: 1) The layout of the image is analysed to find some baselines of the text region. 2) The text region is chopped into components based on the gaps in the baselines. 3) Each component is recognised as several characters by comparing its shape with a trained database. For details of OCR the interested reader is referred to [37].

All three steps of OCR require heavy computation. A series of complicated edits to the image like rotation, segmentation and comparison has to be done. Performing those tasks on the mobile device consumes a lot of energy. For the powerful remote server energy-usage is not a critical metric. In addition, most text images can be stored in small files of at most a few kilobytes. So the amount of data to transmit from the mobile device to the remote server is small. But still the time needed for the transmission depends on the quality of the network connection.

For the experiments a mobile phone (Samsung GT-S7568, Android 4.0) and a server (4 cores: Intel Xeon CPU E5649 2.53GHz) have been used. The mobile phone is placed in a dormitory room and connects to the Internet through Wifi (54Mbps provided by a local Telecom operator). The server is in the lab of the university campus and connects to the Internet through a LAN port of 100M. We have used the Linux command "traceroute" to track the route from the mobile phone to the server. Normally, the route passes 12 hops to reach the destination, and the total round-trip time

---

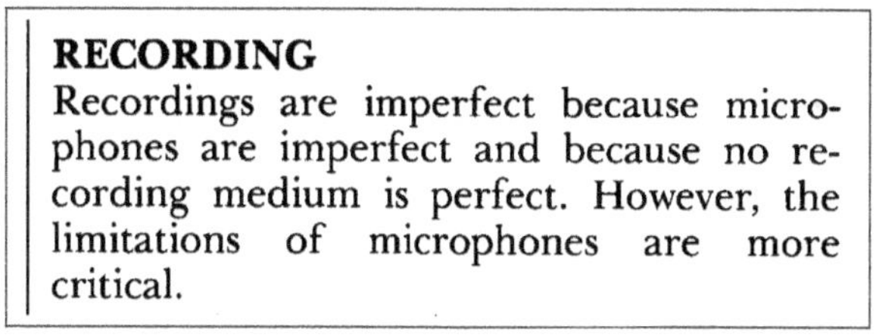

RECORDING
Recordings are imperfect because microphones are imperfect and because no recording medium is perfect. However, the limitations of microphones are more critical.

Figure 1: The image to be recognised

is around 82ms. The offloading engine as introduced in [44] includes an Android Application (App) for the mobile client and a website project for the server. In our experiment, the Tesseract OCR Engine [1] is implemented in both parts of the offloading engine. An image (1160×391px, 8.1 KiB) with a rectangle text region, as shown in Fig. 1, is used for image recognition. Only 100 Bytes are used to represent the decyphered words.

Completion of an offloaded OCR task can be divided into three phases: 1) the Android application transmits the image from the mobile device to the server, 2) the words on the image are recognised using the OCR engine in the server, and 3) the mobile device receives and displays the result from the server. The Offloading Completion Time(OCT) is the time needed to complete the three steps. The same offloading task has been repeated more than 58 000 times in approximately 24 hours in order to observe OCT under the different network conditions. The results are stored in a text file in the mobile device. The memory of the mobile phone used for caching is cleared after the task completion and reused again in the next new task.

In addition, we conducted a different experiment where the image recognition is performed in the mobile device. We call it local execution, as all the processing steps (e.g. analysis, chopping and recognition) are completed by the mobile device itself. The completion time is called Local Completion Time(LCT). The same image Fig. 1 is repeatedly recognised 8 400 times by the local execution. In the next subsection, we will show that although local execution is slower than offloading, it is more stable than the latter.

Fig. 2 shows a scatter plot of all data of the entire 58 000 samples over a 24-hour period starting at 8am on 14th January 2014. Under the assumption of a constant processing time, a large total completion time can be attributed to a long transmission time, i.e. poor network performance. The majority of the samples fall into the range between 980ms and 1380ms, corresponding to the 0.05 and 0.75 quantile of all the samples. Obviously the distribution of the sample values is not identical at different times. While we do not know the reason for systematic changes in network transmission times, there are clearly several types of typical behaviour that should be distinguished.

We have selected three subsets of our observations as indicated by the shaded areas in Fig. 2, each containing 2000 samples, which corresponds to a time window of 40 minutes each. The number of samples is enough to decently fit a distribution and capture one type of network behaviour, the normal, the deteriorated and the bad state.

3.2 Experimental Results

Table 1 shows the mean, the quantiles and the variance of the three subsets. In the *normal* subset the mean completion

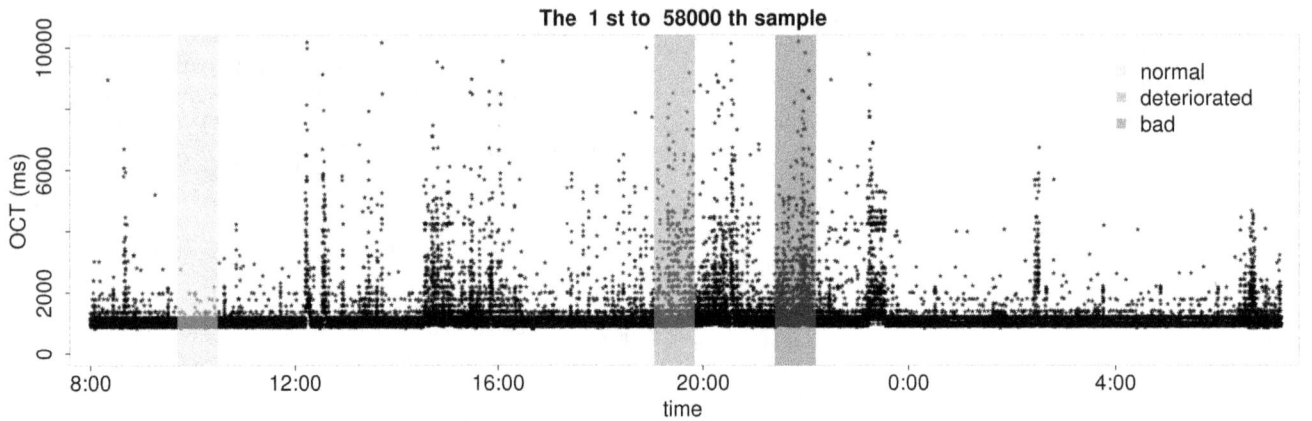

Figure 2: Scatter plot of all OCT samples

time has a low variability, as the 0.9 quantile is only 15% higher than the mean. It is also worth mentioning, that for the given application and setup fast offloading takes in total only half as long as local computation, because remote servers are much faster than mobile devices.

Table 1: Statistics of completion times (msec)

	Normal	Deteriorated	Bad	LCT
mean	1191	1618	2183	2377
0.6-quantile	1171	1466	2075	2382
0.9-quantile	1358	2595	3027	2411
0.99-quantile	1575	5495	7514	2480
variance	14496	80 5861	1680265	1249

Very roughly speaking, it seems like the network degrades most in the early afternoon and in the evening. We do not try to explain this, as finding the cause for network delays is not the scope of this paper. Rather we argue that offloading, as well as a local restart make sense for certain network condition and since we rightfully assume that network conditions change over time a sliding window estimate is needed and appropriate.

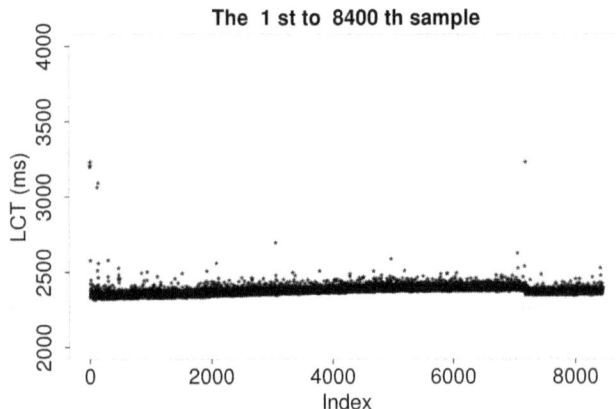

Figure 3: Scatter plot of all LCT samples

It should be noted that on the average, even in poor network condition the offloaded task completes faster than the one that is computed locally. However, for the bad network period, since enough outliers skew the distribution and increase the sample variance, the variability in the data is high enough to justify the use of restart.

The completion time measurement of the local computation (LCT) are shown in Fig. 3. Local computation is usually stable, with very few outliers. Most samples fall into a narrow range between 2338ms and 2411ms, corresponding to the 0.05 and 0.9 quantile.

In summary, in the best case offloading can provide a solution in approximately half the time needed for local processing. On the other hand, local execution times are very stable, albeit longer than processing using offloading, which suffers from high variability and, hence, sometimes takes very long.

3.3 Data Analysis

In this section the sampled data will be analysed to determine whether the theoretical conditions for successful restart are met. It can be shown [42] that restart is beneficial if the task completion time follows a distribution with sufficiently high variance or heavy-tail. Therefore, the distribution of the experimental data and its variability will be determined. The log-log complementary distribution plot is used to illustrate the weight of the tail of the distribution [10].

Fig. 4 shows the completion time of the three subsets and the local completion time versus their complementary cumulative distributions on a log scale. Clearly, for the subset of the bad network state the curve has an approximately constant slope of -2, indicating a heavy tail [10]. For the subset in deteriorated condition the tail has an exponential decay for long task completion times. Therefore in this case we cannot clearly diagnose a heavy-tailed distribution. For the normal subset the decrease is steep, for local computation completion times it is almost infinite. This indicates certainly no heavy tail in the latter two subsets.

Completion times using the local computation are almost constant. There is very little variation in the measurements. This means that once local computation has started restart will certainly not be beneficial. However, during a phase of poor network quality, a local restart may speed up the

6

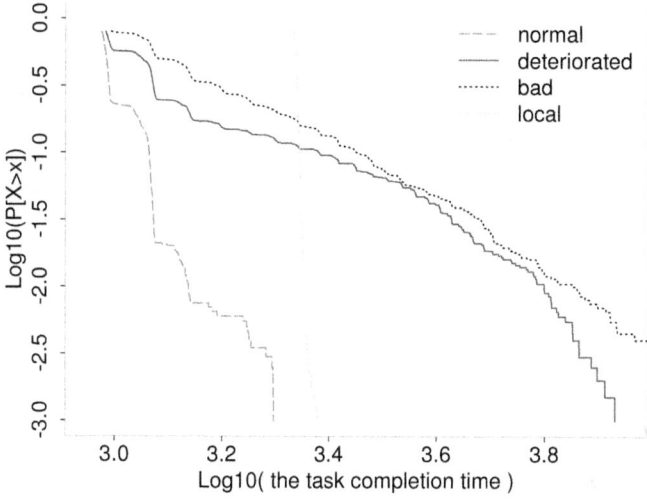

Figure 4: Log-log complementary distribution of the completion time

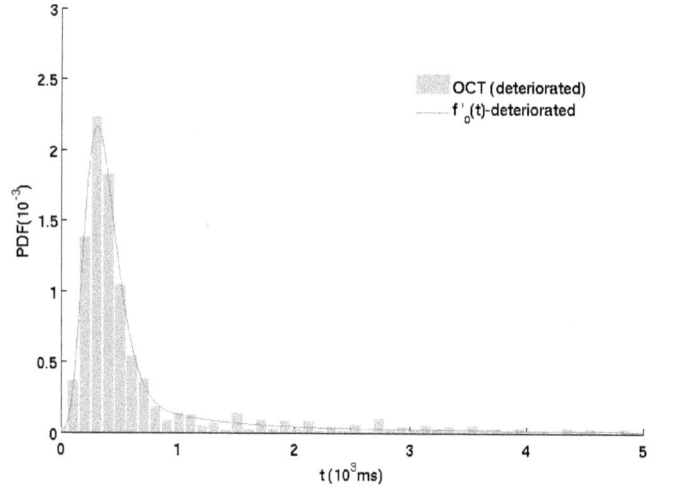

Figure 5: Histogram and PH distribution of the normal subset

solution. This does not yet answer the question what a good choice of the timeout for restart could be.

Fig. 5-7 show the histograms of the three subsets and the density of the fitted distribution. For convenient fitting of phase-type distributions the histograms have been shifted to the origin by subtracting the minimum value from all observations. The distribution fitting will be discussed in the next section.

3.4 Distribution Fitting

In this section we will describe the fitting process for the offloading completion time (OCT) as shown in the histograms and densities in Figs. 5-7. Let the random variable T_o represent OCT of an offloading task without restart. The distribution of T_o is fitted with the Cluster-based fitting algorithm [29] that fits a phase-type (PH) distribution to the data. The fitting procedure uses clustering and fits an Erlang distribution to each cluster. The full distribution is then a mix of those Erlang distributions, a hyper-Erlang distribution.

The hyper-Erlang distribution is suitable for situations where restarts succeed [31]. This distribution takes values from different random variables with different probabilities, for instance, with probability α_i a value from an Erlang distribution with m_i phases and parameter $\lambda_i > 0$, $i = 1, 2, ..., M$. M is the number of clusters. In general, the mixed-Erlang distribution is represented by a vector-matrix tuple $(\boldsymbol{\alpha}, \mathbf{Q})$.

$$\boldsymbol{Q} = \begin{bmatrix} \boldsymbol{Q}_1 & \mathbf{0} & \\ & \ddots & \\ & & \mathbf{0} \\ & & \boldsymbol{Q}_M \end{bmatrix}, \boldsymbol{Q}_i = \begin{bmatrix} -\lambda_i & \lambda_i & \\ & \ddots & \ddots \\ & & -\lambda_i & \lambda_i \\ & & & -\lambda_i \end{bmatrix} \quad (1)$$

$$\boldsymbol{\alpha} = (\underbrace{\alpha_1, 0, ..., 0}_{m_1}, \alpha_2, 0, ..., \underbrace{\alpha_M, 0, ..., 0}_{m_M},) \quad \sum_{i=1}^{M} \alpha_i = 1 \quad (2)$$

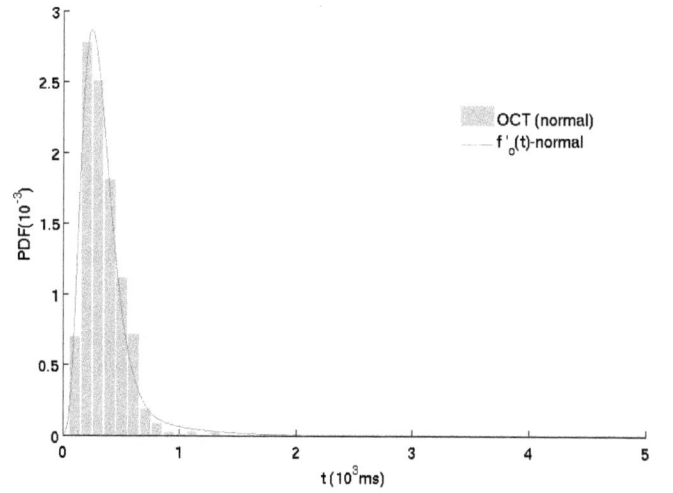

Figure 6: Histogram and PH distribution of the deteriorated subset

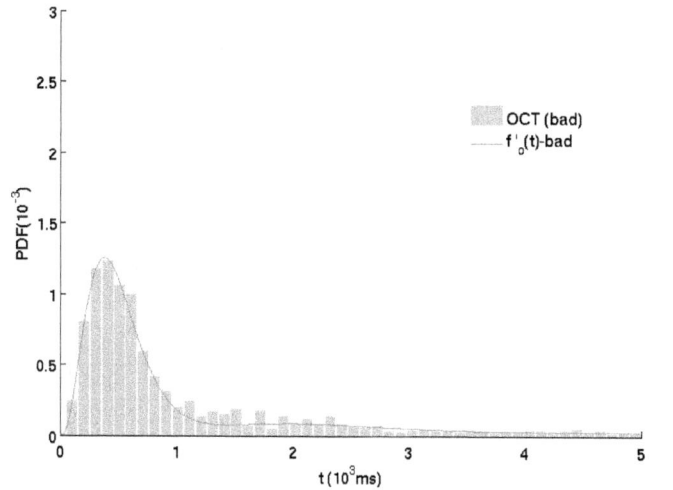

Figure 7: Histogram and PH distribution of the bad subset

$Q_i \in \mathbb{R}^{m_i \times m_i}, i = 1, ..., M$ is a square matrix with size m_i. The probability density function and cumulative distribution function are defined as:

$$f(t) = \boldsymbol{\alpha} e^{\boldsymbol{Q}t}(-\boldsymbol{Q} \cdot \mathbf{I}) \qquad (3)$$

$$F(t) = 1 - \boldsymbol{\alpha} e^{\boldsymbol{Q}t} \cdot \mathbf{I}, \qquad (4)$$

where $\mathbf{I}$ is the column vector of ones with the appropriate size.

Although the hyper-Erlang distribution has exponentially decaying tails, its variance can still be large enough to fulfil the requirements for successful restart as formally introduced in Section 4.1.

Since the completion times of a task have a lower threshold greater zero, as can be seen in Fig. 2 and PH-distributions preferably have a non-zero density at the origin, we have shifted the density $f_o(t)$ to the left by the minimum observed value T^o_{min} for T_o, i.e. $f_o(t) = f'_o(t - T^o_{min})$. This yields $f'_o(t)$ as the PH fitting result of the experimental data shifted to the origin.

Table 2: Hyper-Erlang parameters

T^o_{min}		806

Phase-Type Distribution		
m	λ	α
normal [5, 2, 3]	[0.016, 0.0041, 0.0037]	[0.88, 0.047, 0.073]
det * [3, 6, 2]	[0.00082, 0.0163, 0.0023]	[0.1, 0.7, 0.2]
bad [4, 8, 4]	[0.008, 0.0036, 0.001]	[0.7, 0.15, 0.15]

* det = deteriorated.

Fig. 5-7 show the histograms and the PH results of the shifted T_o of the normal, deteriorated and bad subset. We used three clusters to fit the data, $M = 3$. Since we grouped the data into three categories this seemed to be a natural choice. Of course, one could have chosen more clusters, which might have increased the accuracy of the fit. The parameter results are shown in Table 2. Table 3 shows the error measurement of the PH results of the three subsets. We use the area difference between densities $\triangle f$ and the relative error in the first moment e_1 to measure the error. $\triangle f = \int_0^\infty |\hat{f}(t) - f(t)| dt$ and $e_1 = \frac{|\hat{c}_1 - c_1|}{c_1}$, $f(t)$ denotes the empirical *pdf* of the distribution to be fitted, $\hat{f}(t)$ is the *pdf* of the PH result, c_1 and $\hat{c}_1$ is the first standardized moment of the empirical distribution and of the fitted PH distribution, respectively.

Table 3: Error

	Normal	Deteriorated	Bad
$\triangle f$	0.2783	0.3051	0.2921
e_1	0.1077	0.0262	0.2894

4. OPTIMAL LOCAL RESTART

When using restart one has to decide whether and when to abort a running task and to restart it. Obviously, there is a trade-off between waiting for the offloading task to complete

and terminating the attempt to try again locally. In [42], an iterative solution for an infinite number of possible retries has been derived. In this section, we adopt the solution for computing the optimal timeout from [42] for two tries and a single restart: a first attempt using offloading and a fall back local computation after expiry of the timeout. The efficiency of the method is shown in experiments. In the next section we derive an expression that formulates a condition under which restart in our offloading scenario will be beneficial. In the following section we derive the optimal timeout after which to restart.

4.1 Derivation of the Restart Condition

The theoretical concept of restart applies to random variables for which, first, two successive tries are statistically independent and identically distributed, and, second, new tries abort previous attempts. In the mobile offloading system, the second assumption is certainly met. When the mobile device restarts the task by a local try it abandons the first try on the remote server, where it might continue to run, but will not influence further processing of the restarted task. However, the two successive tries are not drawn from the same distribution, as the computation time in the local device follows a different distribution than the offloading task. The offloading timeout might not be optimal, but completion of the task is guaranteed as the local computation always finishes.

In this section the sampled data will be analysed to determine whether the theoretical conditions for successful restart are met. For a given random variable T describing task completion time restart after a timeout τ is promising if the following condition holds [42]:

$$E[T] < E[T - \tau | T > \tau] \qquad (5)$$

The interpretation of condition (5) means that for restart to be beneficial the expected completion time when restarting from scratch must be less than the expected time still needed to wait for completion. It can be shown [42] that condition (5) holds if the task completion time follows a distribution with sufficiently high variance or heavy-tail.

Remember that T_o represents the offloading completion time OCT of an offloading task without restart. Its density is $f_o(t)$ and its distribution function is $F_o(t)$. Assume τ is the restart time, at which the previous offloading task is aborted and the local computation is issued. Correspondingly, T_l represents the local computation time LCT of the same task, $f_l(t)$ its density and $F_l(t)$ its distribution. We assume that $F_o(t)$ and $F_l(t)$ are both continuous probability distribution functions defined over the domain $[0, \infty)$, such that $F_o(t) > 0$ and $F_l(t) > 0$ if $t > 0$. We introduce T to denote the completion time when a local restart is allowed. We write $f(t)$ and $F(t)$ for its density and cumulative distribution function, respectively. We are interested in the expectation of T using the optimal timeout τ.

$$F(t) = \begin{cases} F_o(t) & (0 \leqslant t < \tau) \\ 1 - (1 - F_o(\tau))(1 - F_l(t - \tau)) & (\tau \leqslant t) \end{cases} \qquad (6)$$

$$f(t) = \begin{cases} f_o(t) & (0 \leqslant t < \tau) \\ (1 - F_o(\tau))f_l(t - \tau) & (\tau \leqslant t) \end{cases} \qquad (7)$$

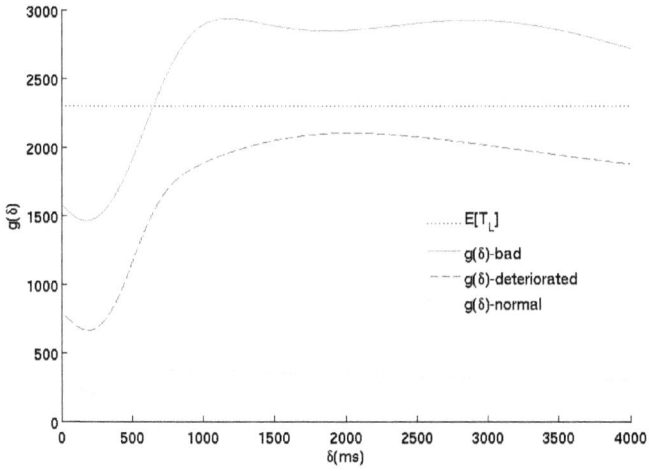

Figure 8: Restart timeout for the different subsets of the data

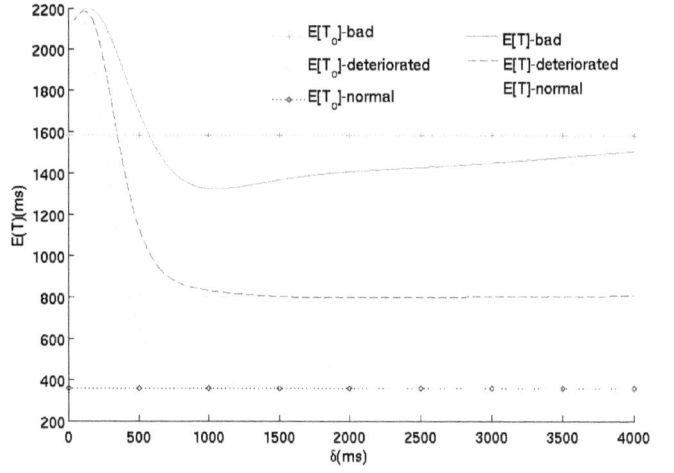

Figure 9: Expectation of OCT with/without the local restart versus τ

Analogous to [42] we define the partial moments $M_n(\tau)$ of the completion time T to determine its expectation $E[T]$.

$$M_n(\tau) = \int_0^\tau t^n f(t)dt = \int_0^\tau t^n f_o(t)dt \qquad (8)$$

The respective densities of T and T_o are identical between 0 and τ, so their partial moments are equal.

$$
\begin{aligned}
E[T^n] &= \int_0^\tau t^n f_o(t)dt + \int_\tau^\infty t^n(1 - F_o(\tau))f_l(t-\tau)dt \\
&= M_n(\tau) + (1 - F_o(\tau)) \sum_{k=0}^n \binom{n}{k} \tau^{n-k} E[T_l^k]
\end{aligned} \qquad (9)
$$

$$E[T] = M(\tau) + (1 - F_o(\tau))(\tau + E[T_l]) \qquad (10)$$

A simple criterion to decide whether to restart or not can be formulated. If there exists an interval S in $[0, \infty)$, where $\tau \in S \Rightarrow E[T] < E[T_o]$, then restart is beneficial. With (10), this condition can be written as the following inequality:

$$E[T_l] < \frac{\int_\tau^\infty t f_o(t)dt}{1 - F_o(\tau)} - \tau \qquad (11)$$

Since the data has been shifted to the origin (11) has to be adjusted to

$$E[T_l] < \frac{\int_{\tau-T_{min}^o}^\infty t f_o'(t)dt}{1 - F_o'(\tau - T_{min}^o)} - (\tau - T_{min}^o) \qquad (12)$$

The optimal restart time is the value of τ where $E[T]$ is minimal. Hence, $f_o(t)$ is the key factor for finding the optimal τ and to take the decision to restart. As introduced in Section 3.3, $f_o(t)$ changes with the network quality. Accurately capturing $f_o(t)$ at run time gives a good solution, but it is a challenge. In the next section, we will introduce a fast method to dynamically approximate $f_o(t)$. Before that, we use the previous experiment data to test the validity of the local restart condition (12).

4.2 The Optimal Restart Timeout

For convenience we use $g(\delta)$ to represent the right hand side of (12), $\delta = \tau - T_{min}^o$, i.e.

$$g(\delta) = \frac{\int_\delta^\infty t f_o'(t)dt}{1 - F_o'(\delta)} - \delta \qquad (13)$$

The potential benefit of the local restart is expressed by $g(\delta)$ and $E[T_l]$ is the threshold to decide whether the local restart is useful or not. If the value of $g(\delta)$ is low, it indicates that the task has a high probability to be completed by offloading and local restart is not helpful. If the value of $g(\delta)$ is high, it indicates that the network condition is poor and the task completion has a high probability to be delayed. In this case restart can be very beneficial to the task.

Fig. 8 shows the result of (13), calculated according to $f_o'(t)$ of the three subsets from Table 2. $E[T_l]$ is calculated based on the data in Fig. 3. Only for values δ for which $g(.)$ is larger than the expected local completion time $E[T_l]$ a retry will be beneficial. It can be seen in Fig. 8 that such values only exist for the curve based on the bad subset of data.

However, Fig. 8 does not allow to determine the optimal restart timeout. We use the expectation of T as a metric to evaluate the system performance under different restart timeouts. The optimal time is found when $E[T]$ is minimal. Equation (10) is used to calculate $E[T]$.

For comparing the system performance with and without the local restart, Fig. 9 shows $E[T]$ and $E[T_o]$ for the three subsets. As expected only $E[T]$-bad benefits from restart and even has a clear minimum under restart. The optimal restart time is found at the value for δ, for which $E[T]$-bad is minimal. We can confirm observations we already made earlier for restart, that when in doubt, one should rather set the timeout too large. A too large timeout may not be optimal, but still better than no restart. While a too small restart timeout can be detrimental to the expected task completion time. Fig. 9 confirms this observation. The figure also shows that none of the other subsets benefit from restart.

Since changes in network conditions and hence the histogram can be expected, a dynamical method is needed. In the next section, we propose a fast and simple method to dynamically update the histogram and to estimate the restart condition directly from the histogram without first fitting a distribution.

5. DYNAMIC RESTART SCHEME

The procedure of fitting a theoretical distribution and computing the optimal restart timeout from this distribution is very expensive in terms of computation cost. Various algorithms and tools exist for fitting PH distributions to empirical data [38, 17, 39, 43], and the fitted distributions approximate the data in many cases very well. For efficiency reasons we use a direct method [30] to estimate $g(\delta)$ and $E[T]$ from the histogram. We dynamically build and update a histogram and then repeatedly determine the optimal restart timeout as discussed in the following subsections.

5.1 Dynamic Histogram

A histogram simply divides up the range of possible observations into intervals, which we call buckets, and counts the number of observations that fall into each bucket. Buckets can have a variable or a constant width; we choose the latter for simplicity. Histograms initially hold too few samples to provide a good approximation of a probability distribution. After collecting data for a while a stationary distribution is represented increasingly well. However, if the distribution changes, old samples will never be dismissed from the histogram and will forever bias the new probability distribution.

There are several options how to handle changes in distribution: the histogram can be repeatedly flushed as to build up a new histogram for the respective current state of the system. This introduces many initial periods with insufficient data. Another option is to transform the buckets into *dripping buckets* that lose samples constantly over time. It is not easy to adjust the dripping speed such that the histogram will hold sufficient but not too many samples at all times [28, 24, 36].

We propose a partial flush which is tuned using two parameters, the total number of samples in the histogram when executing the partial flush and the percentage of samples to equally flush from all buckets.

Algorithm 1 (Initialization for the histogram)

$T_l \leftarrow$ Local_Run()   //*Complete the task by local execution*
$T^o_{min} \leftarrow$ Offload_Run()   //*Complete the task by offloading*
$T^o_{max} = T_l$
$\triangle_B = (T^o_{max} - T^o_{min})/N$ //$\triangle_B$: *The bucket width*
for $i = 1$ to N **do**
    $B_{average}[i] = 0$
    $N_B[i] = 0$
end for
$N_{out} = 0$
$B_{out} = 0$

Algorithm 1 shows the algorithm to initialise the histogram prior to run time. The parameters are the following:

T^o_{min}: The lower bound of the histogram.

T^o_{max}: The upper bound of the histogram.

T_l: The task completion time by local execution.

N: The number of buckets in the histogram.

$B_{average}[i]$: The mean of all the samples in the ith bucket.

$N_B[i]$: The number of samples in the ith bucket.

N_{out}: The number of samples, whose value $> T^o_{max}$.

B_{out}: The mean of all the samples $> T^o_{max}$.

The number of buckets N must be chosen manually. The upper bound of the histogram is determined by the execution time of one local run. The lower bound is given as the execution time of one offloading task. In the course of the experiments there may later be shorter offloading times which will be used as new lower bound and additional buckets will be inserted. These choices are motivated by the purpose of the histogram: to determine the optimal restart timeout the precise shape of the distribution in the tail is not needed.

Algorithm 2 (Recording a new sample)

Local Execution:
1: $T_{temp} \leftarrow$ Local_Run()
2: $T_l = (T_l + T_{temp})/2$
Offloading:
3: $T_{temp} \leftarrow$ Offload_Run()
4: **switch** T_{temp} **do**
5:     **case** $1 : T_{temp} \geqslant T^o_{max}$
6:         $B_{out} = \frac{(B_{out} \times N_{out}) + (T_{temp} - T^o_{min})}{N_{out} + 1}$
7:         $N_{out} + +$
8:     **case** $2 : T_{temp} < T^o_{min}$
9:         $M = \lceil (T^o_{min} - T_{temp})/\triangle_B \rceil$
10:      INSERT(M)
11:      $B_{average}[1] = T_{temp} - T^o_{min}$
12:      $N_B[1] = 1$
13:     **case** $3 : T^o_{min} \leqslant T_{temp} < T^o_{max}$
14:      $j = \lfloor (T_{temp} - T^o_{min})/\triangle_B \rfloor + 1$
15:      $B_{average}[j] = \frac{(B_{average}[j] \times N_B[j]) + (T_{temp} - T^o_{min})}{N_B[j] + 1}$
16:      $N_B[j] + +$
17:
18: **function** INSERT(k)
    //*Insert k empty buckets between T_{temp} and T^o_{min}*
19:     $N = N + k$
20:     $T^o_{min} = T^o_{min} - \triangle_B \times k$
21:     **for** $i = 1$ to N **do**
22:         $B_{average}[i + k] = B_{average}[i] + \triangle_B \times k$
23:         $N_B[i + k] = N_B[i]$
24:     **end for**
25: **end function**

Algorithm 2 shows the algorithm to record a new sample at run time. If the sample comes from local execution, T_l is updated by the mean of its original value and the new sample. Hence, the impact of old samples is reduced and replaced by that of new ones.

If the new sample is produced by offloading, it can be added to the histogram in three ways according to its value. **Case 1**, when new samples are larger than T^o_{max}, they are all added to the *out* bucket. **Case 2**, when a shorter offloading time arrives, M additional buckets are inserted, M is calculated based on the ceiling function shown in line 9. T^o_{min} moves down to include the new sample. Line $21 \sim 24$ adjusts the mean and index of each original bucket accordingly. **Case 3**, when the sample falls into the range between T^o_{min} and T^o_{max}, it is added to the corresponding bucket in the histogram. Fig. 10 is the illustrative diagram of the three cases.

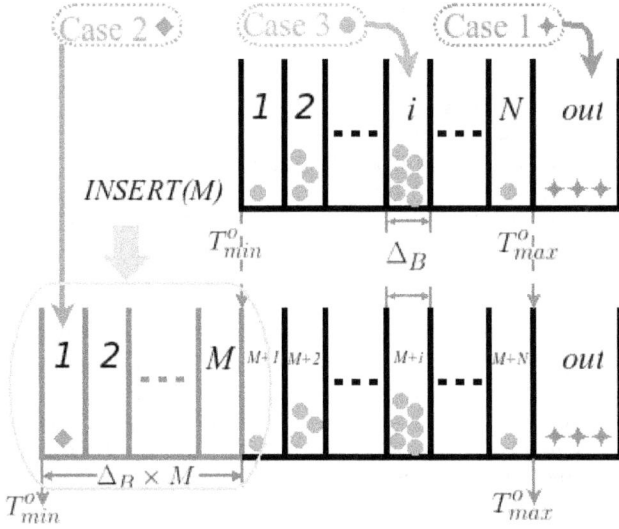

Figure 10: Recording a new offloading sample

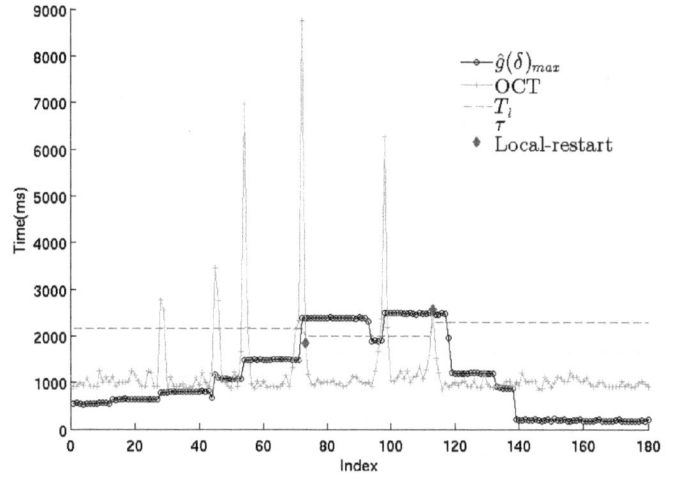

Figure 11: Scatter plot of the dynamic local restart scheme with $N = 20$, $N_{bound} = 100$ and $p = 50\%$.

The partial flush algorithm, shown as Algorithm 3, needs the two new parameters N_{bound} and p:

N_{bound}: threshold to start the update. When the number of samples stored in the histogram exceeds this value, the update algorithm is triggered.

p: percentage of samples to be kept. From each bucket, $(1 - p)/100 * n_i$ samples are removed if the bucket holds a total of n_i samples before the partial flush.

A large number of samples N_{bound} until partial flush leads to a long sampling period. Conversely, a large percentage p indicates that the majority of the samples are kept after updating. This will lead to frequent inexpensive partial flushes. Please note that the mechanism is related to hysteresis as used in the control of queueing systems.

Algorithm 3 (Update for the histogram)

$B = \sum_{i=1}^{N} N_B[i] + N_{out}$
if $B > N_{bound}$ **then**
    $N_B[i] = \lfloor N_B[i] \times p \rfloor$ // i from 1 to N
    $N_{out} = \lfloor N_{out} \times p \rfloor$
end if

5.2 Asymptotically Unbiased Ratio Estimator

The estimate for the optimal restart timeout is based on the asymptotically unbiased ratio estimator [9]. Using the dynamic histogram proposed in the last subsection, an estimator for $g(\delta)$ in equation (13) is:

$$\hat{g}(\delta_i) = \frac{\sum_{j=i}^{N} N_B[j] \cdot B_{average}[j] + N_{out} \cdot B_{out}}{(\sum_{k=i}^{N} N_B[k] + N_{out})(1 - \hat{F_o}'(\delta_i))} - \delta_i \quad (14)$$

We assume that the optimal timeout δ only takes on values $\delta_i = i \times \triangle_B, i = 1, 2, ..., N$. The cumulative distribution function $\hat{F_o}'(\delta_i)$ is estimated as:

$$\hat{F_o}'(\delta_i) = \frac{\sum_{j=1}^{i} N_B[j]}{\sum_{k=1}^{N} N_B[k] + N_{out}} \quad (15)$$

If the maximum estimate $\hat{g}(\delta_i)_{max} > T_l$, the local restart condition (12) is fulfilled. Then, an estimate of $E[T]$ provides the optimal timeout.

$$\hat{E}[T]_{\delta_i} = \hat{M}'(\delta_i) + (1 - \hat{F_o}'(\delta_i))(\delta_i + T_l) + T_{min}^o \quad (16)$$

Remember that we have shifted all data, and the histogram to the origin. Therefore the lower bound T_{min}^o of the histogram should be added to the expectation. The partial moment $\hat{M}'(\delta_i)$ is estimated as:

$$\hat{M}'(\delta_i) = \frac{\sum_{j=1}^{i} N_B[j] \cdot B_{average}[j]}{\sum_{k=1}^{i} N_B[k]} \quad (17)$$

The optimal local restart time can be identified by selecting the value of δ_i, which minimizes $\hat{E}[T]_{\delta_i}$, and the optimal timeout is $\tau = \delta_i + T_{min}^o$. Actually, at run time first the restart condition is evaluated and if it is not satisfied, $\hat{E}[T]_{\delta_i}$ is not determined.

5.3 Evaluation of the Dynamic Restart

In order to evaluate the performance of the dynamic local restart scheme, it is implemented in our mobile offloading engine [44] and evaluated using the OCR application with the same picture as before (cf. Fig. 1). As introduced in Section 3.2, we again conduct measurements over a period of 24 hours from 8:00 on 28th April 2014 and we sampled 54 318 completion times. Using the experiment we then show that our dynamic histogram captures changes in the system and allows the offloading system to react to those in real-time.

Fig. 11 shows a short episode of the whole experiment process. This episode lasts for about 5 minutes (begins at 9:12) and contains 180 successive tasks. A scatter plot of some related parameters of the 180 tasks is shown in Fig. 11. It can be seen that the potential benefit of the local restart, $\hat{g}(\delta)_{max}$, first increases stepwise and then remains constant. After some very long offloading times, $\hat{g}(\delta)_{max} > T_L$, several restarts complete the computation locally.

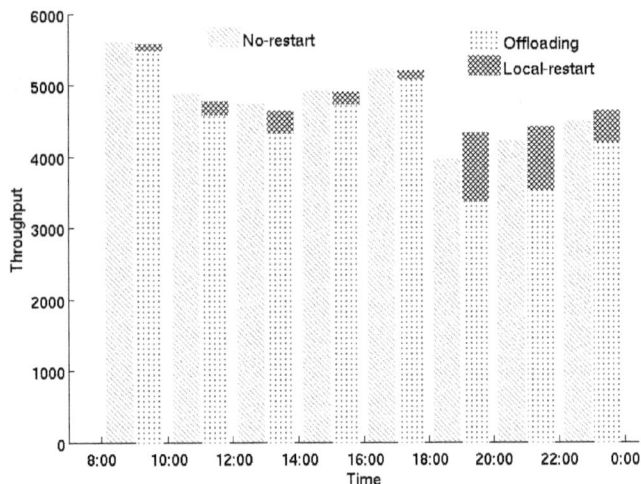

Figure 12: Throughput of different times in a day

For comparing the performance of the scheme with and without the dynamic local restart, the throughput of the two schemes over periods of two hours are shown in Fig. 12. We define the throughput as the number of tasks completed in each period. Here we compare data from the two experiment sessions that took place on different days: the right column in each interval represents the first series of experiments without restart, while the left column shows the new series of experiments using restart. Surprisingly, both columns follow a similar pattern over the day and in most intervals the throughput is almost identical in both experiment series. Only for the last three pairs of columns the dynamic local restart scheme can effectively increase the throughput.

In conclusion, the dynamic local restart scheme can effectively increase the system performance sometimes and does not harm it at any time.

6. CONCLUSION

In this paper, we have introduced a dynamic local restart scheme to improve the performance of the mobile offloading system. Restarting the offloading task again locally in the mobile device at the appropriate moment can reduce its completion time in some cases. First, we introduced an experiment to illustrate the impact of network delays on mobile offloading. Then, we mathematically derived a condition and the optimal timeout for local restart in order to reduce the task completion time. We proposed a dynamic local restart scheme for the mobile offloading system. In this scheme, a dynamic histogram is used to track the variation of the network quality, and the restart condition and the optimal time is estimated with the histogram. Since the normal user might not perform the same task many times in sequence, we have to adjust the method to suit various applications and different tasks. This might be possible by considering more fine-grained metrics such as packet transmission time to base the restart decision on.

7. REFERENCES

[1] tesseract-ocr.
   http://code.google.com/p/tesseract-ocr/.
[2] ALTMAN, E., EL-AZOUZI, R., MENASCHE, D. S., AND XU, Y. Forever young: Aging control for smartphones in hybrid networks. *arXiv preprint arXiv:1009.4733* (2010).
[3] ASMUSSEN, S., FIORINI, P., LIPSKY, L., ROLSKI, T., AND SHEAHAN, R. Asymptotic behavior of total times for jobs that must start over if a failure occurs. *Mathematics of Operations Research 33*, 4 (2008), 932–944.
[4] BALAN, R. K., SATYANARAYANAN, M., PARK, S. Y., AND OKOSHI, T. Tactics-based remote execution for mobile computing. In *Proceedings of the 1st international conference on Mobile systems, applications and services* (2003), ACM, pp. 273–286.
[5] BOBBIO, A., AND TRIVEDI, K. S. Computation of the distribution of the completion time when the work requirement is a ph random variable This work was supported in part by the US Office of Naval Research under Contract no. N3014-88-K-0623, by NASA under Grant NAG-1-70, and by the Italian National Research Council CNR under the project "Material and Devices for Solid State Electronics" Grant no. 86.02177. 61. *Stochastic Models 6*, 1 (1990), 133–150.
[6] CARROLL, A., AND HEISER, G. An analysis of power consumption in a smartphone. In *Proceedings of the 2010 USENIX conference on USENIX annual technical conference* (2010), USENIX Association, pp. 21–21.
[7] CHUN, B., IHM, S., MANIATIS, P., NAIK, M., AND PATTI, A. Clonecloud: elastic execution between mobile device and cloud. In *Proceedings of the sixth conference on Computer systems* (2011), pp. 301–314.
[8] CLARK, C., FRASER, K., HAND, S., HANSEN, J. G., JUL, E., LIMPACH, C., PRATT, I., AND WARFIELD, A. Live migration of virtual machines. In *Proceedings of the 2nd conference on Symposium on Networked Systems Design & Implementation-Volume 2* (2005), USENIX Association, pp. 273–286.
[9] COCHRAN, W. G. *Sampling techniques.* John Wiley & Sons, 2007.
[10] CROVELLA, M. E., TAQQU, M. S., AND BESTAVROS, A. Heavy-tailed probability distributions in the World Wide Web. *A practical guide to heavy tails 1* (1998), 3–26.
[11] CUERVO, E., BALASUBRAMANIAN, A., CHO, D., WOLMAN, A., SAROIU, S., CHANDRA, R., AND BAHL, P. MAUI: making smartphones last longer with code offload. In *Proceedings of the 8th international conference on Mobile systems, applications, and services* (2010), ACM, pp. 49–62.
[12] DEBOOSERE, L., SIMOENS, P., DE WACHTER, J., VANKEIRSBILCK, B., DE TURCK, F., DHOEDT, B., AND DEMEESTER, P. Grid design for mobile thin client computing. *Future Generation Computer Systems 27*, 6 (2011), 681–693.
[13] DONJERKOVIC, D., IOANNIDIS, Y. E., AND RAMAKRISHNAN, R. Dynamic histograms: Capturing evolving data sets. In *Proceedings of the International Conference on Data Engineering* (2000), IEEE Computer Society Press; 1998, pp. 86–86.
[14] FERNANDO, N., LOKE, S. W., AND RAHAYU, W. Mobile cloud computing: A survey. *Future Generation Computer Systems 29*, 1 (2013), 84–106.

[15] FLINN, J., PARK, S., AND SATYANARAYANAN, M. Balancing performance, energy, and quality in pervasive computing. In *Distributed Computing Systems, 2002. Proceedings. 22nd International Conference on* (2002), IEEE, pp. 217–226.

[16] GILBERT, A. C., KOTIDIS, Y., MUTHUKRISHNAN, S., AND STRAUSS, M. Surfing wavelets on streams: One-pass summaries for approximate aggregate queries. In *VLDB* (2001), vol. 1, pp. 79–88.

[17] HORVÁTH, A., AND TELEK, M. Phfit: A general phase-type fitting tool. In *Computer Performance Evaluation: Modelling Techniques and Tools*. Springer, 2002, pp. 82–91.

[18] HUANG, D., ZHANG, X., KANG, M., AND LUO, J. MobiCloud: building secure cloud framework for mobile computing and communication. In *Service Oriented System Engineering (SOSE), 2010 Fifth IEEE International Symposium on* (2010), IEEE, pp. 27–34.

[19] HUERTA-CANEPA, G., AND LEE, D. A virtual cloud computing provider for mobile devices. In *Proceedings of the 1st ACM Workshop on Mobile Cloud Computing & Services: Social Networks and Beyond* (2010), ACM, p. 6.

[20] KEMP, R., PALMER, N., KIELMANN, T., AND BAL, H. Cuckoo: a computation offloading framework for smartphones. In *Mobile Computing, Applications, and Services*. Springer, 2012, pp. 59–79.

[21] KRISTENSEN, M. D. Scavenger: Transparent development of efficient cyber foraging applications. In *Pervasive Computing and Communications (PerCom), 2010 IEEE International Conference on* (2010), IEEE, pp. 217–226.

[22] KULKARNI, V. G., NICOLA, V. F., AND TRIVEDI, K. S. On modelling the performance and reliability of multimode computer systems. *Journal of Systems and Software 6*, 1 (1986), 175–182.

[23] MARINELLI, E. E. Hyrax: cloud computing on mobile devices using MapReduce. Tech. rep., DTIC Document, 2009.

[24] MATIAS, Y., VITTER, J. S., AND WANG, M. Dynamic Maintenance of Wavelet-Based Histograms. In *Proceedings of the 26th International Conference on Very Large Data Bases* (San Francisco, CA, USA, 2000), VLDB '00, Morgan Kaufmann Publishers Inc., pp. 101–110.

[25] MAURER, S. M., AND HUBERMAN, B. A. Restart strategies and Internet congestion. *Journal of Economic Dynamics and Control 25*, 3 (2001), 641–654.

[26] MIETTINEN, A. P., AND NURMINEN, J. K. Energy efficiency of mobile clients in cloud computing. In *Proceedings of the 2nd USENIX conference on Hot topics in cloud computing* (2010), USENIX Association, pp. 4–4.

[27] NICOLA, V., AND TRIVEDI, K. The completion time of a job on multimode systems. *Advances in Applied Probability 19*, 4 (1987), 932–954.

[28] POOSALA, V., HAAS, P. J., IOANNIDIS, Y. E., AND SHEKITA, E. J. Improved histograms for selectivity estimation of range predicates. *ACM SIGMOD Record 25*, 2 (1996), 294–305.

[29] REINECKE, P., KRAUSS, T., AND WOLTER, K. Cluster-based fitting of phase-type distributions to empirical data. *Computers & Mathematics with Applications 64*, 12 (2012), 3840–3851.

[30] REINECKE, P., VAN MOORSEL, A., AND WOLTER, K. A measurement study of the interplay between application level restart and transport protocol. In *Service Availability*. Springer, 2005, pp. 86–100.

[31] RUAN, Y., HORVITZ, E., AND KAUTZ, H. Restart policies with dependence among runs: A dynamic programming approach. In *Principles and Practice of Constraint Programming-CP 2002* (2002), Springer, pp. 573–586.

[32] SATYANARAYANAN, M. Mobile computing. *Computer 26*, 9 (1993), 81–82.

[33] SATYANARAYANAN, M. Pervasive computing: Vision and challenges. *Personal Communications, IEEE 8*, 4 (2001), 10–17.

[34] SATYANARAYANAN, M., BAHL, P., CACERES, R., AND DAVIES, N. The case for vm-based cloudlets in mobile computing. *Pervasive Computing, IEEE 8*, 4 (2009), 14–23.

[35] SHEAHAN, R., LIPSKY, L., FIORINI, P. M., AND ASMUSSEN, S. On the completion time distribution for tasks that must restart from the beginning if a failure occurs. *ACM SIGMETRICS Performance Evaluation Review 34*, 3 (2006), 24–26.

[36] SHRIVASTAVA, N., BURAGOHAIN, C., AGRAWAL, D., AND SURI, S. Medians and beyond: new aggregation techniques for sensor networks. In *Proceedings of the 2nd international conference on Embedded networked sensor systems* (2004), ACM, pp. 239–249.

[37] SMITH, R. An Overview of the Tesseract OCR Engine. In *ICDAR* (2007), vol. 7, pp. 629–633.

[38] TELEK, M., AND HEINDL, A. Matching moments for acyclic discrete and continuous phase-type distributions of second order.

[39] THUMMLER, A., BUCHHOLZ, P., AND TELEK, M. A novel approach for phase-type fitting with the EM algorithm. *Dependable and Secure Computing, IEEE Transactions on 3*, 3 (2006), 245–258.

[40] VAN MOORSEL, A. P., AND WOLTER, K. Analysis and algorithms for restart. In *Quantitative Evaluation of Systems, 2004. QEST 2004. Proceedings. First International Conference on the* (2004), IEEE, pp. 195–204.

[41] VAN MOORSEL, A. P., AND WOLTER, K. Meeting Deadlines through Restart. In *MMB* (2004), pp. 155–160.

[42] VAN MOORSEL, A. P., AND WOLTER, K. Analysis of restart mechanisms in software systems. *Software Engineering, IEEE Transactions on 32*, 8 (2006), 547–558.

[43] WANG, J., LIU, J., AND SHE, C. Segment-based adaptive hyper-Erlang model for long-tailed network traffic approximation. *The Journal of Supercomputing 45*, 3 (2008), 296–312.

[44] WANG, Q., GRIERA JORBA, M., RIPOLL, J. M., AND WOLTER, K. Analysis of local re-execution in mobile offloading system. In *Software Reliability Engineering (ISSRE), 2013 IEEE 24th International Symposium on* (2013), IEEE, pp. 31–40.

Automated Detection of Performance Regressions Using Regression Models on Clustered Performance Counters

Weiyi Shang, Ahmed E. Hassan
Software Analysis and Intelligence Lab (SAIL)
Queen's University, Kingston, Ontario, Canada
{swy, ahmed}@cs.queensu.ca

Mohamed Nasser, Parminder Flora
BlackBerry
Waterloo, Ontario, Canada

ABSTRACT

Performance testing is conducted before deploying system updates in order to ensure that the performance of large software systems did not degrade (i.e., no performance regressions). During such testing, thousands of performance counters are collected. However, comparing thousands of performance counters across versions of a software system is very time consuming and error-prone. In an effort to automate such analysis, model-based performance regression detection approaches build a limited number (i.e., one or two) of models for a limited number of target performance counters (e.g., CPU or memory) and leverage the models to detect performance regressions. Such model-based approaches still have their limitations since selecting the target performance counters is often based on experience or gut feeling. In this paper, we propose an automated approach to detect performance regressions by analyzing all collected counters instead of focusing on a limited number of target counters. We first group performance counters into clusters to determine the number of performance counters needed to truly represent the performance of a system. We then perform statistical tests to select the target performance counters, for which we build regression models. We apply the regression models on new version of the system to detect performance regressions.

We perform two case studies on two large systems: one open-source system and one enterprise system. The results of our case studies show that our approach can group a large number of performance counters into a small number of clusters. Our approach can successfully detect both injected and real-life performance regressions in the case studies. In addition, our case studies show that our approach outperforms traditional approaches for analyzing performance counters. Our approach has been adopted in industrial settings to detect performance regressions on a daily basis.

Categories and Subject Descriptors

D.2.9 [**Software Engineering**]: Management—*Software Quality Assurance (SQA)*

1. INTRODUCTION

Performance assurance activities are an essential step in the release cycle of large software systems [10, 22, 37]. Such activities aim to identify and eliminate performance regressions in each newly released version. Examples of performance regressions are response time degradation, higher than expected resource utilization and memory leaks. Such regressions may compromise the user experience, increase the operating cost of the system, and cause field failures. The slow response time of the United States' newly rolled-out healthcare.gov [4] illustrates the importance of performance assurance activities before releasing a system.

Performance regression detection is an important task in performance assurance activities. The main purpose of performance regression detection is to identify performance regressions, such as a higher CPU utilization relative to the existing version of a system, before releasing a new version of the system. To detect performance regressions, performance analysts conduct performance testing to compare the performance of the existing and new version of a system under the same workload.

However, identifying performance regressions remains a challenging task for performance analysts. One approach is to compare every performance counter across the existing and new versions of the system. However, large software systems often generate thousands of performance counters during performance testing [24, 27]. Comparing thousands of performance counters generated by large software systems is a very time consuming and error-prone task.

Performance engineering research proposes model-based performance regression detection approaches [8]. Such approaches build a limited number of models for a set of target performance counters (e.g., CPU and memory) and leverage the models to detect performance regressions. By examining the results of a small number of models instead of all performance counters, model-based approaches reduce the efforts needed to uncover performance regressions. However, there are major limitations of such model-based approach since performance analysts often select the target performance counters based on their experiences and gut feeling – focusing on a small set of well known counters (e.g., response time). Such ad hoc selection of target counters may lead to the failure to observe performance regressions. For example, selecting CPU as a target counter may miss observing a performance regression for I/O.

In this paper, we propose an automated approach to detect performance regressions by automatically selecting the target performance counters. We first group performance counters into clusters. We use the clusters to determine the number of target performance counters needed to represent the performance of the system. We then leverage statistical tests to select a target performance counter for each cluster. We build one regression model for each target performance counter. The performance models capture the relationships between the performance counters within each cluster. We apply the regression models on data from the new version of the system and measure the modelling error. If the new version of the system does not have any performance regressions, the regression models should model the performance counters in the new version of the system with low modelling error. Larger than usual modelling errors are considered as signs of performance regressions.

To evaluate our approach, we perform two case studies on two large systems: one open-source system and one enterprise system. We find that our approach can cluster performance counters into a small number of clusters. Our approach successfully detects both injected and real-life performance regression in the case studies. In addition, we apply traditional approaches of performance regression detection: comparing every performance counter across both versions and building a model for a single target performance counter. We find that our approach outperforms both traditional approaches in our case studies.

This paper makes three contributions:

1. We develop an automated approach to detect performance regressions by automatically selecting the target performance counters.

2. Our evaluation results show that our approach successfully detects both injected and real-life performance regressions.

3. Our evaluation results show that our approach outperforms traditional approaches for detecting performance regressions.

Our approach is already adopted in an industrial environment and is integrated into a continuous performance testing environment. The environment leverages our approach to flag performance regressions on a daily basis.

The rest of this paper is organized as follows: Section 2 presents prior research for detecting performance regressions and discuses the challenge of current practice. Section 3 presents an example to motivate this paper. Section 4 presents our approach of detecting performance regressions. Section 5 and Section 6 presents the design and results of our case study. Section 7 compares our approach with traditional approaches for detecting performance regressions. Section 8 discusses the threats to validity of our study. Finally, Section 9 concludes the paper.

2. BACKGROUNDS AND RELATED WORK

We now describe prior research that is related to this paper. We focus on performance regression and faults detection approaches that make use of performance counters. There are two dimensions for analyzing performance counters to detect performance regressions: amount of analysis and complexity of analysis (see Figure 1). Performance analysts conduct performance counter analysis either on all counters or on a limited set of counters. On the other dimension, performance analysts can select either simple analysis, such as comparing the mean value of a counter, or complex

analysis, such as building regression models. The choice of the two dimensions makes four types of performance counter based regression detection, as shown in Figure 1. In this section, we discuss prior research based on these four types.

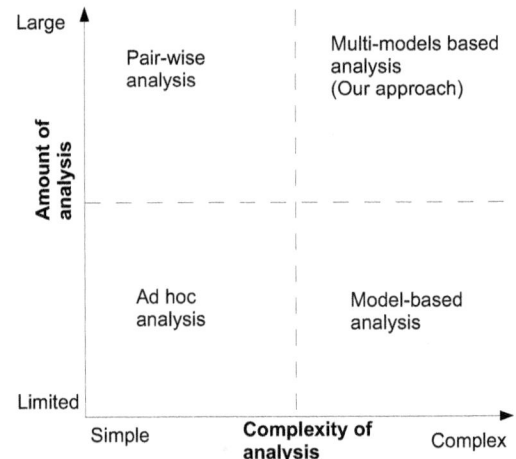

Figure 1: Four types of counter-based performance regression detection.

2.1 Ad hoc analysis

Ad hoc analysis selects a limited number of target performance counters (e.g., CPU and memory) and performs simple analysis to compare the target counters. Heger *et al.* [18] present an approach that uses software development history and unit tests to diagnose the root cause of performance regressions. In the first step of their approach, they leverage Analysis of Variance (ANOVA) to compare the response time of the system to detect performance regressions. The ad hoc approach may fail to detect performance regressions if the target counters do not capture the performance regressions. Moreover, such ad hoc analysis does not detect the change of relationships between counters, such as the relationship between I/O and CPU.

2.2 Pair-wise analysis

Pair-wise analysis leverages simple analysis to compare every performance counter across two versions of a system. Nguyen *et al.* [27–29] conduct a series of studies on performance regressions. They propose to leverage statistical process control techniques, such as control chart [33], to detect performance regressions. In particular, they build a control chart for every performance counter and examine the violation ratio of the same performance counter for a new test. Malik *et al.* [23, 24] propose approaches that cluster performance counters using Principal Component Analysis (PCA). Each component generated by PCA is mapped to performance counters by a weight value. The weight value measures how much a counter contributes to the component. For every counter, a pair-wise comparison is performed on the weight value of each component to detect performance regressions.

There are two major limitations of pair-wise analysis. The first limitation is the large number of performance counters. Nguyen *et al.* and Malik *et al.* state in their research that large software systems have thousands of performance counters [24, 27]. Comparing each performance counter across two versions of a software system is very time consuming and error-prone. Moreover, pair-wise analysis does not capture the complex interplays between counters. A follow-up of Nguyen *et al.*'s research leverages the historical test results to build machine learning models [29]. The machine learning models capture the relationship between counters, as well as their relationship with regression causes. Such models are then used to predict performance regression causes in new tests. However, their approach requires a historical repository of performance tests to build models.

2.3 Model-based analysis

Model-based analysis builds a limited number of models for a set of target performance counters (e.g., CPU and memory) and leverages the models to detect performance regressions. The model-based approach helps us deal with the large number of performance counters and helps compare the relationships between the various counters.

Recent research by Xiong *et al.* [38] proposes a model-driven framework to assist in performance diagnosis in a cloud environment. Their framework builds models between workload counters and a target performance counter, such as CPU. The models can be used to detect workload changes and assist in identifying performance bottlenecks.

Cohen *et al.* [8] propose an approach that builds probabilistic models, such as Tree-Augmented Bayesian Networks, to correlate system level counters and systems' response time. The approach is used to understand the cause to changes on systems' response time. Cohen *et al.* [9] propose that performance counters can be used to build statistical models for system faults. Bodik *et al.* [5] use logistic regression models to improve Cohen *et al.*'s work [8, 9].

Jiang *et al.* [21] propose an approach that calculates the relationship between performance counters by improving the Ordinary Least Squares regression models and using the model to detect faults in a system.

Current model-based approaches still have their limitations. Performance analysts often select the target performance counters based on their experience and gut feeling. They often focus on a small set of well-known counters (e.g., CPU and memory). Such ad hoc selection of target counters may lead to the failure to observe performance regressions (see Section 7).

2.4 Multi-models based analysis

Multi-models based analysis builds multiple models from performance counters and uses the models to detect performance regressions.

Foo *et al.* [12] propose to detect performance regression using association rules. Association rules group historically correlated performance counters together and generate rules based on the results of prior performance tests. Their approach extracts association rules from performance counters generated during performance tests. They use the change to the association rules to detect performance anomalies. The association rules make use of thresholds derived from the analyst's experience (i.e., determining low, medium and high values of counters). The approach requires a historical repository of performance tests to build association rules.

Jiang *et al.* [20] use normalized mutual information as a similarity measure to cluster correlated performance counters. Since counters in one cluster are highly correlated, the uncertainty among counters in the cluster should be lower than the uncertainty of the same number of uncorrelated counters. Jiang *et al.* leverage information theory to moni-

tor entropy of clusters. A significant change in the in-cluster entropy is considered as a sign of a performance fault. During the evaluation of the approach, the authors were able to detect 77% of the injected faults and the faulty subsystems, without having any false positives.

In this paper, we propose an automated approach to detect performance regressions by automatically selecting the target performance counters. Our approach aims to address the limitation of current model-based analysis (see Section 2.3), i.e., the ad hoc selection of target counters. We present our approach in Section 4.

3. A MOTIVATING EXAMPLE

Ian is a performance engineer for a large-scale distributed software system. The system serves millions of users worldwide. Ensuring the efficient performance of the system is a critical job. Therefore, Ian needs to conduct performance testing whenever there is an update to the system, such as adding new features and/or fixing bugs.

A typical performance test consists of the following steps. First, Ian deploys the old version of the system into a testing environment and applies a test workload on the system. The workload is often pre-defined to exercise most of the system's features and is typically similar to the system's workload in the field. While applying the workload, the system is monitored and thousands of performance counters are collected. Second, Ian deploys the new version of the system into the same testing environment and applies the same workload. The new version of the system is monitored in the same manner as the old version. Finally, Ian examines the collected performance counters from both versions of the system in order to uncover any performance regressions in the new version.

To determine whether there exists any performance regressions, Ian adopts a model-based approach. Ian first selects a target performance counter, such as CPU, as dependent variable. The choice of dependent variable is based on Ian's experience (e.g., customer's priorities and prior experience with field problems). In his practice, CPU is by default the dependent variable. Then Ian uses the rest of the performance counters to build a regression model for the CPU counter. Ian applies the model on a new version of the system in order to predict CPU. If the prediction error is high, Ian would report the existence of a performance regression.

However, this model-based approach may not detect all instances of performance regressions. For example, Ian has two sets of performance counters from two versions of the system, shown in Table 1. Ian leverages the model-based approach and the prediction error is less than 7%. Therefore, Ian reports that the new version does not have any performance regressions. However, after the system is updated, users complain that the system is slower than before. To resolve the users' complaints, Ian starts to review the performance counters and finds that there is a big difference between the I/O read counters in the old versus new version. The model-based approach has not captured the I/O read counters, since the model considered that the I/O read counters have low correlation with CPU.

From this example, we observe the following limitations of current model-based approach for detecting performance regressions. First, all too often, one performance counter cannot represent the performance of a system. In Ian's example, he misses the information of I/O read by focusing only on

Table 1: Examples of performance counters from performance testing.

Old version								
Time Stamp	1	2	3	4	5	6	7	8
CPU Privileged	29.17	27.29	29.90	33.23	31.43	30.91	31.15	30.21
CPU User	33.02	29.48	28.23	26.25	26.95	26.22	26.04	29.38
IO read byte/sec	0	0	0	0	0	0	0	0
IO read op/sec	0	0	0	0	0	0	0	0
IO write byte/sec	7,808.09	4,481.75	7,787.79	4,715.79	7,349.50	4,499.50	4,641.17	8,319.15
IO write op/sec	180.36	163.29	174.36	178.87	188.47	192.43	187.91	178.80
Memory Working set	144,867 KB	144,888 KB	146,522 KB	145,920 KB	145,822 KB	145,822 KB	144,364 KB	144,499 KB
Memory Private byte	146,203 KB	146,625 KB	147,763 KB	147,681 KB	147,583 KB	147,587 KB	146,153 KB	146,305 KB

New version								
Time Stamp	1	2	3	4	5	6	7	8
CPU Privileged	29.38	30.52	30.21	33.02	31.77	28.23	29.48	28.02
CPU User	26.98	27.29	31.04	27.92	27.08	28.23	32.29	33.54
IO read byte/sec	175,008.30	176,262.16	177,867.55	178,745.03	181,573.41	174,242.61	165,634.03	163,400.87
IO read op/sec	1,611.37	1,628.83	1,655.19	1,649.85	1,654.89	1,615.44	1,514.00	1,526.93
IO write byte/sec	4,364.58	7,908.74	4,514.13	7,588.77	4,887.06	7,767.46	4,262.85	3,961.54
IO write op/sec	190.99	183.79	188.82	189.32	189.58	186.40	179.88	167.89
Memory Working set	144,499 KB	144,499 KB	144,499 KB	144,753 KB	144,753 KB	145,056 KB	146,874 KB	144,503 KB
Memory Private byte	146,326 KB	146,350 KB	146,379 KB	146,649 KB	146,682 KB	146,981 KB	148,759 KB	146,383 KB

CPU. Second, choosing dependent performance counters are often biased by performance analysts' experiences and gut feelings. In the example, Ian selects CPU based on his experience, while choosing an I/O related counter may have helped him uncover the I/O related regression.

To overcome such limitations, Ian designs an approach that automatically groups performance counters into clusters. He leverages the clusters to determine the number of models that he needs to build. He then leverages statistical tests to determine the dependent variable (i.e., target performance counter) for each cluster and he builds a model to capture the relationships between the counters in each cluster.

In the next section, we present this new approach for detecting performance regression by grouping counters into clusters.

4. APPROACH

In this section, we present our approach for detecting performance regressions. Each subsection corresponds to a step in our approach, as shown in Figure 2. Table 1 shows an example of performance testing results. The performance counters are recorded during the performance testing of the old and new versions a software system. The performance counters are recorded 8 times for each test run. The values of the performance counters at each time stamp are called an observation of the performance counters. To ease the illustration of our approach, we show a running example with only 8 performance counters and 8 observations. However, the number of performance counters and observations is much larger in real-life performance testing. The goal of our approach is to detect whether there are performance regressions in the new version of a system.

4.1 Reducing counters

In the first step, we clean up the performance counters by removing redundant counters or counters with low variance in both new and old tests. We first remove performance counters that have zero variance in both versions of the performance tests. We then perform redundancy analysis [17] on the performance counters in each cluster. The redundancy analysis would consider a performance counter redundant if it can be predicted from a combination of other variables. We use each performance counter as a dependent variable and use the rest of the counters as independent variables to build a regression model. We calculate the R^2 of each model and if the R^2 is larger than a threshold, the current dependent variable (i.e., performance counter) is considered redundant. We then remove the performance counter with the highest R^2 and repeat the process until no performance counters can be predicted with R^2 higher than the threshold. In this step, *I/O read op/sec* and *Memory Working set* are removed, since they can be predicted by *I/O read byte/sec*, and *Memory Private byte*, respectively.

4.2 Clustering performance counters

The second phase of our approach is to group performance counters into clusters based on their similarities. The number of clusters would show the number of models needed to represent the performance of the system, and performance counters in each cluster are used to build a model. This phase in our approach consists of three steps. First, we calculate the dissimilarity (i.e., distance) between every pair of performance counters. Second, we use a hierarchical clustering procedure to cluster the counters. Third, we convert the hierarchical clustering into k clusters (i.e., where each counter is a member of only one cluster).

4.2.1 Distance calculation

Each performance counter is represented by one point in an n-dimensional space (where n is the number of observations of the performance counter). For example, if a performance test runs for an hour and performance counters are recorded every minute, there would be 60 observations of each performance counter for this performance test. To perform clustering, we need to measure the distance between each point in this 60-dimensional space. A larger distance implies a greater dissimilarity between a pair of performance counters. We calculate the distance between every pair of performance counters to produce a distance matrix.

We use the Pearson distance (a transform of the Pearson correlation [15]). While there are many other distance mea-

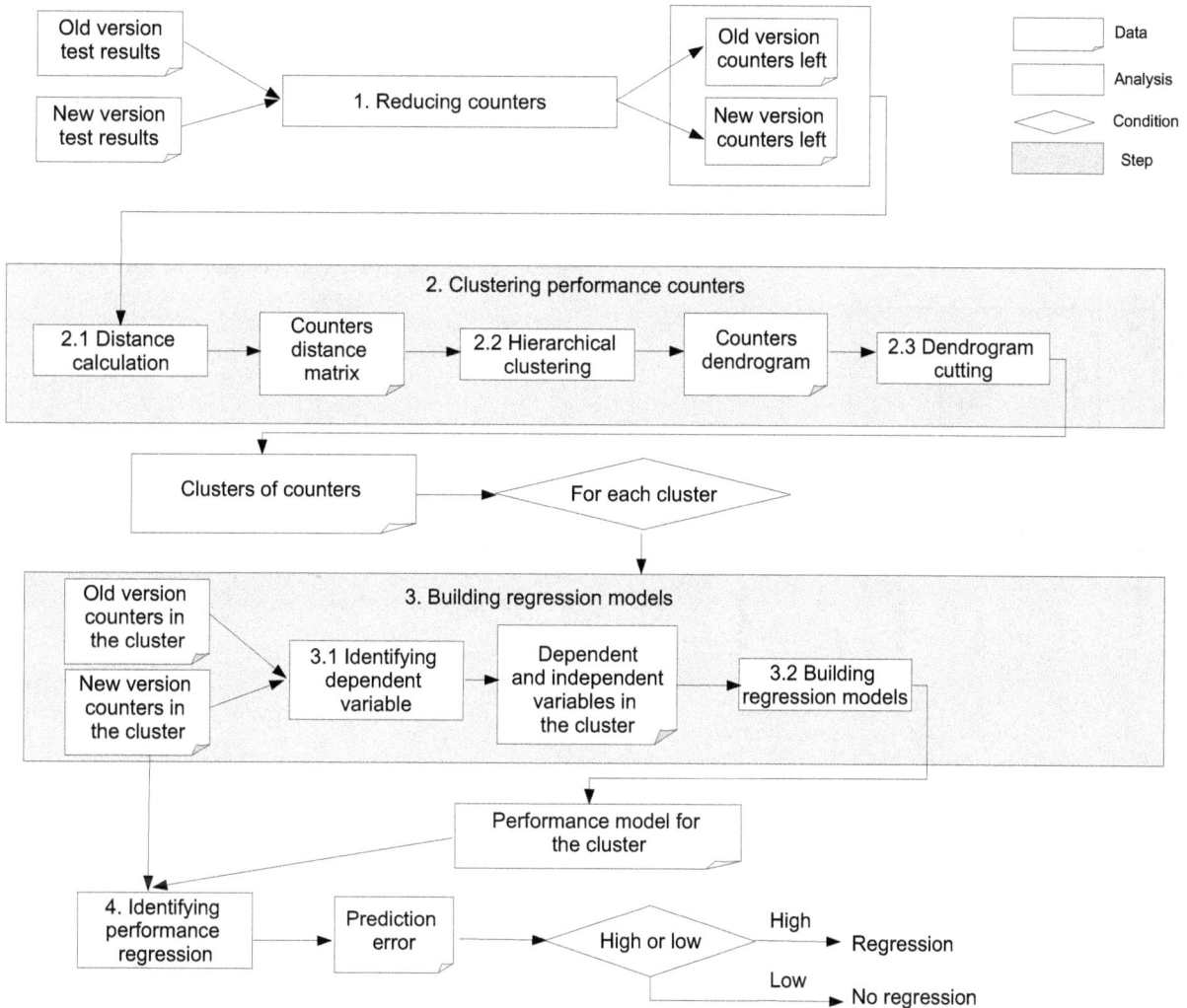

Figure 2: An Overview of Our Approach.

sures [7, 13, 15, 30], we choose Pearson distance since prior research shows that it produces a clustering that is similar to manual clustering [19,32]. Pearson distance also performs well when clustering counters in prior performance engineering research [35].

We first calculate the Pearson correlation (ρ) between two performance counters. ρ ranges from -1 to +1, where a value of 1 indicates that two performance counters are identical, a value of 0 indicates that there is no relationship between the performance counters and a value of -1 indicates an inverse relationship between the two performance counters (i.e., as the values of one performance counter increase, the values of the other counter decrease).

We then transform the Pearson correlation (ρ) to the Pearson distance (d_ρ) using Equation 1.

$$d_\rho = \begin{cases} 1 - \rho & \text{for } \rho \geq 0 \\ |\rho| & \text{for } \rho < 0 \end{cases} \qquad (1)$$

Table 2 shows the distance matrix of our example.

4.2.2 Hierarchical clustering

We leverage a hierarchical clustering procedure to cluster the performance counters using the distance matrix calculated in the previous step. We choose to use hierarchical

Table 2: Distance matrix of our example

	CPU Privileged	CPU User	I/O read byte/sec	I/O write byte/sec	I/O write op/sec
CPU User	0.58				
I/O read byte/sec	0.08	0.80			
I/O write byte/sec	0.90	0.07	0.15		
I/O write op/sec	0.44	0.52	0.73	0.93	
Memory Private/byte	0.84	0.06	0.14	0.12	0.03

clustering in our approach because we do not need to specify the number of clusters before performing the clustering and hierarchical clustering is adopted in prior performance engineering research [35]. The clustering procedure starts with each performance counter in its own cluster and proceeds to find and merge the closest pair of clusters (using the distance matrix), until only one cluster (containing everything) is left. The distance matrix is updated when the two clusters are merged.

Hierarchical clustering updates the distance matrix based on a specified linkage criteria. We use the average linkage, which has been leveraged successfully in prior performance engineering research [35]. When two clusters are merged, the distance matrix is updated in two steps. First, the merged clusters are removed from the distance matrix. Second, a new cluster (containing the merged clusters) is added to the distance matrix by calculating the distance between the new cluster and all existing clusters. The distance between two clusters is the average distance (Pearson distance) between the performance counters of the first cluster and the second cluster [13, 36].

Figure 3 shows the dendrogram produced by hierarchically clustering the performance counters using the distance matrix from our running example from Table 2.

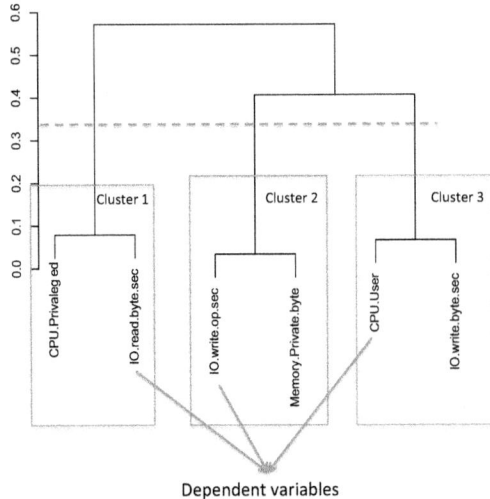

Figure 3: A dendrogram generated by performing hierarchical clustering on our example. The read dashed line in the figure shows where the dendrogram is cut into clusters using the Calinski-Harabasz stopping rule.

4.2.3 Dendrogram cutting

The result of a hierarchical clustering procedure is a hierarchy of clusters, visualized using dendrograms. Figure 3 shows an example of a dendrogram. A dendrogram is a diagram that uses a binary tree to show each stage of the clustering procedure as nested clusters [36].

Dendrogram needs to be cut in order to complete the clustering procedure. The hight of the cut line of a dendrogram represents the maximum accepted amount of intra-cluster dissimilarity within a cluster. After cutting the dendrogram, each performance counter is assigned to only one cluster. Either manual inspection or statistical tests (also called stopping rules) are used to cut dendrograms. Although a manual inspection of the dendrogram is flexible and fast, it is subject to human bias and may not be reliable. We use the Calinski-Harabasz stopping rule [6] to perform our dendrogram cutting. Although there are many other stopping rules [6, 11, 25, 26, 31] available, prior research finds that the Calinski-Harabasz stopping rule performs well when cutting dendrograms produced when clustering performance counters [35].

The Calinski-Harabasz stopping rule measures the similarity within-clusters and the dissimilarity between-clusters. The optimal clustering will have high within-cluster similarity (i.e., the performance counters within a cluster are as similar as possible) and a high between-cluster dissimilarity (i.e., the performance counter from two different clusters are as dissimilar as possible). Using the Calinski-Harabasz stopping rule, we do not need to pre-specify the number of clusters, instead the number of clusters is determined by

the similarity between clusters in the dendrogram. If the distances between performance counters are large, the dendrogram cutting process would generate a large number of clusters. However, in our experiments, we find that the number of clusters generated by our approach is typically small (see Section 6).

We mark a red horizontal dashed line in Figure 3 to show where we cut the example hierarchical cluster dendrogram using the Calinski-Harabasz stopping rule. By cutting the dendrogram, we create three clusters of performance counters. The first cluster contains *CPU Privileged* and *I/O read byte/sec*. the second cluster contains *I/O write op/sec* and *Memory Private byte*. The rest of the performance counters (*CPU User* and *I/O write byte/sec*) are in the third cluster.

4.3 Building models

The third phase of our approach is to build models for each cluster of performance counters. This phase of our approach consists of two steps. First, we identify a dependent counter (i.e., target counter) in each cluster for model building. Second, for each cluster we build a regression models [14] using the performance counters in that cluster.

4.3.1 Identifying dependent variable

In model-based performance regression detection (see Section 2), performance analysts often select the target performance counters based on their experience and gut feeling. They often focus on a small set of well known metrics (e.g., CPU and memory). Such ad hoc selection of target counters may lead to the failure to observe performance regressions (see Section 7).

To address the limitation, we propose an approach to automatically select dependent variables (i.e., target counters). We select the performance counter that has the largest difference between the two versions of the system. We select such a counter as dependent variable since our approach aims to measure the largest difference between two runs of a system. To measure the difference, we use a Kolmogorov-Smirnov test [34] on the distribution of each performance counter across the two versions. The smaller the p-value computed using Kolmogorov-Smirnov test, the more likely the performance counter is non-uniformly distributed across the two versions. We select the performance counter with the smallest p-value computed by Kolmogorov-Smirnov test. We choose to use the Kolmogorov-Smirnov test because it does not have any assumptions on the distribution of the performance counters. *I/O read byte/sec, I/O write op/sec* and *CPU User* are chosen to be the three dependent variables for each cluster in our example.

4.3.2 Building regression models

We build a regression model, where the independent variables are the remaining performance counters in a cluster. We model the dependent variable as a linear function of independent variables. We choose a linear model since it is easier to interpret the model when developers need to identify the root cause of a detected regression.

4.4 Identifying performance regressions

The final phase of our approach is to identify performance regressions using the regression models built in the last phase. We use the average prediction error as a measure of the deviation between two test results. If the average prediction error of a cluster in a new version is larger than a threshold (e.g., 30%), we consider that the new version of the system has a performance regression in the particular cluster. In practice, developers need to learn the best threshold for a particular system based on their experiences of the system. In our example, the average prediction errors are 100%, 4% and 2% in the three clusters. Since 100% prediction error in the first cluster is a large prediction error, we consider that there is performance regression in the new version. Developers should focus on the counters in the first cluster to identify the root cause of the performance regression.

5. CASE STUDY

To study the effectiveness of our approach of detecting performance regressions, we perform case studies with two different large systems with injected performance issues. Both systems were used in prior studies [24, 27]. In this section, we present the subject systems, the workload applied on the systems, the experimental environment and the injected performance issues.

5.1 Subject Systems

5.1.1 Dell DVD Store

The Dell DVD store (*DS2*) is an open-source three-tier web application [2]. *DS2* simulates an electronic commerce system to benchmark new hardware system installations. Performance regressions are injected into the *DS2* code to produce versions of *DS2* with performance issues. We reuse the test results generated by Nguyen *et al.* [27]. The lab setup includes three Pentium III servers running Windows XP and Windows 2008 with 512MB of RAM. The first machine is a MySQL 5.5 database server [3], the second machine is an Apache Tomcat web application server [1], and the third machine is used to run the load driver. During each run, all performance counters associated with the DS2 application server are recorded.

5.1.2 Enterprise Application

The enterprise application (*EA*) in our study is a large-scale, communication application that is deployed in thousands of enterprises worldwide and used by millions of users. Due to a Non-Disclosure Agreement (*NDA*), we cannot reveal additional details about the application. We do note that it is considerably larger than *DS2* and has a much larger user base and longer history. Performance analysts of *EA* conduct performance tests to ensure that the *EA* continuously meets its performance requirements.

5.2 Subject performance tests

We evaluate our approach by running it against performance tests with and without performance regressions.

5.2.1 Dell DVD Store

To have performance tests with and without regressions, the following performance regressions were injected into *DS2*:

- **A: Increasing Memory Usage.** Adding a field to an object increases the memory usage. Because the object is created many times by *DS2*, such a change would cause a large increase of memory usage.

- **B: Increasing CPU Usage.** Additional calculation is added to the source code of *DS2*. The source code

Table 3: Summary of the 10 runs of our approach for the *DS2* system.

Run name	Old Version	New Version	Performance regression symptoms
No regression 1	Good run 1,2,3,4	Good run 5	NA
No regression 2	Good run 1,2,3,5	Good run 4	NA
No regression 3	Good run 1,2,4,5	Good run 3	NA
No regression 4	Good run 1,3,4,5	Good run 2	NA
No regression 5	Good run 2,3,4,5	Good run 1	NA
Regression 1	Good run 1,2,3,4,5	A	Memory usage increase
Regression 2	Good run 1,2,3,4,5	B	CPU usage increase
Regression 3	Good run 1,2,3,4,5	C	Heavier DB requests
Regression 4	Good run 1,2,3,4,5	D	Heavier DB requests
Regression 5	Good run 1,2,3,4,5	E	IO increase

with additional calculation is frequently executed during the performance test.

- **C: Removing column index.** Column index are used for frequently queried columns. Such regression can only be identified during a large-scale performance test since only the workload that exercises the corresponding query would suffer from the performance regression. A column index in the database is removed to cause slower database requests.

- **D: Removing text index.** Similar to **C**, a text index is often used for searching text data in the database. A database text index is removed to cause slower database requests.

- **E: Increasing I/O access time.** Accessing I/O storage devices, such as hard drives, are usually slower than accessing memory. Adding additional I/O access may cause performance regressions. For example, adding unnecessary log statements is one of the causes of performance regressions [16]. Logging statements are added to the source code that is frequently executed in order to introduce this performance regression.

A performance test for *DS2* without any injected performance regressions is run five times. We name these five runs as *Good Run* 1 to 5.

We create ten sets of data. Five sets are with performance regressions and five sets without performance regressions. Each data set has two parts: one part for the new version of the system and another part for the old version of the system. We use *Good Run* 1 to 5 as the old version of the system. We use the five performance tests with injected regressions (A to E) as the new versions of the system. Each set of data without performance regression consists of data from one run from the *Good Run* 1 to 5 as a new version of the system and the rest four runs from the *Good Run* 1 to 5 as old version of the system. We run our approach against the new and old versions of the system. In total, we have five runs of our approach between two versions of *DS2* without performance regression and five runs of our approach between two versions of *DS2* with performance regression. The summary of the ten runs is shown in Table 3.

5.2.2 Enterprise Application

We pick a performance test as a baseline in the test repository of the *EA*. We also pick one performance test without regression and five performance tests with identified regressions. We run our approach between the baseline test and each of the other five tests. Due to the *NDA*, we cannot mention the detailed information of the identified regressions in the performance tests of *EA*. We do note that the identified regressions include CPU, memory and I/O overheads.

6. CASE STUDY RESULTS

In this section, we evaluate our approach through two research questions. For each research question, we present the motivation of the question, the used approach to address the question, and the results.

RQ1: How many models does our approach need to build?

Motivation. Performance regression testing often generates a large number of performance counters, examining every performance counter is time consuming and error prone. On the other hand, model-based performance regression detection approaches often select one performance counter as dependent variable and build one model for the chosen performance counter. However, all too often, one model cannot represent the performance of a software system. Our approach groups performance counters into clusters to determine how many models are needed to represent the performance of a software system. We want to examine the number of clusters that our approach uses to group performance counters. We also want to examine whether the counters used to build regression models in each run of our approach are consistent. If the counters are consistent across different runs, performance analysts can select to use those counters without using our approach.

Approach. We measure the total number of counters in *DS2* and the number of clusters generated from each test. For *EA*, we do not report the total number of performance counters due to *NDA*, but only report the number of clusters generated. However, we do note that the total number of performance counters of *EA* is much larger than *DS2*. We then remove redundant counters in each cluster and identify a target counter for each cluster. We examine whether the counters (target counters and non-redundant independent counters) in each run is consistent.

Results. **Our approach can group performance counters into a small number of clusters.** For the ten runs of our approach on *DS2*, nine runs only have two clusters and one run has four clusters. Such results show that in the nine runs, instead of examining 28 performance counters one-by-one for every performance test, performance analysts only need to build two models and examine two values from the models for each performance test. For the six runs of our approach on *EA*, two to five clusters are generated by our approach. Since *EA* has a much larger number of performance counters, these results show that our approach can group the performance counters into a small number of clusters even when the total number of counters is considerably large.

The counters (target counters and independent counters) used to build regression models in each run of our approach are not consistent. We compare all the counters that are not removed by our variance and redundancy analysis. We find that 5 to 13 counters are used to build models across runs of our approach (i.e., 15 to 23 counters are removed). The removed counters are not the same across runs of our approach. We find that even though nine out of ten runs for *DS2* have two clusters, the clustering results are not the same. Moreover, the clustering results are not the same within the runs with a regression and runs without a regression, respectively. In addition, there is no performance counter that is always selected to be the target counters across runs of our approach. For example, CPU, one of the mostly used performance counters, is only selected twice as a target counter in the ten runs of our approach.

Counters measuring the same type of resource may not result in the same cluster. For example, CPU, memory and I/O are three typical resources in performance testing results. However, our results show that CPU related counters are not clustered together, neither do memory or I/O related counters. For example, in the clustering results of *No regression 1*, the first cluster consists of *ID Process*, *IO Data Bytes/sec* and *IO Read Operations/sec*; while the second cluster consists of *Elapsed Time*, *Page Faults/sec* and *Pool Nonpaged Bytes*.

> *Our approach can group performance counters into a small number of clusters even though the total number of performance counters is large. Results of clustering and removing counters are different across runs of our approach. Performance analysts cannot select a limited number of counters based on experience or based on a small number of runs of our approach, since the results of clustering and removing counters are different across runs of our approach.*

RQ2: Can our approach detect performance regressions?

Motivation. Detecting performance regressions is an important performance assurance task. Deploying an updated a system into with performance regressions may bring significant financial and reputational repercussions. On the other hand, incorrectly detected performance regressions may cause the waste of large amounts of resources. Therefore, we want to evaluate whether our approach can accurately detect performance regressions.

Approach. Our approach is based on a threshold and choosing a different threshold may impact the precision and recall. Hence, we do not report the precision and recall of our approach. Instead, we report the results of our approach, i.e., we build models from an old version and apply the models on a new version of the system and calculate the prediction errors of the models. If the new version of the system does not have any performance regressions, the regression models should model the performance counters in the new version of the system with low prediction errors. On the other hand, if the new version has regressions, applying the models on the new version should generate high prediction errors. Therefore, larger than usual modelling errors are considered as signs of performance regressions. We want to see whether the tests with and without performance regressions have a difference in prediction errors. Since each run of our approach has multiple models and every model has a prediction error, we focus on the largest prediction error in each run of our approach.

Table 4: Prediction errors in each cluster when building regression models for *DS2*. Each model is built using data from an old version and is applied on data from a new version to calculate prediction errors. The largest prediction error in each run is in bold font.

Run Name	Prediction Errors	
No regression 1	3%	9%
No regression 2	3%	6%
No regression 3	11%	4%
No regression 4	4%	4%
No regression 5	6%	5%

Run Name	Prediction Error			
Regression 1	44%		1622%	
Regression 2	916%		2%	
Regression 3	17%	46%	5%	17%
Regression 4	101%		161%	
Regression 5	24%		6%	

Results. **Our approach can detect both the injected performance regressions in *DS2* and the real-life performance regressions in *EA*.** Table 4 shows the prediction errors of our approach on *DS2*. The largest prediction errors in each run without regression is between 4% to 11%, whereas the runs with injected performance regressions have at least one model with a much higher prediction error. The largest prediction errors in each runs with performance regressions is from 24% to 1622%. Table 5 shows that the largest prediction error in the *EA* run without regression is only 3%, while the largest prediction errors in the *EA* runs with real-life regression is 16% to 386%.

Our approach is not heavily impacted by the choice of threshold value. Table 4 and 5 show that the prediction errors generated by our approach have a large difference between the runs with and without performance regressions. For all the largest prediction errors in the *DS2* runs without regression, the *maximum* value is 11%, whereas for all the largest prediction errors in the runs with regressions, the *minimum* value is 24%. For all the largest prediction errors in the *EA* runs, the difference between runs with and without regression is also large. Even though our approach is based on a threshold to detect performance regressions, such large difference in prediction errors (shown in Table 4 and 5) indicate that our approach can successfully detect performance regressions and that the threshold value does not impact the accuracy of our approach. Nevertheless, our experiments highlight the need to calibrate the thresholds based on practitioners' experience since each of the two systems exhibits a different range of prediction errors.

> *Our approach can successfully detect both injected and real-life performance regressions. The threshold value of prediction errors should be calibrated using a good test run (i.e., one with no regressions).*

7. COMPARISON AGAINST TRADITIONAL APPROACHES

In this section, we compare our approach against two traditional approaches: 1) building models against specific performance counters and 2) using statistical tests.

Table 5: Prediction errors in each cluster when building regression models for *EA*. Each model is built using data from an old version and is applied on data from a new version to calculate prediction errors. The largest prediction error in each run is in bold font. The rows with empty cells are the ones with less than five clusters.

Run Name	Prediction Error			
No Regression 1	2%	2%	2%	**3%**

Run Name	Prediction Error				
Regression 1	22%	38%	**94%**		
Regression 2	6%	**16%**			
Regression 3	8%	**386%**	2%	5%	
Regression 4	**65%**	22%	18%		
Regression 5	**55%**	9%	4%	4%	15%

7.1 Comparing our approach with building models for specific performance counters

Prior research often uses performance counters to build models for a specific performance counter (i.e., a target counter) (See Section 2). For example, Xiong *et al.* [38] build regression models for CPU, memory and I/O. Cohen *et al.* [8] build statistical models for a performance counter that measures the response time of the system. However, performance regressions may not have direct impact on the specific target counter. In addition, performance analysts may not have enough good or extensive knowledge to select an appropriate target counter to build a model. On the other hand, our approach automatically identifies the target counters without requiring in-depth knowledge of the system. In this subsection, we compare our approach with building performance models for specific performance counters.

We build two regression models for *DS2* with CPU and memory as target counters, respectively. The *EA* has a performance counter that measures the general load of the system. We build three regression models for the *EA*, using CPU, memory and the load counter of *EA* as target counters, respectively. We measure the prediction error in each model. The results are shown in Table 6 and 7.

Building regression models against specific performance counters may not detect performance regressions. Table 6 and 7 show that even though the prediction errors in the runs without regression are low, some runs with a regression also have low prediction errors. For example, run *Regression 1* in *DS2* has a 0% prediction error when building a model against memory. We examine the counters and find that even though *Regression 1* is injected to introduce a memory overhead, the version with regression uses only 3% more memory than the version without regression. However, the correlations between memory and other counters are different. For example, the correlation between memory and IO Other Bytes/sec is 0.46 in the old version while the correlation is only 0.26 in the new version. In the case study of *EA*, using specific performance counters is even less accurate with real-life regressions. When using CPU and memory, there are cases where prediction errors in the runs with regressions are lower than the runs without regressions. The load counter is typically used in practice for measuring the system performance of *EA*. The prediction error without regressions is 5%, while the two runs with regressions are only

Table 6: Prediction errors when building regression models for specific performance counters in *DS2*. The model is built using data from an old version and is applied on a new version to measure prediction errors.

Run Name	Prediction Error	
	CPU	Memory
No regression 1	1%	0%
No regression 2	1%	0%
No regression 3	1%	0%
No regression 4	1%	0%
No regression 5	1%	0%
Run Name	CPU	Memory
Regression 1	22%	0%
Regression 2	993%	832%
Regression 3	15%	15%
Regression 4	250%	57%
Regression 5	5%	17%

Table 7: Prediction errors when building regression models for specific performance counters in *EA*. The model is built using data from an old version and is applied on a new version to measure prediction errors.

Run Name	Prediction error		
	CPU	Memory	Load counter
Regression 1	27%	11%	45%
Regression 2	16%	3%	7%
Regression 3	0%	6%	12%
Regression 4	19%	9%	147%
Regression 5	641%	3%	7%
Run Name	CPU	Memory	Load counter
No Regression 1	6%	3%	5%

slightly higher (7%). In such cases, it is difficult for performance analysts to determine whether there are any performance regressions. Although one counter in some runs with regression (e.g., CPU in regression 2, DS2) may have high prediction error, developers can only ensure to capture such regression if they build a model for all counters. Otherwise, there is always possibility that we might miss detecting a regression because we selected a wrong target counter.

> *Our approach outperforms the traditional approach of building models for specific counters to detect performance regressions. Using specific counter may miss detecting performance regressions.*

7.2 Comparing our approach with statistical tests

Statistical tests, such as Student T-test, are often used to compare performance counters across performance testing. We use independent two-sample unpaired two-tailed T tests to determine whether the average value of a performance counter in the old and new versions of the system is different. Our null hypothesis assumes that the average values of a performance counter are similar in two versions of the system. Our alternate hypothesis is that the average value of a performance counter is statistically different across the two versions. We reject the null hypothesis when p-values are smaller than 0.05.

Table 8 presents the results of using the T-test when comparing two versions of the system. We find that for *DS2*,

Table 8: Number of performance counters that have significant differences in the two versions. We consider the difference is significant when the p-value of the T-test is smaller than 0.05.

of DS2	
Run Name	# significantly differenced counters
No regression 1	6
No regression 2	3
No regression 3	6
No regression 4	3
No regression 5	6
Regression 1	8
Regression 2	17
Regression 3	21
Regression 4	23
Regression 5	11

of EA	
Run Name	% significantly differenced counters
Regression 1	35%
Regression 2	30%
Regression 3	40%
Regression 4	39%
Regression 5	24%
No regression 1	32%

the runs with regressions have more performance counters with p-values smaller than 0.05 than the runs without performance regressions. However, we notice that the runs in *DS2* without regressions still have 3 to 6 performance counters with significant differences in the two versions. In such case, the performance analysts would need to examine each performance counters to find out that such runs have no regressions.

T-test does not perform well with *EA*. Table 8 shows that the run without regression has 32% of the performance counters with significant difference across both versions, while the runs with regression have 24% to 40% of the performance counters with significant difference. The runs *Regression 2* and *Regression 5* on *EA* have less performance counters with significant differences than the run without regressions (*No regression 1*). Moreover, in the run without regressions, examining 32% of the entire performance counters is still a very time consuming task. Such finding shows that the T-test approach does not work well in practice for identifying performance regressions.

> *T-test does not perform well in practice to detect performance regressions. There are a large number of performance counters with significant differences in the T-test results even though no regressions exist.*

8. THREATS TO VALIDITY

This section discusses the threats to the validity of our study.

External validity

Our study is performed on *DS2* and *EA*. Both subject systems have years of history and there are prior performance engineering research [22, 27, 35] studying both systems. Nevertheless more case studies on other software in other domains are needed to evaluate our approach.

Internal validity

Our approach is based on the recorded performance counters. The quality of recorded counters can impact the internal validity of our study. For example, if none of the recorded performance counters can track the syndrome of a performance regression, our approach would not assist in detecting the regressions. Our approach also depends on building regression models. Therefore, our approach may not perform well where there are a small number of observations of performance counters, since one cannot build a regression model based on a small data set. Our model requires periodically recorded performance counters as input counters. Some event-based performance counters (like response time), need to be transformed (like average response time during the past minute), to be leveraged by our approach.

Although our approach builds regression models using performance counters, we do not claim any causal relationship between the dependent variable and independent variables in the models. The only purpose of building regression models is to capture the relation between performance counters.

Construct validity

Our approach uses the Pearson distance to calculate the distance matrix, uses the average distance to link clusters and uses the Calinski-Harabasz stopping rule to determine the total number of clusters. There are other rules to performance those calculations. Although experiments show that the performance of other rules does not outperform Calinski-Harabasz in performance engineering research [35], choosing other rules may have better results for other systems. We use the p-value from a Kolmogorov-Smirnov test to determine target counters. In practice, multiple counters can all have minimal p-values. To address this threat, we plan to use other criteria, such as effect size, to select the target counter.

Our evaluation is based on comparing the largest prediction errors of the runs with and without performance regression. Our case studies show the large difference of prediction errors between runs with and without performance regression. However, choosing an appropriate prediction error as a threshold is still crucial to achieve high accuracy for our approach. Due to the dissimilarity between large software systems, performance analysts need to choose the best threshold for their systems. Automated identification of a threshold for a system is in our future plan.

We compare our approach with using T-test to compare every performance counter. Although the T-test is widely used to compare two distributions, other statistical tests, such as Mann-Whitney U test, may also be used in practice to compare performance counters. We plan to compare our approach with other statistical tests in future work. We also compare our approach with building regression models against CPU, memory and the load counters for the two subject systems. We plan to compare our approach with building other types of models and using other performance counters to further evaluate our approach.

9. CONCLUSION

Performance regression detection is an important task in performance assurance activities. Detecting performance regressions is still a challenging task for performance analysts. We propose an approach to automatically detect such regressions. Our approach first groups performance counters into clusters. We use the clusters to determine the number of models that we need to build. For each cluster, we leverage statistical tests to select a performance counter (i.e., a

target counter), against which we build a regression model. We use the prediction error to measure the difference between two versions of a system in each cluster. A higher than threshold prediction error is considered a sign of a performance regression. Our approach addresses the challenges of detecting performance regressions in two folds: 1) our approach groups performance counters into clusters to determine how many models are needed to represent the performance of a system, 2) we do not require in-depth system experiences from performance analysts.

The highlights of this paper are:

- We propose an approach to automatically detect performance regressions by building regression models on clustered performance counters.

- Our approach can successfully detect both injected and real-life performance regressions. The accuracy of our approach is not heavily impacted by threshold.

- Our approach outperforms using statistical tests, such as T-test, and building models against one performance counter, such CPU, to detect performance regressions.

Acknowledgement

We would like to thank BlackBerry for providing access to the enterprise system used in our case study. The findings and opinions expressed in this paper are those of the authors and do not necessarily represent or reflect those of BlackBerry and/or its subsidiaries and affiliates. Moreover, our results do not reflect the quality of BlackBerry's products.

10. REFERENCES

[1] Apache tomcat. http://tomcat.apache.org/.

[2] Dell dvd store. http://linux.dell.com/dvdstore/.

[3] Mysql. http://www.mysql.com/.

[4] J. Bataille. Operational Progress Report. http://www.hhs.gov/digitalstrategy/blog/2013/12/operational-progress-report.html, 2013. Last Accessed: 01-Jun-2014.

[5] P. Bodík, M. Goldszmidt, and A. Fox. Hilighter: Automatically building robust signatures of performance behavior for small- and large-scale systems. In *SysML 08: Proceedings of the Third Workshop on Tackling Computer Systems Problems with Machine Learning Techniques*. USENIX Association, 2008.

[6] T. Calinski and J. Harabasz. A dendrite method for cluster analysis. *Communications in Statistics*, 3(1):1–27, Jan 1974.

[7] S.-H. Cha. Comprehensive survey on distance/similarity measures between probability density functions. *International Journal of Mathematical Models and Methods in Applied Sciences*, 1(4):300–307, Nov 2007.

[8] I. Cohen, M. Goldszmidt, T. Kelly, J. Symons, and J. S. Chase. Correlating instrumentation data to system states: A building block for automated diagnosis and control. In *OSDI'04: Proceedings of the 6th Conference on Symposium on Opearting Systems Design & Implementation - Volume 6*, pages 16–16, 2004.

[9] I. Cohen, S. Zhang, M. Goldszmidt, J. Symons, T. Kelly, and A. Fox. Capturing, indexing, clustering, and retrieving system history. In *SOSP '05:*

Proceedings of the Twentieth ACM Symposium on Operating Systems Principles, pages 105–118, 2005.

[10] J. Dean and L. A. Barroso. The tail at scale. *Communications of the ACM*, 56(2):74–80, Feb 2013.

[11] R. O. Duda and P. E. Hart. *Pattern Classification and Scene Analysis*. John Wiley & Sons Inc, 1st edition, 1973.

[12] K. C. Foo, Z. M. Jiang, B. Adams, A. E. Hassan, Y. Zou, and P. Flora. Mining performance regression testing repositories for automated performance analysis. In *Proceedings of the 2010 10th International Conference on Quality Software*, QSIC '10, pages 32–41, 2010.

[13] I. Frades and R. Matthiesen. Overview on techniques in cluster analysis. *Bioinformatics Methods In Clinical Research*, 593:81–107, Mar 2009.

[14] D. Freedman. *Statistical models: theory and practice*. Cambridge University Press, 2009.

[15] M. H. Fulekar. *Bioinformatics: Applications in Life and Environmental Sciences*. Springer, 1st edition, 2008.

[16] H. W. Gunther. *WebSphere Application Server Development Best Practices for Performance and Scalability*, volume 1.1.0. IBM WebSphere White Paper, 2000.

[17] F. E. Harrell. *Regression modeling strategies: with applications to linear models, logistic regression, and survival analysis*. Springer, 2001.

[18] C. Heger, J. Happe, and R. Farahbod. Automated root cause isolation of performance regressions during software development. In *ICPE '13: Proceedings of the 4th ACM/SPEC International Conference on Performance Engineering*, pages 27–38, 2013.

[19] A. Huang. Similarity measures for text document clustering. In *Proceedings of the New Zealand Computer Science Research Student Conference*, pages 44–56, Apr 2008.

[20] M. Jiang, M. Munawar, T. Reidemeister, and P. Ward. Automatic fault detection and diagnosis in complex software systems by information-theoretic monitoring. In *DSN '09: Proceedings of 2009 IEEE/IFIP International Conference on Dependable Systems Networks*, pages 285–294, June 2009.

[21] M. Jiang, M. A. Munawar, T. Reidemeister, and P. A. Ward. System monitoring with metric-correlation models: Problems and solutions. In *ICAC '09: Proceedings of the 6th International Conference on Autonomic Computing*, pages 13–22, 2009.

[22] Z. M. Jiang, A. E. Hassan, G. Hamann, and P. Flora. Automated performance analysis of load tests. In *ICSM '09: 25th IEEE International Conference on Software Maintenance*, pages 125–134, 2009.

[23] H. Malik, H. Hemmati, and A. E. Hassan. Automatic detection of performance deviations in the load testing of large scale systems. In *ICSE '13: Proceedings of the 2013 International Conference on Software Engineering*, pages 1012–1021, 2013.

[24] H. Malik, Z. M. Jiang, B. Adams, A. E. Hassan, P. Flora, and G. Hamann. Automatic comparison of load tests to support the performance analysis of large enterprise systems. In *CSMR '10: Proceedings of the 2010 14th European Conference on Software Maintenance and Reengineering*, pages 222–231, 2010.

[25] G. W. Milligan and M. C. Cooper. An examination of procedures for determining the number of clusters in a data set. *Psychometrika*, 50(2):159–179, Jun 1985.

[26] R. Mojena. Hierarchical grouping methods and stopping rules: An evaluation. *The Computer Journal*, 20(4):353–363, Nov 1977.

[27] T. H. Nguyen, B. Adams, Z. M. Jiang, A. E. Hassan, M. Nasser, and P. Flora. Automated detection of performance regressions using statistical process control techniques. In *Proceedings of the 3rd ACM/SPEC International Conference on Performance Engineering*, ICPE '12, pages 299–310, New York, NY, USA, 2012. ACM.

[28] T. H. D. Nguyen, B. Adams, Z. M. Jiang, A. E. Hassan, M. Nasser, and P. Flora. Automated verification of load tests using control charts. In *APSEC '11: Proceedings of the 2011 18th Asia-Pacific Software Engineering Conference*, pages 282–289, 2011.

[29] T. H. D. Nguyen, M. Nagappan, A. E. Hassan, M. Nasser, and P. Flora. An industrial case study of automatically identifying performance regression-causes. In *MSR 2014: Proceedings of the 11th Working Conference on Mining Software Repositories*, pages 232–241, 2014.

[30] T. V. Prasad. Gene Expression Data Analysis Suite: Distance measures. http://gedas.bizhat.com/dist.htm, 2006. Last Accessed: 11-Jun-2014.

[31] P. J. Rousseeuw. Silhouettes: a graphical aid to the interpretation and validation of cluster analysis. *Journal of Computational and Applied Mathematics*, 20(1):53–65, Nov 1987.

[32] N. Sandhya and A. Govardhan. Analysis of similarity measures with wordnet based text document clustering. In *Proceedings of the International Conference on Information Systems Design and Intelligent Applications*, pages 703–714, Jan 2012.

[33] W. A. Shewhart. *Economic control of quality of manufactured product*, volume 509. ASQ Quality Press, 1931.

[34] J. H. Stapleton. *Models for Probability and Statistical Inference: Theory and Applications*. WILEY, 2008.

[35] M. D. Syer, Z. M. Jiang, M. Nagappan, A. E. Hassan, M. Nasser, and P. Flora. Continuous validation of load test suites. In *Proceedings of the International Conference on Performance Engineering*, pages 259–270, Mar 2014.

[36] P.-N. Tan, M. Steinbach, and V. Kumar. *Cluster Analysis: Basic Concepts and Algorithms*. Addison-Wesley Longman Publishing Co., Inc., 1st edition, 2005.

[37] E. Weyuker and F. Vokolos. Experience with performance testing of software systems: issues, an approach, and case study. *Transactions on Software Engineering*, 26(12):1147–1156, Dec 2000.

[38] P. Xiong, C. Pu, X. Zhu, and R. Griffith. vperfguard: An automated model-driven framework for application performance diagnosis in consolidated cloud environments. In *ICPE '13: sProceedings of the 4th ACM/SPEC International Conference on Performance Engineering*, pages 271–282, 2013.

26

System-Level Characterization of Datacenter Applications

Manu Awasthi, Tameesh Suri, Zvika Guz,
Anahita Shayesteh, Mrinmoy Ghosh, Vijay Balakrishnan
Samsung Semiconductor, Inc.
601 McCarthy Blvd., Milpitas, CA
{manu.awasthi, tameesh.suri, zvika.guz, anahita.sh, mrinmoy.g, vijay.bala}@ssi.samsung.com

ABSTRACT

In recent years, a number of benchmark suites have been created for the "Big Data" domain, and a number of such applications fit the client-server paradigm. A large volume of recent literature in characterizing "Big Data" applications have largely focused on two extremes of the characterization spectrum. On one hand, multiple studies have focused on client-side performance. These involve fine-tuning server-side parameters for an application to get the best client-side performance. On the other extreme, characterization focuses on picking one set of client-side parameters and then reporting the server microarchitectural statistics under those assumptions. While the two ends of the spectrum present interesting results, this paper argues that they are not enough, and in some cases, undesirable, to drive system-wide architectural decisions in datacenter design.

This paper shows that for the purposes of designing an efficient datacenter, detailed microarchitectural characterization of "Big Data" applications is an overkill. It identifies four main system-level macro-architectural features and shows that these features are more representative of an application's system level behavior. To this end, a number of datacenter applications from a variety of benchmark suites are evaluated and classified into these previously identified macro-architectural features. Based on this analysis, the paper further shows that each application class will benefit from a very different server configuration leading to a highly efficient, cost-effective datacenter.

Categories and Subject Descriptors

C [**Computer Systems Organization**]: Performance of Systems; C.4 [**Performance of Systems**]: [Design studies; Performance attributes; Measurement techniques]

Keywords

Performance measurement, Datacenter Performance, Datacenter, Benchmarking, Workload Characterization

1. INTRODUCTION

In recent years, a large amount of the world's compute and storage has been pushed onto back end datacenters. The large scale of these datacenters come at a hefty price–initial setup cost can range anywhere from upwards of US $200 million, and yearly operation cost is on the order of millions [30]. With such a high TCO (Total Cost of Ownership), performance/$ is a first-order design constraint. Tailoring the hardware to the specific set of applications the datacenter is expected to run can save millions of dollars.

The term "Big Data" refers to the explosion in the quantity (and sometimes, quality) of available and potentially relevant data, largely because of the result of recent advancements in data recording and storage [26]. Modern datacenters execute a diverse set of applications on these massive datasets. These applications are collectively referred to as "Big Data" applications. Due to the unprecedented scale of these applications and their highly-distributed nature, the characteristics of "Big Data" applications are significantly different than those of traditional multi-core applications [41]. To gain better understanding of the behavior of these applications, a large body of work has been done in recent years to develop and characterize representative benchmarks for the "Big Data" domain.

A lot of these benchmark suites are focused towards research of the microarchitecture of a single server [34, 27, 41]. While they provide valuable insights into core and chip design, they usually focus on the core [1] microarchitecture analysis. Since most on the microarchitecture research is done using simulators, these "Big Data" benchmarks have been tailored to fit this research model. For example, this leads to decreasing the size of the working set so that the benchmarks can be run within a simulator. This, in turn makes the benchmark not exhibit most of its inherent properties due to which it was chosen as a representative application in the first place.

On the other side of the spectrum, detailed analysis has been published on the client performance of specific applications [13, 7, 6, 9], focusing on tailoring the application for a predefined server architecture. The middle of the spectrum–namely characterizing the behavior of full-scale applications, with representative data sets in a multi-server environment for the purposes of system design is left somewhat unexplored. In this paper, we try to provide a framework for the datacenter designer to make judicious decisions about hardware acquisition based on characterization of realistic

---

[1]This paper uses core and processor interchangeably in the rest of the discussion.

applications. This paper describes the authors' experience in compiling and characterizing a number of representative "Big Data" applications, from different benchmark suites. The authors found that the existing benchmarks, if used *as-is*, are ill-fitted for system and storage architecture research. This is either because they are scaled down to the point where they do not stress the relevant components, or because they are concentrating on studying processor microarchitecture, which is just one of the components of research on system design. The reader is taken through the process the authors went through for tuning the workloads to the environment they are running on, describing how they reason about application scaling, and presenting performance characterization and analysis for several multi-server, real-world applications.

While the results and tuning process presented here should be of interest to any hardware system researcher looking at the "Big Data" domain, they are also valuable outside the realm of pure systems research. Indeed, when trying to decide on specific hardware needed for a new datacenter deployment, server microarchitecture optimizations are of little value. Instead, this paper illustrates how a smaller number of coarse-grained metrics allow for good classification of a workload and are usually enough to make the first order decision about the most important system level bottlenecks for the application. Keeping this context in mind, this paper makes the following contributions:

- The reader is taken through the tuning process of "Big Data" applications, providing an ordered recipe for what should be done, and how.
- Characterization results are presented for several "Big Data" workloads, concentrating on the coarse-grain, per-server, system-level behavior rather than the fine-grained microarchitectural profile.
- The paper illustrates how a few coarse-grained metrics (macroarchitectural properties) are enough to gain understanding of an application's behavior, and explain how these metrics can be obtained.
- Finally, some insights are presented on how to use information about the macroarchitectural properties of applications to intelligently co-locate applications.

The rest of this paper is organized as follows: Section 2 presents an overview of the organization of a modern datacenter, and describes the applications considered in this paper. Section 3 identifies the four macroarchitectural parameters, and provides insights into why these parameters are important. Next, Section 4 presents the characterization methodology and authors' experience on performance tuning of different workloads. Section 5 presents the related work, and Section 6 concludes.

2. DATACENTERS AND APPLICATIONS

Datacenters are broadly classified into three categories: (1) Enterprise, (2) Cloud Computing, and (3) Web 2.0. While they share a common goal of reducing TCO and increasing efficiency of available resources, their application set and requirements are significantly different. As a result, the characteristics and design points of these three deployments are also very different.

- *Enterprise*: These datacenters support corporate and financial environments for primarily one institution.

Such datacenters have a comparatively smaller scales, with low multi-tenancy and a smaller application diversity. Enterprise datacenters mostly run proprietary applications like SAP ERP, Microsoft Sharepoint and Microsoft Exchange.
- *Cloud Computing*: Cloud computing datacenters provide a virtualized computing and storage resources as a service to end users. These datacenters have larger scale and support a bigger class of applications. Examples of Cloud Computing services include Amazon Web Services, Microsoft Azure and Google Compute Engine.
- *Web 2.0*: Web 2.0 datacenters support massively high-volume data and users through vertically integrated application stacks and popular open-source frameworks. Most of the services provided by the likes of Google, Facebook and Yahoo! are hosted on such servers.

This paper focuses on the *Web 2.0* category– a category with an expected Compound Annual Growth Rate (CAGR) of 17.8% [24]. These datacenters typically consist of several types of servers (or server clusters), each of which are designed to execute designated tasks [39]. Figure 1 shows a representative deployment scenario, where the datacenter back-end consists of three distinct layers. Each layer runs a different class of applications and has its distinct set of hardware requirements. The following sections describe each one of these three layers, and describe the applications that have been characterized and analyzed in this paper.

2.1 The Caching Layer

The caching layer is primarily responsible for the performance and response times of the datacenter. The caching layer resides in between the web front-end and the back-end database, and uses large amounts of DRAM capacity to cache frequently used data and reduce the amount of queries hitting the back-end database servers. The reduction in database (DB) queries reduces the pressure on the servers– notably the I/O subsystem– and considerably improves user-experience. Memcache [28]– an open source key-value distributed caching software, is by far the most deployed web caching application in this domain. Section 4.2 presents the authors' experience in tuning Memcache and using it as a representative web caching layer application.

2.2 The Analytics Layer

The analytics layer contains a rich set of applications that analyze huge amount of data (i.e. "Big Data") to extract knowledge and provide value. The majority of "Big Data" applications belong in this layer. These applications can be further classified into two separate groups: *real-time* and *offline*.

Real-Time Analytics: Designed for the most latency sensitive analytics, real-time analytics applications are designed such that they store either the *entire* data set or the *vast majority* of their data set in server memory. Hence, this paradigm of Real-Time Analytics is often referred to as In-Memory Computing (IMC). In the past, their adoption was hampered by high memory acquisition cost, but with the recent decline in DRAM prices and the availability of mature software, IMC is becoming widely used in many datacenter deployments. Indeed, the exponential growth in data and the need for faster turnaround in extracting meaningful

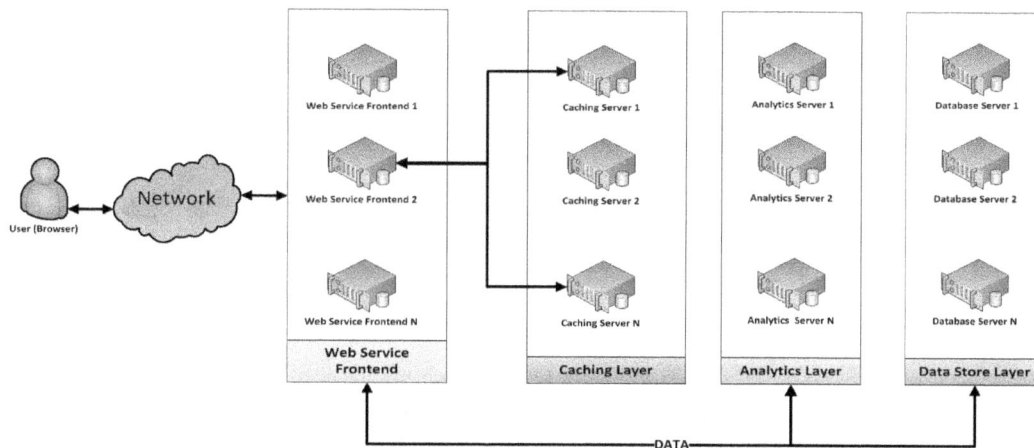

Figure 1: Representative datacenter architecture. A datacenter is composed of several different server tiers.

information is expected to expand adoption of IMC, forecasted to reach over \$13 B by 2018 [18]. Redis [4] and Apache SPARK [15] are two popular open-source, in-memory frameworks. This paper focuses on the Redis framework, which is used in the production stack of several *web 2.0* companies like Twitter, Craigslist, Flickr and Github [21].

Redis [4] is an open-source, in-memory data structure framework that provides an advanced key-value abstraction. Unlike traditional key-value systems where keys are of a simple data type, Redis supports complex data types: keys can contain hashes, lists, sets, and sorted sets. It enables complex atomic operations on these data types; all operations are executed on the server, and the entire dataset is served from the server's DRAM. Data persistence is achieved through frequent syncs to hard-drives, while sharding is used for scaling-out. This abstraction has proved particularly useful for multiple latency-sensitive tasks.

Offline Analytics and Batch Processing: Batch processing of large scale data via distributed computing is a widely used service in contemporary datacenters. These services typically rely on the Map-Reduce computational model, for which Apache Hadoop [1] is the most popular open-source implementation. A Hadoop deployment spans multiple nodes and comprises of multiple modules, including the Hadoop distributed file system (HDFS) for large-scale data storage and the map-reduce programming model for computation. While the computation is slower than an IMC system, the distributed model allows it to process massive amount of data using commodity hardware. It is extensively used by organizations to support analytics like sentiment analysis and recommendation engines on enormous data volumes. This paper studies two popular applications on the Hadoop framework:

- **Nutch** Web search [14, 32] was the first proof-of-concept Hadoop application and remains a good, representative data-intensive distributed application. Nutch is an extensible and scalable open-source web search engine package that aims to index the World Wide Web as effectively as commercial search services.
- **Mahout Data Analytics** is a scalable, open-source machine-learning framework built on top of Hadoop Map-Reduce. It is used to apply machine learning models to massive volumes of data that do not fit the

traditional computational environments. Specifically, our workload uses the bayes classifier algorithm to execute text analysis and clustering on large datasets.

2.3 The Data Store Layer

This layer often comprises of multiple databases that store and serve data back to various applications in the datacenter. Traditionally, relational databases, organized in a row-column format, were used exclusively for data storing. However, since relational databases are both hard to scale out and unfit for unstructured data, contemporary datacenters rely on NoSQL databases to meet the performance requirements at scale. This paper characterizes Cassandra– a popular NoSQL database. Cassandra is designed for write-intensive workloads and targets linear throughput scaling with the number of nodes. The YCSB [25] framework was used as a client for all experiments.

3. MACRO ARCHITECTURAL PARAMETERS FOR SYSTEM WIDE ANALYSIS

This section attempts to provide a framework for system wide analysis of representative datacenter applications. Creation of such a framework is an important step in characterizing these applications with the aim of finding the best hardware configuration for each tier and/or application class. Going through this exercise would be essential for the following scenarios: (i) a new datacenter has to be set up, based on the requirements of the application set of each tier, or (ii) a datacenter installation already exists and the applications running at each tier are well known, but the hardware infrastructure of a particular (or all) tier(s) has to be updated.

A large body of work has been dedicated to characterizing datacenter level applications. Section 5 presents a detailed survey of prior work. However, most of the existing literature is of little use for the said purpose since it highlights one of the two characteristics: (i) client side performance, or (ii) detailed exploration of server microarchitecture. Both of these levels of characterization have value, but looking at application characteristics from a system perspective is much more valuable to the datacenter designer. Getting a complete picture of how a server should be provisioned based on its behavior under real-world use cases is essential to make sure that each server machine can handle all requests, meet QoS and SLA requirements, while still not being *extremely* over-provisioned. In order to make an informed decision, according to the authors' experience, a first level analysis of datacenter applications should be done on a coarser, system-wide level. This section describes the four main macro-architectural resource categories that should be considered while making per-server provision decisions for a particular application/class of applications.

Each macro-architectural resource category is composed of several fine-grained metrics that effectively decide the nature of the application considered with respect to that category. Classifying each application into one or more such categories enables intelligent and cost-effective hardware provisioning. Moreover, since it is in-feasible to list *all* the fine-grained parameters, applications are broadly classified based on their *intensity* of usage of each resource category. The intensity of usage is defined as follows for each resource category.

CPU Intensity CPU utilization provides a broad measure of the amount of work done by the application. It is very important to note *how* the CPU is being utilized. It is entirely possible that some programs have high CPU utilization, while making little forward progress, e.g. in cases where multiple threads of a program are waiting for I/O. Learnings from the application compute requirements provides an effective understanding of the CPU performance requirements and supports informed provisioning decisions about choice of CPUs.

DRAM Intensity At a macro level, this is comprised of two main components: (i) capacity, and (ii) bandwidth. Identifying the dominating component for each application supports effective provisioning trade-offs about DRAM capacity and performance in the server node.

Disk I/O Intensity The two most fundamental components of Disk I/O are (i) access latency, and (ii) bandwidth. Understanding application throughput and sensitivity to each parameter is essential in selecting the correct interface and media for storage provisioning. These may include traditional hard-disk drives (HDDs) or flash-based solid-state disks (SSDs) on standard SATA3 interface, high performance PCIe based SSDs or a combination of some/all of the above.

Network Intensity All nodes in a datacenter communicate over a network, and ethernet is the most commonly deployed technology. Maximum bandwidth of each ethernet port is predefined by the protocol and understanding of sustained and peak application network requirements supports better network provisioning.

Several applications used in production environments representing each tier were evaluated and classified into the four broad categories. Results of characterization experiments suggest that each of the aforementioned tiers of a datacenter have distinct hardware requirements and a uniform, general-purpose hardware allocation across all tiers does not represent an efficient datacenter design. The authors provide a performance architect's perspective of the Web 2.0 applications that over-provisioning hardware in isolation to application requirements does not have any impact on the performance or scalability of the applications, and macro-architectural classification of applications is instrumental in designing and deploying cost efficient datacenters.

4. DATACENTER APPLICATION CHARACTERIZATION

Section 2 postulated that in most cases, matching the application to the right set of hardware resources requires categorizing it into one of four main categories. This section first presents the authors' experiences in installing and running out-of-the-box versions of "Big Data" benchmarks, with the default data sets. Next, the section presents the observations from the default experiments and then compares those results to finely tuned versions of the same applications to highlight the learnings from application tuning. This experience is used to show that stock versions of the considered benchmarks do not stress the *intended* subsystems of a typical server hardware. Based on these experiences, it is also shown that in a datacenter setting, one application can have multiple points of saturation on a server, and the points of saturation are highly dependent on the considered use case.

4.1 Methodology

The configuration used for these studies comprises of a cluster of eight server class machines running Ubuntu 12.04.5. Each server node consists of a dual-socket Intel Xeon E5-2690 processor. There are 8 physical cores on each socket, supporting a total of 32 independent threads per node with hyper-threading. Details of the setup can be found in table 1. The Hadoop setup consisted of seven worker nodes (DataNodes, TaskTrackers) and one master node (NameNode, SecondaryNameNode, JobTracker). The nodes are connected through a 10GbE network. The rest of the workloads use the specified number of nodes as indicated for each configuration. Most client-server style workloads were run as a single client, single server setup, unless otherwise specified.

Table 1: Server node configuration

Processor	Xeon E5-2690, 2.9GHz, dual socket-8 cores
Storage	3× SATA 7200RPM HDDs
Memory Capacity	128 GB ECC DDR3 R-DIMMs
Memory B/W	102.4GB/s (8 channels,DDR3-1600)
Network	10 Gigabit Ethernet NIC
Operating system	Ubuntu 12.04.5
Hadoop version	1.2.1
Memcache version	1.4.13
Cassandra version	2.0.9
Redis version	2.8.12

Benchmarks are evaluated by collecting data from the application, operating system and processor performance counters. High level statistics of application and cluster performance are reported as part of application client or load generator. In addition, collectl [16] is run to monitor system level performance and use its plotting utility colplot [17] to generate graphs.

4.2 Application Tuning

Most of the applications described in prior sections required a significant effort to identify and tune several parameters to emulate real-world use cases. This section summarizes the authors' learnings from the tuning process.

For most cases, if the application fit the client-server paradigm, the goal was to maximize per-client performance, usually measured through metrics like transactions/second (TPS).

Table 2: **Key parameters that had to be tuned for Memcache and Cassandra**

Parameter	Original Value	Tuned Value
Memcache Tuning		
DRAM Size	4 GB	60 GB
Server Threads	4	32
Server TCP Connections	200	4096
Memcslap Clients	1	4
Threads/Client	4	16
Cassandra Tuning		
Commit Log	Same disk as DB	Different disk from DB
Heap Size/JVM Size	Default	600MB/6GB
Concurrent Reads/Writes	Default	64/64
Memtable size	Default	4 GB
Allowed open file handles	Default	32768
YCSB client threads	Default	200
YCSB Database size	Default	128 GB

The server's characteristics are reported after the application tuning has been completed.

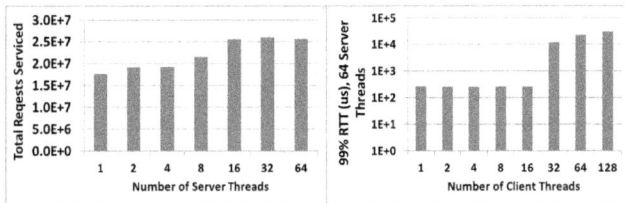

Figure 2: **Memcache performance tuning for number of client and server threads.**

Memcache The Data Caching benchmark provided as a part of CloudSuite benchmark suite was set up using the default parameters suggested in the CloudSuite literature. Over time, the authors realized that to emulate real-world use case, a number of parameters in the benchmark required significant changes. First, CloudSuite instructions [11] prescribe running Memcache with 4 GB memory which can be set using the -m option, and then increasing it to 10 GB for larger working sets. However, experiments on Xeon servers indicated that running Memcache with as much DRAM as possible leads to better client side throughput. This is because of two factors: (i) Larger DRAM capacity implies a larger cache, leading to higher hit rates, and (ii) having more DRAM at hand allows the application to do better memory management by itself. Hence, >90% of the total available DRAM was attached to the Memcache server.

Prior studies [42] indicate poor scalability of Memcache with increase in the number of server threads. However, with the current production version of Memcache, good scalability was observed in client side performance with increasing the number of threads. Client side performance does not begin to degrade until there were enough hardware contexts to run client side threads. As indicated in Figure 2, it was possible to maintain 99th percentile latency of < 1 ms with 32 server threads. This coincides with the E5-2690 Xeon server having 16 physical and 32 SMT threads The number of TCP connections also had to be tuned for both the server and the client. The optimization details are listed in Table 2. This experience led to an exploration of the optimal number of threads on both the server and the client.

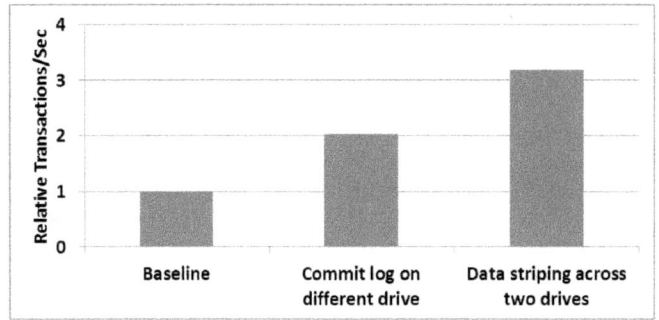

Figure 3: **Optimized Cassandra client side performance for YCSB workload E; parameters in Table 2.**

In order to reap maximum benefits out of a datacenter's Memcache installation, the administrators should ensure the upper limits of TCP connections that both servers and clients are allowed to make. One of the most important changes that the authors had to do to their setup was increase the number of client machines. This was because of two reasons: (i) one physical client was not enough to push the limits of the server, and (ii) no realistic use case could be achieved using a one-server, one-client setup, especially for Memcache [23]. Hence, the experiments were run with four physical clients.

Cassandra Cassandra needs tuning in two different ecosystems: (i) Being a client-server database application, the application server needs to be tuned to make sure that the destructive interference between different components of the application is reduced and the server is given enough physical resources for it to function properly – this will be explained shortly, and (ii) since it is a Java application, the JVM settings need to be tuned. The latter is relatively easy since enough information is publicly available.

For Cassandra-specific configuration parameters, tuning three main ones in accordance with available resources was found to have most impact on performance. The first and the most important optimization was to have the commit log on a different disk than the actual database. Since Cassandra is optimized for extremely fast writes, which are considered complete when they are written (simultaneously) to an on-disk structure called the commit-log (for durability) and also to an in-memory structure called the *Memtable*, which is a write-back cache. The second related optimization is the size of the Memtable. A small Memtable causes frequent writes to disk, affecting overall performance. The authors found that for their setup, 4GB was the most optimal Memtable size, and any further increase led to diminishing returns. Combined, these two optimizations lead to a significant gain in performance (2×, as indicated in Figure 3; left and center bars). This is because the destructive interference between the the two types of disk I/O : one for durability to the commit log and the other to propagate the writes to the database is removed. In addition, striping the database across more than one disk also leads to much better performance – middle and right bars in Figure 3 show that another 1.5× performance benefit can be realized by just allowing Cassandra to stripe data across two HDDs.

Several other, albeit smaller optimizations were also needed for correctness, rather than performance. For example, the maximum number of concurrent open files was increased within Linux to 32768, otherwise Cassandra would fail under heavy load, when Java isn't allowed to open the required number of file descriptors.

Hadoop Hadoop is another good example where a large number of Hadoop, OS and application parameters need to be tuned for best performance on a specific cluster. Number of MapReduce slots, as well as the Java heap size were the first configuration parameters to be tuned. The goal was to maximize resource (CPU, Memory) utilization of the cluster and Hadoop default values are usually too small. Configuring Java heap size is dependent on available memory as well as application characteristics. It was observed that some applications failed to run without sufficiently large heap size/memory and needed to be tuned properly. Several other OS and Hadoop configuration parameters were tuned, including, but not limited to, increasing HDFS block size, increasing `TimeOut` value and sorting parameters like `io.sort.factor` and `io.sort.mb`. More details on Hadoop tuning can be found in prior work [2, 3, 8, 12].

In addition to Hadoop cluster configuration, applications require tuning for best utilization of resources. For the experiments reported in this paper, the number of reduce tasks were configured to take advantage of available reduce slots in the cluster.

Redis Tuning Redis was relatively straightforward. The default configuration file was used, and the limit on concurrent open sockets was increased to 15000 (via ulimit). It was found that a single Redis process cannot saturate the Xeon E5-2690 server. Further process scaling experiments suggested that at least 4 Redis instances were needed to saturate the server.

4.3 Macro Architectural Characterization

This section presents a number of plots for system wide characteristics of application behavior that were generated using colplot. Colplot results for all the benchmarks, for each of the four macro-architectural categories are presented. Analysis of the results show that for a particular benchmark or phase in a benchmark, only *one* of the four categories is interesting. Table 3 provides a legend for understanding the information conveyed by these figures.

4.3.1 Memcache

Memcache was studied in a one server, four client configuration. The Memcache server was started with the parameters described previously in Table 2. A number of key-value combinations were studied, but in the interest of space, results will be reported for key and value sizes of 32 bytes and 25 KB respectively. This particular value corresponds to the *Image Preview* distribution described in [33].

CPU Intensity A well-tuned version of Memcache isn't very compute intensive. Although, if the number of worker threads is made extremely high, the number of context switches between the threads becomes high, and the workload becomes *artificially* compute bound, since most of the time is spent context switching, rather than doing useful work.

DRAM Intensity Since Memcache is essentially an in-memory cache, it is *always* bounded by DRAM capacity, irrespective of the size of key value pairs. Although, for server class machines considered in this study, DRAM bandwidth was *never* the bottleneck – the maximum observed DRAM bandwidth utilization was only 9.3% of peak bandwidth.

Table 3: ColPlot legend

CPU	
User	Percent time spent in user mode (application)
Sys	Percent time spent in system level (kernel)
Wait	Percent time spent idle waiting for an IO request
Memory	
Map	Combines mapped and anonymous memory
Buff	Memory used in system buffers
Cached	Memory in the pagecache, not including SwapCache
Slab	memory allocated to slabs
Inact	memory allocated to process that is no longer running
I/O	
ReadMB	Reads to disk in megabytes
WriteMB	Writes to disk in megabytes
Network	
InMB	Data sent, in megabytes
OutMB	Data received, in megabytes

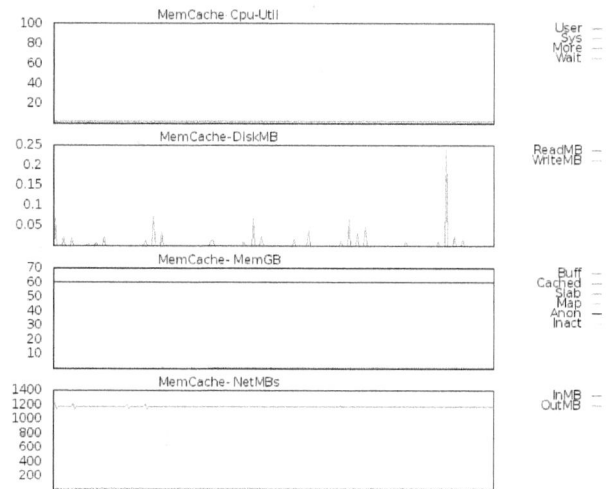

Figure 4: System-wide macro-architectural performance for Memcache.

Disk I/O Intensity Memcache displays close to negligible I/O activity, since all the data is made to fit in the DRAM by design.

Network Intensity Depending on the use case, the line rate (1.25 GB/s) of a 10 Gb ethernet card was achieved in a number of experiments. This tends to be especially true for use cases with larger value sizes, where the relative cost of processing and sending the data over ethernet is amortized over the larger sizes of data being transferred.

4.3.2 Cassandra

The primary bottleneck of a database has traditionally been the server I/O subsystem. NoSQL databases are no different. For Cassandra characterization, the YCSB [25] client was used, which allows users to drive the database with a number of different workloads (workload A - workload F), each varying in the proportion of read, write, insert, read-modify-write, and scan operations. The general profile

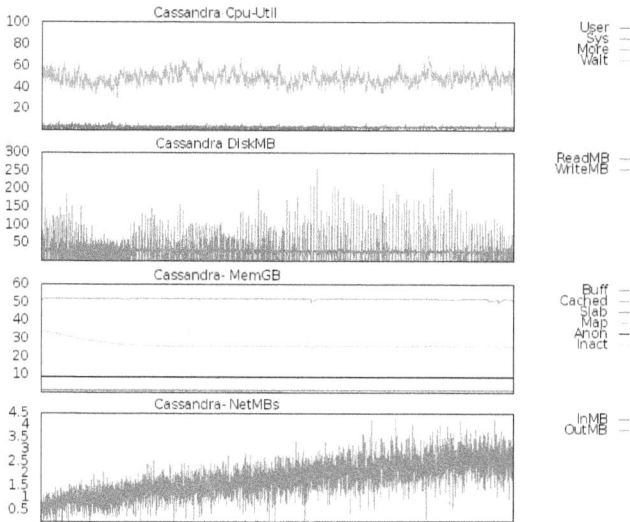

Figure 5: System-wide macro-architectural performance for Cassandra.

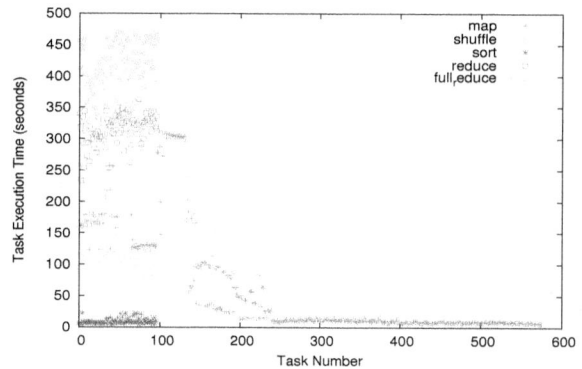

Figure 6: Task execution time for all Map/Reduce tasks in Nutch Indexing.

of Cassandra doesn't change much with the YCSB workload under consideration. It is almost always bottle-necked by I/O, although the degree of saturation varies with the workload. The results for YCSB scan-intensive workload E are illustrated in Figure 5. Next, the characteristics of the workload as a function of previously identified macro-architectural parameters are explained.

CPU Intensity Most of the CPU activity is caused by the server threads waiting for I/O to complete. This can be clearly seen in the CPU summary graphs, where the green part corresponding to *CPU Wait time* dominates – on an average the CPU spends close to 50% of the time waiting for I/O. The rest of the CPU activity is equally divided between the user and kernel. This CPU profile remains similar for other YCSB workloads as well, but the percentage of CPU time spent waiting for I/O is reduced for read intensive workloads, since some of the requests hit in the pagecache of the server DRAM.

DRAM Intensity Cassandra is never bound by DRAM bandwidth, although the servers utilize most of its DRAM capacity, the majority of which is for caching I/O requests in DRAM by the OS. This can be seen in Figure 5, where the most of the DRAM capacity is used by *Cached* and *Anon* types of pages. Some DRAM capacity is also used up by Java, but has not been garbage collected, as indicated by the *Inact* part of the DRAM usage.

Disk I/O Intensity Disk/storage is by far the most exercised system in the Cassandra server. Workload E is a scan intensive workload that requires a lot of random reads from the disk. This behavior leads to a very consistent read throughput of about 50 MB/s from the hard disk drive. Due to the internal commit and compaction operations of Cassandra, spikes in write to disks are seen, which are evidenced by the periodic red spikes in Figure 5. Since the window of time is large (2.5 hours), the write traffic spikes appear as a contiguous phenomenon. Zooming in to the data reveals the correct behavior of the application.

Network Intensity Cassandra under the current test configuration doesn't exercise the network by much. For

workload E, the network traffic is especially small since scan operations cause a large amount of disk I/O, while the amount of data that has to be sent back to the client is small. Hence, the maximum network utilization is around 1% of the peak available bandwidth. For test cases involving multiple clients and read intensive workloads, this utilization becomes better, but doesn't come close to saturating the line rate.

4.3.3 Nutch Indexing

The indexing sub-system of Nutch was studied as included in the HiBench[31] suite. The workload uses the default Linux dictionary file and automatically generates web crawl data where hyperlinks and words follow the Zipfian distribution. Crawl data is read and decompressed during map phase and is converted into inverted index files in the reduce phase. The dataset considered is 10M pages large. Several Map/Reduce parameters were changed to improve performance:

- MapReduce slots; tuned according to CPU count
- Status report timeout; increased to avoid killing jobs pre-mature
- Number of Reduce jobs; originally set to 1, increased to utilize all CPUs
- Map/Reduce Heap size; tuned for DRAM capacity
- Overlap between Map/Reduce jobs; reduced to eliminate undesired impact

Figure 6 shows execution times for all Map/Reduce tasks including execution time of shuffle and sort. Map execution times vary greatly as is expected considering the varying input file sizes and formats. Shuffle time is short, since we reduce Map /Reduce overlap and shuffle starts only after most map jobs have finished. Sort time is insignificant, and Reduce jobs take noticeable time which justifies increasing number of reduce tasks to the highest number of concurrent tasks available on the cluster.

Figure 7 shows system behavior (CPU, disk, memory and network) of a single datanode when running Nutch indexing on the Hadoop cluster.

CPU Intensity: During the map phase, where crawl data is read and decompressed, most CPU cycles are spent waiting for I/O. On the other hand, the reduce phase, where inverted indexes are generated , is very compute intensive.

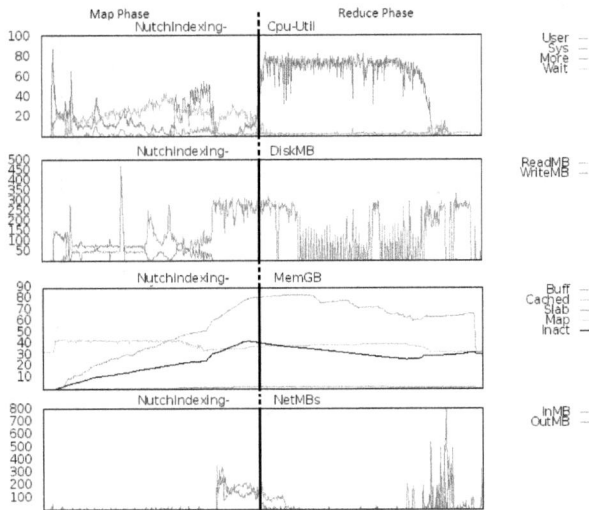

Figure 7: **System-wide macro-arch performance for Nutch indexing.**

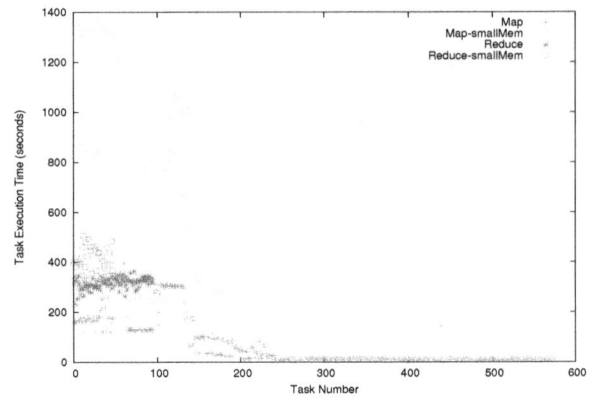

Figure 8: **Execution time sensitivity to total DRAM capacity per node (64 GB vs. 128 GB) for Nutch indexing.**

with up to 80% CPU utilization. Scaling experiments suggest that enabling simultaneous multithreading and utilizing all logical threads (32) in both map and reduce provides the fastest total execution time. Increasing Map/Reduce slots beyond that had no benefits.

DRAM Intensity: An extensive set of memory capacity sensitivity studies were done and it was identified that 1.2 GB memory per map is the optimal capacity for map execution for Nutch. Capacity below that caused failures due to out of heap errors. Experiments also showed undesirable impact of concurrent map/reduce jobs due to resource sharing, including DRAM. To address that, overlap between phases was decreased by increasing the "slow-start" parameter in Hadoop configuration. Figure 8 shows MapReduce execution time sensitivity to DRAM capacity (64 GB vs. 128 GB). As can be seen, increasing the memory capacity to 128 GB from 64 GB leads to reduction in the average execution time per map by about 5×.

Disk I/O Intensity: Nutch reads and transforms a large amount of data leading to high disk read throughput during map, and high write throughput (up-to 250 MB/s) during shuffle and reduce phases. The compression option used on input and output data can impact CPU and Disk I/O intensity.

Network Intensity: Activity on network happens at two distinct phases of execution: at the end of map where all data is shuffled across nodes to prepare for the reduce phase, and also at the end of reduce phase where the inverted index files go over the network to be written back to HDFS. The map phase was mostly data-local which explains the low network activity during that phase. Higher network activity is expected on larger cluster with hundreds or thousands of nodes.

4.3.4 Data Analytics

The Data analytics workload in CloudSuite [27] uses the existing implementation of bayes classification algorithm in Mahout for categorizing documents. Bayes classifier is a simple probabilistic classifier based on the bayes theorem. The

input dataset for categorization is the entire English language Wikipedia articles database (45 GB), which is freely available for download from the Wikipedia Foundation. The training dataset that is used to train the classifier is a subset of the Wikipedia articles (9 GB). This workload represents an offline mode of data analytics, where the training data is used to build the classifier model first, and the input dataset is subsequently used for categorization based on the classifier model. There is no feedback loop to the classifier model. The workload is divided into four phases, in addition to saving the initial Wikipedia-dataset to HDFS.

- The first phase splits the input and training Wikipedia dataset with a pre-defined chunk size across the available nodes in the Hadoop cluster.
- The second phase organizes and further splits the input data (from phase 1) based on predefined categories.
- The third phase builds a classifier model based on the training dataset using the Bayes algorithm. The classifier model is built once within the workload.
- The fourth or classification phase runs each input data split created in the earlier phases against the classifier model to categorize data. Most of the analysis of results in this section pertains to the classification phase.

The results of this study focus entirely on optimizing the execution time of the workload. Figure 9 shows the system-level characterization across the full lifetime of the workload.

CPU Intensity: The classification phase, which categorizes the input dataset, is highly CPU intensive, driving CPU utilization close to peak, as shown in phase 4 of Figure 9. An extensive set of sensitivity and scaling experiments were conducted by mapping map/reduce tasks to varied CPU configurations in each node. Figure 11 shows a subset of map execution time for different concurrent map configurations (8, 16, and 32) per node across the classification phase of the workload. It can be observed that increasing concurrent map tasks past sixteen, leads to 2× increase in execution time per map task. This is due to physical CPU limit of sixteen on the dual-socket Xeon node, even though it supports thirty two threads using hyper-threading. It can be concluded that if shortest execution time is desired, hyper-threading/simultaneous multi-threading (SMT) must be disabled and independent physical CPUs should be used.

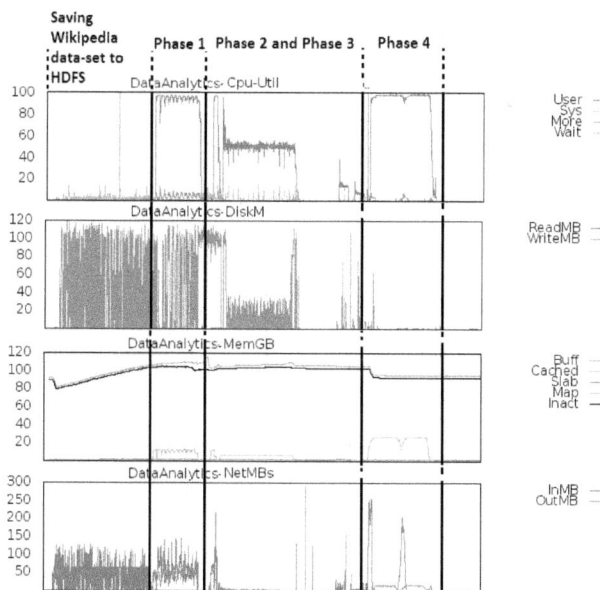

Figure 9: System-wide macro-arch performance for data analytics.

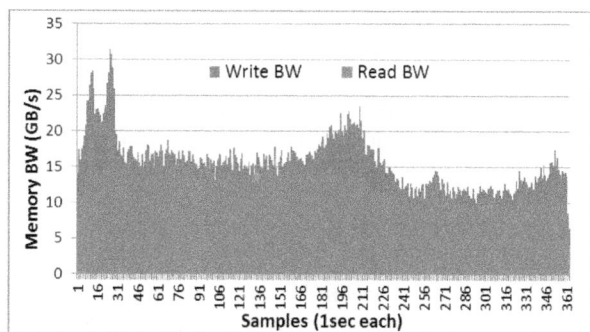

Figure 10: Aggregate memory bandwidth of classification phase in data-analytics.

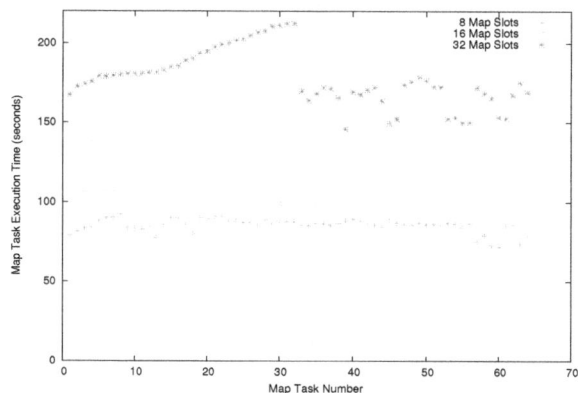

Figure 11: Execution-time sensitivity to Map slots for classification phase in data-analytics.

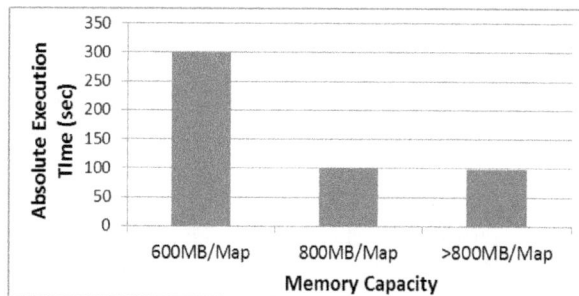

Figure 12: Data-analytics memory capacity scaling.

Although SMT is an effective architectural solution to increase throughput by executing multiple threads on a physical CPU [40], sharing of resources (execution units, caches etc.) leads to slowdown among homogeneous map jobs in a node. In order to achieve maximum map job-level parallelism and lowest time to completion, the Hadoop cluster must be provisioned to support enough independent physical CPUs for concurrent execution of all map jobs (function of the input data-set).

Memory Bandwidth Intensity: Figure 10 shows the aggregate memory bandwidth (including reads and writes) for the classification phase. Overall memory bandwidth utilization for the node is less than 20% of peak memory bandwidth. The DRAM page hit rates were also studied and they average around 80%, suggesting good locality of reference at the memory controller. Read bandwidth is also much higher than write bandwidth. Sensitivity experiments suggest memory bandwidth scales almost linearly with increasing map jobs per node up until all CPUs are fully utilized, although total bandwidth utilization remains less than 20% under full system-load.

Memory Capacity Intensity: An extensive set of memory capacity sensitivity studies were done to identify optimal capacity requirements per map job. Figure 12 shows the average map execution time with a subset of identified scaling memory capacity data points. Experimental results suggest that a minimum of 600 MB of heap space (constrained by physical memory) is required per map job for successful execution, and anything less results in heap memory failures. Increasing memory capacity per map job, 800 MB was identified as the most optimal point. The average execution time of map jobs reduces by 3× - from over 300 s to 100 s by increasing capacity from 600 MB to 800 MB. Scaling memory capacity beyond 800 MB per map does not achieve any performance benefits, as shown in Figure 12. This translates to a total of 25 GB heap space on a node with 32 CPU threads (with SMT enabled). In comparison, each dual socket Xeon server node can support up-to 768 GB of DRAM.

Disk I/O and Network Intensity: Most of the disk I/O activity is recorded in saving the initial Wikipedia dataset on HDFS and the first phase of the workload execution, which includes splitting and writing the updated input and training data on HDFS, as shown in Figure 9. Network traffic is also most prevalent in this phase. The classification phase has intermittent disk and network I/O.

4.3.5 Redis

Redis supports a rich set of data structures and provides various commands to manipulate them. While Redis can

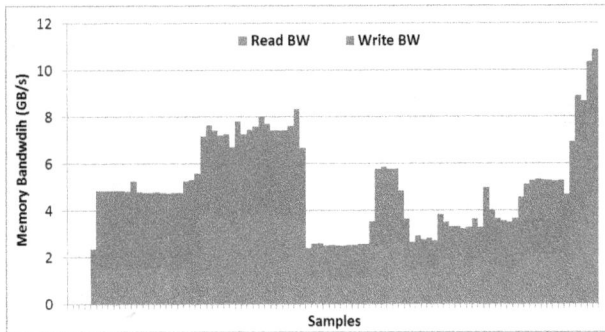

Figure 13: Redis memory bandwidth.

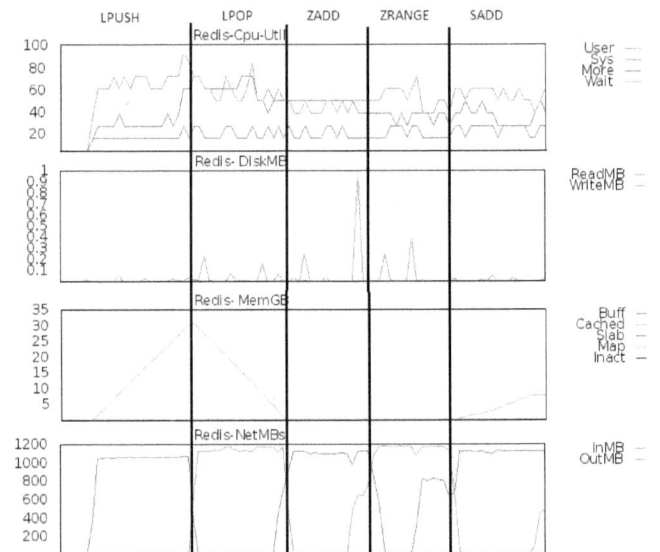

Figure 14: System-wide macro-arch performance for Redis.

also be used as an in-memory cache layer (like Memcache), this paper reports benchmarking results for a set of more complex instructions that are more relevant to the data analytics use-case. Specifically, this paper's benchmark tests utilize lists, sets, and sorted sets, which have all been confirmed to be used extensively in several real-world Redis deployments [19]. Lists are often used to implement job queues and maintain timelines. Sorted sets are naturally used in dashboards, leader boards, and priority queues. Sets are commonly used to maintain unique item lists which is a common task in several real-time analytic applications [5].

Figure 14 shows the macro-architecture characterization of our Redis benchmark. The workload comprises of 5 stages, that are easily distinguishable in the figure: (1) *lpush* inserts new elements to the head of a list. (2) *lpop* returns elements from the head of a list. (3) *zadd* adds an element with a specified score to a sorted set structure. (4) *zrange* - returns a specified range of elements from a sorted set. The workload is set to return the element with the minimal score. Lastly, (5) *sadd* adds an element to Redis set structure. (A set holds an unordered collection of unique elements.)

Network Intensity As can be seen in Figure 14, the server is clearly limited by the network bandwidth: it saturates the 10GbE network link throughout the entire run, while all other resources are lightly used. (lpush, zadd, and sadd saturate the ingress direction, while lpop, and zrange saturate the egress direction).

CPU Intensity CPU load is low for Redis. Even for more compute-heavy operations like zadd and sadd, the network bandwidth is getting saturated without fully utilizing the cores. Moreover, note that the core utilization in Figure 14 is reported for the 4 active cores only. Redis is a single-threaded workload, and 4 Redis instances proved to be enough to saturate the network in all experiments. This means that the majority of cores in the system are practically left idle.

Disk I/O Intensity Since Redis stores all data in memory and serves all requests from memory, there in no meaningful disk traffic. While Redis periodically writes data back to hard-drive to preserve data persistence, this turned out to have minimal performance effect in our experiments.

DRAM Intensity As can be seen in Figure 13, DRAM bandwidth utilization is low (less than 10 GB/s corresponds to less than 10% utilization) throughout the entire run. However, since Redis stores all data in memory, the server memory capacity dictates the maximal database size the application can store. To illustrate the DRAM capacity pressure,

the *lpush* phase stores 32 GB of data to a Redis list structure. The increase in memory capacity can be clearly identified in the memory usage plot in Figure 14. The *lpop* phase later removes all elements from the list, and it can be seen that the memory usage is indeed going down. (The score range is kept limited in the *zadd* phase so the set size is kept minimal. Further increase in the range in the *sadd* test results in an increase of memory capacity usage.)

5. RELATED WORK

There exists a lot of relevant literature on a number of Big Data applications and benchmarks. This section provides an exhaustive list of the most relevant work. The related work is broken down into two main sections: (i) Microarchitectural characterization of servers, and (ii) Client side analysis. A highly specialized characterization work has resulted from the growing popularity of the Hadoop MapReduce framework, focusing on analyzing the system performance from a "job" perspective. Section 5.3 has been dedicated to discussing the relevant job-level characterization efforts.

5.1 Client Side Analysis

Most of the characterization efforts from the industry have focused on comparing client-side performance of products that offer similar features. Netflix uses Cassandra deployed in AWS [10, 13] as a key infrastructure component of its globally distributed streaming product. They have conducted extensive characterization of Cassandra [7, 20]. Most of these studies focused on scalability aspects of Cassandra and measuring client-side throughput in terms of requests serviced per second, as well as client-side response latency. DataStax, one of Cassandra's commercial vendors has provided an extensive study on client side comparisons for many NoSQL databases [9]. This work was an independent extension of the work done in [36] which provided client side comparisons for a number of leading NoSQL databases for one particular use case – application performance management

(APM). Similar scaling studies have been done for Memcache at Facebook [38, 35].

5.2 Server Microarchitectural Characterization

CloudSuite [27] characterization was one of the first works that was done in the field of designing benchmarks for scale-out datacenters. The authors did a great job of identifying representative applications and putting them together as a part of the benchmark suite. They also provide a comprehensive analysis of the workloads, providing results for a number of microarchitectural parameters like L1 and L2 cache hits/misses, instructions per cycle (IPC) and memory/DRAM utilization. However, their analysis stops at the boundary of DRAM, providing very little insight into the I/O behavior of workloads. Given that most applications in the domain are I/O bound, we believe that concentrating workload characterization to just the CPU-Memory subsystem doesn't provide a comprehensive picture of benchmark behavior.

BigDataBench [29, 41] provides a collection of another set of applications that represent datacenter workloads. This work is built on [27] by providing a more comprehensive list of workloads, that cover a broader spectrum of datacenter based services. They also provide representative datasets as a part of the benchmarking suite. The workload analysis done in both these papers has been extremely thorough, and has dealt mostly with analyzing the workloads from the CPU-centric perspective. The analysis has focused on metrics like IPC, MPKI and LLC hit and miss ratios, while not worrying about the client side results.

5.3 Job Level Analysis

A number of other papers have done more comprehensive, per-node analysis of targeted workloads especially for the Hadoop MapReduce framework. However, almost all prior work has focused on carrying out rigorous analysis of *one* subsystem for every workload that they have considered. Abad and Roberts [22] provide a detailed analysis of the storage subsystem for Hadoop based MapReduce jobs. For the Hadoop framework, a number of studies have carried out detailed analysis of the utilization of individual nodes, and of the Hadoop cluster in general. Ren et al. [37] provide a task and job level analysis of a production Hadoop cluster from Taobao Inc.

6. CONCLUSIONS AND FUTURE WORK

This paper presents the authors' experiences and learnings in selecting, setting up and tuning workloads from various published benchmark suites, as well as a few others based on popularity and use cases. The biggest learning that was made from these studies was the fact that a "Big Data benchmark" is a misnomer. The performance of a datacenter application is highly dependent on the test setup, which comprises of a number of moving parts, including, but not limited to the hardware configurations of the server and the client, the characteristics of the network and the fine tuning of the operating system and application settings. Without properly tuning most of the said components, the relevant subsystems of the server will not be stressed.

Secondly, in order to emulate real-world use and deployment cases, it is very important that the application is optimized for providing best performance on the available re-

Table 4: System level bottlenecks for each of the applications under consideration

Workload	Pressure Points
Memcache	DRAM, Network
Cassandra	Disk
Redis	Network
Nutch (Hadoop)	CPU, Disk
Data Analytics (Hadoop)	CPU

sources. This process results in most representative application behavior and characteristics, leading to effective provisioning decisions for each server node.

Even when the application characteristics for the use cases are known, deciding resources for each of the different tiers of a Web 2.0 datacenter is a hard problem. The intent of the designers is to get the maximum performance out of the available resources, be able to handle peak load without buckling under the stress, as well as making sure that the servers are not extremely over-provisioned. Knowing the bottlenecks of different applications will help datacenter architects make the right provisioning trade-offs for each tier of the datacenter. Having a "pressure point matrix" similar to Table 4 will greatly help in making such decisions. For example, if the datacenter is projected to have a big in-memory caching or analytics tier, it would be best to provision servers with adequate network resources, maybe even at the cost of direct attached storage for each server node in that tier.

Furthermore, being able to bin applications according to their pressure points, in a fashion similar to Table 4 would help decide their co-location potential across different tiers of the datacenter. For example, some applications have strict QoS requirements (the caching tier), while others may have relaxed requirements. Knowing the pressure points of different applications, will help make intelligent co-location decisions for different applications. This will lead to designing policies that will result in better utilization of resources across different tiers. We leave such studies for future work.

References

[1] Hadoop. http://hadoop.apache.org.

[2] Intel Distribution for Apache Hadoop Software: Optimization and Tuning Guide. Technical report, Intel.

[3] Optimizing Hadoop Deployments. http://www.intel.com/content/dam/doc/white-paper/cloud-computing-optimizing-hadoop-deployments-paper.pdf.

[4] Redis. http://redis.io/.

[5] Sensor Andrew. http://sensor.andrew.cmu.edu.

[6] Cassandra at Twitter Today. https://blog.twitter.com/2010/cassandra-twitter-today, 2010.

[7] Benchmarking Cassandra Scalability on AWS - Over a million writes per second. http://techblog.netflix.com/2011/11/benchmarking-cassandra-scalability-on.html, 2011.

[8] Hadoop Performance Tuning Guide. Technical report, AMD, 2012.

[9] Benchmarking Top NoSQL Databases. Technical report, DataStax Corporation, February 2013.

[10] Big Data Analytics at Netflix. Interview with Christos Kalantzis and Jason Brown. http://www.odbms.org/blog/2013/02/big-data-analytics-at-netflix-interview-with-christos-kalantzis-and-jason-brown/, 2013.

[11] Data Caching. http://parsa.epfl.ch/cloudsuite/docs/data-caching.pdf, 2013.

[12] Hadoop Job Optimization. Technical report, Microsoft IT SES Enterprise Data Architect Team, 2013.

[13] Nosql at netflix. http://techblog.netflix.com/2011/01/nosql-at-netflix.html, 2013.

[14] Apache Nutch. http://nutch.apache.org, 2014.

[15] Apache Spark – Lightning-fast cluster computing. http://www.odbms.org/blog/2013/02/big-data-analytics-at-netflix-interview-with-christos-kalantzis-and-jason-brown/, 2014.

[16] Collectl. http://collectl.sourceforge.net, 2014.

[17] Collectl Utilities. http://collectl-utils.sourceforge.net, 2014.

[18] In-Memory Computing Market worth $13.23 Billion by 2018. http://www.researchandmarkets.com/research/btkq7v/inmemory, 2014.

[19] Redis Roundup: What Companies Use Redis? http://blog.togo.io/redisphere/redis-roundup-what-companies-use-redis/, 2014.

[20] Revisiting 1 Million Writes per second. http://techblog.netflix.com/2014/07/revisiting-1-million-writes-per-second.html, 2014.

[21] Who's using Redis? http://redis.io/topics/whos-using-redis, 2014.

[22] C. Abad, N. Roberts, Y. Lu, and R. Campbell. A storage-centric analysis of mapreduce workloads: File popularity, temporal locality and arrival patterns. In Proceedings of IISWC, 2012.

[23] B. Atikoglu, Y. Xu, E. Frachtenberg, S. Jiang, and M. Paleczny. Workload Analysis of a Large-scale Key-value Store. In Proceedings of SIGMETRICS, 2012.

[24] companiesandmarkets.com. Global web 2.0 data center market. http://www.companiesandmarkets.com/, 2014.

[25] B. F. Cooper, A. Silberstein, E. Tam, R. Ramakrishnan, and R. Sears. Benchmarking Cloud Serving Systems with YCSB. In Proceedings of SoCC, 2010.

[26] F. X. Diebold. Big Data Dynamic Factor Models for Macroeconomic Measurementand Forecasting. In Eighth World Congress of the Econometric Society, 2000.

[27] M. Ferdman, A. Adileh, O. Kocberber, S. Volos, M. Alisafaee, D. Jevdjic, C. Kaynak, A. D. Popescu, A. Ailamaki, and B. Falsafi. Clearing the clouds: a study of emerging scale-out workloads on modern hardware. In Proceedings of ASPLOS, 2012.

[28] B. Fitzpatric. Memcached - A distributed memory object caching system. http://memcached.org/, 2014.

[29] W. Gao, Y. Zhu, Z. Jia, C. Luo, L. Wang, J. Zhan, J. He, S. Gong, X. Li, S. Zhang, and B. Qiu. BigDataBench: a Big Data Benchmark Suite from Web Search Engines. In Proceedings of ASBD, 2013.

[30] A. Greenberg, J. Hamilton, D. A. Maltz, and P. Patel. The cost of a cloud: Research problems in data center networks. SIGCOMM Comput. Commun. Rev., 39(1):68–73, Dec. 2008.

[31] S. Huang, J. Huang, J. Dai, T. Xie, and B. Huang. The hibench benchmark suite: Characterization of the mapreduce-based data analysis. In ICDE Workshops, 2010.

[32] R. Khare and D. Cutting. Nutch: A Flexible and Scalable Open-source Web Search Engine. Technical report, CommerceNet Labs, 2004.

[33] K. Lim, D. Meisner, A. G. Saidi, P. Ranganathan, and T. F. Wenisch. Thin Servers with Smart Pipes: Designing SoC Accelerators for Memcached. In Proceedings of ISCA, 2013.

[34] P. Lotfi-Kamran, B. Grot, M. Ferdman, S. Volos, O. Kocberber, J. Picorel, A. Adileh, D. Jevdjic, S. Idgunji, E. Ozer, and B. Falsafi. Scale-out processors. In Proceedings of ISCA, 2012.

[35] R. Nishtala, H. Fugal, S. Grimm, M. Kwiatkowski, H. Lee, H. C. Li, R. McElroy, M. Paleczny, D. Peek, P. Saab, D. Stafford, T. Tung, and V. Venkataramani. Scaling memcache at facebook. In Proceedings of NSDI. USENIX, 2013.

[36] T. Rabl, S. Gómez-Villamor, M. Sadoghi, V. Muntés-Mulero, H.-A. Jacobsen, and S. Mankovskii. Solving big data challenges for enterprise application performance management. Proc. VLDB Endow., 5(12):1724–1735, 2012.

[37] Z. Ren, X. Xu, J. Wan, W. Shi, and M. Zhou. Workload characterization on a production hadoop cluster: A case study on taobao. In Proceedings of IISWC, 2012.

[38] P. Saab. Scaling memcached at facebook. https://www.facebook.com/note.php?note_id=39391378919, 2008.

[39] J. Taylor. Facebook scale and infrastructure. http://http://new.livestream.com/ocp/winter2013/videos/9511147, 2013.

[40] D. M. Tullsen, S. J. Eggers, and L. H. M. Simultaneous multithreading: Maximizing on-chip parallelism. In Proceedings of ISCA, 1995.

[41] L. Wang, J. Zhan, C. Luo, Y. Zhu, Q. Yang, Y. He, W. Gao, Z. Jia, Y. Shi, S. Zhang, C. Zheng, G. Lu, K. Zhan, X. Li, and B. Qiu. BigDataBench: A Big Data Benchmark Suite from Internet Services. In Proceedings of HPCA, 2014.

[42] A. Wiggins and J. Langston. Enhancing Scalability of Memcached. Technical report, Intel, May 2012.

Capacity Planning and Headroom Analysis for Taming Database Replication Latency

- Experiences with LinkedIn Internet Traffic

Zhenyun Zhuang, Haricharan Ramachandra, Cuong Tran,
Subbu Subramaniam, Chavdar Botev, Chaoyue Xiong, Badri Sridharan
LinkedIn Corporation
2029 Stierlin Court, Mountain View, CA 94002, USA
{zzhuang, hramachandra, ctran,
ssubramaniam, cbotev, cxiong, bsridharan}@linkedin.com

ABSTRACT

Internet companies like LinkedIn handle a large amount of incoming web traffic. Events generated in response to user input or actions are stored in a source database. These database events feature the typical characteristics of Big Data: high volume, high velocity and high variability. Database events are replicated to isolate source database and form a consistent view across data centers. Ensuring a low replication latency of database events is critical to business values. Given the inherent characteristics of Big Data, minimizing the replication latency is a challenging task.

In this work we study the problem of taming the database replication latency by effective capacity planning. Based on our observations into LinkedIn's production traffic and various playing parts, we develop a practical and effective model to answer a set of business-critical questions related to capacity planning. These questions include: future traffic rate forecasting, replication latency prediction, replication capacity determination, replication headroom determination and SLA determination.

Keywords

Capacity Planning; Espresso; Databus; Database replication

1. INTRODUCTION

Internet companies like LinkedIn handle a large amount of incoming traffic. Events generated in response to user input or actions are stored in a source NoSQL database. Though these events can be directly consumed by simply connecting to the source database where the events are first inserted, today's major Internet companies feature more complicated data flows, and so require database replications to isolate the source database and events consumers (i.e., applications that read the events).

Database replication is needed mainly for the following two reasons. Firstly, the source database may need to be protected from heavy or spiky load. Having a database replication component can fan out database requests and isolate the source database from consumption. Figure 1 illustrates the typical data flow of event generation, replication, and consumption. When users interact with a web page, the corresponding user updates (events) are sent to databases. The events are replicated by a replicator and made available to downstream consumers. Secondly, when Internet traffic is spread across multiple databases or multiple data centers, a converged and consistent data view is required, which can only be obtained by replicating live database events across data centers.

The database replication process has to be fast and incur low latency; this is important both for the benefits of the particular business and for enhanced user experience. Any event replicated by the events replicator has an associated replication latency due to transmission and processing. We define replication latency as the difference in time between when the event is inserted into the source database and when the event is ready to be consumed by downstream consumers. Minimizing the replication latency is always preferred from the business value perspective. While a delayed user update can be a bit annoying (for example, LinkedIn's user profiles fail to show the users' newly updated expertise), other delayed updates can incur additional business cost or reduced business income. For example, with web sites that display customers' paid ads (i.e., advertisements), the number of ads impressions (i.e., the number of times an advertisement is seen) across multiple data centers has to be tightly correlated to the pre-agreed budget. A significantly delayed ads event update will cause additional cost and reduced income for the company that displays the ads.

Keeping a low database replication latency of events is a challenging task for LinkedIn's traffic. The events feature the typical characteristics of Big Data: high volume, high velocity and high variability. These characteristics present tremendous challenge on ensuring low replication latency

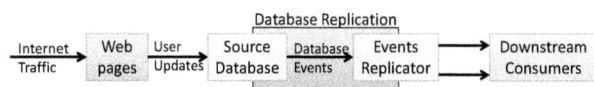

Figure 1: Data flow of database replication

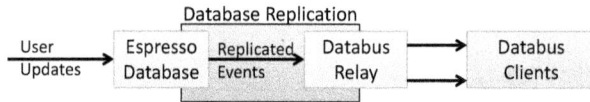

Figure 2: Data flow of LinkedIn Databus replication and consumption

while without significantly over-provisioning the deployment. Though a naive solution to minimizing the replication latency is to provision the capacity based on *maximum* traffic rates, the high-variability feature will incur high business cost associated with the over-provisioning. On the other hand, allowing certain levels of replication latency can significantly reduce business cost. Striking the balance between replication latency and business cost turns out to be a challenging task that requires appropriate capacity planning.

Database replication latency is closely tied to capacity planning. Capacity planning will help understand the current business and operational environment, assess and plan for future application needs based on traffic forecasts. Capacity planning can particularly help reduce the business operation cost. For example, given incoming traffic patterns, we can plan the replication capacity (hardware/software provisioning) so that replication latencies do not exceed business requirements. Though a naive solution is to aggressively provision resources to meet business SLAs (Service Level Agreements) in the worse cases such that the replication capacity always exceeds the foreseen peak traffic rates (for example, maximum replication latencies less than 60 seconds), it would incur unnecessary business cost. On the other hand, based on appropriate capacity planning models, it is possible to significantly reduce business cost without violating business SLAs.

To reduce database replication latency and save business cost, appropriate capacity planning is required. For the problem we attempt to address in this work, we need to understand the relationship among incoming traffic volume, replication capacity, replication latency, and SLAs in order to ensure desired replication latency. In addition, by carefully considering both incoming traffic rate and replication capacity, we can also use capacity planning to foresee future replication latency values given a particular replication processing capacity. Moreover, most Internet companies' traffic also show an ever-growing traffic rate, and we need to improve replication processing capacity to accommodate the traffic increase.

Specifically, the following set of questions need to be answered in the context of capacity planning to tame database replication latency:

- *Future traffic rate forecasting*: Given the historical data of incoming traffic rates, what are the expected traffic rate in the future? This question will also help answering latter questions;

- *Replication latency prediction*: Given the incoming traffic rate and replication processing capacity, what are the expected replication latencies? The values are important to determine the SLA of maximum replication latency;

- *Replication capacity determination*: Given the increased incoming rate and largest allowed replication latencies

(SLA), how much replication capacity do we need to achieve? This will help define replication capacity requirements;

- *Replication headroom determination*: Given the replication capacity and SLA, how much more incoming traffic can we handle? With the current replication capacity, how long (i.e., how many days) will it take before SLA violation? This helps plan for future requirements.

- *SLA determination*: Given the incoming traffic rate and replication processing capacity of today or future, how to determine an appropriate SLA? Apparently, we don't want to over-commit or underestimate the SLA.

Based on our observations into production traffic and various playing parts, in this work we develop a practical and effective model to forecast incoming traffic rates and deduct corresponding replication latency. The model can be used to answer the set of business-critical questions related to capacity planning defined above. In this work, we share how we perform capacity planning by answering the five questions related to capacity planning. These questions offer different aspects of capacity planning and can be applied to different scenarios. We use the models on one of LinkedIn's database replication products to describe the designs and demonstrate usage, but the models can easily be applied to other similar usage scenarios. Moreover, our observations on internet traffic patterns can also help shed light on solving similar capacity planning problems in other areas.

For the remainder of the writing, we first present the various observations regarding our production incoming traffic to motivate our design in Section 2. We then define the problems being addressed in this writing in Section 3. We then present the high level designs in Section 4 and the detailed designs of forecasting in Section 5. Section 6 presents the evaluation results of the proposed designs. We discuss some further relevant questions in Section 7 and share our learned lessons in Section 8. We also present certain related works in Section 9. Finally Section 10 concludes the work.

2. OBSERVATIONS OF LINKEDIN TRAFFIC

In this section, we first give some background of LinkedIn's Databus, then present some observations of our production traffic and deployments. These observations will help our design in later sections.

2.1 LinkedIn Databus

LinkedIn's Databus [7] is a data replication protocol responsible for moving database events across data centers. It can also be used to fan out database usage to reduce the load on source databases. It is an integral part of LinkedIn's data processing pipeline. Replication is performed by the Databus Relay component, which processes incoming database records and makes them ready to be consumed by downstream Databus clients. A simple illustration of the data flow is shown in Figure 2. The raw events are inserted into the source database, LinkedIn's home-grown Espresso [15]. These events are replicated and queued for Databus Relay to consume. Databus Relay fetches and processes the queued events so that the events can be later pulled by clients.

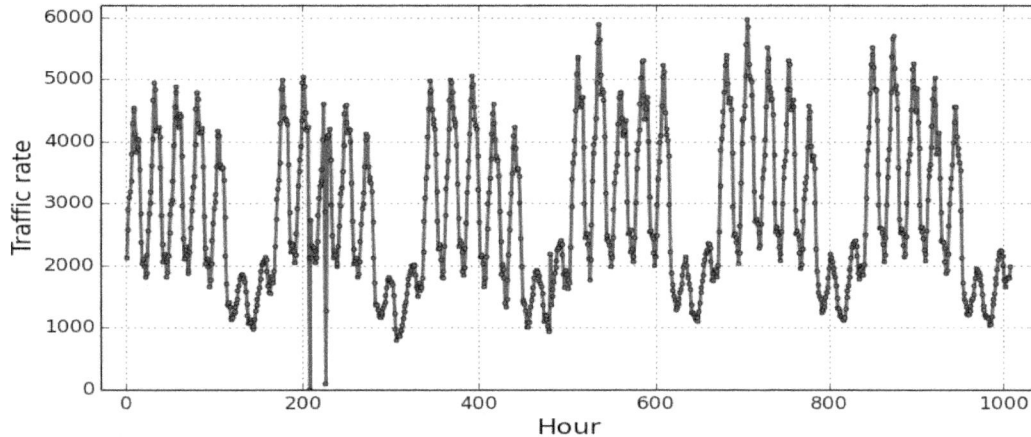

Figure 3: Six weeks (42 days) of incoming traffic (totally 1008 data points; note that two close-to-zero data points are invalid)

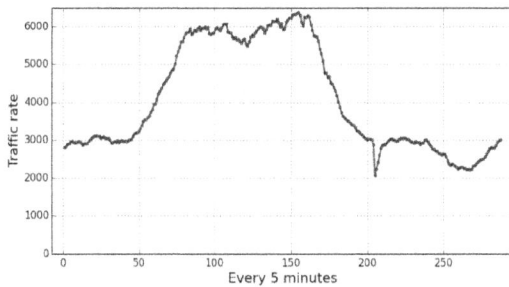

(a) Monday traffic (May 5th, 2014)

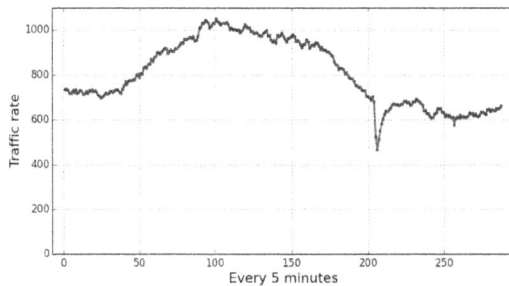

(b) Saturday traffic (May 17th, 2014)

Figure 4: Individual days of traffic (Each data point represents 5 minutes, totally 288 data points)

A critical performance factor is the Databus Relay Lag (i.e., Databus replication latency), which is calculated as the difference in time between when a record is inserted into source Espresso and when the record is ready to be consumed by the Databus clients. The extent of relay lag largely depends on two factors: the rate of incoming raw database events (i.e., the "producing rate" of the events) and the Databus Relay processing capacity (i.e., the "consuming rate" of the events). So if the producing rate is always lower than the consuming rate, there will be no substantial relay lags, other than the event transmission delay which is usually very small. But when the producer over-whelms the consumer, the incoming events will be queued and a non-trivial relay lag will result due to an events queue backlog. To minimize relay lags, appropriate capacity planning is needed after careful consideration of both producing and consuming rates.

2.2 Periodic pattern of incoming traffic rate

We first studied the incoming traffic rate of multiple Espresso instances across many months; our first impression was the strong periodic pattern - the traffic shape is repeated for each day of the week. Figure 3 below shows 42 consecutive days of data for a single Espresso node. The incoming traffic consists of two types of database events: insert and update. Databus Relay processes both types of traffic, so we aggregated the total incoming rate for each minute.

We observed weekly repeating patterns in incoming traffic rates. Every week, the five workdays have much higher traffic rates than the two weekends. Such a weekly pattern repeats with similar traffic shapes. Within a single day, irrespective of being workday or weekend, we found that the traffic rate peaks during regular business hours, while drops to the lowest at night.

2.3 Incoming traffic of individual days

We then studied the periodic pattern of incoming traffic for each day. For each workday and weekend, we noticed that the traffic shape is a well formed curve. In Figure 4, we show the workday of May 5_{th}, 2014 (Monday) and the weekend day of May 17_{th}, 2014 (Saturday).

We observed that the traffic shapes of these two days were quite similar, except for the absolute values of each data point. Specifically, for each day, the peak periods were about 8 hours (that is, 6AM to 2PM in the West Coast, or 9AM to 5PM in the East Coast). Not surprisingly, the workday peak value (6367 records/sec) was much higher than that of weekends (1061 records/sec).

2.4 Relay processing capacity

We also examined the relay processing capacity. The relay processing rate was maximized only when there was a buildup in queued events. To force Databus Relay to work at

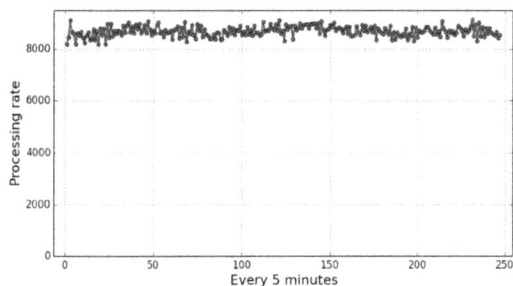

Figure 5: Relay processing rate (Relay capacity)

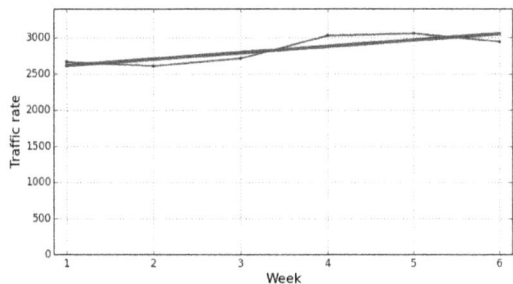

Figure 6: Traffic growth in 6 weeks

full capacity, we rewound the starting System Change Number (SCN) of the relay component to artificially introduce sufficient relay lag. For a particular Databus Relay instance, the replay processing rates over 20 hours of a recent day are plotted in Figure 5.

We observed that the relay processing rate is relatively flat over time. The reason for relative stable relay processing rate is because the processing rate is dominated by the replication protocol, which is relatively constant for each event.

2.5 Growing traffic

We studied the historical data of incoming traffic and found that: (1) overall, the traffic volume grows over time; (2) the traffic for individual days is affected by many factors including weekends, holidays, and production releases. We analyzed the incoming traffic rates for a duration of 6 weeks and plotted the monthly traffic rates in Figure 6. Linear fitting of the curve demonstrates about 20% increase in 6 weeks.

Note that this analysis and graph are based on a particular instance of the Espresso node. We also studied other instances and found that though the exact growth rates differ for different periods and instances, the overall traffic growth rate is quite significant. Even though it is possible to build capacity planning models for each instance for higher accuracy, we want to build a generic model to cover all instances.

2.6 Summary

Our study of LinkedIn's production traffic showed that the database events producing rate (i.e., the incoming traffic rate) follows strong patterns in the form of repeated weekly curves, while the consuming rate (i.e., the replication processing capacity) is relatively constant. Because of varying incoming traffic rates, we used to see that replication la-

tency can accumulate during peak hours when production rate is higher than the relay capacity, and the accumulated replication latency decreases during non-peak hours when the incoming traffic rate is lower than the relay capacity.

The incoming traffic rate keeps growing, thanks to the user and activity growth, so it is important to take into account the traffic growth when doing capacity planning. We need to forecast into future traffic to understand the future replication latency, estimate the capacity headroom, define the replication capacity requirements, and determine SLAs.

3. PROBLEM DEFINITION

In this section, we formally define the problems we attempt to address in this work. We first give the definitions of SLAs (service level agreements); then present the four types problems related to capacity planning.

3.1 Forms of SLA (service level agreements)

SLA is a part of a service contract where a service is formally defined. Thought normally the service contracts are between companies, it can extend to between different divisions inside a company or even between different software components. For instance, a web service component may define a SLA such as maximum call latency being 100 ms, so that the callers (e.g., a web page rendering component) can rely on the SLA to make design choices and further define their SLAs.

The goal of taming the database replication latency is to fulfill SLA, which can come in different forms. A straightforward SLA metric can be expressed as the "largest" replication latency experienced, which is the form we use to describe our designs. For instance, *largest replication latency should not exceed 60 seconds.* However, other forms of SLA metrics are also possible, depending on specific requirements. To give a few examples: (1) certain percentiles (e.g., p99) of all replication latencies in a day, or (2) the duration of replication latencies exceeding certain values. Despite the differences in SLA forms, we believe the underlying mechanisms required to answer the five types of questions in Section 1 are very similar. So in this work, we will use the largest replication latency as the SLA metric to present our solution.

3.2 Problems being addressed

For simplicity in presentation, we fix the time-granularity of the traffic rates to *per-hour* average, but other granularity can be similarly defined. The following variables are needed to define the problems: (1) Relay capacity: $R_{i,j}$ in day d_i and hour h_j, where $0 \leq j \leq 23$; (2) Incoming traffic rate: $T_{i,j}$ in day d_i and hour h_j; (3) Replication latency: $L_{i,j}$ in day d_i and hour h_j; (4) SLA of replication latency: L_{sla}, which is the largest replication latency.

With the above variables, we can formally define the set of the problems we will address in this work:

- *Forecast future traffic rate* Given the historical traffic rate of $T_{i,j}$ of time period P (e.g., past 30 days), what are the future traffic rate $T_{r,k}$, where $r > i_{max}$ in day r and hour k?

- *Determine the replication latency* Given the traffic rate of $T_{i,j}$ and relay capacity $R_{i,j}$, what are the replication latency of $L_{i,j}$?

- *Determine required replication capacity* Given SLA requirement L_{sla} and traffic rate of $T_{i,j}$, what are required relay capacity of $R_{i,j}$?

- *Determine replication headroom* There are two questions: (1) Given the SLA of L_{sla} and relay capacity of $R_{i,j}$, what are the highest traffic rate $T_{i,j}$ it can handle without exceeding SLA? (2) what are the expected date d_k of the previous answer?

- *Determine SLA* There are multiple forms of SLAs that can be determined. In this work we consider two of them: (1) what is the largest replication latency L_{max} in a week; (2) for 99% of time in a week the replication latency should not exceed L_{p99}, what is the L_{p99} value?

4. DESIGN

This section will start with the overview of our design, followed by two models to perform forecasting of future traffic rates. After that, the other four types of questions described in Section 1 will be respectively answered.

4.1 Design overview

Before we jump into the details of the design, it helps to gain a conceptual grasp of the problem we try to address. The extent of relay lag largely depends on two factors: the rate of incoming raw database events and the Databus Relay processing capacity. The Databus Relay is conceptually a queuing system and has the features of a single server, a First-In-First-Out (FIFO) queue, and infinite buffer size. Unlike typical queuing theory problems, in this work, we are more focused on the "maximum" awaiting time of all events at a particular time.

In order to answer all the capacity planning questions, we need to obtain the future traffic rates. We will employ two models for traffic forecasting: Time series model and Regression analysis. Given historical traffic rates of certain period, the time series model will be able to forecast the future rates based on the discovered trend pattern and seasonal pattern. The historical data we can obtain is mostly per-hour based due to current limitations on the storing mechanisms, so for each past day it consists of 24 data points. We also observed that the traffic rates exhibit strong seasonal pattern with period of a week (i.e., 7 days, or 168 hours).

For this type of time series data, typically ARIMA (autoregressive integrated moving average) model [3] is chosen for modeling and forecasting. Due to its design rationales and computation overhead, ARIMA is not suitable for long period seasonality (e.g., 168). In addition, the capacity planning needs to obtain per-hour forecasted data rather than per-day data. Because of this, we are not allowed to aggregate per-hour data into per-day data to reduce seasonality period to 7 (since a week has 7 days). To accommodate the long period seasonality as observed in traffic data and the per-hour forecasting requirements, we propose a *two-step* forecasting model to obtain future per-hour traffic rates. Briefly, it firstly obtain the aggregated traffic volume of each day/week, it then "distribute" (or "convert") the aggregate to each hour inside a day/week. The "conversion" of traffic volume from day/week to hours relies on *seasonal indexes*, which roughly represent the traffic portion of each hour inside a week. Specifically, the model consists of two steps: (1) Step-I of forecasting the average incoming rates *per day*

of future days using ARIMA model and (2) Step-II of forecasting the average rates *per hour* of each future days using seasonal indexes.

Regression analysis is targeted for estimating the relationships among variables. Regression analysis can also be used to forecast and predict. Specifically, for our purpose of forecasting future traffic rate, the independent variable is the time, while the dependent variable is the traffic rate at each time. Such analysis is also referred to as "time series regression". Since we observed strong seasonal pattern with the period of a week, we propose to forecast the average traffic rates of future "weeks" based on historical weekly data. Once we obtained the weekly average, we can then convert the weekly average to per-hour data of within a week using the same step-2 of time series model presented above. Another important reason why we choose *per-week* aggregation is that, regression analysis is based on the assumption that the adjacent data points are not dependent. Compared to finer scale of data points, weekly aggregated data are less dependent on each other. We will discuss more on this in Section 7.

For answering the other three types of capacity-planning related questions, we develop respective mechanisms which utilize numerical calculations and binary-searching. For ease of description, we assume the time granularity is per-hour. Once the traffic rates are obtained, then a numerical calculation method will be used to deduct the relay lags of any time point. Based on the numerically calculated results, the relay capacity required to sustain a particular traffic rate can also be obtained using binary search. The maximum traffic rates as well as the corresponding future dates can also be determined. Finally, examining the deducted replication latencies we can also determine appropriate SLAs.

4.2 Forecasting future traffic rate with ARIMA model

The incoming traffic rates of each time unit are a sequence of observations at successive points in time, hence they can be treated as a time series. We can employ time series method to discover a pattern and extrapolate the pattern into the future. The discovered pattern of the data can help us understand how the values behave in the past; and the extrapolated pattern can guide us to forecast future values.

ARIMA time series forecasting model will be used to predict the incoming rates of any future days. Though it is obvious to see the weekly pattern for our particular time series data, identifying seasonal periods for other time series might not be so trivial. Examining the ACF (Autocorrelation Function) [3], we see a strong signal at 7, indicating a period of 1 week (i.e., 7 days). Based on our investigations into the properties of the traffic data, we decided to use ARIMA(7,1,0) to fit the historical data and forecast the traffic rates of future days, the details will be presented in Section 5.

Answering various capacity planning questions requires the per-hour granularity of traffic rates. To convert the forecasted per-day rate to per-hour rate, we perform time series decomposition. A typical time series consists of three components: trend component, cycle (or seasonal) component and irregular component [3]: $X_t = T_t + S_t + R_t$, where: X_t is the value of the series at time t; T_t is the trend component, S_t is the seasonal component, and R_t is the random effect or irregular component. T_t exists when the time series data

$L_{i,j} = predict(T_{i,j}, R_{i,j})$: // Latency in seconds.
1   // assuming no latency buildup in d_{i-1}, so $L_{i,0} = 0$.
2   for each hour of h_j, where $1 \leq j \leq 24$:
3   if $T_{i,j} > R_{i,j}$: // increase latency buildup
4          $L_{i,j} = L_{i,j-1} + \frac{3600(T_{i,j} - R_{i,j})}{R_{i,j}}$
5   else: //decrease latency buildup if any
6          $L_{i,j} = L_{i,j-1} - \frac{3600(R_{i,j} - T_{i,j})}{R_{i,j}}$
7   if $L_{i,j} < 0$:
8          $L_{i,j} = 0$

Figure 7: Algorithm of predicting replication latency

gradually shift across time; S_t represents repeating patterns (e.g., daily or weekly); while R_t is time-independent and is characterised by two properties: (1) the process that generates the data has a constant mean; and (2) the variability of the values is constant over time.

Time series decomposition can eliminate the seasonal component based on seasonal index, which measures how much the average for a particular period tends to be above (or below) the expected value. Seasonal index is an average that can be used to compare an actual observation relative to what it would be if there were no seasonal variation. In this work, we utilize seasonal index to convert per-day data to per-hour data. Calculating seasonal index requires the setting of seasonal period, which we choose 168 hours (i.e., 1week, or 7 days * 24 hours). Once the seasonal indexes are calculated, each day of data can be "seasonalized" to obtain per-hour data based on the particular day in a week. We will present details in Section 5.

4.3 Forecasting future traffic rate with regression analysis

When regression analysis (i.e., time series regression) is used to forecast future traffic rates, the weekly average values are used instead. Specifically, for the consecutive weekly average traffic rate of W_t, where t is the week id, a trend line (i.e., the linear fitting of W_t) can be obtained in the form of $Y_t = aW_t + b$. The a is the slope of the change, or the growth rate. With the trend line, future weekly average traffic rate W_t can be forecasted.

Future W_t values obtained with time series regression are actually the "deseasonalized" forecast values. To convert to specific hourly rate, W_t needs to be "seasonalized", similar to the process of using ARIMA model. The details of the conversion will be presented in Section 5.

4.4 Predicting replication latency

For a particular day of d_i, assuming the per-hour traffic rate of $T_{i,j}$ and the relay capacity $R_{i,j}$ are known (totally 24 data points). Apparently if the processing capacity is larger than or equal to the incoming traffic rate, or $T_{i,j} \leq R_{i,j}$, no replication latency buildup will result; otherwise, there will be replication latency buildup. We define "peak period" as the time period where the incoming rate exceeds the relay capacity, and "non-peak period" otherwise. For the latency buildup during peak traffic time, it can be gradually consumed during non-peak traffic time when the traffic rate is relatively low. We assume eventually all the latency buildup

$R_{i,j} = capacity(T_{i,j}, L_{sla})$:
    variables:
1    $R_{i,j(min)}$: a $R_{i,j}$ such that $max(L_{i,j}) \geq L_{sla}$
2    $R_{i,j(max)}$: a $R_{i,j}$ such that $max(L_{i,j}) \leq L_{sla}$

1    $R_{i,j(lf)} = R_{i,j(min)}$
2    $R_{i,j(rt)} = R_{i,j(max)}$
3   while $R_{i,j(lf)} < R_{i,j(rt)} - 1$:
4       $R_{i,j(mid)} = \frac{R_{i,j(lf)} + R_{i,j(rt)}}{2}$
5       $L_{i,j} = predict(T_{i,j}, R_{i,j(mid)})$
6   if $max(L_{i,j}) \leq L_{sla}$:
7          $R_{i,j(rt)} = R_{i,j(mid)}$
8   else:
9          $R_{i,j(lf)} = R_{i,j(mid)}$
10 return $R_{i,j(rt)}$

Figure 8: Algorithm of determining replication capacity

will be consumed by the end of non-peak traffic time of any day. This is a reasonable assumption as otherwise the replication latency will continually grow across days, which is unusable scenario for any business logic or SLA definition.

The mechanism to predict replication latency for any hour of a day is based on numerical calculations. Assuming there is no latency buildup from previous day of d_{i-1} (i.e., $L_{i,0} = 0$, for each successive hour h_j where $j > 0$, the traffic rate is compared to relay capacity at h_j. If the incoming rate is higher, it will incur additional replication latency at that time. Otherwise, previous replication latency, if any, will be decreased, as the relay has additional capacity to consume previously built-up latency. The amount of latency change is based on the difference between the two rates, that is, $L_\delta = \frac{T_{i,j} - R_{i,j}}{R_{i,j}}$ hours. This process continues for each hour that follows, and the entire data set of relay lag is constructed. The algorithm is shown in Figure 7.

4.5 Determining replication capacity

Given SLA requirement L_{sla} (i.e., the maximum allowed replication latency) and traffic rate of $T_{i,j}$, we need to obtain the minimum required relay capacity of $R_{i,j}$. Previously we have shown how to predict the replication latency $L_{i,j}$ given $T_{i,j}$ and $R_{i,j}$. For simplicity we denote the process as a function of $predict()$, so we have $L_{i,j} = predict(T_{i,j}, R_{i,j})$. For each day d_i, we can also easily obtain the maximum replication latency of $L_{i,max}$ of $L_{i,j}$, denoted by $L_{i,max} = max(L_{i,j})$.

To find out the relay capacity $R_{i,j}$ that having $L_{i,max} \leq L_{sla}$, we can do a binary searching on the minimum value of $R_{i,j}$. In order to do binary searching, we need to have two base values of $L_{i,j}$ that are below and above L_{sla}, respectively. These two values can be easily found out. With these two base values (denoted by $R_{i,j(min)}$ and $R_{i,j(max)}$, we can perform a binary searching in the value space between them. The time complexity is $log(R_{i,j(max)} - R_{i,j(min)})$. The algorithm is shown in Figure 8.

4.6 Determining replication headroom

Determining replication headroom consists of two questions. Firstly, given the SLA of L_{sla} and relay capacity of

$S_{i,j} = headroom(R_{i,j}, L_{sla})$: // The scaling factor of day d_i
variables:
1 $S_{i,j(min)}$: a $S_{i,j}$ such that $max(L_{i,j}) \leq L_{sla}$
2 $S_{i,j(max)}$: a $S_{i,j}$ such that $max(L_{i,j}) \geq L_{sla}$

1 $S_{i,j(lf)} = S_{i,j(min)}$
2 $S_{i,j(rt)} = S_{i,j(max)}$
3 while $S_{i,j(lf)} < S_{i,j(rt)} - 0.01$:
4      $S_{i,j(mid)} = \frac{S_{i,j(lf)} + S_{i,j(rt)}}{2}$
5      $L_{i,j} = predict(T_{i,j} * S_{i,j(mid)}, R_{i,j(mid)})$
6   if $max(L_{i,j}) \leq L_{sla}$:
7          $S_{i,j(lf)} = S_{i,j(mid)}$
8   else:
9          $S_{i,j(rt)} = S_{i,j(mid)}$
10 return $S_{i,j(lf)}$

Figure 9: Algorithm of determining headroom (scaling factor)

$R_{i,j}$, what are the highest traffic rate $T_{i,j}$ it can handle without exceeding SLA? (2) what are the expected date of the previous answer?

To determine the highest $T_{i,j}$ without compromising L_{sla}, we can again use binary searching. For this purpose, we assume the same shape of traffic rates inside a day, and scale the rate values by multiplying a scaling factor (e.g., 2.0). Specifically, First we find two base scaling factors (denoted by $S_{i,j(min)}$ and $S_{i,j(max)}$, where $S_{i,j(min)}$ will fulfill L_{sla}, while $S_{i,j(max)}$ will exceed L_{sla}. Then binary searching is performed on the $T_{i,j}$ such that $predict(T_{i,j}, R_{i,j}) \leq L_{sla}$. The algorithm is shown in Figure 9.

Once the highest $S_{i,j}$ (denoted by $T_{i,j(h)}$)is obtained, determining the corresponding date will be done by considering the traffic growth rate r, which denotes yearly growth rate. Specifically, with the forecasting model, the traffic rate of day d_k can be obtained and denoted by $\frac{365 S_{i,j}}{r} + d_i$.

4.7 Determining SLA

We have shown above that the replication latency values for each time unit can be obtained if we know the incoming traffic rate and the replication processing capacity. Once the replication latencies are known, determining the appropriate SLA for replication latency is quite straightforward. For the first form of SLA determination (i.e., L_{max}), we can simply iterate through the entire week, find the largest replication

Table 1: The estimates, standard errors, t value and corresponding significance

Lag/Diff.	Estimate	Std. Err.	t	Significance
AR Lag 1	-0.198	0.104	-1.903	0.063
AR Lag 2	-0.312	0.105	-2.983	0.004
AR Lag 3	-0.245	0.107	-2.290	0.026
AR Lag 4	-0.259	0.106	-2.435	0.018
AR Lag 5	-0.284	0.109	-2.611	0.012
AR Lag 6	-0.214	0.106	-2.030	0.047
AR Lag 7	0.655	0.108	6.083	0.000
Difference	1			

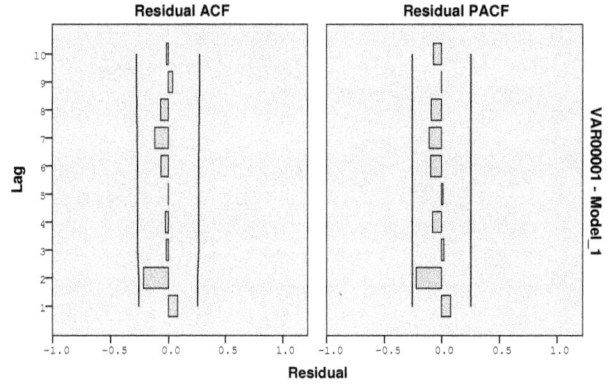

Figure 10: ACF and PACF of ARIMA(7,1,0)

latency value, and assign it to L_{max}. For the second form of SLA determination (i.e., find p99.9 value of L_{p99}, we can apply a adapted binary searching algorithm to find the value of L_{p99}, such that 99% of time the replication latency is below L_{p99}. For simplicity, we will not elaborate on the detailed algorithm.

5. FORECASTING TRAFFIC RATE

In this section, we address the forecasting question by using both time series model and regression analysis model. Both models requires 2 steps: (1) forecasting rate of future days (or weeks) and (2) converting per-day (or per-week) rate to per-hour rate.

5.1 Forecasting using time series model

For 6-weeks of time (i.e., 42 days), the average traffic rate of each hour is plotted in Figure 3. From the figure, we can easily see that the time series is not a *stationary time series*; instead, it exhibits strong *seasonal pattern*. It can be seen to have a weekly seasonal pattern. There is also a trend pattern in the time series which we will discover later. The trend pattern is not easy to spot by human eyes due to two reasons: (1) the trend is shadowed by other patterns (e.g., seasonal patterns); and (2) the trend is not obvious since the shift is slow.

5.1.1 Step-I: Forecasting rate of future days

ARIMA(p,d,q) model needs to know the exact values of (p,d,q). Based on various investigations into the properties of the data, we choose ARIMA(7,1,0). In Figure 10 we show the ACF and PACF of the model, we can see that the model of ARIMA(7,1,0) adequately fits the data.

We obtained the specific parameters (AR lags and difference) of the ARIMA(7,1,0). With confidence interval width of 95%, we show the estimates, standard errors, t value and corresponding significance in Table 1. The stationary R^2 is 0.888.

5.1.2 Step-II: Converting per-day rate to per-hour rate

We will *decompose* the time series to obtain seasonal indexes of each hour in a week (i.e., totally 168 indexes in a week). Calculating the seasonal indexes can be done as follows:

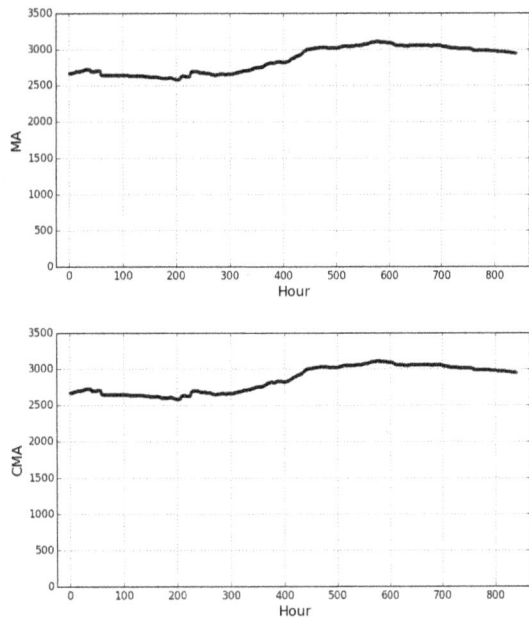

Figure 11: (a) Weekly moving average (MA_t) and (b) centered moving average (CMA_t)

1. *Calculating weekly moving average (MA)*
   $MA_t = \frac{\sum_{i=-63}^{64} X_{t+i}}{168}$. MA_t gives the average weekly traffic rate.

2. *Calculating centered moving average (CMA)* $CMA_t = \frac{MA_t + MA_{t+1}}{2}$. Since the period is an even number (i.e., 168), the moving average values we computed do not correspond directly to the original hours of the time series. This can be resolved by computing the average of the two neighboring averages. The centered moving averages CMA_t represent the trend in the time series and any random variation that was not removed by using moving averages.

3. *Calculating seasonal irregular values* $SII_t = \frac{X_t}{CMA_t}$. Dividing the time series value by the centered moving average, we can get the seasonal irregular values SII_t for each hours.

4. *Calculating seasonal indexes* $SI_t = \overline{SII_t}$. for each of the 168 hours, its seasonal index can be averaged over all corresponding seasonal irregular values. Eventually, we get 168 seasonal indexes SI_t, which are the "scaling" factor of the particular hours.

5. *Adjusting seasonal indexes* $SIndex_t = \frac{SI_t * 168}{\sum_{i=0}^{167} SI_{t+i}}$. Since the average seasonal index should equal 1.00, we need to adjust the seasonal indexes by multiplying 168 and dividing the sum of all unadjusted seasonal indexes.

Once the seasonal indexes are obtained, per-day traffic rate can be easily converted to per-hour rate by "seasonaling" the forecasted data. Specifically, to convert the traffic rate of a forecasted day, let's assume it is the i_{th} day in a week, where $0 \leq i \leq 6$ of a week, say d_i. We use $r_{i,j}$ to denote the forecasted rate of hour j in d_i. For each hour j, we first obtain its in-week hour offsets $h_j = 24i + j$. Then for hour h_j, the per-hour traffic rate is calculated as $d_{i,j} * SIndex_{h_j}$, where $SIndex_{h_j}$ is the corresponding seasonal index for hour h_j.

5.2 Forecasting using regression analysis

The process of forecasting using regression analysis shares the same Step-II with the time series model described above. So we will focus on the Step-I. In Step-I of this model, the per-week traffic rates in future weeks are obtained, which is different from the time series model. The reason for this is the weekly seasonality.

An alternative way of forecasting using regression analysis is to separate the forecasting of each weekday and treat them as independent time series. Specifically, for each of the weekdays (e.g., Monday and Sunday), a separate trending line is obtained. Based on the respective trending lines, the traffic rates of each of the seven weekdays will be forecasted. Though theoretically this treatment should also work, we feel it is a overkill of our problem. In addition, maintaining and processing of seven time series models is a non-trivial tasks.

Once future weekly traffic rates are forecasted, they can be converted to hourly traffic rates using the same seasonal indexes we described before. Specifically, assuming the weekly traffic rate is w, for each hour j ($0 \leq j < 168$) in a forecasted week, the forecasted traffic rate $r_j = w * SIndex_{h_j}$.

In this section, we use the a particular Databus instance to demonstrate the effectiveness of the proposed models when answering the four types of questions in Section 1.

5.3 Some headroom is necessary

Any prediction model with Internet traffic will inevitably have errors for various reasons. The major cause of prediction errors is the high dynamics of Internet traffic. When the prediction underestimates the traffic volume, the actual replication latency will be lower than expected. Note that such underestimation will not violate the performance SLA which is defined based on predicted values. The only cost is over-provisioned computing resources.

However, when the predicted traffic volume is lower than actual value, the performance SLA could be violated. To address this issue, it is absolutely necessary to give certain headroom when determining various metrics such as SLA. The exact amount of headroom given depends on a set of factors including: (1) historical performance of forecasting;

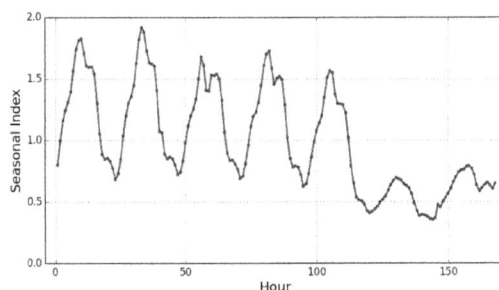

Figure 12: Adjusted seasonal index ($SIndex_t$) (Each hour of the week has a data point, totally 168 data points)

46

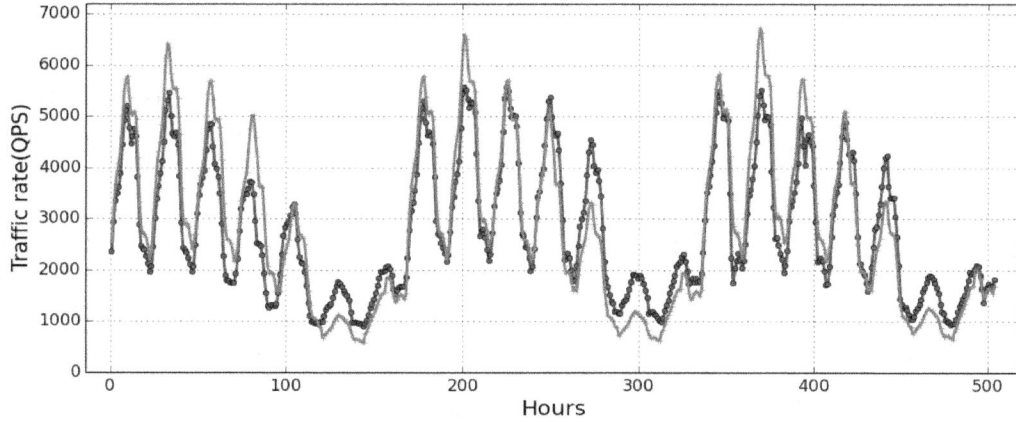

Figure 13: Observed (in blue) and forecasted (in green) hourly traffic using *ARIMA time series* model for 3 weeks

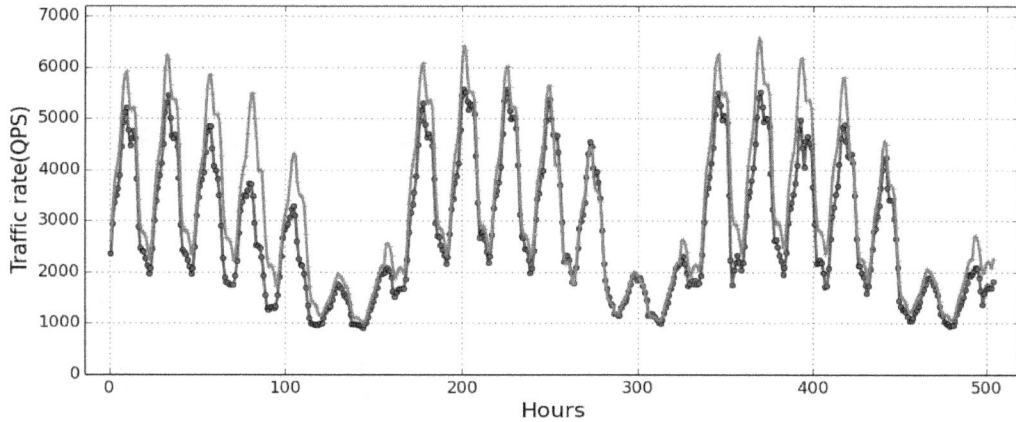

Figure 14: Observed (in blue) and forecasted (in green) hourly traffic using *regression analysis* model for 3 weeks

(2) the consequences (e.g., business cost) of violating SLA; (3) the cost of over-provisioning computing resources. We will not elaborate on this in this writing.

6. EVALUATION

6.1 Future traffic rate forecasting

According to the common practice of forecasting using ARIMA model, the forecasted data length should not exceed half of the historical data length [3]. So with 42 days of historical data, typically up to 21 days into the future can be forecasted using ARIMA model.

We show individual steps of calculating seasonal indexes according to Section 5.1.2. The MA (moving average) and CMA (centered moving average) are shown in Figure 11, respectively. We also show the adjusted seasonal index in Figure 12.

Using both the ARIMA time series model and regression analysis model, we obtained the forecasted hourly traffic rates for the later 21 days. In Figure 13 we show both the observed (raw) values and the forecasted values of ARIMA time series model. Figure 14 shows the results of regres-

sion analysis model. We also evaluated the forecasting accuracy by calculating the root mean square deviation (RMSD). ARIMA model has a RMSD value of 547, while regression analysis gives 578. For comparison, we choose a baseline MA (Moving Average) model which predicts an hour j's traffic rate based on historical data of exactly 1-week ago, that is, $T_{i,j} = T_{i-7,j}$. The corresponding RMSD value is 781, considerably larger than both of our proposed methods. Also note that though for this particular time series data, ARIMA model gives better accuracy, the difference is only about 6%. We also evaluated with other time series, the performance results vary, and both models give quite similar accuracy.

6.2 Replication latency prediction

To understand how well the numerical analysis model predicts replication latencies, we compared the numerically calculated results to observed values in one of our most resource-limited instance. We choose one day of replication latencies for a single Databus Relay instance as the base value. We fed the incoming traffic rates and relay capacity for that Relay instance into the numerical analysis model and then calculated the latencies.

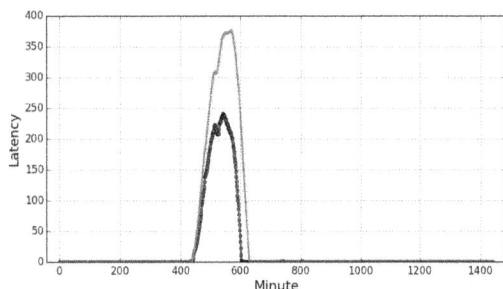

Figure 15: Comparing calculated relay lag to real lag (The shapes of the two curves are similar, the peak values differ by 1.6X.)

The two sets of results are shown in Figure 15. From the figure, we see that these results have almost identical shapes across the time line. The absolute peak values are also very close (i.e., 376 vs. 240, less than 1.6X). Given the data complexities and variations in the production environment (for instance, network bandwidth impact, network latency, cpu and other resource contentions, etc.), we feel the accuracy of the numerical analysis model is satisfactory.

6.3 Replication capacity determination

To determine the replication capacity, we chose a single day and would like to determine the replication capacity needed to ensure a SLA that is defined as the maximum replication latency being 60 seconds.

The average traffic rate of the day is about 2386 event/s. We firstly found that the capacity of 2500 event/s results a maximum latency of 8871 seconds, which violates the SLA. The other base value of capacity being 5000 event/s results in less than 1-second latency. Using the two base values, we perform binary searching. We plotted the min/max/mid values used in the algorithm during the binary searching in Figure 16(a). It only takes 12 steps to finally determine the exact replication capacity needed - 3474 event/s, which results in 57 seconds of replication latency.

6.4 Replication headroom determination

We chose the replication capacity being 5000 event/s and attempted to determine the maximum scaling factor that it can handle without violating the same SLA as defined before (i.e., maximum of 60 seconds). The raw traffic rates (i.e., scaling factor being 1.0) does not violate SLA, while a scaling factor of 2.0 results in more than 8000 second latency. Starting with these two scaling factors, binary searching takes 9 steps to determine the maximum scaling factor is 1.44. Assuming a yearly growth rate of 30%, it will take about 13 months to reach that traffic rate.

6.5 SLA determination

To determine SLAs, let's assume the time period is the entire 3 future weeks and the replication processing capacity is 6000 event/sec, we find the maximum replication latency is about 1135.2 seconds. Based on this, the maximum latency value in an appropriate SLA can be 1136 seconds, that is $L_{max} = 1136$. Correspondingly, we perform binary searching on the percentile values and find the $p99$ value of the SLA $L_{p99} = 850$.

7. DISCUSSION

We now discuss a few interesting issues/aspects in the problems and solutions.

7.1 Strong seasonal pattern of web traffic

LinkedIn's production web traffic shows strong patterns of seasonality, and we believe such seasonality also exists in the traffics other Internet companies. Both strong daily and weekly seasonal patterns are observed. Due to limited data length, in this work we did not study the yearly seasonal pattern. Though such seasonality adds difficulty to capacity planning, the latter actually can potentially take advantage of the seasonality to reduce operation cost and improve the performance. For instance, if the seasonal pattern predicts that the traffic rate will lower down in the next few hours, we might want to shrink the computing resources (e.g., network bandwidth, number of instances) to save operation cost. Similarly, if the traffic rates are expected to increase soon, we can allocate more computing resources to improve the performance. Such dynamic allocation of resources fit well into a cloud computing deployment. We will leave this to future work.

7.2 Forecasting using time series vs. regression analysis

We have presented two methods to forecast future traffic rates: time series model and regression analysis. Both methods then predict hourly traffic rates based on the same seasonal indexes. Though the accuracies of these two methods are quite similar, the design rational for these two methods are *fundamentally* different. Regression analysis assumes little dependency between two neighboring data points (i.e., the traffic rates of two succeeding time), while time series model better fits otherwise. The fact that the outcomes from the two methods are similar suggest the following two characteristics about the data dependency. First, the dependency between neighboring hourly-aggregated data points in our particular production traffic is minor, hence time series model does not gain advantage over regression analysis. Intuitively, since our data points are hourly-aggregated, it is not surprising to see little dependency between two hours. Second, our regression analysis model works on weekly-aggregated data points, which have even less dependency between two neighboring data points. Thus, both ARIMA and regression analysis models suffice in our particular scenario.

7.3 Applying to other areas

Though this work is specific to database replication capacity planning, the observations we made regarding traffic patterns and the models we proposed can help solve similar problems in other areas. For instance, online log processing applications are desired to keep up with the incoming traffic rate. Typical designs/deployments of log processing are fixed, not adaptive to log generation rates. As a result, the processing may incur delays when incoming log generation rates are high. High log generation rates are caused by high traffic rates during peak hours. Similarly, the accumulated delays will decrease during non-peak time. It also has similar capacity planning questions that need to be answered. The characteristics are very similar to those of the database replication process. All the mechanisms we proposed in this work can be applied there.

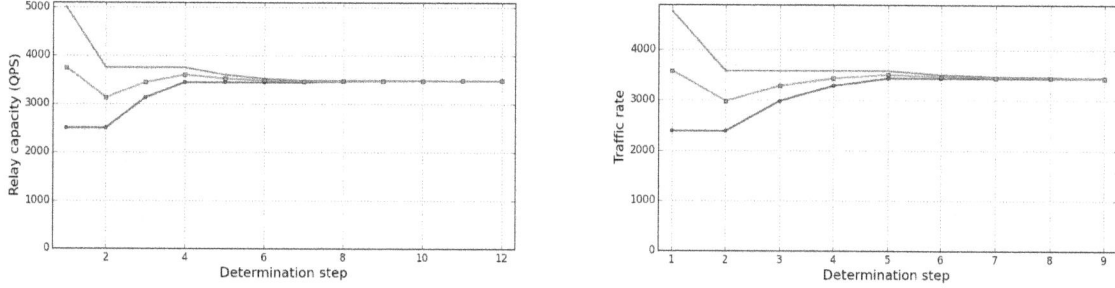

Figure 16: The binary searching steps to determine replication capacity (a) and replication headroom (b)

8. LESSONS LEARNED

During the course of this work, we learned a set of lessons that we would like to share.

8.1 Approximation model works well when the entire data set is not available

When only limited values of incoming traffic are known, while the full curves (i.e., the complete data points corresponding to the incoming traffic rates) are not available, it is difficult to determine the replication latency by performing numerical analysis as presented in Section 4. Partly for this reason, we developed an approximation model to quickly determine the maximum replication latency. This model requires knowing the average traffic rates. Based on average rate, the peak traffic rates can be approximated by scaling the average traffic rate. Based on our experience, for such web-type traffic rates, the rule of thumb is to scale average traffic rate by $1.5X$ to obtain the peak traffic rates.

Once we know the incoming peak traffic rate, we assume the peak hours will last for about 8 hours (which roughly correlates with the length of typical business hours). We denote these 8 hours as "busy period". To estimate the maximum replication latency, we also need to know the non-busy incoming traffic rate. For simplicity, we approximate the non-busy rate by halving the average traffic rate. To gain an idea of these values compared to the entire day's traffic, in Figure 17 we plot the raw traffic rates of the day of April 15th, 2014 for a single instance. Each data point represents a 5-minute average of traffic rate. The thick blue line shows the daily average of the traffic rate, red line is the busy traffic rate, and green line is the non-busy rate.

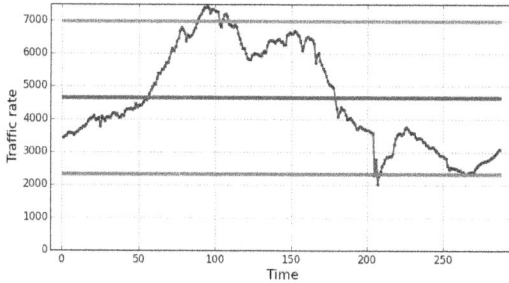

Figure 17: Approximation model (Each data points represents 5 minutes)

Let R_{cap} be the relay capacity (e.g., 6K event/s), T_{avg} be the average incoming traffic rate, T_{busy} be the busy traffic rate, T_{idle} be the non-busy traffic rate, and P be the duration of peak period; we can deduct the maximum replication latency (denoted by La) by $La = \frac{(T_{peak} - R_{cap})P}{R_{cap} - T_{idle}}$. Note that $R_{cap} - T_{idle}$ gives the extra consumption rate that drains the previous latency buildup. Let $T_{busy} = 1.5T_{avg}$ and $T_{idle} = 0.5T_{avg}$. Also assume the time granularity is per second. The equation calculating La in seconds becomes $La = \frac{28800(1.5T_{avg} - R_{cap})}{R_{cap} - 0.5T_{avg}}$.

With the above equation, we can similarly address other capacity planing questions. The corresponding solutions only need a simple linear transformation of variables. Specifically, to determine the needed relay capacity, we use $R_{cap} = \frac{(43200 + 0.5 * La)R_{avg}}{28800 + La}$. To determine the maximum average incoming rate we can handle, we have $T_{avg} = \frac{(28800 + La)T_{cap}}{43200 + 0.5La}$. We evaluated the accuracy of this approximation model by comparing this model to the numerical calculation model, we found that the maximum replication lag obtained by approximation model is about $1.7X$ of that of the numerical calculations. Though it is not quite accurate and only gives the *single* maximum lag, it is a quick way to roughly estimate the worst replication latency. In addition, it does not need the full data set as required by the numerical calculations.

8.2 Internet traffic is highly dynamic, so give enough headroom in capacity planning

Based on our observations into the production traffic, the traffic rates across time can be very dynamic, sometimes bursty. The variability is present in multiple granularities including day, hour and minute. We observed highest variability inside a day. For instance, for the first day in our presented 6-week data, out of 24 data points (hourly aggregated), the mean is 3017, while the standard deviation is 1195. The primary reason for the high variability inside a day is the human activities with regard to business hours.

Even with daily aggregated data of 60 days (totally 60 data points, each for a day), the variability is still high with mean of 2787 and standard deviation of 864. We believe the primary reason is difference between the weekdays and weekends inside a week. Compared to the variability of hourly and daily traffic, the variability inside an hour (i.e., per-minute aggregation) is much smaller. For instance, for a particular workday, we find the maximum variability has the mean of 2484 and standard deviation of 374.

49

Given the high variability of web traffic and the traffic growth trend, it is important to give enough headroom in capacity planning. A careless capacity planning strategy would simply use the average values (e.g., average traffic rate), however, the average value can be significantly misleading due to the dynamic property. For instance, for our 60-day of hourly aggregated traffic, we found that the highest traffic rate can be $2.5X$ of the mean traffic rate.

9. RELATED WORK

This section will present some relevant works in literature.

9.1 Database replication latency

Database replication latencies have been studied in several works. An approach of replicating the commit operations rather than the transactional log is proposed in [12] to reduce replication latency. Database replication latencies in particular applications are also studied [16]. Some other works [2, 1] focus on MySql replication latency and evaluate the latencies of different types of transactions.

9.2 Time Series Model

Time series data are commonly decomposed into trend, season and noise. Noise is often modeled by stationary ARMA (autoregressive moving average) [4, 10] process. Box-Jenkins proposes ARIMA model (differencing) [3], which is a generalization of ARMA model. This model is generally referred to as an ARIMA(p,d,q) model where parameters p, d, and q are non-negative integers that refer to the order of the autoregressive, integrated, and moving average parts of the model respectively. Other models include Holt-Winters (HW) [5] and State Space Model (SSM) [8].

9.3 Forecasting network and Internet traffic

Work in [6] presents both neural networks and two time series (ARIMA and Holt-Winters) to forecast the amount of TCP/IP traffic. [13] found that IP backbone traffic exhibits visible long term trends, strong periodicities and variability at multiple time scales; Work [14] proposes time series based model to forecast when to add more network bandwidth. [11] uses time series model to extract the trends and seasonal patterns from page view data. Other works [9] study the fine-grained time series characteristics of network traffic at an Internet edge network to facilitate anomaly detection.

10. CONCLUSION

In this work we study the problem of taming the database replication latency for LinkedIn Internet traffic. Based on our observations into production traffic and various playing parts, we develop practical and effective models to answer a set of other business-critical questions related to capacity planning. These questions include: future traffic rate forecasting, replication latency prediction, replication capacity determination, replication headroom determination and SLA determination.

11. REFERENCES

[1] *How fast is MySQL replication?* http://www.xaprb.com/blog/2007/10/23/how-fast-is-mysql-replication/.

[2] *Investigating MySQL Replication Latency in Percona XtraDB Cluster.* http://www.mysqlperformanceblog.com/2013/03/03/investigating-replication-latency-in-percona-xtradb-cluster/.

[3] G. E. P. Box and G. M. Jenkins. *Time Series Analysis: Forecasting and Control.* Prentice Hall PTR, Upper Saddle River, NJ, USA, 3rd edition, 1994.

[4] P. J. Brockwell and R. A. Davis. *Introduction to Time Series and Forecasting.* Springer, 2nd edition, Mar. 2002.

[5] C. Chatfield. *The Analysis of Time Series: An Introduction, Sixth Edition (Chapman & Hall/CRC Texts in Statistical Science).* Chapman and Hall/CRC, 6 edition, July 2003.

[6] P. Cortez, M. Rio, M. Rocha, and P. Sousa. *Expert Systems*, 29(2):143–155, 2012.

[7] S. Das, C. Botev, and et al. All aboard the databus!: Linkedin's scalable consistent change data capture platform. SoCC '12, New York, NY, USA, 2012.

[8] J. Durbin and S. J. Koopman. *Time series analysis by state space methods.* Oxford Univ. Press, 2001.

[9] C. James and H. A. Murthy. Decoupling non-stationary and stationary components in long range network time series in the context of anomaly detection. In *Proceedings of the 2012 IEEE 37th Conference on Local Computer Networks (LCN 2012)*, LCN '12, Washington, DC, USA, 2012.

[10] T. H. Lai. Time series analysis univariate and multivariate methods: William w.s. wei, (addison-wesley, reading, ma, 1990). *International Journal of Forecasting*, 7(3):389–390, 1991.

[11] J. Li and A. Moore. Forecasting web page views: Methods and observations. *JMLR (Journal of Machine Learning Research)*, 9(Oct):2217–2250, 2008.

[12] H. Mahmoud, F. Nawab, A. Pucher, D. Agrawal, and A. El Abbadi. *Proc. VLDB Endow.*, 6(9):661–672, July 2013.

[13] K. Papagiannaki, N. Taft, Z.-L. Zhang, and C. Diot. Long-term forecasting of internet backbone traffic. *Trans. Neur. Netw.*, 16(5):1110–1124, Sept. 2005.

[14] K. Papagiannaki, N. Taft, Z.-L. Zhang, and C. Diot. Long-term forecasting of internet backbone traffic. *Trans. Neur. Netw.*, 16(5), Sept. 2005.

[15] L. Qiao, K. Surlaker, S. Das, and et.al. On brewing fresh espresso: Linkedin's distributed data serving platform. In *Proceedings of the 2013 ACM SIGMOD International Conference on Management of Data*, SIGMOD '13, New York, NY, USA, 2013.

[16] P. E. Tun, T. T. Soe, C. Myint, N. N. Ei, M. M. Oo, L. L. Yee, and A. Thida. In *Proceedings of the 3rd International Conference on Communications and Information Technology*, CIT'09, Stevens Point, Wisconsin, USA, 2009. World Scientific and Engineering Academy and Society (WSEAS).

Accurate and Efficient Object Tracing for Java Applications

Philipp Lengauer[1]

Verena Bitto[2]

Hanspeter Mössenböck[1]

[1]Institute for System Software
Johannes Kepler University Linz, Austria
philipp.lengauer@jku.at

[2]Christian Doppler Laboratory MEVSS
Johannes Kepler University Linz, Austria
verena.bitto@jku.at

ABSTRACT

Object allocations and garbage collection can have a considerable impact on the performance of Java applications. Without monitoring tools, such performance problems are hard to track down, and if such tools are applied, they often cause a significant overhead and tend to distort the behavior of the monitored application. In this paper we present a new light-weight memory monitoring approach in which we trace allocations, deallocations and movements of objects using VM-specific knowledge. We strive for utmost compactness of the trace by using a binary format with optimized encodings for different cases of memory events and by omitting all information that can be reconstructed offline when the trace is processed. Our approach allows us to reconstruct the heap for any point in time and to do offline analyses both on the heap and on the trace. We evaluated our tracing technique with more than 30 benchmarks from the DaCapo 2009, the DaCapo Scala, the SPECjvm 2008, and the SPECjbb 2005 benchmark suites. The average run-time overhead is 4.68%, which seems to be fast enough for keeping tracing switched on even in production mode.

Categories and Subject Descriptors

D.3.4 [**Programming Languages**]: Processors—*Memory Management (Garbage Collection)*

General Terms

Performance, Measurement

Keywords

Tracing; Allocations; Garbage Collection; Java

1. INTRODUCTION

Automatic memory management, i.e., garbage collection, has gained wide-spread use because it relieves programmers from the error-prone task of freeing unused memory manually. Moreover, a compacting garbage collector (GC) produces a consecutive, i.e., unfragmented, heap. This makes object allocations simple because new objects are simply appended to the used portion of the heap without an expensive search for a fitting memory block.

However, in today's applications with millions of objects, allocating and collecting objects can easily become a performance bottleneck. Since the details of GC algorithms are hard to understand, developers find it difficult to predict the interaction between the application and the garbage collector. Therefore, diagnosing and fixing memory-related performance problems is a tedious and often futile task.

Some virtual machines (VMs), such as the Java Hotspot^{TM} VM, support the logging of GC statistics, e.g., the collection time or the memory usage before and after garbage collection for individual spaces. While this may help in detecting memory anomalies, it does not help in locating and resolving them.

A common remedy for these issues is to analyze entire heap dumps, which tell developers what objects currently exist and thus give some clue on the reasons for a GC performance degradation. Although a dump contains structural information about the layout of the heap, it lacks information about the origin of the objects, i.e., their allocation site, their allocation time and the thread that allocated them. Furthermore, deallocations can only be detected by comparing two subsequent dumps and finding an object in one but not in the other. Identifying two objects from different dumps as the same is difficult because objects can be moved in the heap and VMs usually do not maintain unique object identifiers. For example, one object could have been reclaimed by the GC while another object of the same type could have been allocated at the same position. These two objects would be indistinguishable in a heap dump. Thus, in order to identify objects uniquely and to capture allocation-specific information we have to trace the actual object allocations.

Most Java VMs support dynamic bytecode instrumentation, enabling an external agent to inject code at each allocation site. However, instrumentation introduces a significant performance overhead because it impedes compiler optimizations, such as escape analysis and inlining. Furthermore, some information about objects cannot be obtained through mere bytecode instrumentation, e.g., the address and the size of an object or the reclamation of an object by the garbage collector. In order to obtain such information, one has to modify or extend the VM.

Ricci et al. [11] describe an approach called *Elephant Tracks* in which they use instrumentation to trace memory events such as object allocations and deallocations. Since they aim for portability between different VMs and garbage collectors, efficiency is not their primary goal. In fact, the overhead of their tracing technique is so big that it changes the behavior of the instrumented program and the GC. One interesting part of their approach is that they compute estimated death times of objects, i.e., the points in time when objects are no longer reachable. Although this is interesting in general, it is not useful for performance monitoring, because even unreachable objects occupy heap space as long as they are not collected and thus influence the GC behavior.

Our approach integrates tracing into the Java Hotspot™ VM so that it has access to all information about objects, their allocation, and how they are treated by the garbage collector. We developed novel techniques for minimizing the tracing overhead. This includes a compact binary trace format in which frequent events are encoded more compactly than less frequent ones, in which certain event data is precomputed at compile time, and in which all information is omitted that can be reconstructed offline when the trace is processed. Based on our traces, we can rebuild the heap for arbitrary points in time, we can detect reoccurring patterns and anomalies in the event stream, and we can reproduce the GC behavior in order to diagnose performance problems.

Our scientific contributions are (1) a compact binary trace format that is largely precomputable at compile time, (2) an efficient tracing mechanism that is built into the Java Hotspot™ VM, and (3) algorithms for reconstructing omitted trace information offline (e.g., object addresses and deallocations). Moreover, we provide (4) an algorithm that is able to rebuild the heap layout based on our traces.

We conducted our research in cooperation with Compuware Austria GmbH. Compuware develops leading-edge performance monitoring tools for multi-tier Java and .NET applications. In their own applications as well as in applications of their customers, high GC times are a problem that currently cannot be resolved with Compuware's tools.

This paper is structured as follows: Section 2 provides an overview of memory management in the Java Hotspot™ VM; Section 3 describes our approach, i.e., the tracing mechanism and the event formats we use; Section 4 presents a detailed evaluation of our approach, including a validation of its soundness as well as a performance evaluation that compares our overhead with those of other tools; Section 5 discusses related work and the state of the art. Section 6 shows future work and potential further usage scenarios and Section 7 concludes the paper.

2. MEMORY MANAGEMENT IN THE HOTSPOT™ VM

The default collector of the Java Hotspot™ VM is the so-called Parallel GC. It is a stop-the-world collector, meaning that all application threads are halted when collecting and resumed afterwards. Using the Parallel GC, the heap is split into two regions: the young generation, which is divided into the eden space and two survivor spaces, and the old generation. Splitting the heap into two generations enables the GC to use a run-time-efficient collection strategy for objects that are likely to die (i.e., young objects) and a

more memory-efficient strategy for objects that are unlikely to die (i.e., old objects). Thus, the run-time-efficient Scavenge algorithm (minor GC) is used for the young generation, whereas the Mark and Compact algorithm (major GC) is used if all spaces need collecting. Both algorithms produce an contiguous, i.e., unfragmented, heap and are highly parallelized.

2.1 Object Allocation

New objects are usually appended at the end of the eden space, which is possible because the eden space is never fragmented. To avoid multiple threads racing for the eden end, every thread uses a separate thread-local allocation buffer (TLAB) that resides within the eden space, and in which objects can be allocated by this thread without the need for synchronization. If a new object does fit into the remainder of a TLAB, the TLAB is retired and a new one is allocated into the eden space. To avoid fragmentation, any remaining space in the old TLAB is filled with an `int[]` when it is retired. This filler object will be collected automatically at the next garbage collection because it is not referenced. Only under rare circumstances, e.g., when a new TLAB cannot be allocated, the object is put into the eden space without a TLAB.

When an object allocation fails, the VM halts all application threads and reclaims unused objects in order to make space for the new object. There are different levels of allocation failures with distinct actions, depending on how often the same allocation already failed.

- Level 1 allocation failures occur if the TLAB is full, and there is neither enough space for another TLAB, nor enough space for the object itself in the eden space. The VM triggers a minor GC (possibly followed by a major GC) and retries to allocate into the eden space.

- Level 2 allocation failures occur if there is still not enough space and a major GC has not been triggered at Level 1. The VM triggers a major GC and retries to allocate into the eden space.

- Level 3 allocation failures occur if there is still not enough space after the major GC or if the object is simply too big for the young generation. Instead of triggering another GC, the VM tries to allocate directly into the old generation.

- Level 4 allocation failures occur only if there is not enough space in the old generation. This means that the VM is running out of memory. Therefore, a more conservative major GC is triggered, clearing all soft references. The allocation is then retried in the eden space.

- Level 5 allocation failures trigger a final attempt to allocate into the old generation. If this fails, an `Out-OfMemoryError` is thrown.

The memory manager provides allocation routines for different kinds of objects, i.e., for instances of any type and for arrays of any size. They allocate objects by first trying to allocate into a TLAB, and, if this fails, act according to the allocation failure level. There are four components which may allocate objects: the interpreter, compiled code, the garbage collector, and the VM itself. The interpreter has a special fast path for allocating instances into a TLAB. The code of this fast path is generated during VM startup and relies on a non-full TLAB. If the TLAB is full or if an array must be allocated, the interpreter has to fall back to the slow path in which it calls one of the generic allocation routines provided by the memory manager. Similarly, compiled code pieces have fast paths for TLAB allocations (both for instances and for arrays). If the TLAB is full, the code falls back to the generic allocation routines (slow path). The garbage collector allocates filler objects (e.g., for retiring TLABs) by directly manipulating the heap. Finally, the VM uses the generic allocation routines for the allocation of so-called universe objects (i.e., objects that are created during VM startup) and for other special cases, e.g., for reflection and cloning.

2.2 Garbage Collection

During a minor GC, all live objects in eden and in one of the survivor spaces are copied into the other (empty) survivor space by following all root pointers into the young generation recursively. When an object has reached a certain age (measured in survived minor GCs), it is "tenured", i.e., copied into the old generation. An object might also be copied directly into the old generation if the survivor space is full or the object is too big. At the end of a minor GC, eden and the source survivor space are considered empty again. Any object that has not been copied is garbage. It is not deallocated explicitly but is implicitly freed when the containing spaces are declared empty. Therefore, the run time of a minor GC depends only on the number of live objects because they have to be evacuated into either one of the survivor spaces or the old generation.

To avoid locking, promotion-local allocation buffers (PLABs) are used for parallel copying into the survivor space and into the old generation. Like TLABs, PLABs are allocated and retired on demand, which might include filling the remainder with a filler object.

In order to avoid that an object is copied twice if two GC threads arrive at that object at the same time, a forward pointer is atomically installed into every copied object. The forward pointer points to the new location of the copied object and is used for detecting whether an object has already been copied as well as for fixing the references to it. If an object has been copied twice by accident, the slower thread then overwrites its copy with an `int[]` and uses the other copy obtained via the forward pointer.

A major GC consists of three phases: mark, summarize, and compact. In the mark phase, the heap is traversed starting with the root pointers and all reachable objects are marked as being alive. The summarize phase computes the new locations of live objects after compaction, whereas the compact phase moves all live objects accordingly and adjusts all pointers. For parallel marking, subsets of the root pointers are handled by different threads; for parallel compaction the heap is split into several small regions. As all objects are moved towards the beginning of the heap during compaction, very old objects, including the universe, tend to accumulate at the beginning of the old generation. As these objects are very unlikely to die in the future, the GC defines a dense prefix at the beginning of the old generation. In this special region, compaction is not performed every time, but dead objects are only overwritten with filler objects.

3. APPROACH

This section presents our tracing approach, i.e., the generation of raw traces as well as the offline post-processing steps required to reconstruct omitted information. Performance results and the impact of individual optimizations will be discussed in Section 4.2.

We modified the Java Hotspot^{TM} VM to capture allocation and GC events. More specifically, we modified the interpreter, the just-in-time compiler, and the garbage collector so that every object allocation and every object move is treated as an event that is written to a dedicated trace file for subsequent analysis.

To reproduce an allocation from the trace, we need to know the object's address, its type, and its size (including the array length if the object is an array), the allocation site, the allocating thread, the allocator (i.e., interpreter, compiled code, GC, or VM), and the allocation mode (i.e., fast path or slow path). To capture object movements by the GC, we need to know the object's old and new address for every move. Furthermore, we need to know if an object was kept alive by the GC without moving it. Every object that is neither moved nor kept alive and is located in a collected space, is reclaimed. Therefore, we do not need dedicated deallocation events but can derive them from other events in the trace. The above information must either be explicitly stored in the trace, or must be reproducible from other events in the trace in combination with the context (i.e., the adjacent events).

Although we extended the Hotspot^{TM} VM, our approach remains applicable to others, because modern VMs and GCs use very similar techniques and algorithms.

3.1 Symbols

Symbolic information such as the allocation site (i.e., class name and method name) and the type name of the allocated object would take up a lot of space if included in every event. Therefore, we map this symbol information to numeric IDs, which are used in the actual events instead. The information corresponding to the IDs is written to a separate symbols file. For every allocation site, the symbols file contains the name of the allocating class (represented by a 2-byte integer), the name of the allocating method, the bytecode index (BCI) of the allocation site, and the ID of the allocated type (represented as a 2-byte integer). For every type, the symbols file contains the name of the type and the size of objects belonging to this class. The size is the actual size for instances, and the element size as well as the header size for arrays. Encoding this information by a single ID keeps the trace file compact. The symbols file is generated on demand during tracing but stabilizes quickly.

3.2 Event Types and Formats

This section describes the format of allocation events and GC events in the trace file.

3.2.1 Allocation Events

Figure 1 shows the format of the most generic (and verbose) allocation event whereas every block is 4 bytes in size. The event type field (1 byte) indicates that the event describes an allocation and contains also the allocator and the allocation mode, e.g., compiled code fast (TLAB) allocation or interpreter slow (eden space) allocation. The allocation site (class, method and BCI) is mapped by an ID in the allocation site field (2 bytes). Although, we support at most 65536 allocation sites, we have never reached this limit because we assign IDs lazily, i.e., only if we observe at least one allocation at that site. The object's address can be determined by the space into which the object was allocated and by an offset that is stored in the relative address field (4 bytes). Since addresses are word-aligned, the space can be encoded in the last 2 bits of the relative address field. If the object is an array, its length is stored in the optional array length / size field (4 bytes). Some instance objects do not have a fixed size, so their size can be encoded in that field instead of the array length. Finally, the optional class field (4 bytes) contains a reference to the type, if it cannot be inferred from the allocation site.

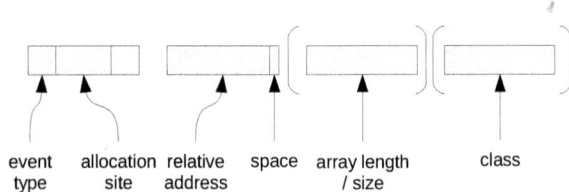

Figure 1: Event format for allocation events

Some of the fields are necessary because their contents cannot always be inferred automatically. For example, the type of the allocated object can usually be inferred from the allocation site, because most sites, can allocate just a single type of objects. However, if a single valid type cannot be determined statically, we use the optional class field to store the type. This can happen if there is no valid allocation site or if different types can be allocated at a specific allocation site. The former occurs when the universe is built by the VM, whereas the latter occurs in multidimensional array allocations. For example, `new int[21][42]` is actually one `new int[21][]` and 21 allocations of kind `new int[42]`. Based on the type information and optionally the array length, we can calculate the size of an object. If the size cannot be derived from the type of the allocated object, the explicit size field is used. This is necessary because the `Class` class contains all static fields of the class it describes. Therefore, the size of a `Class` object, although not being an array, is not fixed but varies depending on the amount of static members. Finally, the allocating thread can be determined from the context, which will be shown in Section 3.3.

This generic allocation event format has potential for optimizations: (1) 16 bytes per allocation event is too big when tracing allocation-intensive applications. (2) Calculating the fields again and again is redundant, because their values usually do not change for a specific allocation site; Figure 2 shows our optimized allocation event format that we use whenever possible, falling back to the generic format only if necessary.

We observed (cf. Section 4.2) that most objects are instances and small arrays, i.e., arrays with a length smaller than 255, which are allocated into the TLAB. Correspondingly, the above mentioned corner cases (i.e., multidimensional arrays and `Class` objects) account only for a small fraction of all objects.

In the optimized format, the first word remains the same, except that we use the previously unused byte for storing the length of small arrays. Moreover, considering only TLAB

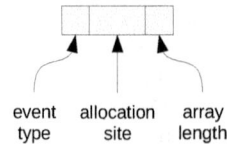

Figure 2: Optimized allocation event format by exploiting continuous TLAB allocations

allocations, there is no need for an explicit object address, since the address can be computed from the TLAB address and previous TLAB allocation events, i.e., the sum of the individual object sizes already allocated into this TLAB (the algorithm to reconstruct the object address is discussed in more detail in Section 4.1). As this event format is not used for large arrays, `Class` objects, multidimensional arrays, and allocations with an unknown allocation site, we can encode everything in a single 4-byte word, without losing any information.

Given this optimized event format and an arbitrary allocation site, the first 3 bytes of the event word can be statically precomputed. This characteristic is used to minimize the run-time performance overhead of allocation events in compiled code, as described in Section 3.4.

3.2.2 GC Events

Figure 3 shows an event denoting that a single object has been moved by the GC, as indicated by the event type field. The from-address and space represent the current object position, whereas the to-address and space are its new location. Although every object movement can be described with such an event, there are several optimized event formats that we use whenever possible in order to keep the trace small and to minimize IO.

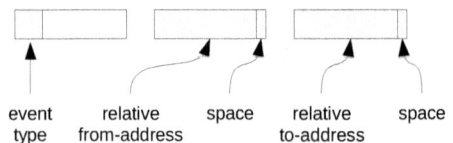

Figure 3: Event format for GC events

During minor GCs, PLABs are placed into the survivor space and the old space to avoid synchronization when moving live objects (cf. Section 2.2). As PLABs are similar to TLABs, we can employ the same technique to calculate the to-address based on the PLAB address and previous object moves into this PLAB. The first optimized event format, shown in Figure 4, takes advantage of this fact. We omit the to-address and only need to know into which space (i.e., survivor space or old space) objects are moved to correctly reconstruct their addresses. If the relative from-address is small enough to fit into the unused 22 bits of the first word, we further compress the event into another 4-byte format. Only if the object is moved without using a PLAB (e.g., because no more PLABs can be allocated or because the object is too big for a single PLAB) we fall back to the above described format.

During major GCs, live objects are moved towards the beginning of the heap (cf., Section 2.2). As the Mark and Compact algorithm does not use PLABs, we cannot omit the

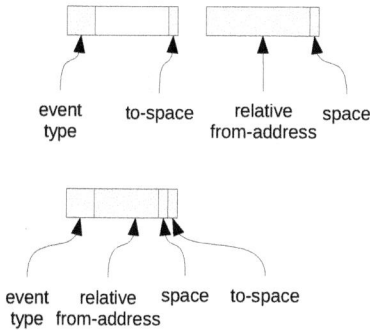

Figure 4: Optimized event format for minor GC events by exploiting continuous PLABs and small addresses

to-address in the same manner as described above. However, we can exploit the fact that objects survive in clusters, because referenced objects are often located next to each other due to their sequential allocation and compaction. Thus, these clusters are moved by the same offset and can therefore be handled more efficiently by the event format shown in Figure 5. This format differs from Figure 3 only in making use of the remaining 24 bits to store the number of adjacent objects moved by the same offset. In combination with the object sizes from the allocation events, we can then reproduce every single move correctly.

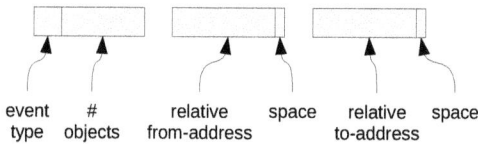

Figure 5: Optimized event format for major GC events by aggregating similar events

3.2.3 Other Events

To support the omission of information in the above mentioned event formats, we capture a number of additional events, such as TLAB and PLAB allocations as well as the start and end of GC runs. TLAB and PLAB allocation events carry the absolute address and the size of the respective thread-local buffer. This information enables computing the relative address of each object allocation or GC move if the address has been omitted. GC start and GC end events carry the absolute address and the size of each space as well as the type, i.e., minor or major. By means of the absolute addresses for each space, we can convert relative object addresses to the correct absolute address. As these events occur infrequently compared to allocation or GC move events, there was no need for compressing the contents or other further optimizations.

3.3 Writing Events to the Trace File

All events described in Section 3.2 have to be written to the trace file. However, writing them one by one would result in an unnecessarily large number of IO operations, stalling application threads. Therefore, we use buffers to collect events before they are written.

Event Buffers.

One simple approach is to store all events in a global event buffer, as shown in Figure 6. However, as today's applications are heavily multi-threaded, the application threads would have to race for the buffer top. This would result in stalling application threads at every event.

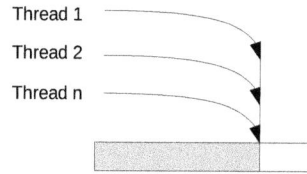

Figure 6: Global buffer for all threads

To avoid multiple threads racing for a single buffer, we assigned a buffer to every thread, as shown in Figure 7. Therefore, every thread can fire events, i.e., store them into its own buffer, without having to synchronize with the other threads. When the buffer is full, it must be written to the trace file, stalling the application thread again.

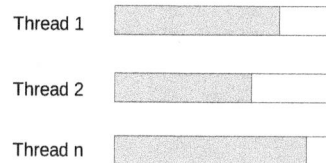

Figure 7: Thread-local buffers

Figure 8 shows how two buffers per thread can be used to avoid stalling application threads for most of the time. A thread always writes to its front buffer until this buffer gets full. Then it swaps its front buffer with its back buffer and continues to write on the new front buffer. The full back buffer is appended to a flush queue. A dedicated worker thread consumes buffers from this queue and writes them to the trace file. The application thread stalls only if the front buffer gets full while the back buffer has not yet been processed by the worker thread. However, our observations showed that only a small number of threads allocate frequently. Therefore, the majority of threads hog buffer space needlessly.

Our final approach, shown in Figure 9, solves this problem by assigning one buffer to each thread on demand, using a flush queue and a worker thread for asynchronous output, as well as a pool of empty buffers. When a thread's buffer gets full, it is appended to the flush queue and a new buffer is requested from the pool of empty buffers. Thus, no application thread consumes buffer space needlessly and threads never have to stall due to full buffers. Moreover, they only have to synchronize on the flush queue and the buffer pool. However, this occurs rarely i.e., only when their own buffer gets full.

Using thread-local event buffers allows us to associate all events in a buffer with a particular thread, avoiding the need for a dedicated thread ID in every event. When a buffer is written to the trace file, it is preceded by a thread ID, thus allowing us to recover this association when the trace file is processed.

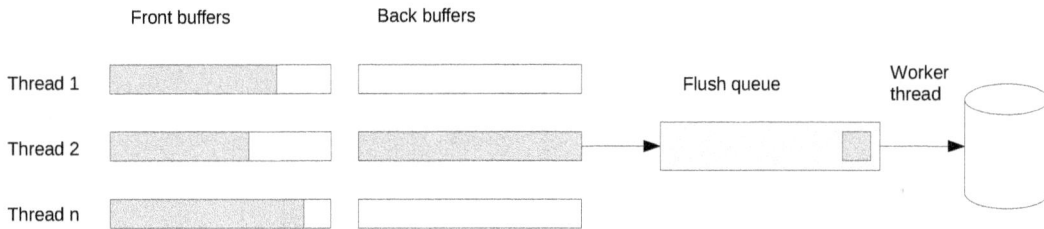

Figure 8: Thread-local front and back buffers

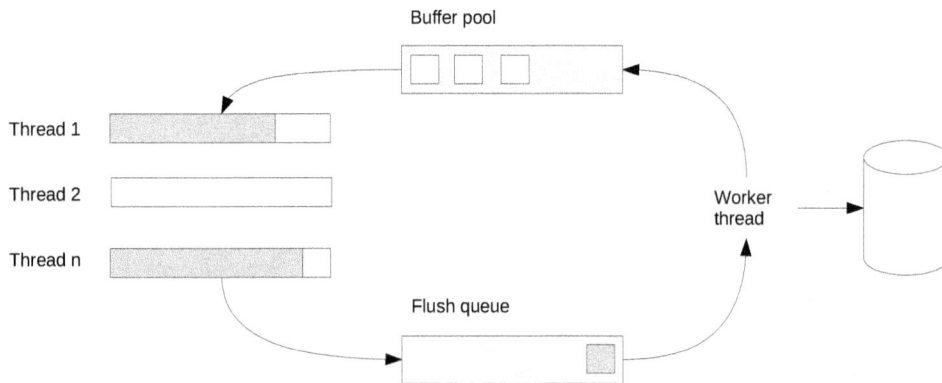

Figure 9: Thread-local buffers with a buffer pool

Buffer Sizes.

We observed that, if threads execute similar tasks, they also have similar allocation frequencies. This can lead to buffer overflows at the same time, and consequently, to performance degradations, because (1) the locks of the flush queue and the buffer pool are contended and (2) the flush queue might overflow itself because the worker thread may not be able to process the buffers fast enough. This problem was overcome by randomizing the individual buffer sizes while leaving the overall size of all buffers the same. As the overall size is the same, buffers are flushed as often as before, but because of the different individual sizes, they are flushed at different points in time.

Event Times.

Since events are collected in thread-local event buffers, their chronological order cannot be recorded if they occur in different threads. We accept that as the price for not having to synchronize the recording of every event. However, we flush all event buffers (even those that are not yet full) before and after every GC run so that the chronological order of events is at least maintained across GC runs. In other words: all events that happended before a GC run occur before the corresponding GC events in the trace file, and all events that happened after a GC run occur after the corresponding GC events. Furthermore, all events that happened in the same thread occur in the correct chronological order.

3.4 Event Capturing

We designed a new VM component (the *Event Runtime*), that is responsible for (1) building an event, (2) writing it to a buffer as well as for (3) appending a full buffer to the flush queue and (4) fetching a new buffer. This section describes

how it is used by other VM components such as the memory manager, the interpreter, compiled code, and the GC.

3.4.1 Allocations in the Memory Manager

Objects allocated by the memory manager are the universe objects (at VM startup) and filler objects (e.g., when retiring TLABs or PLABs). These objects are allocated in native C methods, which we instrumented to call the proper methods of the Event Runtime. Since these objects are not allocated by Java code, no allocation site can be defined. Hence, we use a predefined VM_INTERNAL allocation site and append the type ID in the optional field.

3.4.2 Allocations in the Interpreter

As discussed in Section 2.1, the interpreter allocates instance objects in the fast path. When it processes the allocating bytecode it calls into the Event Runtime to record the allocation event. Since interpreted code is never "hot" (otherwise it would have been compiled) there was no need for optimizing this call.

When the TLAB is full or when the allocated object is an array, the interpreter goes into the slow path and again makes a call into the Event Runtime. In this case, however, the Runtime additionally extracts the method and current BCI from the call stack and records them in the event.

3.4.3 Allocations in Compiled Code

Since hot code is compiled, most objects will be allocated by compiled code (cf. Section 4.2). These allocations are fast because there is a fast path for both instances and arrays of arbitrary lengths. Only if the TLAB is full, a VM routine is called that allocates objects using the generic allocation routines. This is why we designed the event format in a way that we can capture events in the compiled code as fast as possible.

Since the just-in-time compiler knows which allocation site it is currently compiling (i.e., which method and BCI), the value of the optimized allocation event can be inlined into the generated code as a precomputed constant. If the allocation site is an array allocation with less than 255 elements, we just have to add the array length to the precomputed event word. Therefore, the overhead of most allocation events in compiled code is as small as checking whether the event buffer is full (i.e., comparing two pointers), firing the event (i.e., assigning a 4 byte constant to a memory location) and incrementing the top of the event buffer (i.e., incrementing a pointer).

Figure 10 shows C-like pseudo code representing the generated code at every allocation site of an instance object (excluding `Class` allocation sites), whereas Figure 11 shows the generated code for array allocation sites (excluding allocation sites for multiddimensional arrays).

Please note that this code is generated during the translation of an intermediate program representation to machine code, i.e., after optimizations have been applied. Therefore, this code does not impede any optimizations, such as escape analysis or control/data flow analysis. If the buffer is full (or if the array is too big), the Event Runtime is called which is able to handle these cases appropriately. This might include fetching a new buffer or, in the worst case, falling back to the generic allocation event format.

```
Object* o = ...;        //allocation
if(buf->top < buf->end) {
  *(buf->top++) = 0xABCDEF00;
} else {
  allocation_event_slow_path(o);
}
```

Figure 10: Generated code for firing an optimized allocation event for instances

```
Object** a = ...;       //allocation
if(buf->top < buf->end && a->len < 255) {
  *(buf->top++) = 0xABCDEF00 | a->len;
} else {
  allocation_event_slow_path(a);
}
```

Figure 11: Generated code for firing an optimized allocation event for arrays

3.4.4   Allocations in the GC

To avoid fragmentation, the GC allocates objects to fill holes in the heap. This is done by directly manipulating the memory location where the object header will be. We instrumented all sites where the GC creates such filler objects so that they fire proper allocation events. Although filler objects will never survive the next collection (because they are not referenced), they must be tracked in order to calculate the absolute addresses of neighboring objects correctly and to keep our rebuilt heap unfragmented.

3.4.5   Moves in the GC

Whenever the GC moves an object, an appropriate GC move event is fired. If a PLAB is used, e.g., during a minor

GC, one of the fast event formats is used. During a major GC, most GC move events are suppressed and grouped into region events.

4.   EVALUATION

In this section we validate our approach by showing how we can reconstruct omitted information from the trace and consequently rebuild the heap layout. Furthermore, we show that our approach outperforms similar approaches significantly in terms of performance.

4.1   Validation

In order to validate our approach, we defined two categories of tests: Correctness tests are (self-written) applications whose allocation behavior is predictable. For these applications we defined tests in which we check if every single allocation event is recorded in the trace and carries the correct data; Consistency tests check whether the trace is consistent in itself, i.e., whether the heap can be reconstructed. We applied these tests to well-known Java benchmarks described in detail in Section 4.2.

4.1.1   Reconstructing the Heap Layout

Based on the trace file, we can reconstruct the heap layout offline for any point in the execution of the application. This includes information about which objects were alive at that time, as well as where they were located in the heap. To do this, we first parse the symbols file and start with an empty heap before parsing the actual trace file. Each trace file contains an alternating sequence of two phases: the mutator phase and the GC phase. The GC phase starts at a GC start event and ends at a GC end event, whereas the mutator phase is active at all other times.

Mutator Phase.

The first phase is the mutator phase, which consists of object allocations and TLAB allocations. During this phase, we (logically) create a new object for each allocation and store it in a map using the object address as its key. If an event uses the unoptimized event format, this is trivial because the object address is stored in the event explicitly. If an event uses the optimized format, i.e., if the object was allocated into a TLAB and the address was omitted from the trace, the object address must be reconstructed. Thus, we also maintain a map of currently active TLABs using the thread ID as the key. When the address of such an event is reconstructed, we look up the correct TLAB and, consequently, can determine the range in which the object must lie (somewhere in between the TLAB start and the TLAB end).

As objects are allocated sequentially into TLABs, the address of the first object (obj_0) is equal to the address of its TLAB. The address of all subsequent objects (obj_n) can be calculated by adding the size of the previous objects to its address. Figure 12 shows how to incrementally reconstruct object addresses based on previously reconstructed addresses.

As object allocations into a TLAB might also be described by the generic allocation event format, their address must be checked if it lies within the current active TLAB (there might be other reasons for falling back to this format than a non-TLAB allocation). If it lies within the TLAB, the

Heap

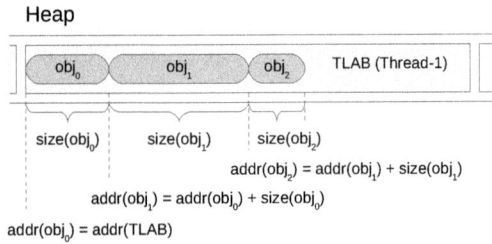

$$addr(obj_n) = \begin{cases} addr(TLAB) & \text{if } n = 0 \\ addr(obj_{n-1}) + size(obj_{n-1}) & \text{else} \end{cases}$$

Figure 12: Algorithm for reconstructing object addresses of TLAB allocations

counters are adjusted as described above, if not, the object is just added to the map with the explicitly stored address.

This algorithm assumes that (1) all allocations are in temporal order within the scope of one thread and that (2) only the owner thread can allocate into a TLAB. Although the former is trivially true because all events are written sequentially to a thread-local buffer and the buffers are flushed in the order they are committed to the flush queue, the latter is false due to filler objects when retiring TLABs in preparation for a GC run.

In this case, all Java threads are suspended and their respective TLABs are retired by a dedicated VM thread. Retiring a TLAB might include allocating a filler object to fill the current TLAB, but, as the VM thread is retiring the TLABs, this allocation is accounted to that thread instead of the owner thread. To make it even worse, due to the lack of temporal ordering among multiple threads, the allocation event of that filler object might be located in the trace before or after the last allocation into the corresponding TLAB.

To deal with filler objects correctly, we detect them while parsing a mutator phase and postpone their processing until the mutator phase is complete. As this filler objects are always of type `int[]` with a `VM_INTERNAL` allocation site allocated by the GC and thus carry an explicit object address, they are easily detectable. Therefore, we process the postponed filler objects when the mutator phase is complete by searching the correct TLAB and assigning the filler to it as described above.

GC Phase.

The second phase is the GC phase, which consists of GC move events, PLAB allocations, and a few object allocations (for filler objects when PLABs are retired). At the end of the mutator phase, the data structure representing the heap can be interpreted as a map of object addresses to object-specific information. When processing a GC move event, the object is copied from the old heap map to a new heap map. In the end, the maps of all collected spaces are cleared and replaced with the new ones (the kind of spaces depend on the kind of GC). Every object which is in the old map but not in the new map has been deallocated.

To reconstruct missing addresses, we use the same technique for PLABs as for TLABs. (cf. Mutator Phase).

When the GC phase has been processed completely (indicated by a GC end event), the heap map is in a valid state and can thus be used for the next mutator phase.

4.1.2 Consistency Tests

The consistency tests are performed while the heap layout is reconstructed from the trace of an application as described above. The tests check certain invariants, e.g., whether the sum of all object sizes in a TLAB matches the TLAB size and whether there are no holes in the heap at each phase change where the heap should be valid. Extensive tests with well-known Java benchmarks (cf. Section 4.2) showed that we can reconstruct the heap for every Java application without restrictions or inconsistencies.

4.2 Performance

In order to measure the overhead of our tracing mechanism we performed measurement on a large number of well-known Java benchmarks such as the DaCapo[1] 2009 benchmark suite [1], the DaCapo Scala[2] benchmark suite [12], the SPECjvm[3] 2008 benchmark suite, and the SPECjbb[4] 2005 benchmark. These suites contain a large variety of programs exhibiting different kinds of allocation and garbage-collection behavior. The DaCapo Scala benchmark suite contributes benchmarks that are not implemented in Java but in Scala, which usually results in a more allocation-intensive behavior. For every benchmark, we chose the largest input available to put more pressure on the memory manager and the garbage collector.

In addition to that, we implemented a benchmark that prints "Hello World" to the standard output. We use this benchmark to measure the overhead we introduce during VM startup and teardown.

Every result we show is the median of 50 runs. For every run, we executed enough warmups in order to JIT-compile all hot methods and to stabilize the caches before measurement.

We ran all measurements on an Intel® Core™ i7-3770 CPU @ 3.40GHz×4 (8 Threads) on 64-bit with 18GB RAM running Ubuntu 13.10 Saucy Salamander with the Kernel Linux 3.11.0-23-generic. All unnecessary services were disabled and the experiments were always executed in text-only mode.

4.2.1 Overhead

Figure 13 shows the run-time overhead of our approach (i.e., lower is better). Every group of bars is one benchmark, whereas the left/red/dark bar is the run time without the tracing mechanism enabled and the right/green/light bar is the run time with the tracing mechanism enabled. Due to large absolute differences in their run times, every benchmark has been normalized with respect to the run time without the tracing mechanism. The crypto, compress, scimark, mpegaudio, factorie, specs and scalatest benchmarks were excluded for space reasons and because they do not show any measurable run-time overhead anyway. The size of a single event buffer has been fixed at 16KB for this experiment.

The results show that the average run time overhead is about 4.68%. Some benchmarks such as tomcat, tradebeans, tradesoap and actors even show a slight speedup. We tracked this reproducible behavior down to the fact that

[1] http://www.dacapobench.org/
[2] http://www.dacapo.scalabench.org/
[3] http://www.spec.org/jvm2008/
[4] http://www.spec.org/jbb2005/

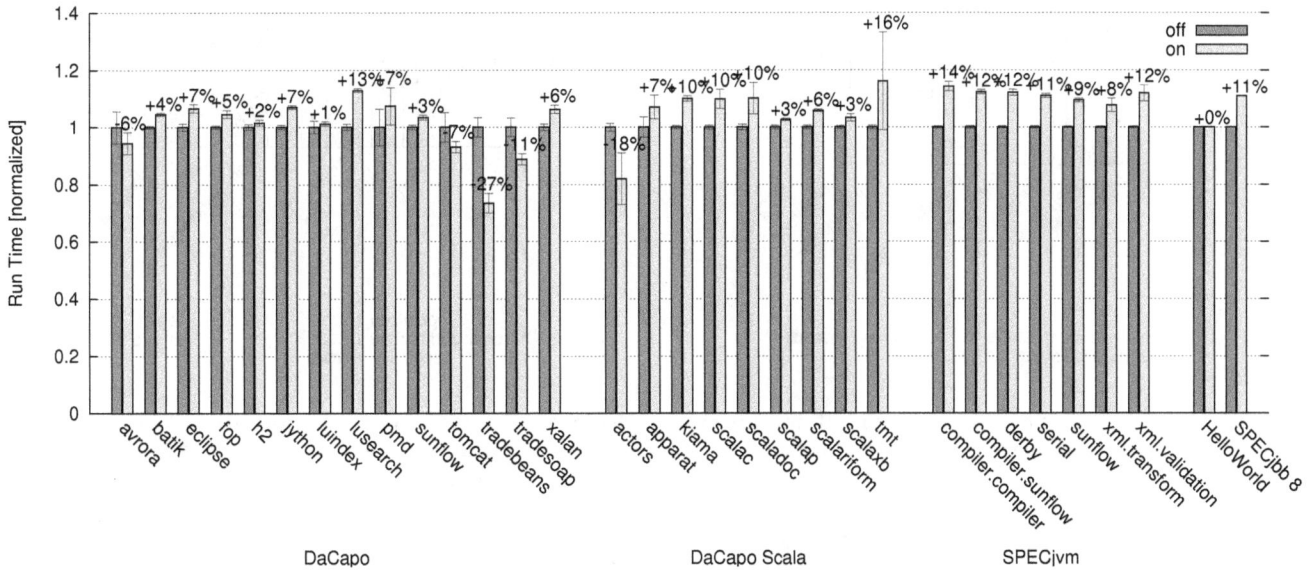

Figure 13: Run time overhead

the slight overhead we introduce when tracing allocations and GC moves causes the compiler to make different optimization decisions, that have an accidental albeit positive influence on the run time.

The overhead observed is significantly lower than similar tracing mechanisms. Figure 14 shows the overhead of *Elephant Tracks* on the DaCapo benchmarks based on [11] (time for tracing allocation and deallocation events without method entry and exit events). Although Elephant Tracks was not built for performance monitoring, it is the tool that is most similar to ours and can be configured to collect almost the same amount of data as we do. Please note the different scale on the y axis and that the overhead on the tradebeans and tradesoap benchmarks is so high that they crash due to internal timeouts with *Elephant Tracks*. The results show that our tracing mechanism outperforms Elephant Tracks significantly.

Although there was no overhead measurable in Java heap size, the non-Java heap rose by 1% due to the event buffers. Furthermore, the code cache (holding all compiled code) grew by 3% due to the additional code generated. These numbers are the same for all benchmarks.

4.2.2 Impact of Optimizations

In order to determine the gain of individual trace optimizations, we compared the benchmark results with and without these optimizations. Here, we will only discuss the most import optimizations in terms of performance impact.

Optimized Allocation Event Formats.

Figure 15 shows the distribution of the types of allocated objects, i.e., instances, small arrays (*length* < 255), and big arrays, of a reduced albeit representative set of benchmarks. As expected, instances and small arrays comprise the by far largest amount of heap objects. Therefore, handling them by a more compact event format makes sense.

Figure 16 shows the distribution of the allocators, i.e., compiled code, interpreter, and the VM. Again, as expected,

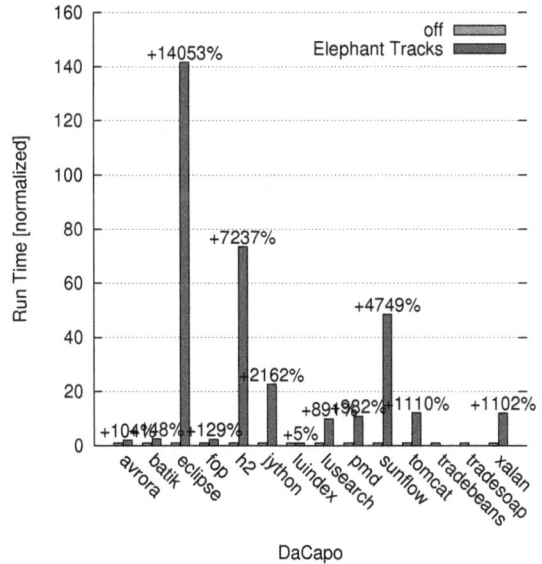

Figure 14: Run time overhead of elephant tracks

after the application is warmed up, almost all allocations were performed by compiled code. The only exception is the HelloWorld benchmark, where all allocations are done during startup by the VM itself or by the interpreter. Therefore, our decision to optimize the tracing of allocations in compiled code pays off.

To summarize, it is obvious that optimizing compiled code for instances and small arrays is of utmost importance. For this reason, we defined optimized and precompilable event formats for these cases as described in Section 3.2.1. Disabling these optimizations and falling back to the unoptimized allocation event format increases the trace size by a factor of 2 to 3 (depending on the ratio between instances and arrays), roughly doubling the overall run-time overhead.

59

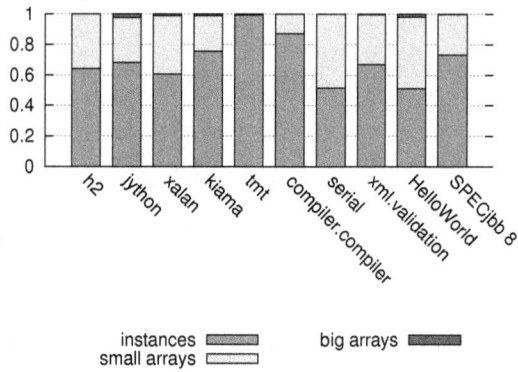

Figure 15: Object type distribution of instances, small arrays, and big arrays (from bottom to top)

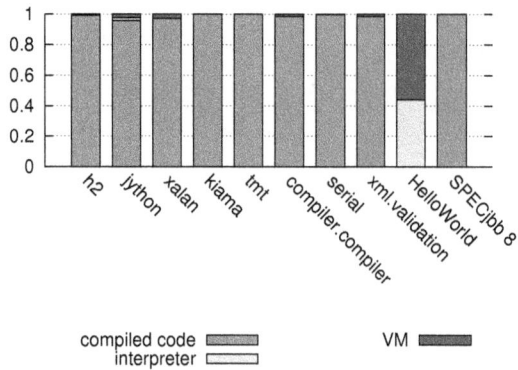

Figure 17: GC event format distribution of optimized, opimized narrow, keep alive, region and generic event formats (from bottom to top)

the pause time of the GC significantly with synchronous IO and large buffers. Furthermore, with large buffer sizes, the non-Java heap size overhead can easily grow to several GBs.

Buffer Management.

Using only a single thread-local buffer produces the same overhead and the same space trade-off as described above (cf. Paragraph Asynchronous IO) because even with asynchronous IO, the thread cannot continue without waiting for the buffer to be flushed. However, using front and back buffers doubles the average overhead compared to our final implementation. Our investigation showed that this is due to the fact that almost every benchmark has allocation-intensive bursts. During these bursts, objects are allocated faster than the buffers can be flushed. In these cases, application threads must be stalled because both, the front buffer is full, and the back buffer has not yet been flushed. As these bursts occur rarely and only affect a limited number of threads at a time, stalling can be avoided by our more flexible buffer management described in Section 3.3.

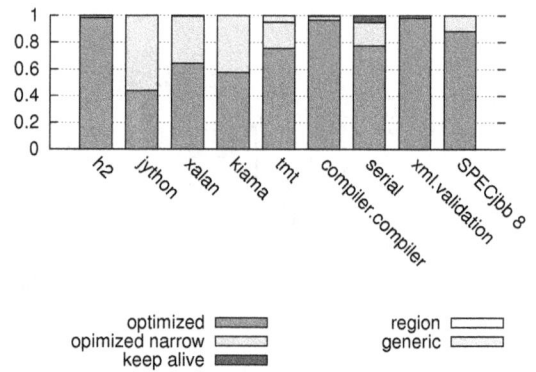

Figure 16: Allocator distribution of compiled code, interpreter, and VM (from bottom to top)

Optimized GC Event Formats.

Figure 17 shows the distribution of the GC event formats used in the benchmarks. We can observe that most events use the optimized event format without the source address; only a few events use the generic (unoptimized) event format (mostly originating from major GCs). The region move event format as well as the generic move event format are used by less than 0.1% of the events in the trace. However, observations have shown that on average at least 300 objects are aggregated into a single region event, meaning that 300 events (900 words) have been replaced by a single event (3 words as well). Furthermore, a significant amount of optimized events can be replaced by their narrow version, cutting the event size in half and consequently reducing buffer overflows and IO.

Asynchronous IO.

The performance impact of asynchronous IO strongly depends on the chosen buffer size. When using synchronous IO, we observed that the run time overhead is multiplied by at least a factor of 5 without changing the buffer size (16KB by default). When the buffers are of much larger size (several MB at least), synchronous IO performs almost as good as asynchronous IO. This is due to the fact that buffer overflows occur only rarely. However, whenever a garbage collection starts or ends, all buffers must be flushed, which increases

Randomized Buffer Sizes.

To evaluate the performance impact of randomized buffer sizes, we measured the lock and wait times when accessing the flush queue. The lock time is the time a thread has to wait for the lock, whereas the wait time is the time spent waiting because the flush queue became full. A high lock time indicates that multiple threads wanted to flush their buffers at the same time, whereas a high wait time suggests that the worker thread could not process the flush queue fast enough. Using randomized buffer sizes reduced the overall run time overhead by 2% on average and the lock time by 5% and wait time by 21% on average.

5. RELATED WORK

There is ample work on how to track down memory-related performance degradations in Java and other managed execution environments. Chilimbi et al. [2] define a binary format for recording memory event traces with the intention to use them as simulation workloads for garbage collector performance tests. However, as their trace format is very flexible and allows for variable-sized fields and custom fields, the trace is not encoded as efficiently as it could be. Harkema et al. [3] create events (not only memory events) by instrumentation and provide an event trace API. Furthermore, they implemented a number of tools on top of this API. Although their events include allocations they lack the granularity of our approach. For example, they do not trace GC events. Hertz et al. [4, 5] generate traces including allocation, deallocation and pointer-update events. They invoke a full GC every n milliseconds to calculate the approximate time of death for an object, whereas the precision depends on n. However, they cannot tell how an object was moved by the GC. Moreover, frequent full collections degrade performance as well as they distort GC behavior. Printezis et al. [10] provide an adaptable framework and API for collecting memory management behavior, including GC behavior. However, they record the behavior for blocks instead of for objects and thus lack object-specific information. Ricci et al. [11] use a combination of bytecode rewriting and JVMTI to build a shadow heap and to generate traces with events such as allocations, deallocations, and pointer updates. However, they produce an overhead of a factor of 3000 for some benchmarks, making this approach unfeasible in production environments. Furthermore, they compute estimated object death times, i.e., the time the last reference to an object is cleared, and not actual deallocations, i.e., the time an object is actually reclaimed by the GC. Although the former might be interesting, it ignores the fact that even unreferenced objects have an impact on the GC behavior. Considering the actual point in time, where they are reclaimed, is therefore more useful for performance monitoring. Finally, Jones et al. [7] offer a detailed study about the correlation of object age, allocation site, program input, and GC performance.

There is also some work on tracing objects in native environments. Although these approaches are only marginally relevant for us, they deserve being mentioned: Janjusic et al. [6] implemented a memory profiling tool that is able to associate each memory access to source-level data structures using binary instrumentation. This enables the programmer to refactor code based on memory access patterns and to simulate cache behavior. Marathe et al. [9] also provide a framework for partial access traces as well as a novel compression algorithm for these traces.

6. FUTURE WORK

This section discusses future work, as well as further potential usage scenarios.

6.1 Compression

As event traces can grow large, we plan to compress them. The event stream can either be compressed on the fly inside the VM (before writing it to the trace file) or by an external phase. Compressing the event stream inside the VM has the advantage that the VM has to write less data which in turn reduces the IO overhead. However, the compression itself will take some time as well, resulting in a trade-off between the quality of the compression (i.e., the resulting size and the run time) and IO time. Additional research and experiments are needed to determine whether an internal compression is beneficial in our case.

6.2 Cyclic Traces

When applications run indefinitely, the trace becomes too large to be kept in a single file or even on a single disk.

Therefore, we plan to overwrite the trace cyclically, so that the last n minutes of the execution are always available for analysis. In other words, the trace must be cut off and restarted in regular intervals. However, cutting off the trace will result in loss of data and, therefore, impede subsequent analysis. Information about previously allocated objects will no longer be available. To solve this problem, we plan to collect all relevant information about objects that are alive at cut points and write it to the beginning of the new trace file. The contents of this information as well as the best suitable cut points are undefined as yet and therefore considered to be future work.

6.3 Pointer Updates

In addition to object allocations and GC moves, we consider tracing also pointer updates. This can either be done at every assignment to a pointer field (which would augment the trace with valuable information about the dynamic behavior of the program but is probably too expensive) or only at major GCs where we could record the current values of pointer fields. Tracing the connections between objects on the heap would open new possibilities for advanced offline analyses such as memory leak detection or the discovery of "tenured garbage" (i.e., dead objects in the old generation that keep other objects in the young generation alive).

6.4 GC Configuration Comparisons

In previous work, we described a technique for automatically tuning the GC by finding optimal GC parameter setting in a black box manner (Lengauer et al. [8]). Object traces will help us to understand why a specific GC configuration is superior to others by providing detailed insights into dynamic behavior of the memory manager and the GC.

6.5 Mining Recurring Patterns in Transactions

Large-scale server applications have to handle a continuous stream of similar requests, i.e., transactions. Transactions can be split into different phases, some of which exhibit exactly the same allocation behavior at every execution. Other phases might follow specific patterns, e.g., the number of allocations of a certain type of objects might depends on a certain transaction parameter. Object traces can be extended with information about transaction boundaries and then mined for recurring patterns of object allocations in relation to transaction parameters. This information can help the developer to understand the performance impact of certain parameters on transactions.

7. CONCLUSIONS

In this paper, we presented the design and the implementation of an efficient tracing mechanism for Java objects, creating a trace file which contains all object allocations and GC moves that occur during the execution of a Java application. We also described a novel and compact event format as well as its efficient generation based on the omission of redundant event data, precomputed event information, and a sophisticated buffering scheme.

Extensive evaluation showed that our approach has a very low run time overhead (4.68%) that is significantly smaller than the overhead reported for other techniques. Furthermore, we showed that our approach can track the full life cycle of every object (i.e., allocations, moves, and deallocations) and allows us to reconstruct the heap layout (i.e., the location of every object) at any point during the execution of an application.

When monitoring applications with large GC pauses or when tuning GC parameters, a trace that reflects the exact behavior of an application can lay the foundation for new tools that help developers in solving memory and GC-related problems.

8. ACKNOWLEDGMENTS

This work was supported by the Christian Doppler Forschungsgesellschaft, and by Compuware Austria GmbH.

9. REFERENCES

[1] S. M. Blackburn, R. Garner, C. Hoffmann, A. M. Khang, K. S. McKinley, R. Bentzur, A. Diwan, D. Feinberg, D. Frampton, S. Z. Guyer, M. Hirzel, A. Hosking, M. Jump, H. Lee, J. E. B. Moss, A. Phansalkar, D. Stefanović, T. VanDrunen, D. von Dincklage, and B. Wiedermann. The DaCapo Benchmarks: Java Benchmarking Development and Analysis. In *Proc. of the Annual ACM SIGPLAN Conf. on Object-oriented Programming Systems, Languages, and Applications*, pages 169–190, 2006.

[2] T. Chilimbi, R. Jones, and B. Zorn. Designing a trace format for heap allocation events. In *Proc. of the 2nd Int'l Symp. on Memory Management*, pages 35–49, 2000.

[3] M. Harkema, D. Quartel, B. M. M. Gijsen, and R. D. van der Mei. Performance monitoring of java applications. In *Proc. of the 3rd Int'l Workshop on Software and Performance*, pages 114–127, 2002.

[4] M. Hertz, S. M. Blackburn, J. E. B. Moss, K. S. McKinley, and D. Stefanović. Error-free garbage collection traces: How to cheat and not get caught. In *Proc. of the 2002 ACM SIGMETRICS Int'l Conf. on Measurement and Modeling of Computer Systems*, pages 140–151, 2002.

[5] M. Hertz, S. M. Blackburn, J. E. B. Moss, K. S. McKinley, and D. Stefanović. Generating object lifetime traces with merlin. *ACM Trans. Program. Lang. Syst.*, 28(3):476–516, May 2006.

[6] T. Janjusic and K. Kavi. Gleipnir: A memory profiling and tracing tool. *SIGARCH Comput. Archit. News*, 41(4):8–12, Dec. 2013.

[7] R. E. Jones and C. Ryder. A study of java object demographics. In *Proc. of the 7th Int'l Symp. on Memory Management*, pages 121–130, 2008.

[8] P. Lengauer and H. Mössenböck. The taming of the shrew: Increasing performance by automatic parameter tuning for java garbage collectors. In *Proc. of the 5th ACM/SPEC Int'l Conf. on Performance Engineering*, ICPE '14, pages 111–122, 2014.

[9] J. Marathe, F. Mueller, T. Mohan, S. A. Mckee, B. R. De Supinski, and A. Yoo. Metric: Memory tracing via dynamic binary rewriting to identify cache inefficiencies. *ACM Trans. Program. Lang. Syst.*, 29(2), Apr. 2007.

[10] T. Printezis and R. Jones. Gcspy: An adaptable heap visualisation framework. In *Proceedings of the 17th ACM SIGPLAN Conference on Object-oriented Programming, Systems, Languages, and Applications*, pages 343–358, 2002.

[11] N. P. Ricci, S. Z. Guyer, and J. E. B. Moss. Elephant tracks: Portable production of complete and precise gc traces. In *Proc. of the 2013 Int'l Symp. on Memory Management*, pages 109–118, 2013.

[12] A. Sewe, M. Mezini, A. Sarimbekov, and W. Binder. Da capo con scala: Design and analysis of a scala benchmark suite for the java virtual machine. In *Proceedings of the 2011 ACM International Conference on Object Oriented Programming Systems Languages and Applications*, OOPSLA '11, pages 657–676, 2011.

Design and Evaluation of Scalable Concurrent Queues for Many-Core Architectures *

Thomas R. W. Scogland
Department of Computer Science
Virginia Tech
tom.scogland@vt.edu

Wu-chun Feng
Department of Computer Science
Virginia Tech
feng@cs.vt.edu

ABSTRACT

As core counts increase and as heterogeneity becomes more common in parallel computing, we face the prospect of programming hundreds or even thousands of concurrent threads in a single shared-memory system. At these scales, even highly-efficient concurrent algorithms and data structures can become bottlenecks, unless they are designed from the ground up with throughput as their primary goal.

In this paper, we present three contributions: (1) a characterization of queue designs in terms of modern multi- and many-core architectures, (2) the design of a *high-throughput, linearizable, blocking, concurrent FIFO queue* for many-core architectures that avoids the bottlenecks and pitfalls common in modern queue designs, and (3) a thorough evaluation of concurrent queue throughput across CPU, GPU, and co-processor devices. Our evaluation shows that focusing on throughput, rather than progress guarantees, allows our queue to scale to as much as *three orders of magnitude* (1000×) *faster* than lock-free and combining queues on GPU platforms and *two times* (2×) *faster* on CPU devices. These results deliver critical insights into the design of data structures for highly concurrent systems: (1) progress guarantees do *not* guarantee scalability, and (2) allowing an algorithm to block can *increase* throughput.

1. INTRODUCTION

Multicore architectures have taken over the CPU market, and many-core accelerators and co-processors, such as GPUs and Intel Xeon Phi, are becoming available to all segments of computing. Each new generation contains more cores, further compounding the demands on the scalability of software. That scalability, more often than not, is governed by the cost of synchronization and communication.

Concurrent data structures have become basic building blocks for the new wave of highly parallel applications, providing intuitive abstractions atop the complexities of low-level synchronization and memory-coherence primitives. The result can be both increased productivity and, when designed well, performance. One of the most ubiquitous of these is the concurrent first-in, first-out (FIFO) queue.[1]

The concurrent queue has been studied extensively over the last four decades. It has gone through a variety of forms – from infinite-array queues [7, 4] to lock-free queues [11, 14] to advanced distributed lock-free [8, 5] or even wait-free [9, 10] variants. As concurrency has increased, so has the contention on concurrent queues and the cost of synchronization, and frequently serialization, in these designs.

Our goal with this paper is to characterize the performance requirements and considerations of concurrent queues in the multi- and many-core era and to create a concurrent queue that is tailored for high throughput, even under extreme contention. Our design and evaluation span CPU, GPU and co-processor architectures using the C, OpenCL, and OpenMP programming models. Specifically, this paper makes the following contributions:

1. A characterization of queue designs in terms of modern multi- and many-core architectures, demonstrating that allowing blocking in high-contention and low-oversubscription environments can improve throughput significantly over non-blocking designs.

2. The design of a linearizable and inspection-compatible, blocking FIFO queue based on the above characterization which is, to our knowledge, the first to combine these properties.

3. A thorough evaluation of our queue in OpenCL and OpenMP, including a comparison with several classic and state-of-the-art concurrent queues and demonstrating up to a 2-fold speedup on CPUs and as much as a 1000-fold speedup on GPUs running more than 1000 concurrent threads.

The rest of the paper is laid out as follows. Section 2 presents the background and setup for our work, including the machine abstraction that we employ to discuss synchronization and threading in OpenCL and OpenMP environments interchangeably. Related work follows in Section 3. Section 4 characterizes the bottleneck points in concurrent queue designs and models their performance in terms

*This work was supported in part by the AFOSR Basic Research Initiative (BRI) via Grant No. FA9550-12-1-044; the NSF Major Research Instrumentation (MRI) program via Grant No. CNS-0960081; and Lawrence Livermore National Laboratory (LLNL-CONF-664304).

---

[1] As we only discuss FIFO queues in this paper, the term *queue* shall be used in place of *FIFO queue* henceforth.

of the atomic-operation throughput of many-core architectures. Section 5 presents the design of our queue and its three interfaces while Section 6 discusses linearizability [7]. Section 7 presents our experimental setup and benchmarks while Section 8 presents the results of our experiments. Section 9 presents concluding remarks and future work.

2. BACKGROUND

In order to discuss the properties of our target architectures in a uniform manner, we first present our abstraction of the concurrency and memory model that we use across devices. This section discusses the abstraction that we employ in this paper in order to discuss OpenMP on CPUs and OpenCL on CPUs, GPUs and co-processors all interchangeably, along with our microbenchmark evaluation of atomic operations that make this possible across each architecture.

2.1 Threading Abstraction

While the threading models of OpenMP and OpenCL are significantly different, they can be reconciled. An OpenCL kernel runs a set of work-groups, each consisting of work-items or, as they are sometimes unfortunately misnamed "threads." We exclusively use the term "work-item" to refer to these throughout this paper. Work-items are usually a single lane of a vector computation, rather than an independent thread of control. In OpenMP, there is no observable equivalent to the work-item, though a single iteration of a loop parallelized by an `omp simd` directive would be closest.

OpenCL does have an equivalent to the OpenMP thread however, but its interpretation changes from device to device. In NVIDIA GPUs, one thread is a "warp," composed of 32 work-items. In AMD GPUs, a thread is a "wavefront" of 32 or 64 work-items. When run on CPUs, work-items may be either operating system threads or individual lanes of vector calculations as on GPUs. For common CPUs, this means each thread may be composed of one to eight work-items. The width of the thread-equivalent used in a compiled kernel in OpenCL can be reliably determined based on the OpenCL 1.1 kernel work group info property "preferred work group size multiple," which is what we use in our implementations. To establish consistent terminology, we use the term *thread* to refer to *OpenMP threads* on the CPU and Xeon Phi or *independent groups of work-items* in OpenCL. Work-items within a thread must execute in lockstep. It is unsafe for more than one work-item in a thread to interact with a concurrent data structure simultaneously. When a thread accesses any queue in this paper, only one work-item is active.

The additional wrinkle is that OpenCL has no mechanism to get the number of threads that actually run concurrently. While a user can request any number of threads, the number that run concurrently can be anywhere from one to the requested number. We add counters as depicted in Figure 1 to all benchmarks to count the number of threads that exist before the first thread finishes execution, which is a reliable upper bound on the number of concurrent working threads regardless of the behavior of the OpenCL runtime.

2.2 Memory Model

CPU models like OpenMP depend on cache-coherent shared memory for correctness. The OpenCL standard does *not* provide a sufficiently strong coherence model or a memory flush that can be used to implement one. The stan-

```
void test(unsigned *num_threads, unsigned *present){
    if(atomic_read(num_threads) != 0)
        return;
    atomic_fetch_and_add(present,1);
    run_benchmark();
    atomic_compare_and_swap(num_threads, 0, atomic_read(present));
}
```

Figure 1: Design of concurrency detection in OpenCL benchmarks

dard states that "there are no guarantees of memory consistency between different work-groups executing a kernel [1]." Writes in different work-groups are only guaranteed to be synchronized at the end of a kernel, and are thus available in subsequent kernels. The standard specifically allows writes to global memory to *never* become visible to other work-groups within a single kernel.

The exception is atomic operations, available since OpenCL 1.1, which are guaranteed to be visible and coherent across work-groups within a kernel as long as all work-groups are executing on the same device. Thus, *every* write and *every* read to global memory that is shared between work-groups *must be atomic* to ensure correctness in OpenCL. In practice, some OpenCL devices support a more coherent memory model than this, but it is not required and several architectures do not. For example, NVIDIA GPUs present a weak coherence model, but offer a fence/flush through the PTX instruction *membar.gl*, but this is not standard OpenCL and must be used carefully. AMD GPUs have similar instructions at the ISA level but inline assembly only accepts the intermediate CAL language, which has no equivalent.

For consistency, we express all algorithms as a set of abstract atomically coherent instructions. In OpenCL, all operations are implemented with explicit atomic intrinsics, including load and store, to maintain coherence. In the CPU implementation, atomic reads and writes are standard load and store instructions, while fetch-and-add (FAA) and compare-and-swap (CAS) use the sequentially consistent memory ordering. The algorithm does not intrinsically require that the ordering be that strong, using the relaxed model on increments with matching acquire and release on reads and exchanges would be sufficient. We use the stronger consistency model because it is the default in OpenCL 2.0 and the only model exposed in OpenCL 1.2, which we used to implement our non-CPU device tests.

3. RELATED WORK

Concurrent queues have been studied for decades, nearly as long as computers with multiple computational units have existed to run them. We will elide some of the early history and refer the reader to the surveys provided by the papers referenced below, especially the Michael and Scott [11] survey, which provides significant discussion of early designs.

Array queues. The array queue proposed by Gottlieb et al. [4] in 1983 is notable for scaling near-linearly to 100 cores in simulation at the time. The Gottlieb queue can scale to as many threads as the hardware can run concurrently due to the use of a a pair of counters to select a location and fine-grained locking on each location in the queue. Unfortunately, however, the Gottlieb queue has been proven to be non-linearizable [2] due to the counters, which can cause the queue to appear empty or full spuriously. Orozco et al. [13] present two related array queues called the Circular Buffer Queue (CB-Queue) and the High-Throughput Queue (HT-

Queue). The CB-queue merges the Gottlieb queue's two counters per side into one and in so doing offers linearizability. In so doing however, the CB-queue loses the ability to detect and return full or empty states to the user. Further, the paper asserts that full and empty status cannot be determined for the CB-queue and provide only blocking enqueue and dequeue calls. Lacking inspection, a closed state, and a non-waiting interface, the CB-queue becomes impractical for any case where the queue may over- or under-flow, as either case may cause an irrecoverable deadlock. The proposed solution to the weaknesses of the CB-Queue is to use the HT-Queue, which regains the ability to detect full and empty by using the same flawed double-counter mechanism employed by the Gottlieb queue.

Contended-CAS queues. Michael and Scott [11] present a pair of unbounded linked-list queues, one lock-free (MS-queue hereafter) and one lock-based. The MS-queue offers a linearizable, lock-free queue using a portable single-word CAS operation and has become the standard unbounded lock-free queue. While this queue has no full state, due to its unbounded nature, it naturally detects empty as a function of the CAS operation, all queues of this and later types support these states without further work, unlike the array queues above. An alternative bounded variant has also been proposed by Tsigas and Zhang (TZ-queue) [14], which uses a slightly different mechanism but performs similarly due to its use of contended CAS for committing operations. Queues like these are also common components of relaxed queues [8, 5]. Relaxed queues reduce contention by relaxing the semantics of linearizability from a strict FIFO queue and spreading the operations across multiple underlying queues.

List of array queues. Morrison et al. [12] combine array and list queues to create the Linked Concurrent Ring Queue (LCRQ). The LCRQ retains lock-freedom while avoiding contended CAS operations in the common case, by using a FAA to select a target element like a blocking array queue might. Since the item selection method is inherently blocking, a dequeuer could get a location and then be forced to wait indefinitely on a slow enqueuer, the LCRQ maintains lock-freedom by allowing threads to skip operations that block for too long, introducing the need for retries. After a certain number of operations, or retries, the underlying concurrent ring queue (CRQ) is closed, requiring enqueuers to allocate and initialize new CRQs and then enqueue them into the LCRQ. The downsides to this approach are the reliance on a double-wide CAS (which while common in x86 is not widely available in mobile or many-core architectures) and the reliance on the potentially frequent and expensive allocation and initialization of new CRQs.

Combining. Hendler et al. [6] embrace the serial nature of lock-free designs and propose a queue that uses coarse-grain locking along with a request-and-assist model called the flat-combining (FC) queue. Since only one thread is actually accessing the queue at any given time, fulfilling requests from other threads, the synchronization overhead and cache coherence traffic are comparatively low. The downside is that the maximum throughput of the FC queue is the maximum throughput of a single thread, regardless of the number of accessors. Even so, the throughput limit is higher than with CAS queues like MS-queue, but it is still bounded to serial performance.

Finally, several of these queues have been evaluated on CUDA GPUs by Cederman et al. [3]. Out of a number of lock-based and two lock-free designs (i.e., MS-queue and TZ-queue), they conclude that for higher concurrency, the two lock-free queue designs are nearly always highest performing. The performance they observe for the MS and TZ queues is similar to that found in our results for the same number of workers on comparable GPUs.

4. QUEUE CHARACTERIZATION

Each queue type's throughput can be modeled in terms of the time each successful operation blocks other operations from succeeding. In essence, the throughput is the average number of times the critical section of each design can be executed per unit of time. In most queues however, there is no explicit critical section where a lock is acquired and released. Rather the critical section is the time spent in a successful atomic operation, or set of operations, required to complete an action on the queue. This section benchmarks the performance of basic atomic operations across CPUs, GPUs and Xeon Phi and then models the scalability and throughput of different queue types in terms of atomic operation throughput.

4.1 Atomic Performance

To understand the scaling behavior of current queues, we must first understand the scalability of atomic operations on modern architectures. We measure the throughput of each atomic operation on a contended memory location for each number of threads. This is accomplished with a set of microbenchmarks in OpenCL that execute each operation 1,000,000 times per thread, not work-item, and for each successful operation increment a 32-bit counter in a register. At the end of the test, each thread's count is written to a separate memory location in global memory to be summed on the host. The throughput is computed as the number of operations completed divided by the time taken to execute the test, not including data movement or host-side setup.

Figure 2 shows the results of our atomic benchmarks for the five atomic primitives that queue designs commonly rely on, especially the compare-and-swap (CAS) and fetch-and-add (FAA) instructions. The CAS test is further broken down into two components because it is the only atomic operation we tested that can fail. For CAS we present the number of operations that were *attempted* per unit time, and the number that actually *succeeded* as separate values. We do not include results for any atomic arithmetic or bitwise operations other than add, but they all perform similarly.

The scalability of the operations on each of the three CPU systems generally follows common knowledge, FAA is faster than successful CAS at high contention by as much as $10\times$. Neither operation scales well however, losing throughput with additional threads on both Intel systems and gaining only marginally on the AMD system. An unexpected result here however was the write/XCHG performance is higher than read and FAA for most thread counts on the AMD Opteron CPU. This is probably due to a difference in the way that the AMD CPUs handle memory invalidation in their coherence protocol, but a full analysis of the cause is beyond the scope of this paper. In the past, the higher cost of CAS has been considered acceptable in order to offer strong progress guarantees in concurrent algorithms, ensuring that at least one thread makes progress at any given time. The full cost of it was also limited by the compar-

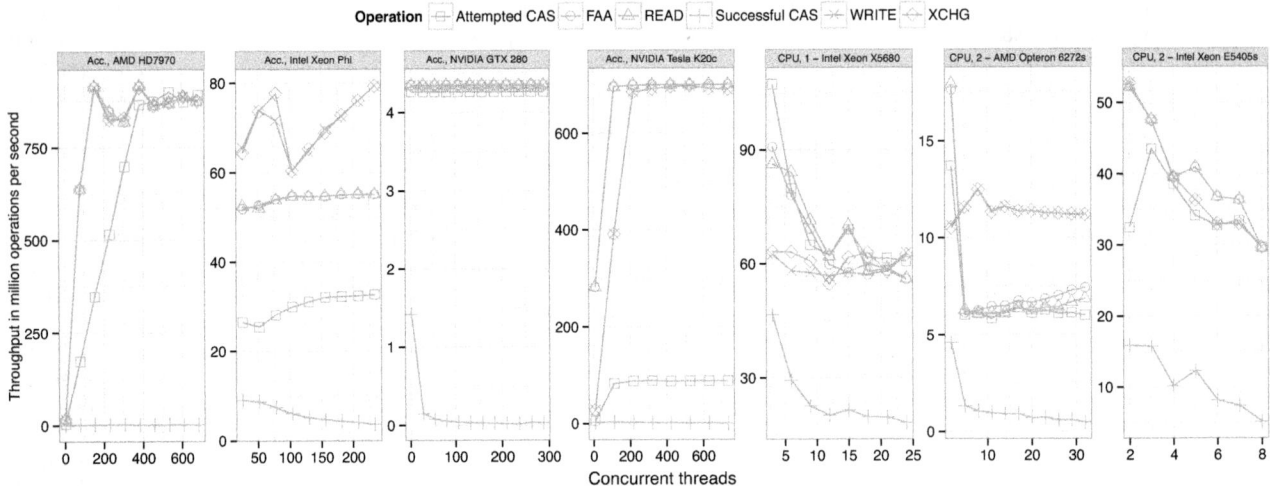

Figure 2: Contended atomic operation throughput, each thread executes its instruction 1,000,000 times, successful CAS represents only the CAS operations that succeed in updating the value

atively small number of threads that could be run concurrently on CPU systems.

On the GPUs and Intel's Xeon Phi FAA, read, write and exchange throughput scale up dramatically as more threads are added, and attempted CAS operations increase as well. Successful CAS throughput does not increase however, in fact it universally falls as the number of threads contending to update the single target value increases. At worst, the difference between successful CAS and FAA expands to 600× with 1000 threads on the AMD 7970. The stark difference between these results is due to the fact that operations such as FAA, read, write, and exchange can be executed completely in the memory controller without any chance of failure or retry. Contending operations are then simply queued there for later execution. On modern hardware, a single memory location can be incremented by FAA *once per cycle* in this fashion. CAS operations can also be handled at the memory controller, but if they fail they cannot retry without returning to the program first. As a result, every failure requires a full round-trip back to the processing core for *every failing thread*, and often an extra read or other logic, before another attempt.

4.2 Queue Throughput Modeling

To evaluate the expected performance of each type of queue across our target architectures, we construct an idealized model of maximum throughput for each type based on its critical operations. We will model the throughput, T, of each queue class in terms of the average latency of the atomic operations used to implement it. By modeling the queues in this way, we can extrapolate their expected scaling behavior as the number of available threads increase in terms of the scaling of their constituent atomics. To simplify the discussion, we treat the arrival distribution and service latency as deterministic and uniform and an arrival rate approaching the throughput. Fixing these allows us to deal directly with the service rate, or the per-operation latency.

Specifically we are going to discuss contended-CAS queues, like the Michael and Scott or Tsigas and Zhang queues; uncontended CAS queues, like the LCRQ or k-fifo queue; combining queues, like the FC-queue; and finally blocking FAA

queues, like the classic array queue of Gottlieb et al. or the CB-queue. Each model is based on an idealized, minimum critical section for each type, and serves as an upper bound on the expected throughput. They do not account for effects of intermixing other operations on the performance of the critical section, which can have significant effects especially on cache-coherent devices. We leave these model extensions to future work.

Contended-CAS queues rely on a CAS operation on a head or tail value to update the queue. We base our model on the canonical MS-queue. The critical section for the MS-queue is the amount of time between a read of the head or pointer value and the completion of a CAS to update it, since the value must not have changed in the intervening period, or the CAS will fail. In addition to the read and CAS, an extra write is required to update the next pointer on an enqueue whereas an extra read to dereference the next pointer is required on dequeue. The resulting max throughput for a given number of threads t, which we will represent as T_t, is modeled in terms of the average latency of read, r_t, write, w_t, and successful contended-CAS, c_t, by Equation 1. In words, two operations, one enqueue and one dequeue, can complete after a period of three reads, one write and two contended-CAS operations.

$$T_t = \frac{2}{(r_t \times 2 + c_t) + (r_t + w_t + c_t)} \qquad (1)$$

An un-contended-CAS queue behaves quite differently from a contended version. They tend to use an FAA instruction to either round-robin between queues, in the case of k-FIFO and similar, or to select a slot in the manner of an array queue, which they then update with CAS for safety but without the failure cost of contended-CAS queues. As a result, the maximum throughput is not dependent on successful CAS latency but rather on attempted CAS latency, since in the best case there are no CAS failures in this type of queue. The enqueue and dequeue are also more symmetrical in this case, since the CAS is used as both a reading and writing operation, and no pointer chasing is required in array-based variants. The resulting model, using C_t and a_t

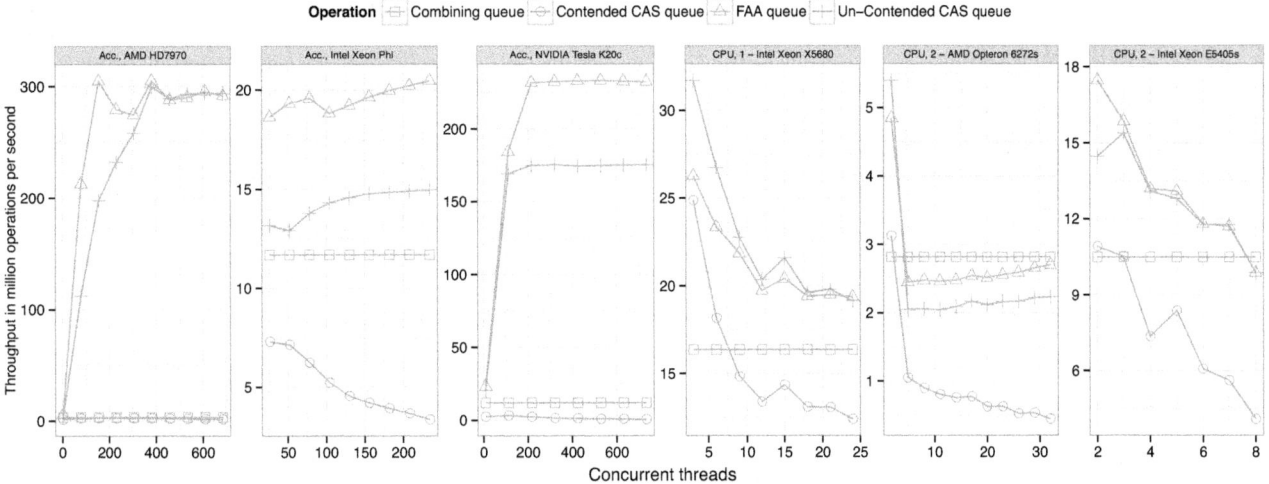

Figure 3: Predicted maximum throughput of each queue for each device and thread count

for average attempted CAS and FAA latency respectively, is presented in Equation 2.

$$T = \frac{1}{a + r + C} \tag{2}$$

The combining queue type is unique in that its throughput is dependent on the latency of reads and writes for *exactly one thread* rather than the throughput a given number of threads is capable of. By using a single thread to perform all operations on the queue at any given time, the maximum throughput at any level of contention is the same. At all numbers of threads we model the combining queue using the atomic latency for one thread in terms of Equation 3. This form is effectively the same as one would use for a serial queue, except that an additional read is performed to determine the operation to perform. This is followed by the operation itself, a read or a write into the queue, and a write to inform the requesting thread of completion.

$$T = \frac{2}{(r_1 + w_1 \times 2) + (r_1 \times 2 + w_1)} \tag{3}$$

Lastly, FAA queues are relatively similar to the un-contended-CAS type in behavior, except that instead of relying on a CAS for the final update they depend on an algorithmic guarantee that the target they receive from the initial FAA will eventually be valid for their use. As a result, the best-case performance is just an add, a read or write depending on the operation, and a write to update the target for the next thread.

$$T = \frac{2}{(a + r + w) + (a + w + w)} \tag{4}$$

The predicted maximum throughput for each design based on the models above and the atomic latency measured in the last section is presented in Figure 3. On the CPUs, it is clear why combining queues have come into favor, since the throughput of a single thread is universally better than that with threads on all cores contending on memory. The contended-CAS type starts as best on all three CPUs with one thread, but universally falls below as the number of threads increases. The un-contended CAS and FAA queue

designs are the most promising for modern high-contention devices such as GPUs however. The prediction for the AMD 7970 and Tesla K20c GPUs show the FAA queue throughput reaching as much as 196 and 377 *times* faster respectively than the contended-CAS queue on the maximum number of threads. Our modeled results show that the bottleneck of contended-CAS-based synchronization becomes progressively more onerous as the number of threads increases, and incurs an unacceptable level of overhead on many-core devices. Despite the fact that the FAA queue shows the best scaling on high thread counts however, as mentioned in Section 3, the existing array or FAA queue variants all lack at least one desirable property of safety or usability.

5. DESIGN

The main goal of our design is to create a queue with as little overhead and as much concurrency as possible while maintaining linearizability and usability. Given the significant throughput advantages demonstrated in Section 4, our goal becomes to produce a linearizable and practical concurrent queue without the need for contended CAS operations in the common case. The CAS operations are normally used to provide a strong progress guarantee, at least non-blocking if not complete lock-freedom, that is highly valuable in environments where oversubscription is common and threads being scheduled out while in critical sections is a significant performance concern. Combining queues have come into being based on the fact that CPUs are less oversubscribed now than they were in the past, and many-core devices such as GPUs often cannot be oversubscribed at all, lacking a context-switching mechanism.

Because oversubscription has become relatively rare in many-core, we propose an array-based blocking queue that, unlike those existing in the literature, offers both inspection of state, in terms of full, empty and number of operations in-flight, and linearizability together. We further support safe interaction with the queue from threads that cannot block, or should deal with full/empty states, by providing two distinct interfaces to the same queue, similar to those offered by communication libraries (e.g., TCP sockets). Each interface has different waiting characteristics: (1) a high-throughput blocking interface and (2) a low-latency non-waiting interface.

5.1 The Queue Structure

Our queue's structure, represented in Figure 4a, is relatively simple, containing head and tail counters as unsigned integers along with arrays of items and IDs. For simplicity we use unsigned integers as the values, but extensions for arbitrary data are trivial.

In order to correctly handle integer rollover, a real concern as 2^{32} queue operations can complete in a matter of seconds on GPUs, we include a `#define` for the maximum id value based on the queue size. The maximum is selected such that when the head or tail roll over to zero, the id value will do the same. The `MAX_ID` value must be at least double the value of `MAX_THREADS+1` and the sum of `MAX_THREADS` and `QUEUE_SIZE`, the `MAX_DISTANCE`, must be less than half of the maximum value representable by the unsigned integer type storing head and tail. All values in the data structure should be initialized to zero.

5.2 The Blocking Interface

Our blocking functions are represented in Figure 4b.[2] Our blocking functions begin by acquiring a ticket for their current transaction by atomically incrementing their respective counters on line 4. A ticket serves to select both the target location, by being modded by `QUEUE_SIZE` on line 5, and the id for the transaction. The ID is the number of times the algorithm has passed through the entire queue's length, calculated by the `GET_ID()` macro, plus one in the dequeue case. Once the target id is equal to the transaction id the current thread effectively holds a lock on that element of the queue and leaves the loop. A value is then either added to or copied from the queue, as appropriate on line 12, and the id safely incremented to preserve consistency across rollover on line 13, which also frees the next transaction on that slot.

Subsequent, or concurrent, calls to the blocking interface receive unique target addresses and ID combinations without retries or waiting, thanks to the FAA. As long as the queue is not full, each enqueue can complete with a constant total of four atomic operations. When the target item is busy, it waits in the loop at line 7 checking for closed status and backing off as appropriate. This can be a truly blocking operation, yielding to the system to wait on a notification, but is implemented as a busy wait in our tests. The CPU version does use a scheduling yield in the backoff routine to allow other threads to proceed however. The ordering imposed by incrementing the target address at each request has the effect of also enforcing fair ordering and preventing individual starvation in this interface short of a thread dying inside a critical section or complete OS starvation of a thread.

Unlike other blocking array queues in the literature, we contend that a closed state is required for usability, and does not interfere with linearizability. Once all items that will exist have been completely enqueued and dequeued, there must be a way to inform the threads blocked in dequeue to exit. The `closed` value in the queue is used for this purpose.

---

[2]Note that the CPU and OpenCL implementations of all of our interfaces are identical save for the addition of memory qualifiers in the OpenCL version. In fact, our evaluation uses a single source version of all queues for both CPU and OpenCL tests, simply compiled with different compilers.

Setting `closed` to true invalidates the queue for all future operations. Closing causes any enqueue or dequeue that is waiting to reverse its ticket acquisition, allowing the status inspection interface to detect when all waiting threads have left, and return immediately with the status `CLOSED`. All subsequent calls also return `CLOSED` without attempting to update the queue. This is equivalent to closing a communication channel like a socket or file descriptor.

5.3 The Non-Waiting Interface

Figure 4c presents our non-waiting interface. Fundamentally, the non-waiting functions are inverted versions of the blocking functions. Rather than immediately reserving a ticket, which could require them to block, the non-waiting functions simply read the value. Having read a ticket, they check whether the current target item is ready on line 7. If the id value indicates the item is busy then acquiring an item at this time would require blocking, so `BUSY` is returned immediately. If the id matches, the thread attempts to acquire the associated target by incrementing the counter with the CAS on line 9. If the CAS fails, the non-waiting function returns `BUSY`, otherwise it has successfully acquired a ready target so it completes its operation and returns `SUCCESS`.

While we implemented the blocking interface completely without CAS, to implement the non-waiting functions in that way is infeasible. Specifically, there is no way to atomically acquire a specific ticket without a conditional atomic or transaction, such as CAS, Load-Linked Store-Conditional, or optimally a compare-and-add. Using an unconditional FAA in place of the CAS would get a ticket, but with no guarantee that it would be the ticket which had been checked ahead of time. While this has the same performance consequences as the contended-CAS queues face, it has the advantage of interleaving with the blocking queue, allowing threads to attempt an operation on the queue safely, or a single thread using the interface persistently to watch for persistent full or empty states and act to remedy them. This cannot be done with other blocking queue designs that preserve linearizability, and is a key benefit to the overall design.

Note that we avoid the use of the terms "wait-free," "lock-free" and "non-blocking" in this section. While these functions do not wait, calls to either `enqueue_nb()` or `dequeue_nb()` will fail if another operation is in progress on the slot they request, or if the queue is full. In a non-full queue, the non-waiting interface does guarantee that at least one thread makes progress at a time, equivalent to the guarantees made by other array-based queues such as the tz-queue.

5.4 The Status Inspection Interface

Much like the CB-queue, our blocking interface does not support returning "full" or "empty" states directly from the enqueue or dequeue functions. While they are not required for a correct concurrent queue, these states are often used to simplify the detection of completion in a concurrent algorithm, and as such are missed when they are unavailable. Rather than re-designing the algorithm to address this weakness however, we design a separate interface that provides checks for these states as well as the number of waiting threads on either end of the queue. The main difficulty in implementing this functionality is that head and tail can *not* be directly compared. There is a distinct chance that one, but not the other, has rolled over causing the less-than or greater-than relationships to be reversed.

```
/* Defines */
#define MAX_ID (UINT32_MAX/(QUEUE_SIZE*2))
/* Maximum possible distance between head and
 * tail for the status inspection interface */
#define MAX_DISTANCE (QUEUE_SIZE \
                    + MAX_THREADS)

/* Macros */
#define GET_ID(X) ((X / QUEUE_SIZE) * 2)
#define INC_SAFE(Q, T, ID) atomic_write( \
                &(Q)->ids[T],\
                ((ID)+1) % MAX_ID)

/* Structures */
typedef struct {
  union {//anonymous pair, allows inspection
    uint64_t combined;
    struct {
      uint32_t head, tail;
    };
  };
  bool closed;
  uint32_t items[QUEUE_SIZE];
  uint32_t ids[QUEUE_SIZE];
} queue_t;
```

```
int enqueue(queue_t *q, uint32_t item) {
  if (atomic_read(&q->closed) != 0)
    return CLOSED;
  uint32_t ticket = atomic_add(&q->tail,1);
  uint32_t target = ticket % QUEUE_SIZE;
  uint32_t id = GET_ID(ticket);
  while(atomic_read(&q->ids[target])!=id){
    if (atomic_read(&q->closed) != 0){
      atomic_sub(&q->tail,1);
      return CLOSED; }
    backoff(); }
  atomic_write(&q->items[target], item);
  INC_SAFE(q, target, id);
  return SUCCESS;
}
```

```
int dequeue(queue_t *q, uint32_t * p) {
  if (atomic_read(&q->closed) != 0)
    return CLOSED;
  uint32_t ticket = atomic_add(&q->head,1);
  uint32_t target = ticket % QUEUE_SIZE;
  uint32_t id = GET_ID(ticket) + 1;
  while(atomic_read(&q->ids[target])!=id){
    if (atomic_read(&q->closed) != 0){
      atomic_sub(&q->head,1);
      return CLOSED; }
    backoff(); }
  *p = atomic_read(&q->items[target]);
  INC_SAFE(q, target, id);
  return SUCCESS;
}
```

```
int enqueue_nb(queue_t *q, uint32_t item) {
  if(atomic_read(q->closed) != 0)
    return CLOSED;
  uint32_t ticket = atomic_read(&q->tail);
  uint32_t target = ticket % QUEUE_SIZE;
  uint32_t id = GET_ID(ticket);
  if(atomic_read(&q->ids[target]) != id)
    return BUSY;//next slot not ready
  if(atomic_cas(&q->tail,
              ticket, ticket+1) != ticket)
    return BUSY;//CAS failed, return
  atomic_write(q->items[target], item);
  INC_SAFE(q, target, id);
  return SUCCESS;//element enqueued
}
```

```
int dequeue_nb(queue_t *q, uint32_t * p) {
  if(atomic_read(q->closed) != 0)
    return CLOSED;
  uint32_t ticket = atomic_read(q->head);
  uint32_t target = ticket % QUEUE_SIZE;
  uint32_t id = GET_ID(ticket);
  if(atomic_read(&q->ids[target]) != id)
    return BUSY;//oldest not ready
  if(atomic_cas(&q->head,
              ticket, ticket+1) != ticket)
    return BUSY;//CAS failed, return
  *p = atomic_read(q->items[target]);
  INC_SAFE(q, target, id);
  return SUCCESS;//element dequeued
}
```

(a) Definitions and Structure   (b) Blocking Interface   (c) Non-waiting Interface

Figure 4: Structure and interfaces to the queue with the volatile keyword removed for space; All "atomic_*" calls map to the corresponding atomic intrinsic

We address this case by establishing the maximum absolute distance possible between head and tail and checking to see if the current distance is greater than that maximum. If this happens, it must be because one counter has rolled over and the distance should be calculated across the rollover point. The maximum distance between head and tail in our queue is the sum of the queue length and the maximum number of threads that are allowed to interact with the queue concurrently. If the maximum distance is less than half the maximum value representable by the counter, single-counter rollover can be reliably detected in this fashion. For a 64-bit unsigned integer, the sum of the queue's length and the maximum concurrent accessors must be less than or equal to $2^{63} - 1$, which we believe is a reasonable limit. If more is required, the size of the counter should be increased.

6. LINEARIZABILITY

To provide a proof of linearizability, we must first define the semantics of our target data structure. Based on instruction ordering our algorithm models a concurrent FIFO queue. When return states, such as empty, full, closed and busy, are included in the requirements for linearizability however, our states do not match. We give our queue the semantics of a *channel queue*: a queue which models a double-sided communication channel, such as is presented by file descriptors and sockets, that can return success, closed, busy, empty or full. If a channel queue is in the closed state then all functions will return closed. If a non-waiting function cannot complete without blocking, busy is returned. All other cases model a concurrent FIFO queue, allowed only to return success, full or empty. In truth, this semantic is more common of concurrent queues in production than the traditional model's restriction to empty, full and success, and is modeled by the interface of the standard BlockingQueue class in Java as well as the interface to the concurrent Wait-ingQueue class proposed for inclusion in the C++1y standard.

Using the techniques and definitions presented by Herlihy et. al. [7], we model access to our concurrent queue as a history h. That history is a potentially infinite series of invocation and response events, representing the beginning and end of calls to functions defining our interface. Any response in h is necessarily preceded by a matching invocation in h but it is valid for an invocation in h to remain pending, lacking a response, at the end of h. Events are said to be ordered in h only if the response of an event e_1 precedes the invocation of an event e_2 and this relation is denoted by $e_1 <_h e_2$. Any pair of events that cannot be compared in this way is said to overlap, and thus may be ordered arbitrarily with respect to one another. The history, h, is linearizable if the strict partial order can be fixed into a total order $\rightarrow_h$ such that the specifications of the object are preserved.

Any history that can be produced by our implementation can be associated with a history mapped onto an auxiliary array of infinite size. Using this auxiliary array, our algorithm guarantees that every enqueue, blocking or non-waiting, will monotonically increase the values of the tail counter and thus insert elements consecutively into the infinite array. In the same way, our dequeues monotonically increase the value of head and consume elements consecutively. Thus all items are dequeued in the same order they were enqueued, or are overlapped. Any element that is added is accounted for, and cannot be removed until it is acquired. Acquisition can only happen in order, preventing any items from being skipped or dequeued before being enqueued. All interleaving between the blocking and non-waiting interface are also in-order, as they acquire and interact with the queue using the same ticket and turn mechanism.

Given these, the only source of non-linearizable behavior possible is from multiple operations waiting on the same target item with the same id. Given our invariant that the

MAX_ID is greater than double MAX_THREADS, this case cannot occur, as ids are not recycled until the queue has been cycled through completely at least MAX_ID times. Given that invariant, even if a queue of length one were to have the maximum number of threads waiting on it, both ordering and fairness are preserved between those accesses.

The above sketches a proof of the key invariant for concurrent queues, that if enqueue(x) < enqueue(y), where x and y are the values enqueued, then dequeue(x) < dequeue(y) or dequeue(x) and dequeue(y) overlap. To simplify reasoning about the ordering, our functions "take effect" at specific points between their invocation and response, but as with any algorithm employing critical sections there is no single instruction that serves as the universal linearization point. Operations are considered to take effect on the status of the queue, observable only through the get_distance() function and its siblings, after committing to the addition or removal of an element by acquiring a ticket with either FAA or incrementing CAS. All enqueue and dequeue operations are ordered in the sequential history by their increment of the id associated with their target item. Any temporary discrepancy in queue structure between invocation and response is protected by the critical region formed between ticket acquisition and id increment.

7. EXPERIMENTAL SETUP

In order to perform our evaluation across a wide range of modern hardware, we have created a version of each queue using both OpenMP and OpenCL. This section will discuss the evaluated queues, our benchmark designs and the hardware evaluated.

7.1 The Queues

In addition to our own, we include implementations of two traditional lock-free queues, the TZ and MS queues, the Flat Combining (FC) queue, and the LCRQ. All queues are implemented to store 32-bit unsigned integers and where memory allocation would normally be necessary use a non-blocking concurrent free-list of appropriately-sized objects that is pre-allocated before each test. The same free-list mechanism is used on both CPUs and GPUs for consistency, and nearly eliminates de-allocation cost but still incurs initialization cost.

Our MS-queue implementation is directly derived from the source code used in the original MS-queue publication [11]. It has been modified minimally to support thread-based rather than process-based parallelism and the memory model presented by OpenCL. The TZ-queue has been faithfully re-implemented using the algorithm and optimizations described in the paper proposing it [14]. The flat combining queue is based on the authors source but reimplemented in C/OpenCL from the original C++. Lastly, the LCRQ is based on the pseudocode in the publication proposing it [12][3]. Our LCRQ implementation deviates in two key ways from the original pseudocode, it includes the spin waiting optimization proposed in the paper, and uses 32 rather than 64 bit values. The value size is changed to allow the algorithm to function on devices that support 64-bit but not

---

[3]We did correct one error in the pseudocode, line 45 should compare (safe,idx,val) rather than (safe,h,val) as the original states, the text description in the original paper agrees with this modification.

128-bit CAS operations. We evaluated the 32-bit version against a 64-bit version of the algorithm and found that the throughput remains within the range of measurement error for all cases.

The OpenCL and OpenMP implementations of each queue share the same source, with only memory location qualifiers, atomics and memory synchronization primitives differentiated through C macros. For all fixed-length queues, the queue length was set at 65,536 elements for the purpose of our evaluation, separate tests with varied sizes did not reveal significant correlation with performance except when using very small sizes, so these results are elided.

7.2 Benchmarks and Methodology

These queue implementations are evaluated across a pair of microbenchmarks designed to measure queue throughput. We define throughput for our evaluation as the number of enqueue and dequeue operations successfully completed per second, or queue operations per second. The first benchmark is a traditional matching enqueue and dequeue benchmark, essentially a balanced producer consumer pattern. All threads execute a loop containing an enqueue, a call to some work, a dequeue, and another call to work. The work between each queue operation is comprised of 100 iterations of addition and multiplication on a value read from and stored back to positions in global memory determined by the value last received from the queue. This work is sufficient to avoid a single thread running through multiple operations without interference, and decreases the performance of the highest throughput implementations by approximately 10% compared to a version without work[4]. Our second benchmark is based on an imbalanced producer/consumer pattern. One in every four threads only enqueues, and the other three only dequeue, these operations are also separated by the same work as in the first benchmark. Both benchmarks are configured to perform as many operations as possible in five seconds and report the number of successful operations. We selected five seconds after running a round of tests ranging from two seconds to a minute and a half per data point and finding that anything over three seconds is sufficient to overcome variance effects across our target platforms.

The OpenMP implementation ends the test by creating an extra thread that sleeps and sets a *done* value, stopping the test after the specified time. OpenCL offers no such mechanism, neither the extra thread nor the sleep. To get around this, we assign one thread to execute a loop performing mathematical operations on its registers for approximately five seconds. Since the number of operations required changes based on the device, the test and sometimes the queue under test, as a result of register usage changes, our run-scripts automatically tune the number of iterations such that each test runs for between 4.95 and 5.5 seconds on all OpenCL platforms. The downside to this approach is that we lose one potential thread, but with throughputs that range up to three orders of magnitude, evaluation using a fixed time rather than a fixed number of operations is essential.

7.3 Devices

Table 1 lists the devices used to conduct our experiments,

---

[4]Some implementations, including LCRQ, perform *better* with the work than without it, as a result of reduced contention on the queue producing fewer CAS retries.

Device	Cores/ device	Threads/ core	Max. threads	Max. achieved
GPUs/Co-processors				
AMD HD5870	20	24	496	140
AMD HD7970	32	40	1280	386
AMD HD7990(one die)	32	40	1280	1020
Intel Xeon Phi P1750	61	4	244	244
NVIDIA GTX 280	30	32	960	960
NVIDIA Tesla C2070	14	32	448	448
NVIDIA Tesla K20c	13	64	832	832
CPUs				
2xAMD Opteron 6272s	16	1	32	32
4xAMD Opteron 6134s	8	1	32	32
2xIntel Xeon E5405s	4	1	8	8
Intel Xeon X5680	12	2	24	24
Intel Core i5-3400	4	1	4	4

Table 1: Target hardware platforms

along with their core counts, the number of thread contexts that can be loaded concurrently on each core, and the maximum hardware threads on the device. Note that the maximum threads listed in the table is the theoretical maximum, and in the case of GPUs is not always achievable due to limitations on available register space. The maximum achieved column lists the largest number of concurrent threads available to our tests, not all queues make it to those values but none make it above. All test systems run Debian Wheezy Linux on a 64-bit 3.2.0 stock kernel. NVIDIA devices use driver version 313.30 and the CUDA 5.0 SDK for OpenCL. AMD GPUs use the AMD APP SDK version 2.8 for OpenCL and the FGLRX version 9.1.11 driver. The Intel Xeon Phi card uses the MPSS gold update 3 driver and firmware. OpenMP tests were compiled with the Intel ICC compiler version 13.0.1 with optimization level 3 and inter-procedural-optimization turned on.

8. RESULTS AND DISCUSSION

We evaluate all queues across all hardware discussed above, with the exception of LCRQ on AMD GPUs because the AMD GPUs do not support bitfields or 64-bit atomic CAS. Since our queue presents two interfaces, we present three different configurations for it. Each is labeled in the figures as "New -" followed by which enqueue and dequeue functions it uses for all enqueues and dequeues in the test. The three configurations are the two homogeneous configurations, paired sets of blocking or non-waiting interface calls, plus a version using the non-waiting dequeue with the blocking enqueue. We expect that the most common use-case would be using the blocking interface for all but one, or perhaps a small number, of threads using the non-waiting interface to detect algorithm completion, which is best represented by the blocking results.

8.1 CPU Performance

The CPU results based on these tests can be found in Figure 5. Each CPU is tested from two threads up to the maximum number of hardware threads supported by the system. In multi-socket systems threads are spread in round-robin fashion across dies using the Intel OpenMP "scatter" affinity policy. While the multi-socket systems tend to maintain or lose throughput as threads are added, the single socket Intel Xeon X5680 gains throughput with each additional thread. This due to the fact that the single CPU only has one memory controller, allowing atomics to be completed without out-of-die coherence overhead. The AMD Opteron 6272 results are also notable for having better performance

in practice than the predicted maximums from Section 4. Since our predictions are based entirely on 100% contentious atomic throughput, our models evidently under-predict for platforms that gain higher throughput of atomic operations when contention is lower.

In terms of the individual queues, in almost all cases the highest throughput comes from our blocking interface, followed by the LCRQ. The TZ and MS queues fare poorly in general across each of the CPUs, their performance degrading with each additional thread due to the increasing CAS retry overhead. On the AMD devices and the Xeon X5680, the FC-queue performs materially better than the classic lock-free variants for the matching enqueue/dequeue benchmark. The FC-queue even gains performance with additional threads on the AMD devices thanks to its comparatively low coherence overhead.

LCRQ's performance on the AMD systems reveals an important characteristic of its design. In the matching enqueue/dequeue test it scales well, performing nearly as well as our blocking interface up to 32-cores. The producer/consumer benchmark, on the other hand, shows LCRQ's performance degrading sharply as more threads are added. This is due to retries and memory initialization overhead caused, not by CAS, but by LCRQ operations skipping slots by marking them unsafe. Whenever an operation times out, as is common in our imbalanced producer/consumer benchmark, the item reserved by that operation is marked unsafe, and it retries potentially marking many more unsafe along the way. This also means that the matching operation on that item must retry. Eventually, the retries cascade into the closing of the CRQ as a whole, forcing initialization of a new CRQ by all threads attempting to enqueue at that time. We employ the optimizations proposed to minimize this behavior, specifically spin waiting before marking a slot unsafe and employing a high starvation cutoff for enqueues, but still observe the problem. The Intel X5680 does not observe this behavior because of those optimizations, but they are insufficient for the multi-socket systems. This condition could be avoided in LCRQ if it were allowed to wait indefinitely for a matching enqueue, but that would make it blocking, and can actually produce deadlocks in the algorithm, since dequeuers might not be aware of the need to move to a new CRQ.

8.2 Effects of Oversubscription

While we designed our queue with no oversubscription in mind, and for architectures where it is often not possible, it is still at least a potential reality in CPU systems. In order to evaluate the effect of oversubscription on throughput we tested all queues with thread counts from two to 128 on a four-core CPU in Figure 6. All queues include a thread yield as part of their back-off routine, immediately allowing another thread to be scheduled in place of the thread which is waiting.

As has been shown in other recent work [12], the FC-queue suffers greatly from oversubscription as a result of the combiner being scheduled out frequently. The lock-free queues, MS, TZ and LCRQ on the other hand perform quite well in this test, as expected since this is the environment they are designed for. Both the MS and LCRQ designs maintain their performance across the full range. On the other hand the TZ-queue and our non-waiting interface tend to perform better than either by between 10 and 75%.

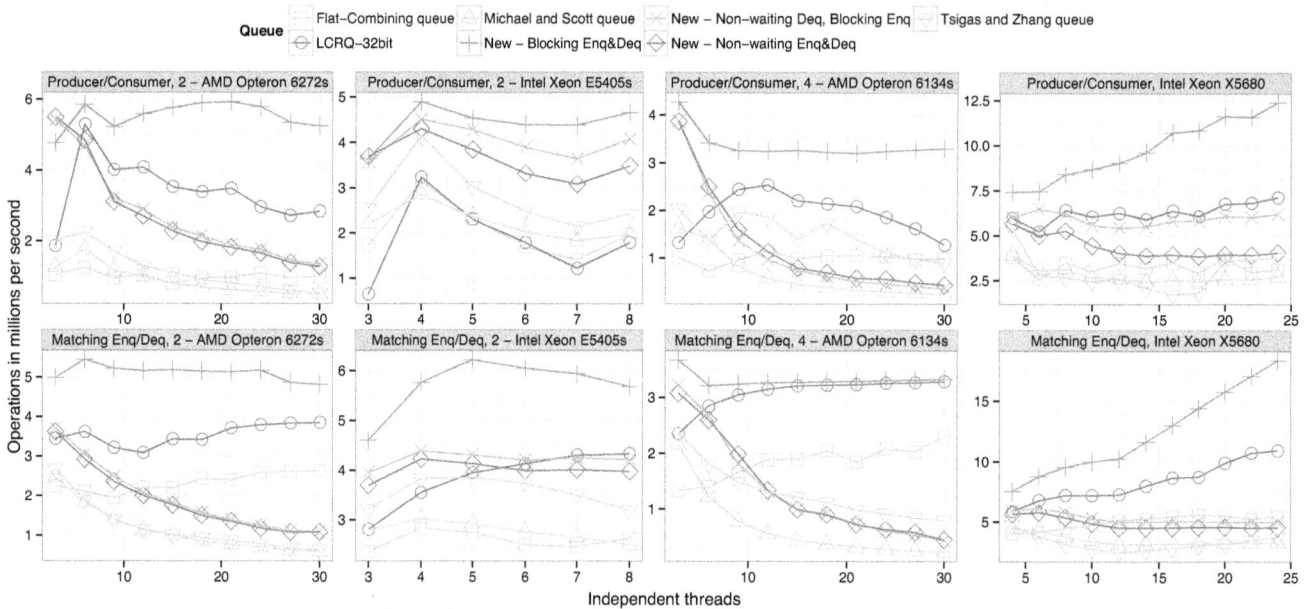

Queue — Flat-Combining queue — Michael and Scott queue — New – Non-waiting Deq, Blocking Enq — Tsigas and Zhang queue — LCRQ-32bit — New – Blocking Enq&Deq — New – Non-waiting Enq&Deq

Figure 5: Throughput on each CPU across thread counts and benchmarks

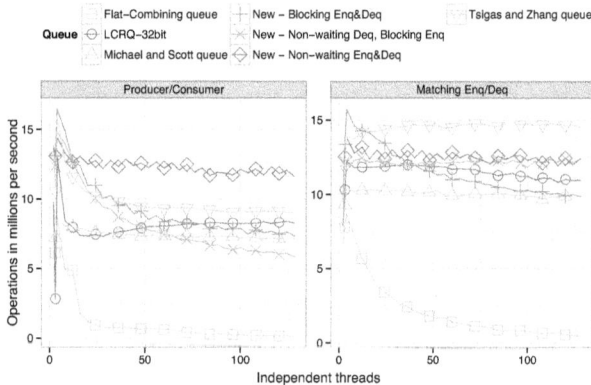

Figure 6: CPU performance when heavily oversubscribed, results of tests running from two to 128 threads on a four core Intel CPU

Finally the blocking interface does lose performance as more threads are added, but not so much as might be expected from a blocking design. Since the blocking is extremely fine-grained, and the potential concurrency extremely high, the blocking interface actually outperforms the MS-queue and maintains 50% of its maximum throughput with $32\times$ more threads than hardware thread contexts.

8.3 Accelerator Performance

This section presents throughput results with the same benchmarks across seven many-core accelerator architectures in Figures 7a and 7b. Please note that unlike the CPU results, the range in performance on the accelerators requires us to use a log-scale for the bandwidth axis on our plots.

The first important difference between the accelerators and CPUs is the sheer number of thread contexts the accelerators support. Even the smallest, the AMD 5870, hosts 140 concurrent thread contexts for most benchmarks, more than four times as many as the CPUs. Recall that this is in threads, not OpenCL work-items, for the number of

work-items multiply the threads on AMD GPUs by 64, and NVIDIA GPUs by 32 to get the full number. The two largest go far higher, with the 7990 reaching 1020 concurrently loaded threads, and the K20c hosting 832 for a total of 65,280 and 26,624 work-items respectively. The Phi device runs the OpenMP benchmark source from the CPU tests, so its 244 threads are standard OpenMP threads.

8.3.1 Matching Enqueue/Dequeue Results

The enqueue/dequeue results on accelerators (Figure 7a) scale more like a single-socket CPU than a multi-socket system. Since the accelerator cores all share a single memory controller, this is expected. The material difference from the CPUs is that each additional thread increases performance noticeably for our blocking interface. On the 7990 the performance scales from 0.585 million operations per second on two threads to 380 million operations per second on 1019 threads. This makes for a $650\times$ increase in throughput for a roughly $509\times$ increase in the number of threads[5]. Similarly, the K20c attains $256\times$ higher throughput with $415\times$ more threads. The cache-coherent Intel Xeon Phi coprocessor scales somewhat less than the GPUs, going from 0.963 Mops/s to 11.462, for a more modest but still significant increase in throughput of $12\times$ for roughly $120\times$ more threads. The exceptions to the rule in terms of scalability are the GTX280 and C2070 NVIDIA GPUs, whose atomic implementations are less mature, and as a result only scale to a fraction of the throughput of the others.

By far the best performing lock-free design across the accelerators is the LCRQ. On the Xeon Phi its performance is nearly indistinguishable from that of our blocking interface. The NVIDIA implementations do not scale to the full number of threads due to LCRQ's high register usage, but for the thread-counts supported the throughput is quite high.

---

[5]The super-linear increase in throughput is not due to any super-linear property of the algorithm, but rather to the fact that the GPU tends to run in a lower performance state when under-utilized.

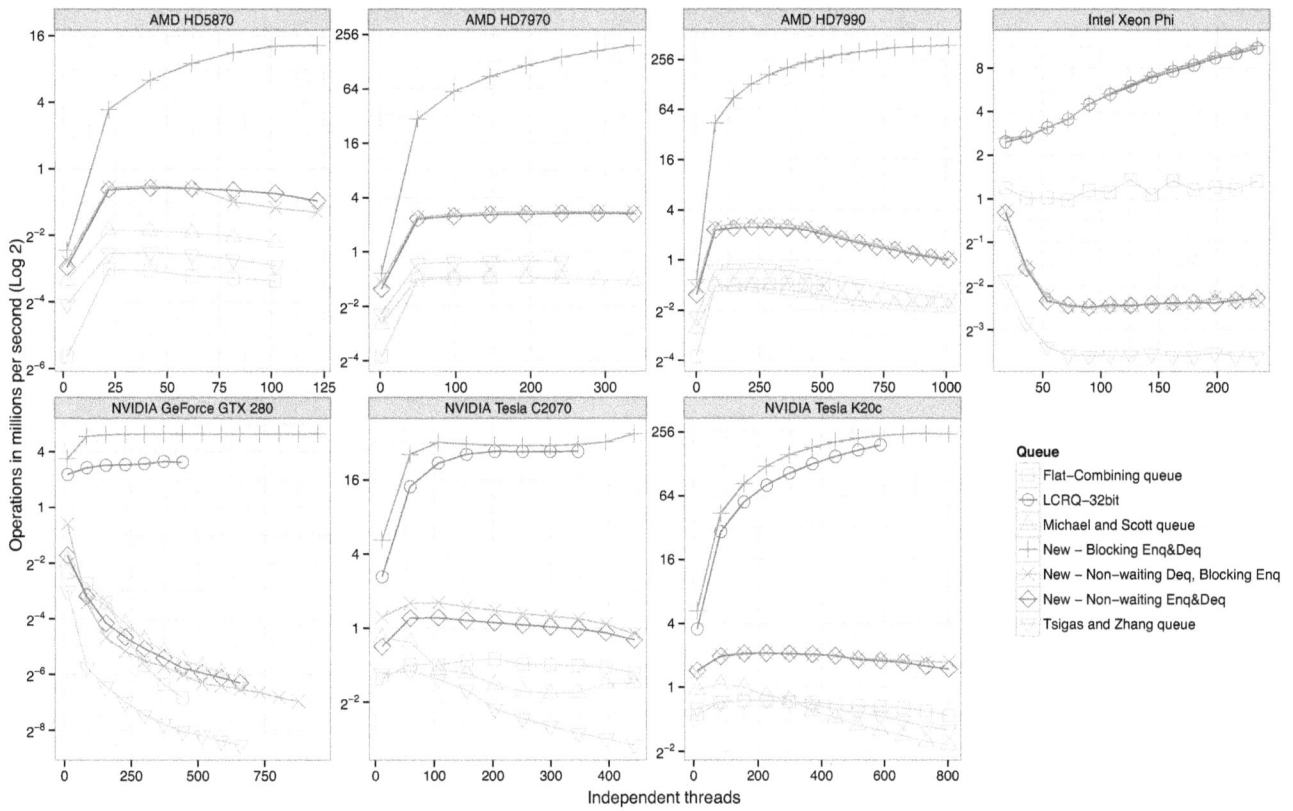

(a) Throughput on each accelerator for the weak-scaling matched enqueue/dequeue benchmark

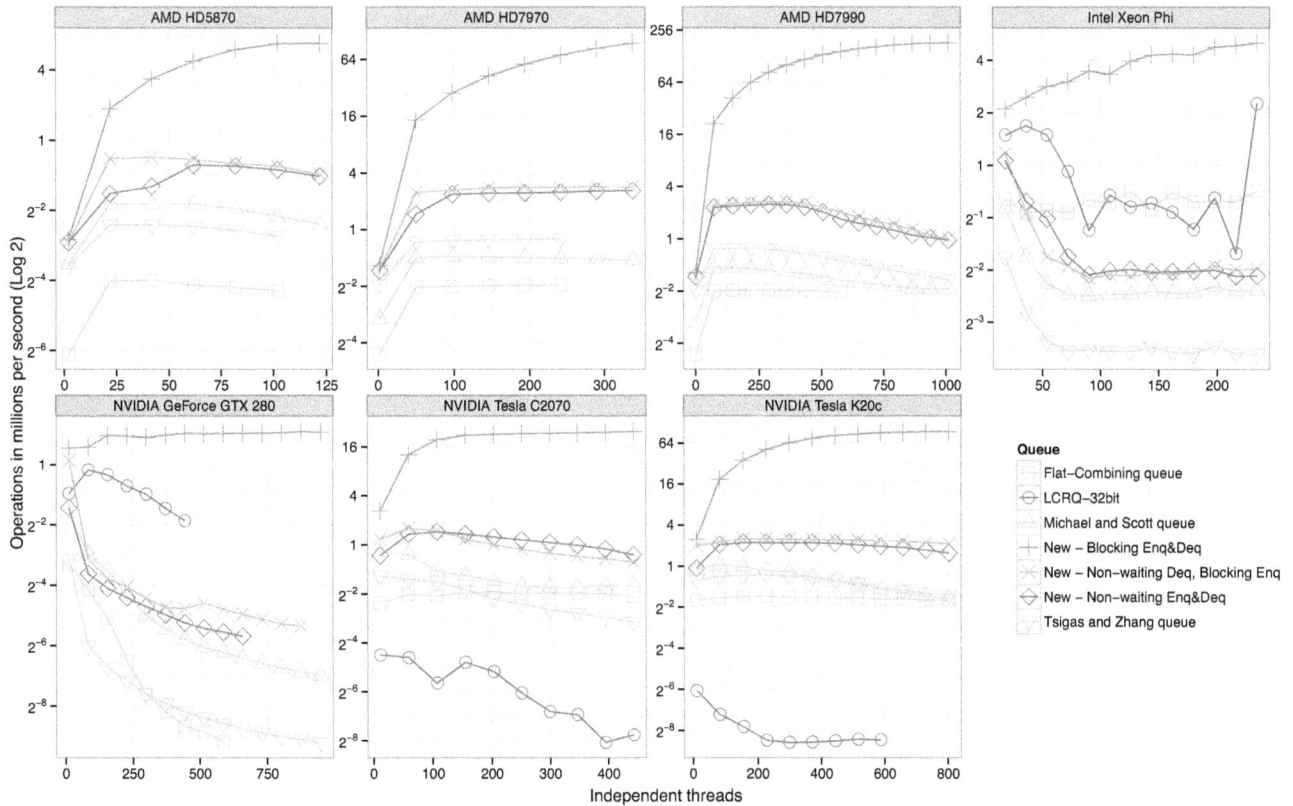

(b) Throughput on each accelerator for the producer/consumer benchmark, of every four threads, one is producer the other three are consumers

Figure 7: Accelerator benchmark results

LCRQ's highest performance on the K20c, at 623 threads, is 201.848 Mops/s, only 16% below the throughput of our blocking interface with the same number of threads.

The contentious-CAS-based queues, FC-queue and our non-waiting interface, tend to lose performance as the number of threads increases and the rate of successful CAS operations drops. The fastest of these, the TZ and our non-waiting design, only achieve 0.342 and 0.994 Mops/s respectively on 1019 threads on the AMD 7990, or $1,112\times$ and $383\times$ lower respectively than the blocking interface in the same test. The K20c results are similar, with TZ performing 0.386 Mops/s and our non-waiting performing 1.357 for differences of $635\times$ and $181\times$ respectively. FC performs similarly to these traditional designs on the GPUs, but achieves $5\times$ better throughput on the cache-coherent Phi, where its cache friendly design offers material benefits. It is worth noting that, while it is not lock free, the non-waiting interface of our queue tends to outperform its counterparts in this space on these architectures, seemingly due to the lower number of instructions per operation.

8.3.2 Producer/Consumer Benchmark Results

Results for the producer/consumer test are presented in Figure 7b. As expected, the producer consumer test shows roughly 50% lower throughput across the board due to using 50% less enqueuers than dequeuers. All queues are affected by the imbalance roughly equally, except LCRQ.

The change in LCRQ results is most visible on the Xeon Phi, where rather than being nearly a match for the blocking interface, it drops to the performance of FC-queue after only 75 threads. Though LCRQ's throughput is variable, it never reaches half of the throughput of the blocking interface in this test on Xeon Phi. On the NVIDIA GPUs, LCRQ is now below the traditional lock-free designs and our non-waiting interface by a factor of 8. LCRQ's performance degrades with each added thread on the k20c, reaching a low of 0.003 Mops/s with 623 threads, where the next lowest, the FC-queue, is 0.322 Mops/s, and the blocking interface performs 91.803 Mops/s, *four orders of magnitude* higher throughput than LCRQ. It is quite apparent that applications of this nature, where consumers and producers are imbalanced, are pathologically bad for LCRQ. None of the other queues are materially affected by the imbalance.

9. CONCLUSIONS

In this paper, we present a characterization of concurrent queue designs across multi- and many-core architectures, and our design of a linearizable, inspection capable, high-throughput FIFO queue engineered for many-core architectures. Our characterization found that, largely due to the serialization caused by CAS operations, either an uncontended CAS design or a FAA-based array queue should scale best. Despite this, there are algorithms that are difficult or impractical to implement on a queue with only a blocking interface that does not allow detection of full or empty states. To address this limitation, our queue design includes both high-throughput blocking and low-latency non-waiting interfaces to customize interactions with the queue on a per-thread or per-interaction basis, both of which are linearizable to the semantics of a "channel queue," as well as a status inspection interface which can reveal full and empty states as well as how many blocking enqueues or dequeues exist. While queues with hard progress guaran-

tees and unbounded size have their benefits, we have shown that focusing on throughput and avoiding retry-based algorithms can produce exceptionally high throughput across a wide range of real-world multi- and many-core hardware. Counter-intuitively, designing an algorithm that allows blocking to occur but increases the maximum concurrency of the structure results in greater throughput. In fact, our evaluation finds that performance can be improved by as much as *1000-fold* for some problems in an environment with more than 1000 concurrent threads.

In the future, we intend to investigate ways to create data structures of this type that are capable of offering some of the progress and safety guarantees of lock-free structures. Our queue might for example serve the purpose that the CRQ serves for the LCRQ data structure. An extension to support blocking, rather than spinning, thread waiting semantics could also be added by exchanging the id-based scheme for another. Further, we believe that this queue could be used to enhance a number of design patterns such as dynamic load-balancing and persistent threading on GPU and fused CPU/GPU architectures.

10. REFERENCES

[1] The OpenCL Specification. https://www.khronos.org/registry/cl/specs/opencl-1.2.pdf, Nov. 2012.

[2] G. E. Blelloch, P. Cheng, and P. B. Gibbons. Scalable Room Synchronizations. *Theory of Computing Systems*, 36(5):397–430, Aug. 2003.

[3] D. Cederman, B. Chatterjee, and P. Tsigas. Understanding the Performance of Concurrent Data Structures on Graphics Processors. *Euro-Par 2012 Parallel Processing*, 2012.

[4] A. Gottlieb, B. D. Lubachevsky, and L. Rudolph. Basic Techniques for the Efficient Coordination of Very Large Numbers of Cooperating Sequential Processors. *Transactions on Programming Languages and Systems*, 5(2), Apr. 1983.

[5] A. Haas, M. Lippautz, T. A. Henzinger, H. Payer, A. Sokolova, C. M. Kirsch, and A. Sezgin. Distributed queues in shared memory: Multicore performance and scalability through quantitative relaxation. In *ACM International Conference on Computing Frontiers*, New York, New York, USA, 2013. ACM Press.

[6] D. Hendler, I. Incze, N. Shavit, and M. Tzafrir. Flat combining and the synchronization-parallelism tradeoff. In *ACM Symposium on Parallelism in Algorithms and Architectures*, June 2010.

[7] M. P. Herlihy and J. M. Wing. Linearizability: A correctness condition for concurrent objects. *Transactions on Programming Languages and Systems*, 12(3):463–492, 1990.

[8] C. M. Kirsch, M. Lippautz, and H. Payer. Fast and scalable, lock-free k-FIFO queues. In *International Conference on Parallel Architectures and Compilation Techniques*, 2012.

[9] A. Kogan and E. Petrank. Wait-free queues with multiple enqueuers and dequeuers. In *Symposium on Principles and Practice of Parallel Programming*, pages 223–234. ACM, 2011.

[10] A. Kogan and E. Petrank. A methodology for creating fast wait-free data structures. In *Symposium on Principles and Practice of Parallel Programming*. ACM, Feb. 2012.

[11] M. M. Michael and M. L. Scott. Simple, fast, and practical non-blocking and blocking concurrent queue algorithms. In *ACM Symposium on Principles of Distributed Computing*. ACM, May 1996.

[12] A. Morrison and Y. Afek. Fast concurrent queues for x86 processors. In *Symposium on Principles and Practice of Parallel Programming*. ACM, Feb. 2013.

[13] D. Orozco, E. Garcia, R. Khan, K. Livingston, and G. R. Gao. Toward high-throughput algorithms on many-core architectures. *ACM Transactions on Architecture and Code Optimization*, 8(4):1–21, Jan. 2012.

[14] P. Tsigas and Y. Zhang. A simple, fast and scalable non-blocking concurrent FIFO queue for shared memory multiprocessor systems. In *ACM Symposium on Parallelism in Algorithms and Architectures*. ACM, July 2001.

Lightweight Java Profiling with Partial Safepoints and Incremental Stack Tracing

Peter Hofer   David Gnedt
peter.hofer@jku.at   david.gnedt@jku.at
Christian Doppler Laboratory on Monitoring and
Evolution of Very-Large-Scale Software Systems
Johannes Kepler University Linz, Austria

Hanspeter Mössenböck
hanspeter.moessenboeck@jku.at
Institute for System Software
Johannes Kepler University Linz, Austria

ABSTRACT

Sampling profilers are popular because of their low and adjustable overhead and because they do not distort the profile by modifying the application code. A typical sampling profiler periodically suspends the application threads, walks their stacks, and merges the resulting stack traces into a calling context tree. Java virtual machines offer a convenient interface to accomplish this, but rely on *safepoints,* a synchronization mechanism that requires *all* threads to park in a safe location. However, a profiler is primarily interested in the running threads, and waiting for all threads to reach a safe location significantly increases the overhead. In most cases, taking a complete stack trace is also unnecessary because many stack frames remain unchanged between samples.

We present three techniques that reduce the overhead of sampling Java applications. *Partial safepoints* require only a certain number of threads to enter a safepoint and can be used to sample only the running threads. With *self-sampling,* we parallelize taking stack traces by having each thread take its own stack trace. Finally, *incremental stack tracing* constructs stack traces lazily and examines each stack frame only once instead of walking the entire stack for each sample. Our techniques require no support from the operating system or hardware. With our implementation in the popular HotSpot virtual machine, we show that we can significantly reduce the overhead of sampling without affecting the accuracy of the profiles.

Categories and Subject Descriptors

C.4 [**Performance of Systems**]: Measurement Techniques

General Terms

Experimentation, Measurement, Performance

Keywords

Java, Profiling, Monitoring, Safepoints, Sampling, Stack Trace, Calling Context Tree

1. INTRODUCTION

Profilers are valuable analysis tools that help performance engineers to understand the behavior of applications and to assess the contribution of individual components to the overall execution time. A profiler observes the execution of an application and measures the run time and/or call frequency of methods to generate an execution profile which indicates those methods where the most time is spent or those that are called most frequently. An engineer can use this information to spot bottlenecks and to apply optimizations where they are most effective. Profiling is also useful to guide compiler optimizations, to determine test coverage, or to identify code that is never used.

In contrast to "flat" profiles that attribute measurements simply to methods, no matter from where they are called, prior research has demonstrated the importance of adding dynamic *calling context* information to profiles [2, 3, 24, 25]. The calling context is the call chain from the root method to the executing method; in other words, it is a *stack trace*. Calling contexts can be merged into a *calling context tree* (CCT, [2]), which differs from a call tree in that it merges identical children (callees) of a node.

In general, there are two approaches for collecting calling contexts. *Instrumenting profilers* insert code snippets in methods to record calls in the CCT. This approach yields an exhaustive CCT, but the instrumentation can introduce significant overhead and distorts the measured method execution times. *Sampling profilers,* on the other hand, periodically interrupt the application to take stack traces and then merge them into the CCT. This approach requires no instrumentation and typically causes significantly less overhead, but it can miss method invocations between samples and therefore results in an approximate CCT with only statistically significant information. Our research focuses on profiling techniques with minimal overhead that are suitable for monitoring production systems, which is why we concentrate on the sampling approach.

The Java Virtual Machine Tool Interface (JVMTI, [18]) offers functionality for sampling calling contexts of Java applications. It is supported by all common Java VM implementations and is therefore used by many Java profiling tools. Implementations of JVMTI rely on *safepoints* for sampling, a mechanism that was originally devised for garbage collection: the Java VM inserts checks for a pending safepoint operation in the application code. When a profiler requests a sample, the VM signals such a pending safepoint operation and then waits for all application threads to reach a safepoint check and park. As soon as all application threads are parked in a safe state, the stack traces can be taken. However, waiting for all threads to park causes significant delays. Parking all threads is often not even necessary because profilers are primarily interested in the threads that are currently running. Furthermore, the compiler can decide to eliminate safepoint checks for performance reasons, which further increases the time that it takes until all threads have parked.

In our previous research, we described a scheduling-aware sampling approach for Java VMs that uses a mechanism of the operating system to copy stack fragments of the running application threads into a buffer for asynchronous analysis [11, 12]. While this approach achieves very low overheads, it requires specific capabilities of the operating system. In this paper, we present an alternative set of techniques that also significantly reduce the overhead of sampling, but are independent of operating systems and hardware. We implemented these techniques in Oracle's HotSpot VM [19], a popular high-performance Java VM.

The main contributions of this paper are:

1. With *partial safepoints* and *self-sampling*, we describe novel techniques that reduce the sampling pause times and that can be used to target those threads that are actually running.

2. We describe a new sampling technique called *incremental stack tracing*. It constructs stack traces lazily instead of walking the entire stack for each sample. Incremental stack tracing examines each stack frame only once and shares the collected data between multiple stack traces.

3. We discuss aspects of our implementation in the HotSpot VM, such as changes to the VM's safepoint mechanism and special cases which must be handled for incremental stack tracing.

4. We provide an extensive evaluation of our techniques, comparing their overheads and their CCTs with those from conventional JVMTI sampling. For the evaluation, we use the DaCapo suite and the Scala Benchmarking Project. We show that our techniques are faster without affecting the accuracy of the CCTs.

The rest of this paper is organized as follows: Section 2 introduces calling context trees as well as profiling with JVMTI using safepoints. Sections 3, 4 and 5 describe our three techniques for reducing the sampling overhead and for targeting only the running threads. Section 6 describes aspects of our implementation. Section 7 evaluates the overheads and the accuracy of our techniques. Section 8 examines related work, and Section 9 concludes this paper.

2. BACKGROUND

2.1 Calling Context Trees

A flat execution profile that only shows the observed methods and their total execution times is of limited value. Often, a performance problem does not originate in the hot methods themselves, but rather in their callers. For example, when profiling shows that a program spends too much time in a sorting method, a developer could conclude that this method is inefficient. However, it could also be the case that the program would rather benefit from better data structures

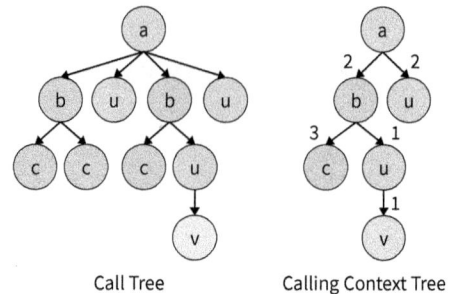

Figure 1: Call tree and calling context tree

that would reduce the necessary amount of sorting. The sorting method could be called from hundreds of locations in the program while the performance problem typically originates in only a few call sites. To identify these call sites and to allow the developer to make changes where they have the most impact, profilers commonly sample entire *calling contexts*, which are stack traces from the executing method to the root method (the entry point of the program or thread).

Profilers typically represent all of the collected calling contexts in a tree structure, like a call tree. Figure 1 shows such a call tree, depicting, among others, multiple calls from *a* to *b*, *b* to *c*, and *a* to *u*. The call tree represents each observed method invocation as a single node, with the caller as its parent. When the execution times of invocations are measured, they can be specified as edge weights. Call trees are an exhaustive representation of all calls of a program's execution, but because each observed call introduces a new node, they quickly grow very large for most programs. Call trees are also less suitable for sampling profilers because these profilers typically cannot distinguish whether a stack frame seen in subsequent samples belongs to the same invocation or to different invocations of a method.

Calling context trees (CCT, [2]) are a more compact structure than call trees. In contrast to call trees, CCTs merge identical children into a single node and thus store identical calling contexts only once. The edge weights specify the number of samples that were merged or the total execution times of all merged samples. A call tree can be converted to a CCT simply by recursively merging sibling nodes representing calls to the same methods and adding up their edge weights. Figure 1 shows a call tree and its corresponding CCT. Since CCTs are more compact while still sufficiently expressive, CCTs are more common in practice.

2.2 Sampling with JVMTI and Safepoints

The Java Virtual Machine Tool Interface (JVMTI) is a native programming interface that allows debuggers, profilers, and similar tools to interact with the Java VM and the application running on top of it [18]. Clients of JVMTI are called *agents* and run in the same process as the Java VM. Agents can invoke JVMTI functions to control the behavior of the application and can register callbacks to receive notifications about application and VM events. For example, an instrumenting Java profiler would be implemented as an agent that subscribes to JVMTI's class loading events and modifies the bytecode of classes when they are loaded.

Typical JVMTI sampling profilers start a separate agent thread that executes a sampling loop. In this loop, the profiler uses the JVMTI function `GetThreadListStackTraces` to obtain stack traces for application threads of interest, and then processes these traces, for example by merging them into a CCT. It then goes to sleep for a certain time, referred to as the sampling interval, before repeating the process.

Because JVMTI offers ready-to-use functionality to accomplish most of the sampling process (i.e., interrupting multiple threads, doing stack walks and decoding the stack frames to an array of method identifiers) sampling agents are straightforward to develop. However, the implementation of JVMTI in the HotSpot VM and in other VMs suffers from problems that affect the performance of sampling agents.

When an agent calls a JVMTI function for taking stack traces, the function does not start its work immediately, but rather enters a task into the work queue of the VM thread. The VM thread can be seen as the main thread of the virtual machine and is different from the application's main thread. Only after higher-priority tasks in the queue have been completed, the VM begins taking stack traces.

In order to safely walk the stacks of application threads, the VM relies on so-called *safepoints*. A safepoint is a state where all application threads are parked to allow safe execution of operations such as garbage collection, deoptimization, or stack walks. To accomplish this, the VM inserts checks for a pending safepoint operation at safe locations in the application code. When the VM thread signals a pending safepoint, each application thread enters a parking state after it runs to its next safepoint check. Threads that are already blocked, such as those that wait for an I/O operation, are always parked in a safe state and only need to enter a safepoint when they become unblocked while the safepoint is still in effect. Once all application threads are parked, the VM thread can safely take stack traces of threads. When the operation has finished, the VM leaves the safepoint, resumes all threads and passes the collected stack traces to the agent.

Figure 2 shows an example of how JVMTI uses safepoints to sample application threads: Thread T_{VM} is the VM thread, the threads T_1, T_2 and T_3 are runnable application threads, and thread T_4 is an application thread which is blocked waiting to receive data via a socket. When the agent requests samples for the threads T_1, T_3 and T_4, the VM thread begins "safepointing", i.e. it signals that a safepoint is pending. Soon after that, thread T_1 reaches its next safepoint check and enters a parking state (indicated by the square and the now dashed line), followed by thread T_3. Thread T_4 does not have to enter a safepoint, since it is already blocked. At this point, thread T_2 delays the process, although no sample was requested for it, and threads T_1 and T_3 remain parked and unproductive. When thread T_3 finally parks and hence, all threads have entered the safepoint, T_{VM} can walk the stacks of the three threads requested by the agent. In the meantime, thread T_4 becomes unblocked because its socket has received data, but instead of resuming its execution, a safepoint check ensures that it also enters a parking state. After the VM thread has finished taking the stack traces, it ends the safepoint and resumes all application threads.

The main problem with using safepoints for sampling is that they affect all Java threads. Even the threads for which no stack trace was requested are required to run to their next safepoint and park until the stack traces have been collected. Hence, the entire application is paused even when only a single thread should be sampled.

Optimizations performed by the JIT compiler can further increase the performance impact of JVMTI sampling. By default, the compiler places safepoints at the exit points

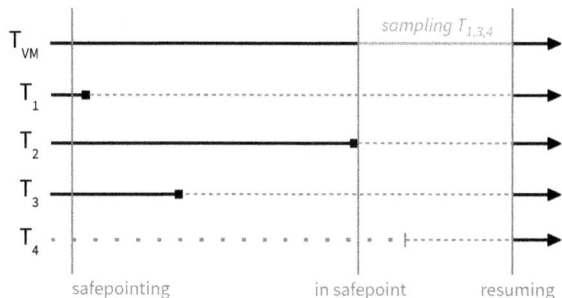

Figure 2: Sampling threads in a safepoint

of methods and at the end of loop iterations. Although the overhead of safepoint checks is very low, it can become significant in hot loops. Safepoints also prevent certain kinds of optimizations because they enforce a particular order of instructions, similar to a memory barrier. Hence, the compiler can decide to move safepoints out of loops to increase performance and can even decide to eliminate safepoint checks in inlined code. With fewer safepoint checks, it can take longer until all threads are parked, and the sampling overhead increases. Eliminating safepoints also means that there are fewer locations where samples can be taken, which can distort the profile.

3. PARTIAL SAFEPOINTS

Global "stop the world" safepoints are acceptable or even necessary for most purposes that they are used for, such as garbage collection and deoptimization. For a profiler, however, it is often sufficient to sample only a subset of the application's threads. In fact, a profiler should focus particularly on the currently running threads because those are the ones that are actively consuming resources. Sampling these threads provides the most insight into where the program spends its time.

However, a sampling profiler that focuses only on running threads cannot be implemented with JVMTI and global safepoints. Although JVMTI supports restricting sampling to a set of threads, a sampling agent cannot determine a priori which threads will be running when the samples are taken. It is the operating system that schedules the threads, and common operating systems do not expose scheduling information to the VM or to an agent. The VM can only keep track of which threads are *runnable* (i.e., ready to run). As an approximation, an agent could request samples for a selection of these threads. Still, this would not significantly decrease the sampling overhead because the safepoint would still affect all the other threads as well.

To target only running threads and to reduce the performance impact of sampling profilers, we implemented a variation of safepoints which we call *partial safepoints*. Partial safepoints require only a certain number of application threads to enter a safepoint state. Samples are then only taken for these threads. We allow the agent to choose the number of threads to sample. By using the number of processors in the system, sampling ideally affects only the running threads. With no scheduling data available, this is a best-effort approach. In practice, some of the system's CPUs might be executing threads from other processes. Also, the operating system might interrupt a thread that was running when the sample was requested, and instead schedule another thread which then enters the partial safepoint in its place. In the worst case, however, a sample is taken of a thread which was runnable, but not actually running, which we consider acceptable.

As soon as the intended number of threads has entered the partial safepoint, the VM can walk their stacks. Because some threads can enter a waiting state and block before reaching a safepoint check, we observe such thread state transitions to avoid a deadlock caused by waiting for more threads than can possibly enter the safepoint. While the stacks are walked, the safepoint must remain in effect. During that time, more threads than anticipated can enter the partial safepoint. Our implementation must consider which threads have entered the safepoint late and must finally resume all of them.

3.1 Waiting Threads

Samples of waiting threads can be useful to locate bottlenecks in locking or to detect inefficient I/O behavior. Threads blocked in a waiting state do not enter a safepoint unless they become unblocked while the safepoint is still in effect. This also applies to Java threads executing native code, where the VM ensures that a thread returning from native code enters a safepoint when one is in effect. Such native calls occur frequently because the Java class library implements I/O operations using native code, and these operations can also block.

We extended our partial safepoints mechanism with an option to take samples also of waiting threads and of threads that are in native code. If this option is active, we determine the number of runnable application threads and the number of threads that are waiting or executing native code, and accordingly divide the number of requested samples between runnable and waiting threads. For example, if a sampling agent requests four samples for an application that has 21 threads, out of which 15 threads are runnable and six threads are waiting or executing native code, our approach will return samples for the first three threads that enter the safepoint, and one sample for another, randomly selected thread.

Figure 3 shows an example of how runnable and waiting threads are sampled with partial safepoints, using a similar scenario as the one shown in Figure 2. In this example, a sampling agent has requested three samples. The VM thread T_{VM} determines that there are three runnable threads and one waiting thread, and hence decides to sample two runnable threads and the waiting thread T_4. T_{VM} then signals a pending safepoint. As soon as two threads, T_1 and T_3, have parked, it takes samples of their stacks and then immediately resumes T_1 and T_3. By the time when thread T_2 reaches its next safepoint check and when T_4 becomes unblocked, the safepoint is no longer in effect, and their execution remains entirely unaffected by sampling.

4. SELF-SAMPLING

With a straightforward implementation of partial safepoints, the safepoint remains in effect while the VM thread walks the stack of each thread to ensure that the stack walks can be done safely. During that time, further threads can enter the partial safepoint. Although these threads will not be sampled, they pause executing code, and the VM must also keep track of them in order to resume them later, all of which causes unnecessary overhead.

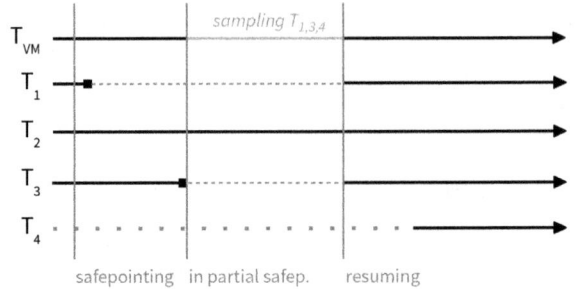

Figure 3: Sampling threads with a partial safepoint

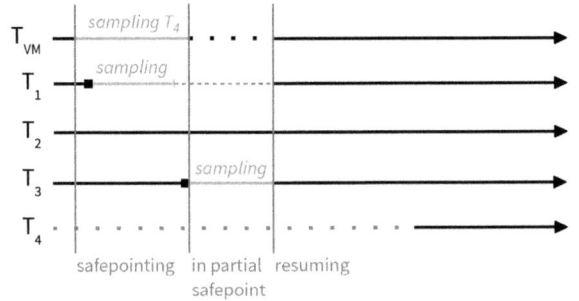

Figure 4: Self-sampling threads in a partial safepoint

To minimize the time the partial safepoint must remain in effect, we combined partial safepoints with a technique that we call *self-sampling*. When a thread enters a partial safepoint, it takes a ticket which tells it whether it is among the threads which should be sampled. If it is, the thread immediately walks its own stack. When the last thread that should be sampled enters the partial safepoint, it notifies the VM thread, which then signals the end of the safepoint so no further threads (which would not be sampled) can enter it. When a thread has completed sampling itself, it places the stack trace in a designated buffer and notifies the VM thread. The VM thread waits until all threads have provided their samples, and then resumes all sampled threads and returns the samples to the agent.

Because blocked threads do not enter a safepoint, they cannot sample themselves. Instead, the VM thread takes their samples, which increases the time the safepoint must remain in effect. However, the VM thread can take the samples while other threads are still running to their next safepoint check.

Figure 4 shows an example of a partial safepoint with self-sampling threads. As in Figure 3, the VM thread T_{VM} inspects the states of the application threads, decides to sample two running threads and the waiting thread T_4, and then signals a pending safepoint. It then immediately begins to take a sample of the waiting thread T_4. Meanwhile, the thread T_1 enters the partial safepoint and examines its ticket. Because it is the first of the two runnable threads that to be sampled, it walks its own stack, places the stack trace in the designated buffer and notifies T_{VM}. When T_3 enters the safepoint, it also examines its ticket and recognizes that it is the second and last of the two runnable threads to be sampled, so it notifies T_{VM}, which signals the end of the safepoint. After T_3 has sampled itself and placed the stack trace in the buffer, it notifies T_{VM} again, which resumes T_1 and T_3 and returns the collected stack traces to the agent.

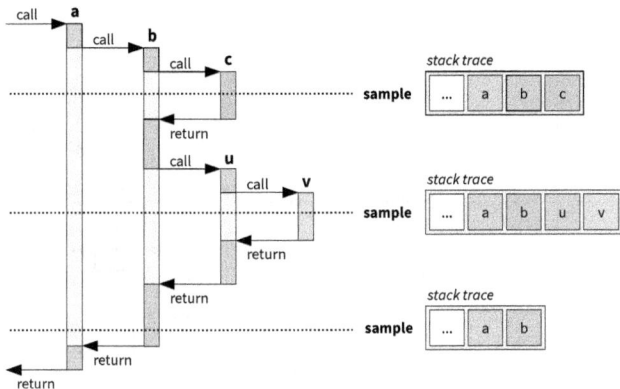

Figure 5: Three samples with complete stack traces

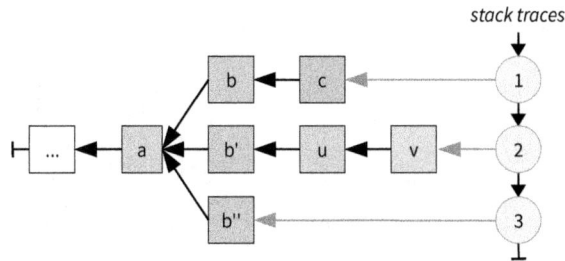

Figure 6: Stack traces in a tree with shared frames

5. INCREMENTAL STACK TRACING

Self-sampling and partial safepoints reduce the time that an application must pause for sampling. To further lower the overall overhead, we looked at the costs of the stack walk. In many cases, the stack frames from the stack base up to a certain stack depth remain unchanged for most of a thread's execution. Nevertheless, these unchanged frames are examined during every stack walk.

Figure 5 shows an example for redundantly sampled frames, starting with a call to the method a. Method a calls b, which in turn calls c. While execution is in c, the profiler takes a sample. The stack walk visits the frames of the three active methods as well as all frames below a. When the profiler takes the next sample in v, c has returned, the frame of b has changed because b continued its execution, and two new frames from the calls to u and v are on the stack. Although the frame of a and all frames below it remained unchanged, the stack walk needlessly walks and decodes them again. When the profiler takes a third sample, the frames of u and v have disappeared and only the frame of b has changed, but the stack walk again visits all other frames as well.

To avoid redundantly sampling frames, stack walks could be limited to a certain number of frames below the frame of the executing method. However, the resulting incomplete stack traces would not be suitable to be correctly merged into a CCT, which has the entry method as its root. Therefore, we devised an approach that builds stack traces incrementally when methods return, and does not examine an unchanged stack frame more than once. We based our technique for incremental stack tracing on an approach that our research group developed for implementing continuations in a Java VM [22]. Similar approaches have also been used to implement incremental scavenging for garbage collection [7].

5.1 Data Structures

To share frame information between stack traces of multiple samples, we store the traces in a tree structure. Figure 6 shows what this tree looks like for the example from Figure 5. We maintain a linked list of *stack trace objects* for the stack traces that were taken, which is shown on the right-hand side of the figure. Stack trace objects are assigned numeric identifiers, which the profiling agent can use to keep track of the stack traces that it has requested. Each stack trace object has a pointer to a *frame object* that represents the stack frame which was on top of the stack when the stack trace was taken. For the first stack trace, which has the identifier 1, this is

the frame object representing the frame for c, for stack trace 2 it is the frame object for v, and for stack trace 3 it is the frame object for b. Each frame object has a pointer to its caller frame object. The frame objects b, b' and b'' refer to the same invocation of b, but the duplication is necessary because the frame objects store different execution positions (i.e., bytecode indices) within the method. This information is useful to a profiler, for example, to distinguish between different call sites in a method.

Frame objects store the details of a captured stack frame in the following attributes:

parent: The pointer to the caller's frame object.

method: An identifier of the Java method that the stack frame belongs to.

bci: The index of the current instruction within the Java bytecode of the method.

The following attributes of a frame object are not intended for the profiler, but are required for capturing frames and managing the tree of frame objects (see the next section).

filled: A value that indicates if the frame object has been filled with valid data, or if it is an empty *skeleton object*.

frame address: The frame's exact location on the stack.

saved return address: Original return address of the callee.

5.2 Capturing Frames

We maintain one list of stack trace objects for each thread. When we take a new stack trace, we first create a new stack trace object and insert it into the respective thread's list. We then create a new frame object for the top frame on the stack, which we call *top frame object (TFO)*. We decode the top frame and fill the TFO with the determined method identifier and bytecode index (see Figure 7 (a)). The *frame address* and the *saved return address* attributes are not required for the TFO. We set the TFO's *filled* attribute and link it with the stack trace object that we created earlier.

In a second step, we deal with the caller frame. The caller frame remains unchanged until the top frame's method returns, so we do not capture it immediately. Instead, we create a *skeleton frame object* for the caller frame that we can fill later, and make this skeleton object the parent of the TFO. We store the caller frame's address (SP_b in Figure 7) in the skeleton object's *frame address* attribute so we can match it to the frame later (see below). To intercept when the top frame's method returns, we patch the top frame's return address on the stack with the address of a piece of trampoline code that we generate during the VM's startup phase. The original return address (RA_c in Figure 7) is stored in the skeleton object's *saved return address* attribute.

When the top method returns, it returns to our trampoline instead of to its caller, and the trampoline in turn calls our stack tracing code. In this code, we decode the caller's frame

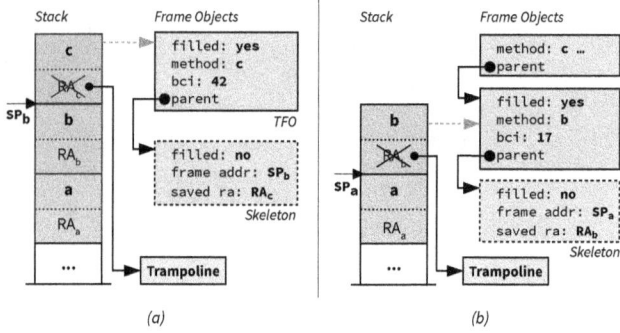

Figure 7: Capturing a frame (a) when taking a sample, and (b) when intercepting a method return

into its skeleton object, patch the caller's return address on the stack, and create another skeleton object for the caller's caller frame (see Figure 7 (b)). Finally, we do the actual return by using the saved return address that we stored in the skeleton object before.

To know which frame object must be filled when we intercept the return of a method, we maintain a thread-local pointer to the next skeleton object that needs to be filled, which we call *current skeleton object (CSO)*. We also use the CSO to implement sharing of frame objects between multiple stack traces. We distinguish the following situations:

Taking a sample. When we take a sample, we create a new TFO and fill it with the decoded top frame. Depending on the CSO, the TFO is treated as follows:

- If the CSO is not set yet, we create a new CSO and make it the parent of the TFO.
- If there already is a CSO, we check whether it refers to the frame of the TFO's caller by comparing their frame addresses. If they match, we make the CSO the parent of the TFO. Otherwise, we create a new CSO and insert it between the TFO and the former CSO.

Intercepting a return. When we intercept a method return, the CSO always refers to the frame object of the caller, so we decode the caller frame into the CSO. We then inspect the CSO's parent:

- If there is no parent, we create a new CSO as the parent of the former CSO.
- If the CSO's parent refers to the frame of the caller's caller, we make that parent the new CSO.
- If the CSO's parent refers to some other frame, we create a new CSO and insert it between the former CSO and its parent.

Figure 8 demonstrates how our technique incrementally builds stack traces for the example from Figure 5. Initially, the list of stack traces is empty and there is no CSO. The stack traces are then built in the following steps (for simplicity, we use the name of the methods to also refer to their frames).

(1) To take the first sample, we create a new TFO and decode the top frame c into it (the object that is filled in each step is highlighted in bold). Because there is no CSO yet, we create a skeleton object for the caller b (skeleton objects are indicated with a dashed frame).

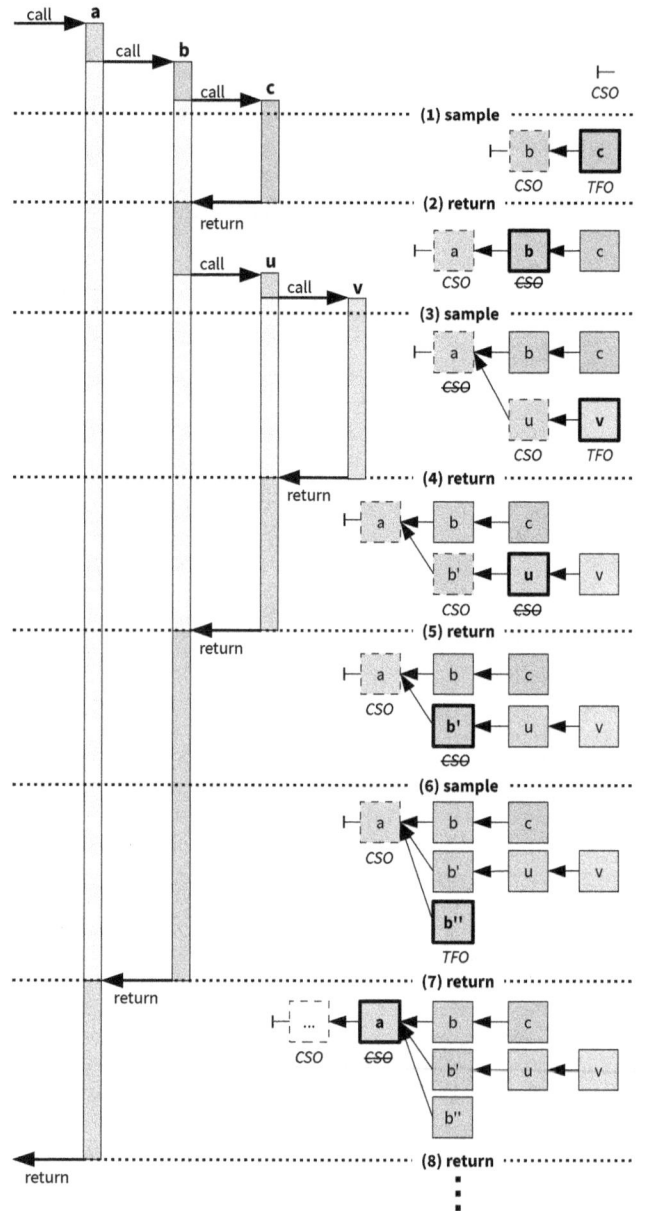

Figure 8: Incremental construction of stack traces

We make the new skeleton object the CSO and also make it the parent of the TFO. Finally, we patch the return address of c and save the original return address in the CSO.

(2) When c returns, the trampoline is executed, and we fill the CSO with the decoded stack frame of b. Because the CSO does not have a parent yet, we create a new skeleton object for a as parent. We then make that skeleton object the CSO, patch the return address of b and do the actual return from c to b.

(3) When we take the second sample, we decode the top frame v into a new TFO. We then check whether the CSO corresponds to the caller frame u. Since the CSO actually corresponds to a, we create a new CSO for u and insert it between a and v. Finally, we patch the return address of v.

80

(4) We intercept the return from v to u and fill the CSO with the decoded frame of u. Because the CSO's parent, which is a, does not match u's caller, which is b, we create a new CSO b' for b and insert it between a and u. We finally patch the return address of u and do the actual return from v to u.

(5) We intercept the return from u to b and fill the CSO with the decoded frame b. Because the CSO's parent, which is a, now corresponds to b's caller, we make the parent the CSO and do not need to create a new one. We also need not patch the return address of b because it was already patched in step (2), and do the actual return from u to b.

(6) When we take a third sample, we fill the top frame b into a new TFO denoted by b''. Because the CSO corresponds to the caller frame a, we make it the parent of the TFO. The return address of b is still patched and does not need to be modified.

(7) We intercept the return from b to a and fill the CSO with the decoded frame a. Since the CSO does not have a parent here, we create a new CSO for a's caller. Because all three stack traces join at the frame object of a, they share this object and all further frame objects below, and we examine their stack frames only once.

5.3 Interface

Typical profiling interfaces, such as JVMTI, offer an operation that walks the stack of a thread and returns a complete stack trace. Our approach does not create such a stack trace right away, but incrementally builds stack traces and requires the profiler to collect them later. Therefore, we devised two operations to use our technique:

sample. The profiler can use the *sample* operation to request a stack trace. It can specify a numeric identifier to assign to the stack trace. The identifiers of stack traces need not be unique, and a profiler can also simply assign timestamps to the stack traces it requests.

retrieve. The profiler can use the *retrieve* operation to collect all requested stack traces for a set of threads. The stack traces are returned in a tree structure that is similar to the described internal representation. When stack traces are still incomplete, the operation examines the remaining frames on the stack, completes the tree and reverts the patched return addresses on the stack. The retrieve operation empties the tree of stack traces kept in the VM. It always enters a full safepoint, but due to its infrequent use, the introduced overhead is negligible.

We implemented these two operations as JVMTI extension methods, which has the advantage that a profiling agent can probe whether the VM supports incremental stack tracing and partial safepoints. Typically, an agent would periodically request samples by calling the *sample* method, and infrequently use the *retrieve* method to collect the stack traces. It can then merge the stack traces into a calling context tree and update the tree's edge weights accordingly. The agent must retrieve the samples of a thread before the thread exits, or otherwise the stack traces would be released together with the thread's resources. It can accomplish this by subscribing to the *ThreadEnd* event that JVMTI offers.

6. IMPLEMENTATION ASPECTS

When we implemented our techniques in the highly optimized HotSpot VM, we had to handle several cases where thread synchronization or taking a correct stack trace is not as straightforward as described in the previous sections.

Frame types. The HotSpot VM starts out by executing Java bytecode in an interpreter, but compiles frequently executed methods to machine code. Therefore, the stack can contain frames of both interpreted and compiled methods, which differ in their layout. Moreover, Java code can call native methods of the VM, which again use different types of frames. When walking stacks and particularly when patching return addresses, we must handle each type of frame differently.

Inlining. The compiler aggressively tries to inline the code of called methods, and attempts to also inline those methods that are called by the inlined callees. Therefore, a particular location in compiled code can actually lie within multiple inlined methods that share a single stack frame. The compiler stores information about inlined methods and their ranges within other methods as metadata. When filling the frame object of a compiled frame, we must read this metadata and create extra frame objects for the inlined methods.

Exceptions. When a method throws an exception which must be handled by a caller, the method does not return in the usual way, using the return address on the stack. Instead, the VM unwinds the stack and pops frames until it reaches a method which can handle the exception. We modified the VM's exception handling code to capture a frame before it is popped from the stack.

Deoptimization. Deoptimization occurs when a method was compiled under an assumption that turned out to be false at runtime [15]. An example is when the compiler omitted a branch in the compiled code because it assumed that it would never be taken. When deoptimization occurs, the stack frame of the compiled method is transformed into one or more interpreted frames, and execution is continued in the interpreter. During this transformation, patched return addresses are lost, so we had to alter the deoptimization code to preserve patched return addresses.

On-stack replacement. For long-running interpreted methods, the VM can decide to compile them on the fly, to transform their interpreted frames into compiled frames, and to continue execution in compiled code. This is called on-stack replacement. Since the resulting compiled frames can have different locations than the interpreted frames, we have to update our data structures in this case.

Safepoint synchronization. The safepoint checks that the HotSpot VM injects into application code simply write a value to a specific page in memory that is called *polling page*. When no safepoint is pending, these writes are inexpensive. To enter a safepoint, the VM thread acquires the global *threads lock* to block thread state transitions, such as when a thread resumes execution after waiting. Next, the VM instructs the operating system to write-protect the polling page. This causes the safepoint checks to trigger page faults in each thread, and the fault handler then parks the thread. The VM finally waits until all threads are parked or are in a safe state guarded by the threads lock.

DaCapo Benchmark Suite [5]	avrora	simulates a microcontroller grid
	fop	transforms an XSL-FO file to PDF
	h2	benchmarks an in-memory database
	jython	executes the pybench benchmark suite
	luindex	indexes a set of documents
	lusearch	searches in a set of documents
	pmd	analyzes Java source code for problems
	sunflow	renders images with raytracing
	tomcat	queries a Tomcat webserver
	tradebeans	trading simulation with database
	tradesoap	trading with SOAP communication
	xalan	transforms XML documents to HTML
Scala Benchmarking Project [21]	actors	trading sample with actors
	apparat	optimizer for ABC, SWC and SWF files
	factorie	deployable probabilistic modeling toolkit
	kiama	language processing
	scalac	Scala language compiler
	scaladoc	Scala documentation tool
	scalap	Scala class file decoder
	scalariform	Scala source code formatter
	scalatest	Testing toolkit for Scala and Java
	scalaxb	XML databinding for Scala
	specs	behavior-driven design framework
	tmt	topic modeling toolbox

Table 1: Set of benchmarks

For partial safepoints and self-sampling, we use a modified safepoint mechanism that waits only until enough threads from the desired set of threads have entered the safepoint, and then immediately unprotects the polling page again. However, other threads can also enter the safepoint during that time. Therefore, before write-protecting the polling page, we set a flag for each thread which indicates whether the thread should sample itself. Threads which have their flag set then sample themselves in the fault handler, while the other threads simply wait for the safepoint to end. When including waiting threads for sampling, we compute the ratio of waiting to runnable threads after acquiring the threads lock, so no threads can change their state.

7. EVALUATION

We evaluated our sampling techniques with the DaCapo 9.12 benchmark suite and the benchmarks of the Scala Benchmarking Project 0.1.0. The DaCapo benchmark suite [5] consists of open source, real-world applications with pre-defined, non-trivial workloads.[1] The Scala Benchmarking Project [21] complements the DaCapo suite with a set of benchmarks based on real-world applications written in the Scala language. Table 1 describes the individual benchmarks.

We compare the overheads and the generated CCTs of the following techniques relative to no sampling:

- Conventional JVMTI sampling
- Self-sampling in Partial Safepoints (SPS)
- Incremental Self-sampling in Partial Safepoints (ISPS)

For that purpose, we implemented two profiling agents that take samples at fixed intervals and build a CCT, one that uses conventional JVMTI, and another one that uses our VM extensions. We enabled sampling of waiting threads

[1] We did not use the DaCapo suite's *batik* and *eclipse* benchmarks because they do not run on OpenJDK 8.

with our techniques to be comparable with JVMTI sampling, which cannot target running threads. We used the number of CPU cores as the number of threads to sample with partial safepoints. Experiments showed that using more threads than that causes considerably more overhead, while using fewer threads does not significantly reduce overhead. The profilers adhere as much as possible to the sampling interval by incorporating the time that elapsed while taking the last sample into the time they wait until taking the next sample.

We chose to execute 30 successive *iterations* of each benchmark with each sampling technique in a single VM instance, and to discard the data from the first 20 iterations to compensate for the VM's startup phase. Hence, our agents track the start and the end of benchmark iterations to extract the metrics and the generated CCT for every iteration. We further executed 10 *rounds* of each benchmark (with 30 iterations each) to ensure the results are not biased by optimization decisions the VM makes in the warm-up phase.

We performed all tests on a system with a quad-core Intel Core i7-3770 processor with 16 GB of memory running Ubuntu Linux 14.04 LTS. To get more stable results, we disabled hyperthreading, turbo boost and dynamic frequency scaling. With the exception of vital system services, no other applications were running while the benchmarks were executed.

7.1 Overhead

Figure 9 shows the median overheads for the benchmarks of the DaCapo suite with all three sampling techniques, using sampling intervals of 10 ms, 1 ms and 0.1 ms. The error bars indicate the first and third quartiles. The *G.Mean* bars show the geometric means for a sampling interval, and their error bars indicate a 50% confidence interval. With 10 ms intervals, JVMTI sampling already has a considerable overhead of more than 10% on average, while that of SPS stays below 3%, and ISPS comes close to 2%. Our techniques have the most impact for the *lusearch, sunflow, tradebeans, tradesoap* and *xalan* benchmarks. We found that these benchmarks have a higher CPU usage or use a larger number of threads than the other benchmarks. In comparison, our techniques have little effect for the *jython* and *luindex* benchmarks, which are mostly single-threaded. Overall, ISPS achieves significantly lower overheads than SPS. Surprisingly, the overhead of JVMTI sampling for *lusearch, sunflow* and *xalan* is lower with 0.1 ms sampling intervals than with 1 ms intervals. This can be explained with the sampling latency, which we examine below.

Figure 10 shows the overheads for the benchmarks of the Scala Benchmarking Project. In contrast to the DaCapo benchmarks, even JVMTI sampling has only 5% overhead with 10 ms sampling intervals. The improvements from our techniques become more significant with 1 ms intervals, where JVMTI sampling has approximately 25% overhead while ISPS achieves less than 10% overhead. One interesting case is *tmt*, where ISPS has more overhead than SPS with 10 ms and 1 ms intervals. The reason is that *tmt* creates a large number of short-lived threads, and the agent must retrieve the samples of each of those threads when they end. The extra effort for this is typically low, but becomes significant in this case. We were unable to measure the overhead of *actors* with JVMTI sampling with 0.1 ms intervals because that benchmark has an internal timeout which causes it to terminate early due to the high overhead.

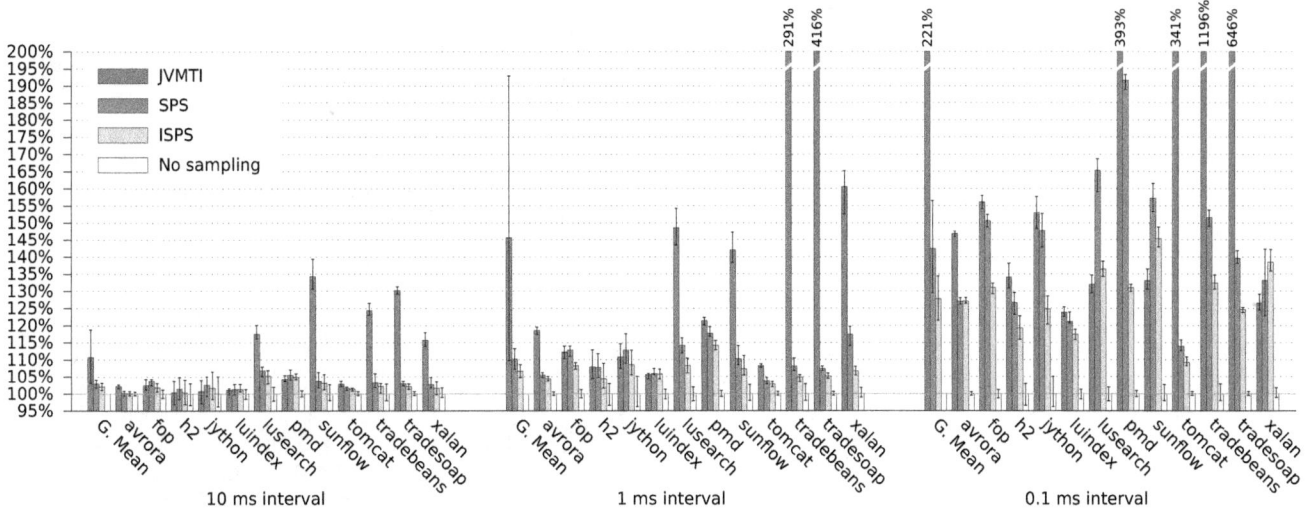

Figure 9: Overhead with the DaCapo benchmark suite using sampling intervals of 10ms, 1ms and 0.1ms

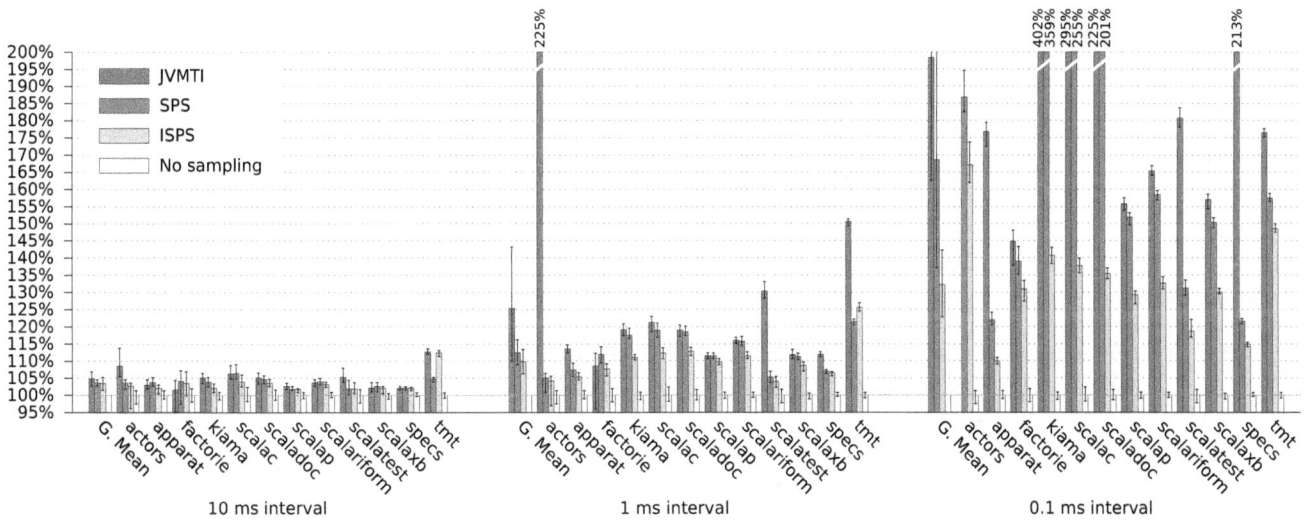

Figure 10: Overhead with the benchmarks of the Scala Benchmarking Project

7.2 Latency

We examined the latency of each sampling technique, which is the time it takes to pause threads and take samples. Figure 11 shows box plots of the latencies for all sampling techniques with 1 ms sampling intervals. The whiskers indicate the 2.5% and 97.5% percentiles. We grouped benchmarks with similar characteristics in *Others*. For all those benchmarks, the latency of JVMTI sampling is low, and SPS and ISPS have slightly lower latencies. For the other shown benchmarks, we found notable differences. *actors, tradebeans* and *tradesoap* use a large number of threads and the median latency with JVMTI sampling is high because it takes longer until all threads have entered a safepoint. The latency with SPS and ISPS is not higher than for all the other benchmarks because these techniques only require some of the threads to enter a safepoint. *lusearch, sunflow* and *xalan* have fewer threads, but they are very CPU-intensive and the compiler aggressively optimizes the hot code and eliminates safepoint checks. While the median latency for those three benchmarks with JVMTI sampling is not excessively high, the latencies fluctuate significantly between samples and can reach more

than 10 ms, which results in fewer taken samples. We found that with CPU-intensive benchmarks, such excessively high latencies occur more often when using shorter sampling intervals, possibly due to scheduling effects. A shorter sampling interval can then yield fewer total samples than a longer interval and actually reduce the overhead compared to a longer interval. This was the case with our overhead measurements with 0.1 ms intervals for those three benchmarks. In comparison, the latency with SPS and ISPS for these benchmarks is not higher than for the other benchmarks and very stable.

7.3 Accuracy

Determining the absolute accuracy of a profiler is challenging: ideally, we would compare a CCT from the profiler against an exact CCT of the same execution. However, such a perfect profile cannot be obtained because all profiling has an effect on the profiled application. While instrumenting profilers can generate a complete CCT with exact call counts, instrumentation significantly slows down short-running methods and interferes with compiler optimizations (particularly

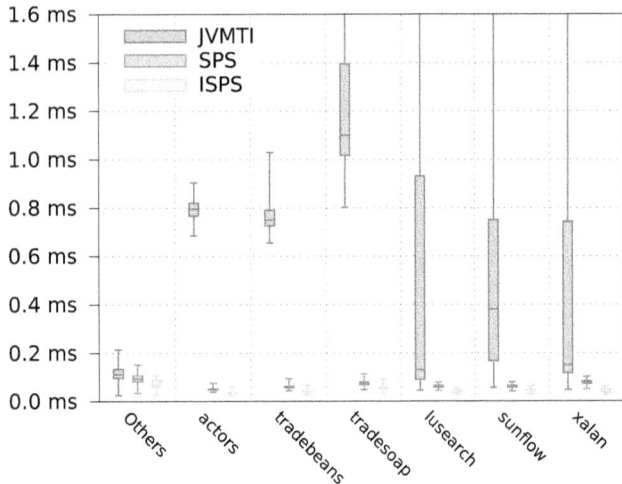

Figure 11: Pause times for selected benchmarks

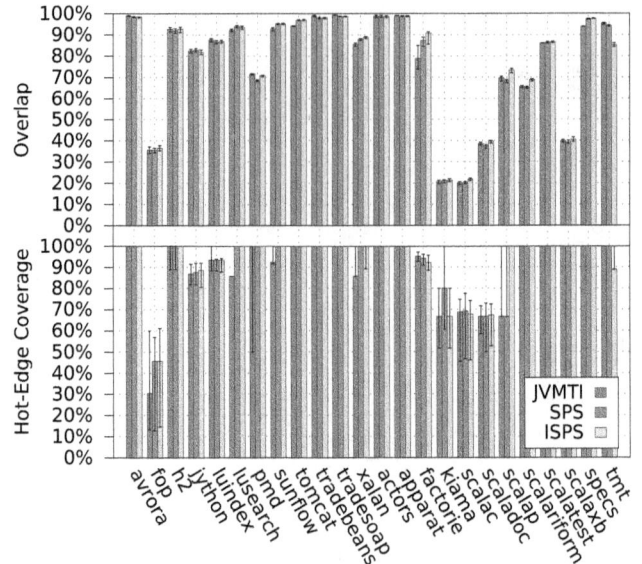

Figure 12: Overlap (top) and hot-edge coverage (bottom) of individual CCTs with average CCT

inlining). Therefore, when using instrumentation to measure execution times, the measured times are not representative for the unaltered application. Instead, we analyze whether each sampling profiler generates similar CCTs for different iterations of the same benchmark. We further construct "averaged" CCTs from different iterations of each benchmark with each profiler and compare them to test whether the profilers agree.

To compare two CCTs with each other, we use the *degree of overlap* and *hot-edge coverage* metrics. The degree of overlap assesses how many edges of the two CCTs are equivalent and how close their edge weights are to each other. It has been described and used extensively in related research [8, 9, 12, 16, 25]. While the degree of overlap reflects all edges of the two CCTs, the hottest edges of a CCT are of particular interest for identifying performance bottlenecks. The hot-edge coverage metric determines whether two CCTs identify a similar set of edges as hot according to a relative threshold and puts less emphasis on the exact edge weights. It was introduced in [25] and is used in [8, 12].

For the results we present below, we used the CCTs that we collected with a sampling interval of 1 ms. However, we found that the results are similar for sampling intervals of 10 ms and 0.1 ms. For each sampling technique and benchmark, we merged the CCTs from every (undiscarded) iteration in all rounds into a single CCT. This merged CCT contains all edges that exist in any of the CCTs, with edge weights that are the sum of the relative edge weights from all CCTs. The merged CCT is thus really the average over all individual CCTs of a benchmark. Some of the benchmarks dynamically generate classes which can be assigned different names in different iterations or rounds, for example call wrappers or web service handlers. We added extra heuristics to our analysis tools to properly match identical generated code when merging CCTs.

Stability Analysis.

The behavior of most benchmarks does not deviate much between iterations and thus, a profiler should produce similar CCTs for different iterations. We determined the stability of the CCTs of a profiler by comparing the CCT of every iteration to the average CCT of each benchmark.

Figure 12 shows the similarity of the individual CCTs with the average CCT by means of their median overlap (top part) and their median hot-edge coverage (bottom part), for all benchmarks and all profiling techniques. We used a threshold of $T = 0.1$ for the hot-edge coverage, which means that we consider an edge to be hot if it is within a tenth of the hottest edge. The error bars indicate the first and third quartiles. The plots demonstrate that for every benchmark, the stability of all three sampling techniques is very similar. They also suggest that the behavior of *fop, kiama, scalac, scaladoc* and *scalaxb* varies significantly between iterations. We found that these benchmarks spend over 40% of their execution time in many different calling contexts, each of which making up less than 0.05% of the overall execution time, in many cases even less than 0.01%. Hence, these calling contexts are seen in only very few samples and even slight shifts in sampling times add up to a significant difference in the resulting overlap. The hot-edge coverage for these benchmarks is significantly better, with the exception of *fop*: it has the shortest execution time of all benchmarks, so the profiler collects the fewest samples, and since it does not have any significantly hot calling contexts, the relative threshold causes a large set of calling contexts to be considered hot.

Our results show that all three sampling techniques produce CCTs that are stable between different iterations of most benchmarks. At the same time, the results demonstrate that the average CCTs are representative for the individual CCTs. However, this does not prove that the CCTs are accurate, since a sampling technique can also repeatedly produce an incorrect CCT.

Comparison between Sampling Techniques.

Figure 13 compares the average CCTs obtained with the three sampling techniques to each other by means of their overlap (top part) and their hot-edge coverage with a threshold of $T = 0.1$ (bottom part). The overlap between the three profiling techniques exceeds 70% for all benchmarks, with the exception of *kiama, scalac* and *scaladoc*. These

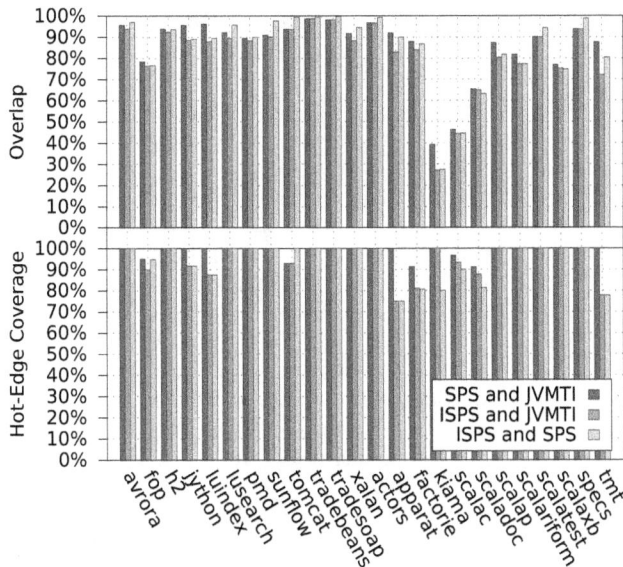

Figure 13: Overlap (top) and hot-edge coverage (bottom) of average CCTs from different sampling techniques

three benchmarks implement recursive-descent parsers with very deep stacks, and their rapidly changing stack depths make it improbable that many calling contexts are captured more than once. The hot-edge coverage plots show that SPS identifies a similar set of hot calling contexts as JVMTI sampling, with over 90% coverage for all benchmarks. We conclude from this that partial safepoints have no negative effect on the accuracy in comparison to sampling all threads. The hot-edge coverage between ISPS and the other two techniques is slightly lower for some benchmarks. The reason are deep stacks which exceed the otherwise adequate limit of 256 frames that we use for SPS and JVMTI sampling. Such a limit is required for the preallocation of data structures and we found that using a limit that is high enough to fit every stack trace significantly increases the overhead even for shallow stacks. While SPS and JVMTI sampling truncate long stack traces, ISPS always provides complete stack traces. While this is actually an advantage of ISPS, it reduces its hot-edge coverage with the other techniques because the complete stack traces do not match their truncated stack traces.

8. RELATED WORK

In this section, we describe previous work on profiling Java applications, on sampling calling context for dynamic analysis, and on analyzing CCTs.

Profiling.

Whaley [24] describes a VM-internal Java profiler which avoids complete stack walks. Unlike incremental stack tracing, it examines stacks eagerly and uses a spare bit in each stack frame's return address to mark if a frame has already been examined. Whaley claims a low overhead of 2-4% at 1000 samples per second, but the used VM performs thread scheduling itself ("green threads"), which permits certain assumptions and direct access to thread states. Green threads are uncommon in modern Java VMs because of their disad-

vantages in systems with multiple CPUs. Our techniques have only slightly more overhead with the high-performance HotSpot VM and work well for multi-processor systems.

Zhuang et al. [25] describe a Java profiler that does not sample stack traces, but instead instruments the code to sample sequences ("bursts") of calls and returns, and uses heuristics to disable and re-enable sampling to reduce redundant samples. The resulting CCTs are claimed to have more than 80% hot-edge coverage and overlap with exhaustive CCTs, but the stated overhead of 20% for 10 ms sampling intervals is significantly higher than that of our techniques.

Binder [4] presents a Java profiler that instruments methods to maintain a shadow method stack and to periodically capture samples of this stack, which he claims is more accurate than JVMTI sampling. Unlike our techniques, this profiler can be implemented in pure Java, but its overhead is much higher and comparable to that of JVMTI sampling.

Inoue and Nakatani [14] describe a Java profiler that uses hardware events to take samples of only the executing method and its stack depth. It builds a CCT through matching stack depths and caller information, and is reported to achieve an overhead of 2.2% at 16000 samples per second. Similarly, Serrano et al. [20] present a Java profiler that uses hardware branch tracing to create partial call traces and attempt to merge them optimally into approximate CCTs, claiming to produce highly accurate CCTs at negligible overhead. Unlike our techniques, both of these techniques require specific hardware and their accuracy can suffer from caller ambiguity.

Dynamic analysis.

Calling context information is also useful for locating data races, memory leaks and other anomalies with dynamic analysis tools. Such tools capture the calling context frequently enough so that continuously maintaining the current calling context is often faster than walking the stack for each sample. Bond and McKinley [6] describe an approach in which they instrument code so that it continuously maintains a probabilistically unique number for the current calling context. This number is then sampled at certain points, such as calls to library methods. A dynamic analysis tool can then compare traces of these samples between executions of a program for anomaly detection. They claim that their approach has an overhead of 3% for such applications. Sumner et al. [23] describe a similar approach for encoding the calling context as a number and report an overhead of 2%. Huang and Bond [13] claim that the accuracy of such approaches does not scale well with program complexity and propose an approach that continuously builds a CCT-like data structure through instrumentation. It creates tree nodes eagerly and relies on a modified garbage collector to release unused nodes and to merge duplicate nodes. Using this technique to add calling context information to a memory leak detector or to a data race detector is claimed to introduce around 30-40% extra overhead. We believe that incremental stack tracing can achieve equivalent or less overhead than these techniques because it also does not walk the stack for each sample, but does not introduce overhead in methods where calling contexts are not needed.

Profile analysis.

The calling context trees of real-world applications can be very large and complex so that it can be difficult to identify performance bottlenecks in them. Moret et al. [17] as well as Adamoli and Hauswirth [1] describe approaches for visualizing and analyzing large and complex CCTs. D'Elia et al. [8] describe algorithms to continuously maintain a "Hot CCT" that includes only hot calling contexts. They claim that it is orders of magnitudes smaller than a regular CCT at comparable accuracy. These algorithms could be used with our sampling techniques to build a memory-efficient profiler. The low overheads of our techniques also make it feasible to enable them in an end-user product or in production systems to gather performance data for real-world usage. Han et al. [10] describe an approach to identify performance problems through pattern mining in vast amounts of performance data, which could be used to analyze data collected this way.

9. CONCLUSIONS AND FUTURE WORK

With partial safepoints, self-sampling and incremental stack tracing, we presented three novel techniques that reduce the overhead of sampling Java applications and allow a profiler to target just the running threads. Unlike many other fast profiling approaches, our techniques require no support from the operating system or from hardware. Experiments with our implementation in the HotSpot Java VM demonstrate that these techniques significantly reduce the sampling overhead while providing high accuracy.

In the future, we intend to look at improvements to the accuracy of Java profiling techniques. For example, when the JIT compiler eliminates safepoint checks to optimize hot code regions, it prevents profilers from taking samples in these regions, which can severely distort the profile of some programs. We consider introducing light-weight "sampling points" which make fewer guarantees about safety than safepoints and therefore do not obstruct compiler optimizations. Instead of eliminating a safepoint check, the JIT compiler could downgrade it to a sampling point check and still produce fast code. We have also experimented with using facilities of the operating system, such as POSIX signals, to interrupt individual threads for sampling with incremental stack tracing. However, patching return addresses on the stack is much more difficult and error-prone when a thread is not in a safepoint, and a correct implementation requires substantial modifications to the VM. Finally, we consider extending incremental stack tracing to track the values of variables. This should be possible at less runtime and space overhead than with exhaustive stack tracing and would be particularly valuable as input for profile-guided optimization.

10. ACKNOWLEDGEMENTS

This work was supported by the Christian Doppler Forschungsgesellschaft, and by Compuware Austria GmbH.

11. REFERENCES

[1] A. Adamoli and M. Hauswirth. Trevis: A context tree visualization & analysis framework and its use for classifying performance failure reports. SOFTVIS '10, pages 73–82. ACM, 2010.

[2] G. Ammons et al. Exploiting hardware performance counters with flow and context sensitive profiling. PLDI '97, pages 85–96. ACM, 1997.

[3] M. Arnold and D. Grove. Collecting and exploiting high-accuracy call graph profiles in virtual machines. CGO '05, pages 51–62. IEEE, 2005.

[4] W. Binder. Portable and accurate sampling profiling for Java. Software: Practice and Experience, 36(6):615–650, May 2006.

[5] S. M. Blackburn et al. The DaCapo benchmarks: Java benchmarking development and analysis. OOPSLA '06, pages 169–190. ACM, Oct. 2006.

[6] M. D. Bond and K. S. McKinley. Probabilistic calling context. OOPSLA '07, pages 97–112. ACM, 2007.

[7] A. M. Cheadle et al. Non-stop Haskell. SIGPLAN Notices, 35(9):257–267, Sept. 2000.

[8] D. C. D'Elia et al. Mining hot calling contexts in small space. PLDI '11, pages 516–527. ACM, 2011.

[9] P. T. Feller. Value profiling for instructions and memory locations. Master's thesis, UC San Diego, 1998.

[10] S. Han et al. Performance debugging in the large via mining millions of stack traces. ICSE '12, pages 145–155. IEEE, 2012.

[11] P. Hofer and H. Mössenböck. Efficient and accurate stack trace sampling in the Java Hotspot virtual machine. ICPE '14, pages 277–280. ACM, 2014.

[12] P. Hofer and H. Mössenböck. Fast Java profiling with scheduling-aware stack fragment sampling and asynchronous analysis. PPPJ '14, 2014. To appear.

[13] J. Huang and M. D. Bond. Efficient context sensitivity for dynamic analyses via calling context uptrees and customized memory management. OOPSLA '13, pages 53–72. ACM, 2013.

[14] H. Inoue and T. Nakatani. How a Java VM can get more from a hardware performance monitor. OOPSLA '09, pages 137–154. ACM, 2009.

[15] T. Kotzmann et al. Design of the Java HotSpot™ client compiler for Java 6. ACM Transactions on Architecture and Code Optimization, 5(1):7, 2008.

[16] P. Moret et al. CCCP: complete calling context profiling in virtual execution environments. PEPM '09, pages 151–160. ACM, 2009.

[17] P. Moret et al. Exploring large profiles with calling context ring charts. WOSP/SIPEW '10, pages 63–68. ACM, 2010.

[18] Oracle. JVM™ Tool Interface version 1.2.1. http://docs.oracle.com/javase/7/docs/platform/jvmti/jvmti.html.

[19] Oracle. OpenJDK HotSpot group. http://openjdk.java.net/groups/hotspot/.

[20] M. Serrano and X. Zhuang. Building approximate calling context from partial call traces. CGO '09, pages 221–230. IEEE, 2009.

[21] A. Sewe et al. Da Capo con Scala: design and analysis of a Scala benchmark suite for the Java virtual machine. OOPSLA '11, pages 657–676. ACM, 2011.

[22] L. Stadler et al. Lazy continuations for Java virtual machines. PPPJ '09, pages 143–152. ACM, 2009.

[23] W. N. Sumner et al. Precise calling context encoding. IEEE Trans. Softw. Eng., 38(5):1160–1177, Sept. 2012.

[24] J. Whaley. A portable sampling-based profiler for Java virtual machines. JAVA '00, pages 78–87. ACM, 2000.

[25] X. Zhuang et al. Accurate, efficient, and adaptive calling context profiling. PLDI '06, pages 263–271. ACM, 2006.

Sampling-based Steal Time Accounting under Hardware Virtualization

Peter Hofer
Christian Doppler Laboratory on Monitoring and Evolution of Very-Large-Scale Software Systems
Johannes Kepler University Linz, Austria
peter.hofer@jku.at

Florian Hörschläger
Johannes Kepler University Linz, Austria
florian.hoerschlaeger@jku.at

Hanspeter Mössenböck
Institute for System Software
Johannes Kepler University Linz, Austria
hanspeter.moessenboeck@jku.at

ABSTRACT

Virtualization enables the efficient sharing of hardware resources among multiple virtual machines (VMs). Because the
physical resources are limited, the scheduler must often suspend one VM to allow some other VM to run. The operating
system in a VM is typically unaware of the suspension and
accounts periods of suspension as CPU time to the executing
application thread. This misrepresentation of resource usage
makes it difficult to tell whether a performance problem is
caused by an actual bottleneck in the application or by the
virtualization infrastructure.

We present a novel approach to compute to what degree the
threads of an application in a virtual machine are affected by
suspension. Our approach does not require any modifications
to the operating system or to the virtualization software.
It periodically samples the system-wide amount of "steal
time" that is reported by the virtualization infrastructure,
and divides it among the monitored threads according to
their CPU usage. With a prototype implementation, we
demonstrate that our approach accounts accurate amounts
of steal time to application threads, that it can be used to
compute the true resource usage of an application, and that
it incurs only negligible performance overhead.

1. INTRODUCTION

Hardware virtualization is commonly used to efficiently
utilize and share hardware resources. The resources of a
physical machine (the *host*) are shared between several virtual
machines (the *guests*). The creation and execution of virtual
machines (VMs) is managed by a *hypervisor*. Each VM has
its own operating system that runs in an isolated execution
domain, which provides reliability and security. VMs can
also be deployed and moved between sites with less effort
than physical hardware.

The number of virtual CPUs of the guests can exceed
the number of physical CPUs of the host. Therefore, the
hypervisor cannot schedule all virtual CPUs on the available
physical CPUs and must temporarily suspend some of them.
Time periods when a virtual CPU is ready to execute, but is
suspended, are referred to as *steal time*.

The amount of steal time is an important indicator for
whether the assigned virtual resources are overprovisioned or
whether the physical resources are insufficient. However, the
operating system in the VM is often not aware of steal time
or does not incorporate it into resource usage accounting
because the concept of steal time does not exist with physical
hardware. When a virtual CPU is suspended, the steal
time is considered active CPU time and counted toward the
resource usage of the currently executing thread. Therefore,
it is difficult for a performance engineer to spot whether a
performance problem is caused by an actual bottleneck in
the application or by virtualization.

In this paper, we present an approach for how a performance analysis tool in an affected VM can estimate to what
degree steal time affects individual application threads. Our
approach relies on the hypervisor to provide the steal time
for the entire VM. We periodically sample this steal time as
well as the CPU usage of threads and then assign fractions
of the steal time to them.

The main contributions of this work-in-progress paper are:

1. We describe a new technique to attribute VM-wide
   steal time to individual application threads. It does
   not require any changes to the hypervisor or to the
   operating system.

2. We present a preliminary evaluation that demonstrates
   that we are able to reliably separate hypervisor steal
   time from the actual CPU usage of application threads
   at negligible performance costs.

2. APPROACH

Hypervisors commonly provide an interface that allows
the operating system or specific guest software in the VM
to detect that they are running in a VM and to interact
with the hypervisor, which can benefit the performance of
the VM. A hypervisor interface typically also exposes steal
time information. However, since the hypervisor has no

knowledge of the processes and threads running within the VM, it accounts steal time only to virtual CPUs as a whole. On this level, steal time is only useful to performance analysis tools as an indicator for how the entire system is affected by virtual CPU suspension.

Our approach works from within the VM and breaks down the steal time provided by the hypervisor to the monitored application threads. We base our approach on the fact that those threads which use the most CPU time (or, to which the most CPU time is attributed) are also the ones that are most affected by the suspension of virtual CPUs. Hence, we divide the steal time among the threads in proportion to the CPU time they have consumed.

When a VM has multiple virtual CPUs, we would ideally determine which threads were executed on each virtual CPU and divide that CPU's steal time among these threads. Unfortunately, common operating systems do not make scheduling information available. However, bare-metal hypervisors often employ a form of co-scheduling in which all virtual CPUs of a VM are scheduled to run on physical CPUs at the same time, which avoids problems such as when one virtual CPU waits for some other virtual CPU that is currently suspended by the hypervisor [1]. With such scheduling, all virtual CPUs of a VM are similarly affected by hypervisor steal time. Other hypervisors simply rely on the host operating system's scheduler, and a fair scheduler should ensure that one ready virtual CPU of a VM is not suspended significantly longer than others. Therefore, we sum up the steal time from all virtual CPUs of the VM and divide it among all threads that consumed CPU time.

The extent of hypervisor suspension in a VM also depends on the load in other VMs and on the host and thus varies over time. To account for this fact, we use a sampling approach and periodically read or compute the following values to account the steal time since the last sample:

$\Delta t_{steal,total}$: The total steal time of all virtual CPUs since the previous sample.

$\Delta t_{cpu,total}$: The total apparent CPU time (including steal time) that was consumed by the VM since the previous sample.

$\Delta t_{cpu}(T)$: The apparent CPU time (including steal time) that was consumed by thread T since the last sample.

The hypervisor and the operating system typically make steal times and CPU times available as total times since the start of the VM or since the start of the thread. Computing the deltas between samples thus requires storing the values that were read in the previous sample. We then use the deltas between samples to divide the steal time among the monitored threads using the following equation for each thread T:

$$\Delta t_{steal}(T) = \Delta t_{steal,total} \frac{\Delta t_{cpu}(T)}{\Delta t_{cpu,total}}$$

The steal time of a process can be computed the same way when the operating system provides a per-process CPU usage that includes all threads. Alternatively, the steal time of each thread of the process can be computed individually and added up, but this can lead to inaccuracies when threads exit between samples.

Figure 1 shows an example of how our approach works in a schedule with three threads $T_{1,2,3}$ executing on three virtual

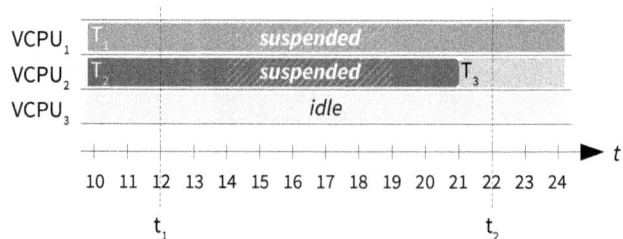

Figure 1: Schedule with three threads on three virtual CPUs

processors $VCPU_{1,2,3}$. Initially, $VCPU_1$ is executing thread T_1, $VCPU_2$ is executing T_2, and $VCPU_3$ is idle. At $t_1 = 12$, we take a first sample. Because we do not have a previous sample, we cannot compute deltas at this point and do not account steal time to the threads. At $t = 14$, the hypervisor suspends both $VCPU_1$ and $VCPU_2$ until it resumes them at $t = 19$. At $t = 21$, the operating system schedules out T_2 on $VCPU_2$ and executes T_3. Finally, at $t_2 = 22$, we take a second sample and compute the deltas to the first sample as follows:

$$\Delta t_{cpu}(T_1) = 10 \qquad \Delta t_{cpu}(T_2) = 9 \qquad \Delta t_{cpu}(T_3) = 1$$
$$\Delta t_{cpu,total} = 10 + 9 + 1 = 20$$
$$\Delta t_{steal,total} = 5 + 5 = 10$$

The time during which the virtual CPUs were suspended is accounted as CPU time to the scheduled threads because the operating system does not consider steal time in its CPU time accounting. Note that $VCPU_3$ was idle, so it does not contribute any steal time, although it was technically suspended. Our approach now computes the following steal times for the individual threads:

$$\Delta t_{steal}(T_1) = 10\frac{10}{20} = 5 \qquad \Delta t_{steal}(T_2) = 10\frac{9}{20} = 4.5$$
$$\Delta t_{steal}(T_3) = 10\frac{1}{20} = 0.5$$

Therefore, T_1 is assigned the correct amount of steal time. Although T_3 was not affected by suspension, it is assigned a small portion of the steal time because it was scheduled briefly at the end of the sampling period. For the same reason, T_2 is assigned slightly less than the actual amount of suffered steal time. However, we expect that such deviations become insignificant with frequent samples.

3. IMPLEMENTATION

We implemented a prototype of our approach that computes the steal time of all threads of a Java application running in a Linux guest under a Linux host with the Kernel-based Virtual Machine (KVM, [7]) as a hypervisor. To integrate our prototype with the Java virtual machine (JVM), we implemented it as an agent that uses the Java VM Tool Interface (JVMTI, [9]).

Linux exposes information about the resource usage of the system, its processes, and its threads via the *procfs* pseudo-filesystem, which is typically mapped to */proc*. The

/proc/stat file provides the resource usage of the entire system, which is broken down into CPU time spent executing application code, CPU time spent in the operating system (mostly on behalf of an application), steal time, and idle time. These times are given in clock ticks since the start of the operating system. Unlike for threads, the system-wide CPU times exclude the steal time. We therefore compute $t_{cpu,total}$ as the sum of all times except the idle time, and use the provided steal time as $t_{steal,total}$. We then use the stored values from the last sample to compute $\Delta t_{cpu,total}$ and $\Delta t_{steal,total}$.

The CPU time of an individual process is available in its */proc/[pid]/stat* file, where *[pid]* is the numeric process identifier. The CPU time of a specific thread of a process is available in */proc/[pid]/task/[tid]*, where *[tid]* is the thread identifier. The times are given in clock ticks since the start of the thread and split up into "regular" user-space ticks and in system ticks. System ticks are time spent in the operating system on behalf of the application. In our implementation, we do not distinguish between user-space ticks and system ticks. Whenever we take a sample, we take their sum and compare it to the stored sum from the last sample to get $\Delta t_{cpu,total}(x)$.

Our JVMTI agent is loaded by the JVM at startup time. During initialization, we create data structures to store the tick counts from /proc that are required to compute the deltas, and to store the accounted steal time for each thread. Our agent registers for JVMTI events so that it is notified when application threads start and end. This enables us to create a record for a thread when it starts and to stop monitoring a thread (but keep its record) when it ends.

When the application is launched, our agent starts a separate thread with a sampling loop. In this loop, we periodically retrieve the system-wide tick counts as well as the tick counts for all existing application threads. We then compute the deltas using the stored values from our records, account the new steal time to the threads, and update our records. At the end of an iteration, the sampling loop pauses for the sampling interval before it takes another sample and attributes the new steal time.

4. EVALUATION

We used our prototype implementation to evaluate the accuracy and the overhead of our approach. We set up KVM virtualization under openSUSE Linux 13.1 on a computer with a quad-core Intel Core i7-4770 processor with 16 GB of memory. To get more stable results, we disabled the hyperthreading, turbo boost and dynamic frequency scaling features. With the exception of essential system services, no other processes were running during our measurements.

We relied on the DaCapo suite [2] for our tests, which consists of non-trivial benchmarks with different multi-threading characteristics[1]. The workload of the benchmarks is constant, so the consumed CPU times are similar between executions. Therefore, we test whether subtracting the accounted steal time results in a similar CPU time as when the benchmarks are not subjected to hypervisor suspension. However, because most benchmarks use thread pools to divide work between threads, the CPU time of individual benchmark threads can vary between executions. Therefore, we compared the total

---

[1]We did not use the DaCapo suite's *batik* and *eclipse* benchmarks because they do not run on OpenJDK 8.

CPU time of all benchmark threads (but excluding threads of the JVM and the sampling thread).

First, we created a VM with four virtual CPUs and installed openSUSE Linux 13.1 and the Oracle Java SDK 8u20 in it. We then executed the DaCapo benchmarks with our JVMTI agent, which we configured to take samples every 50 milliseconds. To reduce the impact of the startup phase of the JVM, we executed 10 successive *iterations* of every benchmark in a single JVM instance. We recorded the total CPU times of all benchmark threads over all iterations. We further executed multiple *rounds* of each benchmark (with 10 iterations each) and took the median total CPU time.

Next, we created a second, identical VM which only executes a tool that continuously generates artificial CPU load by computing checksums in four threads. Therefore, both VMs continuously compete with each other for physical CPU time, and the hypervisor is forced to suspend virtual CPUs. We started this tool in the benchmarking VM as well, so that the suspension of its virtual CPUs affects not only the benchmark threads. Instead, depending on the multi-threading characteristics of each benchmark and on scheduling, suspension affects the benchmark threads and the tool's threads to different degrees over time, which is more likely to expose inaccuracies in our steal time accounting approach. Using this setup, we repeated our measurements.

4.1 Corrected CPU Times

Figure 2 shows the corrected and uncorrected median total CPU times of all application threads for each benchmark. The values of each benchmark are normalized to its median CPU time without extra load. The error bars indicate the 5th and 95th percentiles. The figure demonstrates that the corrected CPU times under load are commonly within a few percent of the CPU times in an idle environment, whereas the uncorrected CPU times under load are typically around twice as large as the CPU times in the idle environment. In some cases, our prototype accounts too much steal time, such as for *avrora* or *tradebeans*. For other benchmarks, the steal time is underestimated, such as for *tomcat*, *tradesoap* and *lusearch*. The reasons seem to be more complex than just differences between the multi-threading characteristics of the benchmarks, because *tradebeans* and *tradesoap* are identical in that regard, but show opposite results. We are investigating these deviations in our ongoing work.

4.2 Overhead

We measured the overhead of our approach by comparing the wall-clock execution times of each benchmark when our agent is enabled and when the agent is not enabled. We performed these measurements in an otherwise idle VM, with no other VMs running. Figure 3 shows the normalized median overheads and the 5th and 95th percentiles for all benchmarks. *fop*, *lusearch* and *sunflow* show a slight median overhead between 0.5% and 1.5%. For *avrora*, *h2* and *tradebeans*, the total execution times with the agent enabled are even 1% to 5% smaller than without the agent, which probably comes from effects that the agent's sampling thread has on scheduling. The other benchmarks did not show any distinctive changes in execution time. The geometric mean of the execution times with steal time accounting is 99.2% of that without steal time accounting. Therefore, we consider the overhead of our approach negligible or even non-existent.

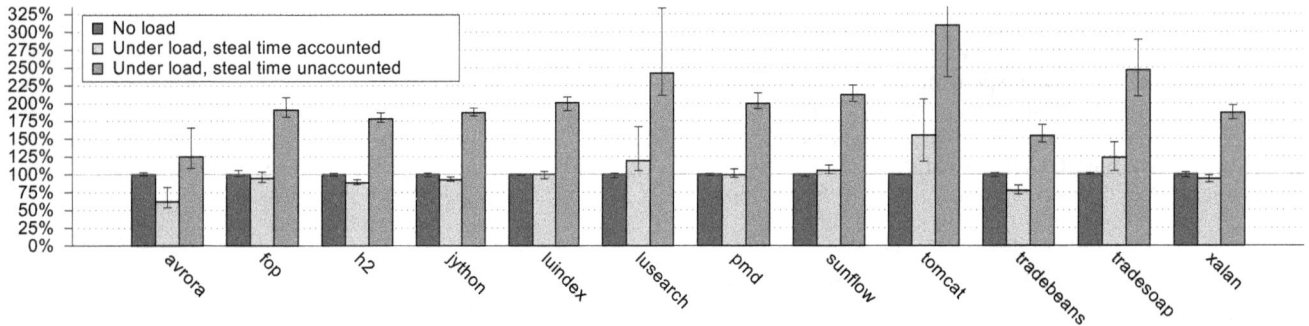

Figure 2: Normalized total CPU time of all application threads with and without accounted steal time

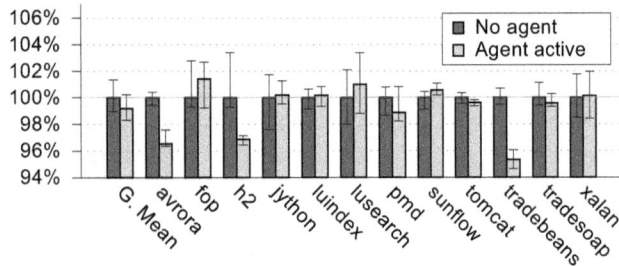

Figure 3: Overhead of the agent

5. RELATED WORK

Timing issues in VMs have been investigated before. Lampe et al. measured the impact of inaccurate timing in publicly available cloud computing services [8]. Johnson et al. describe extensions to the Performance API (PAPI) project which provide more accurate timers and shared resource usage statistics in VMs [5]. However, these extensions only provide system-wide steal time information, and the paper emphasizes the need for per-process steal time accounting. Chen et al. describe a modification to the Xen hypervisor that delivers hypervisor scheduling events to a modified guest operating system which then uses them to correctly account steal time to processes and threads [3]. M. Holzheu proposed a patch for the Linux kernel that detects increases of the per-CPU steal time and accounts them to the scheduled processes and threads [4]. Both approaches require modifications to the operating system or hypervisor, while our approach does not.

6. CONCLUSIONS AND FUTURE WORK

We described a novel approach for determining to what degree application threads in a virtual machine are affected when the hypervisor suspends virtual CPUs. Our approach does not require any modifications to the hypervisor or to the operating system. We implemented our approach for Java applications in a Linux guest with KVM as the hypervisor. An evaluation with the DaCapo benchmarks demonstrated that our approach accurately accounts the system-wide steal time to the application threads at negligible overhead, and that the accounted steal time can be used to compute the application's true execution time on a physical CPU.

As next steps, we plan to extend our prototype with the capability to track *transactions* that execute within a thread, such as individual web requests. Measuring the duration

and resource usage of transactions is a central feature of Application Performance Monitoring (APM) systems such as that from our industry partner Compuware [10]. Suspension can considerably distort these measurements because of the typically short execution time of transactions.

Furthermore, we plan to develop a test suite that generates different deterministic load patterns that we can use to validate our approach in more detail. We also plan to examine the effect of the sampling rate on the accuracy, particularly with different load scenarios. We further consider experimenting with scheduling traces from the Linux perf subsystem [6] for validation.

7. ACKNOWLEDGEMENTS

This work was supported by the Christian Doppler Forschungsgesellschaft, and by Compuware Austria GmbH.

8. REFERENCES

[1] The CPU scheduler in VMware vSphere 5.1. VMware Inc., 2013.

[2] S. M. Blackburn et al. The DaCapo benchmarks: Java benchmarking development and analysis. OOPSLA '06, pages 169–190. ACM, Oct. 2006.

[3] H. Chen et al. XenHVMAcct: Accurate CPU Time Accounting for Hardware-Assisted Virtual Machine. *2010 International Conference on Parallel and Distributed Computing, Applications and Technologies*, pages 191–198, Dec. 2010.

[4] M. Holzheu. [RFC][PATCH v2 4/7] taskstats: Add per task steal time accounting. https://lkml.org/lkml/2010/11/11/271, 2010.

[5] M. Johnson et al. PAPI-V: Performance monitoring for virtual machines. In *ICPP Workshops*, pages 194–199, 2012.

[6] kernel.org. perf: Linux profiling with performance counters. https://perf.wiki.kernel.org/.

[7] A. Kivity et al. KVM: the Linux virtual machine monitor. In *Linux Symposium*, volume 1, pages 225–230, 2007.

[8] U. Lampe et al. The Virtual Margin of Error. *Proc. of CLOSER, 2012*, 2012.

[9] Oracle. JVM^TM Tool Interface version 1.2.1. http://docs.oracle.com/javase/7/docs/platform/jvmti/jvmti.html.

[10] A. Reitbauer et al. *Java Enterprise Performance*. 2012.

Landscaping Performance Research at the ICPE and its Predecessors: A Systematic Literature Review

Alexandru Danciu, Johannes Kroß,
Andreas Brunnert, Felix Willnecker,
Christian Vögele
fortiss GmbH
Guerickestr. 25, 80805 Munich, Germany
{danciu,kross,brunnert,
willnecker,voegele}@fortiss.org

Anand Kapadia, Helmut Krcmar
Chair for Information Systems
Technische Universität München
Boltzmannstr. 3
85748 Garching, Germany
{kapadia,krcmar}@in.tum.de

ABSTRACT

This paper conducts a systematic literature review of papers published in the proceedings of the International Conference on Performance Engineering (ICPE) and its predecessors. It provides an overview of prevailing topics within the community over time. We look at research and contribution facets that have been used to address these topics. Trends are outlined in terms of evaluation methods to validate contributions. The results are complemented with a geographical and organizational dimension. The paper concludes with a look at the top ten contributing countries and organizations for this purpose.

Categories and Subject Descriptors

A.1 [**Introductory and Survey**]; C.4 [**Performance of Systems**]

General Terms

Performance, Theory

Keywords

Systematic Literature Review, Performance Engineering, ICPE, WOSP, SIPEW, Performance Research

1. INTRODUCTION

Many researchers and industry practitioners around the globe have dedicated themselves to performance engineering, due to the complexity of this subject [5]. As a consequence, various workshops and conferences specialized on this field have been established. The principle conference that is focused on the performance of software systems and related questions is the International Conference on Performance Engineering (ICPE). The ICPE was established as a joint meeting of the ACM Workshop on Software and

Performance (WOSP) and the SPEC International Performance Evaluation Workshop (SIPEW). In the scope of this conference, domain experts are invited to present and discuss state-of-the-art research results concerning performance measurement, modeling techniques, benchmark design and run-time performance management [1, 2, 3, 4, 11].

Although research in the field of performance engineering is not in its infancy anymore and numerous papers have already been published, a general overview of prevailing topics and methods within the community does not exist. To the best of our knowledge, there has not been any effort to systematically select, synthesize and review existing literature within the ICPE and its predecessors. Therefore, this gap is addressed in this work.

Performance engineering research at the ICPE and its predecessors is analyzed in a systematic literature review. The first WOSP took place in 1998 followed by six WOSP, one SIPEW and five ICPE events at the time of writing this paper. This work analyzes the proceedings of all these events and captures sixteen years of performance engineering research in total.

2. METHODOLOGY

The systematic literature review in this work is conducted following the guidelines provided by Kitchenham and Charters [8]. According to them, a systematic literature review is a "[...] means of identifying, evaluating and interpreting all available research relevant to a particular research question, or topic area, or phenomenon of interest".

2.1 Research Questions

The initial task in a systematic literature review according to Kitchenham and Charters [8] is the definition of research questions (RQ). RQs in general are central drivers of this research methodology and consequently influence the research process heavily. As part of our study, the following three RQs will be answered:

- **RQ 1: Which topics have been addressed in the papers published at the ICPE (respectively at its predecessors) in the time period from 1998 to 2014?**

The goal of this RQ is to get an overview of different subjects that have been published and discussed at the ICPE, WOSP and SIPEW. Therefore, we investigate which specific topics are addressed more frequently by published papers and how this focus has shifted over the years. The answer for this RQ can be found in Section 3.1.

- **RQ 2: Which research facets, contribution facets and evaluation methods have been used in papers published at the ICPE and its predecessors?**

To answer this research question an overview of research and contribution facets is given in Section 3.2. This helps to get an overview of how researchers try to tackle topics outlined in Section 3.1. Furthermore, evaluation methods are outlined in Section 3.3 that have been used to validate different contribution types. Over the years, different types of evaluation methods have been established in the performance engineering domain. In this paper, methods are analyzed in terms of frequency, applicability to a certain topic and popularity within the performance engineering community.

- **RQ 3: Who are the top ten countries and organizations in terms of the quantity of articles published at the ICPE and its predecessors?**

RQ 3 aims to identify how papers published in the proceedings of the ICPE are distributed among countries and organizations. The resulting analysis includes research and publication activity, from these countries and organizations, at the ICPE and its predecessors from 1998 to 2014. First, the geographical perspective is outlined in Section 3.4. Second, the organizational perspective is adressed in Section 3.5.

2.2 Data Sources and Paper Selection

Only papers that have been published at the ICPE, WOSP and SIPEW were considered in a first step. The initial set of papers contained 471 publications in total. It was predominantly available online in the ACM Digital Library[1] and SpringerLink[2]. Papers with illegible writing due to formatting issues such as overlapping characters were replaced. The replacements were taken from other digital libraries and were then checked on correspondence in order to avoid distorting the outcomes.

After having set a solid base for the research by establishing an initial set of papers, the set needed to be filtered to acquire meaningful results. The filter process was divided into two steps which had been specified with different goals and exclusion criteria. The first exclusion criterion (EC1) to be applied was the removal of all invited talks, keynote addresses and editorial articles, as they did not provide any further benefit for this research. By doing so the initial set could be reduced to 448 papers.

For this research, great focus was set on prevailing topics and evaluation methods. Therefore, the published papers were analyzed in terms of giving information on the formulated RQs which could mainly be found in research, industrial and work-in-progress/vision tracks. As a consequence, all demonstration papers, posters and tutorials were removed from the set (EC2). Papers published in workshops that were held alongside with the ICPE are also not considered. This reduced the set to 388 papers.

After the initial selection of papers, the next step in the systematic literature review is to assess the quality of the primary studies [8]. However, as our goal is to provide a complete overview of the conference, we did not exclude any papers based on quality assessment scores. That is why all 388 papers have ultimately been moved to the data extraction process.

2.3 Data Extraction and Synthesis

Data was extracted from a total of 388 included papers. Due to space limitations, we provide an online accessible list of the papers on our website[3] instead of in this paper. We created a data extraction scheme in an Excel spreadsheet with respect to the previously stated RQs. This proved to be a necessary step as we could easily compute frequencies, filter for relevant information and analyze relationships between the different RQ findings. The scheme is divided into different sections. It contains generic (paper ID, title, authors, type of report, year, conference) as well as specific information (organization, evaluation method, contribution facet, research type facet, lifecycle phase, domain, system under study).

3. RESULTS

In this section results of the systematic literature review are presented. The research questions outlined in Section 2 are answered in a chronological order.

3.1 Topics at the ICPE

Obtaining a deep understanding of topics discussed at a conference and the evolution of these topics over several years is a difficult task. New technologies and trends have a constant influence on topics addressed by researchers. Thus, the focus of the conference is shifting from year to year. The N-Gram analysis is employed in this section to provide a solution to this problem and reveal trends within the conference from 1998 to 2014 [12, 6].

An N-Gram analysis is a technique used in the field of natural language processing for identifying the frequency of the occurrence of words or combinations of words [9]. An N-Gram represents a sequence of n words which is extracted from a body of text. For example, the phrase "software performance management" can be divided into three 1-Grams ("software", "performance", "management"), two 2-Grams ("software performance", "performance management"), and one 3-Gram ("software performance management").

In order to perform the analysis we follow the approach of Soper and Turel [12] and first establish a corpus of text. The corpus consists of the collection of 388 selected articles. All articles were available as PDF documents. We converted each document to a parsable text file. In order to prevent distortion of results we removed in several post-processing steps any unnecessary data such as author information, keyword lists, the bibliography, the appendix, page numbers and citation references. The resulting text files were then grouped by the year of the publication to enable an analysis run for each conference edition.

The N-Gram analysis is supported by a variety of tools. We used the freeware tool AntConc[4] because it is easy to use and well documented. For each analysis run, the user can specify the minimum and a maximum length of N-Grams to be considered. When a sequence of words occurs more frequent than a single word, the sequence receives a higher rank within the analysis results. The results provided by the tool consist of the absolute frequency of each N-Gram. Since

---

[1]http://dl.acm.org/
[2]http://link.springer.com/

[3]http://pmw.fortiss.org/research/icpe/
[4]http://www.antlab.sci.waseda.ac.jp/software.html

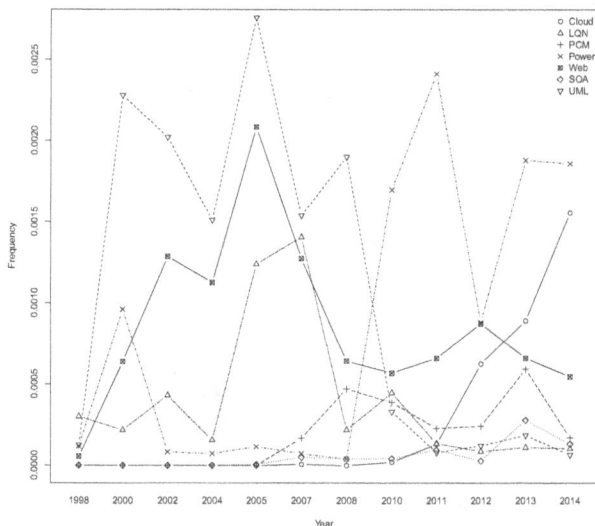

Figure 1: Frequency of terms

the relevance of each N-Gram depends on the size of the text corpus, we calculate relative frequencies and, thus, make the results for each conference edition comparable. Multiple occurrences of the same N-Gram within one article are counted separately. Since word classes such as articles are among the most frequent ones, a filtering needs to be performed to select only content-relevant keywords.

We first performed an analysis for each conference edition to include N-Grams with a minimum length of $n=1$ to include the most frequent keywords and maximum length of $n=4$ to limit the expense for the calculation. The most frequent N-Grams identified during the analysis have a length of $n=1$. However, some of the highest ranked results are of limited value for describing topics addressed by the research. Therefore, words such as *performance, system, software, server, model* or *data* were not considered. The frequency of the occurrence of these keywords remains constant over all conference editions[5]. Some of the most relevant topics and their evolution over time are shown in Figure 1.

The terms *Power* and *Cloud* are among the most frequent N-Grams in 2014. The frequency of the term *Power* first peaked in 2000 and then increased significantly after 2008. The term *Cloud* was first used in 2007 in a context different than cloud computing. Only in 2010 the term was first used in this context and its frequency continued to increase every year. During the transition from WOSP/SIPEW to ICPE between 2008 and 2010 only the terms *Power* and *UML* display a significant change.

To gain more insight on the conference topics we performed a second N-Gram analysis to include N-Grams with a minimum length of $n=2$ and maximum length of $n=4$. The top ten most frequent word combinations identified for each

year at the WOSP/SIPEW and the ICPE are are shown in Tables 1 and 2. The values displayed in the tables represent relative frequencies. Among the most frequent N-Grams in 2014 are *Energy Consumption* and *Power Consumption* having an absolute frequency of 155 and 87 respectively. While used during every edition since 2002, the term *Garbage Collection* is included in 2014 for the first time in the top ten list having 58 occurrences.

3.2 Research and Contribution Facets

This section outlines different kinds of research and contribution facets of papers published in the WOSP/SIPEW and ICPE proceedings. It broadens the understanding of how researchers tried to address topics outlined in Section 3.1. Petersen et al. [10] propose a systematic map to classify and structure studies and their fields in the area of software engineering. For their map and its visualization they categorize studies in the following three different facets:

- Variability context facet - categorization for different topics among studies
- Research facet - classification for the type of research such as evaluations, proposals or experience papers
- Contribution facet - attribution of papers' outcomes such as tools or models

Since we have already analyzed major topics in Section 3.1, the focus here lies on the research and contribution facets. For the research facet, Petersen et al. [10] differentiate between the following research types:

- Validation research - assessment of new techniques with example experiments
- Solution proposal - suggestion of a solution for an existing issue
- Philosophical paper - taxonomy or framework for existing subjects
- Experience paper - personal experience and guide for techniques in practice
- Evaluation research - assessment of already implemented techniques
- Opinion paper - personal opinion about methods and techniques

These categories are used to classify all papers that are included according to our selection in Section 2.2. The results are illustrated in Figure 2. If multiple research types were covered by a given paper, only the focused aspect was considered for the classification. Similarly to Petersen et al. [10], they are presented in a bubble chart showing the number of papers for each category with a corresponding bubble size. The research facets are aggregated per year to give an indication about the progress. Evaluation and validation research are the most common types with a total amount of 109 and 113 each and constantly appear over the years. Solution proposals are also very frequent since the second WOSP in 2000.

Petersen et al. [10] also considered the contribution facet of papers. Such contributions facets are methods, metrics, models, processes or tools [10]. All papers are classified according to their contribution facet. Since multiple papers contain two contribution facets and, thus, are counted twice, the total number of contribution types does not represent the total amount of papers. The results are presented in Figure 3. As before, a bubble chart is used to illustrate the amount of occurrences of each contribution in relation to the year.

---

[5]In 2008, the WOSP and SIPEW were held separately. Due to different profiles of the two workshops, subsuming the papers of both events to one text corpus would not provide consistent results. To avoid a disruption in the course of trends over time the two conferences cannot be both considered separately for the year 2008. Therefore, the SPIEW 2008 was not considered here.

Table 1: Most frequent keyword combinations at the WOSP/SIPEW (values need to be multiplied by 10^{-3})

WOSP 1998		WOSP 2000		WOSP 2002		WOSP 2004	
Queueing Network	0.619	Performance Model	0.792	Response Time	1.459	Response Time	0.644
Software Architecture	0.619	Software System	0.647	Performance Model	0.674	Web Service	0.452
Response Time	0.603	Execution Time	0.485	Autonomous Service	0.514	Performance Analysis	0.431
Task Graph	0.595	Software Architecture	0.477	Performance Analysis	0.409	Performance Model	0.369
Service Time	0.532	Performance Engineering	0.429	Real Time	0.393	Software Performance	0.333
Performance Requirements	0.453	Performance Analysis	0.38	Sequence Diagram	0.382	Operational Profile	0.322
Server Subsystem	0.373	Object Oriented	0.356	Use Case	0.382	Component based	0.312
Mean Service	0.357	Optimal Shutdown	0.356	Web Server	0.371	Class Diagram	0.307
Component Model	0.342	Response Time	0.356	Data Structure	0.321	Content Location	0.27
Use Case	0.334	Service Time	0.348	Data Flow	0.293	Software Component	0.265
WOSP 2005		**WOSP 2007**		**WOSP 2008**		**SIPEW 2008**	
Performance Model	1.308	Response Time	1.143	Performance Model	1	Response Time	1.444
Response Time	0.709	Web Service(s)	0.835	Performance Analysis	0.643	User Behavior	0.565
Software Performance	0.675	Performance Model	0.557	Execution Time	0.634	SPEC CPU	0.532
UML Model	0.579	Queueing Network	0.543	Case Study	0.569	Timing Behavior	0.532
Software System	0.552	LQN Model	0.543	Use Case	0.561	Calling Context	0.5
Redundant Computation	0.539	Performance Engineering	0.44	Software Performance	0.513	Resource Demands	0.424
Software Archtecture	0.396	Service Time	0.418	Performance Modeling	0.48	Context Analysis	0.413
Web Service	0.396	Business Process	0.403	Response Time	0.472	Composite Service	0.402
Acitivity Diagram	0.327	Performance Analysis	0.359	Meta Model	0.391	Trace Context	0.402
Covering Arrays	0.327	Execution Time	0.352	Model Transformation	0.358	Behavior Model	0.391

Table 2: Most frequent keyword combinations at the ICPE (values need to be multiplied by 10^{-3})

ICPE 2010		ICPE 2011		ICPE 2012		ICPE 2013		ICPE 2014	
Response Time	0.842	Response Time	0.66	Response Time	0.694	Response Time	0.963	Energy Consumption	0.856
Non Determinism	0.67	Power Consumption	0.512	File System	0.544	Energy Consumption	0.739	Performance Model	0.685
Page Coloring	0.54	Performance Model	0.403	Software Performance	0.326	Live Migration	0.605	Load Test	0.619
Calling Context	0.439	Power Savings	0.367	Control Charts	0.306	Performance Model	0.534	Power Consumption	0.481
Execution Time	0.425	Product Form	0.358	Web Server	0.292	Performance Regression	0.437	Response Time	0.481
Power Consumption	0.353	Execution Time	0.351	Software System	0.263	Power Consumption	0.355	Execution Time	0.436
Workload Intensity	0.317	Data Center	0.348	Stack Distance	0.263	Time Series	0.348	System Performance	0.381
Data Item	0.288	Delay Tolerant	0.261	Access Control	0.258	Web Server	0.262	Performance Degradation	0.376
Performance Model	0.26	Delay Sensitive	0.232	Monitoring Mechanism	0.238	System Architect	0.239	Performance Metrics	0.359
Performance Signature	0.238	System Performance	0.229	Data Access	0.219	System Performance	0.239	Garbage Collection	0.321

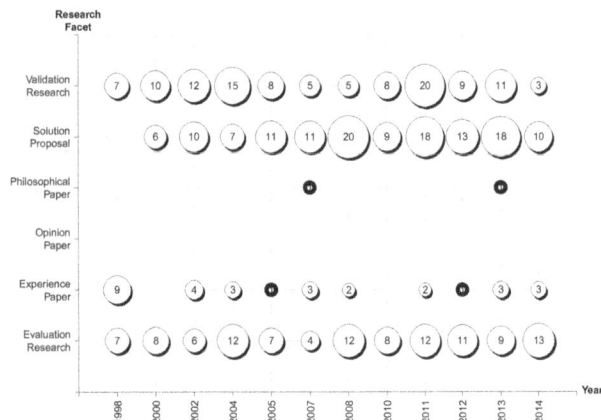

Figure 2: Research facets

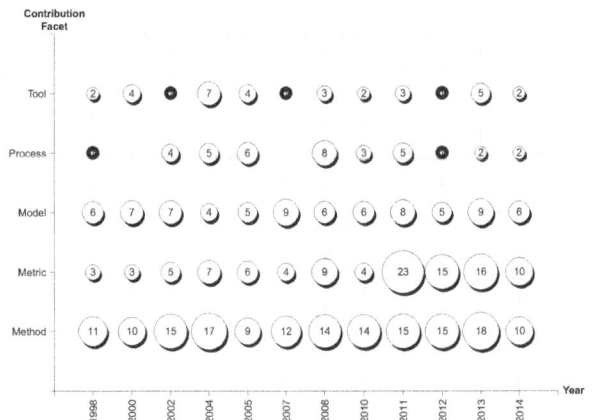

Figure 3: Contribution facets

The results show that each contribution facet is appearing at almost every edition. However, tools as well as processes are the minority group and occur several times not at all or only once per year. Methods represent the majority group and are contributed in 160 papers.

3.3 Evaluation Methods

In this section we investigate evaluation methods used for research and contribution facets outlined in the previous section. The methods are categorized according to the design science theory of Hevner et al. [7]. This theory categorizes evaluation methods based on the validation of IT artifacts. Each of these categories are described in Table 3. According to Hevner et al. [7], these "IT artifacts can be evaluated in terms of functionality, completeness, consistency, accuracy, performance, reliability, usability, fit with the organization, and other relevant quality attributes". All papers are categorized according to these methods and the results are presented in Figure 4. The categorization is based on the evaluation type mentioned by authors of a paper. If multiple evaluation methods were applied in a given paper, only the focused method was considered for the classification.

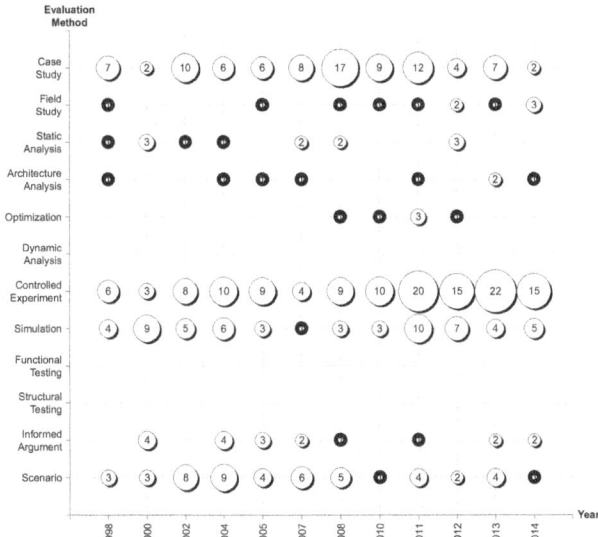

Figure 4: Evaluation methods

Table 3: Design evaluation methods [7]

Category	Method	Paper
1. Observational	**Case Study**: Study artifact in depth in business environment	90
	Field Study: Monitor use of artifact in multiple projects	11
2. Analytical	**Static Analysis**: Examine structure of artifact for static qualities (e.g., complexity)	13
	Architecture Analysis: Study fit of artifact into technical information system architecture	8
	Optimization: Demonstrate inherent optimal properties of artifact or provide optimality bounds on artifact behavior	6
	Dynamic Analysis: Study artifact in use for dynamic qualities (e.g., performance)	0
3. Experimental	**Controlled Experiment**: Study artifact in controlled environment for qualities (e.g., usability)	131
	Simulation: Execute artifact with artificial data	60
4. Testing	**Functional (Black Box) Testing**: Execute artifact interfaces to discover failures and identify defects	0
	Structural (White Box) Testing: Perform coverage testing of some metric (e.g., execution paths) in the artifact implementation	0
5. Descriptive	**Informed Argument**: Use information from the knowledge base (e.g., relevant research) to build a convincing argument for the artifact's utility	19
	Scenarios: Construct detailed scenarios around the artifact to demonstrate its utility	50

The ICPE submissions can be categorized into nine out of twelve distinct evaluation methods: case studies, field studies, static analysis, architecture analysis, optimizations, controlled experiments, simulations, informed arguments and scenarios. No paper was submitted using one of the three remaining categories: functional testing, structural testing and dynamic analysis. It is important to note that Hevner et al. [7] refer to the performance of the artifact itself when he talks about dynamic analysis (e.g., performance). Thus, he does not refer to the performance of a system that is analyzed using the artifact.

The controlled experiment is the most popular evaluation method. 131 of 388 (34%) categorized papers used this evaluation method. The case study is equally popular with a maximum of 17 publications in 2008 and 90 publications (23%) in total. The interest in contributing research with this evaluation method decreases slowly while controlled experiments became more popular recently. A similar development can be observed for scenario based evaluations; both seem to get unpopular while controlled experiments are rising. Today, the most common methods (controlled experiments and case studies) count for over 55% of all papers.

Simulations were popular in the beginning and got a small renaissance in 2011. In the years from 2004 to 2010, this evaluation method was not very popular with only one to three papers per year. In the last years, the interest in simulation based evaluations is again slowly decreasing.

Informed arguments and static analysis are very exotic for ICPE papers. Field studies are rare, even if this method is used more frequently in 2014. We only found eight papers using architecture analysis as evaluation method and six papers in total using optimizations. We see that evaluation methods are more popular that rely on only one artifact, like case studies and controlled experiments. This evaluation popularity is related to the contribution facet of papers submitted to the ICPE. As seen in Section 3.2, model and method contributions are very popular. Such contributions require a case study or experiment as an evaluation. Process or tool contributions are easier evaluated in a field study for example but these contribution types are rare for the ICPE and its predecessors.

3.4 Geographical Perspective

A large number of different countries have contributed to publications over the years. In summary, 33 countries have been involved. Table 4 shows the top ten countries ranked by their total amount of publications. The metric publications includes exclusive as well as joint publications. If, for instance, one paper was published by three authors from USA and one from Germany, the number of publications will be increased by one for both countries since authors from both countries contributed to the publication. Therefore, the total amount of publications in Table 4 is not equal to the total amount of publications of all editions. Furthermore, the share of each country to the total amount of papers is listed.

Table 4: Top 10 contributing countries

Rank	Country	Publications	Share	Cooperation
1	USA	130	33.51%	40
2	Germany	67	17.27%	23
3	Canada	61	15.72%	12
4	Italy	52	13.40%	23
5	UK	41	10.57%	14
6	Spain	20	5.15%	13
7	Australia	9	2.32%	2
	Netherlands	9	2.32%	5
	India	9	2.32%	2
	Switzerland	9	2.32%	5

The first rank is represented by USA with 130 publications followed with a large distance by Germany and Canada with 67 and 61 publications respectively. An analysis of the number of papers published by countries hosting the ICPE indicates that hosting countries publish more papers that on average. Except for three events, the host countries have published twice as many papers than usual.

95

As publications include joint publications between countries, the number of papers in cooperation is listed in Table 4 as well. A remarkable value is presented by Canada, which counts 12 joint publications and, thus, presents the lowest proportion of papers in cooperation in relation to their publications with 20%. In contrast, Spain contributed 13 papers in cooperation and, therefore, has the biggest proportion with 65%.

3.5 Organizational Perspective

The evaluation of the research activity from an organizational perspective is performed in a similar way as in Section 3.4. Table 5 lists the top 10 contributing organizations ranked by the amount of publications. Its listed metrics publications, share and cooperation are defined in the same way as in Table 4, only applied to organizations instead of countries.

Carleton University constitutes the first rank with 38 publications. Rank two and three are placed by Karlsruhe Institute of Technology (KIT) and University of L'Aquila with 24 and 20 publications followed by Imperial College London and University of Rome Tor Vergata with 16 and 12 publications on rank four and five. Beginning from rank six, the remaining organizations count less than ten publications. Although the USA is ranked first by the number of publications, none of the top six organizations belongs to this country.

Table 5: Top 10 contributing organizations

Rank	Organization	Country	Publications	Share	Cooperation
1	Carleton University	Canada	38	9.79%	12
2	Karlsruhe Institute of Technology	Germany	24	6.19%	18
3	University of L'Aquila	Italy	20	5.15%	14
4	Imperial College London	UK	16	4.12%	3
5	University of Rome Tor Vergata	Italy	12	3.09%	5
6	University of Zaragoza	Spain	9	2.32%	4
7	AT&T Labs	USA	8	2.06%	3
7	Hewlett-Packard Laboratories USA	USA	8	2.06%	5
7	University of the Balearic Islands	Spain	8	2.06%	8
10	George Mason University	USA	7	1.80%	3
10	Oracle Corporation USA	USA	7	1.80%	6
10	Performance Engineering Services	USA	7	1.80%	7
10	SAP Research Karlsruhe	Germany	7	1.80%	5
10	University of Oldenburg	Germany	7	1.80%	6

4. CONCLUSION

In this work, we have conducted a systematic review of literature on performance research at the ICPE, WOSP and SIPEW. Most articles published at the WOSP and SIPEW are focused on the system development phase. Since the inception of the ICPE in 2010, an increasing number of papers address the system operation phase which results in a well-balanced conference profile. Our N-Gram analysis revealed a constant shift of the conference focus towards the latest technologies such as cloud computing. Due to this shift, the conference is increasingly addressing the most relevant performance goals for these technologies, e.g., optimizing resource consumption.

The proportion of research and contribution types published has remained constant over the years and only slight shifts can be observed. While metrics are being contributed more frequently since 2011, philosophical papers continue to be underrepresented. The ICPE community would, however, greatly benefit from more research which provides taxonomies for the generated knowledge and summarizes existing findings within the performance engineering field.

Trends found in Section 3.3 show that evaluations based on one IT artifact are very popular nowadays, while evaluations of multiple artifacts or architectures are rare. As contribution type methods and models are very popular, it would be of great benefit to use the results of such research to create tools and processes as well as to evaluate results in broader environments.

The data and conducted analysis in Section 3.4 indicate a positive influence on the number of publications of a country if it is the host of a conference. An explanation for this fact could be an increased amount of submissions due to lower travel costs. In our opinion, the conference organizers should consider this in order to increase the involvement of certain countries.

5. REFERENCES

[1] *WOSP/SIPEW '10: Proceedings of the First Joint WOSP/SIPEW International Conference on Performance Engineering*, New York, NY, USA, 2010. ACM. 488103.

[2] *ICPE '11: Proceedings of the 2nd ACM/SPEC International Conference on Performance Engineering*, New York, NY, USA, 2011. ACM. 594112.

[3] *ICPE '12: Proceedings of the 3rd ACM/SPEC International Conference on Performance Engineering*, New York, NY, USA, 2012. ACM. 594122.

[4] *ICPE '14: Proceedings of the 5th ACM/SPEC International Conference on Performance Engineering*, New York, NY, USA, 2014. ACM. 594142.

[5] A. Brunnert, C. Vögele, A. Danciu, M. Pfaff, M. Mayer, and H. Krcmar. Performance management work. *Business & Information Systems Engineering*, 6(3):177–179, 2014.

[6] S. Demeyer, A. Murgia, K. Wyckmans, and A. Lamkanfi. Happy birthday! a trend analysis on past msr papers. In *Proceedings of the 10th Working Conference on Mining Software Repositories*, MSR '13, pages 353–362, Piscataway, NJ, USA, 2013. IEEE Press.

[7] A. R. Hevner, S. Ram, S. T. March, and J. Park. Design science in information systems research. *MIS Quarterly*, 28(1):75–105, 2004.

[8] B. Kitchenham and S. Charters. Guidelines for performing systematic literature reviews in software engineering. Technical report, Technical report, EBSE Technical Report EBSE-2007-01, 2007.

[9] C. D. Manning and H. Schütze. *Foundations of Statistical Natural Language Processing*. Cambridgeand MA : The MIT Press, 1999.

[10] K. Petersen, R. Feldt, S. Mujtaba, and M. Mattsson. Systematic mapping studies in software engineering. In *Proceedings of the 12th International Conference on Evaluation and Assessment in Software Engineering*, EASE'08, pages 68–77, Swinton, UK, 2008. British Computer Society.

[11] S. Seelam, editor. *ICPE '13: Proceedings of the 4th ACM/SPEC International Conference on Performance Engineering*, New York, NY, USA, 2013. ACM. 594132.

[12] D. S. Soper and O. Turel. An n-gram analysis of communications 2000–2010. *Commun. ACM*, 55(5):81–87, May 2012.

A Performance Tree-based Monitoring Platform for Clouds

Xi Chen and William J. Knottenbelt
Department of Computing
Imperial College London
{x.chen12, wjk}@imperial.ac.uk

ABSTRACT

Cloud-based software systems are expected to deliver reliable performance under dynamic workload while efficiently managing resources. Conventional monitoring frameworks provide limited support for flexible and intuitive performance queries. In this paper, we present a prototype monitoring and control platform for clouds that is a better fit to the characteristics of cloud computing (e.g. extensible, user-defined, scalable). Service Level Objectives (SLOs) are expressed graphically as Performance Trees, while violated SLOs trigger mitigating control actions.

Categories and Subject Descriptors

C.4 [**Computing Systems Organisation**]: Performance of Systems—*Modelling Techniques*

Keywords

Cloud, Benchmarking, Performance, Modelling, Evaluation

1. INTRODUCTION

Active performance management is necessary to meet the challenge of maintaining QoS in cloud environments. In this context, we present a prototype monitoring and control framework for clouds which makes three contributions:

- We outline system requirements for an extensible modular system which allows for monitoring, performance evaluation and automatic scaling up/down control of cloud-based Java applications.

- We present a front-end which allows for the graphical specification of SLOs using Performance Trees (PTs). SLOs may be specified over both live and historical data, and may be sourced from multiple applications running on multiple clouds.

- We demonstrate how our monitoring and evaluation feedback loop system ensures the SLOs of a web application are achieved by autoscaling.

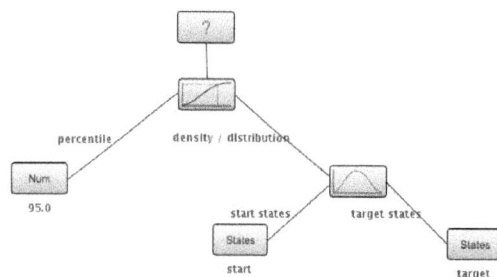

Figure 1: An Example of Performance Tree Query: "what is the 98.0th percentile of the passage time density of the passage defined by the set of start states identified by label 'start' and the set of target states identified by label 'target'?

2. SYSTEM REQUIREMENTS

In this section we present an overview of our system by discussing the requirements for an effective cloud-based monitoring platform and the techniques used to achieve them.

In-depth performance profiling. We require the ability to extract generic metrics on a per-application basis, such as CPU utilisation, memory percentage etc., as well as custom application-specific metrics [6]. This functionality is best delivered through a well-defined API.

Graphical performance query & online/offline evaluation. An important feature which distinguishes our platform from other available tools is the fact we use Performance Trees (PTs) [5, 3] for the comprehensive intuitive, and flexible definition of performance queries and evaluation, while most of the readily available monitoring tools provide users a textual query language [4]. We also incorporate support for historical trend analysis by retaining past performance data. A performance query which is expressed in a textual form as follow can be described as a form of hierarchical tree structure, as shown in Figure 1.

Extensible & Scalable. First, since multiple applications and multi-cloud environments may impose different choices of programming language and monitoring tool, a light-weighted platform independent data format (JSON) is used for monitoring data exchange. Second, all components of our system communicate using a publish-subscribe model, which allows for easy scaling and extensibility. Third, a NoSQL database is used due to ability to support large data volumes found in real-world use-cases. [1]

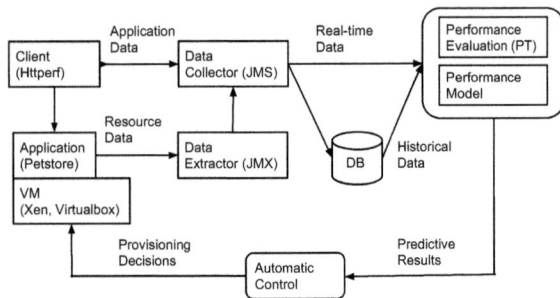

Figure 2: Testbed Architecture

3. PROTOTYPE IMPLEMENTATION

Figure 2 illustrates the prototype of our system. The system is realised as a Java application capable of monitoring and evaluating the performance of a target cloud application, with concurrent scaling of the cloud system so as to meet user-specified SLOs.

The *data collector* (Java Message Service) extracts application metrics, e.g. response time and throughput. This is combined with the output of the *data extractor* (Java Management Extension), which provides hardware-related metrics, i.e. utilisation of each core of the VM, memory bandwidth, etc. The data collector can either feed this data directly into the *performance evaluator* or store it a database for future analysis. The performance evaluator evaluates metrics starting from the leaves of the PTs, and ending with the root, thus producing performance indices which are compared to target measurements for resource management. The *automatic controller* (autoscale) then optimizes the resource configuration to meet the performance targets [2].

4. DEMONSTRATION

4.1 Application and System

Oracle Java Petstore, a common HTTP-based web application, is used to expose a server to high HTTP request volumes which cause intensive CPU activity related to processing of input and output packets. The hypervisor (XenServer 6.2) is running on an a Dell PowerEdge C6220 compute server with two Intel Xeon E5-2690 8-core 2.9 GHz processors and two 1 TB hard drives. The network between each server is 10 Gbps. Each server virtual machine is assigned with on vCPU with 1 to 4 cores, 4 GB memory and one vNIC. Httperf is configured on the other servers to send a fixed number of HTTP requests rate incrementally for each Petstore instance [2].

4.2 GUI and Demo in Action

The user interface contains a dashboard where the user can manage up to 8 different PTs as shown in Figure 3. The graphical nature allows easy comprehension and manipulation by the users, and – thanks to their extensibility – new nodes can be added. The user can design their own PTs, either from scratch or by loading in a saved tree from a file. The user can specify the performance metrics, the application, and the server they want to evaluate. Once the tree has been designed and the evaluation has been started, the

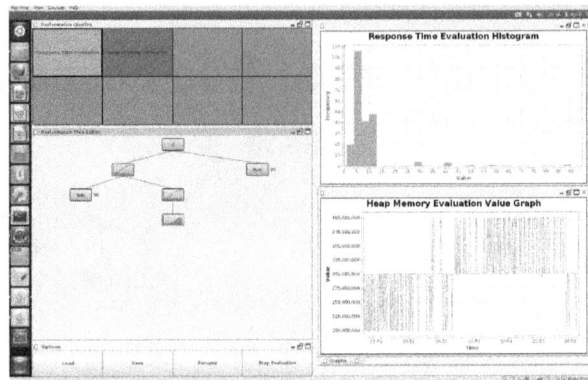

Figure 3: Performance Tree Evaluation Interface: the area on the top left is where the user can manage up 8 different PTs. Two performance evaluations are (a) Is it satisfied that 90% of response time is lower than 10 ms? (b) Is it true that heap memory is lower than 300 MB?

editor receives data from the data collector or the database, which it uses to update the square panel in the GUI. If the performance requirement is violated, this is represented by a red color applied to the evaluation box; otherwise it is green.

Figure 3 illustrates two cases: (a) the monitoring and control of a response-time-related SLO with autoscaling enabled, (b) the monitoring of a memory-consumption-related SLO with autoscaling disabled. In the first evaluation, once the PT detects the SLO is violated, the automatic controller module migrates the server to a larger instance. In this case, the server is migrated from a 1 core to a 2 core instance, so the response time decreases and the SLOs is not violated, represented as a 'green' PT block. The migration time is usually around 8 to 10 secs inside of the same physical machine. In the second case, the 'red' block illustrates the memory-consumption-related SLA is violated since autoscaling is not enabled.

5. REFERENCES

[1] P. Bar, R. Benfredj, U. D. Marks, Jonathon, B. Wozniak, G. Casale, and W. J. Knottenbelt. Towards a monitoring feedback loop for cloud applications. *Proc. MultiCloud'13*, 2013.

[2] X. Chen, C. P. Ho, R. Osman, P. G. Harrion, and W. J. Knottenbelt. Understanding, modelling, and improving the performance of web applications in multicore virtualised environments. *Proc. ICPE' 14*, pages 197–207, 2014.

[3] N. J. Dingle, W. J. Knottenbelt, and T. Suto. PIPE2: A tool for the performance evaluation of generalised stochastic Petri nets. *Proc. ACM SIGMETRICS*, 2009.

[4] F. Gorsler, F. Brosig, and S. Kounev. Performance queries for architecture-level performance models. *ICPE' 14*, 2014.

[5] T. Suto, J. Bradley, and W. Knottenbelt. Performance trees: A new approach to quantitative performance specification. *Proc. MASCOTS*, pages 303–313, 2006.

[6] Q. Zheng, H. Chen, Y. Wang, J. Zhang, and J. Duan. COSBench: cloud object storage benchmark. *Proc. ICPE' 13*, pages 199–210, 2013.

ClusterFetch: A Lightweight Prefetcher for General Workloads

Haksu Jeong
Software R&D Center
Samsung Electronics
Suwon, 443-742, Korea
hks.jeong@samsung.com

Junhee Ryu
Networks Business
Samsung Electronics
Suwon, 443-742, Korea
junhee.ryu@samsung.com

Dongeun Lee
School of Electrical and
Computer Engineering, UNIST
Ulsan 689-798, Korea
eundong@unist.ac.kr

Jaemyoun Lee
Dept. Computer Science &
Engineering
Hanyang University
Ansan 426-791, Korea
jaemyoun@hanyang.ac.kr

Heonshik Shin
Dept. Computer Science &
Engineering
Seoul National University
Seoul 151-744, Korea
shinhs@snu.ac.kr

Kyungtae Kang
Dept. Computer Science &
Engineering
Hanyang University
Ansan 426-791, Korea
ktkang@hanyang.ac.kr

ABSTRACT
Application loading times can be reduced by prefetching disk blocks into the buffer cache. Existing prefetching schemes for general workloads suffer from significant overheads and low accuracy. *ClusterFetch* is a lightweight prefetcher that identifies continuous sequences of I/O requests and identifies the files that trigger them. The next time that the same files are opened, the corresponding disk blocks are prefetched. In experiments, ClusterFetch reduced the launch time, by which we refer to the latency that occurs when a program first runs, by 15.2 to 30.9%, and loading times, meaning the delays that are incurred while additional data is loaded from the disk during program execution, by 15.9%.

Categories and Subject Descriptors
D.4.3 [**Software**]: Operating Systems—*File Systems Management*

General Terms
Design

Keywords
ClusterFetch; Lightweight prefetch; Launch and loading times reduction

1. INTRODUCTION
Prefetching disk blocks effectively reduces subsequent disk access times, allowing applications to load and run more quickly [1, 2]. Successful prefetching depends on the accuracy with which upcoming disk I/O can be predicted, measured by the buffer cache hit-rate [3, 4], and many authors

ICPE'15, Jan. 31–Feb. 4, 2015, Austin, TX, USA.
ACM 978-1-4503-3248-4/15/01.
http://dx.doi.org/10.1145/2668930.2688062

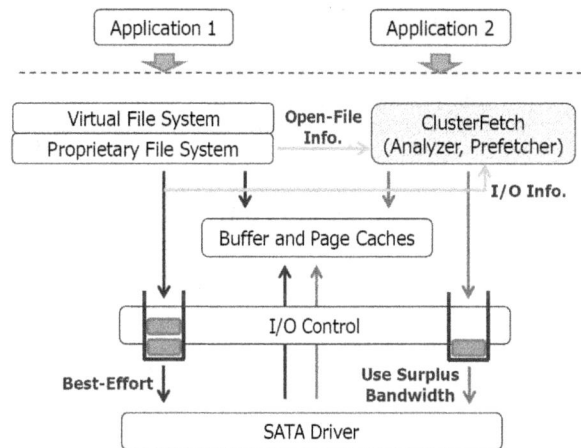

Figure 1: Operation of ClusterFetch.

have tried to improve this accuracy. However, most techniques incur significant memory and CPU overheads, and the predictions they make are not particularly accurate [3, 4]. In addition, existing prefetching approaches have largely focused on reducing application *launch time*, which is the delay in starting a program.

ClusterFetch is a *general-purpose, lightweight* prefetcher that runs within the Linux kernel to reduce the launch time, and also the delays incurred when a program which is already running has to load additional data from disk (i.e. *loading times*). Experiments show reductions of up to 30.9% in launch times and 15.9% in loading times, at the cost of less than 3MB of memory overhead in establishing correlations between disk blocks.

2. DESIGN AND IMPLEMENTATION
Periods during which there is continuous disk I/O, but negligible memory and CPU activity, can be identified by using a circular queue to record every disk I/O operation. For as long as the period between the first and the last entry in the queue is less than a predefined threshold, ClusterFetch

considers the entries to correspond to a period of continuous disk I/O, and stores the identification numbers (IDs) of the blocks that were accessed in a prefetch information file. In addition, ClusterFetch traces the file which triggered the continuous I/O by looking at the log of file opening operations. Then it links this trigger file to an entry in the prefetch information file by setting the sticky permission bit on the trigger file; this bit is available because the current implementation of Linux only uses it when accessing a directory file. Subsequently, whenever the Linux kernel opens the trigger file, the disk blocks corresponding to the IDs written in the prefetch information file are brought into the buffer cache. Thus this scheme is able to detect, and utilize, the correlation between disk blocks with a negligible overhead, unlike many previous prefetching schemes which impose significant memory overhead [4] or generate limited information on block correlation [3].

To avoid prefetching operations delaying I/O from other processes, I/O control process shown in Figure 1 manages the I/O priority of other block requests and prefetch operations. In addition, ClusterFetch provides a control parameter to limit the I/O bandwidth of prefetching operations. Cluster-Fetch also uses native command queuing (NCQ) within the SATA2 standard to maximize I/O throughput. The structure and operation of ClusterFetch are illustrated in Figure 1.

3. EXPERIMENTAL RESULTS AND CONCLUSION

We compared launch and loading times of three popular applications, with and without ClusterFetch. The applications were Eclipse (a development tool), Flightgear (a flight simulator), and Savage 2 (a game), and we measured both cold and warm start times. The results in Table 1 show that our scheme reduce the launch times of Eclipse and Flightgear by 30.9% and 15.2% respectively, and the loading time of Savage 2 by 15.9%, at the expense of the minor overhead incurred in detecting and utilizing the correlation between disk blocks.

Table 1: Effect of ClusterFetch on Launch and Loading Times

Applications	Cold	Warm	ClusterFetch	Reduction
Eclipse (LA)	16.5s	6.1s	11.4s	30.9%
Flightgear (LA)	27.5s	18.9s	23.3s	15.2%
Savage 2 (LO)	22.0s	17.0s	18.5s	15.9%

LA: Launch, LO: Loading

4. ACKNOWLEDGMENTS

This research was supported in part by the Ministry of Science, ICT, and Future Planning (MSIP), Korea, under the Information Technology Research Center support program (NIPA-2014-H0301-14-1044) supervised by the NIPA (National ICT Industry Promotion Agency), in part by the MSIP, Korea, under the IT/SW Creative research Program supervised by the NIPA (National IT Industry Promotion Agency) (NIPA-2013-H0502-13-1061), and in part by the Basic Science Research Program through the National Research Foundation of Korea (NRF) funded by the MSIP (NRF-2013R1A1A105-9188).

5. REFERENCES

[1] JOO, Y., RYU, J., PARK, S., AND SHIN, K. G. Fast: Quick application launch on solid-state drives. In *Proc. FAST'11* (2011), pp. 259–272.

[2] YAN, T., Chu, D., Ganesan, D., Kansal, A., AND Liu, J. Fast app launching for mobile devices using predictive user context. In Proc. *MobiSys'12* (2012), pp. 113–126.

[3] DING, X., JIANG, S., CHEN, F., DAVIS, K., AND ZHANG, X. Diskseen: Exploiting disk layout and access history to enhance I/O prefetch. In *Proc. ATC'07* (2007), pp. 261–274.

[4] LI, Z., CHEN, Z., SRINIVASAN, S. M., AND ZHOU, Y. C-miner: Mining block correlations in storage systems. In *Proc. FAST'04* (2004), pp. 173–186.

GRnet – A tool for Gnetworks with Restart

Katinka Wolter
Freie Universität Berlin
Takustr.9, Berlin, Germany
katinka.wolter@fu-berlin.de

Philipp Reinecke
HP Labs
Bristol
UK
philipp.reinecke@hp.com

Matthias Dräger
Freie Universität Berlin
Takustr.9, Berlin, Germany
matthias.draeger@gmx.net

ABSTRACT

Gnetworks extend standard queueing networks as to include different types of customers or jobs. In addition to ordinary jobs also signals, or negative jobs can arrive to a queue. A signal removes a job from the queue instead of adding one. The interpretation of a signal as retry is very natural and induces semantics to the arrival of a signal. The job that is hit by the signal first leaves the queue but then immediately returns as a new job.

The mathematical specification of Gnetworks with retry has become a cumbersome task. Therefore we present in this tool-demo paper a new tool that will support the specification and analysis of Gnetwork models with retries.

1. INTRODUCTION

In a network of queues with signals (also denoted as a Gnetwork of queues)[2] customers are allowed to change to signals at the completion of their service and signals interact at their arrival into a queue with customers already present in the queue. Signals, or negative customers are never queued. They try to interact with customers and disappear immediately. Note that they may fail to interact with some probability or due to some conditions which are not satisfied. Despite this deep modification of the model, G-networks still preserve the product-form property for the steady-state distribution of some Markovian queueing networks.

In [1] Gnetworks have been used to model queueing systems with restart. The restart of a job is represented as the arrival of a signal that will restart the normal job it interacts with. The model in [1] is fairly general in that it uses phase-type (PH) distributions for the service-time distributions [3], in order to be able to reflect characteristics of real systems.

Unfortunately, the definition of such models is a laborious task, even if the network only consists of very few queues. The tool presented in this paper addresses this shortcoming. It primarily aids in the specification of Gnetwork models

ICPE'15, Jan. 31–Feb. 4, 2015, Austin, Texas, USA.
ACM 978-1-4503-3248-4/15/01.
http://dx.doi.org/10.1145/2668930.2688060

with restart as defined in [1] and solves a class of rather simple models that have only one queue. An extension to real queueing networks with several queues is currently in progress.

2. MODEL SPECIFICATION

The GRnetwork editor is shown in Figure 1. Using drag and drop the model objects can be placed into the editor window and connected following their correct syntax. Most models contain two sources, one for normal jobs and an optional source generating signals. Both sources feed jobs into the queue, or remove and restart them.

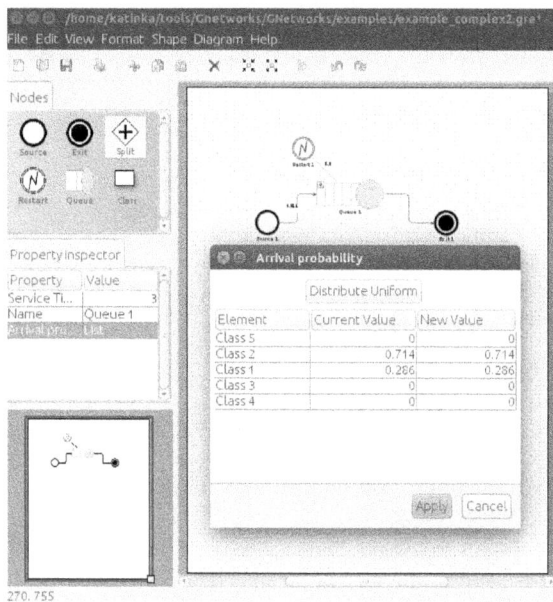

Figure 1: GRnetwork Editor

Figure 2 shows the queue in expanded representation such that the class structure becomes visible. Arriving jobs can be assigned to different classes and jobs can move from one class to the next upon restart. The transitions between classes are shown in the figure. A phase-type (PH) distributed service time distribution is assigned to each job class with service rate μ in each phase and retry success probability α in each phase. In the given example restart signals are accepted with probability 1 by a regular job being served in one of the PH phases. One could refuse restart signals while job service is in a certain phase of the PH distribution. In the simplest case the service time follows an exponential distribution. Any arbitrary PH distribution is possible, e.g. the hyper-erlang distribution fitted to empirical data using HyperStar [4]. Upon completion jobs leave

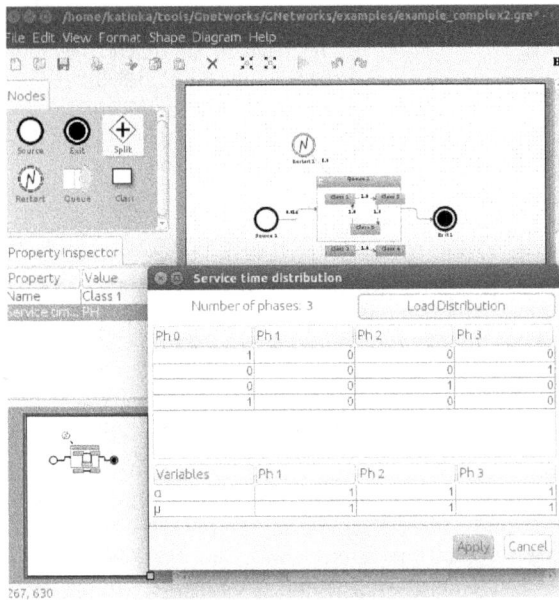

Figure 2: GRnetwork Editor

the queue into the sink. For routing between queues and arrivals from one source into several queues a split object must be used as shown in Figure 4.

3. MODEL ANALYSIS

The model solution provides the utilisation ρ which can be used to compute many metrics of interest. The utilisation can be computed either for a fixed parameter set, or it can be minimised with respect to the restart rate, i.e. arrival rate of signals. Optimisation can be done using a series computation or a Newton algorithm for successive approximation as shown in Figure 3.

Current work extends the tool to several queues as to represent more realistic and more complex systems with job routing between queues. Such a model could be used to study for instance load balancing, as shown in Figure 4.

4. CONCLUSION

We present a tool for editing and solving Gnetworks with restart. The tool will be made available at http://www.mi.fu-berlin.de/inf/groups/ag-tech/projects/Dependable_Systems/index.html.

5. REFERENCES

[1] FOURNEAU, J.-M., WOLTER, K., REINECKE, P., KRAUSS, T., AND DANILKINA, A. Multiple class g-networks with restart. In *Proceedings of the 4th ACM/SPEC International Conference on Performance Engineering* (New York, NY, USA, April 2013), ICPE '13, ACM, ACM, pp. 39–50.

[2] GELENBE, E. Product-form queuing networks with negative and positive customers. *Journal of Applied Probability 28* (1991), 656–663.

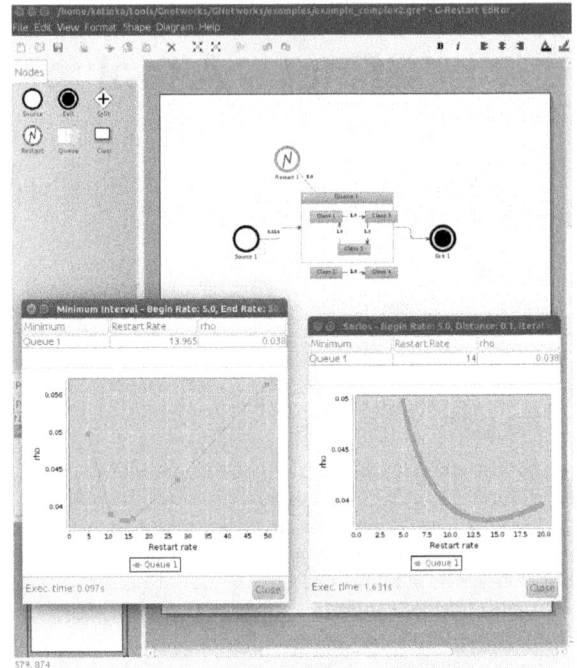

Figure 3: Network solution

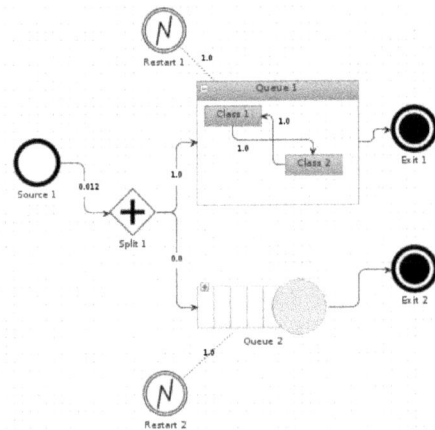

Figure 4: Network with two queues

[3] NEUTS, M. F. *Matrix-Geometric Solutions in Stochastic Models: An Algorithmic Approach.* The Johns Hopkins University Press, 1981.

[4] REINECKE, P., KRAUSS, T., AND WOLTER, K. Hyperstar: Phase-type fitting made easy. In *Quantitative Evaluation of Systems (QEST), 2012 Ninth International Conference on* (sept. 2012), pp. 201 –202.

Using Dynatrace Monitoring Data for Generating Performance Models of Java EE Applications

Felix Willnecker
Andreas Brunnert
fortiss GmbH
Guerickestr. 25
80805 München, Germany
{willnecker,brunnert}
@fortiss.org

Wolfgang Gottesheim
Compuware Austria GmbH
Freistädter Str. 313
4040 Linz, Austria
wolfgang.gottesheim
@dynatrace.com

Helmut Krcmar
Technische Universität
München
Boltzmannstr. 3
85748 Garching, Germany
krcmar@in.tum.de

ABSTRACT

Performance models assist capacity management and planning for large-scale enterprise applications by predicting their performance for different workloads and hardware environments. Manually creating these models often outweighs their benefits. Automatic performance model generators have been introduced to facilitate the model creation. These generators often use custom monitoring solutions to generate the required input data for the model creation. In contrast, standardized application performance management (APM) solutions are used in industry to control performance metrics for productive systems. This work presents the integration of industry standard APM solutions with a performance model generation framework. We apply the integration concepts using the APM solution Dynatrace and a performance model generation framework for Palladio Component Models (PCM).

Categories and Subject Descriptors

C.4 [**Performance of Systems**]: measurement techniques, modeling techniques

General Terms

Measurement, Performance, Prediction

Keywords

Load Testing; Performance Evaluation; Application Performance Management

1. INTRODUCTION

Performance of large-scale enterprise applications (EA) is a critical quality requirement [3]. Application providers and data center operators tend to over-provision capacity to ensure that performance goals are met [11]. This is due to a

ICPE'15, Jan. 31–Feb. 4, 2015, Austin, TX, USA.
ACM 978-1-4503-3248-4/15/01.
http://dx.doi.org/10.1145/2668930.2688061.

lack of tool support for predicting the required capacity of a software system for expected workloads [5]. Performance models and corresponding model solvers or simulation engines can enhance current capacity estimations and therefore increase the utilization of hardware and reduce costs for application operations [2, 7].

The effort of manually creating such performance models often outweighs their benefits [8]. Automatic model generators have been introduced to reduce this effort [4, 2]. These approaches rely on monitoring data from running systems to extract the performance models. Such generated models can be used as input for a simulation engine or an analytical solver to predict the resource utilization, throughput and response time for different workloads and hardware environments.

Monitoring data for the generation of performance models is gathered by either custom solutions or tools from the scientific community [4, 13]. On the other hand, monitoring of large-scale EAs are state of the art technology in practice [9]. Companies use the gathered monitoring data to detect and resolve performance problems in productive environments [10]. This work presents an extension of our existing performance model generation framework to work with industry standard Application Performance Management (APM) solutions. We extend the Performance Management Work Tools (PMWT[1]) model generator to create Palladio Component Models (PCM) based on data collected by the Dynatrace[2] APM solution [1, 12, 6, 4].

2. AUTOMATIC PERFORMANCE MODEL GENERATION FRAMEWORK

In order to use the Dynatrace APM solution we extend the model generation framework presented in [4] and shown in figure 1. This framework uses a custom agent that collects the monitoring data from a running Java EE application. The monitoring data is then processed and aggregated either as comma-separated value (CSV) files and imported into a database or as Managed Beans (MBeans). The aggregated data is input for the model generation. The result is a performance model compliant with the PCM meta-model. The extension proposed in this work allows to use data extracted by standard monitoring frameworks exemplified by a Dynatrace agent for the purpose of performance model

---

[1]http://pmw.fortiss.org/
[2]http://www.dynatrace.com/

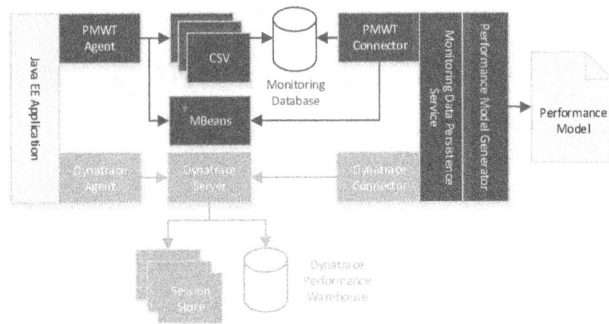

Figure 1: PMWT Performance Model Generation Framework

generation. This agent is attached using runtime options without changes to the instrumented application system's source code. The agent forwards collected data to the Dynatrace server, where detailed traces about method calls and error states are stored in session files for further analysis. Performance metrics derived from these traces are stored in a performance warehouse, and these metrics are typically used by operation engineers as data provider for monitoring dashboards. We extract data from both sources using an extension to our model generation framework called Dynatrace connector.

The Dynatrace connector leverages the representational state transfer (REST) interface of the Dynatrace server to extract detailed monitoring data. This REST interfaces provides, among others, call traces for instrumented operations including their resource demands. The Dynatrace connector is an extension of the monitoring data persistence service that is used by the model generator to access data from different sources. The model generator creates a performance model conforming to the PCM meta-model based on the traces and their average resource demands. The resulting models can then be used for the existing simulation engines and analytical solvers that exist for PCM models [12].

3. CONCLUSION & FUTURE WORK

This work proposed an integration of an industry APM solution with a performance model generation framework. Different input formats and levels of granularity can be processed. The extension shows that the generator and its interface are generally applicable and other APM solutions as generator input are possible. As the Dynatrace solution is in widespread use, the monitoring technology is tested more intensive than custom solutions and in varied operation environments. The generated model can be used to simulate different workloads and therefore enhance the Dynatrace solution with capacity planning capabilities.

As a next step we will further extend an existing prototype for the integration and evaluate it in a case study comparing the results using our PMWT agent and the Dynatrace agent. For the evaluation, we will extract models from a running SPECjEnterprise2010 instance using the two existing data collection approaches. Afterwards, the resulting models are used to predict the utilization, throughput and response time for an increased number of users. The prediction results are compared with measurement for similar workloads on the SPECjEnterprise2010 instance.

4. REFERENCES

[1] S. Becker, H. Koziolek, and R. Reussner. The palladio component model for model-driven performance prediction. *Journal of Systems and Software*, 82(1):3–22, 2009. Special Issue: Software Performance - Modeling and Analysis.

[2] F. Brosig, N. Huber, and S. Kounev. Modeling parameter and context dependencies in online architecture-level performance models. In *Proceedings of the 15th ACM SIGSOFT Symposium on Component Based Software Engineering*, CBSE '12, pages 3–12, New York, NY, USA, 2012. ACM.

[3] A. Brunnert, C. Vögele, A. Danciu, M. Pfaff, M. Mayer, and H. Krcmar. Performance management work. *Business & Information Systems Engineering*, 6(3):177–179, 2014.

[4] A. Brunnert, C. Vögele, and H. Krcmar. Automatic performance model generation for java enterprise edition (ee) applications. In M. Balsamo, W. Knottenbelt, and A. Marin, editors, *Computer Performance Engineering, 10th European Workshop on Performance Engineering*, volume 8168 of *Lecture Notes in Computer Science*, pages 74–88. Springer Berlin Heidelberg, 2013.

[5] A. Brunnert, K. Wischer, and H. Krcmar. Using architecture-level performance models as resource profiles for enterprise applications. In *Proceedings of the 10th International ACM Sigsoft Conference on Quality of Software Architectures*, QoSA '14, pages 53–62, New York, NY, USA, 2014. ACM.

[6] B. Greifeneder. Method and system for processing application performance data ouside of monitored applications to limit overhead caused by monitoring, June 2011. US Patent 7,957,934.

[7] L. Grinshpan. *Solving Enterprise Applications Performance Puzzles: Queuing Models to the Rescue*. John Wiley & Sons, 1st edition, 2012.

[8] S. Kounev. Performance modeling and evaluation of distributed component-based systems using queueing petri nets. *IEEE Transactions on Software Engineering*, 32(7):486–502, 2006.

[9] J. Kowall and W. Cappelli. Magic quadrant for application performance monitoring. *Gartner Research ID G*, 232180, 2012.

[10] H. Koziolek. Performance evaluation of component-based software systems: A survey. *Performance Evaluation*, 67(8):634 – 658, 2010. Special Issue on Software and Performance.

[11] M. Pawlish, A. Varde, and S. Robila. Analyzing utilization rates in data centers for optimizing energy management. In *Green Computing Conference (IGCC), 2012 International*, pages 1–6, June 2012.

[12] R. Reussner, S. Becker, E. Burger, J. Happe, M. Hauck, A. Koziolek, H. Koziolek, K. Krogmann, and M. Kuperberg. The palladio component model. *Journal of Systems and Software*, 82(1):3 – 22, 2009.

[13] A. van Hoorn, J. Waller, and W. Hasselbring. Kieker: A framework for application performance monitoring and dynamic software analysis. In *Proceedings of the 3rd ACM/SPEC International Conference on Performance Engineering*, ICPE '12, pages 247–248, New York, NY, USA, 2012. ACM.

DynamicSpotter: Automatic, Experiment-based Diagnostics of Performance Problems

— Invited Demonstration Paper —

Alexander Wert

Karlsruhe Institute of Technology, Am Fasanengarten 5, Karlsruhe, Germany

alexander.wert@kit.edu

ABSTRACT

Performance problems in enterprise software applications can have a significant effect on the customer's satisfaction. Detecting software performance problems and diagnosing their root causes in the testing phase as part of software development is of great importance in order to prevent unexpected performance behaviour of the software during operation. DynamicSpotter is a framework for experiment-based diagnosis of performance problems allowing to detect performance problems and their root causes fully automatically. Providing different kind of extension points, DynamicSpotter allows for utilizing external measurement tools for the execution of performance tests. Building upon an extensible knowledge base, DynamicSpotter provides means to extend the diagnostic capabilities with respect to detection of additional types of performance problems.

1. INTRODUCTION

The performance of enterprise software systems plays a crucial role for the success of software vendors and operators as it directly affects customer satisfaction. In order to prevent end users from facing performance problems during operation of software applications, performance problems and their root causes need to be identified in the testing phase of a software development process. However in practise, diagnostics of performance problems is a highly manual task which requires significant expertise in performance engineering, rendering frequent, thorough analysis of performance problems impractical.

In this demonstration paper, we introduce DynamicSpotter (DS) [2], a novel framework for automatic, experiment-based diagnostics of performance problems in enterprise software systems. DS automates the execution of performance test series, gathering of measurement data, as well as the analysis of measured data in order to scan fully automatically a system under test (SUT) for known types of performance problems and their root causes. Thereby, DS utilizes existing performance measurement tools for instrumentation of the

ICPE'15, Jan. 31–Feb. 4, 2015, Austin, Texas, USA.
ACM 978-1-4503-3248-4/15/01.
http://dx.doi.org/10.1145/2668930.2693844.

SUT, gathering of measurement data and load generation. Designed for the testing phase of a software development process, DS allows for a frequent, regular execution of diagnostic runs, for instance as part of continuous integration.

DS is an open source tool, which is available on GitHub [2]. DS is designed as an extensible and flexible framework fostering enhancements and extensions by creation of adapters to support the usage of additional measurement tools and detection of additional types of performance problems. In 2014, DS has been reviewed, accepted by the SPEC Research Group and is part of SPEC RG's repository of recommended performance evaluation tools.

2. THE DIAGNOSTICS APPROACH

DynamicSpotter (DS) is a framework for experiment-based, automatic diagnostics of performance problems, combining the concepts of software performance anti-patterns [6] with systematic experimentation. As many performance anti-patterns share common characteristics, they can be structured in a hierarchical way, yielding a taxonomy which covers performance problem types from their high level symptoms to their specific root causes [8, 9]. DS utilizes the taxonomy as a decision tree in order to systematically search for performance problems. For each node of the taxonomy, a detection heuristic is applied which is responsible to decide on the existence of the corresponding performance problem in the SUT. Therefore, a detection heuristic specifies a set of experiments to be executed, the data to be gathered and a set of analysis rules to be applied on the data.

While traversing the taxonomy and applying corresponding detection heuristics for each performance problem, DS generates a report. The report states for each node in the taxonomy whether the corresponding performance problem exists in the SUT and points to the location of the corresponding root cause in the SUT.

3. ARCHITECTURE

The architecture of DynamicSpotter (DS) is depicted in Figure 1. DS requires a *taxonomy on performance problems* and corresponding *detection heuristics* as input which are generic artifacts usually provided by performance experts. Hence, the taxonomy and detection heuristics are intended to be reused in different application contexts of DS. *DS Core* is the main component which is responsible for coordinating the instrumentation of the SUT, the measurement process, gathering and pre-processing measurement data, as well as analyzing data. Furthermore, *DS Core* implements the high level process of iterating a taxonomy on performance prob-

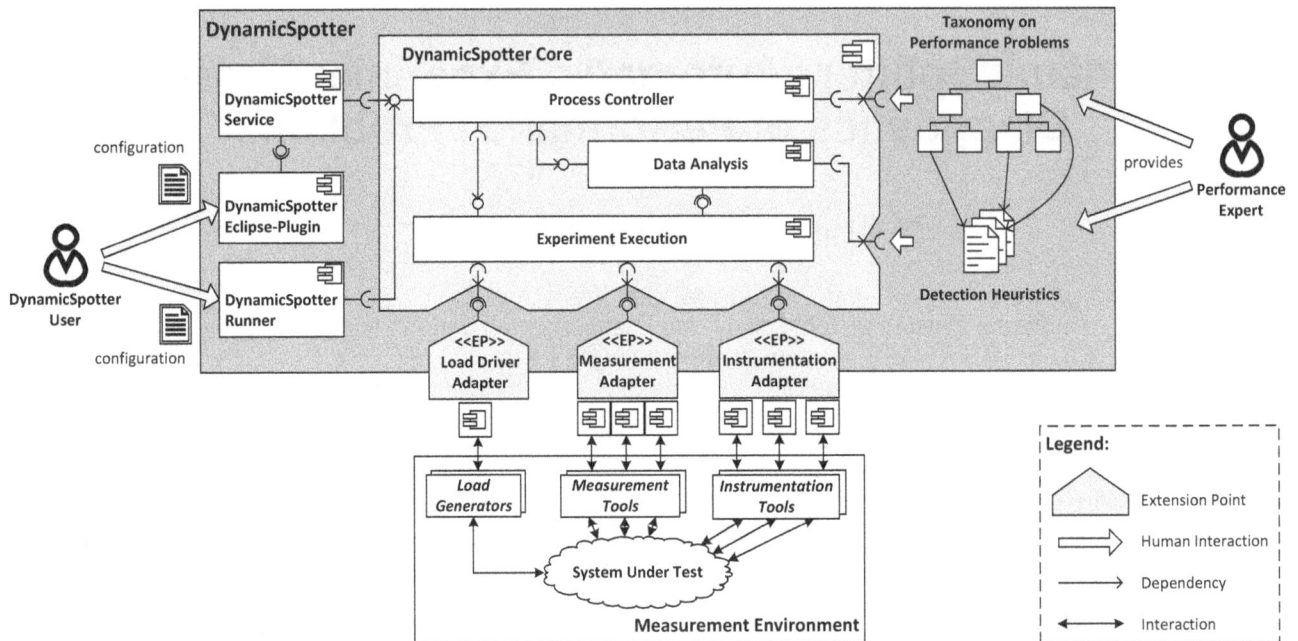

Figure 1: Architecture of DynamicSpotter

lems. The *Experiment Execution* component is responsible for automating experiment execution, while the *Data Analysis* component encapsulates the analysis of measurement data for individual performance problems according to the detection rules defined in the detection heuristics. For each sub-task, DS provides extension points (cf. ≪EP≫ in Figure 1) allowing to provide adapters for specific tools used for instrumentation, monitoring and workload generation:

Load Generator Adapter: This extension point provides means to use existing load generation tools like Apache JMeter [4], Faban [3], etc. for workload generation.

Instrumentation Adapter: This extension point allows to provide adapters for instrumentation tools like DiSL [5], Kieker [7], our own instrumentation tool AIM (Adaptable Instrumentation and Monitoring) [1], etc. Thereby, DS uses a generic instrumentation description model (IDM) to decouple the instrumentation description from the tool realizing it.

Measurement Adapter: A measurement adapter is used to control data collection, as well as to transform and transfer data from the monitoring tools to DS in a common data representation format. Though a specific instrumentation and measurement adapter are often realized within one external tool, they represent conceptually different tasks.

DS may use several instrumentation, measurement, and load generation adapters, whereby the selected set of adapters to be used in a specific application context of DS determines the *Measurement Environment*. In order to run DS, a *DS User* has to describe the *Measurement Environment* in a configuration which is either passed to a headless DS process (*DS Runner*), or the user may prefer an interactive way of creating a configuration for DS using the *DS Eclipse-Plugin*.

4. CONCLUSION & FUTURE WORK

DynamicSpotter (DS) is a framework for experiment-based, fully automatic diagnostics of performance problems in enterprise software systems. DS has been applied in multiple case studies [8, 9] showing promising results with respect to the automation of performance problems diagnostics. As DS is a framework, the diagnostics capabilities highly depend on the detection heuristics available for DS. Currently, heuristics for the detection of software bottlenecks and communication performance anti-patterns are available. Extending the existing set of supported detection heuristics is an important task for future work. Furthermore, we are working on providing additional adapters for common measurement tools (e.g. Kieker [7]).

5. REFERENCES

[1] Aim homepage. http://sopeco.github.io/AIM/.
[2] DynamicSpotter homepage. http://sopeco.github.io/DynamicSpotter/.
[3] Faban homepage. http://faban.org/.
[4] Apache Software Foundation. Apache JMeter homepage. http://jmeter.apache.org.
[5] L. Marek, A. Villazón, Y. Zheng, D. Ansaloni, W. Binder, and Z. Qi. Disl: a domain-specific language for bytecode instrumentation. In *AOSD'11*. ACM, 2012.
[6] C. Smith and L. Williams. Software performance antipatterns; common performance problems and their solutions. In *CMG-CONFERENCE-*, 2002.
[7] A. van Hoorn, J. Waller, and W. Hasselbring. Kieker: A framework for application performance monitoring and dynamic software analysis. In *ICPE'12*. ACM, 2012.
[8] A. Wert, J. Happe, and L. Happe. Supporting swift reaction: automatically uncovering performance problems by systematic experiments. In *ICSE'13*. IEEE Press, 2013.
[9] A. Wert, M. Oehler, C. Heger, and R. Farahbod. Automatic Detection of Performance Anti-patterns in Inter-component Communications. In *QoSA'14*. ACM, 2014.

The Storage Performance Analyzer:
Measuring, Monitoring, and Modeling of
I/O Performance in Virtualized Environments
[Invited Demo Paper]

Qais Noorshams*, Axel Busch*, Samuel Kounev**, Ralf Reussner*

*Karlsruhe Institute of Technology, Germany ([lastname]@kit.edu)
**University of Würzburg, Germany (samuel.kounev@uni-wuerzburg.de)

ABSTRACT
The ever-increasing I/O resource demands pose significant challenges for today's system environments to meet performance requirements. The resource demand effects are even magnified in modern virtualized environments where workloads are consolidated to save hardware and operating costs. Tool-supported analysis approaches can help to understand I/O performance characteristics and avoid I/O performance and interference issues. In this demo paper, we present the Storage Performance Analyzer (SPA) – a tool for automated I/O performance analysis. SPA is equipped with tailored features for virtualized environments allowing to measure, monitor, and model both I/O performance and interference effects in modern environments. SPA is open-source and available for common operating systems.

1. THE SPA APPROACH

The *Storage Performance Analyzer (SPA)* [1] is an approach for the systematic analysis of I/O performance in virtualized environments, which has been successfully applied in our previous work for performance measuring, monitoring, and modeling [2–8]. As illustrated in Figure 1, our SPA framework basically consists of a benchmark harness that coordinates and controls the execution of benchmarks as well as monitors and a tailored analysis library used to process and evaluate the collected measurements.

Measuring. Using integrated I/O benchmarks, SPA coordinates the execution of benchmark runs on possibly multiple targets (e.g, on co-located virtual machines) to obtain measurements of the I/O performance. Currently, we have integrated two benchmarks into our framework, but further benchmarks can be integrated as required. We use the open source *Flexible File System Benchmark*[1] (FFSB) for a fine-grained analysis and the *Filebench* benchmark[2] to emulate mixed application workloads, e.g., a file server workload. After the measurement setup has been configured, the SPA framework first configures the benchmarks, then it executes the target workload, and it finally collects the results.

Monitoring. During the measurement process, the system environment as well as specific targets can be monitored to observe the I/O performance behavior. SPA can activate operating system monitors, such as `blktrace`[3] and `iostat`[4], as well as self-defined monitors, e.g., logging the amount of files the benchmarks produce. The number of executed monitors is not limited and more monitors can be included if needed. If any monitors are activated, SPA starts all monitors before the benchmarks are started. After all benchmarks are finished, SPA stops all monitors and collects the results.

Modeling. The measurement and monitoring results can be processed and analyzed for a variety of purposes, e.g., to identify performance bottlenecks and performance interference effects. The results can also be used for performance modeling. SPA includes analysis libraries enabling fully-automated tuning and modeling using statistical regression techniques.

2. ARCHITECTURE

Components. The benchmarking component, which is implemented in Java, contains a *benchmark controller* that explores the parameter space and coordinates the benchmark runs accordingly. The benchmark controller is connected to the *benchmark driver*, which is an abstraction of the actual benchmark used. In addition, the measurement process can be monitored using a given *monitor driver*. The benchmark controller and the drivers are deployed on a controller machine managing the measurement process. The drivers use an internal *remote execution component* to communicate with the actual benchmark and monitors, which are deployed on the SUT. In our implementation, the remote execution component employs SSH connections, but it could be easily changed to use another connection type. The benchmark controller saves the results using the persistence component.

The performance modeling component is integrated into the open source statistics tool R[5]. The *datastore interface* can load and prepare the data, e.g., by filtering or aggregating data, to evaluate the results. Both the *regression optimization* and the *regression modeling* component can further process this data or use other data specified by the user. The regression optimization component comprises an automated regression parameter tuning process for given training data [3] and uses the *regression techniques* whose

---

[1] https://github.com/FFSB-prime
[2] https://github.com/Filebench-Revise

ICPE'15, Jan. 31–Feb. 4, 2015, Austin, Texas, USA.
ACM 978-1-4503-3248-4/15/01.
http://dx.doi.org/10.1145/2668930.2693845.

---

[3] http://linux.die.net/man/8/blktrace
[4] http://linux.die.net/man/1/iostat
[5] http://www.r-project.org/

implementations are provided by R libraries. The regression modeling component automatically creates the models with the considered regression techniques.

Design Decisions. This design has several advantages: i) Using SSH connections, the VMs deployed on the system under test (SUT), on which the experiments are executed, are not required to have additional software installed as, e.g., in the case of using Java Remote Method Invocation (RMI). Such solutions would require an additional abstraction layer on the VMs, which is often difficult to debug in case of unexpected results. ii) Furthermore, this enables the benchmark controller to take control over the synchronization of the measurements from multiple VMs. The benchmark controller starts the benchmarks simultaneously and does not require, e.g., network time protocol (NTP). iii) Measurement results are saved asynchronously in a lightweight SQLite database that easily supports SQL requests and CSV export for versatile data access. Moreover, SQLite is supported natively and deamonless by many operating systems and programs. iv) The analysis library is integrated into the statistics tool R. The analysis library can be easily extended for new functionality and all functionality of R can be re-used with minimal effort.

3. APPLICATION SCENARIOS

SPA enables a wide range of I/O performance analysis and we used it in the following application scenarios:

1. Identifying and evaluating important performance influences of I/O-intensive applications is a prerequisite for systematic performance analysis [2]. Using such information, the monitoring features of SPA can be used to extract performance characteristics of running I/O-intensive applications in virtualized environments [8].

2. SPA can automatically explore and quantitatively evaluate both workload-specific and system-specific performance influences. This information can in turn be used in an automated process for statistical analysis and regression-based performance modeling [3,5,6]. These models can be used to analyze the system behavior and predict the performance in different scenarios.

3. With understanding the system behavior and performance impact of I/O-intensive workloads, sophisticated model formalisms, e.g., queueing networks or queueing Petri nets, can be applied [4,7]. Creating such models requires increased manual effort, but benefit from usually high predictive power and potential for reuse, since once created, the number of required calibration measurements are relatively low.

4. CONCLUSION

In this paper, we presented SPA – a tool for analyzing the I/O performance of storage systems specifically targeting virtualized environments. The main benefits of SPA are the automated exploration of the configuration space (i.e., the possible configuration parameters are specified and all combinations comprised of benchmarks and monitors are executed automatically) and the built-in support for a synchronized execution on multiple targets (for example virtual machines on separate physical hosts), i.e., multiple benchmarks are started at the same time without manual coordination. While the approach is tailored and pre-packaged for benchmarking and

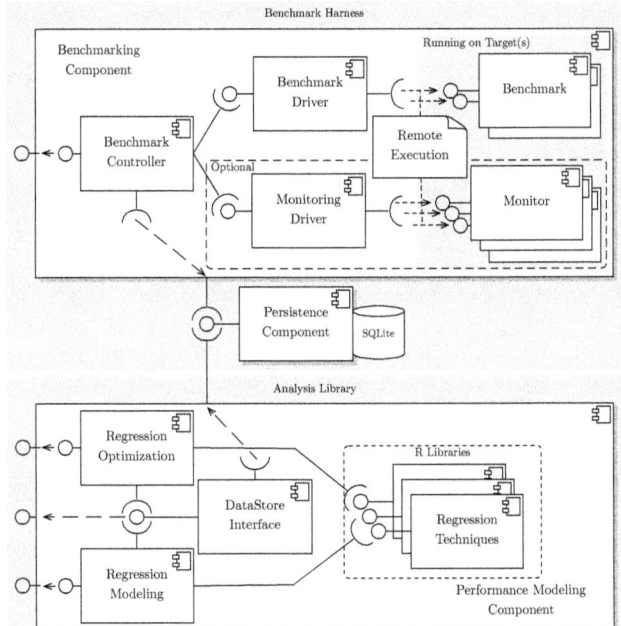

Figure 1: SPA Overview

monitoring the I/O performance of storage systems in both native and virtualized environments, SPA is not limited to a specific domain and can be extended to integrate other benchmarks and monitoring tools. SPA is freely available and can be downloaded from the project page [1] and the SPEC RG Tool Repository: `http://research.spec.org/tools`.

Acknowledgments This work was supported by the German Research Foundation (DFG) under grant No. RE 1674/5-1 and KO 3445/6-1, and the German Federal Ministry of Economics and Energy (BMWI), grant No. 01MD11005 (PeerEnergyCloud). We especially thank the Informatics Innovation Center (IIC) – `http://www.iic.kit.edu/` – for the support of this work.

5. REFERENCES

[1] The Storage Performance Analyzer (SPA). `http://storageperformanceanalyzer.github.io/SPA/`.

[2] Qais Noorshams, Samuel Kounev, and Ralf Reussner. Experimental Evaluation of the Performance-Influencing Factors of Virtualized Storage Systems. In *EPEW '12*.

[3] Qais Noorshams, Dominik Bruhn, Samuel Kounev, and Ralf Reussner. Predictive Performance Modeling of Virtualized Storage Systems using Optimized Statistical Regression Techniques. In *ICPE '13*.

[4] Qais Noorshams, Kiana Rostami, Samuel Kounev, Petr Tůma, and Ralf Reussner. I/O Performance Modeling of Virtualized Storage Systems. In *MASCOTS '13*.

[5] Qais Noorshams, Axel Busch, Andreas Rentschler, Dominik Bruhn, Samuel Kounev, Petr Tůma, and Ralf Reussner. Automated Modeling of I/O Performance and Interference Effects in Virtualized Storage Systems. In *DCPerf '14*.

[6] Qais Noorshams, Roland Reeb, Andreas Rentschler, Samuel Kounev, and Ralf Reussner. Enriching software architecture models with statistical models for performance prediction in modern storage environments. In *CBSE '14*.

[7] Qais Noorshams, Kiana Rostami, Samuel Kounev, and Ralf Reussner. Modeling of I/O Performance Interference in Virtualized Environments with Queueing Petri Nets. In *MASCOTS '14*.

[8] Axel Busch, Qais Noorshams, Samuel Kounev, Anne Koziolek, Ralf Reussner, and Erich Amrehn. Automated Workload Characterization for I/O Performance Analysis in Virtualized Environments. In *ICPE '15*.

Cloud Native Cost Optimization

Adrian Cockcroft
Battery Ventures
Menlo Park, CA, USA

Abstract

For traditional datacenter applications capacity is a fixed upfront cost, so there is little incentive to stop using it once it's been allocated, and it has to be over-provisioned most of the time so there is enough capacity for peak loads. When traditional application and operating practices are used in cloud deployments there are immediate benefits in speed of deployment, automation, and transparency of costs. The next step is a re-architecture of the application to be cloud native, and significant operating cost reductions can help justify the development work. Cloud native applications are dynamic and use ephemeral resources that are only charged for when they are in use. This talk will discuss best practices for cloud native development, test and production deployment architectures that turn off unused resources and take full advantage of optimizations such as reserved instances and consolidated billing.

Categories and Subject Descriptors:
K 6.2 Installation Management
Subjects: Pricing and resource allocation

Keywords
Cloud Native; Cost Optimization; AWS; Netflix; Autoscaling; Reservations; Consolidated Billing

Short Bio

Adrian Cockcroft has had a long career working at the leading edge of technology. He's always been fascinated by what comes next, and he writes and speaks extensively on a range of subjects. At Battery, he advises the firm and its portfolio companies about technology issues and also assists with deal sourcing and due diligence.

Before joining Battery, Adrian helped lead Netflix's migration to a large scale, highly available public-cloud architecture and the open sourcing of the cloud-native NetflixOSS platform. Prior to that at Netflix he managed a team working on personalization algorithms and service-oriented refactoring.

Adrian was a founding member of eBay Research Labs, developing advanced mobile applications and even building his own homebrew phone, years before iPhone and Android launched. As a distinguished engineer at Sun Microsystems he wrote the best-selling "Sun Performance and Tuning" book and was chief architect for High Performance Technical Computing.

ICPE'15, Jan. 31 – Feb. 4, 2015, Austin, Texas, USA.
ACM 978-1-4503-3248-4/15/01..
http://dx.doi.org/10.1145/2668930.2693197

A Constraint Programming Based Hadoop Scheduler for Handling MapReduce Jobs with Deadlines on Clouds

Norman Lim
Dept. of Systems and Computer
Engineering
Carleton University
Ottawa, ON, Canada
nlim@sce.carleton.ca

Shikharesh Majumdar
Dept. of Systems and Computer
Engineering
Carleton University
Ottawa, ON, Canada
majumdar@sce.carleton.ca

Peter Ashwood-Smith
Huawei, Canada
Kanata, ON, Canada

ABSTRACT

A novel MapReduce constraint programming based matchmaking and scheduling algorithm (MRCP) that can handle MapReduce jobs with deadlines and achieve high system performance is devised. The MRCP algorithm is incorporated into Hadoop, which is a widely used open source implementation of the MapReduce programming model, as a new scheduler called the *CP-Scheduler*. This paper originates from the collaborative research with our industrial partner concerning the engineering of resource management middleware for high performance. It describes our experiences and the challenges that we encountered in designing and implementing the prototype CP-based Hadoop scheduler. A detailed performance evaluation of the CP-Scheduler is conducted on Amazon EC2 to determine the CP-Scheduler's effectiveness as well as to obtain insights into system behaviour and performance. In addition, the CP-Scheduler's performance is also compared with an earliest deadline first (EDF) Hadoop scheduler, which is implemented by extending Hadoop's default FIFO scheduler. The experimental results demonstrate the effectiveness of the CP-Scheduler's ability to handle an open stream of MapReduce jobs with deadlines in a Hadoop cluster.

Categories and Subject Descriptors

C.2.4 [**Computer-Communication Networks**]: Distributed Systems. C.4 [**Performance of Systems**]: *performance attributes, modeling techniques*.

Keywords

Resource management on clouds; MapReduce with deadlines; Hadoop scheduler; Constraint programming.

1. INTRODUCTION

Cloud computing has rapidly gained popularity and is now being used extensively by various types of users including enterprises as well as engineering and scientific institutions around the world. Some of the attractive features of the cloud that make it desirable to use include the "pay-as-you-go" model, scalability, and elasticity that lets a user dynamically increase or shrink the number of resources allocated. In cloud computing, hardware resources (including computing, storage, and communication), as well as software resources are exposed as on-demand services, and can be accessed by users over a network such as the Internet.

Cloud computing environments that provide resources on demand are of great importance and interest to service providers and consumers as well as researchers and system builders. Cloud service providers (e.g. Amazon) deploy large pools of resources that include computing, storage, and communication resources for consumers to acquire on demand. An effective resource management technique needs to be deployed for harnessing the power of the underlying resource pool, and efficiently provide resources on demand to consumers. Effective management of the resources on a cloud is also crucial for achieving user satisfaction and high system performance leading to high revenue for the cloud service provider. The important operations performed by a resource manager in a cloud include: *matchmaking* and *scheduling*. The matchmaking operation, when given a pool of requests, determines the resource or resources to be allocated to each request. Once a number of requests are allocated to a specific resource, a *scheduling* algorithm is used to determine the order in which each of the requests are to be executed for achieving the desired system objectives. Both matchmaking and scheduling are performed in a single step in Hadoop [1] by an entity referred to as the Hadoop scheduler in the literature [2]. A further discussion of Hadoop is provided in Section 2.2. Since such a single step operation is performed by the resource manager described in this paper, we refer to it as a Hadoop scheduler.

Two important components of *performance engineering* are performance optimization and performance modeling. One of the goals of this research is to engineer resource management middleware that can make resource management decisions that achieve high system performance, while also maintaining a low processing overhead. This paper describes how optimization theory and constraint programming (CP) [3] is used to devise a matchmaking and scheduling algorithm. Particular emphasis is placed on discussing our design and implementation experience and the performance implications of various system and workload parameters. CP is a well-known theoretical technique used to solve optimization problems, and is capable of finding *optimal* solutions with regards to maximizing or minimizing an objective function (see Section 2.1 for a further discussion).

A majority of the existing research on resource management on clouds has focused mainly on workloads that are characterized by requests requiring a best effort service. In this paper, workloads that comprise of requests with an associated quality of service often specified in a service level agreement (SLA) are considered. Most of the research on resource management for requests characterized by an SLA has only considered: (1) requests requiring service from a single resource and (2) a batch workload comprising a fixed number of requests. The focus of this research is on requests that need to be processed by multiple resources (called *multi-stage* requests) with SLAs specifying a required execution time, an earliest start time (release time), and an end-to-end deadline. Note that in line with the existing Hadoop scheduler [2], the earliest start time of a job is set to its arrival time in this research. Meeting an end-to-end deadline for requests that require processing by multiple system resources increases the complexity of the problem significantly. In addition, this paper considers a workload comprising an open stream of request arrivals (and not a workload with a fixed number of requests) that characterizes typical workloads on cloud data centres. Both the matchmaking and scheduling operations are well known to be computationally hard problems when they need to satisfy user requirements for a quality of service while also considering system objectives, such as high resource utilization and adequate revenue for the service provider.

A popular multi-stage application that is deployed by enterprises and institutions for processing and analyzing very large and complex data sets (for performing Big Data analytics for example) is *MapReduce* [4]. MapReduce, proposed by Google, is a programming model whose purpose is to simplify performing massively distributed parallel processing so that very large data sets can be processed and analyzed efficiently. In such cases, it is necessary to distribute the computation among multiple machines to facilitate parallel processing and reduce the total processing time. One of the benefits of MapReduce is that it provides an abstraction to hide the complex details and issues of parallelization. As its name suggests, the MapReduce programming model has two key functions [4]: *map* and *reduce*. The *map* function accepts a set of input key/value pairs and generates a new set of intermediate key/value pairs. These intermediary key/value pairs are grouped together and then passed to the reduce function, which is typically called the *shuffle* phase. The *reduce* function processes these intermediate key/value pairs to generally produce a smaller set of values.

A typical MapReduce application (or *job*) is comprised of multiple map tasks and multiple reduce tasks as illustrated in Figure 1. Reduce tasks cannot complete their execution until all the map tasks have finished. Many computations can be expressed using the MapReduce programming model. For example, a MapReduce application can be developed to process the logs of web servers to count the number of distinct URL accesses. This type of application is often referred to as a *WordCount* application. In this case, the input into the map function would be the logs of the web servers, and the map function would produce the following intermediate key/value pairs: {URL, 1}. This key/value pair indicates that one instance of a URL is found. Note that the intermediate data set may contain many duplicate key/value pairs (e.g. {www.google.com, 1} can appear multiple times). The reduce function sums all the values with the same key to emit the new data set: {URL, total count}.

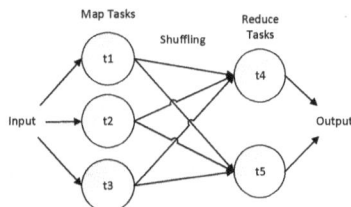

Figure 1. Directed Acyclic Graph for a MapReduce job.

More recently, resource management on clusters that execute MapReduce jobs with an associated completion time guarantee (deadline) has begun receiving attention from researchers (e.g., see [5] to [9]). Executing MapReduce jobs that have an associated end-to-end deadline is required for latency-sensitive applications such as live business intelligence, personalized advertising, spam/fraud detection, and real-time event log analysis applications [5]. By allowing users to specify deadlines, the

system can also prioritize jobs and ensure that time-critical jobs are completed on time. Developing an efficient resource management middleware on such an environment is the focus of attention for this research performed in collaboration with our industrial partners Huawei, Canada.

More specifically, in this paper we focus on devising a scheduler for Hadoop [1] that can effectively perform matchmaking and scheduling of an open stream of MapReduce jobs with SLAs comprising an execution time for the map and reduce tasks, an earliest start time, and an end-to-end deadline. Hadoop is a widely used open source implementation of the MapReduce programming model (discussed in more detail in Section 2.2). The formulation of the matchmaking and scheduling problem of MapReduce jobs with SLAs is achieved using constraint programming (CP) as discussed in Section 3. In our preliminary work [10], a detailed comparison of different resource management approaches based on CP as well as linear programming is presented. The results of the investigation showed the superiority of the CP-based approach implemented and solved using IBM ILOG CPLEX [11], including its more intuitive and simple formulation of constraints, lower processing overhead, and its ability to handle larger workloads.

In addition, our previous work [12] describes a novel *MapReduce Constraint Programming based Resource Management (MRCP-RM)* algorithm that can effectively perform matchmaking and scheduling of an open stream of MapReduce jobs with end-to-end deadlines. Using simulation a performance evaluation of MRCP-RM was conducted that demonstrated its effectiveness in generating a schedule where there is a low number of late jobs. The strong performance of MRCP-RM in simulation experiments has motivated this research that focuses on devising a *revised* version of the MRCP-RM algorithm and implementing the algorithm on a real system (i.e. Hadoop). A new CP-based Hadoop scheduler, named *CP-Scheduler*, which can handle matchmaking and scheduling an open stream of MapReduce jobs with deadlines is devised and implemented. To the best of our knowledge, there is no existing research describing a CP-based scheduler for Hadoop that can handle matchmaking and scheduling an open stream of MapReduce jobs with deadlines. The devising of the CP-Scheduler is based on the objective of providing user satisfaction while achieving high system performance. The main contributions of this paper include:

- A prototype CP-based Hadoop scheduler (called *CP-Scheduler)* for matchmaking and scheduling an open stream of MapReduce jobs with end-to-end deadlines.
  - o A discussion of our experiences and challenges that were encountered in designing and implementing the CP-Scheduler is provided.
- A detailed performance evaluation of the CP-Scheduler was conducted on Amazon EC2. Insights into system behavior and performance are described.
  - o This includes a discussion of the impact of various system and workload parameters on performance and a performance comparison of the CP-scheduler compared to an earliest deadline first (EDF) based Hadoop scheduler, which was implemented by extending Hadoop's default FIFO scheduler.
- Experimental demonstration of the effectiveness of the CP-Scheduler's ability to handle an open stream of MapReduce jobs with deadlines in a Hadoop cluster for a number of different workloads.

The results of this research will be of interest to researchers, cloud providers, as well as developers of resource management middleware for clouds and Hadoop-based systems.

The rest of the paper is organized as follows. In Section 2, background information is provided and related work is discussed. Section 3 discusses the problem formulation and how the MapReduce Constraint Program (MRCP) is devised. The focus of Section 4 is on the design and implementation of the Hadoop EDF and CP based schedulers, and includes a discussion of our experiences and challenges. In Section 5, the results of the experiments performed on Amazon EC2 to evaluate the EDF-Scheduler and CP-Scheduler are presented. Insights into system behavior and performance are described. Lastly, Section 6 concludes the paper and provides directions for future work.

2. BACKGROUND AND RELATED WORK

A brief overview of constraint programming (CP), Hadoop, and Amazon EC2 are provided in Sections 2.1 to 2.3, respectively. In addition, related research is discussed in Section 2.4.

2.1 Constraint Programming (CP)

CP is a theoretical technique for solving optimization problems that was developed by computer science researchers in the mid-1980s using knowledge from artificial intelligence, logic and graph theory, and computer programming languages [3]. A typical CP problem consists of three key parts: decision variables, objective function, and constraints. The *decision variables* are the variables in the CP problem that need to be assigned values. The *objective function* is a mathematical function that generates the value that needs to be optimized (i.e. minimized or maximized). Lastly, the *constraints* are a set of mathematical formulas that restrict the values that the decision variables can be assigned. In summary, when solving a CP problem, a solver will assign values to the decision variables that optimize the objective function, while ensuring that none of the constraints are violated.

2.2 Apache Hadoop

Apache Hadoop [1][13] is an open-source software framework (written in Java) that implements the MapReduce programming model, and is aimed at data-intensive distributed computing applications. Hadoop's software framework contains three sub-frameworks: Hadoop Common, Hadoop Distributed File System (HDFS), and Hadoop MapReduce. *Hadoop Common* provides utility functions including remote procedure call (RPC) and object serialization libraries. *HDFS* and *Hadoop MapReduce* are based on Google's MapReduce programming model [4] and Google's File System (a distributed file system implementation), respectively.

A typical Hadoop cluster comprises a single *master* node and one or more *slave* nodes. In Hadoop 1.2.1, which implements the MapReduce version one (MRv1) architecture, the master node comprises of two entities (which are often called *Hadoop daemons*): *NameNode* and *JobTracker*. Each slave node also consists of two Hadoop daemons: a *DataNode* and a *TaskTracker*. The NameNode and DataNodes are the Hadoop daemons in charge of managing HDFS. Each file that is written to HDFS is split into blocks (64MB by default) and each block is stored on the storage device where a DataNode is running. Each block is replicated multiple times (by default three times) and stored on different DataNodes. It is the job of NameNode to keep track of which DataNode stores the blocks of a particular file (which is called the *metadata* of the HDFS). Another important function of NameNode is to direct DataNodes (slaves) to perform HDFS I/O operations (read, write, delete). DataNodes keep in constant contact with NameNode to receive I/O instructions.

JobTracker is the link between user applications and the Hadoop cluster. In addition, JobTracker is the Hadoop daemon responsible for managing TaskTrackers. Some of the main responsibilities of JobTracker include: initialize jobs and prepare them for execution, determine when the map and reduce tasks of jobs should be executed and which TaskTrackers should execute them (i.e. perform matchmaking and scheduling), as well as monitor all tasks that are currently running. TaskTrackers function as the JobTracker's slaves, and their primary purpose is to execute the map or reduce tasks that they are assigned. Another responsibility of TaskTracker is to periodically send polling/update messages (called *heartbeats*) to JobTracker. If JobTracker does not receive a heartbeat message from a TaskTracker within a specified time period (by default one minute), JobTracker will assume that the TaskTracker has been lost, and re-map all the tasks that was assigned to the lost TaskTracker.

2.3 Amazon EC2

Amazon Elastic Compute Cloud (abbreviated Amazon EC2) is a public cloud that provides Infrastructure-as-a-Service (IaaS). Amazon EC2 allows consumers to launch virtual machines (VMs) called *instances*. After launching these instances, consumers can connect to the instance, and deploy and run their own applications. Amazon EC2 also provides various *instance types*, which are pre-configured VMs that have various predetermined CPU, memory, storage, and networking capacity. The cost of running the instance depends on the type of instance deployed, and users are charged by the hour. As expected, Amazon EC2 provides the benefits of cloud computing including elasticity (scale up/scale down computing capacity dynamically), and pay-as-you-go (no upfront investment).

2.4 Related Work

The focus of this research is on developing resource management techniques for handling MapReduce applications, which are used by many companies and institutions to facilitate Big Data analytics [14]. A representative set of related work is provided next.

In [15] a MapReduce framework for heterogeneous and load-imbalanced environments is described. The research presented in [16] and [17] focuses on a formulation of the MapReduce matchmaking and scheduling problem using linear programming. In these works, the objective is to find a schedule that minimizes the completion time of jobs in the cluster. In [5] the authors present a resource allocation policy based on earliest deadline first (EDF) that attempts to allocate to each job the minimum number of task slots required for completing the job before its deadline. Dong et al. [6], describe a technique that can handle scheduling of MapReduce workloads that contain best-effort jobs as well as jobs with deadlines. Similar to [5], the proposed technique executes jobs at their minimum degree of parallelism to meet its deadline (i.e. attempts to use all of a job's slack time). Mattess et al. [7], propose an approach that uses a cloud to dynamically provision resources to execute MapReduce jobs that cannot meet their deadlines on a local set of resources. Investigation of resource management algorithms for minimizing the cost of allocating virtual machines to execute MapReduce applications with deadlines is presented in [8]. The authors of [9] describe an execution cost model for MapReduce that considers the following job attributes: execution time of the map and reduce tasks, and the size of input data. A scheduler for Hadoop that could handle scheduling a fixed number of jobs was developed based on this concept.

The approaches described in [15], [16], and [17] do not consider jobs with end-to-end deadlines and focus on other aspects of MapReduce jobs. Furthermore, the works described in [5] to [9], which do consider MapReduce jobs with deadlines, use heuristic-based techniques for matchmaking and scheduling the jobs. Handling of workloads comprising an open stream of MapReduce jobs with deadlines is not considered by [6] to [9], which the CP-Scheduler can effectively handle. The existing default schedulers for Hadoop that handle a fixed number of resources do not consider jobs with deadlines. To the best of our knowledge, no existing paper has proposed a CP-based Hadoop scheduler that can effectively perform matchmaking and scheduling of an open stream of MapReduce jobs with end-to-end deadlines on a cluster with a fixed number of processing resources, which is described in this paper.

3. MAPREDUCE CONSTRAINT PROGRAM (MRCP)

The MapReduce Constraint Program (MRCP) is a model of the MapReduce matchmaking and scheduling problem formulated using constraint programming. MRCP was discussed in full detail in our previous work [10]. In this section, a brief summary of MRCP is provided, along with a discussion of the new modifications made in this paper to improve MRCP and make it work with Hadoop. The objective of MRCP is to meet SLAs while achieving high system performance.

Table 1 shows the formulation of the improved MRCP. The inputs required include: a set of MapReduce jobs, J and a set of resources, R, on which to map J. Each job j in J has the following: an earliest start time (s_j), a set of map tasks (T_j^{mp}), a set of reduce tasks (T_j^{rd}), and a deadline (d_j). The tasks t in each job has an estimated execution time in seconds (e_t), and resource capacity requirement (q_t) that specifies the number of resources the task requires to execute (typically set to one for most map and reduce tasks). Note that the estimated task execution times includes the time required to read the input data, and exchange data (e.g. intermediate keys) between the map and reduce phases. The resources are modelled after Hadoop's TaskTrackers. Each resource r in R has a map task capacity (no. of map slots), c_r^{mp}, and a reduce task capacity (no. of reduce slots), c_r^{rd}. The map and reduce task capacity specifies the number of map tasks and reduce tasks, respectively, that the resource can execute in parallel simultaneously.

The decision variables of MRCP are outlined below. Note that the set T contains the tasks for all the jobs in J.

- *Matchmaking*, x_{tr}: a binary variable. If task t is assigned to resource r, $x_{tr}=1$, otherwise $x_{tr}=0$. Each task t in T has an x_{tr} variable for each resource r in R
- *Scheduling*, a_t: an integer variable. Each task t in T, has an a_t variable that specifies the assigned start time of t.
- N_j: a binary variable. If a job j misses its deadline N_j is set to one. Each job j in J has an N_j that is initialized to zero.
- C_j (new): an integer variable that stores the completion time of job j. Each job j in J has a C_j variable.

The objective function of MRCP has been modified from previous work that focused only on the minimization of late jobs. The first part of the objective function minimizes the number of late jobs; whereas, the second part of the objective function minimizes the maximum turnaround time of all jobs. The net effect of the second part of the objective function is to distribute the tasks more evenly among the resources (i.e. load balancing). This is confirmed to be achieved by examining the output schedule generated after MRCP is solved.

A summary of the purpose of each of MRCP's constraints outlined in Table 1 is provided. Constraint (1) states that each task t in the set of tasks, T, can only be assigned to one resource. The second constraint ensures that each job's map task has an assigned start time that is after the job's earliest start time. Constraint (3) enforces that each job's reduce tasks are scheduled to start after

all of the job's map tasks are completed. The fourth constraint, which is a new constraint that was not described in previous work states that the completion time of the job is set to the completion time of the job's latest finishing reduce task. Constraint (5) makes sure that N_j for all the jobs that miss their deadlines is set to one. The next two constraints (6) and (7) are the resource capacity constraints, and enforce that the map and reduce task capacities of each resource are not violated at any point in time. Note that constraints (6) and (7) make use of CP's global constraint function *cumulative*. Lastly, constraints (8)-(10) specify the valid values that the decision variables can be assigned.

Table 1. MapReduce Constraint Program (MRCP)

$$Minimize \left(\sum_{j \in J} N_j + 1 \right) \times max_{j \in J}(C_j - s_j)$$
$$such\ that$$

$$\sum_{r \in R} x_{tr} = 1 \quad \forall t \in T \tag{1}$$

$$(a_t \geq s_j \quad \forall t \in T_j^{mp}) \quad \forall j \in J \tag{2}$$

$$\left(a_{t'} \geq \max_{t \in T_j^{mp}} (a_t + e_t) \quad \forall t' \in T_j^{rd} \right) \forall j \in J \tag{3}$$

$$\left(C_j = \max_{t \in T_j^{rd}} (a_t + e_t) \right) \forall j \in J \tag{4}$$

$$(C_j > d_j \Rightarrow N_j = 1) \quad \forall j \in J \tag{5}$$

$$\big(cumulative((a_t | x_{tr} = 1), (e_t | x_{tr} = 1), (q_t | x_{tr} = 1), \\ c_r^{mp}) \forall t \in T_j^{mp}) \forall r \in R \tag{6}$$

$$\big(cumulative((a_t | x_{tr} = 1), (e_t | x_{tr} = 1), (q_t | x_{tr} = 1), \\ c_r^{rd}) \forall t \in T_j^{rd}) \forall r \in R \tag{7}$$

$$(x_{tr} \in \{0,1\} \quad \forall t \in T) \quad \forall r \in R \tag{8}$$

$$N_j \in \{0,1\} \quad \forall j \in J \tag{9}$$

$$a_t \in \mathbb{Z} \quad \forall t \in T \tag{10}$$

3.1 Implementing and Solving MRCP

The software chosen to solve MRCP is *IBM ILOG CPLEX Optimization Studio v12.5* [11] (abbreviated CPLEX). CPLEX is used because in our preliminary work [10] it was found that it was the most effective (had lower overhead and able to handle larger workloads) in solving MRCP. Before MRCP can be solved by CPLEX's CP solving engine, called the *CP Optimizer* [18], MRCP needs to be implemented (modelled) using CPLEX's *Optimization Programming Language* (OPL) [11]. OPL is an algebraic language that is specifically designed for developing and expressing optimization models. Note that the implementation of MRCP using OPL is referred to as the *OPL model*.

4. HADOOP EDF-SCHEDULER AND CP-SCHEDULER

As indicated in Section 1, a Hadoop scheduler performs both matchmaking and scheduling. This section discusses the design and implementation of two new Hadoop schedulers that can handle matchmaking and scheduling of an open stream of MapReduce jobs with deadlines. The first is the earliest deadline first scheduler, *EDF-Scheduler*, which was devised by extending Hadoop's default FIFO scheduler (see Section 4.2). The second is a more advanced constraint programming based scheduler, called *CP-Scheduler* (see Sections 4.3-4.4), that performs matchmaking and scheduling by solving MRCP, which was discussed in Section 3.1. Our experiences and challenges in implementing these schedulers are discussed. The main challenge encountered is understanding the Hadoop source code and determining which of the Hadoop classes need to be modified to implement the schedulers. A summary of the challenges encountered is provided.

- Determining the Hadoop classes that need to be modified to: (1) support user-specified job deadlines (discussed in Section 4.1), and (2) allow users to define the estimated task execution times of their jobs (see Section 4.3.2).

- Determining how to implement a custom scheduler for Hadoop's JobTracker (see Section 4.2.1). Examining the source code of Hadoop's default FIFO scheduler to learn the intricacies of how job scheduling in Hadoop is performed (discussed in Section 4.2.2).

- The main challenges of implementing the Hadoop CP-Scheduler include: (1) determining how to create the input data for MRCP from Hadoop classes (see Section 4.3.1), (2) integrating IBM CPLEX into Hadoop (see Section 4.3.3), (3) investigating how to handle IBM CPLEX's lack of support for long values to represent timestamps (see Section 4.4.2 and 4.3.1), and (4) developing an approach to ensure that a specific TaskTracker executes the task it has been assigned in the MRCP solution (see Section 4.4.1).

- During testing a bug was discovered where the reduce tasks would stall and take a very long time to complete (discussed in Section 4.4.1.1).

4.1 Adding Support for Job Deadlines in Hadoop

This section discusses the Hadoop classes that were modified to support user-specified job deadlines. First, in Hadoop's `org.apache.hadoop.mapred.JobInProgress` class a new private field, `long deadline`, was added to store a job's deadline. The value stored in the deadline field represents the number of milliseconds elapsed from midnight, January 1, 1970 UTC. The `JobInProgress` (JIP) class represents a MapReduce job that is being tracked by JobTracker. The JIP class maintains all the information for a MapReduce job including: the job's map and reduce tasks, its state (e.g. running, succeeded, failed), as well as accounting information (e.g. launch time and finish time). JIP's deadline field is initialized via the JIP constructor by invoking `conf.getJobDeadline()` where `conf` is an object that is an instance of the `org.apache.hadoop.mapred.JobConf` class, and `getJobDeadline()` is a new method that was implemented in the JobConf class to retrieve the job's deadline.

The `JobConf` class represents a MapReduce job configuration. It is an interface for users to specify the properties (e.g. job name and number of map and reduce tasks) for their MapReduce job before submission to the Hadoop cluster. Two new methods are added to the `JobConf` class: `getJobDeadline()` and `setJobDeadline()`. The method `setJobDeadline(long deadline)` sets the job configuration property, `mapred.job.deadline`, to the supplied parameter. Similarly, the `getJobDeadline()` method is used to retrieve the value assigned to the `mapred.job.deadline` property.

The last Hadoop class that needs to be modified to support user-specified job deadlines is the `org.apache.hadoop.mapreduce.Job` class. The `Job` class is the main user API that is used to create and submit jobs to the Hadoop cluster (more specifically JobTracker). The `Job` class is the user's view of the MapReduce job, and it provides methods to allow the user to create, configure, and submit a job, as well as control its execution, and obtain status information (e.g. state of the job). Similar to the `JobConf` class, the two new methods added to the `Job` class are: `setJobDeadline()`, and `getJobDeadline()`. These two methods in turn invoke `conf.setJobDeadline()` and `conf.getJobDeadline()`, respectively, where `conf` is an instance of a JobConf object. Note that `conf` is one of the private fields of the `Job` class and is initialized when a `Job` object is created. The sequence of calls for setting the deadline of a job is illustrated in the sequence diagram shown in Figure 2.

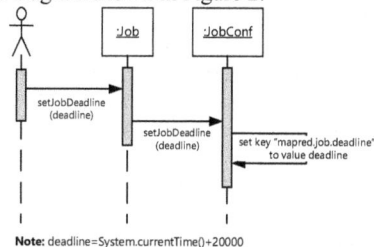

Figure 2. Sequence diagram for `setJobDeadline()`.

4.2 Hadoop EDF-Scheduler

An earliest deadline first scheduler called *EDF-Scheduler* is implemented by extending Hadoop's default FIFO (first-in-first-out) scheduler. This is done to investigate if the naïve solution of using the commonly known EDF policy is effective for handling an open stream of MapReduce jobs with deadlines (see Section 5). This section briefly discusses the key classes that were modified to implement the EDF-Scheduler, but first an overview of how to implement a custom scheduler for Hadoop is discussed in Section 4.2.1, and in Section 4.2.2, a discussion of the key classes of Hadoop's FIFO Scheduler is provided.

4.2.1 Implementing a Custom Hadoop Scheduler

Hadoop provides a pluggable scheduler framework [2] that allows developers to implement custom schedulers using their own scheduling logic and algorithms. The key to implementing a custom scheduler for Hadoop is to extend Hadoop's abstract class `org.apache.hadoop.mapred.TaskScheduler` and implement the abstract method `List<Task> assignTasks(TaskTracker tt)`. The `assignTasks()` method returns a list of tasks (including both map and reduce tasks) that the supplied `TaskTracker` should execute as soon as it receives the list. Note that the returned list can be empty meaning that there are no new tasks to assign to the `TaskTracker` at the moment.

The Hadoop `org.apache.hadoop.mapred.JobTracker` class implements the Hadoop JobTracker daemon, which is responsible for scheduling the tasks of the MapReduce jobs that are submitted. The `JobTracker` class has a `TaskScheduler` private field named `taskScheduler` which stores the reference to the scheduler (e.g. FIFO, EDF or CP) that is used to assign and schedule tasks on TaskTrackers. More specifically, the `JobTracker` class invokes `taskScheduler.assignTasks()` each time JobTracker receives and processes a heartbeat message from a TaskTracker (i.e. within the `JobTracker` class' `heartbeat()` method). Recall that heartbeats are the periodic status messages that TaskTrackers send to JobTracker.

4.2.2 Hadoop FIFO Scheduler

Hadoop's default FIFO scheduler is implemented in the `org.apache.hadoop.mapred.JobQueueTaskScheduler` class (abbreviated JQTS), which extends Hadoop's `TaskScheduler` abstract class. The JQTS class keeps jobs that are ready to execute in priority order and by default, this order is FIFO. There are two other key classes required by JQTS: (1) `JobQueueJobInProgressListener` (JQ-JIPL) and (2) `EagerTaskInitializationListener` (ETIL). The JQ-JIPL class represents the job queue manager, and by default, it sorts the jobs in the queue in FIFO order, but it is possible to implement a custom ordering strategy such as EDF. JQ-JIPL extends Hadoop's abstract class `JobIn`

ProgressListener (JIPL), which is a class that is used by the JobTracker class to listen for when a job's lifecycle in JobTracker changes. The JIPL class has three key methods: jobAdded(), jobRemoved(), and jobUpdated(), which are invoked when JobTracker sees that a job is added, removed, or updated, respectively. For example, when a user submits a job to JobTracker, JQ-JIPL's jobAdded() method is invoked by the JobTracker class to add the submitted job to JQ-JIPL's queue.

The ETIL class prepares a submitted job for execution by initializing/creating the job's tasks. A thread pool with four worker threads is deployed by the ETIL class to concurrently initialize jobs. Similar to JQ-JIPL, the ETIL class also extends the JIPL abstract class. Thus, as soon as a job is submitted to JobTracker, ETIL places the submitted job into its job initialization queue called jobInitQueue (sorted using FIFO by default). The job remains in the queue until there is a worker thread available to initialize the job.

4.2.3 Implementation of Hadoop EDF-Scheduler

The EDF-Scheduler is implemented in a class called EDF_Scheduler (stored in the package org.apache.hadoop.mapred), and is based closely on the implementation of Hadoop's FIFO scheduler (discussed in Section 4.2.2). The major changes that are made are in the JQ-JIPL and ETIL classes. More specifically, in the ETIL class the resortInitQueue() method is modified to sort the queue with priority given to the jobs with an earlier deadline (i.e. earliest deadline first). Moreover, the JQ-JIPL class' JobSchedulingInfo *Comparator* was also modified to place jobs with an earlier deadline first. In Java, a Comparator is an interface used by Java collection objects to sort elements of the collection in a specified order. The JobSchedulingInfo is a *static nested class* of JQ-JIPL that assembles all the necessary job-related information (e.g. job id and deadline) for the EDF-Scheduler to schedule jobs.

4.3 Hadoop CP-Scheduler

Figure 3 shows an overview of the CP-Scheduler being deployed on a Hadoop cluster. There is a single master node and *m* slave nodes (defined in Section 2.2). Users submit jobs to JobTracker which uses the CP-Scheduler to schedule the jobs onto TaskTrackers. CP-Scheduler uses three IBM CPLEX Java library packages (discussed in Section 4.3.3), and performs matchmaking and scheduling by creating a MRCP OPL model and using CPLEX's CP Optimizer (a CP solving engine) to solve the OPL Model (discussed in detail in Section 4.4).

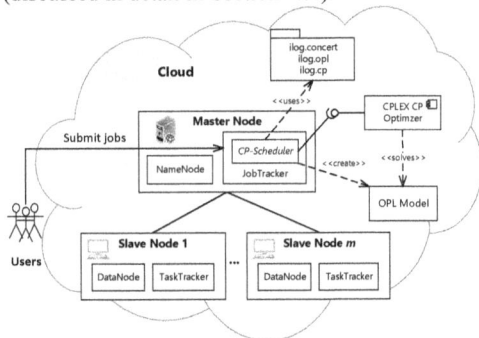

Figure 3. Overview of a Hadoop cluster deploying the CP-Scheduler.

Similar to the EDF-Scheduler the implementation of the *CP-Scheduler* starts with creating a class, called CP_Scheduler (in the package org.apache.hadoop.mapred) which extends Hadoop's TaskScheduler abstract class. In addition, The CP-Scheduler also has two classes: JobQueueManager and JobInitializer that

extend Hadoop's JIPL class, and have similar functionality as the EDF-Scheduler's JQ-JIPL and ETIL classes, respectively.

4.3.1 Entity Classes

The CP_Scheduler class also uses three entity classes: Job_CPS, Task_CPS, and Resource_CPS. These classes represent how the CP-Scheduler views MapReduce jobs, tasks, and TaskTrackers (resources), respectively, and stores the necessary information required by MRCP (discussed in Section 3) for scheduling the MapReduce tasks onto TaskTrackers. An abbreviated class diagram showing the important attributes and methods of the three entity classes is presented in Figure 4. Note that a discussion of the key attributes and methods of the CP_Scheduler class is provided in Section 4.3.

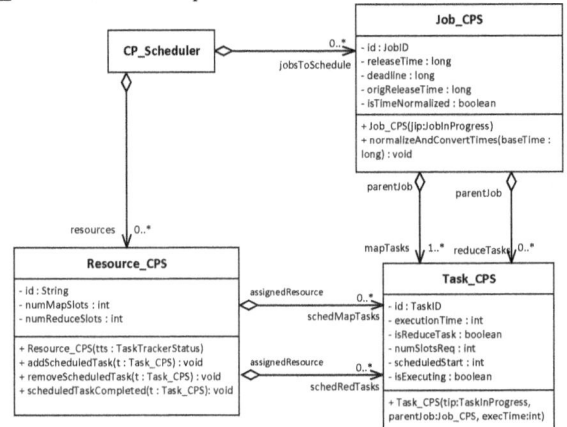

Figure 4. Class diagram (abbreviated) of CP-Scheduler's entity classes.

The Job_CPS class contains information required by the CP_Scheduler to map jobs onto TaskTrackers (resources). This information is retrieved from Hadoop's JobInProgress class, and includes the job's: id, release time, deadline, map tasks, and reduce tasks. Note that both the release time and deadline fields store the number of milliseconds elapsed from midnight, January 1, 1970 UTC. Since the release time field is constantly updated depending on when the job is being scheduled (discussed in Section 4.4), the origReleaseTime field stores the time of when the job is first received by JobTracker. The isTimeNormalized field indicates if the following calculations have been performed: releaseTime = releaseTime – REFERENCE_TIME, and deadline = deadline – REFERENCE_TIME (referred to as *time normalization*). REFERENCE_TIME is a field in the CP_Scheduler class that stores a timestamp which is taken when the CP-Scheduler maps a job for the first time. The job's release time and deadline have to be normalized because CPLEX does not support values of type long (only int is supported). Normalization of the times is discussed in more detail in Section 4.4.2.

The Task_CPS class holds the information that the CP_Scheduler uses for matchmaking and scheduling tasks including: the task's id, estimated execution time (in seconds), task type, and the number of slots (resource capacity) required. This information, except the estimated task execution times (discussed in Section 4.3.2), is retrieved from Hadoop's TaskInProgress class. Once a task has been mapped, its assignedResource and scheduledStart fields are initialized to the resource that the task is scheduled to execute on, and the time the task is to start running, respectively. The isExecuting field is set to true if the task is currently executing.

The Resource_CPS class contains TaskTracker information (retrieved from Hadoop's TaskTrackerStatus class), including:

116

id, the number of map slots, and the number of reduce slots. The tasks that are assigned to the resource are placed in either the `schedMapTasks` list or the `schedRedTasks` list, depending on the task type. Note that both these lists keep tasks sorted by earliest scheduled start time. The methods `addScheduledTask()` and `removeScheduledTask()` are used to add, and remove tasks from the scheduled tasks lists, respectively. The last method, `schedTaskCompleted()`, is called when a task has completed its execution. Completed tasks are moved from the scheduled tasks lists to the completed tasks lists.

4.3.2 Adding Support for Estimated Task Execution Times

One of the inputs that MRCP (discussed in Section 3) requires is the estimated task execution times. Note that the estimation of task execution times can be accomplished by analyzing historical data such as system logs, and workload traces of previously executed tasks (discussed in Section 5.1.2). Similar to how support for job deadlines was added to Hadoop (discussed in Section 4.1), support to allow users to specify the estimated task execution times of their submitted jobs is accomplished by adding two new methods: `setEstimatedTaskExecutionTimes()` and `getEstimatedTaskExecutionTimes()` (abbreviated setET and getET, respectively) to Hadoop's `Job` and `JobConf` classes.

The setET method accepts two parameters: a comma delimitated string of task execution times in seconds (e.g. "2,3"), and the task type (map or reduce). Depending on the task type, the setET method assigns either the `mapred.job.mapTask ExecTimes` property or the `mapred.job.reduceTaskExecTimes` property to the supplied string. The getET method accepts a single parameter the task type (map or reduce), and returns a string array containing the values assigned to the corresponding property.

4.3.3 Integration of IBM CPLEX

As discussed in Section 3.1, MRCP is solved using IBM CPLEX. Therefore, to model and solve MRCP, the CP-Scheduler requires importing IBM CPLEX's Java libraries to make use of the following Java APIs [11]: *ILOG Concert Technology* (abbreviated *Concert*), *ILOG OPL*, and *ILOG CP*. These APIs allow the CP-Scheduler to embed CPLEX's CP Optimizer solving engine and the MRCP OPL model into the `CP_Scheduler` class. To use these APIs, the following CPLEX Java library packages need to be imported: `ilog.concert`, `ilog.opl`, and `ilog.cp`.

Before being able to import the required CPLEX Java libraries, IBM CPLEX v12.5 was installed on the machine where the master node executes. The IBM CPLEX v12.5 JAR (Java archive) file, named `oplall12.5.jar`, was placed in Hadoop's `/hadoop/lib` folder. In addition, a modification is made to Hadoop's `/hadoop/bin/hadoop` script so that the JobTracker would be able to locate the CPLEX libraries. More specifically, the `java.library.path` variable of the `hadoop` script is modified to include the folder `<IBM_CPEX_Install_dir>/opl/bin/x86-64_sles10_4.1`.

Two additional classes that are used by the `CP_Scheduler` for aiding in the integration of CPLEX are: `OPLModelSource` and `OPLModelData`. The former stores the implementation of MRCP written in CPLEX's Optimization Programming Language (OPL), which is referred to as the *OPL model*. The latter class is used by the `CP_Scheduler` class to create the input data for the OPL model. `OPLModelData` extends the OPL APIs `ilog.opl.Ilo CustomOplDataSource` class [11] and converts the `CP_Scheduler`'s *resources* and *jobsToSchedule* lists to a format that the OPL model can read (i.e. generates the OPL model's input sets: *Jobs*, *Tasks*, and *Resources*).

4.4 CP-Scheduler Algorithm

This section provides details on the *CP-Scheduler* algorithm. A class diagram of the `CP_Scheduler` showing its key fields and methods is presented in Figure 5. Note that these fields and methods are discussed in Sections 4.4.1-4.4.3.

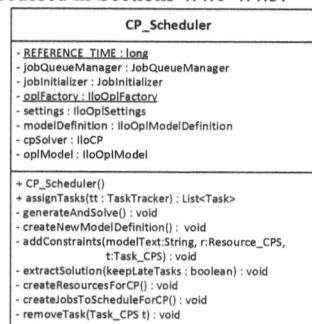

```
┌─────────────────────────────────────────────────┐
│                  CP_Scheduler                     │
├─────────────────────────────────────────────────┤
│ - REFERENCE_TIME : long                           │
│ - jobQueueManager : JobQueueManager               │
│ - jobInitializer : JobInitializer                 │
│ - oplFactory : IloOplFactory                       │
│ - settings : IloOplSettings                        │
│ - modelDefinition : IloOplModelDefinition          │
│ - cpSolver : IloCP                                 │
│ - oplModel : IloOplModel                           │
├─────────────────────────────────────────────────┤
│ + CP_Scheduler()                                   │
│ + assignTasks(tt : TaskTracker) : List<Task>       │
│ - generateAndSolve() : void                        │
│ - createNewModelDefinition() : void                │
│ - addConstraints(modelText:String, r:Resource_CPS, │
│              t:Task_CPS) : void                    │
│ - extractSolution(keepLateTasks : boolean) : void  │
│ - createResourcesForCP() : void                    │
│ - createJobsToScheduleForCP() : void               │
│ - removeTask(Task_CPS t) : void                    │
└─────────────────────────────────────────────────┘
```

Figure 5. Abbreviated class diagram of CP_Scheduler.

4.4.1 assignTasks()

Table 2 shows the CP-Scheduler algorithm which is implemented in the `CP_Scheduler` class' `assignTasks()` method. The input required by the algorithm is a TaskTracker to assign tasks to. The algorithm returns a list of tasks for the supplied TaskTracker to execute (includes both map and reduce tasks). The first step (line 1) is to calculate the currently available map and reduce slots of the supplied TaskTracker (e.g. `availMapSlots = mapCapacity − runningMaps`). The next step (lines 2-3) is to create the `Resource_CPS` list (called `resources`) and `Job_CPS` list (called `jobsToSchedule`), which are required as input to the OPL model. The `createResourcesForCP()` method (abbreviated CR) invokes the `JobTracker` class' `activeTaskTrackers()` method to return a collection of `TaskTrackerStatus` (TTS) objects. The CR method then uses the TTS objects to create `Resource_CPS` objects via its constructor (recall Figure 4). The `createJobsToSchedule ForCP()` method (abbreviated CJ) checks the `JobQueueManager`'s `jobQueue` (a collection of `JobInProgress` objects) for new jobs in the *running* state (i.e. setup is complete and tasks are initialized), and creates a new `Job_CPS` object for each one. If there are new jobs or resources, the `CP_Scheduler`'s `hasNewJob` and `hasNewResources` flags are set to true.

The next step is to check if `CP_Scheduler`'s `jobsToSchedule` list is empty. If this condition is true, then an empty task list is returned (line 4). If either `hasNewJobs` or `hasNewResources` flags are true `CP_Scheduler`'s `generateAndSolve()` method (discussed in Section 4.4.2) is invoked (see lines 5-7). The two flags are used to prevent unnecessarily invoking `generateAndSolve()`when a MRCP solution for the same input (jobs and resources) has already been found. Once a solution is found, the next step (line 8) is to retrieve the assigned map and reduce tasks from the `Resource_CPS` object in `resources` (named `res`) that has the same id as the supplied `TaskTracker`.

In lines 9-19, each available map slot of the supplied `TaskTracker` is assigned the map task with the earliest scheduled start time. This is accomplished by first retrieving the task (a `Task_CPS` object) from `res`, as well as retrieving the task's corresponding `TaskInProgress` (TIP) (lines 10 and 11). Before assigning the task, TIP is checked to see if the task has completed, and if true, the `CP_Scheduler`'s `removeTask()` method is invoked (lines 12-13). The `removeTask()` method performs a number of operations including: moving the task from its assigned resource's scheduled tasks list to the completed tasks list, and moving the task from its parent job's tasks to schedule lists to the completed task lists. Recall that a task's assigned resource and parent job are

Resource_CPS and Job_CPS objects, respectively. Furthermore, removeTask() also checks if the job's mapTasks and reduceTasks lists are empty (i.e. job has completed executing). If this is true, the job's release time is reset to its original release time, and the job is moved from the CP_Scheduler's jobsToSchedule list to the completedJobs list. Otherwise, if the task has not completed executing, the task is assigned to a TaskTracker for execution (lines 14-18). This is accomplished by invoking a new method named obtainSpecificMapTask() (abbreviated OSMT) that is implemented in Hadoop's JobInProgress class. As the name suggests, given a TaskInProgress object, OSMT returns the corresponding Task object (i.e. Task that has the same id). The task that is returned by OSMT is added to the assignedTasks list.

Table 2. CP-Scheduler algorithm (implemented in CP_Scheduler::assignTasks()).

Input: TaskTracker tt
Output: List of Tasks for the supplied TaskTracker to execute, named *assignedTasks*.
1: Get currently available map and reduce slots of *tt*.
2: call *createResourcesForCP()*
3: call *createJobsToScheduleForCP()*
4: if no jobs to schedule **return** empty list
5: if new jobs to schedule **or** new resources in cluster **then**
6:   **call** *generateAndSolve()*
7: end if
8: *res* ← get *Resource_ CPS* object from *resources* with same id as *tt*
9: for each available map slot in *tt* **do**
10:   *Task_CPS t* ← get scheduled map task with earliest start time from *res*
11:   tip ← *t.getTaskInProgress()*
12:   **if** *tip* is complete **then**
13:   **call** *removeTask()*
14:   **else**
15:   *jip* ← t.*getParentJob().getJobInProgress()*
16:   **call** *jip.obtainSpecificMapTask(tip)* **returning** *mapTask*
17:   Add *mapTask* to *assignedTasks*.
18:   **end if**
19: end for
20: Repeat lines 9 to 19 but this time for reduce slots and reduce tasks with one change to Line 14: the new condition is "**else if** all map tasks of *t*'s parent job are completed **then**"
21: return *assignedTasks*

Next, the same logic is executed for the TaskTracker's reduce slots (line 20), except with one change to the *else* statement (line 14). The *else* statement is changed to an *else if* statement, which checks if all the map tasks of the job has completed before assigning reduce tasks (see Section 4.4.1.1). A new obtainSpecificReduceTask() method is implemented in JobInProgress that returns the reduce task (Task object) with the same id as the supplied TIP. Lastly, the assignedTasks list which now contains the tasks that the supplied TaskTracker should execute is returned (line 16).

4.4.1.1 Reduce Task Stalling Problem

During preliminary testing it was found that in some situations the reduce tasks of a job *j* would take a very long time to complete because its map tasks were not being executed in a timely fashion. This can be caused, for example, when the CP-Scheduler schedules the map tasks of a job with an earlier deadline before *j*'s tasks. It was observed that the reason *j*'s reduce task could not finish executing is because not all of *j*'s map

task were finished executing. In fact, it was discovered that Hadoop permits reduce tasks of a job to start executing once a few of its map tasks have finished executing (and does not wait until all the job's map tasks have completed).

One approach to solve this problem is to give execution priority to all of *j*'s map tasks so that they can execute before other tasks. Initially, this approach was used, and implemented by adding constraints to the OPL model that stated that these task should be scheduled to execute at their originally scheduled times (and not be rescheduled). However, further testing showed that this solution is not ideal when it comes to minimizing the number of late jobs because jobs that have an earlier deadline may have to wait for execution. On the other hand, a problem with not ensuring that *j*'s reduce tasks can complete its execution in a timely manner, is that *j*'s reduce tasks will remain idle and unnecessarily consume reduce task slots of TaskTrackers. This can in turn also delay the execution of jobs that already have their map tasks completed. The solution that was used to avoid these problems is to prevent the CP-Scheduler from assigning reduce tasks to TaskTrackers until all the job's map tasks are completed (recall Section 4.4.1). This guarantees that reduce tasks assigned to a TaskTracker can complete its execution.

4.4.2 generateAndSolve()

Table 3 presents CP-Scheduler's generateAndSolve() algorithm whose purpose is to generate the MRCP OPL model, and solve it. The first step is to initialize the CP_Scheduler's REFERENCE_TIME (abbreviated *RT*) if it has not already been done, and initialize the mrcpCurrentTime variable to zero (line 1-3). Recall that *RT* is required to normalize the Job_CPS' release time and deadline fields as discussed in Section 4.3.1. If *RT* has already been initialized, then the mrcpCurrentTime variable is set to the current time minus *RT*, and the value is converted into seconds (lines 4-7). As the name suggests, mrcpCurrentTime is the current time value used when solving MRCP. Recall from Section 4.3.1 that OPL does not support values of type long.

Table 3. CP-Scheduler algorithm, generateAndSolve().

Input: none. **Output:** none.
1: if *REFERENCE_TIME* = -1 **then**
2:   *REFERENCE_TIME* ← *System.currentTimeMillis()*
3:   *mrcpCurrentTime* ← 0
4: else
5:   *mrcpCurrentTime* ← *System.currentTimeMillis()* – *REFERENCE_TIME*
6:   Convert *mrcpCurrentTime* to seconds.
7: end if
8: for each job *j* in *jobsToSchedule* **do**
9:   **call** *j. normalizeAndConvertTimes (REFERENCE_*
10:   *TIME)*
11:   **if** *mrcpCurrentTime > j.getReleaseTime()* **then** *j.setTempReleaseTime(mrcpCurrentTime)*
12: end for
13: call *createNewModelDefinition()*
14: Create a new OPL model and attach the data source containing *jobsToSchedule* and *resources*.
15: Generate and solve the OPL model.
16: call *extractSolution()*

In the next steps (lines 8-12), each job (a Job_CPS object) in CP_Scheduler's jobsToSchedule list has its release time and deadline normalized by invoking Job_CPS' normalizeAndConvertTimes() method (discussed in Section 4.3.1). In addition, each job's release time is updated to mrcpCurrentTime because a job cannot start before mrcpCurrentTime. In line 13, a new OPL model definition is created by invoking CP_Scheduler's createNewModelDefinition() method, which is discussed in Section 4.4.3. After a new model definition has been created, a new OPL model is produced (line 14), and then solved (line 15) using CPLEX. After a solution is found, it is extracted by invoking CP_Scheduler's extractSolution() (line 16). This method retrieves values from MRCP's decision variables: x_{tr} and a_t (discussed in Section 3), and assigns the values to the Task_CPS objects' assignedResource and scheduledStart fields, respectively. In addition, the tasks (Task_CPS objects) that are assigned to a particular resource r (a Resource_CPS object) are added to r's scheduledMapTasks or scheduledRedTasks lists depending on its task type.

4.4.3 createNewModelDefinition()

Table 4 presents the CP-Scheduler's createNewModel Definition() algorithm. The first step is to initialize the variable modelSrc with a string value containing the OPL model's source code, which is obtained from OPLModelSource (discussed in Section 4.3.3) The next step is to process all scheduled tasks (Task_CPS objects) to check the state of the task's corresponding TaskInProgress (TIP) object (lines 2 to 11). If the task's TIP state is *running* then the Task_CPS' isExecuting field is set to true, and the CP_Scheduler's addConstraints() method is called (line 11). This method, as the name suggests, adds a new constraint to modelSrc that specifies the assigned start time, end time, and assigned resource of the task that is currently executing. The purpose of the new constraint is to prevent the solver from scheduling new tasks on the same resource slot during the same time interval. In addition, the task's isExecuting field is also set, which will be passed on to the OPL model (via OPLModelData class), to tell the CP solver that enforcing Constraint 2 is not required for tasks that are already executing. Conversely, if the task's TIP state is *completed* then the CP_Scheduler's remove Task() method (discussed in Section 4.4.1) is invoked (line 9). The final step (line 13) is to create the new OPL model definition object from the updated OPL model source, modelSrc.

Table 4. CP-Scheduler algorithm, createNewModelDefinition().

Input: none. **Output:** none.
1: *modelSrc* ← OPLModelSource.*getSource*()
2: **for** each resource *r* in *resources* **do**
3:   **for** each task *t* in *r.getAllScheduledTasks*() **do**
4:     *tip* ← *t.getTaskInProgress*()
5:     **if** *tip* is currently executing **then**
6:       *t.setCurrentlyExecuting*(true)
7:       **call** addConstraints(*modelSrc, t, r*)
8:     **else if** *tip* is finished executing **then**
9:       **call** *removeTask(t)*
10:     **end if**
11:   **end for**
12: **end for**
13: *modelDefinition* ← Create new OPL model definition using the updated OPL model source, *modelSrc*.

5. PERFORMANCE EVALUATION

This section describes the experiments that were conducted to evaluate the performance of the CP-Scheduler and EDF-Scheduler developed for Hadoop. In addition, a discussion of the experimental results and insights into system performance and behavior are provided.

5.1 Experimental Setup

5.1.1 System

The experiments were performed on an Amazon EC2 Hadoop cluster comprising one master node, and four slave nodes configured to have one map and one reduce slot each. Recall from Section 2.2 and Figure 3 the definitions of the master and slave nodes. Each node is an Amazon EC2 m3.medium instance. The m3.medium instances are *fixed performance instances* that provide a good balance of compute, memory, and network resources. Each m3.medium instance is launched with a 2.5GHz Intel Xeon E5-2670 v2 (Ivy Bridge) CPU, 3.75 GB of RAM, and runs Ubuntu 13.04. The cost of running an m3.medium instance is $0.07 per hour. Our experiments were performed on this cluster because it allowed us to confirm the functionality of the new prototype Hadoop CP-Scheduler by viewing the output of JobTracker and each TaskTracker in real-time. In addition, the chosen cluster fits within our current experimental budget. For future work, the plan is to perform experiments on a cluster with more nodes.

Initially, our experiments used Amazon's t2 instances; however, it was discovered that t2 instances are susceptible to performance degradation over time if the CPU usage is continuously high. This is because t2 instances are *burstable performance instances* and do not provide a fixed (consistent) performance. The t2 instances continuously receive *CPU Credits* at a fixed rated depending on the instance size. A CPU Credit supplies the instance with the performance of a full CPU core for one minute. If the instance is idle, it accumulates CPU Credits whereas the instance consumes CPU Credits when it is active. As a result of this, the m3.medium fixed performance instances are used in the experiments.

5.1.2 Workload

A Hadoop WordCount application (as discussed in Section 1) with three different input data sizes (i.e. *job size*) were used in the experiments: *small:* 3 files (~3MB), *med:* 10 files (~5MB), and *large:* 20 files (~10MB), to investigate the impact of different workload sizes on the performance of the system. The files are e-books (in plain text format) that are obtained from Project Gutenberg (www.gutenberg.org). Note that each job size has a number of map tasks that corresponds to the number of files it has, and one reduce task. For example, the medium workload job comprises ten map tasks and one reduce task. In these experiments, our goal is to use workloads with real input data, which is why e-books from Project Gutenberg were chosen. The number of files in each job was selected so that the cluster could execute the MapReduce job within a reasonable amount of time (small: ~50s, med: ~80s, large: ~100s) when there is no contention for resources. The reasonable execution time of these jobs results in a reasonable run time when conducting experiments with an open stream of job arrivals. The Hadoop/MapReduce framework is used with a variety of different data intensive applications. These include Big Data applications as well as applications processing data with sizes of 10s of megabytes (see [19] for example). This is in line with the size of data files we have experimented with. Analyzing the performance of the CP-Scheduler with other workloads characterized by large volumes of data forms a direction for future research.

A JobSubmitter (which runs on its own m3.medium instance) was implemented in Java to submit an open stream of WordCount jobs at a specified *arrival rate* (λ) to the Amazon EC2 Hadoop cluster. The arrival of jobs was generated using a Poisson process. The earliest start time (s_j) of the jobs is equal to its arrival time, and the job's deadline (d_j) is calculated as the sum of s_j and the maximum execution time of the job multiplied by an execution time multiplier (e_m). The purpose of e_m is to give the job slack time, and it is generated using a uniform distribution within the interval [1, 5]. These parameters for the jobs are generated in a similar manner to [5]. Note that the sample execution times of the jobs are obtained by performing a dry run—executing the jobs on the cluster when there is no resource contention.

Four different types of experiments were performed and each experiment type was conducted for the CP-Scheduler as well as for the EDF-Scheduler. In the first three experiment types, the `JobSubmitter` was configured to submit only a single job type: small, medium, or large. In the fourth experiment type, the `JobSubmitter` submits a mix of the three job types with each job type having an equal probability of being submitted. Note that the `JobSubmitter` is initialized with a predetermined seed for its random number generator so that the same sequence of jobs is submitted during the CP-Scheduler experiments and EDF-Scheduler experiments. Each experiment was run for at least five hours so that the system reached steady state.

5.1.3 Performance Metrics

The performance metrics that are considered in each experiment to evaluate the effectiveness and performance of the schedulers include:

- *Proportion of late jobs (P):* calculated as the ratio of the number of late jobs (N) and the number of jobs executed (NE). Recall that a job j is considered late if its completion time (C_j) is after its deadline (d_j).
- *Average job turnaround time (T):* calculated as $\sum_{j \in J}(C_j - s_j)$ divided by NE.
- *Average matchmaking and scheduling time of a job (O):* calculated as the total time required to perform matchmaking and scheduling of jobs during an experiment divided by NE. Note that O is a measure of the schedulers' processing overhead.

5.2 Experimental Results

5.2.1 Mixed Workload

Figure 6 and Figure 7 demonstrate that CP is able to effectively handle a complex workload with different types of jobs. CP outperforms EDF by a large margin in terms of P (up to 91%) and T (up to 57%). The CP-Scheduler is able to effectively interleave the execution of the tasks of multiple jobs such that jobs do not miss their deadlines. The EDF-Scheduler's poor performance in terms of P and T can be attributed to its focus on only scheduling a single job at a time (i.e. the job with the earliest deadline), and not interleaving the execution of jobs.

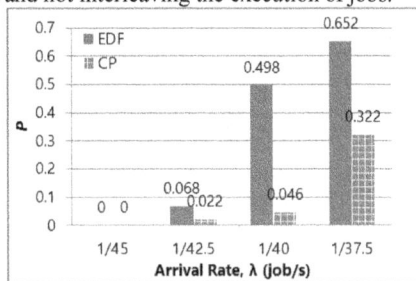

Figure 6. Mixed Workload: P.

The results in Figure 7 show that CP's O is larger (changing from 590ms to 3.5s as λ increases), compared to EDF's O which remains close to 12ms for all λ. CP's O is higher and is observed to increase with λ because the CP-Scheduler requires generating an OPL model that represents MRCP, and solving the OPL model using IBM's CP Optimizer (see Section 4.4). When there are more jobs in the OPL model's input, more time is required to generate and solve the OPL model because of the higher number of decision variables and constraints that need to be processed by the CP Optimizer. On the other hand, EDF's O tends not to change

significantly with λ because the EDF-Scheduler selects the job to schedule by retrieving the first job in its job queue (i.e. the job with the earliest deadline). Although, CP's O is high, the O/T ratio which is an indication of a scheduler's processing overhead in relation to the average job turnaround time, is still relatively low in all cases (less than 0.393%).

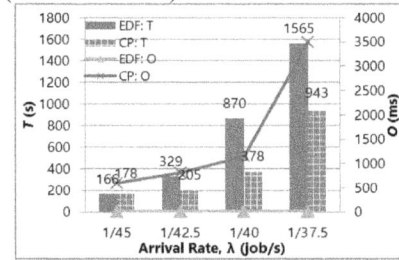

Figure 7. Mixed Workload: T and O.

5.2.2 Small Workload

The experimental results using the small workload are presented in Figure 8 and Figure 9. As shown in Figure 8, CP achieves a much lower P compared to EDF. When $\lambda < 1/17.5$job/s it is observed, that CP achieves a P of less than 0.07 which is close to the lower bound of zero. At $1/22.5$ job/s P is zero for both systems; however, at higher arrival rates CP outperforms EDF and is observed to have a 100% decrease in P. At $\lambda = 1/15$ job/s, both systems exhibit a high P due to high system load (average utilization of resources is 0.92) resulting in a high contention for resources. However, CP still has an approximately 50% lower P compared to EDF. As discussed, the lower P and T of CP can be attributed to MRCP interleaving the execution of jobs to minimize the number of late jobs; whereas, EDF simply schedules the job with the earliest deadline.

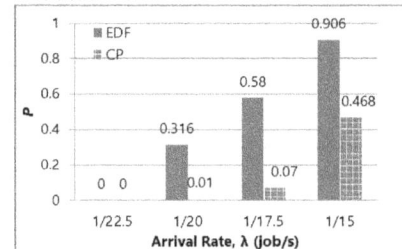

Figure 8. Small Workload: P.

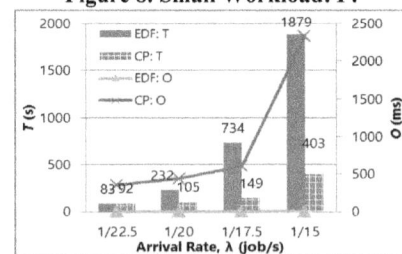

Figure 9. Small Workload: T and O.

Figure 9 shows that CP's T is up to 80% lower than EDF's T, except for when $\lambda = 1/22.5$ job/s. At the lowest arrival rate, CP has a slightly higher (10%) T because of its higher O. When focusing on O it is observed that EDF achieves a much lower O compared to CP. EDF's O is approximately 5ms for all λ, whereas CP's O increases with λ, changing from 350ms to 2.3s. As discussed, the reason for CP's higher O is due to the processing overhead of having to generate and solve MRCP. In comparison to the EDF-Scheduler, the CP-Scheduler puts more effort into deciding which jobs to map in order to minimize P. The benefits of this are captured in the superior performance demonstrated by CP with its lower P while still maintaining an O/T ratio of less than 0.6%.

5.2.3 Medium Workload

Due to the longer execution times of the jobs resulting in a higher load on the system, the λ values used in these experiments are lower than those used for the small workload. Similar to the results of the small workload, CP achieves up to 100% lower P compared to EDF (see Figure 10). In fact, it is observed that CP outperforms EDF by a larger margin when using the medium workload (88% on average) compared to the small workload (78% on average). This shows that the CP-Scheduler is capable of handling jobs with a higher number of tasks more effectively.

In Figure 11, performance trends that are similar to the small workload results are observed: CP has lower T but a higher O compared to EDF. As expected, the O for both the schedulers increase when compared to the small workload case due to the higher number of map tasks in each job. EDF's O increases from 5ms (from the small workload) to approximately 10ms in the medium workload for all λ. On the other hand, CP's O changes from 1.1s to 1.5s as λ increases for the medium workload, compared to 0.3s to 2.3s when the small workload is used. The only case where using the small workload (compared to the medium workload) resulted in a higher O for CP is when λ is at its highest value (1/15 job/s for the small workload and 1/37.5 job/s for the medium workload). This can be attributed to the small workload case having a higher system load (average resource utilization, U is 0.92) compared to the medium workload case where U is 0.89.

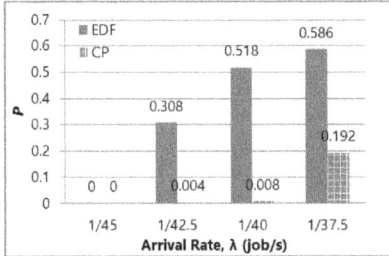

Figure 10. Medium Workload: _P_.

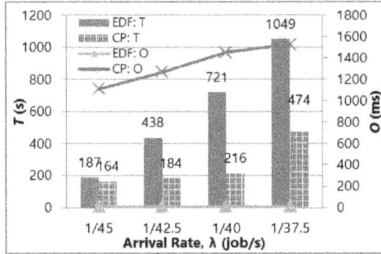

Figure 11. Medium Workload: _T_ and _O_.

Another difference between the medium and small workload results is observed when analyzing the cases where P=0 (i.e. λ =1/22.5 job/s for the small workload, and λ=1/45 job/s for the medium workload). In the medium workload case, CP achieves a lower T compared to EDF, but in the small workload case, the opposite is true. This can be attributed to the fact that in the small workload case, the CP-Scheduler can quickly determine a schedule that minimizes P (the primary objective) without focusing on T (O=352ms). Conversely, for the medium workload case, the CP-Scheduler needs to ensure jobs are executed in a more timely manner in order to minimize P (O=1.1s).

5.2.4 Large Workload

The results of the large workload (see Figure 12 and Figure 13) show CP's largest performance improvement in terms of P and T over EDF. In all cases, CP is able to achieve a P of zero; even when λ= 1/70 job/s where the P that EDF achieves is 0.49.

Furthermore, CP's performance improvement in terms of T is observed to increase from 32% to 100% as λ increases. The cause of the poor performance of EDF is due to the larger workload comprising jobs with more tasks, which results in longer job execution times. Since the EDF-Scheduler does not interleave the execution of jobs, scheduling jobs that have more tasks tends to lead to more late jobs because multiple jobs with closer deadlines can arrive on the system during the execution of the initial job. This shows that the EDF-Scheduler is more suited to handle a fixed number of jobs (closed workload) and cannot effectively handle an open stream of job arrivals. The CP-Scheduler, on the other hand, does interleave the execution of jobs and always attempts to create a new schedule that minimizes the number of late jobs when new jobs arrive on the system.

The performance trend of O when using the large workload is similar the other workloads. CP's O (which increases from 529ms to 765ms with λ) is higher than EDF's O (approximately 16ms for all λ). It is observed that EDF's O increases with the size of the workload because larger workloads comprise jobs with more tasks, and more time is required to map a job with a higher number of tasks compared to a job with fewer tasks. This shows that EDF's O has a direct relationship with the number of tasks in a job (called the _job size_). Conversely, CP's O does not show a similar trend when the size of the workload increases. CP's O depends on the job size, but is also influenced by λ. This can be seen by comparing the results of the medium and large workloads. For all values of λ experimented with, CP's O is observed to be higher for the medium workload in comparison to the large workload. This can be attributed to the higher system load. More specifically, in the medium workload the average resource utilization (U) varies from 0.74 to 0.89 as λ increases from 1/45 to 1/37.5 jobs/s, compared to the large workload where U changes from 0.34 to 0.37 as λ increases from 1/77.5 to 1/70 jobs/s. Note that the values of U in the large workload case are lower because of the lower values of λ used in the experiments.

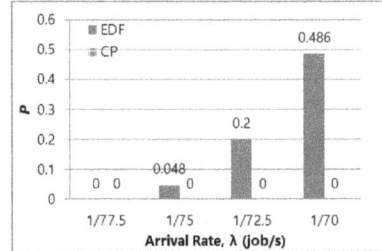

Figure 12. Large Workload: _P_.

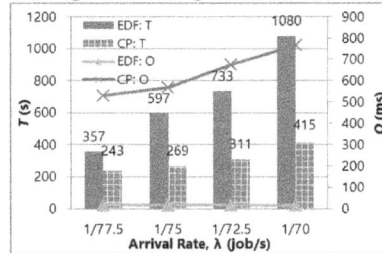

Figure 13. Large Workload: _T_ and _O_.

6. CONCLUSIONS AND FUTURE WORK

The focus of this paper is on engineering resource management middleware that can effectively handle matchmaking and scheduling an open stream of MapReduce jobs with SLAs each of which is characterized by an execution time, an earliest start time, and an end-to-end deadline. The key objective of this research is to achieve high system performance while minimizing resource management overhead. More specifically, a MapReduce constraint programming based matchmaking and scheduling algorithm (MRCP) is devised and solved using IBM CPLEX. Furthermore, a new constraint programming based scheduler for Hadoop, which is a popular open source implementation of the MapReduce programming model, is devised and implemented. The new scheduler for Hadoop, called *CP-Scheduler*, generates and solves an MRCP model to perform matchmaking and scheduling of an open stream of MapReduce jobs with deadlines. Our experiences and the challenges that we encountered in devising the CP-Scheduler and implementing the algorithm in Hadoop are described in this paper. A performance evaluation of the CP-scheduler is conducted on an Amazon EC2 cluster running Hadoop and its performance is compared with that of an EDF-Scheduler, which is implemented by extending Hadoop's default FIFO scheduler. The experimental results demonstrate the CP-Scheduler's effectiveness to map an open stream of MapReduce jobs with deadlines in a Hadoop cluster. Some of the key insights into system behaviour and performance are summarized:

- In all the experiments, the CP-Scheduler generated a schedule that leads to a lower or equal P compared to the EDF-Scheduler, and close to the lower bound of zero when the system utilization is reasonable. The best performance observed is in the large workload experiments where the CP-Scheduler generated a P of zero in all cases. In other experiments, the percentage improvement of the CP-Scheduler's P compared to the EDF-Scheduler's P is observed to be as low as 48% and as high as 100%.

- In most cases, the CP-Scheduler generated a schedule with a lower T compared to the EDF-Scheduler. The CP-Scheduler is outperformed by the EDF-Scheduler by a small margin when the system is lightly loaded (i.e. small workload and small arrival rate, which can be attributed to the CP-Scheduler's O having a larger impact on T.

- Although, the CP-Scheduler demonstrates a much superior P and T in comparison to EDF-Scheduler, this performance improvement is accompanied by an increase in O. However, it is still observed that the ratio O/T for the CP-Scheduler is still very small in all cases experimented with (less than 0.69%).
  - The CP-Scheduler's O depends on the number of tasks in a job (i.e. job size), as well as the job arrival rate, and thus for a given workload type O increases as the job arrival rate increases. Conversely, the EDF-Scheduler's O increases with job size, and remains relatively the same as job arrival rate increases.

Overall, the experimental results show that the CP-Scheduler can effectively perform matchmaking and scheduling of an open stream of MapReduce jobs with deadlines in a Hadoop cluster leading to a schedule with a small proportion of late jobs. The EDF-Scheduler; however, seems to be more suited to handle a fixed (closed) workload because of the fact that it does not interleave the execution of jobs, which can lead to very poor performance on an open system. This can happen, for example, when the execution times of jobs are long and multiple jobs arrive on the system with earlier deadlines (see Section 5.2.4).

For future research, we plan to perform more extensive experiments, which includes experiments that use larger workloads and more nodes. Moreover, techniques for estimating task execution times and handling errors associated with the estimated times warrants further investigation.

7. ACKNOWLEDGMENTS

We are grateful to Huawei, Canada and the Government of Ontario for supporting this research.

8. REFERENCES

[1] The Apache Software Foundation. Hadoop. Available: http://hadoop.apache.org.

[2] Jones, M. 2011. Scheduling in Hadoop. Available: http://www.ibm.com/developerworks/library/os-hadoop-scheduling/

[3] Rossi, F., Beek, P., and Walsh, T. 2008. Chapter 4: Constraint Programming. *Handbook of Knowledge Representation* (2008). 181-211.

[4] Dean, J. and Ghemawat, S. 2004. MapReduce: Simplified data processing on large clusters. *Int'l Symp. on Operating System Design and Implementation* (Dec. 2004). 137–150.

[5] Verma, A., Cherkasova, L., Kumar, V.S., and Campbell, R.H. 2012. Deadline-based workload management for MapReduce environments: Pieces of the performance puzzle. In *Proc. of Network Operations and Management Symposium* (16-20 April 2012). 900-905.

[6] Dong, X., Wang, Y., and Liao, H. 2011. Scheduling Mixed Real-Time and Non-real-Time Applications in MapReduce Environment. *Int'l Conf. on Parallel and Distributed Systems* (7-9 Dec. 2011). 9-16.

[7] Mattess, M., Calheiros, R.N., and Buyya, R. 2013. Scaling MapReduce Applications Across Hybrid Clouds to Meet Soft Deadlines. *Int'l Conf. on Advanced Information Networking and Applications* (25-28 March 2013). 629-636.

[8] Hwang, E. and Kim, K. H. 2012. Minimizing Cost of Virtual Machines for Deadline-Constrained MapReduce Applications in the Cloud. *Int'l Conf. on Grid Computing* (20-23 Sept. 2012).130-138.

[9] Kc, K., and Anyanwu, K. 2010. Scheduling Hadoop Jobs to Meet Deadlines. *Int'l Conf. on Cloud Computing Technology and Science* (Nov. 30 2010-Dec. 3 2010). 388-392.

[10] Lim, N., Majumdar, S., and Ashwood-Smith, P. 2014.Engineering Resource Management Middleware for Optimizing the Performance of Clouds Processing MapReduce Jobs with Deadlines. *Int'l Conf. on Performance Engineering* (Mar. 24-26 2014). 161-172.

[11] IBM. IBM ILOG CPLEX Optimization Studio V12.5 Reference Manual. Available: http://pic.dhe.ibm.com/ infocenter/cosinfoc/ v12r5/index.jsp

[12] Lim, N., Majumdar, S., and Ashwood-Smith, P. 2014. A Constraint Programming-Based Resource Management Technique for Processing MapReduce Jobs with SLAs on Clouds. *Int'l Conf. on Parallel Processing* (Sept 9-12 2014).

[13] White, T. 2011. Hadoop: The Definitive Guide, 2nd Edition. *O'Reilly Media, Inc.,* Sebastopol, CA, USA.

[14] Apache. Hadoop Wiki. Available: http://wiki.apache.org/ hadoop/PoweredBy

[15] Fadika, Z., Dede, E., Hartog, J., and Govindaraju, M. 2012. MARLA: MapReduce for Heterogeneous Clusters. *IEEE/ACM Int'l Symp. on Cluster, Cloud and Grid Computing* (13-16 May 2012). 49-56.

[16] Chang, H., Kodialam, M., Kompella, R.R., Lakshman, T.V. Lee, M., and Mukherjee, S. 2011. Scheduling in mapreduce like systems for fast completion time. *IEEE INFOCOM* (10-15 April 2011). 3074-3082.

[17] Gao, X., Chen, Q., Chen, Y., Sun, Q., Liu, Y., and Li, M. 2012. A Dispatching-Rule-Based Task Scheduling Policy for MapReduce with Multi-type Jobs in Heterogeneous Environments. *ChinaGrid Annual Conference* (20-23 Sept. 2012). 17 -24.

[18] IBM. 2010. Detailed Scheduling in IBM ILOG CPLEX Optimization Studio with IBM ILOG CPLEX CP Optimizer. *White Paper*. IBM Corporation (2010).

[19] Zujie, R., Wan, J., Shi, W., Xu, X., and Zhou, M. 2014. Workload Analysis, Implications, and Optimization on a Production Hadoop Cluster: A Case Study on Taobao. *IEEE Transactions Services Computing* (vol.7, no.2, April-June 2014). 307-321.

An Empirical Performance Evaluation of Distributed SQL Query Engines

Stefan van Wouw[§†], José Viña[§], Alexandru Iosup[†], and Dick Epema[†]

[§]Azavista, the Netherlands
[†]Delft University of Technology, the Netherlands

stefanvanwouw@gmail.com, jose@azavista.com, {a.iosup,d.h.j.epema}@tudelft.nl

ABSTRACT

Distributed SQL Query Engines (DSQEs) are increasingly used in a variety of domains, but especially users in small companies with little expertise may face the challenge of selecting an appropriate engine for their specific applications. Although both industry and academia are attempting to come up with high level benchmarks, the performance of DSQEs has never been explored or compared in-depth. We propose an empirical method for evaluating the performance of DSQEs with representative metrics, datasets, and system configurations. We implement a micro-benchmarking suite of three classes of SQL queries for both a synthetic and a real world dataset and we report response time, resource utilization, and scalability. We use our micro-benchmarking suite to analyze and compare three state-of-the-art engines, viz. Shark, Impala, and Hive. We gain valuable insights for each engine and we present a comprehensive comparison of these DSQEs. We find that different query engines have widely varying performance: Hive is always being outperformed by the other engines, but whether Impala or Shark is the best performer highly depends on the query type.

Categories and Subject Descriptors

D.2.8 [**Software Engineering**]: Metrics—*performance measures*; H.3.4 [**Information Storage and Retrieval**]: Systems and Software—*distributed systems, performance evaluation*; H.4 [**Information Systems Applications**]: Miscellaneous

General Terms

Experimentation; Performance

ICPE'15, Jan. 31–Feb. 4, 2015, Austin, Texas, USA.
Copyright © 2015 ACM 978-1-4503-3248-4/15/01 ... $15.00.
http://dx.doi.org/10.1145/2668930.2688053.

Keywords

Distributed SQL Query Engine; Performance Evaluation; Scalability

1. INTRODUCTION

With the decrease in cost of storage and computation of public clouds, even small and medium enterprises (SMEs) are able to process large amounts of data. This causes businesses to increase the amounts of data they collect, to sizes that are difficult for traditional database management systems to handle. This has led to Hadoop-oriented distributed query engines such as Hive [18], Impala [5], Shark [21], and more recently, Presto [7], Drill [10], and Hive-on-Tez [3]. Selecting the most suitable of these systems for a particular SME is a big challenge, because SMEs are not likely to have the expertise and the resources available to perform an in-depth study. We remove this burden from SMEs by addressing the following research question: *How well do Distributed SQL Query Engines (DSQEs) perform on SME workloads?*

Although performance studies do exist for Distributed SQL Query Engines [1, 6, 8, 9, 15, 21], many of them only use synthetic workloads or very high-level comparisons that are only based on query response time. Our work evaluates performance much more in-depth by reporting more metrics and evaluating more performance aspects. In addition to reporting query response times, we also show scalability and detailed resource utilization. The latter performance aspects are particularly important for an SME in order to choose a query engine.

In order to answer the research question we define a comprehensive performance evaluation method to assess different aspects of query engines. We compare Hive, a somewhat older but still widely used query engine, with Impala and Shark, both state-of-the-art distributed query engines. This method can be used to compare current and future query engines, despite not covering all the methodological and practical aspects of a true benchmark. The method focuses on three performance aspects: processing power, resource utilization and scalability. With the results from this study, system developers and data analysts can make informed choices related to both cluster infrastructure and query tuning.

Using both a real world and a synthetic dataset with queries representative of SME workloads, we evaluate the

Table 1: Overview of Related Work. Legend: Real World (R), Synthetic (S), Modified Workload (+)

Query Engines	Workload	Dataset Type	Largest Dataset	Cluster Size
Hive, Shark [21]	Pavlo+, other	R, S	1.55 TiB	100
Redshift, Hive, Shark, Impala, Tez [1]	Pavlo+	S	127.5 GiB	5
Impala, Tez, Shark, Presto [6]	TPC-DS+	S	13.64 TiB	20
Teradata DBMS [9]	TPC-DS+	S	186.24 GiB	8
Hive, Impala, Tez [8]	TPC-DS/H+	S	220.72 GiB	20
DBMS-X, Vertica [15]	Pavlo	S	931.32 GiB	100
Our Work	**Pavlo+, other**	**R, S**	**523.66 GiB**	**5**

query engines' performance. We find that different query engines have widely varying performance, with Hive always being outperformed by the other engines. Whether Impala or Shark is the best performer highly depends on the query type and input size.

Our main contributions are:

- We propose a method for performance evaluation of DSQEs (Section 4), which includes defining a workload representative for SMEs as well as defining the performance aspects of the query engines: processing power, resource utilization and scalability.

- We define a micro-benchmark setup for three major query engines, namely Shark, Impala and Hive (Section 5).

- We provide an in-depth performance comparison between Shark, Impala and Hive using our micro-benchmark suite (Section 6).

2. RELATED WORK

We wanted to evaluate the major Distributed SQL Query Engines currently on the market using a cluster size and dataset size that is representative for SMEs, but still comparable to similar studies. Table 1 summarizes the related previous works. Some of them run a subset or enhanced version of the TPC-DS benchmark [16] which has only recently been adopted for Big Data analytics in the form of BigBench [9]. Other studies run a variant of the Pavlo et al. micro-benchmark [15] which is widely accepted in the field.

Overall, most studies use synthetic workloads, of which some are very large. Synthetic workloads do not necessarily characterise real world datasets very well. For our work we have also taken a real world dataset in use by an SME. Besides our work, only one other study uses real world datasets [21]. However, like most of the other studies, it only reports on query response times. Our work evaluates performance much more in-depth by reporting more metrics and evaluating more performance aspects including scalability and detailed resource utilization. We argue that scalability and resource utilization are also very important when deciding which query engine will be used by an SME.

3. QUERY ENGINE SELECTION

In this study we initially attempted to evaluate 5 state-of-the-art Distributed SQL Query engines: Drill, Presto, Shark, Impala and Hive. We chose to evaluate these query engines because they are widely used and contributed to by many individuals and companies. All of the engines have

more than 400 forks and more than 1,000 stars on GitHub, except for Drill, which has 188 forks and 298 stars.

We ended up discarding Drill and Presto because these systems lacked required functionality at the time of testing. Drill only had a proof of concept one node version, and Presto did not have the functionality needed to write output to disk (which is required for the kind of workloads we wanted to evaluate).

Shark [21] is a DSQE built on top of the Spark [23] execution engine, which in turn heavily relies on the concept of Resilient Distributed Datasets (RDDs) [22]. In short this means that whenever Shark receives an SQL query, it will convert it to a Spark job, execute it in Spark, and then return the results. Spark keeps all intermediate results in memory using RDDs, and only spills them to disk if no sufficient memory is available. Mid-query fault tolerance is provided by Spark. It is also possible to have the input and output dataset cached entirely in memory.

Impala [5] is a DSQE being developed by Cloudera and is heavily inspired by Google's Dremel [14]. It employs its own massively parallel processing (MPP) architecture on top of HDFS instead of using Hadoop MapReduce as execution engine (like Hive below). One large downside to this engine is that it does not provide fault tolerance. Whenever a node dies in the middle of query execution, the whole query is aborted.

Hive [18] was one of the first DSQEs, introduced by Facebook and built on top of the Hadoop platform [2]. It provides a Hive Meta Store service to put a relational database-like structure on top of the raw data stored in HDFS. Whenever a HiveQL (SQL dialect) query is submitted to Hive, Hive will convert it to a job to be run on Hadoop MapReduce. Although Hive provides mid-query fault tolerance, it relies on Hadoop MapReduce and is slowed down whenever this system stores intermediate results on disk.

4. EXPERIMENTAL METHOD

In this section we present the method of evaluating the performance of Distributed SQL Query Engines. First we define the workload as well as the aspects of the engines used for assessing this performance. Then we describe the evaluation procedure.

4.1 Workload

During the performance evaluation we use both synthetic and real world datasets with three SQL queries per dataset. We carefully selected the different types of queries and datasets to match the scale and diversity of the workloads SMEs deal with.

1) Synthetic Dataset: Based on the benchmark from Pavlo et al. [15], the UC Berkeley AMPLab introduced a general benchmark for DSQEs [1]. We have used an adapted version of AMPLab's Big Data benchmark where we leave out the query testing User Defined Functions (UDFs), since not all query engines support UDF in similar form. The synthethic dataset used by these 3 queries consists of 118.29 GiB of structured server logs per URL (the uservisits table), and 5.19 GiB of page ranks (the rankings table) per website, as seen in Table 2. The uservisits and rankings tables can be joined by matching on the URL field of the web page visited. No other foreign key relationships are present.

Is this dataset representative for SME data? The structure of the data closely resembles the structure of click data

Table 2: Summary of Datasets.

Table	# Columns	Description
uservisits	9	Structured server logs per page.
rankings	3	Page rank score per page.
hotel_prices	8	Daily hotel prices.

Table 3: Summary of SQL Queries.

Query	Input Size GiB	Input Size Records	Output Size GiB	Output Size Records	Tables
1	5.19	90M	5.19	90M	rankings
2	118.29	752M	40	254M	uservisits
3	123.48	842M	$< 10^{-7}$	1	uservisits, rankings
4	523.66	7900M	$< 10^{-2}$	113K	hotel_prices
5	20	228M	4.3	49M	hotel_prices subsets
6	8	94.7M	4	48M	hotel_prices subsets

being collected in all kinds of SMEs. The dataset size might even be slightly large for SMEs, because as pointed out by Rowstron et al. [17] analytics production clusters at *large* companies such as Microsoft and Yahoo have median job input sizes under 13.03 GiB and 90% of jobs on Facebook clusters have input sizes under 93.13 GiB.

On this dataset, we run queries 1 to 3 to test raw data processing power, aggregation and *JOIN* performance respectively. We describe each of these queries below in addition to providing query statistics in Table 3.

Query 1 performs a data scan on a relatively small dataset. It simply scans the whole rankings table and filters out certain records.

Query 2 computes the sum of ad revenues generated per visitor from the uservisits table in order to test aggregation performance.

Query 3 joins the rankings table with the uservisits table in order to test JOIN performance.

2) Real World Dataset: We collected price data of hotel rooms on a daily basis during a period of twelve months between November 2012 and November 2013. More than 21 million hotel room prices for more than 4 million hotels were collected on average every day. This uncompressed dataset (the hotel_prices table) is 523.66 GiB on disk as seen in Table 3. Since the price data was collected every day, we decided to partition the dataset in daily chunks as to be able to only use data of certain collection days, rather than having to load the entire dataset all the time.

Is this dataset representative for SME data? The queries we selected for the dataset are in use by Azavista, an SME specialized in meeting and event planning software. The real world scenarios for these queries relate to reporting price statistics per city and country.

On this dataset, we run queries 4 to 6 to also (like queries 1 to 3) test raw data processing power, aggregation and *JOIN* performance respectively. However, these queries are not interchangeable with queries 1 to 3 because they are tailored to the exact structure of the hotel price dataset, and by using different input and output sizes we test different aspects of the query engines. We describe each of the queries 4 to 6 below in addition to providing query statistics in Table 3.

Query 4 computes average prices of hotel rooms grouped by certain months.

Query 5 computes linear regression pricing curves over a timespan of data collection dates.

Query 6 computes changes in hotel room prices between two collection dates.

3) Total Workload: Combining the results from the experiments with the two datasets gives us insights in performance of the query engines on both synthetic and real world data. In particular we look at how the engines deal with data scans (Query 1 and 4), heavy aggregation (Query 2 and 5), and the JOINs (Query 3 and 6).

4.2 Performance Aspects and Metrics

In order to be able to reason about the performance differences between different query engines, the different aspects contributing to this performance need to be defined. In this study we focus on three performance aspects:

1. *Processing Power*: the ability of a query engine to process a large number of SQL queries in a set amount of time. The more SQL queries a query engine can handle in a set amount of time, the better. We measure the processing power in terms of response time, that is, the time between submitting an SQL query to the system and getting a response. In addition, we also calculate the throughput per SQL query: the number of input records divided by response time.

2. *Resource Utilization*: the ability of a query engine to efficiently use the system resources available. This is important, because especially SMEs cannot afford to waste precious system resources. We measure the resource utilization in terms of mean, maximum and total CPU, memory, disk and network usage.

3. *Scalability*: the ability of a query engine to maintain predictable performance behaviour when system resources are added or removed from the system, or when input datasets grow or shrink. Another way of defining scalability is splitting it in strong, as well as weak scalability. Strong scalability measures the query response time improvement when adding more processors to the cluster while, at the same time, keeping the *total* input size fixed. Weak scalability, on the other hand, measures the query response time when adding more processors, while at the same time increasing the input size such that the amount of data per processor stays constant.

We perform two types of scalability. The first is horizontal scalability (a form of strong scalability), where the total input size is fixed while the number of cluster nodes increases. The second is data input size scalability, where the number of cluster nodes is fixed while the total input size increases. Ideally, the performance should improve proportionally to the amount of resources added (taking the time complexity of the query into account). The performance should only degrade inversely proportional with every unit of input data added (again taking the time complexity of the query into account). In practice this highly depends on the type of resources added as well as the overhead of parallelism introduced.

4.3 Evaluation Procedure

Our procedure for evaluating the DSQEs is as follows: we run each query 10 times on its corresponding dataset while taking snapshots of the resource utilization using the monitoring tool `collectl` [4]. After the query completes, we also store its response time. Note that we run each query in a clean system in a single-tenant environment. No side-effects of queries can affect other queries. When averaging over all the experiment iterations, we report the standard deviation as indicated with error bars in the experimental result figures. Like that, we take into account the varying performance of our cluster at different times of the day, intrinsic to the cloud [13].

The queries are submitted on the master node using the command line tools each query engine provides, and we write the output to a dedicated table which is cleared after every experiment iteration. We restart the query engine under test at the start of every experiment iteration in order to keep it comparable with other iterations.

5. EXPERIMENTAL SETUP

We define a full micro-benchmarking setup by configuring the query engines as well as tuning their data caching policies for optimal performance. We evaluate the most recent stable versions of Shark (v0.9.0), Impala (v1.2.3) and Hive (v.0.12). Many different parameters can influence the query engine's performance. In the following we define the hardware and software configuration parameters used in our experiments.

Hardware: To make a fair performance comparison between the query engines, we use the same cluster setup for each when running the experiments. The cluster consists of 5 `m2.4xlarge` worker Amazon EC2 VMs and 1 `m2.4xlarge` master VM, each having 68.4 GiB of memory, 8 virtual cores and 1.5 TiB instance storage. This cluster has sufficient storage for the real-world and synthetic data, and also has the memory required to allow query engines to benefit from in-memory caching of query inputs or outputs.

The scale of this cluster is comparable to the cluster sizes observed in SMEs and related studies (see Table 1 and [12]). Contrary to other Big Data processing systems, DSQEs (especially Impala and Shark) are tuned for nodes with large amounts of memory, which allows us to use fewer nodes than in comparable studies for batch processing systems to still get comparable (or better!) performance. An additional benefit of this specific cluster setup is the fact it is the same cluster setup used in the AMPLab benchmarks previously performed on older versions of Shark (v0.8.1), Impala (v1.2.3) and Hive (v0.12) [1]. By using the same setup, we can also compare current versions of these query engines with these older versions and see if significant performance improvements have been made.

Software: Hive uses YARN [19] as resource manager while we have used Impala's and Shark's standalone resource managers respectively, because at the time of testing the YARN compatible versions were not mature yet. All query engines under test run on top of a 64-bit Ubuntu 12.04 operating system. We use commonly known best practice configurations without system tuning. Since the queries we run compute results over large amounts of data, the configuration parameters of the distributed file system this data is stored on (HDFS) are crucial. It is therefore imperative that

Table 4: Different ways to configure Shark with caching.

Abbreviation	OS Disk Cache	Input Cache	Output Cache
Cold	No	No	No
OC	No	No	Yes
OSC	Yes	No	No
IC	N/A	Yes	No
OSC+OC	Yes	No	Yes
IC+OC	N/A	Yes	Yes

we keep these parameters fixed across all query engines under test. One of these parameters includes the HDFS block size, which we keep to the default of 64 MiB. The number of HDFS files used per dataset, and how these files are structured and compressed is also kept fixed. While more sophisticated file formats are available (such as RCFile [11]) we selected the Sequence file key-value pair format because unlike the more sophisticated formats this is supported by all query engines, and this format uses less disk space than the plain text format. The datasets are compressed on disk using the Snappy compression type, which aims for reasonable compression size while being very fast at decompression.

Each worker has 68.4 GiB of memory available of which we allow a maximum of 60GiB for the query engines under test. This leaves a minimum of 8 GiB of free memory for other processes running on the same system. By doing this we ensure that all query engines under test have an equal amount of maximum memory reserved for them while still allowing the OS disk buffer cache to use more than 8 GiB when the query engine is not using a lot of memory.

Dataset Caching: Another important factor that influences query engine performance is whether the input data is cached or not. By default the operating system will cache files that were loaded from disk in an OS disk buffer cache. Because both Hive and Impala do not have any configurable caching policies available, we will simply run the queries on these two query engines both with and without the input dataset loaded into the OS disk buffer cache. To accomplish this, we perform a `SELECT` query over the relevant tables, so all the relevant data is loaded into the OS disk buffer cache. The query engines under test are restarted after every query as to prevent any other kind of caching to happen that might be unknown to us (e.g., Impala has a non-configurable internal caching system).

In contrast, Shark has more options available regarding caching. In addition to just using the OS disk buffer caching method, Shark also has the option to use an in-memory cached table as input and an in-memory cached table as output. This completely removes the (need for) disk I/O once the system has warmed up. To establish a representative configuration for Shark, we first evaluate the configurations as depicted in Table 4. OS Disk Cache means the entire input tables are first loaded through the OS disk cache by means of a `SELECT`. Input Cache means the input is first cached into in-memory Spark RDDs. Lastly, Output Cache means the result is kept in memory rather than written back to disk.

Figure 1 shows the resulting average response times for running a simple `SELECT *` query using the different possible Shark configurations. Note that no distinction is made between OS disk buffer cache being cleared or not when a cached input table is used, since in this case Shark does not read from disk at all.

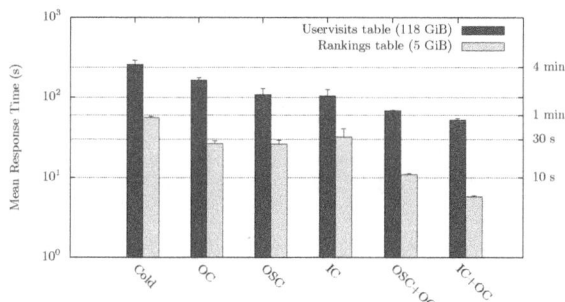

Figure 1: Response time for different Shark caching configurations. Vertical axis is in log-scale.

The configuration with both input and output cached tables enabled (IC+OC) is the fastest setup for both the small and large data set. But the IC+OC and the IC configuration can only be used when the entire input data set fits in memory, which is often not the case with data sets of multiple TBs in size. The second fastest configuration (OSC+OC) only keeps the output (which is often much smaller) in memory and still reads the input from disk. The configuration which yields the worst results is using no caching at all (as expected).

In the experiments in Section 6 we use the optimistic IC+OC configuration when the input data set fits in memory and the OSC+OC configuration when it does not, representing the best-case scenario. In addition the Cold configuration will be used to represent worst-case scenarios.

6. EXPERIMENTAL RESULTS

We evaluate the three query engines selected in Section 3 on the performance aspects described in Section 4.2 using the workloads described in Section 4.1. We evaluate processing power in Section 6.1, resource consumption in Section 6.2, and scalability in Section 6.3.

6.1 Processing Power

We have used the fixed cluster setup with a total of 5 worker nodes and 1 master node as described in Section 5 to evaluate the response time and throughput (defined as the number of input records divided by the response time) of Hive, Impala and Shark on the 6 queries in the workloads. The results of the experiments are depicted in Figure 2. All experiments have been performed 10 times except for Query 4 with Impala since it took simply too long to complete. Only 2 iterations have been performed for this particular query. We used the dataset caching configurations explained in Section 5. For Impala and Hive we used disk buffer caching and no disk buffer caching for the warm and cold situations, respectively. For Shark we used the Cold configuration for the cold situation. In addition we used input and output dataset caching (IC+OC) for the warm situation of queries 1 to 3, and disk buffer caching and output caching (OSC+OC) for the warm situation of queries 4 to 6, since the price input dataset does not entirely fit in memory.

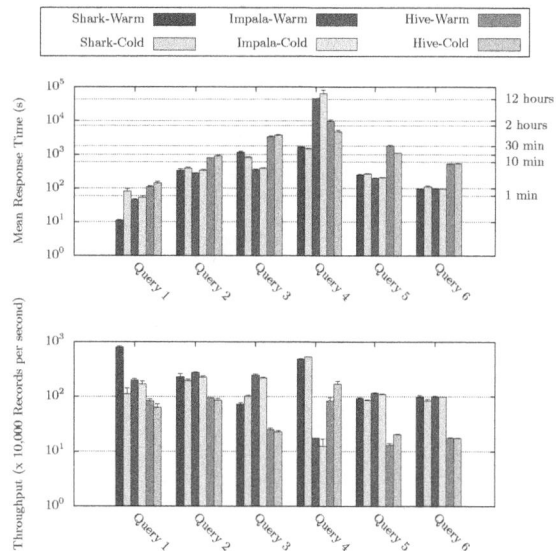

Figure 2: Query Response Time (top) and Throughput (bottom). Vertical axis is in log-scale.

Key Findings:

- Input data caching generally does not cause a significant difference in response times.

- Performance is relatively stable over different iterations.

- Impala and Shark have similar performance and Hive is the worst performer in most cases. There is no overall winner.

- Impala does not handle large input sizes very well (Query 4).

The main reason why Hive is much slower than Impala and Shark is because of the high intermediate disk I/O. Because most queries are not disk I/O bound, data input caching makes little difference in performance. We elaborate on these two findings in more detail in our technical report [20].

In the following we discuss the response times from the 6 queries in a pair-wise manner. We evaluate the data scan queries 1 and 4, the aggregation queries 2 and 5, and the JOIN performance queries 4 and 6 depicted in Figure 2.

1) Scan performance: Shark's response time for query 1 with data input and output caching enabled is significantly better than that of the other query engines (10 seconds vs. 100 seconds for Hive). This is explained by the fact that query 1 is CPU-bound for the *Shark-Warm* configuration, but disk I/O bound for all other configurations as depicted in Figure 3. Since *Shark-Warm* caches both the input and output, and the intermediate data is so small that no spilling is required, no disk I/O is performed at all for *Shark-Warm*.

Results for query 4 for Impala are particularly interesting. The response time of Impala is 12 hours, while the response time of Hive (2 hours) and Shark (30 minutes) are much lower. At the same time, resource utilization of Impala is much lower, as explained in our technical report [20]. No bottleneck can be detected in the resource utilization

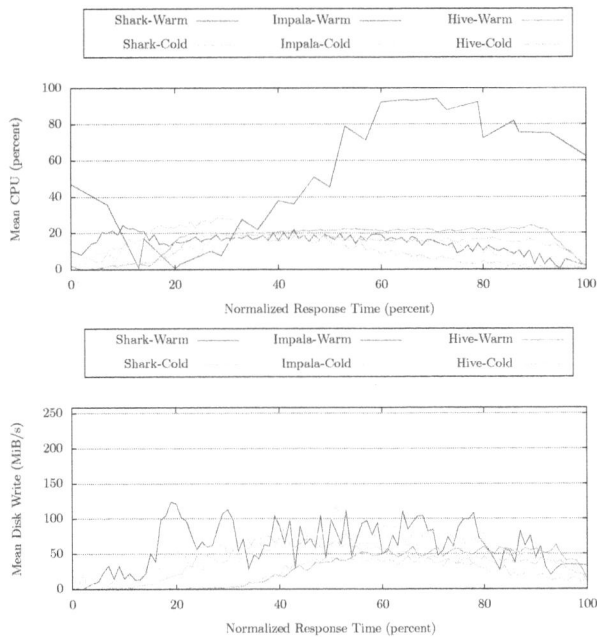

Figure 3: CPU utilization (top) and Disk Write (bottom) for query 1 over normalized response time.

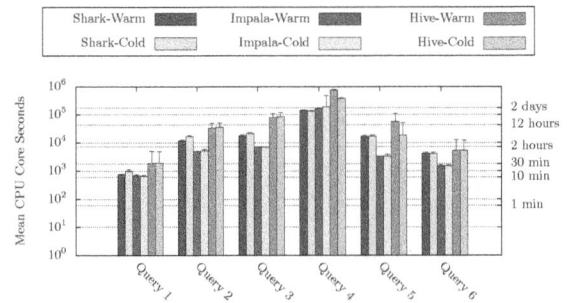

Figure 4: CPU Core Seconds. Vertical axis is in log-scale.

Key Findings:

- Impala is a winner in total CPU consumption. Even when Shark outperforms Impala in terms of response time, Impala is still more CPU efficient (Figure 4).

- All query engines tend to use the full memory assigned to them (See our technical report [20]).

- Disk I/O is as expected significantly higher for the queries without data caching vs. the queries with data caching. Impala has slightly less disk I/O than Shark. Hive ends last (Figure 5).

- Network I/O is comparable in all query engines, with the exception of Hive, which again ends last (Figure 6).

In the following we discuss the resource consumption per query averaged over 5 workers and 10 iterations (50 data-points per average). We show the CPU Core Seconds per query in Figure 4. This shows how much total CPU a query uses during the query execution. The CPU Core Seconds metric is calculated by taking the area under the CPU utilization graphs of all workers, and then multiplying this number by the number of cores per worker (8 in our setup). For example, a hypothetical query running 2 seconds using 50% of CPU uses 1 CPU Second which is equal to 8 CPU Core Seconds in our case. The results in Figure 4 show that the total amount of time required to complete a query on a single core machine can range between 10 minutes (query 1) to more than 2 days (query 4). A query running on Impala is the most efficient in terms of total CPU utilization, followed by Shark. This is as expected since although Shark and Impala are quite close in terms of response time, Impala is written in C/C++ instead of Scala, which is slightly more efficient.

The total disk I/O per query is depicted in Figure 5. It shows that data caching does make a significant difference in the number of disk reads performed. For example, query 1 on Shark requires less than 100 MiB of disk read when caching is enabled, while it requires more than 1 GiB when the cache is cleared. However, as shown in [20], disk I/O is hardly ever the bottleneck. Although the input datasets are entirely cached in the *Shark-Warm* configuration for queries 1 to 3, disk reading still occurs. This can be explained by the fact that Shark writes shuffle output of intermediate stages to the disk buffer cache (which eventually spills to disk). For

logs and no errors are reported by Impala. After re-running the experiments for Impala on query 4 on a different set of Amazon EC2 instances, similar results are obtained, which makes it highly unlikely an error occured during experiment execution. A more in-depth inspection is needed to get to the cause of this problem, which is out of the scope of our work.

2) Aggregation performance: Both the aggregation query 2 and 5 are handled quite well by all the engines. The response time ranges from 5 to 10 minutes. The main reason why even though query 5 has a much smaller input dataset, the response times are close to the ones of query 2 is that this query is relatively much more compute intensive (see Figure 4).

3) JOIN performance: The query engines perform quite similar on the JOIN queries 3 and 6. A remarkable result is that the fully input and output cached configuration *Shark-Warm* starts to perform worse than its cold equivalent when dataset sizes grow. This is explained in more detail in Section 6.3.

6.2 Resource Consumption

Although the cluster consists of both a master and 5 worker nodes, we only evaluate the resource consumption on the workers, since the master is only used for coordination and remains idle the most of the time. For any of the queries the master never used more than 6 GiB of memory (<10% of total available), never exceeded more than 82 CPU Core Seconds (<0.0005% of the workers' maximum), has negligible disk I/O, and never exceeded total network I/O of 4 GiB (<0.08% of the workers' maximum).

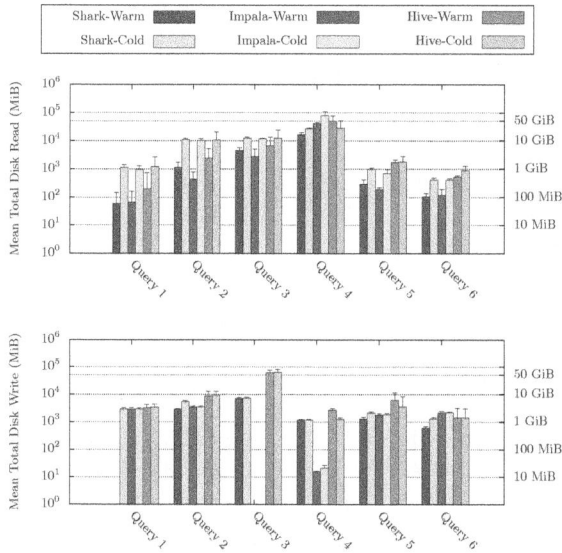

Figure 5: Total Disk Read (top) and Disk Write (bottom). Vertical axis is in log-scale.

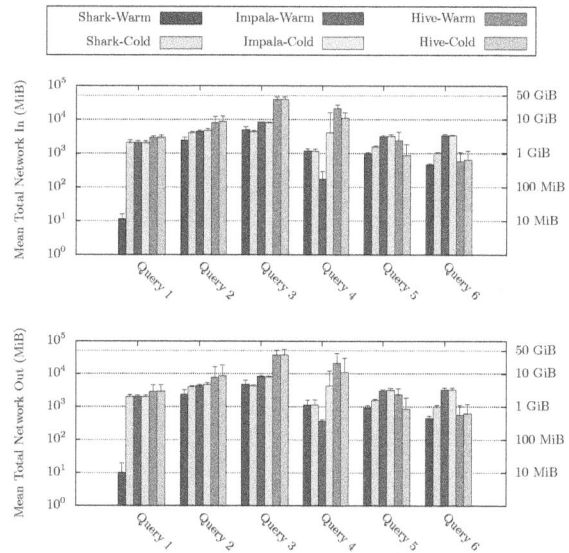

Figure 6: Total Network In (top) and Network Out (bottom). Vertical axis is in log-scale.

queries 4 to 6 less significant differences occur since *Shark-Warm* only uses the OS disk buffer cache mechanism, like Impala and Hive. Note that because the input and output are compressed (compression ratio around 10), generally no more than 10% of the datasets is read or written to disk. Query 1 and 3 have very small output datasets, which makes *Shark-Warm*'s output not visible in the figure for query 1. Similarly for query 3 Impala does not show up at all because Impala does not write intermediate shuffle data to disk.

Figure 6 shows the network I/O per query. Since most network I/O occurs between the workers, the network in and out look similar. Hive has a very variable network output total.

6.3 Scalability

In this section we analyze both the horizontal and the data size scalability of the query engines. We decided to scale horizontally down instead of up because a cluster of 5 nodes of this caliber is already quite expensive for SMEs (more than $7000 a month), and from our experimental results it shows that some queries already do no longer scale well from 4 to 5 worker nodes. We used queries 1 to 3 for data size scaling (since this dataset was already synthetic in the first place) and queries 4 to 6 for horizontal scaling.

Key Findings:

- Both Impala and Shark have good data size scalability on the scan and aggregation queries, whereas the response time has super-linear growth on the JOIN queries as the input size increases. This is as expected, since a JOIN is an operation that requires super-linear time.

- Hive has very good data scalability on all queries, but this is likely due to its large overhead, which dominates the response time at these data input sizes.

- If *Shark-Warm*'s input dataset is too large for its data storage memory, the response time will increase beyond *Shark-Cold* due to swapping.

- Shark and Impala horizontally scale reasonably well on all types of queries up to 3 nodes, whereas Hive only scales well on queries with large input sizes.

- The query engines do not benefit from having more than 3 or 4 nodes in the cluster. Impala even performs worse for query 6 at bigger cluster sizes.

1) Data Size Scalability: The data size scalability of the query engines is depicted in Figure 7. We have sampled subsets from the original dataset of the following sizes: 5%, 10%, 25%, 50%, 75%, 90%, and 100%. We display these along the horizontal axis of the figure in terms of how many times the samples are bigger compared to the 5% sample (1 equals the 5% sample, 20 equals the 100% sample). The vertical axis displays how many times the response time is worse compared to the 5% sample. The colored lines correspond to each of the query engine configurations, whereas the dashed black line depicts the situation where the response time degrades just as fast as the data input size grows. Any query engine performing above this dashed line does not scale very well with the data input size. Query engines performing close to or below the dashed line do scale very well with the input size. Engines that have a much more gentle slope in their performance compared to the dashed line, have their system overhead dominate the response time.

For query 1, all query engines have good data size scalability, but both Shark and Hive have their system overhead dominating the response time. This is because query 1 has a very small input dataset of only 5 GiB. So scalability is not easily shown. For query 2, which has much larger data input size, it shows that both Impala and Shark scale very well. Hive's response time on the other hand, is still being dominated by its system overhead. The query engines have super-linear scalability on query 3, except for Hive, which

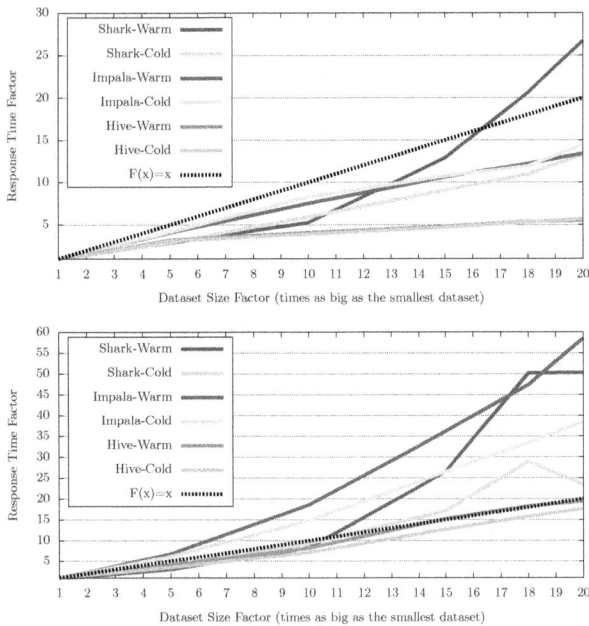

Figure 7: Response time Query 2 (Aggregation; top) and 3 (JOIN; bottom) for different data sizes. Results for Query 1 are in the technical report [20].

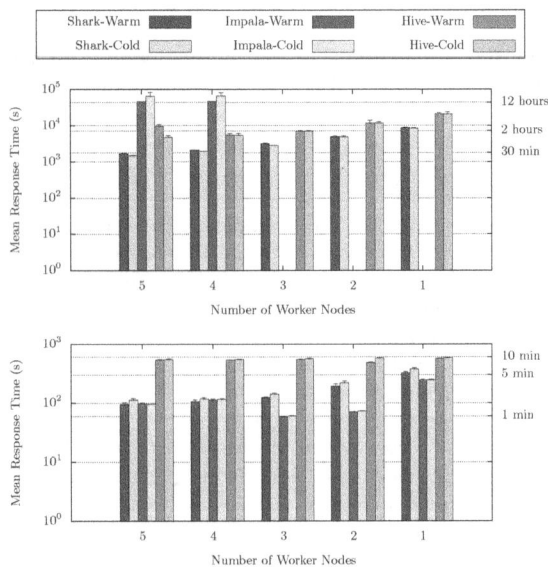

Figure 8: Response time Query 4 (top) and 6 (bottom) for different number of workers (vertical axis is in log-scale). Results for Query 5 are in the technical report [20].

shows close to linear scalability. However, since a JOIN operation takes super-linear time, the response time is expected to grow faster than linearly.

An interesting phenomenom occurs with Shark for query 2 and 3. When the data input size grows and passes 50% of the size of the original dataset (10 on the horizontal axis in the figure), *Shark-Warm* actually starts scaling worse than *Shark-Cold*. This is caused by the fact that Shark allocates only around 34 GiB of the 60 GiB it was assigned for data storage and uses the remaining amount as JVM overhead. This means that the total cluster can only store about 170 GiB of data instead of the 300 GiB it was assigned. The input dataset for query 2 and 3 are close to 120 GiB, which fills some of the worker nodes' fully at the start of query execution. When data exchange occurs between the workers, even more memory is needed for the shuffled data received from the other worker nodes, causing the node to spill some of its input data back to disk.

2) Horizontal Scalability: The horizontal scalability of the query engines is depicted in Figure 8 (note that we are scaling down instead of up). For Impala we only ran 4 and 5 nodes since it already took 12 hours to complete. Both Shark and Hive scale near linearly on the number of nodes. Hive only scales well on query 4 since Hive's Hadoop MapReduce overhead likely outweighs the computation time for query 5 and 6. This is because they have a relatively small input size. Impala actually starts to perform worse on query 6 if more than 3 nodes are added to the cluster. Similarly, both Shark and Impala no longer improve performance after more than 4 nodes are added to the cluster for query 4 and 5 [20].

This remarkable result for horizontal scaling shows that whenever a query is not CPU-bound on a cluster with some number of nodes, performance will not improve any further when adding even more nodes. In the case of network I/O bound queries like query 6, it might even be more beneficial to bind these to a smaller number of nodes so less network overhead occurs.

7. CONCLUSIONS AND FUTURE WORK

In recent years an increasing number of Distributed SQL Query Engines have become available. They all allow for large scale Big Data processing using SQL as interface language. In this work we compare three major query engines (Hive, Impala and Shark) with the requirements of SMEs in mind. SMEs have only little resources available to run their big data analytics on, and cannot afford running a query engine with large overhead.

In this work we have defined an empirical evaluation method to assess the performance of different query engines. Despite not covering all the methodological aspects of a scientific benchmark, this micro-benchmark gives practical insights for SMEs to take informed decisions when selecting a specific tool. Moreover, it can be used to compare current and future engines. The method focuses on three performance aspects: processing power, resource utilization, and scalability.

Using both a real world and a synthetic dataset with representative queries, we evaluate the query engines' performance. We find that different query engines have widely varying performance. Although Hive is almost always outperformed by the other engines, it highly depends on the query type and input size whether Impala or whether Shark is the best performer. Shark can also perform well on queries with over 500 GiB in input size in our cluster setup, while Impala starts to perform worse for these queries. Overall Impala is the most CPU efficient, and all query engines have comparable resource consumption for memory, disk and network. A remarkable result found is that query response time does not always improve when adding more nodes to the cluster. Remaining key findings can be found at the top of every experiment in Section 6.

This work has been an attempt to get insights in DSQE performance in order to make life easier for SMEs picking the query engine that best suits their needs. Query engine performance in a multi-tenant environment has not been evaluated, and is part of future work.

ACKNOWLEDGEMENTS

This research was supported by the Dutch national program COMMIT.

8. REFERENCES

[1] AMPLab's Big Data Benchmark. https://amplab.cs.berkeley.edu/benchmark/. [Online; Last accessed 1st of September 2014].

[2] Apache Hadoop. http://hadoop.apache.org. [Online; Last accessed 1st of September 2014].

[3] Apache Tez. http://tez.apache.org. [Online; Last accessed 1st of September 2014].

[4] Collectl Resource Monitoring. http://collectl.sourceforge.net. [Online; Last accessed 1st of September 2014].

[5] Impala. http://blog.cloudera.com/blog/2012/10/cloudera-impala-real-time-queries-in-apache-hadoop-for-real/. [Online; Last accessed 1st of September 2014].

[6] Impala Benchmark. http://blog.cloudera.com/blog/2014/05/new-sql-choices-in-the-apache-hadoop-ecosystem-why-impala-continues-to-lead/. [Online; Last accessed 1st of September 2014].

[7] Presto. http://www.prestodb.io. [Online; Last accessed 1st of September 2014].

[8] A. Floratou, U. F. Minhas, and F. Ozcan. Sql-on-hadoop: Full circle back to shared-nothing database architectures. *Proceedings of the VLDB Endowment*, 7(12), 2014.

[9] A. Ghazal, T. Rabl, M. Hu, F. Raab, M. Poess, A. Crolotte, and H.-A. Jacobsen. Bigbench: Towards an industry standard benchmark for big data analytics. In *Proceedings of the 2013 international conference on Management of data*, pages 1197–1208, 2013.

[10] M. Hausenblas and J. Nadeau. Apache Drill: Interactive Ad-Hoc Analysis at Scale. *Big Data*, 2013.

[11] Y. He, R. Lee, Y. Huai, Z. Shao, N. Jain, X. Zhang, and Z. Xu. RCFile: A fast and space-efficient data placement structure in MapReduce-based warehouse systems. In *Data Engineering (ICDE), 2011 IEEE 27th International Conference on*, pages 1199–1208, 2011.

[12] T. Hegeman, B. Ghit, M. Capota, J. Hidders, D. Epema, and A. Iosup. The BTWorld Use Case for Big Data Analytics: Description, Mapreduce Logical

[13] A. Iosup, N. Yigitbasi, and D. Epema. On the performance variability of production cloud services. In *Cluster, Cloud and Grid Computing (CCGrid), 2011 11th IEEE/ACM International Symposium on*, pages 104–113, 2011.

[14] S. Melnik, A. Gubarev, J. J. Long, G. Romer, S. Shivakumar, M. Tolton, and T. Vassilakis. Dremel: interactive analysis of web-scale datasets. *Proceedings of the VLDB Endowment*, 3(1-2):330–339, 2010.

[15] A. Pavlo, E. Paulson, A. Rasin, D. J. Abadi, D. J. DeWitt, S. Madden, and M. Stonebraker. A comparison of approaches to large-scale data analysis. In *Proceedings of the 2009 ACM SIGMOD International Conference on Management of data*, pages 165–178, 2009.

[16] M. Poess, R. O. Nambiar, and D. Walrath. Why you should run TPC-DS: a workload analysis. In *Proceedings of the 33rd international conference on Very large data bases*, pages 1138–1149. VLDB Endowment, 2007.

[17] A. Rowstron, D. Narayanan, A. Donnelly, G. O'Shea, and A. Douglas. Nobody ever got fired for using Hadoop on a cluster. In *Proceedings of the 1st International Workshop on Hot Topics in Cloud Data Processing*, page 2. ACM, 2012.

[18] A. Thusoo, J. S. Sarma, N. Jain, Z. Shao, P. Chakka, S. Anthony, H. Liu, P. Wyckoff, and R. Murthy. Hive: a warehousing solution over a map-reduce framework. *Proceedings of the VLDB Endowment*, 2(2):1626–1629, 2009.

[19] V. K. Vavilapalli, A. C. Murthy, C. Douglas, S. Agarwal, M. Konar, R. Evans, T. Graves, J. Lowe, H. Shah, S. Seth, et al. Apache Hadoop YARN: Yet another resource negotiator. In *Proceedings of the 4th annual Symposium on Cloud Computing*, page 5. ACM, 2013.

[20] S. v. Wouw, J. Viña, D. Epema, and A. Iosup. An Empirical Performance Evaluation of Distributed SQL Query Engines: Extended Report. *Delft University of Technology, Tech Rep.*, PDS-2014-002, 2014. http://www.pds.ewi.tudelft.nl/research-publications/technical-reports/2014/.

[21] R. S. Xin, J. Rosen, M. Zaharia, M. J. Franklin, S. Shenker, and I. Stoica. Shark: Sql and rich analytics at scale. In *Proceedings of the 2013 ACM International Conference on Management of Data*, pages 13–24, 2013.

[22] M. Zaharia, M. Chowdhury, T. Das, A. Dave, J. Ma, M. McCauley, M. Franklin, S. Shenker, and I. Stoica. Resilient distributed datasets: A fault-tolerant abstraction for in-memory cluster computing. In *Proceedings of the 9th USENIX conference on Networked Systems Design and Implementation*, pages 2–2, 2012.

[23] M. Zaharia, M. Chowdhury, M. J. Franklin, S. Shenker, and I. Stoica. Spark: cluster computing with working sets. In *Proceedings of the 2nd USENIX conference on Hot topics in cloud computing*, pages 10–10, 2010.

IoTAbench: an Internet of Things Analytics Benchmark

Martin Arlitt
HP Labs
Palo Alto, CA
martin.arlitt@hp.com

Manish Marwah
HP Labs
Palo Alto, CA
manish.marwah@hp.com

Gowtham Bellala
HP Labs
Palo Alto, CA
gowtham.bellala@hp.com

Amip Shah
HP Labs
Palo Alto, CA
amip.shah@hp.com

Jeff Healey
HP Vertica
Cambridge, MA
jeff.a.healey@hp.com

Ben Vandiver
HP Vertica
Cambridge, MA
ben.vandiver@hp.com

ABSTRACT

The commoditization of sensors and communication networks is enabling vast quantities of data to be generated by and collected from cyber-physical systems. This "Internet-of-Things" (IoT) makes possible new business opportunities, from usage-based insurance to proactive equipment maintenance. While many technology vendors now offer "Big Data" solutions, a challenge for potential customers is understanding quantitatively how these solutions will work for IoT use cases. This paper describes a benchmark toolkit called IoTAbench for IoT Big Data scenarios. This toolset facilitates repeatable testing that can be easily extended to multiple IoT use cases, including a user's specific needs, interests or dataset. We demonstrate the benchmark via a smart metering use case involving an eight-node cluster running the HP Vertica analytics platform. The use case involves generating, loading, repairing and analyzing synthetic meter readings. The intent of IoTAbench is to provide the means to perform "apples-to-apples" comparisons between different sensor data and analytics platforms. We illustrate the capabilities of IoTAbench via a large experimental study, where we store 22.8 trillion smart meter readings totaling 727 TB of data in our eight-node cluster.

1. INTRODUCTION

The commoditization of sensors and communication networks is enabling vast quantities of data to be generated by and collected from cyber-physical systems. This "Internet-of-Things" (IoT) makes possible new business opportunities, such as usage-based insurance and proactive equipment maintenance. IDC, a market intelligence firm, estimates that by 2020 there will be over 200 billion Internet-connected "things" installed [20]. For organizations wanting to pursue an IoT business, a question they are immediately faced with is how to store and analyze the vast amount of data that their sensors (i.e., "things") will collect.

A related challenge for these organizations is understanding which Big Data analytics platform will work best for their specific needs. Currently, there are no industry standard benchmarks to aid such organizations in selecting an analytics platform. In this paper we introduce a benchmark toolkit called IoTAbench (Internet of Things Analytics benchmark). IoTAbench is envisioned as a suite of benchmarks, each of which represents a distinct IoT use case. To date we have implemented a benchmark for a smart metering use case. We envision adding other benchmarks (e.g., for building energy management, fleet management, network security, etc.) under the IoTAbench umbrella in the near future.

A key component of our smart metering benchmark is a tool for generating large volumes of synthetic sensor data with realistic properties. To demonstrate the ability of this benchmark to test a Big Data analytics platform, we use IoTAbench to evaluate the performance of the HP Vertica Analytics Platform [17] when used to manage a large IoT dataset.

Our main contributions are: (1) the description of an IoT benchmark (IoTAbench). We intend to contribute our implementation of IoTAbench to facilitate and speed the development of an industry standard IoT benchmark. (2) a realistic synthetic smart meter data generator based on an augmented Markov chain model. (3) the demonstration of IoTAbench to evaluate the performance and scalability of a commercial "Big Data" platform. (4) one of the largest Big Data research studies we are aware of (22.8 trillion readings, 727 TB of data), to help to bridge the divide between Big Data research and practice.[1] (5) a detailed IoT case study of an electric utility with 40 million smart meters (for which we store and analyze the equivalent of more than a decade of data).

The remainder of this paper is organized as follows. Section 2 describes the IoT benchmark we created. Section 3 explains our experimental methodology. Section 4 discusses the results of our experiments. Section 5 examines related work. Section 6 concludes the paper with a summary of our work and possible next steps.

---

[1] We use TB=terabyte= 10^{12} bytes throughout the paper.

2. IoTAbench: AN IoT BENCHMARK

The Internet of Things will encompass a broad range of workloads; we anticipate that an industry standard IoT benchmark will encompass a suite of IoT workloads covering different use cases. This "benchmark suite" approach has been adopted in other industry standard benchmarks such as SPECweb2009, which contained three different workloads (banking, e-commerce and support).[2]

We refer to our benchmark as IoTAbench, the Internet of Things Analytics benchmark. IoTAbench consists of three components: a scalable synthetic data generator; a set of SQL queries; and a test harness. To help guide the initial implementation of IoTAbench, we focused on a single use case - smart metering. The development of additional use cases is left for future work.

2.1 IoT Use Case

In this paper, we focus on one specific use case, *smart metering*. An important step in facilitating more effective use of resources (e.g., electricity, gas, water) is the deployment of more capable meters. Smart metering will enable consumers and producers alike to better understand resource usage, so that actions can be taken to eliminate inefficient use of resources or to alter consumer behavior regarding when resources are consumed. While many resource/utility providers are either considering rollouts of smart meters, in the process of deploying them, or have already installed them, there is still a lot of uncertainty surrounding smart metering. One thing that is clear is that smart metering has the potential to produce enormous volumes of data.

We focus on smart metering as a use case because it is a timely problem. For example, China is rolling out hundreds of millions of smart meters, to enable programs such as Time-of-Use (ToU) billing to raise energy awareness amongst consumers.[3] Similarly, utilities in Europe are rolling out smart meter deployments as part of initiatives to achieve climate change targets such as a 20% increase in energy efficiency across Europe by 2020.[4]

In parallel to the deployment of meters, the utilities must determine how they will store and analyze all of the collected meter data in a sustainable manner. The development of an industry standard benchmark would help utilities make more informed decisions about which analytics platform to use. This is the motivation for our study.

2.2 Synthetic Data Generator

Experimentally evaluating the performance of an analytics platform in a smart metering use case requires access to large volumes of meter data. However, the availability of empirical smart meter data at tera-scale is limited or non-existent. To facilitate testing for an electric utility case study with 40 million smart meters, a compelling option is to generate a large synthetic dataset; however, this can lead to misleading or erroneous results if the synthetic data does not have properties of the empirical data. For example, if synthetic data is generated by duplication, a much higher degree of data compression may be attained. On the other hand, if

[2] http://www.spec.org/web2009

[3] http://www.greentechmedia.com/articles/read/
china-wants-time-of-use-pricing-by-2015-one-meter\
-per-home-by-2017

[4] http://ec.europa.eu/europe2020/targets/
eu-targets/index_en.htm

the synthetic data is completely random, data compression is likely to be poorer than for an empirical dataset. Furthermore, the time to perform analytics on the data can be affected, which would further bias the benchmark results. Thus, it is important to make the synthetic data as realistic as possible. This was our objective.

2.2.1 Generator design

We developed a Markov chain-based realistic synthetic data generator for smart meter data. The objective is to generate time series data of power consumption for any number of users, given the time series for a limited number of users, such that important statistical properties of the generated time series is similar to those of the real time series. We achieve this by simulating the power consumption process as a variant of a Markov chain.

Markov chains are widely used for modeling sequential, stochastic processes. For example, they have been used in the past for generating synthetic data for wind speed [14, 25]. A discrete-time Markov chain consists of a finite number of states, $\mathcal{S} = 1, 2, ..., n$, where state changes occur at discrete time steps; n is the number of states. The transitions between states exhibit the Markov property, that is, given the current state, the next (future) state is conditionally independent of the past states:

$$P(S_{t+1} = j | S_t = i, S_{t-1} = i_{t-1}, ..., S_0 = i_0) = P(S_{t+1} = j | S_t = i) \tag{1}$$

A state transition matrix, P of size $n \times n$, contains all the transition probabilities, where entry P_{ij} corresponds to $P(S_{t+1} = j | S_t = i)$. Furthermore, transition probabilities from a particular state must add to 1, $\sum_j P_{ij} = 1$.

We initially used a Markov chain to generate smart meter data, but the results were poor. This was not surprising, since in addition to the previous state the consumption process depends on several contextual features such as time of day, weather, etc. In order to capture the dependence on these contextual features and incorporate them into the model, we augment the Markov chain model by adding additional inputs. Figure 1 shows an Markov chain augmented with the current hour, H_t, added as an input to each state. The states of the chain are obtained by using fixed-width binning to quantize the consumption in the empirical data. With this modification, the transition to a state now depends on both the previous state and the current hour.

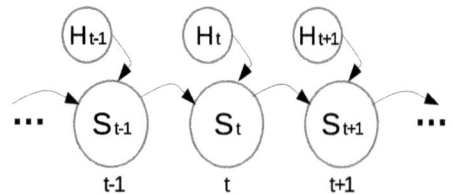

Figure 1: Augmented Markov chain of consumption states.

Using the generator involves two main steps: 1) training the model, which entails learning model parameters from a small empirical data set; and 2) performing a random walk on the augmented chain to generate the synthetic data. We describe each of these in turn.

2.2.2 Model training

Training of the model involves learning two main sets of parameters from the empirical data: 1) the transitional probability matrix (TPM), P; and 2) the probability density functions corresponding to each state. Given the additional time of day dependence, P is now $n \times n \times m$, where n is the number of states, m is the number of hours, and entry P_{ijk} corresponds to the transition probability from state i to state j at hour k; that is, the conditional probability $P(S_{t+1} = j | S_t = i, H_{t+1} = k)$. We use maximum likelihood estimation to estimate the TPM from the empirical data. In many cases, there may not be any empirical data points corresponding to a transition, and the TPM could be sparse. To address this, we use Laplace smoothing, which increases the count for each transition by one so that there are no transitions with zero probability. How sparsity is handled can be used to tune how "different" the generated data is from the empirical.

Even for a moderate n and m, the size of the TPM can be very large. For example, for $n = 50, m = 24$, its size is $n^2m(60,000)$, which is a large number of probabilities and would require a large dataset to estimate robustly. To reduce the number of probabilities, we use Bayes rule and conditional independence assumptions to factor the conditional probability.

$$
\begin{aligned}
&P(S_{t+1} = j | S_t = i, H_{t+1} = k) \\
&\propto P(S_t = i, H_{t+1} = k | S_{t+1} = j) \times P(S_{t+1} = j) \\
&\propto P(S_t = i | S_{t+1} = j) \times P(H_{t+1} = k | S_{t+1} = j) \times P(S_{t+1} = j)
\end{aligned}
\tag{2}
$$

which can be normalized to determine the probabilities. This results in a large drop in the number of probabilities to be estimated. For the above example, the number decreases to $n^2 + nm + n$ (3,750 for the above example), which is a reduction of more than an order of magnitude. For each of the n states, we use a kernel density estimate on the empirical data to compute the probability density function (pdf) corresponding to that state. The estimated pdf, f, at any point x, can be expressed as

$$
f_h(x) = \frac{1}{mh} \Sigma_{i=1}^{m} K\left(\frac{x - x_i}{h}\right)
\tag{3}
$$

where h is the selected bandwidth; m is the total number of points; K is the selected kernel; x_i are the points that fall within that state. We used a Gaussian kernel, although other kernels could also be used. If the number of points, m, is large, a binned kernel density estimate can be used. The bandwidth parameter, h, provides another knob to control the difference between the empirical and generated data. We also estimate the marginal probabilities of each state.

2.2.3 Data generation

Once the Markov chain model parameters are known, the process to generate a synthetic consumption time series involves performing a random walk on the chain. We randomly pick an initial state based on the marginal probability distribution for the starting hour. Then each subsequent state is picked based on the TPM. When a particular state is picked, we generate a consumption value by sampling the pdf of that state. To make this process a bit simpler and faster, we pre-sample a large number of points (over 100,000) from the pdf of each state and save these points. At the time of generation, we uniformly sample from these pre-saved points.

2.2.4 Implementation

Our generator is implemented as two modules. The first is the parameter learning module. We implemented it in R to estimate the model parameters from empirical data in the manner described above. R was chosen for this module since it provides a rich set of analytics packages, such as those for kernel density estimation. The speed of training is not critically important as it only needs to be done once for a particular dataset. The second module is the data generation module; efficiency is important in this step, to enable large datasets (e.g., 100's of TB) to be generated in a timely manner. For this reason, the data generation module is implemented in C. The data generation process is embarrassingly parallel. Thus, our data generation module is multi-threaded, and can be distributed across multiple machines to reduce the time needed to generate large synthetic datasets. We carefully select the random number seeds, such that each thread generates unique results compared to all other threads in the distributed generator. There is no communication between the threads, to improve the scalability of the generator.

Each row in the generator output is a meter reading. The format is:

```
timestamp meter_identifier consumption_value
```

This is the format used in the empirical dataset that we trained our model on. An example reading from the generator is:

```
2015-01-01 13:10:00|12345|103
```

This reading is for January 1, 2015 at 1:10pm from meter 12345. Over the previous 10 minutes the customer used 103 Watts of electricity.

2.2.5 Model validation

To demonstrate the effectiveness of our generator, we trained it on real smart meter data from Ireland.[5] This dataset has about 6,400 timeseries of 1.5 years each. We randomly picked 10% of the timeseries for training. The validation results are based on the entire dataset.

To capture seasonal behavior, we train a separate model for each month. Further, each day of the month is modeled as a mixture model of the current month, previous and next months. We use Gaussian weights with a tunable variance. In these experiments, we picked a variance value such that a month has a non-zero component from the middle of the previous month to the middle of the next month, as shown in Figure 2. While the variance can be varied, this choice worked well.

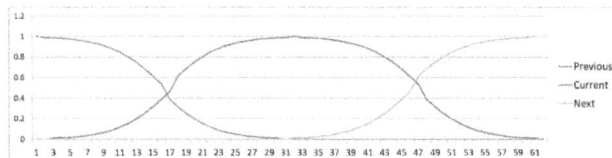

Figure 2: Mixture model weights of the three components over a 60 day period.

[5]http://www.ucd.ie/issda/data/
commissionforenergyregulationcer/

To evaluate the quality of the generated data, we compared the empirical and generated data by looking at their marginal and conditional (by hour, month) probability distributions and the auto-correlation within each time series. All of these matched closely. Figure 3 shows the empirical and synthetic average daily consumption profile for a day in the month of January. These graphs demonstrate visually how the synthetic data captures the aggregate time-of-day patterns in the empirical data. Figure 4 shows the time-series of an entire month of synthetic data. It reveals how the mixture model varies the day-to-day aggregate consumption, and smooths the transition from one month to another. Figure 5 shows that the conditional probability distribution of consumption for two months (January and February) for the empirical (real) and synthetic data are similar. Figure 6 provides a quantitative comparison of the empirical and synthetic datasets. This graph shows summary statistics (mean, median, standard deviation, minimum, maximum) of the empirical and synthetic data for four different months (September - December). This graphs shows that statistically these datasets are quite similar. The biggest difference is in the maximum value, which is always slightly higher in the synthetic data than in the real data; this is because in the TPM, Laplace smoothing introduces a non-zero probability of transition between any two states. This can be tuned depending on how closely a user needs the synthetic data to adhere to the empirical data. Figure 7 shows that the average auto-correlation for empirical and synthetic consumption time series for lags up to 24 hours is comparable. Figure 7(c) shows the auto-correlation of naively generated synthetic data, where the data is sampled independently from the consumption distribution of each hour. Although the summary statistics of this data matched well with the empirical data, as expected, the auto-correlation is not well captured.

Based on these results, we believe that our synthetic data generator provides reasonably realistic sensor data, and therefore enables us to elicit realistic behavior in experimental evaluations of any Big Data analytics platforms that we wish to examine for Internet of Things use cases.

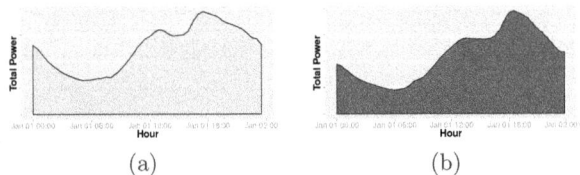

Figure 3: Consumption data for one day in January: (a) empirical; (b) synthetic.

2.3 Benchmark Queries

When embarking on this study, we were not aware of any common set of analyses (i.e., queries) that utility providers plan to run on a large resource consumption dataset. Karnouskos *et al.* state that billing is the current "killer app" [15]; this is also the analysis performed in previous smart metering benchmark studies [2, 13, 21]. Thus, this is one analysis that we consider. However, we wanted to consider additional analyses that might be of interest to utilities that would also stress the system under study in different ways.

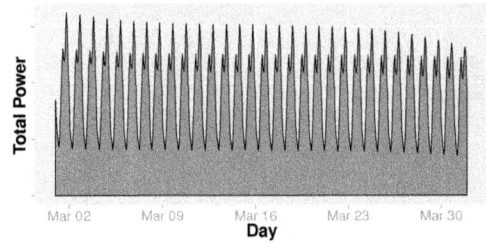

Figure 4: Synthetic consumption data for one month (March).

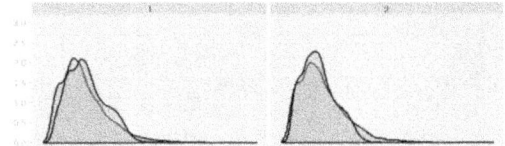

Figure 5: Comparison between power consumption distribution of synthetic and empirical data for January and February.

As shown in Table 1 we designed six distinct analyses: (1) Total readings: counts the total number of readings (i.e., rows) for the given time period. (2) Total consumption: sums the resource consumption for the given time period. (3) Peak consumption: create a sorted list of the aggregate consumption in each ten minute interval[6] in the given time period. (4) Top consumers: create a list of the distinct consumers, sorted by their total (monthly) consumption. (5) Consumption time-series: calculate the time-series of aggregate consumption per ten minute interval in the given time period. (6) Time of Usage Billing: calculate the monthly bill for each consumer based on the time of usage.

Analysis (1) is used primarily as a sanity check, to verify whether the proper amount of sensor data is being stored for the given time period. Analysis (2) determines the aggregate electricity consumption over an extended period of time (e.g., one month). Analysis (3) determines the aggregate electricity consumption in each ten minute interval over a longer duration of time (e.g., one month). It then sorts the results based on the total consumption per interval (highest to lowest). Analysis (4) looks at the aggregate consumption per meter rather than per time interval. It sorts the results based on the total consumption per meter (highest consumption to least consumption). Analysis (5) is similar to Analysis (3), except the results are kept in chronological order. This type of analysis could be used to visualize the aggregate consumption of electricity over time. Lastly, Analysis (6) calculates four "bill determinants" per consumer: the cost for electricity used during off-peak times, the cost for electricity used during peak times, the cost for electricity used during "shoulder" times,[7] and the total cost for the electricity consumed by the consumer (i.e., the sum of the first three bill determinants).

---

[6]Our study assumes the utility's smart meters will record a consumption value every ten minutes. Alternative interval lengths could be used in IoTAbench.

[7]"Shoulder" times refer to the transition period from off-peak to peak usage, as well as the transition period from peak to off-peak usage.

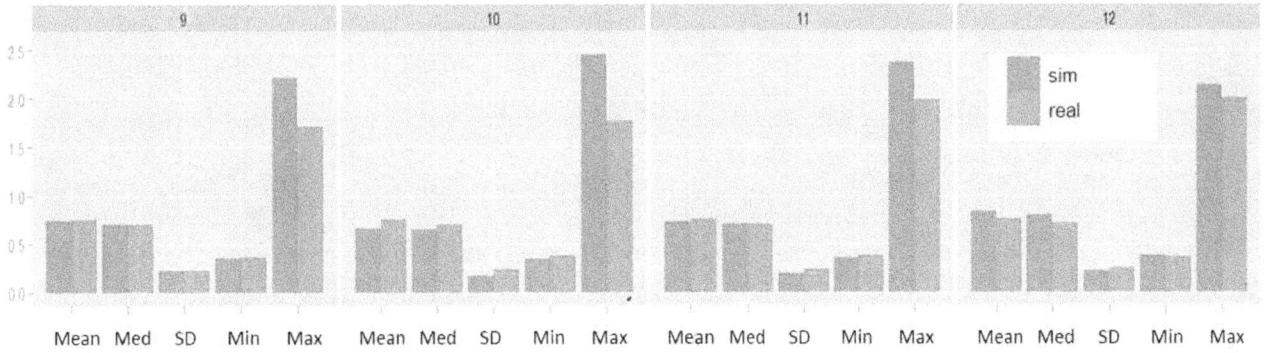

Figure 6: Comparison between summary statistics of synthetic (sim) and empirical (real) data for September through December.

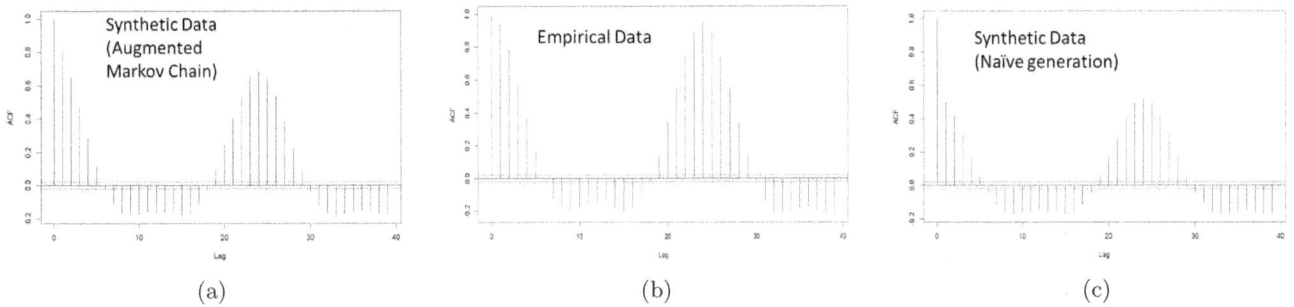

(a) (b) (c)

Figure 7: Comparison between time-series auto-correlation with lags up to 24 hours; (a) IoTAbench data; (b) empirical data; (c) naively generated data.

Obviously, there are virtually an unlimited number of types of information that could be extracted from the dataset; our objective is not to demonstrate all possible queries that could be performed on the dataset. Our six queries are valid examples of information that would be relevant from a business perspective within a utility. These analyses also exercise the system under study in meaningful ways from a performance evaluation perspective. Table 1 compares the composition of the SQL queries used to perform each of the six analyses in the benchmark. In this particular study, three columns are used to store each smart meter reading: ts_key stores a timestamp value (the time the reading was taken), meter_key stores the unique identifier of the meter that prepared the reading, PowerWatts stores the consumption value for the given interval and meter. For example, the Total Readings query ("SELECT COUNT (*)") could use any of the three data columns or other means (e.g., metadata kept on the stored data) to determine the number of readings that are stored in the main table. The decision of how the query is executed is left up to the query optimizer. This query uses a WHERE clause to restrict the analysis to a specific time period; i.e., the month being analyzed. Thus, the WHERE clause makes use of the ts_key column. The Total Readings query does not involve an ORDER BY clause. Overall, the six queries use different numbers and combinations of columns in computing their output. The complexity of the queries also varies quite substantially. Table 1 helps highlight how these queries stress the system under study in different ways, in addition to providing information that is relevant to the business.

2.4 Test Harness

For Big Data studies it is particularly important that all aspects of an experiment be conducted in a systematic fashion. This aids in ensuring that the results are complete, repeatable and completed in as timely a manner as possible. We used a wrapper script around each of the tools we used (e.g., synthetic data generator, SQL client, etc.). We then created a single control script to manage the entire experiment. This control script called the wrapper scripts to invoke the specific tools as they were needed. Our control and wrapper scripts were written in Bash; we used Perl scripts to parse the experimental output. Alternative scripting languages could have provided the same functionality, we used Bash and Perl due to our familiarity with them.

To simplify the management of an experiment, as well as to make it simpler to install and use IoTAbench on a new testbed, we use a single configuration file to store all of the variables. The user edits the configuration file to set up an experiment. IoTAbench then uses the configuration file and a set of template scripts to create the scripts to be used for a specific experiment on the selected testbed.

Based on feedback from utility customers, the smart metering use case assumes batch uploads and analysis of the data. Extending IoTAbench to load and analyze streaming sensor data is ongoing as part of a separate use case.

Table 1: Comparison of benchmark queries.

Query \ Column	SELECT ts_key	meter_key	powerWatts	WHERE ts_key	meter_key	powerWatts	ORDER BY ts_key	meter_key	powerWatts
Total Readings		any		✓					
Total Consumption			✓	✓					
Peak Consumption	✓		✓	✓					✓
Consumption Timeseries	✓		✓	✓			✓		
Top Consumers		✓	✓	✓	✓				✓
Time of Usage Billing		✓	✓	✓	✓			✓	

3. EXPERIMENTAL DESIGN

3.1 Overview

The experiments described in this paper represent a single case study (smart meters) to demonstrate how IoTAbench can be used to experimentally evaluate a Big Data analytics platform.

3.2 System Under Study

Our experiments were run on a cluster of eight HP Pro-Liant DL380p gen8 servers. Each of these 2U servers was configured as follows: two Intel Xeon E5-2670 CPUs (each with eight 2.60 GHz cores, 20 MB cache, 8.00 GT/s QPI), 128 GB RAM, two 300 GB SAS 10K RPM drives, twenty-two 900 GB SAS 10K RPM drives, and two dual-port 10 Gb Ethernet NICs. Red Hat Enterprise Linux Server release 6.4 (Santiago) was the Operating System used on each of these servers. The two 300 GB drives were configured as RAID1, and are used for the Operating System and the database catalog directory. The twenty-two 900 GB drives were configured as RAID10 and used for the database data directory. These servers and the HP 5900AF-48XG 10 Gb network switch connecting them were used exclusively by the system under study during the experiments. On this system we installed the HP Vertica Analytics platform version 7.0.0. The experiments were controlled by a ninth DL380p server.

3.3 Design and Methodology

Table 2 lists the key characteristics of the synthetic dataset used in our study. We assume a fictitious electric utility has 40 million customers (each with their own smart meter). The utility wishes to record the consumption of each customer every 10 minutes. This corresponds to 144 readings per day per customer. The number of customers was selected such that our fictitious utility would be as large as any of the utilities in Europe. The reading interval was chosen based on the shortest interval that we heard a utility ask for (other values we heard utilities ask for were 15, 30 or 60 minutes). We store the consumption value as an integer value, rounded to the nearest Watt (if a utility desired greater precision, that could be handled in a similar manner). This is a general "best practice" for storing large volumes of numeric data. Lastly, in practice it is a common occurrence that some of the meter data is lost before it reaches the analysis platform. Smart meter vendor Itron reports 1% as a common value for how much data is typically missing [13]. Thus, we use that value as a parameter during the generation of the synthetic data.

There are several existing benchmark studies involving the collection and analysis of smart meter data [2, 13, 21]. These studies look at a month in the life of a utility scenarios, as business processes like billing often occur at this

Table 2: Synthetic dataset characteristics.

Characteristic	Setting
Number of customers	40 million
Reading interval	10 minutes
Meter precision	nearest Watt
Missing readings	1%

frequency. For this reason, our smart metering benchmark in IoTAbench uses a monthly scenario for a utility. However, previous studies look at only a single month in the life of a utility; this offers no insights into how the platform will behave over time, as the scale of data that it stores increases. Given the investments utilities must make in the metering infrastructure to collect the fine-grained consumption data, they will want to retain and use data for more than the month it was collected in. To the best of our knowledge, we are the first to explore this issue for Big Data platforms.

Based on the characteristics listed in Table 2, our dataset consists of 5.76 billion readings per day. For a month with 31 days, this is 178.6 billion readings per month. 1% of these are "missing"; in our case, the synthetic data generator never writes them to disk. The platform under study therefore needs to repair the dataset to return to the expected number of readings for the month.

Our experimental methodology is as follows. For each month of data we:

- generate the synthetic dataset for that month

- load the "raw" data into a staging area

- repair the "raw" data and store the repaired data in the main table

- delete the "raw" data and empty the staging area

- analyze the repaired data

This process is continued until the platform runs out of storage space for new data. Once this process finishes, we perform a final step, a "re-analysis" of each month of data. This final step is done to determine if the platform has made any tradeoffs in how it manages the data over time. For example, is older data penalized in an attempt to keep newer data quick to access?

An important feature of the specific platform we tested (HP Vertica Analytics Platform) is the ability to optimize the layout of the data on disk. This requires having a sample of the data for the designer and optionally one or more sample queries to use to calculate the best design to use. In our experiments we ran the designer after the first month of data was loaded, and optimized for the Consumption Timeseries query. With HP Vertica it then automatically stores all subsequent data that is loaded into the optimized layout; i.e., the design only needs to be determined once. In our experiment with one month of data, this optimization step took 5.25 hours. This is a relatively small overhead given the benefits it provides. In addition, the same design could have been obtained using less data, requiring less time. However, since we were using one month of data in all of our other steps, we did for the optimization step as well.

A challenge to address in the development of an industry standard IoT benchmark is how to accommodate "special features" like HP Vertica's Data Designer. While the generation of data and the analysis queries (written in SQL) in IoTAbench should be portable across SQL-enabled Big Data platforms, the queries to load data, repair missing data or optimize the data layout will not. However, if one only considers industry-standard features, the benchmark may not adequately capture the capabilities of the platform. A reasonable tradeoff might be to distinguish between "standard" and "non-standard" performance results, much like publicly-traded companies may report GAAP (Generally Accepted Accounting Principles) and non-GAAP financial results.

4. EXPERIMENTAL RESULTS

4.1 Generator Performance

Since our experiments involve the generation of massive amounts of data, the performance of our synthetic data generator is important. Our implementation takes advantage of the fact that the process is embarrassingly parallel and that our testbed uses a distributed set of multi-core servers.

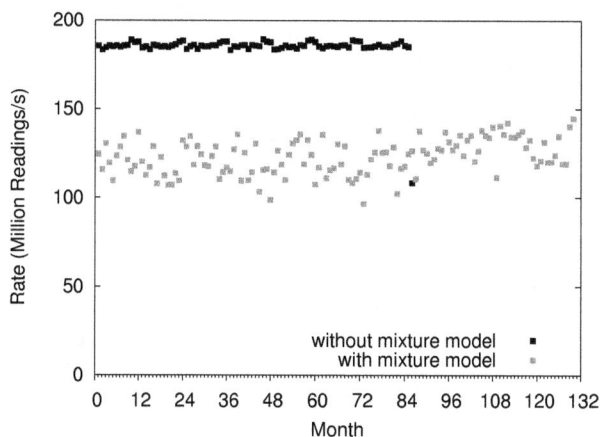

Figure 8: Generator performance.

Figure 8 shows the performance of our generator. Our initial version did not include the mixture model to smooth transitions between months. In version 1 we were able to consistently generate 185 million meter readings/second ($\approx$ 6 GB/s of data). At this rate we could generate a month of data for 40 million meters in about 16 minutes. The addition of the mixture model requires the use of considerably more random numbers, which lowered the average generation rate to 120 million meter readings/second, and made the performance much more variable (the random number generation is a bottleneck). Since this still allowed us to generate a month of data in about 25 minutes, we did not

attempt to alleviate the bottleneck, although that could be a topic of future work.

4.2 Load and Repair Performance

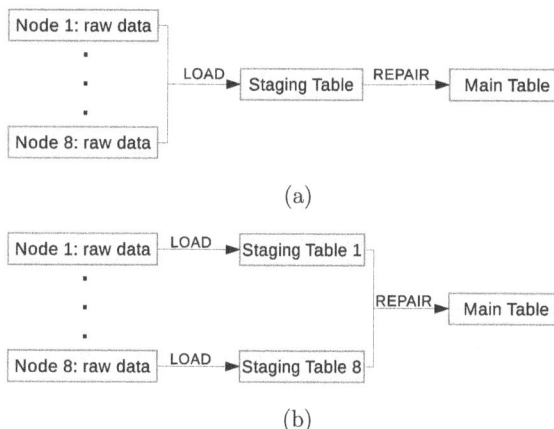

Figure 9: Load implementations considered in our study: (a) scale-up; (b) scale-out.

Figure 9 shows two different load options that we considered. The *scale-up* implementation loads the files on each node into a single staging table. The repair step then reads the raw meter data from the staging table, repairs it, and inserts it in the main table. The *scale-out* implementation involves each cluster node loading the files into a distinct staging table, i.e., one that no other node is directly loading raw data into. The repair step then merges the data from the eight staging tables, repairs it, and inserts the aggregated data into the main table. Once the repaired data is loaded into the main table, the staging area is emptied.

In practice, data is often imperfect. Thus, a Big Data analytics platform must be capable of identifying and repairing data quality issues with the raw data. Since a smart meter use case involves time series data, we perform this step by interpolating any missing values. Defining a more extensive repair methodology is left for future work.

Figure 10(a) shows the rate at which data was loaded into the staging tables. In experiment 1, the scale-out implementation described in Figure 9(a) was used. In experiment 2, each cluster node loads data into a distinct staging table, as explained in Figure 9(b); the scale-out load approach. Figure 10(a) reveals that the scale-out approach offers a significant performance advantage, achieving an average load rate of 39.4 million readings/second compared to an average of 11.7 million readings/second for the scale-up approach, a difference of 3.37x. Figure 10(a) reveals that the load performance of either implementation is quite consistent over time, even as the cluster has used nearly all of the available storage space.[8] There is more variability in the load results when using the scale-out load approach, although this ap-

---

[8] The experiments concluded in the 87th month for the first experiment and in the 131st month for the second experiment. The different durations were due to different data designs affecting how quickly storage space was consumed. We verified that the bottleneck in the scale-up experiment was from loading to the shared staging area, and not from using a different data design.

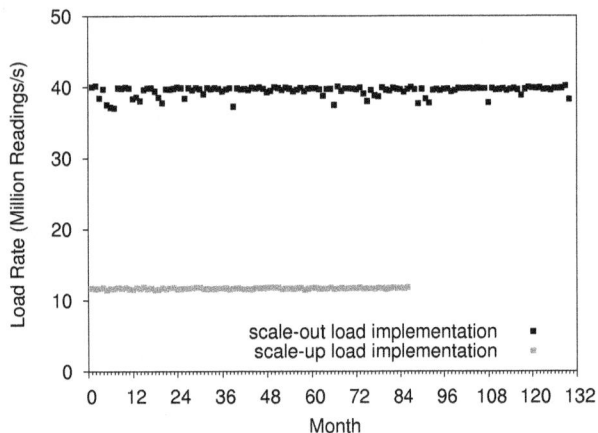

(a)

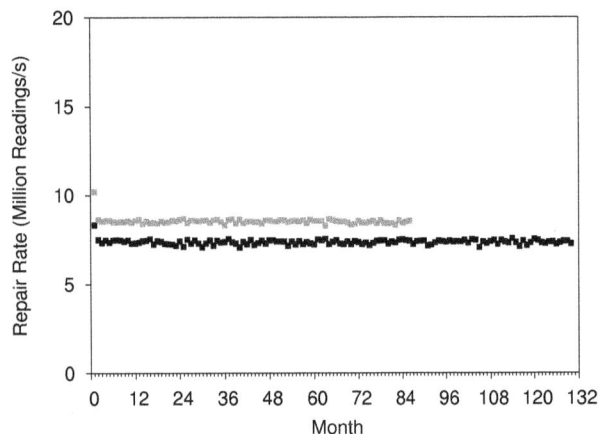

(b)

Figure 10: (a) Load Performance; (b) Repair Performance

proach still has much better overall performance than the scale-up approach.

The repair rate for the two different load approaches is shown in Figure 10(b). For both experiments the repair rate for the first month was higher than for the remaining months; this is due to the data layout being optimized after the first month of data is stored in the main table. Excluding the repair time for the first month, the median repair rate in the first experiment was 8.5 million readings/second, while in the second experiment the median repair rate was 7.4 million readings/second, about 15% slower. There are two potential causes of the slowdown; a) the more efficient encoding method used on the meter_key column in the second experiment requiring more time to compress the data, and b) the need to merge the raw data from eight staging tables before repairing it in the second experiment. We have not attempted to quantify the extent that each of these contributed to the 15% overhead, as this is a relatively small overhead compared to the increased data retention that was achieved and the increased load rate the scale-out approach offers. Overall, we were able to load 22.8 trillion readings and 726.9 TB of data in the second experiment, which Vertica compressed and stored in 65.4 TB of disk space. This is a compression factor of 11.12x (uncompressed size/compressed size). This is substantially more

Table 3: Properties of datasets used in each experiment.

Property	Experiment 1	Experiment 2
Total Readings	15.1 trillion	22.8 trillion
Duration	7 years 2 months	10 years 10 months
Total Size	478 TB	727 TB

data than we were able to load in the first experiment (15.1 trillion readings and 478 TB of data). The primary cause is the improved compression of the meter_key column.

Table 3 summarizes the characteristics of the datasets we used in each experiment. It is important to note that the experiments were run with application-level data redundancy turned on. This means that the system under study retained two copies of the data so that it could withstand the failure of one cluster node. Thus, while our system under study in the second experiment stored 22.8 trillion *distinct* readings, it actually stored 45.6 trillion *total* readings (two copies of each distinct reading, intelligently placed around the cluster to provide the ability to keep the cluster operational in the event of a node failure).[9]

4.3 Analysis Performance

After loading and repairing each month of data the next step in the benchmark is to run a set of analyses on it. IoTAbench cycles through each analysis, then repeats the cycle twice and records the median value. After completing the analysis of the final month of data that the system is able to load, the analyses are re-run on each month of data. This re-analysis step is included in the benchmark to assess whether the Big Data Analytics Platform under study has made any trade-offs that may affect query performance, particularly on older portions of the dataset. The re-analysis step also performs the entire set of benchmark queries, then repeats twice and reports the median query time.

In the remainder of this section we focus on the performance results for Experiment 2, which stored 130 months of data in total.

4.3.1 Total Readings Performance

Figure 11 shows the performance of the Total Readings analysis when run on our system under study. Note that the y-axis is in logarithmic scale, to enable a better comparison of the range of query times. Prior to optimizing the data design, the Total Readings analysis took 23.996 seconds to count 178.6 billion readings. After the re-design, the analysis of the same data (Month 1) took 20.239 seconds. Over the entire 130 months of data (black squares), the median time for this analysis was 19.302 seconds, while the average was 19.165 seconds. For this specific query, the new data layout had only a minimal positive effect on the query times.

There is more than one way to perform most analyses. In this case, "SELECT COUNT(*)" was our initial implementation to determine the number of readings. An alternative method is to use a specific column to use to determine the same result; e.g., "SELECT COUNT(ts_key)". One motivation for considering these different implementations of this simple analysis is that enables one to quantify the implications on query performance of the different encoding

---

[9]In addition to application-level redundancy, our cluster has storage-level RAID 10 redundancy to retain the data in the event of a disk failure.

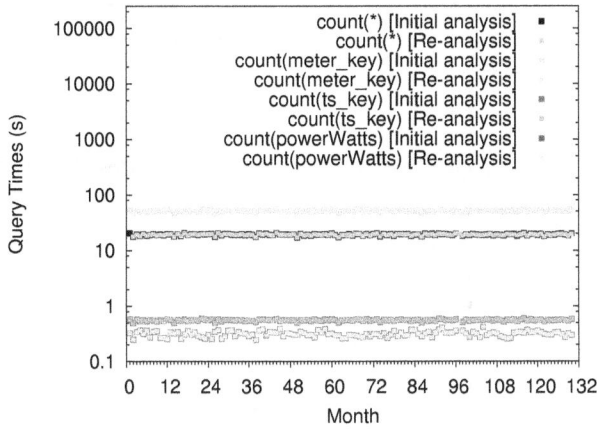

Figure 11: Performance of Total Readings query.

methods used for the different columns. For example, performing this query on the powerWatts column (dark blue squares) took a median time of 310 ms to complete each month. This query took slightly longer on the ts_key column (dark purple squares), averaging 555 ms (558 ms median). The query took the longest on the meter_key column (dark green squares), with a median time of 51.301 seconds. This illustrates the tradeoff for achieving better compression of the meter_key column and the dataset overall; it takes a lot longer to access the meter_key data. As a result, any queries that use this column will encounter this overhead.

Figure 11 also shows the performance results of the Total-Readings query and its variants during the re-analysis stage. Figure 11 shows that the TotalReadings analyses are just as fast in the re-analysis stage. This demonstrates that the system under study performs in a consistent manner as the data sizes grow; i.e., it does not make any tradeoffs to keep queries fast on the most recently added data that might penalize queries involving older data.

4.3.2 Total Consumption

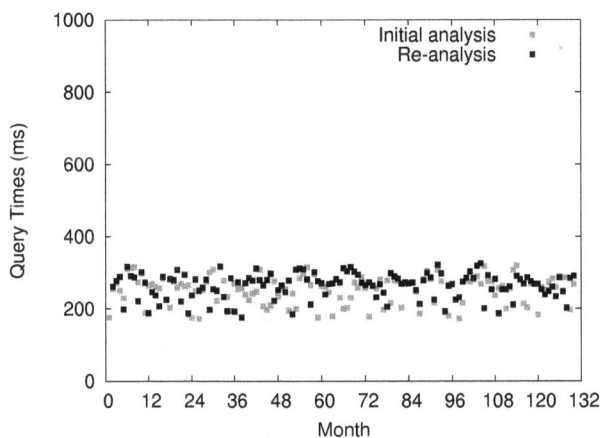

Figure 12: Performance of Total Consumption query.

Figure 12 shows the performance results for the Total Consumption query. Initially, the Total Consumption analysis for the first month of data took 49.813 seconds. After opti-

mizing the data layout, the analysis on the same data took 0.176 seconds. Over the 130 months of data, the average time for this query was 0.249 seconds. In the re-analysis step, the results are quite similar to the performance when the analysis was initially run. The average time for this query was 0.264 seconds. Note that on a linear scale the results appear to have quite a bit of variability in them. This is due at least in part to distributing the query across eight different nodes. Nevertheless, the query times are very low in all cases.

4.3.3 Peak Consumption

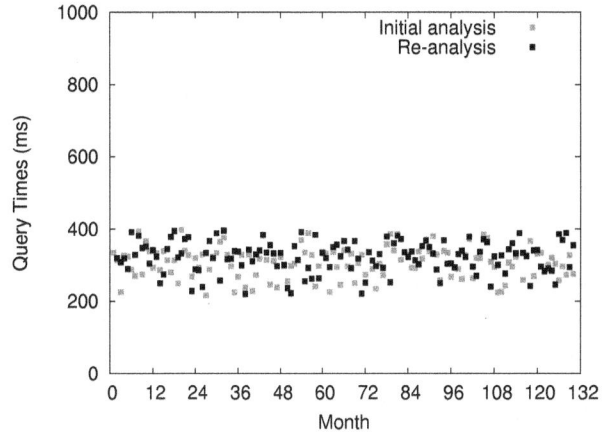

Figure 13: Performance of Peak Consumption query.

Figure 13 shows the results for the Peak Consumption query. The peak consumption analysis took 92.862 seconds prior to the data layout optimization. This was reduced to 0.334 seconds afterward. Across all 130 months, the average was 0.307 seconds. The query times for the re-analysis step are quite consistent with the initial results, with an average time of 0.322 seconds to run the Peak Consumption query.

As shown in Table 1, the Peak Consumption analysis is similar to the Consumption Timeseries query, the only difference being how the results are ordered. After running the experiments we found that there was minimal difference in the performance. Thus, the results in Figure 13 are quite similar to those for the Consumption Timeseries analysis (Figure 14).

4.3.4 Consumption Timeseries Performance

Figure 14 shows the performance of the Consumption Timeseries analysis. The initial query time was 92.639 seconds. After optimizing the data layout, the query time dropped substantially. The median value over 130 months was 0.355 seconds. The low response time and variability both suggest that a user could potentially interact with the data, which could enable real-time exploration of a large sensor dataset. This is a significant result. A month of raw data in our utility use case is nearly 6 TB in size; being able to create an aggregate timeseries from it (e.g., Figure 4) in only a few hundred milliseconds suggests that business analysts could interact with the data, such as visually examining regions of consumption activity that are interesting from a business perspective (e.g., zooming in and out of time periods with

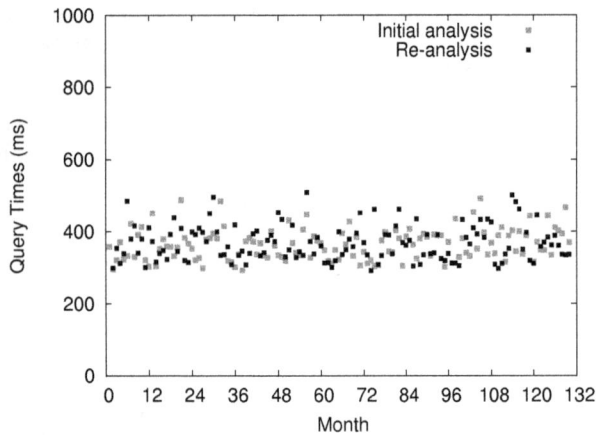

Figure 14: Performance of Consumption Timeseries query.

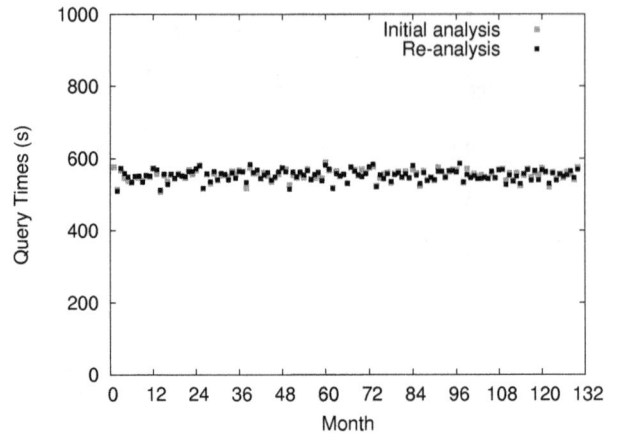

Figure 16: Performance of Time-of-Usage billing query.

abnormal consumption patterns, drilling down into who is contributing to spikes in consumption, etc.).

The re-analysis query times are also shown in Figure 14. Once again, the re-analysis query times are quite similar to the initial query times. The median query time was 0.361 seconds. The variability in the re-analysis results is quite low. These results indicate that a business analyst will be able to interact with historical data about their business in the same way that they can examine current data. This is helpful for identifying emerging trends in their business.

4.3.5 Top Consumers Performance

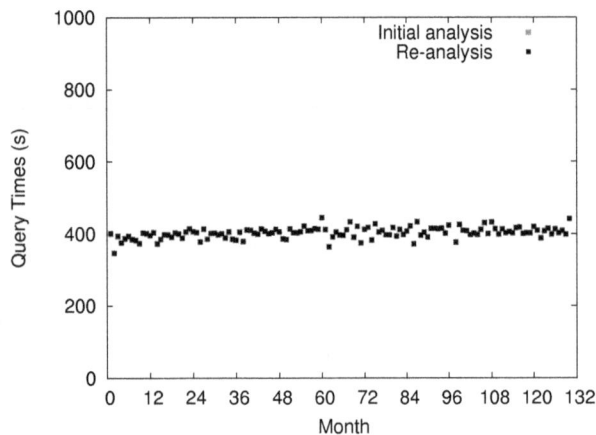

Figure 15: Performance of Top Consumers query.

Figure 15 shows performance results for the Top Consumers analysis. The median query time during the initial analysis was 401.997 seconds. The average re-analysis query time was 408.968 seconds, which is slightly slower (1.7%) than in the initial case, but still relatively the same as when the data was first added to the database.

4.3.6 Time-of-Usage Billing Performance

Our final analysis is Time of Usage Billing. The results are presented in Figure 16. As with Top Consumers, we expected to sacrifice some performance on this query (since

it involves the meter_key column) in order to be able to store a longer duration of data.

The median value over the 130 months was 554.395 seconds. The re-analysis results (also shown in Figure 16) reveal that the query times on older data complete about as quickly as when the queried data was initially added to the database. The median query time for the re-analysis was 555.631 seconds, which is essentially identical to the initial case. This demonstrates that with the system under study, an organization could work with their historical data just like it is new data.

4.3.7 Analyzing the Entire Dataset

Table 4: Benchmark query times over entire dataset.

Query	Time (s)
Total Readings	10.859
Total Readings (ts_key)	10.131
Total Readings (meter_key)	6,673.220
Total Readings (powerWatts)	11.549
Total Consumption	10.636
Peak Consumption	149.034
Consumption Timeseries	155.412
Top Consumers	51,135.932
Time of Usage Billing	54,695.257

As a final exercise, we used IoTAbench to analyze the entire dataset. We modified the benchmark queries so that each would consider the entire dataset (i.e., all 22.8 trillion readings). The query results may not be particularly useful from a business perspective, but the performance results are interesting for understanding whether a "Big Data platform" scales when analyzing a larger dataset. The main modification required to each of the queries was to remove the WHERE clause that filters the data to be considered.

Table 4 provides the results of this exercise. The results can be grouped into three categories. First, two analyses (Total Readings (meter_key) and Top Consumers) had performance that was reasonably close to 130 times the average time they required on a single month of data. These queries involved decompressing the heavily compressed meter_key column, making the query time quite predictable.

The second category includes those where the actual time is much lower than 130 times their average monthly time. This includes Total Readings, Total Readings (ts_key), Total Readings(powerWatts), Total Consumption, and Time of Usage billing. Eliminating the WHERE clause is responsible for at least part of the speedup. For the Time of Usage billing query, the results only need to be sorted once, rather than once per month. The third category are the analyses that take longer than 130 times their monthly average. In this category are Peak Consumption and Consumption Timeseries. These two queries need to keep state on an increasingly larger number of intervals. If a utility wished to search larger intervals (e.g., hours or days) rather than the default ten minute interval when analyzing the entire dataset, then the performance of this sort of analyses may improve. Alternatively, for these queries one could improve the time by issuing each of the monthly queries in sequence and concatenating the results together.

5. RELATED WORK

The most closely related work to ours are white papers from IBM, Microsoft, and Oracle, examining how their products perform for storing, repairing and analyzing smart meter data [2, 13, 21]. Our study uses a dataset that is 2-3 orders of magnitude larger than these studies, uses a larger set of queries, and explores performance and scalability of the system under study in much greater depth.

The "Internet of Things" is a popular topic in research and business circles alike. However, much of the discussion is focused on device features and connectivity issues rather than on managing and analyzing the large datasets that will be collected. The most related work we have come across in this space is by Ding *et al.*, who propose a "statistical database cluster mechanism for Big Data analysis in the Internet of Things" [7]. They provide a small-scale performance evaluation of their framework. Ma *et al.* consider an indexing mechanism for "massive" IoT data in a cloud environment [19]. Their performance evaluation involves four orders of magnitude fewer records that our study.

"Big Data" is a popular topic that overlaps the Internet of Things but spans other areas as well. An issue in the "Big Data" domain is that there are different interpretations of what constitutes "Big". Descriptions of "Big Data" systems in production environments typically mention data sizes in the hundreds of TB to hundreds of PB [27, 4, 17] or trillions to hundreds of trillions of rows [12]. "Big Data" research studies on the other hand tend to work with much smaller datasets, ranging from hundreds of GB [6, 18, 16, 24] to a few TBs [29, 28, 23, 1]. The largest dataset we have seen used in an existing "Big Data" study is 16 TB [9]. We attempt to bridge the gap between research and production in our paper, working with a dataset that is three-quarters of a PB in size on a modest-sized cluster.

Benchmarking is another related domain. There are a number of groups like SPEC[10] and TPC[11] that create industry standard benchmarks. At this time we are not aware of any industry standard IoT benchmarks. BigBench is a recent effort to create an industry standard benchmark for the "Big Data" domain [11]. That work considers a broader scope than we are; however, there may be an opportunity to collaborate with them. Other recent works include a social graph benchmark [3] and benchmarks for cloud services [5, 26, 22]. While these could potentially be used to benchmark "Big Data" applications, they are not specifically focused on IoT applications.

There is a long history of research on predicting electricity load curves and the factors that affect them. For example, Gellings and Taylor developed a simulation model of a utility's load shape in 1981 [10]. 70 years ago, Dryar described a method to predict the effect of weather on a utility's load [8]. The key difference between such works and ours is that we are generating the loads for individual households that once aggregated provide the desired utility load.

6. CONCLUSIONS

This paper introduced a benchmark called IoTAbench for evaluating Big Data analytics platforms for the Internet of Things. To generate a large data set with realistic properties, we used our Markov chain-based synthetic data generator. To demonstrate the potential for IoTAbench to benchmark Big Data IoT applications, we considered a smart metering use case, and evaluated the HP Vertica 7 Analytics platform for a scenario involving an electric utility with 40 million meters.

To our knowledge, this is one of the largest Big Data research studies to date, involving 22.8 trillion distinct readings and 727 TB of raw data. In our opinion, this work helps bridge the divide between "Big Data" research and practice. In other words, we provide practitioners with insights into a platform managing sensor data at production scale, and simultaneously demonstrate to other researchers a methodology to follow to conduct their research at production scale. It is important to note that this work was done on an eight-node cluster, not a cluster of hundreds or thousands of servers as is often mentioned in discussions of production environments.

We would like to contribute our tools and experience towards the creation of an industry standard IoT benchmark suite. We plan to identify additional IoT applications and sensor data types to include as part of that suite.

Acknowledgments

The author would like to thank Priya Arun, Cullen Bash, Sue Charles, Carlos Felix, John Gearen, Meichun Hsu, Uri Kogan, Harumi Kuno, Oliver Moreno, Brad Morrey, Alison Reynolds, Stewart Robbins, Mark Slavin, and Min Xiao for their constructive feedback and assistance.

---

[10] http://www.spec.org
[11] http://www.tpc.org

7. REFERENCES

[1] A. Aji, F. Wang, H. Vo, R. Lee, Q. Liu, X. Zhang, and J. Saltz. Hadoop-GIS: A high performance spatial data warehousing system over MapReduce. In *Proceedings of the VLDB Endowment*. VLDB Endowment, August 2013.

[2] AMTSybex and IBM. Sink or swim with smart meter data management. September 2011.

[3] T. Armstrong, V. Ponnekanti, D. Borthakur, and M. Callaghan. LinkBench: a database benchmark based on the Facebook social graph. In *SIGMOD 2013*, pages 1185–1196. ACM, June 2013.

[4] D. Borthakur. Petabyte scale databases and storage systems at Facebook. In *SIGMOD 2013*. ACM, June 2013.

[5] B. Cooper, A. Silberstein, E. Tam, R. Ramakrishnan, and R. Sears. Benchmarking cloud serving systems with YCSB. In *SoCC'10*, June 2010.

[6] E. Dede, Madhusudhan, D. Gunter, R. Canon, and L. Ramakrishnan. Performance evaluation of a MongoDB and Hadoop platform for scientific data analysis. In *ScienceCloud 2013*, June 2013.

[7] Z. Ding, X. Gao, J. Xu, and H. Wu. IOT-StatisticDB: A general statistical database cluster mechanism for big data analysis and the Internet of Things. In *IEEE Internet of Things*. IEEE, August 2013.

[8] H. Dryar. The effect of weather on the system load. *AIEE Transactions*, 63(12):1006–1013, December 1944.

[9] A. Floratou, N. Teletia, D. Dewitt, J. Patel, and D. Zhang. Can the elephants handle the NoSQL onslaught? In *Proceedings of the VLDB Endowment*, pages 1712–1723. VLDB Endowment, August 2012.

[10] C. Gellings and R. Taylor. Electric load curve synthesis - a computer simulation of an electric utility load shape. *IEEE Transactions on Power Apparatus and Systems*, PAS-100(1):60–65, January 1981.

[11] A. Ghazal, T. Rabl, M. Hu, F. Raab, M. Poess, A. Crolotte, and H. Jacobsen. BigBench: towards an industry standard benchmark for big data analytics. In *SIGMOD 2013*, pages 1197–1208. ACM, June 2013.

[12] A. Hall, O. Bachmann, R. Bussow, S. Ganceanu, and M. Nunkesser. Processing a trillion cells per mouse click. In *Proceedings of the VLDB Endowment*, pages 1436–1446. VLDB Endowment, August 2012.

[13] Itron and Microsoft. Benchmark testing results: Unparalleled scalability of Itron Enterprise Edition on SQL Server. May 2011.

[14] D. Jones and M. Lorenz. An application of a Markov chain noise model to wind generator simulation. *Mathematics and Computers in Simulation*, 28:391–402, 1986.

[15] S. Karnouskos, P. G. da Silva, and D. Illic. Assessment of high-performance smart metering for the web service enabled smart grid. In *ICPE 2011*, March 2011.

[16] M. Kaufmann, A. Manjili, R. Vagenas, P. Fischer, D. Kossmann, F. Farber, and N. May. Timeline index: A unified data structure for processing queries on temporal data in SAP HANA. In *SIGMOD 2013*. ACM, June 2013.

[17] A. Lamb, M. Fuller, R. Varadarajan, N. Tran, B. Vandiver, L. Doshi, and C. Bear. The Vertica analytic database: C-store 7 years later. In *Proceedings of the VLDB Endowment*, pages 1790–1801. VLDB Endowment, August 2012.

[18] P. Larson, C. Clinciu, C. Fraser, E. Hanson, M. Mokhtar, R. Rusanu, and M. Saubhasik. Enhancements to SQL server column stores. In *SIGMOD 2013*. ACM, June 2013.

[19] Y. Ma, J. Rao, W. Hu, X. Meng, X. Han, Y. Zhang, Y. Chai, and C. Liu. An efficient index for massive IOT data in cloud environment. In *CIKM'12*, October 2012.

[20] C. MacGillvary, V. Turner, and D. Lund. Worldwide Internet of Things (IoT) 2013-2020 forecast: Billions of things, trillions of dollars. *IDC*, pages 1–22, October 2013.

[21] Oracle. Meter-to-cash performance using Oracle Utilities applications on Oracle Exadata and Oracle Exalogic. January 2012.

[22] S. Patil, M. Polte, K. Ren, W. Tantisiriroj, L. Xiao, J. Lopez, G. Gibson, A. Fuchs, and B. Rinaldi. YCSB++: benchmarking and performance debugging advanced features in scalable table stores. In *SoCC'11*, October 2011.

[23] A. Pavlo, E. Paulson, A. Rasin, D. Abadi, D. DeWitt, S. Madden, and M. Stonebraker. A comparison of approaches to large-scale data analysis. In *SIGMOD 2009*. ACM, June 2009.

[24] V. Raman, G. Attaluri, R. Barber, and N. Chainani. DB2 with BLU acceleration: so much more than just a column store. In *Proceedings of the VLDB Endowment*. VLDB Endowment, August 2013.

[25] D. Shamshad, M. Bawadi, W. Hussin, T. Majid, and S. Samusi. First and second order Markov chain models for synthetic generation of wind speed time series. *Energy*, 30:693–708, 2005.

[26] Y. Shi, X. Meng, J. Zhao, X. Hu, B. Liu, and H. Wang. Benchmarking cloud-based data management systems. In *CloudDB'10*, October 2010.

[27] J. Shute, R. Vingralek, B. Samwel, B. Handy, C. Whipkey, E. Rollins, M. Oancea, K. Littlefield, D. Menestrina, S. Eliner, J. Cieslewicz, I. Rae, T. Stancescu, and H. Apte. F1: A distributed SQL database that scales. In *Proceedings of the VLDB Endowment*. VLDB Endowment, August 2013.

[28] P. Wong, Z. He, and E. Lo. Parallel analytics as a service. In *SIGMOD 2013*, pages 25–36. ACM, June 2013.

[29] R. Xin, J. Rosen, and M. Zaharia. Shark: SQL and rich analytics at scale. In *SIGMOD 2013*. ACM, June 2013.

Enhancing Performance Prediction Robustness
by Combining Analytical Modeling and Machine Learning*

Diego Didona[1], Francesco Quaglia[2], Paolo Romano[1], Ennio Torre[2]
[1]INESC-ID / Instituto Superior Técnico, Universidade de Lisboa
[2] Sapienza, Università di Roma

ABSTRACT

Classical approaches to performance prediction rely on two, typically antithetic, techniques: Machine Learning (ML) and Analytical Modeling (AM). ML takes a black box approach, whose accuracy strongly depends on the representativeness of the dataset used during the initial training phase. Specifically, it can achieve very good accuracy in areas of the features' space that have been sufficiently explored during the training process. Conversely, AM techniques require no or minimal training, hence exhibiting the potential for supporting prompt instantiation of the performance model of the target system. However, in order to ensure their tractability, they typically rely on a set of simplifying assumptions. Consequently, AM's accuracy can be seriously challenged in scenarios (e.g., workload conditions) in which such assumptions are not matched. In this paper we explore several hybrid/gray box techniques that exploit AM and ML in synergy in order to get the best of the two worlds. We evaluate the proposed techniques in case studies targeting two complex and widely adopted middleware systems: a NoSQL distributed key-value store and a Total Order Broadcast (TOB) service.

1. INTRODUCTION

Predicting the performance of applications and systems is a primary concern for various purposes such as capacity planning, elastic scaling and anomaly detection. Existing approaches to performance prediction typically rely on two, antithetic, techniques, namely Analytical Modeling (AM) and Machine Learning (ML).

AM has been, for decades, the reference technique to carry out performance evaluation and prediction of computing platforms, in a wide range of application contexts (see, e.g., [43, 20]). AM takes advantage of available expertise on the internal dynamics of systems and/or applications, and encodes such knowledge into a mathematical model aimed at capturing how (tunable) parameters map onto performance. AM techniques typically require no or minimal training in order to operatively carry out predictions in the target scenario, and have been shown to achieve a good overall accuracy. On the other hand, in order to be instantiated and/or be made tractable, AMs typically rely on simplifying assumptions on how the modeled system and/or its workload behave. Their accuracy can hence be seriously challenged in scenarios (i.e., areas of the features' space or specific workload conditions) in which such assumptions are not matched.

ML-based modeling lies on the opposite side of the spectrum, given that it requires no knowledge about the target system/application's internal behavior. Specifically, ML takes a black box approach that relies on observing the system's actual behavior under different settings in order to infer a statistical behavioral model, e.g., in terms of delivered performance. Over the last years, ML techniques have become more and more popular as tools for performance prediction of complex systems. Two are the main reasons behind this trend. On one side, the ever-increasing complexity of modern computing architectures represents a challenge for the accuracy of existing white box modeling techniques. On the other side, difficulties arise when employing white box models in virtualized, multi-tenant Cloud Computing environments, where details about the infrastructure physically hosting the application are normally (intentionally) hidden away from the users, restricting the possibility of employing detailed white box models for relevant parts of the system (e.g., the interconnection/networking infrastructure).

However, ML-based approaches are not the silver bullet for the problem of performance prediction. Their key drawback is that the accuracy they can reach strongly depends on the representativeness of the dataset used during the initial training phase. In fact, predictions targeting areas of the features' space that have not been sufficiently explored during the training process have typically very poor accuracy [2]. Unfortunately, the space of all possible configurations for a target application grows exponentially with the number of variables (a.k.a. features in the ML terminology) that can affect its performance — the so called *curse of dimensionality* [1]. Hence, in complex systems comprising large ecosystems of hardware and software components, the cost of conducting an exhaustive training process, spanning all possible input configurations, can quickly become prohibitive. Overall, pure ML approaches appear as not fully suited for contexts, like the Cloud, in which it is relevant

*This work has been supported by FCT - Fundação para a Ciência e a Tecnologia through PEst-OE/EEI/LA0021/2013, project specSTM (PTDC/EIA-EIA/122785/2010) and project GreenTM EXPL/EEI-ESS/0361/2013

to promptly build models capable of determining configurations that guarantee optimal performance (and consequently resource usage).

In this paper we explore the problem of how to combine white and black box performance modeling and prediction methodologies by proposing and evaluating three techniques based on the common idea of building an ensemble of different methodologies. By exploiting AM and ML in synergy, we aim at building a performance model that is more *robust*, i.e., less prone to error than a model based on any of the two techniques implemented alone. The gray box techniques that we propose serve this purpose in a twofold fashion: *i*) by incorporating some ML component, they allow for increasing the prediction accuracy over time as new data from the operational system are collected; *ii*) by relying on a pre-built analytical performance model, they can be instantiated with a lower training time than conventional, pure ML-based predictors.

Particularly, we take inspiration from the literature on ensembles of ML models, which has been targeted at studying how to combine multiple black box ML techniques, and propose three algorithms that allow for the synergistic use of AM and ML models:

- *K Nearest Neighbors (KNN)*: during the learning process, this algorithm evaluates the accuracy that can be achieved by the selected AM model(s) of the target system and by one (or several) black box ML approaches (e.g., Decision Trees, Artificial Neural Networks, Support Vector Machines) in points of the features' space that were not included in the training sets used to build the ML-based learners (namely, a *validation set*). When used to predict the performance achievable in a configuration c, the average error achieved by the AM model(s) and by the ML-based learner(s) across the K Nearest Neighbors configurations belonging to the validation set is used to determine which prediction method to choose.

- *Hybrid Boosting (HyBoost)*: in this technique a chain (possibly of length one) of ML algorithms is used to learn the residual errors of some AM. The intuition is that the function that characterizes the error of the AM may be learned more easily than the original target function that describes the relation between input and output variables. With this approach, the actual performance prediction in operative phases is based on the output by AM, adjusted by the error corrector function.

- *Probing (PR)*: The idea at the basis of this algorithm is to use ML to perform predictions exclusively on the regions of the features' space in which the AM does not achieve sufficient accuracy (rather than across the whole space). To this end two learners are exploited. Initially a classifier is used to learn in which regions of the features' space the AM incurs a prediction error larger than some predetermined threshold. In these regions, a second black box regressor is trained to learn the desired performance function.

All of the above algorithms allow for reducing the performance model instantiation time compared to pure ML techniques. In fact, either (i) the employed ML predictors do not need to reach extremely high precision across the whole features' space — given that they are complemented by white-box predictors (as it occurs in KNN) that can normally provide good accuracy in broad areas of the features' space; or (ii) they are targeted at estimating a function, namely the error curve associated with AM, which can be simpler (i.e., require less samples) to learn than the actual performance function (as it occurs in HyBoost); or (iii) they need to be trained only in circumscribed regions of the features' space (as it occurs in PR), which again can reduce the number of samples to be observed during the training phase.

Also, the structure of the framework is open to the possibility of using a family of AM techniques of recent interest (see, e.g., [12]), where parametric meta-models (requiring fewer assumptions on the target system than classical analytical models, hence widening their applicability) are fast trained, in order give rise to the actual AM instance suited for the target system. This has been shown to be doable by relying on a very reduced amount of samples of the real system behavior. Hence, the same (or a reduced portion) of training data that are used for the ML models envisioned in our framework, could be also used to carry out the meta-model training phase.

We assess the validity of our proposal through an extensive experimental evaluation carried out in two different application domains: throughput prediction of a popular open-source NoSQL distributed key-value store, Red Hat's Infinispan [25], and response time prediction of a total order broadcast service, a key building block for fault-tolerant replicated systems.

Our experimental results show that the best performing of our proposed techniques can reduce the Root Mean Square Error on average by about 40% with respect to AM and ML, with maximum gains that extend up to a factor 3× vs AM and 5× vs ML. On the other hand, they also show that none of the proposed ensemble techniques outperforms all the others in all the considered scenarios, and that their accuracy is strongly dependent on the correct determination of their internal meta-parameters. In this work we extensively investigate this issue and we highlight various interesting trade-offs that affect the parameters' tuning of the proposed algorithms.

The remainder of the paper is organized as follows. Section 2 discusses related work. In Section 3 we provide some background on ML techniques, which will form the basis for the comprehension of our proposal. The three innovative ensemble algorithms are presented in Section 4. The experimentation-based evaluation of the effectiveness of our proposals is provided in Section 5. Finally, Section 6 concludes the paper.

2. RELATED WORK

The body of literature on solutions relying either on AM or ML to predict applications' performance is extremely vast [29, 10, 35, 23, 8, 39, 42, 40]. On the other hand, to the best of our knowledge, only a few approaches rely on the synergistic exploitation of AM and ML. We group them in the discussion depending on how the combination of the two techniques is achieved.

Estimate and model. These works rely on ML to perform workload characterization and to estimate the service demand of the requests in the system. Next, this information is used to instantiate an AM, e.g. based on queuing theory. Techniques employed to identify the parameters' values for the AM include regression [44, 9], clustering [34], Genetic Programming [18] or a combination of Kalman Filters and autoregressive models [45]. As ML is only employed to characterize the workload, the accuracy of these solutions is ultimately dependent on the accuracy of the adopted AM technique. The ensemble techniques proposed in our work, on the other hand, rely on ML to correct the inaccuracies of an analytical model, and can hence improve accuracy over time, as new sampling data is collected from the system being modeled.

Divide and conquer. This technique consists in building performance models of individual parts of the entire system, which are either based on AM or on ML. The sub-models are then combined according to some formula in order to achieve the prediction curve of the system as a whole. We find applications of this technique in the context of performance modeling of distributed transactional applications [14, 16] and response time prediction of Map-Reduce jobs [22]. In the former case, AM is employed to capture the effects of data and CPU contention on performance, whereas ML is employed to forecast response time of network-bound operations. In the latter one, AM is exploited to compute some performance metrics that are input features for the ML predictor.

The solution we propose in this work is fully complementary with respect to the divide and conquer approach. In fact, performance predictors resulting from the adoption of this technique can still show the limitations typical of the base AM and ML techniques at their core (resp. inaccuracies due to approximations and lengthy training phases). Our solution is specifically aimed at mitigating such limitations, by relying on ensembles of learners to increase accuracy (e.g., by discarding the output of some AM/ML predictor in specific operating points) while jointly reducing the cost of the training process. We demonstrate the effectiveness of our proposal by considering the divide and conquer-based model presented in [16] as the reference performance predictor for the NoSQL transactional platform case study.

Bootstrapping. This technique, which has been applied in various contexts ranging from automatic resource provisioning to anomaly detection, consists in relying on an AM predictor to generate an initial synthetic training set for the ML, with the purpose of avoiding the initial, long profiling phase of the target application under different settings [15]. Then, the ML is retrained over time in order to incorporate the knowledge coming from samples collected from the operational system [38, 32, 37, 33].

With respect to this solution, that only employs the AM to generate the initial training set for the ML, our ensemble-based forecasting techniques maintain the AM as a base predictor, and exploit different ML-based techniques to train complementary black box models aimed at correcting the AM's inaccuracies.

In a previous work [13], we have explored the possibility to infer at runtime, via a single ML, a *corrective function* that, applied to the output of some AM predictor, is able to increase the overall accuracy. The HyBoost ensemble that we propose in this work improves over that solution, partic-

ularly by allowing for the combination of multiple learners to compensate for the error of the base AM.

Generally speaking, one (additional) common shortcoming of the above discussed literature solutions is that they rely on a single ML in combination with an AM. This represents a major limitation to the degree of accuracy and predictive power that AM and ML, combined, could achieve: in fact, several independent results in the ML field identify in models' diversity and heterogeneity the key means to build a robust and accurate model with low training time [17, 4]. Our results back and extend this claim: by investigating different techniques of combining white box and black box models, relying in their turn on the exploitation of several MLs, not only we do assess the benefits of combining the two techniques, but we show evidence that there is not a single hybrid ensemble model that always outperforms the others.

Finally, it is worthy to note that nothing prevents our framework to be usable for combining ML with other kinds of white box predictors like simulation models. Although in principle these are generally considered as more expensive (in terms of time for being solved) as compared to AM ones, the vast literature on high performance parallel simulation techniques provides a good support for instantiating simulators allowing to promptly evaluate the behavior of complex systems (thanks to speedups by parallel runs [11, 3]). This would lead to the availability of white box simulation models with features that are still complementary to ML ones, such as reduced instantiation time, leading not to subvert the possibility to reach the actual targets of our proposal when employed as an alternative to AM in the presented ensemble algorithms.

3. BACKGROUND ON ML MODELING

Before presenting the proposed gray box ensemble techniques, we recall some basic concepts on ML-based techniques and introduce terminology that will be used in the remainder of the paper.

From a mathematical perspective, a ML algorithm, noted γ, is a function defined over a set, called *training set* and noted $D_{tr} = \{< \mathbf{x}, y >\}$, where $\mathbf{x} = < x_1, \ldots, x_n >$ is a point in a $n-$dimensional space, called *features' space* and noted F, and y is the value of some unknown function $\phi : F \to C$. In this paper we consider the case in which the co-domain C of function ϕ is the set $\mathbb{R}$ of real numbers, namely we consider a *regression* problem. The proposed techniques can however be straightforwardly adapted to cope with problems, known under the name of *classification* problems, in which the co-domain of ϕ is discrete.

The output of a ML algorithm γ is a function, called *model* and noted Γ, which represents an approximator of function ϕ over the features' space F. More precisely, a model $\Gamma : F \to C$ takes as input a point $\mathbf{x} \in F$, possibly not observed in D_{tr}, and returns a value $\hat{y} \in C$. The process of building a model using a ML algorithm γ over a given training set is also called training phase.

The literature on ML has proposed a number of alternative statistical approaches to infer the model Γ given a training set D_{tr}, like Decision Trees (DT), Artificial Neural Network (ANN) and Support Vector Machines (SVM). Independently of the specific approach used to derive Γ, these techniques pursue the same objective: minimizing the error of Γ on the training set, while preserving the ability to generalize the information observed during the training phase in order to provide accurate estimations of ϕ even in regions of the features' space that were not observed during the training phase.

Various definitions of error can be adopted to evaluate this trade-off, and, more in general, the accuracy of a prediction model (independently of whether it adopts a black or white methodology). In this paper we adopt as error function the Root Mean Square Error (RMSE), whose definition we recall in the following. Given a set of actual values $y_i \in Y$ and of corresponding predictions $\hat{y}_i \in \hat{Y}$, with $\hat{y}_i, y_i \in C$, the RMSE of $\hat{Y}$ with respect to Y is defined as:

$$RMSE(\hat{Y}, Y) = \sqrt{\sum_{\hat{y}_i \in \hat{Y}} \frac{(\hat{Y}_i - Y_i)^2}{|\hat{Y}|}}$$

4. GRAY BOX ENSEMBLE ALGORITHMS

In this Section we present the three different algorithms that exploit ML techniques in ensemble with a white box analytical model, denoted as Γ_{AM}. Before presenting the proposed techniques, we provide a generic mathematical formalization of Γ_{AM}.

Analogously to a ML-based model, an analytical model Γ_{AM} is a function $F_{AM} \to C$, which can be queried to predict the performance of the modeled system $\hat{y} = AM(\mathbf{x})$ over a given configuration $x \in F_{AM}$. For simplicity, we will assume in the following that $F_{AM} = F_{ML}$ and refer to them by simply using the notation F. In other words, we assume that the domain F_{AM} over which the analytical model Γ_{AM} is defined coincides with the features' space, noted F_{ML}, used by the ML techniques that will be used to learn a correction function for Γ_{AM}. In practice, this assumption is not strictly required, and we simply require that the variables defining the features' space are observable, i.e., they can be measured in the target system. For instance, the white box model AM may actually use a smaller subset of the variables defining the features' space of the black box learners used in ensemble with AM. This could happen, for instance, if the AM were not to account for a set of parameters, say $P \notin F_{AM}$, whose effects on system's performance may be too hard to model explicitly via analytical models. The parameters in P could, however, be incorporated in the features' space F_{ML}, so as to keep their value into account when learning the target function.

The key difference of an analytical model Γ_{AM} with respect to a ML-based model Γ is that the latter is obtained by running a ML algorithm over a training set D_{tr} (i.e., $\Gamma = \gamma(D_{tr})$). Hence, whenever new observations are incorporated in the training set, yielding an updated training set $D'_{tr} \supseteq D_{tr}$, an updated version of the ML-based model $\Gamma' = \gamma(D'_{tr})$ can be computed by training the ML-based learner on D'_{tr}.

Conversely, an analytical model Γ_{AM} incorporates *a priori* domain knowledge on the target system, and it does not require a training phase nor can be dynamically updated. In other words, we consider the analytical model Γ_{AM} to be a static/immutable object, which cannot be updated based on the feedback obtained from the target system.

One may note that analytical models typically rely on a number of internal parameters, which can be used to calibrate the model's output. Such parameters could be updated, via fitting techniques [26], in order to minimize the error achieved by the AM over the set of performance sam-

---

Algorithm 1 K Nearest Neighbors

```
 1: Set Γ = ∅                                    ▷ Set of models to use
 2: Set γ = {γ₁, ..., γ_M}                       ▷ Set of ML regressors
 3: Set D_val = ∅                                       ▷ Validation set
 4:
 5: function INIT(Analytical Model Γ_AM, Training Set D_tr)
 6:     Γ = {Γ_AM}                        ▷ Initialize with the AM model
 7:                            ▷ Build the training set for ML regressors
 8:     Set D_regr = StatifiedSample(D_tr)
 9:                        ▷ Use a disjoint data set as Validation set
10:     D_val = D \ D_tb
11:     for m = 1 → M do
12:         Γ_m = γ_m(D_tb)                      ▷ Train m-th regressor
13:         Γ = Γ ∪ {Γ_m}
14:     end for
15: end function

16: function FORECAST(x_s)
17:     Set D_k={<x_i,y_i>∈KNN(x_s, D_val) s.t. ||x_i,x_s|| < c}
18:     for each Γ_i ∈ Γ do
19:         RMSE[i] = compute RMSE of model Γ_i on set D_k
20:     end for each
21:     μ = argmin RMSE[i]         ▷ Find learner with lowest RMSE
             i=1...M
22:     return Γ_μ(x_s)
23: end function
```

---

ples gathered over time from the target system. Also, as discussed in Section 2, gray box performance modeling techniques based on the *divide-and-conquer* approach, couple analytical and ML-based models targeting different, but dependent, subcomponent of the system. Whenever the ML-based models are updated, this leads to changes of the input parameters for the white box analytical models. From this perspective, hence, these gray box techniques can be seen as equivalent to white box analytical models whose internal parameters can be dynamically adjusted.

It is worth noting that, by assuming the analytical model Γ_{AM} to be an immutable object, we can ensure that the proposed techniques can also be employed in case Γ_{AM} can be dynamically updated. To this end, it simply suffices to treat the updated white box model $\Gamma_{AM'}$ as a new/different model. On the other hand, having not to impose such an assumption, we would allow the usage of techniques (e.g., ensemble techniques designed for "re-trainable" ML-based learners) that may not be applicable in case the analytical model was actually static.

As already mentioned, we present in the following three ensemble techniques that pursue the same objectives (minimizing training time and achieving an accuracy better or comparable to that of both black and white box techniques) using different algorithmic approaches. In the light of the above considerations, the proposed techniques can be seen as instances of ensemble techniques for ML-based learners, specialized for the case in which one of the learning algorithms in the ensemble outputs always the same model, namely the one coded in the AM formulas, which is essentially independent of the actual ML training set.

4.1 K Nearest Neighbors

The pseudo-code of the first presented technique, which we call K Nearest Neighbors (KNN), is reported in Algorithm 1. This technique relies on an analytical model, noted Γ_{AM}, and on a set γ of M alternative prediction models, noted $\gamma_1, \ldots, \gamma_M$. These predictors in γ should be selected to maximize model diversity, which can be achieved in various ways. A first technique consists in considering different ML algorithms, e.g., DT and ANN. One can also train each learner γ_i using a different training set, with the purpose of specializing the various models to predict performance in different regions of the features' space. Model diversity can also be promoted by using different analytical models (focused on capturing different systems' dynamics), or even alternative modeling techniques such as simulation.

The KNN algorithm is initialized via the INIT function, by providing Γ_{AM} and a data set of samples, $D_{tr} = <\mathbf{x}_i, y_i>$, which conveys information on the performance $y_i \in C$ of the target system over a set of observed configurations $\mathbf{x}_i \in F$. The data set D_{tr} is not entirely used to train the set Γ of regressors. Conversely, D_{tr} is split into two disjoint data sets, namely D_{regr} and D_{val}.

D_{regr} is used as training set for the learners in Γ, and it should be obtained by extracting a random subset amounting to a percentage p_{regr} of D_{tr}. In order to enhance the representativeness of the samples included in D_{regr}, the process of extraction of D_{regr} from D_{tr} is performed by means of the stratified sampling technique [2], which ensures that the distribution of the values $y_i \in C$ is the same in the two sets.

D_{val} is obtained as the complementary subset of $D_{regr} \in D_{tr}$, which ensures the disjointness of the two sets D_{regr} and D_{val} by construction. The D_{val} is used at query time (Function FORECAST), when one wants to predict the expected performance of the target system, noted y_s, in the configuration $\mathbf{x}_s$. To this end, it is first computed the set D_k that contains the k nearest neighbors $\{\mathbf{x}_1,\ldots,\mathbf{x}_k\} \in D_{val}$ within distance c from point $\mathbf{x}_s$. The samples in D_k, for which we have available also the corresponding actual performance, are then used to compute the average accuracy of each of the models in the set Γ (Line 19). This allows for determining the model, noted γ_μ in the pseudo-code (Line 21), which is expected to maximize prediction accuracy in the region surrounding $\mathbf{x}_s$. Based on this geometrical interpretation, the c parameter can be interpreted as a cut-off threshold, which allows discarding samples of the validation set that are too far away from $\mathbf{x}_s$ and which may not be representative of the target configuration $\mathbf{x}_s$.

The relevance of ensuring the disjointness of D_{val} and D_{tr} can be understood by recalling that samples $\mathbf{x} \in D_{tr}$ are used to train the regressors in Γ. Estimating the accuracy of these models using the same samples that were used to derive the models during the training phase would lead to significantly overestimate the accuracy achievable by, so called, over-fitted models, i.e., models that minimize (or even nullify) the error with respect to the configurations observed during the training phase, but which are unable to generalize and thus incur large errors even in regions in the proximity of points contained in the training set.

4.2 Hybrid Boosting

The second algorithm we present applies a well-known technique from the literature on ensembles of black box learners, which is known as Boosting [2]. In particular, as we are considering a regression problem (whereas the boosting technique was defined for classification problems), we draw inspiration from the *Adaptive Logistic Regression* technique [19]. This is a boosting algorithm that was originally conceived to operate with ML-based regressors, and which we adapted to support the joint usage of one analytical model and of a set of black box learners.

Algorithm 2 Hybrid Boosting

```
1: Set γ^red = {γ₁^red,...,γ_M^red}         ▷ ML regressors for residue pred.
2: Set Γ^red = {Γ₁^red,...,Γ_M^red}         ▷ Models for residue pred.
3: Set Γ^per = {Γ₀^per, Γ₁^per,...,Γ_M^per}  ▷ Models for perf. pred.
4:
5: function INIT(Analytical Model Γ_AM, Training Set D_tr)
6:     Γ₀^per = Γ_AM              ▷ Set the AM as the 1ˢᵗ predictor
7:     for m = 1 → M do
8:         D_m = ∅
9:         for each <x_n,y_n> ∈ D_tr
10:            y_{m,n} = y_n − Γ_{m−1}^per(x_n)   ▷ Compute the residual error
11:            D_m = D_m ∪ <x_n, y_{m,n}>    ▷ of previous learner
12:        end for each
13:        Γ_m^red = γ_m^red(D_m)         ▷ Train on the residuals
14:        β_m = argmin_β Σ_{n=1}^N y_n − (Γ_{m−1}^per(x_n) + βΓ_m^red(x_n))
15:        Γ_m^per = Γ_{m−1}^per + β_m Γ_m^red   ▷ Set the m-th predictor
16:    end for
17: end function
18:
18: function FORECAST(x_s)
19:    return Γ₀^per(x_s) + Σ_{m=1}^M β_m Γ_m^red(x_s)
20: end function
```

The pseudo-code of this technique, which we name Hybrid Boosting (HyBoost), is reported in Algorithm 2. In addition to the analytical model Γ_{AM}, also in this case we assume the availability of a set of M regressors based on machine learning techniques, which we denote γ^{red}. Unlike in KNN, however, these learners are not used to build alternative models of the performance of the target system. Conversely, the learners are stacked in a chain (i.e., an ordered set) and used to learn the error (residue) introduced by the previous learner in the chain.

More in detail, HyBoost uses two (ordered) sets of predictive models, noted Γ^{red} and Γ^{per}, composed by, respectively, m and $m+1$ models. The first model in Γ^{red}, i.e., Γ_1^{red}, is obtained by training the first regressor γ_1^{red} with a training set D_i that characterizes the error (defined as the difference between the actual and predicted value) of the analytical model Γ^{AM} for each point in the original training set D_{tr}. Any other model Γ_i^{red}, with $i \in [1, M]$, is trained to learn the prediction error of the model Γ_{i-1}^{per}, which incorporates the knowledge of the AM and of the first $i-1$ ML-based learners by means of the following recurrence equation (Line 15):

$$\Gamma_m^{per} = \Gamma_{m-1}^{per} + \beta_m \Gamma_m^{red}$$

where β_m is a coefficient (computed in Line 14) such that the cumulative training error of the resulting m-stage regressor is minimized.

The key intuition at the basis of this algorithm, as already hinted, is that learning the residual errors of an analytical model may be easier than learning the original function for which we are trying to build a robust predictor. Also Hy-Boost, analogously to KNN, can exploit machine learners using different algorithms. Moreover, it may be further extended and optimized using well-known techniques in the literature on boosting ML-algorithms, such as adaptively weighting the elements in the training set of the i-th learner in order to focus it on minimizing its fitting error on samples over which the $i-1$-th learner incurred the largest errors.

4.3 Probing

We named the last of the three presented techniques *Probing*, and we reported its pseudo-code in Algorithm 3. This approach, which to the best of our knowledge has no direct

Algorithm 3 Probing

```
1:  Classifier γ_cls                    ▷ Detects when Γ_AM is wrong
2:  ClassificationModel Γ_cls
3:  Regressor γ_reg            ▷ Learns φ in areas where Γ_AM is wrong
4:  RegressionModel Γ_reg
5:  Set D_bad, D_cls, D_good = ∅              ▷ Initialize data sets
6:
7:  function INIT(Analytical Model Γ_AM, Training Set D_tr)
8:      for each < x_n,y_n >∈ D_tr
9:          if |(y_n − Γ_AM(x_n))/y_n| ≥ c then
10:             D_bad = D_bad ∪ {< x_n, y_n >}
11:             D_cls = D_cls ∪ {< x_n,"bad">}
12:         else
13:             D_cls = D_cls ∪ {< x_n,"good">}
14:         end if
15:     end for each
16:     Γ_cls = γ_cls(D_cls)              ▷ Train the "good/bad" classifier
17:     Γ_reg = γ_reg(D_bad) ▷ Train the regressor for samples in D_bad
18: end function

19: function FORECAST(x_s)
20:     if Γ_cls(x_s) ="bad" then
21:         return Γ_reg(x_s)
22:     else
23:         return Γ_AM(x_s)
24:     end if
25: end function
```

correspondence in the literature on ensembles of ML-based learners, uses 2 ML-based learners:

1. a classification algorithm, noted γ_{cls}, to learn *where* (i.e., in which regions of the features' space) the analytical model is not sufficiently accurate (based on a parametric threshold c over the absolute percentage error);

2. a regression algorithm, noted γ_{reg} which is trained to learn the function ϕ describing the performance of the target systems exclusively in the regions in which the analytical model does not achieve adequate accuracy.

To this end, during the initialization phase, each sample $< x_i, y_i >$ in the training set is classified as either "good" or "bad" based on the absolute percentage error achieved by the analytical model when queried for x_i (Lines 8-15). In addition, whenever a sample $< x_i, y_i >∈ D_{tr}$ is classified as bad, it is included in the data set D_{bad} that is used to train the black box regressor γ_{reg}.

When queried to predict the performance of the system on configuration x_s, it is first determined, using the classification model Γ_{cls} whether the analytical model Γ_{AM} is expected to achieve good or bad accuracy, and use, accordingly, either Γ_{AM} or the black box model Γ_{reg}.

The intuition underlying this technique is that, if the errors of the AM are focused in restricted and easily identifiable regions (via Γ_{cls}), one can then specialize the training phase of a black box learner exclusively on those regions. By narrowing the scope in which the ML-based learner Γ_{reg} is used to the regions of high error for Γ_{AM}, the complexity of the function that needs to be learnt via ML may be reduced, which may ultimately benefit the accuracy of Γ_{reg}.

5. EVALUATION

This section is devoted to assess the effectiveness of the proposed gray box modeling techniques by means of an extensive experimental evaluation based on two case studies on middleware systems: the Appia Group Communication Toolkit [28] and a popular open-source distributed key-value

store, Infinispan [25] by Red Hat. For each middleware platform, we consider two recently proposed performance prediction models [14, 32], which we use as a first baseline and which we combine with different ML approaches (Decision trees, Neural Networks and SVM) via the proposed gray box techniques.

We start by presenting the two case studies, and the corresponding performance models in Section 5.1. In Section 5.2 we evaluate the impact of the key parameters of the presented gray box modeling techniques on their accuracy. Finally, Section 5.3 focuses on comparing the accuracy and training/querying time of the proposed solutions and of a number of alternative performance modeling approaches.

5.1 Case studies

In order to evaluate experimentally the effectiveness and the sensitivity to parameters of the gray box ensemble methods discussed in the previous section, we consider two case studies: *i*) response time prediction of a Sequencer-based Total Order Broadcast (STOB) service, implemented in Appia [28] and *ii*) throughput prediction of an application deployed over a popular distributed transactional key-value data store, Red Hat's Infinispan (v. 5.2) [25]. We consider these two middleware systems for two main reasons. First, because of their relevance and wide adoption, they allow to demonstrate the viability of the proposed techniques when applied to mainstream software. Second, because of the diversity of the corresponding performance prediction problems: the features' spaces of the two case studies have very different dimensionality (2 for STOB vs 7 for Infinispan), and the corresponding analytical models exhibit different distribution of errors. This allows us to evaluate the proposed solutions in very heterogeneous scenarios, increasing the representativeness of our experimental study.

STOB primitive. Total Order Broadcast (TOB) [21] is a primitive that allows a group of processes to achieve consensus on a common delivery order of messages that can be broadcast (possibly concurrently) by processes in this group. TOB is a fundamental building block at the basis of a number of fault-tolerant replication mechanisms for databases [30], transactional memory [7] and highly-available objects [27]. TOB algorithms based on sequencer processes (STOB) [28] are probably among the most widely deployed TOB protocols, as they achieve the minimum bound on message latency for the TOB problem. In failure-free runs of the

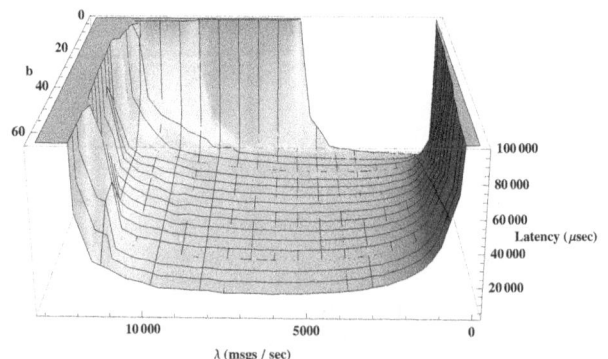

Figure 1: Response time of the STOB service

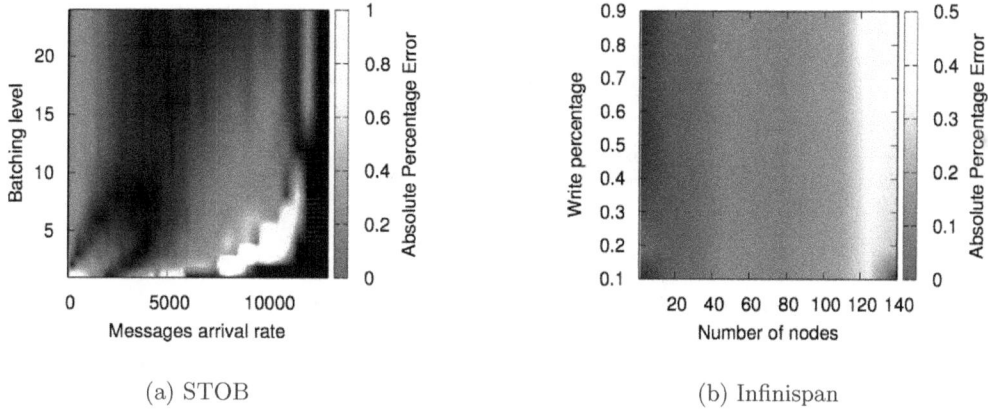

(a) STOB   (b) Infinispan

Figure 2: Error distribution of Γ_m of the two case studies.

STOB algorithm, if no processes leave or join the group, the processes agree on the identity of a single process, before starting to totally order broadcast (TO-Bcast) messages. Such a process, called *sequencer*, has the role to impose a common total order of delivery on messages to all processes in the group. A total order broadcast of a message is supported via the execution of a plain broadcast of the message by the sender process. When a process receives a message from the network, however, it cannot immediately deliver it to the application. In order to guarantee group-wide agreement on the final delivery order, in fact, it has first to wait to receive from the sequencer the corresponding *sequencing* message, and to ensure that all previously ordered messages have been delivered. The batching level, denoted in the remainder as b, defines how many messages the sequencer waits to receive before generating a sequencing message. Setting b to 1 ensures minimal latency at low load; at high load, however, higher values of batching lead to amortize the cost of sequencing each message, and allow the sequencer to sustain higher throughput.

The AM adopted in this work as white box predictor of the latency of a STOB algorithm has been proposed in [32], in order to automate the tuning of the batching level in function of the message arrival rate λ. This is a relatively simple model, which represents the sequencer node as a $M/M/1$ queue [24], and, based on purely analytical methods, computes the STOB message delivery as the traversal time of a client in the queue.

This case study is interesting because, although the parameters characterizing the system's behavior are only two (message arrival rate and batch size), the resulting performance function (shown in Figure 1) exhibits non-linear behavior. This is typical of queuing systems [24], as the response time quickly grows to infinite when the message arrival rate approaches the maximum service rate sustainable by the sequencer (given the current batching level b). It is well known that most ML techniques can be challenged when faced with functions having accentuated non-linear behaviors. Moreover, the error distribution of the corresponding analytical model is particularly interesting as the error looks generally low, except for a very specific zone of the input parameters' space. Such localized error is depicted in

Figure 2(a), where the the messages arrival rate is on the x-axis and the batching level on the y-axis.

Infinispan. NoSQL data stores have emerged as reference data platforms for the Cloud: they adopt less expressive data models than the classic relational one, and opt for simpler, yet more scalable, paradigms, as in key-value stores; moreover, in order to enhance performance, these systems typically maintain data fully in-memory and rely on replication as their primary mechanism to ensure fault-tolerance and data durability. Infinispan is a popular NoSQL data store which, analogously to other recent cloud platforms [6, 36], provides support for strong consistency via the abstraction of atomic transactions.

Predicting the performance of such platforms is far from being a trivial task, as it is impacted by several factors: contention on physical (i.e., CPU and network) and logical (i.e., data) resources, characteristics of the transactional workload (e.g., conflict likelihood and transactional mix) and configuration of the platform itself (e.g., scale and replication degree). This case study is, thus, an example of a modeling/learning problem defined over a very vast dimensional space (spanning 7 dimensions in our case) and characterized by a very complex performance function.

The reference model that we employ as base predictor for this case study is PROMPT [16]. PROMPT relies on the divide-and-conquer approach described in Section 2. On one hand, it exploits the knowledge of the concurrency and replication scheme (e.g., Two-Phase Commit) employed by the data platform to capture the effects of workload and platform configuration on CPU and data contention via a white box analytical model. On the other hand, it relies on ML to predict latencies of network bound operations.

Overall, besides involving a much wider features' space, this case study is particularly interesting as it allows us to evaluate the effectiveness of our approach also when used in combination with another gray box modeling technique. In Figure 2(b) we also visualize, again by means of a heat-map, the error distribution of PROMPT, obtained by projecting the features' space over two dimensions, namely number of nodes in the system (on the x-axis) and percentage of write transactions (on the y-axis). It can be noted that the error distribution of PROMPT is more diffuse than for the case of

(a) Training set 20% and 30%

(b) Training set 50% and 80%

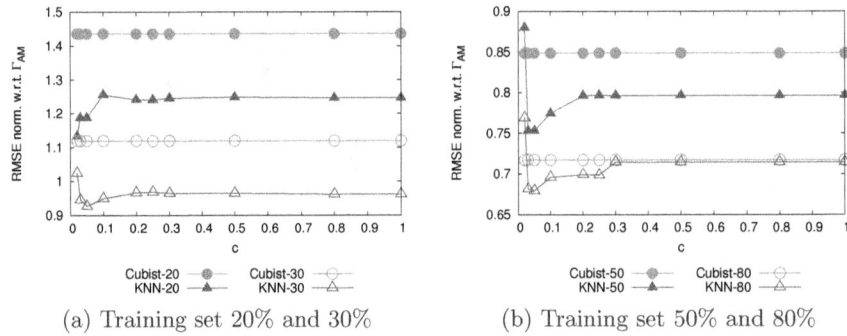

Figure 3: Sensitivity analysis of KNN w.r.t. the c parameter (STOB)

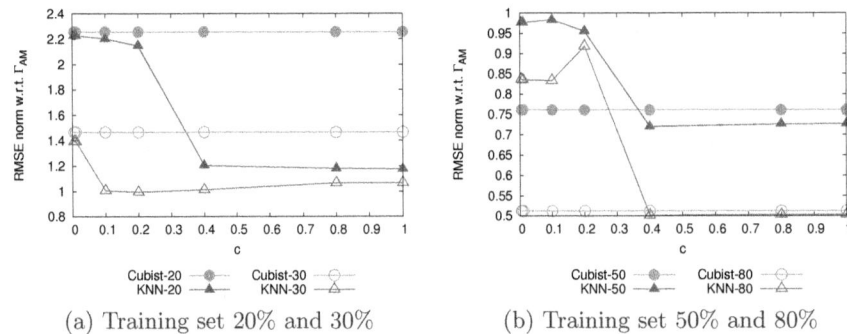

(a) Training set 20% and 30%

(b) Training set 50% and 80%

Figure 4: Sensitivity analysis of KNN w.r.t. the c parameter (Infinispan)

STOB (see Figure 2(a)), which was characterized by intense spikes in clearly circumscribed regions of the features' space.

Experimental dataset and test bed[1]. For the STOB case study, we consider a data set containing a total of five hundred observations drawn from a cluster of 10 machines equipped with two Intel Quad-Core XEON at 2.0 GHz, 8 GB of RAM, running Linux 2.6.32-26 server and interconnected via a private Gigabit Ethernet. In the experiment performed to collect the samples, the batching level was varied between 1 and 24, and 512-byte messages were injected at arrival rates ranging from 1 msgs/sec to 13K msgs/sec.

As for the transactional application case study, we consider a dataset composed by approximately five hundred samples, collected by deploying Infinispan on a cloud infrastructure composed by 140 Virtual Machines (VM) equipped with 1 Virtual CPU and 2GBs of RAM; each VM runs a Fedora 17 Linux distribution with kernel 3.3.4- 5.fc17.x86 64. The physical infrastructure hosting the cloud is composed by 18 physical servers equipped with two 2.13 GHz Quad-Core Intel(R) Xeon(R) processors and 32 GB of RAM and interconnected via a private Gigabit Ethernet; the employed virtualization software is Openstack Folsom.

The considered application is a porting of YCSB [5], the *de facto* standard benchmark for key-value stores, which has been modified in order to support transactions. The generated workloads are A, B and F: workload A has a mix of 50/50 reads and writes, and models a session store recording recent actions; workload B is the one of a photo tagging

application, which contains a 95/5 reads/update mix; workload F models a user database, in which records are first read and modified within a transaction. In order to generate a wider set of workloads, we also vary the number of reads and writes performed by transactions between 1 and 5. Finally, we consider two different data access patterns: Zipfian, i.e., the popularity of data items follows the zipf distribution (with zipfian constant 0.7), and Hot Spot, according to which the x% of the data accesses are biased towards the y% of the data items (with $x = 99$ and $y = 1$ in our case); the data set is always composed of 500K keys. The samples relevant to the application's throughput are collected while varying workloads and the data platform configuration, deployed on a number of nodes, noted N, ranging from 2 to 140 and set up with a replication factor in the set $\{1, 2, 3, \frac{N}{2}, N\}$.

5.2 Analysis of Parameters' Sensitivity

In this section we evaluate the sensitivity of the proposed ensemble techniques with respect to their key parameters, namely the cut-off threshold c (for KNN and Probing) and the number M of black-box learners exploited in the ensemble. We consider as baselines, in this phase, the performance models described in Section 5.1, as well as a state of the art ML-based regressor, Cubist [31]. Cubist adapts and extends the popular C4.5 decision tree classification algorithm to cope with regression problems, by interpolating arbitrary functions by means of peace-wise linear functions. The choice of Cubist as reference base learner for the results presented in this section is due to the fact that, at least in the considered case studies, Cubist consistently resulted to be the most accurate individual (non-ensembled) ML tech-

---

[1]Dataset in Weka format and source code are available at https://github.com/EnnioTorre/CombiningMultiplePredictors

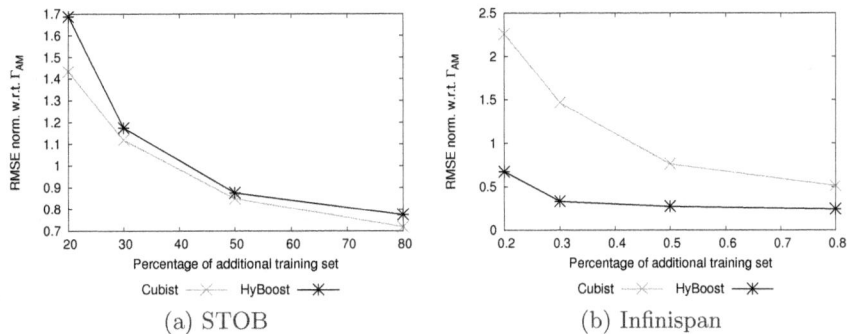

(a) STOB   (b) Infinispan

Figure 5: Evaluating the accuracy of HyBoost.

nique, when compared to (Weka's implementations of) ANN and SVM[2].

In order to quantify accuracy of the compared alternatives, we select as metric the RMSE normalized with respect to the RMSE of the performance models described in Section 5.1. Whenever we assume the availability of a given training set D_{tr}, we always compute the RMSE over a disjoint test set that comprises all the elements in the entire data set but the ones in D_{tr}.

KNN. Figure 3 and Figure 4 show the normalized accuracy achieved by KNN while varying the cut-off parameter c for the case, respectively, of STOB and Infinispan. Each plot reports results obtained by letting KNN and Cubist observe two percentages of the training set, namely: 20% and 30% in Figures 3(a) and 4(a); 50% and 80% in Figures 3(b) and 4(b). In this experiment we configured KNN to use at most $k = 10$ neighbors, and a single black-box regression model, Γ, which is built by using Cubist.

The plots highlight that the optimal settings of the c parameter is quite different in the two case studies. In particular, for STOB the experimental data clearly show that small cut-off values (on the order of 1% to 5%) are preferable to larger ones. The opposite is true for the Infinispan's case study, where the cut-off parameter that provides optimal accuracy is around 40%. This can be explained by considering that the performance function ϕ that needs to be learnt in the STOB case study is highly non-linear and defined over a small bi-dimensional space. Indeed, given the low dimensionality of the features' space, this data set allows for a quite dense (and hence accurate) sampling of ϕ. Such a dense sampling, combined with the fact that ϕ is subject to quick variations, implies that, by increasing the cut-off parameter, one also increases the probability of including in the set of points D_k (which, we recall, is used to estimate the accuracy of the various prediction models) samples belonging to regions of F in which ϕ exhibits very different dynamics. On the other hand, given the much higher dimensionality of F for the case of Infinispan (and the correspondingly much sparser sampling of F provided by the considered data set), using large cut-off values does pay off, as it increases the likelihood of finding suitable neighbors.

In the negative case, being most of the points in the training set quite far apart, for a large fraction of the queries (especially with low percentages of training set), no suitable neighbor is found — in which case, KNN uses, as fall-back, the analytical model.

Overall, both Figures highlight that KNN, when properly tuned, consistently outperforms both the analytical models and the regression models built by Cubist with gains that are more consistent, at low percentage values of the training set, with respect to Cubist, and, vice-versa, more accentuated with respect to the analytical models for higher percentage values of the training set.

HyBoost. The internal parameters of HyBoost are M, namely the depth of the chain of black-box learners that are used to learn a correction function for Γ_{AM}, and the ML algorithms that compose such chain. We experimented with chains of learners of length up to 10 and considered ensembles of black-box learning algorithms including Cubist, Neural Networks and SVM. We present, however, results only with $M = 3$, as the results have shown that, both with STOB and Infinispan, using additional learners did not have any added value on the accuracy. We argue that this depends on the fact that the error function of the ensemble composed by Γ_{AM} and by one ML-based regressor was extremely irregular, hence resulting not easy to learn using additional black-box regressors.

Therefore, we report, in Figure 5, the RMSE (again normalized with respect to the RMSE of Γ_{AM}) achieved by HyBoost while varying the percentage of samples observed during the training phase. The plots highlight remarkable differences between the performances achieved by HyBoost in the two considered case studies. With Infinispan, HyBoost yields substantial improvements with respect to both Γ_{AM} and Cubist, with maximum gains for 30% of training set where it reduces the RMSE by a factor 3x with respect to PROMPT and 5x with respect to Cubist. As for STOB, instead, the error function of the analytical model, as shown in Figure 2(a), is strongly non-linear and irregular, and, consequently, the chain of corrective MLs fails in effectively compensating for Γ_{AM}'s inaccuracies.

Probing. In Figure 6 and Figure 7 we report the results of a study aimed at assessing the sensitivity of Probing with respect to the cut-off parameter c for the case, respectively, of STOB and Infinispan. Let us analyze first the case of Infinispan, where we can see that, with small training sets, this method yields the best results with high cut-off values, i.e.,

---

[2]It stems from the no-free-lunch-theorem [41] that no ML algorithm can universally outperform all the others. Hence, we do not exclude that for specific parameters' tunings, ANN, SVM, or any other alternative ML algorithm may outperform Cubist.

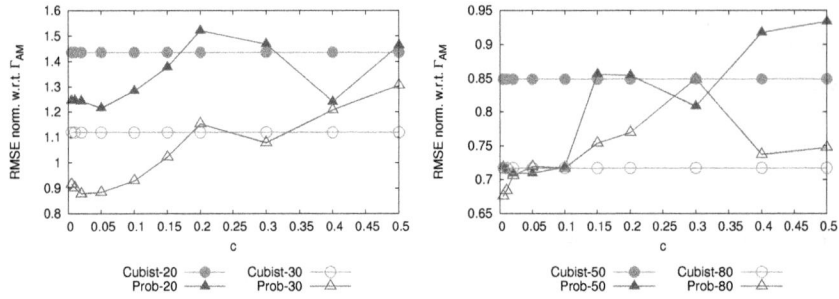

Figure 6: Sensitivity analysis of Probing w.r.t. the c parameter (STOB)

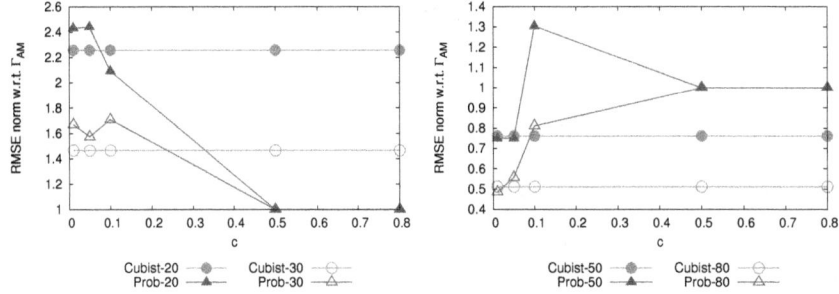

Figure 7: Sensitivity analysis of Probing w.r.t. the c parameter (Infinispan)

greater than 50%. This is indeed expectable, considering that, after having observed only a few samples in the training set it is very hard to build a reliable black-box model in a scenario with such a high dimensional features' space. It follows that in this scenario and for this setting of c, Probing will always query the analytical model. This also explains why Probing performs exactly like Γ_{AM} in these cases. For larger percentages of training sets, the optimal configuration is instead obtained for very small values of c, i.e., close to 1%. With such a configuration, clearly the ML regressor is used most of the times, as the prediction error of Γ_{AM} will be larger than 1% for the vast majority of the points in D_{TR}. Hence we may observe performance very close to those of the ML in this case. Overall, in the Infinispan scenario, Probing never really manages to outperform significantly both the white box and the black box approaches. A possible explanation can be found in Figure 2(b). As already mentioned, the error distribution of Γ_{AM} is extremely disperse in this scenario. In these conditions, generalizing rules capable of accurately determining when to use Γ_{AM} or the black-box learner is quite a challenging task for Γ_{cls}.

As already mentioned, instead, in the case of STOB, Γ_{AM} exhibits a much more irregular error distribution that, however, exhibits high values only in a clearly localized portion of the features' space. This simplifies considerably the problem of classifying automatically the regions in which the white box model is expected to achieve good/bad accuracy — explaining why Probing performs so much better in this scenario with respect to the case of Infinispan. Concerning the optimal tuning of c, the STOB scenario confirms what our results had already highlighted for Infinispan, when using relatively large training sets (50% and 80%): picking low cut-off values, and trusting consequently more the ML,

is the optimal strategy. Somewhat surprisingly, picking very low cut-off values (and hence trusting excessively the ML) is the most rewarding strategy also when considering small training sets in STOB. This may be explained by considering that since in this case ϕ is relatively simple, the ML could already learn a very robust approximator of ϕ, which can hardly be further improved by exploiting Γ_{AM}.

5.3 Mutual Comparison

So far, the proposed ensemble techniques have been only evaluated individually. This section compares their mutual performance, assuming that each ensemble technique is using the optimal parameter values determined in the previous section[3].

Figure 8 compares the three proposed gray box ensemble techniques with respect to each other, to Γ_{AM} and to a pure black-box model built using Cubist. The left plot reports the results obtained for STOB. In this scenario, KNN and Probing are the two techniques that deliver the best results, consistently outperforming both Γ_{AM} and Cubist when the percentage of training set used to initialize the ensemble is larger than or equal to 30%. Conversely, HyBoost exhibits quite disappointing performance in this use case. As already discussed above, the cause of these differences is imputable to the strong non-linearity of the error distribution of Γ_{AM}, which HyBoost tries unsuccessfully to learn via ML techniques. On the other hand, as the regions in which Γ_{AM}

---

[3]The correct settings of these parameters can be identified recurring to the standard methodology used to tune the internal parameters of ML-based algorithms: performing a parameter's sweep during the training phase, and using cross-validation to evaluate the accuracy achieved when using a candidate parameter configuration over a test set disjoint from the training set used to initialize the ensemble [2].

154

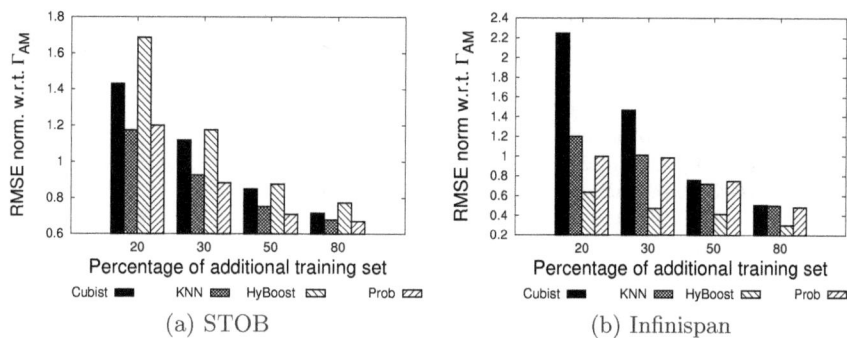

(a) STOB   (b) Infinispan

Figure 8: Mutual comparison between KNN, HyBoost and Probing.

incurs the largest errors are relatively circumscribed, solutions like KNN and Probing, which are based on the idea of determining in which regions to use which learner, result the most effective.

The landscape changes significantly in the Infinispan case study. Here, HyBoost is by far the most effective technique, reducing RMSE on average by a 2x factor vs Γ_{AM} and a 3x factor vs Cubist. KNN and Probing, instead, fail to achieve significant gains with respect to both the baselines, although normally remaining competitive with the best of the two across the entire spectrum of considered training set percentage values. The reason underlying these results is again identifiable by looking at the error distribution of Γ_{AM}, which, as shown in Figure 2(b), varies slowly in this case and exhibits pronounced linear trends.

Overall, these results suggest two main considerations. *No one size fits all*: None of the proposed techniques was able to consistently outperform all others in all the considered scenarios. This result is indeed not surprising if one takes into account seminal results, such as the no-free-lunch-theorem [41], which states precisely the impossibility of building a universal statistical learning technique. It is therefore imperative not to blindly rely on any of the proposed ensemble techniques, but to always verify, using cross-validation during the training phase, the actual effectiveness of each technique based on the problem at hand.

The error distribution of Γ_{AM} is crucial: Our experimental study suggests that one of the key factors that affects the performance of the proposed solutions is the "shape" of the error distribution of Γ_{AM}. A natural research question triggered by this finding is whether it is possible to identify rigorous conditions under which each of the proposed ensemble algorithms is favored. Another, probably even more interesting, question is whether one could intentionally introduce biases in the design of analytical models to make them more amenable to be used within a gray box ensemble such as the ones proposed in this work. For instance, one may prefer a simpler, yet globally less accurate analytical model, if it could be guaranteed (even probabilistically) that the error distribution of the adopted model was easier to learn using techniques like HyBoost.

6. CONCLUSIONS

In this paper we explored the problem of how to combine white and black box performance modeling methodologies by proposing and evaluating three techniques that aim at

taking the best of the two worlds, namely avoid incurring the drawbacks (e.g., non-minimal errors in specific operative conditions) of any individual technique, while minimizing the time for instantiating a reliable performance model of the target system/application.

Our proposal is aligned with the needs arising in modern computing systems, namely (a) their extremely high complexity and the reliance on virtualization, factors that tend to be adverse to white box, e.g., analytical, performance modeling techniques (e.g., given that system internal operations may be not perfectly known, hence being difficult to be reliably expressed in term of their behavior via analytical formulas), and (b) the need for timely instantiating scenario-specific performance models, which can then be used for prompt optimization of the usage of, e.g., Cloud rented resources. The latter requirement is particularly challenging for black box approaches based on machine learning, given that the building of reliable machine learning predictors generally requires lengthy training phases, leading to delays in the actual optimization based on the performance model.

We evaluated the effectiveness of our proposals by relying on case studies related to two highly relevant open-source middleware platforms, namely a key-value data store and a group communication system. We feel our proposal stands as a relevant achievement in terms of the construction of supports for coping with the problem of performance (and hence resource usage) optimization of highly complex computing systems.

7. REFERENCES

[1] R. Bellman. *Dynamic Programming*. Princeton University Press, Princeton, NJ, 1957.

[2] C. M. Bishop. *Pattern Recognition and Machine Learning (Information Science and Statistics)*. 2007.

[3] C. D. Carothers and K. S. Perumalla. On deciding between conservative and optimistic approaches on massively parallel platforms. In *Winter Simulation Conference*, 2010.

[4] R. Caruana et al. Ensemble selection from libraries of models. In *Proc. of ICML*, 2004.

[5] B. F. Cooper et al. Benchmarking cloud serving systems with ycsb. In *Proc. of SOCC*, 2010.

[6] J. C. Corbett et al. Spanner: Google's globally-distributed database. In *Proc. of OSDI*, 2012.

[7] M. Couceiro et al. D2stm: Dependable distributed software transactional memory. In *Proc. of PRDC*, 2009.

[8] M. Couceiro et al. A machine learning approach to performance prediction of total order broadcast protocols. In *Self-Adaptive and Self-Organizing Systems (SASO), 2010 4th IEEE International Conference on*, pages 184–193. IEEE, 2010.

[9] P. Desnoyers et al. Modellus: Automated modeling of complex internet data center applications. *ACM Trans. Web*, 6(2):8:1–8:29, June 2012.

[10] P. Di Sanzo et al. On the analytical modeling of concurrency control algorithms for software transactional memories: The case of commit-time-locking. *Perform. Eval.*, 69(5):187–205, May 2012.

[11] P. Di Sanzo et al. A framework for high performance simulation of transactional data grid platforms. In *Proc. of SIMUTools*, 2013.

[12] P. Di Sanzo et al. Regulating concurrency in software transactional memory: An effective model-based approach. In *Proc. of SASO*, 2013.

[13] D. Didona et al. Identifying the optimal level of parallelism in transactional memory applications. *Computing*, 2013.

[14] D. Didona et al. Transactional auto scaler: Elastic scaling of replicated in-memory transactional data grids. *ACM Trans. Auton. Adapt. Syst.*, 9(2):11:1–11:32, July 2014.

[15] D. Didona and P. Romano. On Bootstrapping Machine Learning Performance Predictors via Analytical Models. *ArXiv e-prints*, Oct. 2014.

[16] D. Didona and P. Romano. Performance modelling of partially replicated in-memory transactional stores. In *Proc. of MASCOTS*, 2014.

[17] T. G. Dietterich. Ensemble methods in machine learning. In *Proc. of MCS Workshop*, 2000.

[18] M. Faber and J. Happe. Systematic adoption of genetic programming for deriving software performance curves. In *Proc. of ICPE*, 2012.

[19] J. H. Friedman. Stochastic gradient boosting. *Comput. Stat. Data Anal.*, 38(4):367–378, Feb. 2002.

[20] V. Grassi et al. On the optimal checkpointing of critical tasks and transaction-oriented systems. *IEEE Trans. Software Eng.*, 18(1):72–77, 1992.

[21] R. Guerraoui and L. Rodrigues. *Introduction to Reliable Distributed Programming*. Springer-Verlag New York, Inc., 2006.

[22] H. Herodotou et al. No one (cluster) size fits all: automatic cluster sizing for data-intensive analytics. In *SOCC*, 2011.

[23] D. Jiang et al. Autonomous resource provisioning for multi-service web applications. In *Proc. of WWW*, 2010.

[24] L. Kleinrock. *Queueing Systems*, volume I: Theory. Wiley Interscience, 1975.

[25] F. Marchioni and M. Surtani. *Infinispan Data Grid Platform*. Packt Publishing, 2012.

[26] D. W. Marquardt. An algorithm for least-squares estimation of nonlinear parameters. *SIAM Journal on Applied Mathematics*, 11(2):431–441, 1963.

[27] H. Meling et al. Jgroup-arm: A distributed object group platform with autonomous replication management. *Softw. Pract. Exper.*, 38(9):885–923, July 2008.

[28] H. Miranda et al. Appia: A flexible protocol kernel supporting multiple coordinated channels. In *ICDCS*, 2001.

[29] G. Pacifici et al. Performance management for cluster-based web services. *Selected Areas in Communications, IEEE Journal on*, 23(12):2333–2343, 2005.

[30] F. Pedone et al. The database state machine approach. *Journal of Distributed and Parallel Databases and Technology*, 14:2003, 1999.

[31] J. R. Quinlan. Rulequest Cubist. http://www.rulequest.com/cubist-info.html, 2012.

[32] P. Romano and M. Leonetti. Self-tuning batching in total order broadcast protocols via analytical modelling and reinforcement learning. In *Proc. of ICNC*, 2011.

[33] D. Rughetti et al. Analytical/ml mixed approach for concurrency regulation in software transactional memory. In *Proc. of CCGRID*, 2014.

[34] R. Singh et al. Autonomic mix-aware provisioning for non-stationary data center workloads. In *Proc. of ICAC*, 2010.

[35] R. Singh et al. Analytical modeling for what-if analysis in complex cloud computing applications. *SIGMETRICS Perform. Eval. Rev.*, 40(4):53–62, Apr. 2013.

[36] Y. Sovran et al. Transactional storage for geo-replicated systems. In *SOSP*, 2011.

[37] G. Tesauro et al. On the use of hybrid reinforcement learning for autonomic resource allocation. *Cluster Computing*, 2007.

[38] E. Thereska and G. R. Ganger. Ironmodel: Robust performance models in the wild. *SIGMETRICS Perform. Eval. Rev.*, 36, June 2008.

[39] B. Trushkowsky et al. The scads director: scaling a distributed storage system under stringent performance requirements. In *Proc. of FAST*, 2011.

[40] L. Wang et al. Fuzzy modeling based resource management for virtualized database systems. In *MASCOTS*, 2011.

[41] D. H. Wolpert. The lack of a priori distinctions between learning algorithms. *Neural Comput.*, 8(7):1341–1390, Oct. 1996.

[42] J. Xu et al. On the use of fuzzy modeling in virtualized data center management. In *Proc. of ICAC*, 2007.

[43] P. S. Yu, D. M. Dias, and S. S. Lavenberg. On the analytical modeling of database concurrency control. *J. ACM*, 40(4):831–872, 1993.

[44] Q. Zhang et al. A regression-based analytic model for dynamic resource provisioning of multi-tier applications. In *ICAC*, 2007.

[45] T. Zheng et al. Integrated estimation and tracking of performance model parameters with autoregressive trends. In *Proc. of ICPE*, 2011.

A Comprehensive Analytical Performance Model of DRAM Caches

Nagendra Gulur,
Mahesh Mehendale
Texas Instruments
Bangalore, India
nagendra@ti.com,
m-mehendale@ti.com

Ramaswamy Govindarajan
Indian Institute of Science
Bangalore, India
govind@serc.iisc.ernet.in

ABSTRACT

Stacked DRAM promises to offer unprecedented capacity, and bandwidth to multi-core processors at moderately lower latency than off-chip DRAMs. A typical use of this abundant DRAM is as a large last level cache. Prior research works are divided on how to organize this cache and the proposed organizations fall into one of two categories: (i) as a *Tags-In-DRAM* organization with the cache organized as small blocks (typically 64B) and metadata (tags, valid, dirty, recency and coherence bits) stored in DRAM, and (ii) as a *Tags-In-SRAM* organization with the cache organized as larger blocks (typiclly 512B or larger) and metadata stored on SRAM. *Tags-In-DRAM* organizations tend to incur higher latency but conserve off-chip bandwidth while the *Tags-In-SRAM* organizations incur lower latency at some additional bandwidth. In this work, we develop a unified performance model of the DRAM-Cache that models these different organizational styles. The model is validated against detailed architecture simulations and shown to have latency estimation errors of 10.7% and 8.8% on average in 4-core and 8-core processors respectively. We also explore two insights from the model: (i) the need for achieving very high hit rates in the metadata cache/predictor (commonly employed in the *Tags-In-DRAM* designs) in reducing latency, and (ii) opportunities for reducing latency by load-balancing the DRAM Cache and main memory.

1. INTRODUCTION

Stacked DRAMs offer unprecedented capacity and bandwidth by allowing many layers of DRAM storage to be vertically stacked up and enabling access to these cells via high bandwidth channels [25]. The on-chip integration also reduces latency compared to off-chip DRAM storage. While the capacity of stacked DRAM (100s of MB) is far higher than SRAM (a few MB), the DRAM storage is still not sufficient to hold the entire working set of multi-core workloads. Thus the stacked DRAM is typically employed as a large last-level cache, backed by main memory. The main memory could be made up of DRAM or non-volatile technologies such as PCM [24] or STT-MRAM [14]. In this scenario, the DRAM Cache organization plays a pivotal role in processor performance since it

services the bulk of the memory requests coming from the last-level SRAM cache (abbreviated *LLSC* in the rest of this paper).

Due to their large capacity, DRAM Caches require a large amount of metadata (tags, valid, dirty, recency, coherence bits). The size of this metadata can run into megabytes (for example, a 256MB Cache with 64B blocks and 4B metadata per block needs 16MB for metadata). Two different organizational styles have been proposed to manage metadata: *Tags-In-SRAM* and *Tags-In-DRAM*. *Tags-In-SRAM* organizations [12,13] reduce the metadata overhead by using larger cache blocks (typically 512B or larger). The (small-sized) metadata is maintained on SRAM. However, the larger block size may waste off-chip bandwidth by fetching un-used data. In *Tags-In-DRAM* organizations [11, 16, 19], the metadata is stored alongside data in DRAM Cache rows (pages). This organization incurs a higher access latency since both tags and data have to be accessed from DRAM. Thus a small metadata cache/predictor is typically employed to reduce or avoid DRAM Cache accesses for tags.

In this work, we develop a unified analytical performance model of the DRAM Cache that spans both these styles of organizations taking into account key parameters such as cache block size, tag cache/predictor hit rate, DRAM Cache timing values, off-chip memory timing values and salient workload characteristics. The model estimates average miss penalty and bandwidth seen by the *LLSC*. Through detailed simulation studies, we validate this model for accuracy, with resulting latency estimation errors of 10.7% and 8.8% on average in 4-core and 8-core workloads respectively. Using the model we draw two interesting and useful insights:

Role of Tag Cache/Predictor: We show that the hit rate of the auxiliary tag cache/predictor (abbreviated *Tag-Pred*) is crucial to overall latency reduction. We also show that this tag cache (*Tag-Pred*) needs to achieve very high hit rate in order for the *Tags-In-DRAM* designs to out-perform *Tags-In-SRAM* designs.

Tapping Main Memory Bandwidth: Counter to intuition, we show that performance can be improved by sacrificing DRAM Cache hits to a certain extent. Sacrificing the hits allow balancing the utilization of on-chip (DRAM Cache) and off-chip memory bandwidth which can lead to overall latency reduction.

2. BACKGROUND

2.1 DRAM Cache Overview

By virtue of stacking and the inherent density of DRAM, a DRAM cache provides a large capacity (typically 64MB to even gigabytes) offering an unprecedented opportunity to hold critical workload

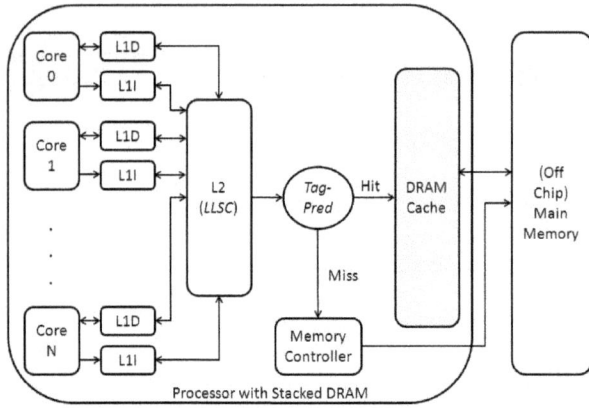

Figure 1: Overview of a Multi-core Processor with DRAM Cache

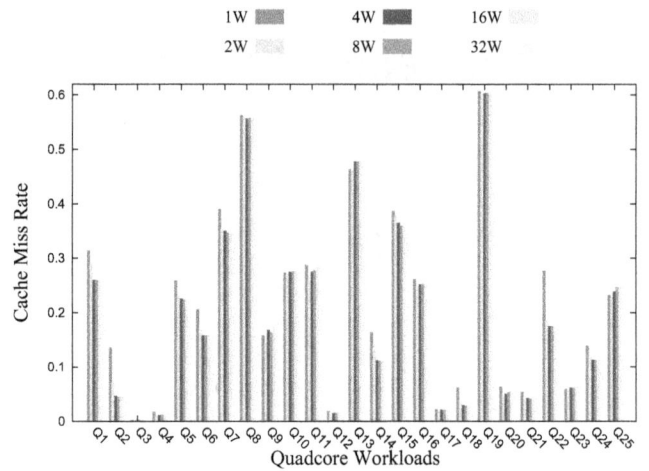

Figure 2: Impact of Set Associativity on DRAM Cache Hit Rate

data on chip. The DRAM cache is typically organized as a last level shared cache behind a hierarchy of SRAM caches. A DRAM cache offers such large capacity caches at lower power unlike L1, L2 caches that are implemented using SRAM. However DRAM cache design requires careful attention to access latency since a typical DRAM access requires activating a row of cells, sensing the stored charge on these capacitors and finally transmitting the sensed data over a bus. Since row activation has drained the corresponding capacitors, a *precharge* operation is required to restore the charge back on these capacitors.

Figure 1 provides an organizational overview of a multi-core processor comprising 2 levels of SRAM caches, followed by a DRAM Cache and off-chip main memory. The DRAM Cache services misses and write-backs from the last level SRAM Cache (*LLSC*). A *Tag-Pred* is typically employed to make a quick decision of whether to access the DRAM Cache (if the data is predicted to be present in it) or go directly to main memory.

The logical organization and functionality of DRAM caches is similar to traditional SRAM caches. For the purposes of this work, we assume that it is organized as a N way set-associative cache with block size that is B_s times the size of the CPU LLC block size. Note that $B_s = 1$ models *Tags-In-DRAM* organizations while larger values (typically $B_s = 8$ or 16) model *Tags-In-SRAM* organizations. DRAM Cache misses fetch the cache block from main memory. We assume a writeback cache and that only dirty sub-blocks are written back upon eviction. This assumption reflects the real-world implementation that DRAM Caches use - namely, when a dirty block is evicted, only the portions that are actually dirty (modified) are written to main memory. For example, a cache organized at 512B block size ($B_s = 8$) will write back only those 64B sub-blocks that are modified. This is done to conserve bandwidth and energy in the main memory system.

Since the data is on DRAM the access incurs high latency (comprising row activation, column access, and finally precharge) and thus several data layout organizations have been evaluated [11–13, 16, 19]. We summarize the key design considerations below that we need to take into account in the model.

Metadata Storage: The large capacities offered by DRAM caches incur high metadata (tags, valid, dirty bits, recency, coherence bits etc) storage requirements which can run into multiple megabytes. Obviously committing this much storage in SRAM is costly and energy expensive[1]. *Tags-In-DRAM* organizations [11,16,19] propose

---

[1]The tag storage overhead may even exceed the total size of the last-level SRAM cache.

to store the set metadata in the same DRAM rows as data thereby ensuring that one DRAM row activation is sufficient to retrieve both tags and data. In case of a DRAM cache miss, the latency of access is a sum of the DRAM cache tag look up time followed by the main memory access time. Since this degrades the access latency of cache misses, nearly all of these organizations propose the use of a *tag cache/predictor* structure (*Tag-Pred*) in SRAM to quickly evaluate if the access is a hit in the cache.

In the *Tags-In-SRAM* organizations [12,13] the metadata is held in SRAM and provides faster tag lookup. Typically, these organizations employ large block sizes (typically 1KB or larger) to reduce storage overhead.

Cache Block Size: Typically upper-level caches (L1, L2) employ a small block size ($\approx$ 64B or 128B) to capture spatial locality as well as to ensure low cost of a line fill. With large DRAM caches however larger block sizes may be gainfully employed to reduce metadata storage overhead (especially when it is on SRAM) as well as to leverage inherent spatial locality in workloads.

Set Associativity: A *k-way* mapped cache organizes each set to hold k blocks of data. Larger values of k reduce potential conflicts caused by addresses mapping to the same sets. However, in the context of DRAM caches, we find that associativity does not have a significant bearing on hit rate – an observation that other researchers have also made [10, 19]. Figure 2 plots the cache miss rates achieved at six different associativites (1-way, 2-way, 4-way, 8-way, 16-way, and 32-way) for several quad-core workloads in a 128MB cache. Except for workloads Q2 and Q22 that show noticeable miss rate reduction from 1-way to 2-way, all the others show no significant reduction with higher associativity (average reduction in miss rate in the 32-way organization over the direct-mapped organization is 4.3%). Thus, in our model *we assume that the hit rate is independent of set associativity.*

Row-Buffer Hit Rate: If accesses map to currently open pages in DRAM cache banks, then they can be serviced quickly (termed *row-buffer hits*). Row-buffer hit rate is governed by spatial locality in the access stream as well as by how adjacent cache blocks are mapped to DRAM cache sets and pages. Exploiting locality plays an important role in overall latency reduction.

The above design aspects interact to influence arrival rate, cache hit rate, DRAM row-buffer hit rate and thus the resulting latencies at the cache and main memory. Next we present an overview of the underlying DRAM performance model that we use in this work.

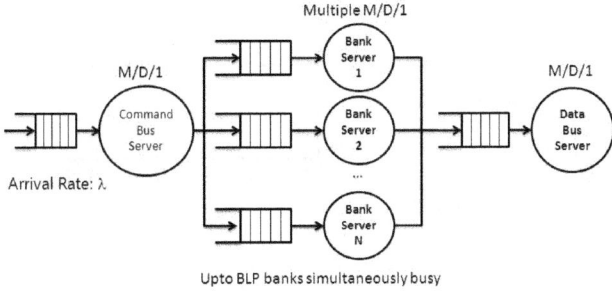

Figure 3: Queuing Model of Memory Controller as a 3-Stage Network of Queues

2.2 ANATOMY Overview

Our proposed performance model of the DRAM Cache is based on *ANATOMY* - an analytical model of memory performance in [7]. *ANATOMY* is the substrate for the DRAM Cache model that we develop in this work. *ANATOMY* has two key components that work together:

- A queuing model of memory that models in detail the key technological characteristics and design choices. The service times in this queuing model are parameterized by workload characteristics.
- A trace based analytical model that estimates key workload characteristics, namely arrival rate, row-buffer hit rate (RBH), bank-level parallelism (BLP) and request spread (S), that are used as inputs to the queuing model to estimate memory performance.

The queuing model of *ANATOMY* considers a memory system $\mathcal{M}$ with M memory controllers. Each controller has a single channel and manages a memory system consisting of D DIMMs, each consisting of R ranks, and each rank having B banks. In this work, we do not model the rank parameters in detail [2] and treat that there is a total of $N = D \times R \times B$ banks. Each channel has a command bus and data bus.

We summarize the actions from the time a request reaches the memory controller to the time the required data is sent back. The controller selects one of several queued requests based on a scheduling policy. For simplicity, we assume the *FCFS* scheduling policy here but as demonstrated in [7], other schedulers can be incorporated into the model. The controller has to issue a series of commands to the memory to perform access (read/write). Thus the command bus is a "server" that each request uses for one or more cycles. Once a command is issued, the memory bank to which that command was addressed performs the requested operation (precharge, row activation or column access). During this time the memory bank is busy and can not service other commands. Each bank is thus modeled as a server. Since there are N banks in the memory system, we model them as N servers. Finally, once the memory bank has put the data on the memory bus, the burst of data reaches the memory controller taking a few bus clock cycles. This final step of data transfer is modeled as the third stage server. An overview of this 3-stage network-of-queues model is presented in Figure 3. A system with multiple memory controllers is modeled using a 3-stage network for each controller.

2.2.1 3-stage Network of Queues Model

Each server is modeled as an $M/D/1$ server, where the inter-arrival times are assumed to be exponentially distributed and the service time is deterministic[3].

2.2.2 Stage 1: Command Bus

The command bus server captures issuing of necessary commands to the memory banks. We assume that the inter-arrival times of memory requests are exponentially distributed with a mean $\frac{1}{\lambda}$. As we consider multi-programmed workloads (details in Section 4), considering the interleaved nature of memory requests from the various programs, the assumption that the arrival process is Markovian is a reasonable approximation. The arrival rate λ is a characteristic of the application/workload and is estimated from a trace of memory requests issued by the *LLSC*. As explained earlier, based on whether an access turns into a row-buffer hit or a miss, the command bus issues either one (column access) or three (precharge, row-activate and column access) commands respectively to the corresponding DRAM bank. The time required to send any one command is fixed, and equal to one cycle of memory clock (t_{CK}). Hence the average service time at the command bus can be approximated as a function of Row-buffer Hit rate (RBH), the fraction of requests that experience a row-buffer hit. RBH is primarily a workload characteristic with some design parameters like page size affecting it. For a given RBH value of R, the average service time required by the command bus is $(R \times 1 + (1 - R) \times 3) \times t_{CK}$. Since RBH is a workload specific constant, the average service time required can be treated as fixed.

Using the queuing theory result for the $M/D/1$ queue [17], the queue delay at the command bus is given by:

$$QD_{Cmd\_Bus} = \frac{1}{2\mu_{cmd}} \frac{\rho_{cmd}}{(1 - \rho_{cmd})} \qquad (1)$$

where $\mu_{cmd} = \frac{1}{(R \times 1 + (1-R) \times 3) \times t_{CK}}$ and $\rho_{cmd} = \frac{\lambda}{\mu_{cmd}}$.

2.2.3 Stage 2: Memory Banks

The bank servers take into account the key memory technology-specific timing parameters as well as the inherent parallelism present in a multi-bank memory.

In real memory systems, the number of banks that operate in parallel depends to a great extent on the amount of parallelism found in the memory accesses made by the workload. This workload characteristic is commonly referred to as Bank Level Parallelism (BLP) [4]. Note that in real memory, the requests are queued at the memory controller in bank-specific queues [20] until the bank becomes available. The functioning of each bank is assumed to be independent of other banks[5]. Thus we treat this stage as a collection of M/D/1 queues operating in parallel (rather than as a single $M/D/N$ queue). Multiple $M/D/1$ servers enable modeling the concurrency of many banks simultaneously servicing requests.

As the service time of stage 1, the command bus server, is really small, we make the simplifying assumption that the input process at the second stage is also Markovian [17], with the same mean λ. Since the memory system typically has more banks (N) than currently active (B), a fraction of the incoming requests may go to idle banks. Such requests do not have to queue up as their banks are idle. This fraction of requests that go to idle banks is called the *Request Spread* (denoted S). Thus only the rest of the requests

---

[2]We observe that the rank parameters, such as the rank-to-rank switching delay do not significantly affect the memory performance.

[3]While the output of an $M/D/1$ process is not Markovian, in practice this approximation works well (see [17])

[4]Some of the memory design choices also have an impact on BLP.

[5]Except for peak-power limiting timing constraints such as T_{FAW}, the banks operate pretty much independently.

(fraction $(1 - S)$) incur queueing delays. Thus the average arrival rate to each busy bank is modeled as: $\lambda_{busy\_bank} = \frac{((1-S)*\lambda)}{B}$.

Next, we consider the average service time of a request in one of the banks. The service time depends on whether the actual request turns into a row-buffer hit or miss. In the case of a row-buffer hit, the time required is the column access latency (t_{CL}). If the access turns into a row-buffer miss, then the time required is a sum of the time required to complete precharge (t_{PRE}), activate (t_{ACT}) and column access (t_{CL}). Hence with the application locality being characterized by a RBH of R, the average service time for a request is $(t_{CL} \times R + (t_{PRE} + t_{ACT} + t_{CL}) \times (1 - R))$.

The important thing to note regarding the service time computations is that the values for t_{CL}, t_{PRE} and t_{ACT} are technology specific. Hence choice with respect to technology (like DDR3, DDR4, PCM or STT-MRAM) can be captured here by choosing appropriate latencies for the various actions. Thus our DRAM Cache model supports different types of main memory models - not just DRAM.

The queue delay at each bank is given by:

$$QD_{Bank} = \frac{1}{2\mu_{bank}} \frac{\rho_{bank}}{(1 - \rho_{bank})} \quad (2)$$

where $\mu_{bank} = \frac{1}{(R \times t_{CL} + (1-R) \times (t_{PRE} + t_{ACT} + t_{CL}))}$ and $\rho_{bank} = \frac{\lambda_{busy\_bank}}{\mu_{bank}}$.

2.2.4 Stage 3: Data Bus

Data is transferred to/from the memory in a burst. A data burst leverages the open row-buffer and a large burst amortizes the cost of the row activation. The size of the burst (measured in number of clock cycles) is denoted BL. This data transfer takes a fixed time of $BL \times t_{CK}$.

The queue delay at this stage is given by:

$$QD_{Data} = \frac{1}{2\mu_{data}} \frac{\rho_{data}}{(1 - \rho_{data})} \quad (3)$$

where $\mu_{data} = \frac{1}{BL \times t_{CK}}$ and $\rho_{data} = \frac{\lambda}{\mu_{data}}$.

2.2.5 Estimation of Workload Characteristics

The four workload characteristics (λ, R, B, S) are estimated from a time-annotated trace of memory requests issued by the last-level cache (*LLSC* in our case). Details of these estimations and their accuracy are presented in [7].

2.2.6 ANATOMY Summary

The *ANATOMY* performance model provides an estimate of average latency and peak bandwidth as a function of the memory technology, memory organization and workload characteristics. The average latency is given by:

$$
\begin{aligned}
Lat_{Avg} = \quad & \frac{1}{\mu_{Cmd\_Bus}} + QD_{Cmd\_Bus} \\
+ \quad & \frac{1}{\mu_{bank}} + QD_{Bank} \\
+ \quad & \frac{1}{\mu_{data}} + QD_{Data} \quad (4)
\end{aligned}
$$

The peak bandwidth achievable by the memory system (per controller) is limited by the smallest of the three service stages and is given by:

$$Peak\_BW = min\left(\mu_{Cmd\_Bus}, N * \mu_{bank}, \mu_{data}\right) \quad (5)$$

The model was validated against detailed simulations of 4-, 8- and 16-core workloads with average errors of $8.1\%, 4.1\%, 9.7\%$ respectively.

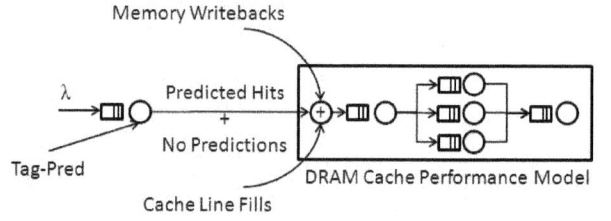

Figure 4: *ANATOMY* augmented with the Tag Cache/Predictor (*Tag-Pred*) Server

3. MODEL

Our model is based on the *ANATOMY* performance model. We first present the construction of the DRAM Cache model that provides an analytical estimation of latency seen at the *LLSC*. This model covers both the *Tags-In-SRAM* and the *Tags-In-DRAM* organizations. Next, we extend the model to achieve optimal latency by bypassing a fraction of DRAM Cache accesses.

3.1 DRAM Cache Model

The DRAM Cache is modeled as an instance of the *ANATOMY* model since the cache is a DRAM comprised of channels, ranks, banks and rows/columns of cells. Thus all the ingredients of the 3-stage network-of-queues formulation are applicable to the cache model. We further specialize the *ANATOMY* model by taking into account the following design considerations:

3.1.1 Metadata Storage and Hit/Miss Determination:

We model the *Tag-Pred* in front of the DRAM Cache as an M/D/1 server with service rate $\mu_{pred} = \frac{1}{t_{pred}}$. We extend *ANATOMY* by modeling this server in front of the 3-stage DRAM queuing model as shown in Figure 4. Since t_{pred} is typically very small, the output of this server can be approximated as Markovian [17]. The total latency of this server is given by: $L_{Pred} = t_{pred} + QD_{pred}$

With probability h_{pred} this server makes a prediction (cache hit/miss). We assume that the predictor does not make false-positive or false-negative predictions. Thus a fraction $(1 - h_{pred})$ of the requests do not get predicted. For such requests, the DRAM Cache is first looked up, and if it is a cache miss, only then the main memory is accessed. This assumption reflects real-world implementations since the cost of a wrong prediction is expensive[6].

Observe that this model includes both the *Tags-In-SRAM* as well as the *Tags-In-DRAM* organizations. For the *Tags-In-SRAM* organizations, since tags are stored on SRAM the tag look up is like a perfect predictor with $h_{pred} = 100\%$ and t_{pred} depends on the tag store size. For the *Tags-In-DRAM* organizations, the predictor's h_{pred} and t_{pred} parameters can be set to the values proposed in literature [11, 16, 19].

As we show in Section 5.3, the performance of the *Tag-Pred* plays a critical role in overall hit latency and is an important parameter governing the decision on metadata storage location.

3.1.2 Modeling the Effects of DRAM Cache Block Size:

The DRAM Cache performance is influenced by a block size factor B_s which denotes the number of *LLSC* blocks that corresponds to one DRAM Cache block. Recall that DRAM Cache blocks may be larger than CPU L1, L2 cache blocks and thus we let B_s denote the ratio of DRAM Cache block size to CPU L2 Cache block size.

---

[6]In case of accesses to dirty cache blocks, an incorrect prediction can lead to incorrect program execution.

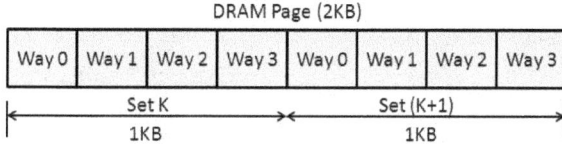

Figure 6: Set Data Layout in DRAM Pages

For instance, with a 64B line size in the L2 cache and a 512B line size in the DRAM Cache, we have $B_s = 8$. Note that B_s is always a power of 2.

Block Size and Cache Hit Rate: Larger block sizes improve cache hit rate if the workload exhibits sufficient spatial locality to utilize larger contiguous chunks of data. In a bandwidth-neutral model, *every doubling of block size halves the DRAM Cache miss rate*. If this condition holds, then block size does not influence bandwidth. In such a model knowing the DRAM Cache hit rate at the CPU cache block size organization is sufficient to estimate the hit rates at other block sizes. Specifically, if h_1 is the cache hit rate when the cache is organized at the *LLSC* block size (i.e., $B_s = 1$) then the cache hit rate h_2 at twice the block size (i.e., $B_s = 2$) is given by: $h_2 = h_1 + \frac{(1-h_1)}{2}$. Generalizing, at a block size factor B_s times the *LLSC* block size, the cache hit rate under the bandwidth-neutral model is given by:

$$h_{b_s} = 1 - \frac{(1-h_1)}{B_s} \qquad (6)$$

This model provides a useful way to understand the role of DRAM Cache block size. If miss rates do indeed halve with doubling of block size, then the cache should be organized at larger block sizes to leverage efficient line fills and lower metadata overhead. On the other hand, if miss rates did not halve with doubling of block size, then larger block sizes are wasteful of bandwidth and cache space.

Figures 5a through 5d plot the observed miss rates (bars) as well as the "ideal" (labeled "theoretical" in the figure) miss rates under the bandwidth-neutral model (lines) for 4 quad-core workloads. It shows that workloads Q5 and Q10 follow the empirical miss-rate-halving rule quite closely while workloads Q7 and Q22 tend to deviate from this model (their miss rates fall by less than half with doubling block size).

On average, this rule resulted in average cache hit rate estimation errors of 16.2% and and 14.5% in 4, and 8-core workloads respectively. Thus the rule provides a reasonable approximation for cache hit rate estimation at different block sizes. It also helps to determine whether a workload is bandwidth efficient at larger block sizes or not by comparing the workloads's actual miss rate at a large block size with the estimated miss rate.

Block Size and RBH: Larger block sizes improve *RBH* in general by capturing spatio-temporal locality in the workloads' accesses. In order to understand this interaction, we first present the data layout of cache blocks in DRAM Cache pages.

The data blocks corresponding to the ways of a set are mapped to contiguous locations in the same DRAM page. This is done in order to ensure that the cache controller can access the correct DRAM row as soon as the set index has been identified. This reduces access latency as well as keeps the set index to DRAM page mapping quite simple. Depending on the associativity of the cache, one or more sets could be mapped to the same page. For example, Figure 6 shows a 2KB DRAM page holding data for 2 sets, in a 4-way set-associative cache organized at 256B block size. The 4 ways of set K occupy the first 1KB of the DRAM page while the 4 ways of the set $(K+1)$ occupy the next 1KB of the page.

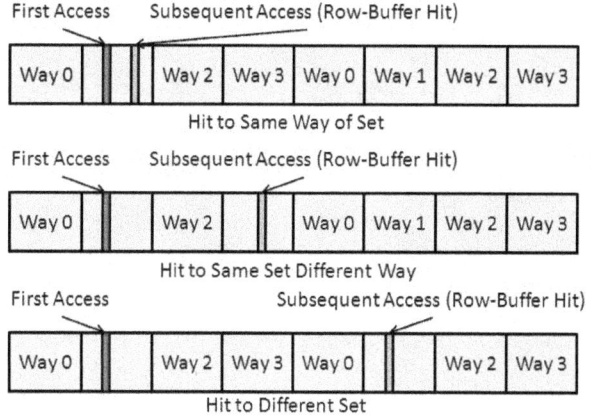

Figure 7: Row-Buffer Hit Scenarios in DRAM Caches

In this mapping, a cache hit is also a row-buffer hit (denoted RBH_{hit}) under the following scenarios:

R.1 A subsequent access to the DRAM bank maps to the same DRAM cache way that initially opened that page.

R.2 A subsequent access to the DRAM bank maps to the same cache set (but a different cache way) that initially opened that page.

R.3 A subsequent access to the DRAM bank maps to a different cache set that is mapped to the same page.

These scenarios are illustrated in Figure 7. Condition [R.1] occurs whenever the DRAM cache block size is larger than the *LLSC* block size and the CPU accesses possess spatial locality. For example, with an *LLSC* block size of 64B, a single DRAM cache block of 512B may get multiple accesses successively.

Since the physical addresses of the different ways in a set are not contiguous (contiguous addresses at cache block size granularity map to contiguous sets), the probability of getting a row-buffer hit due to condition [R.2] is quite low. This follows because each DRAM bank holds data for several millions of cache blocks and the probability of getting a subsequent access to a different block of the *same* is set is very small.

Condition [R.3] can again arise from spatial locality since consecutive cache block addresses map to consecutive sets and thus a neighboring cache block may be resident in the same page at the time the page was opened.

Thus the row-buffer hits in a DRAM cache page are limited by the spatial locality that a page can capture. Hence we estimate RBH_{hit} using a smaller "effective" page size E_P that is computed as $E_P = B \times S$ where B is the cache block size and S is the number of sets per DRAM Cache page. In the above example, $E_P = 256 \times 2 = 512B$. This effective page size is used to estimate RBH_{hit} using the reuse distance methodology from *ANATOMY*. Figure 8 shows the actual and estimated RBH_{hit} in several quad-core workloads for a 128MB 2-way associative 256B block-size cache with an underlying DRAM page size of 2KB. The average error in RBH_{hit} estimation is $< 3\%$ across 4- and 8-core workloads indicating that the modeling of an "effective page size" is a reliable method for DRAM Cache RBH_{hit} estimation.

3.1.3 Row Buffer Hits during Cache Line Fills:

In Section 3.1.2 we provided an estimate of the RBH_{hit} observed in the DRAM Cache due to cache hits. Here, we account

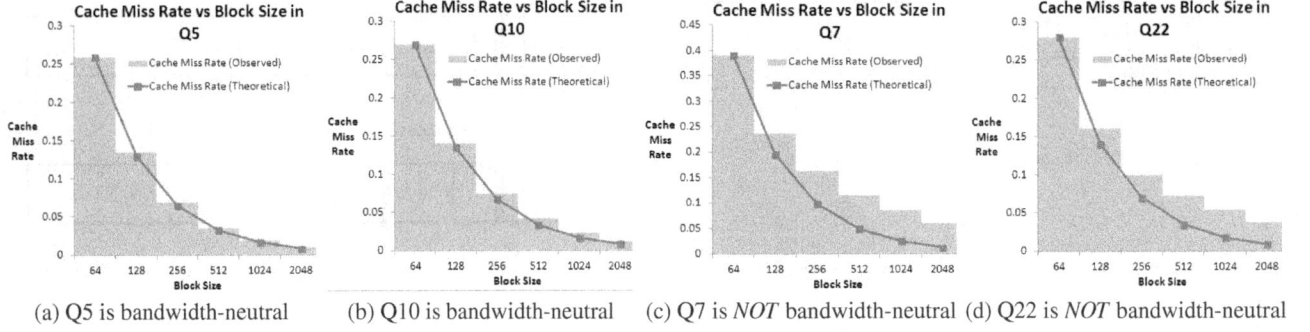

(a) Q5 is bandwidth-neutral   (b) Q10 is bandwidth-neutral   (c) Q7 is *NOT* bandwidth-neutral   (d) Q22 is *NOT* bandwidth-neutral

Figure 5: Miss Rate versus Block Size in a 128MB DRAM Cache

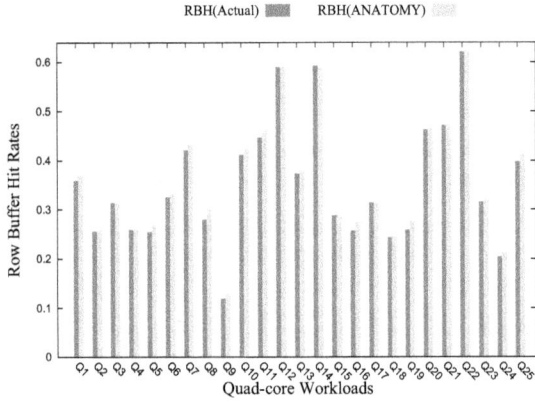

Figure 8: Row-Buffer Estimation Accuracy

for the row buffer hits seen during line fills. Note that we modeled a line fill of a DRAM cache block in terms of B_s *LLSC* block sized accesses. These accesses have high spatial locality and thus have a very high row-buffer hit rate since they are typically serviced back to back. At each cache miss, we assume that the first access is a row-buffer miss (mildly pessimistic) followed by $(B_s - 1)$ row-buffer hits. This results in an RBH_{miss} of $\frac{(B_s-1)}{B_s}$ for cache misses.

Combining with the RBH estimate obtained in Section 3.1.2 for cache hits, we can obtain the overall RBH as:

$$RBH_{cache} = RBH_{hit} * h_{cache} + RBH_{miss} * (1 - h_{cache}) \quad (7)$$

3.1.4 DRAM Cache Access Rate:

The access rate seen at the DRAM Cache is a sum of several streams of accesses (see Figure 4). In the below discussion, we assume that the arrival rate from the LLSC is λ (comprising both misses and writebacks).

Predicted DRAM Cache Hits: With a predictor hit rate of h_{pred} and a DRAM cache hit rate of h_{cache}, the cache sees an average arrival rate $\lambda * h_{cache} * h_{pred}$ of incoming requests.

No Predictions (Tag Look-Up) A fraction $(1 - h_{pred})$ of requests are not predicted and go to the DRAM Cache. This contributes an arrival rate of $\lambda * (1 - h_{pred})$ to the cache. These requests cause tag accesses on the DRAM cache for hit/miss evaluation and thus need to be counted in the overall traffic to the cache.

DRAM Cache Line Fills: At a rate $\lambda * (1 - h_{cache})$, cache misses cause line fills into the DRAM Cache. Each line fill brings B_s times the *LLSC* cache block size worth of data. We model this by scaling the cache access rate by B_s. This leads to an additional arrival rate $\lambda * (1 - h_{cache}) * B_s$ to the cache[7].

DRAM Cache Writebacks: A fraction w of the DRAM Cache misses result in dirty writebacks from the DRAM Cache. These writebacks also contend for the same DRAM Cache resources - namely the command bus, banks and data bus. Thus this adds another arrival rate term $\lambda * (1 - h_{cache}) * w$. Note that w is measured in *LLSC* cache block granularity to model real world implementations wherein only the dirty sub-blocks of large blocks are written back to main memory.

These interactions effectively cause the total arrival rate at the DRAM Cache to be:

$$
\begin{aligned}
\lambda_{cache} = \quad & \lambda * [h_{cache} * h_{pred} + (1 - h_{pred}) \\
+ \quad & (1 - h_{cache}) * B_s + (1 - h_{cache}) * w] \quad (8)
\end{aligned}
$$

It is worth highlighting that it is important to model all the above components of the arrivals seen at the DRAM Cache for a correct modeling of its latency. In particular, cache line fills constitute a significant additional traffic to the cache (particularly when the cache miss rate is high and B_s is large). We discuss this further in the Results section (Section 5).

3.1.5 Summing Up the Model

In summary, the model simply adds a predictor server at the head of the *ANATOMY* model to account for the tag hit/miss prediction time. It also adjusts the arrival rate seen at the DRAM Cache to take into account the additional traffic caused by tag lookups, line fills and writebacks as shown in Equation 8. The model requires $t_{pred}, h_{pred}, h_{cache}, B_s$ and w as inputs. Table 2 summarizes how these parameters are obtained.

Among the workload characteristics that *ANATOMY* requires, λ_{cache} and RBH_{cache} are computed as presented earlier. The estimation of the other inputs (BLP B, and Request Spread S) is not affected by use of the DRAM as a cache.

The model estimates the average cache access latency using λ_{cache} (from Equation 8) and RBH_{cache} (from Equation 7) along with the rest of the *ANATOMY* workload inputs B, S.

---

[7]Alternately, we could model this fill-stream as a different class of requests requiring a larger service time.

162

$$L_{Dram\_Cache} = \quad \frac{1}{\mu_{Cmd\_Bus}} + QD_{Cmd\_Bus}$$
$$+ \quad \frac{1}{\mu_{bank}} + QD_{Bank}$$
$$+ \quad \frac{1}{\mu_{data}} + QD_{Data} \quad (9)$$

3.1.6 Extension to Main Memory

A similar analysis holds for the main memory model. The main memory sees traffic contributed by:

Cache Misses: A fraction $\lambda * (1 - h_{cache})$ of incoming requests cause cache line fills. These are read requests on the main memory. Each line fill brings B_s times the *LLSC* block size worth of data. We model this by scaling the memory access rate by B_s. This leads to an additional arrival rate $\lambda * (1 - h_{cache}) * B_s$ to the memory.

Cache Writebacks: A fraction w of the DRAM Cache misses result in dirty writebacks from the DRAM Cache. These writebacks create an additional arrival rate term $\lambda * (1 - h_{cache}) * w$ to the memory.

It may be observed that the main memory arrival rate is not affected by the tag/predictor hit rate since the predictor's role is only to avoid DRAM Cache lookups for tags and not to eliminate any accesses to the main memory. The total arrival rate at memory is given by:

$$\lambda_{mem} = \quad \lambda * (1 - h_{cache}) * B_s$$
$$+ \quad \lambda * (1 - h_{cache}) * w \quad (10)$$

We can derive the latency estimate L_{Mem} of main memory similar to Equation 9. RBH, BLP, and Request Spread S of the memory are estimated from a trace of accesses issued to it by the *Tag-Pred* and the DRAM-Cache. In Section 5.2 we validate the accuracy of these estimates.

3.1.7 Average LLSC Miss Penalty

The average latency seen by *LLSC* misses can now be estimated as a sum of the following weighted contributions made by L_{Dram_Cache} and L_{Mem}:

- *Predicted Hits:* A fraction $(h_{pred} * h_{cache})$ of all the arrivals from the *LLSC* are sent to the DRAM Cache for cache hit processing. The weighted average latency of such requests is:

$$L_{Dram\_Cache}^{Pred\_Hits} = (h_{pred} * h_{cache}) * L_{Dram\_Cache} \quad (11)$$

- *Predicted Misses:* A fraction $(h_{pred} * (1 - h_{cache}))$ of all the arrivals from the *LLSC* are sent to memory for fetching full DRAM Cache blocks for filling them into the DRAM Cache as line fills. The weighted average latency of such requests is:

$$L_{Mem}^{Pred\_Misses} = (h_{pred} * (1 - h_{cache})) * L_{Mem} \quad (12)$$

- *Un-Predicted Hits:* A fraction $((1 - h_{pred}) * h_{cache})$ of all the arrivals from the *LLSC* are unpredicted and turn out to be hits in the DRAM Cache. The weighted average latency of such requests is:

$$L_{Dram\_Cache}^{Unpred\_Hits} = ((1 - h_{pred}) * h_{cache}) * L_{Dram\_Cache} \quad (13)$$

- *Un-Predicted Misses:* A fraction $((1 - h_{pred}) * (1 - h_{cache}))$ of all the arrivals from the *LLSC* are unpredicted and turn out to be misses in the DRAM Cache. This requires two rounds of accesses. The first access to the DRAM Cache to resolve the request as a miss, followed by access to the main memory. The weighted average latency of such requests is:

$$L_{Dram\_Cache\_Then\_Mem}^{Unpred\_Misses} = \quad ((1 - h_{pred}) * (1 - h_{cache}))$$
$$* \quad [L_{Dram\_Cache} + L_{Mem}] \quad (14)$$

The overall average latency L_{LLSC} is given by:

$$L_{LLSC} = L_{Dram\_Cache}^{Pred\_Hits} + L_{Mem}^{Pred\_Misses}$$
$$+ L_{Dram\_Cache}^{Unpred\_Hits} + L_{Dram\_Cache\_Then\_Mem}^{Unpred\_Misses}$$
$$+ L_{pred}$$
$$(15)$$

Note that the last term accounts for the *Tag-Pred* lookup latency.

3.2 Load-Balancing the Cache with Main Memory

The above model reveals the opportunity for an architecture optimization - balancing the load at the DRAM Cache and main memory. At high DRAM Cache hit rates, the cache gets almost all the traffic from the *LLSC*. This causes significant contention at the DRAM Cache incurring queuing delays and increased waiting times. In such a scenario, a better use of the idle main memory could be made by diverting some of the cache traffic to it[8]. Thus we present a *load balancing* model that minimizes the average latency by identifying the optimal fraction of requests to divert to main memory.

For purposes of the model, we assume that the *Tag-Pred* is enhanced to divert a fraction f_{mem} of the predicted hits and misses to the main memory. In case of cache misses, the diverted accesses are like *cache bypasses* - they directly return the fetched data to the *LLSC* without performing cache line fills into the DRAM Cache. We further assume that all the diverted requests are only for *clean* cache blocks.

We can now estimate the new arrival rates and average latencies of the cache and memory as with the standalone model.

3.2.1 Traffic to the DRAM Cache

The arrival rate at the cache is now a sum of predicted hits sent to the cache (fraction: $h_{pred} * h_{cache} * (1 - f_{mem})$), un-predicted accesses (fraction: $(1 - h_{pred})$), cache line fills (fraction: $h_{pred} * (1 - h_{cache}) * (1 - f_{mem}) * B_s + (1 - h_{pred}) * (1 - h_{cache}) * B_s$), and write-backs (fraction: $(h_{pred} * (1 - h_{cache}) * (1 - f_{mem}) + (1 - h_{pred}) * (1 - h_{cache})) * w$). The resulting arrival rate λ_{cache} is:

$$\lambda_{cache} = \lambda * [h_{pred} * h_{cache} * (1 - f_{mem})$$
$$+ (1 - h_{pred})$$
$$+ h_{pred} * (1 - h_{cache}) * (1 - f_{mem}) * B_s$$
$$+ (1 - h_{pred}) * (1 - h_{cache}) * B_s$$
$$+ h_{pred} * (1 - h_{cache}) * (1 - f_{mem}) * w$$
$$+ (1 - h_{pred}) * (1 - h_{cache}) * w] \quad (16)$$

The average DRAM Cache access latency L_{Dram_Cache} can be obtained from Equation 9.

---

[8]This is valid only if the cache did not hold a more recent copy of the data.

3.2.2 Traffic to the Main Memory

The arrival rate at the main memory is now a sum of predicted hits sent to the memory (fraction: $h_{pred} * h_{cache} * f_{mem}$), memory reads for cache line fills (fraction: $h_{pred} * (1 - h_{cache}) * (1 - f_{mem}) * B_s + (1 - h_{pred}) * (1 - h_{cache}) * B_s$), misses that bypass the cache (fraction: $h_{pred} * (1 - h_{cache}) * f_{mem}$), and write-backs (fraction: $(h_{pred} * (1 - h_{cache}) * (1 - f_{mem}) + (1 - h_{pred}) * (1 - h_{cache})) * w$). The resulting arrival rate λ_{mem} is estimated similar to Equation 10.

The average main memory access latency L_{Mem} can be obtained similar to Equation 9.

3.2.3 Optimal f_{mem}

In order to estimate the average latency, we first estimate the latency of each type of request processing:

- *Predicted Hits sent to the DRAM Cache:* A fraction $(h_{pred} * h_{cache} * (1 - f_{mem}))$ of all the arrivals from the *LLSC* are sent to the DRAM Cache for cache hit processing. The weighted average latency of such requests is:

$$L^{Pred\_Hits}_{Dram\_Cache} = (h_{pred} * h_{cache} * (1 - f_{mem})) * L_{Dram\_Cache}$$
(17)

- *Predicted Hits diverted to the main memory:* A fraction $(h_{pred} * h_{cache} * f_{mem})$ of all the arrivals from the *LLSC* are diverted to memory for hit processing. The weighted average latency of such requests is:

$$L^{Pred\_Hits}_{Mem} = (h_{pred} * h_{cache} * f_{mem}) * L_{Mem}$$
(18)

- *Predicted Misses that bypass the cache:* A fraction $(h_{pred} * (1 - h_{cache}) * f_{mem})$ of all the arrivals from the *LLSC* are sent to memory for fetching the *LLSC* requested block. These requests do not initiate DRAM Cache fills. The weighted average latency of such requests is:

$$L^{Pred\_Misses\_Bypassed}_{Mem} = (h_{pred} * (1 - h_{cache}) * f_{mem}) * L_{Mem}$$
(19)

- *Predicted Misses that are cached:* A fraction $(h_{pred} * (1 - h_{cache}) * (1 - f_{mem}))$ of all the arrivals from the *LLSC* are sent to memory for fetching full DRAM Cache blocks for filling them into the DRAM Cache as line fills. The weighted average latency of such requests is:

$$L^{Pred\_Misses\_Cached}_{Mem} = (h_{pred} * (1 - h_{cache}) * (1 - f_{mem})) * L_{Mem}$$
(20)

- *Un-Predicted Hits:* This is the same as in Equation 13 above.

- *Un-Predicted Misses:* This is the same as in Equation 14.

The overall average miss penalty $L_{LLSC}(f_{mem})$ seen by the *LLSC* is a sum of the above weighted latencies similar to Equation 15. Treating this as a function of the single variable f_{mem}, we can numerically minimize $L_{LLSC}(f_{mem})$ at some f^*_{mem}. The value f^*_{mem} defines the optimal distribution of cache requests to the main memory in order to minimize overall average latency. It should be noted that this optimal f^*_{mem} depends on the configurations of the DRAM Cache and main memory. Changes to the cache organization and/or the main memory will require re-computing f^*_{mem}.

To emphasize, this set up has taken into account both the cache and memory performance models into a single hybrid model that allows estimation of a global minimum latency. In Section 5.4 we explore this load-balancing opportunity in real systems and demonstrate that this can lead to as much as 74% reduction in average latency.

Processor	3.2 GHz OOO Alpha ISA
L1I Cache	32kB private, 64B blocks, Direct-mapped, 2 cycle hit latency
L1D Cache	32kB private, 64B blocks, 2-way set-associative, 2 cycle hit latency
L2 Cache (LLSC)	For 4/8 cores: 4MB/8MB, 8-way/16-way, 128/256 MSHRs, 64-byte blocks, 7/9 cycles hit latency
Tags-In-DRAM (AlloyCache)	For 4/8 cores: 128MB/256MB, **Direct-Mapped**, **64-byte blocks**, 80-byte tag+data burst, Cache Memory in 2/4 Channels, Total of 16/32 DRAM banks, 2KB page, 128-bit bus width, 1.6GHz, CL-nRCD-nRP=9-9-9
Tag-Pred	A 2-way Set Associative Tag Cache For 4/8 cores: 48KB/96KB, (Design similar to that in [11])
Tags-In-SRAM	For 4/8 cores: 128MB/256MB, **2-Way Set Associative, 1024-byte blocks**, Cache Memory in 2/4 Channels, Total of 16/32 DRAM banks, 2KB page, 128-bit bus width, 1.6GHz, CL-nRCD-nRP=9-9-9
Memory Controller	For 4/8 cores: 1/2 off-chip data channels Each MC: 64-bit interface to channel, 256-entry command queue FR_FCFS scheduling [20], open-page policy Address-interleaving: row-rank-bank-mc-column
Off-Chip DRAM	For 4/8 cores: 4GB/8GB main memory using: DDR3-1600H, BL (cycles)=4, CL-nRCD-nRP=9-9-9 in 2/4 ranks, 16/32 banks Refresh related: T_{REFI} of 7.8us and T_{RFC} of 280nCK

Table 1: CMP configuration

4. EXPERIMENTAL SETUP

We evaluate the accuracy of the proposed model by comparing the model-predicted latency with results from detailed simulations. Using multiprogrammed workloads running on the GEM5 [3] simulation infrastructure, we obtained the observed latency for the configurations listed in Table 1. For quad-core workloads, timing simulations were run for 1 billion instructions on each core after fast-forwarding the first 10 billion instructions to allow for sufficient warm-up. As is the norm, when a core finishes its timing simulation, it continues to execute until all the rest of the cores have completed[9]. In case of 8 and 16-core workloads, due to the amount of simulation time required, we collected statistics on timing runs of $500M$ and $250M$ instructions per core respectively. In all cases, the total instructions simulated across all the cores amount to more than 4B.

We obtained the DRAM Cache model inputs (h_{pred}, h_{cache}, w) using a trace-based DRAM cache simulator. This (un-timed) simulator simulates the various *Tags-In-SRAM* and *Tags-In-DRAM* organizations. Traces collected from GEM5 simulations of 4, and 8-core architectures running for 75 billion instructions on each core were supplied as input to this cache simulator. This has resulted in 120M – 450M accesses to the DRAM cache, with an average of $310M$ DRAM cache accesses per workload. t_{pred} is obtained from the CACTII tool [23] with 22nm technology. All the other workload parameters are estimated as in *ANATOMY*. For completeness, Table 2 lists the relevant parameters used in the model, their sources and when they are obtained/updated.

Our workloads are comprised of programs from SPEC 2000 and SPEC 2006 benchmark [9] suites. The 4, and 8-core multiprogrammed workloads are listed in Table 3. These benchmarks were carefully combined to create high, moderate and low levels of memory *intensity*[10] in the chosen workloads to ensure a representative mix. Workloads marked with a "*" in Table 3 have high memory intensity (*LLSC* miss rate $\geq 10\%$). We also measured the footprints of these workloads in terms of the number of distinct $64B$

---

[9]The statistics are collected only during the first 1 Billion instructions.

[10]Intensity was measured in terms of the last-level SRAM cache miss rate.

Parameter	Source	Update Frequency
B_s	Input to the model	For each DRAM Cache block size explored
h_{pred}	(Un-timed) Cache Simulator	For each predictor organization and size
t_{pred}	CACTII tool [23]	For each predictor table size
λ	From *LLSC* trace, as in *ANATOMY*	Once per workload
λ_{cache}	Estimated using Equation 8	For each DRAM Cache size and B_s
h_{cache}	(Un-timed) Cache Simulator	For each DRAM Cache size and B_s
w	(Un-timed) Cache Simulator	For each DRAM Cache size and B_s
RBH_{cache}	Estimated using Equation 7	For each DRAM Cache size, B_s and cache page size
BLP_{cache}, S_{cache}	From *LLSC* trace, as in *ANATOMY*	For each DRAM Cache size, B_s and number of DRAM Cache banks
λ_{mem}	Estimated using Equation 10	For each DRAM Cache size and B_s
RBH_{mem}	Trace of misses from DRAM cache, as in *ANATOMY*	For each main memory configuration (Banks and Page Size)
BLP_{mem}, S_{mem}	Trace of misses from DRAM cache, as in *ANATOMY*	For each main memory configuration (Banks and Page Size)
DRAM Cache and Memory Timing Values	Input to the model. Obtained from JEDEC specification	For each memory technology/device type

Table 2: Sources of model parameters

Quad-Core Workloads
*Q1:(462,459,470,433), *Q2:(429,183,462,459), *Q3:(181,435,197,473), Q4:(429,462,471,464), *Q5:(470,437,187,300), *Q6:(462,470,473,300), *Q7:(459,464,183,433), Q8:(410,464,445,433), Q9:(462,459,445,410), *Q10:(429,456,450,459), Q11:(181,186,300,177), Q12:(168,401,435,464), Q13:(434,435,437,171), *Q14:(444,445,459,462),Q15:(401,410,178,177), Q16:(300,254,255,470), *Q17:(171,181,464,465), Q18:(464,450,465,473), *Q19:(453,433,458,410), Q20:(462,471,254,186),Q21:(462,191,433,437), Q22:(197,168,179,187), Q23:(401,473,435,177),Q24:(416,429,454,175) Q25:(254,172,178,188)

Eight Core Workloads
E1:(462,459,433,456,464,473,450,445), *E2:(300,456,470,179,464,473,450,445), *E3:(168,183,437,401,450,435,445,458), *E4:(187,172,173,410,470,433,444,177), E5:(434,435,450,453,462,471,164,186), E6:(416,473,401,172,177,178,179,435), *E7:(437,459,445,454,456,465,171,197), E8:(183,179,433,454,464,435,444,458), *E9:(183,462,450,471,473,433,254,168), *E10:(300,173,178,187,188,191,410,171), *E11:(470,177,168,434,410,172,464,171), E12:(459,473,444,453,450,197,175,164), E13:(471,462,186,254,465,445,410,179), *E14:(187,470,401,416,433,437,456,454), *E15:(300,458,462,470,433,172,191,471),E16:(183,473,401,435,188,434,164,427)

Table 3: Workloads

blocks accessed. The average memory footprints in 4-core and 8-core workloads are 990MB and 2.1GB respectively. We also found that on average 87% of all the DRAM cache misses are due to capacity/conflict. Thus our workloads are sufficiently exercising the DRAM cache.

The details of our architecture configurations are summarized in Table 1. We simulate two typical configurations: a *Tags-In-DRAM* configuration based on the *AlloyCache* [19] organization, and a *Tags-In-SRAM* configuration based on the *FootprintCache* [12] organization.

5. RESULTS

We first validate the accuracy of estimating key model input parameters. Next we perform end-to-end validation of the *Tags-In-DRAM* and *Tags-In-SRAM* designs in Section 5.2 and show that the average *LLSC* miss penalty is estimated with good accuracy. Finally, we use this validated model to explore two important cache organizational topics in Sections 5.3 and 5.4.

5.1 Validation of the model input parameters

In this section, we validate the accuracy of the estimated model input parameters. We only focus on two parameters - λ_{cache} and RBH_{cache} - as the other parameters are either trivially computed from the cache access trace (λ, h_{pred}, h_{cache}, write-back rate w) or their estimates have already been validated for accuracy in the baseline study presented in *ANATOMY* [7] (Bank-Level Parallelism BLP, and Request Spread S). The validations used both the *Tags-In-DRAM* and *Tags-In-SRAM* organizations.

5.1.1 Exponential Inter-Arrival Times

We validated the assumption of exponential inter-arrival times seen by the cache (with a mean of $\frac{1}{\lambda_{cache}}$ where λ_{cache} is computed using Equation 8) by comparing the actual inter-arrival times observed in the detailed simulations against the theoretical distribution. Using the Chi-$square$ goodness-of-fit test [18] with 30 degrees of freedom, the average p-values[11] for 4, and 8-core workloads are 0.03, and 0.01 respectively, denoting reasonably high confidence of match between the actual and theoretical distributions.

5.1.2 Estimating RBH_{cache}

We compared RBH_{cache} estimated using Equation 7 with the actual RBH in simulations and obtained very low average errors of 4.3% and 3.7% in 4-core and 8-core workloads.

5.2 End-to-End Model Validation

Having validated the accuracy of the parameters, we demonstrate that the overall model provides accurate estimates of the *LLSC* miss penalty.

5.2.1 Validation of the Tags-in-DRAM Model:

We use the *AlloyCache* [19] organization to validate the accuracy of *Tags-In-DRAM* model. The *AlloyCache* organizes the cache as direct-mapped 64B blocks with metadata and data co-located in the same DRAM pages. We implemented the *SAM* (Serial Access Model) in our simulator, wherein the cache is first probed for hit/miss detection and subsequently a miss is sent to the main memory. Thus every *LLSC* access is sent to the cache for hit/miss evaluation. Since no predictor is used, we set h_{pred} and t_{pred} both to 0. In order to incur lower DRAM latency, the *AlloyCache* uses a larger data burst of 80 bytes to read both the tag and data associated in a single access. *ANATOMY* framework incorporates this by setting the data bus server's bus length (BL) value to 5 clock cycles (see Section 2.2.4). Further, since the DRAM cache uses 64B block size, the block size factor $B_s = 1$. Estimates for h_{cache}, and w were obtained by simulating traces on the DRAM Cache simulator. We estimate RBH_{cache}, λ, λ_{cache}, and λ_{mem} as discussed in Section 3.1. Additional *ANATOMY* inputs namely BLP and Request Spread S are estimated from the memory access trace. These estimates are used to compute the estimated latency L_{LLSC} as in Equation 15.

Figures 9a and 9b report the errors in the estimation of L_{LLSC} when compared to results from detailed simulation of the *Alloy-*

---

[11]p-value is a statistical measure of deviation of the actual distribution from the hypothesis.

Cache Size (MB)	Block Size (B)	Tag Store Size (MB)	Access Latency (cycles)
64	64	4	10
64	256	1	6
64	512	0.5	4
128	64	8	12
128	256	2	8
128	512	1	6
512	64	32	16
512	256	8	12
512	512	4	10

Table 4: SRAM Tag Storage Size and Latency

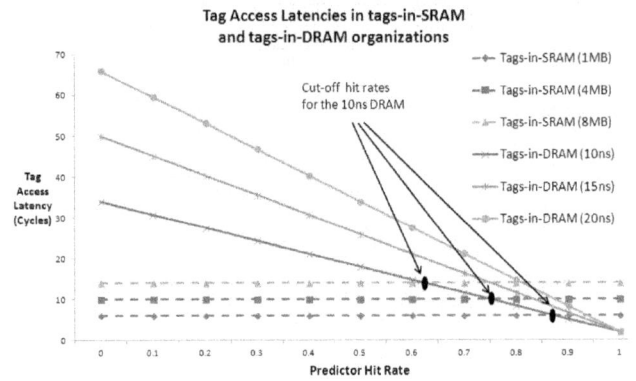

Figure 11: Comparing tag latencies of SRAM and DRAM tags

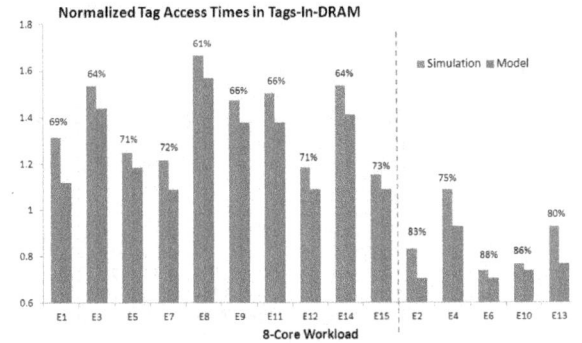

Figure 12: Tag Access Times in Eight-Core Workloads

Cache in quad and 8-core configurations[12]. The averages of (absolute) errors are 10.8% and 9.3% respectively showing that the model captures key architectural elements reasonably well.

5.2.2 Validation of the Tags-in-SRAM Model:

We use a configuration similar to the proposal in [12] wherein 1024B blocks are employed with the metadata stored on SRAM. For simplicity, we omitted the feature of bypassing *singleton* blocks[13] in both the simulation and in the model. We set t_{pred} to the latency estimate provided by CACTII [23] (see Section 5.3) and h_{pred} to 1.0. We also set $B_s = 16$ since each DRAM Cache block is $16\times$ the size of the *LLSC* block. The rest of the model parameters are estimated as indicated above in Section 5.2.1.

Figures 10a and 10b report the errors in latency estimation of the *Tags-In-SRAM* model when compared to results from detailed simulation in quad and 8-core configurations. The averages of (absolute) errors are 10.5% and 8.2% respectively.

Averaged over both the *Tags-In-DRAM* and *Tags-In-SRAM* configurations, the model has average errors of 10.7% and 8.8% in quad and 8-core configurations respectively. These results indicate that the proposed model accurately captures the salient properties of a wide range of DRAM Cache organizations. Thus the model can be used as an analytical tool for rapid exploration of different cache organizations. In Sections 5.3 and 5.4 we use the model to explore two important design considerations.

5.3 Insight 1 - Can Tags-In-DRAM designs outperform Tags-In-SRAM?

We quantitatively argue that *Tags-In-SRAM* designs generally outperform *Tags-In-DRAM* designs except when the *Tag-Pred* can achieve very high hit rates. Table 4 lists the tag storage size and associated access latency for various DRAM Cache sizes and block sizes (assuming a 4B tag overhead per block) when tags are held on SRAM. The latency estimates are obtained from CACTII [23] at 22nm using high performance cells. Cycles are in units of a 3.2GHz clock. This corresponds to the tag access latency (t_{pred}) in *Tags-In-SRAM* designs.

In case of *Tags-In-DRAM*, the average tag access time may be expressed as:

$$t_{tag}^{tags-in-dram} = h_{pred} * t_{pred} + (1 - h_{pred}) * t_{dram\_cache} \quad (21)$$

Note that this equation does not take any contention at the *Tag-Pred* or at the DRAM cache into account and thus provides an aggressive estimate for the tag access time. Figure 11 plots $t_{tag}^{tags-in-dram}$ as a function of h_{pred} at 3 different DRAM access latencies (t_{dram_cache} set to 10ns, 15ns, 20ns) and $t_{pred} = 2$ (i.e., prediction in 2 cycles).

---

[12]A negative error indicates that the model estimated a higher latency than observed from simulation.

[13]Singleton blocks are defined to be those 1024B blocks that receive only one access to a 64B sub-block when they are cache-resident.

For comparison the fixed tag access latency of the *Tags-In-SRAM* designs are also plotted for 3 different tag store sizes (1MB, 4MB, 8MB) (using latency estimates from Table 4). The intersections of the *Tags-In-DRAM* lines (solid) with the *Tags-In-SRAM* lines (dotted) denote the *cut-off* predictor hit rates - lower hit rates suffer higher latencies in the *Tags-In-DRAM* organization. This reveals the importance of achieving high prediction rates - for example, even with a fast DRAM Cache access time of 10ns, the predictor needs to achieve a hit rate in excess of 75% to outperform a 4MB *Tags-In-SRAM* organization.

We verified this claim by measuring the tag access latencies in detailed simulations of the *Tags-In-DRAM* configuration with predictor (refer Table 1) and comparing them to estimated tag access latencies (from Equation 21). Figure 12 plots these latencies normalized to the tag access time of the *Tags-In-SRAM* organization. The values on top of the bars are the h_{pred} values. 10 out of 15 workloads (grouped to the left of the vertical dashed line) have higher tag access latency in the *Tags-In-DRAM* design than in the *Tags-In-SRAM* design. The model predicts this correctly except for workload E4. In workloads $E2$, $E6$, $E10$ and $E13$, the h_{pred} values are low (all below 75%) while in the other workloads, the h_{pred} values are high, confirming the analysis presented above.

Thus we conclude that the use of this auxiliary tag hit/miss prediction structure in SRAM is beneficial only when the predictor achieves a high enough prediction rate to outperform the SRAM tag look up time.

5.4 Insight 2 - Bypassing the Cache Results in Overall Latency Reduction

In this section, we show that contrary to the expectation that higher cache hit rates are always better, it is often helpful to di-

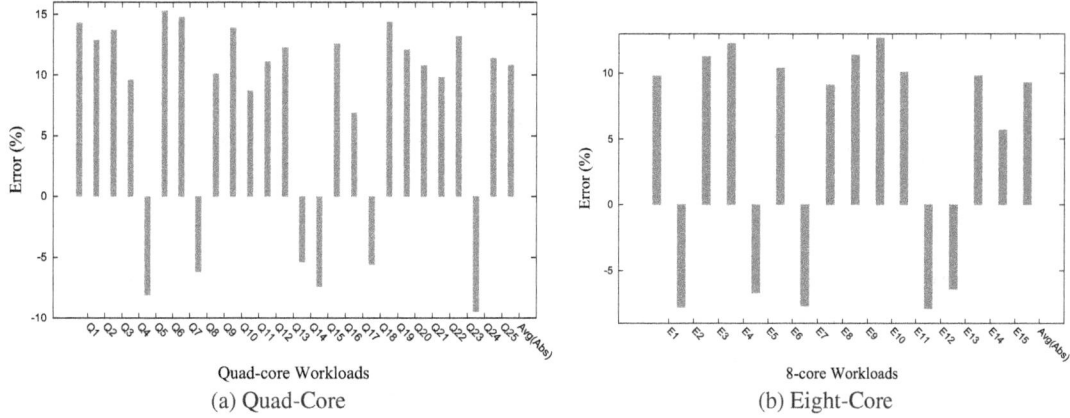

(a) Quad-Core   (b) Eight-Core

Figure 9: *Tags-In-DRAM* Model Validation: Errors in *LLSC* Miss Penalty (L_{LLSC}) Estimation

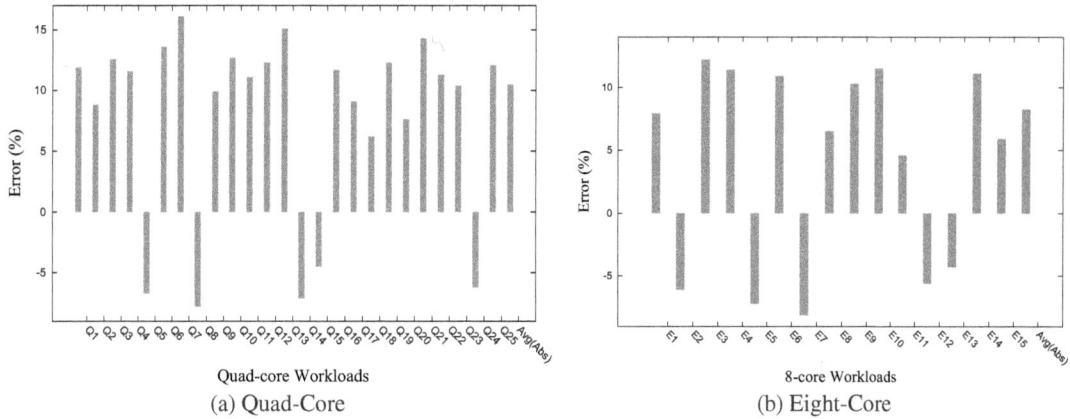

(a) Quad-Core   (b) Eight-Core

Figure 10: *Tags-In-SRAM* Model Validation: Errors in *LLSC* Miss Penalty (L_{LLSC}) Estimation

vert a fraction of cache accesses to the main memory. Even though the latency of an individual access to the DRAM Cache is lower than that of main memory, a high arrival rate to the cache builds up congestion at the cache banks causing longer waiting times. Under such conditions, we show that our experimental evaluation corroborates the model's prediction of the existence of a fraction $f^*_{mem}, 0 < f^*_{mem} < 1$, that results in lower L_{LLSC} than with $f_{mem} = 0$ (sending all the requests to the cache).

We explore the results on two *Tags-In-SRAM* 128MB direct-mapped cache organizations, one with a block size of 64B and the other with a block size of 512B. Figures 13a and 13b show the observed and model-predicted *LLSC* latencies in quad-core workload $Q1$ as f_{mem} is varied from 0 to 1 in steps of 0.1 for two cache block sizes. It is evident that there is an optimal distribution of requests across the cache and main memory that results in the least *LLSC* miss penalty. From Figure 13a, we observe that the queuing contention has a lesser impact at the 64B block size (since $B_s = 1$ and the cost of a line fill is not high) and the cache bypass reduces the latency by a maximum of 16% at $f_{mem} = 0.2$.

In Figure 13b, we observe that at both the extremes ($f_{mem} = 0$ and $f_{mem} = 1$) the average latency steeply increases. In fact, the latency experienced with no bypass ($f_{mem} = 0$) is worse than when the DRAM Cache is not even used ($f_{mem} = 1$). This is due to the high cost of cache line fills (filling 512B). Recall that when the cache is bypassed, only the requested 64B is fetched and re-

turned to the *LLSC*. Employing an optimal distribution ($f_{mem} = 0.3$) reduces latency by as much as 74% compared to the baseline ($f_{mem} = 0$). In all cases, very high bypass rates should be avoided since they lead to increased congestion at the slower main memory. Similar results are observed in the other quad and eight-core workloads.

These results reveal the opportunity for architecture enhancement wherein the *Tag-Pred* structure could observe the queuing delays and latencies at the cache and main memory and adaptively estimate the optimal f^*_{mem} to improve system performance.

6. RELATED WORK AND CONCLUSIONS

While both cache [1, 4, 5, 8, 21] and DRAM [2, 6, 15, 22, 26, 27] models exist, no prior analytical model has taken into account the interactions that result from using DRAM as a substrate for cache functionality. In particular, our work encompasses the entire DRAM Cache design space spanning *Tags-In-SRAM* and *Tags-In-DRAM* organizations taking into account the key underlying architectural issues of how metadata is accessed, the role of cache block size, and RBH and the significance of the *Tag-Pred*.

By comparing the model with detailed multi-core simulations, we showed that the model predicts latency accurately, achieving average errors of 10.7% and 8.8% in 4 and 8-core workloads respectively. The model offers two insights: one, the tag cache/predictor has to achieve very high hit rate in *Tags-In-DRAM* designs to out-

(a) Block size 64B	(b) Block Size 512B

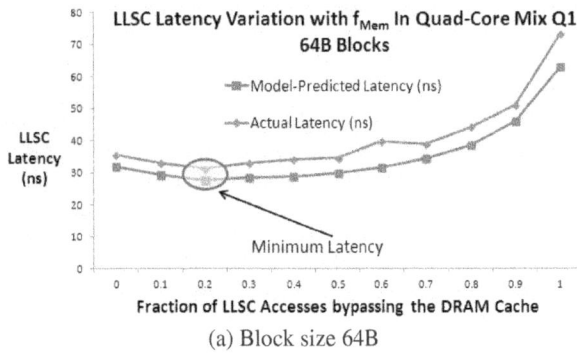

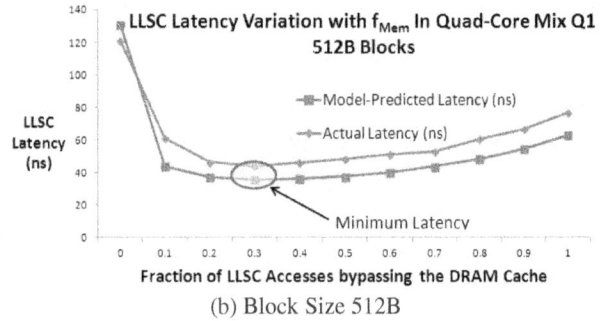

Figure 13: Latency variation with f_{mem} in Quad-core Workload $Q1$ at two block sizes

perform *Tags-In-SRAM* designs, and two, bypassing a fraction of DRAM cache accesses results in overall *LLSC* miss penalty reduction. The model thus serves as a practical analytical tool for rapid design space exploration of DRAM Cache designs.

7. REFERENCES

[1] A. Agarwal, J. Hennessy, and M. Horowitz, "An analytical cache model," *ACM Trans. Comput. Syst.*, 1989.

[2] J. H. Ahn, M. Erez, and W. J. Dally, "The design space of data-parallel memory systems," in *SC*, 2006.

[3] N. Binkert, B. Beckmann, G. Black, S. K. Reinhardt, A. Saidi, A. Basu, J. Hestness, D. R. Hower, T. Krishna, S. Sardashti, R. Sen, K. Sewell, M. Shoaib, N. Vaish, M. D. Hill, and D. A. Wood, "The gem5 simulator," *SIGARCH Comput. Archit. News*, 2011.

[4] X. E. Chen and T. M. Aamodt, "Hybrid analytical modeling of pending cache hits, data prefetching, and mshrs." in *MICRO*, 2008.

[5] ——, "Modeling cache contention and throughput of multiprogrammed manycore processors." *IEEE Trans. Computers*, 2012.

[6] H. Choi, J. Lee, and W. Sung, "Memory access pattern-aware DRAM performance model for multi-core systems," in *ISPASS*, 2011.

[7] N. Gulur, M. Mehendale, R. Manikantan, and R. Govindarajan, "Anatomy: An analytical model of memory system performance," *SIGMETRICS*, 2014.

[8] A. Hartstein, V. Srinivasan, T. R. Puzak, and P. G. Emma, "On the nature of cache miss behavior: Is it v2?" *J. Instruction-Level Parallelism*, 2008.

[9] J. L. Henning, "Spec cpu2006 benchmark descriptions," *SIGARCH Comput. Archit. News*, 2006.

[10] M. D. Hill, "A case for direct-mapped caches," *Computer*, 1988.

[11] C.-C. Huang and V. Nagarajan, "Atcache: Reducing dram-cache latency via a small sram tag cache," in *PACT*, 2014.

[12] D. Jevdjic, S. Volos, and B. Falsafi, "Die-stacked dram caches for servers: Hit ratio, latency, or bandwidth? have it all with footprint cache," in *Proceedings of the 40th Annual International Symposium on Computer Architecture*, ser. ISCA '13. New York, NY, USA: ACM, 2013, pp. 404–415.

[13] X. Jiang, N. Madan, L. Zhao, M. Upton, R. Iyer, S. Makineni, D. Newell, Y. Solihin, and R. Balasubramonian, "Chop: Adaptive filter-based dram caching for cmp server platforms." in *HPCA*.

[14] E. Kultursay, M. T. Kandemir, A. Sivasubramaniam, and O. Mutlu, "Evaluating stt-ram as an energy-efficient main memory alternative." in *ISPASS*. IEEE, 2013.

[15] F. Liu et al, "Understanding how off-chip memory bandwidth partitioning in chip multiprocessors affects system performance," in *HPCA-16*, 2010.

[16] G. H. Loh and M. D. Hill, "Efficiently enabling conventional block sizes for very large die-stacked dram caches," in *Proceedings of the 44th Annual IEEE/ACM International Symposium on Microarchitecture*, ser. MICRO-44, 2011.

[17] C. D. Pack, "The output of an m/d/1 queue," *Operations Research , Vol. 23, No. 4*, 1975.

[18] R. L. Plackett, "Karl pearson and the chi-squared test," *International Statistical Review (ISI) 51(1):59-72*, 1983.

[19] M. K. Qureshi and G. H. Loh, "Fundamental latency trade-off in architecting dram caches: Outperforming impractical sram-tags with a simple and practical design," in *Proceedings of the 2012 45th Annual IEEE/ACM International Symposium on Microarchitecture*, ser. MICRO-45, 2012.

[20] S. Rixner, W. J. Dally, U. J. Kapasi, P. Mattson, and J. D. Owens, "Memory access scheduling," *SIGARCH Comput. Archit. News*, 2000.

[21] G. E. Suh, S. Devadas, and L. Rudolph, "Analytical cache models with applications to cache partitioning," in *Proceedings of the 15th International Conference on Supercomputing*, 2001.

[22] G. Sun et al, "Moguls: a model to explore the memory hierarchy for bandwidth improvements," in *ISCA-38*, 2011.

[23] S. J. E. Wilton and N. P. Jouppi, "Cacti: An enhanced cache access and cycle time model," *IEEE Journal of Solid-State Circuits*, vol. 31, 1996.

[24] H.-S. P. Wong, S. Raoux, S. Kim, J. Liang, J. P. Reifenberg, B. Rajendran, M. Asheghi, and K. E. Goodson, *Proceedings of the IEEE*, 2010.

[25] D. H. Woo, N. H. Seong, D. L. Lewis, and H.-H. S. Lee, "An optimized 3d-stacked memory architecture by exploiting excessive, high-density tsv bandwidth." 2010.

[26] G. L. Yuan et al, "A hybrid analytical DRAM performance model," 2009.

[27] M. Zhou, Y. Du, B. R. Childers, R. Melhem, and D. Mosse, "Writeback-aware bandwidth partitioning for multi-core systems with pcm," in *PACT*, 2013.

Systematically Deriving Quality Metrics for Cloud Computing Systems

Matthias Becker*　　　Sebastian Lehrig†　　　Steffen Becker†

{matthias.becker|sebastian.lehrig|steffen.becker}@{*uni-paderborn|†informatik.tu-chemnitz}.de

*Heinz Nixdorf Institute　　　†Software Engineering Chair
University of Paderborn, Paderborn, Germany　　Chemnitz University of Technology, Chemnitz, Germany

ABSTRACT

In cloud computing, software architects develop systems for virtually unlimited resources that cloud providers account on a pay-per-use basis. Elasticity management systems provision these resources autonomously to deal with changing workload. Such changing workloads call for new objective metrics allowing architects to quantify quality properties like scalability, elasticity, and efficiency, e.g., for requirements/SLO engineering and software design analysis. In literature, initial metrics for these properties have been proposed. However, current metrics lack a systematic derivation and assume knowledge of implementation details like resource handling. Therefore, these metrics are inapplicable where such knowledge is unavailable.

To cope with these lacks, this short paper derives metrics for scalability, elasticity, and efficiency properties of cloud computing systems using the goal question metric (GQM) method. Our derivation uses a running example that outlines characteristics of cloud computing systems. Eventually, this example allows us to set up a systematic GQM plan and to derive an initial set of six new metrics. We particularly show that our GQM plan allows to classify existing metrics.

Categories and Subject Descriptors

D.2.8 [**Software Engineering**]: Metrics—*Performance measures*; D.2.11 [**Software Engineering**]: Software Architectures—*Languages*

Keywords

cloud computing; scalability; elasticity; efficiency; metric; SLO; analysis; GQM

1. INTRODUCTION

In cloud computing, software architects develop applications on top of compute environments being offered by cloud providers. For these applications, the amount of offered resources is virtually unlimited while elasticity management systems provision resources autonomously to deal with changing workloads. Furthermore, providers bill pro-

visioned resources on a per-use basis [1]. As a consequence of these characteristics, architects want their applications to use as few resources as possible in order to save money while still maintaining the quality requirements of the system. Quality properties that focus directly on these aspects are scalability, elasticity, and efficiency [9].

These quality properties need to be quantified for requirements engineering and software design analysis by means of suitable metrics. For instance, cloud consumers and cloud providers need to negotiate service level objectives (SLOs), i.e., metrics and associated thresholds [7]. Such SLOs have to consider characteristics like changing workloads ("how fast can an application adapt to a higher workload?") and pay-per-use pricing ("how expensive is serving an additional consumer?"). However, no established metrics for requirements/SLO engineering and software design analysis exist. Current metrics assume knowledge of implementation details as they focus on the application at run-time [9] and lack a systematic derivation making such limitations explicit.

In literature, classical performance-oriented metrics [4] like response time and throughput are insufficient for situations relevant for cloud computing applications. First, they do not take changing workloads into account, e.g., metrics to describe reaction times to system adaptations are missing. Second, the degree to which systems match resource demands to changing workloads cannot be quantified. More recent work [9] proposes metrics for such characteristics that assume knowledge of implementation details like resource handling. These metrics are inapplicable when such knowledge is unavailable, e.g., in early design phases and for SLOs.

To cope with these lacks, we systematically derive an initial set of scalability, elasticity, and efficiency metrics using the goal question metric (GQM) method [15]. First, we illustrate the characteristics of cloud-aware applications using a running example scenario and, subsequently, derive metric candidates from this scenario. Second, by generalizing our metric candidates, we develop a first set of six metrics. Third, we show that our GQM plan allows to systematically classify existing metrics and makes their limitations explicit.

This paper contributes our systematic GQM plan, including classifications of our six and related work metrics.

This short research paper is organized as follows. Section 2 gives definitions of the considered quality properties and Sec. 3 introduced the running example system and its requirements. The system is implemented as cloud-aware application. In Sec. 4, we systematically derive a set of new metrics using the GQM method. In Sec. 5, we put our metrics in relation to existing metric proposals in literature and classify these metrics using our GQM plan in Sec. 6. Finally, Sec. 7 concludes the paper and highlights future work.

2. DEFINITIONS

Because we distinguish scalability, elasticity, and efficiency throughout our paper, we first give the definitions of these properties based on the work of Herbst et al. [9]: "**Scalability** is the ability of the system to sustain increasing workloads by making use of additional resources" [9]; "**Elasticity** is the degree to which a system is able to adapt to workload changes by provisioning and deprovisioning resources in an autonomous manner, such that at each point in time the available resources match the current demand as closely as possible" [9]; and "**Efficiency** expresses the amount of resources consumed for processing a given amount of work" [9]. We use these definitions throughout this paper to derive metrics for each quality property. In the next section, we exemplify these definitions based on our running example.

3. MOTIVATING EXAMPLE

As an example scenario, we consider a simplified online bookshop. An enterprise assigns a software architect to design this shop, given the following requirements:

R_{fct}: **Functionality** In the shop, customers shall be able to browse and order books.

R_{scale}: **Scalability** The enterprise expects an initial customer arrival rate of 100 customers per minute. It further expects that this rate will grow by 12% in the first year, i.e., increase to 112 customers per minute. In the long run, the shop shall therefore be able to handle this increased load without violating other requirements.

R_{elast}: **Elasticity** The enterprise expects that the context for the bookshop repeatedly changes over time. For example, it expects that books sell better around Christmas while they sell worse around the holiday season in summer. Therefore, the system shall proactively adapt to anticipated changes of the context, i.e., maintain a response time of 3 seconds or less as well as possible. For non-anticipated changes of the context, e.g., peak workloads, the system shall re-establish a response time of 3 seconds or less within 10 minutes once a requirement violation is detected.

R_{eff}: **Efficiency** The costs for operating the bookshop shall only increase (decrease) by $0.01 per hour when the number of customers concurrently using the shop increases (decreases) by 1. In other words, the marginal cost of the enterprise for serving an additional customer shall be $0.01.

Requirements R_{scale}, R_{elast}, and R_{eff} are typical reasons to operate a system in an elastic cloud computing environment [9], i.e., an environment that autonomously provisions the required amount of resources to cope with contextual changes. Thus, the software architect designs the shop as a 3-layer Software as a Service (SaaS) application operating in a rented Infrastructure as a Service (IaaS) cloud computing environment that provides replicable virtual servers (see Fig. 1). The three layers involve the typical layers of web applications: presentation, application, and data layer.

The architect designs each SaaS layer such that it can consume a higher/lower quantity of IaaS services to sustain changing workloads. Technically, he ensures that each SaaS layer can be replicated and load-balanced over additional IaaS virtual servers (scale-out) or be removed again (scale-in). Therefore, properties like scalability (R_{scale}), elasticity

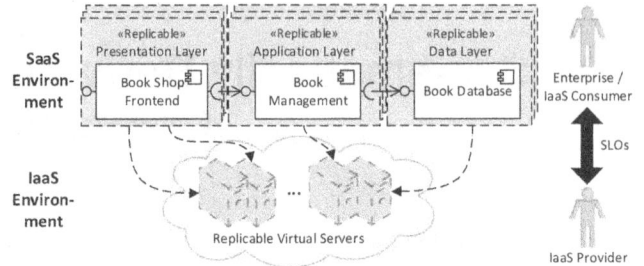

Figure 1: Overview of the simplified online bookshop.

(R_{elast}), and efficiency (R_{eff}) of the bookshop are inherently coupled with corresponding properties of the underlying IaaS environment. The enterprise (IaaS consumer) and the IaaS provider have, thus, to agree on measurements and thresholds for these properties. Typically, consumer and provider achieve an agreement based on negotiated SLOs as exemplified by R_{scale}, R_{elast}, and R_{eff}. However, currently there is a lack of agreed-on metrics for scalability, elasticity, and efficiency in the context of cloud computing. This lack results in too few SLOs or SLOs that cannot be quantified and checked by cloud consumers. In consequence, there is the risk that requirements R_{scale}, R_{elast}, and R_{eff} cannot be fulfilled due to a non-anticipated (and contractually uncheckable) behavior of the underlying IaaS environment.

4. DERIVING METRICS WITH GQM

We derive our metrics with the goal question metric (GQM) method [15] in a systematic top-down fashion by first defining the goal to analyze cloud computing system designs, e.g., for design analysis or SLO specification (conceptual level). Second, we formulate questions that help achieving the goal (operational level). Finally, we identify metrics that allow us to answer the questions (quantitative level).

4.1 Goal

Table 1 shows the goal in form of the GQM goal definition template. The metrics we want to define in this paper shall help to analyze (purpose) the scalability, elasticity, and efficiency (issue) of cloud computing system designs (object) from the viewpoint of a software architect (viewpoint).

Note that the derived metrics are not necessarily generalizable or applicable for different objects or viewpoints. For example, cloud computing vendors may perceive the efficiency of cloud system software different than software architects and, thus, need different metrics.

Table 1: Goal definition according to GQM plan

Purpose	Analyze
Issue	the scalability, elasticity, and efficiency of
Object	cloud computing system designs
Viewpoint	from a software architect's viewpoint

4.2 Questions

Next, we define questions that help achieving our defined goal. We define questions for each quality property separately. All questions are indicator questions for the according quality property as defined in Sec. 2.

Questions for Scalability.

According to the definition, scalability is an *ability*, i.e., a system is either scalable or it is not. Hence, we define questions whether a system is able to fulfill its requirements under increasing workload. Moreover, the increase rate of the workload can be a relevant context factor.

$Q1_{scale}$ Does the system fulfill its requirements when the workload increases (from workload WL_X to WL_Y)?

$Q2_{scale}$ Does the system fulfill its requirements when the workload increases with rate R (from workload WL_X to WL_Y within time t)?

Questions for Elasticity.

Elasticity is, according to the definition, the degree to which a system is able to autonomously adapt to workload changes. Thus, we define questions that consider the time it takes for the system to adapt.

$Q3_{elast}$ How often does the system violate its requirements under workload WL_X in time period Δt?

$Q4_{elast}$ From a point the system violates its requirements, how long does it take before the system recovers to a state in which its requirements are met again?

Questions for Efficiency.

Efficiency relates the amount of demanded resources to the amount of work requested. Hence, we formulate questions that ask for this relation.

$Q5_{eff}$ How close to the actual resource demand can the system align the resource provisioning?

$Q6_{eff}$ What is the amount of resources, autonomously provisioned by the system, for a given workload WL_X?

4.3 Metrics

In this section, we summarize general requirements for metrics and concrete requirements for cloud computing system metrics. We then derive our metrics that answer the questions from Sec. 4.2 in two steps. In the first step, we derive exemplary metrics (EM) for scalability, elasticity, and efficiency for the example system in Sec. 3. In the second step, we generalize these metrics to answer the questions for arbitrary cloud computing systems.

4.3.1 Requirements for Derived Metrics

The metrics we define have to meet four typical characteristics of metrics [7] in order to be applicable by software architects: (1) *quantifiability*, (2) *repeatability*, (3) *comparability*, and (4) *easy obtainability*. Additionally, we require our metrics to be (5) *context dependent* to reflect the context dependency of cloud computing systems. Figure 2 shows parts of the context that impact the quality of a cloud computing system as a feature diagram. This context covers the system's workload, i.e., work and load, and deployment, i.e., replication of components, processor speed, memory size, network speed, etc. This entire context is subject to change at run-time in a typical cloud computing environment. Hence, metrics need to have a context parameter to enable the comparison of implementations in different contexts. For example, system S_A may have less SLO violations

per minute with workload WL_X (context) but more SLO violations per minute with workload WL_Y (different context) compared to system S_B.

4.3.2 Derived Metrics from Example Scenario

In this section, we define exemplary metrics (EM) that can be used to answer the questions from Sec. 4.2. In this section, we restrict these metrics to evaluate whether the requirements for the example scenario in Sec. 3 are fulfilled. In Sec. 4.3.3, we generalize these metrics for arbitrary cloud computing systems.

The first requirement R_{fct} in our example scenario is a general requirement that defines the basic functionality of the bookshop. However, metrics for functional requirements are out of the scope of this paper.

Exemplary Scalability Metrics.

R_{scale} specifies the system's required scalability, i.e., the system's ability to make use of additional resources at increasing workloads. Hence, this requirement is dependent on the context, e.g., the load specified as arrival rates. The book enterprise has to specify arrival rates, e.g., by estimating current sales, sale trends, and seasonal sale variability.

The bookshop's software architect checks whether the designed system fulfills requirement R_{scale} by evaluating questions $Q1_{scale}$ and $Q2_{scale}$ for this design. A metric EM_{scale}, defined as the maximum workload the system can handle without violating requirement R_{scale}, answers question $Q1_{scale}$. For example, the software architect can measure this metric by predicting the performance for the bookshop design with the increased workload of 12% as expected by the book enterprise (predictions can, e.g., be conducted using queuing networks, c.f. [14]).

The enterprise does not specify at which rate the workload increases, e.g., linearly or exponentially. Therefore, to answer question $Q2_{scale}$, the bookshop's software architect needs a metric EM_{rate}, defined as the rate a system can scale up to a certain maximum workload. For example, the software architect can measure this metric by predicting the performance of the bookshop design under increasing workload, e.g., a linear increasing workload of one additional customer per month. Afterwards, the architect can discuss the quantified requirement with the enterprise.

Exemplary Elasticity Metrics.

R_{elast} specifies the bookshop's required elasticity, i.e., the degree to which the bookshop is able to adapt to workload changes by autonomously provisioning and deprovisioning cloud resources. In general, these workload changes (context) can be either anticipated or impossible to anticipate. As described in Sec. 3, the enterprise can anticipate variability of the bookshop's customers demand, i.e., the enterprise estimates to sell more books around Christmas than in mid-summer. Other short-term variations of the workload cannot be anticipated, e.g., peak workloads.

The bookshop's software architect can evaluate whether R_{elast} is fulfilled by answering questions $Q3_{elast}$ and $Q4_{elast}$ for the bookshop design. The cloud computing system can potentially cope with both, anticipated and non-anticipated, workload variability. However, considering the fact that resources can be available with delay, the system will likely violate requirement R_{elast} until the time additionally provisioned resources are available. A metric EM_{viol}, defined as

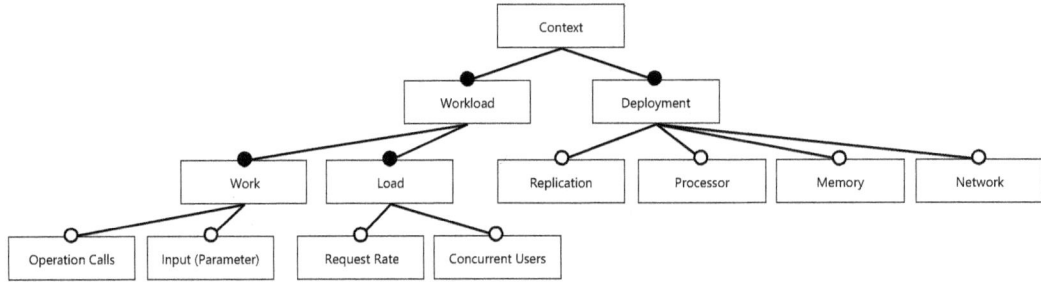

Figure 2: Feature diagram showing aspects of context.

number of requirement violations for a given workload, is a mean for the software architect to answer question $Q3_{elast}$. A metric EM_{adapt}, defined as the time between detection of a requirement violation and the time when the requirement is fulfilled again, e.g., by autonomous resource provisioning, answers question $Q4_{elast}$. For example, the bookshop's architect can measure both metrics, EM_{viol} and EM_{adapt}, by simulating the bookshop's autonomous behavior using self-adaptive queuing networks [2].

Exemplary Efficiency Metrics.

R_{eff} specifies the required efficiency of the bookshop regarding its resource consumption. The bookshop's autonomous provisioning and deprovisioning adapts the resource consumption to the bookshop's workload, i.e, the workload is important context here as well. Furthermore, the operation costs of the bookshop depend on this resource consumption as the enterprise has to pay for the cloud resources in a pay-per-use fashion.

The software architect can evaluate whether the R_{eff} is fulfilled by answering questions $Q5_{eff}$ and $Q6_{eff}$. A metric EM_{close} can be defined as the difference between the bookshop's amount of provisioned resources for a workload WL_X and the minimum amount of resources required to cope with that workload WL_X without violating the stated requirements. The bookshop's software architect can use this metric to answers question $Q5_{eff}$. A metric EM_{prov}, defined as the amount of resources provisioned for a workload WL_X, answers question $Q6_{eff}$. Whereas the marginal costs can be calculated directly from the metric EM_{prov}, EM_{close} supports the software architect to determine whether the required marginal costs are achievable. Again, both metrics can be measured by simulating the bookshop's autonomous behavior under variable workload, for example.

4.3.3 Generalized Metrics

We define initial new metrics that we derived from the six exemplary metrics (EM) from the previous subsection. For each metric, we define the corresponding quality property it quantifies, what is being measured, on which contextual properties the measurement depends, and the scope and unit of the measurement result. To guarantee objectivity, our metrics rely only on externally observable properties of a system, e.g., costs per time. Reproducibility is guaranteed by specifying the contextual properties on which the metric depends. Thus, context dependency is also guaranteed. By defining the measurement result's scope as ordinal numbers, we guarantee that the metric reflects a testable quantification of the quality property. Additionally, we pro-

vide a small example for each metric. Table 2 summarizes the following generalized metrics.

Scalability Metrics.

Scalability Range (ScR) Based on EM_{scale}, we define scaling range as a scalability metric that reflects a cloud computing system's ability to achieve its SLOs in a certain workload range, e.g., a range of request rates. For each single workload within this range, the system achieves its SLOs. The workload range is defined as a maximum workload. For example, a perfectly scalable system S_A can scale up to a infinite request rate, i.e., $ScR_{S_A} = \infty \; req/min$. A less scalable system, for example, scales up to a request rate of 112 requests per minute, i.e., $ScR_{S_B} = 112 \; req/min$.

Scalability Speed (ScS) Based on EM_{rate}, we define scalability speed ScS as a workload range with a maximal change rate in which a system can scale. This metric is a scalability metric which additionally considers the rate at which a system can scale. That is, the metric defines that a system is able to achieve its SLOs at each time when the workload changes at a maximal changing rate. The rate is defined by a maximum workload and an increase rate. For example, a scalable system can scale up to a request rate of 112 req/min with a linear increase rate of 1 additional requests per month, i.e., $ScS_{S_A} = (112 \; req/min, 1 \; req/month)$.

Elasticity Metrics.

Mean Time To Quality Repair ($MTTQR$) We derive the mean time to quality repair metric from EM_{adapt}, the measure how quickly a system can adapt to workload changes. It is a measure for elasticity and depends on a workload delta, i.e., the increase/decrease between two workloads. $MTTQR$ defines the mean time a system needs to re-establish its SLOs when the workload increases/decreases for a defined workload delta specified as factor (real number). Hence, $MTTQR$ is measured in time units. Since it defines a mean time, $MTTQR$ is specific for a specified time frame in which the mean is calculated. For example, with the same workload increase factor of 1.2, a perfectly elastic system will adapt itself to the increasing workload within zero time, i.e., $MTTQR_{S_A,1d}(1.2 \; req/s) = 0 \; min$. A less elastic system, e.g., will need a mean time of 10 min (calculated over one day) to adapt itself to increasing workload after it detects the workload increase, i.e., $MTTQR_{S_B,1d}(1.2 \; req/s) = 10 \; min$.

Number of SLO violations ($NSLOV$) The number of SLO violations in a defined time interval is derived from EM_{viol}. This metric measures elasticity of a system. The workload delta is specified as a factor (real number) as well.

Table 2: Derived quality property metrics for cloud computing systems

Metric	Unit	Example
Scalability Metrics		
Scalability Range (ScR)	max	The system scales up to 112 req./min
Scalability Speed (ScS)	(max, rate)	The system scales up to 112 req./min with linear increase rate 1 req./month
Elasticity Metrics		
Number of SLO Violations ($NSLOV$)	1/[time unit]	42 SLO (response time) violations in 1 hour
Mean Time To Quality Repair ($MTTQR$)	[time unit]	30 seconds for an additional 10 requests/hour
Efficiency Metrics		
Resource Provisioning Efficiency (RPE)	$[0, \infty]$	10% more resources than actual resource demand
Marginal Cost (MC)	[monetary unit]	$1.00 for an additional 100 requests/hour

$NSLOV$ reflects how often a system violates its SLOs when workload changes at a given rate, measured as a real number. For example, with a workload increase factor of 1.2, a perfectly elastic system would have 0 SLO violations per request, i.e., $NSLOV_{\mathcal{S}_A}(1.2\ req/s) = 0$. In contrast, a non-elastic system will violate its SLO for each request, i.e., $NSLOV_{\mathcal{S}_A}(1.2\ req/s) = 1$.

Efficiency Metrics.

Resource Provisioning Efficiency (RPE) We define resource provisioning efficiency (RPE) as a metric to measure a system's efficiency in a specified workload delta based on EM_{close}. That is, the metric measures the mismatch between actual resource utilization and resource demand while the workload is changing. We measure this mismatch in percentage, i.e., as a real number. A perfectly efficient system will adapt its resource demand exactly to the resource demand at all times. For example, if the workload increases with factor 1.2 the system will provision exactly that amount of additional resources required to cope with this additional workload, i.e., $RPE_{\mathcal{S}_A}(1.2\ req/s) = 0$.

Marginal costs (MC) We derive the *marginal costs* for a specified workload delta from EM_{prov}. Marginal costs are the operation costs to serve one additional workload unit, thus, measuring the efficiency of a cloud computing system. For example, the operation costs to serve 20% additional requests per second (factor 1.2) can be $1.00 for system $\mathcal{S}_A$, i.e., $MC_{\mathcal{S}_A}(1.2) = \$1.00$.

5. RELATED WORK

In this section, we present related work that also targets metrics for scalability, elasticity, and efficiency in the context of cloud computing and SLO specification. Where applicable, we classify found metrics using our GQM plan in Sec. 6.

In the area of **scalability metrics**, Bondi [5] further divides scalability into structural scalability ("ability to expand in a chosen dimension without major modification") and load scalability ("ability of a system to perform gracefully as the offered traffic increases"). In terms of this classification, we focus on load scalability in our work. However, in contrast to Bondi, we also provide concrete metrics for load scalability and apply these to the cloud computing context. Duboc et al. [6] formally define scalability requirements and provide a method to analyze a software model for scalability obstacles. A scalability obstacle could also be defined and detected using our metrics. In contrast to the approach from Duboc et al., our metrics are closer to SLOs

in their current form. Jogalekar and Woodside [11] present a scalability metric for general distributed systems. Their scalability metric also includes an efficiency measure. In our work, we distinguish between scalability and efficiency as two different metrics. Furthermore, in contrast to Jogalekar and Woodside, our metrics are focused on cloud computing environments with their particular characteristics.

Herbst et al. [9] provide a set of **elasticity metrics** based on speed and precision (w.r.t. avoiding under- and overprovisioning) of scale-in and -out. Because their goal is a benchmarking methodology for elasticity, they can assume full knowledge about the resource usage of the benchmarked application. However, in our case, we assume that this knowledge is unavailable because details on resources are implementation decisions. In contrast, we consider requirements specified between cloud consumer and provider. This lack of knowledge necessarily leads to different metrics as by Herbst et al., e.g., considering SLO violations instead of resource usage transparent to consumers. Folkers et al. [8] and Islam et al. [10] both provide elasticity metrics that meet this requirement regarding knowledge. However, they lack the distinction between elasticity and efficiency because they both use cost metrics for elasticity, thus, eliminating the possibility to investigate both properties in separation.

Roloff et al. [12] define basic **efficiency metrics** for high performance computing in cloud computing environments. They define cost efficiency as the product of costs per hour and average performance. In contrast to our work, they neglect the context, e.g., actual workload, and only take the average performance. Berl et al. [3] address energy efficiency in all technical components of cloud computing, e.g., servers, networks as well as network protocols. We do not address energy efficiency directly but only resource provisioning efficiency in this paper. Investigating whether efficient provisioning of resources positively correlates with energy efficiency is left as future work.

These related works focus on single quality properties. In contrast, the Cloud Services Measurement Initiative Consortium (CSMIC) provides a standard **measurement framework**, called the Service Measurement Index (SMI), that covers all quality properties considered important for cloud computing [13]. CSMIC particularly provides metrics for these quality properties, intended to be used by cloud consumers and cloud providers. Their framework allows for a structured classification of quality properties, similar to our GQM plan. However, CSMIC does not address the deviation of their suggested metrics, thus, leaving open what limitations come with their metrics and whether other metrics are feasible as well.

6. CLASSIFICATION OF METRICS IN RE-LATED WORK

In this section, we classify metrics identified in related work (Sec. 5) by relating these metrics to the questions of our GQM plan. In doing so, we show that we can systematically make assumptions and limitations of existing metrics explicit. Note that we classify only a few related metrics, for illustration.

Scalability metric by Jogalekar and Woodside [11]
Jogalekar and Woodside provide a scalability metric that can directly be used to answer $Q1_{scale}$ ("Does the system fulfill its requirements when the workload increases (from workload WL_X to WL_Y)?"). They use workload as the main input context factor to their metric, thus, complying to our scalability question. As an output, they determine a productivity factor that states whether system requirements can be fulfilled (using a threshold for this factor). Also this idea complies to our question. However, to calculate the productivity factor, they require knowledge about the operation costs for a given workload. In contrast, we do not limit our scalability metrics to this knowledge about costs and require it for elasticity metrics only.

Elasticity and efficiency metrics by Herbst et al. [9]
Herbst et al. provide metrics that consider speed and precision (w.r.t. avoiding under- and overprovisioning) of scale-in and -out. Their ideas on speed can be used to answer our elasticity question $Q4_{elast}$ ("From a point the system violates its requirements, how long does it take before the system recovers to a state in which its requirements are met again?"). However, to detect requirement violations, they assume to have already an implemented system at hand; design-time (e.g., simulation-based) approaches do not work with their metric. Their ideas on precision fit to our elasticity question $Q5_{eff}$ ("How close to the actual resource demand can the system align the resource provisioning?"). Again, their metric requires an implemented system to determine the actual resource usage.

7. CONCLUSION

In this short research paper, we argue for the need of novel metrics for quality properties of cloud computing systems. Using the GQM method, we systematically derive an initial set of six metrics for scalability, elasticity, and efficiency. Moreover, by using our GQM plan, we classify existing metrics to make their limitations explicit.

Our systematically derived metrics help software architects, requirements engineers, testers, etc. to design and analyze cloud computing systems. Our GQM plan helps them to consider limitations of such metrics during these tasks.

Future work is directed towards the development of analysis methods and tools that enable software architects to verify the fulfillment of scalability, elasticity, and efficiency requirements of their cloud computing applications already at design time. Understanding limitations of metrics is essential for this purpose.

8. ACKNOWLEDGMENTS

This work is supported by the German Research Foundation (DFG) within the Collaborative Research Centre "On-The-Fly Computing" (SFB 901). The research leading to these results has received funding from the European Union Seventh Framework Programme (FP7/2007-2013) under grant no 317704 (CloudScale).

9. REFERENCES

[1] M. Armbrust, A. Fox, R. Griffith, A. D. Joseph, R. Katz, A. Konwinski, G. Lee, D. Patterson, A. Rabkin, I. Stoica, and M. Zaharia. A view of cloud computing. *Commun. ACM*, 53(4):50–58, Apr. 2010.

[2] M. Becker, S. Becker, and J. Meyer. SimuLizar: Design-time modelling and performance analysis of self-adaptive systems. In *Proceedings of Software Engineering 2013 (SE2013), Aachen*, 2013.

[3] A. Berl, E. Gelenbe, M. Di Girolamo, G. Giuliani, H. De Meer, M. Q. Dang, and K. Pentikousis. Energy-efficient cloud computing. *The Computer Journal*, 53(7):1045–1051, 2010.

[4] G. Bolch, S. Greiner, K. S. Trivedi, and H. de Meer. *Queueing Networks and Markov Chains: Modeling and Performance Evaluation With Computer Science Applications*. 1998.

[5] A. B. Bondi. Characteristics of scalability and their impact on performance. In *WOSP '00*, pages 195–203, New York, NY, USA, 2000. ACM.

[6] L. Duboc, E. Letier, and D. S. Rosenblum. Systematic elaboration of scalability requirements through goal-obstacle analysis. *IEEE Transactions on Software Engineering*, 39(1):119–140, Jan. 2013.

[7] T. Erl, Z. Mahmood, and R. Puttini. *Cloud Computing: Concepts, Technology & Architecture*. Prentice Hall, 2013.

[8] E. Folkerts, A. Alexandrov, K. Sachs, A. Iosup, V. Markl, and C. Tosun. Benchmarking in the cloud: What it should, can, and cannot be. In *TPCTC*, pages 173–188, 2012.

[9] N. R. Herbst, S. Kounev, and R. Reussner. Elasticity: What it is, and What it is Not. In *ICAC '13*, 2013.

[10] S. Islam, K. Lee, A. Fekete, and A. Liu. How a consumer can measure elasticity for cloud platforms. In *Proceedings of the 3rd ACM/SPEC International Conference on Performance Engineering*, ICPE '12, pages 85–96, New York, NY, USA, 2012. ACM.

[11] P. Jogalekar and M. Woodside. Evaluating the scalability of distributed systems. *IEEE Trans. Parallel Distrib. Syst.*, 11(6):589–603, June 2000.

[12] E. Roloff, M. Diener, A. Carissimi, and P. Navaux. High performance computing in the cloud: Deployment, performance and cost efficiency. In *CloudCom '12*, pages 371–378, 2012.

[13] J. Siegel and J. Perdue. Cloud services measures for global use: The service measurement index (smi). In *SRII Global Conference (SRII), 2012 Annual*, pages 411–415, July 2012.

[14] C. U. Smith. *Performance engineering of software systems*. Software Engineering Institute series in software engineering. Addison-Wesley, 1990.

[15] R. van Solingen, V. Basili, G. Caldiera, and H. D. Rombach. *Goal Question Metric (GQM) Approach*. John Wiley & Sons, Inc., 2002.

Subsuming Methods: Finding New Optimisation Opportunities in Object-Oriented Software

David Maplesden
Dept. of Computer Science
The University of Auckland
dmap001@aucklanduni.ac.nz

John Hosking
Faculty of Science
The University of Auckland
j.hosking@auckland.ac.nz

Ewan Tempero
Dept. of Computer Science
The University of Auckland
e.tempero@auckland.ac.nz

John C. Grundy
School of Software and Electrical Engineering
Swinburne University of Technology
jgrundy@swin.edu.au

ABSTRACT

The majority of existing application profiling techniques aggregate and report performance costs by method or calling context. Modern large-scale object-oriented applications consist of thousands of methods with complex calling patterns. Consequently, when profiled, their performance costs tend to be thinly distributed across many thousands of locations with few easily identifiable optimisation opportunities.

However experienced performance engineers know that there are repeated patterns of method calls in the execution of an application that are induced by the libraries, design patterns and coding idioms used in the software. Automatically identifying and aggregating costs over these patterns of method calls allows us to identify opportunities to improve performance based on optimising these patterns.

We have developed an analysis technique that is able to identify the entry point methods, which we call subsuming methods, of such patterns. Our offline analysis runs over previously collected runtime performance data structured in a calling context tree, such as produced by a large number of existing commercial and open source profilers.

We have evaluated our approach on the DaCapo benchmark suite, showing that our analysis significantly reduces the size and complexity of the runtime performance data set, facilitating its comprehension and interpretation. We also demonstrate, with a collection of case studies, that our analysis identifies new optimisation opportunities that can lead to significant performance improvements (from 20% to over 50% improvement in our case studies).

Categories and Subject Descriptors

D.3.4 [**Programming Languages**]: Processors—*Optimization*; D.2.5 [**Software Engineering**]: Testing and Debugging—*Debugging aids*

General Terms

Performance,Measurement

Keywords

dynamic performance analysis, profiling, subsuming methods, runtime bloat

1. INTRODUCTION

Performance is a crucial and often elusive attribute for modern applications. Trends such as mobile application development, where resources are limited, cloud deployment, where running costs are directly impacted by software efficiency, and online solutions, where low latency response times are key, means that software performance analysis is often a vital part of software engineering today. Enabled by the increase in hardware capacity over the last three decades, the size and complexity of software has increased to a similar or even greater extent [13]. This growing scale of the software under development means that analysing and improving the performance of these systems has become increasingly difficult.

Many of the challenges faced when analysing the performance of modern large-scale systems are exacerbated by specific characteristics of object-oriented software. Following object-oriented principles tends to lead to applications with inter-procedural rather than intra-procedural control flow and a great number of methods. Additionally many object-oriented methodologies focus on developer productivity, producing maintainable and flexible software, and promoting componentisation and reuse. As a result most applications are built from reusable generalised frameworks and leverage established design patterns, making them very layered and complex.

For example, a Java service-oriented application might implement SOAP web services using the apache Axis web service framework, running in the apache Tomcat servlet engine and using the Hibernate persistence framework to access a relational database. This approach means that the handling of even the simplest request in these framework-based applications goes through many layers and will require hundreds, maybe thousands, of method calls to complete [17]. This excessive activity to achieve seemingly simple results is a problem that has become known as *runtime bloat* [26].

It makes the applications difficult to profile and it has led many large scale object-oriented applications to suffer from chronic performance problems [15].

Traditional application profilers provide method-centric feedback on where an application is consuming resources, in particular memory allocation and execution time. Therefore profiling the extremely complex runtime behaviour exhibited by these large-scale object-oriented applications typically reports resource costs that are thinly distributed across a large number of methods, and results in a massive dataset that is very difficult to interpret. This also means that compile time and dynamic runtime optimisation approaches struggle to mitigate runtime bloat because of the lack of easily identifiable optimisation targets [26].

This is the challenge that we are interested in: how can we provide more useful feedback on the performance of large-scale object-oriented applications so that it can be improved? How can we help software engineers to reduce runtime bloat?

Our key insight in this paper is that there are repeated patterns of method calls induced by the libraries and design idioms used in the implementation of the software. These repeated patterns represent coherent units of aggregation for the resource costs recorded by traditional profilers. We show that identifying and aggregating performance costs over these repeated patterns will facilitate a better understanding of the performance characteristics of the software and highlight new, high potential candidates for optimisation that would led to useful performance improvements.

One of our key goals is to *automatically* identify the key repeated patterns of method calls. It is not practical to manually detect these patterns in a large-scale application with complex runtime behaviour spanning thousands of methods.

Our approach to identifying these repeated patterns of method calls is to identify the key methods, which we call the *subsuming methods*, in the application that represent the entry point or root of these repeated patterns. The other methods we call the *subsumed* methods and we attribute their execution costs to their parent subsuming method.

The main contributions of this paper are:

- We introduce the concept of automatically identifying repeated patterns of method calls in an application profile and using them to aggregate performance costs.
- We describe *subsuming methods*, a specific technique for identifying the entry points to repeated patterns of method calls.
- We define a novel metric, minimum dominating method distance, used to help identify subsuming methods.
- We demonstrate that our approach can be applied efficiently to large scale software.
- We empirically evaluate our approach over standard benchmarks to characterise the typical attributes of subsuming methods.
- We demonstrate the utility of subsuming methods in several case studies.

The remainder of this paper is structured as follows. Section 2 motivates our work and presents background information. Section 3 covers related work. Section 4 describes our approach. Section 5 presents an evaluation using the DaCapo benchmark suite and several case studies. Section 6 discusses the results of our evaluation and areas of future work. We conclude in Section 7.

2. MOTIVATION AND BACKGROUND

Traditional profiling tools typically record measurements of execution cost per method call, both inclusive and exclusive of the cost of any methods they call. Usually of the most interest are the top exclusive cost methods, known as the *hot* methods. The cost measurements are usually captured with calling context information, that is, the hierarchy of active methods calls leading to the current call, and are aggregated in a calling context tree.

A calling context tree (CCT) records all distinct calling contexts of a program. Each node in the tree has a method label representing the method call at that node and has a child node for each unique method invoked from that calling context [3]. Therefore the method labels on the path from a node to the root of the tree describe a distinct calling context. For multithreaded programs containing multiple execution entry points a virtual root node is used to collate the multiple traces into a single tree. A CCT is an intermediate representation in the spectrum of data structures that trade off size for richness of information. It retains more information than either a flat method level aggregation of data (also known as a vertex profile), which discards all calling context information, or a dynamic call graph (also known as an edge profile), which retains only a single level of calling context information. It is more compact than a full call tree, which captures every unique method invocation separately but grows in size linearly with the number of method calls and hence is unbounded over time.

For example the small program in Example 1 will generate the CCT shown in Figure 1. Table 1 shows the aggregated costs for each method assuming the per-call costs given in column one. The per-call costs are arbitrary numbers that we have assumed to complete the example.

The objective of performance profiling is to identify sections of source code that are performance critical, as these represent optimisation opportunities. The simplest approach to this is to identify the hot methods — methods with the highest exclusive cost. This is easily done by aggregating the performance data in the CCT for each method i.e. creating a flat method profile as in Table 1.

Example 1

```
1:      void main() {          13:     void b() {
2:          a();               14:         c();
3:          a();               15:         c();
4:          b();               16:         x();
5:      }                      17:         x();
6:                             18:     }
7:      void a() {             19:
8:          b();               20:     void c() {
9:          y();               21:         x();
10:     }                      22:     }
11:                            23:
12:     void x() { ... }       24:     void y() { ... }
```

Table 1: Costs for Example 1

Method	Per-call	Invocations	Exclusive	Inclusive
main	3	1	3	71
a	2	2	4	50
b	4	3	12	54
c	1	6	6	24
x	3	12	36	36
y	5	2	10	10

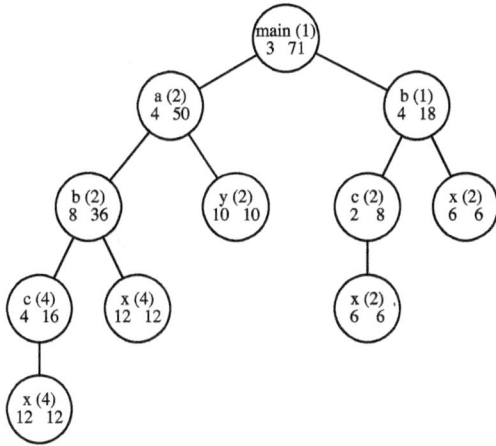

Figure 1: CCT for Example 1

The numbers shown for each node are the invocation count, exclusive cost, and inclusive cost for that node. Each node maintains the aggregated totals for a calling context.

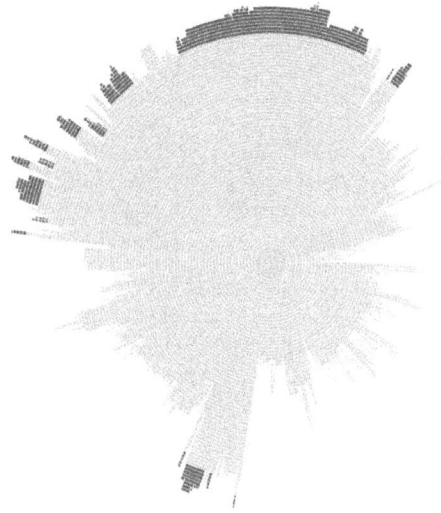

Figure 2: Usages of formatDouble in fop

Unfortunately the list of hot methods often isn't useful because the identified methods are difficult to optimise or avoid. For example Table 2 shows the top ten hot methods from a case study (discussed in section 5.1.1) we completed on the `fop` benchmark from the DaCapo-9.12-bach benchmark suite [8]. The `fop` benchmark is a relatively small library used in many applications for applying XSL-FO stylesheets to XML documents to produce PDF or other formatted output. Only one of the top ten hot methods is actually a method in the `fop` codebase, all the others are support methods from the Java runtime library, methods that are heavily used and already well optimised. Also the method calls typically occur a large number of times within the CCT, each occurrence representing a different calling context in which the method was invoked. This makes it difficult to target the code that calls the method in order to avoid invoking the costly method. Finally, by the time we reach the fifth method we are considering methods using less than 2% of the total execution time, so even if we could remove this cost completely the benefit would be minor.

Apart from investigating hot methods, another common approach to identifying performance critical code is to perform a top-down search of the CCT, looking for a compact

Table 2: Top 10 hot methods in the fop benchmark

Method	Occ.	% Exc.	% Inc.
sun.misc.FloatingDecimal.dtoa	348	6.904	9.428
java.text.DigitList.set	374	5.266	6.166
java.text.DecimalFormat.subformat	374	3.123	5.614
org.apache.fop.fo.properties.			
PropertyMaker.findProperty	1501	2.471	11.675
sun.nio.cs.US_ASCII$Encoder.encode	568	1.795	1.796
sun.misc.FloatingDecimal.countBits	348	1.563	1.563
java.util.HashMap.hash	10663	1.512	3.534
java.lang.String.equals	4620	1.454	1.454
java.util.HashMap.getEntry	6081	1.348	4.950
java.lang.String.indexOf	3343	1.300	1.300

Occ. - is the number of occurrences of the method in the full CCT i.e. the number of distinct calling paths that lead to the method call

sub-tree that has a high total cost. The sub-tree should be compact so that it represents a constrained piece of dynamic behaviour that can be understood and optimised. If such a sub-tree even exists, finding it within a large CCT is difficult; nodes near the root of the CCT, which have high total costs, encompass very large sub-trees and nodes near the leaves of the CCT, which are compact, have low total costs.

Consequently traditional hot method analysis and top-down searches are often ineffective with a large CCT, and they can grow very large for object-oriented programs. The CCT generated by the relatively small `fop` benchmark contained over six hundred thousand nodes, real-world applications can create CCTs with tens of millions of nodes [10].

However there does exist within the `fop` benchmark a clear cut performance optimisation opportunity. A single method, `org.apache.xmlgraphics.ps.PSGenerator.formatDouble`, accounts for (by inclusive cost) over 26% of the total execution time. Figure 2 is a calling context ring chart [18, 1] visualising the full CCT with all the occurrences of this method and its sub-trees highlighted. The chart depicts the CCT as a series of concentric rings broken into segments, each segment representing a node in the CCT with the root node in the centre. Moving away from the middle each segment is divided into a new segment for each child node, so nodes deeper in the CCT are further away from the middle and leaf nodes in the CCT have no surrounding segments. The arc length covered by each segment is proportional to the inclusive cost of the associated calling context, so the more cost the sub-tree rooted at a node accounts for the longer the ring segment. Figure 2 illustrates the fact that `formatDouble` occurs in multiple locations deep within the CCT and in aggregate accounts for a significant amount of the total execution time.

The `formatDouble` method uses `java.text.NumberFormat` (Java's general purpose floating point number formatter) for producing a simple three decimal place format. It induces the same expensive pattern of method calls each time it is used, but that cost is distributed over a number of low-level string manipulation and floating decimal inspection methods. Once we have found this method it is easy to see it represents just the sort of opportunity we are looking for, a compact repeated pattern of method calls that accounts for a significant proportion of the overall cost, but finding it amongst the full CCT or deducing it from the list of low-level hot methods is difficult.

This is a classic example of the type of runtime bloat experienced by many large-scale object oriented applications. The use of a conveniently available and powerful generic library routine has a significant performance impact that is later difficult to detect amongst the mass of performance data produced when the application is profiled. We were able to refactor this method to use a much more specialised approach that drastically reduced its relative cost, improving the overall execution cost of the benchmark by 22%. Our aim is to help identify these types of opportunities.

3. RELATED WORK

There is a significant body of work into investigating software performance that we cannot adequately describe here due to space limitations. This includes extensive research into model-based performance prediction methods that are complementary to our empirical performance analysis approach and many papers on novel performance data collection (profiling) approaches that are applicable to object-oriented software (e.g. [4, 6, 7, 20]). Typically these data collection approaches are either striving for lower overheads, better accuracy or better contextual information (e.g. argument, loop or data centric profiling). By contrast our work is focussed on improving the analysis rather than the collection of performance data.

The most closely related work to ours in terms of its motivation is the existing research into runtime bloat [26]. Generally they have focussed on memory bloat (excessive memory use)(e.g. [9, 5]) or they have taken a data-flow centric approach [16, 17], looking for patterns of inefficiently created or used data structures, collections and objects [22, 25, 27, 24, 28, 19]. This includes approaches specifically looking at the problem of object churn, that is the creation of a large number of short-lived objects [11, 12]. In contrast, we investigate a control-flow centric approach, searching for repeated inefficient patterns of method calls.

Also related are approaches to aggregating calling context tree summarised performance data [14, 23]. These are based on grouping by package and class name, aggregating methods below a certain cost threshold into the calling method or the manual specification of aggregation groupings. None of these approaches attempt to *automatically* detect repeated patterns of method calls.

4. SUBSUMING METHODS

Our aim is to identify repeated patterns of method calls within the CCT over which we can aggregate performance costs. The intuition behind idea this is two-fold:

1. Consolidating costs within the CCT in this way reduces the size and complexity of the tree, making it easier to interpret to discover performance bottlenecks.
2. The traditional unit of aggregation, individual methods, often identifies bottlenecks that are difficult to optimise. By contrast a pattern of methods calls is more likely to encapsulate a range of behaviour that contains optimisation opportunities.

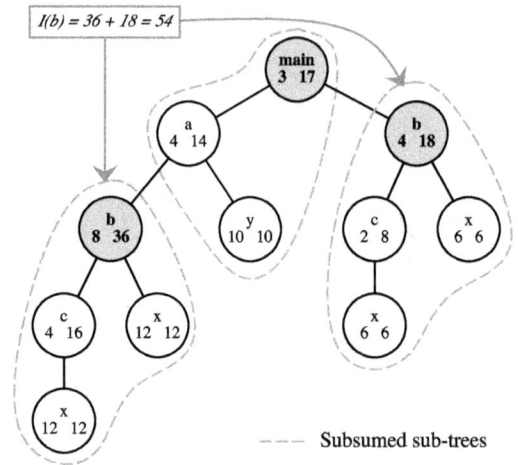

Figure 3: Subsumed subtrees for Example 1
We have chosen *main* and *b* as subsuming methods. The numbers shown for each node are the exclusive and induced costs at that node.

Our approach to consolidating costs within the CCT is to identify the methods that are the most interesting from a performance standpoint and use these to identify consolidation points within the tree, we call these the *subsuming* methods. All other methods we call *subsumed* methods and we attribute their costs to their parent node in the CCT. We attribute costs recursively upwards until we find a node labeled with a subsuming method, where the costs are aggregated. We call this cost the `induced cost` for the node as it represents the cost induced by the subsuming method at that node. Figure 3 illustrates the subsuming concept using the CCT from our earlier example. Here we have chosen methods *b* and *main* as our subsuming methods (the method at the root of the CCT always becomes a subsuming method).

Each node labeled with a subsuming method becomes the root of a subsumed subtree and represents a pattern or block of code consisting of itself and the nodes it subsumes, either directly or transitively through other subsumed nodes. The induced cost of a subsuming method is the sum of the induced costs for all the nodes in the tree labeled with that method. In our example the total induced cost for method *b* is $36 + 18 = 54$. As the exclusive cost of each CCT node is consolidated into exactly one subsuming node (and each node is labeled with exactly one method) the sum of the induced costs of all the subsuming methods equals the total cost of the CCT. Effectively the subsuming methods form a new way of partitioning the CCT at a coarser granularity than the initial method level partitioning.

This approach can be used to subsume any type of resource cost recorded in the CCT, or multiple costs at once. Typically these costs are execution time, invocation count or memory allocations but our approach can be applied to any recorded cost value.

More formally: Let V be the set of nodes in the CCT. Let M be the set of methods of the application, used as labels of nodes in the CCT. Let $S \subseteq M$ be the set of subsuming methods. Let function $l(v) : V \rightarrow M$ denote the method label of a node v and function $c(v) : V \rightarrow \mathbb{R}$ denote the cost.

Then we define $nodes(m) = \{v : v \in V, l(v) = m\}$ i.e. the subset of V that have the label m, and the induced cost for a node $v \in V$:

$$i(v) = c(v) + \sum_{c \in child(v)} \begin{cases} 0 & c \in S \\ i(c) & c \notin S \end{cases}$$

and the induced cost for a method $m \in S$:

$$I(m) = \sum_{v \in nodes(m)} i(v)$$

4.1 Identifying Subsuming Methods

Our approach is based upon identifying a subset of the methods in an application that are interesting from a performance standpoint i.e. the subsuming methods. Using different sets of subsuming methods leads to different results and potentially different insights into application performance. In this paper we have considered two characteristics of methods in order to define a set of subsuming methods that give us interesting and useful results. We are confident that there are many other approaches to selecting the subsuming methods that would also be effective. We discuss some of these in section 6. The two characteristics are:

Methods that induce only a very limited range of behaviour at runtime. These methods are not interesting from a performance standpoint because they tend to be simple code that is difficult to optimise. We have used the height of the method as a measure of the range of behaviour it induces. The height of a method is the maximum height of any sub-tree within the CCT rooted at a node labeled by the method. For example the height of method a from our earlier example is 3 (see Figure 4). The trivial case is a leaf method that never calls any other method and therefore has a height of zero.

More formally the height $h(v)$ of any node $v \in V$ is:

$$h(v) = \begin{cases} 0 & |child(v)| = 0 \\ \max_{c \in child(v)}(1 + h(c)) & |child(v)| > 0 \end{cases}$$

and the height $H(m)$ of any method $m \in M$ is:

$$H(m) = \max_{v \in nodes(m)} h(v)$$

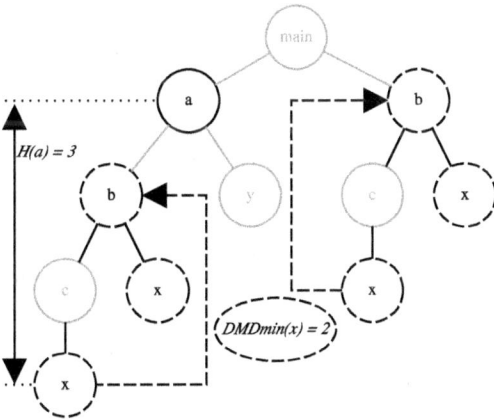

Figure 4: CCT for Example 1 showing height and DMD_{min}

Methods that are called in a very constrained set of circumstances. Specifically each call to the method can be traced back to a nearby *dominating* method, a distinct calling method responsible for its invocation. A dominating method appears in the call stack for every invocation of the dominated method i.e. if a method p dominates a method m, then any call to m is preceded by a call to p and followed by the return of that same call to p. Whilst potentially interesting from a performance standpoint these dominated methods are generally less interesting than the dominating method, as the dominating method is always invoked shortly before and encapsulates their invocation.

We have used the distance from a method to its nearest dominating method as a measure of this characteristic. The trivial case is when a method is only ever called from a single call site i.e. every occurrence of the method within the CCT has the same parent method. In this case that single parent will be the dominating method and the dominating method distance will be 1.

Formally for methods p and m, we say p is a dominating method of m (or p dominates m) if $p \neq m$ and $\forall v \in nodes(m)$ there exists a node $n \in V$ such that $l(n) = p$ and n is an ancestor of v in the CCT. By definition this means that the method label assigned to the root node dominates all other methods. Hence every method except the root method is guaranteed to have at least one dominating method i.e. the root method.

We define a distance function for the dominating method p of a method m as:

$$dmd(p, m) = \max_{v \in nodes(m)} d(p, v)$$

where $d(p, v)$ is the length of the path from node v to the first ancestor node n such that $l(n) = p$ (such an ancestor node must exist otherwise, by definition, p does not dominate m). We call this the dominating method distance (DMD) for m to p.

The minimum DMD for a given method m then is:

$$dmd_{min}(m) = \min_{p \in M} dmd(p, m)$$

i.e. the smallest DMD amongst all the dominating methods of m. Figure 4 illustrates the minimum DMD for method x from Example 1. Table 3 lists the dominating method and dmd_{min} for each method from Example 1.

Table 3: Height and dmd_{min} **for Example 1**

Method	Height	Dominating Method	dmd_{min}
main	4	–	–
a	3	main	1
b	2	main	2
c	1	b	1
x	0	b	2
y	0	a	1

Using our height and dmd_{min} attributes we can define a condition for identifying subsuming methods by specifying a bound on the minimum height and/or dmd_{min} a method must have in order to be considered subsuming i.e. we can define that all subsuming methods must have a height greater than H_{bound} and dmd_{min} greater than D_{bound}:

$$S = \{m : m \in M, H(m) > H_{bound}, dmd_{min}(m) > D_{bound}\}$$

It is also straightforward to efficiently implement an interactive analysis where these bounds can be dynamically changed as we need to only recalculate the induced costs after changing these bounds.

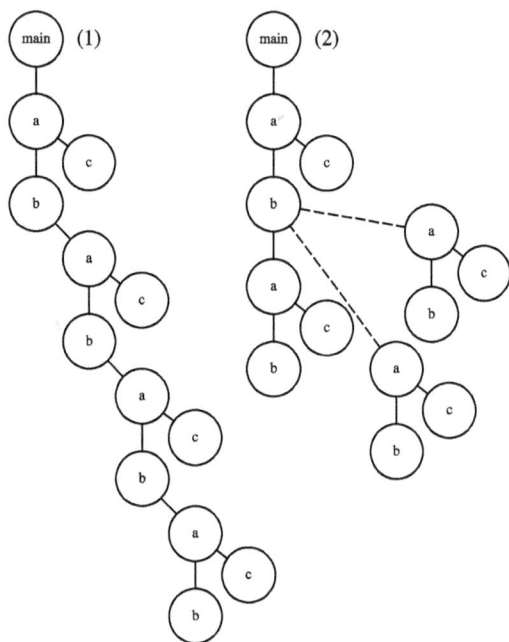

Figure 5: CCT before (1) and after (2) the recursive adjustment

4.2 Adjusting for recursive calls

Our discussion so far has ignored the impact of recursive calling patterns on the CCT and its subsequent analysis. Even conceptually simple recursive algorithms can result in very deeply nested call paths. These create subtrees with very large heights and dominating method distances that we would like to reduce to a single representative repetition of the recursion.

To achieve this we identify and reduce these recursive call paths in the CCT before we perform our height and DMD calculations. That way we can calculate the height and DMD in the adjusted tree to ensure our subsuming characterisation appropriately adjusts for recursion. We then perform our induced cost calculation on the original tree to ensure we aggregate the full costs from the tree. To build the adjusted tree we traverse the original tree from the root node downwards calculating, at each node, the ancestor node that we want to use as the adjusted parent. We perform an in-order traversal of the original tree to ensure that all ancestor nodes of the current node have already been added to the adjusted tree. Figure 5 illustrates this recursive adjustment with a simple example. There is a recursive path from method a to method b back to method a. We find each repetition of the sequence after the first and insert it as a child of that first sequence. The exact algorithm we use is detailed in the next section.

4.3 Implementation

We have developed a tool which implements our subsuming methods analysis. The tool takes as input a CCT representing a captured execution profile. We represent a CCT using a typical tree data structure made up of Nodes as detailed in Listing 1. Each Node has a Method label, a cost, a

link to its parent and a list of children, all of which are populated when the CCT is input. Each Method has a populated list of the Nodes it is associated with, i.e. for all Nodes n it is true that $n.method.nodes.contains(n)$. The remaining fields in the Node and Method data structures are the ones that we calculate as part of our analysis. There is a Method object for each distinct method used by the application at runtime. In practice our Method object has fields for the method's name, owning class and signature, but these are not important for the description of the algorithms that follow. The root Node of the tree has a `null` parent.

Algorithm 1 Data-structures

    class Tree
        Node *root*
        List<Method> *methods*

    class Node
        Method *method*
        integer *cost*
        Node *parent*
        List<Node> *children*
        Node *adjustedParent*
        List<Node> *adjustedChildren*
        integer *height*
        integer *induced*

    class Method
        List<Node> *nodes*
        integer *maxHeight*
        integer *minDMD*
        integer *induced*

This input data can be obtained from a number of different open-source or commercial profilers that capture CCT structured profiles. We have implemented adapters for the popular commercial tool JProfiler and the open-source profiler JP2. We have also implemented a tool which will parse a series of thread dumps captured from a running JVM and build from them a rough statistical CCT profile. The details of these adapters are not interesting for the current discussion except to highlight the fact that our approach can be used in conjunction with a number of existing profiling tools and frameworks for a variety of languages and platforms.

The first algorithm we apply is the recursive reduction process shown in Listing 2. It traverses the CCT finding and then linking each node with its adjusted parent. To find the adjusted parent for a node we scan back through its ancestor nodes looking for the last two nodes with the same method label as the current node. We then compare the two subpaths, from the current node to the most recent occurrence of the same method and from the most recent to the second most recent occurrence of the method, and if they match we set the adjusted parent to be the parent of the most recent occurrence of the method, effectively removing the last repetition of the recursion. We do this scanning process not in the original tree but in the adjusted tree, meaning that earlier repeats of the recursion have already been removed, therefore all consecutive repetitions of the same recursion are reduced to a single occurrence.

The result of this algorithm is the adjusted tree with repeated recursive call patterns reduced to a single instance

Algorithm 2 Reduce Recursive Paths

function REDUCERECURSIVEPATHS(Node n)
   $n.adjustedParent \leftarrow$ FINDADJUSTEDPARENT(n)
   $n.adjustedParent.adjustedChildren.add(n)$
   for all Node c in $n.children$ **do**
      REDUCERECURSIVEPATHS(n)

function FINDADJUSTEDPARENT(Node $current$)
   Node $match1 \leftarrow$ **null**, $match2 \leftarrow$ **null**
   Node $n \leftarrow current.parent$
   while $n \neq$ **null** & $match2 =$ **null do**
      if $n.method = current.method$ **then**
         if $match1 =$ **null then**
            $match1 \leftarrow n$
         else
            $match2 \leftarrow n$
      $n \leftarrow n.adjustedParent$
   if $match1 =$ **null**$\|match2 =$ **null then**
      return $current.parent$
   Node $n1 \leftarrow current.parent$
   Node $n2 \leftarrow match1.adjustedParent$
   while $n1 \neq match1$ & $n2 \neq match2$ **do**
      if $n1.method \neq n2.method$ **then**
         return $current.parent$
      $n1 \leftarrow n1.adjustedParent$
      $n2 \leftarrow n2.adjustedParent$
   if $n1 \neq match1$\|$n2 \neq match2$ **then**
      return $current.parent$
   return $match1.adjustedParent$

Algorithm 4 Calculate Minimum DMD

function MINDMD(Method m)
   $m.minDMD \leftarrow \infty$
   Node $n \leftarrow m.nodes.getFirst()$
   $n \leftarrow n.adjustedParent$
   while $n \neq$ **null do**
      integer $dist \leftarrow$ DMD($n.method, m$)
      if $dist < m.minDMD$ **then**
         $m.minDMD \leftarrow dist$
      $n \leftarrow n.adjustedParent$

function DMD(Method p, Method m)
   integer $dmd \leftarrow 0$
   for all Node n in $m.nodes$ **do**
      integer $dist \leftarrow$ DISTANCE(p, n)
      if $dist > dmd$ **then**
         $dmd \leftarrow dist$
   return dmd

function DISTANCE(Method m, Node n)
   integer $dist \leftarrow 0$
   while true do
      $dist \leftarrow dist + 1$
      $n \leftarrow n.adjustedParent$
      if $n =$ **null then**
         return ∞
      if $n.method = m$ **then**
         return $dist$

as illustrated earlier in Figure 5. Note that every node from the original tree is included in the adjusted tree, so they contain the same number of nodes, all that has happened is that some nodes have been moved so they are inserted as the child of a node that was previously an ancestor higher in the tree, potentially reducing the overall height of the tree.

Once we have built our adjusted tree we use it to calculate the height of each node. This is a simple traversal (Listing 3) where we recursively calculate the height of each child and set our height to be one more than the maximum child's height. We also update the maximum height of the method associated with each node.

Next we calculate the minimum DMD for each method using the algorithm in Listing 4.

This is the most complex algorithm in our approach. The basic idea is to calculate the DMD for each method m to each of its dominating methods and find the smallest of these values to be the minimum DMD for m. However finding all the dominating methods for a method may be costly, so we

take advantage of the fact that each dominating method must exist on the call path for every node n that is labeled with m. This means we can choose any node labeled with m and we only need check the methods that are the labels of its ancestors in the CCT. In our implementation the method minDMD takes the first node labeled with m and walks back up the ancestor nodes to the root of the tree using the associated methods as candidate dominating methods. The method DMD calculates the dominating method distance from m to p and returns ∞ if p does not in fact dominate m.

Once we have the height and minimum DMD calculated for each method we can traverse the original tree and calculate the induced costs (Listing 5). For each node we calculate the induced cost of each child node and add it to the current node's induced cost if the child is labeled with a subsumed method. We also add the cost to the aggregated induced cost for the associated method.

Algorithm 3 Calculate Height

function CALCULATEHEIGHT(Node v)
   $v.height \leftarrow 0$
   for all Node c in $v.adjustedChildren$ **do**
      CALCULATEHEIGHT(c)
      if $c.height + 1 > v.height$ **then**
         $v.height \leftarrow c.height + 1$
   if $v.height > v.method.maxHeight$ **then**
      $v.method.maxHeight \leftarrow v.height$

Algorithm 5 Calculate Induced Cost

function CALCULATEINDUCEDCOST(Node n)
   $n.induced \leftarrow n.cost$
   for all Node c in $n.children$ **do**
      CALCULATEINDUCEDCOST(c)
      if ISSUBSUMEDMETHOD($c.method$) **then**
         $n.induced \leftarrow n.induced + c.induced$
   $n.method.induced \leftarrow n.method.induced + n.induced$

function ISSUBSUMEDMETHOD(Method m)
   return $(m = java.lang.Method.invoke())\|$
   $((m.maxHeight \leq H_{bound})$&$(m.minDMD \leq D_{bound}))$

As mentioned earlier the basis of our `isSubsumedMethod` check is a simple test of the already calculated maximum height and minimum DMD values against user defined constant values. The only extension to this that we have added is special handling for `java.lang.Method.invoke()` so that it is always marked as a subsumed method. Many Java libraries and frameworks make extensive use of reflection for various functionality. This means that `invoke` typically occurs in a large number of different contexts within a CCT, resulting in a large minimum DMD, and usually has a nontrivial height, as the methods being called via reflection are often non-trivial. Therefore without adding it as a special case it will often be listed as a subsuming method when in fact it is rarely interesting from a performance standpoint.

4.4 Implementation Efficiency

An important aspect of our approach is its efficiency. We are able to practically apply our approach to captured calling context tree profiles generated from large scale applications.

In terms of required space all the algorithms from the previous section operate on precisely the data structures we outlined without requiring anything more than the small constant number of variables they declare. For our data structures the space used is a constant amount of space for each node and method record plus the space required for the lists of child references. As each of these (the number of nodes, methods and total number of children) is bounded by the number of nodes in the CCT the space required for our representation is proportional to the size of the CCT.

Of course a number of the algorithms are recursive in nature and may generate a number of call stack frames but the recursion depth is bounded by the height of the CCT. Therefore the overall space requirements for processing a CCT with n nodes and a height of h is $O(n + h)$, which is equivalent to $O(n)$ given that $h \leq n$.

The recursive adjustment algorithm traverses every node in the tree but the calculation done at each node in findAdjustedParent uses only two loops each of which iterates over, at most, the ancestors of the current node. Hence findAdjustedParent has a worst case time proportional to the height of the original CCT and, since it is called once for each node in the CCT, the cost of building the adjusted tree is $O(n \times h)$. Given that for all but the most extremely unbalanced trees (which are very unlikely for CCTs of nontrivial applications) h is proportional to $\log n$ the average cost is $O(n \log n)$.

The height calculation is a simple constant time calculation for each node in the tree, so $O(n)$.

The minimum DMD calculation is the most expensive algorithm we undertake. For a CCT with n nodes, a height of h and m methods:

> minDMD is called m times.
> The loop in minDMD iterates at most h times.
> $\implies$ DMD is called at most h times for each method m.
> Now DMD calls distance once for each node labeled with m
> $\implies$ in total distance is called at most h times for each node in the CCT
> $\implies$ distance is called at most $h \times n$ times.
> The method distance is also $O(h)$ as the number of iterations for the loop it uses is bounded by the height of the CCT

> $\implies$ entire algorithm is $O(h \times h \times n)$.
> As before h is proportional to $\log n$ for all but the most unbalanced trees so the minimum DMD calculation is $O(n \log^2 n)$

Finally, assuming the `isSubsumedMethod` check is a constant time operation, the induced cost calculation, is a simple constant time calculation for each node in the CCT and is therefore $O(n)$. In our case the `isSubsumedMethod` check simply compares the already calculated height and minimum DMD to constant values.

5. EVALUATION

In order to evaluate our subsuming methods approach we have captured CCT profiles of the 14 benchmark applications in the DaCapo-9.12-bach suite [8] and applied our subsuming methods analysis to those captured profiles. Using the results of those experiments we have undertaken:

- A study of the characteristics of subsuming methods
- An empirical evaluation of the analysis time required
- Three detailed case studies that describe real problems found by our tool in the benchmark applications

All benchmarks were run with their default input size. All experiments were run on a quad-core 2.4 GHz Intel Core i7 with 8 GB 1600 MHz DDR3 memory running Mac OS X 10.9.3. We used Java SE Runtime Environment (build 1.7.0_40-b43) with the HotSpot 64-Bit Server VM (build 24.0-b56, mixed mode).

To capture the CCT profiles for each benchmark we used the open-source JP2 profiler developed at the University of Lugano [20, 21]. Our subsuming methods analysis can be applied to any CCT structured profile data but the JP2 profiler appealed to us for our experiments because it measures execution cost in terms of a platform independent metric, namely the number of bytecode instructions executed, which makes the captured profiles accurate, portable, comparable and largely reproducible. The only reason for variation in the profiles across multiple runs is non-determinism in the application or in the JVM (often related to thread scheduling in multi-threaded applications).

For the majority of the benchmarks we ran JP2 with the DaCapo-9.12-bach suite in the fashion outlined in the most recent JP2 paper [20], only adding our own custom 'dumper' which is used at program exit to serialise the captured JP2 profile to the binary CCT format our tool takes as an input. The framework activates the JP2 profiling using a callback mechanism that the DaCapo benchmark harness provides, so that the captured JP2 profiles include only the benchmark application code and not the benchmark harness. However we found that this approach only activated profiling for the thread that actually called the benchmark harness callback and any threads it subsequently created. For the client/server benchmarks (`tomcat`, `tradebeans` and `tradesoap`) and the benchmarks with background worker threads that were initialised before the main benchmark starts (`eclipse` and `xalan`) using the benchmark harness callback meant the captured profile included only a small fraction of the actual benchmark activity. Therefore for these 5 benchmarks we used our own wrapper which activated profiling for the entire run of the benchmark.

The results of our experiments on the DaCapo suite are summarised in Table 4. We ran and analysed each benchmark 5 times. Because of the very low variation between

Table 4: Results for DaCapo benchmarks when Subsuming Methods have height and $DMD_{min} > 4$

Benchmark	Instr Count (millions)	CCT Node Count			Method Count			$S(e)$	$S(i)$	$S(*)$	Analysis Time (ms)
		All	Subsuming	Ratio	All	Sub.	Ratio				
avrora	8393.98	176646.6	7158.0	4.05%	2189.0	74.0	3.38%	2	4	16	839.2
batik	2413.90	573887.0	48218.4	8.40%	6616.0	416.8	6.30%	0	2	18	3870.4
fop	863.41	628750.8	71429.8	11.36%	6709.4	345.0	5.14%	5	1	14	4512.4
luindex	2767.65	207279.0	7186.6	3.47%	2667.0	162.0	6.07%	3	1	16	980.0
lusearch	8121.91	59987.2	3850.2	6.42%	1726.0	73.0	4.23%	3	3	15	482.6
pmd	2272.56	4845777.8	1226270.6	25.31%	4573.2	266.2	5.82%	7	2	12	38424.4
sunflow	49626.02	299438.2	7666.4	2.56%	2341.6	106.0	4.53%	0	4	16	1087.2
xalan	8556.75	439529.6	38988.8	8.87%	4506.4	278.0	6.17%	1	5	15	2742.6
tradebeans	22799.24	8024512.8	1117675.8	13.93%	29111.6	2465.2	8.47%	6	4	10	52801.4
tradesoap	24768.51	8693078.0	1229925.6	14.15%	29913.8	2553.2	8.54%	4	1	15	62061.4
h2	12745.53	138520.2	17010.6	12.28%	1969.8	102.2	5.19%	4	3	13	1171.4
jython	12289.34	18982647.8	2667036.6	14.05%	5794.4	441.0	7.61%	7	1	12	215782.6
eclipse	67468.64	20670484.0	2942069.0	14.23%	16793.2	1841.0	10.96%	2	2	16	195120.6
tomcat	4067.95	2623250.6	357123.6	13.61%	13494.8	1025.2	7.60%	2	3	15	13823.2
Minimum				2.56%			3.38%	0	1	10	
Lower Quartile				6.91%			5.15%	2	1.25	13.25	
Median				**11.82%**			**6.12%**	3	2.5	**15**	
Upper Quartile				14.02%			7.61%	4.75	3.75	16	
Maximum				25.31%			10.96%	7	5	18	

$S(e)$ – The number of the top 20 subsuming methods that were also in the top 20 exclusive cost methods
$S(i)$ – The number of the top 20 subsuming methods that were also in the top 20 inclusive cost methods
$S(*)$ – The number of the top 20 subsuming methods that **did not** appear in either the top 20 exclusive or inclusive cost methods

each run our table only lists the average measurements across the 5 runs for each benchmark.[1] We characterised all methods with a height and minimum DMD greater than four as subsuming methods. We chose to use four as our threshold as it represents a relatively small distance in the CCT that can be readily visualised but still allows us to subsume a significant proportion of methods. We have also experimented with other small values and they generally return very similar results. The proportion of methods subsumed slowly increases as the threshold increases in an unsurprising manner.

The results show that:

- Across the benchmarks a median of 6.12% of all methods were subsuming methods
- The median size of the subsuming CCT was 11.82% of the size of the full CCT
- The median value for $S(*)$ was 15.

$S(*)$ measures the number of the top 20 subsuming methods (by induced cost) that did **not** appear in either the top 20 inclusive cost or the top 20 exclusive cost methods i.e. they represent code locations not directly highlighted by traditional measures. A median value of 15 implies 75% of the top 20 subsuming methods represented new potential optimisation opportunities. The compression results (only 6.12% of all methods and 11.82% of all CCT nodes were subsuming) demonstrate that subsuming methods analysis produces a CCT that is greatly reduced in size and has far fewer unique methods to inspect. We feel this substantially eases the task of interpreting the performance data.

We recorded the time taken to complete the analysis for each of our benchmarks. Note that this was the offline analysis time, it did not include the time taken to execute and profile each benchmark, only the time taken to parse and

load the previously recorded profile data and apply our subsuming methods analysis. In section 4.4 we analysed the efficiency of our analysis and showed that it was practical to apply our analysis to large sets of performance data. Here we have the empirical data to support that claim, even the largest of our data sets was able to be analysed in under 4 minutes. The graph in Figure 6 shows the relationship between the number of nodes in the CCT and the required analysis time. The fit line we have plotted is of the form $y = a + bx \log^2(x)$ where a and b are constants and x and y are the CCT node count and analysis time respectively. The

[1]https://www.cs.auckland.ac.nz/~dmap001/subsuming has more details and complete results.

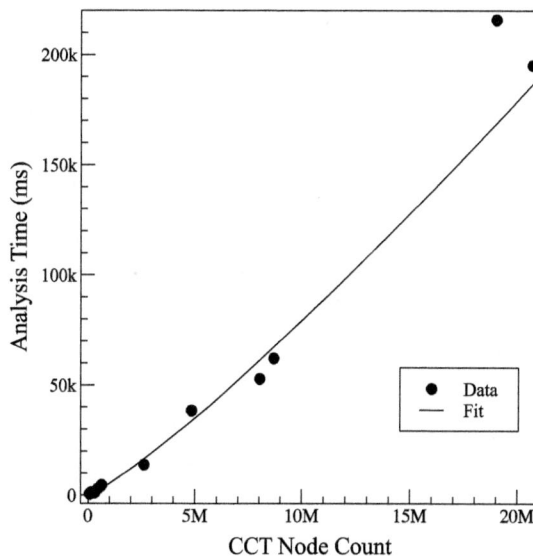

Figure 6: Analysis Time vs CCT Size

fit line indicates that the measured analysis time is very close to our theoretical complexity of $O(n \log^2 n)$.

5.1 Case Studies

We have undertaken a number of case studies to demonstrate the utility of using subsuming methods in performance analysis. Each of these case studies is based on one of the individual benchmarks from the DaCapo suite. Due to space limitations we have only been able to present a limited number of the case studies here. All of the analysis and implementation of improvements for all of the case studies was completed within a single week on code bases with which we were unfamiliar, highlighting the fact that the subsuming methods approach rapidly facilitated useful improvements in the benchmark code.

5.1.1 Case Study: fop

Our first case study, introduced earlier in section 2, is on the `fop` benchmark. As we described earlier the method `org.apache.xmlgraphics.ps.PSGenerator.formatDouble` accounts for over 26% of the total cost of the benchmark. This method uses a `java.text.NumberFormat` to convert a double into a Java string with a 3 decimal place format. Having identified this costly method we have been able to implement a highly customised version that performs the same transformation much more efficiently, leading to an overall improvement in the benchmark of 22%.

The difficult part of this optimisation was identifying the opportunity i.e. that `PSGenerator.formatDouble` was inefficiently using Java's general purpose number formatting library. We found this opportunity almost immediately using subsuming methods. The top subsuming method in our analysis, with an induced cost of 13.6% (and inclusive cost of over 26%), is `java.text.DecimalFormat.format`. Inspecting the callers of this method we find that it is being called over 99% of the time by `java.text.NumberFormat.format` which in turn is being called over 98% of the time by `PSGenerator.formatDouble`. In short it takes only a brief time inspecting the top subsuming method in the benchmark to highlight the `PSGenerator.formatDouble` method. All that remains is to inspect the source code for the `PSGenerator` class to identify the opportunity that exists to fix the inefficient formatting code.

5.1.2 Case Study: h2

The second case study is the `h2` benchmark that runs a series of SQL load tests via JDBC against the H2 pure Java relational database implementation.

The second highest subsuming method by induced time in the benchmark is `org.h2.jdbc.JdbcResultSet.getString`, with an induced cost of nearly 16% and inclusive cost of over 25%. This method is called repeatedly whilst processing the results of SQL queries to retrieve the individual values for each row and column. It performs the relatively simple task of retrieving the Java object value at a particular index in the result set and converting it to a Java string. There are two major inefficiencies in the implementation that we were able to fix. Firstly it performs a very expensive validity check (including testing whether the associated database connection is still valid) on every call, even though the results for the current row have already been retrieved into memory and accessing them does not require any use of the underlying database connection. Secondly the string conversion for date and timestamp columns relies on an inefficient `java.sql.Timestamp.toString` implementation. More than 40% of the method time is spent in `Timestamp.toString` even though less than 10% of the columns in the database are dates or timestamps. We were able to fix both of these issues by patching the H2 code to avoid the expensive validity check and the call to `Timestamp.toString`, which we replaced with our own string conversion routine. These fixes combined to reduce the cost of `JdbcResultSet.getString` by 66% and the overall cost of the benchmark by 17%.

5.1.3 Case Study: tomcat

Our final case study is on the `tomcat` benchmark. Tomcat is a popular Java HTTP web server and servlet engine implementation. Using subsuming methods analysis highlights two significant optimisation opportunities in the benchmark, though neither is an inefficiency in the Tomcat server codebase. These are real optimisation opportunities in terms of the benchmark itself, but are probably atypical in terms of how Tomcat is used in other scenarios. Nevertheless they are real problems in this benchmark that we were able to find and fix and the fact that they may be atypical implies that the `tomcat` benchmark itself may not be a great representation of a typical Tomcat server deployment.

The first opportunity is `org.dacapo.tomcat.Page.fetch`, which is the implementation of a HTTP client that drives the benchmark by sending a series of HTTP requests to the Tomcat server. Three of the top four subsuming methods by induced cost are being called by this method. In total the `Page.fetch` method has an inclusive cost of 49% of the entire benchmark. Checking the implementation reveals some major inefficiencies in processing the received HTTP responses. The responses (received initially as a stream of bytes) are converted to a Java string, this string is then converted back into a byte array to calculate an MD5 checksum for the response and compare it to an expected result. The string version of the response is then also formatted with platform specific line endings (using a regular expression search and replace) in preparation to be written to a local log file, but the response is only actually written to the log file in exceptional circumstances (such as when the checksum doesn't match the expected result). We changed the implementation to calculate the MD5 checksum directly from the received bytes and only create the string encoded response with platform specific line endings when actually necessary. This reduces the cost of `Page.fetch` by over 65%.

The second optimisation opportunity we identified from inspecting the list of top subsuming methods when sorted by inclusive time. As we briefly discussed in section 2 when working with the full list of methods (i.e. not filtered to just the subsuming methods) the list of top inclusive time methods is rarely helpful. It is naturally dominated by the methods near the root of the CCT and in large-scale object-oriented applications with large CCTs and deep calling hierarchies there are a large number of framework methods that come to dominate the list. When filtered to just the subsuming methods however, because one of our criteria for subsuming methods (namely requiring a non-trivial minimum DMD) naturally excludes methods used in a predictable fashion, the list better provides a succinct overview of the most costly interesting sub-trees in the CCT.

In the case of the `tomcat` benchmark the list allows to quickly find that `JspCompilationContext.compile`, which is the seventh method on the list, accounts for over 28% of the cost of the benchmark (`Page.fetch`, at 49%, was second on the list behind only `java.lang.Thread.run`). We were able to quickly confirm that this represented the time the benchmark was spending compiling requested JSP resources first into Java servlets and then into Java bytecode. However JSP resources can be precompiled. Doing this reduces the time being spent in the jasper compiler during the benchmark by 89%. The time was not completely eliminated because there was one JSP property group defined by Tomcat's example web application which relied on runtime properties and therefore triggered a recompilation of the associated JSP.

Neither of these optimisations were problems in the Tomcat server implementation, which is a mature and extensively tuned application, but they were both inefficiencies in the profiled benchmark that our subsuming methods approach allowed us to rapidly find and address. The combination of the two improvements produced a cost reduction in the benchmark of over 57%.

5.1.4 *Summary of Case Studies*

In our case studies we have been able to demonstrate the ability of subsuming methods analysis to aid in the identification of patterns of expensive methods calls that can then be optimised. Each case study highlighted a unique set of opportunities that were able to be addressed in different ways. For `fop` we were able to replace a powerful but inefficient generic library with a highly specialised approach. In the `h2` benchmark we removed unnecessary work (the validity checks) and optimised a poor `toString` implementation. In the `tomcat` benchmark we again removed unnecessary work in the client harness and avoided the cost of compiling JSP pages at runtime by precompiling them. All of these opportunities were readily found by investigating the results of the subsuming methods analysis.

6. DISCUSSION

Subsuming methods is a novel idea that provides additional insight into the runtime behaviour and performance of object-oriented applications. It enables us to discover new optimisation opportunities that are not apparent by inspecting the hot methods of an application. We regard it as a complementary approach, it provides the most benefit when used in conjunction with existing approaches to interpreting performance data (such as hot methods, calling context ring charts [18, 1] and using multiple context sensitive views [2]). It has the advantage of being efficient to apply as an offline analysis over data that can be obtained using a range of profiling tools. This means the approach is applicable in a range of performance investigations, from execution time and memory allocation profiling to more detailed analyses such as memory access patterns and CPU pipeline stalling instructions. It is also applicable in a range of runtime contexts, from detailed experimental performance analysis in dedicated test environments to the analysis of low overhead sampling profiles from production systems.

In section 4.1 we presented a particular approach for identifying subsuming methods, but there are other techniques that would complement or enhance our current approach. For example we are interested in using more sophisticated static analysis techniques, such as cyclomatic complexity measures, rather than height, as a measure of the range

of behaviour a method induces. We also plan to investigate using static analysis to identify subsuming methods in other ways, such as identifying classes that implement key interfaces or hold key controlling roles in an application.

One of the weaknesses of our current approach is that methods such as `java.lang.Method.invoke`, whose child method calls are determined by their parameter values and that are used in a large number of different calling contexts, may get highlighted as subsuming methods. In actual fact it is some ancestor method higher up the call chain that is 'responsible' for the cost of the child method calls as it constructed the parameter values to pass to the method. It is a straightforward problem to work around for specific cases but we are interested in developing a general heuristic or approach for identifying these methods.

The evaluation we have presented in this paper is based upon empirical results and case studies from the DaCapo benchmark suite. We chose to use the benchmark suite as it provides a good range of different runtime behaviours from an independent source. The benchmarks in the suite are not ideal as examples of large-scale applications but our results have been encouraging and indicate that our approach should scale up well to handle the software found in industry that motivated our work. We have recently completed an industrial case study in which we applied our approach to a real-world large-scale application with promising results.

7. CONCLUSION

Experienced software engineers know that there are repeated patterns of method calls within a profiled application, induced by the design patterns and coding idioms used by the software, which represent significant optimisation opportunities. In this paper we have presented an approach to assist in automatically detecting these repeated patterns. By identifying the key *subsuming* methods within the calling context tree profile we are able to discover new optimisation opportunities not readily apparent from the original profile data. Our approach is implemented as an efficient offline analysis that can be applied to previously collected data from existing tools and environments. This makes it practical to apply, even for large-scale live production systems, and a useful additional tool for a wide range of performance investigations.

8. ACKNOWLEDGMENTS

We would like to thank the anonymous reviewers for their helpful comments and suggestions.

David Maplesden is supported by a University of Auckland Doctoral Scholarship and the John Butcher One-Tick Scholarship for Postgraduate Study in Computer Science.

9. REFERENCES

[1] A. Adamoli and M. Hauswirth. Trevis: A Context Tree Visualization & Analysis Framework and its Use for Classifying Performance Failure Reports. *Proc. of the 5th Int'l Symp. on Software Visualization - SOFTVIS '10*, pages 73–82, 2010.

[2] L. Adhianto, J. Mellor-Crummey, and N. R. Tallent. Effectively presenting call path profiles of application performance. *39th Int'l Conf. on Parallel Processing Workshops*, pages 179–188, 2010.

[3] G. Ammons, T. Ball, and J. R. Larus. Exploiting hardware performance counters with flow and context sensitive profiling. *Proc. of the ACM SIGPLAN Conf. on Programming Language Design and Implementation - PLDI '97*, pages 85–96, 1997.

[4] M. Arnold and P. Sweeney. Approximating the calling context tree via sampling. *IBM TJ Watson Research Center*, 2000.

[5] S. Bhattacharya, M. G. Nanda, K. Gopinath, and M. Gupta. Reuse, Recycle to De-bloat Software. *Lecture Notes in Computer Science*, 6813:408–432, 2011.

[6] W. Binder. A Portable and Customizable Profiling Framework for Java Based on Bytecode Instruction Counting. *Lecture Notes in Computer Science*, 3780:178–194, 2005.

[7] W. Binder. Portable and accurate sampling profiling for Java. *Software: Practice and Experience*, 36(6):615–650, 2006.

[8] S. M. Blackburn, R. Garner, C. Hoffmann, A. M. Khan, K. S. McKinley, R. Bentzur, A. Diwan, D. Feinberg, D. Frampton, S. Z. Guyer, M. Hirzel, A. Hosking, M. Jump, H. Lee, J. E. B. Moss, A. Phansalkar, D. Stefanovic, T. VanDrunen, D. von Dincklage, and B. Wiedermann. The DaCapo Benchmarks: Java Benchmarking Development and Analysis. *Proc. of the 21st annual ACM SIGPLAN Conf. on Object Oriented Programming Systems Languages and Applications - OOPSLA '06*, pages 169–190, 2006.

[9] A. E. Chis, N. Mitchell, E. Schonberg, G. Sevitsky, P. O. Sullivan, T. Parsons, and J. Murphy. Patterns of Memory Inefficiency. *Lecture Notes in Computer Science*, 6813:383–407, 2011.

[10] D. C. D'Elia, C. Demetrescu, and I. Finocchi. Mining hot calling contexts in small space. *Proc. of the 32nd ACM SIGPLAN Conf. on Programming Language Design and Implementation - PLDI '11*, pages 516–527, 2011.

[11] B. Dufour, B. G. Ryder, and G. Sevitsky. Blended analysis for performance understanding of framework-based applications. *Proc. of the 2007 Int'l Symp. on Software Testing and Analysis - ISSTA '07*, pages 118–128, 2007.

[12] B. Dufour, B. G. Ryder, and G. Sevitsky. A scalable technique for characterizing the usage of temporaries in framework-intensive Java applications. *Proc. of the 16th ACM SIGSOFT Int'l Symp. on Foundations of Software Engineering - SIGSOFT '08/FSE-16*, pages 59–70, 2008.

[13] J. Larus. Spending Moore's Dividend. *Communications of the ACM*, 52(5):62–69, 2009.

[14] S. Lin, F. Ta'iani, T. C. Ormerod, and L. J. Ball. Towards Anomaly Comprehension: Using Structural Compression to Navigate Profiling Call-Trees. *Proc. of the 5th Int'l Symp. on Software Visualization - SOFTVIS '10*, pages 103–112, 2010.

[15] N. Mitchell, E. Schonberg, and G. Sevitsky. Four Trends Leading to Java Runtime Bloat. *IEEE Software*, 27(1):56–63, 2010.

[16] N. Mitchell, G. Sevitsky, and H. Srinivasan. The diary of a datum: an approach to modeling runtime complexity in framework-based applications. *Library-Centric Software Design - LCSD'05*, page 85, 2005.

[17] N. Mitchell, G. Sevitsky, and H. Srinivasan. Modeling Runtime Behavior in Framework-Based Applications. *Lecture Notes in Computer Science*, 4067:429–451, 2006.

[18] P. Moret, W. Binder, D. Ansaloni, and A. Villazón. Visualizing Calling Context Profiles with Ring Charts. *5th IEEE Int'l Workshop on Visualizing Software for Understanding and Analysis - VISSOFT '09*, pages 33–36, 2009.

[19] K. Nguyen and G. Xu. Cachetor: detecting cacheable data to remove bloat. *Proc. of the 2013 9th Joint Meeting on Foundations of Software Engineering - ESEC/FSE 2013*, pages 268–278, 2013.

[20] A. Sarimbekov, A. Sewe, W. Binder, P. Moret, and M. Mezini. JP2: Call-site aware calling context profiling for the Java Virtual Machine. *Science of Computer Programming*, 79:146–157, 2014.

[21] A. Sarimbekov, A. Sewe, W. Binder, P. Moret, M. Schoeberl, and M. Mezini. Portable and accurate collection of calling-context-sensitive bytecode metrics for the Java virtual machine. *Proc. of the 9th Int'l Conf. on Principles and Practice of Programming in Java - PPPJ '11*, page 11, 2011.

[22] O. Shacham, M. Vechev, and E. Yahav. Chameleon: Adaptive Selection of Collections. *Proc. of the ACM SIGPLAN Conf. on Programming Language Design and Implementation - PLDI '09*, pages 408–418, 2009.

[23] K. Srinivas and H. Srinivasan. Summarizing application performance from a components perspective. *Proc. of the 10th European Software Engineering Conf. held jointly with 13th ACM SIGSOFT Int'l Symp. on Foundations of Software Engineering - ESEC/FSE-13*, pages 136–145, 2005.

[24] G. Xu. Finding reusable data structures. *Proc. of the ACM Int'l Conf. on Object Oriented Programming Systems Languages and Applications - OOPSLA '12*, page 1017, 2012.

[25] G. Xu, N. Mitchell, M. Arnold, A. Rountev, E. Schonberg, and G. Sevitsky. Finding low-utility data structures. *Proc. of the ACM SIGPLAN Conf. on Programming Language Design and Implementation - PLDI '10*, pages 174–186, 2010.

[26] G. Xu, N. Mitchell, M. Arnold, A. Rountev, and G. Sevitsky. Software Bloat Analysis: Finding , Removing , and Preventing Performance Problems in Modern Large-Scale Object-Oriented Applications. *Proc. of the FSE/SDP Workshop on the Future of Software Engineering Research - FoSER 2010*, pages 421–425, 2010.

[27] G. Xu and A. Rountev. Detecting inefficiently-used containers to avoid bloat. *Proc. of the ACM SIGPLAN Conf. on Programming Language Design and Implementation - PLDI '10*, pages 160–173, 2010.

[28] D. Yan, G. Xu, and A. Rountev. Uncovering performance problems in Java applications with reference propagation profiling. *34th Int'l Conf. on Software Engineering (ICSE)*, pages 134–144, 2012.

Enhancing Performance And Reliability of Rule Management Platforms

Mark Grechanik
University of Illinois at Chicago
Chicago, IL 60607
drmark@uic.edu

B. M. Mainul Hossain
University of Illinois at Chicago
Chicago, IL 60607
bhossa2@uic.edu

ABSTRACT

RulE Management Platforms (REMPs) enable software engineers to represent programming logic as conditional sentences that relate statements of facts. A key benefit of REMPs is that they make software adaptable by burying the complexity of rule invocation in their engines, so that programmers can concentrate on business aspects of highly modular rules. Naturally, rule-driven applications are expected to have excellent performance, since REMP engines should be able to invoke highly modular rules in parallel in response to asserting different facts. In reality, it is very difficult to parallelize rule executions, since it leads to the loss of reliability and adaptability of rule-driven applications.

We created a novel solution that is based on obtaining a rule execution model that is used at different layers of REMPs to enhance the performance of rule-driven applications while maintaining their reliability and adaptability. First, using this model, possible races are detected statically among rules, and we evaluate an implementation of our abstraction of algorithms for automatically preventing races among rules. Next, we use the sensitivity analysis to find better schedules among simultaneously executing rules to improve the overall performance of the application. We implemented our solution for JBoss Drools and we evaluated it on three applications. The results suggest that our solution is effective, since we achieved over 225% speedup on average.

Categories and Subject Descriptors

D.2.10 [**Software Engineering**]: Design—*Representation*; I.2.4 [**Knowledge Representation Formalisms and Methods**]: Representations—*Rule-Based*; C.4 [**Performance of Systems**]: Reliability, availability, and serviceability

General Terms

Algorithms, Performance, Experimentation

Keywords

concurrency; parallelism; rule-driven application; expert system

1. INTRODUCTION

Widely used in different software applications (e.g., anti-money-laundering, fraud detection, network monitoring, stock exchange trading, insurance claim management, and risk assessment) [65, 63, 53, 77], *RulE Management Platforms (REMPs)* allow software engineers to represent programming logic as conditional sentences that relate statements of facts (i.e., rules) using high-level declarative languages [14, 29, 38, 41]. New facts are inferred in REMPs automatically using *modus ponens*. An example of a rule is "if an insurance customer filed a claim for over $1Mil and this customer is 30 year old or younger, then the insurance premium should be increased by 20% for this customer." Once the facts "an insurance customer filed a claim for over $1Mil" and "this customer is 30 year old or younger" are asserted, this rule is fired (or invoked) by the underlying REMP engine and a new fact is produced, i.e., the insurance premium for this customer is increased by 20%. The popularity of REMPs is partially explained by the ease of designing and maintaining the highly modular logic of rules [35, 39, 42, 47, 59, 17, 10]. Different stakeholders can independently design and deploy rules for *Rule-driven APplications (RAPs)* that run on top of REMPs, making RAPs highly *adaptable* to frequent changes in business requirements in today's dynamic world.

REMPs have become very important in the age of *big data*—collections of large-sized data sets that contain useful patterns and rules. Programmers often encode into RAPs patterns and rules that are extracted from big data (e.g., rules that describe increases in insurance premiums for customers with some risky behavior), so that these rules are invoked in business processes. RAPs are pervasive, they are used by many major insurance companies, government agencies, and various non-profit organizations [65, 33, 38]; for example, they are used to check for fraud for 90% of all credit card transactions in the USA in real time [65]. The market for REMP engines alone is estimated to be growing at the annual rate of 10.5%, reaching $1 Billion worldwide [38].

1.1 Background on REMPs

A key property of REMPs is that they encapsulate the control flow that includes fact inference and rule firing logics, while enforcing a fundamental separation of concerns of the control flow and the rule business logic. REMPs enable software engineers to concentrate on reasoning about higher-level business logic that they encode in rules without worrying about low-level details of rule invocations by effectively delegating this job to REMP engines. With this separation of concerns, RAPs are highly adaptable to changing requirements, since stakeholders simply add new rules as independent modules to RAPs and the underlying REMP engines ensure that these rules are fired when these conditions are met.

In a model for rule-based programming, rules can be viewed as decision points in some business process [46]. Martin Fowler views a rule-based computational model for REMPs as an alternative to the imperative model where sequences of `if-then` statements with conditionals and loops are evaluated in a strictly defined order. Having many `if-then` conditions results in a hard-to-maintain and inefficient code that is not *adaptable* to frequent changes in business requirements [26]. Moreover, since the conditional expressions of `if-then` statements must be evaluated by the runtime system, some overhead is incurred. In contrast, using rules replaces `if-then` statements with an optimized network of rule invocations that are controlled by the REMP engine. In addition, burying the complexity of reasoning about executions of multiple nested `if` statements inside the REMP engine enables stakeholders to write easy-to-comprehend rules that are more efficiently executed by REMPs, since runtime evaluation of many conditional expressions is avoided. Rules are often simple and they rarely contain complex nested loops and conditional statements [30, pages 495-558]; we use this insight to offer lightweight analysis to detect and prevent data races. Many problems naturally fit this model, since their solutions are often expressed using `if-then` rules.

Using the REMP model, it is easy to maintain and evolve RAPs, since rules often do not depend on one another [26, 51, 46, 55]. Adding new rules and replacing old rules does not require recompilation of the entire RAP's source code. Stakeholders can maintain different rules independently and these rules can be added to RAPs without regard to one another. Since rules are easy-to-comprehend and highly modular, it is easy to make changes to complex RAPs to enable large organizations to modify complex business processes inexpensively, hence RAPs are highly adaptable [30, pages 370].

1.2 Drawbacks of the REMP Model

These benefits have the other side. RAPs contain highly diverse rules, and it makes their analysis very difficult. Our investigation of dozens of open-source multithreaded Java applications showed that applications spawn many threads that execute a small subset of the application's methods, and still it is very difficult to reason about even a small number of concurrently executing methods [31].

In contrast, consider a RAP at a major insurance company that has over 30,000 different rules, many of which are written by different stakeholders. Our analysis showed that at any point hundreds to thousands of rules could be fired concurrently. "No one has any idea if there are conflicting rules when a new one is added" is a comment left on a programming forums that discuss pros and cons for using rules in applications [69]. "Rules should not be used if they are strongly connected Java files" is the other comment left on a different programming forum [70]. Redhat portal specifies: "Rules engines are not really intended to handle workflow or process executions nor are workflow engines or process management tools designed to do rules" [60]. These drawbacks highlight what happen when dependencies are introduced among rules – suddenly, they lose adaptability and they become very difficult to maintain and evolve. Hiding the logic that deals with these dependencies inside the REMP engine is a way to free stakeholders from dealing with the accidental complexity of explicitly coded dependencies among rules, thus ensuring adaptability of RAPs.

1.3 The PAR Model

A fundamental problem of REMPs that we address in this paper lies at the intersection of *Performance, Adaptability and Reliability (PAR)* that is shown in Figure 1. Recall that in today's rapidly changing business requirements, software adaptability is a critical element that ensures success [71, 16, 45, 25]. For example, an

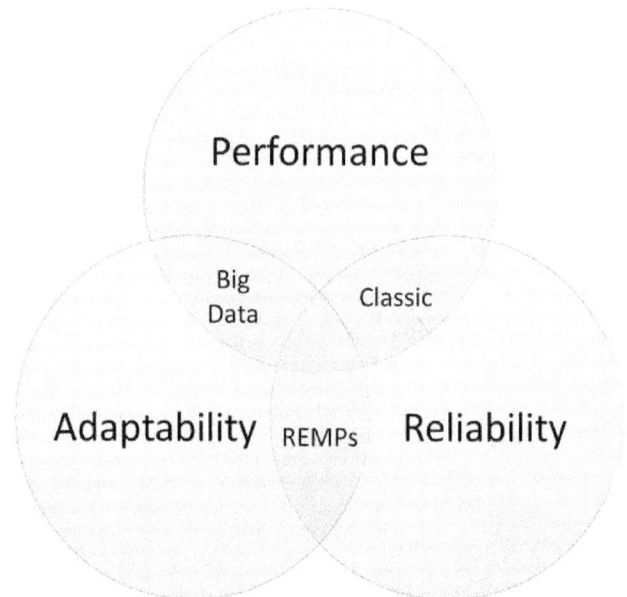

Figure 1: The PAR model.

efficient but inflexible software application makes it very difficult for businesses to refocus their effort on new revenue-generating opportunities. REMPs provide software adaptability by burying the complexity of rule invocation in REMP engines and enabling stakeholders to concentrate on business aspects of highly modular rules. Unlike RAPs, in "classic" software applications, modularity and adaptability are often sacrificed while optimizing these applications for performance and reliability [8]. With advent of big data and cloud computing, the focus shifted somewhat towards the intersection of adaptability and performance while sacrificing reliability, where applications are created from modular components (e.g., RapidMiner, Weka) that use machine learning and data mining algorithms to compute somewhat incorrect and approximate results fast and if needed, quickly change the configurations of these applications. New methodologies known as probabilistic programming and cloud accelerators put emphasis on computing approximate results faster and applying quick program repair techniques to allow buggy programs to complete calculations at the expense of reliability [23, 21, 22, 11, 52, 61, 64, 18].

Naturally, RAPs are expected to have excellent performance, since REMP engines should be able to invoke highly modular declarative rules in parallel in response to asserting different facts [75, 32, 30]. In some exceptional cases it is straightforward to do so, e.g., checking for credit card transaction fraud is done by invoking rules in parallel, since they almost never produce any side effects. However, in general, it is difficult to parallelize executions of rules.

Early languages for REMPs were purely declarative [41], however, over years, tight integration of RAPs with legacy systems made vendors mix imperative and declarative constructs [38, 53, 65, 33]. For example, programmers can define facts by assigning values to global variables. Prominent examples of open source REMPs with mixed languages include CLIPS [76], JESS [39] and JBoss Drools [5, 13], where C functions and Java methods are used in rules (see an example in Figure 2). Commercial REMPs with mixed language constructs include BizTalk by Microsoft [36] and Fusion by Oracle [27]. These and other REMPs fire rules sequentially [67], e.g., Oracle Fusion documentation states: "Rules fire sequentially, not in parallel. Note that rule actions often change the set of rule activations and thus change the next rule to fire" [58]. Thus, the results of the computations depend on the order of rule executions, i.e., if executing rules in parallel may lead to different results for the same input values (i.e., facts) and for the same environment configuration, hence the loss of reliability.

Not only do many REMPs execute RAPs sequentially, but also programmers are often restricted from using locks to handle concurrent accesses to resources from different RAPs to prevent races. Locks introduce complex dependencies among rules, thereby defeating the separation of concerns and eventually the adaptability of RAPs [56]. For example, waiting on locks to be released overrides the control flow computed by the underlying REMP engines. Clearly, programmers should be able to write their code for rules without worrying about races, and REMP engines should take care of rule firing and preventing data races at the same time. Thus, *a fundamental problem of REMPs is how to enhance the performance of RAPs without sacrificing their adaptability and reliability*, i.e., to move REMPs into the center of the PAR area in Figure 1.

1.4 Our Contributions

Our novel solution for enhancing *PErformance and Reliability for ruLe-driven ApplicaTiOns (PERLATO)* connects separate layers or REMPs in a way that enable us to solve the fundamental problem of REMP. First, we obtain a rule execution model from a RAP that approximate different execution scenarios by using the `if-then` structure of rules by analyzing their antecedents and consequents. To do that, we statically analyze conditions in antecedents of rules and possible ways that rules can be triggered by approximating the control flow in consequents. As a result of this analysis, we obtain constraints that can be solved using constraint solvers to obtain dependencies among rules. Second, the obtained rule execution model is used in PERLATO to detect races statically among these rules effectively and efficiently. A key idea is that if the rule execution model shows that some rules cannot run concurrently (e.g., one rule is triggered based on the constraint $x > y$ and the other rule is triggered based on the constraint $x < y$, where x and y some variables), the complexity of the data race analysis can be significantly reduced.

Next, the rule execution model and locking strategies for a given RAP are passed to the REMP engine, so that it can precompute an execution schedule for rules in a RAP to optimize the performance of the RAP. This is the essence of a *cross-layer design* where we pass the information that we compute at the application layer deep into the REMP engine layers to schedule rules in a way that lets faster executing rules proceed sooner and a longer executing rule to wait until other faster executing rules finish, so that some performance can be gained by reducing an average waiting time. Using a scheduler to enforce a specific order of rule execution is our novel way to optimize the performance of the RAP that addresses the issue of reliability, since the REMP engine will enforce locking and scheduling leading to the same results of executions for the same input data and environment configuration. This paper makes the following contributions.

- With PERLATO, we show how to parallelize rule execution automatically inside REMP engines without requiring programmers to use locks. Our tool and results are available at http://www.cs.uic.edu/~drmark/perlato.htm.

- Using sensitivity analysis [62], we show how to compute *symbiotic* schedules (i.e., co-scheduling conflicting jobs to achieve higher speedup [24, 68]) of execution of rules that have concurrent accesses to resources.

- We implemented PERLATO for JBoss Drools, an open-source enterprise-level REMP [5, 13] and we evaluated PERLATO on three RAPs. The results suggest that PERLATO is effec-

```
rule "Rule-Credit" salience 10                          1
when                                                    2
    $cashflow : Cashflow( $account:account,             3
    $date : date, $amount : amount,                     4
    type==Cashflow.CREDIT )                             5
    not Cashflow(account==$account,date<$date)          6
then                                                    7
    //some code                                         8
    $account.setBalance(                                9
        $account.getBalance()+$amount);                 10
    retract($cashflow);                                 11
end                                                     12
rule "Rule-Debit" salience 1                            13
when                                                    14
    $cashflow : Cashflow( $account : account,           15
    $date : date, $amount : amount,                     16
    type==Cashflow.DEBIT )                              17
    not Cashflow(account==$account,date<$date)          18
then                                                    19
    //some code                                         20
    if($account.getBalance()>$amount){                  21
        $account.setBalance(                            22
        $account.getBalance()-$amount); }               23
    else { new BlockedAccount($cashflow); }             24
    retract($cashflow);                                 25
end                                                     26
```

Figure 2: An example of debit and credit rules from a banking RAP that concurrently modify an account balance.

tive and efficient, since we achieved up to 225% speedup on average without observing any races.

- Summarily, we extend the theory of REMPs by enhancing their performance and reliability while preserving adaptability of RAPs without violating the separation of concerns between REMP engines and high-level rules.

2. THE PROBLEM

In this section, we provide a motivating example, discuss interplays between the components of the PAR model, and give the problem statement.

2.1 Motivating Example

Consider account debit and credit rules[1] that are shown in Figure 2 – they are similar to over 30,000 rules that an insurance claim handling RAP comprises at a major insurance company. The headers of the rules that are located in line 1 and line 13 contain the names of these rules, `Rule-Credit` and `Rule-Debit` correspondingly, and their *saliences*, with which programmers define priorities that the REMP engine should give to rules when choosing to execute them. The design idea of specifying the value of salience equal to 1 for rule `Rule-Debit` versus value 10 for rule `Rule-Credit` is to ensure that the REMP engine will first deposit money to the account before it subtracts an amount when both rules are triggered, thus preventing overdrafts in some cases.

Suppose that a bank user debits her account and a web store credits this account at the same time. Correspondingly, two `Cashflow` objects will be created that will trigger these rules by matching antecedents in the `when` parts of these rules in lines 2–6 and lines 14–18. The condition `not Cashflow` ensures that there is no

---
[1]http://docs.jboss.org/drools/release/5.2.0.
Final/drools-expert-docs/html/ch09.html

189

`Cashflow` object with an earlier date. In the end of the consequence part of the rule, the object `Cashflow` is retracted in line 11 and line 25 to ensure that it will not trigger rules any more. To handle overdrafts, the object of type `BlockedAccount` is created in line 24, and this fact will trigger some rules that handle overdrafts. Declarations of all classes are not shown here for simplicity.

Since JBoss Drools engine executes rules sequentially, there are no concurrency bugs in this example. However, doing so worsens the performance of RAPs. Code in lines 8, 11, 20, 24, and 25 can be executed in parallel, since locks are required only for the method `setBalance` in lines 9–10 and 21-23 to prevent a data race to update the value of the concurrently modified variable `account`. While it seems straightforward to parallelize the execution of rules and let programmers use locks, it would lead to serious problems.

2.2 Parallelism Interferes With Saliences

Since REMP engines execute rules sequentially, there are no concurrency bugs in our motivating example, but the performance of the RAP is much worse when compared with unrestricted parallel execution of rules. In a gedanken experiment, let us assume that a REMP engine executes rules in parallel, (e.g., one rule per thread) and lock objects are used to synchronize concurrent accesses. Since code in different rules (i.e., threads) locked by the same object cannot interleave, one thread will execute and the other thread will suspend execution until the first thread release the lock. However, this standard practice in multithreaded programming leads to serious challenges when applying it to RAPs – dependencies are introduced among different rules, leading to lost adaptability and making it very difficult to maintain and evolve RAPs.

Parallelizing rules and using synchronization locks interfere with salience values. Consider the situation when conditions of two or more rules are satisfied. These rules are fired, and during executing these rules more facts are asserted and `when` conditions of rules are satisfied, which leads to firing other rules until there are no more rules whose conditions are satisfied. The set of rules whose conditions are satisfied at any given time is called the *conflict set*. REMP engines employ different strategies for conflict resolution [41, pages 85-87], most popular of which are *random*, where rules are chosen to fire at random and *recent*, where rules are ranked higher if they use data that have been most recently created or modified in memory. These strategies work in conjunction with the values of salience, which programmers specify for some rules, and there lies a challenge.

Consider our example in Figure 2 and suppose that both rules are triggered at the same time. According to the higher value of salience, the rule `Rule-Credit` should be give a higher priority (e.g., by giving it a larger time slice to execute) by JBoss Drools (i.e., the REMP engine) before the rule `Rule-Debit`. However, the lock object may be reached faster in the rule `Rule-Debit`, after which the rule `Rule-Credit` will be put on hold to wait until the object is released. In this scenario, using a lock object effectively overrides the intention of the programmer to give the priority to the rule `Rule-Credit`. Moreover, a new `BlockedAccount` object that is created in line 17 may trigger more rules in the RAP that otherwise will not be triggered if the order of executing these rules would be different, i.e., no account overdraft occurs. Given the large number of possible interleavings among tens of thousands of rules in a RAP, it is very difficult to reason about interactions between saliences and synchronization lock mechanisms. Therefore, it is not enough to introduce locks to prevent races, rules must be scheduled in a way to preserve priority invariants that are embedded into saliences of these rules.

2.3 Reliability Meets Performance In REMPs

Loss or reliability of RAPs comes from two sources: different orders in which rules are executed by the REMP engines for consecutive runs of the same RAP with the same input facts and races between parallelized executions of rules. Recall from Section 1.3 that the Oracle Fusion documentation warns that rule actions often change the set of rule activations and thus change the next rule to fire. It is contrary to the classic example in the parallelism and concurrency theory, where two or more threads concurrently execute the same set of instructions (e.g., increment a variable) and as long as locks are applied correctly w.r.t. the atomicity assumptions, the result of the execution is always the same for the same input data. Adjusting this example to REMPs, we view a rule as a thread and these rules/threads execute different sets of instructions, some of which may spawn additional threads of execution based on the order in which program variables are assigned values in different threads. Reasoning about such complicated scenarios is difficult.

We studied two large insurance systems where REMP engines were allowed to execute rules in parallel. Performance is paramount for these systems and the reliability may be of lesser importance (e.g., a precise oracle is not known for an insurance quote or risk assessment due to the time-dependent nature of input data). Sometimes, it is more important that a RAP computes an approximately correct result fast like in the case of determining if a credit card transaction is fraudulent [12]. Since the user does not know what the correct result should be (e.g., a precise insurance quote), the user does not perceive any loss of reliability for a slightly different result. *However, when the system produces different results consecutively for the same computational task using the same input data, it is a serious problem, since it reduces the confidence of the users in the RAP and it impacts negatively their perception about the reliability of the RAP.*

Consider a situation where the user obtains an insurance quote from a RAP of some insurance company, then the user shops around, compares different quotes and comes back to the RAP from that insurance company to purchase the insurance. This time, when entering the same data the user will get a different quote. The loss of reliability comes from the fact that the execution order for different instructions can be affected by multiple factors beyond the control of stakeholders: input/output loads that lead to high variability in times that some instructions take to execute, the CPU load, RAM fragmentation and the frequency with which garbage collector is run, essentially, running other concurrent processes that steal CPU cycles and make RAP instructions execute longer. All in all, sometimes even slight changes in the non-functional parameters of the environment (e.g., paging on demand) for executing RAPs result in different orders of instruction interleavings that lead to different results, hence the loss of reliability. It is our goal to ensure reliability while parallelizing the execution of rules.

Even if locks could be used, it is difficult for programmers to make correct atomicity assumption and deal with *unserializable* executions, i.e., a property for the concurrent execution of several operations where their effect is not equivalent to that of a serial execution of these operations [49, 43, 48]. In our motivating example in Figure 2, it may be relatively easy to see that the code between lines 21–23 should be treated as atomic; however, for tens of thousands of rules that are written by different programmers, it is difficult to determine correct atomicity assumptions. Recall from Section 1.2 that stakeholders often do not have an idea how rules interact in a RAP. It is highly likely that even if programmers used synchronization locks in RAPs, which would defeat their adaptability, races would still remain and RAPs will not be reliable.

2.4 The Problem Statement

Our goal is to achieve with a high degree of automation the following multiple conflicting objectives: 1) enable REMPs to execute rules in RAPs in parallel; 2) do not violate the separation of concerns in REMPs by requiring programmers to use synchronization lock mechanisms for concurrent accesses to shared resources; 3) prevent races in parallelized RAPs without explicit using of locking mechanisms by programmers; 4) enable reliable executions by guaranteeing that the same RAP outputs the same values for the same input facts under the same hardware and software configurations, and 5) choose an effective schedule for executing rules that concurrently access the same resources to improve the overall performance of RAPs.

We aim to make PERLATO sound, i.e., to ensure the absence of races. It means that our solution should be conservative, since it assumes that all accesses to external resources (e.g., network, files, databases) are concurrent, and all statically unresolved references to variables in some rule are considered concurrent with all unresolved references to resources in other rules. At the same time, the execution of RAP should be parallelized to achieve a speedup when compared with the baseline approach when executions of all rules are sequentialized. In general, it is an NP-complete problem to detect all races [15]. There are many approaches for enabling race detection and protecting shared resources automatically using locks [9]. Once read-write and write-write concurrent accesses to resources among rules are identified, these approaches can be used to define synchronization of rules around these concurrent accesses.

It is not our goal to use these approaches in PERLATO, but to abstract them to study how much they can contribute to improving performance and reliability of RAPS. Since we use a sound conservative approach that leads to false positive conflicts, too many of them may lead to less than optimal parallelization strategies for RAPs. Our insight is that a point of attack is based on using a rule execution model that can eliminate many infeasible scenarios when rules cannot be instantiated concurrently based on contradictions among their antecedents.

3. OUR SOLUTION

In this section, we discuss key ideas of our solution, explain the architecture of PERLATO, give an algorithm for synchronizing concurrent accesses to resources in REMPs, and describe how we select schedules for parallelization of rules.

3.1 Key Ideas

Our key idea is threefold. First, we obtain a rule execution model, which is an overapproximation of the actual behavior of RAP. Our goal is to determine rules with concurrent accesses to the same resources that cannot be executed at the same time due to contradictions in their antecedents. Using this model, read-write and write-write concurrent accesses to resources are obtained from rules in RAPs statically. Naturally, there will be false positives, since our analysis can miss contradictions in rule antecedents. Since our goal is to make PERLATO a sound approach, we will make conservative approximations about read-write and write-write concurrent accesses to resources among rules, which may negatively affect the speedup that is achieved by parallelizing the execution of rules. However, as we show in Section 4, we achieve significant speedup even with this conservative approach.

We consider three abstract levels to synchronize rules based on the scope: rule-level, atomic section level, and a single operation which accesses a resource (or variable) concurrently. Rule-level synchronization has the coarsest granularity – the entire rule is locked by a REMP when executed and other conflicting rules wait

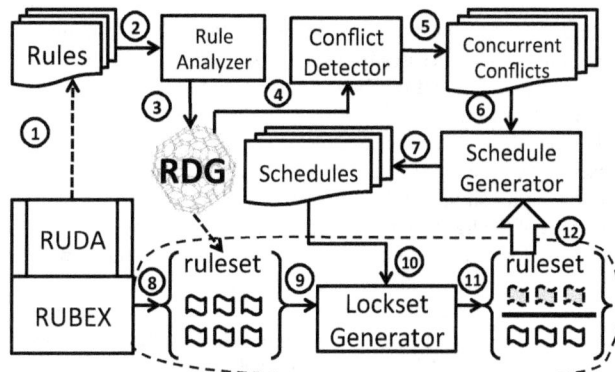

Figure 3: PERLATO's architecture and workflow.

upon completion of the executing rule. With atomic synchronization, a REMP places the lock before the first conflicting operation for a rule and holds this lock until the last conflicting operation is executed. Finally, the finest granularity of synchronization is when the lock is acquired before a conflicting operation access a shared variable and released right after it is executed. We experiment with these synchronization levels and we show in Section 4 that speedup is significant between rule and atomic synchronization levels.

The third part of our idea is to schedule executions of rules around synchronization locks, so that the same results will be consistently outputted if the same RDA is executed with the same input values under the same hardware/software configuration. That is, we impose a complete order among all rules that are fired and are in the working memory (i.e., a special memory region in REMPs where fired rules are placed for execution) that have conflicts with one another and this order is imported and used by REMPs for subsequent executions of the RAPs. We show in Section 4 that ordering rules with read-write and write-write concurrent accesses to resources guarantees the consistency of output results and achieves a speedup of up to 25% for atomic level synchronization level when the same RAP is executed with the same input values under the same hardware/software configuration.

3.2 PERLATO Architecture

The architecture of PERLATO is shown in Figure 3. Solid arrows show command and data flows between components, dashed arrows show relations between components and the block arrow with the label (12) indicates a feedback loop; numbers in circles indicate the sequences of operations in the workflow. The input to PERLATO is the set of rules of the RAP, and it is specified with the dashed arrow labeled (1). The RAP is hosted and run on top of a REMP. The output of PERLATO is the scheduled rule set that is specified with the arrow labeled (11).

We use a lightweight static analysis for detecting read-write and write-write concurrent accesses to resources among rules. Recall from Section 1.1 that rules are often simple and they rarely contain complex nested loops and conditional statements; in addition, recall from Section 1 that only few rules access resources concurrently. The latter makes sense; too many dependencies among rules defeat a goal of using a REMP in the first place, since stakeholders will not be able to obtain benefits that we discussed in Section 1.1. Therefore, our insight is to use lightweight context-insensitive interprocedural analysis to resolve references to objects and their fields. To do that, we construct and traverse a *control-flow graph (CFG)* of the RAP. When traversing the CFG we obtain a list of all objects and their fields that are referenced in rules. We perform virtual-call resolution using static class hierarchy analysis, and we take a conservative approach by accounting for all references of methods that can potentially be invoked. We also automatically assign concurrent accesses to all unresolved references including network calls, file and database accesses. This conservative approach catches all races, but it also produces false positives that will reduce the performance of PERLATO. However, even with this conservative baseline the performance of PERLATO improves the state-of-the-art significantly as we show in Section 5.

As part of the lightweight static analysis, the Rule Analyzer (2) inputs rules and then produces (3) a rule execution model which (4) is used by the Conflict Detector (5) to obtain read-write and write-write concurrent accesses to resources, i.e., Concurrent Conflicts, which are the input (6) to the Schedule Generator that uses a race detection algorithm (7) to output Schedules for synchronization locks for handling these concurrent accesses within the REMP engine. This information is buried within the REMP engine thus preventing additional accidental complexity.

The dynamic phase of PERLATO starts with executing the RAP on top of the REMP where some facts are asserted and (8) a rule set is computed that includes the rules that are triggered by the asserted facts. At this point, this rule set is supplied (9) into the Lockset Generator along with (10) the precomputed Schedules that uses a locking strategy to output (11) a partitioned rule set (it is shown with the thick horizontal line that separated rules with dashed line border on top and solid border rules on the bottom). This top section of the rule set contains rules that can be executed in parallel and the bottom section contains rules whose execution order is defined based on the precomputed schedule. At this point, REMP continues to execute rules of the RAP. The REMP engine periodically applies sensitivity analysis [62] during RAP maintenance phases (e.g., regression testing) to perturb schedules and determine a better one that can improve the performance thus (12) realizing a feedback loop.

3.3 PERLATO Lockset Algorithm

Our algorithm for generating execution schedules and synchronization locks is shown in Algorithm 1. Our goal is to abstract existing race detection algorithms, so that we can roughly evaluate the bounds in performance improvements that these algorithms can give. Algorithm 1 consists of two procedures: the procedure `ComputeLockset` that determines sets of locks for each pair of rules with read-write and write-write concurrent accesses to resources and the procedure `AtomicLocks` that computes atomic syncronization locks for all pairs of rules with concurrent accesses. We give the algorithm only for atomic levels because rule-based and shared variable-based lock levels are trivial to compute.

The algorithm's procedure `ComputeLockset` takes as its input the set of all rules in the RAP with read-write and write-write concurrent accesses to resources, $\mathcal{R}$ and it outputs sets of locks for each pair of rules, (L_{ij}^s, L_{ij}^e). A key idea of this procedure is to compute the set of lock starts, L_{ij}^s and lock exits, L_{ij}^e for the rule r_i assuming that it executes concurrently with some other rule, r_j. This algorithmic procedure consists of two nested loops between Lines 3–14. For each pair of rules, r_i and r_j the set of conflicts is computed in Line 6 where it is placed in the variable V_{ij}. If at least one of these rules accesses a shared variable with the write access (see Line 7), we compute the locations of accesses to these variables within the rule in Lines 8–12. Correspondingly, we update the values of (L_{ij}^s, L_{ij}^e) for these rules. Once the loops finish, the procedure terminates. As a results, all locks are computed conservatively for all combinations of read-write and write-write concurrent accesses in rule pairs.

The algorithm's procedure `AtomicLocks` in Line 17 that takes as its input the set of rules for which lock sets are computed by the

---

Algorithm 1 Obtaining atomic synchronization locks for rules.

```
 1: ComputeLockset( Set of rules R )
 2:   V ← ∅ {Initialize the set of conflicts}
 3:   for all r_i ∈ R do
 4:     L_ij^s ← ∅, L_ij^e ← ∅ {Initialize the values of lock sets for each
           pair of rules to empty. L^s designates where the lock is placed
           and L^e where it ends in the rule r_i when it is executed with
           the rule r_j.}
 5:     for all r_j ∈ R ∧ r_i ≠ r_j do
 6:       V_ij ← conflict(r_i, r_j)
 7:       if access(V_ij, r_i) = W ∨ access(V_ij, r_J) = W then
 8:         if loc(r_i, V_ij) < loc(r_i, L_ij^s) then
 9:           L_ij^s ← V_ij
10:         else if loc(r_i, V_ij) > loc(r_i, L_ij^e) then
11:           L_ij^e ← V_ij
12:         end if
13:       end if
14:     end for
15:   end for
16:   return (L_ij^s, L_ij^e)
17: AtomicLocks( Set of rules R )
18: for all r_i ∈ R do
19:   L_i^s ← END_OF_RULE_i, L_i^e ← START_OF_RULE_i
20:   for all r_j ∈ R ∧ r_i ≠ r_j ∧ conflict(r_i, r_j) ≠ ∅ do
21:     if L_i^s > loc(r_i, L_ij^s) then
22:       L_i^s ← L_ij^s
23:     end if
24:     if L_i^e < loc(r_i, L_ij^e) then
25:       L_i^e ← L_ij^e
26:     end if
27:     if r_i ∉ S then
28:       S ↦ S ∪ r_i
29:     end if
30:   end for
31: end for
32: return S, L_i^s, L_i^e
```

---

procedure `ComputeLockset`, $\mathcal{R}$ and it outputs sets of atomic locks for each rule, r_i, L_i^s and L_i^e and the sequence, S for entering atomic sections protected by lock sets for rules with concurrent accesses to resources. Lines 18–32 in Algorithm 1 specify the body of the procedure `AtomicLocks`. For each rule, the lock indicators L_i^s and L_i^e are initialized in Line 19. While iterating through all rules in the triggered rule set, $\mathcal{R}$ in Lines 20–31, the procedure computes the minimum size atomic section of shared variables that that are concurrently accessed by other rules and this section will be protected by synchronization locks within the REMP engine. We sort rules in a random order; precedence is given to rules with higher values of salience; among rules with the same salience we sort them in a random order and assign unique sequence integers to them and we use these integers to add rules to the sequence set S in Lines 27–29 that is used in a rule scheduler within the REMP engine. The algorithm terminates when all rules are explored.

3.4 Achieving Reliability By Determining And Enforcing Schedules In REMPs

Recall the example from Section 2.3 that shows the loss of reliability in REMPs, where the user of an insurance RAP runs it twice with the same inputs and obtains a different quote. Our idea is to determine execution schedules for conflicting rules for RAPs, so that rule saliences are respected.

Our idea of computing optimal execution schedules to enforce the same results for executing the RAP with the same input data is based on our observation that a REMP engine usually hosts one RAP, since industrial RAPs are big and mission critical, and it is impractical to run more than one such RAP on top of a REMP engine. In contrast, the schedulers of operating system kernels do not preempt processes to avoid race conditions, since it is not feasible to find an optimal context switching schedule quickly for multiple processes and the overhead of doing it is prohibitive. However, in the case of REMPs it is possible to precompute an execution schedule for a RAP using our rule execution model and the REMP engine will use it to both improve the performance and guarantee reliability without requiring stakeholders to change their existing programming practices.

THEOREM 1. *If the RAP is executed two or more times with the same input values and the same environment configuration, then PERLATO preserves the output values for this RAP.*

PROOF. The proof is by contradiction. Let us assume that two executions of the same RAP using the same starting states produced different output values. Since the starting state is the same, it would mean that the execution orders $S^m \neq S^{m+1}$ or the interleavings of instructions are different for executing rules. However, race detection algorithmic procedures from Algorithm 1 guarantee that every possible conflict is protected by locks, thus preventing instruction interleavings within atomic sections that are protected by the same locks. Moreover, the scheduler will ensure that the order of rule execution is always the same for the same starting states for the same RAP. Therefore, the same values are produced for both executions leading to the same output values, hence the contradiction. □

3.5 Symbiotic Scheduling

Recall from Section 1 that *symbiotic* scheduling is co-scheduling conflicting jobs to achieve higher speedup of execution of rules that have concurrent accesses to shared resources. Symbiotic scheduling is widely used in the schedulers of simultaneous multithreading processors [24, 68]), and we apply it in PERLATO to determine if it is possible to improve the performance of RAPs over time.

Our idea is the following. Using sensitivity analysis [62], we permute the order that is computed in Algorithm 1 in which conflicting rules are scheduled to access resources concurrently using synchronization locks. For our motivating example that is shown in Figure 2 we will change the order of rules `Rule-Debit` and `Rule-Credit`. A goal of this operation is to obtain samples of alternative orders of executions that may give us clues if scheduling of rules can be changed to improve the overall performance of the RAP. Of course, this exercise should be done independently from live production execution of RAPs, so that the consistency of the output values will not be violated. We suggest that this exercise can be done as part of acceptance testing of RAPs. We experiment with symbiotic scheduling and show that the overall performance of RAPs can be improved by up to 20% in Section 5.

4. EXPERIMENTAL EVALUATION

In this section, we pose research questions (RQs), explain our methodology and variables and discuss threats to validity.

4.1 Research Questions

We seek to answer the following research questions.

RQ1: Is PERLATO effective in achieving higher speedups?

RQ2: Is finer granularity locking strategy more effective in obtaining higher speedup for RAPs?

RQ3: Is symbiotic scheduling effective in obtaining higher speedups?

The rationale for RQ1 is to compare the elapsed time it takes to execute RAPs using the baseline approach with the original JBoss Drools sequential rule execution engine to the elapsed time it takes to execute these RAPs using parallel versions of JBoss Drools. Our goal is to show that PERLATO is more effective than this baseline approach. The rationale for RQ2 is determine if finer granularity locking leads to much higher speedups. Recall that PERLATO allows three types of locking strategies: **R**ule-level locking were all concurrent accesses in a given rule are protected using synchronization lock objects as the rule is about to execute and released only after the REMP engine finishes executing the rule; **A**tomic locking that is shown in Algorithm 1 where the section of the rule code is locked starting with the first concurrent access and this lock is released with the last concurrent access; and finally, the resource- or **V**ariable-level locking where each operation that uses concurrently shared variables is surrounded with a lock/unlock commands. Using rule-level locking is the simplest locking strategy, but it may lead to unnecessary waits by other rules with concurrent accesses; and the variable-level locking strategy seems to be most efficient, but it may leads to the increased frequency of deadlocks. Answering RQ2 will help programmers select an optimal locking strategy. Finally, the rationale behind RQ3 is to determine if symbiotic scheduling results in higher speedups for RAPs versus the baseline approach where the schedule is computed by Algorithm 1.

4.2 Subject Applications

We evaluate PERLATO on three RAPs, each of which has been developed by five to eight graduate students as part of their master project work and taking a graduate course on distributed object programming at the University of Illinois at Chicago. Characteristics of the subject RAPs are shown in Table 4. The number of concurrently accesses variable is small, and it is expected to be small, since it is an indication of good rule design. Each subject RAP uses a database, and we report information about databases in the last three columns. With our conservative static analysis the numbers of false positive are large percentagewise, even though their absolute values are small. It is more important to determine how they affect the speedup that can be achieved with parallelizing the JBoss Drool engine.

4.3 Methodology

We aligned our methodology with the guidelines for statistical tests to assess randomized approaches in software engineering [2]. Since parallel execution with different input facts may result in different speedups, several executions with different inputs for subject RAPs are required to answer the RQs. Our goal is to collect highly representative samples of runs when applying different approaches, perform statistical tests on these samples, and draw conclusions from these tests. Since our experiments involve the probability of obtaining different speedups when executing subject RAPs with different input facts, it is important to conduct the experiments multiple times to pick the average to avoid skewed results. For each subject RAP, we ran each experiment 50 times with each approach to obtain a good representative sample.

Our first set of experiment is to obtain baseline indicators of the performance of the sequential and fully parallelized JBoss Drools engine. Recall that the state-of-the-art implementation is sequential and a fully parallelized version does not use any synchronization locks. Even though the latter implementation does not prevent any races, it gives us an upper bound on the performance of RAPs.

The second set of experiments involve using synchronization locks at the **R**ule, **A**tomic (computed using Algorithm 1), and **V**ariable

Table 1: Characteristics of the subject applications: their code name and the full name are shown in the first and the second columns respectively followed by the lines of code, *LOC* column. The next column, *Rules*, shows the total number of rules followed by the total number of shared variables, S_{var} that may be accessed concurrently from different rules. The next column shows the total number of false positives, *FPs* detected through static analysis, then the maximum number of rules, R_{max} that concurrently accessed at least one variable and the minimum number of rules, R_{min} that concurrently accessed at least one variable. Last three columns show the number of tables in the database that the RAPs access, the number of rows and the number of columns in those tables.

Application	Name	LOC	Rules	S_{var}	FPs	R_{max}	R_{min}	Tables	Rows	Cols
EEWS	Early Epidemic Warning System	4,029	13	8	4	6	2	6	1,005,918	27
TAXC	TAX Calculator	13,215	23	5	2	8	2	28	179,372,032	89
IMS	Insurance Management System	17,249	79	5	1	33	27	10	1,076,550	78

levels. Intuitively, we expect that the performance of RAPs should be better than the one of the sequential rule execution but lower when compared to the fully parallelized JBoss Drools engine.

For symbiotic scheduling, we perform 50 runs for each set of input facts using different permutations of schedules for each run, and then we compute the average elapsed execution time and the variance for each run from the average execution time. Then, we select a schedule that has the least sum of variances for different sets of input facts.

4.4 Variables

We have three independent variables: the subject RAP, the approach (DROOLS or PERLATO), and sets of input facts for each RAP. For the approach DROOLS we have two types of experiments: sequential and parallel version of the engine. For PER-LATO, there are three types of experiment: the **R**egular or baseline, where a subject RAP is run using the rule-level synchronization, the experiment with the **A**tomic-level synchronization that enables concurrent execution of unsynchronized parts of rules from subject RAPs, and finally, the experiment with **V**ariable synchronization that enables RAPs to execute with the highest concurrency.

We measure the performance of RAPs as the elapsed execution time, and it is a dependent variable. Using its values we obtain speedups for PERLATO when compared with the baseline sequential JBoss Drools engine. We repeated each experiment 10 times. Thus, the total number of experiments is equal to three RAPs × (three types (R,A,V) for PERLATO + two types (Seq and Par) for DROOLS) × three sets of input facts × 50 times = 2,250 experiments. We report statistical results.

4.5 Hypotheses

We introduce the following null and alternative hypotheses to evaluate how close the means are for speedups for different approaches. We seek to evaluate the following hypotheses at a 0.05 level of significance.

H_0 The primary null hypothesis is that there is no difference in the values of speedup between R, A, and V approaches for all subject RDAs.

H_1 An alternative hypothesis to H_0 is that there is statistically significant difference in the values of speedups between R, A, and V approaches for all subject RDAs.

Once we test the null hypothesis H_0, we are interested in the directionality of means, μ, of the results of control and treatment groups. We are interested to compare the effectiveness of the R, A, and V approaches vs one another.

H1 (Speedup of R versus A). The effective null hypothesis is that $\mu_R = \mu_A$, while the true null hypothesis is that $\mu_R \leq \mu_A$. Conversely, the alternative hypothesis is $\mu_R > \mu_A$.

H2 (Speedup of R versus V). The effective null hypothesis is that $\mu_R = \mu_V$, while the true null hypothesis is that $\mu_R \leq \mu_V$. Conversely, the alternative hypothesis is $\mu_R > \mu_V$.

H3 (Speedup of A versus V). The effective null hypothesis is that $\mu_A = \mu_V$, while the true null hypothesis is that $\mu_A \leq \mu_V$. Conversely, the alternative is $\mu_A > \mu_V$.

The rationale behind the alternative hypotheses to H1–H3 is that finer granularity locking may lead to higher speedups. These alternative hypotheses are motivated by our belief that finer granularity locking may not necessarily lead to statistically significant increase of speedups, given the complexity of even small RAPs and dependencies among their rules that are introduced by locks.

4.6 Threats to Validity

A threat to the validity of this experimental evaluation is that our subject programs are relatively small; it is difficult to find large open-source RAPs. Large RAPs may have millions of lines of code and use databases whose sizes are measured in thousands of tables and attributes. Those RAPs may have different characteristics compared to our smaller subject programs. On the one hand, increasing the size of RAPs to millions of lines of code is unlikely to affect the time and space demands of our analyses because PERLATO only considers conflicts among concurrently accessed variables, and by the nature of rule-based programming, rules do not share many variables. Thus, the majority of the source code of RAPs is ignored in the conflict analysis, which is focused on concurrent accesses to shared variables among rules. Evaluating this impact is a subject of future work.

Additional threats to validity of this study is that we used graduate students as programmers who created RAPs, and this task should be tackled by professional programmers. However, many of these students have at least one year of professional programming experience, thereby reducing this threat to validity. The other threat to validity is that we tried to avoid complex logics, and we issued instructions to students to restrict the subject RAPs by writing rules under the default agenda group `MAIN` of drools and also by writing rules without many complicated attributes such as `ruleflow-group`, `activation-group`, `date-expires`.

Finally, recall that our conflict analysis is conservative and there are many false positives. Improving the precision of this analysis may also improve the overhead of PERLATO. It is also unclear how well PERLATO will perform on many different and diverse RAPs, so this is a threat to external validity of our results.

5. RESULTS

In this section, we report the results of the experiment and evaluate the null hypotheses. We use one-way ANOVA and t-tests for paired two sample for means to evaluate the hypotheses that we stated in Section 4.5. Results of our experiments are provided in Table 2. We used ANOVA to evaluate the null hypothesis H_0 that

Table 2: PERLATO experimental results. The first four columns specify the name of the RAP, the sequence number for collections of input facts that are inputs for the RAPs, the number of asserted facts and the total number of fired rules during the execution of the RAPs. Next columns report average, median, minimum, and maximum execution times for two types of approaches (DROOLS and PERLATO). Two types of DROOLS approach are (sequential and parallel) and three types of PERLATO approach are rule level, atomic level and variable level for 50 execution runs of each experiment.

Application	Input Set	Facts	Rules Fired	Approach	Type	Avg	Med	Min	Max	σ^2
EEWS	1	246896	1088	DROOLS	Seq	32.22	32.08	31.559	35.358	0.4
					Par	9.52	9.27	8.267	11.789	0.87
				PERLATO	Rule	13.44	13.6	10.927	14.911	0.99
					Atomic	10.85	10.82	10.21	11.867	0.14
					Variable	10.67	10.67	10.21	11.359	0.06
	2	334220	1454	DROOLS	Seq	42.31	42.12	41.508	43.322	0.21
					Par	11.62	11.53	10.299	14.126	0.85
				PERLATO	Rule	18.86	19.02	15.794	21.549	2.07
					Atomic	15.62	15.58	15.016	16.476	0.11
					Variable	15.08	15.02	14.24	16.689	0.21
	3	247113	572	DROOLS	Seq	19.51	19.44	18.906	21.115	0.24
					Par	6.05	6.19	3.947	8.242	1.32
				PERLATO	Rule	8.33	8.22	7.025	9.442	0.42
					Atomic	7.24	7.13	6.837	8.259	0.13
					Variable	6.79	6.76	6.662	7.165	0.02
TAXC	1	16	95	DROOLS	Seq	20.4	20.32	20.023	20.97	0.06
					Par	19.52	19.52	19.115	20.072	0.07
				PERLATO	Rule	19.71	19.69	19.232	20.657	0.13
					Atomic	19.62	19.61	19.144	20.227	0.08
					Variable	19.55	19.52	19.077	20.161	0.08
	2	22	162	DROOLS	Seq	42.48	42.48	41.553	43.63	0.32
					Par	34.27	34.6	31.866	36.019	1.13
				PERLATO	Rule	36.87	36.83	36.016	37.812	0.19
					Atomic	36.86	36.77	36.007	37.775	0.21
					Variable	36.8	36.74	35.972	37.698	0.23
	3	10	66	DROOLS	Seq	11.78	11.73	11.549	12.344	0.04
					Par	9.85	9.87	9.116	10.314	0.05
				PERLATO	Rule	9.93	9.9	9.641	10.431	0.03
					Atomic	9.91	9.92	9.145	10.342	0.04
					Variable	9.98	9.97	9.309	10.761	0.06
IMS	1	17	124	DROOLS	Seq	8.58	8.59	8.102	8.838	0.01
					Par	2.42	2.42	1.543	3.721	0.11
				PERLATO	Rule	3.08	3.06	2.862	3.618	0.02
					Atomic	3.07	3.08	2.809	3.598	0.02
					Variable	4.46	4.44	4.35	4.736	0.01
	2	75	550	DROOLS	Seq	60.02	60.02	58.883	61.681	0.44
					Par	11.86	11.97	7.074	16.414	4.51
				PERLATO	Rule	10.94	11.05	9.41	12.579	0.42
					Atomic	10.02	10.04	9.242	10.948	0.23
					Variable	15.79	15.78	15.499	16.362	0.01
	3	120	880	DROOLS	Seq	37.76	37.66	37.502	39.536	0.09
					Par	23.29	24.51	15.33	27.849	10.26
				PERLATO	Rule	19.7	19.73	18.43	21.88	0.55
					Atomic	18.78	18.69	17.022	21.016	1.1
					Variable	32.73	32.92	30.445	34.785	0.99

the variation in an experiment is no greater than that due to normal variation of individuals' characteristics and error in their measurement. The results of ANOVA confirm that there are large differences between the groups for R, A, and V for RAPs as shown in Table 3. Based on these results we can reject the null hypothesis for RAPs EEWS and IMS and we accept the alternative hypothesis H_1. We accept the null hypothesis for the application TAXC. One explanation for TAXC is that the code for rules that concurrently access variables contains very few statements that can be executed in parallel; as a result, R, A, and V synchronization lock

approaches do not lead to increased parallelism and subsequently, higher speedup values.

Not surprisingly, the speedup is the highest between the fully unsynchronized parallel execution and fully sequential execution – the maximum speedup is close to 600%, with races, of course. However, an average speedup is 225% across three subject RAPs for all three synchronization approaches. These numbers are in the ballpark of the reported results from a major insurance company whose REMP is fully parallelized and where synchronization was

Table 3: Results of ANOVA tests for sets of input facts.

RAP	Input	F	F_{crit}	p	Test H_0
EEWS	1	77.3	4.4	$\approx 6.2 \cdot 10^{-8}$	Accept
	2	65.6	3.35	$\approx 4.3 \cdot 10^{-11}$	Accept
	3	31.3	3.35	$\approx 9.2 \cdot 10^{-8}$	Accept
TAXC	1	1.97	3.35	0.16	Reject
	2	0.19	3.35	0.83	Reject
	3	2,41	3.35	0.1	Reject
IMS	1	789.6	3.35	$\approx 1.1 \cdot 10^{-24}$	Accept
	2	256.5.6	3.35	$\approx 2.7 \cdot 10^{-18}$	Accept
	3	789.6	3.35	$\approx 1.1 \cdot 10^{-24}$	Accept

Table 4: Results of experiments with symbiotic schedules.

Application	Input	Best Schedule	Avg	Var
EEWS	1	10.489	10.4	0.01
	2	15.339	15.19	0.06
	3	6.923	6.95	0.01
TAXC	1	19.428	19.57	0.05
	2	36.028	36.8	0.06
	3	9.286	9.55	0.09
IMS	1	3.084	2.76	0.01
	2	9.297	9.43	0.06
	3	17.409	17.32	0.82

experimentally tried at our request. Interestingly, the company suggested that they may go with a higher speedup and tolerate incon.

To test the null hypothesis H1, H2, and H3 we applied two t-tests for paired two sample for means, for elapsed execution times for different experiments. Based on these results we reject the null hypotheses H1 and H3, and we accept the alternative hypotheses that say that **atomic-level synchronizations result in higher speedups than using rule and variable-level synchronization locks**. The hypothesis H2 is accepted, leading us to conclude that **using variable-level synchronization locks does not lead to higher speedups when compared with rule-level synchronization locks**. Possible explanations include a significantly increased overhead of locking on the variable level and greater difficulty to find an optimal schedules for rule executions.

The results of experiments for computing an optimal symbiotic schedule are shown in Table 4 for 10 independent runs of subject RAPs with schedules that are randomly permuted. These results suggest that it is possible to identify an optimal schedule among rules that concurrently access resources that are protected by using synchronization objects. Obtaining sample runs for computing a symbiotic schedule with different permuted schedules can be done during testing of RAPs. Of course, more research is needed to investigate this issue, and we report preliminary results in this paper.

Summary. Based on our experimental results, we can answer affirmatively to RQ1 that PERLATO is effective in increasing speedup for subject RAPs and to RQ3 that symbiotic scheduling is effective in obtaining higher speedup for RAPs. However, our answer is negative to RQ2, since we determined that a finer granularity locking strategy is not more effective in speeding up RAPs.

6. RELATED WORK

Related work to PERLATO consists of two sections: research on detecting and eliminating races in multithreaded applications and research for improving reliability of rule-driven applications. We believe that our work is the first at the intersection of these two important areas.

There is a multitude of research in detecting and preventing races in multithreaded applications and we concentrate on related work that goes beyond race detection in multithreaded Java and C++

applications. There is an excellent survey for race detection and prevention techniques [9], however, it does not discuss RAPs. Neither does a paper on taxonomy of race conditions mentions REMPs [37]. Our ideas of fast and large-scale race detection are related to RacerX [20], however, it is unclear how RacerX can be applied to RAPs. Recent work includes partial detection and prevention of certain races in Ajax applications [1], file systems [73], workflow applications [72], relational databases [28, 40], and web services [79], however, no work is done in rule-driven applications. CARISMA is a recent work that is related to PERLATO, where dynamic race detectors explore multiple thread schedules of a multithreaded program over the same input to detect data races [78]. In contrast, PERLATO uses a combination of static and dynamic analysis among rules in RAPs, however, ideas of CARISMA are complementary to PERLATO. An interesting use of thread scheduling for executing multiple replicas of the program may lead to prevention of data races, and we may research the application of this approach to RAPs in future work [74].

The contribution of the software engineering community to rule-based programming is limited. Weyuker et al published one of first papers where an algorithm is presented for reliability testing of rule-based systems [3]. Same authors published a paper eight years later on estimating CPU utilization in rule-based systems [4]. Some approaches on testing knowledge systems use the ideas of rule-based development [54, 44, 34, 6], however, we know of no papers that investigated races in RAPs using the fundamental notion of separation of concern like we do in PERLATO. A related area of research investigates checking consistency and completeness of rule-based expert systems [57, 50, 19]. An idea of using control and data flow in testing RAPs was proposed by Barr [7], but it was never applied to deal with races. Some approaches deal with error checking and bug finding in RAPs[66]. However, these approaches do not address races in RAPs.

7. CONCLUSION

RulE Management Platforms (REMPs) are widely used in enterprise applications in which programming logic is represented using *rules*, which are executed sequentially by REMPs. We created a novel solution that is based on obtaining a rule execution model that is used at different layers of REMPs to enhance the performance of rule-driven applications while maintaining their reliability and adaptability. First, using this model, possible races are detected statically among rules, and we evaluate an implementation of our abstraction of algorithms for automatically preventing races among rules. Next, we use the sensitivity analysis to find better schedules among simultaneously executing rules to improve the overall performance of the application. We implemented our solution for JBoss Drools and we evaluated it on three applications. The results suggest that our solution is effective, since we achieved over 225% speedup on average.

Acknowledgments

This work is supported by NSF CCF-1217928, CCF-1017633, and Microsoft SEIF. We warmly thank Chen Fu and Andrea Bonisiol for their contributions at the initial stage of the project.

8. REFERENCES

[1] T. J. Albert, K. Qian, and X. Fu. Race condition in ajax-based web application. ACM-SE 46, pages 390–393, New York, NY, USA, 2008. ACM.

[2] A. Arcuri and L. C. Briand. A practical guide for using statistical tests to assess randomized algorithms in software engineering. In *ICSE*, pages 1–10, 2011.

[3] A. Avritzer, J. P. Ros, and E. J. Weyuker. Reliability testing of rule-based systems. *IEEE Softw.*, 13(5):76–82, Sept. 1996.

[4] A. Avritzer, J. P. Ros, and E. J. Weyuker. Estimating the cpu utilization of a rule-based system. WOSP '04, pages 1–12, New York, NY, USA, 2004. ACM.

[5] M. Bali. *Drools JBoss Rules 5.0 Developer's Guide*. Packt Publishing, 2009.

[6] V. Barr. Applications of rule-base coverage measures to expert system evaluation. In *Journal of Knowledge Based Systems*, pages 411–416. Press/ MIT Press, 1998.

[7] V. Barr and D. V. Barr. Rule-based system testing with control and data flow techniques, 1996.

[8] D. S. Batory, R. Gonc_c alves, B. Marker, and J. Siegmund. Dark knowledge and graph grammars in automated software design. In *SLE*, pages 1–18, 2013.

[9] N. E. Beckman. A survey of methods for preventing race conditions, 2006.

[10] A. Ben-David. Rule effectiveness in rule-based systems: A credit scoring case study. *Expert Syst. Appl.*, 34(4):2783–2788, May 2008.

[11] J. Bornholt, T. Mytkowicz, and K. S. McKinley. Uncertain<t>: A first-order type for uncertain data. In *ASPLOS*, pages 239–248, 2014.

[12] E. A. Brewer. Towards robust distributed systems (abstract). PODC '00, pages 7–, New York, NY, USA, 2000. ACM.

[13] P. Browne. *JBoss Drools Business Rules*. Packt Publishing, 2009.

[14] B. G. Buchanan and R. O. Duda. Principles of rule-based expert systems. Technical report, Stanford University, Stanford, CA, USA, 1982.

[15] S. Carr, J. Mayo, and C.-K. Shene. Race conditions: a case study. *J. Comput. Sci. Coll.*, 17(1):90–105, Oct. 2001.

[16] L. Chung, K. Cooper, and A. Yi. Developing adaptable software architectures using design patterns: An nfr approach. *Comput. Stand. Interfaces*, 25(3):253–260, June 2003.

[17] R. Dazeley, P. Warner, S. Johnson, and P. Vamplew. The ballarat incremental knowledge engine. In *Proceedings of the 11th PKAW*, PKAW'10, pages 195–207, Berlin, Heidelberg, 2010. Springer-Verlag.

[18] B. Demsky and M. C. Rinard. Goal-directed reasoning for specification-based data structure repair. *IEEE Trans. Software Eng.*, 32(12):931–951, 2006.

[19] R. Djelouah, B. Duval, and S. Loiseau. Validation and reparation of knowledge bases. In *Proceedings of the 13th ISMIS '02*, ISMIS '02, pages 312–320, London, UK, UK, 2002. Springer-Verlag.

[20] D. Engler and K. Ashcraft. Racerx: effective, static detection of race conditions and deadlocks. SOSP '03, pages 237–252, New York, NY, USA, 2003. ACM.

[21] H. Esmaeilzadeh, A. Sampson, L. Ceze, and D. Burger. Architecture support for disciplined approximate programming. In *ASPLOS*, pages 301–312, 2012.

[22] H. Esmaeilzadeh, A. Sampson, L. Ceze, and D. Burger. Neural acceleration for general-purpose approximate programs. In *MICRO*, pages 449–460, 2012.

[23] H. Esmaeilzadeh, A. Sampson, L. Ceze, and D. Burger. Neural acceleration for general-purpose approximate programs. *IEEE Micro*, 33(3):16–27, 2013.

[24] S. Eyerman and L. Eeckhout. Probabilistic job symbiosis modeling for smt processor scheduling. In *ASPLOS*, pages 91–102, 2010.

[25] M. Fayad and M. P. Cline. Aspects of software adaptability. *Commun. ACM*, 39(10):58–59, Oct. 1996.

[26] M. Fowler. Should i use a rules engine? *martinfowler.com*, Jan. 2009.

[27] H. Gaur and M. Zirn. *Oracle Fusion Middleware Patterns*. Packt Publishing, 2010.

[28] S. Ghandeharizadeh and J. Yap. Gumball: a race condition prevention technique for cache augmented sql database management systems. DBSocial '12, pages 1–6, New York, NY, USA, 2012. ACM.

[29] J. C. Giarratano and G. Riley. *Expert Systems: Principles and Programming*. Brooks/Cole Publishing Co., Pacific Grove, CA, USA, 1989.

[30] J. C. Giarratano and G. D. Riley. *Expert Systems: Principles and Programming*. Brooks/Cole Publishing Co., Pacific Grove, CA, USA, 2005.

[31] M. Grechanik, C. McMillan, L. DeFerrari, M. Comi, S. Crespi-Reghizzi, D. Poshyvanyk, C. Fu, Q. Xie, and C. Ghezzi. An empirical investigation into a large-scale java open source code repository. In *ESEM*, 2010.

[32] A. Gupta, C. Forgy, A. Newell, and R. Wedig. Parallel algorithms and architectures for rule-based systems. In *Proceedings of ISCA*, ISCA '86, pages 28–37, Los Alamitos, CA, USA, 1986. IEEE Computer Society Press.

[33] K. Harris-Ferrante and S. Forte. Hype cycle for p&c insurance. *Gartner*, July 2009.

[34] R. Hartung and A. Hρ akansson. Automated testing for knowledge based systems. KES'07/WIRN'07, pages 270–278, Berlin, Heidelberg, 2007. Springer-Verlag.

[35] D. Heckerman and E. Horvitz. The myth of modularity in rule-based systems. *CoRR*, abs/1304.3090, 2013.

[36] J. Hedberg, K. Weare, and M. la Cour. *MCTS: Microsoft BizTalk Server 2010 (70-595) Certification Guide*. Packt Publishing, 2012.

[37] D. P. Helmbold and C. E. McDowell. A taxonomy of race conditions. Technical report, University of California at Santa Cruz, Santa Cruz, CA, USA, 1994.

[38] S. D. Hendrick. Worldwide business rules management systems 2009-Ü2013 forecast update and 2008 vendor shares. *IDC*, Oct. 2009.

[39] E. F. Hill. *Jess in Action: Java Rule-Based Systems*. Manning Publications Co., Greenwich, CT, USA, 2003.

[40] J. M. Hughes and H. Bolinder. Testing a database for race conditions with quickcheck: none. Erlang '11, pages 72–77, New York, NY, USA, 2011. ACM.

[41] P. Jackson. *Introduction to Expert Systems, 3rd Edition*. Addison-Wesley, 1999.

[42] R. J. K. Jacob and J. N. Froscher. A software engineering methodology for rule-based systems. *IEEE Trans. on Knowl. and Data Eng.*, 2(2):173–189, June 1990.

[43] G. Jin, L. Song, W. Zhang, S. Lu, and B. Liblit. Automated atomicity-violation fixing. In *Proceedings of the 32nd ACM SIGPLAN conference on Programming language design and implementation*, PLDI '11, pages 389–400, New York, NY, USA, 2011. ACM.

[44] J. D. Kiper. Structural testing of rule-based expert systems. *ACM Trans. Softw. Eng. Methodol.*, 1(2):168–187, Apr. 1992.

[45] L. Lahav. Hobbes framework: An adaptable solution to web-driven applications. *Comput. Stand. Interfaces*, 25(3):271–274, June 2003.

[46] B. A. Lieberman. Requirements for rule engines. *IBM DeveloperWorks*, Nov. 2012.

[47] L. Lin, S. M. Embury, and B. C. Warboys. Facilitating the implementation and evolution of business rules. ICSM '05, pages 609–612, Washington, DC, USA, 2005. IEEE Computer Society.

[48] S. Lu, S. Park, E. Seo, and Y. Zhou. Learning from mistakes: a comprehensive study on real world concurrency bug characteristics. *SIGPLAN Not.*, 43(3):329–339, Mar. 2008.

[49] S. Lu, S. Park, and Y. Zhou. Finding atomicity-violation bugs through unserializable interleaving testing. *IEEE Trans. Softw. Eng.*, 38(4):844–860, July 2012.

[50] S. Lukichev. Improving the quality of rule-based applications using the declarative verification approach. *Int. J. Knowl. Eng. Data Min.*, 1(3):254–272, Dec. 2011.

[51] S. Luypaert. Rule engines in java: Jboss drools. *Java, JBoss Drools*, July 2010.

[52] A. Mccallum, K. Schultz, and S. Singh. Factorie: Probabilistic programming via imperatively defined factor graphs. In *In Advances in Neural Information Processing Systems 22*, pages 1249–1257, 2009.

[53] D. W. McCoy. Taking the mystery out of business rule representation. *Gartner*, Mar. 2009.

[54] T. Menzies and B. Cukic. On the sufficiency of limited testing for knowledge based systems. ICTAI '99, pages 431–, Washington, DC, USA, 1999. IEEE Computer Society.

[55] C. Moran. Does your project need a rule engine? *Java Developer's Journal*, June 2004.

[56] R. H. B. Netzer and B. P. Miller. What are race conditions?: Some issues and formalizations. *ACM Lett. Program. Lang. Syst.*, 1(1):74–88, Mar. 1992.

[57] T. A. Nguyen, W. A. Perkins, T. J. Laffey, and D. Pecora. Checking an expert systems knowledge base for consistency and completeness. IJCAI'85, pages 375–378, San Francisco, CA, USA, 1985. Morgan Kaufmann Publishers Inc.

[58] Oracle. Oracle fusion middleware user's guide for oracle business rules. *Oracle Documentation,http://docs.oracle.com/cd/E21764_01/integration.1111/e10228/intro.htm*, May 2011.

[59] S. Purohit and K. Jamdaade. Rule based system to facilitate the immunity of hiv/aids patients using ayurveda therapy. CUBE '12, pages 226–234, New York, NY, USA, 2012. ACM.

[60] redhat. Why use a rule engine? *Customer Portal,https://access.redhat.com/site/documentation/en-US/JBoss_Enterprise_SOA_Platform/4.2/html/JBoss_Rules_Manual/sect-JBoss_Rules_Reference_Manual-Why_use_a_Rule_Engine.html*, Feb. 2013.

[61] D. Roy. Probabilistic-programming.org. *http://probabilistic-programming.org/wiki/Home*, Feb. 2014.

[62] A. Saltelli, M. Ratto, T. Andres, F. Campolongo, J. Cariboni, D. Gatelli, M. Saisana, and S. Tarantola. *Global Sensitivity Analysis: The Primer*. Wiley-Interscience, Hoboken, NJ, Feb. 2008.

[63] W. Schulte and J. Sinur. Rule engines and event processing. *Gartner*, Mar. 2009.

[64] S. Sidiroglou-Douskos, S. Misailovic, H. Hoffmann, and M. C. Rinard. Managing performance vs. accuracy trade-offs with loop perforation. In *SIGSOFT FSE*, pages 124–134, 2011.

[65] J. Sinur. The art and science of rules vs. process flows. *Gartner*, Mar. 2009.

[66] C. Sinz, T. Lumpp, J. Schneider, and W. Küchlin. Detection of dynamic execution errors in {IBM} system automation's rule-based expert system. *Information and Software Technology*, 44(14):857 – 873, 2002.

[67] S. Smith and A. Kandel. *Verification and Validation of Rule-Based Expert Systems*. CRC Press, Inc., Boca Raton, FL, USA, 1994.

[68] A. Snavely, D. M. Tullsen, and G. M. Voelker. Symbiotic jobscheduling with priorities for a simultaneous multithreading processor. In *SIGMETRICS*, pages 66–76, 2002.

[69] stackoverflow. Rules engine - pros and cons. *stackexchange,http://stackoverflow.com/questions/250403/rules-engine-pros-and-cons/398389#398389*, Dec. 2008.

[70] stackoverflow. When should you not use a rules engine? *stackexchange,http://stackoverflow.com/questions/775170/when-should-you-not-use-a-rules-engine*, Nov. 2011.

[71] N. Subramanian and L. Chung. Software architecture adaptability: An nfr approach. IWPSE '01, pages 52–61, New York, NY, USA, 2001. ACM.

[72] X. Sun, A. Agarwal, and T. S. E. Ng. Attendre: mitigating ill effects of race conditions in openflow via queueing mechanism. ANCS '12, pages 137–138, New York, NY, USA, 2012. ACM.

[73] P. Uppuluri, U. Joshi, and A. Ray. Preventing race condition attacks on file-systems. SAC '05, pages 346–353, New York, NY, USA, 2005. ACM.

[74] K. Veeraraghavan, P. M. Chen, J. Flinn, and S. Narayanasamy. Detecting and surviving data races using complementary schedules. SOSP '11, pages 369–384, New York, NY, USA, 2011. ACM.

[75] C.-C. Wu. Parallelizing a clips-based course timetabling expert system. *Expert Syst. Appl.*, 38(6):7517–7525, June 2011.

[76] R. M. Wygant. Clips - a powerful development and delivery expert system tool. *Comput. Ind. Eng.*, 17(1):546–549, Nov. 1989.

[77] M. G. Yunusoglu and H. Selim. A fuzzy rule based expert system for stock evaluation and portfolio construction: An application to istanbul stock exchange. *Expert Syst. Appl.*, 40(3):908–920, Feb. 2013.

[78] K. Zhai, B. Xu, W. K. Chan, and T. H. Tse. Carisma: a context-sensitive approach to race-condition sample-instance selection for multithreaded applications. ISSTA 2012, pages 221–231, New York, NY, USA, 2012. ACM.

[79] J. Zhang, S. Su, and F. Yang. Detecting race conditions in web services. AICT-ICIW '06, pages 184–, Washington, DC, USA, 2006. IEEE Computer Society.

Exploiting Software Performance Engineering Techniques to Optimise the Quality of Smart Grid Environments

Catia Trubiani
Gran Sasso Science Institute
L'Aquila, Italy
catia.trubiani@gssi.infn.it

Anne Koziolek
Karlsruhe Inst. of Technology
Karlsruhe, Germany
koziolek@kit.edu

Lucia Happe
Karlsruhe Inst. of Technology
Karlsruhe, Germany
lucia.happe@kit.edu

ABSTRACT

This paper discusses the challenges and opportunities of Software Performance Engineering (SPE) research in smart-grid (SG) environments. We envision to use SPE techniques to optimise the quality of information and communications technology (ICT) applications, and thus optimise the quality of the overall SG. The overall process of Monitoring, Analysing, Planning, and Executing (MAPE) is discussed to highlight the current open issues of the domain and the expected benefits.

Categories and Subject Descriptors

C.4 [**Performance of Systems**]: Modeling techniques

Keywords

Smart grid environment; software performance engineering; quality optimisation

1. INTRODUCTION

An intelligent power distribution system, Smart Grid (SG), is a modernized electrical grid that uses information and communications technology (ICT) to gather and act on information in an automated fashion to improve the efficiency and economics, dependability and security, and resilience of the whole life cycle of electric energy[1] from generation and transmission to distribution and consumption of electricity [13]. SG is a term used to describe the broad scope of interdependent systems where ICT plays a crucial role that will bring significant economical and environmental benefits to consumers, organisations and countries deploying ICT-intensive SG technologies.

---

[1]Electric energy is called just "energy" throughout this paper. We also use the common terms "produce (electric) energy" and "consume (electric) energy" etc. while it is clear that energy is never created or lost, but always just converted to other forms of energy.

ICPE'15, Jan. 31–Feb. 4, 2015, Austin, Texas, USA.
Copyright © 2015 ACM 978-1-4503-3248-4/15/01 ...$15.00.
http://dx.doi.org/10.1145/2668930.2695532.

SG environments are complex, real-world aware systems of systems that must integrate and interoperate across a broad spectrum of heterogeneous business and operation domains involving multiple enterprises and customers. Numerous technological innovations will be required to enable smart grid environments. These innovations will come from multiple fields and disciplines including real world aware systems of systems, modelling, analysis, optimisation, security, silicon technology, and physical science [10]. Existing deployments of SG technology (e.g., Grid4EU[2] and SmartWatts[3]) operate only with few participants. However to meet the requirements for large scale deployments we have to evaluate in advance scalability of these technologies and ability to provide required processing capabilities. An estimation in [11] indicates that an overwhelming data would be generated by Smart Meters (SMs), 22GB of data per day from 2 million customers with 30s measurement rate per each SM.

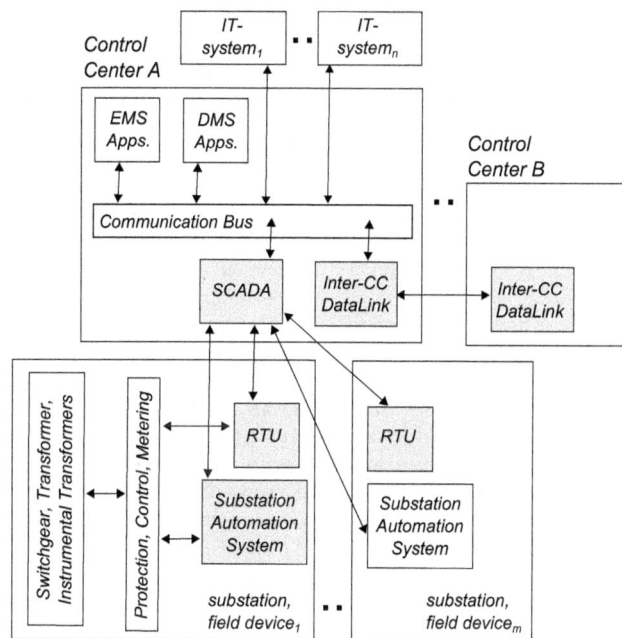

Figure 1: Smart grid environments - basic concepts.

In this paper we focus on ICT aimed at facilitating the distribution of power energy to improve the management of

---

[2]http://www.grid4eu.eu
[3]http://www.smartwatts.de

smart grid supply and demand. In particular we are interested to evaluate the quality of smart grid environments that brings novel challenges to the power grid engineers, such as the assessment of the suitable architecture that fits the metering system requirements (size and rate of measurement messages) or the tradeoffs involved to efficiently engineer the power distribution when of example the goal is to reduce the large-scale deployment cost.

Figure 1 reports the basic concepts [1] of an SG environment we target in this paper: (i) control centers (CC) need to handle unprecedented operational demands, (ii) substation field devices include remote terminal units (RTU) and substation automation systems that communicate with SCADA (system control and data acquisition). Goal of this paper is to provide a vision of the ICT challenges and opportunities of research in the area of designing high-quality SG environments. In particular, we envision to evaluate how the use of software performance engineering (SPE) techniques [12] can contribute to optimise the quality of ICT in SG environments. The MAPE (Monitoring, Analysing, Planning, and Executing) process is introduced to highlight the current open issues of the domain and the expected benefits.

The paper is organised as follows. Section 2 presents related work. Section 3 reports the challenges the SG domain entails, Section 4 discusses our vision towards the optimisation of SG environments. Section 5 provides our conclusions and plans for future research.

2. RELATED WORK

This section reports the surveys on smart grid communication infrastructures where motivations, requirements and challenges (in the context of optimising the quality of smart grid environments) have been sketched.

In [14] emerges the necessity of a control system and particularly a communication infrastructure that must be designed to adjust the performance metrics on the basis of the energy production as well as of the power distribution. Smart grid environments are required to meet the ever increasing efficiency challenges by harnessing modern information technologies to enable a communication infrastructure that provides monitoring and control capabilities.

In [5], smart grid security challenges are discussed. Such challenges basically concern the protection of smart metering data against unauthorized access and repudiation. Security solutions are required on different levels: end to end secure communication protocols need to be used, hardware components (e.g., smart meters) need to withstand physical attacks, the grid needs to detect forged/hacked components, etc. Hence, it arises the common challenge to design a system that will balance the trade-off between security and performance, i.e. use adequate security strength while minimizing its performance and cost overheads.

In [10] the quality-of-service (QoS) is highlighted as a cross-cutting issue of a grid-wise interoperability framework, and the monitoring of power distribution is indicated as an emerging area that will gain in importance as the fraction of renewable energy into the grid increases. Current monitoring systems must be adapted to become reporting systems performing prediction and optimisation functionalities.

Our previous work in smart grid environments includes the following contributions: (i) in [3] we proposed a methodology to assess the impact of different system parameters on the survivability of distribution automation power grids; (ii)

in [7] we presented a mapping from a common information model to a holistic survivability analysis which allows to predict the survivability of distribution circuits with respect to power equipment and communication failures; (iii) in [9] we introduced a phased recovery survivability model that allows to assess the effect of backup power, demand response programs and effectiveness of distributed generation on survivability metrics.

3. SPE CHALLENGES OF THE SMART GRID

In this section we collect the challenges for SPE in the context of SG environments. We have identified three areas of issues that make the SG a particularly challenging domain for SPE, namely (a) that SG systems span multiple domains, (b) that SG systems are critical infrastructures, and (c) that SG systems are data intensive systems, as explained below.

Systems span multiple domain. The overall SG system covers a multitude of domains, from the physical generation, transmission and distribution of energy (governed by the laws of electromagnetism and analysed using differential equations) to the prediction of human end user demand and their response to incentives such as price signals. In many of these domains, timing is an issue but it is not feasible to capture all these timing aspects in an overall timing model. Thus, the challenge is to meaningfully decompose the system into scenarios amenable to timing analysis and in particular, for us as SPE researchers, to identify and delineate the scenarios related to software performance.

In doing so, the main challenge is to define the border of such scenarios. When studying the performance of control centre systems (cf. Fig 1) we need both to (1) capture the workload of the surrounding SG system properly and conversely (2) investigate what the impact of the determined software system performance is on the rest of the system. In particular, for the impact of the software system performance on the rest of the system, it is important to determine whether transient behaviour of the software part are relevant as well. Here, it may be the case that (a) any violation of a response time threshold may lead to undesired effects in the rest of the system (hard real time), that (b) certain amount of violation can be tolerated (e.g. in only 95% of cases within a defined time window the response time needs to be below the threshold (e.g. soft real time, firm real time, or due to user expectations) or that (c) only the average is relevant and no transient behaviour needs to be analysed.

For example, regarding metering and aggregation of data in substation automation systems, real-time monitoring of electricity usage permits accurate analysis of demands and allows to plan for higher efficiency in energy consumption dependent on real-time pricing. The SG technologies operate dependent on a huge number of meters and sensors and these synchronised technologies include fault detection systems (i.e., Fault Location Acquisition Reporter) or real-time monitoring systems (i.e., Phasor Measurement Units) using precision time down to microseconds.

Systems are critical infrastructures. As smart grids systems are critical infrastructures, the quality characteristics reliability and security are highly important. Performance is related to all these properties as performance degradation is often an indicator of system instability. Thus, additional performance requirements and scenarios may be derived from reliability, security, and cost requirements. This is most evident for reliability, where, on the one hand, the failure of a system to react in a certain time span may cause additional failures (as described above) but also, on the other hand, where failure scenarios such as electrical equipment failure might lead to changed workload conditions for the control centre systems. If the control centre systems in such contingency cases are not able to handle the workload, this might cause a propagation of the failure to other areas of the SG. As well as metering measurements collected by control centre and substations or other devices actually substitute the heart beat signalling and are used for fault detection.

For example, a disruption of multiple power lines due to a storm might cause sudden changes in the available generated power and its price, so that smart meters in the affected area (which are a special kind of field devices not shown in Fig. 1) might need to communicate intensively with the control centre to renegotiate and optimize their power consumption contracts. Furthermore, analysis results how well the control centre systems perform provides feedback to failure propagation analysis.

Also in security scenarios, performance is relevant. For systems running with constant load a performance signature for diverse attacks (e.g., DOS, MITM or SQL injection) can be identified. On the one hand, intruders might try to mask their attacks by causing more traffic in the system, causing workload that is higher than expected. Thus, attack prevention strategies might lead to additional performance requirements and scenarios. Similarly strategies using performance tests can be developed to detect or harden system against security attacks.

For example, forged signals being sent to a SCADA system need to be detected quickly enough so that the system does not become instable or at least to minimize the impact of the attack (and the potential blackouts), as e.g. considered by Esfahani et al. [4].

Systems are data intensive. As smart grid systems aim to optimize power generation, transmission, and distribution on all levels, enormous amounts of data will potentially be generated, transmitted, and analysed. Here, there is a trade-off between accurate analysis of the system state and performance. Perfectly accurate analysis and load prediction might require to transmit and analyse the detailed consumption patterns of individual houses or even devices. However, the increased processing effort of such detailed data may not pay off and it might be more desirable overall to aggregate the data in a meaningful fashion. Of course, another reason to avoid such detailed data are privacy concerns, which we do not discuss here further. To estimate the effect of more detailed or less detailed data on the sizing of the control centre systems and the networking infrastructure, performance prediction approaches are required. For SPE, we see an additional challenge in that many SPE methods and tools focus on control flow, less on data flow. Enhancing SPE methods and tools by models for data flow might be required to make them applicable for this challenge.

For example, SCADA systems collect the information about the state of the grid and in relation to data logging all data must be time stamped (performed by RTU within few milliseconds) in order to determine the correct sequence of events. With the granularity and scale of the future SG to provide for this operation the ICT challenges and synchronisation among diverse SG operations are much more complex.

4. RESEARCH VISION

This section discusses our vision to use SPE techniques to optimise the quality of ICT applications, and thus optimise the quality of the overall SG.

As stated in Section 3, SG systems are data intensive and critical systems that span on multiple domains, hence ICT applications need to manage a huge amount of data over heterogeneous devices and networks. As outlined in [8], there exist several challenges and needs to improve the quality of SG environments, such as new materials and alternative clean energy sources, advanced power electronics and devices, advanced computing and control methodologies, intelligent technologies, etc. It is unrealistic that ICT applications can automatically embed these techniques, human intervention is needed to design and validate the SG technologies and devise the refactorings that can be applied.

Figure 2 reports the MAPE process [6] at work in SG: an inner loop is identified to deal with ICT applications that can be automatically reconfigured with a set of pre-defined and non-invasive refactorings (e.g. the redeployment of a software component), whereas an outer loop is meant to consider the human intervention in the optimisation process (e.g. add a server for the SCADA system). The basic activities of the MAPE process are: (i) Monitoring, i.e. the most relevant energy-related services of software systems are monitored; (ii) Analysing, i.e. the QoS status of software systems is estimated to predict in advance their processing capabilities; (iii) Planning, i.e. if energy-related services suffer or will suffer from poor performance, then design alternatives are devised and compared; (iv) Executing, i.e. the selected design alternatives are actually realized to improve the processing capabilities.

Figure 2: MAPE process at work in SG.

The monitoring activity is of key relevance and it is shared between the inner and the outer MAPE loop (see Figure 2): we aim to collect all the knowledge that help us to build a set of software models for the ICT infrastructure underlying the SG. Since SG are data intensive systems, as anticipated in Section 3, such software models need to embed not only the control flow but also the data flow is relevant. In fact, the data flow may influence the behavioural patterns of energy-related services that may include the possibility to aggregate data with different strategies. All these features need to be modelled to better characterise the software systems and its quality properties. Besides this, we also assume that the software models include the available hardware resources, i.e. platforms deploying energy-related services and communication networks along with their features, e.g. processor speed, network rate, etc.

Since SG systems span on multiple domains, it is necessary to identify a set of energy-related services of software systems that contribute to the quality of SG. For example, substation automation systems (see Figure 1) are aimed to provide protection, control, and metering of data while guaranteeing a high efficiency of the substation field devices. Real-time monitoring of these services help to identify their characteristics as well as the workload to which they are subjected thus to figure out the needed software and hardware resources of systems implementing such services.

Due to the complexity of SG systems, that include the physical generation, transmission and distribution of energy, the energy-related services are subjected to high variable, non-stable, and usually bursty workloads. In fact, natural factors (such as the wind or the sun) affect the expected energy generation, and consequently its transmission and distribution. Furthermore, natural disasters (such as a storm) suddenly require an higher energy provision depending on the criticality of the event to manage. Therefore, the real-time monitoring need to be further detailed with some contextual information (e.g. catastrophic event happening) of SG, thus to provide lower and upper bounds approximating the variability of workloads. In this way, we are able to evaluate scalability issues of ICT applications.

In order to apply model-based performance prediction techniques it is necessary to annotate the software model with quantitative data, i.e. the demand of software services (e.g. the number of requests to cpu/disk devices) as well as their usage (e.g. the number of service invocations). Furthermore, it is necessary to specify the required quality properties (e.g. the reliability of a software component, the confidentiality of some data). In fact, SG systems are critical infrastructures and other quality characteristics (such as reliability, security, and costs) are highly important and must be evaluated. In this way, the values of performance indices coming from the solution of the initial software model can be compared to the ones obtained for the same model: (i) without considering other quality properties, (ii) with different design alternatives improving other quality properties (e.g. reliability, security) and (iii) even with different design alternatives improving the same quality property. Such comparisons help software engineers to quantify the impact of improving other quality properties while meeting performance requirements.

Our goal is to consider multiple quality criteria of SG (such as reliability, security and costs), thus to support trade-off decisions and use multi-criteria optimization methods [2].

5. CONCLUSION

In this paper we envision the usage of SPE techniques for the ICT infrastructure underlying SG thus to optimise its quality. We identified challenges of SPE in the context of smart grids. First, smart grids span multiple domains, so it is necessary to collaborate between such different domains to identify the relevant performance scenarios. Second, smart grids are critical infrastructures, so the connection to other dependability attributes such as reliability and security should be considered. Third, smart grids are data-intensive systems, so models will need to consider data flow as well. Monitoring, Analysing, Planning, and Executing (MAPE) activities are discussed to highlight the current open issues of the domain and the expected benefits. We showed that ICT applications built for SG environments offer very promising challenges for SPE research.

As future work we plan to include the experience gained by SG experts, as this additional knowledge contributes to improve the MAPE process. Finally, SPE techniques must be experimented in real-world smart grids in order to assess their benefits.

6. REFERENCES

[1] Power system control and associated communications - reference architecture for object models, services and protocols. Technical report, International Electrotechnical Commission, 2003.

[2] A. Aleti, B. Buhnova, L. Grunske, A. Koziolek, and I. Meedeniya. Software architecture optimization methods: A systematic literature review. *IEEE Trans. Software Eng.*, 39(5):658–683, 2013.

[3] A. Avritzer, S. Suresh, D. S. Menasché, R. M. M. Leão, E. de Souza e Silva, M. C. Diniz, K. S. Trivedi, L. Happe, and A. Koziolek. Survivability models for the assessment of smart grid distribution automation network designs. In *ICPE*, pages 241–252, 2013.

[4] P. M. Esfahani, M. Vrakopoulou, G. Andersson, and J. Lygeros. A tractable nonlinear fault detection and isolation technique with application to the cyber-physical security of power systems. In *CDC*, pages 3433–3438, 2012.

[5] Z. Fan, P. Kulkarni, S. Gormus, C. Efthymiou, G. Kalogridis, M. Sooriyabandara, Z. Zhu, S. Lambotharan, and W. H. Chin. Smart grid communications: Overview of research challenges, solutions, and standardization activities. *CoRR*, abs/1112.3516, 2011.

[6] B. Jacob, R. Lanyon-Hogg, D. K. Nadgir, and A. F. Yassin. *A Practical Guide to the IBM Autonomic Computing Toolkit*. ibm.com/redbooks, 2004.

[7] A. Koziolek, L. Happe, A. Avritzer, and S. Suresh. A common analysis framework for smart distribution networks applied to survivability analysis of distribution automation. In *International Workshop SE-SmartGrids*, pages 23–29, 2012.

[8] F. Li, W. Qiao, H. Sun, H. Wan, J. Wang, Y. Xia, Z. Xu, and P. Zhang. Smart transmission grid: Vision and framework. *IEEE Trans. Smart Grid*, 1(2):168–177, 2010.

[9] D. S. Menasché, R. M. M. Leão, E. de Souza e Silva, A. Avritzer, S. Suresh, K. S. Trivedi, R. A. Marie, L. Happe, and A. Koziolek. Survivability analysis of power distribution in smart grids with active and reactive power modeling. *SIGMETRICS Performance Evaluation Review*, 40(3):53–57, 2012.

[10] M. Rosenfield. The smart grid and key research technical challenges. In *VLSI Technology (VLSIT), 2010 Symposium on*, pages 3–8, 2010.

[11] M. Shargal and D. Houseman. The big picture of your coming smart grid, 2009. Online http://www.smartgridnews.com/artman/publish/commentary/The_Big_Picture_of_Your_Coming_Smart_Grid-529.html.

[12] C. U. Smith and L. G. Williams. *Performance Solutions: A Practical Guide to Creating Responsive, Scalable Software*. Addison-Wesley, 2001.

[13] U.S. Department of Energy. Smart Grid / Department of Energy. Retrieved 2012-06-18.

[14] Y. Yan, Y. Qian, H. Sharif, and D. Tipper. A survey on smart grid communication infrastructures: Motivations, requirements and challenges. *Communications Surveys Tutorials, IEEE*, 15(1):5–20, 2013.

Generic Instrumentation and Monitoring Description for Software Performance Evaluation *

Alexander Wert[1], Henning Schulz[2], Christoph Heger[1], Roozbeh Farahbod[2]
[1]Karlsruhe Institute of Technology, Am Fasanengarten 5, Karlsruhe, Germany
[2]SAP AG, Vincenz-Priessnitz-Strasse 1, Karlsruhe, Germany
alexander.wert@kit.edu, henning.schulz@sap.com, christoph.heger@kit.edu,
roozbeh.farahbod@sap.com

ABSTRACT

Instrumentation and monitoring plays an important role in measurement-based performance evaluation of software systems. To this end, a large body of instrumentation and monitoring tools exist which, however, depend on proprietary and programming-language-specific instrumentation languages. Due to the lack of a common instrumentation language, it is difficult and expensive to port per se generic measurement-based performance evaluation approaches among different application contexts. In this work-in-progress paper, we address this issue by introducing a performance-oriented, generic meta-model for application-independent and tool-independent description of instrumentation instructions. Decoupling the instrumentation description from its realization in a concrete application context, by a concrete instrumentation tool allows to design measurement-based performance evaluation approaches in a generic and portable way.

1. INTRODUCTION

Many performance engineering tasks entail measurement-based analysis of the application under test (AUT), such as performance troubleshooting, capacity planning, performance regressions testing, etc [11]. Most of these tasks employ instrumentation and monitoring (IaM) tools to retrieve performance data from the AUT. There is a large body of different IaM tools with different, proprietary and programming-language-specific configuration languages.

Though many measurement-based performance engineering tasks are conceptually transferable from one application context to another, the lack of a common, generic and abstract configuration language for the IaM tools renders portability of established performance engineering processes among different AUTs (potentially based on different technologies) impractical. On the one hand, in many performance engineering projects multiple, different IaM tools are used,

requiring expertise in different instrumentation languages and a way of keeping different instrumentation descriptions consistent. Furthermore, introducing a new IaM tool entails tedious migration of existing instrumentation descriptions. On the other hand, without a common instrumentation language, applying conceptually similar instrumentation and monitoring instructions on different contexts (i.e., projects) implies tedious analysis of the target AUT in order to create AUT-specific instrumentation descriptions for each concrete context.

Existing languages for the description of instrumentation instructions [2,3,5,7] either lack abstraction from technical implementation details, are programing-language-specific, or are not designed for measurement-based performance evaluation. As such, they are not sufficient to enable generic description of instrumentation instructions, which can be reused among different application contexts.

In this work-in-progress paper we present the Instrumentation Description Model (IDM) which is a generic meta-model for describing instrumentation and monitoring instructions in an AUT-independent, IaM-tool-independent way for the purpose of software performance engineering. Primarily designed for AUTs implemented in object-oriented, managed programing languages, IDM instances can be reused even in different environments, such as Java or .NET. We show the conceptual relationship between IDM, potential AUTs and existing IaM tools. Furthermore, we discuss the main design goals for IDM and describe the semantics of the individual model elements.

2. INSTRUMENTATION DESCRIPTION

In this section, we explain the context of IDM, discuss the main design goals for an abstract instrumentation description model and show how we realized these goals by explaining IDM in detail. Finally, we show an example of an instantiation of IDM.

2.1 Giving the Context

The main goal of IDM is to decouple the instrumentation and monitoring descriptions from their realization in a concrete managed-language-based context. Hereby, concrete context means both the application under test (AUT) and the instrumentation and monitoring (IaM) tools used to instrument the AUT.

IDM is a meta-model for the specification of instrumentation descriptions (IDM instances). An IDM instance can reference concrete parts of a specific AUT (e.g. concrete methods), generic concepts common in most AUTs (e.g. the

*The research leading to these results has received funding from the DFG grant RE 1674/6-1.

concept of a database interface), or both. An IDM instance is generically reusable among different contexts (AUTs and IaM tools) if it only comprises instrumentation description entities which reference generic concepts without referencing AUT-Specific parts. Specific instrumentation engine are responsible for mapping generic concepts to concrete implementations of the AUT. For instance, in the context of Java, a Java instrumentation engine would map the concept of a database interface to the JDBC API. Hereby, it is irrelevant how a specific instrumentation engine realizes the instrumentation described by an IDM instance, whether through static code analyses, load-time weaving [5] or even dynamically adaptable instrumentation [1]. Existing IaM tools can be adapted to use IDM by providing an adapter which interprets and translates IDM instances to the tool-specific and context-specific specification.

2.2 Design Goals for IDM

In order to address the issues mentioned in Section 1, we identified the following design goals for IDM:

Abstraction. In order to reuse instrumentation descriptions in different contexts, we need a meta-model which allows to abstract from the specifics of individual run-time environments, programming languages and concrete AUTs. However, if an AUT-specific instrumentation is required, the meta-model has to provide means to describe an AUT-specific instrumentation, too.

Orthogonality. An instrumentation instruction has basically two dimensions: *Where* to instrument (in the following called *scope*), and *How* to instrument (which *probes* to inject). Since entities of both dimensions can be comprehensive, definitions of scopes and probes need to be independently reusable. Therefore, as far as reasonable, probes need to be independent of scopes, and vice versa.

Composability. In order to provide a flexible and expressive way of describing instrumentation instructions, the meta-model needs to be composable. Besides the orthogonality of probes and scopes, individual model elements should cover basic, minimalistic aspects of the AUT and the measurement data of interest. In this way, instrumentation descriptions can be kept simple (e.g. in order to keep the measurement overhead low), while advanced descriptions can be composed when needed.

Focus. An instrumentation description language with a clear focus on a domain allows to define expressive models while reducing complexity and effort of model creation. Our focus lies on performance evaluation which guides the definition of probes (i.e. data to measure).

2.3 IDM in Detail

Following the design goals (cf. Section 2.2), we created IDM as depicted in Figure 1. In general, IDM can be partitioned along two dimensions. Hereby, we distinguish between *sampling* and *instrumentation* on the first dimension, and between *scopes* and *probes* (cf. orthogonality principle, Section 2.2) on the second dimension. Sampling is the process of periodically retrieving information from a certain resource (e.g. CPU utilization, Disk I/O, etc.) while instrumentation is used to retrieve measurement data (e.g. response times) from the control flow of the AUT. While scopes describe which resource to monitor, respectively where in the code to instrument, probes define what should be measured.

The `IaM Description` is the root element of IDM, constituting a container for `Instrumentation Entities` and `Sampling Entities` which are explained in the following.

2.3.1 Instrumentation

An `Instrumentation Entity` comprises an `Instrumentation Scope` (i.e. *where* to measure) and a set of `Measurement Probes` (i.e. *what* to measure). We distinguish different types of scopes:

Synchronization Scope. This scope covers all points in the AUT, where synchronization of threads occurs due to a lock on a passive resource. In particular, this scope covers all lock acquisition events and lock release events.

Method Enclosing Scope. This is an abstract scope, providing a common parent element for all scopes which cover a set of individual methods or method calls. Entities of this scope type comprise two parts: a *before-method-execution* and an *after-method-execution* part.

Method Scope. The Method Scope is the most direct way to specify a set of methods to be instrumented. Hereby, the methods are identified by a set of `method patterns` (method names with potential wild-cards). A Method Scope covers all methods (except for constructors) whose full qualified names match a specified pattern.

Constructor Scope. Covers the instrumentation of all constructors of the target classes. Analogously to the method patterns the target classes are specified by name patterns.

Allocation Scope. Covers all code statements where an object of the target classes is allocated. By contrast to the `Constructor Scope`, this scope does not instrument any constructor, but only their invocation.

Modifier Scope. The Modifier Scope allows to specify a set of modifiers (e.g. `public`, `private`, etc.) to describe a scope of all methods whose modifiers match all specified modifiers of the scope.

API Scope. Conceptually, an `API Scope` covers all methods of an *abstract API* whose implementing methods shall be instrumented. An *abstract API* represents a conceptual interface for which concrete APIs consist in most modern, managed programing languages (e.g. Java, .NET, etc.). In the current version, IDM supports the following five API scopes: The `Entry Point API` covers all entry points into a server application (e.g. in Java: Servlets, HTTP handlers, etc.). The `Messaging API` covers all ways of the target context to realize remote communication (e.g. in Java: JMS, RMI, etc.). The `Database API` and the `OR Mapping API` need to be mapped to the concrete standard API of the target context for managing a database connection (e.g. JDBC in Java), respectively concrete API for realizing an object-relation mapping (e.g. JPA in Java). Finally, the `Logging API` covers standard interfaces for logging (e.g. log4j, slf4j).

Trace Scope. The `Trace Scope` allows to instrument the whole dynamic trace (i.e. call tree) originating from the methods covered by the `sub-scope`.

The `Method`, `Allocation` and `Constructor Scope` provide a application-specific way of specifying a scope. Application-specific definition of instrumentation instructions may be useful in some application scenarios where the AUT is know and reuse of the instrumentation descriptions is not important. However, in an evolving environment, where IaM tools may be replaced, or common measurement-based performance evaluation approaches need to be applied on several AUTs,

sampling

Sampling Scope — 1 — scope

CPU | Memory | Disk | Network — processes

Sampling Entity — delay : int

probes 1..* — Sampling Probe — Utilization | Capacity

Process Spec — hostName : String — procId : int

processes *

Restriction — globalRestriction — 0..1 — localRestriction

IaM Description — sampling entities * — instrumentation entities *

instrumentation

Instrumentation Scope — scope — 1 — Instrumentation Entity — probes 1..* — Measurement Probe

exclude | include *

Method Enclosing Scope — 1 — sub-scope

Syncronization Scope | Trace Scope | Modifier Scope (mods : String [*])

API Scope — Entry Point API | Messaging API | Database API | OR Mapping API | Logging API

application-specific scopes: Method Scope (patterns : String [*]) | Allocation Scope (patterns : String [*]) | Constructor Scope (patterns : String [*])

generic scopes

inv: self.entity.scope.oclIsKindOf(Database API) — DB Query

inv: self.entity.scope.oclIsKindOf(Syncronization Scope) — Queue Length | Waiting Time

inv: self.entity.scope.oclIsKindOf(Method Enclosing Scope) — Response Time | Memory Footprint | Trace ID | CPU Time

scopes (i.e. where to instrument) | probes (i.e. what to measure)

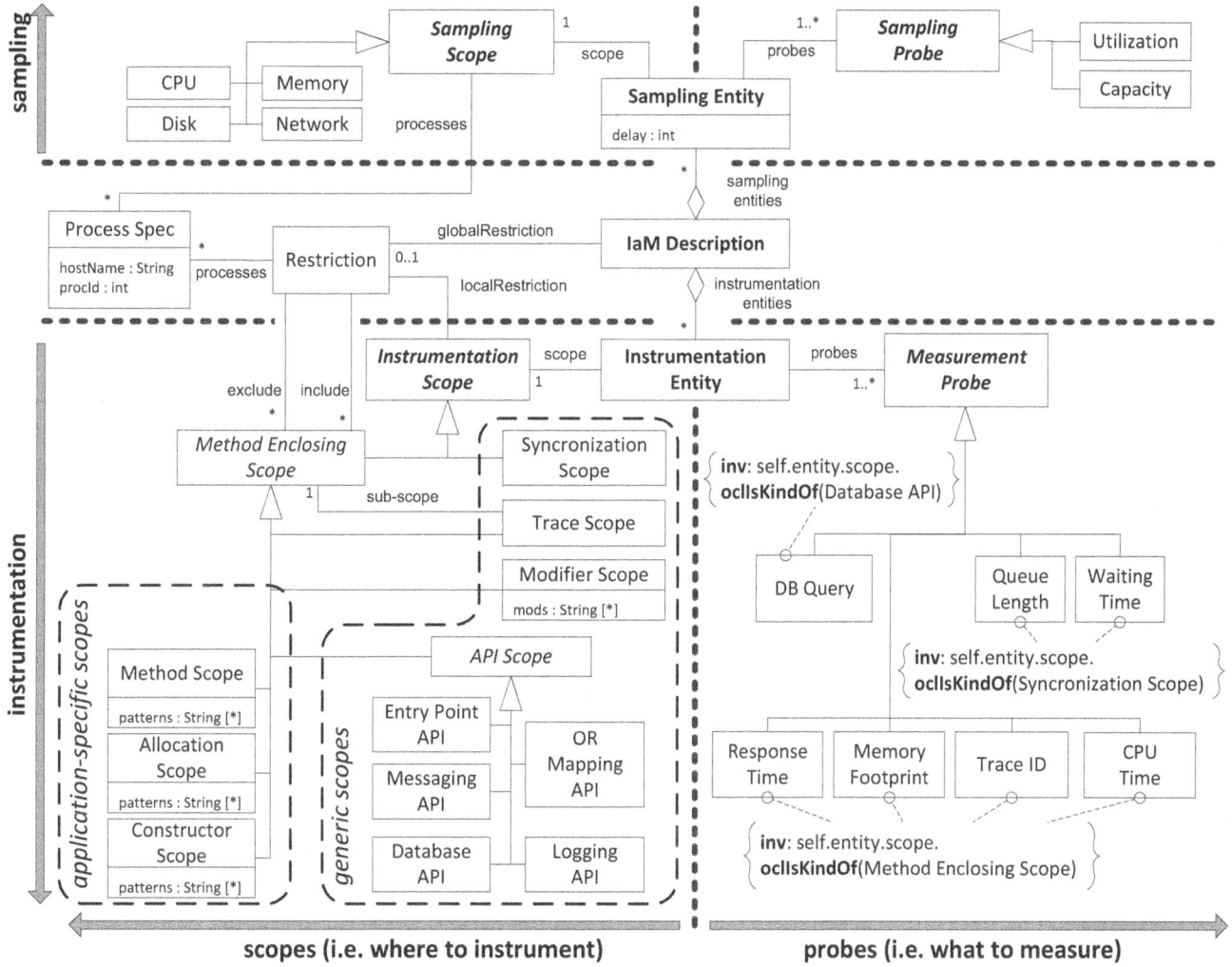

Figure 1: Instrumentation Description Model (IDM)

purely generic instrumentation descriptions are required. To this end, IDM provides the remaining scopes (Synchronized, Trace, Modifier and API Scope), which allow to describe scopes in an AUT-independent way.

Following the composability principle (cf. Section 2.2), an Instrumentation Scope can be further refined by a local Restriction. In particular, a Restriction allows to limit a scope to a set of processes (specified by a host name and process id) and a set of excluded, respectively included, scopes. Hereby, the restriction has the following semantics: Let us assume that M is the set of all methods in the AUT, S is the set of methods defined by a scope X (without regarding the restrictions), and In_i, Ex_j are the inclusive, respectively exclusive, scopes of the restriction for X. Then, the scope X is resolved to the following set of methods:

$$X = S \cap \left(\bigcap_i In_i \right) \cap \left(\bigcap_j M \setminus Ex_j \right) \qquad (1)$$

Additionally to the local restrictions, an IaM Description can have a global Restriction which applies to all Instrumentation Entities.

Orthogonally to the Instrumentation Scope, an Instrumentation Entity comprises a set of Measurement Probes specifying the data to be retrieved from the corresponding scope. Although the probes are orthogonal to the scopes, not all probes are reasonably applicable with all scopes. Therefore, we define some restrictions (expressed as OCL statements) limiting the applicability of certain probes to corresponding sub-sets of scopes. In particular, Response Time, Memory Footprint, Trace ID and CPU Time can be measured from all Method Enclosing Scopes. Waiting Time and Queue Length can be retrieved from the Synchronization Scope. Finally, the SQL statement of an executed DB Query can be retrieved from a Database API scope.

2.3.2 Sampling

A Sampling Entity is specified by a delay (in ms) determining the sampling frequency, exactly one sampling scope (e.g. CPU, Memory, Disk or Network), and a set of sampling probes (e.g. Utilization and Capacity). The Capacity probe stands for the absolute capacity of the corresponding resource, e.g. the absolute clock rate of a CPU, the network bandwidth or total memory. The Sampling Scope can be further restricted to a set of operating system processes

205

(`Process Spec`) specified by a host name and a process id. In this way one could monitor for instance the CPU utilization of a single process instead of the overall CPU utilization.

2.4 IDM Instance Example

Figure 2 shows an exemplary, target application-independent, however, Java-specific IDM instance. On the sampling side of the `IaM Description`, the IDM instance specifies sampling of the utilization of all CPUs with a frequency of 2Hz (cf. `delay=500ms`). On the instrumentation side the goal is

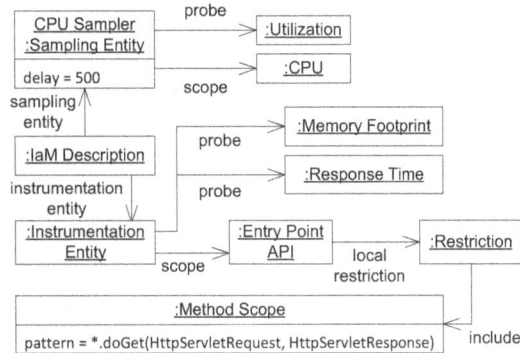

Figure 2: An exemplary IDM instance

to capture the response times and memory footprints (cf. `probes`) of all `doGet(...)` methods (cf. inclusive restriction) of all Java Servlets (covered by the `Entry Point API`). Note, the method pattern `*.doGet(...)` as part of the restriction is the only Java-specific entity in this example.

3. RELATED WORK

As instrumentation is a cross-cutting concern, most instrumentation languages and tools are based on ideas of aspect oriented programming (AOP) [6]. AspectJ [5] is an implementation of AOP in Java comprising its own language for instrumentation definition. AspectJ (similarly to IDM) distinguishes between where to instrument (pointcuts) and how to instrument (advices), which is specified in a Java-like syntax. Josh [3] is an AspectJ-like language introducing a mechanism for defining custom pointcut designators in Java. SCoPE [2] is an AspectJ compiler allowing to provide user-defined analysis-based pointcuts. DiSL [7] is a domain-specific instrumentation language. Relying on concepts of AOP, DiSL provides high level language constructs based on Java and Java annotations to describe instrumentation instructions for an AUT. Providing an open join point model, DiSL is able to instrument any region of Java bytecode, ranging from methods through loops to single statements. All muti-purpose, AOP-based languages [2,3,5,7] inherently lack a focus on performance evaluation, requiring additional definition of probe-code. Furthermore, AOP-based languages are specific to the target programing language they are designed for, rendering general, language-independent reuse of instrumentation descriptions impossible.

Kieker [9] is a framework for continuous monitoring and performance analysis of software utilizing existing AOP solutions for instrumentation. Although Kieker does not comprise its own instrumentation language, it provides AOP advices for measurement-based performance evaluation simplifying

the definition of performance-oriented instrumentation descriptions. Though Kieker supports different programing languages, descriptions of instrumentation instructions are programing-language-specific.

The Java Performance Measurement Framework (JPMF) [8] introduces a generic interface for definition of performance events in Java. In this way JPMF decouples the occurrence of an event (cf. scope in IDM) from the measurement of performance data (cf. probes in IDM). Primarily designed for Java, JPMF is programming-language-specific.

4. CONCLUSION

In this paper, we presented a novel instrumentation description model (IDM) for the purpose of measurement-based performance evaluation of managed-language-based applications. IDM allows to describe instrumentation and monitoring instructions in an application-independent and monitoring-tool-independent way, enabling portability of instrumentation instructions and, thus, a more generic applicability of different measurement-based performance evaluation approaches.

Though the presented IDM is the current state of ongoing research, it gives an insight on a common, generic instrumentation description language, constituting a potential standard for different, performance-oriented instrumentation tools like Kieker [9] or SPASS-meter [4]. So far, we used IDM to create generic instrumentation descriptions for measurement-based, automated diagnostics of performance problems [10]. To this end, we created a Java instrumentation engine [1] which directly uses IDM descriptions as input.

Furthermore, we are currently working on adapters for Kieker which translate an IDM instance to corresponding Java or .NET instrumentation configurations for Kieker. We plan to extend the current version of IDM by further scopes and probes to provide a more comprehensive language.

5. REFERENCES

[1] Aim: Adaptable instrumentation and monitoring. visited: October 2014. http://sopeco.github.io/AIM.

[2] T. Aotani and H. Masuhara. Scope: an aspectj compiler for supporting user-defined analysis-based pointcuts. In *AOSD'07*, pages 161–172. ACM, 2007.

[3] S. Chiba and K. Nakagawa. Josh: an open aspectj-like language. In *AOSD'04*, pages 102–111. ACM, 2004.

[4] H. Eichelberger and K. Schmid. Flexible resource monitoring of java programs. *JSS*, 93:163–186, 2014.

[5] G. Kiczales, E. Hilsdale, J. Hugunin, M. Kersten, J. Palm, and W. G. Griswold. An overview of aspectj. In *ECOOP'01*. Springer, 2001.

[6] G. Kiczales, J. Lamping, A. Mendhekar, C. Maeda, C. Lopes, J.-M. Loingtier, and J. Irwin. *Aspect-oriented programming*. Springer, 1997.

[7] L. Marek, A. Villazón, Y. Zheng, D. Ansaloni, W. Binder, and Z. Qi. Disl: a domain-specific language for bytecode instrumentation. In *AOSD'12*. ACM, 2012.

[8] Q-ImPrESS. Java performance measurement framework, January 2011. http://www.q-impress.eu/wordpress/wp-content/uploads/2011/01/D6.1-Annex-Guidelines-and-Tool-Manuals_Final_version.pdf.

[9] A. van Hoorn, J. Waller, and W. Hasselbring. Kieker: A framework for application performance monitoring and dynamic software analysis. In *ICPE'12*. ACM, 2012.

[10] A. Wert, J. Happe, and L. Happe. Supporting swift reaction: automatically uncovering performance problems by systematic experiments. In *ICSE'13*. IEEE, 2013.

[11] M. Woodside, G. Franks, and D. C. Petriu. The future of software performance engineering. In *FOSE'07*. IEEE, 2007.

Introducing Software Performance Antipatterns in Cloud Computing Environments: Does it Help or Hurt?*

Catia Trubiani
Gran Sasso Science Institute
L'Aquila, Italy
catia.trubiani@gssi.infn.it

ABSTRACT

Performance assessment of cloud-based big data applications require new methodologies and tools to take into consideration on one hand the volume, the variability and the complexity of big data, and on the other hand the intrinsic dynamism of cloud environments. To this end, we introduce software performance antipatterns as reference knowledge to capture the well-known bad design practices that lead to software products suffering by poor performance.

This paper discusses some of the challenges and opportunities of research while introducing software performance antipatterns in cloud computing environments. We present a model-based framework that makes use of software performance antipatterns to improve the Quality-of-Service (QoS) objectives of cloud-based big data applications.

Categories and Subject Descriptors

C.4 [**Performance of Systems**]: Modeling techniques, Performance Attributes; D.2.8 [**Software Engineering**]: Metrics—*performance measures*

Keywords

Software Performance Antipatterns; Cloud Computing Environments; Big Data Applications

1. INTRODUCTION

Cloud computing environments offer a variety of solutions and services to their customers in fact they provide new opportunities while performing the service provisioning, i.e. the capability of acquiring and releasing resources on demand. However, beside the advantages, cloud computing introduced new issues and challenges. In particular, the heterogeneity of the services offered while dealing with big data applications makes the process of identifying a deployment solution that minimizes costs and guarantees Quality-of-Service (QoS) very complex.

In last years many EU projects were targeting cloud environments and their quality assessment, for example:

- *Artist* (http://www.artist-project.eu) aims to migrate legacy software to gain improved performance from the service provisioning of cloud infrastructures;
- *MODAClouds* (http://www.modaclouds.eu/) aims to provide a run-time environment that guarantees QoS for applications deployed on multi-Clouds;
- *CloudScale* (http://www.cloudscale-project.eu/) aims to provide an engineering approach for building scalable cloud applications and services;
- *Cloud-TM* (http://www.cloudtm.eu/) aims to provide a data-centric middleware platform facilitating development and abating costs of cloud applications;
- *PaaSage* (http://www.paasage.eu/) aims to provide an open source integrated platform to support both design and deployment of Cloud applications;
- *SeaClouds* (http://www.seaclouds-project.eu/) aims to guarantee agility after deployment by considering different aspects of the cloud development life-cycle.

All these projects confirm the growing interest for cloud environments not only in the academic field, but also in the industry. In fact, many existing issues have not been fully addressed by academic research, and new challenges keep emerging from industry applications. Automated service provisioning, virtual machine migration, server consolidation, energy management, traffic management and analysis, data security, etc. are cited as key features of cloud computing that also represent the major barriers to broader adoption [7, 28].

This paper is focused on the cloud capability to provide automated service provisioning (i.e. the ability of acquiring and releasing resources on demand) while dealing with big data applications. The goal of a cloud provider is to allocate and de-allocate resources from the cloud to satisfy the QoS while minimizing their operational costs. However, it is not obvious how a cloud provider can achieve this objective. In the context of big data applications it is even more difficult to determine the migration of services, as well as allocating and de-allocating resources from the infrastructure offered by the cloud. In fact, services are conceived as abstract specifications, typically defined and managed by third party organizations, aimed at modeling dynamic and complex business workflows [1].

*This work has been developed in the context of the Microsoft Azure Research Award for the project DESPACE (DEtecting and Solving Performance Antipatterns in Cloud Enviroments).

In this context we propose to introduce Software Performance Antipatterns (SPA) [21] to drive the process of deploying big data applications on cloud-based environments. The rationale of using performance antipatterns is two-fold: on the one hand, a performance antipattern identifies a bad practice in the big data application that negatively affects the performance indices, thus to support the identification of performance flaws; on the other hand, a performance antipattern definition includes a solution description that lets the software architect devise refactoring actions, thus it aims to improve the system performance.

Goal of this paper is to discuss the challenges and opportunities of research in the area of using performance antipatterns in cloud computing environments. In particular, we propose a model-based framework (named *SPA-CloudMeter*) that makes use of software performance antipatterns to optimise the QoS of big data applications deployed on cloud environments. To this end, we focus on modelling, analysis, and feedback software performance engineering activities to highlight the current open issues of the domain and the expected benefits.

The paper is organised as follows. Section 2 presents related work. Section 3 discusses the research vision of our model-based framework that aims to estimate the benefit of using SPA in cloud computing environments. Finally Section 4 concludes the paper with remarks for future research.

2. RELATED WORK

In the last decades software architects have proposed and implemented several concepts and best practices to build highly scalable applications. However, due to ever-growing datasets, unpredictable traffic, and the demand for faster response times these concepts need to be adapted in the context of cloud computing. The business and technical benefits of cloud computing as well as the issues and challenges of architecting cloud-based systems have been formulated and discussed in [13, 26].

In literature a variety of solutions have been provided to the individual challenges, e.g. virtual machine migration, server consolidation, energy management, traffic management and analysis, etc. [28]. In this paper we focus on the challange of automated service provisioning that is not a new problem. Dynamic resource provisioning has been studied extensively in the past [25, 29, 9, 3, 12]. These approaches typically involve: (i) constructing a performance model that predicts the number of application instances required to handle the demand, in order to satisfy quality requirements; (ii) predicting future demand and determining resource requirements using the performance model. However, to the best of our knowledge, none of the existing approaches proposes the usage of performance antipatterns as support for the automated service provisioning. Several approaches have been recently introduced to specify and detect code smells and antipatterns [16, 10, 20, 27, 18]. They range from manual approaches, based on inspection techniques [22], to metric-based heuristics [14, 17], using rules and thresholds on various metrics [15] or Bayesian Belief Networks [11].

Our previous work in software performance antipatterns includes the following latest contributions: (i) in [4] we tackled the problem of providing a more formal representation by introducing first-order logic rules that express a set of system properties under which an antipattern occurs; (ii) in [24] we introduced a methodology to rank performance antipatterns and optimise the solution process; (iii) in [23] we explored the synergies in the process of combining performance antipatterns with bottleneck analysis; in [6] we introduced a model-driven approach to broaden the detection of software performance antipatterns at runtime.

3. SPA-CLOUDMETER

This section presents the model-based framework, named *SPA-CloudMeter*, we propose to introduce software performance antipatterns for improving the QoS of big data applications deployed on cloud environments.

Figure 1 schematically represents the operational steps of our *SPA-CloudMeter* framework: in the *modelling* phase, an application model is built to design the software and hardware artifacts for the big data application under study; in the *analysis* phase, a QoS model is built to monitor the software and hardware cloud resources employed by the big data application, and such model is solved to obtain QoS results of interest; in the *feedback* phase, the QoS results are interpreted and, if necessary, antipattern-based refactoring actions are devised with the goal to improve (from a performance perspective) the application under study.

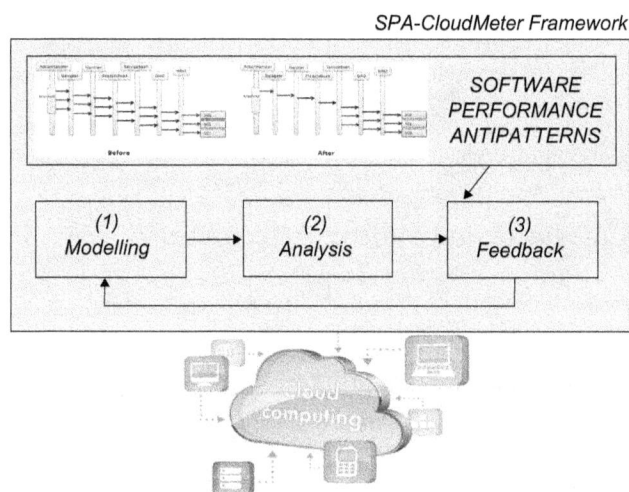

Figure 1: SPA-CloudMeter framework.

A preliminary step consists in the specification of cloud-related antipatterns. In fact, big data applications deployed on cloud environments include new performance related challenges, and practitioners continuously highlight more advanced pattern problems, e.g. for *Hadoop*[1] and *Cassandra*[2]. We are investigating the problems that have an analogy with the high-level specifications of the performance antipatterns we considered up to now [21]. For example, we found that some practitioners found that Hadoop map/reduce is not efficient for data locality, i.e. the more data nodes and data implies the less locality, especially larger clusters tend not to be complete homogeneous and data distribution and placement is not optimal. This latter problem is very similar to the *Circuitous treasure hunt* antipattern [21] that basically refer to software applications retrieving data in a not efficient way, i.e., such applications retrieve data from a first location, use those results to search in a second location, and so on until the ultimate results are obtained.

---

[1] http://hadoop.apache.org/
[2] http://cassandra.apache.org/

The first work-in-progress activity is the specification of the performance antipatterns, in the context of big data applications deployed on cloud environments, we are able to handle. Inspired by the DECOR method [15], we identified the following operational steps to specify antipatterns in the cloud computing context: (i) *Domain Analysis*: key concepts are identified in the text-based descriptions of reports provided by experienced big data technologists in their summits. They form a unified vocabulary of reusable concepts to describe bad practices and their solution; (ii) *Specification*: the concepts, which constitute a vocabulary, are combined to systematically specify performance antipatterns; (iii) *Processing*: the specifications are translated into operational ones that can be directly applied for the detection.

The second work-in-progress activity is the specification of QoS properties, in the context of big data applications deployed on cloud environments, we are able to analyse. In [2] we presented a graph of relationships highlighting the dependencies among some QoS attributes. In the cloud computing context we started focusing on performance and security that are related by a *trade-off* relationship, hence we aim to quantify the performance degradation incurred to achieve certain security requirements. From our previous work [5, 19] we experimented that the values of indices coming from the solution of the performance model (i.e. the one that includes security aspects) can be compared to the ones obtained for the same model (i) without security solutions, (ii) with different security mechanisms and (iii) with different implementations of the same security mechanism. Such comparisons help software designers to decide whether it is feasible to introduce/modify/remove security strategies on the basis of the stated performance requirements.

Modelling. SPA-CloudMeter allows to model big data applications deployed on cloud computing environments by specifying their functionalities, i.e. software and hardware services and their provisioning. It is necessary to model what are the application's software and hardware resources (e.g. software components, active virtual machines, hypervisors, etc.) and their expected resource demand or consumption. Key features of this domain are: for big data applications the volume, the variability and the complexity of data software services need to manage; for cloud computing environments the dynamic behaviour of hardware services that have the ability to scale workload peaks. In case of dynamic deployment of software services it is necessary to explicitly model elastic methodologies for hardware services while avoiding premature resource release. Finally, it is fundamental to model the security properties of software and hardware services as well to devise strategies suitable to protect them against not authorised accesses.

Analysis. SPA-CloudMeter allows to transform the big data application and the cloud computing environment model along with their security settings into a performance model. The performance indices [8] we expect to calculate are: the system response time, the throughput of software resources, and the utilization of hardware resources. All these indices contribute to quantify the QoS of the modelled big data application deployed on the cloud computing environment. QoS analysis results have to be interpreted in order to detect, if any, performance problems. Once performance problems have been detected (with a certain accuracy) somewhere in the application model, solutions have to be applied to remove those problems. A performance flaw originates

from a set of unfulfilled requirement(s), such as the estimated average response time of a software service is higher than the required one. In case of unfulfilled requirement(s), our framework makes use of software performance antipatterns as reference knowledge to capture the well-known bad design practices that lead to software products suffering by poor performance.

Feedback. SPA-CloudMeter allows to detect and solve software performance antipatterns. In particular, antipattern-based rules interrogate the model elements to look for occurrences of the corresponding antipattern, whereas antipattern-based refactoring actions can be applied on the model elements with the final goal to improve (from a performance perspective) the application under analysis. The feedback operational step takes as input an application model (AM) and a set of performance results (PR), and it is constituted by two main operational steps. First, the detection of performance antipatterns is performed on the AM application model by running the antipatterns operational specifications, and it returns the detected antipattern instances with the list of suspicious model elements involved in them. Second, the solution of performance antipatterns is performed on the AM application model by using the antipattern-based refactoring actions that are a set of design alternatives suggested by the detected antipatterns. This step returns a set of refactored AM application models (AM_1', ..., AM_n') where the detected antipatterns have been removed, and each of these models undergo the same process of the initial model hence their analyses lead to a corresponding set of performance results (PR_1', ..., PR_n').

Note that the process of solving performance antipatterns includes further issues that may hurt the application under study. For example, a certain number of antipatterns cannot be unambiguously applied due to incoherencies among their solutions. It may happen that the solution of one antipattern suggests to split a software resource (with a high volume of data) into three finer grain resources, while another antipattern at the same time suggests to merge the original resource with another one (with a low volume of data). These two actions obviously contradict each other, although no pre-existing requirement limits their application. Even in cases of no explicit conflict between antipattern solutions, coherency problems can be raised from the order of application of solutions. In fact the result of the sequential application of two (or more) antipattern solutions is not guaranteed to be invariant with respect to the application order. Criteria must be introduced to drive the application order of solutions in these cases. Furthermore, antipattern-based refactoring actions do not a priori guarantee performance improvements, because the entire process is based on heuristic evaluations.

Summarizing our SPA-CloudMeter framework provides the following contributions: (i) specifying software performance antipatterns for cloud computing environments; (ii) modelling the activity flow in the specification of big data applications deployed on cloud environments; (iii) defining metrics and indices to evaluate the QoS of such applications; (iv) devising feedback strategies to optimise software and hardware services. SPA-CloudMeter currently considers only performance and security goals of big data applications deployed on cloud computing environments, however it can be extended to other quality criteria such as reliability, availability, etc., thus to support trade-off decisions.

4. CONCLUSION

In this paper we presented the research vision of a model-based framework that makes use of software performance antipatterns to optimise the quality of big data applications deployed on cloud environments. Modelling, analysis, and feedback activities have been discussed to highlight the current open issues of the domain and the expected benefits. We showed that both big data applications and cloud computing environments offer very promising challenges for research. As future work it is necessary to implement the SPA-CloudMeter framework for the performance assessment of real-world systems, thus to estimate its effectiveness.

5. REFERENCES

[1] A. Barker, C. D. Walton, and D. Robertson. Choreographing web services. *IEEE T. Services Computing*, 2(2):152–166, 2009.

[2] S. Becker, L. Happe, R. Mirandola, and C. Trubiani. Towards a methodology driven by relationships of quality attributes for qos-based analysis. In *ICPE*, pages 311–314, 2013.

[3] P. Bodík, R. Griffith, C. Sutton, A. Fox, M. Jordan, and D. Patterson. Statistical machine learning makes automatic control practical for internet datacenters. In *HotCloud*, 2009.

[4] V. Cortellessa, A. Di Marco, and C. Trubiani. An approach for modeling and detecting software performance antipatterns based on first-order logics. *Software and System Modeling*, 13(1):391–432, 2014.

[5] V. Cortellessa and C. Trubiani. Towards a library of composable models to estimate the performance of security solutions. In *WOSP*, pages 145–156, 2008.

[6] A. Di Marco and C. Trubiani. A model-driven approach to broaden the detection of software performance antipatterns at runtime. In *International Workshop FESCA*, pages 77–92, 2014.

[7] A. Greenberg, J. Hamilton, D. Maltz, and P. Patel. The cost of a cloud: Research problems in data center networks. *Computer Communications Review*, 2009.

[8] R. Jain. The Art of Computer Systems Performance Analysis. *SIGMETRICS Performance Evaluation Review*, 19(2):5–11, 1991.

[9] E. Kalyvianaki, T. Charalambous, and S. Hand. Self-adaptive and self-configured cpu resource provisioning for virtualized servers using kalman filters. In *ICAC*, pages 117–126, 2009.

[10] F. Khomh, M. D. Penta, Y.-G. Guéhéneuc, and G. Antoniol. An exploratory study of the impact of antipatterns on class change- and fault-proneness. *Empirical Software Engineering*, 17(3):243–275, 2012.

[11] F. Khomh, S. Vaucher, Y.-G. Guéhéneuc, and H. A. Sahraoui. Bdtex: A gqm-based bayesian approach for the detection of antipatterns. *Journal of Systems and Software*, 84(4):559–572, 2011.

[12] J. Kirschnick, J. Alcaraz Calero, L. Wilcock, and N. Edwards. Toward an architecture for the automated provisioning of cloud services. *Communications Magazine, IEEE*, 48(12):124–131, 2010.

[13] H. C. Lim, S. Babu, J. S. Chase, and S. S. Parekh. Automated control in cloud computing: challenges and opportunities. In *Workshop on Automated control for datacenters and clouds (ACDC)*. ACM, 2009.

[14] R. Marinescu. Detection strategies: Metrics-based rules for detecting design flaws. In *ICSM*, pages 350–359, 2004.

[15] N. Moha, Y.-G. Guéhéneuc, L. Duchien, and A.-F. L. Meur. Decor: A method for the specification and detection of code and design smells. *IEEE Trans. Software Eng.*, 36(1):20–36, 2010.

[16] N. Moha, F. Palma, M. Nayrolles, B. J. Conseil, Y.-G. Guéhéneuc, B. Baudry, and J.-M. Jézéquel. Specification and detection of soa antipatterns. In *ICSOC*, pages 1–16, 2012.

[17] R. Oliveto, F. Khomh, G. Antoniol, and Y.-G. Guéhéneuc. Numerical signatures of antipatterns: An approach based on b-splines. In *European Conference on Software Maintenance and Reengineering (CSMR)*, pages 248–251, 2010.

[18] R. Peters and A. Zaidman. Evaluating the lifespan of code smells using software repository mining. In *European Conference on Software Maintenance and Reengineering (CSMR)*, pages 411–416, 2012.

[19] R. J. Rodríguez, C. Trubiani, and J. Merseguer. Fault-Tolerant Techniques and Security Mechanisms for Model-based Performance Prediction of Critical Systems. In *ISARCS*, 2012.

[20] D. Romano, P. Raila, M. Pinzger, and F. Khomh. Analyzing the impact of antipatterns on change-proneness using fine-grained source code changes. In *Working Conference on Reverse Engineering (WCRE)*, pages 437–446, 2012.

[21] C. U. Smith and L. G. Williams. More New Software Performance Antipatterns: Even More Ways to Shoot Yourself in the Foot. In *Computer Measurement Group Conference*, pages 717–725, 2003.

[22] G. Travassos, F. Shull, M. Fredericks, and V. R. Basili. Detecting defects in object-oriented designs: using reading techniques to increase software quality. In *ACM SIGPLAN conference on Object-oriented programming, systems, languages, and applications*, pages 47–56, 1999.

[23] C. Trubiani, A. Di Marco, V. Cortellessa, N. Mani, and D. C. Petriu. Exploring synergies between bottleneck analysis and performance antipatterns. In *ICPE*, pages 75–86, 2014.

[24] C. Trubiani, A. Koziolek, V. Cortellessa, and R. Reussner. Guilt-based handling of software performance antipatterns in palladio architectural models. *Journal of Systems and Software*, 95:141–165, 2014.

[25] B. Urgaonkar and A. Chandra. Dynamic provisioning of multi-tier internet applications. In *ICAC*, pages 217–228. IEEE Computer Society, 2005.

[26] J. Varia. Amazon Web Services - Architecting for the Cloud: Best Practices, May 2010.

[27] A. F. Yamashita and L. Moonen. Do code smells reflect important maintainability aspects? In *ICSM*, pages 306–315, 2012.

[28] Q. Zhang, L. Cheng, and R. Boutaba. Cloud computing: state-of-the-art and research challenges. *J. Internet Services and Applications*, 1(1):7–18, 2010.

[29] Q. Zhang, L. Cherkasova, and E. Smirni. A regression-based analytic model for dynamic resource provisioning of multi-tier applications. In *ICAC*, 2007.

Green Domino Incentives: Impact of Energy-aware Adaptive Link Rate Policies in Routers

Cyriac James
University of Calgary, Canada
cyriac.james@ucalgary.ca

Niklas Carlsson
Linköping University, Sweden
niklas.carlsson@liu.se

ABSTRACT

To reduce energy consumption of lightly loaded routers, operators are increasingly incentivized to use Adaptive Link Rate (ALR) policies and techniques. These techniques typically save energy by adapting link service rates or by identifying opportune times to put interfaces into low-power sleep/idle modes. In this paper, we present a trace-based analysis of the impact that a router implementing these techniques has on the neighboring routers. We show that policies adapting the service rate at larger time scales, either by changing the service rate of the link interface itself or by changing which redundant heterogeneous link is active, typically have large positive effects on neighboring routers, with the downstream routers being able to achieve up-to 30% additional energy savings due to the upstream routers implementing ALR policies. Policies that save energy by temporarily placing the interface in a low-power sleep/idle mode, typically has smaller, but positive, impact on neighboring routers. Best are hybrid policies that use a combination of these two techniques. The hybrid policies consistently achieve the biggest energy savings, and have positive cascading effects on surrounding routers. Our results show that implementation of ALR policies can contribute to large-scale positive domino incentive effects, as they further increase the potential energy savings seen by those neighboring routers that consider implementing ALR techniques, while satisfying performance guarantees on the routers themselves.

Categories and Subject Descriptors

C.2.0 [**Computer-communication Networks**]: General—*Data communications*; C.2.6 [**Computer-communication Networks**]: Internetworking—*Routers*

Keywords

Energy Efficiency; Adaptive Link Rate; Energy Proportional Computing; Router Performance

1. INTRODUCTION

Internet routers are typically over provisioned and operate at low utilization, leaving much room for energy savings. Motivated by increasing energy prices and high CO_2 emissions (associated with non-green energy, for example), different Adaptive Link Rate (ALR) policies and techniques [10, 14, 16] have been proposed to reduce energy consumption when routers are lightly loaded.

Depending on hardware capability, ALR policies can operate at different time scales. Over larger time scales (e.g., order of minutes), the operator can save energy by adapting the active service rate of interfaces based on the estimated utilization. At the granularity of tens of microseconds, a router can save energy by toggling between an active high-power mode and a low-power idle mode, during which some interface components are put to temporary sleep.[1] This finer granularity allows decisions to be made based on the current packet arrival pattern and queue occupancy.

In general, ALR policies attempt to scale the energy usage based on the current traffic load. Ideally, routers should be energy proportional [3]. In this case, idle router interfaces do not consume any power and the energy consumption is proportional to the load. While policies that use low-power idle modes can be implemented within the recent Energy Efficient Ethernet (EEE) standard [10] and the feature is already available in the market (e.g., Cisco Catalyst 4500E switches), achieving proportional energy usage without significant delay penalties is typically not possible with the current state of the art hardware. It should also be noted that techniques have been proposed to allow "near" proportional energy consumption using non-proportional hardware available today. For example, eBond [18] uses redundant heterogeneous links coupled with energy-aware bonding to save energy. With this approach, a low-bandwidth link is used when the router is lightly loaded, allowing the regular high-bandwidth link to be turned off. With hardware expected to become increasingly energy proportional, it is therefore important to consider the impact of implementing ALR policies on both proportional and nonproportional systems.

Although many ALR policies have been proposed and evaluated, not much is known about the effect that a router applying ALR techniques has on the performance and po-

---

[1]Throughout the paper we will use *low-power idle mode* and *sleep mode* interchangeably. We will also use a relatively broad definition of ALR policies, which include both policies that adapt the rate itself and policies that enter such low-power mode, for which the service rate is zero.

tential energy savings of neighboring routers. As these techniques are being increasingly deployed, it is important to understand the impact such deployment may have on the overall end-to-end system. For example, are there global performance or energy penalties associated with routers greedily minimizing their own energy usage? And, perhaps more importantly, does the potential energy savings on other routers increase or decrease with the implementation on one router?

In this paper, we use trace-driven simulations to analyze the effects that ALR policies used on one router have on neighboring routers. We first develop a simple evaluation framework, that allows us to evaluate different classes of ALR policies. Our framework captures the basic tradeoffs between *energy usage* and *per-router packet delay* for each of the policy classes. Using trace-based simulations, we then evaluate policies under a wide range of traffic patterns, and provide insights with regards to the energy-delay tradeoff effects these policies have on neighboring routers.

The model developed for our evaluation framework captures the energy and delay characteristics of two general ALR policy classes, and hybrids thereof. The first policy class, *rate switching policies*, saves energy by adapting the (maximum) service rate of the outgoing interfaces. Referring to the above discussion, we note that rate switching can be implemented either by adapting the service rate of a single interface [14] or by implementing heterogeneous bonding [18]. The second policy class, *active/idle toggling policies*, saves energy by temporarily placing the interface into a low-power idle mode when there are no (or few) packets to process. Finally, the hybrid policy class adjusts the active service rate based on long-term measurements and also use active/idle toggling to save energy at shorter time scales.

Motivated by an end-to-end client-server scenario, we use both edge and core network traffic traces, and consider simulation scenarios in which (i) the traffic is aggregated at routers with increasingly higher capacities, (ii) the traffic is dispersed on its way towards the edge of the network, and (iii) cases with varying degrees of traffic multiplexing. Particular attention is given to the average energy savings and the tail of the per-router packet delays, as values such as the 99th percentile often are important in practice.

Our results provide a quantitative comparison of the relative impact different policies have on neighboring routers under different workload scenarios and traffic patterns. We find significant differences in the possible energy savings at neighboring routers. The savings are largest on upstream interfaces close to the edge, which typically carry a larger fraction small packets, but reduce with increased multiplexing of packet streams. Perhaps most interestingly, for all three policy classes, we observe that implementing ALR policies in upstream routers allows downstream routers to achieve higher energy savings than is possible if the upstream routers do not use ALR. While the additional improvements in energy savings is greatest for rate switching, which can achieve up-to 30% additional energy savings, the other two policy classes can also achieve up-to 5-10% additional energy savings.

These results suggest that greedy energy savings on one router can have multiplicative benefits. First, they reduce the energy usage on the router itself. Second, they increase the potential energy savings possible on neighboring routers, further incentivizing implementation of ALR techniques. With the largest energy savings and significant energy savings improvements, our findings make a strong case for the more advanced hybrid policies, when possible. Of course, it is important to also note that the basic rate switching and active/idle toggling policies can provide significant advantages on their own, and should hence not be ignored. Particularly as hardware constraints and availability of utilization and packet-level queueing information may differ between routers and operators.

The remainder of this paper is organized as follows. Section 2 sets the context, describes the state of the art, and the policies analyzed in the paper. Section 3 presents the system model and datasets used to evaluate the impact of implementing different policies. Section 4 presents our performance and energy implication analysis. Finally, Section 5 concludes the paper with a discussion of our findings.

2. BACKGROUND AND RELATED WORK

2.1 End-to-End Path and Energy Usage

HTTP is responsible for a majority of the Internet traffic [24]. To understand the overall energy usage of present day networks and the impact one router's actions have on that of the next router along the path, we first consider a Web request being sent between a home user and a server in a modern datacenter. Today, the big players are (i) building big data centers in places where electricity and network bandwidth are cheap, and/or (ii) moving the content closer to the end user by using CDNs or putting their own servers in the datacenters operated by the ISPs. This means that some traffic will be served close to the end user, while other traffic will need to traverse the entire end-to-end path. Such end-user generated traffic is aggregated as it moves into the core networks and then disperse again as it moves closer to the particular datacenter serving the request. Naturally, the HTTP response takes a similar but reverse path.

Along its path, a typical Internet packet traverse many routers, operated by different operators or Autonomous Systems (AS), each with its separate administrative domain and policies. For example, a simple IP-to-AS mapping [26] analysis that we performed on 1,000 randomly selected traceroutes from the Route Views project[2] suggests that an average packet may see 13.1 routers and 4.2 ASes. With many operators along the path, the choices made by one operator will clearly impact others. Even within an AS, the choices made on one router will impact neighboring routers.

Taking a birds-eye view, edge networks consume 70-80% of the total network energy, and core networks the remaining 20-30% [4], with the difference explained by the edge being responsible for 95% of the network elements [4,5]. However, recent studies [25] combined with a doubling in traffic volumes every 18 months [37], suggest that the energy shares will be comparable around year 2021. These numbers show that it is important to consider energy saving implications on both core and edge network routers.

2.2 Adaptive Link Rate Policies

In 2003, Gupta and Singh [16] first discussed Adaptive Link Rate (ALR) as a plausible energy efficient solution for wired networks. Building on technologies such as Dynamic Voltage Scaling [34], they argue that apart from implement-

---

[2]U. of Oregon, Route Views project. `http://www.routeviews.org/`

ing these techniques in the line card, the main challenges may be determining (i) when to change the link rates and (ii) what are the performance implications on the network. Since then, many ALR techniques and policies have been proposed that address (i) by adapting the link rate based on traffic measures such as queue sizes, link utilization, or a combination thereof [10,14,16]. However, not much is known about (ii) and the impact that a router implementing ALR techniques may have on neighboring routers. Addressing this question is our primary contribution.

In this paper, we consider two general classes of ALR policies, and a hybrid thereof.

- **Rate switching:** With rate switching, the active link rate μ is varied (linearly, stepwise, or by any other function) depending on the traffic load, with rate changes typically happening over time scales of minutes. We consider a general policy class, but note that the service rate changes can be implemented in many ways, including solutions using a single interface or heterogeneous bonding [18].

- **Active/idle toggling:** With active/idle toggling policies, the interface operates on a much finer time granularity and frequently toggle between a low-power idle mode and a high-power active mode. A router interface switch to low-power idle mode when there are no packets to serve, and switch back to active mode when L bytes have been queued. Typically, there will be a time delay Δ before the interface is activated and can start serving the queued packets.

- **Hybrid:** A general hybrid policy adjusts the active service rate μ on long-term basis (e.g., order of minutes), and uses active/idle toggling with a threshold L to save energy at shorter time scales. To restrict ourselves to a single protocol parameter, we consider an example policy with a very small threshold $L = \epsilon$, such that the interface always is activated when a new packet arrives. A discussion on the impact of this parameter choice is provided in Section 4.2.

2.3 Energy Savings

Implementations based on the first two general policy classes above have been evaluated for a wide range of systems. Most papers that discuss ALR techniques at the core network have focused on the use of sleep-based energy-aware traffic engineering techniques [7,8,30,33] that allow some interfaces to go to sleep temporarily. On the other hand, end hosts, access networks, and edge technologies have been evaluated under both rate switching and active/idle toggling techniques [2,13,14,17]. Trace-driven simulations [14,15] and hardware prototypes [36] have been used to study the impact of switching times and policies on the energy consumption when implementing ALR techniques in the Ethernet. It has also been shown that finer time granularity is needed for bursty traffic, such as Internet traffic [27,35]. Other works have considered the impact on higher layer protocols such as TCP [19].

Despite this body of work, there is very limited work studying the impact of ALR techniques on neighboring routers. This question is particularly important as routers do not operate in isolation and implementation of these "green" techniques on one or more routers will impact the overall network

performance, as measured by the packet delivery delays, for example, as well as the potential energy savings others may be able to achieve without sacrificing performance.

Perhaps most closely related is the work by Nedevschi et al. [28], which simulate the end-to-end performance (measured in terms of end-to-end packet delay and loss) of the network as a whole, when ALR techniques are applied to intermediate routers/switches along the end-to-end path. In contrast, we study the impact ALR techniques have on neighboring routers, allowing us to provide insights into how the use of ALR techniques may affect neighboring routers' potential benefits of using ALR and their decision to use ALR techniques. A broader class of policies also allow us to capture differences and similarities across policy classes.

2.4 Standardization and State of the Art

The recent Energy Efficient Ethernet (EEE) standard [1, 10], called *IEEE 802.3az*, is based on an active/idle toggling framework by Hays [20], and defines the signaling that is required between the transmitter and the receiver when the former toggles back-and-forth between a Lower Power Idle (LPI) mode and an active mode. The standard does not define policies to determine when to change mode, but it has been suggested that the default wakeup time typically should be approximately equal to the transmission time of the maximum length packet in the particular link [1]. For example, for a 1 Gbps link, it takes ≈ 0.01 ms to send a 1500 byte packet. Based on simulations done in lab environment, the expected power saving for IEEE 802.3az enabled Cisco Catalyst 4500E, a 384 1000Base-T port switch, is 74% [1]. It should also be noted that standard Gigabit Ethernet interfaces already support multiple data rates (e.g., 10 Mbps, 100 Mbps and 1 Gbps) using the auto-negotiation feature, which can be utilized for implementing *rate switching*.

3. SYSTEM MODEL AND DATASETS

3.1 Basic Router Model

For the purpose of our trace-driven evaluation we use the router model developed by Hohn et al. [21]. The model assumes a First-In-First-Out (FIFO) queueing policy, was developed and validated using real traffic, and ratifies the commonly held assumption that the output buffer is the bottleneck in popular store-and-forward routers that implements virtual output queueing (to avoid head-of-line blocking). Typically, the switch fabric is overprovisioned and very little queueing happens at the incoming interfaces. With very small switch fabric delays (typically $10 - 50$ μs) and by focusing on the tail of the delay distribution, for which acceptable delay constraints may be of the order of milliseconds or above, the model only considers the queueing delay on the outgoing interface and the transmission delay. Finally, motivated by the low loss context and that line cards often can accommodate up to 500 ms worth of traffic, the model assumes an infinite buffer size.[3] Under these assumptions, the delay d_k experienced by the kth packet in an *always-on* router with service rate μ is

$$d_k = [d_{k-1} - (t_k - t_{k-1})]^+ + \frac{l_k}{\mu}, \qquad (1)$$

---

[3] For our experiments, we are typically interested in 99th-percentile per-router delays below 10^2 ms.

where $[y]^+ = \max(y, 0)$, and t_k is the arrival time of the kth packet of length l_k. For additional details on the model, we refer the interested reader to the original paper [21].

3.2 Policy Model

We next extend the router model to capture the performance under the three general ALR policies, defined in Section 2.2. Assuming that the service rate does not change during service of a packet, rate switching, between non-zero service rates, is easily modeled by giving each packet k an individual service rate μ_k. To capture the active/idle toggling aspect we introduce two additional parameters Δ and L, where L is the pre-defined threshold parameter used by the active/idle policy and Δ is the time that it takes to activate the link again after being in the low-power idle mode.

Given these assumptions, a general hybrid policy that allows active/idle toggling should (i) switch to low-power idle mode when there are no packets to serve, and (ii) switch back to active mode when L bytes have been queued. The delays of such a policy can be modeled as follows:

$$d_k = \begin{cases} \Delta + W_k + \sum_{n=k'}^{k} \frac{l_n}{\mu_n}, & \text{if } t_k \text{ during idle} \\ [d_{k-1} - (t_k - t_{k-1})]^+ + \frac{l_k}{\mu_k}, & \text{otherwise,} \end{cases} \tag{2}$$

where W_k is the waiting time until the interface goes active after a packet k arrive at the interface when it is in low-power idle mode, calculated as $W_k = (t_{k''} - t_k)$, k' is the first (lead) packet that arrives during an idle period, and k'' is the packet that takes the interface out of low-power idle mode. We note that the lead packet during an idle period satisfies the condition $t_{k'} > t_{k'-1} + d_{k'-1}$ and that the packet that takes the interface out of low-power idle mode can be calculated as $k'' = \min_{k''}\{k''|k'' \geq k' \cap \sum_{n=k'}^{k''} l_n \geq L\}$.

As previously argued, we only consider policies for which the *active* service rate μ changes on the order of minutes and therefore (at finer time granularity) use a constant service rate $\mu_k = \mu$. For our active/idle policy, we always use the full link rate $\mu = \mu^{max}$, but simulate the policy for different thresholds L. For the hybrid policy, we pick a threshold $L = \epsilon$ smaller than the size of the smallest packet, and simulate the policy with different active service rates $\mu \leq \mu^{max}$.

3.3 Energy Model

Motivated by advancements in Dynamic Voltage Scaling and measurements of existing routers [18], we model the power usage $P_a(\mu)$ of a link with active link rate μ, using a simple linear model between the minimum and maximum service rate:

$$P_a(\mu) = P_a^{min} + (P_a^{max} - P_a^{min})\frac{\mu - \mu^{min}}{\mu^{max} - \mu^{min}}, \tag{3}$$

where P_a^{max} is the maximum active energy usage per time unit (power) when the router interface operates at maximum service rate μ^{max}, and P_a^{min} is the power usage when the interface operate at lowest possible service rate μ^{min}. In general, this power is lower bounded by the power usage P_s in sleep (low-power idle) mode; i.e., $P_s \leq P_a^{min}$.

Ideally, future routers will be energy proportional [3]. For this to be the case the energy usage should be proportional to the computing/service provided. This would imply that (i) the power usage P_a when in active mode is proportional to the service rate μ, (ii) the power usage P_s when in sleep

mode is 0, and (iii) the activation time Δ and activation energy is 0.

Unfortunately, routers are not yet fully energy proportional. First, the interfaces often consume a significant amount of power (w.r.t to the maximum power) when it is not processing any traffic or when in various sleep modes. In some cases, an interface even consume a significant amount of power when it is down or when the cable is unplugged [18]. Second, there are non-negligible time delays and energy costs associated with activating an interface in the case of routers with active/idle toggling features [1,31]. In the short term, very few circuits in the physical layer can be turned off (put to sleep) during the low-power idle mode, resulting in modest energy savings.[4] Hence, we make a pessimistic assumption that $P_s = P_a^{min}$, by raising the value of P_s, and $\mu^{min} = 0$. (We note that this assumption also is valid for the best-case scenario in which routers are energy proportional and $P_s = P_a^{min} = 0$.) Furthermore, we assume that the activation time Δ is constant and that the activation energy is proportional to the power usage $P_a(\mu)$ in active mode and the activation time Δ. Under these assumptions, the total energy usage is equal to

$$T_a P_a(\mu) + T_s P_s + c N_a \Delta P_a(\mu), \tag{4}$$

where T_a is the total time in active mode, T_s is the total time in sleep mode, N_a is the number of times the interface have been activated, and c is a constant capturing the energy penalty associated with turning on the interface. When $c = 0$ there is no energy cost associated with the activation time, and when $c = 1$ the energy usage is the same as when active.

3.4 Traffic Model

To model the traffic seen at consecutive routers, we use a basic model with two layers of back-to-back routers. Each of the routers in the first layer is assumed to have m_{in} input interfaces, m_{out} output interfaces, and each outgoing interface sees $1/m_{out}$ of the traffic from each of the incoming interfaces. The corresponding number of interfaces for the second set of routers are n_{in} and n_{out}. The packets from the output interfaces of the first set of routers become input sequence of packets to the second set of routers.

For each interface, we use a separate packet trace. To decide which packets to forward to each output interface, we leverage the destination addresses in the Internet Protocol (IP) headers. More specifically, we identify m_{out} (or n_{out}) blocks of IP addresses, each consisting of many IP prefixes, such that on average each block has the same fraction of total traffic. We then forward the traffic of each separate block to individual interfaces. While the IP addresses in the traces have been anonymized with Crypto-PAN [12], we note that Crypto-PAN is prefix preserving and therefore allow us to capture the longest-prefix-based routing used by typical store-and-forward routers, used on the Internet.

For simplicity, we restrict our analysis to the case of routers with the same number of incoming and outgoing interfaces; i.e., when $m_{in} = m_{out} = m$ and $n_{in} = n_{out} = n$. Under this abstraction, we look at scenarios in which the traffic is increasingly aggregated ($m > n$), is dispersed as it is moving towards the edge ($m < n$), and symmetric scenarios with different degrees of multiplexing (i.e., different values

---

[4]In the long run, the expectation is that advanced hardware technologies will allow energy savings up to 80% [1].

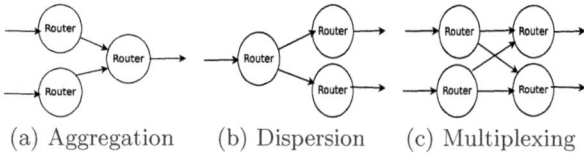

(a) Aggregation (b) Dispersion (c) Multiplexing

Figure 1: Modified tandem queue model.

of $m = n$). Figure 1 provides an overview of three basic example scenarios: 2×1, 1×2, and 2×2.

We note that most routers have few interfaces, suggesting that m and n typically are small. Furthermore, as the load across interfaces typically is highly skewed, with most of the traffic being directed to a small subset of the interfaces, the insights of small m and n may be applicable even for routers with many interfaces.

3.5 Packet Traces

Simulating an $m \times n$ topology, we use mn packet traces. Each trace is fed into a separate incoming interface of the m first-layer routers, each relaying $1/n^{\text{th}}$ of their traffic to each of the n second-layer routers.

For the core, we use packet traces collected at a core router connected to a trans-pacific link, labeled *samplepoint-F*, in the WIDE Internet (MAWI) dataset[5] [9]. The traces are collected between 14:00 and 14:15 (local time) each day of January 2013. For the edge, we use traces from the Waikato Internet Traffic Storage (WITS) project[6] [11], labeled Waikato VIII, and are collected from an edge router of a university network. For simplicity, we use the same 15 minute time-of-day period as used for the core. Appendix A provides a more detailed characterization of the traces.

4. PERFORMANCE ANALYSIS

4.1 Methodology overview

This section presents our simulation results. Using the packet traces and simulation methodology described in Section 3.5, both the delay (Section 3.2) and the energy usage (Section 3.3) associated with each policy are measured over the simulation duration. Throughout our analysis we use an initial warm-up period, and do not include the initial packets in our statistics. Unless stated otherwise, we conservatively use $c = 1$ in our evaluation.

Both the energy usage and the per-packet routing delay are measured variables, which depend on the traffic pattern and the protocol parameters used by each protocol. To capture the general performance tradeoff between these variables, we run a sequence of simulations with the same workload, but in which we vary the main system parameters associated with each policy. In the case of the rate switching policy and the hybrid policy, different energy-delay tradeoffs are achieved by running simulations with different active service rate μ (and hence also $P_a(\mu)$). In contrast, the energy-delay tradeoff seen by the active/idle toggling policy is determined by the byte threshold L. To illustrate these tradeoffs, Figure 2 shows the 99-percentile per-router packet delay, as a function of the corresponding protocol parameter. The results are for the outgoing edge traffic (Section 3.5),

---

[5]MAWI, http://mawi.wide.ad.jp/mawi/, June 2013.
[6]WITS, http://www.wand.net.nz/wits/, June 2013.

and as per the EEE standard specifications, in all cases, we use Δ equal to the packet processing time (≈ 0.01 ms) of the largest possible packet when operating at maximum link capacity μ^{max}.

Furthermore, in later sections, where we show results for a particular delay (e.g., the energy saving or improvement in energy savings as a function of the delay; Figures 6, 7, 8 and 9) we must perform a binary search over the primary policy parameter (link rate or threshold value, that control the delay-energy tradeoff) for the achieved delay. By identifying the delay-energy pair (both measured variables) when the two scenarios or policies see the same delay (but different energy usage or energy savings), that provide a fair head-to-head comparison for a given target delay. In these cases, we call the "per-router packet delay" seen by a packet (at a single router) the "target per-router packet delay".

4.2 Single Router Energy Analysis

Before our analysis of back-to-back routers, we first present results for a single router implementing each of the three basic policy classes, defined and modeled in Sections 2.2 and 3.2, respectively. For clarity, we only present example results illustrating the relative performance and/or energy savings with each policy. Furthermore, for the single-router case presented in this section, we use $m = n = 1$.

Figure 3 shows a head-to-head comparison of the normalized energy usage of the different policies, as a function of the 99-percentile per-router packet delay. Normalization is done with regards to the regular energy usage when operating at maximum power P_a^{max}. Results are presented for 15 minute example traces on the core (dir-A) and edge router (outgoing). The "proportional" cases assume $P_s = P_a^{min} = 0$. (Here, $c = 0$ for both the active/idle toggling and hybrid policy.) This case is motivated by future hardware improvements, as well as software solutions achieving energy proportionality with non-proportional hardware. For the "conservative" cases, we use $c = 1$ and some of the most pessimistic parameter values that we observed in the profiling literature [1, 18, 19, 31]; all values reported by Hähnel et al [18]. For the 1 Gbps edge router we used $P_s = P_a^{min} = 1.35$ W and $P_a^{max} = 1.92$ W. For the 10 Gbps core router, the corresponding values are 7.88 W and 8.10 W, respectively.

When implementing rate switching and hybrid policies on non-proportional hardware, these policies typically can only select rates from a pre-defined set of link rates. While we show results for the full range of delay values, in practice, the tradeoff curves for these policies are therefore expected to be stepwise. As such, the presented results only illustrate approximate energy-delay tradeoffs.

Typical systems likely would see savings in-between the "proportional" (Figures 3(a) and 3(b)) and "conservative" (Figures 3(c) and 3(d)) extremes for a foreseeable future. While the big difference between the possible energy savings using energy proportional hardware and the conservative hardware specs may appear disheartening at first, it is important to remember that systems such as eBound [18], can achieve energy proportional savings using non-proportional hardware. In fact, we argue that eBond [18] could easily be extended to use active/idle toggling on each link, allowing also the hybrid policy to be implemented with current hardware. The proportional scenarios can provide insights on the potential performance of such systems.

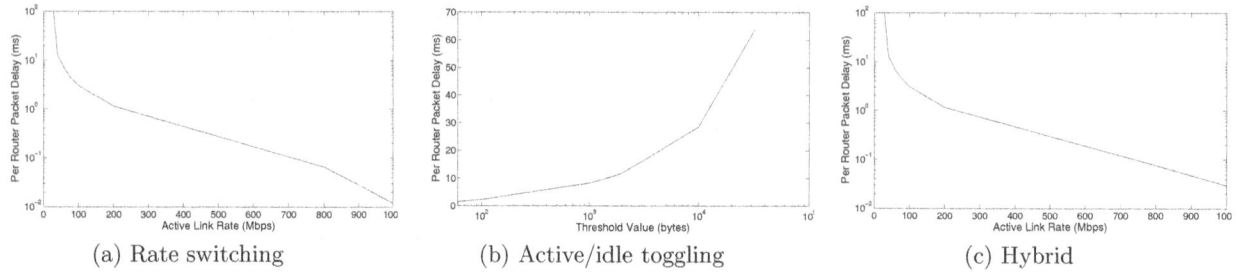

(a) Rate switching   (b) Active/idle toggling   (c) Hybrid

Figure 2: Impact on the 99-percentile per-router packet delay when varying the main parameter of each policy.

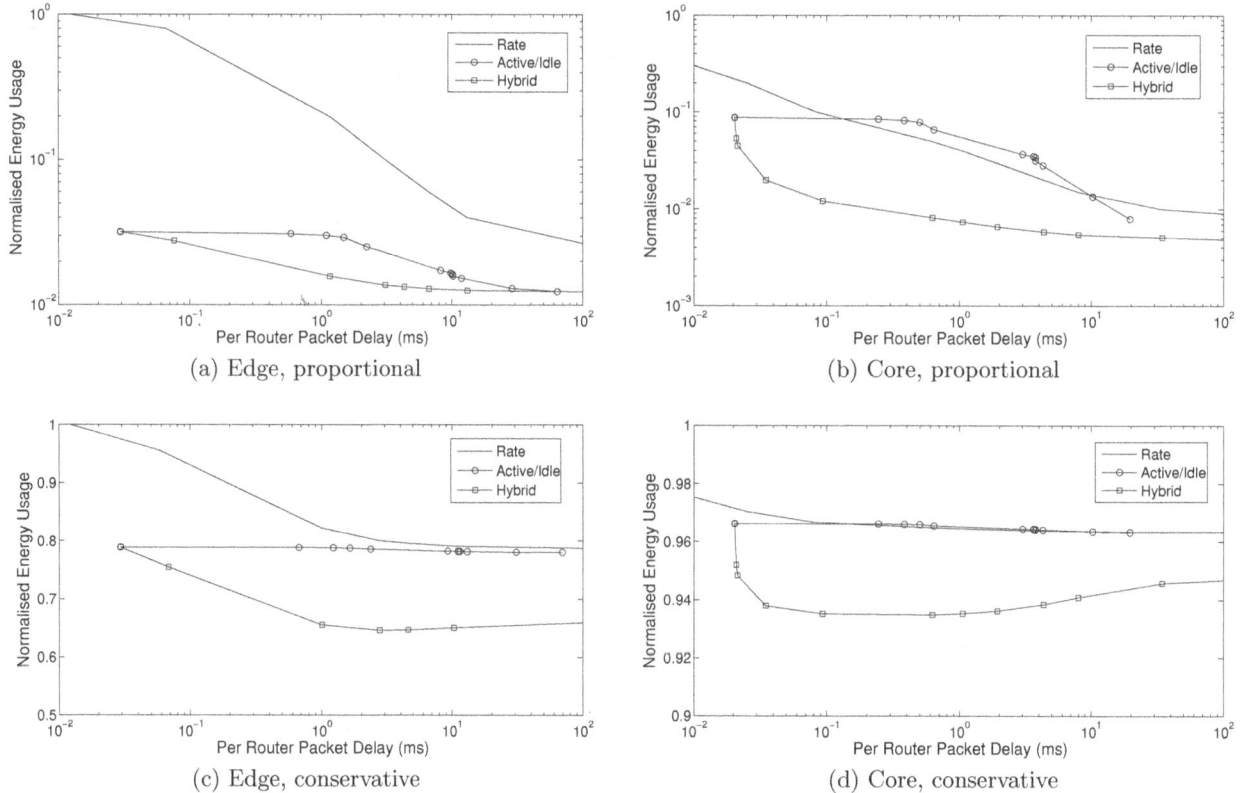

(a) Edge, proportional   (b) Core, proportional

(c) Edge, conservative   (d) Core, conservative

Figure 3: Normalized energy usage for each policy, under four example scenarios.

We note that the particular hybrid policy used in our simulations, similar to the other policies, is restricted to use a single protocol parameter. With this observation in mind, it is interesting that the biggest energy savings consistently (across scenarios) are achieved by the hybrid policy. While most of the energy savings come from the active/idle part of the policy, these results show that it is better to adjust the active rate μ (at a larger time scale) and turn the interface back on (to active mode) as soon as one receives a single packet, than to use the maximum link rate and adjust the byte threshold L (as done by the active/idle policy).

Note that an optimal hybrid policy that optimizes over both L and μ would do even better. For example, the increase in energy usage for the hybrid policy under high delays is due to additional queueing caused by low link rates. (In the limit, the performance of the hybrid policy would converge to that of the rate switching policy.) For these de-

lays, it would be better to use the rate used for the local minimum on the curve and instead increase the byte threshold L.

4.3 Back-to-Back Rate Switching Example

Applying ALR techniques can affect the per-router packet delays and potential energy savings of neighboring routers. In this section, we use a simple example scenario to illustrate how two back-to-back routers can be affected. Here, rate switching is implemented on one or both of the routers.

Figure 4 shows the CDF of the per-router packet delay seen at each of the two routers, for three example configurations. The first corresponds to the default configuration, in which both interfaces operate at maximum capacity. In the second configuration, the link rate of both routers are decreased by a factor 12.5, and in the third configuration only the link rate of the first is decreased. We note that the tail delays (upper percentiles) are significantly lower on the second router, especially for the cases when the link rates of the first router are reduced. In fact, we often observe a decrease in tail delays on the second router just by lowering the service rate on the first router. This illustrates that rate switching can have positive effects on neighboring routers.

At this point, it should be noted that the reduction in tail delays depend on the traffic patterns observed in our packet traces. In fact, at first, a reduction can appear somewhat contrary to what may be suggested by traditional two-stage tandem queue models [6, 29]. For example, Burke's theorem [6] suggests that two consecutive M/M/m queues with independent service times can be treated independently, and any scaling in the service rates of the first router should not benefit the second router. Furthermore, when the service times are the same at the two routers and the routers are lightly loaded (e.g., $\rho < 0.6$), the second M/M/1 → M/1 router would typically see higher delays [29]. This can be explained by queued jobs on the first router typically arriving during service of a very large job, which because of the bigger job size also will be queued at the second router too; this time for an even longer time duration. However, as discussed in Appendix A, in contrast to assumptions common in these studies, for all our traces, the packet size distributions are well approximated by a bimodal distribution (Figure 10(b)), and service times are highly correlated both with regards to back-to-back packets (Table 1) and processing at consecutive routers [21].

When discussing the related tandem-queue literature, it should be noted that both a richer set of service time distributions and correlated service times have been considered (e.g., [29, 32]). However, often these studies use continuous service time distributions and potentially miss effects of the bimodal packet-size distribution and the inter-packet correlations seen in real network traces. For example, Sandmann [32] recently simulated the end-to-end packet delays through a series of queues, with correlated service times drawn from "general" (but continuous) service time distributions. While their results provide interesting insights into the relative impact as the load of the system changes from light-to-heavy load, the simulations also suggest that under light load correlated service times typically result in an increase in the end-to-end delays. In contrast, we typically observe a decrease both under light and heavy load.

To help explain how the above properties can result in a decrease in the delay seen on the second router, consider a simple 1×1 model with two packet sizes: large and small. Furthermore, assume that both routers have the same link capacity. In this special case (i) no queueing of large packets will happen on the second router, and (ii) all small packets queued behind a large packet on the first router will be queued for the difference in processing time of a large and small packet on the second router. These delays corresponds to the rightmost (maximum delay) points of the R_2 curves in Figure 4. Under these circumstances, the first router can see much larger delays, as packets can be queued behind more than one large packet. The somewhat larger median values, are due to small packets arriving to an otherwise empty system during processing of a large packet. These packets see a smaller delay on the first router, but would not greatly affect the average, which is dominated by the tail values. For most of our analysis we focus on the tail.

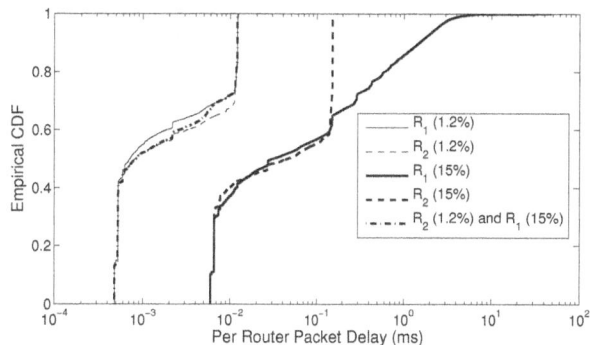

Figure 4: CDF of the per-router delay on two back-to-back routers R_1 (solid lines) and R_2 (dotted lines) when one or both their link rates are adjusted to different alternative link utilizations (shown in label). (Outgoing edge trace.)

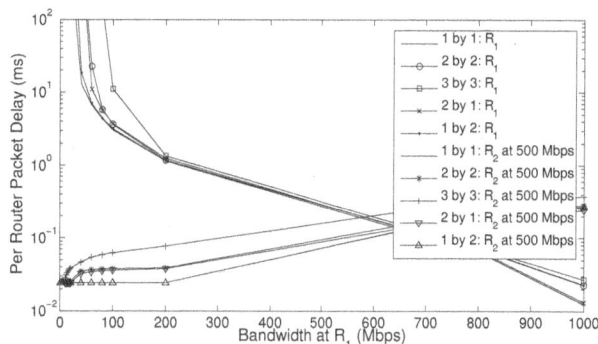

Figure 5: The 99-percentile per-router packet delays for each of the two routers (R_1 and R_2), under different link rates (shown on x-axis for R_1 and in the label for R_2) and scenarios (label).

To look closer at the interplay between the back-to-back routers, we next consider the per-router packet delays under different degrees of multiplexing. Figure 5 shows the 99-percentile delays observed at the two routers (R_1 and R_2) as a function of the link rate of the outgoing interfaces of the first router (x-axis), for different link rates of the outgoing interfaces of the second router. We again note that the more rate constrained (higher link utilization) the first router (R_1) is, the smaller the delays on the second router (R_2) become, at the cost of higher delays on the first router. Furthermore, for most of the cases, the delays on the second router are lower than the delays observed on the first router when the two routers have the same link rate (in this case 500 Mbps). In these cases, the combined per-packet delay (summed over the two routers) is dominated by the per-packet delay on the first router.

Motivated by the above observations, we next consider the potential energy savings when applying rate switching at both routers. Figure 6 shows the energy savings on each of the two routers for different degrees of multiplexing. All energy savings are calculated relative to the case when the router interfaces operate at full link capacity. For this and the remaining analysis, we focus on the proportional case.

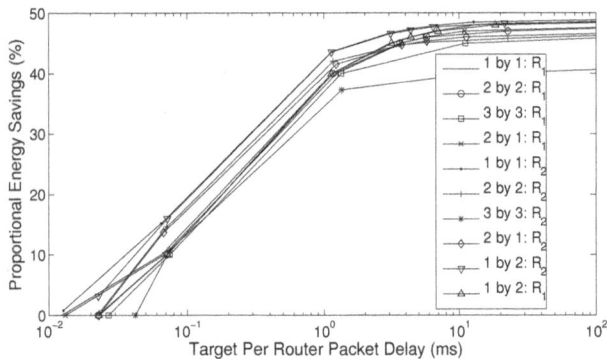

Figure 6: Energy savings for 99-percentile target per-router packet delays, under different scenarios (shown in label).

While there are regions for which the savings are greater on the first router, we note that the delay region for which the energy savings are larger for the second router are substantial. With the exception for the 3x3 case, the savings are always bigger for the second router. For the 3x3 case, there is a significant amount of multiplexing adding randomness at the second router that is not present on the first set of routers (regardless if ALR is used or not). This results in a significant delay penalty, especially under high utilizations.

4.4 Cascading Energy Improvements

The example in the previous section illustrates two types of energy improvements. First, downstream routers often see larger energy savings than upstream routers. Second, and perhaps more interestingly, the downstream routers themselves typically are able to achieve larger energy savings with ALR methods when the upstream routers also implement ALR methods, compared to if the upstream routers do not. This suggest that implementing ALR methods can help further incentivize neighboring routers to implement ALR methods, potentially leading to positive cascading effects.

In this section, we characterize this second type of multiplicative improvements. Under different scenarios and ALR policies, we quantify the improvements in energy savings at router R_2 that can be contributed to implementing ALR techniques at router R_1. We define the improvement in energy savings as the difference between (i) the energy savings that router R_2 can make when router R_1 is implementing the given ALR method, and (ii) the energy savings that router R_2 can make when router R_1 does not implement ALR.

Figure 7 shows the improvements for the edge and core traces when using the rate switching policy. We note that the largest improvements are observed for the outgoing edge traffic (the case with the smallest packets and lowest utilization) when multiplexing is low. For the 1x1 case, additional energy savings of up-to 30% are possible for all traces.

Also for the active/idle toggling policy (Figure 8(a)) and the hybrid policy (Figure 8(b)) we observe significant improvements, although smaller than the peak improvements observed for the rate switching policy. The two sharp peaks in improvements observed for some of the active/idle policy curves correspond to threshold values of approximately the same size as large and small packet, respectively. As exemplified by the delay-shift of the peaks in Figure 9, this effect causes the peaks to be shifted depending on the uti-

lization. Different utilizations cause the peaks to occur for different delay values. Relative to the active/idle policy, we also see that the hybrid policy shows relatively smaller but consistent improvements across workloads.

Finally, we note that while there are cases under low utilizations where ALR techniques can result in reduced energy savings (although still savings), these regions are much smaller and not the regions for which the ALR methods are likely to operate (such as to ensure good energy savings). For example, for intermediate 99-percentile per-router packet delays (between approximately 0.025 ms and 10 ms, for example) the improvements are positive for all policies and workloads considered.

5. DISCUSSION AND CONCLUSION

ALR policies and techniques can provide significant energy savings (e.g., Figure 3), providing strong incentives for operators to implement them into their routers. In this paper, we present a trace-based analysis of the impact that a router implementing these techniques has on neighboring routers. Looking at three general policy classes, each with their own hardware and monitoring constraints, we show that (i) ALR policies of each class have positive impact on the potential energy savings of neighboring routers, and (ii) the absolute energy savings at neighboring routers significantly depends on workload scenario and traffic patterns.

Tying back with our discussion of the end-to-end path of a packet, we note that the biggest savings are achieved at upstream interfaces close to the edge. These streams typically carry a relatively larger fraction small packets (e.g., TCP acks and HTTP requests) and can hence benefit more from ALR policies. However, these savings reduce with increased multiplexing of packet streams.

The biggest improvements in energy savings are achieved with rate switching policies. These policies can result in up-to 30% additional energy savings (Figure 7) on the neighboring downstream routers. These results suggest that a greedy energy savings on one router can have green cascading effects and provides further incentive to implement these policies at a large scale.

While hardware that allows active/idle toggling can achieve great energy savings (Figure 3), the multiplicative effects of these policies are somewhat smaller, although still positive (Figure 8(a)). Perhaps most attractive are the hybrid policy, which achieves the largest energy savings (Figure 3), and have positive effects on neighboring routers (Figure 8(b)). In the absence of energy-proportional hardware, we envision that effective hybrid policies could be implemented by combination of heterogeneous bonding [18], with active/idle toggling (based on the EEE standard [10]) implemented on each redundant link. Future work will consider the implications of large-scale deployment and the interaction with higher layer protocols [22]. More complex router models and an investigation of the variability (beyond our 99-percentile analysis) also present promising directions for future work.

6. ACKNOWLEDGEMENTS

This work was supported by funding from Center for Industrial Information Technology (CENIIT). We thank Martin Arlitt and Anirban Mahanti for helpful discussion on this work, and Rahul Hiran for helping us with the IP-to-AS mappings used in Section 2.1.

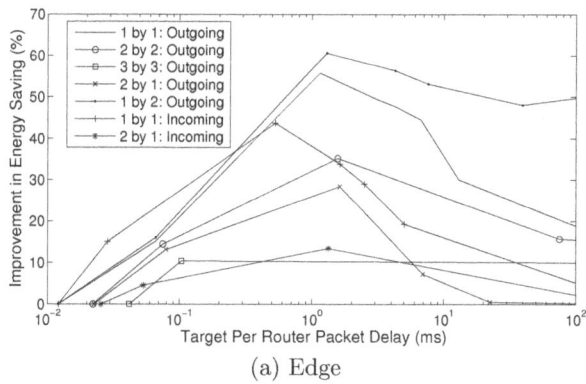

(a) Edge

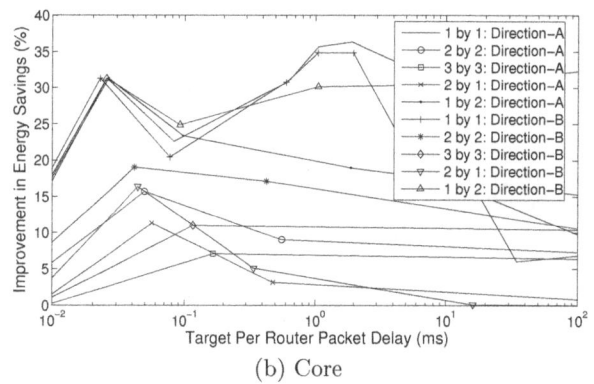

(b) Core

Figure 7: Improvements in energy savings on the second router, when using rate switching, under different scenarios and directions (shown in label).

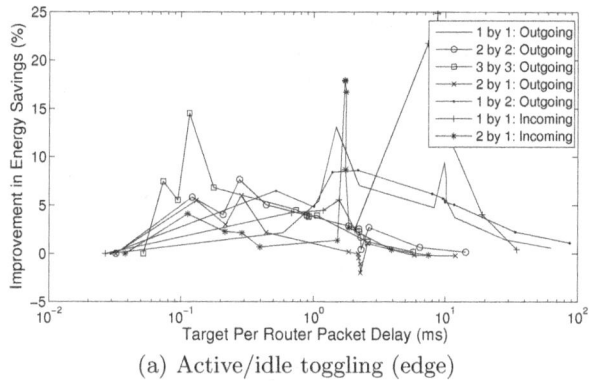

(a) Active/idle toggling (edge)

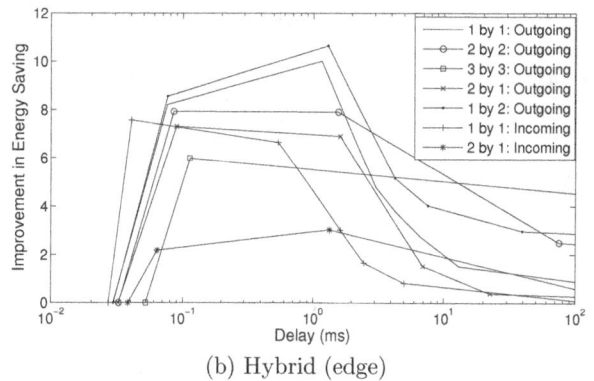

(b) Hybrid (edge)

Figure 8: Improvements in energy savings on the second router, when using the active/idle policy and the hybrid policy, under different scenarios and directions (shown in label).

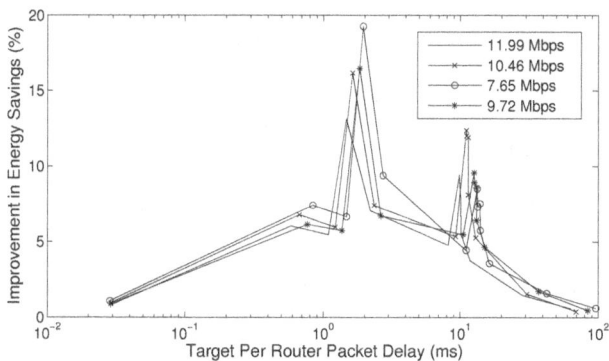

Figure 9: Impact of utilization on the improvements in energy savings on the second router, when using active/idle toggling with different link rates (shown in label).

7. REFERENCES

[1] Ieee 802.3az energy efficient ethernet: Build greener networks. *White Paper from Cisco and Intel* (2011).

[2] ANANTHANARAYANAN, G., AND KATZ, R. H. Greening the switch. In *Proc. OSDI* (2008).

[3] BARROSO, L., AND HOLZE, U. The case for energy-proportional computing. *IEEE Computer 40*, 12 (April 2007), 33–37.

[4] BOLLA, R., BRUSCHI, R., DAVOLI, F., AND CUCCHIETTI, F. Energy Efficiency in the Future Internet: A Survey of Existing Approaches and Trends in Energy-Aware Fixed Network Infrastructures. *IEEE Communications Survey and Tutorials 13*, 2 (2011), 223–244.

[5] BOLLA, R., DAVOLI, F., CHRISTENSEN, K., CUCCHIETTI, F., AND SURESH, S. The potential impact of green technologies in next-generation wireline networks: Is there room for energy saving optimization? *IEEE Communications Magazine 49*, 8 (Aug 2011), 80–86.

[6] BURKE, P. J. The output of a queueing system. *Operations Research 4*, 6 (1956), 699–704.

[7] CHIARAVIGLIO, L., MELLIA, M., AND NERI, F. Energy-aware backbone networks: A case study. In *Proc. IEEE GreenComm* (2009).

[8] CHIARAVIGLIO, L., MELLIA, M., AND NERI, F. Reducing power consumption in backbone networks. In *Proc. IEEE ICC* (2009).

[9] CHO, K., MITSUYA, K., AND KATO, A. Traffic data repository at the WIDE project. In *Proc. USENIX ATC* (2000).

[10] CHRISTENSEN, K., REVIRIEGO, P., NORDMAN, B. ANDBENNETT, M., MOSTOWFI, M., AND MAESTRO, J. Ieee 802.3az: The road to energy efficcient ethernet. *IEEE Communications Magazine 48*, 11 (2010), 50–56.

[11] CLEARY, J. G. Wand project at university of waikato, nz. In *Proc. HPN: Measurements and Analysis Collaborations Workshop* (1999).

[12] FAN, J., XU, J., AMMAR, M. H., AND MOON, S. B. Prefix-preserving ip address anonymization: measurement-based security evaluation and a new cryptography-based scheme. *Computer Networks* (Oct. 2004), 253–272.

[13] GUNARATNE, C., CHRISTENSEN, K., AND NORDMAN, B. Managing energy consumption costs in dektop PCs and LAN switches with proxying, split tcp connections, and scaling of link speed. *International Journal of Network Management 15* (Sept. 2005), 297–310.

[14] GUNARATNE, C., CHRISTENSEN, K., NORDMAN, B., AND SUEN, S. Reducing the energy consumption of ethernet with an adaptive link rate (alr). *IEEE Trans. on Computers 57*, 4 (April 2008), 448–461.

[15] GUPTA, M., GROVER, S., AND SINGH, S. A feasibility study for power management in LAN switches.

[16] GUPTA, M., AND SINGH, S. Greening of the internet. In *Proc. ACM SIGCOMM* (2003).

[17] GUPTA, M., AND SINGH, S. Dynamic ethernet link shutdown for energy conservation on ethernet links. In *Proc. IEEE ICC* (2007).

[18] HÄHNEL, M., DÖBEL, B., VÖLP, M., AND HÄRTIG, H. ebond: energy saving in heterogeneous R.A.I.N. In *Proc. e-Energy* (May 2013).

[19] HANAY, Y. S., LI, W., TESSIER, R., AND WOLF, T. Saving energy and improving TCP throughput with rate adaptation in ethernet. In *Proc. IEEE ICC* (2012).

[20] HAYS, R. Active/idle toggling with low-power idle. *Presentation for IEEE 802.3az Task Force* (Jan 2008).

[21] HOHN, N., PAPAGIANNAKI, K., AND VEITCH, D. Capturing router congestion and delay. *IEEE/ACM Trans. on Networking 17*, 3 (June 2009), 789–802.

[22] HUANG, T.-Y., HANDIGOL, N., HELLER, B., MCKEOWN, N., AND JOHARI, R. Confused, timid, and unstable: Picking a video streaming rate is hard. In *Proc. IMC* (2012).

[23] KLEINROCK, L. *Communications Nets: Stochastic Message Flow and Delay.* McGraw Hill, 1964.

[24] LABOVITZ, C., IEKEL-JOHNSON, S., MCPHERSON, D., OBERHEIDE, J., AND JAHANIAN, F. Internet inter-domain traffic. In *Proc. ACM SIGCOMM* (2010).

[25] LANGE, C. Energy-related Aspects in Backbone Networks. In *Proc. ECOC* (2009).

[26] MAO, Z. M., REXFORD, J., WANG, J., AND KATZ, R. H. Towards an accurate as-level traceroute tool. In *Proc. ACM SIGCOMM* (2003).

[27] MEISNER, D., GOLD, B. T., AND WENISCH, T. F. Powernap: Eliminating server idle power. In *Proc. ASPLOS* (2009).

[28] NEDEVSCHI, S., POPA, L., IANNACCONE, G., RATNASAMY, S., AND WETHERALL, D. Reducing network energy consumption via sleeping and rate-adaptation. In *Proc. NSDI* (2008).

[29] PINEDO, M., AND WOLFF, R. W. A comparison between tandem queues with dependent and independent service time. *Operations Research 30*, 3 (1982), 464–479.

[30] RESTREPO, J., GRUBER, C., AND MACHOCA, C. Energy profile aware routing. In *Proc. IEEE GreenComm* (2009).

[31] REVIRIEGO, P., CHRISTENSEN, K., RABANILLO, J., AND MAESTRO, J. An initial evaluation of energy efficient ethernet. *IEEE Communications Letters 15* (May 2011), 578–580.

[32] SANDMANN, W. Delays in a series of queues with correlated service times. *Journal of Networks and Computer Applications 35* (2012), 1415–1423.

[33] TUCKER ET AL., R. Energy Consumption in IP Networks. *ECOC* (2008).

[34] WEISER, M., WELCH, B., DEMERS, A., AND SHENKER, S. Scheduling for reduced cpu energy. In *Proc. USENIX OSDI* (1994).

[35] WIERMAN, A., ANDREW, L. L. H., AND TANG, A. Power-aware speed scaling in processor sharing systems. In *Proc. IEEE INFOCOM* (2009).

[36] ZHANG, B., SABHANATARAJAN, K., GORDON-ROSS, A., AND GEORGE, A. Real-time performance analysis of adaptive link rate. In *Proc. IEEE LCN* (2008).

[37] ZHANG, G. Q., YANG, Q. F., AND CHENG, T. Z. Evolution of the internet and its cores. *New Journal of Physics 10*, 12 (2008), 1–11.

APPENDIX

A. TRACE CHARACTERIZATION

To better understand our results, we must first understand the traffic traces. Figure 10 provides a high-level characterizing of the packet traces. Figure 10(a) shows the empirical Cumulative Distribution Function (CDF) of the packet inter-arrival times seen for ten example days. While common packet sizes and queueing at prior routers result in some frequent inter-arrival times (see curve steps), similar to many other traces collected over shorter time periods, the distributions are exponential in nature, with the general curve shapes being well-fitted by straight lines on lin-log scale.

Figure 10(b) shows the empirical CDF of the packet sizes, with traffic traces broken down by both location and direction. In all cases the observed distributions are bimodal in nature, with most packets being either small (less than 100 bytes) or large (1400-1500 bytes). We call the remaining packets medium sized (100-1400 bytes). While day-to-day variations are observed, the most significant differences are between measurements associated with different location and direction. For example, the outgoing (upstream) traffic at the edge has the largest fraction small packets, and the incoming (downstream) traffic at the edge has the largest fraction big packets. With HTTP being the dominant traffic type [24], this is expected, as the campus users close to the edge likely are consumers. Many of the big packets correspond to data traffic, whereas the small packets going in the opposite direction often will include TCP acknowledgements and HTTP requests.

We next consider the packet-size correlation between back-to-back packets. Table 1 shows the probability of a pair of consecutive packets being of certain packet sizes. In particular, we show the probability that a packet of a certain size category (small, medium, or large) is proceeded by a packet

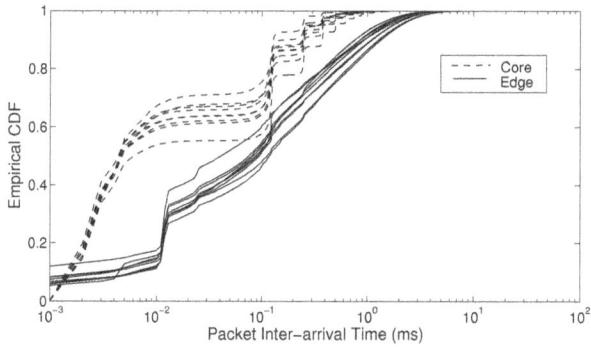

(a) Inter-arrival times

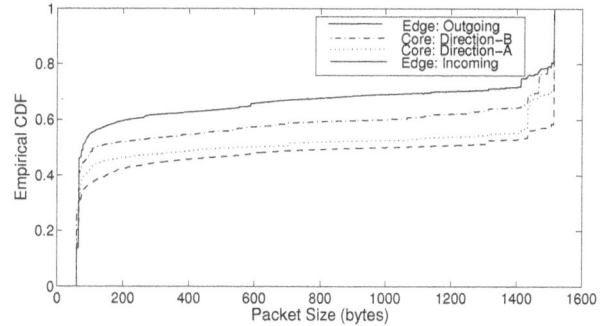

(b) Packet sizes

Figure 10: Empirical Cumulative Distribution Functions (CDFs) of the packet inter-arrival times and packet sizes, for different traces (shown in labels).

(a) Edge, outgoing

	Small	Medium	Large
Small	0.39	0.11	0.04
Medium	0.10	0.06	0.03
Large	0.05	0.02	0.20

(b) Edge, incoming

	Small	Medium	Large
Small	0.24	0.09	0.06
Medium	0.09	0.10	0.07
Large	0.06	0.07	0.24

(c) Core, direction A

	Small	Medium	Large
Small	0.29	0.07	0.08
Medium	0.06	0.04	0.05
Large	0.10	0.04	0.27

(d) Core, direction B

	Small	Medium	Large
Small	0.23	0.05	0.07
Medium	0.04	0.02	0.04
Large	0.08	0.03	0.45

Table 1: Packet-size probabilities of back-to-back packets.

belonging to one of the same categories. As expected, we observe significant correlations, with 58-70% of the packets following a packet belonging to the same size category (sum across the diagonals). When we only consider the packets that arrive at the time there is queueing, the bias is even higher. For example, in the case of a single router with transmission rate 1Gbps, approximately 76-77% of the queued packets see a packet of the same size ahead of them in the queue.

When doing this study, we originally wanted to build on traditional two-stage tandem queue models [6, 32]. Unfortunately, these studies typically makes simplifying assumptions that does not match our workloads, including assumptions about exponential service times, independent service times [29], or independent queues [23]. In contrast, the above results show that the real packet traces used in this study include correlations (e.g., Table 1), has bimodular packet size distribution (e.g., Figure 10(b)), and has packet-dependent processing times (proportional to the packet sizes [21], which typically remains fixed along the end-to-end path). For these reasons, we find that some of the observations are different from what would have been predicted by these queuing models.

Analysis of the Influences on Server Power Consumption and Energy Efficiency for CPU-Intensive Workloads

Jóakim v. Kistowski
University of Würzburg
joakim.kistowski@
uni-wuerzburg.de

Hansfried Block
Fujitsu Technology Solutions
GmbH
hansfried.block@
ts.fujitsu.com

John Beckett
Dell Inc.
john_beckett@dell.com

Klaus-Dieter Lange
Hewlett-Packard Company
klaus.lange@hp.com

Jeremy A. Arnold
IBM Corporation
arnoldje@us.ibm.com

Samuel Kounev
University of Würzburg
samuel.kounev@
uni-wuerzburg.de

ABSTRACT

Energy efficiency of servers has become a significant research topic over the last years, as server energy consumption varies depending on multiple factors, such as server utilization and workload type. Server energy analysis and estimation must take all relevant factors into account to ensure reliable estimates and conclusions. Thorough system analysis requires benchmarks capable of testing different system resources at different load levels using multiple workload types. Server energy estimation approaches, on the other hand, require knowledge about the interactions of these factors for the creation of accurate power models. Common approaches to energy-aware workload classification categorize workloads depending on the resource types used by the different workloads. However, they rarely take into account differences in workloads targeting the same resources. Industrial energy-efficiency benchmarks typically do not evaluate the system's energy consumption at different resource load levels, and they only provide data for system analysis at maximum system load.

In this paper, we benchmark multiple server configurations using the CPU worklets included in SPEC's Server Efficiency Rating Tool (SERT). We evaluate the impact of load levels and different CPU workloads on power consumption and energy efficiency. We analyze how functions approximating the measured power consumption differ over multiple server configurations and architectures.

We show that workloads targeting the same resource can differ significantly in their power draw and energy efficiency. The power consumption of a given workload type varies depending on utilization, hardware and software configuration. The power consumption of CPU-intensive workloads does not scale uniformly with increased load, nor do hardware or software configuration changes affect it in a uniform manner.

Categories and Subject Descriptors

C.4 [**Computer Systems Organization**]: Performance of Systems—*Performance attributes*

General Terms

Benchmarking, Workload, Energy Efficiency

Keywords

SPEC, SERT, Power, Workload Characterization, Energy Efficiency, Metrics, Utilization

1. INTRODUCTION

The energy efficiency of servers has become a significant issue as data center energy consumption has risen dramatically over the past decade. In 2010, the U.S. Environmental Protection Agency (U.S. EPA) estimated 3% of all electricity consumed in the US to be used in running data centers [8]. According to a New York Times study from 2012, data centers worldwide consume about 30 billion watts per hour. This is equivalent to the approximate energy output of 30 nuclear power plants [1].

This leads to an increasing pressure on hardware vendors to design systems with a high energy efficiency. Equally, software developers are tasked with the design and development of energy efficient applications.

Conventional end-user hardware makes use of device power-saving states to reduce energy consumption. Such states enable significant power savings during system idle times. Servers, however, are rarely fully idle. Instead they often serve requests that arrive at low frequencies leading to a steady load at a low-resource utilization level [2]. Furthermore, servers in data centers nowadays have to deal with highly variable application load intensities [17], translating into varying resource utilization levels. Therefore, considering the energy efficiency exhibited by a server at different load levels is equally as important as considering the server's efficiency at peak load.

To enable the design of energy efficient data centers and software systems, methods for the reliable measurement and estimation of server energy efficiency are needed. These methods must be able to accurately measure and estimate energy efficiency for a variety of workloads and load levels. The authors of [12] state that fine granular energy estimation models in particular are highly dependent on the type of workload for which energy is estimated.

As a result, many models for energy estimation classify workloads by the type of resources used. Models, such as the models proposed in [10, 3] decompose workloads to derive their respective CPU, memory, and storage I/O usage in order to obtain accurate power estimates based on device utilization and load levels. Utilization-based models, however, rarely take into account the effect of different types of workloads that use the same resource type. CPU-heavy workloads, for example, can lead to different power usage characteristics depending on their use of different instructions, caches, and so on.

Current approaches to model such effects make use of performance counters for the estimation of power usage based on the type of instructions [4]. Performance counters are, however, difficult to measure and classify, especially if the approach is to be extended over different machines with different architectures. As a result, we see the need to classify workloads that use the same resource type, based on their power and energy-efficiency characteristics at multiple load levels.

In this paper, we show the impact of different CPU-heavy workloads on the power consumption and energy efficiency of servers. For this evaluation, we employ the SERT provided by the Standard Performance Evaluation Corporation (SPEC). SERT is a tool suite for the measurement and analysis of server energy efficiency using different worklets exercising different aspects of the system under test (SUT) under multiple load levels. We employ SERT's seven CPU worklets to measure and characterize the power consumption and energy efficiency of these workloads over a range of at least 10 load levels. We present the measurement results of 20 selected machines, featuring three different CPU architectures.

The goal of this paper is to gain insight into the different classes of CPU workloads and how they vary in power consumption and energy efficiency at different load levels.

The major contributions of the paper are:

1. We explore the differences in power consumption and energy efficiency of different CPU worklets over a range of target load levels.

2. We demonstrate that different workloads utilizing the same resource (CPU) can have a significantly different energy draw. We analyze and characterize the changes in the energy efficiency of these workloads over multiple target load levels.

3. We explore the impact of different hardware and software configurations, including different architectures on the energy curves over target load levels.

Our measurements show that different CPU-heavy workloads exhibit significant differences in power consumption. These differences also translate directly to differences in the workload energy efficiency. Comparison of different hardware architectures and the introduction of hardware bottlenecks also shows a non-trivial relationship between power consumption and efficiency, as it introduces complexities in system performance without necessarily affecting the power draw in the same manner. We also debunk common assumptions such as constant operating system power overhead and maximum energy efficiency at full utilization.

The remainder of this paper is structured as follows: Section 2 introduces SERT, its architecture, and measurement approach. Section 3 then introduces the CPU workloads contained in SERT. Section 4 details the considered SUTs, and our measurement approach. Following that, Section 5 details the measurement results and describes the workloads power and energy-efficiency behavior over different load levels, architectures, and hardware and software configurations. We conclude the paper in Section 6.

2. SERT

SERT has been developed by the SPEC OSG Power Committee as a tool for the analysis and evaluation of the energy efficiency of server systems. Its design and development goals and process have been introduced in [8].

In contrast to energy-efficiency benchmarks, such as Joule-Sort [13], SPECpower_ssj2008 [6], and the TPC-Energy benchmarks [11], SERT is not intended to be used as a benchmark for a single system energy efficiency score. It does not aim to generate specific end user workloads, but instead provides a set of focused synthetic micro-workloads called worklets that exercise selected aspects of the Server (or System) Under Test (SUT). Specifically, the worklets have been developed to exercise the processor, memory and storage I/O subsystems, and may be combined into various configurations running serially or in parallel to provide "system" tests as part of a larger workload.

For each of the server components to be stressed, SERT offers a range of worklets designed to exercise the targeted component in a different manner. This allows for thorough analysis of system energy behavior under different workload types designed to target the same component. As an example, the CryptoAES worklet profits from both specialized instruction sets, as well as better CPU to memory connectivity, whereas the SOR worklet primarily scales with processor frequency.

SERT and its worklets are designed for the measurement of system energy efficiency at multiple load levels. This sets it further apart from conventional performance benchmarks, such as SPEC CPU [5], which targets maximum load and performance. A detailed description of SERT memory worklets and their applicability can be found in [7]. A detailed description of the storage I/O worklets and their properties can be found in [9].

2.1 Workload Calibration

According to [2], servers nowadays spend most of their time in a CPU utilization range between 10% and 50%. As a result, server energy-efficiency evaluation tools should support testing at different load levels. SERT offers functionality to do this.

SERT contains a test harness named Chauffeur which, among other tasks, handles the task of calibrating the workload to run at target load levels. To this end it runs each worklet in a calibration mode to determine the maximum transaction rate that the worklet can achieve on the SUT. For each Target Load Level (e.g., 100%, 75%, 50%, 25%), Chauffeur calculates the target transaction rate and derives the corresponding mean time from the start of one transaction to the start of the next transaction. During the measurement interval, these delays are randomized using an exponential distribution that statistically converges to the desired transaction rate. As a result, lower target loads consist of short bursts of activity separated by periods of inactivity.

2.2 Tool Architecture

SERT's measurements are controlled by a **controller** system. This system runs the Chauffeur harness, the reporter, the optional graphical user interface, and instances of the SPEC PTDaemon.

Chauffeur is the framework on which SERT is built. It handles both the coordination with the SUT director triggering the execution of worklets, as well as the communication with other controller-internal components, such as the PTDaemon and the reporter.

The Reporter generates the final report on measured and derived results including performance and energy measurements, as well as energy-efficiency scores.

The SPEC PTDaemon is a tool that allows network-based communication with a host connected to power and temperature measurement devices. PTDaemon supports a range of SPEC-approved devices, all featuring a maximum measurement uncertainty of 1% or better.

SERT requires at least one power analyzer and one temperature sensor. The power analyzer measures the wall power of the entire SUT, while the temperature sensor verifies the validity of measurements by assuring that all experiments are conducted under similar environmental conditions.

SERT also provides a graphical user interface (GUI) for easy test-run execution.

All SERT hardware and software components and their relationships to one another are illustrated in Fig. 1.

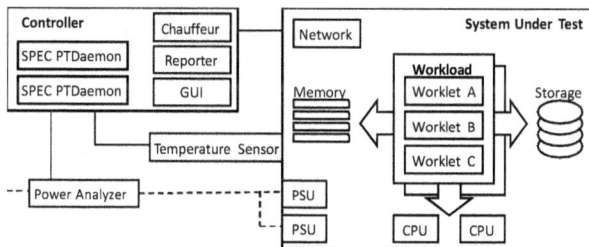

Figure 1: SERT Architecture [15]

3. CPU WORKLETS

This paper focuses on the characterization of worklets and their effect on system energy efficiency at different load levels. We focus on CPU-heavy worklets as CPUs offer a clear definition of different utilization levels and the calibration of a worklet's execution frequency offers a highly accurate method of reaching a given target load. Note that all load levels in this paper are workload specific loads, as they signify the number of executing transactions in relation to the maximum possible transaction rate without performance loss. This load definition offers the advantage of being platform independent and thus allowing better comparability of utilization based power and energy efficiency over multiple architectures, workloads, and machine types.

The SERT design document [15] defines CPU worklets through the following properties:

- A worklet requires consistent processor characteristics per simulated "user" regardless of the number of processors, cores, enabled threads, etc.
- At the 100% load level, the performance bottleneck is the processor subsystem.

- A worklet's performance should increase with increasing amount of processing resources, such as the number of physical CPUs, the number of cores, possibly the number of logical processors, higher clock rate, larger available cache, lower latency, and faster interconnect between CPU sockets.

SERT features a total of seven different CPU worklets, which we describe in short in this section. The performance metric employed for each of these worklets is throughput measured in transactions per second. Each CPU worklet is executed at a target load 25%, 50%, 75%, and 100% per default. For more detailed analysis, we have reconfigured our SERT runs to use 10% load level interval steps.

1. **Compress**: Implements a transaction that compresses and decompresses data using a modified Lempel-Ziv-Welch (LZW) method following an algorithm introduced in [18]. It finds common substrings and replaces them with a variable size code. This is deterministic and it is done on-the-fly. Thus, the decompression procedure needs no input table, but tracks the way the initial table was built.

2. **CryptoAES**: Implements a transaction that encrypts and decrypts data using the AES or DES block cipher algorithms using the Java Cryptographic Extension (JCE) framework.

3. **LU**: Implements a transaction that computes the LU factorization of a dense matrix using partial pivoting. It exercises linear algebra kernels (BLAS) and dense matrix operations.

4. **SHA256**: Utilizes standard Java functions to perform SHA-256 hashing and encryption/decryption transformations on a byte array. This byte array is perturbed by one byte for each transaction.

5. **SOR** (Jacobi Successive Over-Relaxation): Implements a transaction that exercises typical access patterns in finite difference applications, for example, solving Laplace's equation in 2D with Drichlet boundary conditions. The algorithm exercises basic "grid averaging" memory patterns, where each $A(i,j)$ is assigned an average weighting of its four nearest neighbors.

6. **SORT** Implements a sorting algorithm, which sorts a randomized 64-bit integer array during each transaction.

7. **XMLValidate**: Implements a transaction that exercises Java's XML validation package *javax.xml.validation*. Using both SAX and DOM APIs, an XML file (.xml) is validated against an XML schemata file (.xsd). To randomize input data, an algorithm is applied that swaps the position of commented regions within the XML input data.

4. MEASUREMENT METHODOLOGY

We measure all results according to the SPEC Power and Performance Benchmark Methodology [16]. The devices are setup and configured as required by SERT (see Section 2.2). The controller with the Chauffeur harness runs on an external machine, while the worklets are executed on the JVM within the SUT. We employ a Hioki 3334 Power Analyzer for most power measurements. A Digi Watchpart/H temperature sensor monitors the environmental temperature to ensure that it ranges between 22 and 23 °C for the duration of all test runs.

For the purpose of this paper, we have modified SERT's default configuration to execute measurements at intervals of 10% load levels, instead of the usual 25%. We confirm the expressiveness of results obtained using this configuration by comparing one set of measurements taken with 10% load intervals to a measurement series with 50 data-points for each worklet, differing by 2% in load. Detailed results of this measurement series are discussed in Section 5.1.4.

4.1 Systems under Test

We use a number of similar systems to explore the different bottlenecks that influence CPU-heavy worklets and cause differing power behavior. These systems are based on a Fujitsu PRIMERGY RX300S7 2 socket system using Intel Sandy Bridge processors. Our baseline configuration is shown in Table 1. Almost all servers feature two 8-core processors, with two hardware threads each. As a result, the workload features 32 threads with affinity to each of the virtual cores.

	RX300S7_RHEL6.4 _E5-2690_8x8GB
PSU Output Power	450 W
Number of Sockets	2
CPU name	Intel Xeon E5-2690 (Sandy Bridge)
Cores per CPU	8
Threads per Core	2
CPU frequency	2.9 GHz (3.3 GHz Turbo)
Memory Type	8GB 2Rx4 PC3L-12800R ECC
Number of DIMMs	8
Operating System	Red Hat Enterprise Linux Server 6.4 (Santiago)
JVM	Oracle HotSpot 1.7.0_51-b13

Table 1: Baseline Server Configuration

For our basic configuration, we introduce multiple variation points. We vary either the processor, the number of DIMMs, the DIMM size, or the operating system. The alternate operating system to the Linux Server is the Windows Server 2008 R2 Enterprise Edition OS.

When varying the processor, the following processors are used: Intel Xeon E5-2620, E5-2643, and E5-2650L. The Xeon E5-2643 and E5-2620 processors vary the number of available cores, having 4 and 6 cores per socket, respectively. The Intel Xeon E5-2650L processor features an identical number of cores as the baseline E5-2690 (8 cores per socket), having a reduced frequency of 1.8 GHz (up to 2.3 GHz with Turbo).

The number of DIMMs varies between 2, 8, and 24, whereas DIMM capacity is either 8 or 16 GB.

For comparison with other architectures, we also employ Fujitsu PRIMERGY RX600S6, Fujitsu PRIMERGY RX200S8, Dell PowerEdge R720 servers, and an AMD Opteron based HP ProLiant DL385p Gen8 machine. The Fujitsu PRIMERGY RX200S8 and Dell PowerEdge R720 servers are introduced in detail in Sections 5.4 and 5.5. The PRIMERGY RX600S6 Servers feature 4 processor sockets, each

carrying an Intel Xeon E7-4870 Westmere-EX CPU at 2.4 GHz (up to 2.8 GHz with Turbo) processing frequency with 10 cores each and 2 hardware threads per core.

4.2 Normalized Power/Efficiency Values

For each measurement interval, we measure the amount of dispatched and completed work units, the interval's length, the average power use, load level, and environmental temperature. In this paper, we focus on the performance, power, and efficiency metrics in relation to the load level at which they were measured.

As the goal of this paper is the characterization of distinctive power and energy efficiency behavior measured at different load levels for different CPU heavy workloads under different platforms and platform configurations, we display the measured power-load and energy efficiency-load curves in a manner that allows for easy comparison. To achieve this, we normalize all power and energy efficiency measurements to the minimum value for each load level based curve. As a result, all measurements feature a normalized power or efficiency value of one for the smallest CPU load interval. This approach allows for easy comparison of the measurements corresponding to different target load levels, as each measurement now displays the ratio between the measurement at the respective load level and the measurement at the minimum load level.

5. EXPERIMENTAL ANALYSIS

In this section, we show and analyze the measurement results. First, we discuss the differences between CPU worklets when run on the same machine. Next, we compare the performance and power of each worklet under different machine configurations. We then go into detail on configuration changes that have a significant impact on power consumption. Finally, we categorize the different types of power and energy efficiency per load curves.

5.1 Power Consumption Differences between CPU Workloads

We first compare the power consumption of the different CPU worklets on our baseline system before comparing their overall energy efficiency. Following that, we provide an outlook on how these inter-worklet differences can be affected using other system configurations.

5.1.1 Power Consumption

Figure 2 shows the power consumption of SERT's CPU worklets on the baseline system (see Table 1). The power consumption for the worklets differs the least at 10% load level with average power draw ranging between 118.3 W for SOR and 126 W for the XMLValidate worklet. The 100% target load level features a larger total difference in power consumption of 87.6 W. The worklet using the most power here is again XMLValidate with a power draw of 431.4 W, and the least power is again drawn by SOR at 343.8 W. XMLValidate is not always the biggest power consumer though, nor does SOR always consume the least power. Between 30% and 90% load, XMLValidate is replaced by CryptoAES as the biggest power consumer, and SHA256 consumes less power than SOR in the range between 30% and 70% load. Even though worklets' power consumption differences are most pronounced at full utilization, it is notable that significant differences of power draws do exist at lower utilization

RHEL6.4_E5-2690_8x8GB Power

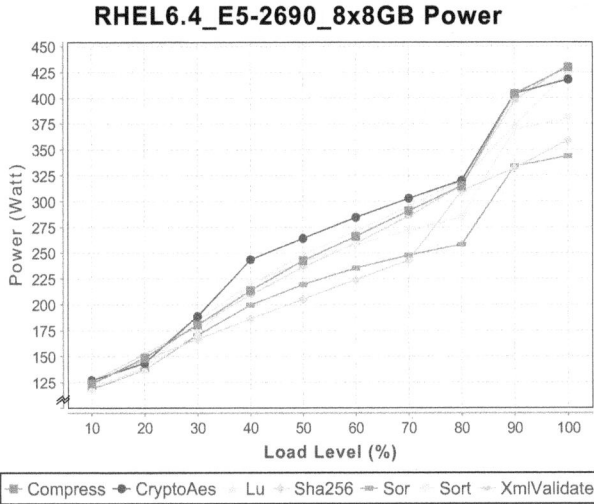

Figure 2: Power Consumption on Baseline Server

ranges. For instance, at 40% load, the biggest power consumer (CryptoAES, 243.5 W) draws 57.1 W more than the smallest power consumer (SHA256 186.4 W).

The power / load curves display a similar pattern for all seven worklets. At lower load levels, power draw increases in an either linear or slightly concave manner. After this gradual power increase, we can observe a drastic rise in power draw between the 80% and 90% load intervals. Exceptions are the SHA256 and LU worklets. SHA256's sudden power increase is located between the 70% and 80% intervals, whereas LU features a longer linear increase in power consumption between 80% and 100%. In most cases, after the sudden increase in power consumption, the power increase reverts back to a similar shape as for the lower load levels.

RHEL6.4_E5-2690_8x8GB Performance

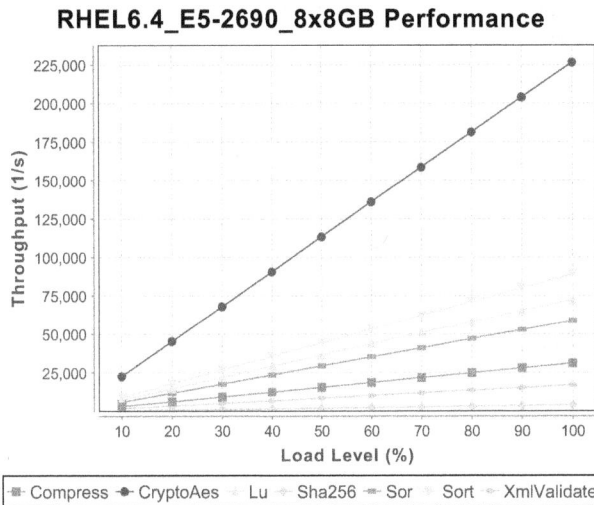

Figure 3: Throughput on Baseline Server

5.1.2   Energy Efficiency

Energy efficiency for CPU worklets is measured in throughput/power [15]. SERT achieves the different target load levels by scaling the number of executed transactions per unit of time. As a result, the throughput of the different worklets

rises linearly with CPU utilization (see Fig. 3). Throughput per load level differs greatly depending on the actual worklet, as each worklet type induces different loads on the target CPU. To enable comparability, the energy efficiency displayed in Fig. 4 applies the normalization approach introduced in Section 4.2.

RHEL6.4_E5-2690_8x8GB Throughput/Power

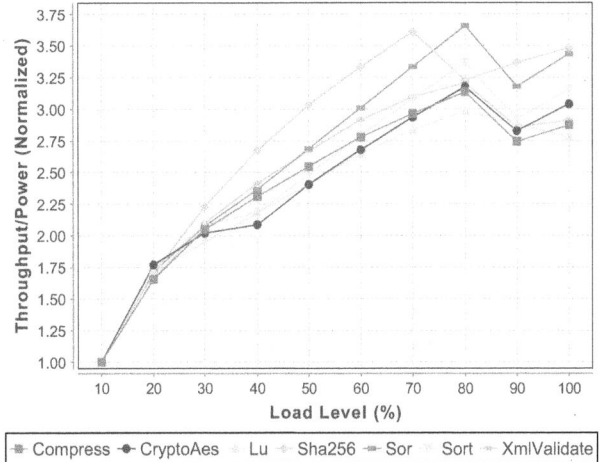

Figure 4: Energy Efficiency on Baseline Server.

Due to the linear nature of the throughput increase over the load intervals, energy efficiency mirrors the observations made for the pure power measurements.

Energy efficiency increases steadily, as long as the throughput increases faster than the power consumption. The sudden rise in power consumption between the 80% and 90% load mark, however, features a power demand that exceeds the linear increase in throughput, thus leading to a slight drop in energy efficiency. This observation contradicts the common assumption of maximum energy efficiency at full machine load. Observations of a "U"-shaped energy efficiency curve [14], though more accurate, also do not picture the entirety of the energy-efficiency curve, as energy efficiency increases again at the 90% load level.

The LU and CryptoAES worklets feature a relatively steep rise in power consumption between 20% and 40% load. As a result, the increase in energy efficiency is slightly diminished at these intervals.

5.1.3   Worklet Comparison for Lower CPU Frequency

Lower CPU frequencies have some effect on the worklets' normalized power consumption. Fig. 5 shows the normalized power consumption for SERT's CPU worklets on a server in which the CPUs have been exchanged with Intel Xeon E5-2650L processors. These processors feature the same number of cores and hardware threads as the Xeon E5-2690, which was installed in the baseline system. They do, however, work at a reduced base frequency of 1.8GHz compared to the 2.9GHz of the Xeon E5-2690.

While the power / load curves bear some overall similarity to the curves on the baseline server, we can make some additional observations from this measurement.

First, we can see that the sudden rise in power consumption between the 80% and 90% measurement intervals, while still notable, is not as steep as it was in the previous case.

A new observation is that the concave segment of the

RHEL6.4_E5-2650L_8x8GB Power

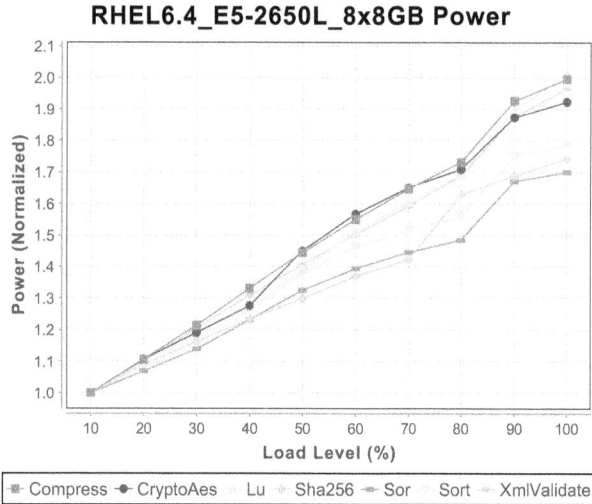

Figure 5: Normalized Power Consumption on Server with Xeon E5-2650L Processor

RHEL6.4_E5-2690_8x8GB Power

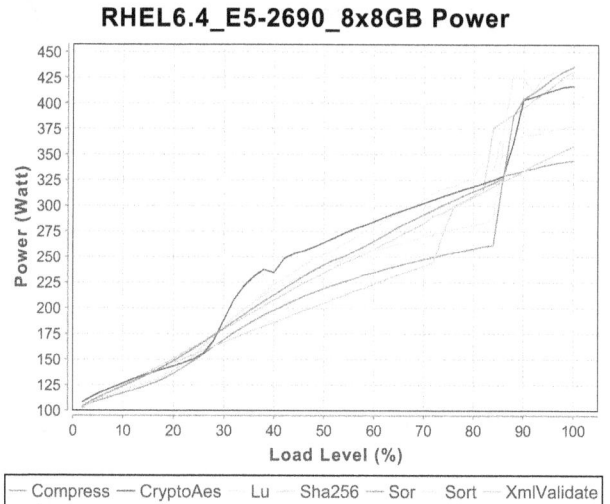

Figure 6: Power Consumption of the Baseline Server Measured at 2% Load Intervals

power / load curve does not start directly at the 10% load level. Instead, a linear segment leading up to the concave curve is clearly visible for all worklets. CryptoAES demonstrates this best with a linear segment leading up to the 40% load mark, followed by a concave curve segment up to the 80% load level. Knowing that this effect exists, we can also find it when revisiting the original measurement on the baseline system. Here, the concave function begins at an earlier point. In most cases, the linear segment terminates at the 20% load level.

5.1.4 Accuracy of Measurements at 10% Utilization Intervals

The majority of measurements in this paper show the power consumption and energy efficiency measured at 10% CPU load intervals. From this, we extrapolate functions and curves approximating the energy behavior of the considered servers when subjected to CPU heavy workloads.

To verify that 10% load intervals can lead to representative insights on the overall behavior of the machine's power consumption at different load levels, we perform one series of measurements at the fine granularity of 2% load intervals. Fig. 6 shows the results of those measurements.

Compared to the measurements at 10% load intervals in Fig. 2, we can confirm all of our observations in Section 5.1. A slow rise in power consumption is followed by a concave curve segment starting around the 20% load level in most cases. This segment then ends with a steep linear increase in power consumption usually occurring between the 80% and 90% load levels, which again is followed by a continuation of the increase of the previous segment.

While confirming the previous observations, the finer granularity of load intervals also reveals some additional insights. Most notably, the LU and CryptoAES worklets exhibit instances of short decreases in power use for some load level increases. These effects are repeatable over several measurements and warrant some further research.

5.2 Per Workload Results

We analyze the impact of varying the system architecture and configuration on the power consumption and energy ef-

ficiency of selected worklets. More specifically, we evaluate the behavior of CryptoAES, SHA256, and SORT as they deviate the most from the observed power pattern on our baseline machine. They are also representative of most deviations, which occur on our selected SUTs.

5.2.1 CryptoAES

For CryptoAES, the amount of available memory channels has a significant impact on the power draw caused by the worklet. When increasing the baseline machine's amount of RAM to 24 DIMMs, each with a capacity of 16 GB, the function characterizing power consumption over load changes little. The only visible difference is a slight reduction in the relative difference between power consumption at 10% and 100% load, resulting in a slightly smaller normalized power consumption in Fig. 7. This effect can be attributed to the increase in constant system power draw caused by the additional DIMMs.

CryptoAES Power

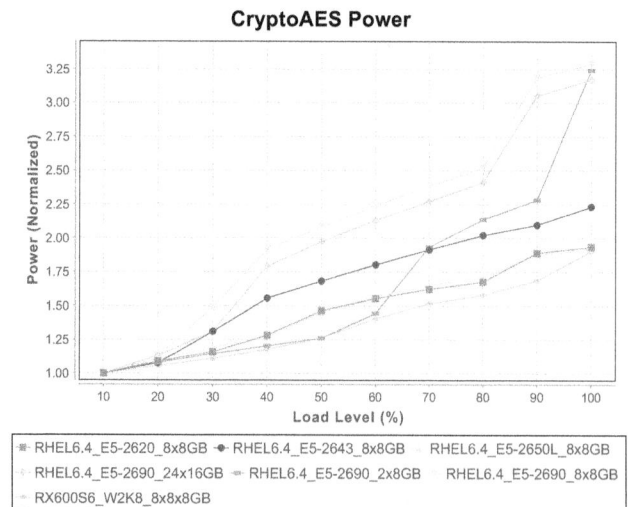

Figure 7: Normalized Power Consumption of Different Servers Running CryptoAES

Decreasing the amount of available RAM to two DIMMs,

however, has a far more drastic effect. The normalized power draw does not increase as heavily at early load stages, as all DIMMs are already under high load due to the smaller constant power overhead. This effect is mitigated at 100% load, as the CPU power consumption outweighs the memory effects.

Exchanging the processor also impacts the power draw of CryptAES. The use of processors with lower clock rates or fewer cores lowers the difference between the power draw at low vs. full load. Both the Intel Xeon E5-2650L with its 8 cores at 1.8 GHz and the Xeon E5-2620L with its 6 cores at 2.0 GHz demonstrate this effect well. Both show a decreased difference in power consumption between load levels, yet both still follow the same curve shape as the baseline system.

Running CryptoAES on a Xeon E5-2643 quad-core processor, however, results in a different power / load function, as the steep rise in power consumption between the 80% and 90% load level seems to be missing. Instead, we can only observe a minor increase at the 90% to 100% level.

Running CryptoAES on a four socket system using Windows results in the smallest normalized difference between low vs. full load power draw. This can easily be attributed to the higher constant energy costs of keeping a four socket system running. Considering the system's energy efficiency in Fig. 8, we can see a dramatic difference in energy efficiency, which is due to the high combined performance potential of 40 cores. Generally speaking, larger systems tend to feature higher constant power draw. This leads to poor energy efficiency at lower load levels. In return, these systems are capable of far greater performance at high load levels, increasing their energy efficiency at those levels.

CryptoAES Throughput/Power

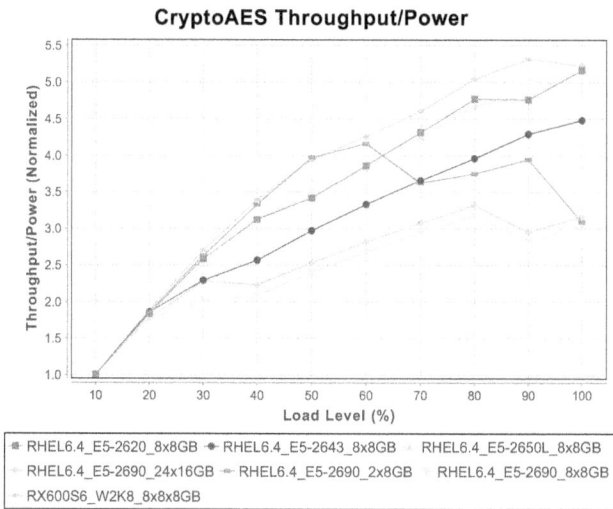

RHEL6.4_E5-2620_8x8GB   RHEL6.4_E5-2643_8x8GB   RHEL6.4_E5-2650L_8x8GB
RHEL6.4_E5-2690_24x16GB   RHEL6.4_E5-2690_2x8GB   RHEL6.4_E5-2690_8x8GB
RX600S6_W2K8_8x8x8GB

Figure 8: Normalized Energy Efficiency of Different Servers Running CryptoAES

Evaluation of energy efficiency also confirms that CryptoAES requires a minimal number of available memory access channels. Using 2 DIMMs only results in greater energy efficiency for CPU load of 60% and less. At higher load levels, however, the memory bottleneck leads to a decrease in performance and causes efficiency to drop.

Even though the 16 x 24GB RAM configuration of our baseline system shows smaller differences in power consumption, it does show a slight increase in normalized energy efficiency. This is to be expected as performance increases with

the additionally provided memory channels. The addition of more DIMMs does however also lead to a decrease in effective memory frequency from 1600 MHz to 1066 MHz. As a result, the increase in normalized efficiency is only minimal.

5.2.2 SHA256

Experiments with the SHA256 worklet confirm most of the observations made for CryptoAES, with some key differences. The overall shape of the power / load curves still matches the previously observed shapes, with the four socket Windows system showing the smallest differences between the load levels. The Windows system also displays a different power scaling behavior over load. We discuss the differences in power scaling of SERT's worklets for different operating systems in Section 5.3.

SHA256 Power

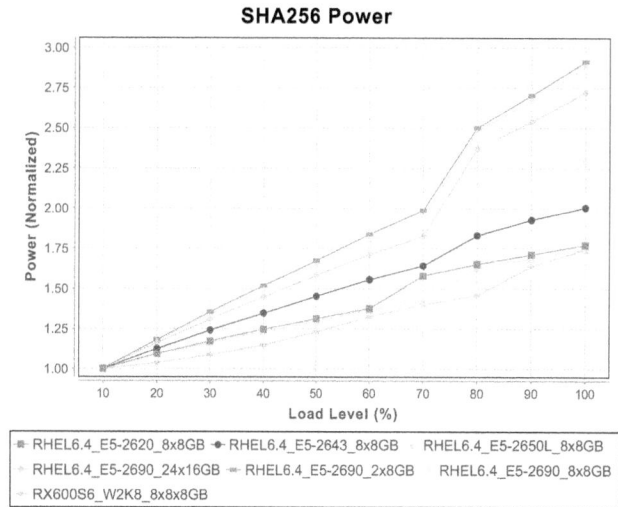

RHEL6.4_E5-2620_8x8GB   RHEL6.4_E5-2643_8x8GB   RHEL6.4_E5-2650L_8x8GB
RHEL6.4_E5-2690_24x16GB   RHEL6.4_E5-2690_2x8GB   RHEL6.4_E5-2690_8x8GB
RX600S6_W2K8_8x8x8GB

Figure 9: Normalized Power Consumption of Different Servers Running SHA256

A key difference in SHA256 and CryptoAES is found in the way in which power consumption over load scales depending on the number of installed DIMMs. For CryptoAES, a minimum number of memory access channels is necessary for high performance and energy efficiency. An insufficient number of memory channels also leads to significant deviations in power behavior. SHA256 shows little dependency an RAM connectivity. It has little impact on power, with smaller numbers of DIMMs only causing a slightly lower constant power overhead. It also has no significant impact on energy efficiency, as seen in Fig. 10.

Another new observation is the deviation between the normalized power consumption of SHA256 using the Xeon E5-2620 and 2650L processors. Both processors still behave similarly, yet show difference in normalized power at 70% load, with the E5-2620 system having its steep increase in power consumption between the 60% and 70% intervals, and the E5-2650L system increasing its energy draw at the 70% to 80% interval. This deviation is not surprising, as the processors feature different numbers of cores and processor clocks.

Running on the Xeon E5-2643 processor, SHA256 also features a smaller sudden increase between the 70% and 80% load levels. Other than CryptoAES running on the same processor, it does show some increase at this level. This increase is, however, not as pronounced as it is on the other

229

system configurations.

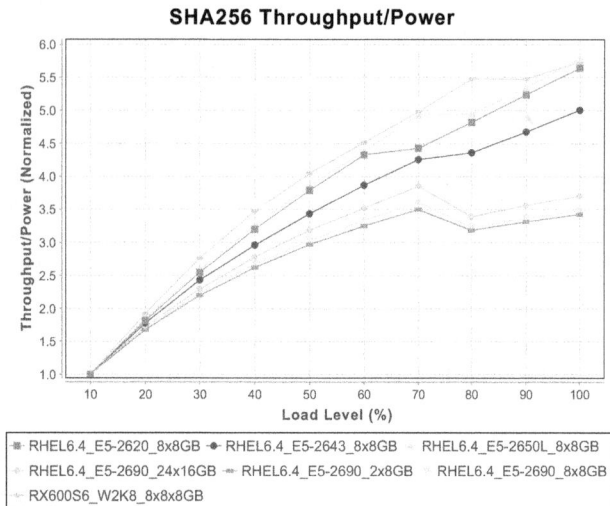

Figure 10: Normalized Energy Efficiency of Different Servers Running SHA256

The normalized worklet energy efficiency in Fig. 10 provides another observation for the Xeon E5-2620 and E5-2650L processors. While systems with these processors exhibit smaller differences in power consumption than the baseline system, they show greater differences in energy efficiency, matching the energy efficiency range of the 4 socket system.

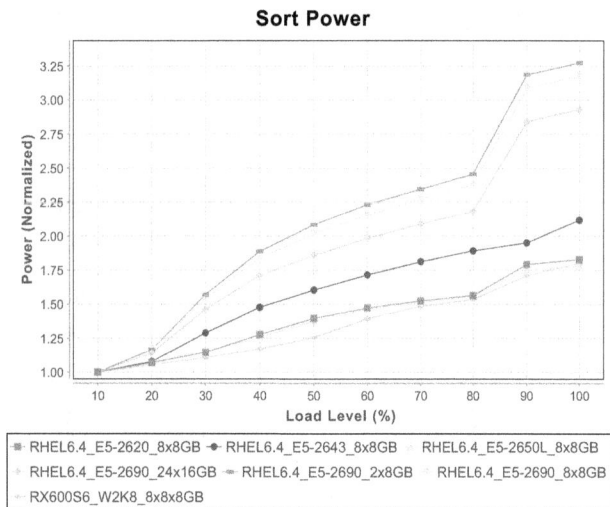

Figure 11: Normalized Power Consumption of different Servers running Sort

5.2.3   Sort

The Sort worklet presents a mix of the observations from CryptoAES and SHA256. Sort's normalized power consumption (see Fig. 11) mirrors CryptoAES for the system running Xeon E5-2643 processors, as the power over load function features only a slight additional increase in power consumption at the 90% to 100% load interval.

Similarly to SHA256, however, Sort shows little RAM dependency featuring a similar normalized power consumption for the different RAM configurations of the baseline system.

The biggest difference between Sort and the other worklets is the observation that the concave segment of the power function is far more pronounced. It is also clearly visible for all system configurations with the exception of the 4 socket Windows system.

5.2.4   Conclusions

Our analysis of the impact of hardware configurations on worklet power consumption and energy efficiency has revealed several insights. Our experiments confirmed that a greater number of hardware components decreases the relative difference between maximum and minimum power consumption, as these components introduce an additional constant power draw. These systems have a lower energy efficiency at low load levels, in return they feature greater efficiency at high load.

The relative differences between power draw at low vs. high load are also smaller for processors with fewer cores and lower clock rates. We have also demonstrated that bottlenecks, in our case a memory access bottleneck, have significant impact on both power consumption and energy efficiency.

5.3   Effect of Operating System

Common power models such as [3] often assume a constant power overhead created by the respective operating system. As a result, operating systems can be compared with respect to the amount of constant power overhead they induce.

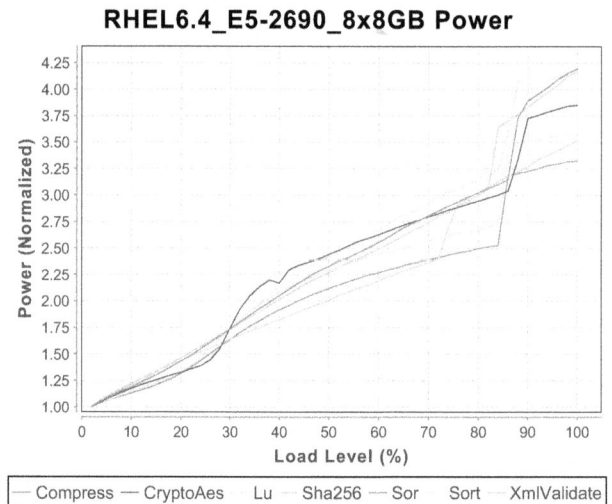

Figure 12: Normalized Power Consumption on Baseline Server Running Linux

We test this assumption by executing our CPU worklets on both Linux and Windows Server systems. Fig. 12 shows the normalized power consumption of our baseline system running Linux using load level intervals of 2%, whereas Fig. 13 shows the normalized power consumption of the same server running Windows Server 2008 R2 as its operating system.

Both figures show that a constant power overhead per operating system is a gross oversimplification of the diverse power behaviors.

On Linux, the different worklets exhibit a range of different power / load curves. Windows, on the other hand, creates a more uniform power draw. Workloads still differ in their power consumption, specifically in the rate of power increase with increasing utilization. The shape of the power / load curve, however, is very similar for each worklet. This relatively uniform manner of power over load increase results in smaller normalized power differences between the worklets at lower load levels. These differences in normalized power then increase with higher load levels.

W2K8_E5-2690_8x8GB Power

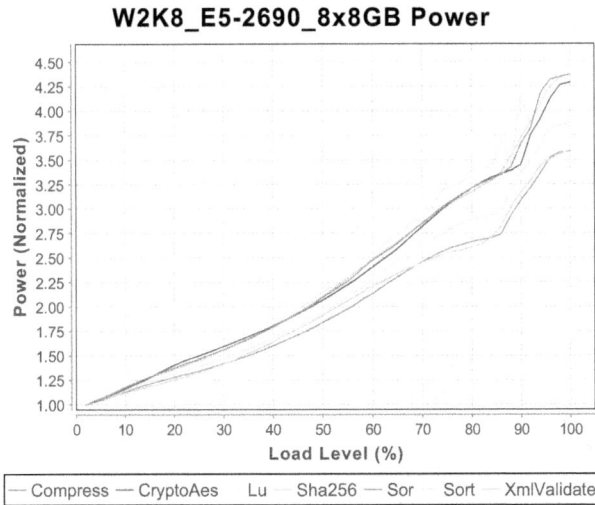

Figure 13: Normalized Power Consumption on Baseline Server Running Windows Server 2008 R2

The only worklets deviating from the common scheme are Compress and CryptoAES, which show a lesser increase than the other worklets at the 90% load level.

Overall, the power / loadation curve on Windows can be approximated using an exponential increase in power draw over load. Deviations from this exponential curve are less pronounced and less diverse than on the Linux system. We can still observe a slightly concave part overlapping the exponential curve between the 50% and 80% load levels. This deviation is clearly visible for the SHA256 and SOR worklets. The visibility of this deviation differs between architectures. The four socket Windows system, running Westmere-EX processors (see Figures in Section 5.2), for example, demonstrates a greater deviation from the exponential curve than the baseline system. Compared to the non-Windows system, however, the base function of power over load follows an exponential pattern, which it does not on the Linux system.

An additional measurement series of SERT's CPU worklets on the baseline system running Windows Server 2012 also confirmed the results of our comparison and are shown in Fig. 14. Windows Server 2012 features smaller changes to the exponential base power over load function compared to Windows Server 2008 R2. As a result, the concave deviations of worklet power as described above are not as pronounced.

Concluding, we find that differences in power draw over load cannot be approximated using a constant power overhead per operating system. Operating systems are not simply "better" or "worse" in their impact on power. Power draw differs depending on worklet and load level, with power over load being approximated by completely different functions.

5.4 Effect of Processor Architecture

We now evaluate the effect of the processor architecture

W2012_E5-2690_8x8GB Power

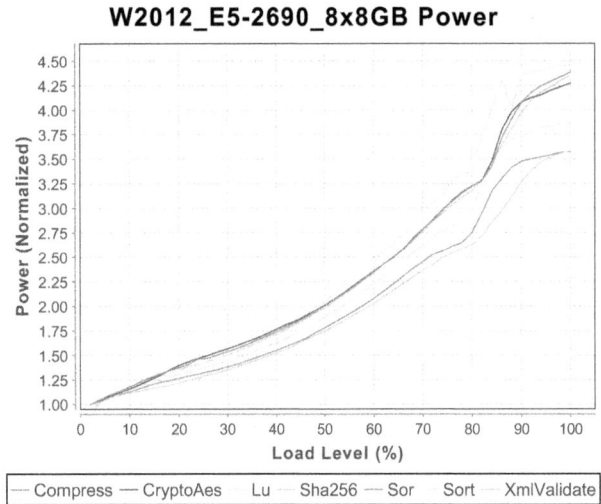

Figure 14: Normalized Power Consumption of the Baseline System Running Windows Server 2012

on the character of the power over load function on both Linux and Windows. We run the Windows comparison on our baseline Fujitsu system with its Intel Sandy Bridge type processor and on a Fujitsu PRIMERGY RX200S8 with 8 core Intel Xeon E5-2667v2 processors at 3.3 GHz (3.6 GHz with Turbo). Both systems feature 8x8 GB RAM and two processor sockets. The Xeon E5-2667v2 processor was selected as it is also an 8 core processor with an only slightly higher clock frequency.

Sort,SOR,LU Windows Server 2012 Power

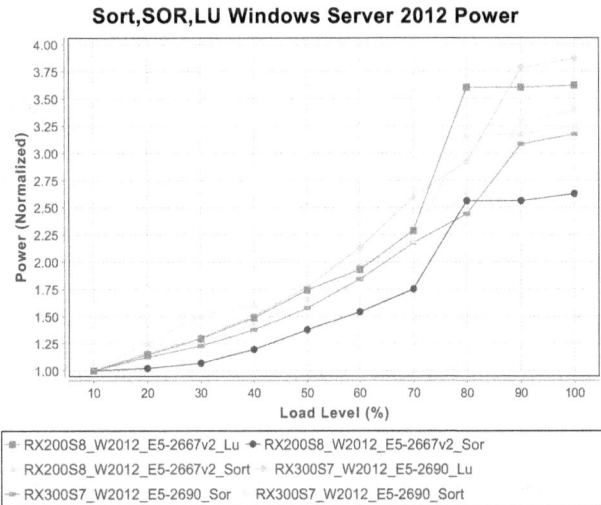

Figure 15: Normalized Power Consumption of the Baseline Sandy Bridge System and an Ivy Bridge System, both Running Windows Server 2012

Linux CPU architecture comparisons are performed on a Dell PowerEdge R720 system, also using the same two processors and 8x8 GB RAM. These systems run Red Hat Enterprise Linux 6.5. Dell BIOS power management has been disabled on those systems to enable an accurate accounting of the effects of operating system power management functionality.

For better visibility we present the results for the Sort, SOR, and LU worklets. The differences between these worklets are representative when comparing SERT's CPU worklet power consumption over the two architectures.

Comparison of the worklet's power draw on Windows (see Fig. 15) shows, that power consumption tops out far earlier for all worklets on the E5-2667v2 processor. On Sandy Bridge power consumption stops its exponential increase at 90% load. Ivy Bridge, on the other hand, features an only minimal increase starting at 80% load. Another visible deviation is found for the Sort worklet, which features a bigger deviation from the exponential base pattern on the E5-2667v2 CPU than on the older E5-2690. Deviations of this kind are also visible on Sandy Bridge for other worklets (such as LU), yet occur at higher load levels than the Sort deviation on the E5-2667v2.

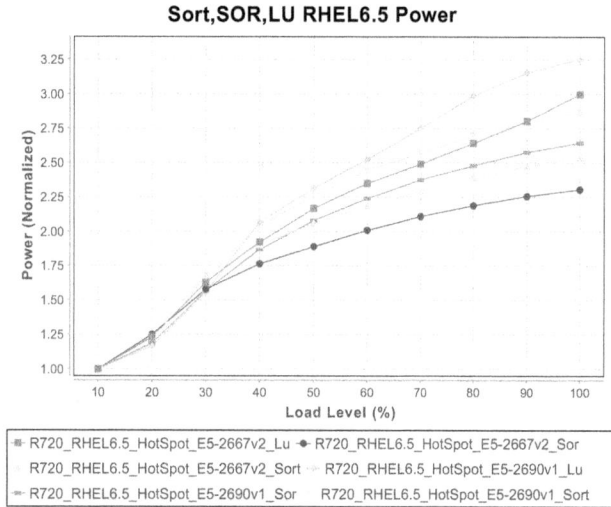

Figure 16: Normalized Power Consumption of a Sandy Bridge System and Ivy Bridge System, both Running Linux

The power consumption of the worklets on Linux (see Fig. 16) shows only small differences between the processor architectures. LU features a more linear power increase over load on Ivy Bridge, with a slight additional increase around 90% load. Differences between power consumption at 10% and 100% load are also not as large overall. The curve shapes are relatively similar, however.

Notably, the Dell R720 system running RHEL 6.5 does not show the steep rise in power consumption around the 80% load mark that was measured on the systems in Section 5.2 running RHEL 6.4. In our previous measurements, we already observed the absence of this sudden increase when using the Intel Xeon E5-2643 processor (see Fig. 7). The RHEL 6.4 measurements using the Xeon E5-2690 processor, however, did feature the increase after the concave function segment.

We also evaluate the shape of the power curve for an AMD Opteron based system on an HP ProLiant DL385p Gen8 machine, running Windows Server 2008R2 (Fig. 17) with two AMD Opteron 6320 processors (8 cores each) at 2.8 GHz (3.3 GHz with Turbo) and 8 x 8 GB of RAM. This curve shows major differences with the power curves of other architectures. It is still clearly a power curve as measured on a Windows system, as it features the characteristic exponential power increase over utilization also measured on the Intel systems. The sudden increase in power around the 80%

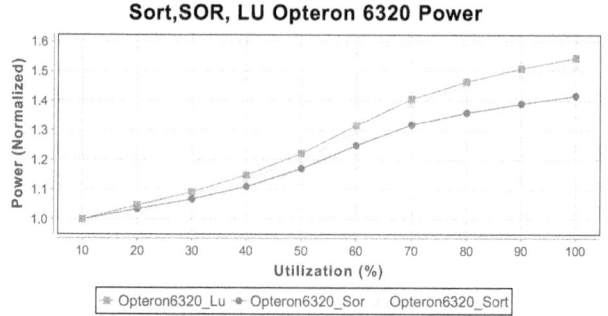

Figure 17: Normalized Power Consumption of an AMD Opteron based System, running Windows Server 2008R2

load level, however, is missing and is replaced by a concave function segment beginning at 60% load.

5.5 Effect of JVM

Similarly to our exploration of operating system impact on the power / load function, we also measure the impact of the Java Virtual Machine (JVM). For these measurements we employ a Dell PowerEdge R720 machine equipped with two Intel Xeon E5-2667v2 processors and 8 DIMMs of 8 GB DDR3 memory at 1866 MHz.

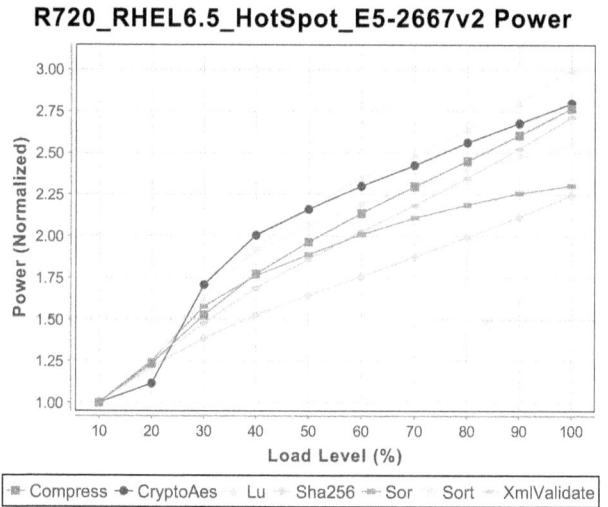

Figure 18: Normalized Power Consumption of Dell PowerEdge Running the Oracle HotSpot JVM

Fig. 18 shows the worklets' normalized power consumption running on Oracle's HotSpot JVM and Fig. 19 shows the worklets' power consumption on IBM's J9 JVM. The choice of JVM does not have as significant of an impact on the overall curve shape as the choice of operating system. Some differences are visible though.

Small changes can be observed in the consumption of the LU, Compress, and XMLValidate worklets. For the LU worklet, the concave function segment is flattened out at higher load levels, when using the J9 JVM. As increase in power consumption drops slightly on HotSpot, J9 features a linear rise. Compress and XMLValidate feature the return of the segment with a steep increase in power consumption following the concave segment on J9. This effect was visible for our HotSpot measurements on the Sandy Bridge

232

architecture on RHEL 6.4, but has almost completely disappeared on RHEL 6.5. Running the worklets on J9 results in this increase returning in some cases between the 90% and 100% load level. The reverse can be observed for the LU worklet. LU features a minimal increase in the rise of power consumption between the 90% and 100% load level on HotSpot. This effect is not visible on J9.

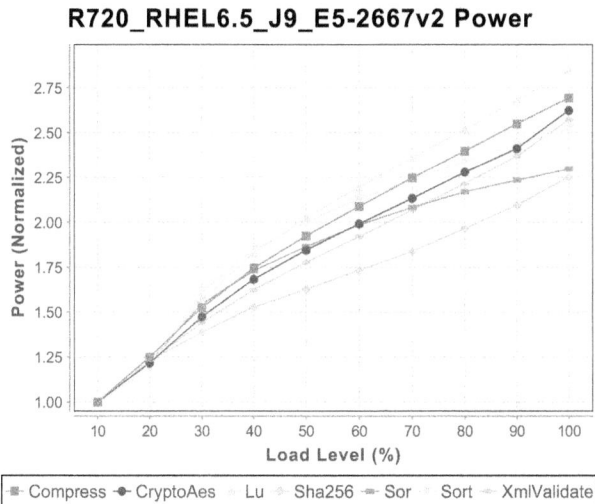

R720_RHEL6.5_J9_E5-2667v2 Power

Figure 19: Normalized Power Consumption of Dell PowerEdge Running IBM's J9 JVM

The biggest differences, however, can be observed for the CryptoAES worklet. Newer versions of HotSpot feature integrated AES support with a significant performance boost. This has an impact on both energy efficiency and power consumption. At low load, normalized power consumption is higher on HotSpot, indicating a steeper increase. The consumption levels out towards higher utilization levels, as the observations for the LU worklet repeat. On HotSpot, the concave segment of the worklet's power over load function is more pronounced, whereas it seems almost linear on J9. For CryptoAES this effect is even stronger and more visible than for LU. Additionally, CryptoAES features the steep increase in power draw at the 90% to 100% level, whereas it does not on HotSpot.

We confirmed our observations of worklet differences depending on JVM with a second measurement series using an Intel Xeon E5-2697v2 12 core processor. This second measurement series confirmed all of our observations except for one. The slight additional increase in power consumption of LU at the 80% to 100% load interval on HotSpot is missing on the E5-2697v2 system. Instead, it continues the concave power curve in the same manner as CryptoAES and Compress.

Our measurements for the power consumption of the two JVMs confirm that JVMs influence power consumption indirectly, mostly through their impact on worklet performance and support of hardware and operating system features as they do not provide additional power management mechanisms.

5.6 Characteristic Power / Utilization Curves

Over the course of our measurements, we have observed two distinct types of power over load curves, depending on the server's operating system. Within these types the power over load behavior of worklets can be approximated by piecewise mathematical functions:

- **Linux**: Power consumption over load on Linux follows a similar pattern for all CPU-heavy workloads: Functions approximating this power consumption start with a linear segment followed by a concave segment. The concave segment is optionally followed by a steep increase in power consumption around the 80% load level. After this sudden increase the concave segment resumes.
- **Windows**: Power consumption on Windows resembles an exponential function. This exponential base function can be modified by a concave deviation, usually between the 40% and 80% load levels.

The form in which these basic function templates are realized then depends on the workload type and the hardware configuration. These factors influence both the load levels at which each function segment begins and terminates, as well as the actual power output at these points.

Most notably, the concave function segments on all platforms can be pronounced with differing strengths. They can be clearly visible, as it is for CryptoAES and Sort, but they can also be almost non-existent, resulting in a linear function for the Linux case or the default exponential function on Windows.

5.6.1 Characteristic Energy-Efficiency / Utilization Curves

Due to SERT's linear calibration of target load levels through the number of dispatched transactions, the shape of the function approximating energy efficiency is a direct mirror of the worklet's power draw.

This direct correlation changes once specific bottlenecks or architectures with different performance attributes are introduced. As both of these factors significantly influence the overall system performance at each load level, the energy efficiency is affected as well.

In our experiments, we observed this change when comparing the 2 socket and 4 socket systems. The 4 socket system features significantly more CPU cores of a different architecture, leading to different performance characteristics. As a result its energy efficiency deviates greatly from the 2 socket system.

The effect of bottlenecks can be easily observed for the CryptoAES worklet using only two DIMMs of RAM. The under-saturation of available memory channels leads to hardware contention for memory access and causes a smaller increase in performance for each amount of additional power. As a result, efficiency drops at higher load levels.

6. CONCLUSIONS

In this paper, we demonstrate the need for characterization of server workload energy consumption and efficiency at multiple resource load levels. Specifically, the characterization of power consumption of CPU-intensive workloads is an open field of research.

We demonstrate that different workloads using CPU as their primary resource can feature significant differences in power consumption and energy efficiency. They are also affected differently by changes in the hardware and software configuration.

We characterize the power over CPU load, as well as energy efficiency over CPU load of these workloads and explore the effect of the execution environment and configuration changes on the workloads' power characteristics. Specifically, we derive two characteristic power over load functions and notice that the operating system is the major decider between these two functions.

We also explore the effect of different architectures and hardware configurations on workload power and energy efficiency, showing how they impact the character of power consumption over load. Changes in hardware configuration have a bigger impact when evaluating the overall energy efficiency instead of pure power consumption. This is especially true when considering architecture changes, as they cause shifts in performance behavior, which are reflected in the energy efficiency metric.

Several common assumptions on server energy efficiency are called into question as part of this paper. We show that the assumption of constant operating system power overhead is a gross oversimplification of the complex impact operating systems have on the system's power consumption. We also show that the assumption of maximum energy efficiency at full utilization is equally wrong in many cases, as many workloads exhibit their maximum efficiency at 80% utilization. The "U"-shape of energy efficiency curves, which is found in other literature [14] is also an oversimplification as efficiency does not always decrease monotonically after its maximum peak. We also show that the choice of Java Virtual Machine impacts power consumption mostly through secondary factors, such as performance improvements, and we demonstrate that workload specific hardware bottlenecks have a major, but non-trivial impact on power consumption and energy efficiency.

7. ACKNOWLEDGMENTS

The authors also wish to acknowledge current and past members of the SPECpower Committee who have contributed to the design, development, testing, and overall success of SERT: Sanjay Sharma, Nathan Totura, Mike Tricker, Greg Darnell, Karl Huppler, Van Smith, Paul Muehr, David Ott, Cathy Sandifer, Jason Glick, Ashok Emani, and Dianne Rice, as well as the late Alan Adamson and Larry Gray.

SPEC and the names SERT, SPEC PTDaemon, and SPECpower_ssj are registered trademarks of the Standard Performance Evaluation Corporation. Additional product and service names mentioned herein may be the trademarks of their respective owners.

8. REFERENCES

[1] C. Babcock. NY Times data center indictment misses the big picture. 2012.

[2] L. Barroso and U. Holzle. The Case for Energy-Proportional Computing. *Computer*, 40(12):33–37, Dec 2007.

[3] R. Basmadjian, N. Ali, F. Niedermeier, H. de Meer, and G. Giuliani. A Methodology to Predict the Power Consumption of Servers in Data Centres. In *Proceedings of the 2Nd International Conference on Energy-Efficient Computing and Networking*, e-Energy '11, pages 1–10, New York, NY, USA, 2011. ACM.

[4] F. Bellosa. The Benefits of Event: Driven Energy Accounting in Power-sensitive Systems. In *Proceedings of the 9th Workshop on ACM SIGOPS European Workshop: Beyond the PC: New Challenges for the Operating System*, EW 9, pages 37–42, New York, NY, USA, 2000. ACM.

[5] J. L. Henning. SPEC CPU2000: measuring CPU performance in the New Millennium. *Computer*, 33(7):28–35, Jul 2000.

[6] K.-D. Lange. Identifying Shades of Green: The SPECpower Benchmarks. *Computer*, 42(3):95–97, March 2009.

[7] K.-D. Lange, J. A. Arnold, H. Block, N. Totura, J. Beckett, and M. G. Tricker. Further Implementation Aspects of the Server Efficiency Rating Tool (SERT). In *Proceedings of the 4th ACM/SPEC International Conference on Performance Engineering*, ICPE '13, pages 349–360, New York, NY, USA, 2013. ACM.

[8] K.-D. Lange and M. G. Tricker. The Design and Development of the Server Efficiency Rating Tool (SERT). In *Proceedings of the 2Nd ACM/SPEC International Conference on Performance Engineering*, ICPE '11, pages 145–150, New York, NY, USA, 2011. ACM.

[9] K.-D. Lange, M. G. Tricker, J. A. Arnold, H. Block, and C. Koopmann. The Implementation of the Server Efficiency Rating Tool. In *Proceedings of the 3rd ACM/SPEC International Conference on Performance Engineering*, ICPE '12, pages 133–144, New York, NY, USA, 2012. ACM.

[10] A. Lewis, S. Ghosh, and N.-F. Tzeng. Run-time Energy Consumption Estimation Based on Workload in Server Systems. In *Proceedings of the 2008 Conference on Power Aware Computing and Systems*, HotPower'08, pages 4–4, Berkeley, CA, USA, 2008. USENIX Association.

[11] M. Poess, R. O. Nambiar, K. Vaid, J. M. Stephens Jr, K. Huppler, and E. Haines. Energy benchmarks: a detailed analysis. In *Proceedings of the 1st International Conference on Energy-Efficient Computing and Networking*, pages 131–140. ACM, 2010.

[12] S. Rivoire, P. Ranganathan, and C. Kozyrakis. A Comparison of High-level Full-system Power Models. In *Proceedings of the 2008 Conference on Power Aware Computing and Systems*, HotPower'08, pages 3–3, Berkeley, CA, USA, 2008. USENIX Association.

[13] S. Rivoire, M. A. Shah, P. Ranganathan, and C. Kozyrakis. JouleSort: A Balanced Energy-efficiency Benchmark. In *Proceedings of the 2007 ACM SIGMOD International Conference on Management of Data*, SIGMOD '07, pages 365–376, New York, NY, USA, 2007. ACM.

[14] S. Srikantaiah, A. Kansal, and F. Zhao. Energy Aware Consolidation for Cloud Computing. In *Proceedings of the 2008 Conference on Power Aware Computing and Systems*, HotPower'08, pages 10–10, Berkeley, CA, USA, 2008. USENIX Association.

[15] Standard Performance Evaluation Corporation. Server Efficiency Rating Tool (SERT) Design Document. http://spec.org/sert/docs/SERT-Design_Document.pdf.

[16] Standard Performance Evaluation Corporation. SPEC Power and Performance Benchmark Methodology. http://spec.org/power/docs/SPEC-Power_and_Performance_Methodology.pdf.

[17] J. G. von Kistowski, N. R. Herbst, and S. Kounev. Modeling Variations in Load Intensity over Time. In *Proceedings of the 3rd International Workshop on Large-Scale Testing (LT 2014), co-located with the 5th ACM/SPEC International Conference on Performance Engineering (ICPE 2014)*. ACM, March 2014.

[18] T. Welch. A Technique for High-Performance Data Compression. *Computer*, 17(6):8–19, June 1984.

Measuring Server Energy Proportionality

Chung-Hsing Hsu and Stephen W. Poole
Computer Science and Mathematics Division
Oak Ridge National Laboratory
Oak Ridge, Tennessee, USA
{hsuc,spoole}@ornl.gov

ABSTRACT

In performance engineering, metrics are often used to track the progress over time. Concerning the potential bias of using a single metric, performance engineers tend to use multiple metrics for reasoning. However, this approach has its own challenges. In this work we study one of the challenges in the context of analyzing trends in server energy proportionality. We examine a wide range of metrics for measuring energy proportionality, trying to determine which metrics are essential and which are redundant. We do this by comparing the trend curves of the metrics for the published results of the SPECpower_ssj2008 benchmark. While the context is specific, the proposed analysis method is quite general. We hope that this method would help us do performance engineering more effectively.

Categories and Subject Descriptors

C.4 [**Computer Systems Organization**]: Performance of Systems—*measurement techniques, performance attributes*; D.2.8 [**Software Engineering**]: Metrics—*performance measures*

General Terms

Design, Measurement, Performance, Standardization

Keywords

Metrics; Energy proportionality; SPECpower

1. INTRODUCTION

In performance engineering, metrics are often used to track the progress over time. Concerning the potential bias of using a single metric, performance engineers tend to use multiple metrics for reasoning. However, this approach has its own challenges. For example, what if two metrics give the opposite indications? How does one evaluate the added

value of each metric? In this work we study the latter problem in the context of analyzing the progress in server-level energy proportionality.

In an energy-proportional server, the power consumption of the server is proportional to its load. When the server is idle, the server would ideally consume no power. As the load increases, the server consumes gradually more power. In 2007, Barroso and Hölzle made a case why this is important [1]. Specifically, most servers in a data center stay at low utilization levels most of the time in order to accommodate occasional load spikes. Unfortunately, a traditional server has low energy efficiency at low utilization levels. An energy-proportional server, in contrast, has the same peak energy efficiency across all utilization levels. While this new server design does not address the issue of low utilization, it alleviates its consequence. As the annual energy cost for a server surpasses its purchase cost [2], more and more efforts have been made to improve server-level energy proportionality (e.g., [11,14]).

Seven years have passed, and there have been some studies analyzing trends in server energy proportionality (e.g., [6,7, 13,14]). Many of these studies use the SPECpower_ssj2008 benchmark results published by the Standard Performance Evaluation Corporation (SPEC). However, they use different metrics because there is no consensus on how to measure energy proportionality. In this work we examine these metrics as well as several other new metrics, trying to determine which metrics are similar in their evaluation of server energy proportionality. To the best of our knowledge, this has never been done before.

In this work metrics can be similar empirically or analytically. We determine whether two metrics are *empirically* similar by calculating the correlation between two time series, each of which is derived from one metric applied to the common historical data archive. The higher the correlation, the more similar the metrics empirically. We say that two metrics are *analytically* similar if we can establish a mathematical equation between them. Empirical similarity gives us a hint on the possible analytical similarity. A new metric has no added value if it is similar to an existing metric.

Taking the aforementioned approach with the data being all 459 SPECpower_ssj2008 benchmark results published by SPEC until June 2014, we have found that the metric EP [7] can be considered as a good metric for measuring server energy proportionality. We have also established a mathematical relationship between EP and the overall score of the SPECpower_ssj2008 benchmark set forth by SPEC. The relationship allows us to understand how much improve-

ICPE'15, Jan. 31–Feb. 4, 2015, Austin, Texas, USA.
Copyright © 2015 ACM 978-1-4503-3248-4/15/01 ...$15.00.
http://dx.doi.org/10.1145/2668930.2688049.

ment in energy efficiency comes from improvement in energy proportionality. The paper also argues for the importance of another aspect of energy proportionality, linearity. This aspect is often overlooked but it impacts the potential for achieving the greatest energy proportionality at cluster level. Since none of existing linearity metrics provides this kind of insight, the paper calls for the development of a good linearity metric in the context of energy proportionality.

The rest of the paper is organized as follows. Section 2 provides information on how trends in server energy proportionality were studied in the past. The method for analyzing the empirical similarity of two metrics is detailed in Section 3. Section 4 shows how the method can be used to reach the conclusion that EP is a good metric. Sections 5 highlights the many ways to measure the linearity aspect of server energy proportionality, and Section 6 discusses why they all fail to provide important insight relating to cluster-level energy management. Section 7 concludes the paper with some future research directions.

2. RELATED WORK

This section describes how trends in server energy proportionality were studied in the past. Two key elements of these studies are the *data* and *methods* used for analysis. We discuss each element in details.

2.1 The SPECpower_ssj2008 Benchmark

To study trends in server energy proportionality, many past studies [6, 7, 13, 14] use the SPECpower_ssj2008 benchmark results published by the Standard Performance Evaluation Corporation (SPEC). This benchmark takes the approach of graduated workload [3], thus allowing energy proportionality to be measured. Specifically, the benchmark measures the performance and power of eleven load levels from zero to 100% of a given server's full capacity to process business transactions with a server side Java application.

The results published by SPEC are arguably the best data available for analyzing trends in server energy proportionality. Many other power benchmarks [5] have very limited data, making it impossible to do any meaningful trend analysis. For example, GBench implements graduated workload but does not have much data [10]. The Green500 [4] has more data, but its workload does not have any sense of graduated workload, making it impossible to measure energy proportionality. In addition, there are serious concerns about its measurement bias [8]. In contrast, the SPEC-published results may have less measurement bias. In order for a result to be published by SPEC, a set of rigorous run rules must be complied with, including the proper setup for taking the measurements.

SPEC maintains an archive [1] of all the results it has published since December 2007. The archive currently contains over 450 results from major server vendors such as Acer, Dell, Fujitsu, HP, Huawei, and IBM. As the previous studies, our study also uses these results for trend analysis.

2.2 Measuring Energy Proportionality

Any trend analysis of energy proportionality requires a measure of energy proportionality. Unfortunately there is no consensus on what metric should be used. As a result,

the previous studies differ mainly in the metric each uses for quantifying energy proportionality.

Historically, server energy proportionality has been measured by the difference in power between the 0% load level and the 100% load level [1]. In this paper we call this metric DR (Dynamic Range) [14]:

$$DR = \frac{P(1) - P(0)}{P(1)} \qquad (1)$$

where $P(\ell)$ represents the power consumption (in watts) of a server at load level ℓ, $0 \le \ell \le 1$. DR is between 0 and 1, with 1 being fully energy-proportional.

Another commonly used metric is called EP (Energy Proportionality) [7]. Like DR, EP is between 0 and 1, with 1 being fully energy-proportional. In contrast to DR, EP accounts for the power usage in intermediate load levels:

$$EP = 2 - \frac{\int_0^1 P(\ell)\, d\ell}{\int_0^1 P_E(\ell)\, d\ell} \qquad (2)$$

where

$$P_E(\ell) = P(1) \cdot \ell \qquad (3)$$

represents the power-consumption behavior of the fully energy-proportional server, i.e., the EP (also DR) of $P_E(\ell)$ is 1.

Some metrics measure energy disproportionality instead. For example, the metric IPR (Idle-to-peak Power Ratio) [13],

$$IPR = \frac{P(0)}{P(1)}, \qquad (4)$$

is also between 0 and 1, but the IPR of $P_E(\ell)$ is 0. In fact, IPR and DR are duals, i.e., IPR + DR = 1.

Some metrics measure nonlinearity because the geometrical interpretation of $P_E(\ell)$ is a line. For example, the metric LD (Linear Deviation) [14] quantifies the deviation from a linear function $P_L(\ell)$:

$$LD = \frac{\int_0^1 P(\ell)\, d\ell}{\int_0^1 P_L(\ell)\, d\ell} - 1 \qquad (5)$$

where

$$P_L(\ell) = P(0) + [P(1) - P(0)]\ell \qquad (6)$$

represents a particular power-consumption behavior. A server is called superlinearly energy-proportional if LD > 0 and sublinearly energy-proportional if LD < 0. Geometrically, sublinearity occurs when the curve $P(\ell)$ lies under the line $P_L(\ell)$. The LD of $P_E(\ell)$ is 0, so is that of $P_L(\ell)$.

Another metric, LDR (Linear Deviation Ratio) [13], measures the deviation differently:

$$LDR = \max_\ell^{|\cdot|} \left(\frac{P(\ell)}{P_L(\ell)} - 1 \right) \qquad (7)$$

where $\max^{|\cdot|}$ is the maximum by absolute-value comparison so as to retain the sign of the maximum value. Like LD, LDR distinguishes between superlinearity and sublinearity. The LDR of $P_E(\ell)$ is 0, so is that of $P_L(\ell)$.

This paper will discuss the similarity of these metrics and whether new metrics are still needed.

3. THE ANALYSIS METHOD

How can one tell that the insights from two metrics are the same? This section will present a method that casts

[1] http://www.spec.org/power_ssj2008/results/

the problem as computing the similarity of two time series called *trend curves* in this paper. This method is in contrast to visual analysis used in the previous studies.

Define a trend curve as a sequence of n elements sorted according to some temporal order. Each metric has a corresponding trend curve. In this work, the trend curve of a metric contains $n = 459$ elements, and each element holds the metric value for one SPECpower_ssj2008 benchmark result. For example, the EP value for a benchmark result can be approximated via the trapezoidal rule for integration as

$$\text{EP} \approx 2 - \sum_{j=1}^{m-1} (\ell_j - \ell_{j-1}) \left[\frac{P_{j-1} + P_j}{P_{m-1}} \right] \quad (8)$$

where the result contains $m = 11$ data points $\{(\tau_j, P_j)\}$, $0 \leq j \leq m - 1$ and $\tau_0 < \tau_1 < \ldots < \tau_{m-1}$, describing the performance and power behavior of a server. These data points are viewed as the samples of $P(\ell)$ where $P(\ell_j) = P_j$ for $\ell_j = \tau_j / \tau_{m-1}$. The value of a metric can then be calculated based on these samples.

The similarity of two trend curves $\vec{u} = (u_1, u_2, \ldots, u_n)$ and $\vec{v} = (v_1, v_2, \ldots, v_n)$ can be computed using Pearson's r:

$$r(\vec{u}, \vec{v}) = \frac{\sum_i (u_i - \bar{u})(v_i - \bar{v})}{\sqrt{\sum_i (u_i - \bar{u})^2} \sqrt{\sum_i (v_i - \bar{v})^2}} \quad (9)$$

where

$$\bar{u} = \frac{1}{n} \sum_i u_i \quad \text{and} \quad \bar{v} = \frac{1}{n} \sum_i v_i. \quad (10)$$

Pearson's r measures the strength of the linear relationship between variables $\vec{u}$ and $\vec{v}$ based on the data $\{(u_i, v_i)\}$. It ranges from -1 to 1, with -1 (or 1) being a perfect negative (or positive) linear relationship and 0 no linear relationship. One nice property of this measure is that the two trend curves do not have to be on the same scale, thereby allowing us to study a larger set of metrics.

According to our method, the trend curves of DR and EP have a similarity (or linear correlation) of 0.91. In other words, the two curves are similar but not identical. This justifies the existence of both metrics.

3.1 Verification

Now consider visual check. Figure 1 shows the two trend curves. We see that server energy proportionality has stagnated since 2009 according to DR. In contrast, there was a uplift in 2012 according to EP. In other words, EP captures the uplift that DR does not. On the other hand, DR provides an insight that the *early* improvement in EP can be correlated to the widening dynamic range of the power. Therefore, both metrics are valuable, and EP can be considered better for the current time. This exercise also shows that the proposed method enables us to determine whether two metrics provide different insights or not. The uplift in 2012 has been attributed to the result of using dynamic processor over-clocking (e.g., Intel Turbo Boost) [6].

In fact, we can establish a mathematical relationship between EP and DR as follows:

$$\text{EP} \approx 2 - (2 - \text{DR})(\text{LD} + 1) \quad (11)$$

where LD is a nonlinearity measure. This equation indicates two ways to increase EP: to increase DR or to decrease LD. Since the trend in DR has stagnated since 2009, much of the *later* improvement in EP comes from the decrease in

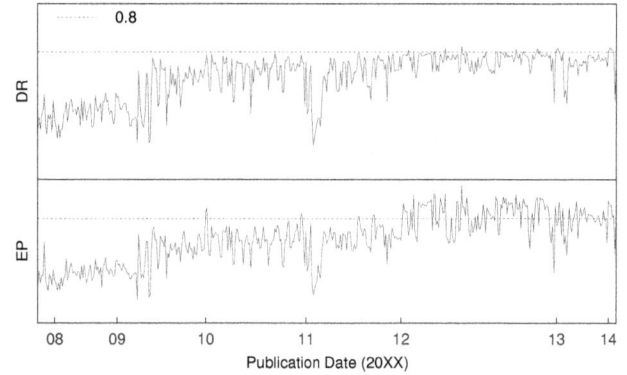

Figure 1: The trend curves of DR and EP.

LD. Wong and Annavaram noted that DR and LD can affect EP [14], but here we establish the math form for that observation. This exercise also shows how empirical similarity can give us a hint on the possible analytical similarity.

4. METRICS BASED ON DEVIATION

In this section and next, we examine a series of metrics for measuring server energy disproportionality. The metrics discussed in this section all measure the deviation from the behavior described by $P_E(\ell) = P(1) \cdot \ell$.

Given a set of m samples $\{(\ell_j, P_j)\}$, the following are a few possible metrics for measuring the deviation:

$$\text{L}_\infty = \max_j |\varepsilon_j|, \quad (12)$$

$$\text{L}_1 = \sum_j |\varepsilon_j|, \quad (13)$$

and

$$\text{L}_2 = \sqrt{\sum_j |\varepsilon_j|^2}, \quad (14)$$

where

$$\varepsilon_j = \frac{P_j - P_E(\ell_j)}{P(1)}. \quad (15)$$

These are common deviation metrics, but we are not aware of any previous work that uses one of these metrics to evaluate energy disproportionality.

Based on our method, these metrics are very similar to each other. The curves of L_∞ and L_1 have the least similarity which is 0.98. In fact, these metrics can be viewed as the dual of EP. Mathematically, we can establish the following relationship between EP and L_1:

$$\text{EP} \approx 1 - \frac{2\text{L}_1}{m-1}. \quad (16)$$

In summary, EP is a good energy-proportionality metric because metrics L_∞, L_1, and L_2 do not add any new insight.

4.1 The Impact to Energy Efficiency

Ryckbosch et al. [7] compared EP with the overall score (SCR) of the SPECpower_ssj2008 benchmark. While SCR is a metric for measuring server energy *efficiency*, its calculation involves the power numbers at multiple load levels

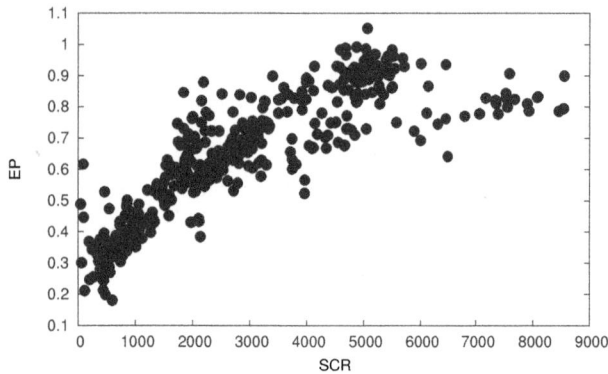

Figure 2: The imperfect correlation between metrics SCR and EP.

and thus includes some notion of energy proportionality:

$$SCR = \frac{\sum_j \tau_j}{\sum_j P_j}. \qquad (17)$$

Through visual analysis, Ryckbosch et al. noted that SCR correlates well with EP, but not perfect. A server with a high EP does not necessarily have a high SCR, and vice versa. Figure 2 shows this imperfect correlation. Using our method, the correlation can be quantified as 0.83.

In fact, we can do more. Through some mathematical manipulation, we can establish the following relationship:

$$SCR \approx \left(\frac{\tau_{10}}{P_{10}}\right)\left(\frac{1.1}{2.1 - EP}\right). \qquad (18)$$

This equation indicates two ways to increase SCR: to improve the performance-power ratio at the 100% load level or to improve EP. Since the improvement in EP has stagnated since 2012, much of the recent improvement in SCR has come from the increasing performance-power ratio at the 100% load level.

5. METRICS BASED ON LINEARITY

In this section we examine metrics for measuring nonlinearity. We start by comparing metrics LD and LDR.

Based on our method, the similarity of the two metrics is only 0.85. So both metrics are valuable. We are unable to establish a mathematical equation connecting them. However, we have found that their dissimilarity is largely due to the different *design* bias. In the following we will discuss where they are similar and dissimilar.

On the similarity side, both metrics indicate the same trend. As shown in Figure 3, the metric values were mostly positive in 2007–2011. Beginning 2012, more negative values have appeared. This timing matches what we have discussed earlier about the EP's uplift in 2012. Clearly, these curves provide additional evidence on why the uplift occurs. They also supplement Equation (11) by showing that LD not only decreases but also falls below zero. In other words, modern servers show more sublinear energy proportionality.

On the dissimilarity side, the two metrics treat the deviation at the same load level unequally. LDR weighs more on deviations at low load levels. In contrast, LD treats deviations at all load levels equally. Specifically, both metrics

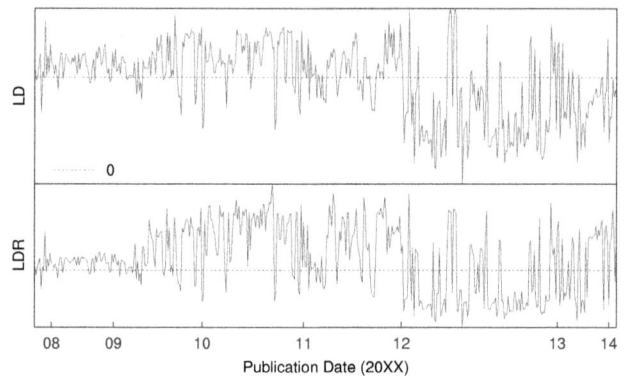

Figure 3: The trend curves of LD and LDR.

can be rewritten as

$$LD \approx \frac{2}{(m-1)(IPR+1)} \sum_j \frac{P_j - P_L(\ell_j)}{P(1)}. \qquad (19)$$

and

$$LDR \approx \max_j \frac{|\cdot|}{IPR + (1 - IPR)\ell_j} \cdot \frac{P_j - P_L(\ell_j)}{P(1)}. \qquad (20)$$

While both metrics calculate the deviation from the same linear function $P_L(\ell)$ as

$$\varepsilon_j = \frac{P_j - P_L(\ell_j)}{P(1)}, \qquad (21)$$

LDR weighs more on deviations at low load levels. Due to their different weight assignments, the trend curves of LD and LDR become somewhat dissimilar.

In terms of insight, Varsamopoulos et al. [13] noted two trends in LDR: one positive trend and one negative trend. However, the positive trend in LD is not as obvious in Figure 3. In other words, LDR shows the continuing difficulty in achieving sublinear energy proportionality at low load levels. LD shows that either sublinearity occurs at more load levels or sublinearity becomes higher or both.

Probably a better way to gain the above kind of insight is to look into the *range* of the deviations at various load levels. Using Equation (21) as the deviation measure, Figure 4 shows the maximum and minimum of these deviations. We see that both extremes tend to have the same sign before 2013. They are either all positive or all negative. Starting 2013, the maximum is positive and the minimum is negative. In other words, curve $P(\ell)$ and line $P_L(\ell)$ intersect.

This insight has led us to study the impact of the shape of $P(\ell)$. The next section will discuss how it plays an important role in achieving great *cluster-level* energy proportionality.

5.1 Other Possible Metrics

The rest of this section shows that there are many other ways to measure linearity or nonlinearity. Table 1 lists a sample of them in three different types. The first two types are related to curve fitting. For the first type, we see that many functional forms can be used to describe the curve, and fitness or function parameter can be used to measure linearity. For the second type, linearity is measured in terms of complexity. A line is expected to be modeled by a simple function with a good fitness (or numerical accuracy). The more complex the function, the more nonlinear the curve.

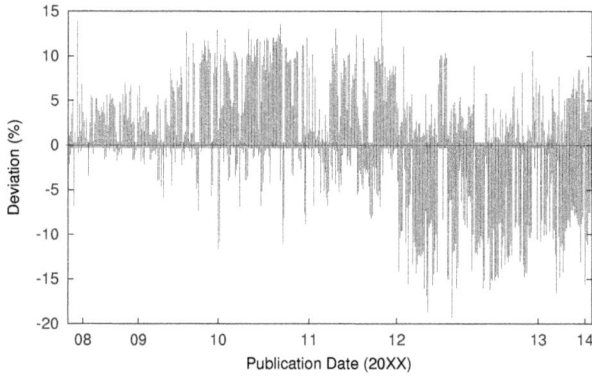

Figure 4: The range of the linearity deviations based on Equation (21).

The third type comes from image processing. In image processing applications, a line is often needed to be recognized. There are also many ways to recognize the line pattern. AO is considered to be one of the most effective methods for this task [9]. AO assumes the curve as a piecewise-linear function which passes through all data points $\{(\ell_j, P_j)\}$. Since there are 11 points, there are 10 line segments in this curve. AO uses the average of all the normal unit vectors of these line segments to measure linearity.

According to our method, the trend curves of these metrics are different from each other, except that the curves of RMSE and MAPE have a similarity of 0.99. We have tried other correlation measures such as Spearman's ρ and Kendall's τ, but none helped. Smoothing the curves before computing their similarity helped but not much. We were only able to derive a high similarity of POW and COE using the median trend-lines of their curves.

More importantly, we cannot associate any of these metrics with implications on how to improve energy proportionality. As we will discuss in the next section, a metric that characterizes the shape of $P(\ell)$ may provide such insight.

6. IS LINEARITY IMPORTANT?

This section tries to justify the importance of a good shape of $P(\ell)$ that the existing metrics may have overlooked. We start with the shape of $P_E(\ell) = P(1) \cdot \ell$.

Consider a cluster of homogeneous servers. Curve $P_E(\ell)$ has two properties that affect cluster-level energy management. The property of $P(0) = 0$ affects server provisioning. Servers can be added at any time without power penalty. The property of linearity affects load distribution. Load can be distributed in any way without power penalty. In the case of two servers, this means there are many ways to serve the input load level of 0.8 with the same amount of aggregate power usage, whether it be one server at the 0.8 load level, two servers at the 0.4 load level each, or two servers at the 0.2 and 0.6 load levels respectively.

In reality, the first property is not met by any real server. In other words, any server that is on will introduce some power penalty. To achieve better energy proportionality, cluster management can use the Packing scheme which provisions a minimum number of servers to handle the input load level. In the case of two servers, provisioning one server at the 0.8 load level consumes the least power.

For a cluster of s servers, the following formula calculates the cluster-level energy proportionality $\widehat{EP}$ if managed by the Packing scheme:

$$\widehat{EP} = 1 - \frac{1 - EP}{s}. \quad (22)$$

Assume each server is very energy disproportional, say $EP = 0.1$. A cluster of 100 such servers with the Packing scheme can easily achieve the cluster-level energy proportionality of 0.9, and this applies to all shapes of $P(\ell)$.

The above formula is only correct in the ideal scenario in which servers can be provisioned instantaneously. According to a simulation-based study done by Wong and Annavaram [15], $\widehat{EP}$ saturates around 0.8 in more realistic scenarios. They suggested to forego dynamic server provisioning and distribute the input load evenly among all servers. Using this Uniform scheme, $\widehat{EP}$ is equivalent to EP. Since some of modern servers have their EP greater than 0.8 (see Figure 1), the Uniform scheme effectively improves cluster-level energy proportionality.

The Uniform scheme is sometimes optimal. In the case of two servers, the scheme will provision two servers at the 0.4 load level each. If the server behavior can be described as $P(\ell) = 0.2 + 0.8 \cdot \ell^2$, then the total power usage based on this scheme is the lowest. In fact, the Uniform scheme remains optimal if $P(\ell)$ depicts a *convex* curve. Once the curve is not convex, the optimality will not be guaranteed. This is where the shape of $P(\ell)$ can impact how to achieve the best cluster-level energy proportionality.

As we continue to create solutions, such as [12, 15], to further improve server energy proportionality, we may need to consider its impact on the complexity of achieving near-optimal cluster-level energy management. If linearity is desired, we should increase its weight when creating these new solutions. If convexity is desired, we need metrics that can capture this. Metric LD falls short because LD < 0 does not imply that $P(\ell)$ is convex. If curve $P(\ell)$ and line $P_L(\ell)$ intersect, $P(\ell)$ is definitely not convex.

In short, we are lacking metrics that can provide insight on the good shapes of $P(\ell)$ for enabling simple yet effective cluster-level energy management.

7. CONCLUSIONS AND FUTURE WORK

This paper starts with the question of how to evaluate the added value of each metric when multiple metrics are used during performance engineering. This is important because a high degree of redundancy in results hinders the efficiency in gaining insight. This paper presents a general method to address the question. The method is demonstrated in the context of analyzing trends in server energy proportionality. It enables the identification of a good energy-proportionality metric from which more focused studies, such as mathematical relationships, can be conducted. While the identified metric is considered better than other existing metrics, this paper argues that the metric fails to capture an important aspect of server energy proportionality, linearity. The paper outlines why this aspect is also equally important and concludes that none of the existing metrics has captured it in a satisfactory manner.

Obviously, the lack of a good linearity metric is one of several directions for the future work. In addition, the argument provided in the paper is rather analytical. Simulation-based studies can be conducted to further strengthen the

Table 1: The many ways to measure linearity. SEG uses piecewise linear functions of different line segments. COD and AO measure linearity, and all the other metrics measure nonlinearity.

Name	Definition	Notes	Range
Type 1: Fitting by the least squares method			
COD	$[r(\vec{\ell}, \vec{P})]^2$		$[0,1]$
RMSE	$\sqrt{\frac{1}{m}\sum_j \left[\frac{P(\ell_j)-P_j}{P_{m-1}}\right]^2}$	$P(\ell) = c_0 + c_1 \cdot \ell$	$[0,1]$
MAPE	$\frac{1}{m}\sum_j \frac{|P(\ell_j)-P_j|}{P_j}$		$[0,\infty]$
POW	α	$P(\ell) = c_0 + c_1 \cdot \ell^\alpha$	$[0,\infty]$
COE	c_2	$P(\ell) = c_0 + c_1 \cdot \ell + c_2 \cdot \ell^2$	$[0,\infty]$
Type 2: Finding the smallest k such that RMSE is below 0.01			
DEG	k	$P(\ell) = \sum_{i=0}^{k} c_i * \ell^i$	$[0, m-1]$
SEG	k	$P(\ell) = c_0 + c_1 * x + \sum_{i=2}^{k} c_i * |x - \beta_i|$	$[1, m]$
Type 3: Recognizing pattern in planar point sets			
AO	$\frac{1}{m-1}\sqrt{(\sum_j \frac{-s_j}{\sqrt{s_j^2+1}})^2 + (\sum_j \frac{1}{\sqrt{s_j^2+1}})^2}$	$s_j = \frac{P_{j+1}-P_j}{\ell_{j+1}-\ell_j}, 0 \le j < m$	$[2/\pi, 1]$

argument. If linearity is indeed very critical, new server designs will need to be judged based on this aspect as well. In terms of trend analysis, one idea is to approximate $\{(\ell_j, P_j)\}$ with a curve, measure the energy proportionality of the curve, and see if it makes any difference.

8. ACKNOWLEDGMENTS

This work was supported by the Extreme Scale Systems Center at Oak Ridge National Laboratory and funded by the United States Department of Defense. This manuscript has been authored by UT-Battelle, LLC, under Contract No. DE-AC05000R22725 with the U.S. Department of Energy. The United States Government retains and the publisher, by accepting the article for publication, acknowledges that the United States Government retains a non-exclusive, paid-up, irrevocable, world-wide license to publish or reproduce the published form of this manuscript, or allow others to do so, for the United States Government purposes.

9. REFERENCES

[1] L. Barroso and U. Hölzle. The case for energy-proportional computing. *IEEE Computer*, 40(12):33–37, Dec. 2007.

[2] C. Belady. In the data center, power and cooling costs more than the IT equipment it supports. *Electronics Cooling Magazine*, Feb. 2007.

[3] L. Gray, A. Kumar, and H. Li. Workload characterization of the SPECpower_ssj2008 benchmark. In *SPEC International Performance Evaluation Workshop*, June 2008.

[4] The Green500 list: Environmentally responsible supercomputing. http://www.green500.org.

[5] C. Hsu, J. Kuehn, and S. Poole. Towards efficient supercomputing: Searching for the right efficiency metric. In *International Conference on Performance Engineering*, Apr. 2012.

[6] C. Hsu and S. Poole. Revisiting server energy proportionality. In *International Workshop on Power-Aware Systems and Architectures*, Oct. 2013.

[7] F. Ryckbosch, S. Polfliet, and L. Eeckhout. Trends in server energy proportionality. *IEEE Computer*, 44(9):69–72, Sept. 2011.

[8] T. Scogland, C. Steffen, T. Wilde, F. Parent, S. Coghlan, N. Bates, W. Feng, and E. Strohmaier. A power-measurement methodology for large-scale, high-performance computing. In *International Conference on Performance Engineering*, Mar. 2014.

[9] M. Stojmenović, A. Nayak, and J. Zunic. Measuring linearity of planar point sets. *Pattern Recognition*, 41(8):2503–2511, Aug. 2008.

[10] B. Subramaniam and W. Feng. GBench: Benchmarking methodology for evaluating the energy efficiency of supercomputers. In *International Supercomputing Conference*, June 2012.

[11] B. Subramaniam and W. Feng. Towards energy-proportional computing for enterprise-class server workloads. In *International Conference on Performance Engineering*, Apr. 2013.

[12] B. Subramaniam and W. Feng. Enabling efficient power provisioning for enterprise applications. In *International Symposium on Cluster, Cloud and Grid Computing*, May 2014.

[13] G. Varsamopoulos, Z. Abbasi, and S. Gupta. Trends and effects of energy proportionality on server provisioning in data centers. In *International Conference on High Performance Computing*, Dec. 2010.

[14] D. Wong and M. Annavaram. Scaling the energy proportionality wall with KnightShift. *IEEE Micro*, 33(3):28–37, May/June 2013.

[15] D. Wong and M. Annavaram. Implications of high energy proportional servers on cluster-wide energy proportionality. In *International Symposium on High-Performance Computer Architecture*, Feb. 2014.

Slow Down or Halt: Saving the Optimal Energy for Scalable HPC Systems

Li Tan and Zizhong Chen
University of California, Riverside
{ltan003, chen}@cs.ucr.edu

ABSTRACT

The presence of pervasive slack provides ample opportunities for achieving energy efficiency for HPC systems nowadays. Regardless of communication slack, classic energy saving approaches for saving energy during the slack otherwise include *race-to-halt* and *CP-aware slack reclamation*, which reply on power scaling techniques to adjust processor power states judiciously during the slack. Existing efforts demonstrate *CP-aware slack reclamation* is superior to *race-to-halt* in energy saving capability. In this paper, we formally model our observation that the energy saving capability gap between the two approaches is significantly narrowed down on today's processors, given that state-of-the-art CMOS technologies allow insignificant variation of supply voltage as operating frequency of a processor scales. Experimental results on a large-scale power-aware cluster validate our findings.

Categories and Subject Descriptors

D.4.1 [**Operating Systems**]: Process Management—*Scheduling, Multiprocessing/multiprogramming/multitasking*

Keywords

energy; power; DVFS; HPC; critical path; slack; scalable

1. INTRODUCTION

Power and energy efficiency are now of great concern when the launching date of exascale computers is approaching. Power and energy consumption of a supercomputer nowadays have been rapidly increasing due to expansion of its size and duration in use. The US Department of Energy has set up a goal of 20 MW for the exascale computers targeted in the year around 2020 [2]. The advancement of hardware and software solutions have greatly improved power and energy efficiency of High Performance Computing (HPC), where the pervasive slack during runs of task-parallel applications is regarded as an important source for achieving power and energy savings, regardless of various performance boosting techniques (e.g., load balancing [4] and work stealing [5]) for decreasing the slack as much as possible.

Slack generally refers to a time period when one hardware component waits for another due to imbalanced throughput and utilization. For instance, CPU usually waits for data to be ready from memory for memory intensive applications, in accordance with the fundamental memory hierarchy. Typical examples of slack include load imbalance, network latency, communication delay, memory and disk access stalls, etc. Energy saving opportunities can be exploited during the slack of runs of task-parallel HPC applications, since the peak performance of hardware components that are not fully utilized during the slack is not necessary. Software-controlled hardware solutions such as Dynamic Voltage and Frequency Scaling (DVFS) techniques have been extensively leveraged to mitigate energy costs by appropriately scaling power states of the hardware without incurring performance loss for the HPC applications [6] [10] [9].

Critical Path (CP) is one particular task trace from the beginning task of a task-parallel HPC run to the ending one, with the total slack of zero. Any delay on tasks on the CP increases the total execution time of the application, while *appropriately slowing down* the processors where the application is running by dilating tasks off the CP into their slack, or *halting* tasks off the CP during their slack individually without further delay, does not cause performance loss as a whole. Energy savings can be achieved effectively by both approaches with negligible performance loss.

In this paper, we discuss energy saving capability of two classic energy saving approaches, and formally calculate and compare energy savings from both solutions. Previous formal proof shows that *CP-aware slack reclamation* beats *race-to-halt* in terms of energy efficiency [7] [8]. We demonstrate that for DVFS on state-of-the-art architectures, supply voltage of a processor scales much less than its operating frequency, the energy saving gap between the two approaches is narrowed down significantly. We also provide preliminary experimental evaluation to validate our observations.

2. CLASSIC ENERGY SAVING STRATEGIES

Existing energy efficient approaches that save energy strategically during slack of HPC runs can essentially be categorized into two types: race-to-halt and CP-aware slack reclamation. Next we illustrate how they work in different ways.

2.1 Energy Saving for Communication

Slack from communication is an important source of energy savings. Consider a HPC run on a distributed-memory system based on message passing, reduction of energy consumption can be achieved by reducing frequency and voltage of computing components such as CPU and GPU for

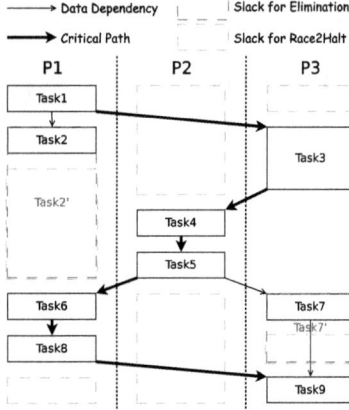

Figure 1: DAG Notation of Slack Handling of Two Energy Saving Solutions for a 3-Process HPC Run.

Table 1: Notation in Energy Efficiency Analysis.

E	Total nodal energy consumption of all components
P	Total nodal power consumption of all components
$P_{dynamic}$	Dynamic power consumption in the running state
$P_{leakage}$	Static/leakage power consumption in any states
T	Execution time of a task at CPU peak performance
T'	Slack of executing a task at CPU peak performance
A	Percentage of active gates in a CMOS-based chip
C	The total capacitive load in a CMOS-based chip
f	Current CPU working frequency
V	Current CPU supply voltage
V'	Supply voltage of components other than CPU
I_{sub}	CPU subthreshold leakage current
I'_{sub}	non-CPU component subthreshold leakage current
f_m	Available frequency assumed to eliminate T' without using frequency approximation
V_h	The highest supply voltage set by DVFS
V_l	The lowest supply voltage set by DVFS
V_m	Supply voltage corresponding to f_m set by DVFS
n	Ratio between execution time and slack of a task

large-message MPI communication, since generally execution time of such operations barely increases at a low-power state of the computing hardware during the communication slack. We adopt this *scheduled communication* [10] strategy for communication slack. However, the next two classic energy saving approaches are intended in particular for slack arising from non-communication, i.e., mostly, computation.

2.2 Race-to-halt

As the name suggests, *race-to-halt* is a DVFS scheduling strategy that enforces hardware components (e.g., CPU and GPU) to *race* when workloads are ready for processing, and to *halt* when no workloads are available, as the area covered by green dashed boxes shown in Figure 1. Specifically, *race* refers to execute workloads with the maximum performance, i.e., at the highest frequency and voltage of processors, until the finish of the workloads, while *halt* means to slow down processors to the minimum frequency and voltage, i.e., the lowest power state for energy saving purposes, from the end of the precedent workload to the start of the subsequent workload. This straightforward approach can effectively save energy without incurring performance loss.

2.3 CP-aware Slack Reclamation

Another critical strategy of saving energy during the slack is to reclaim slack by *appropriately* slowing down tasks that are not on the Critical Path (CP) of an execution trace of a HPC run. Per the definition of CP, it is implied that any delay on tasks on the CP also delays the application as a whole, while *appropriately* dilating tasks off the CP into their slack individually without overflowing slack, does not increase the total execution time of the application, as prolonged tasks in blue dashed boxes shown in Figure 1. Energy savings can thus be achieved from scaling down frequency/voltage for dilating tasks off the CP into their slack without performance degradation. This solution is based on CP detection. Energy efficient DVFS scheduling decisions for slack reclamation are determined among tasks on/off the CP.

3. ENERGY SAVING CAPACITY ANALYSIS

Existing work demonstrates that under a time constraint, slowing down a processor can reduce energy consumption the most, compared to completing a task as fast as possible and completing a task using combination of discrete frequencies [7] [8]. However, the gap between energy saving capability of *race-to-halt* and *CP-aware slack reclamation* shrinks, since

state-of-the-art CMOS technologies allow insignificant variation of supply voltage as operating frequency of a processor scales. Next we formalize that the two approaches can be comparable in energy saving capability. Given the following two energy saving strategies, towards a task t with an execution time T and slack T' at the peak CPU performance, we calculate the total nodal system energy consumption for both strategies, i.e., $E(\mathsf{S}_1)$ and $E(\mathsf{S}_2)$ formally below:

- Strategy I (Race-to-halt): Execute t at the highest frequency f_h until the end, and then switch to the lowest frequency f_l, i.e., run in T at f_h and in T' at f_l;
- Strategy II (CP-aware Slack Reclamation): Execute t at the optimal frequency f_m with which T' is eliminated, i.e., run in $T + T'$ at f_m (For simplicity in the later discussion, assume T' can be eliminated using available frequency f_m without frequency approximation).

For simplicity, let us assume the tasks for the use of DVFS are compute-intensive (memory-intensive tasks can be discussed with minor changes in the model), i.e., $T + T' = nT$, when $f_m = \frac{1}{n}f_h$, where $1 \le n \le \frac{f_h}{f_l}$. Consider the nodal power consumption P, we model it formally as follows:

$$P = P^{CPU}_{dynamic} + P^{CPU}_{leakage} + P^{other}_{leakage} \quad (1)$$
$$P_{dynamic} = ACfV^2 \quad (2)$$
$$P_{leakage} = I_{sub}V \quad (3)$$

Substituting Equations 2 and 3 into Equation 1 yields:

$$P = ACfV^2 + I_{sub}V + I'_{sub}V' \quad (4)$$

In our scenario, $P^{other}_{leakage} = I'_{sub}V'$ is independent of CPU voltage and frequency scaling, and thus can be regarded as a constant in Equation 4, so we denote $P^{other}_{leakage}$ as P_c for simplicity. Further, although subthreshold leakage current I_{sub} has an exponential relationship with threshold voltage, results presented in [11] indicate that I_{sub} converges to a constant after a certain threshold voltage value. Without loss of generality, we treat $P^{CPU}_{leakage} = I_{sub}V$ as a function of supply voltage V only. Thus, we model the nodal energy consumption E_{node} for both strategies individually below:

$$E(\mathsf{S}_1) = \overline{P(\mathsf{S}_1)} \times T + \overline{P'(\mathsf{S}_1)} \times T'$$
$$= (ACf_hV_h^2 + I_{sub}V_h + P_c)T + (ACf_lV_l^2 + I_{sub}V_l + P_c)T'$$
$$= AC(f_hV_h^2T + f_lV_l^2T') + I_{sub}(V_hT + V_lT') + P_c(T+T') \quad (5)$$

$$E(\mathsf{S}_2) = \overline{P(\mathsf{S}_2)} \times (T + T')$$
$$= (ACf_mV_m^2 + I_{sub}V_m + P_c)(T + T')$$
$$= ACf_mV_m^2(T + T') + I_{sub}V_m(T + T') + P_c(T + T') \quad (6)$$

242

Table 2: Frequency-Voltage Pairs for Different Processors (Unit: Frequency (GHz); Voltage (V)).

Gear	AMD Opteron 2380		AMD Opteron 846 and AMD Athlon64 3200+		AMD Opteron 2218		Intel Pentium M		Intel Pentium 4 HT 530		Intel Xeon E5 2687W		Intel Core i7-2760QM	
	Freq.	Volt.	Freq.	Volt.	Freq.	Volt.	Freq.	Volt.	Freq.	Volt.	Freq.	Volt.	Freq.	Volt.
0	2.5	1.300	2.0	1.500	2.4	1.250	1.4	1.484	3.0	1.430	3.1	1.200	2.4	1.060
1	1.8	1.200	1.8	1.400	2.2	1.200	1.2	1.436	N/A	N/A	N/A	N/A	2.0	0.970
2	1.3	1.100	1.6	1.300	1.8	1.150	1.0	1.308	N/A	N/A	N/A	N/A	1.6	0.890
3	0.8	1.025	0.8	0.900	1.0	1.100	0.8	1.180	2.1	1.250	1.2	0.840	0.8	0.760

We obtain the difference between energy costs of both strategies by subtracting Equation 5 from Equation 6:

$$E(\mathsf{S}_2) - E(\mathsf{S}_1) = AC\left((f_m V_m^2 - f_h V_h^2)T + (f_m V_m^2 - f_l V_l^2)T'\right) + I_{sub}\left((V_m - V_h)T + (V_m - V_l)T'\right) \quad (7)$$

Denote the first term as ΔE_d and the second term as ΔE_l. Substituting the assumption that $T' = (n-1)T$ and $f_m = \frac{1}{n}f_h$ into both terms yields simplified formulae:

$$\Delta E_d = AC\left(\left(\frac{1}{n}f_h V_m^2 - f_h V_h^2\right)T + \left(\frac{1}{n}f_h V_m^2 - f_l V_l^2\right)(n-1)T\right)$$

$$= AC\left(\left(\frac{1}{n}f_h V_m^2 - f_h V_h^2\right)T + \left(\frac{n-1}{n}f_h V_m^2 - (n-1)f_l V_l^2\right)T\right)$$

$$= ACT\left(f_h\left(V_m^2 - V_h^2\right) - (n-1)f_l V_l^2\right) \quad (8)$$

$$\Delta E_l = I_{sub}\left((V_m - V_h)T + (V_m - V_l)(n-1)T\right)$$

$$= I_{sub}T\left(nV_m - V_h - (n-1)V_l\right) \quad (9)$$

Given the fact that voltage has a positive correlation with (i.e., not strictly proportional/linear to) frequency (scaling up/down frequency results in voltage up/down accordingly as shown in Table 2), from Equation 8 we conclude that ΔE_d is a monotonically decreasing function for n, where the maximum 0 is attained when $n = 1$, i.e., when slack T' equals 0. Although generally $\Delta E_d \leq 0$, state-of-the-art CMOS technologies allow insignificant variation of voltage as frequency scales (see Table 2). Consequently the term $V_m^2 - V_h^2$ within ΔE_d is not a large value. Moreover, the ratio between the highest frequency and the lowest one determines the upper bound of n, so the term $(n-1)f_l V_l^2$ is not significant either. Equation 9 indicates that ΔE_l is a non-monotonic function for n, since V_m decreases as n increases.

Example. From the operating points of different processors shown in Table 2, we can calculate numerical energy savings for different n values for a specific processor, and thus quantify energy efficiency of the two approaches. For instance, for AMD Opteron 2218 processor, given a task with the execution time T and slack $0.25T$, i.e., $n = 1.25$, for eliminating the slack, 1.8 GHz is adopted as the working frequency for running the task, and thus $\Delta E_d = ACT \times (2.4 \times (1.15^2 - 1.25^2) - (1.25 - 1) \times 1.0 \times 1.1^2) = -0.8785 \times ACT$; $\Delta E_l = I_{sub}T \times (1.25 \times 1.15 - 1.25 - (1.25 - 1) \times 1.1) = -0.0875 \times I_{sub}T$; $E(\mathsf{S}_2) - E(\mathsf{S}_1) = \Delta E_d + \Delta E_l = -0.8785 \times ACT - 0.0875 \times I_{sub}T < 0$. We can see that with slightly higher energy costs, Strategy I is comparable to Strategy II in energy efficiency.

4. SCALABILITY ANALYSIS

Regardless of energy saving capability, a scalable energy efficient solution prevails for today's supercomputers. Due to the nature of slowing down processors during identified slack instead of switching to an idle mode, *CP-aware slack reclamation* can be superior to *race-to-halt* in terms of power scalability. We next use an example to illustrate the case.

Consider a IBM Blue Gene/Q configured cluster that has a power range from 9 MW at full load (e.g., running the High Performance LINPACK benchmark) to 0.1 MW when idle. Assume a CPU-bound and load-imbalanced application is running on the cluster, where 1% of nodes need to run 10% longer than other nodes. When 99% of nodes have completed their tasks and been placed into an idle mode by *race-to-halt*, the total system power costs amount to around 0.2 MW (0.1 MW × 0.99 + 9 MW × 0.01) for the rest 10% execution time, when there is a huge drop from 9 MW to 0.2 MW in the total system power. The case is even worse if the power variation happens within a loop. If the interval of power variation is small enough, the power gap can be absorbed in the capacitors on the motherboard or in the nodal power supply. Otherwise the huge power spike will be reflected on the transmission lines, which jeopardizes the hardware reliability of the whole system. The case is however greatly mitigated if the load is balanced, or the load imbalance is caused by inevitable data dependencies among tasks, without considering the effect of looping.

5. EXPERIMENTAL EVALUATION

In this section, we validate our findings aforementioned. We applied both energy saving solutions individually to an MPI implementation of one widely used numerical linear algebra operation Cholesky factorization to assess their energy efficiency empirically. Experiments were performed on a large-scale power-aware cluster ARC, equipped with an 40 GB/s Infiniband switch and consisting of 108 computing nodes with two 8-core AMD Opteron 6128 processors (totalling 1728 cores) and 32 GB RAM running 64-bit Linux kernel 2.6.32. The range of CPU frequency on ARC was {0.8, 1.0, 1.2, 1.5, 2.0} GHz. The total of static and dynamic power consumption was measured using Watts up? PRO [3] power meter, which is shared by three ARC nodes. Thus the power consumption measured is the total value of three nodes. CPU frequency scaling was implemented via CPUFreq [1] which directly modifies CPU frequency system configuration files. We did not utilize the whole cluster but only a 16 × 16 process grid (totalling 256 cores), which is sufficient to demonstrate solid power results. Next we present preliminary results on power and performance efficiency of the two approaches for the target HPC runs.

Power Savings. First we evaluate the capability of saving power from the two energy efficient approaches, taking Cholesky factorization running on the ARC cluster for example, where power consumption is measured by sampling at a constant rate through the execution of the application. Figure 2 depicts the total system power consumption of three nodes (out of sixteen nodes in use) running the application with the two approaches individually using a 160000 × 160000 global matrix. Here we present time durations of the first few iterations, where the core loop performs alternating computation and communication with decreasing execution time of each iteration, as the remaining unfactorized matrix shrinks. Thus we can see that for all curves, from left to right, the durations of computation (i.e., the peak power values) decrease as the factorization proceeds.

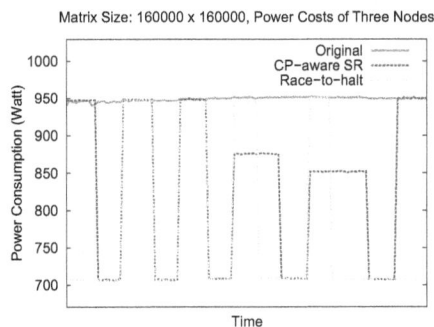

Figure 2: Power Costs of Cholesky Factorization with Two Energy Saving Solutions on Cluster ARC.

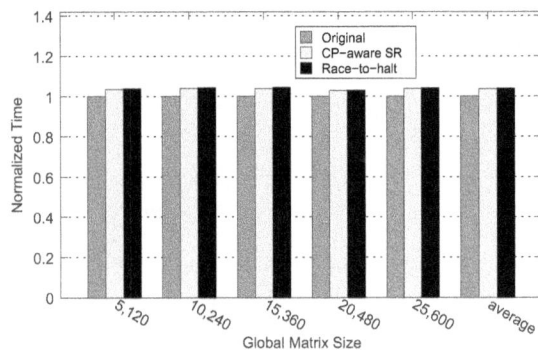

Figure 3: Performance of Cholesky Factorization with Two Energy Saving Solutions on Cluster ARC.

The three runs manifest three different power variation patterns. The *original* run used the same highest CPU frequency for computation and communication, resulting almost constant power costs around 950 Watts. The *CP-aware slack reclamation* approach slowed down computation to eliminate slack, while the *race-to-halt* approach lowered down CPU performance to the minimum scale for all durations other than computation. Both approaches employed the lowest CPU frequency during communication, i.e., the five low-power durations around 700 Watts, and resumed the peak CPU performance when computation started.

Energy saving solutions only slow down processors during communication are semi-optimal. Thus both *CP-aware slack reclamation* and *race-to-halt* are expected to utilize computation slack for further energy savings. The difference lies in that the former requires detection of CP and calculation of the extent of slowing down per the amount of slack, while the latter only needs to know when the slack arises, which is much easier to implement and deploy. Figure 2 demonstrates that *CP-aware slack reclamation* succeeded to lower power states down to an intermediate scale, i.e., the two medium-power durations around 850 Watts during the third and the fourth computation as the blue line shows. Whereas *race-to-halt* observed when the computation started and ended, and utilized the peak CPU performance when it started and switched to the lowest power state immediately when it ended. Moreover, the nature of *race-to-halt* also guarantees no high-power states are employed during the waiting durations resulting from load imbalance and data dependency, i.e., the two low-power durations in green where the application started and ended.

Performance Trade-off. Both energy saving approaches incur minor performance loss while achieving considerable power savings. Figure 3 illustrates slow-down of the two approaches compared to the original runs. The time overhead on employing *CP-aware slack reclamation* and *race-to-halt* are negligible: 3.5% and 3.9% on average respectively. Besides the time overhead on employing the DVFS techniques, additional performance loss is caused by both approaches individually. Detection of CP and slack and frequency calculation (in some cases frequency approximation is also needed) are necessary to perform *CP-aware slack reclamation*. *Race-to-halt* requires to monitor the completion of tasks to determine the appropriate timing for power state switching. Generally the time overhead incurred by both approaches are acceptable in a message-passing HPC environment.

6. FUTURE WORK

The debate between energy efficiency of *CP-aware slack reclamation* and *race-to-halt* is an ongoing issue as hardware technologies advance. We intend to model and generalize both solutions for more scientific applications and present complete empirical evidence to validate our observations. We also plan to apply improved solutions on emerging accelerated architectures for gaining the optimal energy savings.

7. REFERENCES

[1] *CPUFreq - CPU Frequency Scaling.* https://wiki.archlinux.org/index.php/CPU_Frequency_Scaling

[2] *US DOE Exascale Computing Initiative 2012.* http://science.energy.gov/~/media/ascr/ascac/pdf/meetings/aug12/2012-ECI-ASCAC-v4.pdf.

[3] *Watts up? Meters.* https://www.wattsupmeters.com/.

[4] T. Davies, C. Karlsson, H. Liu, C. Ding, and Z. Chen. High performance linpack benchmark: A fault tolerant implementation without checkpointing. In *ICS*, pages 162–171, 2011.

[5] J. Dinan, D. B. Larkins, P. Sadayappan, S. Krishnamoorthy, and J. Nieplocha. Scalable work stealing. In *SC*, page 53, 2009.

[6] V. W. Freeh and D. K. Lowenthal. Using multiple energy gears in MPI programs on a power-scalable cluster. In *PPoPP*, pages 164–173, 2005.

[7] T. Ishihara and H. Yasuura. Voltage scheduling problem for dynamically variable voltage processors. In *SC*, pages 197–202, 1998.

[8] N. B. Rizvandi, J. Taheri, and A. Y. Zomaya. Some observations on optimal frequency selection in DVFS-based energy consumption minimization. *Journal of Parallel Distributed Computing*, 71(8):1154–1164, Aug. 2011.

[9] B. Rountree, D. K. Lowenthal, B. R. de Supinski, M. Schulz, V. W. Freeh, and T. Bletsch. Adagio: Making DVS practical for complex HPC applications. In *ICS*, pages 460–469, 2009.

[10] B. Rountree, D. K. Lowenthal, S. Funk, V. W. Freeh, B. R. de Supinski, and M. Schulz. Bounding energy consumption in large-scale MPI programs. In *SC*, pages 1–9, 2007.

[11] Y. Taur, X. Liang, W. Wang, and H. Lu. A continuous, analytic drain-current model for DG MOSFETs. *IEEE Electron Device Letters*, 25(2):107–109, Feb. 2004.

Defining Standards for Web Page Performance in Business Applications

Garret Rempel

MNP Consulting

2500-201 Portage Ave

Winnipeg, MB, Canada R3B 3K6

1-204-924-7503

garret.rempel@mnp.ca

ABSTRACT

Distinctions between standalone computer applications and web-based applications are becoming increasingly blurry, and client-server communication is being used as a part of everyday computing. This is resulting in user expectations of web page performance converging with their expectations of standalone application performance. Existing industry standards for web page performance are widely varied and inconsistent, and standards based on surveying users are especially so. We illustrate this inconsistency with examples from published literature and industry studies.

Considering a specific class of web-based applications (high usage, minimal overhead, business web applications), we attempt to define a set of industry standards by conducting a case study of an implementation of an industry-leading software suite. We measure the application's performance over time and contrast its performance with the frequency of reported end-user performance complaints. Taking these measurements, we define a specific set of measurable performance standards that, when met, would achieve a high level of performance satisfaction among a large percentage of users.

Based on our examination of existing industry standards, we know there are limitations in users' ability to define consistent performance requirements. Here we present a method that proposes to produce a set of performance requirements through a user interview process that closely matches the performance standards defined by the case study. We then examine the results achieved by applying this method to a comparable web application within the same company as the case study to demonstrate that the requirements produced match the performance observations of the case study analysis.

Categories and Subject Descriptors

D.2.1 [**Software Engineering**]: Requirements/Specifications – *Elicitation methods, Methodologies;* D.2.8 [**Software Engineering**]: Metrics – *Performance measures;* H.1.2 [**Models and Principles**]: User/Machine Systems – *Human factors, Software psychology.*

General Terms

Measurement, Performance, Human Factors, Standardization

Keywords

Performance; industry standards; requirements; case study; methodology; web applications

1. INTRODUCTION

We are seeing a convergence between standalone applications and the web, which includes traditional and mobile platforms. Cloud computing, network data storage, and sharing information between desktop and mobile devices is becoming ubiquitous and transparent. In many cases it is difficult for a user to know when they are interacting with a piece of technology as to whether it is operating in a standalone manner or if it is communicating with the web [22]. Thus a user's expectations of the performance of their consumer electronics are converging across all platforms and technology. As web browsers and web enabled applications become a dominant platform [25], users expect to be able to do the same things and have the same performance regardless of their technology choices [1]. This convergence in technology means that applying traditional Human-Computer Interface (HCI) standards to web technology is becoming more relevant and important.

Currently there are widely varying opinions on what constitutes an acceptable web page load time. These opinions range from over 30 seconds to less than 1 second, depending on who is espousing the standard and what methodology they have followed to obtain it. There are three main categories of studies in performance literature that establish standards: Physiological Measurements, Empirical Studies, and Surveys.

Physiological Measurements examine physical thresholds or reactions of the human body that are independent of a users' decision-making process. These measurements are effective at providing limits to the level of optimization required to make something 'good enough' and defining thresholds of human perception that, once crossed, further improvement has limited or no additional benefit.

Empirical Studies typically measure the duration of time between the start of a web page request and a point in time when a user chooses to abort the request prematurely (hereafter referred to as "abandonment"). Empirical studies use a variety of tools and testing methodologies to impose known delays and measure when and how many participants abandon their task. They do not directly attempt to measure a participant's emotional state, but rely on measuring concrete actions or decisions that a participant makes as a result of exceeding their wait time tolerance.

Empirical studies are effective at evaluating strategies to overcome or mitigate poor performance by comparing those strategies against a baseline to determine how effective they are at delaying or negating user abandonment.

Surveys typically ask participants to evaluate their emotional reaction, frustration level, or satisfaction level based on page performance as part of an empirical study. They may also ask participants to provide a self-evaluation of how long they will wait before they become frustrated or abandon a web page (their 'wait time tolerance'). The most significant limitation to surveys is that they are subject to a participant's perception and rely on a participant's ability to self-evaluate and quantify an undependable emotional state that can be impacted by many factors [24]. These studies are important however, since "frustration" and "satisfaction" are both emotional reactions that strongly influence user perception of the credibility [6] and quality of a system [3].

1.1 Physiological Measurements

Studies conducted on human interactions with computer systems have given us reasonable upper and lower bounds for several classes of interactions based on their purpose. One of the most widely-cited results is Miller's (1968) powers-of-10 thresholds of 0.1s, 1.0s, and 10s [13] that places limits on a person's perception of instantaneous reaction (0.1s), their continuity of thought (1.0s), and ability to keep their attention focused on the dialogue of interaction (10s) [15].

In terms of conversational interaction with a system, the acknowledgement of "knowledge of results" peaks in effectiveness for simple responses at 0.5s with an upper limit of 2.0s, and delays of more than 4.0s indicate a break in the thread of communication. This is also compatible with the result that distractions can interfere with information being held in short-term memory, and the effects of distractions on short-term memory rapidly increase once a person is aware that they are waiting. This awareness of waiting typically begins to occur in as little as 2 seconds [13].

A further study on gaze fixation demonstrates that a display with multiple independently loading components will result in person fixating on the components that load quickest. A page with a slowly (8s) loading banner advertisement that occupies 23% of the screen space will only receive 1% of a person's attention time, while the same advertisement will receive 20% of a person's attention time when they are only exposed to the screen after rendering has completed [16].

These results indicate the unintended consequences of first-impression response time optimization (as opposed to fully rendered response time optimization). If the most important information is not among the earliest to display onscreen, a person is less likely to give it the attention that it requires. In addition, if unimportant information is rendered earlier than important information, the likelihood increases of becoming distracted and that distraction interfering with their short-term memory and the continuity of their thought process.

1.2 Empirical Studies

The primary focus of this class of study has been to measure the average (mean or median) time that a user will wait while expecting a response before abandoning the process (their 'wait time tolerance'). For systems designed for public consumption, these studies provide an important upper bound on web page response time performance where abandonment is a significant and measurable negative outcome. Several of these studies also

evaluate the effectiveness of providing feedback to the user while they are waiting as a tactic for delaying abandonment by communicating with the user that an error has not occurred and something is happening behind the scenes.

These studies have approached the question of abandonment in a variety of methods and have produced a wide range of results and recommendations from less than 2 seconds [14][24] up to 41s [19]. The most constrained result (<2s) is from Shneiderman (1984) and is regarding the pace of human-computer interaction and predates public access to the internet [14]. However, as expectations for offline and online computing converge, this result becomes important to consider as we can observe a steady decrease in the duration of time a person is willing to wait among online-specific studies as shown in Table 1.

Table 1: Wait Time Tolerances for Online-Specific Empirical Studies

Study	Year	Wait Time Tolerance (in seconds)
Bickford [2]	1997	8.5
Ramsay [19]	1998	41
Selvidge* [23]	1999	30
Hoxmeier* [10]	2000	12
Galleta, Henry, McCoy, and Polak* [8]	2002	4-8
Nah [14]	2004	2-4

*These studies included a survey component in an attempt to quantify the impact on user satisfaction levels caused by introducing fixed delays into the rendering process.

The study conducted by Nah (2004) is of particular interest as the conclusions she presents regarding wait time tolerances most closely agrees with Shneiderman's (1984) conclusions regarding human-computer interactions. Specifically, Nah states that "the findings from this study suggest that most users are willing to wait for only about two seconds for simple information retrieval tasks on the Web." [14] She also directly references the results obtained by Shneiderman (1984) and Miller (1968) as comparable findings. However, her conclusions are based upon a method that involves iterative testing and are drawn from her observation that each test subject's wait time tolerance decreases with subsequent failures. Her result is that a person's wait time tolerance converges towards 2s *after experiencing multiple failures* (shown in Table 2).

Table 2: Wait Time Tolerances Measured by Nah (2004)

Without Feedback	Mean	Median	Mode
First Response Failure	13s	9s	5-8s
Second Response Failure	4s	3.6s	2-4s
Third Response Failure	3.3s	2.5s	2-3s
With Feedback	**Mean**	**Median**	**Mode**
First Response Failure	37.6s	22.6s	15-16s, 20-22s, 45-46s
Second Response Failure	17s	8.4s	2-3s
Third Response Failure	6.7s	4.3s	2-3s

Nah's (2004) conclusion that 2s is the 'tolerable' threshold for web page performance is not necessarily supported by the evidence. Her method of providing instantaneous responses to successful page requests interspersed with three pages which fail by never providing a response, she is conditioning her subjects to expect one of two outcomes when clicking a link: instantaneous success, or failure. Therefore she is proving that *when conditioned*, a subject's ability to determine whether or not a page will succeed or fail trends towards 2s by their third failure.

A much more important observation from Nah's (2004) study is when a subject is given a defined task to accomplish (load a web page), 50% of the subjects will abandon that task within 9s (measured by the median wait time tolerance of the First Response Failure, no feedback). It is also telling to observe that poor performance will *decrease* a subject's wait time tolerance. A perceived failure to load a web page due to poor performance will cause a person to more quickly abandon subsequent requests.

For business purposes, the results of these studies are important in establishing a maximum response time limit for web pages to load. They do not however, provide a conclusive target for response times, as typically a business would intend to achieve a much lower abandonment rate than 50%. In order to establish reasonable performance goals, they must be based on people's subjective reactions since a business typically intends to achieve a high rate of satisfaction, and a negligible rate of abandonment due to performance.

1.3 Surveys

Of the three categories of performance studies, surveys provide the most subjective and ambiguous results as they rely on respondents being capable of objectively self-assessing or estimating their own emotional reaction to web page performance. It is also well-established that a person's threshold for frustration and wait time tolerance are impacted by many variables [24]. Methodology also plays an important part of assessing survey results, as some surveys that use a multiple-choice structure may be subject to Central Tendency Bias or Position Bias, wherein respondents will prefer options presented in the middle or at the beginning of a list unless they hold very strong opinions on the question being presented [9].

Notable results from surveys on emotional reactions that are conducted within an empirical study framework result in recommendations that range from 30s [23], to 12s [10], to 4-8s [8]. Results from non-empirical standalone surveys include 8s [27] (which provides no justification for using the threshold of 8s), 4s [11], and 2s [7]. The conclusions drawn from these surveys, much like the empirical studies, are based upon average (mean or median) answers provided by the respondents [20]. Comparing conclusions, we can also see an unusually rapid drop in performance expectations by respondents, a drop that does not appear to correspond with an equivalent improvement in consumer connectivity. In regards to the JupiterResearch (2006) and Forrester (2009) surveys, the results as given show a drop of 50% in performance expectations (from 4s to 2s). However, broadband penetration in the United States only increased from 20.3% to 25.5% between Q4 2006 and Q4 2009 [17] and 16.9% to 23.1% for the entire OECD survey region. Since expectations of web page performance are primarily influenced by experience, it is unlikely that the expectation of web page response times would drop so significantly on average over the same timeframe. This is also supported by research that shows that the average web page size has continuously increased since 2003, and from 312KB

to 507KB (62.5%) between 2008 and 2009 alone [26]. This increase continues to appear until we see an average size of 1510KB in 2014 [5]. This increase in web page size is only partially offset by improving connectivity and has resulted in a net *increase* in typical web page loading times over that time period.

Re-examining the results published by JupiterResearch (2006) and Forrester (2009) by examining their high percentile responses and combining those results along with an additional survey conducted by Rempel (2014), we can see a significantly more consistent and useful result. Combining the three surveys produces a conclusion that at least 90% of respondents would be satisfied with response times of 1s or less, and at least 80% of respondents would be satisfied with response times of 2s or less. Additionally, on average we would expect a satisfaction level of 99% with response times of 1s or less, and 90% with response times of 2s or less [20].

1.4 Findings

Studying the subject of industry standards as they apply to web page performance, it is apparent that there is a lack of consistency in the way the topic is studied, measured, and the conclusions that are drawn. There are however, a few observations that can be made that are useful from a business perspective.

As traditional applications, the web, and mobile devices converge, the expectations that people have in terms of web performance will converge with their expectations of traditional human-computer interfaces. Therefore it is reasonable to consider that original HCI research by Miller (1968) can serve as a gold standard for performance targets, even if they are not widely achievable.

- The threshold for instantaneous feedback is <0.1s.
- The threshold for train of thought (typical web request-response interaction) is <1.0s.
- The threshold for complex operation is <10.0s.

In addition, wait time tolerance improves when dynamic feedback is presented. There is a case to be made for using 2s as a threshold as referenced by Miller (1968), Shneiderman (1984), Nah (2004), and Forrester (2009) with varying levels of support. It is reasonable to suggest that 2s be used as an upper bound for basic, non-instantaneous transactions, and that any transactions that consistently take longer than 2s should take advantage of feedback techniques to avoid user abandonment. Operations that are known to exceed 10s should include additional feedback or pre-operation estimates of expected wait time to improve a person's engagement with the system and ease potential frustration.

It is also important to note that *consistency* in performance is important, and that page interactions should not deviate outside of 25% to 200% of the mean [24] to avoid anxiety or frustration caused by unexpected or unusual variances in response time.

2. CASE STUDY

This section describes a study that was performed on an internal business web application in production in order to examine user feedback (complaints) about system performance as compared to actual performance metrics gathered on the system. This study differs from the previously described studies in that it is a passive, unsolicited study of actual user behavior and satisfaction levels in a real life situation, instead of a study comprised of volunteers or survey respondents.

2.1 System Under Scrutiny

The system being studied is the primary client information tracking and incident reporting system of an international company and is recognized as an industry-leading platform, supported by a reputable international vendor. The system is used by 1,200 users in offices spanning 5 time zones, from the east coast to the west coast of Canada and the United States. Many of the system's users are required to use this application as part of their primary duties, often while actively communicating with their customers, while using the application to perform data entry that their customers are providing over the phone or in person. During the course of a business day, peak usage has been measured at 800 simultaneous logins and 50,000 page requests per hour over a four-hour window. On an average weekday, the system receives 440,000 page requests and peaks at 510,000 page requests on the busiest day of the week. The system also receives approximately 10,000,000 page requests per month.

This web application has several advantages as a subject for study:

- The period of time under scrutiny includes initial go-live, as well as several months of stabilization in which systemic performance problems were observed.

- The system's users are motivated and encouraged to report impressions of poor performance via a centralized service desk.

- Users do not have any recourse to abandon the application as no alternatives exist to provide workarounds to problems they encounter.

As a business application, the system has been designed as a high-efficiency system. All secondary requests to acquire resources from a web page are made to the same server that the web application is hosted on, eliminating the need for secondary DNS lookups or additional connections to be established. Resources in use are also very minimal and are cached by the browser after the initial request. Page structures are also very simple and there are no javascript commands issued with the onload directive, resulting in a very fast render time.

2.2 Methodology

The time period of this study is January 2012 through May 2012, as well as October 2013, all of which encompasses:

- Initial go-live of the system.

- A period of systemic performance problems.

- Incremental improvements in system performance as patches are released and performance defects are resolved.

- A comparative period (October 2013) in which the system is stable, performance is optimized, and no further patches are being developed for the system.

In order to establish an upper bound for server communication time, a load generation tool was used to generate a known sequence of requests to an identical production support server using a fixed interval between the end of one request and the beginning of the next over a period of four hours. This process was conducted from an agent local to the system's host server on the same local subnet, and repeated from an agent deployed in an office in the furthest geographic location from the host server (Southern California). The number of completed requests was compared between the two runs to determine an upper bound for communication latency between the two locations. This test sequence was repeated at different times of the day and days of the week and the results averaged to produce an expected communication latency margin for each request.

The developer tools in Google's Chrome browser were used to obtain a random sampling of requests and analyze the duration of time required to parse and render the final result of the page. These timings were weighted and averaged to determine the expected render time for each request.

The production server was instrumented to record and log the interval between receipt of each request and transmission of the final response. These logs were aggregated and analyzed across every request made to the server to generate a count of requests by hour and by day into 0.5s response time buckets.

Service desk logs were examined to obtain the number of issue tickets opened (complaints) related to perceived performance problems with the web application and correlated with the measured performance of the web application.

2.3 Findings

2.3.1 Communication Latency

To calculate the margin of communication latency that exists for remote locations, we executed the same test plan over a fixed duration from an agent local to the host server and from one that is remote. The request frequency was then analyzed to calculate the margin that existed between the two tests. This process was performed three times at different times of the day and different days of the week to reduce the impact of network traffic on the results. The following calculation was used to calculate the communication latency.

Let r be the number of completed requests, t be the total time of the test in seconds, and a be the average time between requests (which is the sum of the fixed think time plus the measured average response time of all requests). Let R represent the test execution from the remote agent, and L represent the test execution from the local agent. The communication latency at the remote agent is defined by:

$$M = a_L - [(r_R \cdot t_L \cdot a_L) / (r_L \cdot t_R)]$$

This value is averaged over multiple iterations, producing a final calculated average communication latency of 0.481 seconds.

2.3.2 Render Time

To calculate an estimated render time margin, Google's Chrome browser developer tools were used to analyze the network timeline of a series of page request / responses. Prior to the test, the browser's cache was cleared in order to evaluate the difference in time between an initial request to the server, and a request where resources had already been cached.

Prior to resource caching being completed, secondary resource requests and rendering time required up to 0.190s to process between receipt of the initial server response and the final load event being fired. All subsequent requests (once the resource cache was established) required between 0.004s to 0.047s to complete rendering. This resulted in an effective average of 0.026s.

2.3.3 Aggregated Response Percentiles

The aggregated server processing times provided by server instrumentation have been adjusted by adding a 0.5s margin to account for the measured average communication latency and rendering and the result is shown in Table 3. The values presented in the table are the percent of requests during each month that completed within the specified time constraint. Major percentile thresholds are color-coded so that measurements that fall below the 85th percentile are red, below the 90th percentile are orange, below the 95th percentile are yellow, and 95th percentile and above are green.

Table 3: Server Processing Percentiles with Rendering and Latency Margins

	Jan 2012	Feb 2012	Mar 2012	Apr 2012	May 2012	Oct 2013
	Percent of Requests Completed within Range					
< 1.0 s	64.43	63.82	59.98	67.87	69.06	70.22
< 1.5 s	80.65	79.62	76.18	81.57	83.76	87.27
< 2.0 s	87.47	86.18	82.83	87.17	89.62	92.17
< 2.5 s	91.40	90.40	87.32	91.01	93.37	97.81
< 3.0 s	93.64	92.72	89.94	92.76	95.27	
< 3.5 s	94.94	94.12	91.65	93.82	96.29	
< 4.0 s	95.82	95.09	92.94	94.82	97.00	
< 4.5 s	96.51	95.88	94.05	96.01	97.66	
< 5.0 s	97.11	96.57	95.02	96.83	98.23	

From this information we can observe four distinct phases of application performance: Go-live (Jan / Feb 2012), Decay (Mar 2012), Optimization (Apr / May 2012), and Stable (Oct 2013). These four periods are mirrored by the level of complaints issued to the service desk over perceived performance problems during the same timeframes as shown in Table 4.

Table 4: Performance Complaints to Service Desk

	Jan 2012	Feb 2012	Mar 2012	Apr 2012	May 2012	Oct 2013
Complaints*	17	20	22	21	13	0

*Jan-May monthly values are estimated based on reported number of complaints received/week.

There is a clear connection between the number of service desk complaints issued about performance and the aggregated web page performance percentiles of the system. As performance decays (illustrated by major percentile thresholds dropping into lower response time buckets), the number of complaints increases. Conversely as the performance level of the system increases, the number of complaints drops until a certain level is reached at which point no new performance complaints are forthcoming.

Reorienting the results from Table 4 in order to show response time levels for each major percentile, Table 5 and Figure 1 compare the four phases of application performance and how they changed over time.

Although the number of actual performance complaints made to the service desk appears small, the number of unhappy users is typically much larger than the number that will issue a formal complaint. In a public consumer system, only 1 out of 26 unhappy customers will lodge a formal complaint, while many of the remaining customers will simply never return [4][18]. Because of the nature of this system being an internal business system, it is possible that the number of unhappy users who do not complain is smaller. However, regardless of the actual factor involved, the number of complaints is a good indicator of user satisfaction.

Table 5: Response Time Levels for Major Percentiles by Phase

Percentile	Go-live (Jan/Feb 2012)	Decay (Mar 2012)	Optimization (Apr/May 2012)	Stable (Oct 2013)
80th	<1.5s	<2.0s	<1.5s	<1.5s
85th	<2.0s	<2.5s	<2.0s	<1.5s
90th	<2.5s	<3.5s	<2.5s	<2.0s
95th	<4.0s	<5.0s	<3.0s/<4.5s	<2.5s
Complaints per Month	*18.5*	*22*	*17*	*0*

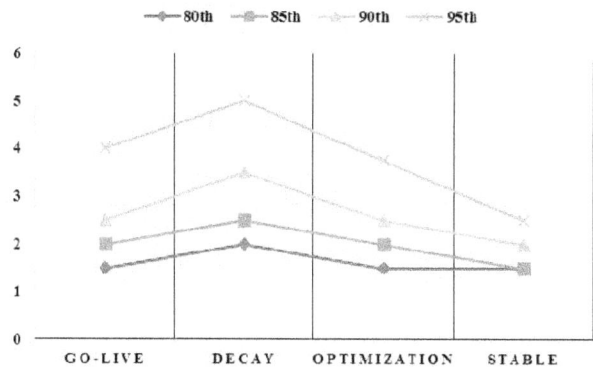

Figure 1. Response Time Levels for Major Percentiles by Phase

Based on this study we have sufficient information to set performance goals for future systems that may be implemented at this corporation as follows:

- 95% of all page requests must be completed within 2.5s.

- 90% of all page requests must be completed within 2.0s.

- 85% of all page requests must be completed within 1.5s.

3. GATHERING PERFORMANCE REQUIREMENTS PROCESS

Given the wide discrepancy in web page performance standards that use a survey as part of its data gathering process, and the wide spread in responses (0.5s to 60s) given when respondents were asked to provide their own estimate for their wait time tolerance [20], it is uncertain whether performance requirements can be reasonably obtained through an interview process with business users for a new web application. If two business users were interviewed independently for performance requirements without guidance, it is entirely possible that their response time targets could range from <0.5s to <30s. This section describes an effort to refine the process of establishing performance requirements by presenting guidelines to business users prior to soliciting their input, in an effort to create a set of performance requirements that closely match the results generated by the case study. To match the case study results, on aggregate we would need to see 95% of all web page requests achieve an end-to-end response time of 2.5s or less. To meet this target and to stay in line with prior studies of a <2s standard, we would require a majority of page performance targets be set at <2s. A limited number of pages may have larger performance targets depending on function and still meet these guidelines. Pages with larger performance targets can also be candidates for alternate feedback strategies to improve end user perception [2][14].

3.1 Response Time Performance Categories

In this attempt to establish performance requirements for a new application, a set of performance requirement categories were established with assistance from system developers to define examples. Each performance requirement category (shown in Table 6) had four components, a definition (with examples), a target response time level, a maximum response time level, and a stability measurement (a percentile value to be used to measure against the target). Percentiles are used to measure web page performance instead of an average response time in order to provide a better bound on the page performance and smooth out any spikes in measured response times [12][21]. It is also used to provide a comparable metric to our server processing time measurements as defined in the prior case study.

Table 6: Performance Requirement Categories

Category Name	Target Response Time	Maximum Response Time	Stability (Percentile)
Basic Operations Ex. Most Standard Pages or Simple Operations	<2 s	<2 s	95th
Complex or Ambiguous Search or Save Operations Ex. Major Save Operations, Large Result Set Searches	<5 s	<5 s	90th
Integration or Major Calculation Operations Ex. Upload Documents, Synchronous Interfaces, Complex Calculations	<5 s	<15 s	85th
Heavyweight Operations Extremely Complex Calculation and Data Processing Operations, Resource Intensive Interfaces	<10 s	<30 s	85th

To evaluate the performance of a specific web page or operation after a test cycle, its measured response time performance is compared to the target and maximum response times defined in its category. A page is considered to have passed under a typical load when:

- Its percentile response time measurement meets or betters the target response time.

- Its overall maximum response time measurement meets or betters the maximum response time.

A page is considered to have passed under maximum peak load when:

- Its percentile response time measurement meets or betters the maximum response time.

3.2 Requirement Definition Process

In the example presented in the previous case study, the functional requirements of the system defined 259 distinct web pages or operations in the system that could be evaluated for performance. The performance requirement categories were presented to the business users and they were then given instructions to categorize each page into one of the pre-defined performance categories whenever possible. They were also instructed that if there was sufficient reason that a page could not be placed into one of the categories, the business could create new performance requirements for that page. At the end of the process, the pages were categorized by the business as shown in Table 7.

Table 7: Business User Allocation of Web Pages into Response Time Categories

Category Name	# of Pages	% of Total Pages
Basic Operations	222	85.71
Complex or Ambiguous Search or Save Operations	29	11.20
Integration or Major Calculation Operations	1	0.39
Heavyweight Operations	7	2.70

Calculating the weighted average performance target response time value for all of the pages in the system produced a value of 2.56s, and the weighted average performance maximum response time value was 3.14s.

During the next stage of the requirements process, the business users were asked to weight the web pages and operations based on number of requests per day. These weightings were used during a performance test cycle to simulate production workload. The test results were analyzed based on the number of page requests made to each of the pages and the results are shown in Table 8.

Table 8: Performance Testing Page Request Frequency by Response Time Category

Category Name	# of Page Requests During Test Cycle	% of Total Page Requests
Basic Operations	353,737	89.54
Complex or Ambiguous Search or Save Operations	33,550	8.49
Integration or Major	2,942	0.74

Calculation Operations		
Heavyweight Operations	4,819	1.21

Performing a similar calculation as was done for the number of web pages, based on the number of actual page requests, the weighted average performance target response time value for all of the pages in the system was 2.37s, and the weighted average performance maximum load time value was 2.69s.

If achieved in a production environment, the requirements presented here closely correspond to the desired performance target of achieving 95% of all web page requests in under 2.5s, and matches the calculated wait time tolerance level of the users of this type of system, in this particular company, as illustrated in the above case study.

4. CONCLUSIONS

Industry performance standards are widely variable and inconsistently structured and researched. However, a careful study of a web application that exists in a controlled environment shows that the actual wait time tolerance of the users in the study closely aligns with the most popular performance recommendations of <2s.

By using this case study to pre-define performance target categories with assistance from business analysts and system developers, business users with no particular training or experience with performance requirements were able to independently define performance requirements that closely aligned with the observed optimal performance state of an existing production application.

5. ACKNOLWEDGEMENTS

The author has benefited from discussions with Glenn Hemming.

6. REFERENCES

[1] Anderson, J. 2012. The Web Is Dead? No. Experts expect apps and the Web to converge in the cloud; but many worry that simplicity for users will come at a price. *Pew Research Center's Internet & American Life Project*. Retrieved August 8, 2014, from Pew Research Center: http://www.pewinternet.org/files/old-media/Files/Reports/2012/PIP_Future_of_Apps_and_Web.pdf

[2] Bickford, P. 1997. Worth the Wait. *Netscape's Developer Edge, Netscape Communications (online)*, Mountain View, CA, USA (1997). Retrieved August 8, 2014, from Archive.org: http://web.archive.org/web/20040913083444/http://developer.netscape.com/viewsource/bickford_wait.htm

[3] Bouch, A., Kuchinsky, A., and Bhatti, N. 2000. Quality is in the eye of the beholder: meeting users' requirements for Internet quality of service. In *Proceedings of the SIGCHI conference on Human Factors in Computing Systems* (CHI '00). ACM, New York, NY, USA, 297-304. DOI=10.1145/332040.332447 http://doi.acm.org/10.1145/332040.332447c

[4] Digby, J. 2010. 50 Facts about Customer Experience. *Return on Behavior Magazine (online)*. Retrieved August 8, 2014, from Archive.org: https://web.archive.org/web/20140210221957/http://returnon behavior.com/2010/10/50-facts-about-customer-experience-for-2011/

[5] Everts, T. 2014. State of the Union, Ecommerce Page Speed & Web Performance. Retrieved August 8, 2014, from Radware: http://www.webperformancetoday.com/2014/04/29/spring-2014-state-union-ecommerce-page-speed-web-performance-infographic/

[6] Fogg, B.J., Marshall, J., Laraki, O., Osipovich, A., Varma, C., Fang, N., Paul, J., Rangnekar, A., Shon, J., Swani, P., and Treinen, M. 2001. What makes Web sites credible?: a report on a large quantitative study. In *Proceedings of the SIGCHI Conference on Human Factors in Computing Systems* (CHI '01). ACM, New York, NY, USA, 61-68. DOI=10.1145/365024.365037 http://doi.acm.org/10.1145/365024.365037

[7] Forrester Consulting. 2009. eCommerce Web Site Performance Today; An Updated Look At Consumer Reaction To A Poor Online Shopping Experience. Retrieved August 8, 2014, from Damco Group: http://www.damcogroup.com/white-papers/ecommerce_website_perf_wp.pdf

[8] Galletta, D.F., Henry, R., McCoy, S. and Polak, P. 2004. Web Site Delays: How Tolerant are Users?, *Journal of the Association for Information Systems*: Vol. 5: Iss. 1, Article 1. http://aisel.aisnet.org/jais/vol5/iss1/1

[9] Gingery, T. 2009. Survey Research Definitions: Central Tendency Bias. Retrieved August 8, 2014, from Cvent: http://survey.cvent.com/blog/market-research-design-tips-2/survey-research-definitions-central-tendency-bias

[10] Hoxmeier, J.A. and DiCesare, C. 2000. System response time and user satisfaction: an experimental study of browser-based applications. *Proceedings of the Americas Conference on Information Systems*, (Long Beach, CA, USA, 2000), Association for Information Systems, 140-145. http://citeseerx.ist.psu.edu/viewdoc/summary?doi=10.1.1.99.2770

[11] JupiterResearch 2006. Retail Web Site Performance; Consumer Reaction to a Poor Online Shopping Experience. Retrieved August 8, 2014, from Akamai: http://www.akamai.com/dl/reports/Site_Abandonment_Final_Report.pdf

[12] Meier, J.D., Farre, C., Bansode, P., Barber, S. and Rea, D. 2007. Performance Testing Guidance for Web Applications, *Microsoft Patterns & Practices (Chapter 15 – Key Mathematic Principles for Performance Testers)*. Retrieved August 8, 2014, from MSDN: http://msdn.microsoft.com/en-us/library/bb924370.aspx

[13] Miller, R.B. 1968. Response time in man-computer conversational transactions. In *Proceedings of the December 9-11, 1968, fall joint computer conference, part I* (AFIPS '68 (Fall, part I)). ACM, New York, NY, USA, 267-277. DOI=10.1145/1476589.1476628 http://doi.acm.org/10.1145/1476589.1476628

[14] Nah, F. 2004. A Study on Tolerable Waiting Time: How Long Are Web Users Willing to Wait?, *Behaviour and Information Technology*, (Lincoln, NE, USA, 2004), Vol. 23, No. 3 (May 2004). Retrieved August 8, 2014 from

University of Nebraska-Lincoln:
http://cba.unl.edu/research/articles/548/download.pdf

[15] Nielsen, J. *Usability Engineering*. Morgan Kaufmann Publishers Inc., San Francisco, CA, USA, 1993.

[16] Nielsen, J. 2010. Website Response Times. Retrieved August 8, 2014, from Nielsen Norman Group: http://www.nngroup.com/articles/website-response-times/

[17] OECD 2013. Historical penetration rates, Fixed and Wireless broadband, G7 (June 2013). Retrieved August 8, 2014, from OECD Broadband Portal: http://www.oecd.org/sti/broadband/1i-BBPenetrationHistorical-G7-2013-06.xls

[18] Quinn, P. 2014. The Customer Complaint Iceberg. Retrieved August 8, 2014 from PeoplePulse: http://www.peoplepulse.com.au/Customer-Experience.htm

[19] Ramsay, J., Barbesi, A. and Preece, J. 1998. A psychological investigation of long retrieval times on the world wide web, *Interacting with Computers* (1998), 10(1), 77-86. DOI=10.1016/S0953-5438(97)00019-2 http://iwc.oxfordjournals.org/content/10/1/77.abstract

[20] Rempel, G. 2014. Web Performance Standards: Finding Value in User Surveys. Retrieved August 8, 2014, from Mincing Thoughts: http://mincingthoughts.blogspot.com/2014/07/web-performance-standards-finding-value.html

[21] Rhea, R. 2012. Performance Test Best Practices With Rational Performance Tester. Retrieved August 8, 2014, from IBM DeveloperWorks: https://www.ibm.com/developerworks/community/groups/service/html/communityview?communityUuid=a9ba1efe-

b731-4317-9724-a181d6155e3a#fullpageWidgetId=W5f281fe58c09_49c7_9fa4_e094f86b7e98&file=b3e1526b-8981-4e42-826d-d8eadc569a13

[22] Schindler, E. 2007. The Convergence of Desktop, Web and Mobile Clients. Retrieved August 8, 2014, from CIO: http://www.cio.com/article/2437560/developer/the-convergence-of-desktop--web-and-mobile-clients.html

[23] Selvidge, P. 1999. How long is too long for a website to load?. *Usability News*, 1(2). Retrieved August 8, 2014, from Archive.org: http://web.archive.org/web/20020404143111/http://psychology.wichita.edu/surl/usabilitynews/1s/time_delay.htm

[24] Shneiderman, B. 1984. Response time and display rate in human performance with computers. *ACM Comput. Surv.* 16, 3 (September 1984), 265-285. DOI=10.1145/2514.2517 http://doi.acm.org/10.1145/2514.2517

[25] Wang, H., Moshchuk, A. and Bush, A. 2009. Convergence of Desktop and Web Applications on a Multi-Service OS. In *HotSec '09*, (Montreal, CA, 2009). https://www.usenix.org/legacy/event/hotsec09/tech/full_papers/wang.pdf

[26] Web Site Optimization 2014. Average Web Breaks 1600K. Retrieved August 8, 2014, from WebSiteOptimization: http://www.websiteoptimization.com/speed/tweak/average-web-page/

[27] Zona Research Inc. 1999. The Economic Impacts of Unacceptable Web-Site Download Speeds. Retrieved August 8, 2014, from WebPerf: http://www.webperf.net/info/wp_downloadspeed.pdf

NUPAR: A Benchmark Suite for Modern GPU Architectures

Yash Ukidave*, Fanny Nina Paravecino*, Leiming Yu*, Charu Kalra*, Amir Momeni*,
Zhongliang Chen*, Nick Materise*, Brett Daley*, Perhaad Mistry[†]and David Kaeli*

*Electrical and Computer Engineering, Northeastern University, Boston, MA

[†]Advanced Micro Devices Inc. (AMD), Boxborough, MA

{yukidave, fninaparavecino, ylm, ckalra, amomeni, zhonchen, nmaterise, bdaley,
kaeli}@ece.neu.edu, Perhaad.Mistry@amd.com

ABSTRACT

Heterogeneous systems consisting of multi-core CPUs, Graphics Processing Units (GPUs) and many-core accelerators have gained widespread use by application developers and data-center platform developers. Modern day heterogeneous systems have evolved to include advanced hardware and software features to support a spectrum of application patterns. Heterogeneous programming frameworks such as CUDA, OpenCL, and OpenACC have all introduced new interfaces to enable developers to utilize new features on these platforms. In emerging applications, performance optimization is not only limited to effectively exploiting data-level parallelism, but includes leveraging new degrees of concurrency and parallelism to accelerate the entire application.

To aid hardware architects and application developers in effectively tuning performance on GPUs, we have developed the *NUPAR* benchmark suite. The *NUPAR* applications belong to a number of different scientific and commercial computing domains. These benchmarks exhibit a range of GPU computing characteristics that consider memory-bandwidth limitations, device occupancy and resource utilization, synchronization latency and device-specific compute optimizations. The *NUPAR* applications are specifically designed to stress new hardware and software features that include: nested parallelism, concurrent kernel execution, shared host-device memory and new instructions for precise computation and data movement. In this paper, we focus our discussion on applications developed in CUDA and OpenCL, and focus on high-end server class GPUs. We describe these benchmarks and evaluate their interaction with different architectural features on a GPU. Our evaluation examines the behavior of the advanced hardware features on recently-released GPU architectures.

Categories and Subject Descriptors

D.1.3 [**Programming Techniques**]: Concurrent Programming—*Parallel programming*; D.2.8 [**Software Engineer-**

ing]: Metrics—*Performance measures*; H.5.2 [**Information Interfaces and Presentation**]: User Interfaces—*Benchmarking*

General Terms

Profiling, Performance Measurement, Benchmarking,

Keywords

Benchmark suite, GPUs, CUDA, OpenCL

1. INTRODUCTION

Heterogeneous computing using accelerators such as multi-core CPUs, GPUs, and FPGAs has gained a lot of traction in recent years. The programmability and performance of the GPUs have increased to support a range of throughput-oriented workloads belonging to various scientific domains. The availability of mature software frameworks has helped GPUs become a commonly used device in throughput computing.

In more recent accelerator platforms we are beginning to see applications that come with stricter timing constraints, stringent resource requirements, opportunities for concurrent execution and irregular memory access patterns. Many of these applications have been successfully moved to GPU platforms [33]. Programming frameworks such as CUDA, OpenCL, and OpenACC have introduced new features that address many of these challenges on GPUs. Modern GPU architectures constantly evolve by adding support for such advanced constructs introduced in the programming frameworks. The performance of applications on GPUs can improve dramatically if these programming features are used efficiently. It is essential to provide researchers with a proper set of benchmarks that can appropriately exercise such advanced features, to consider hardware and software performance tradeoffs on different GPU platforms, and to identify performance bottlenecks and evaluate potential solutions.

Researchers have developed a number of benchmark suites to study different aspects of a GPU architecture [7, 10, 16, 31]. The goals of a benchmark suite can vary depending on the class of system they target. As GPU systems have evolved, older benchmark suites gradually become less relevant. This evolution calls for the development of a new generation of GPU benchmarks that target modern GPU architectures using advanced programming frameworks.

In this paper, we provide *NUPAR*, a novel benchmark suite to equip architects and application designers with appropriate workloads to evaluate the performance of the emerging class of GPUs. We incorporate a set of real-world applications that appropriately exercise advanced architectural features of the GPUs. The applications have been developed using features from CUDA and OpenCL frameworks [1, 17]. The *NUPAR* suite provides eight different applications spanning seven different computing domains. The nature of computation for each application is different, providing a mix of behaviors. The properties of the applications include real-time constraints, memory-bound operations, compute-bound execution, heavy synchronization, and concurrent execution. Each application highlights one or more advanced architectural features of the GPU according to the nature of their computation. The application kernels are optimized to better utilize the GPU architecture.

The applications written in CUDA can be easily ported to OpenCL, and vice versa. CUDA and OpenCL programming models are quite similar to each other in many respects. The OpenCL model is based on a Compute Device that consists of Compute Units with Processing Elements. These Compute Units are equivalent to CUDA's Streaming Multiprocessors, which contain CUDA cores. In OpenCL, a host program launches kernel with *work-items* (vs. *threads* in CUDA) over an index space. These work-items are further grouped into *work-groups* (vs. *thread blocks* in CUDA). Furthermore, both have similar device memory hierarchies abstracted into different address spaces. However, CUDA is currently supported on NVIDIA GPUs and multicore CPUs [32], whereas OpenCL is supported on many different heterogeneous devices including many GPUs, multi-core CPUs and FPGAs.

We evaluate the CUDA workloads on an NVIDIA K40 and OpenCL workloads on an AMD Radeon HD 7970 GPU. We measure speedup against a GPU-accelerated baseline that is unoptimized. We use NVIDIA's Visual Profiler [23] for profiling CUDA applications and AMD's CodeXL [3] for profiling OpenCL applications.

The major contributions of this paper include:

- we introduce a new benchmark suite to study advanced architectural features of modern GPUs,

- we provide benchmarks that can cover a wide range of computation models, exercising properties common in emerging heterogeneous applications, and

- we utilize these benchmarks to exercise advanced architectural features on GPUs to illustrate their impact on the performance of applications.

The remainder of this paper is organized as follows. Section 2 covers the motivation for our work. In Section 3, we describe the architectural and programming features that we are targeting in our applications. Section 4 introduces the applications chosen from various domains that are included in *NUPAR*. Section 5 discusses our evaluation methodology. In Section 6, we discuss experimental results using the benchmarks. Section 7 provides a comparison between different programming frameworks. Section 8 surveys related work and Section 9 concludes the paper and considers directions for future work.

2. MOTIVATION

NVIDIA Devices	NVIDIA C2070	NVIDIA K40
Microarchitecture	Fermi	Kepler
Fabrication	40nm	28nm
Compute Capability	2.0	3.5
CUDA Cores	448	2880
Core Frequency	575 MHz	745 MHz
Memory Bandwidth	144 GB/s	288GB/s
Peak Single Precision FLOPS	1288 GFlops	4290 GFlops
Peak Double Precision FLOPS	515.2 GFlops	1430 GFlops

Table 1: Evolution of NVIDIA GPU architecture from Fermi to Kepler.

AMD Devices	Radeon HD 5870	Radeon HD 7970
Microarchitecture	Evergreen	Southern Islands
Fabrication	40nm	28nm
Stream Cores	320	2048
Compute Units	20	32
Core Frequency	850 MHz	925 MHz
Memory Bandwidth	153.6 GB/s	264 GB/s
Peak Single Precision FLOPS	2720 GFlops	3789 GFlops
Peak Double Precision FLOPS	544 GFlops	947 GFlops

Table 2: Evolution of AMD GPU architecture from Evergreen to Southern Islands.

GPUs have increased in performance, architectural complexity and programmability over the years. This trend can be observed in various generations of GPUs from different vendors [21]. Table 1 shows how NVIDIA GPUs have improved from Fermi to Kepler microarchitecture in terms of their compute capability, architectural complexity, and memory bandwidth. Table 2 shows similar improvements that have been made in AMD's Southern Islands generation of GPUs over its predecessor. Not only have the GPUs evolved in terms of sophistication and capabilities, but the programming frameworks have evolved dramatically to support the hardware changes in the GPU architectures.

Previous benchmark suites have been developed specifically to understand the performance of the GPU devices. The Rodinia suite provides a set of GPU programs targeting multi-core CPU and GPU platforms based on the *Berkeley dwarf* taxonomy [7]. Rodinia benchmarks highlight architectural support for memory-bandwidth, synchronization and power consumption. Another important GPU benchmark suite is the Parboil suite. Parboil provides GPU workloads which exercise architectural features of GPUs such as floating point throughput, computational latency and cache effectiveness [31]. Both of these benchmark suites have served the GPU architectural research community well over many years. In contrast to Rodinia and Parboil, the Scalable Heterogeneous Computing (SHOC) [10] benchmark suite provides a range of low-level benchmarks based on scientific computing workloads. The Valar benchmark suite emphasizes the host-device interaction on Accelerated Processing Units (APUs) and between multi-core CPUs and discrete GPUs [16]. The workloads provided in the Valar suite utilize multiple command-queue/streams features of a true heterogeneous programming framework that combines CPUs and GPUs.

Unfortunately, the available GPU benchmark suites do not provide that can applications to properly stress the latest architectural features appearing on GPUs. Some of these features include concurrent kernel execution, dynamic parallelism, unified memory hardware, improved double precision and atomic instructions. Many of these features are already supported in the new CUDA-6 and OpenCL 2.0 standards. These advances in runtime systems and architectures have motivated us to assemble a new benchmark suite that focuses attention on the latest architectural features on GPUs. These real world applications belong to a diverse set of domains and perform computations to stress different combinations of these new features. This allows us to study the impact of each architectural feature. Architects are no longer fully responsible for identifying why a particular benchmark achieves a larger advantage than another benchmark when studying a particular architectural feature. We have identified the characteristics of each benchmark, and users can leverage this guidance as they explore the benefits of each new feature.

3. USE OF ARCHITECTURAL AND PROGRAMMING FEATURES FOR OPTIMIZATION

As mentioned in Section 2, today's programming frameworks and architectures have rapidly evolved to enable new programming patterns and improve performance. In this section, we describe some of the new architectural and programming features that we target with our applications. Traditionally, optimizations applied to GPU workloads consist of effective memory management techniques and use of sophisticated algorithms to leverage the parallelism offered by GPUs. As new architectural features are being delivered to the market, it is important that application developers understand the nature of these features so that they can reap the full benefits of them when developing their applications.

The number of features appearing in new GPU devices go well beyond the few that are summarized in this section. Most of these features are available on both CUDA and OpenCL frameworks using similar programming nomenclature.

3.1 Nested Parallelism

Nested parallelism is defined as the process of launching child threads from a parent thread. A child kernel performing the same or different computation can be launched using a thread from its parent kernel. Dynamic Parallelism is an extension to the CUDA and OpenCL programming models. It provides the user with constructs to implement nested thread-level parallelism. The ability to create and control workloads directly from the GPU avoids the need to transfer execution control and data between the host and the device. This reduces the overhead of invoking a GPU kernel from the host CPU. Dynamic Parallelism also offers applications the flexibility to adapt thread assignments to cores during runtime. Nested Parallelism enables the execution pattern of the application to be determined at runtime (i.e., dynamically) by the parent threads executing on the device. Additionally, since child threads can be spawned by a kernel, the GPU's hardware scheduler and load balancer are utilized dynamically to support data-driven applications.

Nested parallelism provides several performance and programmability benefits. First, recursive execution, irregular loop structures, and other complex control-flow constructs that do not conform to a single-level of task-level parallelism can be more transparently expressed. Moreover, the overhead of data transfers between kernel launches, as well as PCIe traffic, can be reduced or avoided in some cases since flow control transfers can be implemented in a single kernel. Furthermore, hierarchical algorithms can be written, where the data from a parent kernel computation is used to decide how to partition the next lower level of the computation.

3.2 Concurrent Kernel Execution

Concurrent kernel execution allows multiple kernels to execute simultaneously on the GPU. An application can launch multiple kernels containing no inherent data dependency to execute concurrently. Modern GPU architectures partition the compute resources of the GPU to enable concurrent execution. This partitioning is implemented by introducing multiple hardware queues which acquire compute resources to execute the queued kernels. Concurrent Kernel Execution can improve GPU utilization and improve the occupancy of the GPU. It can also increase cache efficiency by launching kernels which operate on the same input data.

The Hyper-Q feature was introduced by NVIDIA on their Kepler GK110 architecture devices [24]. Multiple CUDA streams get mapped to different hardware queues, which can schedule the execution of kernels on the device concurrently. Hyper-Q permits up to 32 simultaneous, hardware-managed, concurrent executions, if the kernels have no data dependency and the GPU has enough compute resources to support such execution. NVIDIA Fermi architecture GPUs map CUDA streams to a single hardware queue. This can introduce false dependencies between kernels from different streams. Such false dependencies can be avoided by using the Hyper-Q feature. Applications that were previously limited by false dependencies can see a performance increase without changing any code. The multiple streams of the applications are handled by separate hardware queues and data-independent kernels can be executed concurrently.

AMD introduced Asynchronous Compute Engines (ACE) on their GPUs as a hardware queue to schedule workloads on different compute units [15]. Work from different OpenCL command queues is mapped to different ACE units on the AMD hardware. The ACE units support interleaved execution of compute kernels on the GPU.

3.3 Memory Management

3.3.1 Shared Memory

On a GPU, shared memory is much faster than global memory. By accessing shared memory, kernels can take advantage of the lower latency provided by shared memory, and at the same time save global memory bandwidth. Moreover, shared memory can be used to avoid non-coalesced memory accesses. Applications can issue loads/stores in shared memory to reorder non-coalesced addressing.

3.3.2 Texture Memory

Texture memory is implemented on the GPU as specialized RAM that is designed for fast reads of texture data. This memory is cached in a *texture cache*, which makes a texture fetch very fast on a cache hit and costs one memory read from the device memory on a miss. The texture cache is optimized for 2D spatial locality, so the best performance can be achieved if threads in a warp read 2D texture addresses that are close together. Also, texture memory has a constant latency for streaming fetches.

Reading texture memory has four benefits over issuing reads to global or constant memory:

1. When applications exhibit 2D spatial locality, they suffer from a performance bottleneck introduced by increased global or constant memory accesses. In such cases, higher bandwidth can be achieved using texture memory fetches.

2. Address calculations are performed using dedicated hardware units.

3. Packed data may be broadcast to separate variables in a single operation.

4. Texture-memory based instructions provide an easy conversion of 8-bit and 16-bit integers to 32-bit floating-point values.

3.3.3 Page-Locked Host Memory

When applications use pageable memory to carry out data transfers between a host and a device, allocation of a block of *page-locked memory* is necessary. The allocation is followed by a host copy from pageable memory to a page-locked block, the data transfer, and then deallocation of the page-locked memory after the transfer. The overhead on the host for this process can be reduced when page-locked memory is directly used.

Using Page-locked host memory has three benefits:

1. Data transfers between page-locked memory and device memory can be performed concurrently with kernel execution.

2. Page-locked memory can be mapped into the address space of the device, which can avoid frequent data transfers between the host and the device.

3. Bandwidth between page-locked memory and device memory is higher on systems with a front-side bus.

3.4 Specialized Intrinsic Function

3.4.1 Warp Shuffle Functions

Warp shuffle functions exchange a variable between threads within a warp without the use of shared memory. All active threads simultaneously perform exchanges to transfer 4 bytes per thread per function call. The *SHFL* instruction was introduced in the CUDA programming model to implement warp shuffle.

3.4.2 Mathematical Intrinsic Functions

Compared to standard mathematical functions, *intrinsic functions* trade accuracy for execution speed. They execute faster since they are mapped to fewer native instructions. Intrinsic functions may also cause some differences when handling special cases such as half precision computations, divide-by-zero operations and rounding operations for transcendental functions. Therefore, standard mathematical functions are often selectively replaced by intrinsic functions in order to achieve better performance, and at the same time, generate acceptable results.

Application	Dwarf Taxonomy	Domain
Connected Component Labeling	Unstructured Grid	Object Detection
Level Set Segmentation	Structured Grid	Image Segmentation
Spectral Clustering	Spectral Method, Dense Linear	Clustering
Mean-shift Object Tracking	N-Body Method	Computer Vision
Periodic Greens Function	Dynamic programming	Electromagnetics
Infinite Impulse Response Filter	Branch and Bound	Signal Processing
Local Kernel Density Ratio	Dense Linear, Unstructured Grid	Feature Extraction
Finite-difference Time-domain	Dynamic programming	Electromagentics

Table 3: *NUPAR* applications with corresponding dwarf taxonomy and computation domain.

3.4.3 Atomic Functions

An *atomic function* performs a read-modify-write atomic operation on a 32-bit or 64-bit word. An atomic operation is guaranteed to be performed without interference from other threads. In other words, this address can be accessed exclusively by one thread until the operation is complete.

4. THE NUPAR BENCHMARK SUITE

The Berkeley dwarves offer benchmark application guidelines that have been used as a guiding set of principles for parallel computing benchmarks [4]. However, with the advent of GPU computing, a number of computational barriers have been overcome, enabling researchers to push the limits of applications that were previously inhibited by computing capabilities or resources. In order to stress these new parallel architecture capabilities, *NUPAR* presents eight sophisticated applications implemented using CUDA and OpenCL. Each application represents one or more dwarves. Table 3 lists the applications, along with their corresponding dwarves and general application domains.

4.1 Applications

4.1.1 Connected Component Labeling (CCL)

Connected Component Labeling (CCL) is a well-known labeling algorithm that is commonly used for object detection. The accuracy of the labeling process can greatly impact the fidelity of the overall object detection task. Typically, CCL performs two passes over a binary image, analyzing every pixel in an attempt to connect multiple pixels based on their position. If the current pixel is not a part of the background, then its label is determined by comparing the labels of neighboring pixels. The North and West side pixels are considered first to determine the label of a particular pixel. Once labeled, the contiguous pixels with same label are assigned the same component [36].

Our *Accelerated CCL* (ACCL) implementation uses two scanning phases [22]. The first phase scans the image in parallel in a row-wise fashion to find contiguous pixels in

Application	Programming Framework	Typical Bottleneck in an Unoptimized implementation	Optimizations Applied
CCL	CUDA	Nested loop with dependencies	Dynamic Parallelism
LSS	CUDA	Sequential execution of instances of same kernel	Dynamic Parallelism, Hyper-Q
SC	CUDA	Global Memory Bandwidth Utilization	Hyper-Q
IIR	CUDA	Synchronization Stall, Execution Dependency	Shuffle Instruction
LoKDR	CUDA	Sequential execution of data-independent kernels	Dynamic Parallelism, Hyper-Q, Local Memory
MSOT	OpenCL	Global Memory Bandwidth	Local Memory, -cl-mad-enable
PGF	OpenCL	Intensive Floating Point Operations	Math Intrinsics, Vector Types
FDTD	OpenCL	Intensive global memory accesses	Local Memory, Texture Memory

Table 4: Characterization of *NUPAR* applications and potential areas for optimization.

the same row that can be assigned the same label. It also creates an intermediate matrix to store the labels of each component. The second phase merges the components previously found and updates the respective labels using child threads(*dynamic parallelism*).

4.1.2 Level Set Segmentation (LSS)

Level set is an algorithmic approach commonly used in image segmentation. The goal is to partition an image into regions of interest. Using LSS, a curve is implicitly described by the level set of a multivariate surface. One significant advantage of using the level set method is that the curve can easily handle topological changes, including merges and breaks [25].

We employ the version of level set algorithm described by Shi *et al.*as the basis of our CUDA GPU implementation [29]. Points in the discretized grid are characterized in four ways: i) in L_{in} (immediately inside the curve), ii) in L_{out} (immediately outside the curve), iii) in the interior of the curve but not in L_{in}, and iv) in the exterior of the curve but not in L_{out}. Evolving the contour is simply a matter of switching points from L_{in} to L_{out} or vice versa. *Dynamic parallelism* allows us to switch points using child kernel calls, thus eliminating the need to communicate with the CPU during the image segmentation process. Additionally, multiple instances of the parent kernel can be run concurrently by utilizing NVIDIA's *Hyper-Q*, which enables more than one image to be processed at the same time.

4.1.3 Spectral Clustering (SC)

Among the many choices to perform cluster analysis, *spectral clustering* is commonly used for non-convex structures. One key advantage of spectral clustering is its ability to cluster data that is connected, but potentially sparse and unclustered within convex boundaries [20].

The spectral clustering algorithm included in *NUPAR* is a matrix-based implementation which is well-suited for GPUs. We define 4 steps present in the algorithm based on the Ng-Jordan-Weiss approach [20]: (1) form the affinity matrix, (2) apply Laplacian normalization, (3) run an eigen solver and (4) cluster using k-means. Using multiple kernels, we can leverage the latest features offered by the CUDA framework such as: *Hyper-Q and pinned memory*. Our parallel approach uses a tile-based approach and *Hyper-Q* allows execution of concurrent kernels over different tiles. *Dynamic parallelism* is used to compute the nearest cluster during the k-means step. *Pinned memory* leverages the higher bandwidth between host memory and the device memory.

4.1.4 Mean-shift Object Tracking (MSOT)

Mean-shift is an algorithm for tracking non-rigid objects in a sequence of images. The mean-shift algorithm uses the color histogram of the target object in the current frame, and iteratively searches the neighborhood in the next frame to find the location whose color histogram is closest to the target. The Bhattacharyya coefficient is used to measure the distance between two histograms [9].

We implement the Mean-shift algorithm using multiple levels of granularity with OpenCL. At a coarse-grained level, the program tracks multiple objects at the same time. The program also calculates the histogram for the neighbors of each object to reduce the total number of iterations and therefore the execution time. Working at a fine-grained level, the histogram calculation is distributed to the work-items in a work-group. Each work-item calculates a portion of the histogram – we use a reduction method to compute the overall histogram. We also use a lookup table to reduce the memory size and shared memory usage. With our parallel approach, we can modify the work-group/work-item ratio in order to stress a specific GPU architecture.

4.1.5 Periodic Green's Function (PGF)

The *Periodic Green's Function* is a discrete implementation of the continuous function used in the integral equation (IE) to solve computational electromagnetics (CEM) problems by application of the Method of Moments (MoM) [30]. In its standard representation, the PGF involves a slowly converging series of free space Green's Function. When applying a windowed summation method, we are able to compute the PGF several million times for different points in the lattice [6]. This accelerated function evaluation fits into a larger array integral equation designed to parallelize infinitely periodic electromagnetic problems. When the problem of interest involves infinite periodic structures, the PGF provides a fast and efficient method to solve CEM problems with a windowed summation method, requiring the evaluation of the PGF on the order of several million times. Our OpenCL GPU code achieves the best performance when the number of PGF evaluations is large, as we assign each work-item a unique call to the PGF.

When considering alternative data types, we chose `double2` for our complex output type to improve the global memory store efficiency and improve memory transfers from the device to the host. In an effort to reduce the computational cost of the large number of transcendental functions and multiply-add calculations, we replace these functions with their equivalent math intrinsic calls and use the "cl-finite-math-only" compiler flag during clBuildProgram.

4.1.6 Infinite Impulse Response Filter (IIR)

Finite Impulse Response (FIR) and *Infinite Impulse Response* (IIR) are used in signal processing applications such as speech and audio processing. IIR is preferred to FIR if some phase distortion is either tolerable or unimportant.

Application	Baseline Implementation	Application Input	Baseline GPU
CCL	CUDA with less workload on child kernels	5 Images (512 x 512)	NVIDIA K40
LSS	CUDA with fewer threads per child kernel	Over 256 (512 x 512) Images	NVIDIA K40
SC	CUDA with serial kernel call(non-Hyper-Q)	Tile Basis of 900 elements (Only first two kernels)	NVIDIA K40
IIR	CUDA with Shared Memory Use (without *SHFL* instruction)	Input 1024 (floats) 128 Channels, 256 parallel biquad filters/channel	NVIDIA K40
LoKDR	CUDA with serial kernel calls (non-Hyper-Q) and no nested parallelism	Input data set with 7129 features and 99 samples	NVIDIA K40
MSOT	OpenCL without shared memory and cl-mad-enable	10 objects tracked over 120 frames	AMD Radeon 7970
PGF	OpenCL without cl-finite-math-only and fma, hypot	Number of PGF Evaluations = 3 million, FFT Sample Rates = (120,120,120)	AMD Radeon 7970
FDTD	Naive OpenCL without use of local and Texture memory	(nx, ny, nz) = (240, 80, 80), (dx, dy, dz) = (0.005, 0.005, 0.005)	AMD Radeon 7970

Table 5: Baseline configuration for each *NUPAR* application and associated input datasets.

Due to its nature, IIR performs a smaller number of calculations per time step than FIR.

Our parallel implementation of IIR [26] starts by decomposing the transfer function into parallel second-order IIR sub-filters. Each sub-filter reduces the waiting period for the next output calculation. A multi-channel high order IIR should improve IIR filtering efficiency on a GPU [28].

We have implemented a parallel IIR using the CUDA framework, leveraging the *shuffle (SHFL)* instruction on the Kepler architecture to achieve a fast summation to produce the output signal. Each channel's coefficients are cached in constant memory along with the input signal. Filtering multiple channels works in a block-wise fashion (i.e., the number of channels is equal to the number of blocks launched on the GPU). Our grid configuration attempts to stress GPU occupancy by increasing the number of channels.

4.1.7 Local Kernel Density Ratio (LoKDR) for Feature Selection

Selecting the best set of features is an important step in all machine learning tasks. The focus is to determine and choose features relevant for classification and regression of the given data. Our next application presents a non-parametric evaluation criterion for filter-based feature selection to enhance outlier detection [5]. The method identifies the subset of features that represents the inherent characteristics of the normal dataset, while also identifying features to filter out outliers.

Our CUDA application utilizes GPUs for computation of the *K-nearest neighbors* in a dataset. These kernels have to be launched for each feature and each set of features to determine outliers. Data parallelism offered by the computation is nicely exploited using the GPU. Computation includes kernels to compute the distance between pairs of points in the data set and includes sorting of the k-nearest neighbors. We utilize *dynamic parallelism* and develop a pipelined approach for outlier detection for each feature. *Hyper-Q* is used to facilitate concurrent execution of these pipelined kernels. Computations launched for different features are also executed concurrently.

4.1.8 Finite-Difference Time-Domain (FDTD)

The *Finite-Difference Time-Domain* (FDTD) method is a widely-used computational method for solving Maxwell's equations in many electromagnetics problems. FDTD is a grid-based marching-in-time algorithm that calculates the electric and magnetic fields over every cell in a computational domain at each time step [18].

When using FDTD, the entire computational domain needs to be divided into a number of Yee cells whose size must be sufficiently small to resolve smaller electromagnetic wavelength and smaller geometrical features in the model. A medium-sized computational domain can often lead to days or even weeks of solution time. Thus, we employ GPUs as a highly multi-threaded data-parallel processor to accelerate FDTD simulation. In our implementation of FDTD, up to 35 kernels are launched for the computation based on the size of the input.

For each iteration, we advance the time by Δt, which is a configurable unit for the benchmark. FDTD computes the H(magnetic) and E(electric) fields for each cell. Then, the computation advances time by Δt and begins the next iteration. A leap-frog integration scheme is used to compute the H and E values of each cell. The value at time t is dependent on the previous value at time step $t-\Delta t$, and thus sequential iterations cannot be run in parallel. However, the computation of each cell at a specified time t is independent of other cells, and so can be run in parallel.

5. EVALUATION METHODOLOGY

Next, we describe the platforms used for evaluating the performance of the *NUPAR* applications, implemented in either CUDA or OpenCL. The baseline used for evaluating each application is also described in this section.

5.1 Evaluation Platforms

The NVIDIA K40 and the AMD Radeon HD 7970 GPUs are used to evaluate the *NUPAR* applications developed using CUDA and OpenCL, respectively. These platforms are comparable in terms of clock rate, number of cores, peak bandwidth and FLOPS. Table 6 compares the specifications

	NVIDIA	AMD
Device Name	K40	HD7970
GPU Architecture	Kepler	Southern Islands
Peak Single Precision FLOPS (Gflops)	4291	3789
Peak Bandwidth (GB/s)	288	264
Streaming Cores	2880	2048
Clock Rate (MHz)	876	925
Global Memory (GB)	12	3
L2 Cache (KB)	1536	768
Constant Memory (KB)	64	128
Shared Memory Per Block (KB)	48	64
Warp/Wavefront Size	32	64

Table 6: Architectural specifications of GPU platforms used for evaluation.

of these two GPU platforms. The CUDA workloads are profiled using NVIDIA's Visual Profiler. AMD's CodeXL profiler is used for profiling OpenCL workloads. The applications supporting CUDA were developed for the CUDA-6 version of the programming framework. The OpenCL applications were developed for both OpenCL 1.2 and OpenCL 2.0 versions. The OpenCL 2.0 applications utilize modern features described in Section 3. Due to the unavailability of platforms supporting OpenCL 2.0 during the time of development of this paper, the evaluation of applications on OpenCL 2.0 has not been performed yet. The current evaluations of the OpenCL applications are done with the OpenCL 1.2 version of the programming framework.

5.2 Baselines

The *NUPAR* suite focuses on exercising new GPU architectural and programming features. Each application in the *NUPAR* benchmark suite has been optimized using one or more features to tackle an inherent bottleneck present in the unoptimized implementation. To evaluate the *NUPAR* workloads, each application is compared with an unoptimized implementation as its baseline. The SC workload uses Hyper-Q as an optimization feature. This workload is compared with the same CUDA implementation with serial kernel calls instead of using Hyper-Q. The CCL and LSS workloads are also compared with a CUDA version that places less workload on child kernels and uses fewer threads per child kernel, respectively. The baseline for MSOT and FDTD use their original OpenCL implementations, their optimized runs use shared or texture memory and the `cl-mad-enable` optimization. Table 5 summarizes the baselines used for evaluating each application.

6. EXPERIMENTAL RESULTS

In this section, we evaluate the performance of the *NUPAR* applications on the platforms described in Section 5. We also investigate the performance benefits obtained when applying the optimizations described in Section 3.

6.1 Computational Characteristics of NU-PAR Applications

Each of the *NUPAR* applications stresses different architectural features on the GPU or in the updated programming models. We characterize the behavior of the applications based on seven factors: *i) Global memory bandwidth utilization, ii) Occupancy, iii) Register Utilization, iv) Local/Shared memory usage, v) Control Flow/Divergence, vi) Cache utilization,* and *vii) ALU usage.*

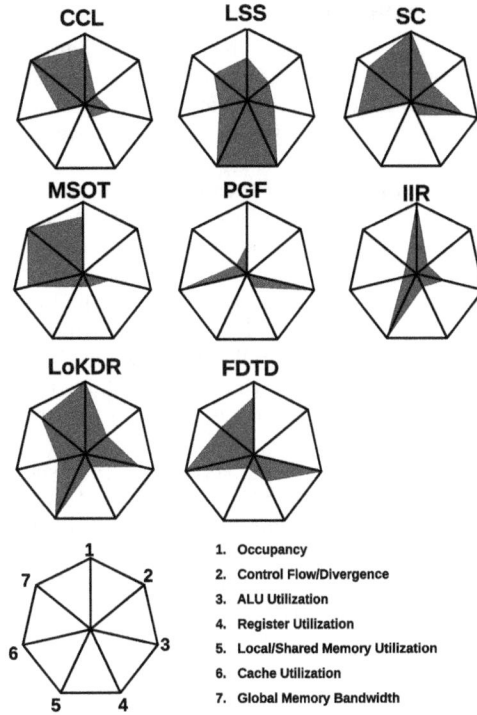

1. Occupancy
2. Control Flow/Divergence
3. ALU Utilization
4. Register Utilization
5. Local/Shared Memory Utilization
6. Cache Utilization
7. Global Memory Bandwidth

Figure 1: Kiviat-charts describing computational characteristics of *NUPAR* applications.

Figure 1 presents a Kiviat-chart to clearly characterize the different architectural features exercised by each *NUPAR* application. Each axis of the Kiviat diagram denotes a different feature. The values for each architectural feature are obtained using the profiling tools described in Section 5. The values show the percent utilization for each architectural feature. The applications from the *NUPAR* suite exhibit diversity in their characteristics, as seen in Figure 1. For example, the *CCL, SC, MSOT, and LoKDR* applications show heavy utilization of the global memory bandwidth, whereas *PGF and FDTD* utilize the cache on the GPU. Local/shared memory performance can be evaluated using the *LSS, IIR and LoKDR* applications.

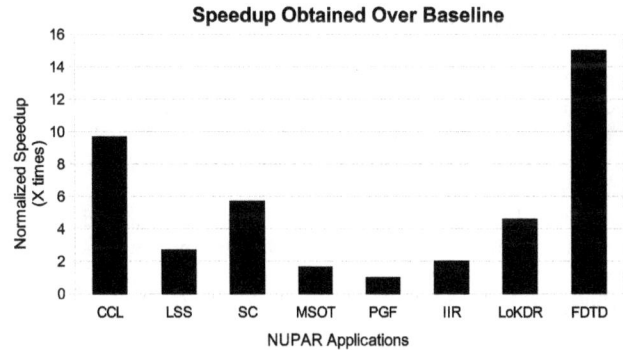

Figure 2: Normalized speedup of *NUPAR* applications over their corresponding baseline.

6.2 Speedup Analysis

We evaluate the speedup obtained by the *NUPAR* applications after applying the optimizations required to sensitize the new architectural features that were described in Section 3. The baseline for each application is described in Table 5.

The speedup obtained by the benchmark applications is shown in Figure 2. The average speedup observed for all applications is 5.1x. The *FDTD* sees the greatest speedup by using local memory and texture memory available on the GPU. Applications such as *MSOT* and *PGF* benefit by using optimized multiply-add instructions for integer and floating point operations. Dynamic parallelism is used in *CCL* to cache the data for sub-kernels on the device without transferring intermediate results back to the host and then back to the device. *CCL* achieves an overall speedup of 9.7x by launching multiple image processing kernels simultaneously. *LoKDR* also sees a 4.3x speedup using NVIDIA's Hyper-Q, which allows for concurrent execution of data-independent kernels. Similarly, a speedup of 5.9x is seen for *SC* and speedup of 2.3x is seen for *LSS* when using Hyper-Q and dynamic parallelism. *IIR* utilizes the *SHFL* intrinsic for performing inter-thread memory operations and sees a speedup of 2.2x.

Figure 3 shows the pre-optimization (baseline) and post-optimization resource utilization mix of the *NUPAR* applications. *LSS* and *LoKDR* experience an increase of 19% in occupancy, improvements in cache utilization by 7%, and a rise in ALU utilization by 9% on average after applying the optimizations. For *SC*, the occupancy increases from 74% to 92% by using the Hyper-Q feature. As observed, an increase in occupancy is tied to a more efficient use of the cores through concurrent kernel execution using Hyper-Q. For the *IIR* benchmark, the use of the *SHFL* instruction increases the number of blocks that can be allocated on each stream processor. This leads to an 18% improvement in occupancy, and an increase in cache utilization from 21% to 26%, and an increase in ALU utilization from 22% to 28% for the *IIR* application.

6.3 Performance of Nested Parallelism

Nested parallelism is described in Section 3 and is referred to as *Dynamic Parallelism* by the CUDA and OpenCL programming frameworks. Many classes of algorithms (e.g., *CCL* and *LoKDR*) can potentially benefit from *Dynamic Parallelism*. *CCL* requires thread-level parallelism to reduce the overhead of updating labels of multiple components that belong to the same object during its detection of connected components. Similarly, *LoKDR* utilizes dynamic parallelism to detect outliers by calculating the distance between the nearest neighbors. The overhead of launching kernels to perform the distance calculation is reduced through dynamic parallelism.

We evaluate the speedup obtained using nested parallelism for the *CCL*, *LSS* and *LoKDR* applications. Figure 4 shows the speedup obtained for these applications when varying the number of threads per child kernel. We observe that we achieve more speedup as we increase the number of threads per child kernel. This can be attributed to the increase in overall occupancy of the GPU. Increasing the number of threads for the child kernel reduces the effective number of child kernel launches. This avoids the

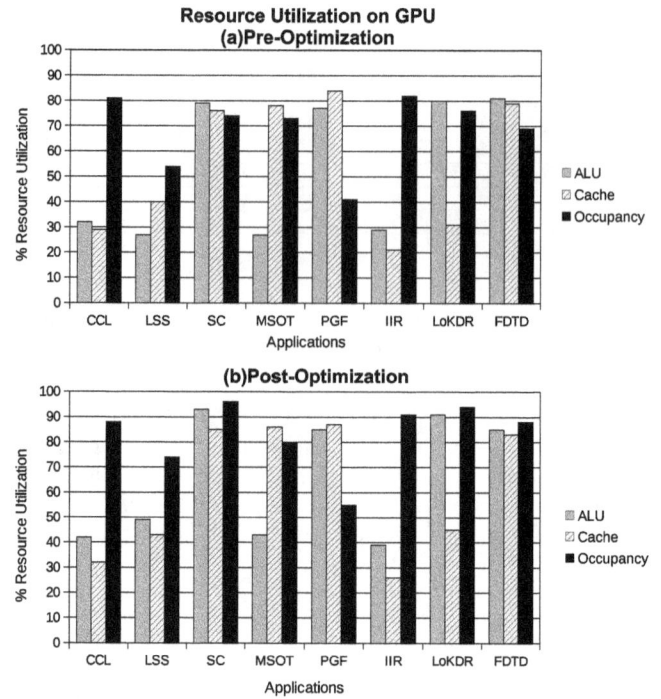

Figure 3: Resource utilization of the *NUPAR* applications, (a) Pre-Optimization and (b) Post-Optimization.

overhead of launching multiple child kernels on the GPU. An increased number of threads per child kernel results in higher ALU utilization for these three applications, as illustrated in Figure 3b. The peak speedup reported by *CCL*, *LSS* and *LoKDR* is 13.9X, 5.8X and 6.2X, respectively. The *CCL*, *LSS* and *LoKDR* applications can be used to evaluate how the number of threads per child kernel impacts the performance when using dynamic parallelism.

The communication between the threads of the parent kernel and child kernel can be carried out only using global memory for dynamic parallelism. Applications such as *CCL*, *LSS and LoKDR* impose a heavy communication penalty due to communication between the parent and child threads. Figure 5 shows the throughput obtained for accessing data between parent and child kernels while varying the number of threads per child kernel. Figure 5 shows that our CUDA implementation for *CCL*, *LSS* and *LoKDR* achieves higher global memory throughput as we increase the work on the child kernel. The average global memory throughput achieved by *CCL*, *LSS* and *LoKDR* is 14.6 Gb/s, 16.1 Gb/s and 15.3 Gb/s, respectively. The number of coalesced global memory accesses increases as we increase the number of threads for a kernel. The efficient utilization of the global memory load/store unit results in a clear improvement in global memory throughput. These benchmarks can be used to judge the global memory throughput of the GPU.

6.4 Utilizing Concurrent Kernel Execution

Concurrent kernel execution is an important feature supported by modern GPUs, as described in Section 3. NVIDIA GPUs utilize the new Hyper-Q mechanism and AMD GPUs use the ACE (Asynchronous Compute Engine) units to man-

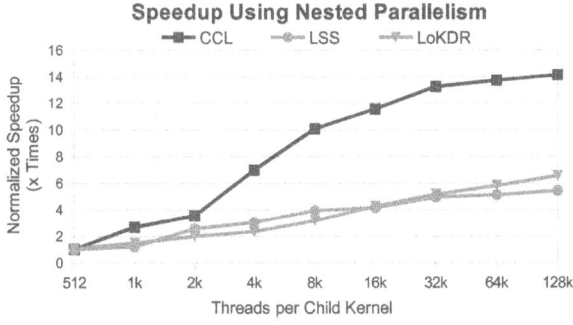

Figure 4: Speedup obtained using nested parallelism for *CCL*, *LSS* and *LoKDR*. Speedup is reported while varying the number of threads per child kernel.

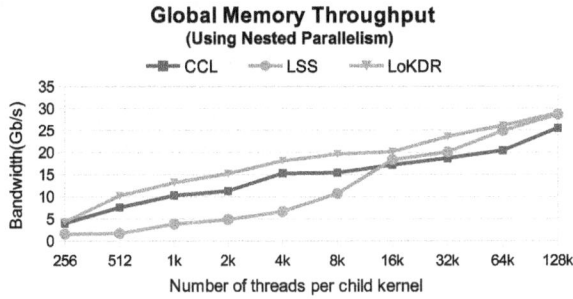

Figure 5: Evaluation of global memory throughput for parent-child kernel communication for *CCL*, *LSS* and *LoKDR* using nested parallelism.

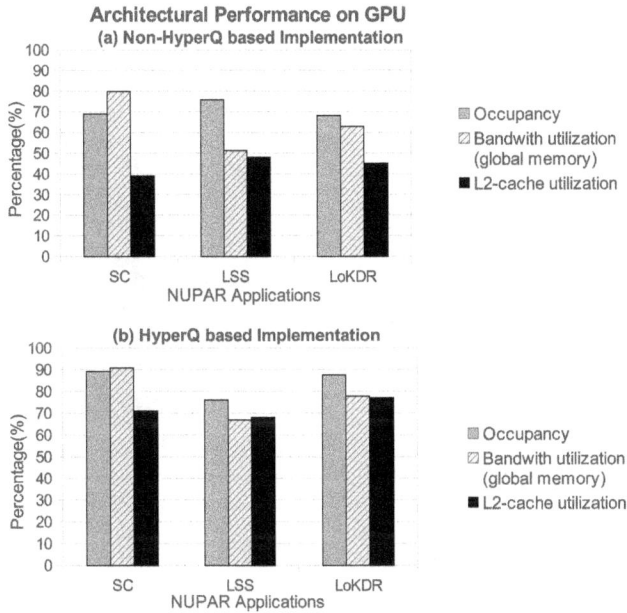

Figure 6: Comparison of architectural performance of NUPAR applications on GPUs for (a) Non-Hyper-Q based implementation and (b) Hyper-Q based implementation

age concurrent kernel execution. We explore the performance of this class of features using three different applications from the *NUPAR* suite: *SC, LSS, LoKDR*.

The occupancy improvement of any implementation that uses multiple streams depends on the resources utilized by each stream. As seen in Figures 6a and 6b, *LSS* and *LoKDR* do not find any improvement in occupancy. This is because the kernels executed in each stream have already saturated the available resources. *SC* exploits a new level of parallelism exposed by Hyper-Q, since each stream occupies less than 70% of the GPU when executed sequentially.

Concurrent execution of kernels on the GPU using Hyper-Q also results in improved L2 cache utilization. We can see in Figure 6 that applications such as *LoKDR* and *LSS* see an improvement of 32% and 20% in cache utilization, respectively. The overall cache utilization of all the kernels launched by the application is recorded using the profiler tools. Hyper-Q facilitates concurrent execution of kernels which operate on same input data (e.g., *LoKDR*), which results in an overall improvement in cache utilization.

We have also studied the global memory bandwidth utilization for all three applications. Figure 6 shows the positive impact of Hyper-Q on the memory efficiency. Hyper-Q helps concurrent kernels keep the load/store units on the GPU busy. This improves global memory bandwidth utilization of the GPU. The *LoKDR* and *LSS* applications experience an increase greater than 15% in terms of global memory bandwidth utilization. The *SC* application already has high global memory bandwidth utilization and does not show a significant improvement in bandwidth utilization when using Hyper-Q. These three applications can also be used to test queuing mechanisms on the GPU by using concurrent execution of kernels.

6.5 Specialized Intrinsics and Instructions

Programming frameworks such as CUDA and OpenCL from time to time introduce specialized intrinsic functions and compiler optimizations for improving performance of complex computations. Intrinsic functions provide the user with the ability to perform complex math calculations efficiently, including execution of transcendental operations, square-root operations and atomic operations. Different compiler optimizations can leverage new GPU hardware features and carry out operations using special instructions.

For cases where a potential reduction in accuracy is tolerable, fast math operation intrinsics can be turned on during GPU code generation. Use of these intrinsics shrinks the size of the executable binaries by reducing the number of instructions executed on the GPU. The *NUPAR* applications, such as *MSOT* and *PGF*, use the fast-math intrinsics for compile-time optimizations.

MSOT uses the `-cl-mad-enable` optimization option, which leverages special instructions for multiply-add operations. The impact on a range of performance factors is shown in Table 7. Using the `-cl-mad-enable` switch reduces vector register usage per work-item by 87%. This results in an increase in the number of active waves, which enhances the kernel occupancy by 60%. The improvement in such factors is responsible for the 1.9x speedup obtained by *MSOT*, as seen in Figure 2. Besides the computational speedup, the occupancy ratio also affects the kernel execution time and can be improved by reducing the amount of

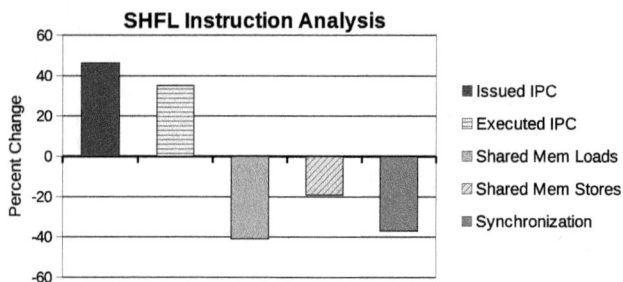

Figure 7: Percentage change in performance metrics due to the use of *SHFL* instruction in *IIR* application over the baseline.

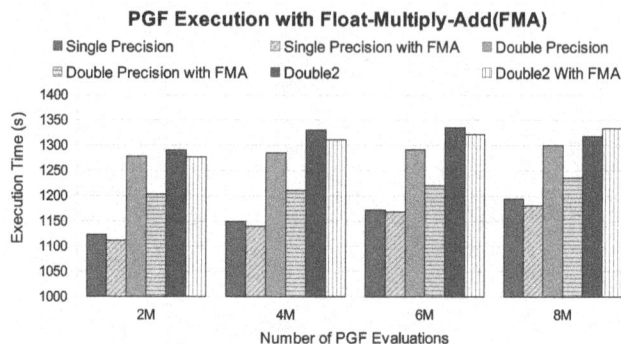

Figure 8: Kernel time comparison of PGF for 2 to 8 million PGF evaluations using different precision types to represent the complex output of the PGF.

shared memory usage. NVIDIA's Kepler architecture provides new *SHFL* (shuffle) instructions as an efficient solution for fast intra-warp communications. The use of the *SHFL* reduces shared memory usage. Though inter-warp communication still requires some shared memory, the total amount of shared memory used could ideally be lowered by 32 times [1]. As a result, the number of instructions and barriers for *SHFL* are less than the number of instructions using shared memory.

The *IIR* consists of multiple parallel biquad filters. The output signal is produced by summing up the independent biquads results for each time step. The Parallel reduction used in *IIR* is an ideal fit for the shuffle instructions. It is required for summation among the threads where each thread functions as a biquad filter. We observe a 2.1x speedup in kernel execution time when launching 128 channels for a parallel IIR program. We use the *nvvp* profiler to extract the related performance counters for the execution of *IIR*. As shown in the Figure 7 (which includes the selected performance counters), the *SHFL* instruction increases the Instructions Per Cycle (IPC) by 35%. The number of synchronizations is reduced by 38% and the shared memory usage (load/store) drops by 30% on an average.

Performance Counters	Un-Optimized	Optimized
Vector Registers per Work-item	167	22
Number of waves limited by vector registers	40	4
Number of active waves	4	28
Occupancy	10.00%	70.00%

Table 7: Comparison of performance counters for un-optimized and optimized versions of MSOT.

Floating point performance is an important metric to evaluate overall GPU performance. Double precision optimizations are included in the vendor-specific implementations of many FFT and linear algebra routines. We include the periodic Green's function which requires millions of floating point calculations per iteration for evaluating the double precision performance of the GPU.

We use the fused-multiply-add (FMA) optimization to evaluate floating point performance of the GPU using the *PGF* application. Figure 8 shows the execution time of the *PGF* application when varying the number of *PGF* evaluations. The analysis is done for *Single Precision, Double Precision and Double2* variables, with and without FMA support. As observed in Figure 8, the computations using

single precision variables and using FMA yield the best execution performance. Double precision operations use two single precision registers and operations are performed by specialized double precision units on modern GPUs. An average slowdown of 9.3% is observed due to the use of double precision over single precision. FMA optimizations force the hardware to utilize instructions for the specialized double precision units on the GPU. The double precision performance with FMA shows an average speedup of 3.9% over the regular double precision execution.

We also tested the performance of the *PGF* with the `double2` complex output data type. As seen in Figure 8, the `double2` evaluation shows a minor loss in performance as compared to the real and imaginary `double` kernel code. The differences between the two versions are exaggerated due to the scaling of the Y-axis in Figure 8.

7. DISCUSSION

NUPAR covers eight applications across a wide spectrum of domains. The features described in Section 3, such as Nested Parallelism, Concurrent Kernel Execution, Shared memory, and Texture memory are available on both the OpenCL and CUDA frameworks. In *NUPAR*, we use features implemented in CUDA 6. The same features are also available on OpenCL 2.0, and can be implemented when hardware supporting OpenCL 2.0 is available [17]. Table 8 demonstrates the features available in OpenCL 2.0 and CUDA 6. Nested Parallelism is referred to as *Dynamic Parallelism* in both CUDA and OpenCL terminologies. Concurrent Kernel Execution is referred to as *Hyper-Q* in CUDA. The OpenCL 2.0 specification also incorporates Shared Virtual Memory and Pipe-based communication channels as advanced features. Shared Virtual Memory is known as unified virtual addressing in CUDA terminology and was introduced in CUDA-4. The advanced constructs such as *SHFL* are only supported on CUDA architectures developed by NVIDIA.

The new architectures developed using the HSA (Heterogeneous System Architecture) standard will provide advanced features such the shuffle intrinsic [27]. HSA also supports other new features, such as the Architected Query Language (AQL), a simple job queuing mechanism which handles the memory transfers and kernel execution. Another important feature for Inter-Kernel Communication known as *Pipes* is supported on HSA and OpenCL 2.0, but is not

	CUDA 6	OpenCL 2.0
Nested Parallelism	✓	✓
UVA	✓	✓
Concurrent Kernel Execution	✓	-
Inter-Kernel Communication	-	✓
Atomics	✓	✓

Table 8: Comparison of Programming Features Between CUDA 6 and OpenCL 2.0

yet part of the CUDA standard. The present HSA standards for GPUs and accelerators are supported by many vendors such as AMD, ARM, Qualcomm, Samsung, and Imagination. Many of the features introduced in HSA and OpenCL 2.0 will be supported on hardware provided by all of these vendors. The *NUPAR* suite can be used for evaluating the performance of this new class of GPUs.

8. RELATED WORK

Several benchmark suites have been developed in the past for evaluating the performance and architectural characteristics of GPU systems. Rodinia [7] and Parboil [31] benchmark suites target GPUs and multi-core CPUs using CUDA. However, their scope is limited to traditional GPU architectures and do not exercise the newer hardware features of modern GPUs and other accelerators. The *NUPAR* suite fulfills this requirement of GPU benchmarks by targeting modern heterogeneous systems. SHOC is a scalable benchmark suite implemented in CUDA and OpenCL to measure the performance and stability of both NVIDIA and AMD platforms [10]. Valar also targets both AMD and NVIDIA devices, while focusing on evaluating the interaction between host and device in heterogeneous systems [16]. We developed the *NUPAR* suite for CUDA and OpenCL to provide the user with programming flexibility. Volkov and Demmel have benchmarked linear algebra applications using CUDA on NVIDIA GPUs [34]. *NUPAR*, however, covers a larger spectrum of applications. CUDA-NP proposes a compiler-level solution to leverage nested parallelism for GPGPU applications [35]. Y. Liang et al. demonstrate a performance improvement over Hyper-Q using their technique which allows spatial and temporal multitasking on GPUs [8]. But they do not provide researchers with a set of applications to evaluate these features on the GPUs.

Another common way to benchmark GPUs includes measurement of frames per second (FPS) achieved by computationally demanding games such as *Crysis* [11]. Also, proprietary GPU benchmark softwares such as 3DMark are designed to determine the performance of GPUs using DirectX [2]. Other parallel benchmark suites for CPUs that have been developed include MediaBench [14] for multimedia applications, BioParallel [12] for biomedical applications, and MineBench [19] for data mining applications. These benchmark suites target a specific application domain and do not provide a diverse range of workloads. Lonestar is an attempt to extract amorphous data-parallelism from graph-based real world applications [13]. *NUPAR* is distinct from these works as it primarily targets modern GPUs using OpenCL and CUDA and provides a set of diverse applications to highlight changes in the evolving GPU architectures.

9. CONCLUSION AND FUTURE WORK

In this paper, we have introduced the *NUPAR* benchmark suite designed to provide a rich set of parallel programs to study the performance of emerging architectural features and programming constructs targeting modern heterogeneous platforms. The applications help the user judge the performance of the new class of GPUs and accelerators with features such as nested parallelism, concurrent kernel execution and advanced computational and memory instructions. We provide eight publicly available implementations of real-world applications belonging to different scientific domains. The applications are developed using both CUDA and OpenCL programming frameworks. The paper characterizes the different applications according to the architectural features stressed by such applications. We also highlight the performance obtained by the use of different architectural optimizations as described in the paper.

We plan to support the *NUPAR* applications on different OpenCL-compatible platforms including FPGA platforms and embedded SoCs from vendors such as Qualcomm and NVIDIA. We would like to extend the *NUPAR* suite to include applications developed for graphics and for interoperable compute-graphics. We are planning to add additional applications which utilize the unified virtual memory model introduced in CUDA 6 and OpenCL 2.0. The benchmark suite is available for download *https://code.google.com/p/nupar-bench/*.

Acknowledgments

This work was supported in part by a NSF CISE award CSR-1319501. We would like to thank the HSA foundation for their gift to support this work. We would also thank AMD and Nvidia for providing hardware to conduct this work. We thank Fatemeh Azmandian for her help with the *LoKDR* application development.

10. REFERENCES

[1] CUDA C Programming Guide. *NVIDIA Corporation, Feb*, 2014.

[2] 3DMark. http://www.futuremark.com/benchmarks.

[3] AMD. Accelerated Parallel Processing: OpenCL programming guide. *URL http://developer. amd. com/sdks/AMDAPPSDK/documentation*, 2011.

[4] K. Asanovic, R. Bodik, B. C. Catanzaro, J. J. Gebis, P. Husbands, K. Keutzer, D. A. Patterson, W. L. Plishker, J. Shalf, S. W. Williams, et al. The landscape of parallel computing research: A view from berkeley. Technical report, Technical Report UCB/EECS-2006-183, EECS Department, University of California, Berkeley, 2006.

[5] F. Azmandian, A. Yilmazer, J. G. Dy, J. A. Aslam, and D. R. Kaeli. Gpu-accelerated feature selection for outlier detection using the local kernel density ratio. In *Proceedings of the 2012 IEEE 12th International Conference on Data Mining*, pages 51–60. IEEE Computer Society, 2012.

[6] O. P. Bruno, S. P. Shipman, C. Turc, and V. Stephanos. Efficient Evaluation of Doubly Periodic Green Functions in 3D Scattering, Including Wood Anomaly Frequencies. *Arxiv*, 1307.1176:80–110, 2013.

[7] S. Che, M. Boyer, J. Meng, D. Tarjan, J. W. Sheaffer, S.-H. Lee, and K. Skadron. Rodinia: A benchmark suite for heterogeneous computing. In *Workload Characterization, 2009. IISWC 2009. IEEE International Symposium on*, pages 44–54. IEEE, 2009.

[8] D. Chen, H. P. Huynh, R. S. M. Goh, and K. Rupnow. Efficient gpu spatial-temporal multitasking. *IEEE Transactions on Parallel and Distributed Systems*, page 1, 2014.

[9] D. Comaniciu, V. Ramesh, and P. Meer. Real-time tracking of non-rigid objects using mean shift. In *Proceedings IEEE Conference on Computer Vision and Pattern Recognition. CVPR 2000 (Cat. No.PR00662)*, volume 2, pages 142–149, 2000.

[10] A. Danalis, G. Marin, C. McCurdy, J. S. Meredith, P. C. Roth, K. Spafford, V. Tipparaju, and J. S. Vetter. The scalable heterogeneous computing (shoc) benchmark suite. In *Proceedings of the 3rd Workshop on General-Purpose Computation on Graphics Processing Units*, pages 63–74. ACM, 2010.

[11] C. Frankfurt. Crysis. http://www.crysis.com, 2007.

[12] A. Jaleel, M. Mattina, and B. Jacob. Last level cache (llc) performance of data mining workloads on a cmp-a case study of parallel bioinformatics workloads. In *High-Performance Computer Architecture, 2006. The Twelfth International Symposium on*, pages 88–98. IEEE, 2006.

[13] M. Kulkarni, M. Burtscher, C. Casçaval, and K. Pingali. Lonestar: A suite of parallel irregular programs. In *Performance Analysis of Systems and Software, 2009. ISPASS 2009. IEEE International Symposium on*, pages 65–76. IEEE, 2009.

[14] C. Lee, M. Potkonjak, and W. H. Mangione-Smith. Mediabench: a tool for evaluating and synthesizing multimedia and communicatons systems. In *Proceedings of the 30th annual ACM/IEEE international symposium on Microarchitecture*, pages 330–335. IEEE Computer Society, 1997.

[15] M. Mantor and M. Houston. AMD Graphics Core Next. In *AMD Fusion Developer Summit*, 2011.

[16] P. Mistry, Y. Ukidave, D. Schaa, and D. Kaeli. Valar: A benchmark suite to study the dynamic behavior of heterogeneous systems. In *Proceedings of the 6th Workshop on General Purpose Processor Using Graphics Processing Units*, pages 54–65. ACM, 2013.

[17] A. Munshi. The OpenCL Specification 2.0. *Khronos OpenCL Working Group*, 2014.

[18] T. Namiki. A new fdtd algorithm based on alternating-direction implicit method. *Microwave Theory and Techniques, IEEE Transactions on*, 47(10):2003–2007, 1999.

[19] R. Narayanan, B. Ozisikyilmaz, J. Zambreno, G. Memik, and A. Choudhary. Minebench: A benchmark suite for data mining workloads. In *Workload Characterization, 2006 IEEE International Symposium on*, pages 182–188. IEEE, 2006.

[20] A. Y. Ng, M. I. Jordan, Y. Weiss, et al. On spectral clustering: Analysis and an algorithm. *Advances in neural information processing systems*, 2:849–856, 2002.

[21] J. Nickolls and W. J. Dally. The gpu computing era. *IEEE micro*, 30(2):56–69, 2010.

[22] F. Nina-Paravecino and D. Kaeli. Accelerated connected component labeling using cuda framework. In *Computer Vision and Graphics (ICCVG), 2014 International Conference on*, 2014.

[23] NVIDIA. Visual Profiler, 2011.

[24] NVIDIA. NVIDIA's Next Generation CUDA Computer Architecture Kepler GK110. 2012.

[25] S. Osher and J. A. Sethian. Fronts propagating with curvature dependent speed: algorithms based on hamilton-jacobi formulations. *Journal of Computational Physics*, 79(1):12–49, 1988.

[26] B. Porat. *A course in digital signal processing*, volume 1. Wiley New York, 1997.

[27] P. Rogers. Heterogeneous system architecture overview. In *Hot Chips*, 2013.

[28] J. Schmidt. A Flexible IIR Filtering Implementation for Audio Processing. *Technicolor Research & Innovation, GTC*, 2014.

[29] Y. Shi and W. C. Karl. A fast implementation of the level set method without solving partial differential equations. *Boston University, Department of Electrical and Computer Engineering*, 2005.

[30] S. Singh, W. F. Richards, J. R. Zinecker, and D. R. Wilton. Accelerating the convergence of series representing the free space periodic green's function. *Antennas and Propagation, IEEE Transactions on*, 38(12):1958–1962, 1990.

[31] J. A. Stratton, C. Rodrigues, I.-J. Sung, N. Obeid, L.-W. Chang, N. Anssari, G. D. Liu, and W.-m. W. Hwu. Parboil: A revised benchmark suite for scientific and commercial throughput computing. *Center for Reliable and High-Performance Computing*, 2012.

[32] J. A. Stratton, S. S. Stone, and W. H. Wen-mei. Mcuda: An efficient implementation of cuda kernels for multi-core cpus. In *Languages and Compilers for Parallel Computing*, pages 16–30. Springer, 2008.

[33] W. Sun and R. Ricci. Augmenting Operating Systems With the GPU. 2011.

[34] V. Volkov and J. W. Demmel. Benchmarking gpus to tune dense linear algebra. In *Proceedings of the 2008 ACM/IEEE conference on Supercomputing*, page 31. IEEE Press, 2008.

[35] Y. Yang and H. Zhou. Cuda-np: realizing nested thread-level parallelism in gpgpu applications. In *Proceedings of the 19th ACM SIGPLAN symposium on Principles and practice of parallel programming*, pages 93–106. ACM, 2014.

[36] H. Zhao, Y. Fan, T. Zhang, and H. Sang. Stripe-based connected components labelling. *Electronics Letters*, 46:1434–1436, October 2010.

Automated Workload Characterization for I/O Performance Analysis in Virtualized Environments

Axel Busch*, Qais Noorshams*, Samuel Kounev†,

Anne Koziolek*, Ralf Reussner*, Erich Amrehn‡

*Karlsruhe Institute of Technology, Karlsruhe, Germany (email: [lastname]@kit.edu)
†University of Würzburg, Würzburg, Germany (email: samuel.kounev@uni-wuerzburg.de)
‡IBM Research & Development, Böblingen, Germany (email: amrehn@de.ibm.com)

ABSTRACT

Next generation IT infrastructures are highly driven by virtualization technology. The latter enables flexible and efficient resource sharing allowing to improve system agility and reduce costs for IT services. Due to the sharing of resources and the increasing requirements of modern applications on I/O processing, the performance of storage systems is becoming a crucial factor. In particular, when migrating or consolidating different applications the impact on their performance behavior is often an open question. Performance modeling approaches help to answer such questions, a prerequisite, however, is to find an appropriate workload characterization that is both easy to obtain from applications as well as sufficient to capture the important characteristics of the application. In this paper, we present an automated workload characterization approach that extracts a workload model to represent the main aspects of I/O-intensive applications using relevant workload parameters, e.g., request size, read-/write ratio, in virtualized environments. Once extracted, workload models can be used to emulate the workload performance behavior in real-world scenarios like migration and consolidation scenarios. We demonstrate our approach in the context of two case studies of representative system environments. We present an in-depth evaluation of our workload characterization approach showing its effectiveness in workload migration and consolidation scenarios. We use an IBM SYSTEM Z equipped with an IBM DS8700 and a SUN FIRE system as state-of-the-art virtualized environments. Overall, the evaluation of our workload characterization approach shows promising results to capture the relevant factors of I/O-intensive applications.

Categories and Subject Descriptors

C.4 [**Performance of Systems**]: Measurement techniques, Modeling techniques; D.2.8 [**Software Engineering**]: Metrics—*performance measures*

Keywords

I/O; Storage; Workload; Characterization; Virtualized; Performance

1. INTRODUCTION

Today, I/O-intensive applications support major processes of many organizations in their daily business. Workloads as mail servers, file servers, and video servers show highly I/O-intensive workload profiles, cf. [6, 14]. Their huge data volumes require high-performing dedicated external storage infrastructures. To reduce hardware costs, energy consumption, and administration costs, applications are increasingly deployed in virtualized environments. Current forecasts predict a global virtualized server market growth of 31 % until 2016 [20]. At the same time, the amount of stored digital data will double every two years until 2020 [11]. 40 % of this data will be stored or processed in the cloud. Further, a consolidation of dedicated storage systems into a shared storage infrastructure is under way, cf. [28, 21]. Nevertheless, consolidating several applications on one shared infrastructure introduces complex performance implications due to mutual interference.

To allow the consolidation of applications and services while respecting Service Level Agreements (SLAs), predicting the performance implications becomes a crucial factor. Such a prediction, however, requires tailored performance models that in turn require a significant amount of expertise to create the models. Even when such performance modeling approaches are applied, it is unclear which exact workload parameters are required as input since different approaches use different parameters [17, 18, 30]. Furthermore, it is often unclear how to obtain the parameters for given applications and if they are even sufficient to describe them [10].

To address this discrepancy, in this paper, we develop an automated workload characterization approach to extract workload models [16] that are representations of the main aspects of I/O-intensive applications in virtualized environments. Using the relevant workload parameters identified in previous work [23] as basis, we present a formalized and automated workload characterization approach for running I/O-intensive workloads in virtualized environments. We have tailored our approach to enable a non-invasive and lightweight monitoring, yet with a level of abstraction such that the parameters are practically obtainable.

To evaluate our approach, we perform a comprehensive evaluation to demonstrate its workload modeling performance for common business workloads. We present two case studies showing how our approach can be used for performance analysis. In the case studies, we demonstrate how to use the workload description for measurement-based performance predictions in two scenarios. Our first case study is focused on evaluating the quality of the workload characterization. We execute two representative workloads on a state-of-the-art IBM mainframe system to show the workload model performance of our approach. The second case study demonstrates how it can be used in migration and consolidation scenarios. To draw conclusions on the performance of a given application, typical approaches involve the installation and setup of the application to be analyzed. The installation sequence of complex applications can be very challenging or even infeasible due to legal constraints. Using our approach, the migration of complex workloads can be conducted in a predictable manner. Once the workload is modeled, a given workload can be emulated on arbitrary hardware. The installation and setup of the actual application under test on the target system is not necessary. Thus, characterizing a workload for performance model generation can be performed with less effort. Two scenarios address this area: In the migration scenario, we show the prediction of the performance behavior of a certain workload on a SUN FIRE system by means of the extracted workload data. The second scenario addresses a consolidation scenario that extends the migration scenario by considering two different workloads. In this scenario, we use a second virtual machine to execute both workloads on one machine in parallel. The consolidation scenario demonstrates the ability of our approach to predict the performance behavior of consolidated workloads in a virtualized environment.

In summary, the contribution of this paper is a formalized and fully-automated methodology for workload characterization specifically targeted at I/O-intensive applications in virtualized environments without requiring invasive or proprietary monitoring tools. In contrast to related work, we perform an extensive validation of this methodology: i) We perform a detailed evaluation using representative application workloads to show the effectiveness of our approach in different scenarios with state-of-the-art server hardware. ii) We show that our approach can be used for performance prediction in a migration scenario. iii) Finally, we show the use of the approach in a workload consolidation scenario.

This paper is organized as follows: Section 2 describes our workload characterization approach. We present a formalization of our characterization methodology and introduce the automation of our approach. Section 3 describes the experimental setup, i.e., the systems under study as well as the software environment for our measurements. Section 4 presents the two case studies evaluating our characterization approach as well as migration and consolidation scenarios. Section 5 presents related work. We finish with a conclusion in Section 6.

2. CHARACTERIZATION APPROACH

A high-level view of our workload characterization approach is shown in Figure 1. The high-level workload, e.g., a file upload, is processed by a certain I/O-intensive business application, e.g., a file server system. From a storage point of view, this high-level workload is transformed into a low-level

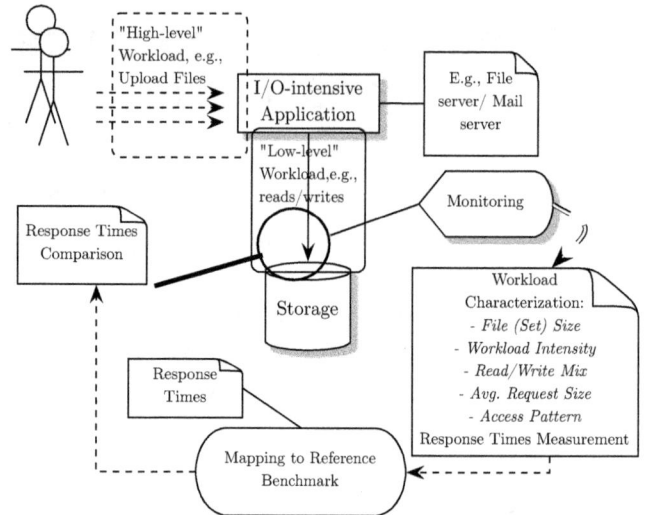

Figure 1: Workload Characterization Approach

workload comprised of a sequence of read and write requests. This low-level workload is analyzed by our approach. Using monitoring tools allow to extract the requests' properties, i.e., the workload parameters of the model. The workload model is described by a set of metrics that quantify the various workload parameters. In our approach, the workload model is described by a set of storage-specific metrics that quantify the workload. Once extracted, the workload properties are mapped to a reference benchmark. As a reference benchmark, we use the *Flexible File System Benchmark*[1] (FFSB). Using the reference benchmark, we emulate the original low-level workload on the target system.

A simple capture-replay mechanism would not be sufficient in terms of flexibility. In contrast to a capture-replay mechanism, emulating a workload allows to vary the desired parameters (i.e., file size, workload intensity,...). Therefore, different scenarios, e.g., scaling scenarios, become possible.

For validation, we calculate the prediction error between the workload's response times and the reference benchmark. Thus, conclusions on the performance of the extraction sequence become possible.

The contribution of our approach is the formalized and fully-automated characterization methodology for I/O-intensive workloads.

2.1 Workload Characterization

In this section, we describe and formalize the set of workload metrics that we consider for our workload model. In [23], a set of performance-influencing factors in virtualized storage environments was identified. Further, in [22, 24] this set was used as a basis for their performance model. Since our approach is targeted at virtualized systems, we use a subset of these factors for our workload characterization. They respect the limited monitoring possibilities as well as the limited control on system settings. In addition, they represent an adequate level of abstraction for our specific goals.

The set of influencing factors can be divided into two classes, the workload and system factors. In this work, we concentrate on the basic parameters of a workload mix,

---

[1] http://github.com/FFSB-prime

cf. Figure 2. In the following, we describe our selected set in detail:

- *File size:* Physically allocated space on disk per file. It determines the limits for sequential requests.
- *File set size:* Total physically allocated space on disk. This value influences locality of requests, caching algorithms, and data placement strategies.
- *Workload intensity:* We approximate the workload intensity as the number of threads running in parallel.
- *Request mix:* Proportion between read and write requests.
- *Avg. request size:* Average size of each request processed by the storage system.
- *Request access pattern:* Requests can access data on the disk sequentially or randomly.

In the following, we present the set of metrics we use to measure the performance-influencing factors. Our intention is to monitor the respective parameters over time and to obtain the mean values over the measurement period. Our monitoring tools capture discrete values over time periodically. Thus, we approximate the integral over time to a summation of discrete values used to calculate the mean values.

The *file size* may change significantly over time. Operations like creation of new files, deletion of files from the file set, adding or removing data to existing files influence the file size. Let $[0, T], T > 0$ be the observation period. To capture the changes of the file sizes over time, we propose

$$fileSize^{avg} = \int_0^T \frac{\sum_{\iota=1}^{n(t)} \phi^\iota(t)}{T \cdot n(t)} dt \qquad (1)$$

$$= \lim_{|\Delta| \to 0} \sum_{k=1}^{\tau} \frac{\sum_{\iota=1}^{n(x_k)} \phi^\iota(x_k)}{T \cdot n(x_k)} \cdot \Delta t_k \qquad (2)$$

$$\approx \frac{1}{F} \sum_{t=1}^{F} \frac{\sum_{\iota=1}^{n(t)} \phi^\iota(t)}{n(t)}, \qquad (3)$$

where $\phi^\iota(t)$ is the size of the ι-th file at time t and $n(t)$ is the number of files at time t, F is the number of actual measurement points in the observation period, $\dot{\mathcal{P}} := \{([t_{k-1}, t_k], x_k), 1 \leq k \leq \tau\}$ is a tagged partition of the interval $[0, T]$, i.e., $0 = t_0 \leq x_1 \leq t_1 \leq x_2 \leq \ldots \leq x_\tau \leq t_\tau = T$, $\Delta t_k := t_k - t_{k-1}$, and $|\Delta| := \max_k(\Delta t_k), k \in \{1, \ldots, \tau\}$. In Equation (1) to Equation (3), the integral is transformed to the Riemann sum using $\dot{\mathcal{P}}$ and approximated equidistant points in time.

The *file set size* is a highly changing value in a typical workload life cycle. Thus, again, we propose to measure a set of samples of the file set size over time.

$$fileSetSize^{avg} = \int_0^T \frac{\sum_{\iota=1}^{n(t)} \phi^\iota(t)}{T} dt \qquad (4)$$

$$= \lim_{|\Delta| \to 0} \sum_{k=1}^{\tau} \frac{\sum_{\iota=1}^{n(x_k)} \phi^\iota(x_k)}{T} \cdot \Delta t_k \qquad (5)$$

$$\approx \frac{1}{F} \sum_{t=1}^{F} \sum_{\iota=1}^{n(t)} \phi^\iota(t) \qquad (6)$$

In a typical workload, the number of clients changes over time. We capture the number of clients accessing the system over time to capture the *workload intensity*. The workload

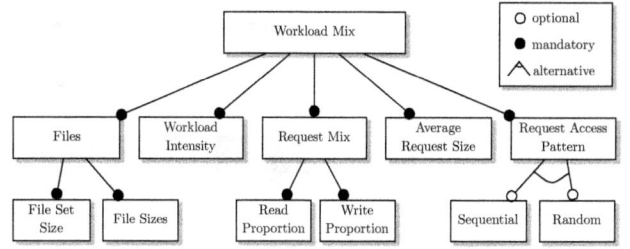

Figure 2: Performance-Influencing Factors (cf. [23])

intensity, here, can be easily adjusted to use, e.g., the number of requests per second.

$$workloadIntensity^{avg} = \int_0^T \frac{\chi(t)}{T} dt \qquad (7)$$

$$= \lim_{|\Delta| \to 0} \sum_{k=1}^{\tau} \frac{\chi(x_k)}{T} \cdot \Delta t_k \qquad (8)$$

$$\approx \frac{1}{F} \sum_{t=1}^{F} \chi(t), \qquad (9)$$

where $\chi(t)$ is the workload intensity (i.e., number of threads, requests per second) at time t.

The *request mix* is captured by the following: Let Γ_0 and Γ_1 be the sets of all observed read and write request sizes:

$$requestMix = \frac{|\Gamma_0|}{|\Gamma_0| + |\Gamma_1|} \qquad (10)$$

The *average request size* allows reasoning about the amount of data the storage systems compute in one go. We calculate the average request size for read and write requests as follows:

$$requestSize^{read} = \frac{\sum_{j=0}^{|\Gamma_0|-1} \Gamma_{0,j}}{|\Gamma_0|} \qquad (11)$$

$$requestSize^{write} = \frac{\sum_{j=0}^{|\Gamma_1|-1} \Gamma_{1,j}}{|\Gamma_1|} \qquad (12)$$

Request access pattern: Data is organized in a fixed length of sequences of bytes, i.e., blocks. When an application requests an amount of data, one or several blocks are accessed in one go. If the accessed blocks of two requests are adjacent, we refer to these requests as sequential, even if they are offset in time. Storage systems often implement algorithms to optimize such sequential requests. They recognize requests whose blocks are consecutive on disk, even if they are interrupted by other requests. This case can easily happen in applications with many execution threads. To detect sequential requests, we propose Algorithm 1, illustrated in Figure 3 and explained below.

Our algorithm determines the percentage of requests that are accessed sequentially. To do so, we search for requests whose block access boundaries are adjacent to each other. The initial observation space comprises all occurred requests from potentially different threads. To distinguish between read and write access patterns, the request space is divided into one read and one write sequence.

Figure 3 illustrates the idea of the algorithm. One request accesses one or several blocks but is depicted as one box, regardless of its size. In the illustration, we depicted sequential accesses using the same pattern. The algorithm compares

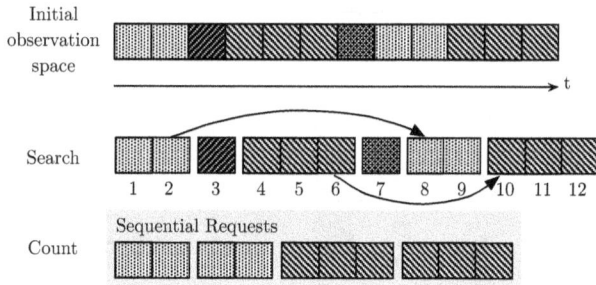

Figure 3: Access Pattern Recognition Algorithm Illustration

each request to all following requests and thus detects that requests 1, 2, 8, and 9 are sequential, as they access consecutive blocks. Additionally, it detects that requests 4, 5, 6, 10, 11, and 12 are sequential.

Algorithm: The algorithm's input parameter is a list of n pairs. A pair is defined as $R_i := (block\_start, block\_end)$, where $0 \leq block\_start \leq block\_end$ represents the start and end block number of the i-th request access. The algorithm compares the end block numbers of one request with the start block numbers of the following requests to search for sequential requests. It outputs the proportion of sequential requests in the observation space.

To improve run time and avoid overestimation of sequential requests, we enhanced the algorithm's performance by dividing the observation space into i subsets S_i. Hence, the complexity of our algorithm results in $O(n)$ at best and $O(\omega \lceil \frac{n}{\omega} \rceil^2)$ at worst.

$$S_i := \begin{cases} \{R_{i \cdot \lceil \frac{n}{\omega} \rceil}, \ldots, R_{(i+1) \cdot \lceil \frac{n}{\omega} \rceil - 1}\}, & (i+1)\lceil \frac{n}{\omega} \rceil \leq n \\ \{R_{i \cdot \lceil \frac{n}{\omega} \rceil}, \ldots, R_{n-1}\}, & else \end{cases}$$
(13)

where $i \in \{0, \ldots, \omega - 1\}$ and ω is the number of used subsets. The result access pattern ratio is the average of Algorithm 1's result for each subset:

$$accPatternRatio(R) = \frac{\sum_i getAccPat(S_i)}{\omega}$$

$$accPattern(R) = \begin{cases} sequential, & accPatternRatio(R) \geq 0.5 \\ random, & else \end{cases}$$
(14)

Our approach avoids overestimation of sequential requests: Sequential requests that are far away from each other in the observation space are not included in the access pattern ratio $accPatternRatio$.

Similar request access pattern heuristics do not respect sequential requests if they are not directly followed up, but interrupted by a non-sequential request, cf. [12]. Our approach respects this and allows a configuration of the observation space using an observation window.

2.2 Characterization Automation

To automate the proposed workload characterization approach, we have extended a tool to automatically execute a workload and obtain its parameters by observing the set of relevant metrics. The tool, called Storage Performance Analyzer (SPA) [3], is a software that supports fully-automatic systematic performance measurements and monitoring of storage system properties. Its architecture allows to analyze

---

Algorithm 1 Access Pattern Recognition Algorithm

Configuration:
$R \leftarrow$ Sequence of request pairs
$req \leftarrow$ Number of requests
$req\_seq \leftarrow 0$

Function getAccPat(R):
  while $i < req$ **do**   // Iterate through requests
    for j such that $i < j < req$ **do**
      $block\_end = R_{i2}$ // End block of request R_i
      $block\_start = R_{j1}$ // Start block of request R_j
      if $block\_end = block\_start$ **then**
        $req\_seq \leftarrow req\_seq + 2$ // Count both R_i, R_j
        $R \leftarrow R \setminus \{R_i, R_j\}$
        continue while;
      end if
    end for
    $i \leftarrow i + 1$
  end while
  return $\frac{req\_seq}{req}$

---

arbitrary application workloads. Alternatively, it supports the integration of workload generators, e.g., benchmarks.

Performing manual steps is highly error-prone. SPA supports automatic measurements and therefore allows a coordinated execution of the original workloads. To enable the extraction of workload parameters, the **benchmark controller** was extended to support the synchronized and parallel execution of several workloads and to distinguish these parallel workloads when monitoring. The actual execution, i.e., execute start and stop commands and gathering of log files, of the particular workload is realized by the **benchmark driver** component. For our monitoring goals, we extended the tool architecture by adding a monitor component, cf. class diagram in Figure 4.

The core of the monitor component is the **monitor driver**. It controls the monitoring tools to be prepared, started and stopped on the system under test, as well as processing its measurement values, i.e., extracting a metrics set. The class diagram shows several concrete monitor drivers, e.g., **FilesizeMonitorDriver**, which is an implementation of the abstract monitor driver class. **IndependentVariables** stores the configuration parameters of the monitoring tools. To extract request block relevant metrics, we use BLKTRACE [7] in SPA.

BLKTRACE is a block layer I/O tracing tool. Since it collects data on the application layer it is executed on the system under test. Using BLKTRACE, we obtain detailed disk request trace information. The powerful tracing mechanism of BLKTRACE allows conclusions about request properties. The raw data of BLKTRACE is used to extract the actual request block relevant workload parameter metrics.

Our experiment setup is shown in Figure 5. A controller machine starts and coordinates the benchmark and monitoring tools on the system under test (SUT), which is accessed using an SSH connection. After each successful workload execution the controller machine collects the raw measurement data from the SUT and extracts the workload parameters from the raw data. Finally, the results are stored in an SQLite database.

The measurement execution sequence works as follows: i) a preparation phase that performs an initial warm up, ii) a workload execution and monitoring phase, iii) a phase that

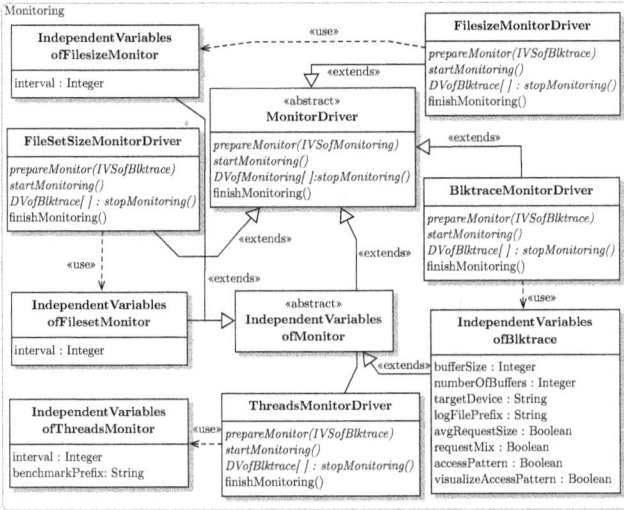

Figure 4: Class diagram of the monitor component

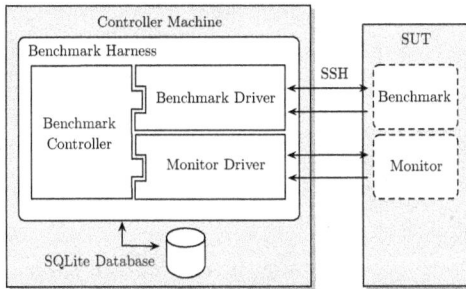

Figure 5: Experimental Setup Overview

stops monitoring and collects the measurement results from the SUT, vi) a finishing phase that finalizes the workload and monitors execution.

The parallel execution of several workloads and monitors further increases the requirements for a coordinated execution: An overlapping preparation and monitoring phase would lead to displaced characterization results. Therefore, the preparation phase must be finished before the monitoring process is started, which is automatically ensured by SPA's coordination process.

3. EXPERIMENTAL SETUP

3.1 Systems Under Study

For our case studies, we use an IBM SYSTEM z equipped with an IBM DS8700 storage system and a separate SUN FIRE X4440 server system to evaluate how our approach performs in migration and consolidation scenarios.

For our experiments, we consider the IBM SYSTEM z and the IBM DS8700 storage system as a representative virtualized environment. Both machines represent a high-end virtualized environment for critical business applications. Figure 6 shows the conceptual design of both systems.

The *Processor Resource/System Manager* (PR/SM) allows a mapping of physical to virtual resources and thus enables CPU and storage virtualization. The PR/SM hypervisor manages logical partitions (LPAR) and allocates hardware

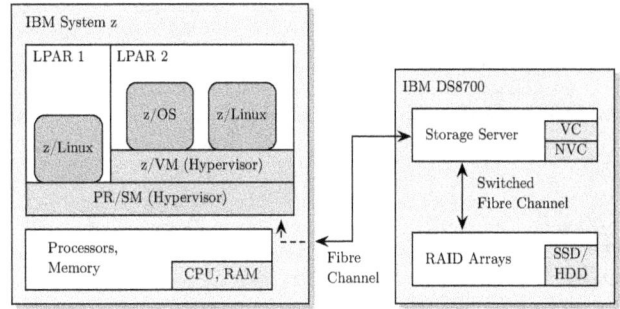

Figure 6: Conceptual design of IBM System z and DS8700

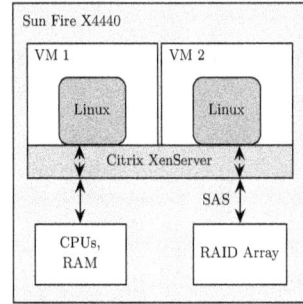

Figure 7: Conceptual design of Sun Fire X4440

component classes (e.g. CPU, RAM, I/O) to each LPAR. An LPAR represents an independent resource container that runs applications on a Linux operating system or the z/VM hypervisor. z/VM provides an execution environment for different operating systems separated from the underlying hardware. The allocated resource class can be accessed by the LPARs either exclusively or in a shared manner. SYSTEM z itself is connected to the storage system by a Fibre Channel.

The *IBM DS8700 storage system* manages I/O operations (e.g., read and write operations) using a processor complex, which contains both volatile (50 GB) and persistent (2 GB) (non-volatile) cache memory. The storage system supports a set of pre-fetching and destaging algorithms to increase the I/O performance. Write requests are cached in the volatile cache as well as in the non-volatile cache, but are destaged to the underlying RAID system asynchronously. Similar to write requests, read requests are served and cached in the volatile cache memory. Thus, recurring accesses are served by the cache, while others are served by the RAID system. The system tries to predict further reads and holds data as long as possible in its cache memory. Each processor complex can access the disk subsystem via two separate switched Fibre Channel networks (cf. [27]).

The characterization environment is set up in a z/Linux LPAR environment with 2 CPUs (more precisely, *Integrated Facilities for Linux*) and 4 GiB of memory. The storage system's partition uses the *ext4* file system. For I/O scheduling, we use a first-come, first-served (FCFS) scheduling policy.

For our migration and consolidation scenarios, we use a SUN FIRE X4440 x64 server system. It contains 4 times 2.4 GhZ AMD Opteron 6 core processors and 128 GB of memory. The storage back end is a RAID system with 8 *Serial Attached SCSI* (SAS) devices with 300 GB each. It contains a write cache that allows buffering incoming write requests. The guest operating system is virtualized using a Citrix XenServer. Figure 7 shows the SUN FIRE design in detail.

The consolidation scenario runs in two separate virtual machines on the SUN FIRE system. Both of the virtual machines use six CPU cores and 2 GiB of memory each. The virtual machine instances access a shared RAID system. For all measurements the *ext4* file system is used. Again, for I/O scheduling, the FCFS scheduling policy is used.

3.2 Software Environment

Our software environment comprises two benchmarks and one monitoring tool: We use the FILEBENCH benchmark to generate the original workloads to be analyzed. To this end, we enhanced SPA adding a benchmark driver to allow automated execution of FILEBENCH.

FILEBENCH[2] [2] is a storage system benchmark and is widely used in the performance modeling community [17, 4, 9, 19]. It supports emulation of common business workloads such as mail server and file server workloads. Its workload modeling language allows a fine-grained workload construction. Hence, FILEBENCH achieves a realistic representation of the emulated workloads. Furthermore, we use GNU_SOURCE configuration to focus the measurements on the storage performance and to take caching effects of the storage system into account.

For validation, we use the open source FFSB benchmark. FFSB is a file system performance benchmarking tool. Our set of considered workload parameters can be mapped to FFSB's workload configuration parameters. Thus, FFSB is highly suitable to be used as a reference benchmark in our methodology. Additionally, we use the response times of FFSB as a basis to validate the characterization performance.

All benchmarking and measurement steps were executed 20 times for 300 seconds to achieve statistical robust values. Each run is prepared by a warm up period of 60 seconds.

4. CASE STUDIES

In this section, we present our case studies. In the first case study, we apply the workload characterization approach to two different workloads. In the second case study, we perform a migration scenario followed by a consolidation scenario in the context of the considered workloads.

To assess the quality of our workload characterization approach, we compare the response times of the original FILEBENCH workload with the response time of the reference benchmark FFSB, which is supposed to emulate the original workload. As a metric in this comparison, we calculate the prediction error per run as follows. Let $RT_i \in \mathbb{R}$ be the average response times of FILEBENCH and FFSB for one workload in run i, then,

$$RT_i^{err} = \left| \frac{RT_i^{Filebench} - RT_i^{FFSB}}{RT_i^{FFSB}} \right| \qquad (15)$$

4.1 Case Study I: Workload Characterization

We show how our approach can be applied in practice and evaluate its effectiveness. We consider two different types of workloads: a mail server and a file server workload. The approach of Section 2 is realized by a four step process, illustrated in Figure 8.

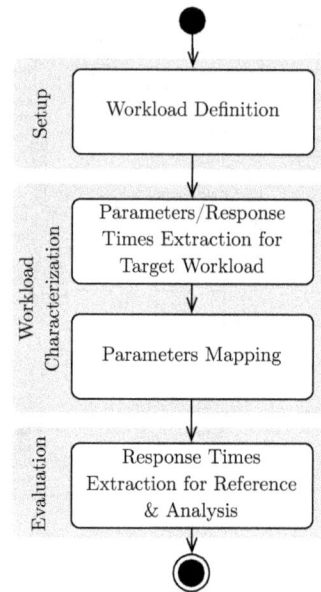

Figure 8: Execution steps in case study I

In the first step the original workload to be analyzed is specified, i.e., mail server and file server. In the second step, SPA is used to execute the original workload and collect measurements, gathering and aggregating the raw data and extracting the workload parameters. Additionally, the response times per operation are stored to allow validation of the results.

In step 3, we map the determined workload parameters to our reference benchmark. Finally, in step 4, SPA runs the reference benchmark workload configuration and extracts the response times per operation and we compare them to the response times of the original workload to assess the workload model accuracy.

Workload Definition.

Mail server and file server are basically mixed read/write workloads. They comprise a sequence of composite read and write operations. The following list gives an overview of the used operations:

- *readwholefile/writewholefile:* Both operations process one randomly chosen file as a whole, i.e., the complete file is accessed at once.

- *appendfilerand: Appendfilerand* appends a certain amount of data to the end of a file chosen randomly from the target directory.

- *openfile: Openfile* opens a file for read or write access. It supports different options to allow a random selection of a file from the target directory.

- *closefile: Closefile* simply closes a file.

- *createfile: Createfile* creates a new file in the target directory. The initial file size is 0 B.

- *deletefile:* The *deletefile* operation deletes a randomly chosen file in the target directory.

- *statfile:* The *statfile* operation accesses to the meta information of a file.

	Mail server	Std. dev.	File server	Std. dev.
File Size	16.62 KiB	0.74 KiB	129.76 KiB	3.91 KiB
File Set Size	683.68 MiB	58.37 MiB	1163.49 MiB	5.91 MiB
Workload Intensity	16 Threads	0 Threads	50 Threads	0 Threads
Request Size Read	14 151.17 B	31.63 B	105 152.00 B	166.67 B
Request Size Write	15 639.04 B	81.59 B	80 473.09 B	190.77 B
Request Mix	55.96 %	0.11 %	41.85 %	0.37 %
Access Pattern Ratio (Read)	28.74 %	0.52 %	97.00 %	2.30 %
Access Pattern Ratio (Write)	57.24 %	1.22 %	99.23 %	0.27 %

Table 1: Obtained metrics and standard deviations for FILEBENCH mail and file server workload

Listing 1: Mail Server Workload

```
    File set:
      - number of files = 50000
      - mean file size = 16 KiB
      - file preallocation = 80%
5   Threads:
      - 16 (default)
    Operations:
      - deletefile
      - createfile
10    - appendfilerand, mean req size = 16
          KiB
      - closefile
      - openfile,
      - readwholefile
      - closefile
15    - openfile
      - appendfilerand, mean req size = 16
          KiB
      - closefile
      - openfile
      - readwholefile
20    - closefile
```

Listing 2: File Server Workload

```
    File set:
      - number of files = 10000
      - mean file size = 128 KiB
      - file preallocation = 80%
5   Threads:
      - 50 (default)
    Operations:
      - createfile
      - writewholefile
10    - closefile
      - openfile
      - appendfilerand, mean req size = 16
          KiB
      - closefile
      - openfile
15    - readwholefile
      - closefile
      - deletefile
      - statfile
```

Different sequences of these operations are possible. These define the workload that the thread instance executes in a

	Mail server	File server
File Size	17.0 KiB	130.0 KiB
Number of Files	41 201	9 169
Running Threads	16 Threads	50 Threads
Block Size Read	14 336 B	104 960 B
Block Size Write	15 872 B	80 384 B
Read Size	14 336 B	104 960 B
Write Size	15 872 B	80 384 B
Read Weight	56 %	42 %
Write Weight	44 %	58 %
Access Pt. Read	random	sequential
Access Pt. Write	sequential	sequential

Table 2: FFSB configurations for emulated mail server and file server workload

loop until the run time limit is reached. The *mail server* and *file server* operation sequences are shown in Listings 1 and 2, respectively.

Workload Parameters Extraction.
In this section, we extract the parameters of the application's workloads. Our workload characterization provides stable results all over our metrics set. Table 1 shows a comparison between the different metrics and the standard deviations of both of the considered workload scenarios. The file set size, file size, workload intensity, request mix and access pattern metrics exhibit low standard deviations. The request sizes exhibit low standard deviations in the dimensions of the actual measurement values. Figures 9, and 10 show the workload model parameter results graphically.

Workload Parameters Mapping.
The beforehand obtained workload parameters of both workloads are used to create corresponding configurations for the FFSB benchmark. As FFSB does not directly offer our set of workload metrics, we need to map our metrics to the FFSB configuration parameters. We round the request size parameters to a multiple of 512 Bytes. Table 2 shows the final FFSB parameters.

Response Time Extraction.
In this section, we show the extracted FILEBENCH and FFSB response times for both the mail server and file server workloads. For the mail server workload, we obtain a mean response time for the read requests of 0.98 ms and 0.83 ms for the write requests. Here, the read and write response times each are comprised of two operations. Figure 11 shows the FILEBENCH response times in detail.

For the file server workload, we observe a mean application layer response time of 11.21 ms for the read requests and

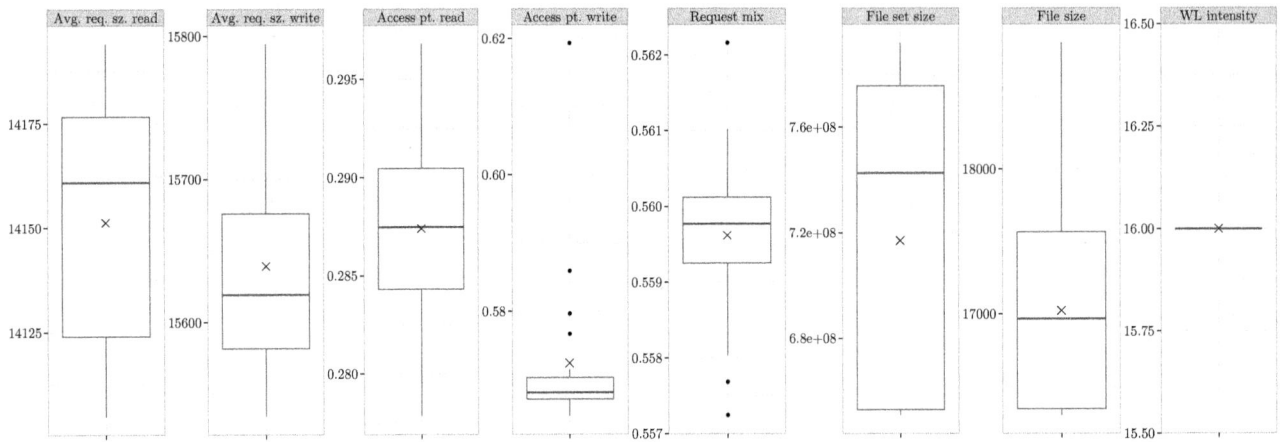

Figure 9: FILEBENCH mail server workload parameters (units cf. Table 1)

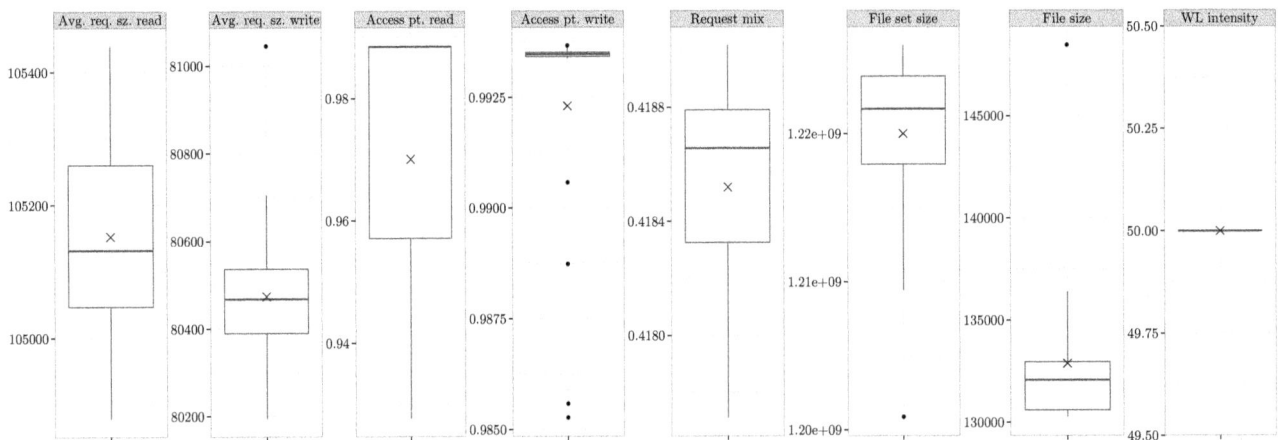

Figure 10: FILEBENCH file server workload parameters (units cf. Table 1). The box marks the 25- to 75-percentile, the fat line is the median, the cross is the mean value, and whiskers mark the lowest (resp. highest) value still within 1.5 times the interquartile range of the lower (resp. higher) quartile.

11.65 ms for the write requests. Here, the write response time is comprised of two operations. Emulating the mail server configuration by FFSB, we obtain a read response time of 0.81 ms, while the mean standard deviation ($\overline{\sigma}$) is 2.78 ms[3]. The write response time of the mail server workload is on average 1.29 ms ($\overline{\sigma} = 2.94$ ms).

The emulated file server configuration exhibits a mean read response time of 11.67 ms ($\overline{\sigma} = 21.13$ ms). The mean write response time of the mail server workload is 18.48 ms ($\overline{\sigma} = 20.77$ ms). The response time's standard deviations in both workload scenarios result in about double the height of the actual response time values. Compare Figure 12 for the detailed FFSB response times.

Response Time Analysis.
To evaluate the accuracy of our characterization approach, we compare the response times of FILEBENCH with the response times of the corresponding FFSB workload configuration. Figure 13 shows the obtained prediction errors.

Mail server: In the case of the mail server workload, the mean read prediction error per run is in the range of [17.01, 25.87] %. For writes, the error is in the range of [31.25, 38.54] %. Overall, the mean prediction error over all runs is 20.82 % for read requests and 35.72 % for write requests. Considering the very low absolute response times of this workload, these are stable results.

File server: For the file server workload's read requests response times, we observe errors in the range of [1.18, 9.62] %. The write request errors are in the range of [33.89, 41.06] %. Overall, the mean prediction error for read requests is 3.93 %, while the mean prediction error for write requests is 36.96 %.

Summary.
Our first case study demonstrates the performance of our workload characterization approach and its ability to capture the performance-relevant aspects of the analyzed original workloads. The slightly higher prediction error for write operations is caused by a higher standard deviation of the characterized request sizes. Our reference benchmark FFSB

---

[3]$\overline{\sigma}$ averages the standard deviations of each of the 20 runs.

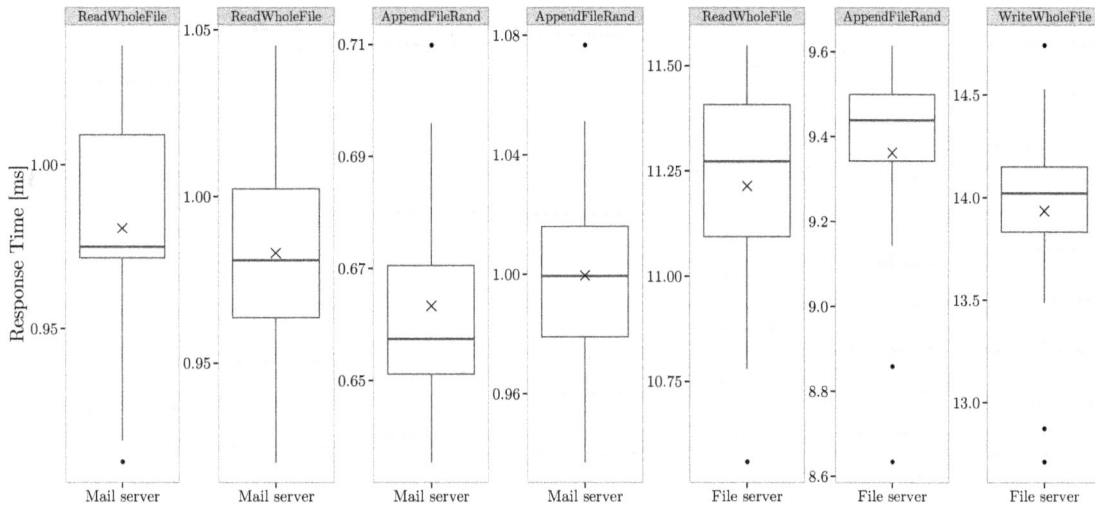

Figure 11: FILEBENCH mail server and file server response times

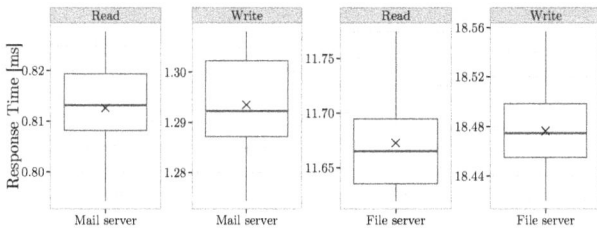

Figure 12: FFSB mail server and file server response times

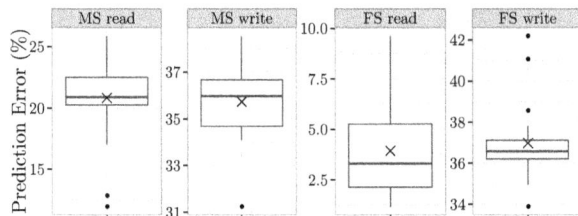

Figure 13: FILEBENCH mail and file server prediction error

emulates constant request sizes, and therefore we use mean sizes of the requests as input. Although the prediction errors for write requests are slightly higher, the errors stay in the same dimension. Overall, the workload model accuracy is sufficient for most applications and provides an adequate characterization of the analyzed workload behavior.

4.2 Case Study II: Migration & Consolidation

In Section 4.1, we extracted the workload parameters of a mail server and a file server workload. In this case study, we use the obtained parameters to predict the performance impact of migrating and consolidating the workloads to a SUN FIRE server system.

Again, we use FILEBENCH as our original workload generator and FFSB as reference benchmark. Figures 14 and 15 illustrate the considered scenarios.

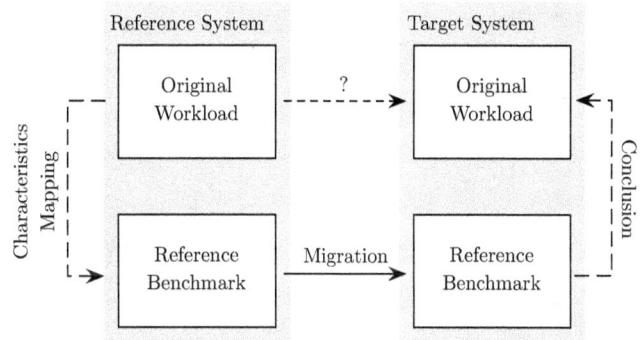

Figure 14: Migration scenario procedure

Workload Migration.

In our workload migration scenario, we show how to move a certain workload to another system. We model the workload as before and map the workload parameters to the reference benchmark. Then, we execute the migration step: We emulate the modeled workload on the target system using the reference benchmark, which allows us to evaluate the impact of the migration on the application response times. Figure 14 illustrates the procedure.

In this scenario, we use the IBM SYSTEM z as reference system and the SUN FIRE as target system. Like before, we use FILEBENCH as workload generator and FFSB as reference benchmark. We use the obtained workload parameters that are described in Section 4.1. In this scenario, we concentrate on the file server workload. For evaluation, we additionally measure the FILEBENCH response times of the file server workload on the SUN FIRE system, so that we can calculate the prediction error for the workload response times.

Workload Consolidation.

The goal of the consolidation scenario is to predict the performance of two different workloads that are executed on the same machine at the same time based on workload models obtained in isolation. To do so, we characterize the workloads separately and map the obtained workload parameters to the reference benchmark. Then, both reference benchmark

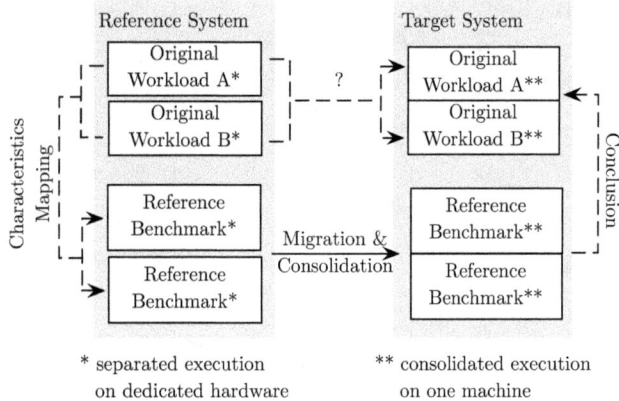

Figure 15: Consolidation scenario procedure

Workload	Operation	Resp. Time	Std. dev.
File server	ReadWholeFile	67.21 ms	0.55 ms
	AppendFileRand	34.96 ms	0.44 ms
	WriteWholeFile	31.68 ms	0.47 ms
FS + MS	AppendFileRand	85.00 ms	2.08 ms
		30.57 ms	0.87 ms
		29.94 ms	0.69 ms
	WriteWholeFile	93.43 ms	2.46 ms
	ReadWholeFile	139.48 ms	2.56 ms
		47.67 ms	1.22 ms
		46.11 ms	1.20 ms

Table 3: Details of FILEBENCH operations response times averaged the 20 runs. The standard deviation refers to the 20 mean response times of the 20 runs.

instances are migrated to the target systems and are run consolidated, i.e., at the same time, but in separated VMs. Figure 15 illustrates this scenario.

In this consolidation scenario, again, we use the IBM SYSTEM Z as reference system and the SUN FIRE as target system. Here, we use the workload model to predict the performance behavior when consolidating the two workloads at the same time on the SUN FIRE system. Again, we use the obtained mail server and file server workload parameters of Section 4.1. For the FFSB configuration, we use the same emulated mail server and file server configurations as in Section 4.1, cf. Table 1. For the evaluation, we again extract the FILEBENCH response times of the mail server and file server consolidated workloads on the SUN FIRE system. Again, we calculate the prediction error of the workload response times.

Response Times.
In our migration scenario, for the FILEBENCH file server workload, we obtain a mean response time of 67.21 ms, while the standard deviation (σ) is 0.55 ms for the read and 33.32 ms ($\sigma = 0.45$ ms) for the write requests. Here, the write mean response time is comprised of two operations.

For the consolidated scenario, we obtain a mean response time of 77.75 ms ($\sigma = 0.95$ ms) for the read and 59.71 ms ($\sigma = 1.02$ ms) for the write requests. Here, the read response

time is comprised of three, while the write response time is comprised of four operations. For response time details of particular operations, cf. Table 3.

The FFSB mean response times for the file server workload is 55.29 ms ($\overline{\sigma} = 20.61$ ms) for the read and 42.21 ms ($\overline{\sigma} = 14.49$ ms) for the write operations. For the consolidated scenario, we obtain 89.34 ms for the read and 79.12 ms for the write operations. Figures 16(a), and 16(b) show the FILEBENCH and FFSB scenario response times in detail.

Response Time Analysis.
As in Section 4.1, we use Equation (15) to calculate the prediction error.

Migration scenario: The prediction error of the file server workload that we used for the migration scenario shows a read error in the range of $[19.12, 28.02]\%$, and a write error in the range of $[12.77, 24.12]\%$, respectively. Overall, we obtain a mean prediction error of 21.59% for read operations and 20.98% for write operations.

Consolidation scenario: For the consolidation scenario, we obtain a read error of $[9.23, 17.32]\%$, and a write error of $[21.46, 28.28]\%$. Overall, we obtain a mean prediction read error of 12.95%, while the mean write error is 24.51%. Figure 17 illustrates the prediction error for both scenarios.

Summary.
Both scenarios demonstrate the performance of our automated workload characterization approach when migrating and consolidating workloads. Our experiments cover low response times less than 30 ms, and comparatively long response times of more than 140 ms. Still, we obtain stable measurements and low prediction errors of less than 25% for both of the considered scenarios.

5. RELATED WORK
The related work presented in this paper can be classified into three groups. The first group focuses on the area of workload characterization. Here, Gulati et al. [13], performed a study about the effects of running several workloads (i.e., a set of top-tier enterprise applications) on a shared set of I/O devices. They used a VMWare ESX server hypervisor for virtualization. They analyzed the effects of shared I/O devices while observing the behavior of workloads in isolation and in a consolidated scenario.
For their isolated workload characterization they used isolated RAID systems for each of the workloads. For their consolidated characterization they merged the isolated RAID systems into one big array. In contrast to our work, the set of workload metrics they used is more hardware related. Their analysis and conclusions concentrate on the impact of consolidating workloads with different workload access patterns. Further, they concentrate on consolidation of hard drives, but not on applications.

Ahmad et al. [5] studied the performance of storage subsystems. Here, they modeled native as well as virtualized machines. For their measurements they used several disk microbenchmarks (e.g., Iometer, Perfmon). For their characterization they concentrated on the throughput of the storage system for different block sizes, access patterns and read-/write ratios. Using the throughput of the applications they compared the native vs. virtualized performance. In a first case study, they used a capture-replay mechanism to model a

(a) FILEBENCH scenario response times

(b) FFSB scenario response times

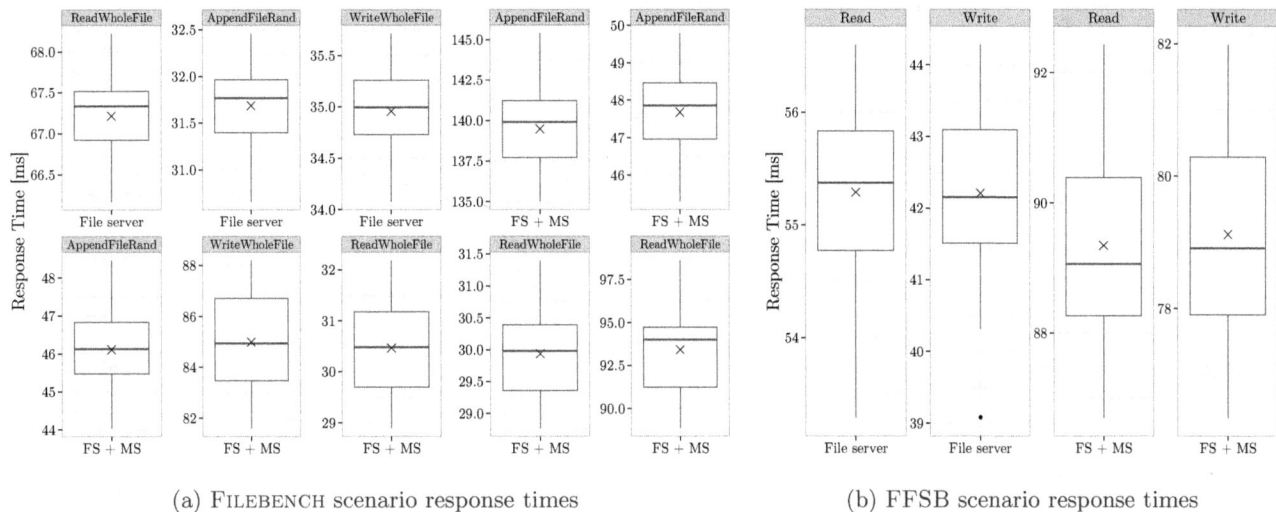

Figure 16: Scenarios: Migration and consolidation scenario response times

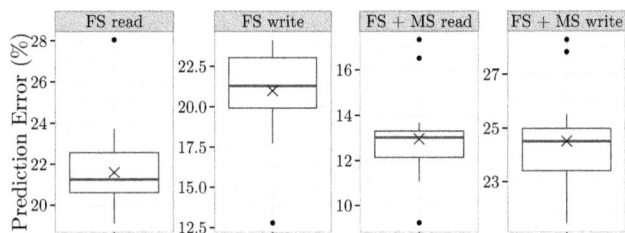

Figure 17: Scenarios prediction error

file server workload. In a second case study, they modeled a commercial mail server system. In a later work [4], they used online histograms to model several FILEBENCH workloads. For their characterization approach they used a metrics set comprising I/O, CPU and workload intensity metrics.

Kavalanekar et al. [15] modeled several workloads, e.g., mail server and file server workloads, using the *Event Tracing for Windows* (ETW) instrumentation. They showed a metrics set for their characterization and use histograms and standardized distributions for the metric's representation. Their approach is tailored for the ETW instrumentation and uses long-term traces as input data.

Wang et al. [30] used a machine learning model CART (Classification And Regression Tree) that uses a binary decision tree to predict the storage device performance for a particular workload on a particular device. Their first approach used parameters of each disk request, i.e., its request description like arrival time differences between two requests or distances between two consecutive block accesses to predict the request/response time. The second approach used workload-level parameters like burstiness, read/write ratio, locality metrics, arrival rate and request size.

Finally, Tarasov et al. [26] extracted a workload model using I/O traces. They use their model to transfer the workload, captured by the traces, to a benchmark, i.e. FILEBENCH. Finally, they replayed the captured workload using this benchmark.

All works in this group do not consider predicting the workload behavior on a different system or in consolidation scenarios.

The second group describes performance-influencing factors and performance metrics. Wang et at. [29] developed a statistical model to capture burstiness and spatio-temporal correlation of disk and memory accesses. They used entropy plots to represent burstiness and spatio-temporal correlation.

Ruemmler and Wilkes [25] analyze disk access patterns using disk request traces. In contrast to our work, Ruemmler and Wilkes do not respect sequential requests that are offset in time.

The third group concentrates on performance model generation. Here, Kraft et al. [18, 17] analyzed the influences of consolidated virtual environments on the response time behavior of storage systems. They used two approaches to model the I/O performance of consolidated virtual machines: First, they used homogeneous workloads in two virtual machines. In a second approach, they performed measurements for a consolidation of heterogeneous workloads. To do so, they used the FFSB benchmark as well as the FILEBENCH benchmark. They rely on low level response times obtained by BLKTRACE.

Benevenuto et al. [8] developed several performance prediction models. They used open queueing models to predict the performance of applications in a XEN virtualized environment. For their model creation process they collected metrics for performance prediction model design and validation.

In contrast to the above, our workload characterization approach is a formalized and automated methodology that allows a characterization of I/O-intensive workloads using relevant parameters and enables a performance behaviour prediction on a different system and in consolidation scenarios.

6. CONCLUSIONS

We presented a fully-automated workload characterization approach that allows a systematic derivation of a workload model by capturing the major performance-relevant workload parameters. We presented our experimental methodology and the workload modeling process. We demonstrated the approach's quality on an IBM SYSTEM z mainframe system equipped with a DS8700 storage system using two different workloads. On average, we achieved a prediction error of 12.38 % for the read requests and 36.34 % for the write requests.

Additionally, we studied migration and consolidation scenarios using a SUN FIRE server system. The migration scenario demonstrated the ability of migrating an already modeled workload to a different system. The consolidation scenario showed the performance of our approach in virtualized environments, when moving two workloads modeled in isolation to a shared system. The migration scenario exhibits an adequate prediction error of 21.59 % for read and 20.98 % for write requests, respectively. Consolidating two prior isolated workloads results in adequate prediction errors of 12.95 % for read requests, and 24.51 % for write requests. Overall, we showed the practical relevance of our workload characterization approach, as well as its capabilities in migration and consolidation scenarios. Even though the overall prediction errors may be higher than with applying standard performance modeling techniques, the error rates are sufficient for a low-overhead, first estimation of the workload performance behavior without applying full-blown modeling formalisms or physically migrating the whole software stack.

In general, our approach is designed as a lightweight technique to evaluate the workload performance impact of an I/O-intensive software application on different platforms without requiring to actually install the whole software application. It is especially beneficial in cases that prohibit creating explicit performance models due to, e.g., time and budget constraints. As a further application scenario, our workload characterization can be used as a basis for performance modeling approaches. Existing applications can be characterized automatically and mapped to the input of the performance models, thus increasing the applicability of the performance models as well as eliminating the need for specialized performance models for a given software application.

7. ACKNOWLEDGMENTS

This work was partially funded by the German Research Foundation (DFG) under grant No. RE 1674/5-1 and KO 3445/6-1. We thank the Informatics Innovation Center (IIC) - http://www.iic.kit.edu/ - for providing the technical systems IBM SYSTEM z and IBM DS8700 storage system.

8. REFERENCES

[1] FFSB. http://sourceforge.net/projects/ffsb/, 2004.
[2] Filebench. http://sourceforge.net/apps/mediawiki/filebench/, 2011.
[3] Storage performance analyzer. http://sdqweb.ipd.kit.edu/wiki/SPA/, 2013.
[4] I. Ahmad. Easy and efficient disk i/o workload characterization in vmware esx server. IEEE Computer Society, 2007.
[5] I. Ahmad, J. M. Anderson, A. M. Holler, R. Kambo, and V. Makhija. An analysis of disk performance in VMware ESX Server virtual machines. IEEE Computer Society, 2003.
[6] M. Armbrust, A. Fox, R. Griffith, A. D. Joseph, R. Katz, A. Konwinski, G. Lee, D. Patterson, A. Rabkin, I. Stoica, and M. Zaharia. A view of cloud computing. ACM, 2010.
[7] J. Axboe, A. Brunelle, and N. Scott. blktrace - linux man page. http://linux.die.net/man/8/blktrace, 2006.

[8] F. Benevenuto, C. Fernandes, M. Santos, V. A. F. Almeida, J. M. Almeida, G. J. Janakiraman, and J. R. Santos. Performance models for virtualized applications. Springer, 2006.
[9] G. Casale, S. Kraft, and D. Krishnamurthy. A model of storage i/o performance interference in virtualized systems. ICDCSW, 2011.
[10] R. C. Chiang and H. H. Huang. Tracon: interference-aware scheduling for data-intensive applications in virtualized environments. New York, NY, USA, 2011. SC'11.
[11] J. Gantz and D. Reinsel. The digital universe in 2020: Big data, bigger digital shadows, and biggest growth in the far east. IDC, 2012.
[12] B. Gregg. Dtrace tools: iopattern. http://www.dtracebook.com/index.php/Disk_IO:iopattern, Jul-2005. [Online; accessed 21-Aug-2013].
[13] A. Gulati, C. Kumar, and I. Ahmad. Storage workload characterization and consolidation in virtualized environments. VPACT, 2009.
[14] V. Kasavajhala. Solid State Drive vs. Hard Disk Drive Price and Performance Study. Technical report, Dell Technical White Paper. Dell PowerVault Storage Systems, 2011.
[15] S. Kavalanekar, B. Worthington, Q. Zhang, and V. Sharda. Characterization of storage workload traces from production windows servers. IISWC, 2008.
[16] S. Kounev. Wiley encyclopedia of computer science and engineering - chapter software performance evaluation. Wiley-Interscience and John Wiley & Sons Inc., 2009.
[17] S. Kraft. Performance models of storage contention in cloud environments. *Journal of Software and Systems Modeling (SoSyM)*, 2012.
[18] S. Kraft, G. Casale, D. Krishnamurthy, D. Greer, and P. Kilpatrick. IO performance prediction in consolidated virtualized environments. ICPE, 2011.
[19] S. Kundu, R. Rangaswami, A. Gulati, M. Zhao, and K. Dutta. Modeling virtualized applications using machine learning techniques. SIGPLAN/SIGOPS, 2012.
[20] I. R. Limited. Global server virtualization market 2012-2016. http://www.rnrmarketresearch.com/global-server-virtualization-market-2012-2016-market-report.html, 2013. [Online; accessed 19-Aug-2013].
[21] L. McLaughlin. Virtualization in the enterprise survey: Your virtualized state in 2008. *CIO Magazine*, 2008.
[22] Q. Noorshams, D. Bruhn, S. Kounev, and R. Reussner. Predictive Performance Modeling of Virtualized Storage Systems using Optimized Statistical Regression Techniques. ICPE '13, 2013.
[23] Q. Noorshams, S. Kounev, and R. Reussner. Experimental Evaluation of the Performance-Influencing Factors of Virtualized Storage Systems. Springer Berlin Heidelberg, 2013.
[24] Q. Noorshams, K. Rostami, S. Kounev, P. Tůma, and R. Reussner. I/O Performance Modeling of Virtualized Storage Systems. MASCOTS, 2013.
[25] C. Ruemmler and J. Wilkes. Unix disk access patterns. Hewlett-Packard Laboratories, 1993.
[26] Tarasov, Kumar, Ma, Hildebrand, Povzner, Kuenning, and Zadok. Extracting flexible, replayable models from large block traces. FAST'12, 2012.
[27] R. Vaupel. *High Availability and Scalability of Mainframe Environments using System z and z/OS as example.* 2012.
[28] W. Vogels. Beyond server consolidation. ACM, 2008.
[29] M. Wang, A. Ailamaki, and C. Faloutsos. Capturing the spatio-temporal behavior of real traffic data. Elsevier Science Publishers B. V., 2002.
[30] M. Wang, K. Au, A. Ailamaki, A. Brockwell, C. Faloutsos, and G. Ganger. Storage device performance prediction with cart models. MASCOTS, 2004.

Can Portability Improve Performance? An Empirical Study of Parallel Graph Analytics

Ana Lucia Varbanescu,
Merijn Verstraaten, Cees de Laat
University of Amsterdam
The Netherlands
{a.l.varbanescu,m.e.verstraaten,delaat}@uva.nl

Ate Penders, Alexandru Iosup,
Henk Sips
Delft University of Technology
The Netherlands
{a.b.penders, a.iosup, h.j.sips}@tudelft.nl

ABSTRACT

Due to increasingly large datasets, graph analytics—traversals, all-pairs shortest path computations, centrality measures, etc.—are becoming the focus of high-performance computing (HPC). Because HPC is currently dominated by many-core architectures (both CPUs and GPUs), new graph processing solutions have to be defined to efficiently use such computing resources. Prior work focuses on platform-specific performance studies and on platform-specific algorithm development, successfully proving that algorithms highly tuned to GPUs *or* multi-core CPUs can provide high performance graph analytics. However, the portability of such algorithms remains an important concern for many users, especially the many companies without the resources to invest in HPC or concerned about lock-in in single-use parallel techniques.

In this work, we investigate the functional portability and performance of graph analytics algorithms. We conduct an empirical study measuring the performance of 3 graph analytics algorithms (a single code implemented in OpenCL and targeted at many-core CPUs *and* GPUs), on 3 different platforms, using 11 real-world and synthetic datasets. Our results show that the code is functionally portable, that is, the applications can run unchanged on both CPUs and GPUs. The large variation in their observed performance indicates that portability is necessary not only for productivity, but, surprisingly, also for performance. We conjecture that the impact of datasets on performance is too high to allow platform-specific algorithms to outperform the portable algorithms by large margins, *in all cases*. Our conclusion is that portable parallel graph analytics is feasible without significant performance loss, and provides a productive alternative to the expensive trial-and-error selection of one algorithm for each (graph,platform) pair.

Categories and Subject Descriptors

C.4 [**Computer Systems Organization**]: Performance of Systems; D.1.3 [**Software**]: Concurrent Programming

Keywords

Parallel Graph Analytics; Portability; OpenCL; GPU; Multi-core processors; Many-core processors

1. INTRODUCTION

While graph processing is at the core of a large variety of applications, from path finding in maps and networks to bioinformatics, from circuit floor planning to text and speech analysis, it is probably large social and professional networks, like Facebook and LinkedIn, that have brought graph analytics back into the spotlight. Given the extreme scales of the datasets that need to be analyzed, as well as the more extensive analysis that needs to be performed, graph analytics has become a high-performance computing (HPC) concern. This trend is probably best proven by the intense activity and fast changes happening in the Graph500[1] ranking, as well as in the adoption of graph traversals as important benchmarks [6] and drivers for irregular algorithms programming paradigms [26].

At the same time, the state-of-the-art in high performance computing is massive parallel processing, backed up by a large variety of parallel platforms ranging from graphical processing units (GPUs) to multi-core CPUs and Xeon Phi. Because traditional graph processing algorithms are known for their parallelism-unfriendly features - data-dependency, irregular processing, bad spatial and temporal locality [1] - a lot of work has focused on developing GPU-specific [17, 29, 5, 24], multi-core CPU-specific [2], or even vendor-specific [7, 27] algorithms. *None* of these algorithms is portable between different families of platforms. This platform lock-in is undesirable for users that want to make the best use of their resources for longer than a couple months - e.g., small and medium enterprises (SMEs). Moreover, as graph processing workloads increase in size, single-node platforms quickly become unfeasible, and multi-node solutions such as clusters and clouds must be used to tackle "big-data" graphs [35]. For productivity reasons, such platforms must rely on some degree of software stability. We argue in this work that code portability is one way towards this stability, and we show that the performance of such a scenario is, for the specific case of graph analytics, sufficient.

Programming models such as OpenCL[2] allow users to write functionally portable programs for massively parallel architectures with controlled performance losses (if any) compared to native solutions such as CUDA or OpenMP [15, 30]. In our study, we use OpenCL to implement three well-known graph analytics workloads - breadth-first search traversal (BFS), all-pairs shortest path computation (APSP), and betweenness centrality calculation (BC). We test the performance of these 3 algorithms on 3 platforms using 11 real-life and synthetic datasets, and we observe a large diversity in our results: no (platform, algorithm) pair wins for all datasets, and no (graph, platform) pair is superior for all algorithms. In other words, given a graph and an algorithm, one needs to empirically determine which platform is the best performing one. Having port-

---

[1] http://www.graph500.org
[2] https://www.khronos.org/opencl/

able code enables this choice on any graph and any platform, and it is agnostic to platform heterogeneity in multi-node systems.

The contribution of this work is three-fold:

1. We present three parallel graph analytics workloads implemented in OpenCL (Section 3) and prove their functional portability.

2. We provide empirical evidence that performance depends significantly on *three factors*: datasets, algorithms and data structures, and platforms (Section 4).

3. We show empirical evidence that portability can improve performance (Section 4) and discuss the operational impacts, for real-life users, of the trade-off between performance and portability.

2. BACKGROUND

In this section, we present the two families of hardware used for this study and OpenCL, our programming model of choice.

2.1 The architectures: CPUs vs. GPUs

In 2007, the bundle of parallelism and multiple cores has been proposed as *the* solution to increase performance. Since then, a large variety of architectures - including Cell/B.E., the GPGPU many-cores, multi-core and many-core CPUs, and the Fusion architectures - have been proposed, discussed, benchmarked, upgraded, and/or dismissed. Currently, the HPC community focuses mostly on multi-core CPUs and many-core accelerators (GPUs).

Multi-core CPUs are architectures that combine a few homogeneous cores (curently, 6 to 8, but slowly increasing over the years), additionally augmented with hardware multi-threading. These cores are complex architectures, much like the traditional CPUs. The memory system uses relatively deep cache hierarchies (2-3 levels), with both per-core and shared caches, as well as shared global memory. In terms of parallelism, multi-cores have little restrictions, allowing both symmetric and asymmetric multi-threading applications. Fine-grain parallelism is exploited by vector units. Finally, multi-cores are stand-alone systems, and the mapping of threads to cores is typically delegated to an operating system and/or a runtime system.

By contrast, Graphics Processing Units (GPUs) have hundreds to thousands simple processing elements (called "threads" by NVIDIA and "processing units" (PUs) by OpenCL), which can be further grouped in core-like entities (called "streaming multi-processors" by NVIDIA and "compute units" by OpenCL). The memory model is based on a large shared global memory, augmented with private and distributed local memories. Using a relaxed memory model, GPUs require the users to address memory consistency issues. In terms of parallelism, GPUs focus on massively data-parallel applications. Thus, programmers write the operations one thread needs to perform, and launch a sufficient (typically large) number of threads. Thread mapping and scheduling are done very efficiently by the hardware. GPUs are typically used as accelerators, to process compute-intensive tasks offloaded to them by a "host" device.

To summarize, GPUs are aiming at speeding-up massively data parallel applications, while multi-core CPUs are typically a better option for more complex parallel processing patterns (e.g., asymmetric multithreading or pipelining). As graph processing seems to be neither of the two [1], we use both CPUs and GPUs in our evaluation, in the (indirect) search of a clear winner in terms of performance.

2.2 The programming model: OpenCL

Proposed in 2008 (by the KHRONOS group), OpenCL aims to tackle the platform diversity problem by offering a common hardware model for all multi- and many-core platforms. The user programs this "virtual" platform, and the resulting source code is portable on any OpenCL compliant platform[3].

An OpenCL program has two types of code: the kernel(s), which are the basic unit of computation to be executed on one or more OpenCL devices, and the host program, which is executed on the host. A host program defines the context for the kernels and manages their execution. Note that the device and the host - and consequently the kernel and the host program - have separate memory spaces: any communication between them needs to be explicit.

A compute kernel can be thought of as similar to a C function which specifies the computation that each thread (i.e., *work-item* in OpenCL terminology) needs to perform. The threads can be grouped in *work-groups*, which allow for synchronization and shared memory. On the host side, the programmer needs to write the host code, which, besides application-specific initialization, needs to setup the OpenCL context, choose a running configuration for the kernel (i.e., the number of work-items and the size of the work-groups), copy data to the device (if needed), launch the kernels, and copy the results of the kernel.

The strongest point of OpenCL is its functional portability, a result of using a *common platform model* as a virtual middleware. This separates the design and implementation concerns: *programmers* are only concerned with designing a parallel application for the given platform model, while it is the responsibility of the *hardware vendors* to provide good OpenCL drivers to map the platform to real hardware. Portability is the main reason for which we chose OpenCL for our work: we want to avoid comparing different algorithms and/or implementations for CPUs and GPUs.

3. APPLICATIONS

We study three common graph processing algorithms: breadth first search (BFS), all-pairs shortest paths computation (APSP), and betweenness centrality computation (BC). When implementing these algorithms, we opted for a controlled parallelism increase: each algorithm attempts to add extra parallelism on top of the previous one. Thus, APSP uses BFS, and BC uses both APSP and BFS. While this is not the best implementation in terms of performance, it is definitely a valid one (i.e., it leads to correct results), and allows us to better isolate the impact of algorithm parallelism in the overall performance. We will address the performance concerns in more detail in Section 4.

We further note that the graph representation we have chosen is edge-based - i.e., the graph is represented as a list of edges (similar to the representation found in SNAP[4]. Moreover, our implementation does not attempt to reconstruct the graph, nor to transform it to a different representation (such as adjacency lists or adjacency matrix). Instead, we use the edge-based representation directly in our parallel BFS, which propagates further into APSP and BC.

3.1 Breadth First Search (BFS)

A BFS traversal explores a graph level by level. Given a graph $G = (V, E)$, with V its collection of vertices and E its collection of edges, and a source vertex s (considered as the only vertex on

---

[3]Currently (December 2014), these devices have hardware drivers and compiler back-ends: AMD, NVIDIA, and ARM GPUs, AMD's multi-core CPUs and APUs, Intel's CPUs and Intel's Xeon Phi, the Cell/B.E, and Altera's FPGAs

[4]http://snap.stanford.edu/snap/

level 0), BFS systematically explores edges outgoing from vertices at level i and places all their destination vertices on level $i + 1$, *if* these vertices have not been already discovered at prior levels (i.e., the algorithm has to distinguish *discovered* and *undiscovered* vertices to prevent infinite loops).

In a BFS that accepts an edge list as input, an iteration over the entire set of edges is required for each iteration. By a simple check on the source vertex of an edge, the algorithm can determine which edges to traverse, hence which destination vertices to place in the next level of the resulting tree.

Our parallel BFS works by dividing the edge list into sub-lists, which are processed in parallel (see the kernel listed in Algorithm 3): each thread will traverse its own sub-list in every iteration. Synchronization between levels is mandatory to insure a full exploration of the current level before starting the next one.

When mapping this parallel kernel to OpenCL, each thread is mapped to an work-item. As global synchronization is necessary, we implement a two-layer barrier structure: first at work-group level (provided by OpenCL), then between work-groups (implemented in-house). This solution limits the synchronization penalty - see [25], Chapter 3 for more details, or check Algorithms 1 and 3 in the Appendix.

3.2 All Pairs Shortest Paths (APSP)

The problem of finding the minimal distance between all pairs of nodes in a graph is called All-Pair Shortest Paths (APSP). The APSP algorithm gets a graph $G = (V, E)$ and computes, for each pair of vertices $(u, v) \in V$, the shortest path from u to v. The length of a path is the sum of its constituent edges.

There are multiple algorithms for computing APSP. For example, Johnson's algorithm [16] uses the Bellman-Form algorithm [3, 10] to remove negative edges and then applies Dijkstra's algorithm [23, 32] for finding the shortest paths. Another approach is based on dynamic programming, as shown by the Floyd-Warshall algorithm [9]. This algorithm gradually builds the full paths by choosing a next best step in each iteration.

In this work, we see APSP as a collection of $N = |V|$ shortest path problems, where N is the number of vertices in the graph. By systematically performing a BFS traversal (see Algorithm 2 in the Appendix) for each shortest path problem (using different source vertices), we solve the full query. Note that all the BFS traversals are kept independent (i.e., we do not implement any optimizations) in order to increase the parallelism level of the APSP algorithm as compared with the BFS one.

To parallelize APSP, one could adopt three strategies: (1) execute each BFS in parallel, and loop over all N vertices sequentially, (2) execute each BFS sequentially (i.e., in a single thread), and run all N instances of BFS concurrently, or (3) a mixed approach, where each BFS is parallelized itself, and more BFS instances are executed in parallel. We choose option (3), as it maps best to the two-layer parallelism of OpenCL: each BFS is parallelized per work-group, and concurrent work-groups run multiple BFS's in parallel. To achieve the full APSP, each workgroup has to sequentially iterate over an own sub-list of BFS sources (for more details, please check Algorithm 4 in the Appendix).

Note that this design choice also reduces the complexity of our BFS synchronization, replaced now by the built-in work-group synchronization. However, statically assigning groups of vertices to work-groups can lead to high imbalance between work-groups, potentially leading to low platform utilization. Improving this point is mandatory for a better performing BFS, but less important for our parallelism analysis (a complete analysis of all these options is presented in [25], Chapter 4).

3.3 Betweenness Centrality (BC)

Centrality analysis provides detailed information about the impact of individual vertices in a graph structure, by measuring the "influence" a vertex has on the connectivity of the graph.

A widely used BC algorithm, by Freeman [11], searches all the shortest paths between any two vertices and assigns a degree of betweenness (between 0 and 1) to the intermediate vertices. An intermediate vertex has a degree of 1 if and only if all the shortest paths between two other vertices pass through it, and 0 if no shortest path passes through it. The BC index of a vertex v is the sum of degrees of betweenness for all pairs of vertices (see equation 1) whose shortest connection passes through v. Here, σ_{st} denotes the total number of shortest paths between s and t, and $\sigma_{st}(v)$ the count of shortest paths that pass through v.

$$BC(v) = \sum_{s \neq t \neq v \in V} \frac{\sigma_{st}(v)}{\sigma_{st}} \qquad (1)$$

To calculate the BC of a graph, we compute the number of shortest paths between pairs of vertices, remember the vertices on each of these paths, and determine the ratio of shortest paths passing through each vertex in the graph. This procedure is repeated for all pairs of vertices in the graph, with $(s, t) = (t, s)$, and the pair-dependencies are accumulated per vertex.

When implementing this algorithm, we distinguish three steps: (i) a traversal to get the total number of shortest paths for a pair of vertices, (ii) computing all ratios of (shortest) paths passing each vertex for a pair of vertices, and (iii) adding the derived pair-dependencies (i.e., the ratios of shortest paths) for each vertex to its BC value. This sequence of steps is repeated for computing pair-dependencies of all vertices for the different pairs of vertices, allowing us to use the same strategy as for APSP: we iterate (partially in parallel) over steps (i), (ii) and (iii) for each vertex.

A BFS is used for step (i), to derive the total number of shortest paths for a pair of vertices. Based on a technique presented in [4], we also use a reverse BFS traversal (i.e., a *bottom-up BFS*) to accumulate the ratios of the counts for the intermediate vertices in step (ii). At each step of the bottom-up BFS, the score $\delta_{s\bullet}(v)$ of vertex v is computed as the accumulated score of all individual children of v, as seen in Equation 2. Finally, we retrieve the pair-dependency values assigned to the vertices in the previous step and add them all to compute the final BC value of each vertex (step (iii)). For more details, on this implementation, please refer to [25], Chapter 5.

$$\delta_{s\bullet}(v) = \sum_{c : v \in Parent(c)} \frac{\sigma_{sv}}{\sigma_{sc}} \cdot (\delta_{s\bullet} + 1) \qquad (2)$$

To summarize, our implementation uses one APSP that includes $2 \cdot N$ BFS traversals, allowing us to build upon the existing implementations of these kernels (for implementation details, Algorithm 5 is available in the Appendix).

4. EXPERIMENTAL RESULTS

In this section we describe our experiments and discuss their results, focusing on qualifying the impact of algorithms, datasets, and architectures on performance.

4.1 Experimental Setup

Due to the portability of OpenCL, we are able to use the same implementations of BFS, APSP, and BC for two different families of architectures: multi-core CPUs and GPUs. The platforms we have used for our experiments are presented in Table 1. For all our CPU experiments, we have used Intels's OpenCL SDK, version

Table 1: The hardware platforms used for the experiments.

Name	Memory	Bandwidth	PUs
CPU: Intel Xeon E5620	24 GB	25.6 GB/s	8×2
GPU: Tesla C2050	3 GB	144 GB/s	14×32
GPU: GeForce GTX480	1.5 GB	177.4 GB/s	15×32

"PUs" stands for processing units (CPU hardware threads or GPU threads). It is computed as the number of "cores" (CPU cores or GPU multiprocessors) $\times$ the number of threads per core.

2.0. For the GPU experiments, we have the OpenCL implemntation from NVIDIA CUDA 5.0.

The results presented in this work focus on the performance of the kernels of each of these algorithms. We note that the overhead due to the data transfer between the host (CPU) and the device (GPU) is not included. This overhead is only significant for BFS (due to its low-processing nature). Indeed, for BFS, when including the data transfer overhead, more datasets show better overall peformance for the CPU instead of the GPU (namely, 1M, ES, 64K, WV, and 4K). However, taking this overhead into account does not change *the variability* of the results which, as seen below, is the most important observation in all our experiments. Moreover, we believe that in realistic scenarios, BFS, APSP, and BC are not computed in isolation, but rather used in more complex pipelines and/or iterative applications. In these cases, the one-time overhead of data copying can be ignored.

4.2 Datasets

As datasets, we chose eleven graphs covering a large spectrum of variants in terms of numbers vertices and edges, diameters, and in/out edge ratios. Our datasets are of three types: (i) synthetic graphs, i.e. randomly generated graphs with predetermined properties, (ii) real world graphs, i.e. subsets of existing networks like road networks, social media networks, and email exchange networks, and (iii) pathological graphs, i.e. artificial graphs reflecting the expected worst and best case performance of the BFS, namely a chain of vertices and a star. The three synthetic datasets we use are from the Rodinia benchmark [6], and the remaining six real world datasets are from the SNAP repository [20]. The properties of all our 11 datasets are presented in Table 2.

4.3 BFS results

We execute our OpenCL implementation on the three different hardware platforms and measure its execution time for all the 11 datasets and present our results in Figure 1[5]. Note that the results are normalized to the slowest platform.

We point out that he slowest and the fastest platforms are not always the same, showing high variability with the dataset and the platform. We further make the following observations. First, the performance difference between the CPU and the GPUs is similar: either the CPU outperforms both GPUs, or the other way around. Furthermore, GTX always shows a higher performance than Tesla, which is due to the larger bandwidth of the former, an important advantage for memory-bound kernels such as BFS. For large graphs, the performance gap can be as large as 20%, indicating that Second, different graphs show very different preferences for platforms. For example, for WT, the GPUs significantly outperforms the CPU. CR and SW, on the other hand, perform best on the CPU. Three, and last, the sizes of the graphs do not show any immediate correlation

---

[5]A full overview of all the results is beyond the scope of this paper - therefore, more details can be seen in [25], Chapter 3

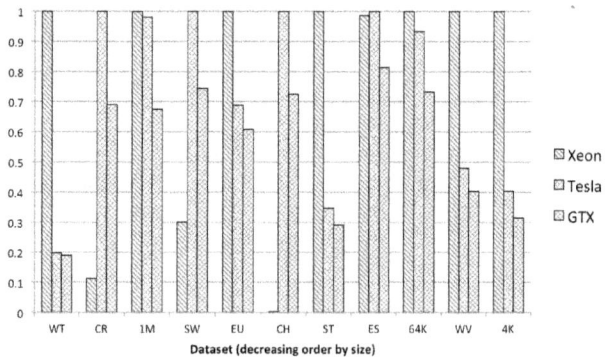

Figure 1: Parallel BFS performance for the Xeon CPU, the Tesla GPU, and the GTX GPU. The execution time is normalized compared with the slowest platform, which shows a relative performance of 1.

with the execution time. For example, the execution time difference between WT and CR is an order of magnitude, despite a mere 20% difference in size. This gap is probably explained by the BFS traversing the node with the maximum numbers of connections (over 100,000 - see Table 2).

Overall, BFS is very sensitive to low parallelism in the input dataset: graphs with low connectivity between nodes are not be able to fully exploit parallel platforms, and their performance is not significantly improved when compared with reference sequential implementations. This behavior is illustrated best by the Chain and Star graphs, which show extreme low and high performance, respectively.

To verify whether we introduced this chaotic behavior through our edge-based implementation, we compare the performance of our edge-based BFS with that of a vertex-based BFS, also implemented in OpenCL, and included in the Rodinia benchmark suite [6]. The results, presented in Figure 2, show large performance discrepancies between the two implementations, with no clear winner. This in turn means that not only is performance significantly dependent on the structure of the dataset, but it is also very sensitive to implementation choices such as graph representation.

In summary, BFS and its parallelism are dominated by the amount of parallelism available in the dataset. Furthermore, being a memory-bound application, using platforms with higher bandwidth can bring additional performance. Finally, using a platform that exceeds the parallelism of the graph (i.e., its average or max connectivity) will lead to severe platform underutilization and, consequently, the gap between the achieved and expected performance will increase.

4.4 APSP results

Figure 3 shows the performance results for our APSP implementation in OpenCL.

We make the following observations. First, the GPUs clearly outperform the CPU for all datasets. The achieved speedups are between 1.4 and 11.4 for GTX, and between 1.2 and 6.8 for Tesla. This gain is a direct consequence of the increased parallelism of our APSP algorithm, which matches the massively-parallel GPUs much better than the CPU. Second, we note that the two GPUs perform similarly, with an advantage for the GTX. This is not surprising, given that our APSP is, in fact, a massively concurrent execution of the BFS, which also shows better performance for the GTX card.

In summary, these results reflect the fact that our choice for im-

Table 2: The datasets used in our experiments. *D*, *AVG* and *MAX* represent the diamter, the average and maximum number of vertex connections, respectively.

Graph name	Vertices	Edges	D	AVG	MAX	Source
Wikipedia Talk Network (WT)	2,394,385	5,021,410	9	4.19	100,032	SNAP
California Road Network (CR)	1,965,206	5,533,214	850	5.63	24	SNAP
Random 1M (1M)	1,000,000	5,999,970	11	12.00	36	Rodinia
Stanford Web Graph (SW)	281,903	2,312,497	740	16.41	38,626	SNAP
EU Email Communication (EU)	265,214	420,045	13	3.17	7,636	SNAP
Chain 100K (CH)	100,000	99,999	99,999	2.00	2	synthetic
Star 100K (ST)	100,000	99,999	2	2.00	99,999	synthetic
Epinions Social Network (ES)	75,879	508,837	13	13.41	3,079	SNAP
Random 64K (64K)	65,536	393,216	9	12.00	48	Rodinia
Wikipedia Vote Network (WV)	7,115	103,689	7	29.15	1,167	SNAP
Random 4K (4K)	4,096	24,576	7	12.00	38	Rodinia

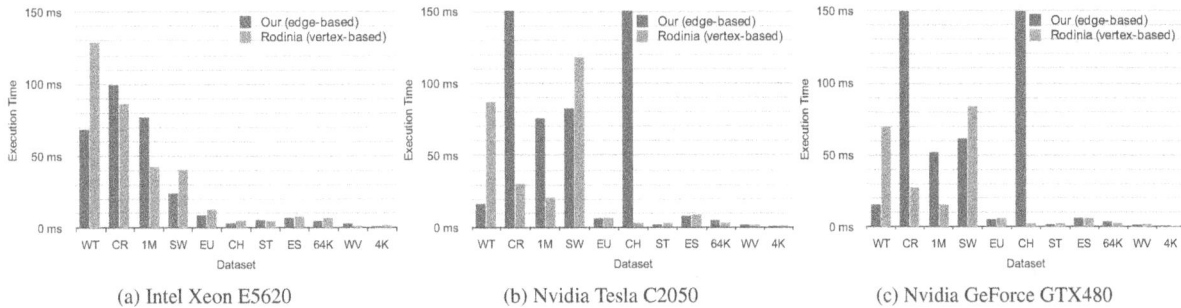

(a) Intel Xeon E5620   (b) Nvidia Tesla C2050   (c) Nvidia GeForce GTX480

Figure 2: Comparison of the performance of BFS, for an edge-based versus a vertex-based graph representation: our implementation, and the OpenCL implementation from Rodinia, respectively.

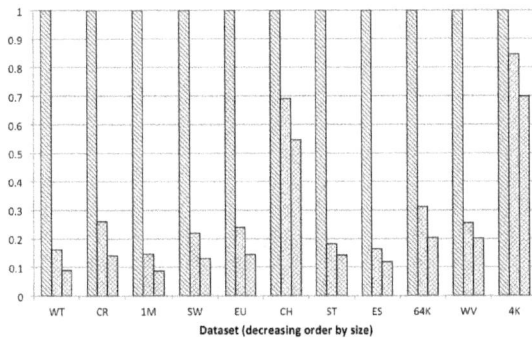

Figure 3: Parallel APSP performance for the Xeon CPU, the Tesla GPU, and the GTX GPU.The results are normalized to the slowest platform, which shows a relative performance of 1.

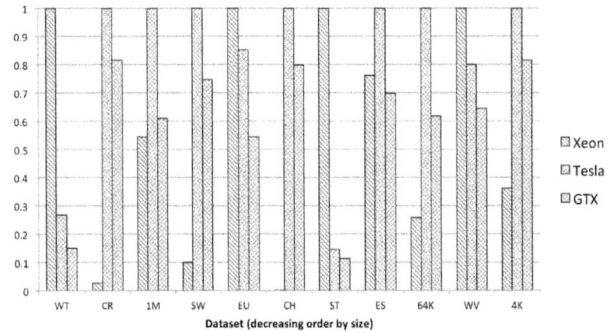

Figure 4: Parallel BC performance for the Xeon CPU, the Tesla GPU, and the GTX GPU. The results are normalized to the slowest platform, which shows a relative performance of 1.

plementing APSP exposes a lot more parallelism than BFS, This increase is directly visible in the kernel performance: the GPUs outperform the CPUs in all cases. For this APSP implementation, "more parallel" architectures handle larger graphs better, as the performance of the kernel is dominated by the number of iterations needed to calculate the whole APSP.

4.5 BC results

The performance comparison for computing betweenness centrality on our three platforms is presented in Figure 4.

As the core algorithm of our betweenness centrality is the APSP calculation, we expected the GPUs to outperform the CPU. Instead,

we see again different platforms performing best for different workloads.

To clarify this apparent contradiction, we recall that our BC implementation first does a BFS from a vertex v, determining the depth of every other vertex. Then it performs a bottom-up traversal from every vertex back to the root v, annotating every vertex with path information. This bottom-up traversal takes the same number of iterations as the initial BFS. After this the algorithm iterates over every vertex, updating their betweenness score. Like APSP, this process is done for every vertex. This is why we expected, naïvely, to see a graph similar to that of APSP, given that BC effectively does twice the number of traversals of APSP plus another $|V|$ traversals of all vertices. However, the results shown in Figure 4 do not confirm this expectation. This behavior comes from the fact that, unlike APSP, BC has to update the state of a vertex multiple times during the traversals. These updates are done using atomic operations to avoid race conditions. Doing many parallel traversals can result in high contention at these atomic operations, reducing the performance. Because the atomic operations are much more expensive on GPUs than on CPUs, the performance penalty is much more significant, relative to the rest of the computation, for the GTX and Tesla.

To verify this intuition we replaced the atomic operations with non-atomic ones - this produces incorrect results, but eliminates the contention. Indeed, when we ran the algorithm on our datasets graph, we saw a significant reduction in runtime for the GPU platforms, confirming that the contention due to atomic operations is having a significant impact on the performance of BC on the GPUs.

4.6 Performance per platform

We revisit our experimental results, and present them clustered per platform. Thus, Figure 5 presents the results for the Xeon CPU and the GTX GPU. Presented this way, our results demonstrate the impact of incremental complexity on the two different families of platforms[6].

We make the following observations. First, for the CPU, the increase in complexity leads to an increase in execution time. Not surprisingly, the APSP takes a lot longer than the BFS, given the scale of the graphs and the limited number of available cores (16). Futhermore, BC takes twice longer than APSP, due to the double reuse of APSP inside the BC algorithm. Note that the differences in performance are not the same between data sets, since they differ in sizes and structure.

Second, for Nvidia GeForce GTX480, the performance differences between the three algorithms vary a lot. For example, for the *CR* data set, the fraction of the increase in the execution time between BFS and APSP is similar to that between APSP and BC. However, for the *WT* data set, the difference between BFS and APSP is much larger than that between APSP and BC. These results show that the GPUs (again, we see the same behavior for NVIDIA Tesla) are much more sensitive to the structure of the data set. We note that the GPU performance gap between the APSP and BC is in general very large. We believe this is an effect of the data dependencies for BC calculations: the ratios of each of the shortest paths needs to be derived and accumulated for all vertices (i.e., each ratio depend on the ratios of the neighboring vertices).

Third, we note the different behaviors between the CPUs and GPUs: the differences in dataset size and structure affect the platforms *in different ways*. We see this as additional proof for considering a graph processing workload as an (algorithm, dataset) pair, and potentially choose a matching target using the characteristics of the pair, and not of the algorithm in isolation.

4.7 Performance in Meps

A "traditional" measure for high-performance graph processing is *edges per second (eps)* - i.e., how many edges are traversed by the graph processing application in one unit of time (1s). *eps* offers a normalized view of performance, as it implicitly takes into account the size (through normalization) and the structure of the graph (which impacts the execution time)[7].

An accurate measurement of the number of edges traversed in total would require the addition of several counters inside the al-

gorithms, which might in turn change the algorithm behavior. Therefore, we choose to estimate the EPS for each of the algorithms by using the theoretical number of edges they would traverse (i.e., based on the algorithm itself).

For BFS, multiply the diameter D of the graph (which approximates the number of iterations) with the number of edges $M = |E|$ (which approximates the number of edges visited in each iteration - i.e., all of them) and divide by the execution time of the BFS (T_{BFS}):

$$EPS_{BFS} = \frac{D \cdot M}{T_{BFS}} \qquad (3)$$

For APSP, we use multiple BFS searches, hence we can use a similar approach for computing the EPS: we multiply the diameter of the graph (D) with the number of edges (M) and with the number of shortest path searches ($N = |V|$). This number of edges traversed is then divided by the execution time of the APSP (T_{APSP}):

$$EPS_{APSP} = \frac{D \cdot M \cdot N}{T_{APSP}} \qquad (4)$$

For BC, the metric is more difficult to calculate (i.e. it uses an APSP and additional computations to derive the centrality values). In section 4.5, we see that the computations for the centrality values require backtracking of the shortest paths, making it similar to traversing the search tree, in terms of traversal steps. Hence, for simplicity, we can reduce this to an APSP to find the shortest paths in the graph and an APSP to backtrack these shortest path in deriving the centrality values. This simplification allows us to derive a formula for the eps of BC: we multiply the diameter of the graph (D) with the number of edges (M) and with the number of shortest path searches (N), this is divided by the execution time of the BC (T_{BC}). This value is then multiplied by two, resulting in:

$$EPS_{BC} = 2 \cdot \frac{D \cdot M \cdot N}{T_{BC}} \qquad (5)$$

Figure 6 presents the performance of BFS, APSP, and BC in *Meps*.

We make the following observations: First, APSP shows the best *eps*, regardless of the platform or data set. This is because the algorithm we have chosen for APSP is a massively parallel one, and, in combination with the edge-based representation of the graph, it is suitable for the chosen parallel platforms. Second, for BC, the number of edges traversed/processed per second is lower, due to the additional complexity of the computation performed to determine the BC coefficients.

Third, we note again the different behavior of the two hardware platforms. For the GPUs, a large performance gap is visible between APSP and the rest, caused by the large potential of parallelism of our algorithm. For the CPU, the gap is smaller due to coarser level of parallelism in the system. The only graph that breaks the pattern is *ST*, which seems to favor fine-grained parallelism also for the BC algorithm.

Overall, although *eps* provides normalized performance against the graph size, it remains insufficient for quantifying/qualifying the impact of the dataset structure on the overall performance of the algorithm. In other words, *eps* can be used to compare different implementations of the same algorithm, but provides too little insight into matching workloads to platforms.

---

[6]We only show the CPU and GTX 480 behavior due to because the Tesla performance trends are very similar to those of the GTX.

[7]This is also the metric used in Graph500.

(a) NVIDIA GTX480

(b) Intel Xeon E5620

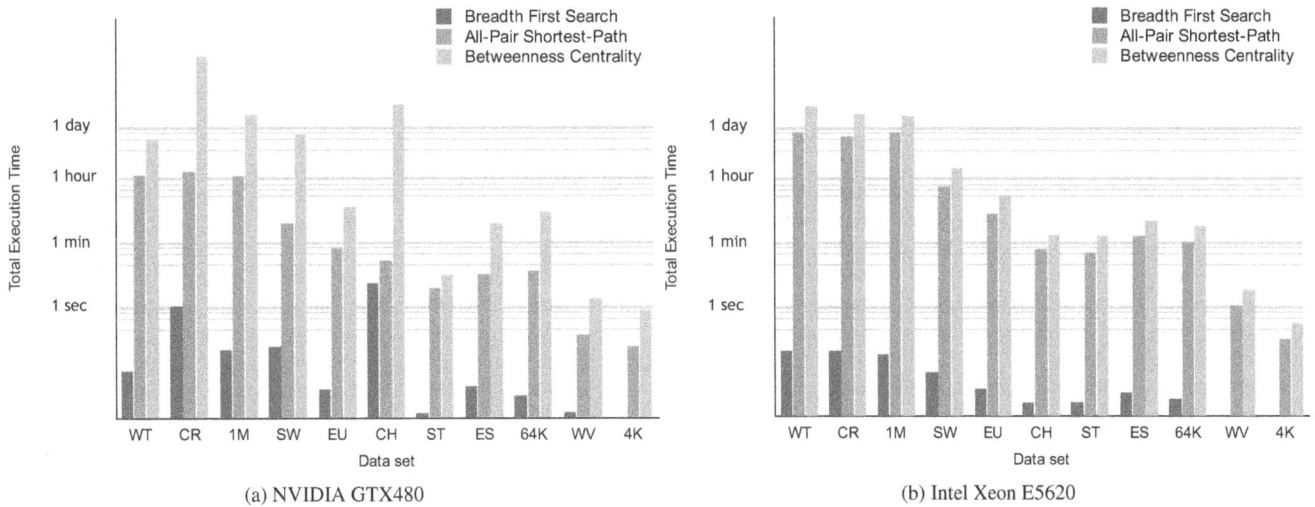

Figure 5: The performance of our BFS, APSP, and BC (logarithmic scale) for the GTX and Xeon platforms.

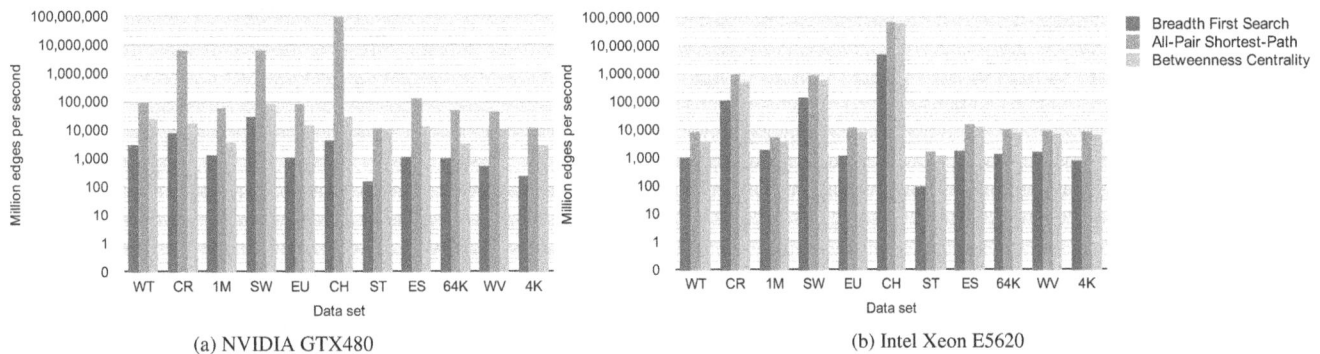

(a) NVIDIA GTX480

(b) Intel Xeon E5620

Figure 6: Million edges per second for the BFS, APSP, and BC algorithms, grouped per dataset.(logarithmic scale).

5. RELATED WORK

We discuss in this section two different related work fields: modern studies of parallel graph processing, targeted at multi- and many-core architectures, and studies on performance portability.

Work on parallel graph processing stands out by its specific approaches: improved parallel algorithms, tuning parallel algorithms to effectively use of modern parallel hardware, or building high-level programming solutions to hide parallelism from programmers.

For example, previous work improves the throughput of graph searches (based on BFS) on parallel systems by data partitioning and message compression [33]. The queuing of visited graphs vertices (also seen in BFS) have been replaced in [19] with *bags*, allowing splitting and merging of queued operations such that they can operate in parallel. For a centrality algorithm, recent work [21] replaces the SSSP algorithm, used to calculate the pair-dependencies for all pairs, with a BFS algorithm (as suggested in other work [4]), and gain additional performance. Finally, work presented in [7, 27] shows how exploiting the lowest-level specifics of hardware archiecture can lead to a high performance algorithm for graph processing, which will outperform most of the competition, yet it will not work efficiently on any other machine than the one it is designed for.

Using GPUs to accelerate graph processing has also been tried, by adapting traditional graph analysis to heterogeneous systems [8]. In [14, 31], the quantify the performance gain of GPU-enabled graph analysis against the sequential version. The GPU shows significant performance improvement for different algorithms, but dataset impact is not quantified. In [17, 29], graph algorithms are adapted for GPU execution by reordering operations and data accesses.

All these examples show that the research on modern architectures for graph analysis focuses on *specific algorithms*, and their improvement for a *specific environment*. In contrast to our work, none of these studies quantifies the impact of the datasets on the achieved performance, nor does it address the portability of the approaches to a new/different generation of parallel architectures. While the latter is, for many of them, out of the scope of their research, the former is mandatory for a better understanding of the observed performance.

An alternative approach to using CPUs and GPUs for graph processing has emerged in the form of dedicated programming systems. MEDUSA [37] and TOTEM [12] are two examples of systems take into account some of the properties of the datasets to schedule, at runtime, the computation of a graph analysis algorithm on the different components of a heterogeneous system. TOTEM is further improved in [13] with a systematic CPU-GPU partitioning algorithm that takes into account, at runtime, the characteristics of the dataset and the hardware. Ultimately, we share the goal of matching datasets with architectures, but this scheduling-driven approach in [13] does not pay enough attention to the algorithm; we believe an analytical model that mixes dataset, algorithm, and platform will be more useful in the context of portability.

The second dimension of our work is related to performance and portability (in the context of OpenCL), a controversial concept in the current landscape of parallel processing. Several empirical studies on performance portability [28, 18, 34] have shown, for different mixes of applications and platforms (all including GPUs and CPUs), that OpenCL provides a good basis for performance portability. We note, however, that (1) none of the used benchmarks were irregular applications, and (2) no dependence of the performance on the dataset has been studied. Similar approaches in [36, 30] have taken a more proactive approach, and showed how OpenCL applications can be improved in terms of performance portability. Again, no discussion on irregular algorithms or dataset performance dependency is included.

Another way to achieve portability is to build platform-agnostic algorithms. In [26], the authors introduced the notion of *amorphous data parallelism*, an attempt to parallelize highly irregular algorithms by exposing the fine-grained parallelism within the algorithm, which in turn can scale better with the available hardware parallelism. Several studies on using amorphous data parallelism on GPUs have looked at the performance of graph algorithms [5, 24]. However, these studies take the use of a GPU as a given, and do not compare the GPU performance against CPU performance. As our results demonstrate several cases when CPUs outperform GPUs, such a comparison is necessary to prove the portability and the high performance of these solutions.

This brief survey of related work demonstrates that performance portability and parallel graph processing have been, so far, disjoint. In this context, our work is the first to combine them in claiming that performance portability assessment for irregular applications must take all three variables - dataset, application, and platform - into account. We finally argue (claim indirectly supported by the work in [12, 13]) that portability allows for better usage of heterogeneous platforms, contributing to an overall increase in performance, especially in the context of large scale datasets.

6. CONCLUSION

Graph processing is one of the pillars of big data analysis, and it becomes a real challenge for high performance computing and its multi-layer massively parallel architectures of today (multi-core CPUs and GPUs). Many different parallel graph analytics algorithms have been proposed, all addressing the specific needs of one hardware platform or another, and achieving good performance for various datasets *on their target platform*. However, these solutions are rarely evaluated, in terms of performance gain/loss in comparison with different parallel platforms [22] and using a truly wide variety of graphs. Without such an evaluation, users' have little flexibility in their choices: platform comes first.

We argue that a landscape with so many different flavors of graph analytics algorithms and such incomplete evalution, is difficult to navigate by regular users that want to focus more on productivity and efficiency than on software development and platform updates. For such users, our work has showed that using relatively simple, portable graph algorithms, one can make use of most of their in-house resources without code changes. Due to the strong dependency of graph analytics (such as BFS, APSP, and BC) on the structure of the datasets, the performance loss *across different types of graphs is not significant* - i.e., depending on the algorithm and dataset, the right platform to be used can be a GPU, a CPU, or a combination of the two. By having the same implementation for both types of platforms (and many others, given the portability of OpenCL), users can easily maintain a single codebase, and perform a simple empirical check to find the right platform for a new dataset. In this sense, portability can offer a performance

boost by providing multiple platform options: for algorithms such as BFS and BC, over 40% of our tests show a CPU outperforming the GPUs. We acknowledge that this approach might not offer the best ever performance for a (platform,dataset,algorithm) at hand, but we argue none of the alternatives will. The only option for finding the absolute best remains a trial-and-error sweep to rank *all* the existing solutions, a prohibitively expensive, low-productivity approach given the tens of alternatives.

To summarize, our results have shown that graph analytics portability (using OpenCL) is feasible for CPUs and GPUs. Our portable algorithms provide additional performance opportunities by simply allowing alternative execution platforms to be used. We observed that such flexibility pays off: we gained significant performance in more than 40% of the cases we tested, by simply replacing a GPU with a CPU.

Our future work will focus on two directions: performance improvement and analytical modeling. On the short term, we aim to improve the performance of these portable implementations by generalizing the findings of the most promising platform-specific solutions (see Section 5). On the longer term, we aim to build models of impact of both platforms and datasets characteristics on the performance of the graph analytics workloads. Using such models, we aim to predict the best platform for a given (dataset,algorithm) pair for portable, platform-agnostic algorithms.

References

[1] A. LUMSDAINE, D. GREGOR, B. H., AND BERRY, J. W. Challenges in parallel graph processing. *Parallel Processing Letters 17* (2007).

[2] AGARWAL, V., PETRINI, F., PASETTO, D., AND BADER, D. A. Scalable graph exploration on multicore processors. In *SC* (2010), pp. 1–11.

[3] BELLMAN, R. On a routing problem. *Quarterly of Applied Mathematics, vol. 16* (1958), 87–90.

[4] BRANDES, U. A faster algorithm for betweenness centrality. *Journal of Mathematical Sociology 25* (2001), 163–177.

[5] BURTSCHER, M., NASRE, R., AND PINGALI, K. A quantitative study of irregular programs on gpus. In *Workload Characterization (IISWC), 2012 IEEE International Symposium on* (2012), IEEE, pp. 141–151.

[6] CHE, S., BOYER, M., MENG, J., TARJAN, D., SHEAFFER, J. W., LEE, S. H., AND SKADRON, K. Rodinia: A benchmark suite for heterogeneous computing. *The 2009 IEEE International Symposium on Workload Characterization, IISWC'09* (2009), 44–54.

[7] CHECCONI, F., AND PETRINI, F. Massive data analytics: The graph 500 on ibm blue gene/q. *IBM Journal of Research and Development 57*, 1/2 (2013), 10.

[8] DINNEEN, M. J., KHOSRAVANI, M., AND PROBERT, A. Using opencl for implementing simple parallel graph algorithms. *Conference on Parallel and Distributed Processing Techniques and Applications, PDPTA'11* (2011).

[9] FLOYD, R. W. Algorithm 97: Shortest path. *Communications of the ACM* (1962), 345.

[10] FORD, L. R., AND FULKERSON, D. R. Flows in networks. *Princeton University Press* (1962).

[11] FREEMAN, L. C. Centrality in social networks conceptual clarification. *Social Networks* (1978), 215.

[12] GHARAIBEH, A., COSTA, L. B., SANTOS-NETO, E., AND RIPEANU, M. A yoke of oxen and a thousand chickens for heavy lifting graph processing. *The 21st international conference on Parallel architectures and compilation techniques, PACT'12* (2012), 345–354.

[13] GHARAIBEH, A., COSTA, L. B., SANTOS-NETO, E., AND RIPEANU, M. On graphs, gpus, and blind dating: A workload to processor matchmaking quest. In *IPDPS* (2013), pp. 851–862.

[14] HARISH, P., AND NARAYANAN, P. J. Accelerating large graph algorithms on the gpu using cuda. *HiPC'07 Proceedings of the 14th international conference* (2007).

[15] J. FANG, A. L. V., AND SIPS, H. A comprehensive performance comparison of cuda and opencl. *The 40th International Conference on Parallel Processing, ICPP'11* (2011).

[16] JOHNSON, D. B. Efficient algorithms for shortest paths in sparse networks. *Journal of the ACM 24 issue 1* (1977).

[17] KATZ, G. J., AND JR, J. T. K. All-pairs shortest-paths for large graphs on the gpu. *23rd ACM SIGGRAPH/EUROGRAPHICS symposium on Graphics hardware* (2008), 47–55.

[18] KOMATSU, K., SATO, K., ARAI, Y., KOYAMA, K., TAKIZAWA, H., AND KOBAYASHI, H. Evaluating performance and portability of opencl programs. In *The Fifth International Workshop on Automatic Performance Tuning* (June 2010).

[19] LEISERSON, C. E., AND SCHARDL, T. B. A work-efficient parallel breadth-first search algorithm (or how to cope with the nondeterminism of reducers). *Computer Vision and Pattern Recognition, CVPR'10* (2010), 2181–2188.

[20] LESKOVEC, J. Stanford network analysis platform (snap). *Stanford University* (2006).

[21] MADDURI, K., EDIGER, D., JIANG, K., BADER, D. A., AND CHAVARRIA-MIRANDA, D. A faster parallel algorithm and efficient multithreaded implementations for evaluating betweenness centrality on massive datasets. *The 2009 IEEE International Symposium on Parallel and Distributed Processing, IPDPS'09* (2009), 1–8.

[22] MERIJN VERSTRAATEN, ANA LUCIA VARBANESCU, C. D. L. State-of-the-art in graph traversals on modern arhictectures. Tech. rep., University of Amsterdam, August 2014.

[23] N. EDMONDS, A. BREUER, D. G., AND LUMSDAINE, A. Single-source shortest paths with the parallel boost graph library. *The Ninth Implementation Challenge: The Shortest Path Problem* (2006).

[24] NASRE, R., BURTSCHER, M., AND PINGALI, K. Data-driven versus topology-driven irregular computations on gpus. In *Parallel & Distributed Processing (IPDPS), 2013 IEEE 27th International Symposium on* (2013), IEEE, pp. 463–474.

[25] PENDERS, A. Accelerating Graph Analysis with Heterogeneous Systems. Master's thesis, PDS, EWI, TUDelft, December 2012.

[26] PINGALI, K., NGUYEN, D., KULKARNI, M., BURTSCHER, M., HASSAAN, M. A., KALEEM, R., LEE, T.-H., LENHARTH, A., MANEVICH, R., MÉNDEZ-LOJO, M., ET AL. The tao of parallelism in algorithms. *ACM SIGPLAN Notices 46*, 6 (2011), 12–25.

[27] QUE, X., CHECCONI, F., AND PETRINI, F. Performance analysis of graph algorithms on p7ih. In *ISC* (2014), pp. 109–123.

[28] RUL, S., VANDIERENDONCK, H., D'HAENE, J., AND DE BOSSCHERE, K. An experimental study on performance portability of opencl kernels. In *Application Accelerators in High Performance Computing, 2010 Symposium, Papers* (2010), p. 3.

[29] S. HONG, S. K. KIM, T. O., AND OLUKOTUN, K. Accelerating cuda graph algorithms at maximum warp. *Principles and Practice of Parallel Programming, PPoPP'11* (2011).

[30] SHEN, J., FANG, J., SIPS, H., AND VARBANESCU, A. Performance gaps between openmp and opencl for multi-core cpus. In *Parallel Processing Workshops (ICPPW), 2012 41st International Conference on* (Sept 2012), pp. 116–125.

[31] SRIRAM, A., AND GAUTHAM, K. Evaluating centrality metrics in real-world networks on gpu. *High Performance Computing, HiPC'09 Student Research Symposium 2009* (2009).

[32] U. MEYER, V. O. Design and implementation of a practical i/o-efficient shortest paths algorithm. *10th Workshop on Algorithm Engineering and Experiments, ALENEX'09* (2009), 85–96.

[33] UENO, K., AND SUZUMURA, T. Highly scalable graph search for the graph500 benchmark. *The 21st international symposium on High-Performance Parallel and Distributed Computing, HPDC'12* (2012), 149–160.

[34] VAN DER SANDEN, J. Evaluating the performance and portability of opencl. Master's thesis, TU Eindhoven, 2011.

[35] VARBANESCU, A. L., AND IOSUP, A. On many-task big data processing: From GPUs to clouds.

[36] YAO ZHANG, M. S. I., AND CHIEN, A. A. Improving performance portability in opencl programs. In *International Supercomputing Conference 2013* (2013).

[37] ZHONG, J., AND HE, B. Medusa: Simplified graph processing on gpus. *17th ACM SIGPLAN symposium on Principles and Practice of Parallel Programming, PPoPP'12* (2012), 283–284.

APPENDIX

A. THE BFS, APSP, AND BC ALGORITHMS

In this section we include all the pseudocode samples that illustrate our sequential and parallel (i.e., OpenCL) implementations of BFS, APSP, and BC.

Our sequential BFS is presented in Algorithm 1.

Algorithm 1 Edge-based BFS implementation for graph $G = (V, E)$, using start vertex s; $N = |V|$ is the number of vertices and $M = |E|$ is the number of edges.

1: **function** ENDGEBASED_BFS(E, s)
2:     $Q \leftarrow \emptyset$
3:     **for** $e \in E$ **do**
4:       $e \leftarrow UNVISITED$
5:     **end for**
6:     $add(Q, s)$
7:     $changed \leftarrow 1$
8:     **while** $changed = 1$ **do**
9:       $changed \leftarrow 0$
10:      **for** $e \in E, e = UNVISITED$ **do**
11:        **if** $Source(e) \in Q$ **then**
12:          $add(Q, Dest(e))$
13:          $e \leftarrow VISITED$
14:          $depth[Dest(e)] \leftarrow depth[Source(e)] + 1$
15:          $changed \leftarrow 1$
16:        **end if**
17:      **end for**
18:     **end while**
19: **end function**

Our sequential APSP is presented in Algorithm 2.

Algorithm 2 A BFS-based APSP implementation. R is the result as a collection of distances between pairs of vertices.

1: **function** APSP_USING_BFS(V)
2:     $R \leftarrow \emptyset$
3:     **for** $v \in V$ **do**
4:       $BFS(V, v)$
5:       **for** $u \in V$ **do**
6:         **if** $v \neq u$ **then**
7:           $Add(R, Distance(v, u))$
8:         **end if**
9:       **end for**
10:     **end for**
11: **end function**

Our parallel BFS is presented in Algorithm 3.
Our parallel APSP is presented in Algorithm 4.
Our parallel BC algorithm is presented in Algorithm 5.

Algorithm 3 Parallel BFS implementation in OpenCL, for graph $G = (V, E)$ and start vertex s; $E_{thread} \subseteq E$ is the edge list assigned to this thread (PU); operations preceded by *atomic* are executed atomically; *barrier*() is a global barrier.

1: **function** KERNEL_BFS(E, s)
2:     $Q_i \leftarrow \{s\}$
3:     $hasNextLevel \leftarrow 1$
4:     $i \leftarrow 0$ ▷ Set Current Level
5:     **while** $hasNextLevel = 1$ **do**
6:       **for** $e \in E_{thread}, e = UNVISITED$ **do**
7:         **if** $Source(e) \in Q_i$ **then**
8:           ▷ Attempt to lock.
9:           **while** ($atomic(CAS(Dest(e), 0, 1))$)
10:          ▷ Lock succeeded.
11:           $add(Q_{i+1}, Dest(e))$
12:           $e \leftarrow VISITED$
13:           $depth[Dest(e)] \leftarrow depth[Source(e)] + 1$
14:          ▷ Unlock.
15:           $atomic(Dest(e) \leftarrow 0)$
16:           $atomic(hasNextLevel \leftarrow 1)$
17:         **end if**
18:       **end for**
19:       $i \leftarrow i + 1$ ▷ Increase Level
20:       $barrier()$ ▷ Level Synchronization
21:     **end while**
22: **end function**

Algorithm 4 Our parallel APSP implementation in OpenCL, for graph $G = (V, E)$, with R being the result distance matrix, $V_g group \subseteq V$ being the sources list assigned to this work-group, and $E_{thread} \subseteq E$ being the edge list assigned to this work-item.

1: **function** KERNEL_APSP(E, V)
2:     **for** $s \in V_g group$ **do**
3:       $Q_i \leftarrow \{s\}$
4:       $hasNextLevel \leftarrow 1$
5:       $i \leftarrow 0$ ▷ Set Current Level
6:       **while** $hasNextLevel = 1$ **do**   ▷ Begin BFS
7:         **for** $e \in E_{thread}$ **do**
8:           **if** $e = UNVISITED$ & $Source(e) \in Q_i$ **then**
9:             $add(Q_{i+1}, Dest(e))$
10:            $e \leftarrow VISITED$
11:            $R[s][Dest(e)] \leftarrow depth[Source(e)] + 1$
12:            $atomic(hasNextLevel \leftarrow 1)$
13:          **end if**
14:         **end for**
15:         $i \leftarrow i + 1$ ▷ Increase Level
16:         $barrier()$ ▷ Level Synchronization
17:       **end while**   ▷ End BFS
18:       $barrier()$
19:     **end for**
20: **end function**

Algorithm 5 Our parallel BC implementation in OpenCL, for graph $G = (V, E)$, with BC be the resulting vector containing the betweenness centrality scores for all the vertices in V.

```
 1: function KERNEL_BC(E, V)
 2:     for s ∈ V_group do
 3:         Q_i ← {s}
 4:         σ ← ∅                                                           ▷ Path Count
 5:         δ ← ∅                                                           ▷ Pair-Dependency
 6:         hasNextLevel ← 1
 7:         i ← 0                                                           ▷ Set Current Level
 8:         while hasNextLevel = 1 do                                       ▷ Step II
 9:             for e ∈ E_thread do
10:                 if e = UNVISITED & Source(e) ∈ Q_i then
11:                     add(Q_{i+1}, Dest(e))
12:                     e ← VISITED
13:                     σ[Dest(e)] ← σ[Dest(e)] + σ[Source(e)]
14:                     atom_xchg(hasNextLevel, 1)
15:                 end if
16:             end for
17:             i ← i + 1                                                   ▷ Increase Level
18:             barrier()                                                   ▷ Level Synchronization
19:         end while
20:         i ← i - 2
21:         while i > 1 do                                                  ▷ Step III
22:             for e ∈ E_thread do
23:                 if Source(e) ∈ Q_i & Dest(e) ∈ Q_{i+1} then
24:                     delta ← (σ[Source(e)]/σ[Dest(e)]) · (δ[Dest(e)] + 1)
25:                     atom_add(δ[Source(e)], delta)
26:                 end if
27:             end for
28:             i ← i - 1
29:             barrier()                                                   ▷ Level Synchronization
30:         end while
31:         for v ∈ V do                                                    ▷ Step IV
32:             if v ≠ r then
33:                 atomic(BC[v] ← BC[v] + δ[v])
34:             end if
35:         end for
36:     end for
37: end function
```

Utilizing Performance Unit Tests
To Increase Performance Awareness

Vojtěch Horký   Peter Libič   Lukáš Marek

Antonín Steinhauser   Petr Tůma

Department of Distributed and Dependable Systems
Faculty of Mathematics and Physics, Charles University
Malostranské náměstí 25, Prague 1, 118 00, Czech Republic

{horky,libic,marek,steinhauser,tuma}@d3s.mff.cuni.cz

ABSTRACT

Many decisions taken during software development impact the resulting application performance. The key decisions whose potential impact is large are usually carefully weighed. In contrast, the same care is not used for many decisions whose individual impact is likely to be small – simply because the costs would outweigh the benefits. Developer opinion is the common deciding factor for these cases, and our goal is to provide the developer with information that would help form such opinion, thus preventing performance loss due to the accumulated effect of many poor decisions.

Our method turns performance unit tests into recipes for generating performance documentation. When the developer selects an interface and workload of interest, relevant performance documentation is generated interactively. This increases performance awareness – with performance information available alongside standard interface documentation, developers should find it easier to take informed decisions even in situations where expensive performance evaluation is not practical. We demonstrate the method on multiple examples, which show how equipping code with performance unit tests works.

Categories and Subject Descriptors

D.2.6 [**Programming Environments**]: Interactive environments; D.2.8 [**Metrics**]: Performance measures; D.4.8 [**Performance**]: Measurements

General Terms

Performance, Measurement, Documentation

Keywords

performance documentation; performance awareness; performance testing; Java; JavaDoc

1. INTRODUCTION

The software development process can be perceived as a stream of decisions that gradually shape the final implementation of the initial requirements. Each of the decisions presents multiple options, such as choosing between available libraries, selecting appropriate algorithms and internal data structures, or adopting a particular coding style. The concerns affecting the decision are also many, ranging from cost or efficiency to complexity and maintainability, and the developers are expected to keep these concerns in balance.

The decisions that drive the development process also have a very different potential impact. Some decisions – for example whether to use a filesystem or a database to store persistent application data – are likely to have a major impact. Other decisions – for example whether to use a short integer or a long integer for a local counter variable – are likely to have a minor impact.

The perceived impact determines how the individual decisions are treated. Faced with a major-impact decision, the developer would deliberate carefully and use techniques such as modeling or prototyping to justify the eventual choice. In contrast, large-scale deliberation is not appropriate for minor-impact decisions, where the developer is more likely to simply fall back on an educated guess.

We illustrate the examples of several such choices on an imagined XML processing application. Listing 1 shows two functionally equivalent methods that accept a DOM tree [12] with purchase records as input and provide totals spent per user as output. Listing 1.a shows one developer using XPath [42] to navigate the DOM tree and `HashMap` to store the totals, whereas Listing 1.b shows another developer choosing a sequence of getters for navigation and `TreeMap` for storage.

The impact of choices from Listing 1 is likely perceived as minor rather than major.[1] As such, the decisions would not be made after a large-scale deliberation – choosing XPath might simply appear straightforward to a developer who has used XPath in the past, and choosing TreeMap might be similarly straightforward for a developer who thinks the totals will eventually be printed in a sorted sequence.

---

[1] But special circumstances can lend importance even to otherwise innocuous choices – for example, the code can be used in a hot loop, or availability of certain packages can be limited.

```
Map<String, Double> get(Document doc) {          Map<String, Double> get(Document doc) {
    Map<String, Double> result                      Map<String, Double> result
        = new HashMap<>();                              = new TreeMap<>();

    XPathExpression<Element> expr                   List<Element> purchases
        = XPathFactory.instance().compile(              = doc.getRootElement()
        "/rec/purchase", Filters.element());            .getChildren("purchase");

    for (Element e : expr.evaluate(doc)) {          for (Element e : purchases) {
        String customer                                 String customer
                = e.getChildText("customer");                   = e.getChildText("customer");
        double price = Double.parseDouble(              double price = Double.parseDouble(
                e.getChildText("price"));                       e.getChildText("price"));
        Double sum = result.get(customer);              Double sum = result.get(customer);
        if (sum == null) sum = price;                   if (sum == null) sum = price;
        else sum += price;                              else sum += price;
        result.put(customer, sum);                      result.put(customer, sum);
    }                                               }

    return result;                                  return result;
}                                                }
```

(1.a) XPath and HashMap   (1.b) Getters and TreeMap

Listing 1: Alternative implementations of imagined XML processing.

We focus on situations where the developer relies on insight to avoid large-scale deliberation. Ideally, the developer would correctly identify decisions whose impact will be minor and use educated guesses to make reasonably appropriate choices. For obvious reasons, we want to avoid situations where the developer fails to recognize that a choice deserves deliberation. We also want to avoid situations where the developer makes individually innocuous choices whose detrimental impact accumulates. Recent work on sources of software bloat suggests that such choices are common and can have a major impact on performance [33, 43, 44].

One way to avoid the bad situations is by making sure the developer can be reasonably aware of the concerns affecting each decision. For some concerns, this awareness often comes naturally with experience – simply by virtue of reading and maintaining code, the developer will have ample opportunities for feedback on criteria related to code readability and maintainability. Additional information can be provided by tools such as CheckStyle [5] or FindBugs [21].

The situation is different where awareness concerns software performance. Recognizing poor performance requires knowing what performance should be expected, and that information can only come from prototyping and measurement – in fact, the very kind of large-scale activities the developer wants to avoid. Apart from actively experimenting, the developer is therefore likely to receive feedback on software performance only when it is obviously insufficient.[2]

Our goal is to provide the developer with easily accessible information on software performance that is relevant to the software under development and thus increase performance awareness. This should in turn decrease the chance that the developer would make a poor choice due to lack of insight into performance.

We meet our goal by utilizing performance unit tests, introduced in detail in [4, 20]. When a performance unit test accompanies a particular software artefact, we use the workload generation component of the unit test to execute perfor-

mance measurements and present the measurement results alongside the documentation for that artefact. Modern development environments such as Eclipse [14] make locating artefact documentation as easy as pointing with mouse to the artefact of interest, our solution extends the same comfort to locating performance information. Same as the unit tests, the performance information can be collected remotely on the target deployment platform and the workload can be adjusted to focus on relevant information.

In compact points, our contribution starts with identifying the documentation potential of performance unit tests and providing the technical design used to generate the performance documentation. Furthermore, we explore the benefits of our solution on multiple experimental examples. Rather than solving a particular technical issue, we provide a mechanism that helps build performance awareness – our contribution therefore carries the implied promise of improved software development process, with smaller room for mistakes due to lack of developer insight.

We start our presentation by introducing the performance unit tests in Section 2 and the motivating scenarios in Section 3. The technical design needed to generate the performance documentation is discussed in Section 4, followed by experimental evaluation in Section 5. Related work discussion and conclusion close the paper.

2. PERFORMANCE UNIT TESTS

Our mechanism for generating performance documentation uses code provided by performance unit tests, we therefore present the basic elements of the performance unit test design as the necessary context. We consider performance unit tests as described in [4, 20], using tools developed for the Java platform.

The general structure of a performance unit test is depicted on Figure 1. It is similar to the structure of a functional unit test, which usually consists of the setup, execution, validation and cleanup phases [1, 22]. In the setup phase, the workload for the system under test is prepared and the system under test is put into initial test state. In the

---

[2]And experiments carry their own risks [2, 17, 9].

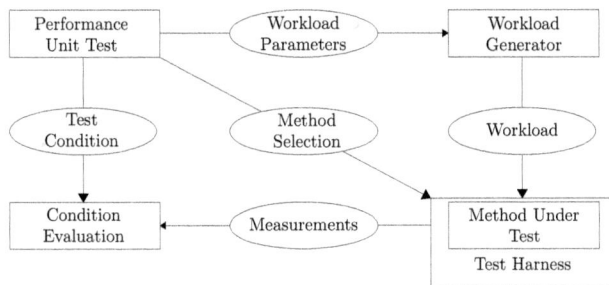

Figure 1: Performance unit test structure.

```
for i ← 1 .. sample count do
    test arguments ← GENERATOR(workload parameters)
    start the measurement
    for all args ← test arguments do
        MEASUREDMETHOD(args[0], args[1], ...)
    end for
    stop the measurement
    store the result
end for
```

Listing 2: Repeated measurement with workload generator.

execution phase, the system under test is subjected to the previously prepared workload and the performance is measured. In the validation phase, the observed performance is evaluated against the test criteria. The cleanup phase takes care of preparing for the next test, if any.

Two notable distinctions between performance and functional unit tests are the separation of the workload generator and the test criteria evaluation.

In the setup phase, the unit test code prepares the sequences of input arguments, which will be used in the execution phase to invoke the method under test. In effect, the input arguments determine the unit test workload, we therefore refer to this code as the *workload generator*. Technically, the generator is a standalone method that returns the `Iterable<Object[]>` type. Each `Object[]` contains arguments for a single method invocation, used in a manner similar to the `invoke()` method from the `java.reflection` package.

Making the workload generator a standalone method has two reasons. The first reason is code reuse – we can use the same generator for different unit tests when those tests use the same workload. The second reason is related to the performance measurements. By preparing the workload before the execution phase, we minimize the disruptive influence. We can also easily repeat the test multiple times to obtain more robust results. This process is illustrated in Listing 2.

The measurement results are evaluated against the test criteria using statistical hypothesis testing. The criteria is described in a formalism called Stochastic Performance Logic (SPL) [4], which defines the performance of a method as a random variable with a probability distribution that reflects the *workload parameters*. Workload parameters are arbitrary parameters that characterize the workload, given as arguments to the workload generator – examples of workload parameters used in this paper include sizes of collections to be measured, frequencies of individual collection operations, or sizes of generated graphs.

3. MOTIVATING SCENARIOS

The goal of this paper is to investigate the possibility of turning unit tests into performance documentation and to resolve the many issues associated with the technical side of this goal. To illustrate the benefits of our solution, we use multiple experimental examples.

3.1 Case 1: Navigating DOM Tree

Our first example returns to Listing 1, where an XPath query is used to retrieve the content of relevant document nodes. The code is written assuming a fixed document structure and an infrequent execution. A similar situation can exist for example in applications that read their configuration from an XML file.

Two major approaches for accessing values stored in an XML file are using SAX or using DOM. With SAX, the content is presented as arguments to content handlers during parsing. With DOM, the content is available after parsing in the form of an object tree. Here, we assume DOM was chosen over SAX for simplicity.[3]

With the content in the DOM tree, the developer can select a particular element using XPath, illustrated on Listing 1.a, or using a sequence of getters, illustrated on Listing 1.b. The former alternative appears more flexible – for example, the query string can be easily replaced with a more readable symbolic constant or modified to describe a more complex selection. In contrast, the latter alternative appears more straightforward – the developer may suspect that getters are simple and therefore efficient. With knowledge about performance of the two alternatives, the developer can make an informed choice.

3.2 Case 2: Choosing A Collection

Our example from Listing 1 also involves choosing a collection implementation. The two alternative implementations of the `get` method both return a `Map` object, however, Listing 1.a uses a `HashMap` and Listing 1.b a `TreeMap`. Syntactically, the two alternatives are very similar, we can therefore assume the developer would decide based on criteria such as overhead or performance.

Again, a similar situation can arise in most applications that use collections. As an extension of the example from Listing 1, we also consider an imagined online store where each commodity has a list of attributes. These attributes describe optional properties of each commodity, for example the screen dimensions for computer monitors or the storage capacity for disks. The commodity descriptions reside in a database, our scenario deals with choosing the collection implementation used for caching the commodity attributes in memory. The choice should reflect these observations:

- The attribute names are strings, values are objects.
- The attributes are few, typically fewer than ten.
- Some attributes are queried more often than others.
- Some attributes are used as searching criteria.
- The attributes are rarely updated.

The choices available in these scenarios are many, starting with the classes of the `java.util` package in the Java Class Library. There, the obvious choice is one of the available implementations of `Map<String, Object>`. However, a simpler list of pairs can be used as well – with the most

---

[3]For the same reason, we assume the developer would not attempt using JAXB.

queried attributes kept in front, this choice can turn out to be more efficient than a map. The spectrum of choices is further extended by external collection implementations in libraries such as PCJ [36], Guava [19] or Trove [40].

3.3 Case 3: Choosing A Library

For the third example, we consider the common task of choosing among multiple libraries with similar purpose. In our experiment, we examine GRAL [18], XChart [41] and JFreeChart [27], three open source libraries that offer graph plotting functions. The task at hand is generating image files with line charts of up to 10000 data points, we assume the developer found all three libraries functionally sufficient and needs to choose one.

As with the other examples, we do not mean to suggest that the developer should use performance as the sole factor guiding the decision. We do believe, however, that knowledge of performance should be used alongside other factors – in this case for example the quality of the library documentation or the maturity of the library code base – in reaching the decision. With other things being equal, performance should not be sacrificed needlessly.

4. TURNING TESTS INTO DOCUMENTATION

Assuming we have a component reasonably covered by performance unit tests, we now look at the issues involved in generating performance documentation for such component. The primary output of a performance unit test is the pass or fail status.[4] This extremely condensed output is useful in automated build environments, however, it is also backed by the individual measurements collected during the test execution, which provide detailed information on the observed performance of the component under test and therefore constitute component performance documentation.

Unfortunately, distributing the measurements collected by the performance tests as a part of the component documentation is not a simple endeavour. Although some projects regularly publish their performance test results, the reports are limited to summaries – major examples of such activities include the Open Benchmarking Site [35], which offers summaries for several thousand test results, or the ACE+TAO+ CIAO Distributed Scoreboard [38], which provides results of selected performance tests across the entire project history.

One of the reasons why performance measurements are not provided together with the documentation is the measurement duration. The measurements required to generate a complete performance documentation would take too long for even a moderately sized projects – even for the testing purposes, the performance unit tests need to be run on carefully selected test cases only [20].

Another factor is the volume of the measurement data collected. The study in [20], where the tests have covered about 20 % of code, has produced several hundreds of kilobytes of compressed measurement data, easily an order of magnitude more than the size of the byte code tested.

Finally, the performance measurements are platform-dependent. Although [20] shows that relative performance can

---

[4]To be completely accurate, the test in our tool implementation can also return a third status that indicates the test does not yet have enough data to decide on the test condition.

```
class LinkedList {
    @Generator ("LinkedListGen#contains")
    public boolean contains (Object obj) {
        /* ... */
    }
}
```

Listing 4: Binding workload generator generator with the measured method.

be a reasonably stable property across platforms, the difference in absolute numbers generally makes it difficult to relate the measurement results collected on one platform to the expected performance on other platforms.

4.1 Using Workload Generators

Section 2 has introduced the unit test structure, in which the workload generator prepares the input arguments for test execution based on the specified workload parameters. Listing 3 contains an example generator code that prepares arguments for invoking the `LinkedList.contains()` method in a sequence that produces a given number of hits and misses. The workload parameters – the size of the list and the number of hits and misses – are specified as the generator inputs. Briefly, the generator first prepares the underlying list, on which the `contains()` method will be invoked. Next, the arguments of the individual invocations are prepared, first for hits (the invocation looks for a random integer from a range that is known to be in the list) and then for misses (the invocation looks for an integer beyond the range known to be in the list).

Although the generator prepares the arguments for individual method invocations in a form reminiscent of the `invoke()` method arguments from the `java.reflection` package, our tool for performance unit tests does not rely on reflection to execute the workload. Instead, the tool generates code that extracts the arguments (unboxing and recasting as necessary) and then performs a standard method invocation. This is because reflection introduces a disruptive overhead.

We use the workload generators to generate the performance documentation on-the-fly on the application developer side. This helps overcome the outlined challenges – rather than having the component provider collecting and distributing measurements, the application developers run the selected measurements of interest locally. Our performance unit test framework also supports remote testing, with the measurements performed on a remote deployment platform rather than on the build system itself, this makes it possible to display results directly relevant to the deployment platform.

4.2 Associating Generators With Methods

To generate a performance documentation for a method, we need to locate the workload generator associated with that method. In the performance unit tests, the association relies on annotations, as illustrated in Listing 4. In certain situations, such as when testing proprietary code, it is not easily possible to attach the annotation directly to the measured method. When this is the case, we introduce a helper class that defines an empty method with the same signature and attach the generator to this method instead, as illustrated in Listing 5.

```
class LinkedListGen {
    public Iterable<Object[]> contains (int size, int hits, int nohits) {
        ArrayList<Object[]> result = new ArrayList<> (hits + nohits);
        LinkedList<Integer> list = new LinkedList<> ();
        for (int i = 0 ; i < size ; i++) {
            list.add (new Integer (i));
        }

        Random rnd = new Random ();
        for (int i = 0 ; i < hits ; i++) {
            Integer searchFor = rnd.nextInt (size);
            Object[] args = new Object[] { list, searchFor };
            result.add (args);
        }
        for (int i = 0 ; i < nohits ; i++) {
            Integer searchFor = new Integer (size + i);
            Object[] args = new Object[] { list, searchFor };
            result.add (args);
        }

        return result;
    }
}
```

Listing 3: Generator for invoking the contains() method of a linked list.

```
@TestHelper (
    for = java.util.LinkedList.class)
class LinkedListHelper {
    @Generator ("LinkedListGen#contains")
    public boolean contains (Object obj) { }
}
```

Listing 5: Binding workload generator with the measured method through a helper class.

In the straightforward example from Listing 4, we can locate the generators that can be used with a particular method simply by enumerating the method annotations. In the example from Listing 5, the situation can be likened to propagating documentation across an interface-implementation relationship. The annotation information is kept in byte code, the generators can therefore be located even for methods in packages that are distributed in compiled form.

Complex performance unit tests require workloads that invoke multiple methods of a component. In these cases, we use a special-purpose test method that executes the individual component methods and associate the generator with this special-purpose method. Listing 6 shows such a special-purpose method, used by a unit test of a graph plotting library – the workload uses the library to create an image file of given dimensions that shows given data points using a line plot, this requires calls to multiple library methods.

The example from Listing 6 makes associating the generator with individual component methods more difficult, we therefore use extra ShowWith* annotations that specify classes and methods whose performance the test exercises.

The use of helper methods shown Listing 5 and Listing 6 requires searching for the classes that implement these methods. To reduce the search time, we assume the developer would specify a separate class path to be searched.

4.3 Limiting Measurement Time

To avoid the issues with test execution duration, we expect that the performance documentation would be gener-

ated on demand, much in the same way as the JavaDoc [24] documentation is displayed on demand when the developer selects a particular method. To react quickly enough in an interactive environment, we need to execute the measurements in a short time frame. There are situations where this is clearly not possible, for example when even a single invocation of the measured method takes a long time to complete. When the measurement method executes in reasonable time, we also need the workload generator to prescribe a short enough workload.

As a complication, the requirement of relatively short workloads conflicts with the need to make the performance unit tests reliable – robust results are known to require long measurements, possibly with multiple restarts and multiple compilations [9, 17, 29]. This tendency was also reflected in our initial performance unit test experiments [20], where the workload generator design tended to put test robustness first and test duration second. This resulted in execution times inapplicably long for an interactive measurement context.

We aim to solve this issue by gradually updating the presented results. The very first time a developer displays the documentation for a method, we only measure the method for a short period of time, limiting both the scale of workload parameters used and the number of measurement repetitions performed. After displaying the initial results, further measurements are collected on the background and the initial results are gradually refined – a finer scale of the workload parameters is used and the measurements are repeated more times. Because the measurement results are preserved, this only happens when a method documentation is first examined.

Figure 2 illustrates the effect of gradually updating the presented results on a workload that measures the duration of the LinkedList<Integer>.contains() method when looking for an element that does not exist in the collection. We see that a very short measurement – 1 second – reveals the general linear complexity trend, but does not run long enough for runtime optimizations to occur. A slightly longer measurement – 5 seconds – suffices to present stable results

```
@Generator (...)
@ShowWithClass (de.erichseifert.gral.plots.XYPlot.class)
@ShowWithMethod ("de.erichseifert.gral.io.plots.DrawableWriter#write")
void plotLinesToPng (DataTable data, OutputStream output, int width, int height) {
    DrawableWriterFactory factory = DrawableWriterFactory.getInstance ();
    DrawableWriter writer = factory.get ("image/png");
    XYPlot plot = new XYPlot (data);
    LineRenderer lines = new DefaultLineRenderer2D ();
    lines.setSetting (LineRenderer.COLOR, Color.BLUE);
    plot.setLineRenderer (data, lines);
    writer.write (plot, output, width, height);
}
```

Listing 6: Special-purpose test method for a plotting library. Exceptions omitted.

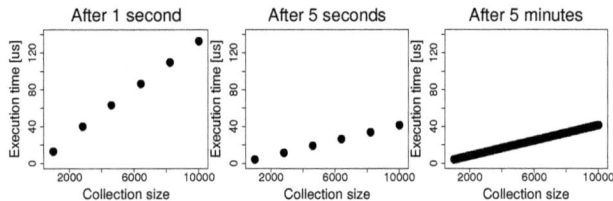

Figure 2: Improving the precision over time.

for six workload parameter values. A measurement of 300 seconds is safely enough to collect stable measurements for 100 workload parameter values.

A more complex issue concerns our very ability to create workload generators that can drive short measurements. Most measurements must execute in a loop to provide reasonable results (for many reasons – for example to execute a representative workload, to trigger runtime optimization, or to compensate for measurement noise or measurement overhead). When the method invocations in the measurement loop change the measured object state, the collected measurements may no longer reflect the intended workload. For example, it is difficult to write a workload generator that would measure the time to add an element to a collection of particular size without invoking any other collection operation – with each measurement repetition, the collection would grow and the measurement would no longer apply to the initial collection size. A specific solution is required for each particular situation – in the collection example, we can simply measure the time to add and remove an element in the same loop, because this workload variation does not grow the collection as the measurement progresses.

4.4 Presenting Measurement Results

The workload produced by a workload generator depends on both the implementation of the generator and the supplied workload parameters. When selecting the measurement and presenting the results, we therefore need to provide both the description of the generator and the description of the workload parameters.

We rely on the fact that each generator is simply a method of a class and therefore can be documented using JavaDoc. JavaDoc can be used to capture the description of the whole generator as well as the description of the individual workload parameters, which are simply arguments to the generator method. The advantage is that the developer writing the workload generator uses a standard documentation tool. The disadvantage is that the comments are not preserved

when compiling into byte code, the documentation may thus not be available in packages distributed in compiled form.

To address the issue of packages distributed in compiled form, we add extra annotations that can be used to describe the workload parameters in a compact manner, as shown on Listing 7. The annotations serve dual purpose – besides being used when JavaDoc is not available, they also describe the axes of the measurement result plots together with valid parameter ranges.

4.5 Realistic Measurement Context

So far, we have considered measurements collected using workload generators originally designed for performance unit tests. When associated with a component, these generators produce workloads that the component developer considered useful to test – these can be common workloads for the component, workloads that exhibit interesting behavior, or even workloads that target a particular performance regression. However, these workloads can still substantially differ from the workload expected by the application developer. They are also designed to be executed in relative isolation, which makes them similar to classical micro benchmarks.

Correctly interpreting a micro benchmark result is tricky – even with a reasonable workload, the micro benchmark still executes under conditions that can be very different from those in the eventual application. This is not an issue for the performance unit tests, which are designed with the knowledge of the benchmark execution conditions. It is, however, a potential issue when trying to interpret the micro benchmark result with the application conditions in mind. Although our tool permits adding custom workload generators that can remedy this issue, the surest way to determine the behavior of a component in an application is still by measuring it in the application.

Our work on performance awareness in component systems [3] suggests a solution. We use the DiSL framework [31] to instrument the component inside the application and collect measurements in much the same way as with the performance unit tests – except now, the workload is generated by the application itself rather than the workload generator. To determine the workload parameters required for presenting the measurements, we employ sizers as an inverse complement to generators – where the generator produces workload given the relevant parameters, the sizer produces the parameters while observing the workload.

5. EXPERIMENTAL EVALUATION

The ultimate aim of our approach is to improve performance awareness among software developers so that they

```
/** Generator for testing Collection.contains() method.
 *
 * @param size Size of the underlying collection.
 * @param hits Number of searches that hit.
 * @param nohits Number of searches that miss.
 */
@Generator("Collection.contains() with mix of hits and misses.")
public Iterable<Object[]> contains(
        @Param("Collection size", min=10) int size,
        @Param("Searches that hit", min=0) int hits,
        @Param("Searches that miss", min=0) int nohits) {
    /* ... */
}
```

Listing 7: Generator documentation with annotations.

can write more efficient code. With this aim in mind, the evident method of experimental evaluation is to conduct a study that would test whether developers with access to performance documentation write more efficient code. We investigate this evaluation method next, however, it turns out the study is too expensive to be practical. We therefore turn to additional methods of examining our approach, looking at whether reasonably realistic use cases can be found, and whether real software can benefit.

We have executed our experiments on a 2.33 GHz machine with two quad core Intel Xeon E5345 processors and 8 GB of memory, running Fedora Linux with kernel 3.9.9, glibc 2.16-33 and OpenJDK 1.7.0-25, all in 64 bit mode. The libraries used in the experiments were JDOM 2.0.5 [26] with Jaxen 1.1.6 [25], GRAL 0.9 [18], XChart 2.3.0 [41] and JFreeChart 1.0.17 [27].

Our experimental implementation includes a complete performance unit test framework for Java [39]. The framework supports for workload generators attached through annotations, local and remote measurement, result collection and processing. We have not yet implemented the user interface integration envisioned in our approach, specifically the workload generator and workload parameter selection and the integrated result display features. The graphs shown here are produced manually from the measurement data.

5.1 Developer Awareness Study

To test whether developers with access to performance documentation write more efficient code, we design an experiment where multiple developers are given the same implementation task, and the performance of the resulting implementations is compared. In terms of hypothesis testing, we postulate the following null hypothesis: availability of performance documentation during software development has no impact on the eventual implementation performance. Our independent variable is the availability of performance documentation, our dependent variable is the execution time of the resulting implementation.

With limited resources to hire professional developers, our test subjects are volunteer computer science students. The students have completed a Java Programming class and participated in an Advanced Java Programming class, the average self assessment of the relevant programming language skills is 3.5 on a scale of 1 to 5. The students were not told the purpose of the experiment beyond the bare minimum needed to ask for consensus.

As the implementation task, we choose XML processing with the JDOM library, for which we have developed the performance unit tests in [20]. The students were asked to implement an application that accepts a DocBook [11] file on the standard input and produces a list of cross references grouped per section on the standard output. This is a reasonably simple task – our reference solution has less than 200 LOC– yet it provides opportunity for exercising multiple different uses of the JDOM library and the standard collections.

We have assigned the task to 39 students split into three equal-sized groups – one control group and two test groups. The control group was given the standard JDOM library documentation, the two test groups were given two versions of documentation augmented with performance information, one strictly correct and one deliberately misleading. In both versions, methods relevant to the task were identified together with possible alternatives. In the first test group, the true performance measurements of all methods were provided, with the intent to guide the students towards more efficient implementation. In the second test group, the performance measurements of the fastest and the slowest methods in some alternatives were switched, to guide the students towards less efficient implementation.

The experiment results suffered from high attrition rate. Of the 39 students, only 12 have submitted implementations that have passed minimum correctness tests. The attrition rates have not differed greatly between the three groups, suggesting low general motivation to complete the task rather than bias particular to individual groups.

More importantly, the execution times of the implementations have exhibited very high variance. On a test input of 80 MB, the fastest implementation has finished in 3.28 s, but the slowest implementation has not finished in one day. The median execution time was 5.38 s. The high variance prevents making statistically significant rejection of the null hypothesis at reasonable scales – even if we filter out the execution times that exceed one minute as anomalies, the variance remains such that a two-sided t-test at the 5% confidence level would only spot average differences above 6.13 s. Our approach does not aspire at performance improvements of such a large relative magnitude.

Given that our approach targets minor-impact decisions, we believe it could be considered successful if it brought average performance improvement in the order of tens of percent. We can use the common sample size estimation methods to guess the required experiment size. In statistical terms, we consider the probability P that the sample average performance $\bar{X}$ estimates the true mean performance μ with a relative error exceeding δ, and we want P to remain at a reasonably low confidence level α: $P((\bar{X}-\mu)/\mu) \geq \delta) = \alpha$. Under normality assumptions, reasonable for this particular lower bound computation, we can estimate the minimum sample size $n = (z_\alpha^2 * \sigma^2)/(\delta^2 * \mu^2)$ [34]. For our experiment results, α set to 5% and δ set to 10%, this suggests a minimum of 2397 students per group, or 128 students per group if we again filter out the execution times that exceed one minute as anomalies.

Our study did not provide sufficient data to rule on whether our approach indeed helps improve performance awareness among software developers, however, it did point out another important observation – a direct evaluation of the possible effect would require a study with a minimum of several hundred participating developers. It is possible that some aspects of the experiment can help reduce this number. For example, using more experienced developers or constraining the assignment may reduce the execution time variance, however, neither solution is without drawbacks. Before considering this more expensive evaluation, we therefore turn to additional methods of examining our approach.

5.2 Evaluating Motivating Scenarios

To see whether reasonably realistic use cases can be found, we evaluate our approach in the context of the motivating scenarios from Section 3. For each scenario, we show what the generated performance documentation would reveal and discuss how the information relates to the eventual developer decision.

The exact shape of the performance documentation depends on the available workload generators. It is rather unlikely that a generator would address a particular scenario directly – for example, when a scenario calls for comparing the performance of two collection implementations on a particular workload, it would be ideally addressed by a workload generator that can drive both collection implementations with that exact workload. Having a performance unit test with such a workload generator would seem too much of a coincidence, we are more likely to have workload generators that drive individual collection implementations in some other – possibly similar – workloads. We discuss this issue with each scenario too.[5]

5.3 Case 1: Navigating DOM Tree

In this scenario, the developer considers whether to navigate a DOM tree using a sequence of getters or using XPath. The choice with sequence of getters relies on the `Element.getChild()` method. Internally, the method is fairly complex, using a lazy element name filter and a cache of filter results – we can therefore reasonably assume the component developer would equip the method with a performance unit test that makes sure both the lazy filtering and the result caching work. This suggests a workload generator that calls the `getChild()` method on an element with a variable number of children and a variable position of the matching child, coupled with a performance unit test that makes sure the `getChild()` timing does not depend on the child count when the matching child position stays constant. The

---

[5]For the curious reader, we have also evaluated the alternatives from Listing 1. On 10000 purchase records of 1000 customers, Listing 1.a takes an average 304 ms to complete, Listing 1.b completes in an average of 12 ms. The best combination uses a sequence of getters and `HashMap` in 7 ms.

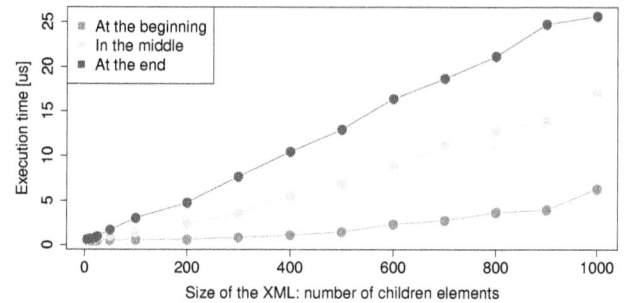

Figure 3: Measurements of `Element.getChild()` for varying child count and selected matching child position.

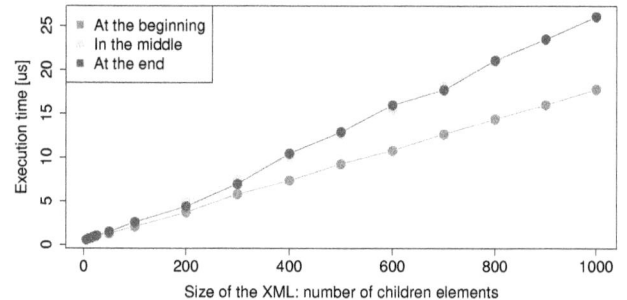

Figure 4: Measurements of XPath query for varying element count and selected matching element position. Compilation amortized over 100 queries.

measurement results collected using such a generator are on Figure 3.

For the alternative choice with XPath, we do not have to hypothesize what workload generator can be reasonably available. The developers that use Jaxen, the XPath engine used in our experiments, have already implemented a simple performance benchmark [6] that measures the time needed to execute a query that locates a unique node in various positions of a tree with a given size. We have implemented the corresponding workload generator, the measurement results are on Figure 4.

Equipped with the information from Figures 3 and 4, the developer can properly balance the difference in performance with other concerns. In particular, the information helps notify the developer of some performance realities that are not self evident, for example the linear dependency between the `getChild()` time and the position of the matching child among siblings.

5.4 Case 2: Choosing A Collection

In the second scenario, the developer decides what collection to use to store a relatively small number of variable attributes. Evaluating the performance of a collection implementation against a particular workload is a common endeavor, we therefore assume the evaluation would provide a workload generator. Our implementation of such a workload generator accepts basic workload parameters – the initial size of the collection, the number of operations to perform, and the relative frequencies of individual operations in the workload. The operations are inserting and removing an element, iterating over the collection, and two versions of searching the collection (one that searches for an existing

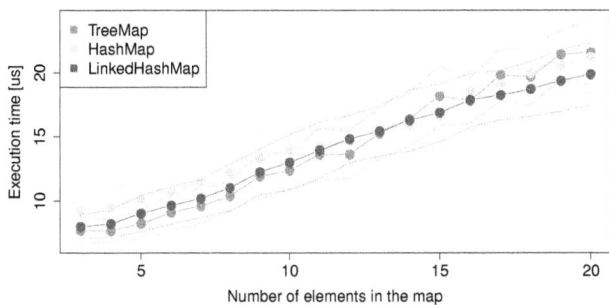

Figure 5: Measurements of operation mix on Map<String, String> collections. Average time, dotted lines at 3σ.

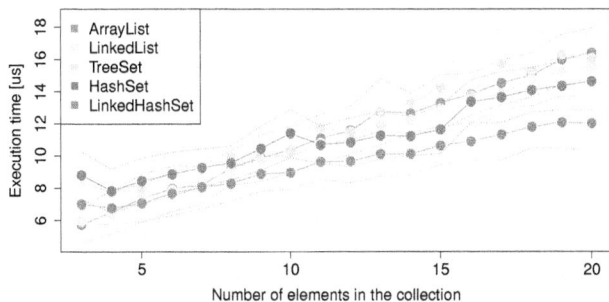

Figure 6: Measurements of operation mix on Collection<String> collections. Average time, dotted lines at 3σ.

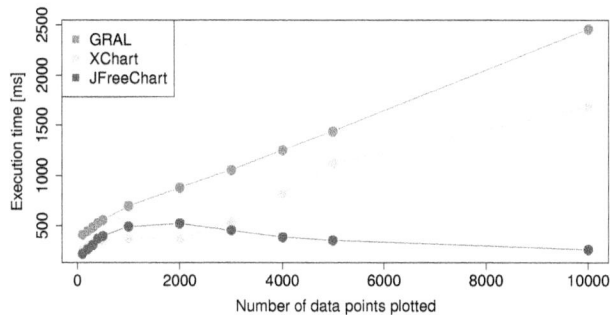

Figure 7: Measurements of line plot creation time. Image dimension 800×600 points.

element and one that searches for an element that does not exist).

Ideally, the generator would also permit specifying the type of the collection elements (the type parameter of the collection type). So far, we have not tackled the issue of specifying a type as a workload parameter, and instead assume multiple workload generators would be present – one for each type for a small set of common types. Figure 5 shows the measurements on a workload suggested in the scenario, that is, a mix of one-third iterations, one-third successful searches, one-third unsuccessful searches on the Map<String,String> type. The figure can help the developer realize that in this scenario, all three collections perform reasonably well, with perhaps a small saving to be made by using LinkedHashMap.

Among other likely concerns in the choice of a collection is the memory overhead [33]. This might lead the developer to also look at the performance of collections that do not implement the Map interface – after all, for the collection sizes suggested in the scenario, searching an array might not be much slower than searching a sophisticated collection. The developer can look at the same workload on the Collection<String> type, with results shown on Figure 6. The results would suggest that for small collections, trading memory requirements for performance by using arrays is potentially feasible.

5.5 Case 3: Choosing A Library

In the last scenario, the developer needs to select among different graph plotting libraries. Although we cannot expect the libraries to provide workload generators matching our needs exactly, we assume each library would provide tests demonstrating typical usage – as a matter of fact, the library developers can use the examples distributed with the

library documentation, because the amount of additional work required to turn the examples into generators is low.

In our scenario, the developer would look at workload generators that plot line charts. The workload parameters of the generators can differ from library to library, the developer will thus be presented with separate results rather than the combined result plot we present here. The generator we use creates a PNG image with a line chart, the workload parameters were the image dimensions and the number of data points. Figure 7 offers a comparison of the three libraries under consideration.

As another example of an interesting behavior, the dependency on Figure 7 is not strictly monotonous. This behavior correlates with the line plot appearance – with too many data points, the lines merge into larger blotches that are easier to compress.

5.6 Evaluating Existing Projects

Although our motivating scenarios were inspired by real code, they are not from real projects. Lacking the means to involve a sufficient number of external developers, we instead examine the existing projects ourselves, looking for opportunities for performance improvement based on performance documentation. Many of our performance unit tests were developed for the JDOM library [20], we have therefore looked for open source projects that use JDOM.

We have used the Ohloh[6] open source project tracking site to look for projects that import classes from the JDOM library package, locating roughly 100 projects. We did not consider projects that are simply too big to evaluate, such as the Eclipse development environment. We have also excluded projects that use JDOM merely to read their configuration files, because in such projects the performance improvement is unlikely to matter. Finally, some projects did not build on our experimental platform. The following sections document cases of performance improvement.

5.7 Project 1: Buildhealth

Buildhealth[7] is a utility that parses the reports of common software development tools, such as JUnit or FindBugs, to create a build health summary. Many of the parsed reports are stored in XML and Buildhealth uses JDOM for their analysis. The individual modules for parsing the reports often use XPath. Our performance documentation reveals high initial cost associated with XPath compilation, we have therefore decided to replace simple XPath expressions – such

---

[6]http://www.openhub.net
[7]https://github.com/pescuma/buildhealth

Table 1: Buildhealth results

	Original	No XPath	Cached XPath
Repeated	938.3 ms	908.4 ms	929.8 ms
Ant task	2.23 s	2.16 s	–
Standalone	2.52 s	2.40 s	–

Table 2: METS downloader results

	XPath	Nested `getChildren`
Total time	120.2 s	120.4 s
`getImageURLs`	131.5 ms	27.4 ms

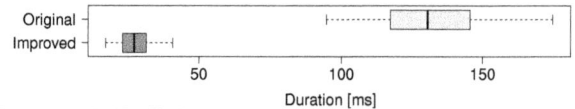

Figure 9: METS downloader, the `getImageURLs` method.

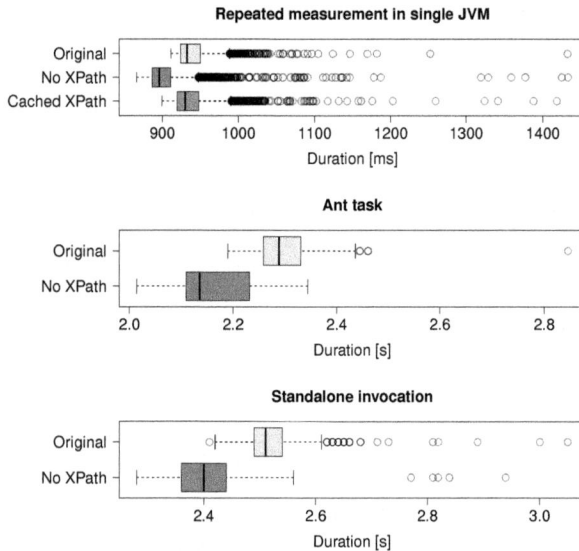

Figure 8: Buildhealth

as selecting all children of given name – with more efficient but less versatile API calls. The changes were a few lines in size and done within minutes.

We do not analyze other qualities of the modification, such as code readability or maintainability. Without doubt, complex XPath expressions would be very difficult to replace in a similar manner, however, in this case the expressions were sufficiently simple to justify the change.

We have evaluated the performance effect of our changes in three different settings. All concern the processing time of JUnit reports for the Apache Ant project, the size of the report files is approximately 4 MB. The average execution times are in Table 1, boxplots are displayed in Figure 8.

The first of the three settings serves to explain the performance effect of our changes. To filter out the usual warm up effects, we run the core of the Buildhealth utility in an artificial loop. Besides the original and the modified versions of the utility, we also show the performance when the compiled XPath expression is cached. The results indicate the part of the performance improvement due to XPath compilation, the API calls used by the modified version of the utility are faster than even compiled XPath.

In the second of the three settings, we have executed Buildhealth as an Ant task. Using the `ProfileLogger`[8] support, we have measured only the time needed to execute Buildhealth, without the overhead of the Ant invocation.

In the third setting, we have measured the total time to execute Buildhealth. This setting is the most realistic, but it does not allow us to filter the warm up effects, which are therefore included in this and further results. Overall, the changes have improved performance of the utility on our

data by about 5 %, which can be considered a success especially given that the modifications were small and performed without deep knowledge of the source code.

5.8 Project 2: METS Downloader

The METS (Metadata Encoding and Transmission Standard) is a "standard for encoding descriptive, administrative, and structural metadata regarding objects within a digital library" [32]. To facilitate downloading METS documents recursively (with referenced files), an unofficial downloader exists.[9]

The downloader uses XPath to extract the list of referenced images that need to be downloaded. Technically, the XPath expression selects a `link` attribute from elements nested in certain order. Motivated by the same information as in the previous project, we have replaced this XPath expression with a series of nested loops iterating over the individual child elements. The modification is located in the `getImageURLs` method of the `MetsDocument` class.

Table 2 shows both the total execution time of the downloader and the execution time of the `getImageURLs` method, measured on about 67 MB of data from the UCB library site. While the impact on the overall performance – which is influenced much more by the network latency and throughput – is negligible, the method alone executes in one fifth of the original time, as also illustrated on Figure 9.

5.9 Project 3: Dynamic Replica Placement

For our last project, we have chosen a prototype implementation[10] that accompanied a paper about dynamic replica placement in CDN [8]. Again guided by our performance documentation, we have replaced a recursive document traversal based around the `getChildren` method with a single iteration over elements returned by the `getDescendants` method in one of the included tests.

The results are displayed in Table 3 and in Figure 10. The modifications were again relatively small, we were able to improve the total execution time by 2 % and the affected method alone by 6 %.

6. DISCUSSION AND RELATED WORK

In our evaluation, we have demonstrated the kind of information that performance documentation can provide to the software developer. We have also shown that real software projects do contain the kind of code constructs that lead to

---

[8] http://ant.apache.org/manual/listeners.html#ProfileLogger

[9] The sources are available from https://svn.thulb.uni-jena.de/repos/maven-projects/mets-downloader, we are not aware of an official project homepage.

[10] https://code.google.com/p/dynamicreplicaplacement

Table 3: CDN simulator test results

	getChildren	getDescendants
Total time	1.93 s	1.89 s
Processing alone	744.3 ms	700.3 ms

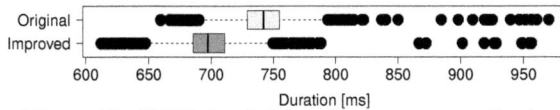

Figure 10: CDN simulation, the `process` method.

needless performance loss and that can be easily fixed. Additionally, we saw that even on an assignment that is short and thus limited in the number of decisions taken during development, the performance of individual implementations can vary significantly.

On the down side, our evaluation is not comprehensive – while we did show cases where our approach is useful, we did not quantify the share of those cases in some representative sample of software development activities. One can easily observe that such quantification will require long term effort and should be expected to deliver results in the form of developer acceptance or rejection, rather than hard numbers. Towards this goal, we continue to develop and improve our prototype tools.

We can also see several potential drawbacks of our approach. Obviously, when the performance unit tests are constructed improperly, the derived performance documentation can provide misleading information. Interpreting measurements is also a skill that requires some experience – in this context, we can only argue that the developers should be trusted to acquire that skill, and eventually develop best practices for writing the documentation.

In a broader view, we should also stress that performance documentation is not a substitute for efficient algorithms. While it can warn the developer of unexpected complexity in the used code, our approach complements, rather than replaces, the need to choose proper algorithms and architectures. Along the same lines, our approach complements techniques such as profiling or parameter tuning, which are useful at other software development stages.

There is also the question of costs vs benefits. Where we point out that our approach increases performance awareness, it also brings costs associated with developing the unit tests and executing the measurements. Possibly, the performance information can draw the developer attention away from other topics, which might have more impact on the overall software performance. Again, these are likely issues that are best evaluated through practice – we can draw a parallel with functional unit testing, which has been shown to improve software quality without adding extra costs [15].

On the related work side, much work has been dedicated to enriching interface specifications with non-functional properties, which often include performance metrics. One such example is the performance-enabled WSDL [13], which adds requirements and assumptions about performance of web services. Where the existing work focuses on automatic service selection at runtime, we aim at providing performance relevant information to the developer.

An important aspect of approaches that extend the interface description is the choice of metrics for quantifying performance. One possible approach is to devise a portable metric that summarizes the performance as a platform-independent value. For example, JavaPSL [16], used for detecting performance problems in parallel applications, normalizes the values to $[0, 1]$ to simplify comparison. The performance unit tests in [4] also rely on relative comparison to tackle the platform-dependent nature of the measurements. In contrast, the approach described here provides platform-specific information in absolute numbers.

As a practically useful extension, we also consider measuring more than just the execution time of a specific method. Of eminent interest are the memory-related metrics such as heap consumption or cache utilization. The basic idea is a straightforward extension of this paper, however, the technical process of defining and collecting the memory-related metrics presents specific challenges especially for the separation of the workload generator from the measured method.

In a broader context, our work also complements the research effort in the performance adaptation domain. We have touched on the issue of choosing a suitable collection implementation, which is addressed in depth by the Chameleon tool [37] – the tool observes access patterns on individual collections and, based on a set of static rules, issues recommendations on which collection implementation to use. The problem of choosing from multiple available implementations was explored for example in the context of selecting the best parallel algorithm [45]. Other frameworks address the need for adaptive configuration [10] and other situations. What these approaches have in common is that the developer has to be aware of the potential for dynamic adaptation to attempt the adaptation in the first place. Our work improves the awareness of the likely performance of individual software components and therefore helps the developer identify the adaptation opportunities to be explored in detail.

On the benchmarking side, our work is also related to the existing benchmarking tools, especially those in the micro benchmark category. Among such tools for Java are jmh [28], Japex [23] or Caliper [7]. These projects allow the developer to mark a method as a benchmark and collect the results. Our approach stands apart especially in using the unit test code and in integrating the performance evaluation into the interactive software development process.

7. CONCLUSION

Our work seeks to improve the perception of typical software performance that the software developers form in their work. We propose a system where performance unit tests acquire dual purpose – besides evaluating a component, the unit tests also serve to generate performance documentation for application developers that use the components. Our approach facilitates building software architectures where the performance of individual components can be easily examined and where the decisions that steer the development process can take this performance into account.

We have illustrated the potential use of performance documentation on multiple examples, each accompanied by measurements carried out using a real performance unit test tool. We believe the potential benefits of our approach parallel those of functional unit testing, and although such benefits are difficult to quantify experimentally [30], we find it reasonable to expect that a better-informed developer makes fewer wrong decisions.

Among the plethora of performance optimization opportunities, we see the contribution of our approach especially with the many low profile decisions. An experienced developer should not make major performance mistakes often, however, that same developer can make a conscious decision to ignore the performance impact of low profile decisions simply for the sake of fast development. Better performance awareness reduces the need for this particular sacrifice. We also provide more chances to recognize situations where advanced performance solutions, such as dynamic adaptation or manual optimization, are warranted by the potential performance benefit.

Acknowledgements

This work was partially supported by the Charles University institutional funding and the EU project ASCENS 257414.

8. REFERENCES

[1] K. Beck. *Simple Smalltalk Testing*. Cambridge University Press, 1997.

[2] A. Buble, L. Bulej, and P. Tuma. CORBA benchmarking: a course with hidden obstacles. In *Proc. IPDPS 2003 PMEOPDS*, 2003.

[3] L. Bulej, T. Bures, V. Horky, J. Keznikl, and P. Tuma. Performance awareness in component systems: Vision paper. In *Proc. COMPSAC 2012 CORCS*, 2012.

[4] L. Bulej, T. Bures, J. Keznikl, A. Koubkova, A. Podzimek, and P. Tuma. Capturing Performance Assumptions using Stochastic Performance Logic. In *Proc. ICPE 2012*. ACM, 2012.

[5] O. Burn et al. *Checkstyle*, 2014. http://checkstyle.sf.net.

[6] M. Böhm and J.-J. Dubray. *Dom4J performance versus Xerces / Xalan*, 2008. http://dom4j.sf.net/dom4j-1.6.1/benchmarks/xpath.

[7] *Caliper: Microbenchmarking framework for Java*, 2013. http://code.google.com/p/caliper.

[8] Y. Chen, R. H. Katz, and J. D. Kubiatowicz. Dynamic replica placement for scalable content delivery. In *Proc. IPTPS 2002*. Springer, 2002.

[9] C. Click. The Art of Java Benchmarking. http://www.azulsystems.com/presentations/art-of-java-benchmarking.

[10] C. Ţăpuş, I.-H. Chung, and J. K. Hollingsworth. Active Harmony: Towards automated performance tuning. In *Proc. SC 2002*. IEEE, 2002.

[11] *DocBook*, 2014. http://www.docbook.org.

[12] *Document Object Model*, 2005. http://w3.org/DOM.

[13] A. D'Ambrogio. A WSDL extension for performance-enabled description of web services. In *Proc. ISCIS 2005*. Springer, 2005.

[14] *Eclipse*, 2014. http://www.eclipse.org.

[15] M. Ellims, J. Bridges, and D. Ince. The economics of unit testing. *Empirical Software Engineering*, 11(1), 2006.

[16] T. Fahringer and C. S. Júnior. Modeling and detecting performance problems for distributed and parallel programs with JavaPSL. In *Proc. SC 2001*. ACM, 2001.

[17] A. Georges, D. Buytaert, and L. Eeckhout. Statistically rigorous Java performance evaluation. In *Proc. OOPSLA 2007*. ACM, 2007.

[18] *GRAL*, 2014. http://trac.erichseifert.de/gral.

[19] *Guava: Google Core Libraries for Java 1.6+*, 2014. http://code.google.com/p/guava-libraries.

[20] V. Horký, F. Haas, J. Kotrč, M. Lacina, and P. Tůma. Performance Regression Unit Testing: A Case Study. In *Proc. EPEW 2013*. Springer, 2013.

[21] D. Hovemeyer and W. Pugh. Finding bugs is easy. *SIGPLAN Not.*, 39(12), Dec. 2004. http://findbugs.sf.net.

[22] IEEE standard for software unit testing. *ANSI/IEEE Std 1008-1987*, 1986.

[23] *Japex Micro-benchmark Framework*, 2013. https://java.net/projects/japex.

[24] *Javadoc Tool*, 2014. http://www.oracle.com/technetwork/java/javase/documentation/index-jsp-135444.html.

[25] *Jaxen*, 2013. http://jaxen.codehaus.org.

[26] *JDOM*, 2013. http://www.jdom.org.

[27] *JFreeChart*, 2013. http://www.jfree.org/jfreechart.

[28] *JMH: Java Microbenchmark Harness*, 2014. http://openjdk.java.net/projects/code-tools/jmh.

[29] T. Kalibera, L. Bulej, and P. Tuma. Benchmark precision and random initial state. In *Proc. SPECTS 2005*, 2005.

[30] L. Madeyski. *Test-Driven Development: An Empirical Evaluation of Agile Practice*. Springer, 2010.

[31] L. Marek et al. DiSL: a domain-specific language for bytecode instrumentation. In *Proc. AOSD 2012*, 2012.

[32] *Metadata Encoding and Transmission Standard*, 2014. http://www.loc.gov/standards/mets.

[33] N. Mitchell and G. Sevitsky. The causes of bloat, the limits of health. In *Proc. OOPSLA 2007*. ACM, 2007.

[34] *NIST/SEMATECH e-Handbook of Statistical Methods*, 2014. http://www.itl.nist.gov/div898/handbook.

[35] *OpenBenchmarking.org: An Open, Collaborative Testing Platform For Benchmarking & Performance Analysis*, 2014. http://openbenchmarking.org.

[36] *Primitive Collections for Java*, 2003. http://pcj.sf.net.

[37] O. Shacham, M. Vechev, and E. Yahav. Chameleon: Adaptive selection of collections. In *Proc. PLDI 2009*. ACM, 2009.

[38] *ACE+TAO+CIAO+DAnCE Distributed Scoreboard*, 2014. http://www.dre.vanderbilt.edu/scoreboard.

[39] *SPL Tools*, 2013. http://d3s.mff.cuni.cz/software/spl.

[40] *Trove*, 2012. http://trove.starlight-systems.com.

[41] *Xeiam XChart*, 2014. http://xeiam.com/xchart.jsp.

[42] *XML Path Language (XPath) 2.0*, 2010. http://w3.org/TR/xpath20.

[43] G. Xu, M. Arnold, N. Mitchell, A. Rountev, and G. Sevitsky. Go with the flow: Profiling copies to find runtime bloat. In *Proc. PLDI 2009*. ACM, 2009.

[44] G. Xu et al. Software bloat analysis: Finding, removing, and preventing performance problems in modern large-scale object-oriented applications. In *Proc. FoSER 2010*. ACM, 2010.

[45] H. Yu, D. Zhang, and L. Rauchwerger. An adaptive algorithm selection framework. In *Proc. PACT 2004*. IEEE, 2004.

On the Road to Benchmarking BPMN 2.0 Workflow Engines

Marigianna Skouradaki[*]
Dieter H. Roller
Frank Leymann
Institute of Architecture and Application Systems
University of Stuttgart
Germany
{skouradaki, dieter.h.roller, leymann}
@iaas.uni-stuttgart.de

Vincenzo Ferme[*]
Cesare Pautasso
Faculty of Informatics
University of Lugano
Switzerland
firstname.lastname@usi.ch

ABSTRACT

Workflow Management Systems (WfMSs) provide platforms for delivering complex service-oriented applications that need to satisfy enterprise-grade quality of service requirements such as dependability and scalability. In this paper we focus on the case of benchmarking the performance of the core of WfMSs, Workflow Engines, that are compliant with the Business Process Model and Notation 2.0 (BPMN 2.0[1]) standard. We first explore the main challenges that need to be met when designing such a benchmark and describe the approaches we designed for tackling them in the Bench-Flow project[2]. We discuss our approach to distill the essence of real-world processes to create from it processes for the benchmark, and to ensure that the benchmark finds wide applicability.

Categories and Subject Descriptors

H.4.1 [**Information Systems Applications**]: Office Automation—*Workflow management*; K.6.2 [**Management of Computing and Information Systems**]: Installation Management—*Benchmarks*; D.2 [**Software Engineering**]: Metrics—*Performance measures*

General Terms

Benchmarking, Workflow Engine Performance, BPMN 2.0

1. INTRODUCTION

Performance benchmarking is an established practice that helps to drive the continuous improvement of technology by

---

[*]Corresponding authors

[1]http://www.omg.org/spec/BPMN/2.0/

[2]http://www.iaas.uni-stuttgart.de/forschung/projects/benchflow.php

setting a clear standard in measuring and assessing performance. Only recently there have been some proposals for benchmarks of service oriented architecture middleware tools (e.g., SOABench [2]). In this paper we focus on one specific kind of middleware: Workflow Engines (WfEs), which can be used for business process automation and service composition. For WfEs there is not yet a currently accepted benchmark, even if standard workflow modeling languages such as BPMN 2.0 are widely used in academia and industrial practice. A possible explanation on this deficiency can be given by the inherent architectural complexity of WfEs and the very large number of parameters affecting their performance.

The main challenges we identify in benchmarking a real-world WfE are: (a) Collecting real-world process models; (b) Synthesing the benchmark workload out of real-world processes; (c) Designing the benchmark environment; (d) Assessing and selecting the BPMN 2.0 engines to be tested; (e) Characterising workloads of different actors; (f) Defining expressive Key Performance Indicators (KPIs).

In this paper, we introduce the BenchFlow approach for benchmarking WfEs. Its main goal is to address the aforementioned challenges, by defining the first benchmark for WfEs. In particular, it targets engines supporting BPMN 2.0 because, as we are going to show in this paper, this standard has gained a noticeable impact on the market.

2. BENCHMARK DESIGN

Given the challenges and complexity of benchmarking WfEs, we follow an iterative project management approach to design and release the benchmark. With each iteration, we enhance both the completeness and real-world representativeness of the benchmark, while taking advantage of early results to steer the BenchFlow project direction. We are currently planning to perform three iterations during the project's lifespan.

1st Iteration: runs a performance stress test on two selected WfEs, with both micro-benchmarks, to measure specific features of WfEs, and a workload mix that reflects all elements of the BPMN 2.0 Core[3], to simulate real-world behaviours. According to Muehlen and Recker [15] supporting BPMN 2.0 Core should already have a good coverage of the process models' regular usage of BPMN 2.0 constructs.

---

[3]http://www.omg.org/bpmn/Samples/Elements/Core_BPMN_Elements.htm

Actors interacting with the System Under Test (SUT) are omitted in this phase. In real-life executions the WfE uses the actors' think time to spread its load, while at this case the WfE must execute all the incoming activities immediately. For this reason this stress test responds to the worst case scenario for the WfE performance. In this iteration throughput (i.e., processes executed/time unit) is used as KPI.

2nd Iteration: targets to more open source and proprietary systems, with load, soak, and spike tests as performance tests [14], as well as the performance stress test from the 1st iteration. To get a step closer to real-life conditions, simple actor workload models are added in this iteration. The workload mix is also more complex in terms of structures, parallelism, and interaction with external services (e.g., JMS, web services), and BPMN 2.0 non-core activities. More KPIs measured in order to better address the new types of tests (e.g., latency, utilization, etc.) [16].

3rd Iteration: the sample of WfEs is further extended. The workload represents more complex interactions of the actors with the SUT. The impact of monitoring to the WfE performance will be assessed, as monitoring is a very common feature for WfEs. The workload mix will be more complex in structure, parallelism, and BPMN 2.0 elements (complete BPMN 2.0 set). Fault-models are also part of this workload mix. Finally the set of measured KPIs will be completed by offering the possibility to the user to select custom KPIs.

3. ADDRESSING THE CHALLENGES

3.1 Collect Real-World Process Models

In order to come up with a benchmark that correctly reflects the usage of a WfE in the real world, we need to collect as many process models representing real-world scenarios as necessary. Because "process equals product" [11] most companies and business organisations are not willing to share their process models with academic researchers to protect their intellectual property and their competitive advantage. To encourage sharing of the models we have signed confidentiality agreements with several companies and implemented a tool for obfuscating and anonymizing process models [20].

Without requesting models with a focus on a specific modelling language we have managed to collect 8363 models within four months from: the IBM Industry Models collection[4], the BPM Academic Initiative[5], companies we contacted and research projects we are involved in. More specifically, our collection contains: 1% WS-BPEL, 4% EPC, 7% YAWL, 24% Petri Net, and 64% BPMN Models, where 2/3 are BPMN 2.0. The large number of BPMN 2.0 models found in the collection supports our choice of developing a benchmark for the most recent standard process modelling language (BPMN 2.0).

3.2 Process Synthesis

The process models we have collected reflect a wide diversity of models (complex, long running, highly parallel etc.). In order to keep the benchmark close to real world we intend to accompany the default workload set, with a workload generator. Figure 1 depicts the methodology for

[4] http://www-01.ibm.com/software/data/industry-models/
[5] http://bpmai.org/BPMAcademicInitiative/

the generation of the workload, which uses the following four phases:

Process Fragment Discovery: Addresses the automatic discovery of the most frequently reoccurring structures in a collection of process models. As BPMN 2.0 models can be seen as an attributed directed graph this problem can be reduced to frequent pattern discovery or subgraph discovery that are specification problems of graph/subgraph isomorphism. This problem is NP-Hard [5] and thus it is imperative to define an efficient methodology for discovering the similar structures. The sub-graphs are calculated with a naive algorithm approach, and clustered according to frequency of appearance. The ones with a frequency above a threshold are included in a new repository.

Process Fragment Refinement: The extracted parts are stored in the form of sliced BPMN 2.0 code. Their refinement as "Process Fragments" (namely, process parts of relaxed completeness) [19] will make this code reusable. We are initially focusing on Schumm's definition but we will tailor it to our needs. For example in BPMN 2.0, an event gateway followed by events could be considered as a fragment even if it does not include an activity. "Process Fragments" can be used to synthesize processes that will represent the existing collection.

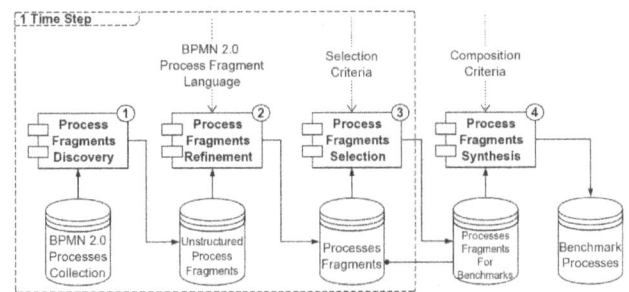

Figure 1: Workload Generation Methodology

Process Fragments Selection: All process fragments will not necessarily be of benchmark interest. This phase automatically selects fragments that satisfy benchmark related criteria that are calculated according to a set of process model metrics [13, 3]. The selected fragments are stored in a separate repository that is a subset of the initial process fragment repository.

Process Fragments Synthesis: Synthesizes the process fragments into processes according to composition criteria that are given by the user and stores them in a repository. For example, when the selection criteria ask for a process with depth $\leq$ N and M external interactions, the appropriate fragments are chosen to synthesise it. Phases 1-3 may only be executed one time, as it is not needed to extract the fragments every time.

3.3 Design the Benchmarking Environment

A carefully designed benchmarking environment and an efficient and flexible deployment mechanism are fundamental in order to guarantee the quality of the benchmark. Portability, scalability, simplicity, vendor neutrality, repeatability, and efficiency are characteristics that any reliable benchmark should demonstrate [6, 9]. We setup the benchmarking environment on different physical machines on the same local network, and deploy different actors and components of the WfE on them. To obtain a "clean" measurement of the WfE performance we must separate it to the maximum possible degree from the external interferences (e.g. DBMS server and Web Services). Figure 2 gives an overview of the BenchFlow benchmark environment and how different components and main actors of the WfE are deployed on different machines.

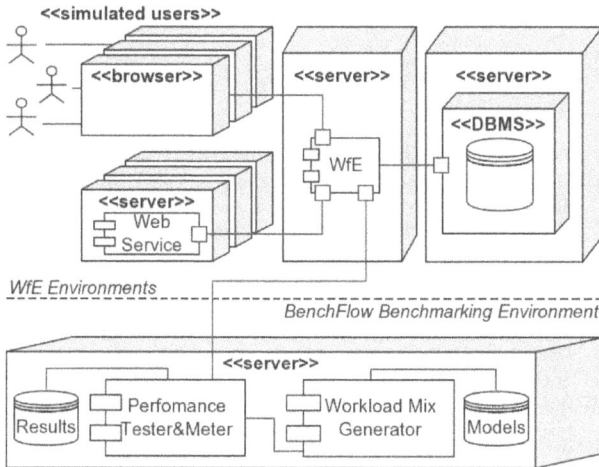

Figure 2: Benchmarking Environment Deployment

BenchFlow offers different types of performance tests (see Section 2), allowing the configuration of the workload mix (through the *Workload Mix Generator* component), the WfE under test, the characteristics of the interacting actors and the computed KPIs. Moreover it generates workload-configurable actors [Req. (1)] as the dual of benchmark processes and test configurations using a model-driven approach. This means we need to ensure a flexible deployment mechanism [Req. (2)], e.g., what is offered by tools such as Vagrant[6], a tool for managing virtual machines via a simple to use command line interface, or Docker[7], a tool for creating and working with containers to deploy complex applications. Docker fits our needs because it guarantees a sufficient level of isolation and a quick start up. It is more lightweight and requires less resources in contrast to the virtual machines approach implemented by Vagrant. Docker also allows to configure the hardware resources of different machines in a flexible way [Req. (3)], so we can use it to switch between test configurations. After the deployment, BenchFlow runs the tests using the interfaces exposed by the WfE, injecting the load as configured by the test configuration. Given that the interfaces exposed by the WfEs are heterogeneous (non-standard APIs), we map them to a common, uniform access mechanism [Req. (4)] to guarantee the best level of scalability of the benchmarking environment so that the effort to benchmark a new WfE is minimised. BenchFlow also ensures that the initial state of the different components is the same for every execution (frozen initial conditions) [Req. (5)], and verifies the environment [Req. (6)] to ensure the fulfilment of the conditions needed to execute a reliable

benchmark. During or at the end of the test executions, BenchFlow collects the data to compute KPIs in a reliable way. Depending on the options of the SUT, data to compute KPIs are collected during the test executions, using tools like Faban[8] and JMeter[9], or exploiting the log generated by the WfE, which are retrieved and analysed at the end of the test execution. Moreover BenchFlow collects system performance metrics from every environment shown in Figure 2, such as CPU, memory and bandwidth usage, while minimising the invasiveness of the measurements [Req. (7)]. These metrics allow us to check for external interferences during the benchmark measurement, and guarantee the same environment conditions for each benchmarked engine.

3.4 BPMN 2.0 Engines Assessment

The WfEs that participate in the benchmark need to fulfill the following requirements: a) support at least the BPMN 2.0 Core, b) be testable in order to automate the benchmark executions. Testability means that the WfE exposes APIs to interact with it at least to: b.1) deploy a process; b.2) request to start the process execution; b.3) access pending user, manual and receive tasks, intermediate catching message and signal events; b.4) access the process execution log; and c) be still in active development.

We have conducted a survey among the existing WfEs that support BPMN 2.0, gathering the following information from the discovered products' Web sites and release notes. Our search found both proprietary and open source products. We have found 19 systems in active development that support BPMN 2.0. The complete list is omitted for space reasons but available online[10].

The release date of the first version supporting BPMN 2.0 has been used to visualize the trend of the number of systems in active development that support BPMN 2.0 over time (cf. Figure 3). In addition to show the rapid adoption of the standard (released in January 2011), this trend shows that the time is ripe for developing a benchmark for it.

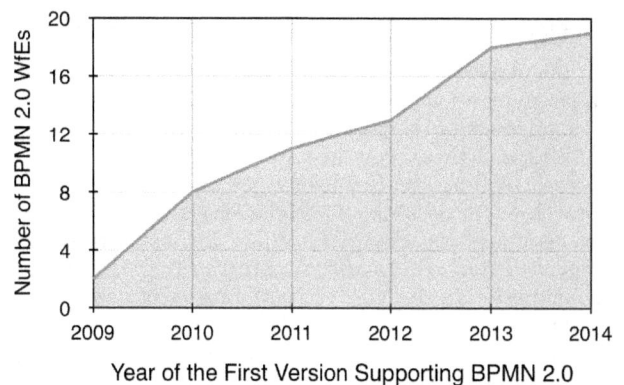

Figure 3: Trend of the Number of WfEs Supporting BPMN 2.0

The systems are written in different programming languages (PHP, Javascript, Java, etc.). This heterogeneity of programming languages makes it particularly challenging to

---

[6]http://www.vagrantup.com
[7]https://www.docker.com

[8]http://faban.org
[9]http://jmeter.apache.org
[10]https://en.wikipedia.org/wiki/List_of_BPMN_2.0_Engines

compare their performance. We have found it surprisingly difficult to determine the level of testability of a given WfE (req. (b)) without actually installing it and looking for the necessary APIs, since these are rarely documented on the corresponding websites. For the same reason, we need to run a compliance test for the BPMN 2.0 standard as done for BPEL WfEs in [8], in order to assess the req. (a).

4. RELATED WORK

To the best of our knowledge BenchFlow is the first benchmark that specifically targets BPMN 2.0 WfEs. There is a widely recognised need for introducing such a benchmark [22, 18], which would enable the evaluation of performance of different research prototypes and commercial products in meaningful conditions.

SOABench [2] can be seen as an initial step to provide a performance assessment and comparison framework of SOA middleware systems. It features automatic generation and execution of testbeds for benchmarking BPEL WfEs. However SOABench assumes that the performance of a BPEL WfE can be reduced to its response time. OpenESB [21] and Din et al. [4] use a simple synthetic process to run the benchmark. ActiveVOS [1] and Intel Cape Clear [10] perform a load testing of a proprietary system with two real process models.

Roller [17] and FACTS [12] perform load testing using one real-world process to stress an open source and a proprietary WfE. Both of these works invoke external services through their processes. Hackman et al. [7] benchmarks BPEL WfEs using 12 kernels processes. The benchmark performs a baseline test that measures the latency and the memory utilisation of two open source WfEs.

BenchFlow is different considering: a) the number and heterogeneity of the WfEs under test, b) the growing complexity of the workload mix, and c) the type of performance tests that will observe a broader spectrum of raw performance metrics and aggregate them into meaningful KPIs.

5. CONCLUSION AND FUTURE WORK

In this paper we discussed critical aspects of the design of a benchmark for BPMN 2.0 WfEs that will help towards the comparison of the performance characteristics of different WfEs and therefore stimulate further research in this important middleware technology. We presented our initial approach to tackle some of the challenges that one meets when designing a benchmark for WfEs. Our goal is to start a discussion on our benchmarking approach within the community, interested in studying the performance of middleware for workflow and business process management and come up with a well-designed, widely accepted and usable benchmark for assessing, comparing and further improving the performance of BPMN 2.0 WfEs.

Acknowledgements

This work is funded by the Swiss National Science Foundation and the German Research Foundation with the BenchFlow (DACH Grant Nr. 200021E-145062/1) project.

6. REFERENCES

[1] Active Endpoints Inc. Assessing ActiveVOS performance, 2011. http://www.activevos.com/content/developers/technical_notes/assessing_activevos_performance.pdf.

[2] D. Bianculli, W. Binder, and M. L. Drago. SOABench: Performance evaluation of service-oriented middleware made easy. In *Proc. of ICSE'10 - Volume 2*, pages 301–302, 2010.

[3] J. Cardoso. Business process control-flow complexity: Metric, evaluation, and validation. *International Journal of Web Services Research*, 5(2):49–76, 2008.

[4] G. Din, K.-P. Eckert, and I. Schieferdecker. A workload model for benchmarking BPEL engines. In *Proc. of ICSTW'08*, pages 356–360, 2008.

[5] M. Dumas, L. García-Bañuelos, and R. M. Dijkman. Similarity search of business process models. *IEEE Data Eng. Bull.*, 32(3):23–28, 2009.

[6] J. Gray. *The Benchmark Handbook for Database and Transaction Systems*. Morgan Kaufmann, 2nd edition, 1992.

[7] G. Hackmann, M. Haitjema, C. Gill, and G.-C. Roman. Sliver: A BPEL workflow process execution engine for mobile devices. In *Proc. of ICSOC'06*, pages 503–508. Springer, 2006.

[8] S. Harrer, J. Lenhard, and G. Wirtz. BPEL conformance in open source engines. In *Proc. of SOCA'12*, pages 1–8, 2012.

[9] K. Huppler. The art of building a good benchmark. In *Performance Evaluation and Benchmarking*, pages 18–30. Springer, 2009.

[10] Intel and Cape Clear. BPEL scalability and performance testing. White paper, 2007.

[11] F. Leymann. Managing business processes via workflow technology. In *Proc. of VLDB 2001*, pages 729–, 2001.

[12] A. Liu, Q. Li, L. Huang, and M. Xiao. Facts: A framework for fault-tolerant composition of transactional web services. *IEEE Trans. on Services Computing*, 3(1):46–59, 2010.

[13] J. Mendling. *Metrics for Process Models: Empirical Foundations of Verification, Error Prediction, and Guidelines for Correctness*. Springer, 2008.

[14] I. Molyneaux. *The Art of Application Performance Testing: Help for Programmers and Quality Assurance*. O'Reilly, 2009.

[15] M. Z. Muehlen and J. Recker. How much language is enough? theoretical and practical use of the business process modeling notation. In *Proc. of CAiSE'08*, pages 465–479, 2008.

[16] C. Röck and S. Harrer. Literature survey of performance benchmarking approaches of BPEL engines. Technical report, Otto-Friedrich University of Bamberg, 2014.

[17] D. H. Roller. *Throughput Improvements for BPEL Engines: Implementation Techniques and Measurements applied in SWoM*. PhD thesis, University of Stuttgart, 2013.

[18] N. Russell, W. M. van der Aalst, and A. Hofstede. All that glitters is not gold: Selecting the right tool for your BPM needs. *Cutter IT Journal*, 20(11):31–38, 2007.

[19] D. Schumm, D. Karastoyanova, O. Kopp, F. Leymann, M. Sonntag, and S. Strauch. Process fragment libraries for easier and faster development of process-based applications. *CSSI*, 2(1):39–55, 2011.

[20] M. Skouradaki, D. Roller, C. Pautasso, and F. Leymann. BPELanon: Anonymizing BPEL processes. In *Proc. of ZEUS'14*, pages 9–15, 2014.

[21] Sun Microsystems. Benchmarking BPEL service engine, 2007. http://wiki.open-esb.java.net/Wiki.jsp?page=BpelPerformance.html.

[22] B. Wetzstein, P. Leitner, F. Rosenberg, I. Brandic, S. Dustdar, and F. Leymann. Monitoring and analyzing influential factors of business process performance. In *Proc. of EDOC'09*, pages 141–150, 2009.

Impact of Data Locality on Garbage Collection in SSDs: A General Analytical Study

Yongkun Li[†], Patrick P. C. Lee[‡], John C. S. Lui[‡], Yinlong Xu[†]
[†]School of Computer Science and Technology, University of Science and Technology of China
[‡]Department of Computer Science and Engineering, The Chinese University of Hong Kong
[†]{ykli,ylxu}@ustc.edu.cn, [‡]{pclee,cslui}@cse.cuhk.edu.hk

ABSTRACT

Solid-state drives (SSDs) necessitate garbage collection (GC) to erase data blocks and reclaim the space of invalidated data, and GC inevitably introduces additional writes due to data relocation. The performance of GC, which is quantified by cleaning cost or write amplification, is critical to the overall performance of SSDs. However, characterizing GC performance is complicated by the general implementations of GC algorithms and the complex data locality characteristics of real-world workloads. This paper presents a *general* analytical study to characterize the performance impact of data locality on a general family of GC algorithms. We develop probabilistic models to address two fundamental issues: (1) What is the impact of data locality on the performance of locality-oblivious GC? (2) How can data locality be leveraged to improve the performance in locality-aware GC? We further conduct extensive trace-driven simulations on real-world workloads to validate the findings of our models.

Categories and Subject Descriptors

B.3.3 [**Memory Structures**]: Performance Analysis and Design Aids; D.4.2 [**Operating Systems**]: Storage Management—*Garbage collection*; G.3 [**Probability and Statistics**]: Probabilistic algorithms

General Terms

Performance;Theory;Algorithms

Keywords

SSDs; Garbage Collection; Trade-off; Data Locality

1. INTRODUCTION

NAND-flash-based solid-state drives (SSDs) provide performance gains over traditional hard-disk drives (HDDs) in I/O throughput, energy efficiency, and reliability, and thus have seen wide adoption in mainstream storage systems. SSDs have distinct I/O characteristics from HDDs.

An SSD organizes data into *blocks*, each containing a number of fixed-size *pages*. Reads and writes are performed on pages. To write new data, an SSD must identify a *clean* page to program and mark the programmed page as *valid*; to update existing data, an SSD uses an *out-of-place* approach that first programs the data to a new clean page and then marks the original page as *invalid*. Invalid pages can only be reset to clean pages by an erase operation, which must be performed on the whole block. Thus, an SSD regularly performs *garbage collection* (GC) to erase blocks so as to reclaim the space of invalid pages. A physical constraint is that each SSD block can only tolerate a finite number of erase operations before wearing out.

The design of a GC algorithm, which specifies the strategy of choosing a block to erase, determines the performance of an SSD. Specifically, a GC algorithm relocates all valid pages to a different free block with clean pages and hence incurs additional writes. Its performance, often quantified as *cleaning cost* [17] or *write amplification* [12], affects the performance of normal read/write operations in the foreground. Since an SSD block can wear out, a GC algorithm is often designed to improve GC performance (e.g., by erasing the block with the fewest valid pages), while avoiding over-wearing a particular SSD block. It is shown that the trade-off between performance and durability can be realized via different parametric configurations of a general family of GC algorithms [17].

The analysis of general GC algorithms becomes challenging when taking into account the heterogeneity of storage workloads. Specifically, real-world storage workloads are known to exhibit high *data locality*, where some stored data is frequently accessed (i.e., hot), while the rest is rarely accessed (i.e., cold) [23]. It is a common consensus that separating the placement of hot/cold data can improve GC performance [11, 14]. However, general non-uniform workloads can be more complex and exhibit different degrees of hotness/coldness. Their implications on different implementations of GC algorithms remain an open issue. To characterize the GC performance of SSDs, measurement studies (e.g., trace-driven simulations) can be used, yet they suffer from the efficiency problem due to the variety of workloads and the wide choices of GC implementations. On the other hand, analytical modeling is easy to be parameterized and generally needs less running time. However, analytical studies on GC in the literature (see §7) often lack generality, and do not explicitly address the relationships between different types of workloads and different implementations of GC algorithms.

In this paper, we propose a general analytical model that formally characterizes the impact of data locality on the cleaning performance of a general family of GC algorithms, with emphasis on taking into account the generality of both data locality characteristics and implementations of GC algorithms. We make the following contributions:

- We first formalize the notion of data locality. From the study of real-world traces, we observe that real-world workloads exhibit the properties of *clustering* (i.e., only a small proportion of address space is accessed) and *skewness* (i.e., accesses to different parts of address space vary significantly). We formulate a general workload model that classifies the regions of address space into different types of access frequencies, so as to capture both the clustering and skewness.

- We present probabilistic models that analyze the cleaning behaviors for *locality-oblivious GC*, whose implementation builds on a family of GC algorithms called the *Greedy Random Algorithm (GRA)*. GRA can achieve the performance of GREEDY, RANDOM and those in between through a tunable parameter. We formally show that data locality may severely degrade GC performance, and the influence becomes more significant when GRA moves from RANDOM to GREEDY.

- We further extend our model to study the performance of *locality-aware GC*, which incorporates data locality information into the GC design. Based on the knowledge that data pages have different types of access frequencies, we analyze the design strategy of *data grouping*, which stores different types of data pages in separate regions of an SSD.

- We conduct extensive trace-driven simulations using the SSD simulator [1]. We validate the accuracy of our model in performance characterization. We evaluate both locality-oblivious GC and locality-aware GC through several real-world traces from different storage environments, and confirm our findings derived from our analytical model. We also study the performance-durability trade-off of GC algorithms via trace-driven simulations.

The remaining of the paper proceeds as follows. In §2, we formulate the problem of analyzing the impact of data locality on GC performance. In §3, we present probabilistic analysis on the cleaning behaviors of locality-oblivious GC, and study the impact of data locality. In §4, we focus on locality-aware GC, and study the impact of data grouping. In §5, we validate our analysis via trace-driven simulations and identify the implications of our model. In §6, we present trace-driven simulation results under real-world traces. In §7, we review related work, and finally in §8, we conclude the paper.

2. PROBLEM FORMULATION

In this section, we formulate the problem of analyzing the impact of data locality on the performance of GC algorithms. We first present an SSD model. Based on the analysis of real-world storage traces, we then propose a new model that can capture the data locality of workloads. Finally, we define the metrics for quantifying the performance of GC algorithms.

2.1 SSD Model

We consider an SSD with N physical blocks with k pages each. Recall from §1 that a block consists of a combination of valid, invalid, and clean pages. Since an SSD reserves blocks for GC and bad block management [19], its advertised capacity as viewed by the logical address space is generally smaller than its physical capacity. We define the proportion of reserved blocks as the *spare factor* S. That is, NS blocks are reserved, and we call them *spare blocks*. Since the logical address space only spans $N(1 - S)$ blocks, increasing S implies less available storage space, yet it reduces write amplification since each block contains fewer valid pages on average. Thus, S is a critical parameter to GC performance.

To support out-of-place updates (see §1), an SSD maintains address mappings between logical and physical pages in a software layer called *flash translation layer (FTL)*. In this work, we assume that address mapping is implemented in the *page level* since it potentially achieves the best I/O performance [9], although it can also be realized in the block level [22] or hybrid form [6, 15, 21]. Note that page-level address mapping is also assumed in prior analytical work [3, 7, 12, 26, 27].

With page-level address mapping, we consider the following write and GC implementations, which are also used by previous analytical studies (see §7). At any time, there is one special block called the *write frontier*. All page writes, such as external writes (due to workload) and internal writes (due to GC), are directed to the write frontier, and pages are sequentially written to the write frontier. When all clean pages in the write frontier are used up, the write frontier is *sealed* and no more writes are permitted until a clean block is selected as the write frontier. Thus, an SSD contains three types of blocks at any time: (1) the write frontier (containing valid, invalid, and clean pages), (2) sealed blocks (without any clean pages), and (3) clean blocks (with clean pages only). When the number of clean blocks drops below a certain threshold, GC will be triggered to perform the following steps: (1) select a sealed block, (2) write all valid pages from the selected sealed block to the write frontier, and (3) erase the selected block. To fully utilize the available spare blocks, we set the threshold as small as possible, so GC is triggered only when the SSD no longer contains any clean physical block after the write frontier is allocated, and GC stops when at least one clean block is reclaimed.

2.2 Workload Model

We propose a workload model to characterize data locality in real-world storage workloads. To motivate the characterization, we first analyze eight real-world I/O traces collected from different storage environments (see §6.1 for details). Since read requests do not affect the GC performance, we focus on write requests only, and accessing a page means that the data in this page is updated. We configure the volume size of an SSD as the maximum logical page number being accessed, and measure the distribution of the access frequency of logical pages for each I/O trace. Here, the access frequency of a logical page is defined as the total number of writes to this page during the whole period of executing a workload. Figure 1 depicts the distributions of four traces, while the remaining traces also share similar trends (which are not shown in the interest of space). We make two observations. First, if we measure the proportion of pages which have *at least one access*, it only accounts for a small por-

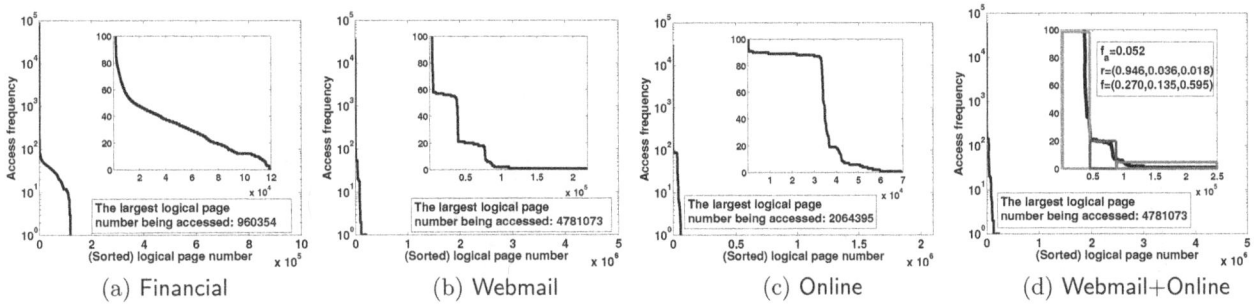

Figure 1: Distributions of access frequency of logical pages for four different real-world workloads. The logical page numbers in the x-axis are sorted in descending order of access frequencies.

tion of the entire logical address space. For example, for the Financial, Webmail, Online, and Webmail+Online traces, the proportions of accessed pages are only 12.4%, 4.6%, 3.3%, and 5.2%, respectively. This reflects a high degree of *clustering* in the workloads. Secondly, among the accessed pages, the number of times that each page is accessed varies significantly. For example, the highest access frequencies of pages in these four traces are around 9.1×10^4, 3.8×10^4, 3.1×10^4, and 6.0×10^4, respectively, implying that some pages are re-accessed frequently. This reflects high *skewness* of the workloads.

We formulate our workload model based on our trace analysis as follows. To model the clustering property, we define a proportion f_a of the logical address space that gets accessed as the *active region*, while the remaining logical address space as the *inactive region*. The active (inactive) region contains all active (inactive) logical pages. With page-level address mapping, each active (inactive) logical page is mapped to an active (inactive) physical page. In our analysis, we do not distinguish the physical and logical pages explicitly, and we simply refer to them as active or inactive pages. Thus, the number of active pages over an SSD is $N(1-S)kf_a$.

Since a real workload usually accesses only a very small proportion of the address space of the SSD, to model the clustering property, we let the active and inactive pages be mapped to separate blocks in the physical address space. That is, the region of the active pages can be taken as the working set of the workload. We call the blocks containing only inactive pages *inactive blocks*, and they must be sealed as they are also occupied by valid data which never gets updated during the whole period of executing the workload. We call the remaining sealed blocks *active blocks*, which may contain both valid and invalid pages.

To model the skewness property, we further classify the active pages into n *access types*. Let $\mathbf{r} = (r_1, ..., r_n)$ and $\mathbf{f} = (f_1, ..., f_n)$ be the vectors, such that type-i (where $1 \leq i \leq n$) pages are uniformly accessed by a proportion r_i of requests which account for a proportion f_i of active pages of the logical address space, and we have $\sum_{i=1}^{n} r_i = \sum_{i=1}^{n} f_i = 1$. Without loss of generality, we assume that $\frac{r_1}{f_1} \geq \frac{r_2}{f_2} \geq \cdots \geq \frac{r_n}{f_n}$. A larger ratio $\frac{r_i}{f_i}$ means that a type-i page is on average accessed by more requests, so our assumption implies that type-1 pages are the hottest, while type-n pages are the coldest. To summarize, we can characterize a workload by the parameters $(f_a, n, \mathbf{r}, \mathbf{f})$, as illustrated in Figure 2.

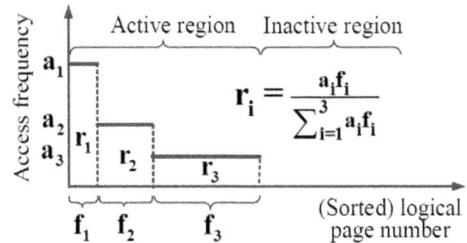

Figure 2: Illustration of our workload model with $n = 3$.

We show via examples how to map a workload to our model. The uniform workload can be modeled by setting $f_a = 1$, $\mathbf{r} = (1)$ and $\mathbf{f} = (1)$. A non-uniform hot/cold workload [7,27], such as 80/20 workload, can be modeled by setting $f_a = 1$, $n = 2$, $\mathbf{r} = (0.8, 0.2)$, and $\mathbf{f} = (0.2, 0.8)$. We can also model a more fine-grained workload by setting a larger n. For instance, for the Webmail+Online workload in Figure 1(d), the proportion of active pages f_a is 0.052, and the embedded figure in Figure 1(d) shows the distribution of access frequency of active pages only. We can choose $n = 3$ and set the thresholds as 20 and 5. That is, pages that are accessed by no less than 20 times are classified as type-1, other pages that are accessed by no less than 5 times are classified as type-2, and the remaining active pages are of type-3. Under this setting, the parameters $\mathbf{r}$ and $\mathbf{f}$ can be measured as $\mathbf{r} = (0.946, 0.036, 0.018)$ and $\mathbf{f} = (0.270, 0.135, 0.595)$.

Note that our workload model differs from the traditional $\mathbf{r}$–$\mathbf{f}$ model in [23] (which is also used in prior analytical studies [7,27]) in that the latter does not consider the clustering property (i.e., it sets $f_a = 1$). Our workload model can be viewed as a generalized $\mathbf{r}$–$\mathbf{f}$ model in [23], and it enables us to model a wider range of real-life I/O workloads.

Our analysis considers the entire period of executing a workload. Note that we focus on write requests only, we let L be the total number of single-page writes in the entire workload. To guarantee the statistical significance, we assume that L is sufficiently larger than the capacity of the logical address space, i.e., $L \gg Nk(1-S)$.

2.3 Performance Metric

Given the SSD and workload models, our analysis focuses on the metric *cleaning cost* $C(alg)$, which quantifies the performance of a GC algorithm alg. Let M be the total number of GC operations that have been performed on an SSD, v_j (where $1 \leq j \leq M$ and $0 \leq v_j \leq k$) be the number of valid pages moved from the erased block to the write frontier in the j-th GC operation. Mathematically, we define the cleaning cost as the total number of internal page writes in all GC operations. That is,

$$\mathcal{C}(alg) = \sum_{j=1}^{M} v_j. \qquad (1)$$

Note that the cleaning cost equivalently models write amplification [12], which is often defined as the average number of internal page writes per external user write.

In this paper, we study two classes of GC designs, namely *locality-oblivious GC* and *locality-aware GC*. Locality-oblivious GC does not consider data locality in the design. We analyze how data locality influences the cleaning cost of GC algorithms under this category. See §3 for details. Locality-aware GC aims to include the workload characteristics defined by $(f_a, n, \mathbf{r}, \mathbf{f})$ into the design. We consider the design strategy of *data grouping*, which stores the data pages of different access types separately in an SSD. See §4 for details.

3. LOCALITY-OBLIVIOUS GC

In this section, we propose a *probabilistic analysis framework* on a family of locality-oblivious GC algorithms. The framework enables us to quantify the cleaning cost. We then study some special cases of GC algorithms.

3.1 General Analysis Framework

We consider a family of locality-oblivious GC algorithms, which we call the *Greedy Random Algorithm (GRA)*. The operations of GRA are defined by a *window size* parameter d (where $1 \le d \le N$): each time when GC is triggered, we first select d sealed blocks that have the smallest number of valid pages as candidates (random tie-breaking is used if multiple blocks contain the same number of valid pages); then we uniformly select a block from these d candidate blocks for GC. We use d to denote an implementation of a GC algorithm when the context is clear. In particular, if $d = 1$, then GRA always selects the sealed block containing the smallest number of valid pages for GC, and we call it the *GREEDY* algorithm. On the other hand, if $d = N$, then GRA uniformly selects a sealed block among all physical blocks, and we call this special GRA the *RANDOM* algorithm. We see that GREEDY locally minimizes the cleaning cost as it always write the fewest valid pages in each GC, while RANDOM maximizes the evenness of erasures on blocks as it in essence has all blocks evenly erased. Therefore, GREEDY and RANDOM represent the two *extreme points* in the design space of GC algorithms [17], and GRA operates at the points between GREEDY and RANDOM via the tunable window size parameter.

We now describe the dynamics of the physical blocks in locality-oblivious GC. Figure 3 depicts the states of physical blocks in an SSD right after a clean block is allocated as the write frontier. Recall that GC is triggered when the SSD has no clean block left (see §2.1). Both active blocks and inactive blocks may be chosen for GC according to d: if an inactive block is selected, then k additional page writes are always required as the block contains all valid pages that are not updated; otherwise, if an active block is chosen for GC, then the number of additional page writes is a random variable. Let $\overline{C}_a(d)$ be the average number of all valid pages in the block, and $\overline{C}_i(d)$ be the average number of type-i (where

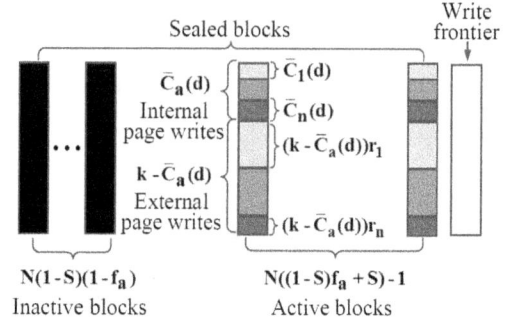

Figure 3: States of blocks right after a clean block is allocated as the write frontier.

$1 \le i \le n$) valid pages in the block. We have $\overline{C}_a(d) = \sum_{i=1}^{n} \overline{C}_i(d)$.

Our GRA analysis makes the following approximation: the d candidate blocks are chosen from the d blocks that are sealed in the earliest time, since the earlier sealed blocks should contain fewer valid pages on average. We note that all writes are designated to the unique write frontier without differentiating the type of updated pages in the case of locality-oblivious GC. Suppose that $n \ll k$, which is expected since we have $k \ge 64$ in commodity SSDs and n is small. Then every sealed block should likely contain *all* n types of pages (see Figure 3). Since our workload model assumes that all pages of the same access type have the same probability of being accessed and updated, we expect that an earlier sealed block has more pages of each type invalidated and hence fewer valid pages overall. In particular, GREEDY can be approximated by the first-in-first-out (FIFO) algorithm, which reclaims blocks following their order of being sealed.

In the following, we analyze the cleaning cost of GRA for general window size d. We refer readers to Appendix for the proofs of all theorems in this paper.

THEOREM 1. *The cleaning cost of GRA with window size d is*

$$\mathcal{C}(d) = \left[L/(k - \overline{C}(d)) \right] \overline{C}(d), \quad (1 \le d \le N), \qquad (2)$$

where $\overline{C}(d)$ denotes the average cleaning cost in each GC and it is

$$\overline{C}(d) = \begin{cases} \overline{C}_a(d), & \text{if } d \le N_a, \\ (N_a/d)\overline{C}_a(d) + (1 - N_a/d)k, & \text{otherwise,} \end{cases} \qquad (3)$$

where $N_a = N((1 - S)f_a + S) - 1$ denotes the number of active blocks. As $N \to \infty$, $\overline{C}_a(d)$ can be computed via Equations (4) and (5) if $1 \le d \le N_a$, and $\overline{C}_a(d) = \overline{C}_a(N_a)$ if $d > N_a$.

$$\overline{C}_a(d) = \sum_{i=1}^{n} \overline{C}_i(d), \qquad (4)$$

$$\overline{C}_i(d) = \frac{r_i(k - \overline{C}_a(d))(1 - P')^{N_a - d}}{1 + P' \times d - (1 - P')^{N_a - d}}, \qquad (5)$$

where $P' = \frac{r_i(k - \overline{C}_a(d))}{(N_a + 1)(1 - S')k f_i}$ and $S' = \frac{S}{(1 - S)f_a + S}$.

Remarks: S' denotes the spare factor of the active region and P' represents the average conditional probability that an active block has a type-i page invalidated for each external page write given that it accesses a type-i page. Equation (5) shows that *the cleaning cost of GC may be affected by data locality, including both clustering and skewness*, which can be reflected by the parameters f_a, r_i's and f_i's. We will further discuss this impact for different values of d in more detail in the following subsections. ∎

Theorem 1 provides a general framework to derive the cleaning cost of GRA for general window size d. However, Equation (5) in Theorem 1, which characterizes the average number of type-i valid pages containing in each active block to be reclaimed, i.e., $\overline{C}_i(d)$, is still too complicated to solve. Since d varies from one to infinity as N goes to infinity, to further simplify the equation so as to efficiently derive the cleaning cost of GRA, we consider the following cases for d: (1) $d = o(N)$, i.e., $\lim_{N\to\infty}\frac{d}{N} = 0$, (2) $d \geq N_a$, and (3) $d = \alpha N_a$ ($0 < \alpha < 1$) where α is a constant. Note that GREEDY ($d=1$) and RANDOM ($d=N$) are included in the first two cases. In the following, we focus on the average cleaning cost in each GC, i.e., $\overline{C}(d)$, because the cleaning cost can be derived based on Theorem 1 given $\overline{C}(d)$.

3.2 GRA with Window Size $d = o(N)$

Consider the case where $d = o(N)$, which also includes the scenario of GREEDY ($d=1$). Equation (5) can be further simplified when N goes to infinity.

THEOREM 2. *As $N \to \infty$, the average cleaning cost $\overline{C}(d)$ of GRA with window size $d = o(N)$ is the unique solution of Equation (6) in the range $[0, k]$*[1].

$$\overline{C}(d) = \sum_{i=1}^{n} \left[(k - \overline{C}(d))r_i \right] / \left[e^{A_i} - 1 \right], \quad (6)$$

where $A_i = \frac{r_i(k-\overline{C}(d))}{(1-S')kf_i}$ and $S' = \frac{S}{(1-S)f_a+S}$.

Remarks: It shows that the cleaning cost of GREEDY is related to the clustering and skewness within the workload, which can be reflected by the parameters f_a, r_i's and f_i's. In particular, we have the following observations from Equation (6). First, the cleaning cost increases as the active region size increases, since Equation (6) is a monotone increasing function with respect to f_a. Formally, if we take $\overline{C}(d)$ as a function of f_a and take the derivative with respect to f_a on both sides of Equation (6), then we can show that the derivative of $\overline{C}(d)$ is greater than zero. Second, the cleaning cost increases if the workload possesses skewness. To check this observation, we fix $r_i = 1/n$, and study different distributions of f_i's, where $f_1 \leq f_2 \leq \cdots \leq f_n$. If we define $g(f_i) = (k - \overline{C}(d))r_i/(e^{\frac{(k-\overline{C}(d))r_i}{(1-S')kf_i}} - 1)$, then we can see that $g(f_i)$ is a convex function with respect to f_i. Thus, we have $\sum_{i=1}^{n} g(f_i) \geq ng((\sum_{i=1}^{n} f_i)/n) = ng(1/n)$. This inequality indicates that if f_i's are not equal, which corresponds to some skewed workload as we fix $r_i = 1/n$, then the cleaning cost increases. In other words, the cleaning cost is the lowest when the workload has no skewness (i.e., when f_i's are equal). ∎

Note that when $r_i = f_i$ ($\forall i = 1, 2, \cdots, n$), the workload changes to uniform access to blocks in the active region. We can derive the cleaning cost of GREEDY as well as GRA with window size $d = o(N)$. In fact, this case was well studied in previous work, e.g., [7], and Theorem 2 derives the same results, which we state in Corollary 1.

---
[1] The equation can be efficiently solved using Newton's method.

COROLLARY 1. *If the pages in the active region are uniformly accessed, as $N \to \infty$, the average cleaning cost of GREEDY (as well as GRA with window size $d = o(N)$) is*

$$\overline{C}(d) = -W_0\left(-\frac{1}{1-S'}e^{-\frac{1}{1-S'}} \right) / \left[\frac{1}{(1-S')k} \right], \quad (7)$$

where $S' = \frac{S}{(1-S)f_a+S}$ and $W_0(\cdot)$ is one branch of Lambert's W function (where $W_0(x) \in [-1, 0]$ for $x \in [-\frac{1}{e}, 0]$).

3.3 GRA with Window Size $d \geq N_a$

Now we focus on the case when $d \geq N_a$, which includes the scenario of RANDOM where $d = N$.

THEOREM 3. *As $N \to \infty$, the average cleaning cost $\overline{C}(d)$ of GRA with window size d where $d \geq N_a$ is*

$$\overline{C}(d) = (1 - NS/d)k. \quad (8)$$

Remarks: Theorem 3 shows that the average cleaning cost of RANDOM is independent of both the clustering and skewness within the workload. The reason is that $\overline{C}_a(d)$ remains unchanged regardless of parameters f_a, **r** and **f**. ∎

3.4 GRA with Window Size $d = \alpha N_a$

We now consider values of d which are smaller than the number of active blocks N_a, but can scale with N_a. We let $d = \alpha N_a$ (where α is a constant with $0 < \alpha < 1$), which means that the window size d is comparable to the number of active blocks. In this case, the average cleaning cost of GRA can be derived as follows.

THEOREM 4. *As $N \to \infty$, the average cleaning cost $\overline{C}(d)$ of GRA with window size $d = \alpha N_a$ is the unique solution of Equation (9) in the range $[0, k]$*[1].

$$\overline{C}(d) = \sum_{i=1}^{n} \left[(k - \overline{C}(d))r_i \right] / \left[(1 + \alpha A_i)e^{(1-\alpha)A_i} - 1 \right], \quad (9)$$

where $A_i = \frac{r_i(k-\overline{C}(d))}{(1-S')kf_i}$ and $S' = \frac{S}{(1-S)f_a+S}$.

Remarks: Note that Equation (9) is also a monotone increasing function of f_a. If we fix $r_i = 1/n$, then each summation term in the right hand side of Equation (9) is also a convex function of f_i. Therefore, Equation (9) has the same implications as those in Equation (6). That is, the relationship between the cleaning cost and data locality is the same for GRA with window size $d < N_a$. ∎

4. LOCALITY-AWARE GC

In this section, we consider the case of locality-aware GC, and analyze a design strategy leveraging on data locality. Since it is a general consensus that cleaning cost of GC algorithms may be reduced when data can be differentiated [11, 14] and a workload includes $n + 1$ types of data pages, it is of interest to study the performance of GC that exploits data locality using *data grouping*, which differentiates different types of data pages and stores them separately in different regions in an SSD. In particular, we analyze how data grouping influences the performance of GC in SSD, and how much is the influence for workloads with different degrees of locality? We assume that we have the complete priori information about the workload so as to take full advantage of hot/cold information.

We first illustrate the architecture of an SSD with data grouping. To perform locality-aware GC, we divide the

309

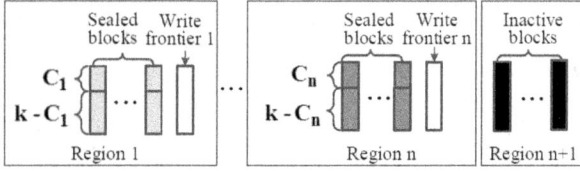

Figure 4: System architecture with data grouping.

whole storage space into $n + 1$ regions, and let the last region keep the inactive data so that this region never gets accessed. For other n regions, each region keeps only one type of data pages and performs GC independently, so it has a separate write frontier for handling writes directed to that region. Without loss of generality, we assume that region 1 stores the hottest data while region n stores the coldest data. Note that logical pages in each of the first n regions are randomly and uniformly accessed because of data grouping. Hence, the first n regions can be considered as n independent sub-systems, each of which is fed with a uniform workload. The architecture of an SSD with data grouping can be further illustrated in Figure 4. Here, since each region is fed with a uniform workload, it only contains one type of data. In particular, we denote C_i as the average cleaning cost in region i $(1 \le i \le n)$.

Note that the purpose of considering data grouping is to leverage data locality in improving the GC performance, and the analysis in §3 shows that GREEDY outperforms GRA with a general window size under the uniform workload (i.e., when $f_a = 1$ and $n = 1$). Therefore, in the interest of space, we assume that GREEDY is used for GC in each region for locality-aware GC.

Since there are NS spare blocks in total and $n + 1$ separate regions with data grouping, one implementation issue of locality-aware GC is how many spare blocks should be allocated to each region. The allocation of spare blocks to each region may influence the cleaning cost. To study the impact of different allocations, we analyze the cleaning cost of GC with a given allocation $\mathbf{b} = (b_1, b_2, \cdots, b_n)$, where b_i denotes the proportion of spare blocks allocated to region i. We have $0 \le b_i \le 1$ and $\sum_{i=1}^{n} b_i = 1$. Note that since no request goes to region $n + 1$, we do not need to allocate spare blocks to it. Given the allocation of $\mathbf{b}$, the total number of physical blocks in region i is $N(1 - S)f_a f_i + NSb_i$ $(1 \le i \le n)$, which we denote as N_i. Now we can derive the cleaning cost of locality-aware GC, and the result is stated in Theorem 5.

THEOREM 5. *Given the spare block allocation* $\mathbf{b}$ *where proportion* b_i *of spare blocks are allocated to region* i $(1 \le i \le n)$ *and* $\sum_{i=1}^{n} b_i = 1$ $(0 \le b_i \le 1)$, *the cleaning cost* $\mathcal{C}$ *of locality-aware GC are*

$$\mathcal{C} = \sum_{i=1}^{n} \left[Lr_i/(k - C_i) \right] C_i,$$

where $C_i = -W_0\left(-\frac{1}{1-S_i}e^{-\frac{1}{1-S_i}}\right)/\left[\frac{1}{(1-S_i)k}\right]$ *as* $N \to \infty$ *and* $S_i = Sb_i/[(1 - S)f_a f_i + Sb_i]$.

Remarks: Theorem 5 shows that the allocation of spare blocks, $\mathbf{b}$, affects the cleaning cost of locality-aware GC. The most significant allocation is the one that minimizes the cleaning cost, which we denote as $\mathbf{b}_c^*$. We will further

show the performance improvement of cleaning cost for $\mathbf{b}_c^*$ in §5.3 via numerical analysis.

Note that the design strategy of data grouping exploits data locality by eliminating the skewness within a workload. In particular, it separates a highly-skewed workload into multiple uniform workloads with no skewness so as to reduce the cleaning cost (see §5.2 for the impact of skewness). ■

5. MODEL VALIDATION AND IMPLICATIONS

In this section, we conduct model analysis to study the impact of data locality and the implications of locality awareness on the GC design. We first validate our model using the SSD simulator [1]. Based on our model, we then study the impact of data locality and architectural design.

5.1 Model Validation

Since the analysis of locality-aware GC builds on locality-oblivious GC and each region of the SSD in the locality-aware GC corresponds exactly to the case of locality-oblivious GC under uniform workload, our model validation focuses on locality-oblivious GC only with respect to different workloads. To speed up our simulation, we consider a small-scale SSD that contains one flash chip composed of 8 planes with 1024 blocks each. We configure each block with 64 pages of size 4KB each. We use the default timing parameters set by the simulator. We set the spare factor $S = 0.1$ (i.e., the logical address space is 90% of the physical address space).

We generate multiple synthetic workloads to drive our simulation. Since read requests do not affect GC, we generate write requests only. Specifically, for each workload, we generate 5M write requests, which suffice to make all active pages get enough number of accesses so to guarantee the statistical significance. Each request has size of 4KB, which aligns with the page size. We specify a workload based on the parameterizing $(f_a, n, \mathbf{r}, \mathbf{f})$. Here, we consider two types of workloads: (a) *skewed workload*, in which we have 20% of active pages accessed by 80% of requests by setting $f_a = 0.1$, $n = 2$, $\mathbf{r} = (0.8, 0.2)$ and $\mathbf{f} = (0.2, 0.8)$; and (b) *fine-grained workload*, in which we set a larger value of n by fixing $f_a = 0.1$, $n = 4$, $\mathbf{r} = (0.4, 0.3, 0.2, 0.1)$ and $\mathbf{f} = (0.2, 0.2, 0.3, 0.3)$.

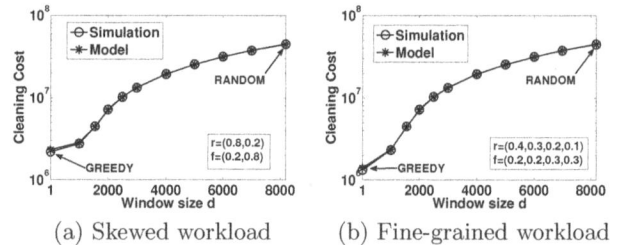

(a) Skewed workload   (b) Fine-grained workload

Figure 5: Model validation for locality-oblivious GC.

Figure 5 shows both the model and simulation results based on the above workloads. Each data point in a curve corresponds to GRA with a particular value of d, which increases from the leftmost point (i.e., GREEDY) to the rightmost point (i.e., RANDOM). Our model accurately characterizes the cleaning cost under different workloads. In particular, comparing the model and simulation results for a given value of d, the cleaning costs differ by no more than

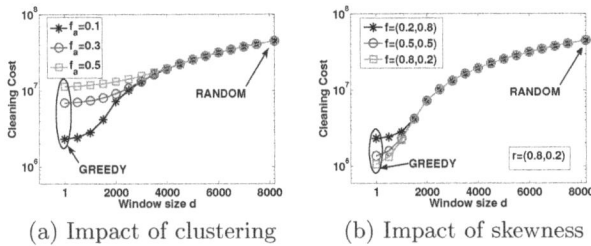

(a) Impact of clustering   (b) Impact of skewness

Figure 6: Impact of data locality on locality-oblivious GC.

7%, and it is no more than 1% in most cases. We also validate other types of workloads, such as different values of f_a. The model and simulation results conform to each other. In the interest of space, we do not present the results here.

5.2 How Data Locality Affects Locality-oblivious GC?

We use our model to obtain numerical results, and study how data locality affects the GC performance. Here, we focus on locality-oblivious GC. To study the impact of data locality, we consider a given GC implementation by fixing the window size d of GRA, and examine its changes of cleaning cost under different workloads.

Figure 6(a) shows the impact of clustering by varying $f_a = 0.1$, 0.3, and 0.5, which determines the proportion of the active region, while fixing the skewness with $n = 2$, $\mathbf{r} = (0.8, 0.2)$, and $\mathbf{f} = (0.2, 0.8)$. Figure 6(b) studies the impact of skewness, and we fix $\mathbf{r} = (0.8, 0.2)$, and vary $\mathbf{f} = (0.2, 0.8)$ (which is the most skewed workload), $\mathbf{f} = (0.5, 0.5)$, and $\mathbf{f} = (0.8, 0.2)$ (which is equivalent to the non-skewed workload). From the figures, we see that cleaning cost increases as either the clustering or skewness increases. Moreover, the increase is more pronounced for a smaller d, and GREEDY shows the most increase. For example, in Figure 6(b), the cleaning cost of GREEDY increases from 1.063×10^6 to 2.314×10^6 when we increase skewness by varying from $\mathbf{f} = (0.8, 0.2)$ to $\mathbf{f} = (0.2, 0.8)$. As d increases, both the impact of clustering and skewness on the cleaning cost vanishes. In particular, data locality within a workload, including both clustering and skewness, has a significant impact on GREEDY, but has no impact on RANDOM.

5.3 Will Locality Awareness Help?

We now analyze via our model the performance of locality-aware GC with data grouping (see §4), and study if it improves over locality-oblivious GC.

Figure 7(a) shows the impact of different spare block allocations on GC performance. Here we consider the skewed workload with $f_a = 0.1$, $n = 2$, $\mathbf{r} = (0.8, 0.2)$ and $\mathbf{f} = (0.2, 0.8)$. Each data point (asterisk) corresponds to a particular allocation $\mathbf{b} = (b_1, 1 - b_1)$, where the leftmost data point ($\mathbf{b}_c^* = (0.432, 0.568)$) minimizes the cleaning cost, and the rightmost data point ($\mathbf{b}_w^* = (0.862, 0.138)$) shows the same performance of locality-oblivious GC with GREEDY, which is marked as square. That is, there is no performance gain for locality-aware GC under the block allocation $\mathbf{b}_w^*$. So we focus on the range of allocations from $\mathbf{b}_c^*$ to $\mathbf{b}_w^*$, and other data points are obtained by varying b_1 from 0.432 to 0.862 with a step size of 0.02. The figure shows that data grouping may efficiently reduce the cleaning cost. For ex-

ample, it can be reduced from 2.31×10^6 to 0.53×10^6 with a proper configuration of the spare blocks in each region.

Figures 7(b) and 7(c) show the impact of clustering and skewness on locality-aware GC, respectively. In Figure 7(b), we vary $f_a = 0.1$, 0.3, and 0.5, while fix the skewness within the workload with $n = 2$, $\mathbf{r} = (0.8, 0.2)$ and $\mathbf{f} = (0.2, 0.8)$. In Figure 7(c), we fix $f_a = 0.1$, $\mathbf{r} = (0.8, 0.2)$, and vary from $\mathbf{f} = (0.2, 0.8)$ to $\mathbf{f} = (0.5, 0.5)$. For each workload, we consider the block allocations varying from $\mathbf{b}_c^*$ to $\mathbf{b}_w^*$ as in Figure 7(a). From Figure 7(b), we see that when the active region size increases, the relative change of cleaning cost decreases. For instance, when $f_a = 0.1$, the cleaning cost under the allocation of $\mathbf{b}_w^*$ (which is 2.31×10^6) is 4.36 times higher than that under the allocation of $\mathbf{b}_c^*$ (which is 0.53×10^6), while this ratio decreases to 2 when $f_a = 0.5$. However, Figure 7(c) shows that the relative change of cleaning cost increases if the workload is more skewed. This can be observed from that the difference of the cleaning cost between the allocations of $\mathbf{b}_c^*$ and $\mathbf{b}_w^*$ is larger when $\mathbf{f} = (0.2, 0.8)$. Even though skewness worsens the cleaning performance of GREEDY for locality-oblivious GC (see Figure 6(b)), it improves the performance of locality-aware GC. That is, incorporating locality awareness into GC design is more significant for workload with higher skewness.

5.4 Summary of Findings

We summarize the implications from our model analysis.

- Data locality affects the performance of locality-oblivious GC with a given implementation (i.e., GRA with a fixed d): (1) cleaning cost increases when either the active region size or the skewness increases, (2) the increase is more pronounced for a smaller window size. In particular, data locality has the most significant impact on GREEDY, but has no impact on RANDOM.

- Locality-aware GC reduces the cleaning cost through data grouping, while the performance improvement depends on the proper allocation of spare blocks. Data locality also affects the performance of locality-aware GC in different ways: (1) if the active region size increases, the relative change of cleaning cost decreases; (2) if the workload has higher skewness, the relative change increases, and so locality awareness is more important if the workload is more skewed.

6. TRACE-DRIVEN EVALUATION

In this section, we conduct trace-driven evaluation on the GC performance under real-world workloads, using the SSD simulator [1]. The goals of our evaluation are two-fold. First, we further validate the implications of our model under real-world workload traces. Second, we show the significance of locality awareness on the GC design.

6.1 Evaluation Setup

We have collected eight real-world workload traces to drive our evaluation. Since read requests do not affect the GC performance, we focus on write-intensive traces. The traces can be categorized into three types of environments:

- Financial [25]: It is an I/O trace of an online transaction process application. We select the write-intensive one Financial1.spc in the repository.

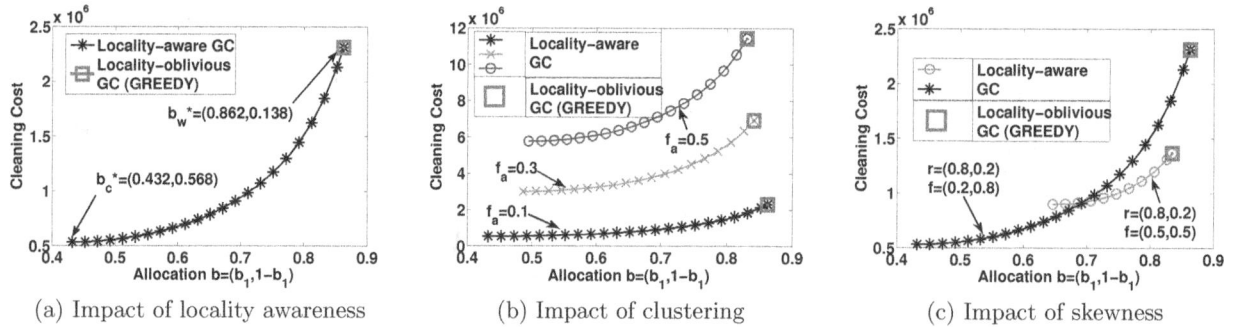

(a) Impact of locality awareness   (b) Impact of clustering   (c) Impact of skewness

Figure 7: Performance of locality-aware GC.

Traces	Total # of single-page writes	Volume size	Proportion of accessed pages
Financial	4.9 M	4 GB	12.4%
Webmail	6.4 M	18 GB	4.6%
Online	4.2 M	8 GB	3.3%
Webmail+Online	10.6 M	18 GB	5.2%
stg_0	5.2 M	2 GB	3%
prxy_0	23.8 M	2 GB	2%
proj_0	41.0 M	2 GB	3.2%
prn_0	18.1 M	2 GB	2.4%

Table 1: Statistics of traces.

- Webmail, Online, Webmail+Online [28]: The three traces describe workloads in a university department. Webmail describes the workload of a mail server, Online describes a coursework management workload on Moodle, and Webmail+Online is the combination of Webmail and Online.

- prxy_0, prn_0, proj_0, stg_0 [20]: The four traces are collected from an enterprise data center. The original set of traces cover 36 volumes in total. We choose four of them that have high write-to-read ratios and a sufficiently large number of write requests.

Table 1 summarizes the statistics of traces. We fix the page size as 4KB and align the requests in each trace to be a multiple of the page size. As shown in the table, each trace consists of millions of single-page writes. We then determine the volume size (i.e., the capacity of the logical space) of each trace by multiplying the largest logical page number among all requests with the page size and rounding it up to the next multiple of gigabytes. For the Financial trace, we ignore the requests with application-specific unit numbers ASU1, ASU3, and ASU5 as they lead to an extremely large volume size. As shown in Table 1 Webmail and Webmail+Online have a large volume size, while the data-center traces [20] have a much smaller volume size. By measuring the proportion of logical pages that are accessed by at least one write request, we see that all write requests only access a very small portion of the logical space for all traces (i.e., f_a is small), with up to only 12.4% as shown in Table 1. We use this characteristic to motivate our workload model formulation (see §2.2).

We configure the SSD simulator for our evaluation as follows. We note that each flash chip in an SSD typically operates independently with its own I/O bus, and performs GC on its own blocks independently of other flash chips. Thus, when we evaluate a GC algorithm under a given workload,

we feed the trace to an SSD with only one flash chip so as to preserve the statistics of the workload. We set each block with the number of pages $k = 64$, and configure the SSD capacity (i.e., the total number of blocks) according to the volume size of each trace, and the spare factor which is set as $S = 0.2$. We focus on page-level address mapping, and assume that the SSD is fully utilized initially, and locality pages are mapped sequentially to physical pages. Thus, each write request to a page corresponds to an update. The full initial state is the default setting of the SSD simulator, and we use it to stress-test the I/O performance of the SSD. Note that the SSD contains a proportion S of spare blocks that have no data initially. To eliminate the influence of these spare blocks, we first warm up the simulator with 10M write requests that uniformly access the pages of the entire logical address space. Afterwards, we drive our evaluation with the real-world traces.

6.2 Impact of Data Locality on Cleaning Cost

Locality-oblivious GC: We first evaluate the cleaning cost of locality-oblivious GC. We consider different GC implementations by configuring GRA with $d = 1$, $\frac{N}{2}$, $\frac{3N}{4}$, and N, where N is the total number of physical blocks. Note that $d = 1$ and $d = N$ correspond to GREEDY and RANDOM, respectively. Since the workload size varies from traces, for ease of comparison, we normalize the cleaning cost as the number of internal page writes caused by GC over the number of external page writes containing in the workload. This normalized cleaning cost can be interpreted as write amplification [12] minus one.

Figure 8(a) shows the results. We see that the performance of locality-oblivious GC manifests in two ways. First, RANDOM gives the worst performance in terms of cleaning cost and GREEDY achieves the best performance. In fact, a trade-off between performance and durability exists for GRA with different values of d, and we show the trade-off in §6.3. Second, we observe that among different GC implementations, GREEDY has the most varying cleaning cost across different workloads. Its normalized cleaning cost varies from 1.6 to 2.46. RANDOM has the least variance in cleaning cost, as also indicated by our analysis (see §3).

Locality-aware GC: Now we evaluate the cleaning cost of locality-aware GC. Our implementation assumes the complete knowledge of the workload, so that we can evaluate the best achievable design of a GC algorithm. Specifically, we fix the number of regions n, and then measure the access frequency of each data page so as to separate data pages into n regions and obtain the corresponding parameters $\mathbf{r}$ and $\mathbf{f}$,

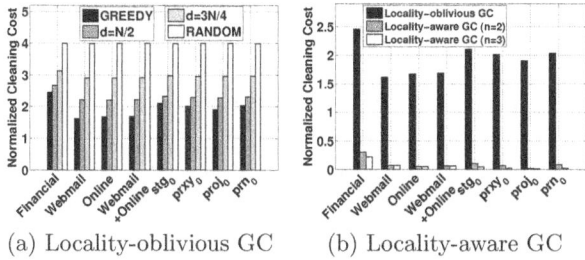

(a) Locality-oblivious GC   (b) Locality-aware GC

Figure 8: Cleaning cost of GC algorithms.

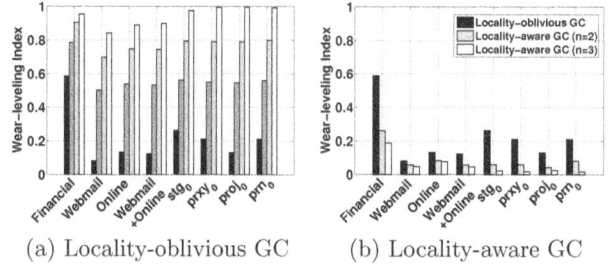

(a) Locality-oblivious GC   (b) Locality-aware GC

Figure 9: Wear-leveling index of GC algorithms.

as defined in §2.2. In terms of the spare block allocation for each region, since different allocations lead to different performance results (see §4), we focus on the one minimizing the cleaning cost.

We consider two scenarios of data grouping: (1) we separate data pages into $n = 2$ types, one of which has data pages accessed by at least 10 times and another has data pages accessed by less than 10 times; (2) we separate data pages into $n = 3$ types, which have data pages accessed by no less than 50 times, less than 50 but no less than 10 times, and less than 10 times, respectively. For comparison, we also plot the cleaning cost of GREEDY in locality-oblivious GC.

Figure 8(b) shows the cleaning cost of locality-aware GC for different traces. First, compared to locality-oblivious GC, cleaning cost can be *significantly reduced with data grouping*, e.g., by more than 87% for locality-aware GC with $n = 2$. The reduction can even reach up to 99% for the proj_0 trace. Note that we can achieve further reduction, although marginal, if we separate data pages into three types.

6.3 Impact of Data Locality on GC Design Trade-off

As stated in [1, 17], GC design poses a trade-off between performance and durability of an SSD. In this subsection, we show the performance-durability trade-off of GC design and study the impact of data locality on it.

Recall that we use the cleaning cost as defined in Equation (1) to represent the performance of GC algorithms. For durability, we define another metric, namely *wear-leveling index* $\mathcal{W}(alg)$.

$$
\mathcal{W}(alg) = \left[N \sum_{i=1}^{N} \left(\frac{n_i}{\sum_{i=1}^{N} n_i} \right)^2 \right]^{-1}
$$
$$
= \left(\sum_{i=1}^{N} n_i \right)^2 \Big/ \left(N \sum_{i=1}^{N} n_i^2 \right),
$$

where n_i $(1 \le i \le N)$ is the number of erasures performed on block i. The intuition of $\mathcal{W}(alg)$ is that it quantifies the fairness among n_i's, so it characterizes how *evenly* blocks are erased throughout all GC operations. Note that we have $0 < \mathcal{W}(alg) \le 1$, where $\mathcal{W}(alg) = 1$ means all blocks receive the same number of erasures.

Figure 9 shows the wear-leveling index of different GC algorithms for both locality-oblivious GC and locality-aware GC. By combining the results in Figure 8, we see that the design trade-off manifests in two ways for locality-oblivious GC. First, the trade-off exists in GRA with different values of d. For a given trace, RANDOM gives a large wear-leveling index but introduces high cleaning cost, while GREEDY in-

curs low cleaning cost but has a small wear-leveling index. Second, the trade-off exists among different traces. For instance, GREEDY shows the highest cleaning cost and wear-leveling index under the Financial trace, which spans the largest active region (i.e., f_a is the largest) as indicated in Table 1. From our analysis, a larger f_a implies higher cleaning cost (see Figure 6). For locality-aware GC, when cleaning cost decreases, the wear-leveling index also decreases (by 28% to 77% as shown in Figure 9(b)). It is thus important to deploy a dedicated wear-leveling technique orthogonal to locality-aware GC.

6.4 Summary

The above evaluation results show that the impact of data locality varies across different GC algorithms. For locality-oblivious GC, data locality significantly influences the performance of GREEDY, but has negligible impact on RANDOM. We demonstrate that locality-aware GC can efficiently reduce the cleaning cost. We also show that the GC design poses a trade-off between cleaning and wear leveling, and the design trade-off exists under all workloads.

7. RELATED WORK

NAND-flash-based SSDs have received much attention in both industrial and academic communities. Several aspects are studied such as write performance optimization [2,10,24], reliability analysis [16], and lifetime extension [5,18]. In particular, Gal *et al.* [8] survey the algorithms and data structures of flash memory. Chen *et al.* [4] and Jung *et al.* [13] reveal the intrinsic characteristics and system implications of SSDs through extensive empirical measurements. Agrawal *et al.* [1] study different design trade-off issues for SSDs using a trace-driven simulator.

Since the cleaning operation introduces additional writes (also known as write amplification) that are critical to SSD performance, several studies analyze the cleaning performance of GC algorithms. For example, Hu *et al.* [12] propose a probabilistic model to analyze a windowed greedy algorithm that erases the block with the fewest valid pages among the least-recently-used blocks. Bux *et al.* [3] analyze the greedy algorithm under uniform workload. Desnoyers [7] analyzes the greedy algorithm under both uniform and non-uniform workloads. Van Houdt [26] develops a mean field model to derive the write amplification for various GC algorithms under uniform workload, and later extends the model for hot/cold workload [27]. Yang and Zhu [29] further employ the mean field model to analyze the performance of various hotness-aware GC algorithms. Li *et al.* [17] also propose a mean field model to analyze different GC algorithms for

SSDs, with the emphasis on modeling the trade-off between cleaning and wear leveling.

Unlike most previous studies, our work focuses on studying the impact of data locality on the cleaning performance of different GC implementations, and makes the following differences. First, we consider more general workloads, with different levels of hotness/coldness, by modeling both clustering and fine-grained skewness. Second, we analyze a family of locality-oblivious GC algorithms and consider a more general implementation of locality-aware GC, which supports the separation of data pages in more fine-grained levels. Finally, we conduct trace-driven simulations to validate our analysis and the findings of our model. In summary, our work complements the previous studies by addressing more general deployment scenarios through both analytical modeling and trace-driven simulations.

8. CONCLUSIONS

We develop analytical models to characterize the impact of data locality on the GC performance of SSDs. We first formalize a workload model to capture data locality (i.e., clustering and skewness) evidenced by the trace analysis of real-life I/O workloads. We then integrate the workload model into GC performance analysis, and study two classes of GC designs: locality-oblivious GC and locality-aware GC. In locality-oblivious GC, we analyze the cleaning cost of a family of GC algorithms. We show that as the active region size increases, the cleaning cost increases, and a more skewed workload also increases the cleaning cost. Furthermore, we extend our analysis for locality-aware GC. We show that data grouping can reduce the cleaning cost, and the reduction is more significant if the workload is more skewed, which shows the importance of locality awareness. Finally, we conduct extensive trace-driven simulations to validate the accuracy and findings of our models. The main focus of our work is to analytically study how data locality influences the cleaning performance of various GC algorithms so as to guide the GC design, while we leave the actual design of locality-aware GC algorithms that exploit workload locality and adapt to workload dynamics as future work.

9. ACKNOWLEDGMENTS

The work of Yongkun Li was supported in part by National Nature Science Foundation of China under Grant No. 61303048, and the Fundamental Research Funds for the Central Universities under Grant No. WK0110000040.

10. REFERENCES

[1] N. Agrawal, V. Prabhakaran, T. Wobber, J. D. Davis, M. Manasse, and R. Panigrahy. Design Tradeoffs for SSD Performance. In *Proc. of USENIX ATC*, Jun 2008.

[2] A. Birrell, M. Isard, C. Thacker, and T. Wobber. A Design for High-performance Flash Disks. *ACM SIGOPS Oper. Syst. Rev.*, 41(2):88–93, Apr 2007.

[3] W. Bux and I. Iliadis. Performance of Greedy Garbage Collection in Flash-based Solid-state Drives. *Performance Evaluation*, Nov 2010.

[4] F. Chen, D. A. Koufaty, and X. Zhang. Understanding Intrinsic Characteristics and System Implications of Flash Memory based Solid State Drives. In *Proc. of ACM SIGMETRICS*, Jun 2009.

[5] F. Chen, T. Luo, and X. Zhang. CAFTL: A Content-aware Flash Translation Layer Enhancing the Lifespan of Flash Memory Based Solid State Drives. In *Proceedings of USENIX, FAST*, 2011.

[6] T.-S. Chung, D.-J. Park, S. Park, D.-H. Lee, S.-W. Lee, and H.-J. Song. System Software For Flash Memory: A Survey. In *Proc. of Int. Conf. on Embedded and Ubiquitous Computing*, Aug 2006.

[7] P. Desnoyers. Analytic Modeling of SSD Write Performance. In *Proceedings of SYSTOR*, Jun 2012.

[8] E. Gal and S. Toledo. Algorithms and Data Structures for Flash Memories. *ACM Computing Surveys*, 37(2):138–163, Jun 2005.

[9] A. Gupta, Y. Kim, and B. Urgaonkar. DFTL: A Flash Translation Layer Employing Demand-based Selective Caching of Page-level Address Mappings. In *Proc. of ACM ASPLOS*, Mar 2009.

[10] A. Gupta, R. Pisolkar, B. Urgaonkar, and A. Sivasubramaniam. Leveraging Value Locality in Optimizing NAND Flash-based SSDs. In *Proc. of USENIX FAST*, 2011.

[11] J.-W. Hsieh, T.-W. Kuo, and L.-P. Chang. Efficient Identification of Hot Data for Flash Memory Storage Systems. *ACM TOS*, Feb 2006.

[12] X.-Y. Hu, E. Eleftheriou, R. Haas, I. Iliadis, and R. Pletka. Write Amplification Analysis in Flash-based Solid State Drives. In *Proc. of SYSTOR*, May 2009.

[13] M. Jung and M. Kandemir. Revisiting Widely Held SSD Expectations and Rethinking System-level Implications. In *Proc. of ACM SIGMETRICS*, Jun 2013.

[14] H.-S. Lee, H.-S. Yun, and D.-H. Lee. HFTL: Hybrid Flash Translation Layer based on Hot Data Identification for Flash Memory. *IEEE Trans. on Consumer Electronics*, 55(4):2005–2011, 2009.

[15] S.-W. Lee, D.-J. Park, T.-S. Chung, D.-H. Lee, S. Park, and H.-J. Song. A Log Buffer-based Flash Translation Layer Using Fully-associative Sector Translation. *ACM TECS*, 6(3), Jul 2007.

[16] Y. Li, P. P. C. Lee, and J. C. S. Lui. Stochastic Analysis on RAID Reliability for Solid-State Drives. In *Proc. of IEEE SRDS*, 2013.

[17] Y. Li, P. P. C. Lee, and J. C. S. Lui. Stochastic Modeling of Large-Scale Solid-State Storage Systems: Analysis, Design Tradeoffs and Optimization. In *Proc. of ACM SIGMETRICS*, 2013.

[18] Y. Lu, J. Shu, and W. Zheng. Extending the Lifetime of Flash-based Storage through Reducing Write Amplification from File Systems. In *Proc. of USENIX FAST*, 2013.

[19] Micron Technology. Bad Block Management in NAND Flash Memory. Technical Note, TN-29-59, 2011.

[20] D. Narayanan, A. Donnelly, and A. Rowstron. Write off-loading: Practical power management for enterprise storage. *ACM TOS*, 4(3):10:1–10:23, Nov 2008.

[21] C. Park, W. Cheon, J. Kang, K. Roh, W. Cho, and J.-S. Kim. A Reconfigurable FTL (Flash Translation Layer) Architecture for NAND Flash-based Applications. *ACM TECS*, 7(4):38:1–38:23, Aug 2008.

[22] Z. Qin, Y. Wang, D. Liu, and Z. Shao. Demand-based Block-level Address Mapping in Large-scale NAND Flash Storage Systems. In *Proc. of IEEE/ACM/IFIP CODES+ISSS*, Oct 2010.

[23] M. Rosenblum and J. K. Ousterhout. The Design and Implementation of a Log-structured File System. *ACM Trans. Comput. Syst.*, 10(1):26–52, Feb 1992.

[24] A. Soga, C. Sun, and K. Takeuchi. NAND Flash Aware Data Management System for High-speed SSDs by Garbage Collection Overhead Suppression. In *IEEE 6th International Memory Workshop (IMW)*, May 2014.

[25] Storage Performance Council. http://traces.cs.umass.edu/index.php/Storage/Storage, 2002.

[26] B. Van Houdt. A Mean Field Model for a Class of Garbage Collection Algorithms in Flash-based Solid State Drives. In *Proc. of ACM SIGMETRICS*, Jun 2013.

[27] B. Van Houdt. Performance of Garbage Collection Algorithms for Flash-based Solid State Drives with Hot/cold Data. *Performance Evaluation*, 70(10):692 – 703, Sep 2013.

[28] A. Verma, R. Koller, L. Useche, and R. Rangaswami. SRCMap: Energy Proportional Storage using Dynamic Consolidation. In *Proc. of USENIX FAST*, Feb 2010.

[29] Y. Yang and J. Zhu. Analytical Modeling of Garbage Collection Algorithms in Hotness-aware Flash-based Solid State Drives. In *Proc. of IEEE MSST*, June 2014.

APPENDIX

Proof of Theorem 1 in §3.1: Since the proportion of active region in logical space is f_a, the number of active blocks is $N_a = N((1-S)f_a+S) - 1$. We consider two cases.
Case 1: $d \leq N_a$. Based on the argument that the blocks that are sealed earlier should contain fewer valid pages on average, we can make an approximation that the d candidate blocks are chosen from the d blocks that are sealed in the earliest time. Thus, only active blocks have the chance of being selected for GC if $d \leq N_a$. Moreover, an active block can be reclaimed at the j-th ($j = N_a - d + 1, N_a - d + 2, \cdots, \infty$) GC instant since it has been sealed, and the corresponding probability is $\frac{1}{d}(1-\frac{1}{d})^{j-(N_a-d)-1}$. Note that $\overline{C}_a(d)$ denotes the average number of valid pages in an active block to be reclaimed under GRA with selection window size d. Among these $\overline{C}_a(d)$ pages, the average number of type-i pages is denoted by $\overline{C}_i(d)$. We have $\overline{C}_a(d) = \sum_{i=1}^n \overline{C}_i(d)$. To simplify the presentation, let us drop the notation d when the context is clear. Since each GC needs to write back $\overline{C}_a$ valid pages on average, each clean block can only handle $k - \overline{C}_a$ external page writes. Therefore, a sealed block is reclaimed after handling $(j-1)(k - \overline{C}_a)$ external page writes on average if it is reclaimed by the j-th GC. For each external page write, it updates a type-i page with probability $\frac{r_i}{N(1-S)f_a k f_i} = \frac{r_i}{(N_a+1)(1-S')k f_i}$ where $N_a = N((1 - S)f_a + S) - 1$ and $S' = \frac{S}{(1-S)f_a+S}$. The physical meaning of S' is that it represents the spare factor of a sub-system without inactive blocks. Now $\overline{C}_i$ can be characterized by the following equation.

$$\overline{C}_i = (\overline{C}_i + (k-\overline{C}_a)r_i) \sum_{j=N_a-d+1}^{\infty} \left[\frac{1}{d}\left(1-\frac{1}{d}\right)^{j-(N_a-d)-1} \times \right.$$
$$\left. \left(1 - \frac{r_i}{(N_a+1)(1-S')k f_i}\right)^{(j-1)(k-\overline{C}_a)} \right]$$
$$= (\overline{C}_i + (k-\overline{C}_a)r_i)(1-P')^{N_a-d}\left[\frac{1}{(1+P' \times d)}\right], \text{(as } N \to \infty)$$

where $P' = \frac{r_i(k-\overline{C}_a)}{(N_a+1)(1-S')k f_i}$. Thus, $\overline{C}_i$ is derived as in Eq. (5). Now the average cleaning cost incurred by reclaiming an active block is $\overline{C}_a = \sum_{i=1}^n \overline{C}_i$. Since inactive blocks will never be chosen for GC as $d \leq N_a$, we have $\overline{C} = \overline{C}_a$.
Case 2: $d > N_a$. There are N_a active blocks and $d - N_a$ inactive blocks in the window of d candidate blocks, and each of them is chosen for GC with equal probability, so the probabilities of reclaiming an active and an inactive block in each GC are N_a/d and $(d - N_a)/d$, respectively. Note that reclaiming an inactive block always incurs k page writes. Thus, the average cleaning cost in each GC can be derived as $(N_a/d)\overline{C}_a(d) + [(d-N_a)/d]k$. Note that all active blocks are in the window and uniformly selected for GC, which is

equivalent to the case where $d = N_a$, so $\overline{C}_a(d)$ can also be derived via Equations (4)-(5) by replacing d with N_a.

Given the average cleaning cost $\overline{C}(d)$, the write frontier can only handle $k - \overline{C}(d)$ external page writes during one GC. Therefore, the total cleaning cost caused by GC is $[L/(k - \overline{C}(d))]\overline{C}(d)$.

Proof of Theorem 2 in §3.2: Since $d = o(N)$, according to Equation (5), as $N \to \infty$, $\overline{C}_i(d)$ can be transformed to $\overline{C}_i(d) = [(k - \overline{C}_a(d))r_i]/(e^{A_i} - 1)$, where $A_i = r_i(k - \overline{C}(d))/[(1 - S')k f_i]$ and $S' = S/((1 - S)f_a + S)$. Therefore, the average cleaning cost in each GC, $\overline{C}(d)$, can be easily derived as

$$\overline{C}(d) = \sum_{i=1}^n (k - \overline{C}(d))r_i/(e^{A_i} - 1). \quad (10)$$

To show the uniqueness of the solution in Equation (10), we only focus on $\overline{C}(d) \in [0, k]$. We let $f(x) = \sum_{i=1}^n (k - x)r_i/(e^{A_i(x)} - 1) - x$, where $A_i(x) = r_i(k - x)/[(1 - S')k f_i]$ and $x \in [0, k]$. We have $f(0) > 0$, and $\lim_{x \to k^-} f(x) < 0$. By checking the first-order derivative of $f(x)$, we have $f'(x) < 0$. So Equation (10) has a unique solution in $[0, k]$.

Proof of Corollary 1 in §3.2: Since $r_i = f_i$ ($i = 1, 2, \cdots, n$), Equation (6) can be rewritten as $\overline{C}(d) = ke^{-[k-\overline{C}(d)]/[(1-S')k]}$, which can be solved in terms of Lambert's W function as $\overline{C}(d) = -W\left(-\frac{1}{1-S'}e^{-\frac{1}{1-S'}}\right)/\left[\frac{1}{(1-S')k}\right]$. Note that $S' < 1$, we have $-\frac{1}{1-S'}e^{-\frac{1}{1-S'}} \geq -1/e$, so Lambert's W function $W(\cdot)$ is a real valued function and has two branches. One branch defines a single-valued function $W_0(\cdot) \geq -1$, while the other branch has $W_1(\cdot) \leq -1$. In our case, since $\overline{C}(d) \leq k$, we restrict Lambert's W function to the higher branch $W_0(\cdot)$, and we obtain the results as claimed.

Proof of Theorem 3 in §3.3: As $N \to \infty$, we have $N_a \to \infty$, since $d \geq N_a$, based on Eq. (5), we have

$$\overline{C}_i(d) = r_i(k - \overline{C}_a(N_a))/\left[\frac{r_i(k - \overline{C}_a(N_a))}{(N_a+1)(1-S')k f_i}N_a\right] = (1-S')k f_i.$$

Therefore, $\overline{C}_a(d) = (1 - S')k$ and $\overline{C}(d)$ can be derived as $\overline{C}(d) = (N_a/d)(1 - S')k + (1 - N_a/d)k = (1 - NS/d)k$.

Proof of Theorem 4 in §3.4: Since $d = \alpha N$, as $N \to \infty$, Equation (5) can be simplified as $\overline{C}_i(d) = [(k - \overline{C}_a(d))r_i]/[(1 + \alpha A_i)e^{(1-\alpha)A_i} - 1]$, where $A_i = r_i(k - \overline{C}_a(d))/[(1 - S')k f_i]$. Now $\overline{C}(d)$ can be easily derived via $\overline{C}(d) = \overline{C}_a(d) = \sum_{i=1}^n \overline{C}_i(d)$. For the proof of uniqueness, it is the same as that in Theorem 2.

Proof of Theorem 5 in §4: Since the workload in each region is uniform, based on Corollary 1, we can derive the average cleaning cost in each GC, and we denote it as C_i for region i. We have $C_i = -W_0\left(-\frac{1}{1-S_i}e^{-\frac{1}{1-S_i}}\right)/\left[\frac{1}{(1-S_i)k}\right]$, where $S_i = Sb_i/[(1-S)f_a f_i + Sb_i]$. Note that the workload contains L page writes, and proportion r_i of them go to region i, so the total number of GCs in region i is $\frac{Lr_i}{k-C_i}$ as each GC can only handle $k - C_i$ external page writes. Therefore, the total number of page writes issued by GC in region i is $\frac{Lr_i}{k-C_i}C_i$, and the total cleaning cost is the sum of all page writes issued by GC in all regions. So we have $\mathcal{C} = \sum_{i=1}^n \frac{Lr_i}{k-C_i}C_i$.

A Framework for Emulating Non-Volatile Memory Systems with Different Performance Characteristics

Dipanjan Sengupta[1,2], Qi Wang[1,3], Haris Volos[1], Ludmila Cherkasova[1], Jun Li[1],
Guilherme Magalhaes[4], and Karsten Schwan[2]

[1]Hewlett-Packard Labs, [2]Georgia Institute of Technology, [3]The George Washington University,
[4]Hewlett-Packard

[2]dsengupta6@gatech.edu, [3]interwq@gwu.edu, [1,4]{haris.volos, lucy.cherkasova, jun.li,
guilherme.magalhaes}@hp.com, [2]karsten.schwan@cc.gatech.edu

ABSTRACT

Exponential increase of online data and a corresponding growth of data-centric applications (Big Data analytics) forces system architects to revisit assumptions and requirements of the future system design. New non-volatile memory (NVM) technologies, such as Phase-Change Memory (PCM) and HP Memristor offer significantly improved latency and power efficiency compared to flash and hard drives. Many future systems are expected to have both DRAM and NVM. This can radically change system and software design, and enable new style of Big Data processing applications. However, the commercial unavailability of new NVMs technologies and uncertainty of their performance characteristics make it difficult to assess new system software stacks and to study their performance impact on future workloads. To bridge this gap and encourage an early design phase, we are building a DRAM-based performance emulation platform[1], called *NVMpro*, that leverages features available in commodity hardware, to emulate different latency and bandwidth characteristics of future NVM technologies. *NVMpro* enables an efficient and accurate emulation of a wide range of NVM latencies and bandwidth characteristics for performance evaluation of emerging byte-addressable NVMs and their impact on applications performance without modifying or instrumenting their source code.

Categories and Subject Descriptors: C.4 [Computer System Organization] Performance of Systems, D.2.6.[Software] Programming Environments.

General Terms: Measurement, Performance, Design.

Keywords: Performance modeling, benchmarking, profiling, performance counters, memory throttling

1. INTRODUCTION

Emerging byte-addressable, non-volatile memory technologies such as phase-change-memory and memristors offer an alternative to disk for persistence and provide performance within the order of magnitude of DRAM. Forward-looking projects like Firebox [7] and HP's The Machine [6] envision future scale-out machines that have enormous amount of non-volatile memories (NVMs). There are many open questions about possible system software design with NVMs such as:

- Shall we consider DRAM as a caching layer for NVM?
- Shall we build systems with two types of memory: DRAM (fast) and NVM (slow)?
- Given two memory types, how shall we design new applications to benefit from this memory arrangement and decide on the efficient data placement?
- How sensitive the applications are to different ranges of NVM access latency and bandwidth?

Apparently, many design and data placement decision might depend on the *performance characteristics (latency and bandwidth)* of future NVMs. However, NVMs are not commercially available yet, and a few existing hardware prototypes [8, 9] have limited accessibility. Therefore, there is a high need for an emulation platform that mimics performance characteristics of different NVM technologies for assisting researchers in design of new software stacks for emerging NVMs and studying their performance on future workloads (without modifying or instrumenting the application source code).

In this work, we introduce a novel performance emulation platform, called *NVMpro*, that we are implementing on top of existing DRAM to emulate **different performance characteristics** of future NVM technologies. *NVMpro* utilizes several features available in commodity hardware to "slow down" DRAM and emulate a wide range of NVM latencies and bandwidth characteristics that can be used for performance evaluation of emerging byte-addressable NVMs. Thus, we **are not** after an accurate simulation of NVM functionality, but rather after emulating the NVM performance characteristics.

Since the next-generation NVMs are not currently available, it is a non-trivial task to assess the effectiveness of our approach and accuracy of performance models used in the emulator design. In order to achieve "physically slower" memory, we perform our experiments on a multi-socket machine with different access latencies for local and remote DRAM. In our validation experiments, we analyze a set of specially designed memory-intensive applications and SPEC CPU2006 benchmarks. The completion times of the test applications in the emulation platform are on average within 5% of the measured ones on the remote memory configuration. The remainder of the paper presents our results in more detail.

2. MEMORY PERFORMANCE MODEL

In this section, we discuss subtleties in emulating NVM using DRAM and the requirements for separately mimicking two performance characteristics of NVM when compared to DRAM: lower memory bandwidth and higher latency.

Bandwidth Model.

We emulate bandwidth by leveraging the DRAM thermal control feature available in commodity processors to limit available memory bandwidth similarly to other efforts [9].

---

[1]This work was originated during Dipanjan Sengupta and Qi Wang internship at HP Labs.

Specifically, we utilize thermal control registers found in the integrated memory controller of modern Intel Xeon processors [1] to programmatically throttle DRAM bandwidth in a per channel basis. The configuration registers we used are *THRT_PWR_DIMM_[0:2]*, and we use the *setpci* command to programmatically configure these thermal control registers.

Latency Model.

Unlike DRAM bandwidth, which can be programmatically controlled in modern processors as described above, modelling NVM latency is more challenging as commodity hardware does not provide a similar knob to physically control the DRAM latency. Therefore, we employ *a software-based solution* for emulating memory latency. As software introduces a very high overhead for slowing down each individual memory access, we instead *focus on modelling average application perceived latency* to be close to NVM latency. The **key idea** of the model is to dynamically inject software created delays to account for higher NVM latency of combined memory accesses. We avoid the overhead of instrumenting every memory access by adopting a coarse grain approach, in which we divide the application lifetime into time intervals called *epochs* and by inserting appropriate delays at the end of each epoch. Our emulator monitors and collects application's compute and memory characteristics for a given epoch using *hardware performance counters*, and at the end of each epoch it dynamically injects an appropriate amount of software delay in the application. The length of the epochs (and their frequency) is configurable. Figure 1 shows the memory access pattern of an application before and after the introduction of additional memory delay.

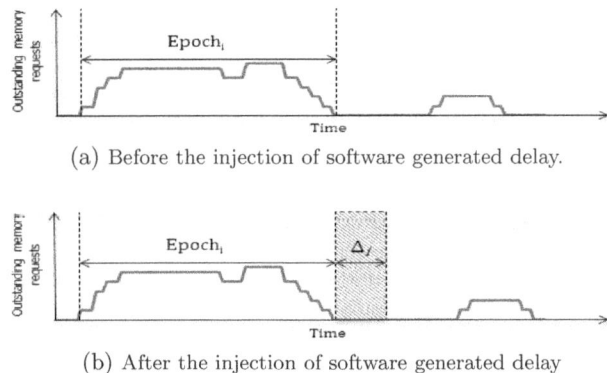

(a) Before the injection of software generated delay.

(b) After the injection of software generated delay

Figure 1: Emulation of NVM latency by injecting software delay at the end of each epoch.

The proposed model has two inter-related aspects: the logic behind the calculation of the additional delay for a given epoch, and the construction of the epochs, i.e., defining the size and frequency of these epochs.

For a *single threaded application* the epoch creation is as simple as creating the *fixed-size* intervals, but for multi-threaded applications it is more complex because of inter-thread dependencies and communications. In this work, we demonstrate our approach by considering a single threaded application model. (However, we have the model extention for the multi-threaded case, which is under performance evaluation.) In our model, we use the following denotations:

- NVM_{lat} - the average NVM access latency (in *ns*).
- $DRAM_{lat}$ - the average DRAM access latency (in *ns*).
- M_i - the total number of memory references going to the memory system in epoch i.
- LDM_STALL_i - the total number of processor stall cycles caused by serving memory requests in epoch i.

- Δ_i - software delay injected at the end of epoch i.

A very *simple* memory model for emulating the NVM latency is to count the total number of memory references made in a given epoch and multiply it by a difference in the average NVM and DRAM latencies. But the point to note is that not all the memory references issued by the application are served by DRAM, because some of the references are served by the processor's private caches and/or shared last level cache. Moreover, the hardware prefetching in modern processors can further reduce the memory references actually going and being served from DRAM. Therefore, we need to count only those memory references that *miss the caches* and are actually served from memory (M_i). So the additional delay for a particular epoch i can be defined as

$$\Delta_i = M_i \cdot (NVM_{lat} - DRAM_{lat}) \qquad (1)$$

This *simple* model works correctly if we assume that all the memory references are issued serially to DRAM one after another. However, this assumption does not hold for most modern processors that support multiple memory requests to be issued and served in parallel. This feature is also known as *memory level parallelism (MLP)*. Figure 2 shows pictorially different memory reference processing patterns, that require injecting different delays for emulating a slower NVM latency.

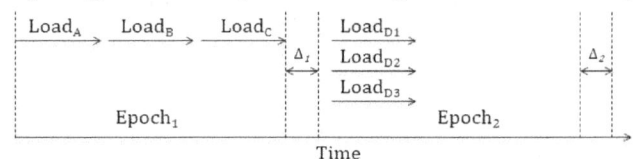

Figure 2: Impact of memory level parallelism on calculating the software delay injected at the end of each epoch.

We can observe that $Load_A$, $Load_B$, and $Load_C$ are issued serially in $Epoch_1$, and therefore, Eq. 1 correctly models the additional delay for this epoch. However, in $Epoch_2$, this *simple* model over-estimates the additional delay by a factor of 3, because of not considering the impact of MLP during memory reference processing (MLP=3 in this epoch). Therefore, to account for MLP we should approximate the average number of *sequential* memory accesses for computing the additional delay in a given epoch i as follows:

$$\Delta_i = \frac{LDM\_STALL_i}{DRAM_{lat}} \cdot (NVM_{lat} - DRAM_{lat}) \qquad (2)$$

Therefore, using only one hardware performance counter that measures LDM_STALL_i, the equation Eq. 2 computes the additional delay per epoch.

3. EVALUATION

In this section, we evaluate the accuracy of the proposed approach by using a set of specially designed memory-intensive applications and SPEC CPU2006 benchmarks.

Experimental Testbed.

Our emulation platform is implemented and evaluated on the dual-socket system with **Intel Xeon E5-2450** processor that supports up to 3 DDR3 channels and a total of 16 *two-way* hyper-threaded cores running at 2.1 GHz. Cache sizes of L1I, L1D, L2 and L3 are 32 KB, 32 KB, 256 KB and 20 MB respectively, and the total amount of DRAM is 32 GB.

Validating Accuracy of Memory Bandwidth Emulation.

As bandwidth emulation is solely based on hardware features, we are primarily interested in verifying that the memory bandwidth can be indeed controlled through the thermal control registers.

Figure 3 shows the memory bandwidth measured using *copy* kernel of STREAM benchmark [5] for varying thermal control register values. The measured memory bandwidth changes linearly as a function of specified register values, until the application's maximum attainable bandwidth is reached.

As DRAM memory bandwidth can be controlled *linearly* using thermal control registers, we conclude that the desired bandwidth for NVM can be realized with good accuracy.

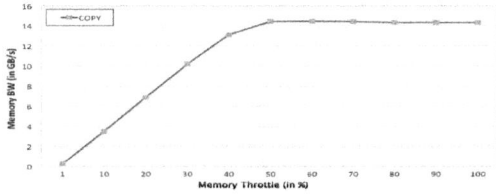

Figure 3: Relationship between memory throttling using thermal control registers and memory bandwidth of STREAM benchmark (*copy* kernel).

Approach for Validating Memory Latency Emulation.

Validating the memory latency model requires comparing the application performance as predicted by the performance model to the application performance as measured on real hardware with "physically slower" (higher-latency) memory. This validation is non-trivial as commodity hardware platforms do not support configuring different memory latencies. The lack of such hardware feature has served as a primary motivation for our software emulation approach.

To validate our model against physically increased memory latency, we leverage the different access latencies of local and remote DRAM in a multi-socket machine as follows. We create two different configurations for our experiments:

- *Conf_1* - a single socket is used for executing applications, i.e., processor and memory from the same socket;

- *Conf_2* - a processor from one socket and remote memory from the other socket are configured to run the same applications. We use the *numactl* tool to bind the experiment's computation on the local socket and force the experiment to use memory from the remote socket: this way we can physically increase memory latency.

First, we run a set of latency-sensitive experiments on *Conf_1* with *NVMpro* which injects software created delays based on the proposed memory latency model to mimic the latency of remote socket memory. Thus, we specify the *NVM latency* as the average latency to access remote socket memory. The *epoch size is 10 milliseconds* in all our experiments. We use Linux *perf* monitoring tool [2] to monitor the raw processor events needed by our latency model including memory stall cycles (LDM_STALL), and last level cache hit and miss ratios (LLC_HIT, LLC_MISS).

Then for validation and comparison, we measure application completion times executed on *Conf_2* (without *NVMpro*).

Applications and Benchmarks.

Pointer-Chasing Microbenchmark: We designed a memory-latency bound microbenchmark with a configurable degree of memory parallelism. The microbenchmark creates a pointer chain as an array of 64-bit integer elements. The contents of each element dictate which one is read next; each element is read exactly once. We choose the array size to be much larger than the size of the last-level cache so that each element's memory access results in a cache miss that is guaranteed to be served from memory.

The microbenchmark is *memory-latency sensitive* because the next element to be accessed is determined only after the current access completes. The microbenchmark can also create *multiple* independent chains to experiment with *different degrees of memory parallelism*. During each iteration the microbenchmark accesses the current element of each chain before proceeding with the next element. This results in multiple parallel memory requests as element accesses from different chains are independent. To minimize memory accesses due to TLB misses, we configure the virtual memory subsystem to use 2 MB hugepages.

SPEC CPU2006 Bench: We use twenty applications from the SPEC CPU2006 [4] benchmark suite that offer a broad and representative coverage of real applications with diverse compute and memory characteristics.

Validating Accuracy of Memory Latency Emulation.

Pointer-Chasing Microbenchmark. Figure 4 compares the additional execution times of the pointer-chasing microbenchmark as estimated by our latency model (Eq. 2 used by the emulator) on *Conf_1* and the actual additional execution times measured by running the same benchmark on *Conf_2* compared against the base line execution on *Conf_1*[2]. The X-axis reflects the memory level parallelism of the microbenchmark, which is defined by the number of independent memory accesses issued by microbenchmark at each iteration.

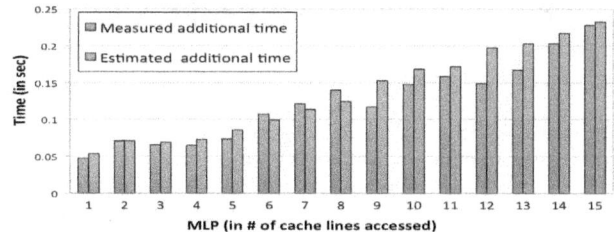

Figure 4: Comparison between the *measured* additional execution time in *Conf_2* vs *estimated* delay with the emulation platform in *Conf_1* for Xeon E5-2450-based system.

We observe that our model very closely matches the measured additional times. The average absolute error is 4.6%, and the minimum and maximum errors are being 0.16% and 11% respectively. This validates the correctness and high accuracy of the proposed model.

SPEC CPU2006 Benchmark. Figure 5 shows the LLC misses per 1000 instructions across the executed benchmarks in the suite. This signifies the *memory intensity* of different benchmark applications, i.e., how often they access the memory system. We can observe that *mcf*, *omnetpp*, and *milc* have a relatively high LLC miss rate, and they are memory-intensive, while applications like *hmmer*, *h264*, etc., have very low memory intensity and are rather compute-intensive.

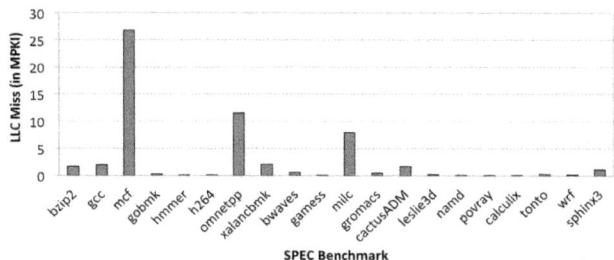

Figure 5: LLC miss of various SPEC benchmarks.

---

[2] All the experiments are performed five times, and the measurement results are averaged. This comment applies to all results in this section.

In order to formally evaluate the accuracy of the designed memory model we compute the *prediction error* as follows:

$$error = \frac{|CT_{native}^{remote} - CT_{emulated}^{remote}|}{CT_{native}^{remote}} \quad (3)$$

where CT_{native}^{remote} is the measured application completion time when benchmarks are executed (without the emulator) on the memory allocated in remote socket (i.e., *Conf_2*), and $CT_{emulated}^{remote}$ is the measured application completion time when benchmarks are executed with *NVMpro* emulator on memory allocated in local socket (i.e., *Conf_1*) while **emulating** the memory latency of the remote socket.

Figure 6 depicts the accuracy results of the validation experiments. We can observe that for most benchmarks the errors for measured vs estimated execution times are low with an average and maximum errors of 1.8% and 5.36% respectively. As a sanity check, we also analyzed a variability of benchmarks' completion times without the emulator: the measured completion times are very consistent (less than 2% of corresponding average completion times).

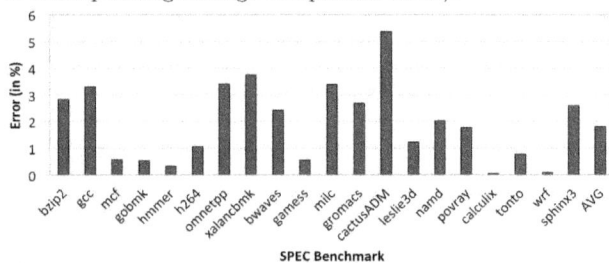

Figure 6: Validating the emulation accuracy for various SPEC benchmarks on Xeon E5-2450 system.

These experiments validate that the proposed memory model not only mimics the NVM performance specification but also achieves it with a high accuracy.

4. RELATED WORK

Several previous projects attempted to emulate performance of NVRAM using DRAM. Dulloor et al. [9] describe an emulation platform that requires special hardware and firmware. Similar to our approach, they inject delays derived using a simple stall model. However, they rely on special hardware hooks to monitor the amount of time a core is not committing instructions. Instead, we base our model on performance counters commonly available in commodity processors.

Pelley et al. [12] make use of *offline analysis* using the PIN binary instrumentation tool to estimate the average number of cache misses per program regions. Then they use the cache miss estimates to introduce additional delay during actual runs on bare metal. Instead, we focus on an *online model* that does not require the extra step of offline analysis.

Finally, Volos et al. [15, 14] emulate only NVRAM write-latency by injecting a software created delay, whenever a programmer explicitly flushes a cache line out of the processor. The memory latency model presented in our paper extends the earlier model by injecting delays to account for slow NVRAM reads.

Previous work [11] has proposed that DRAM bandwidth throttling can be used for impacting the application perceived latency (as a result of created resource contention). This method can only be applied if the application's bandwidth requirement is higher than the throttled bandwidth, and there is a difficulty with achieving an accurate latency "slowdown" using this method. Moreover, this assumption is not true for latency-bound applications whose bandwidth requirements are very small. In contrast, our approach decouples latency emulation from bandwidth emulation.

There is a body of works that utilize performance counters for analyzing application memory performance. Green governor model [10] monitors the last level cache (LLC) misses and memory stall cycles. They multiply average memory latency by LLC misses to get an estimated time spent in memory. However, this model ignores memory-level parallelism, which might lead to an over estimate of the actual memory time. Recent work [13], proposes a memory model based on *miss handling status register (MSHR)* introduced in AMD processors. However, these performance counters are not readily available in other platforms (e.g., Intel).

5. CONCLUSION

In this work, we introduce a novel platform, called *NVMpro* for emulating NVM systems with different performance characteristics. *NVMpro* offers two performance knobs for changing NVM's bandwidth and NVM's latency. The experiments with specially designed memory-intensive applications and SPEC CPU2006 benchmarks on the multi-socket machine show that the emulation platform supports a high degree of accuracy: the completion times of emulated applications are within 5% (on average) of the measured ones.

To control memory latency we implemented a software-based solution that injects a pre-computed delay in the stream of memory references to achieve a desirable (average perceived) NVM latency. The solution is based on the memory model that leverages hardware performance counters. The counters are read with *perf* tool at specified time intervals to dynamically compute the additional delay to inject. As the *perf* tool uses a system call to monitor the events, there is an overhead associated with crossing the user-kernel protection boundary. To minimize this overhead, we are exploring an alternative implementation for reading performance counters directly via RDPMC instruction [3]. Our next steps also include extending the emulator for multi-threaded applications by taking into account synchronization primitives.

6. REFERENCES

[1] Intel Xeon Processor E5-1600/2400/2600/4600 (E5-Product Family.) http://www.intel.com/content/dam/www/public/us/en/documents/datasheets/xeon-e5-1600-2600-vol-2-datasheet.pdf.
[2] Perf. https://perf.wiki.kernel.org/index.php/Main_Page.
[3] RDPMC– Read Performance Monitoring Counters. http://www.rcollins.org/p6/opcodes/RDPMC.html .
[4] SPEC CPU2006. https://www.spec.org/benchmarks.html.
[5] STREAM benchmark: http://www.cs.virginia.edu/stream/.
[6] With The Machine, HP May Have Invented a New Kind of Computer. http://www.businessweek.com/articles/2014-06-11/with-the-machine-hp-may-have-invented-a-new-kind-of-computer.
[7] K. Asanovic. FireBox: A Hardware Building Block for 2020 Warehouse-Scale Computers. In *Proc. of FAST*, 2014.
[8] A. M. Caulfield, A. De, J. Coburn, T. I. Mollov, R. K. Gupta, and S. Swanson. Moneta: A High-performance Storage Array Architecture for Next-generation, Non-volatile Memories. In *Proc. of MICRO'43*, 2010.
[9] S. R. Dulloor, S. Kumar, A. Keshavamurthy, , P. Lantz, D. Reddy, R. Sankaran, and J. Jackson. System Software for Persistent Memory. In *Proc. of EuroSys*, 2014.
[10] S. Eyerman and L. Eeckhout. A Counter Architecture for Online DVFS Profitability Estimation. *IEEE Transactions on Computers*, 59(11), 2010.
[11] H. Hanson and K. Rajamani. What Computer Architects Need to Know about Memory Throttling. In *Proc. of ISCA*, 2010.
[12] S. Pelley, T. F. Wenisch, B. T. Gold, and B. Bridge. Storage Management in the NVM Era. In *Proc. of PVLDB*, 2013.
[13] B. Su, J. L. Greathouse, J. Gu, M. Boyer, and Z. Wang. Implementing a Leading Loads Performance Predictor on Commodity Processors. In *Proc. of Usenix ATC*, 2014.
[14] H. Volos, S. Nalli, S. Panneerselvam, V. Varadarajan, P. Saxena, and M. M. Swift. Aerie: Flexible File-System Interfaces to Storage-Class Memory. In *Proc. of EuroSys*, 2014.
[15] H. Volos, A. J. Tack, and M. M. Swift. Mnemosyne: Lightweight persistent memory. In *Proc. of ASPLOS 16*, ASPLOS '11, 2011.

Towards a Performance Model Management Repository for Component-based Enterprise Applications

Andreas Brunnert, Alexandru Danciu
fortiss GmbH
Guerickestr. 25
80805 Munich, Germany
{brunnert,danciu}@fortiss.org

Helmut Krcmar
Technische Universität München
Boltzmannstr. 3
85748 Garching, Germany
krcmar@in.tum.de

ABSTRACT

This work introduces a Performance Model Management Repository (PMMR) for component-based enterprise applications. A PMMR is a central server that allows managing performance model components in corporate environments. A key challenge when using performance models in such environments is to distribute, update and maintain them. Especially, when software components represented in performance models are under the control of different teams in an organization. Additional problems arise as soon as release cycles for their components are not synchronized. A PMMR helps to address these challenges by introducing a central repository in which different performance model component versions can be managed and maintained. Such capabilities support the collaboration of distributed teams as they can manage their performance model components independently from each other. Performance models of specific component versions can be combined into one performance model as required for the current performance evaluation. We propose to build such a PMMR using the capabilities provided by the Palladio Component Model (PCM) as meta-model and the EMFStore as underlying versioning repository.

Categories and Subject Descriptors

C.4 [**Performance of Systems**]: measurement techniques, modeling techniques

General Terms

Measurement, Performance

Keywords

Performance Model Repository, Performance Evaluation, Palladio Component Model, Enterprise Application, Component-based Performance Model

ICPE'15, Jan. 31–Feb. 4, 2015, Austin, Texas, USA.
Copyright is held by the owner/author(s). Publication rights licensed to ACM.
ACM 978-1-4503-3248-4/15/01 ...$15.00.
http://dx.doi.org/10.1145/2668930.2695526.

1. INTRODUCTION

Performance models are still not in widespread industry use as of today [12, 11]. One of the most cited reasons for this lack of adoption is that the effort required to create performance models often outweighs their benefits [6, 9]. To reduce the modeling effort, several approaches to automatically generate performance models based on static and dynamic analysis have been proposed [2, 6, 15].

An additional challenge for applying performance models in industrial practice is the organizational complexity in corporate IT environments [5, 14]. Performance modeling is especially demanding for component-based enterprise applications as soon as components are under the control of different teams within one or more organizations. Performance models can thus only be created through the cooperation of these teams. It gets even worse if they adhere to different release cycles for their components. In such a scenario it is challenging to keep a performance model consistent and in sync with changes that occur in parallel.

The Performance Model Management Repository (PMMR) concept proposed in this work addresses these organizational challenges. Its primary purpose is that of an integration server for performance models to support the collaboration of distributed teams within an organization (see Figure 1). A PMMR contains architecture-level performance models which represent performance-relevant aspects of a software architecture separately from workload and hardware environment. Only performance-relevant aspects of software architecture are managed in a PMMR. Performance-relevant aspects of component-based enterprise applications are represented by component-based performance models (CBPM). CBPMs represent software components, their relationships, operation behavior and resource demands. A PMMR allows to manage software components in CBPMs independently from each other.

2. PERFORMANCE MODEL MANAGEMENT REPOSITORY

The realization of a PMMR is driven by several research questions. This work in progress paper focuses on the following three:

1. Which existing methodologies and technologies can be used for implementing the PMMR concept?

2. How can the relationships of components and their corresponding versions be represented in a PMMR?

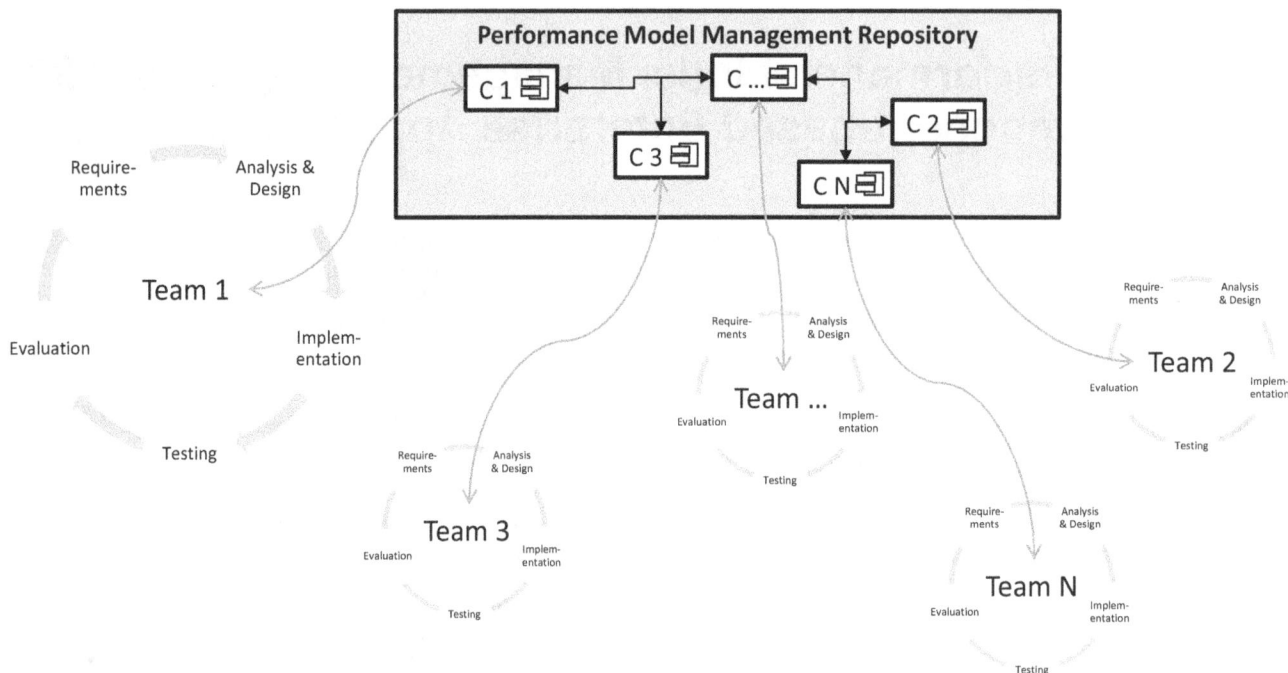

Figure 1: Conceptional architecture of a Performance Model Management Repository (PMMR)

3. How can a PMMR handle resource demand specifications in performance model components that are derived from different hardware environments?

To address the first research question, we propose the use of the Palladio Component Model (PCM) as meta-model for the component performance models managed in a PMMR [3]. A PMMR prototype is being developed on top of the PCM modeling environment (Palladio-Bench[1]) as PMMR client and the EMFStore as PMMR server [8]. Using the PCM modeling methodology and corresponding technologies allows to extend an existing modeling environment and avoids the need to introduce a new one.

PCM is designed with specific organizational roles in mind and consists of several model layers [3, 11]. One of the main models within the meta-model is the PCM repository model. The PCM repository model contains the components of a system, their operation behavior and resource demands as well as their relationships. The content of the PCM repository model is created by component developers. These repository model components are combined into a system model by system architects. A so called deployer can afterwards specify the available servers and resources (e.g., central processing unit (CPU) cores) in a resource environment model. An allocation model specifies how the repository model elements are mapped to these servers. A domain expert specifies the workload on the system represented by the other PCM model layers in the PCM usage model.

All PCM model layers apart from the repository model are intended to represent specific application scenarios. The repository model, on the other hand, is intended to contain reusable components for different application scenarios [3,

11]. The basic purpose of a PCM repository model and a PMMR are thus quite similar. However, the PCM repository model itself can nowadays not address the challenges mentioned in the introduction. PCM repository models are represented by single files that are hard to maintain by different teams concurrently. The result of this difficulty is that multiple PCM repository models with outdated component specifications exist, as multiple component versions need to be maintained at the same time by different teams. The PMMR extends the repository model concept in order to manage repository model components independently.

The PCM meta-model is based on the Eclipse Modeling Framework (EMF)[2]. All PCM-based performance models therefore conform not only to the PCM meta-model but also to the Ecore meta-model defined by EMF. We are leveraging this capability by using the EMFStore, which already implements the required versioning features for models based on the Ecore meta-model. The advantage of using EMFStore compared to other versioning systems is that it is designed to support the semantic versioning of models. Instead of working with textual representations of the models in existing systems such as Apache Subversion (SVN)[3], EMFStore uses the Ecore model elements and their relationships to manage models stored in a repository. For example, a structural change between two model versions is not represented as multiple lines in their textual representation. EMFStore rather stores the change in the Ecore model itself [8].

Users can access, analyze and edit models in the EMFStore using the EMF Client Platform (ECP)[4]. ECP supports collaborative editing of model versions using multiple clients at the same time. By using ECP as a plugin for the Palladio-

---

[1]http://www.palladio-simulator.com/

[2]http://www.eclipse.org/modeling/emf/
[3]http://subversion.apache.org/
[4]http://www.eclipse.org/ecp/

Bench, model versions in a repository are directly accessible to performance analysts [4]. A PMMR can thus be seen as an organization-wide replacement of the PCM repository model. System architects, deployers and domain experts in distributed teams can use component model versions in a PMMR to build their PCM model cases on demand.

To allow for a comparison of different component model versions, we are also leveraging the fact, that the generated performance models are based on EMF. By using the EMF-Compare framework[5], the differences between two model versions can be analyzed. Such capabilities allow for efficient version-to-version comparisons, to evaluate the performance impact of changes introduced in a specific component version [4].

The second research question is concerned with the representation of PMMR component relationships. Performance model component relationships are specified in PCM by their dependencies. Components in PCM repository models can *require* one or more other components to be usable. As these components are managed independently from each other in a PMMR, these *require* references now need to respect the specific version of a component. A meta-model extension is therefore necessary to specify these relationships across component versions in a PMMR. The Palladio-Bench also needs to be extended to support the user while interacting with different component versions.

Another reason for the difficulty of representing the component relationships is that the PMMR content can be derived from static (e.g., software designs) or dynamic (e.g., runtime measurements) analysis. It is very important to ensure that software components that are dependent on each other in a software architecture are represented in a compatible way in a PMMR. The easiest way to ensure this, is to agree on a common abstraction level for representing software systems in performance models. Following Wu and Woodside [18], we suggest that software systems represented in a PMMR should reflect the actual component subdivision in terms of encapsulated sets of functionality.

A PMMR only contains PCM repository model components in different versions. However, the PCM repository model components can contain resource demands (i.e., CPU or hard disk drive (HDD) demands) that are specified relative to a specific hardware resource. A PMMR should therefore be able to handle the heterogeneity of hardware environments on which different components are deployed. To handle different hardware environments and, thus, to address research question three, all resource demands of repository model components stored in a PMMR are specified relative to a common baseline. Following Menascé and Almeida [13], this common baseline is specified by benchmark scores for hardware resources supported by the PCM meta-model (i.e., CPU, HDD).

Using these benchmark scores in a PMMR allows to transform the resource demands specified in repository model components during PMMR check-ins and PMMR check-outs. Users can specify benchmark scores for all hardware resources referenced by repository model components they are intending to check-in or to check-out. These benchmark scores are then used during check-in to calculate the baseline resource demands relative to the common baseline benchmark scores. For one specific resource type (e.g., CPU)

the resource demand ($r_{baseline}$) relative to a baseline hardware resource benchmark score ($b_{baseline}$) during check-in is calculated as shown in Equation 1. In this equation, $r_{checkinvalue}$ denotes the resource demand in a component model that a user checks-in to a PMMR. The benchmark score of the hardware resource used to derive the resource demand, which is also given by the user during check-in, is specified by $b_{checkinbenchmarkvalue}$:

$$r_{baseline} = \frac{b_{baseline}}{b_{checkinbenchmarkvalue}} * r_{checkinvalue} \quad (1)$$

During check-out, the resource demand for the user ($r_{checkoutvalue}$) is calculated relative to the benchmark score provided by the user ($b_{checkoutbenchmarkvalue}$) as follows:

$$r_{checkoutvalue} = \frac{b_{checkoutbenchmarkvalue}}{b_{baseline}} * r_{baseline} \quad (2)$$

This calculation is possible for different hardware resources. For CPU benchmarks it is important that the benchmark can evaluate the performance of a single core (e.g., SPEC CPU2006[6]), otherwise it is much harder to adapt the resource demand from one server to another. Without such a transformation, users of PMMR components would need to know which hardware resources have been used to derive resource demands for the component models. This approach simplifies the reuse of component performance models. If resource demands are estimated instead of measured [15] and no benchmark scores are available, we propose the use of the baseline benchmark scores during check-in and checkout. The check-in and check-out capabilities of ECP for models in the EMFStore need to be extended to support this transformation process.

3. RELATED WORK

Several approaches for versioning model artifacts exist in literature [1]. However, these approaches do not address the specific requirements which arise from the versioning of performance models of individual components.

The work that is most closely related to the PMMR concept is the Performance Knowledge Base (PKB) introduced by Woodside et al. [17]. The PKB is broader in its scope. It is envisioned as central performance repository. The authors propose to store measurement and model prediction results in a PKB instead of the models itself. In this way the PMMR concept differs from the PKB idea as it is designed so that performance models can be stored in it directly. It is not intended to be used as result repository. However, Woodside et al. [17] also note that the PKB should allow to build performance models on demand. These models should be built based on the current state of parameters and a so called model base that builds the foundation for modeling a system.

Koziolek [11] also argues that central performance model repositories (called model libraries) "... *could allow rapid performance predictions ...*". However, the author does not propose a solution for the realization of such a repository.

4. CONCLUSION AND FUTURE WORK

The proposed approach enables distributed (or even cross-organizational) teams to contribute and maintain perfor-

---

[5]http://www.eclipse.org/emf/compare/

[6]http://www.spec.org/cpu2006/

mance models concurrently and provides access to a coherent and consistent model of interrelated components.

Future work includes a better integration of existing approaches that support the performance evaluation of component-based enterprise applications using the PCM meta-model with the PMMR concept. For example, an approach proposed in [7] supports developers with insights on the response times of the component they are currently developing by employing the PCM meta-model. The response time of components is calculated based on component reuse and could therefore be derived using the PMMR. As explained in Section 2, existing performance evaluation approaches using PCM need to agree on a common abstraction level for representing software components in performance models before they can be managed by a PMMR.

Another challenge for future work is to define at which level performance models can be abstracted to reduce the amount of components that need to be represented in a performance model. For example, if someone evaluates a specific enterprise application, one might not be interested in a detailed representation of all dependencies of an existing component used by the current application. It would thus be an interesting research direction to evaluate how detailed white-box and high-level black-box models for the same component can be stored in a PMMR [10]. A black-box representation could, for example, only represent the response time behavior of a component in a specific deployment scenario [16]. Whereas a white-box representation would model the component behavior in detail including its dependencies to other components. Clients of a PMMR should be able to choose between such representations during check-out time.

Once the PMMR prototype is completely implemented, it will be evaluated in an experimental setup to validate the feasibility of the approaches described in this work. Afterwards, the PMMR prototype needs to be evaluated in a corporate environment to validate the intended improvements.

5. REFERENCES

[1] K. Altmanninger, M. Seidl, and M. Wimmer. A survey on model versioning approaches. *International Journal of Web Information Systems*, 5(3):271–304, 2009.

[2] S. Balsamo, A. Di Marco, P. Inverardi, and M. Simeoni. Model-based performance prediction in software development: A survey. *IEEE Transactions on Software Engineering*, 30(5):295 – 310, 2004.

[3] S. Becker, H. Koziolek, and R. Reussner. The palladio component model for model-driven performance prediction. *Journal of Systems and Software*, 82(1):3 – 22, 2009.

[4] A. Brunnert and H. Krcmar. Detecting performance change in enterprise application versions using resource profiles. In *Proceedings of the 8th International Conference on Performance Evaluation Methodologies and Tools*, VALUETOOLS '14, New York, NY, USA, 2014. ACM.

[5] A. Brunnert, C. Vögele, A. Danciu, M. Pfaff, M. Mayer, and H. Krcmar. Performance management work. *Business & Information Systems Engineering*, 6(3):177–179, 2014.

[6] A. Brunnert, C. Vögele, and H. Krcmar. Automatic performance model generation for java enterprise edition (ee) applications. In M. S. Balsamo, W. J.

Knottenbelt, and A. Marin, editors, *Computer Performance Engineering*, volume 8168 of *Lecture Notes in Computer Science*, pages 74–88. Springer Berlin Heidelberg, 2013.

[7] A. Danciu, A. Brunnert, and H. Krcmar. Towards performance awareness in java ee development environments. In S. Becker, W. Hasselbring, A. van Hoorn, S. Kounev, and R. Reussner, editors, *Proceedings of the Symposium on Software Performance: Descartes/Kieker/Palladio Days 2014*, pages 152–159, November 2014.

[8] M. Koegel and J. Helming. Emfstore: A model repository for emf models. In *Proceedings of the 32nd ACM/IEEE International Conference on Software Engineering - Volume 2*, ICSE '10, pages 307–308, New York, NY, USA, 2010. ACM.

[9] S. Kounev. *Performance Engineering of Distributed Component-Based Systems - Benchmarking, Modeling and Performance Prediction*. Shaker Verlag, Ph.D. Thesis, Technische Universität Darmstadt, Germany, Aachen, Germany, 2005.

[10] S. Kounev, F. Brosig, and N. Huber. The descartes modeling language. Technical report, Universität Würzburg, Institut für Informatik, 2014.

[11] H. Koziolek. Performance evaluation of component-based software systems: A survey. *Performance Evaluation*, 67(8):634–658, 2010.

[12] M. Mayer, S. Gradl, V. Schreiber, H. Wittges, and H. Krcmar. A survey on performance modelling and simulation of sap enterprise resource planning systems. In *The 10th International Conference on Modeling and Applied Simulation*, pages 347–352. Diptem Universitá di Genoa, 2011.

[13] D. A. Menascé and V. A. F. Almeida. *Capacity Planning for Web Services: Metrics, Models, and Methods*. Prentice Hall, Upper Saddle River, New Jersey, 2002.

[14] A. Schmietendorf, E. Dimitrov, and R. R. Dumke. Process models for the software development and performance engineering tasks. In *Proceedings of the 3rd International Workshop on Software and Performance*, WOSP '02, pages 211–218, New York, NY, USA, 2002. ACM.

[15] C. Smith. Introduction to software performance engineering: Origins and outstanding problems. In M. Bernardo and J. Hillston, editors, *Formal Methods for Performance Evaluation*, volume 4486 of *Lecture Notes in Computer Science*, pages 395–428. Springer Berlin Heidelberg, 2007.

[16] A. Wert, J. Happe, and D. Westermann. Integrating software performance curves with the palladio component model. In *Proceedings of the third joint WOSP/SIPEW international conference on Performance Engineering*, ICPE '12, pages 283–286, New York, NY, USA, 2012. ACM.

[17] M. Woodside, G. Franks, and D. C. Petriu. The future of software performance engineering. In *Future of Software Engineering (FOSE)*, pages 171–187, Minneapolis, MN, USA, 2007.

[18] X. Wu and M. Woodside. Performance modeling from software components. *SIGSOFT Softw. Eng. Notes*, 29(1):290–301, 2004.

Automated Reliability Classification of Queueing Models for Streaming Computation

Jonathan C. Beard, Cooper Epstein, and Roger D. Chamberlain
Dept. of Computer Science and Engineering
Washington University in St. Louis
{jbeard,epsteinc,roger}@wustl.edu

ABSTRACT

When do you trust a model? More specifically, when can a model be used for a specific application? This question often takes years of experience and specialized knowledge to answer correctly. Once this knowledge is acquired it must be applied to each application. This involves instrumentation, data collection and finally interpretation. We propose the use of a trained Support Vector Machine (SVM) to give an automated system the ability to make an educated guess as to model applicability. We demonstrate a proof-of-concept which trains a SVM to correctly determine if a particular queueing model is suitable for a specific queue within a streaming system. The SVM is demonstrated using a micro-benchmark to simulate a wide variety of queueing conditions.

Categories and Subject Descriptors

D.4.8 [**Performance**]: Measurements, Modeling and Prediction, Queuing Theory

1. INTRODUCTION

Stochastic modeling is essential to the optimization of high performance stream processing systems. The optimization of streaming systems can require the application of several different stochastic models within a single system. Each one must be carefully selected so that assumptions inherent to the model do not make the model diverge significantly from reality. Some streaming systems (such as RaftLib [9]) can spawn tens to hundreds of queues, each potentially with a unique environment and characteristics to model. Approximating an optimal queue size at run-time is clearly not possible manually when microsecond-level decisions are required. This paper outlines a proof-of-concept for an approach when fast modeling decisions are necessary. We will briefly outline the approach to training and using a SVM for deciding when and when not to apply a simple $M/M/1$ queueing model [7] to a particular queue in the context of a streaming computation. Evaluation is given for selection of this queueing model

for a variety of conditions simulated via micro-benchmark on a multitude of hardware platforms.

Stream processing is a compute paradigm that views an application as a set of compute kernels connected via communications links or "streams" (example shown in Figure 1). Streaming languages include StreamIt [12], S-Net [6], and others. Stream processing is increasingly used by multi-disciplinary fields with names such as computational-x and x-informatics (e.g., biology, astrophysics) where the focus is on safe and fast parallelization of a specific application [8, 13]. Many of these applications involve real-time or latency sensitive big data processing necessitating usage of many parallel kernels on several compute cores.

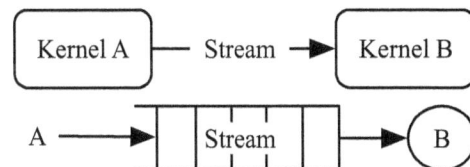

Figure 1: The top image is an example of a simple streaming application with two compute kernels (labeled A & B). Each compute kernel could be assigned to any number of compute resources (e.g., processor core, graphics engine). The communications stream connecting A & B could be allocated to a variety of resources depending on the nature of A & B (e.g., heap, shared memory or network interface). We are interested in the queueing behavior that results from the communications between compute kernels A & B. The bottom image is the resulting queue with arrival process A (emanating from compute kernel A) and server B. For more complex systems this becomes a queueing network.

Optimizing or reducing the communication overhead within a streaming application is often a non-trivial task, it is however central to making big data and stream processing successful. When viewing each compute kernel as a "black-box," a major tuning knob at the application's disposal is the buffer (queue) size between kernels. A classic way to size a buffer is to run each compute kernel in isolation with the expected workload, derive the service rate and distribution, then use this data to select a queueing model to inform the correct buffer size. Modern streaming systems such as RaftLib support online queue optimization. Parameters such as service process distribution are difficult to determine online. Clearly, the classic method is inadequate for this circumstance. Another approach could use branch and bound searching, but it can consume significant time (much spent reallocating buffers). A more efficient online approach is to make an educated guess as to which model to use for each queue and solve for the buffer size. If the service rate of the kernel is known, we contend (and show evidence for) that a sufficiently trained SVM can select the correct model quickly, avoiding bounding search and possibly negating the need for process distribution determination.

A SVM is a method to separate a multi-dimensional set of data into two classes by a separating hyperplane. Theoretical details are covered by relevant texts on the subject [14] A SVM labels an observation (represented by a set of attributes to identify it) with a learned class label based on the solution to Equation (1) [5] (note: dual form given, $\mathbf{e}$ is a vector of all ones of length l, Q is an $l \times l$ matrix defined by $Q_{i,j} \leftarrow y_i y_j K(x_i, x_j)$ and K is a kernel function, specific symbolic names match those of [3]). A common parameter selected to optimize the performance of the SVM is the penalty parameter for the error term C (value discussed in Section 3.1).

$$\min_{\boldsymbol{\alpha}} \quad \frac{1}{2} \boldsymbol{\alpha}^T \mathbf{Q} \boldsymbol{\alpha} - \mathbf{e}^T \boldsymbol{\alpha} \tag{1}$$
$$\text{subject to} \quad 0 \leq \alpha_i \leq C, i = 1, \ldots, l,$$

$$K(x, y) = e^{-\gamma \|x - y\|^2}, y > 0. \tag{2}$$

Utilizing 76 features (shown in Figure 2) easily extracted from a system, we show that a machine learning process can identify where a model can and cannot be used. Each one of the input features can be determined *a priori*. We also assume that the mean service rate (i.e., rate of data consumption by the kernel) can be determined either statically or online, while the application is executing. In order to map all 76 attributes into features we use a Radial Basis Function (RBF, [10], Equation (2)) represented as K. The parameter, γ is commonly optimized separately in order to maximize the performance of the SVM and kernel combination (value of γ also discussed in Section 3.1).

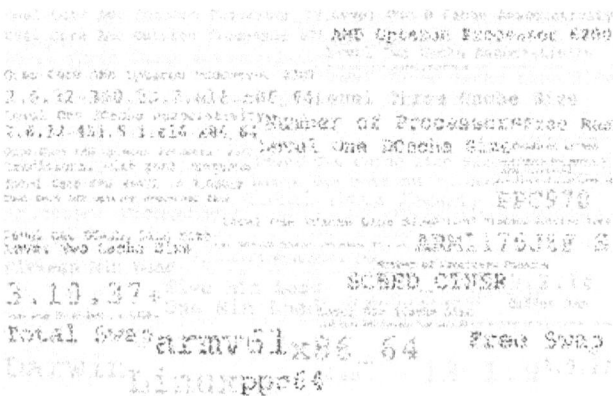

Figure 2: Word cloud depicting features used for machine learning process with the font size representing the significance of the feature as determined by [4].

Kernel learning methods such as SVM have been utilized in diverse pattern recognition fields such as handwriting recognition and protein classification [2]. This work does not seek to add new techniques to SVM or machine learning theory, rather we are focused on expanding the application of these methods to judging the applicability of stochastic performance models to real-world scenarios in streaming computation. Results are shown that demonstrate that our SVM approach appears to be applicable with respect to multiple operating systems and hardware types, at least for the micro-benchmark conditions.

2. ASSUMPTIONS & PITFALLS

The stochastic mean queue occupancy models our SVM will be trained for are steady state models. Applications whose performance is not well characterized by mean behavior are not good candidates without modifications of our approach. First, we assume that the applications under test have executed long enough so that the queue occupancies observed are at steady state. Second, our investigation will be constrained to applications for which the computational behavior is independent of the input set or does not vary dramatically as a function of the input. In future work we plan to modify our approach that will perhaps enable characterization of some non-steady state behavior.

Architectural features of a specific platform such as cache size are used as features for this work. As such we assume that we can find them either via literature search or directly by querying the hardware. Platforms where this information is unknown are avoided, and there is a surfeit of platforms where this information is knowable.

Implicit within most stochastic queueing models (save for the circumstance of a deterministic queue) is the strict relegation of server utilization ρ to be less than one for a finite queue occupancy. It is expected that the SVM should be able to find this relationship based upon the training process. It is shown in Section 3.2 that this is indeed the case. We also assume that the SVM is not explicitly told what the actual service time distributions are of the compute kernels modulating data arrival and service.

Changes in service time distribution can drastically effect the queue occupancy characteristics of an individual queue. Traditionally a change in distribution would necessitate a quantification of that distribution before moving forward with a different type of model. We hypothesize that by training the SVM with a variety of distributions that the SVM can identify regions where the models under consideration can be used and where they cannot. This is not to say that the SVM as trained will be successful in all cases. We'll examine some edge cases in the results. It is possible that the SVM as trained might not generalize to distributions that did not exist in the training data.

3. EVALUATION

In order to train the model with as much data as possible and evaluate the method with some known parameters, a set of micro-benchmarks (see topology in Figure 1) with synthetically generated workloads is used. A synthetic workload for each compute kernel is composed of a simple busy-wait loop whose looping is dependent on a random number generator (either exponential, Gaussian, deterministic or a mixture of multiple distributions). Upon completion of work, a nominal "job" (data element) is emitted from "A" to "B" via the connecting stream. Each job is the same size for each execution of the micro-benchmark (8-bytes). The micro-benchmark applications have been authored in C/C++ using the RaftLib framework and are compiled with g++ using the -O1 optimization flag for their respective platforms. These applications are executed on a variety of x86 commodity hardware with a range of Linux and OS X operating systems.

3.1 Methodology

Our SVM will be used to classify the micro-benchmark queues with "use" or "don't use" for the $M/M/1$ analytic queueing model. Before the SVM can be trained as to which set of attributes to assign to a class, a label must be provided. The labeling function is described by Algorithm 1. For our labeling function $l \leftarrow 5$. A percentage based function for l could also have been used. Empirically measured mean queue occupancy is used for labeling purposes. Observation data is divided into two distinct sets via a uniform random process. Approximately 20% of the data is used for training the SVM, the remainder is used for testing. The set training set has the following specifications: server utilization ranges from close to zero to greater than one and distributions vary widely (a randomized mix of Gaussian, deterministic, and the model's expected exponential distribution as well as some mixture distributions).

Algorithm 1 Class assignment algorithm

---

if |observed occupancy − predicted occupancy| $\leq l$ **then**
    class ← use
else
    class ← don't use
end if

The micro-benchmark data (and attributes) are linearly scaled in the range $[-1000, 1000]$ (see [11]). This tends to cause a slight loss of information, however it does prevent extreme values from biasing the training process. It also has the added benefit of reducing the precision necessary for the representation. Once all the data are scaled, there are a few SVM specific parameters that must be optimized in order to maximize classification performance (γ and C). We use a branch and bound search for the best parameters for both the RBF Kernel ($\gamma \leftarrow 4$) and for the penalty parameter ($C \leftarrow 32768$). The branch and bound search is performed by training and cross-validating the SVM using various values of γ and C for the 20% set of training data discussed above. The SVM framework is sourced from LIBSVM [3].

3.2 Results

The SVM classifies a set of platform and compute kernel specific attributes with one of two labels, "use" or "don't use" with respect to a $M/M/1$ stochastic queueing model. The SVM is trained on data labeled with these two binary categories via Algorithm 1. To evaluate how well the SVM classifies a queueing system, we'll compare the known (but not to the SVM) class labels compared to those predicted by the SVM. If the queueing model is usable and the predicted class is "use" then we have a true positive (TP). Consequently the rest of the error types true negative (TN), false positive (FP) and false negative (FN) follow the obvious corollaries.

As enumerated in Table 1, the SVM correctly predicts (TP or TN) 88.1% of the test instances for the $M/M/1$ model. Overall these results are quite good compared to manual selection [1]. Not only do these results improve the mean queue occupancy predictions, they are far faster than manually interpreting the parameters of the queueing system to select a model. The average per example classification time is in the microsecond range. Our results suggest that this process can be effective for online model selection for the $M/M/1$ model.

Table 1: Overall classification predictions for micro-benchmark data.

Model	# obs.	TP	TN	FP	FN
$M/M/1$	39392	66.60%	21.60%	11.70%	0.20%

Server utilization (ρ) informs a classic, simple test to determine if a mean queue length model is suitable. At high ρ it is likely that the $M/M/1$ models will diverge widely from reality. It is assumed that the SVM should be able to discern this intuition from its training without being given the logic via human intervention (a key point in training the SVM to take the place of human intervention). Figure 3 shows a box and whisker plot for the error types separated by ρ. As expected the middle ρ ranges offer the most true positive results. Also expected is the correlation between high ρ and true negatives. Slightly unexpected was the relationship between ρ and false positives.

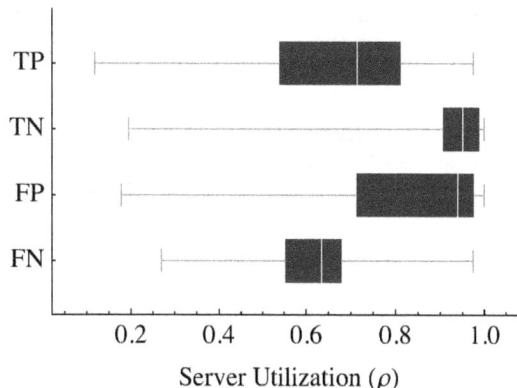

Figure 3: Summary of true positive (TP), true negative (TN), false positive (FP), false negative (FN) classifications for the $M/M/1$ model of the micro-benchmark data by server utilization ρ.

Directly addressing the performance and confidence of the SVM is the probability of class assignment. Given the high numbers of TP and TN it would be useful to know how confident the SVM is in placing each of these feature sets into a category. Probability estimates are not directly provided by the SVM, however there are a variety of methods which can generate a probability of class assignment [15]. We'll use the median class assignment probability for each error category as it is a bit more robust to outliers than the mean. This results in the following median probabilities: TP = 99.5%, TN = 99.9%, FP = 62.4% and FN = 99.8%. The last number must be taken with caution given that there are only 79 observations in the FN category. For the FP it is good to see that these were low probability classifications on average, perhaps with more training and refinement these might be reduced. Calculating probabilities is expensive relative to simply training the SVM and using it. It could however lead to a way to reduce the number of false positives. Placing a limit of $p = .65$ for positive classification reduces false positives by an additional 95% for the micro-benchmark data. Post processing based on probability has the benefit of moving this method from slightly conservative to very conservative if high precision is required, albeit at a slight increase in computational cost.

In Section 2 we noted that one potential pitfall of this method is the training process. What would happen if the model is trained with too few distributions? To test this hypothesis a set of the training data from a single distribution (the exponential) is used and divided into two sets, 20% for training and 80% for testing. The exponential only training data is used to train a SVM which is then tested on the testing exponential only data (results shown in Table 2). Second, the SVM trained with only exponential micro-benchmark data is used to classify data from distributions other than exponential (note: no data used to train is in the test set). These results are shown in Table 2. Two trends are apparent: training with a single distribution increases the accuracy when attempting to classify data with that distribution and lack of training diversity increases the number of false positives for the distributions not seen during the training process. Unlike the false positives seen earlier, these are high confidence predictions meaning that post processing for probability will not significantly improve predictions. Training with as many distributions as possible is essential to improving the generalizability of our method.

Table 2: % for SVM predictions with SVM trained only with servers having an exponential distribution.

Dist.	# obs.	Model	TP	TN	FP	FN
exp.	3249	$M/M/1$	53.0	31.2	15.7	.092
many	6297	$M/M/1$	55.8	0.0	44.2	0.0

4. CONCLUSIONS & FUTURE WORK

We have shown an approach for using a SVM to classify a stochastic queuing model's reliability in the context of a streaming system (varying hardware platform, application, operating system and environment). Across multiple hardware types, operating systems and micro-benchmark applications it has been shown to produce fairly good reliability estimates for the $M/M/1$ stochastic queueing model.

This work does not assume the availability of knowledge of the actual distribution of each compute kernel. Manually determining these distributions and retraining the SVM improves the classification rate to 96.6%. One obvious path for future work is faster and lower overhead process distribution estimation. As a work in progress paper, we did not explore the limits of generalization or the impact of online model selection to the efficiency (and performance) of the RaftLib framework. In conclusion we have shown a proof-of-concept for automated stochastic model selection using a SVM. We have shown that it can be done, and our limited testing suggests it works relatively well.

5. ACKNOWLEDGMENTS

This work was supported by Exegy, Inc., and VelociData, Inc. Washington University in St. Louis and R. Chamberlain receive income based on a license of technology by the university to Exegy, Inc., and VelociData, Inc.

6. REFERENCES

[1] J. C. Beard and R. D. Chamberlain. Analysis of a simple approach to modeling performance for streaming data applications. In *Proc. of IEEE Int'l Symp. on Modelling, Analysis and Simulation of Computer and Telecommunication Systems*, pages 345–349, Aug. 2013.

[2] C. J. Burges. A tutorial on support vector machines for pattern recognition. *Data Mining and Knowledge Discovery*, 2(2):121–167, 1998.

[3] C.-C. Chang and C.-J. Lin. LIBSVM: A library for support vector machines. *ACM Trans. on Intelligent Systems and Technology*, 2:27:1–27:27, 2011.

[4] Y.-W. Chen and C.-J. Lin. Combining SVMs with various feature selection strategies. In *Feature Extraction*, pages 315–324. Springer, 2006.

[5] C. Cortes and V. Vapnik. Support-vector networks. *Machine Learning*, 20(3):273–297, 1995.

[6] C. Grelck, S.-B. Scholz, and A. Shafarenko. S-Net: A typed stream processing language. In *Proc. of 18th Int'l Symp. on Implementation and Application of Functional Languages*, pages 81–97, 2006.

[7] L. Kleinrock. *Queueing Systems. Volume 1: Theory*. Wiley-Interscience, New York, NY, 1975.

[8] W. Liu, B. Schmidt, G. Voss, and W. Muller-Wittig. Streaming algorithms for biological sequence alignment on GPUs. *IEEE Trans. on Parallel and Distributed Systems*, 18(9):1270–1281, Sept 2007.

[9] RaftLib. http://www.raftlib.io. Accessed November 2014.

[10] B. Schölkopf and A. J. Smola. *Learning with Kernels: Support Vector Machines, Regularization, Optimization, and Beyond*. MIT Press, Cambridge, MA, 2002.

[11] D. M. Tax and R. P. Duin. Support vector data description. *Machine learning*, 54(1):45–66, 2004.

[12] W. Thies, M. Karczmarek, and S. Amarasinghe. StreamIt: A language for streaming applications. In R. Horspool, editor, *Proc. of Int'l Conf. on Compiler Construction*, volume 2304 of *Lecture Notes in Computer Science*, pages 49–84. 2002.

[13] E. J. Tyson, J. Buckley, M. A. Franklin, and R. D. Chamberlain. Acceleration of atmospheric Cherenkov telescope signal processing to real-time speed with the Auto-Pipe design system. *Nuclear Inst. and Methods in Physics Research A*, 585(2):474–479, Oct. 2008.

[14] V. N. Vapnik and V. Vapnik. *Statistical Learning Theory*, volume 2. John Wiley & Sons, New York, NY, 1998.

[15] T.-F. Wu, C.-J. Lin, and R. C. Weng. Probability estimates for multi-class classification by pairwise coupling. *The Journal of Machine Learning Research*, 5:975–1005, 2004.

The CloudScale Method for Software Scalability, Elasticity, and Efficiency Engineering: a Tutorial*

Sebastian Lehrig   Steffen Becker

{sebastian.lehrig|steffen.becker}@informatik.tu-chemnitz.de

Software Engineering Chair
Chemnitz University of Technology, Chemnitz, Germany

ABSTRACT

In cloud computing, software engineers design systems for virtually unlimited resources that cloud providers account on a pay-per-use basis. Elasticity management systems provision these resource autonomously to deal with changing workloads. Such workloads call for new objective metrics allowing engineers to quantify quality properties like scalability, elasticity, and efficiency. However, software engineers currently lack engineering methods that aid them in engineering their software regarding such properties.

Therefore, the CloudScale project developed tools for such engineering tasks. These tools cover reverse engineering of architectural models from source code, editors for manual design/adaption of such models, as well as tools for the analysis of modeled and operating software regarding scalability, elasticity, and efficiency. All tools are interconnected via ScaleDL, a common architectural language, and the CloudScale Method that leads through the engineering process. In this tutorial, we execute our method step-by-step such that every tool and ScaleDL are briefly introduced.

Categories and Subject Descriptors

D.2.8 [**Software Engineering**]: Metrics—*Scalability, Elasticity, Efficiency*; D.2.9 [**Software Engineering**]: Management—*Software quality assurance (SQA)*; D.2.11 [**Software Engineering**]: Software Architectures—*Architectural analysis*

Keywords

Tutorial; CloudScale; Cloud Computing; Software; Analysis; Scalability; Elasticity; Efficiency; Metrics; Method; Engineering

*The research leading to these results has received funding from the European Seventh Framework Programme (FP7/2007-2013) under grant no 317704 (CloudScale).

1. MOTIVATION

In cloud computing, software engineers develop applications on top of compute environments being offered by cloud providers. For these applications, the amount of offered resources is virtually unlimited while elasticity management systems provision resources autonomously to deal with changing workloads. Furthermore, providers bill provisioned resources on a per-use basis [1]. As a consequence of these characteristics, engineers want their applications to use as few resources as possible in order to save money while still maintaining the quality requirements of the system. Quality properties that focus directly on these aspects are scalability, elasticity, and efficiency [2].

These quality properties need to be quantified for software engineering by means of suitable metrics. For instance, cloud consumers and cloud providers need to negotiate service level objectives (SLOs), i.e., metrics and associated thresholds [5]. Such SLOs have to consider characteristics like changing workloads ("how fast can an application adapt to a higher workload?") and pay-per-use pricing ("how expensive is serving an additional consumer?"). However, no established engineering methods and tools supporting metrics for the mentioned quality properties exist. Current methods assume knowledge of implementation details as they focus on the application at run-time [6].

In literature, methods and tools with support for classical performance-oriented metrics [3] like response time and throughput are insufficient for situations relevant for cloud computing applications. First, they do not take changing workloads into account, e.g., metrics to describe reaction times to system adaptations are missing. Second, the degree to which systems match resource demands to changing workloads cannot be quantified. More recent work [6] proposes initial metrics for such characteristics that assume knowledge of implementation details like resource handling. Therefore, these metrics are inapplicable when such knowledge is unavailable, e.g., in early software engineering phases such as the software design phase. Accordingly, no existing method/tool has an appropriate support for software engineers that want to analyze scalability, elasticity, and efficiency properties at the design time of software applications.

To cope with this lack, we developed tools for such engineering tasks in the context of the CloudScale project [4]. These tools cover reverse engineering of architectural models from source code, editors for manual design/adaption of such models, as well as tools for the analysis of modeled and operating software regarding scalability, elasticity, and efficiency. We derived metrics for such properties in our previous work [2]. All tools are interconnected via ScaleDL, a common architectural language, and the CloudScale Method that leads through the engineering process.

The contribution of this tutorial paper is an example-based, step-by-step execution of our method such that every tool and ScaleDL are briefly introduced. Our method and tools eventually help software engineers in engineering cloud computing applications. Most interesting, we go beyond classical performance metrics like response time and highlight challenges in cloud computing settings where engineers have to plan for changing workloads and dynamic resource allocation.

This paper is organized as follows. In Sec. 2, we introduce our running example. Afterwards, we use this example to walkthrough our CloudScale Method in Sec. 3. Sec. 4 concludes the paper and gives an outlook on future work.

2. EXAMPLE SCENARIO

A software engineer of a company offers a book store as a Software-as-a-Service (SaaS) solution. The shop has been used for 15 years. An increase in load is now expected as a consequence of a new business strategy of selling novel cloud scalability books. The manager wants the engineer to ensure that the system – after modernization – can sustain this increased load.

Based on the general business strategy of the company, the engineer suggests the manager a modern cloud computing solution. However, the manager has heard of others that were disappointed by migrating to the cloud. The manager is concerned about short term issues such as unacceptable response times. In addition, he wants to know what the new system's operation will cost in the long term (considering the expected increase in users).

The engineer has heard that CloudScale [4] has some useful tools to analyze systems regarding such issues. Therefore, he plans to apply these tools and to provide the manager with detailed analysis results, allowing the manager to get rid of unpleasant surprises.

The engineer starts with the following. There is already an existing book store implementation which is implemented in the classical three layer architectural style (we show a screenshot of the client UI). This implementation has currently certain service level objectives (SLOs; e.g., 2 seconds response time limit). He plans to move this implementation to Amazon EC2 as one of the popular cloud computing infrastructures. However, he does not know whether features like autoscaling will eventually provide the needed user capacity (because he does not know whether his SaaS layer scales). As he also has no experience in building cloud computing systems, he is also unable to tell without either implementing the system and doing costly tests or without applying an engineering method like CloudScale's.

In the next section, we examine each step the engineer conducted to achieve his goals in detail. After the execution of these steps, the engineer is able to build a guaranteed scalable, elastic, and efficient system while answering all other questions of the manager. Source code and models of the book store and for all steps are available at our web page[1]. (Note: Our so-called "Cloud Book Store" is based on a legacy implementation of the TPC-W benchmark.)

[1]http://www.cloudscale-project.eu/results/
showcase/; Last accessed at 2014/11/29

3. USING THE CLOUDSCALE METHOD

The engineer learns about the CloudScale method[2]. He also learns that this method is configurable to support multiple use cases. His use case is a modernization task. For this task, the following sequence of activities is recommended:

1. extract a model of the existing application,

2. refine the extracted model with resource demands,

3. analyze the model,

4. spot HowNotTos & resolve with HowTos,

5. reanalyze, and

6. implement, test, and operate when OK.

The following subsections now lead the engineer through applying these steps; potentially guided by a dedicated CloudScale tool. All of these tools are included within the CloudScale Environment[3].

3.1 Extractor: Extract Model from Code

The Extractor is a tool for reverse-engineering (partial) ScaleDL models from Java source code. ScaleDL allows to specify inter-connected components and their behavior, hardware resources, user behavior, and special annotations needed for scalability, elasticity, and efficiency analyses. Extractor supports the first part of ScaleDL (inter-connected components and their behavior).

Based on its clustering algorithm, the Extractor summarizes Java classes in such components and their interfaces (ScaleDL Repository model). For example, the book store source code involves ~50 classes that Extractor summarizes to ~20 software components. Extractor particularly links such components via connectors (ScaleDL System model). Thanks to such models, engineers can get a good overview of existing software, even if documentation is unavailable.

The engineer follows our screencast for extraction[4]. In our experience, such extractions take only a few minutes, even for larger systems (> 1 million LOC). For extracting ScaleDL models that provide a good overview, engineers commonly have to try several extractions with varying parameters for the clustering algorithm. These parameters are explained in our screen cast as well.

3.2 ScaleDL Editors: Refine & Calibrate

Because the Extractor only provides a partly specified ScaleDL model, the engineer has to refine the previously extracted model.

First, he needs to annotate resource demands using our ScaleDL editors. Therefore, the engineer takes an example behavior specification of a component, measures the needed resource demands for that behavior, and puts them into the model. Our Analyzer series of screen casts explains resource demand measurement in detail (see same page as the Extractor screen cast).

[2]http://www.cloudscale-project.eu/results/method/;
Last accessed at 2014/11/29

[3]http://www.cloudscale-project.eu/results/
environment/; Last accessed at 2014/11/29

[4]http://www.cloudscale-project.eu/results/
screencasts/; Last accessed at 2014/11/29

The engineer repeats resource demand measurement for all quality-relevant component behaviors. In our experience, this process takes a maximum of 2 weeks for half a million lines of code; for the complete cloud book store it took 1 week for an inexperienced engineer.

Second, the engineer adds usage scenarios to the model. For getting the information he needs for these models, he asks the manager for the expected load evolution. He models this evolution using the ScaleDL Usage Evolution editor. The editor comes with a self-explanatory wizard.

3.3 Analyzer: Analyze

Once finished with ScaleDL's Usage Evolution model, the engineer runs CloudScale's analysis tool – the Analyzer. On our screen casts page, we demonstrate how and which results can be obtained using the Analyzer. For example, we show predicted response times and connect them to previously stated SLOs.

In our running example, the engineer may observe scalability issues: the system capacity (in terms of the maximum number of users the system can cope with) is insufficient. He may also observe too many SLO violations in Analyzer's results.

3.4 Spotter: Spot HowNotTos & Resolve with HowTos

Because the engineer observed too many SLO violations, he wants to investigate the root causes for these using CloudScale's Spotter. Spotter detects scalability, elasticity, and efficiency anti-patterns utilizing information from the source code, extracted models, and/or the system in operation. Such anti-patterns are provided in CloudScale's catalogue of HowNotTos[5]. Our screen casts about CloudScale's Spotter exemplify the detection of the one lane bridge anti-pattern. This anti-pattern is also detected by our engineer.

Therefore, the engineer looks up the Simplified SPOSAD HowTo (in the CloudScale catalogue for best practices[6]). Based on this HowTo, he resolve the found issue resulting in a new implementation and model.

3.5 Analyzer: Reanalyze

The architect reanalyzes the new model created based on the Simplified SPOSAD HowTo. He particularly investigates the differences to the previous analysis.

The analysis results indicate a success, which means that the engineer now can also pay attention to other metrics generated, e.g., operational costs (checking this long-term concern was asked for by the manager). In our recent works, we describe supported metrics [2] and their integration into CloudScale's Analyzer [7].

3.6 Implement, Test & Operate

After the engineer achieved satisfying analysis results, he implements the planned system according to the modified model. In our scenario, the implementation is fine, testing does not show any issues any more, and operation really costs what has been predicted. The manager and the engineer are happy now.

4. CONCLUSIONS

In this tutorial paper, we apply the CloudScale method step-by-step on a running example. For each step, we point to relevant resources allowing to reproduce our descriptions. In particular, the running example is available at our web page[7].

This tutorial helps software engineers to learn our method and to get familiar to our tools and languages for engineering cloud computing applications. Our engineering method goes beyond classical performance metrics like response time and supports challenges in cloud computing settings where engineers have to plan for changing workloads and dynamic resource allocation.

In our future work, we will polish our tools and reduce some remaining manual effort in using them. Where feasible, we will extend our screen casts such that every step will finally be exemplified in detail. Regarding HowTos and HowNotTos, we plan to extend our catalogues as we now have the infrastructure in place. We also recently moved core parts of our tools to GitHub to make it easier for others to contribute[8]. The CloudScale project ends September 2015 – until then, we plan to finalize these tasks.

5. REFERENCES

[1] M. Armbrust, A. Fox, R. Griffith, A. D. Joseph, R. Katz, A. Konwinski, G. Lee, D. Patterson, A. Rabkin, I. Stoica, and M. Zaharia. A view of cloud computing. *Commun. ACM*, 53(4):50–58, Apr. 2010.

[2] M. Becker, S. Lehrig, and S. Becker. Systematically deriving quality metrics for cloud computing systems. In *Proceedings of the 6th ACM/SPEC International Conference on Performance Engineering*, ICPE '15, New York, NY, USA, 2015. ACM. Accepted for publication.

[3] G. Bolch, S. Greiner, K. S. Trivedi, and H. de Meer. *Queueing Networks and Markov Chains: Modeling and Performance Evaluation With Computer Science Applications*. 1998.

[4] G. Brataas, E. Stav, S. Lehrig, S. Becker, G. Kopcak, and D. Huljenic. CloudScale: Scalability Management for Cloud Systems. In *4th Int. Conf. on Performance Engineering*. ACM, Apr. 2013.

[5] T. Erl, Z. Mahmood, and R. Puttini. *Cloud Computing: Concepts, Technology & Architecture*. Prentice Hall, 2013.

[6] N. R. Herbst, S. Kounev, and R. Reussner. Elasticity: What it is, and What it is Not. In *Proceedings of the 10th International Conference on Autonomic Computing (ICAC 2013), San Jose, CA, June 24–28*, 2013.

[7] S. Lehrig and M. Becker. Approaching the Cloud: Using Palladio for Scalability, Elasticity, and Efficiency Analyses. Technical Report 2014/05, Proceedings of the Symposium on Software Performance 2014, University of Stuttgart, Faculty of Computer Science, Electrical Engineering, and Information Technology, Nov. 2014.

---

[5] http://cloudscale.xlab.si/wiki/index.php/ HowNotTos:_Anti-Patterns; Last accessed at 2014/11/29
[6] http://cloudscale.xlab.si/wiki/index.php/HowTos; Last accessed at 2014/11/29

[7] http://www.cloudscale-project.eu/results/ showcase/; Last accessed at 2014/11/29
[8] https://github.com/CloudScale-Project; Last accessed at 2014/11/29

How to Build a Benchmark

Jóakim v. Kistowski
University of Würzburg
joakim.kistowski@
uni-wuerzburg.de

Jeremy A. Arnold
IBM Corporation
arnoldje@us.ibm.com

Karl Huppler
karl.huppler@gmail.com

Klaus-Dieter Lange
Hewlett-Packard Company
klaus.lange@hp.com

John L. Henning
Oracle
john.henning@oracle.com

Paul Cao
Hewlett-Packard Company
paul.cao@hp.com

ABSTRACT

Standardized benchmarks have become widely accepted tools for the comparison of products and evaluation of methodologies. These benchmarks are created by consortia like SPEC and TPC under confidentiality agreements which provide little opportunity for outside observers to get a look at the processes and concerns that are prevalent in benchmark development. This paper introduces the primary concerns of benchmark development from the perspectives of SPEC and TPC committees. We provide a benchmark definition, outline the types of benchmarks, and explain the characteristics of a good benchmark. We focus on the characteristics important for a standardized benchmark, as created by the SPEC and TPC consortia. To this end, we specify the primary criteria to be employed for benchmark design and workload selection. We use multiple standardized benchmarks as examples to demonstrate how these criteria are ensured.

Categories and Subject Descriptors

C.4 [**Computer Systems Organization**]: Performance of Systems—*Performance attributes*

General Terms

Measurement, Performance, Standardization

Keywords

SPEC; TPC; SPECpower_ssj2008; SERT; SPEC CPU

1. INTRODUCTION

Standardized benchmarks have become widely accepted tools for the comparison of software and hardware products. They are also regularly used for the evaluation of methodological approaches to problems in multiple fields of computer science and beyond.

In order to be accepted for standardization, benchmarks must meet a host of quality criteria. Benchmarks candidates must undergo a process of several steps, including the definition of measurement methodologies, workload selection, and a number of rigorous benchmark acceptance tests. Benchmark inception, development, and acceptance, however, are conducted under consortia confidentiality agreements, with little opportunity for outside observers to profit from the processes that these consortia have developed over time. Being unable to access these processes, calls for benchmark development processes have become louder [6]. We address this situation by offering this paper as a description of the processes for benchmark inception, development, testing, release, and support for the SPEC and TPC consortia.

As part of this work, we provide a definition of the term "benchmark" in the context of performance evaluation. Note that we differentiate between benchmarks with the purpose of product comparison and rating tools, which are intended for standardized measurements as part of a product development or evaluation process. We explain the differences between the three types of benchmarks: specification-based, kit-based, and hybrid. We also present the properties and criteria that any quality benchmark or rating tool must fulfill. For this, we focus on the properties that workloads of quality benchmarks must meet. We present multiple examples of standardized benchmarks and demonstrate how these benchmarks ensure the specific quality criteria.

The remainder of this paper is structured as follows: Section 2 presents our benchmark and rating tool definitions, it also explains the three benchmark types. Section 3 presents the properties of good benchmarks. The paper concludes in Section 4.

2. WHAT IS A BENCHMARK

Before discussing the development process of a benchmark, we define what a benchmark is. We also explain the difference between major types of benchmarks.

2.1 Definition of Benchmark

We define a benchmark as a "Standard tool for the competitive evaluation and comparison of competing systems or components according to specific characteristics, such as performance, dependability, or security".

This definition is a variation of a definition provided in [12] with a focus on the competitive aspects of benchmarks, as that is the primary purpose of standardized benchmarks as developed by SPEC and TPC.

We define tools for the non-competitive system evaluation and comparison as *rating tools*. Rating tools are primarily intended for a standardized method of evaluation for research purposes, regulatory programs, or as part of a system improvement and development approach. Rating tools can also be standardized and should generally follow the same design and quality criteria as benchmarks. SPEC's Server Efficiency Rating Tool (SERT), e.g., has been designed and developed using a similar process as the SPECpower_ssj2008 benchmark.

2.2 Types of Benchmarks

Computer benchmarks typically fall into three general categories: specification-based, kit-based, and a hybrid between the two. Specification-based benchmarks describe functions that must be achieved, required input parameters and expected outcomes. The implementation to achieve the specification is left to the individual running the benchmark. Kit-based benchmarks provide the implementation as a required part of official benchmark execution. Any functional differences between products that are allowed to be used for the benchmark must be resolved ahead of time and the individual running the benchmark is typically not allowed to alter the execution path of the benchmark.

Specification-based benchmarks begin with a definition of a business problem to be simulated by the benchmark. The key criteria for this definition are the relevance topics discussed in section 3 and novelty. Specification-based benchmarks have the advantage of allowing innovative software to address the business problem of the benchmark by proving the specified requirements of the new implementation [5]. On the other hand, specification-based benchmarks require substantial development prior to running the benchmark, and may have challenges proving that all the requirements of the benchmark are met.

Kit-based benchmarks may appear to restrict some innovative approaches to a business problem, but have the significant advantages of providing near "load and go" implementations that greatly reduce the cost and time required to run the benchmarks. For kit-based benchmarks, the "specification" is used as a design guide for the creation of the kit. For specification-based benchmarks, the specification is presented as a set of rules to be followed by a third party who will implement and run the benchmark. This allows for substantial flexibility in how the benchmark's business problem will be resolved - a principal advantage for specification-based benchmarks.

A hybrid of these may be necessary if the majority of the benchmark can be provided in a kit, but there is a desire to allow some functions to be implemented at the discretion of the individual running the benchmark.

While both specification-based and kit-based methods have both been successful in the past, current trends have favored kit-based development.

3. WORKLOAD PROPERTIES

Workload designers must balance several, often conflicting, criteria in order to be successful. Several factors must be taken into consideration, and trade-offs between various design choices will influence the strengths and weaknesses of the workload. Since no single workload can be strong in all of these areas, there will always be a need for multiple workloads and benchmarks [8].

It is important to understand the characteristics of a workload and determine whether or not it is applicable for a particular situation. When developing a new workload, the goals should be defined so that choices between competing design criteria can be made in accordance with those goals to achieve the desired balance. Several researchers and industry participants have listed various desirable characteristics of benchmarks [3, 4, 8, 1, 2, 11, 7]. The contents of the lists vary based on the perspective of the author and their choice of terminology and grouping of characteristics, but most of the concepts are similar. The key characteristics can be organized in the following groups, which will be discussed in more detail in the next sections:

- **Relevance** How closely the benchmark behavior correlates to behaviors that are of interest to consumers of the results
- **Reproducibility** The ability to consistently produce similar results when the benchmark is run with the same test configuration
- **Fairness** Allowing different test configurations to compete on their merits with-out artificial limitations
- **Verifiability** Providing confidence that a benchmark result is accurate
- **Usability** Avoiding roadblocks for users to run the benchmark in their test environments

All benchmarks are subject to these same criteria, but each category includes additional issues that are specific to the individual benchmark, depending on the benchmark's goals.

3.1 Relevance

"Relevance" is perhaps the most important characteristic of a benchmark. Even if the workload was perfect in every other regard, it will be of minimal use if it doesn't provide relevant information to its consumers. Yet relevance is also a characteristic of how the benchmark results are applied; benchmarks may be highly relevant for some scenarios and of minimal relevance for others. For the consumer of benchmark results, an assessment of a benchmark's relevance must be made in context of the planned use of those results. For the benchmark designer, relevance means determining the intended use of the benchmark and then designing the benchmark to be relevant for those areas [10]. A general assessment of the relevance of a benchmark or workload involves two dimensions: the breadth of its applicability, and the degree to which the workload is relevant in that area. For example, an XML parsing benchmark may be highly relevant as a measure of XML parsing performance, somewhat relevant as a measure of enterprise server application performance, and not at all relevant for graphics performance of 3D games. Conversely, a suite of CPU benchmarks such as SPEC CPU2006 may be moderately relevant for a wide range of computing environments. The behavior illustrated in these examples is generally true: benchmarks that are designed to be highly relevant in a specific area tend to have narrow applicability, while benchmarks that attempt to be applicable to a broader spectrum of uses tend to be less meaningful for any particular scenario [4].

Scalability is an important aspect of relevance, particularly for server benchmarks. Most relevant benchmarks are multi-process and/or multi-threaded in order to be able to take advantage of the full resources of the server [8]. Achieving scalability in any application is difficult; for a benchmark, the challenges are often even greater because the benchmark is expected to run on a wide variety of systems with significant differences in available resources. Benchmark designers must also strike a careful balance between avoiding artificial limits to scaling and behaving like real applications (which often have scalability issues of their own).

3.2 Reproducibility

Reproducibility is the capability of the benchmark to produce the same results consistently for a particular test environment. It includes both run-to-run consistency and the ability for another tester to independently reproduce the results on another system.

Ideally, a benchmark result is a function of the hardware and software configuration, so that the benchmark is a measure of the performance of that environment; if this were the case, the benchmark would have perfect consistency. In reality, the complexity inherent in a modern computer system introduces significant variability in the performance of an application. This variability is introduced by several factors, including things such as the timing of thread scheduling, dynamic compilation, physical disk layout, network contention, and user interaction with the system during the run [4]. Energy efficiency benchmarks often have additional sources of variability due to power management technologies dynamically making changes to system performance and temperature changes affecting power consumption.

Benchmarks can address this run-to-run variability by running for long enough periods of time to include representative samples of these variable behaviors. Some benchmarks require submission of multiple runs with scores that are near each other as evidence of consistency. Benchmarks also tend to run at steady state, unlike more typical applications which have variations in load due to factors such as the usage patterns of users.

The ability to reproduce results in another test environment is largely tied to the ability to build an equivalent environment. Industry standard benchmarks require results submissions to include a description of the test environment, typically including both hardware and software components as well as configuration options. Similarly, published research that includes benchmark results generally includes a description of the test environment that produced those results. However, in both of these cases, the description may not provide enough detail for an independent tester to be able to assemble an equivalent environment.

Hardware must be described in sufficient detail for another person to obtain identical hardware. Software versions must be stated so that it is possible to use the same versions when reproducing the result. Tuning and configuration options must be documented for firmware, operating system, and application software so that the same options can be used when re-running the test. TPC benchmarks require a certified auditor to audit results and ensure compliance with reporting requirements. SPEC uses a combination of automatic validation and committee review to establish compliance.

3.3 Fairness

Fairness ensures that systems can compete on their merits without artificial constraints. Because benchmarks always have some degree of artificiality, it is often necessary to place some constraints on test environments in order to avoid unrealistic configurations that take advantage of the simplistic nature of the benchmark.

Benchmark development requires compromises among multiple design goals; benchmarks developed by a consensus of experts is generally perceived as being more fair than a benchmark designed by a single company [1]. While "design by committee" may not be the most efficient way to develop an application, it does require that compromises are made in such a way that multiple interested parties are able to agree that the final benchmark is fair. As a result, benchmarks produced by organizations such as SPEC and the TPC (both of which are comprised by members from companies in the industry as well as academic institutions and other interested parties) are generally regarded as fair measures of performance.

Benchmarks require a variety of hardware and software components to provide an environment suitable for running the benchmark. It is often necessary to place restrictions on what components may be used. Careful attention must be placed on these restrictions to ensure that the benchmark remains fair. Some restrictions must be made for technical reasons. For example, a benchmark implemented in Java requires a Java Virtual Machine (JVM) and an operating system and hardware that supports it. A benchmark that performs heavy disk IO may effectively require a certain number of disks to achieve acceptable IO rates, which would therefore limit the benchmark to hardware capable of supporting that number of disks.

Benchmark run rules often require hardware and software to meet some level of support or availability. While this restricts what components may be used, it is actually intended to promote fairness. Because benchmarks are by nature simplified applications, it is often possible to use simplified software to run them; this software may be quite fast because it lacks features that may be required by real applications. For example, enterprise servers typically require certain security features in their software which may not be directly exercised by benchmark applications; software that omitted these features may run faster than software that includes them, but this simplified software may not be usable for the customer base that the benchmark is targeted to. Rules regarding software support can be a particular challenge when using open source software, which is often supported primarily by the developer community rather than commercial support mechanisms.

Both of these situations require a careful balance. Placing too many or inappropriate limits on the configuration may disallow results that are relevant to some legitimate situations. Placing too few restrictions can pollute the pool of published results and, in some cases, reduce the number of relevant results because vendors can't compete with the "inappropriate" submissions. Portability is an important aspect of fairness. Achieving portability with benchmarks written in Java is relatively simple; for C and C++, it can be more difficult [3].

Benchmark run rules often include stipulations on how results may be used. These requirements are intended to promote fairness when results are published and compared, and often include provisions that require certain basic information to be included any time that results are given. For example SPECpower_ssj2008 requires that if a comparison is made for the power consumption of two systems at the 50%

target load level, the performance of each system at the 50% load level as well as the overall ssj_ops/watt value must also be stated. SPEC has perhaps the most comprehensive fair use policy which further illustrates the types of fair use issues that benchmarks should consider when creating their run rules [9].

3.4 Verifiability

Within the industry, benchmarks are typically run by vendors who have a vested interest in the results. In academia, results are subjected to peer review and interesting results will be repeated and built upon by other researchers. In both cases, it is important that benchmark results are verifiable so that the results can be deemed trustworthy.

Good benchmarks perform some amount of self-validation to ensure that the workload is running as expected, and that run rules are being followed. For example, a workload might include configuration options intended to allow researchers to change the behavior of the workload, but standard benchmarks typically limit these options to some set of compliant values which can be verified at runtime. Benchmarks may also perform some functional verification that the output of the test is correct; these tests could detect some cases where optimizations (e.g. experimental compiler options) are producing incorrect results.

Verifiability is simplified when configuration options are controlled by the benchmark, or when these details can be read by the benchmark. In this case, the benchmark can include the details with the results. Configuration details that must be documented by the user are less trustworthy since they could have been entered incorrectly.

One way to improve verifiability is to include more details in the results than are strictly necessary to produce the benchmark's metrics. Inconsistencies in this data could raise questions about the validity of the data. For example, a benchmark with a throughput metric might include response time information in addition to the transaction counts and elapsed time.

3.5 Usability

Most users of benchmarks are technically sophisticated, making ease of use less of a concern than it is for more consumer-focused applications. There are, however, several reasons why ease of use is important. One of the most important ease of use features for a benchmark is self-validation. This was already discussed in terms of making the benchmark verifiable. Self-validating workloads give the tester confidence that the workload is running properly.

Another aspect of ease of use is being able to build practical configurations for running the benchmark. For example, the current top TPC-C result has a system under test with over 100 distinct servers, over 700 disk drives and 11,000 SSD ash modules (with a total capacity of 1.76 petabytes), and a system cost of over $30 million USD. Of the 18 non-historical accepted TPC-C results published between January 1, 2010 and August 24, 2013, the median total system cost was $776,627 USD. These configurations aren't economical for most potential users [4].

Accurate descriptions of the system hardware and software configuration are critical for reproducibility, but can be a challenge due to the complexity of these descriptions. Benchmarks can improve ease of use by providing tools to assist with this process.

4. CONCLUSIONS

This paper provides an insight into the benchmark development criteria as employed be the SPEC and TPC consortia. We provide a definition for benchmarks and rating tools, differentiating between benchmarks for competitive purposes and rating tools for research purposes, regulatory programs, or as part of a system improvement and development approach. We explain the differences between the three major types of benchmarks: specification-based, kit-based, and hybrid. Finally, we describe the major quality criteria of industrial benchmarks: relevancy, repeatability, fairness, verifiability, and usability, including examples on how the criteria are ensured in standardized benchmarks.

5. REFERENCES

[1] R. García-Castro and A. Gómez-Pérez. Benchmark Suites for Improving the RDF(S) Importers and Exporters of Ontology Development Tools. In Y. Sure and J. Domingue, editors, *The Semantic Web: Research and Applications*, volume 4011 of *Lecture Notes in Computer Science*, pages 155–169. Springer Berlin Heidelberg, 2006.

[2] J. Gustafson and Q. Snell. HINT: A new way to measure computer performance. In *System Sciences, 1995. Proceedings of the Twenty-Eighth Hawaii International Conference on*, volume 2, pages 392–401 vol.2, Jan 1995.

[3] J. L. Henning. SPEC CPU2000: measuring CPU performance in the New Millennium. *Computer*, 33(7):28–35, Jul 2000.

[4] K. Huppler. The Art of Building a Good Benchmark. In R. Nambiar and M. Poess, editors, *Performance Evaluation and Benchmarking*, volume 5895 of *Lecture Notes in Computer Science*, pages 18–30. Springer Berlin Heidelberg, 2009.

[5] K. Huppler and D. Johnson. TPC Express - A New Path for TPC Benchmarks. In R. Nambiar and M. Poess, editors, *Performance Characterization and Benchmarking*, volume 8391 of *Lecture Notes in Computer Science*, pages 48–60. Springer International Publishing, 2014.

[6] K. Sachs. *Performance Modeling and Benchmarking of Event-Based Systems*. PhD thesis, TU Darmstadt, 2010. SPEC Distinguished Dissertation Award 2011.

[7] S. E. Sim, S. Easterbrook, and R. C. Holt. Using Benchmarking to Advance Research: A Challenge to Software Engineering. In *Proceedings of the 25th International Conference on Software Engineering*, ICSE '03, pages 74–83, Washington, DC, USA, 2003. IEEE Computer Society.

[8] K. Skadron, M. Martonosi, D. I. August, M. D. Hill, D. J. Lilja, and V. S. Pai. Challenges in Computer Architecture Evaluation. *Computer*, 36(8):30–36, Aug. 2003.

[9] Standard Performance Evaluation Corporation. SPEC fair use rule. http://www.spec.org/fairuse.html.

[10] Standard Performance Evaluation Corporation. SPEC Power and Performance Benchmark Methodology. http://spec.org/power/docs/SPEC-Power_and_Performance_Methodology.pdf.

[11] F. Stefani, A. Moschitta, D. Macii, and D. Petri. FFT benchmarking for digital signal processing technologies. In *17th IMEKO World Congress*, 2003.

[12] M. Vieira, H. Madeira, K. Sachs, and S. Kounev. Resilience Benchmarking. In K. Wolter, A. Avritzer, M. Vieira, and A. van Moorsel, editors, *Resilience Assessment and Evaluation of Computing Systems*, XVIII. Springer-Verlag, Berlin, Heidelberg, 2012. ISBN: 978-3-642-29031-2.

DOs and DON'Ts of
Conducting Performance Measurements in Java

Vojtěch Horký   Peter Libič   Antonín Steinhauser   Petr Tůma

Department of Distributed and Dependable Systems
Faculty of Mathematics and Physics, Charles University
Malostranské náměstí 25, 118 00 Praha 1, Czech Republic
{horky,libic,steinhauser,tuma}@d3s.mff.cuni.cz

ABSTRACT

The tutorial aims at practitioners – researchers or developers – who need to execute small scale performance experiments in Java. The goal is to provide the attendees with a compact overview of some of the issues that can hinder the experiment or mislead the evaluation, and discuss the methods and tools that can help avoid such issues. The tutorial will examine multiple elements of the software execution stack that impact performance, including common virtual machine mechanisms (just-in-time compilation and garbage collection together with associated runtime adaptation), some operating system features (timers) and hardware (memory) – although the focus will be on Java, some of the take away points should apply even in a more general performance experiment context.

Categories and Subject Descriptors

D.4.8 [**Performance**]: Measurements; D.2.8 [**Metrics**]: Performance measures

General Terms

Performance, Measurement

Keywords

performance measurement; performance evaluation; Java

1. INTRODUCTION

Some quarter century ago, a programmer using a linked list could rely on its performance being fairly transparent. The timing of the individual list operations could be computed merely by considering their algorithmic complexity together with the timing of the individual algorithmic steps, whose source – perhaps in Pascal – was compiled into known assembly instructions with known durations.

Today, programmers do not have that luxury. The same list – this time perhaps written in Java – is repeatedly com-

piled in multiple stages by adaptive compilers, it is not easy to figure out which assembly instructions will eventually be used to execute the list operations, and even if it were, the instructions do not have predictable durations anymore.

In absence of performance transparency, performance experiments become an attractive alternative. Rather than guessing what performance a linked list may exhibit, a programmer can simply measure it. The same approach is adopted in many similar situations – system administrators may use small scale performance experiments to determine optimal machine settings, computer scientists back their research into software performance with experimental evaluation, and so on.

Intuitively, performance experiment results should represent the ground truth in software performance – after all, what can give a better idea of true software performance than an experiment that measures that very performance ? In truth, however, the very lack of performance transparency that makes performance experiments useful can also make them very much misleading. Even when the measurements themselves report the true performance, which is not always a given, the lack of performance transparency means it is difficult to interpret the measurements and to extrapolate the interpretation beyond the experiment.

There is much evidence that it is easy to unwittingly conduct performance experiments that produce tricky results [6, 7, 4, 8, 21, 3, 14]. On contemporary execution platforms, even small scale performance experiments are turning from an easy and reliable way of evaluating software performance into a difficult exercise of tracking a multitude of technical details that must be dealt with even in otherwise very simple scenarios.

The goal of this tutorial is to help practitioners – programmers, administrators, researchers – who need to evaluate software performance by providing a compact technical overview of the essential problems and the available solutions in performance experiments. By way of a disclaimer, we acknowledge that our work does not tackle the core problem of insufficient performance transparency, but it may help execute performance experiments with less effort and more trust in the results.

The tutorial focuses on contemporary desktop environments running Java. Outside this environment, the content is mostly relevant in general, but the technical particulars can obviously differ. Due to space constraints, this tutorial paper contains only a dense list of topics that we believe deserve attention, together with references to related resources. The tutorial will explore the topics in more depth where appropriate.

2. WARMING UP: FAST AND STEADY

Perhaps the most well-known issue related to performance experiments is warm up. The term refers to the fact that software performance can be influenced by one-time artifacts, often visible shortly after software start. When the goal of the experiment is to examine sustainable performance, measurements influenced by these warm up artifacts need to be recognized and discarded.

Understanding the sources of the warm up artifacts is essential. Contrary to expectations, the warm up time can be very long, and observing a long period of steady performance does not necessarily imply all warm up is done. Besides the start of an experiment, the warm up artifacts can also appear between individual experimental stages, especially if these involve changes in workload.

Two major sources of the warm up artifacts discussed in the first tutorial section are class loading and just-in-time compilation. Other sources are discussed later.

2.1 Class Loading

Java code is loaded class by class on demand, where demand is first use, not first declaration [16]. Class loading disrupts performance both directly, because execution cannot proceed until the required classes are loaded, and indirectly, because some compiler optimizations are based on assumptions related to presence or absence of classes.

Once loaded, classes are rarely collected, because of many links that connect the classes to other objects, with the exception of classes loaded by the anonymous class loader.

2.2 Just-In-Time Compliation

Java program is first compiled statically from source code into bytecode. Bytecode is the portable representation that the Java Virtual Machine (JVM) loads and executes. Although it is possible to execute the bytecode in an interpreter, it is more common to compile bytecode into native code, which executes directly. This is done by Just-In-Time (JIT) compiler.

Triggering compilation. Inherent to JIT compilation is the trade off between initial performance loss, due to executing the compilation, and later performance gain, due to executing the compiled code. The JVM is therefore selective in submitting code for JIT compilation – only methods that have been observed to execute often enough are compiled with complex optimizations.

JIT compilation can be configured with various levels of optimization and include various levels of profiling code that enable better optimization later. Current JIT compilers use tiered JIT compilation, where methods gradually move towards higher compilation levels. A common criterion for triggering a compilation is the number of times a method was invoked or the number of times a loop iterated. Thresholds for lower compilation levels default to values around thousands, thresholds for higher compilation levels to values around tens of thousands. The thresholds can be adjusted [18].

Inlining methods. Inlining is an optimization performed by the JIT compiler which replaces method calls by method bodies where appropriate. The immediately obvi-

ous but relatively small benefit of inlining is removing the call overhead. More importantly, inlining improves other optimizations by providing more code to work on.

Whether inlining happens depends on multiple factors, especially the size of the method to be inlined (hence instrumentation influences inlining) and the ability of the JIT compiler to determine the method call target (hence class loading influences inlining).

A performance experiment may inline both more and less than desired or expected. Sometimes it is possible to control inlining or display inlining decisions [18, 19].

Determinism. The exact result of JIT compilation depends on many timing factors. Multiple executions of the same performance experiment will not necessarily exhibit the same JIT behavior and therefore will not use the same code. Support for making the behavior of JIT compilation deterministic is not yet common [5, 1], in absense of such support multiple JVM executions can be used to examine the possible spectrum of experiment behaviors.

Initial performance. So far, we have considered experiments that examine sustainable performance. When initial rather than sustainable performance is of interest, multiple JVM executions are required. Warm up artifacts exist even in this context, for example the very first execution is likely to fetch data from disk, while the subsequent executions will benefit from disk cache. Even the opposite can be true, when all but the first execution pay the cost of flushing the disk cache left dirty by the previous execution.

3. TOO SMART: MORE COMPILATION

In a performance experiment, the dangers of JIT compilation are not only that it progresses gradually or that it is not deterministic, but also that it may be rather sensitive to minute differences between the performance experiment and the real environment the experiment approximates. As a result, the experiment may see optimizations systematically different from reality.

3.1 Optimizing Experiment Workload

It is common for a performance experiment to repeat the measured code multiple times. Also, a performance experiment often cares only about the timing, throwing away the result that would be used in reality. Without careful coding, this may lead to optimizations such as moving loop-invariant parts of the measured code out of the measurement loop, simplifying the measured code through constant propagation from outside the measurement loop, merging multiple iterations of the measured code by loop unrolling and common subexpression elimination, and more.

The black hole support in JMH is particularly helpful in efficiently preventing similar optimizations [21, 19].

As the flip side of the same coin, a performance experiment should not attempt to measure isolated code that would not be isolated in reality.

3.2 Polymorphic Invocation

Calls whose target address is difficult to predict entail overhead at the processor instruction level. Optimizations used to make polymorphic invocations predictable include class hierarchy analysis and target caching. Both are possibly sensitive to performance experiment conditions, such as loading or exercising a relatively limited subset of classes.

3.3 Optimization Fallback

Compared to static compilers, performance experiments with dynamic compilers require a subtly different mindset. Where a static compiler needs to prove a particular optimization correct before using it, a dynamic compiler may optimize tentatively and surround the optimized code with a test that guards the correctness prerequisites. When the guard fails, the assumptions are corrected and compilation redone.

To guarantee realistic optimizations, a performance experiment must emit workload that violates unrealistic compiler assumptions. This may entail taking unusual branches, throwing unexpected exceptions, or loading and exercising classes that are not otherwise essential to the workload.

3.4 On Stack Replacement

Normally, a method compiled at lower optimization level is replaced by a method at higher optimization level between calls. This poses a problem for methods with long loops, where the more optimized version may wait long for the less optimized version to exit.

Replacement of an executing method is possible but may require converting stack layout and limiting available optimizations. Both may impact the performance experiment.

4. MANAGED MEMORY

Java heap uses garbage collection (GC) with many performance implications. Importantly, a performance experiment must decide whether the GC cost should be included or avoided. Using large enough heap and forcing collections between iterations may avoid most GC costs, but from the practical perspective, including GC cost may provide more relevant results.

Heap size. Heap size has significant impact on GC cost [2]. Adaptive heuristics that tune heap size are therefore complicating performance experiments [15, 12].

Heap content. A performance experiment may generate heap content that is less diverse than reality. When using a large heap, most objects are in the young generation, with better locality and fewer references between generations. Experiments that discard results between iterations lower GC costs by reducing live data. Collections between iterations may also encounter few live objects, making GC cheaper.

Sometimes, comparing workloads with different allocation behavior is needed. Additional allocations exhaust allocation buffers (TLAB) sooner, causing more slow-path allocations and more young collections. In turn, this pushes more objects into the old generation. This often leads to higher GC costs.

Many changes to the heap content also impact the behavior of weak reference types.

Optimized allocation. Using escape analysis or escape detection, JVM can allocate objects on stack rather than on heap [17]. As a side effect, measurement may turn stack allocation into heap allocation [11]. This increases the allocation cost and disables some potential optimizations.

Storing measurements. The measurements are often stored on the same heap that the workload uses. This again impacts heap content, in particular when storing the measurements in dynamic structures such as lists. The very

presence of a long list may decrease the throughput of parallel collectors, because the list must be traversed sequentially, also part of the list will likely be in the young generation, with impact as above.

Dynamic structures suffer from bloat that may not be immediately apparent [13]. Using an array instead of a dynamic structure is less flexible, but may be more efficient and more predictable, especially when the array items are primitive.

When necessary, it is possible to store measurements outside the heap, using native memory through JNI or through the sun.misc.unsafe API.

5. PARALLELISM

When collecting data from more threads, proper workload synchronization is essential. Where blocking is reasonable, the java.util.concurrent API may suffice. In some cases, it is necessary to keep workload threads running and only synchronize their data collection phases.

Biased locking. Parallel workload often involves synchronization. Synchronization may be heavily optimized in favor of certain common cases, such as the same thread repeatedly acquiring a lock without contention [20]. To assess realistic synchronization performance, a performance experiment must therefore use realistic contention.

Synchronization optimizations may exhibit anomalies due to internal implementation details. For example, biased locking is disabled for certain time after JVM start, and does not work for objects whose identity hashcode was queried [20].

Memory sharing. Contemporary architectures utilize multiple levels of memory caches, some local to cores, some shared among cores. Although JVM may use thread local allocation buffers (TLAB) to prevent threads on different cores from allocating data near each other, various workload patterns may lead to excessive cache traffic.

Particularly disruptive issue is that of false sharing, where unrelated variables occupy the same cache line. Modifying such variables from multiple cores generates needless cache coherency traffic whose reason is difficult to discern at source code level. In artificial (especially extremely regular) workloads, similar effects may occur with internal JVM structures, such as card tables.

Randomizing workload parameters tends to reduce the chance of encountering performance anomalies due to artificial memory sharing patterns.

NUMA. On NUMA architectures, memory access performance depends on node locality. Automated partitioning of data to improve locality is a technically difficult problem [22]. Solutions that avoid some worst-case scenarios include thread-local allocations and interleaving data in shared heap spaces [17].

6. SENSORS

Besides paying attention to how the workload of a performance experiment behaves, we also need to pay attention to the sensors used to measure the workload. Perhaps the most obvious sensor is the time source.

Timing accuracy. The most easily accessible time source in Java is calling System.nanoTime. The exact behavior of this method is platform-dependent, for example Open-

JDK 8 on Linux queries the CLOCK_MONOTONIC system clock, OpenJDK 8 on Windows uses the QueryPerformance-Counter call. These are both high precision time sources, however, on older systems the same method can use microsecond or millisecond granularity sources.

Internally, the high precision time sources may use hardware counters with unknown or varying frequency. Such sources are callibrated against counters with known frequency but possibly lower accuracy, this callibration can yield slightly different frequency estimate on each initialization. Also, the CLOCK_MONOTONIC system clock is subject to adjustments on systems with NTP or PTP support, even during measurement.

Performance counters. Hardware performance event counters are another important sensor in performance experiments. Querying the counters from Java requires making native calls, possibly through JNI. The associated overheads may limit usefulness. Libraries for accessing these and other sensors from Java are also available [9].

7. MISCELLANEA

The tutorial will also touch on other topics that we do not describe in detail now. Some diverse examples include anomalous optimization behavior on loop constructs that do not qualify as counted due to choice of the loop control type, caching of some boxed primitive values and impact on memory allocation behavior, overhead associated with invoking native code through JNI, and effects of thermal budget on turbo boosting and frequency scaling [10].

Acknowledgements

This work was partially supported by the Charles University institutional funding and the EU project ASCENS 257414.

8. REFERENCES

[1] Azul. Zing JVM, 2014. http://www.azulsystems.com/products/zing/virtual-machine.

[2] S. M. Blackburn, P. Cheng, and K. S. McKinley. Myths and realities: The performance impact of garbage collection. SIGMETRICS '04/Performance '04. ACM, 2004.

[3] S. M. Blackburn et al. Wake up and smell the coffee: Evaluation methodology for the 21st century. *Commun. ACM*, 51(8), Aug. 2008.

[4] A. Buble, L. Bulej, and P. Tůma. CORBA benchmarking: a course with hidden obstacles. In *PDPS*, April 2003.

[5] A. Georges, L. Eeckhout, and D. Buytaert. Java performance evaluation through rigorous replay compilation. In *OOPSLA*. ACM, 2008.

[6] J. Y. Gil, K. Lenz, and Y. Shimron. A microbenchmark case study and lessons learned. In *SPLASH Workshops*. ACM, 2011.

[7] B. Goetz. Java theory and practice: Anatomy of a flawed microbenchmark, 2005. http://www.ibm.com/developerworks/java/library/j-jtp02225/.

[8] D. Gu, C. Verbrugge, and E. M. Gagnon. Relative factors in performance analysis of Java virtual machines. ACM, 2006.

[9] V. Horký. Java microbenchmark agent, 2014. http://github.com/d-iii-s/java-ubench-agent.

[10] Intel. Intel Turbo Boost technology, 2014. http://www.intel.com/content/www/us/en/architecture-and-technology/turbo-boost/turbo-boost-technology.html.

[11] P. Libič, L. Bulej, V. Horký, and P. Tůma. On the limits of modeling generational garbage collector performance. In *ICPE*. ACM, 2014.

[12] P. Libič, P. Tůma, and L. Bulej. Issues in performance modeling of applications with garbage collection. In *QUASOSS*. ACM, 2009.

[13] N. Mitchell and G. Sevitsky. The causes of bloat, the limits of health. In *OOPSLA*. ACM, 2007.

[14] T. Mytkowicz, A. Diwan, M. Hauswirth, and P. F. Sweeney. Producing wrong data without doing anything obviously wrong! In *ASPLOS*. ACM, 2009.

[15] Oracle. Memory management in the Java HotSpot virtual machine, 2006. http://www.oracle.com/technetwork/java/javase/memorymanagement-whitepaper-150215.pdf.

[16] Oracle. The Java® virtual machine specification, 2013. http://docs.oracle.com/javase/specs/jvms/se7/html/jvms-5.html.

[17] Oracle. Java HotSpot virtual machine performance enhancements, 2014. http://docs.oracle.com/javase/7/docs/technotes/guides/vm/performance-enhancements-7.html.

[18] Oracle. Java invocation documentation, 2014. http://docs.oracle.com/javase/8/docs/technotes/tools/unix/java.html.

[19] Oracle. Java microbenchmarking harness (OpenJDK: jmh), 2014. http://openjdk.java.net/projects/code-tools/jmh/.

[20] Oracle. Synchronization (HotSpot internals for OpenJDK), 2014. http://wikis.oracle.com/display/HotSpotInternals/Synchronization.

[21] A. Shipilev. Java microbenchmark harness (the lesser of two evils). Presented at Devoxx, 2013.

[22] M. Tikir and J. Hollingsworth. NUMA-aware Java heaps for server applications. In *IPDPS*, 2005.

Hybrid Machine Learning/Analytical Models for Performance Prediction: a Tutorial*

Diego Didona and Paolo Romano

INESC-ID / Instituto Superior Técnico, Universidade de Lisboa

ABSTRACT

Classical approaches to performance prediction of computer systems rely on two, typically antithetic, techniques: Machine Learning (ML) and Analytical Modeling (AM).

ML undertakes a black-box approach, which typically achieves very good accuracy in regions of the features' space that have been sufficiently explored during the training process, but that has very weak extrapolation power (i.e., poor accuracy in regions for which none, or too few samples are known).

Conversely, AM relies on a white-box approach, whose key advantage is that it requires no or minimal training, hence supporting prompt instantiation of the target system's performance model. However, to ensure their tractability, AM-based performance predictors typically rely on simplifying assumptions. Consequently, AM's accuracy is challenged in scenarios not matching such assumptions.

This tutorial describes techniques that exploit AM and ML in synergy in order to get the best of the two worlds. It surveys several such hybrid techniques and presents use cases spanning a wide range of application domains.

1. INTRODUCTION

Performance modeling of applications and systems is a critical requirement in tasks like anomaly detection, optimization, capacity planning, and, with the advent of Cloud computing, automatic resource provisioning.

Analytical Modeling (AM) has been for decades the reference technique in this context [11, 12, 20, 21]. AM relies on exploiting *a-priori* knowledge of the internal dynamics of target applications/systems in order to express the input/output relation by means of a set of analytical equations. For this reason, AM modeling is often referred to as *white box modeling*. The most appealing feature of AM is that, once instantiated, a white box model exhibits a good

*This work has been supported by FCT - Fundação para a Ciência e a Tecnologia through PEst-OE/EEI/LA0021/2013, project specSTM (PTDC/EIA-EIA/122785/2010) and project GreenTM EXPL/EEI-ESS/0361/2013

accuracy when working in *extrapolation*. That is, AM is capable of predicting several Key Performance Indicators (KPI) for a wide set of application's workload, input parameters and characteristics of the underlying hosting platform. Yet, AM comes with the downside of relying on assumptions and approximations (necessary to ensure the analytical tractability of the model) that can hamper prediction's accuracy.

The successful application of AM technique has been progressively challenged over the last years, primarily due to two main causes: *i*) the ever increasingly complexity of applications makes it increasingly difficult to derive detailed AMs capable of capturing all the dynamics and relations that map characteristics of an application/system onto KPIs; *ii*) the advent of Cloud Computing has led applications to be deployed over virtualized infrastructures, whose details are typically intentionally hidden. This limited knowledge about the underlying platform poses serious challenges to the derivation of accurate white box models.

Fortunately, the last years have also witnessed the maturing of research in the area of Machine Learning (ML) [1], which resulted into the development of a wide range of freely-available high quality ML toolkits [15]. This has led a growing number of researchers to explore the possibility of using ML techniques to build *black box* predictors of complex computer systems [16, 18, 19]. Black box modeling is antithetic with respect to its white box counterpart: it relies on inferring the input/output relationships that map application's and system's characteristic onto the target KPI, and on encoding such relationships via statistical models. Such models are built on the basis of a so called *training phase*, during which the application is tested with different workloads and parametrized with different configurations, with the purpose of observing the corresponding achieved performance. The most appealing property of such modeling approach is that it is sufficient to identify *which* are the inputs –a.k.a. features– of the performance functions, and the ML algorithm will take care of inferring *how* they map to the target KPI, without exploiting any additional knowledge about the application.

Unfortunately, ML does not represent the "silver bullet" for the performance modeling problem, as the lack of *a priori* information about the target application/system does come with a price. The accuracy of ML-based performance predictors, in fact, ultimately depends on the representativeness of the input/output samples collected during the training phase. In order to exhaustively cover the whole space of possible inputs, the training phase should sweep all combinations of possible workloads and system configurations.

Unfortunately, the cardinality of the resulting set grows exponentially with the number of input features, making it cumbersome, or even impossible, to carry out an exhaustive training phase for complex systems. As a result, black box models typically delivers a very good accuracy when working in *interpolation*, i.e., in regions of the features' space that they have been sufficiently explored; conversely, their accuracy is typically poor when working in extrapolation.

Gray box modeling [5, 6, 4, 8, 7, 10, 14, 9, 3] has emerged in the last years as an attempt to achieve the best of the AM and ML world. It relies on exploiting both methodologies, in order to compensate the weaknesses of the one with the strengths of the other. In particular, gray box modeling aims at making performance predictors more robust to the limitations of the two base methodologies by *i*) inheriting from ML-based models the ability to progressively enhance the accuracy of the performance predictor as new data from the operational system are collected; *ii*) requiring, like AM models, little or no training time in order to instantiate a performance predictor. Different gray box methodologies have been proposed, targeting very diverse techniques to combine AM and ML. In this paper we overview the most prominent approaches that have been proposed in literature. This document is intended to be a companion of the ICPE15 tutorial, which will cover this topic in deeper detail.

The next section is devoted at introducing some basic concepts and terminology on ML. Section 3 describes the three most prominent gray box modeling methodologies, whereas Section 4 overviews example applications for each of these methodologies. Finally, Section 5 concludes the paper and discusses open research questions in the area of gray box modeling.

2. BACKGROUND ON MACHINE LEARNING

Machine Learning deals with the construction and study of systems that can learn from data [1]. In this section we are going to provide basic background on ML focused on Supervised Learning and Reinforcement Learning, which are the ML techniques that are most frequently employed in the domain of performance modeling. We shall also introduce two of the most commonly used ML algorithms, namely Decision Trees and Support Vector Machines.

Supervised Learning (SL) is the task aimed at learning the relation between a set of input parameters, called *input features*, and a set of outputs, called *target features*. More formally, a supervised machine learner infer a function (also called model) $\phi : X \rightarrow Y$ based on the observed output corresponding to a set $\tilde{X} \subset X$, called *training set*. Such a function can be exploited to predict the output value y corresponding to values of the input parameters that are not present in the training set. If the codomain of the ϕ function is continuous, then the learner is defined *regressor*. If it is discrete, then the learner is defined *classifier*; in this case, the values that the output can assume are called *classes*.

Two of the most prominent Supervised Learning algorithms are Decision Trees (DT) and Support Vector Machines (SVM) [1].

DTs [1] structure their model as a tree: each interior node of the tree corresponds to one of the input variables; edges from a parent to a child are labeled with a predicate about the value of the input feature relevant to the parent node. In the case of DT classifiers, each leaf represents the class of the target feature; in the case of regressors, it is a function of the input values.

SVMs [1] map the points of the training set over a multi-dimensional space W such that elements in the same class occupy a specific portion of that space and are as far away as possible from elements of other classes. Although introduced to solve classification problems, SVMs have been extended to be used also as regressors [1].

Reinforcement Learning (RL) is the branch of ML that investigates the issue of how an *agent* should perform actions in an environment in order to maximize a cumulative *reward*. One of the most important issues in reinforcement learning techniques is the trade-off between exploration and exploitation: in absence of an explicit model capable of determining *a priori* the optimality of an action over another one, the agent must explore the environment in order to gather feedback on the rewards of the action. A RL algorithm aims to identify which and how many exploration steps should be performed in order to maximize the long-term reward (typically modeled as an unknown random variable). When applied to the domain of self-tuning, RL techniques are used to implement a controller that is in charge of determining the optimal configuration for a system. In this context, the environment is represented by the set of tunable parameters and external factors (e.g., the workload) and the reward is defined as a function of some target KPI.

3. GRAY BOX MODELING TECHNIQUES

Existing works in the area of gray box performance modeling and optimization can be grouped in three different classes, which we call *Boostrapping*, *Divide-and-conquer*, and *Ensembling*. We overview each of them in the following.

Bootstrapping. This technique relies on an AM in order to produce a *synthetic* training set over which a black box learner is initially trained. This training set is composed of $< input, output >$ tuples where the input normally spans different workload metrics and platform configurations, and the corresponding output is obtained by querying the analytical model. As this set is obtained without actually gathering samples from the operational system, this technique allows for significantly reducing the time necessary an initial black-box leaner (e.g., based on DT or SVM). Clearly, the performance function inferred by the ML will be very similar to the one encoded in the AM and, as such, it will inherit also its possible inaccuracies. However, as $< input, output >$ tuples are collected from the actual system (e.g., while it is running in production), such synthetic training set can be complemented with *real* samples. The ML can be, thus, periodically re-trained over time, in order to benefit from this additional knowledge and compensate for possible inaccuracies of the original AM.

This technique has been implemented in solutions integrating analytical models both with RL [13, 9] and SL algorithms [14, 10], and has been applied for data centers management [13, 14] and applications optimization [10, 9]. A recent detailed study of the bootstrapping technique investigates the design space of such technique and highlights some pitfalls that may arise in its implementation [7].

Divide and conquer. This approach consists in building specialized models, for different components of the target system, that rely either on AM or on ML; such models are then coupled to carry out the performance prediction about the behavior of the overall system. Normally, AM is exploited to capture performance of components whose internal dynamics are known and easy to monitor; ML, conversely, is typically employed to predict the behavior of components whose internals are hidden (and, thus, not observable), or whose performance dynamics are too complex to be accurately captured via analytical methods.

This approach has been implemented for modeling performance of distributed transactional Cloud data platforms, where details of the underlying physical architecture is hidden by the virtualization layer; it has been integrated in hybrid models encompassing both queueing-theory based AMs [5, 8] as well as simulation-based ones [3].

Ensembling. This technique entails combining the outputs of multiple AMs and MLs according to different schemes. Various implementations have been proposed, which differ in the way the base models are combined to produce the final performance prediction of the target KPI.

One approach we find in literature [4, 6] consists in building an AM to predict the target KPI; then, a chain of M black box learners is progressively trained not on the KPI itself, but on the residual prediction errors of the previous model. In this way, the i-th model learns a corrective function that compensates for the inaccuracies of the chain composed by previous $i-1$ models.

Other solutions rely on building a battery of independent predictors for the target KPI; at query time, only the predictor that is estimated to be the most reliable for a given input i is employed to carry out the final prediction. All the ensemble-based predictors that we are aware of carry out this decision based on the expected accuracy of the individual learners in the "proximity" of the target input i, but adopt different notions of proximity. Existing approaches include solutions that partition statically the input space (based on some *a-priori* knowledge) and assign different partitions to each model [2], techniques that employ a classifier to determine which predictor to use or that pick the most accurate learner over the k nearest neighbors of the target input in the training set [6] .

4. APPLICATIONS

This section is devoted to presenting in greater detail one use case for each of the gray box modeling methodologies described in the previous section.

4.1 Divide and conquer

For this category we present Transactional Auto Scaler (TAS) [5]. We choose this use case as, to the best of our knowledge, it represents the first implementation of such gray box modeling methodology.

TAS is a performance model for replicated transactional Cloud data stores; a transactional data store is a platform that allows applications deployed over it to perform atomic operations on shared data in spite of concurrent accesses via the *transaction* abstraction [17]. In a replicated transactional platform, there are multiple machines (a.k.a. nodes) that host the same data set, and each node maintains a local copy of it. Whenever a transaction completes its execution, it starts a distributed *commit* phase during which it contacts all the nodes in the systems to determine the final outcome for the transaction, i.e., commit or abort. In the former case

the transaction completes successfully, otherwise it needs to be aborted and restarted.

TAS captures the effect of data and CPU contention by means of white box models: it models the CPU of different nodes using queuing theory in order to compute the response time of CPU-bound operations, like reading or writing data; moreover, it also models each datum as a queue, in order to compute the probability for two transactions to abort due to conflicting accesses on the same data. On the other hand, TAS exploits ML, specifically DTs, in order to predict the execution time of network-bound operations, i.e., the distributed commit phase. As already discussed, the rationale behind this choice is that the virtualization layer of Cloud environments hides the physical details of the hosting infrastructures; it is, thus, extremely cumbersome to derive a network performance model without knowing, for example, the network topology according to which physical machines are organized.

The two models are built independently, but they are solved according to an iterative scheme that couples them in order to predict the overall execution time of a transaction. First, the AM is queried to produce an estimate of some intermediate performance variables that are among the input features of the ML, e.g., the rate at which commit procedures are initiated; then, the ML is queried to produce a prediction of the network-bound operations execution times, which is in turn needed by the AM to compute the overall response time of a transaction. This two steps are repeated until the difference in the transactions response time computed in two consecutive iterations becomes marginal.

Bootstrapping. We choose as representative for this methodology IRONModel [14], which is a performance modeling framework for anomaly detection in data centers.

IRONModel relies on a set of AMs that are built to predict the expected behavior of components in a data center, from routers to storage systems. The synthetic training sets generated starting from these models are given in input to a DT, which ultimately serves all the performance prediction queries. Note that, unlike other use cases in which any ML could be employed, IRONModel specifically relies on DTs because of their characteristic to produce a model that is interpretable by humans; this is an important requirement for anomaly detection and data centers management.

This black box model is exploited not only to perform what-if analysis, but it is also periodically queried so at to monitor whether the behavior of a component deviates from its normalcy. Upon detecting such a deviation, an alarm is triggered, which is handled by the system administrator. If the anomalous behavior is not recognized to be caused by a bug or a failure of a sub-component, and it is, then, a regular but unforeseen behavior of the target component, then the system administrator performs the following operations: *i*) she examines the logs about the utilization patterns of the target component, in order to detect and isolate workloads of the target component that caused the anomalous performance; *ii*) she sets-up experiments aimed at reproducing such workloads and conditions, and schedules them to be run either immediately, if the current workloads can be redirected to other components in the data center, or as soon as they can be executed in isolation, e.g., at night; *iii*) once the experiments are completed, the logs encoding the measured input/output relation is given as input to the DT, which is re-trained in order to update its rule-set and properly predict the component's behavior that was regarded as anomalous.

Ensemble. The use case chosen as example for this methodology is Chorus, a model ensemble tool for self-management in data centers. Chorus' performance predictor relies on ensembles of both black and box models. Chorus' white box models are typically simple, as they are designed to capture the target system's behavior in well specified operational conditions, for example in cases in which the workload is CPU bound, disk bound or memory bound. Black box models include both SVMs, as well as simpler regressive models (linear, polynomial or exponential functions), whose parameters are determined by fitting the output of the various models to the data in the training set.

Chorus is trained by performing the following steps. First of all, the input space is partitioned into R disjoint regions. Then, an immutable validation set D_v is generated, starting from some input/output observations; such set is used to evaluate the accuracy of the overall performance model and to stop the training phase when a target average accuracy has been achieved. The training set D_t is expanded incrementally in rounds, until the stopping criterion is met. At each round, the accuracy of the M models is evaluated by means of k-fold cross validation on D_t. This entails partitioning D_t into k bins $D_{t,1} \ldots D_{t,k}$ and then, iteratively for $i = 1 \ldots k$, training the models over $D_t \setminus D_{t,i}$ and evaluating its accuracy against $D_{t,i}$. The models are then sorted on a per region basis, according to the achieved accuracy in predicting performance for samples falling in a given region.

Once trained, Chorus serves a query for an input sample belonging to region $r \in R$ by returning the output of the most accurate performance predictor for r.

5. CONCLUSIONS AND DISCUSSION

Analytical Modeling and Machine Learning are typically regarded as two alternative methodologies to model performance of computer systems and applications. In this paper we have overviewed three different hybrid modeling methodologies, which leverage on both AM and ML to get the best of the two worlds, namely reducing the model's training time and increasing its accuracy as new training data become available.

While research on AM and ML has already reached maturity, investigation on hybrid methodologies is still at its infancy. A recent work [6] has shown that none of such techniques outperforms the others in terms of accuracy for every application and for every training data set. An interesting research line to pursue, in the light of this result, is to identify which characteristics of the applications being modeled, or of the AM and ML techniques employed for modeling may lead a given hybrid methodology to outperform the others.

Another interesting issue to investigate is whether it is possible to fruitfully combine further the described methodologies, with the goal of building a unique, more accurate, meta-hybrid model.

6. REFERENCES

[1] C. M. Bishop. *Pattern Recognition and Machine Learning (Information Science and Statistics).* 2007.

[2] J. Chen et al. Model ensemble tools for self-management in data centers. In *Proc. of ICDE Workshops*, 2013.

[3] P. Di Sanzo et al. A flexible framework for accurate simulation of cloud in-memory data stores. *ArXiv e-prints*, Dec. 2014.

[4] D. Didona et al. Identifying the optimal level of parallelism in transactional memory applications. *Springer Computing Journal*, 2013.

[5] D. Didona et al. Transactional auto scaler: Elastic scaling of replicated in-memory transactional data grids. *ACM Trans. Auton. Adapt. Syst.*, 9(2):11:1–11:32, July 2014.

[6] D. Didona et al. Enhancing Performance Prediction Robustness by Combining Analytical Modeling and Machine Learning. In *Proc. of ICPE*, 2015.

[7] D. Didona and P. Romano. On Bootstrapping Machine Learning Performance Predictors via Analytical Models. *ArXiv e-prints*, Oct. 2014.

[8] D. Didona and P. Romano. Performance modelling of partially replicated in-memory transactional stores. In *Proc. of MASCOTS*, 2014.

[9] P. Romano and M. Leonetti. Self-tuning batching in total order broadcast protocols via analytical modelling and reinforcement learning. In *Proc. of ICNC*, 2011.

[10] D. Rughetti et al. Analytical/ml mixed approach for concurrency regulation in software transactional memory. In *Proc. of CCGRID*, 2014.

[11] Y. C. Tay. *Analytical Performance Modeling for Computer Systems.* Morgan & Claypool Publishers, 2013.

[12] L. Kleinrock *Queueing Systems, Theory, Volume 1.* Wiley Interscience, 1975.

[13] G. Tesauro et al. On the use of hybrid reinforcement learning for autonomic resource allocation. *Cluster Computing*, 2007.

[14] E. Thereska and G. Ganger. Ironmodel: Robust performance models in the wild. In *Proc. of SIGMETRICS*, 2008.

[15] M. Hall et al. The WEKA Data Mining Software: An Update. *SIGKDD Explor. Newsl.*, 11(1) 10–18, June 2009.

[16] M. Couceiro et al. A machine learning approach to performance prediction of total order broadcast protocols. In *Proc. of SASO*, 2010.

[17] P. Bernstein and E. Newcomer Principles of Transaction Processing: For the Systems Professional *Morgan Kaufmann Publishers Inc.*, 1997

[18] M. Couceiro et al. Chasing the optimum in replicated in-memory transactional platforms via protocol adaptation. In *Proc. of DSN*, 2013

[19] A. Ganapathi et al. Predicting Multiple Metrics for Queries: Better Decisions Enabled by Machine Learning. In *Proc. of ICDE*, 2009

[20] J. Padhye et al. Modeling TCP throughput: A simple model and its empirical validation. *SIGCOMM Comput. Commun. Rev.*, 28(4) 303-314, Oct. 1998.

[21] P. Di Sanzo et al. On the analytical modeling of concurrency control algorithms for software transactional memories: The case of commit-time-locking. Performance Evaluation 69(5), May, 2012

LT 2015: The Fourth International Workshop on Large-Scale Testing

Zhen Ming Jiang,
York University
Toronto, Canada
zmjiang@cse.yorku.ca

Andreas Brunnert
fortiss GmbH
Munich, Germany
brunnert@fortiss.org

ABSTRACT

Many large-scale software systems (e.g., e-commerce websites, telecommunication infrastructures and enterprise systems, etc.) must service hundreds, thousands or even millions of concurrent requests. Large-scale testing includes all different objectives and strategies of testing large-scale software systems using load. Large-scale testing is a challenging area and industry has invested large amount of resources into this. Yet, there are few academic research efforts devoted to large-scale testing. In this workshop, we intend to bring together industrial practitioners and researchers to establish and grow an academic research community around this important and practical research topic.

Categories and Subject Descriptors

C.4 [**Performance of Systems**]: measurement techniques, modeling techniques; D.2.8 [**Software Engineering**]: Metrics—*performance measures*; D.2.5 [**Software Engineering**]: Testing and Debugging

General Terms

Performance; Measurement; Verification

Keywords

large-scale testing; performance; reliability; scalability; dependability; software performance engineering; application performance management

1. INTRODUCTION

Large-scale software systems must service thousands (e.g., enterprise applications) or even millions (e.g., e-commerce websites like Amazon) of concurrent users every day. Many field problems of these systems are due to their inability to scale to field workloads, rather than feature bugs. In addition to conventional functional testing (e.g., unit and integration testing), these systems must be tested with large

volumes of concurrent requests (called the *load*) to ensure the quality of these systems. Large-scale testing includes all different objectives and strategies of testing large-scale software systems using load. Examples of large-scale testing include live upgrade testing, load testing, high availability testing, operational profile testing, performance testing, reliability testing, stability testing and stress testing.

Large-scale testing is a difficult task requiring a great understanding of the system under test [8]. Practitioners face many challenges such as tooling (choosing and implementing the testing tools), environments (software and hardware setup) and time (limited time to design, test, and analyze). Yet, little research is done in the software engineering domain concerning this topic. Industry has been focused primarily on creating tools to automatically drive specified load into the system under test (e.g., LoadRunner [6] and Apache JMeter [2]). Large-scale testing is gaining more importance, as an increasing number of systems (on-premise and/or cloud-based systems) are designed to serve thousands or millions of users.

2. SCOPE

LT 2015 [4] includes the following two tracks of submissions: **technical papers** (maximum 4 pages) and **extended abstracts** for industry talks (maximum 700 words). The technical papers follow the standard ACM SIG proceedings format [1] and are submitted through EasyChair. Topics of interest include, but not limited to the following:

- Efficient and cost-effective test executions

- Rapid and scalable analysis of the test results

- Case studies and experience reports on large-scale testing

- Large-scale testing on emerging systems (e.g., adaptive/autonomic systems or cloud services)

- Taxonomies of testing large-scale software systems

- Large-scale testing in the context of agile software development process

- Using performance models to support large-scale testing

- Building and maintaining large-scale testing as a service

- Efficient test data management for large-scale testing

3. WORKSHOP OBJECTIVES

LT 2015 intends to bring together researchers, practitioners and tool developers to discuss the challenges and opportunities of conducting research on large-scale testing.

4. WORKSHOP PROGRAM FORMAT

LT 2015 is a one-day workshop. The workshop participants consist of a mixture of academic and industrial researchers. A big emphasis of this workshop is to make the workshop interactive with many discussion slots assigned throughout the schedule.

The workshop has two keynote talks:

- **"Load Testing Elasticity and Performance Isolation in Shared Execution Environments"** by Professor Samuel Kounev from University of Würzburg;

- **"Challenges, Benefits and Best Practices of Performance Focused DevOps"** by Wolfgang Gottesheim from Compuware.

In addition, it also includes presentations from technical papers and industrial talks. Finally, there is a panel, which brings together industrial practitioners and academic researchers to discuss the opportunities and challenges associated with large-scale testing.

5. CONCLUSIONS

Large-scale testing is a required testing procedure to ensure the performance and scalability of the software systems, which are used by thousands or millions of users simultaneously. LT 2015 provides a forum for software engineering researchers and practitioners to discuss the challenges and opportunities of large-scale testing.

6. WORKSHOP ORGANIZERS

Zhen Ming (Jack) Jiang [3] is an Assistant Professor at the Department of Electrical Engineering and Computer Science, York University, Canada. Prior to joining York, he worked at BlackBerry's Performance Engineering Team for over half a decade. His research interests lie within Software Engineering and Computer Systems, with special interests in software performance engineering, mining software repositories, source code analysis, software architectural recovery, software visualizations and debugging and monitoring of distributed systems. Some of the tools resulted from his research are already adopted and used in practice on a daily basis to monitor and debug the health of several large-scale commercial software systems. He is the co-founder and co-organizer of the annually held International Workshop on Large-Scale Testing (LT), formally called International Workshop on Load Testing Large-Scale Software Systems. He is the recipient of several best paper awards including

ICSE 2013, WCRE 2011 and MSR 2009 (challenge track). He received his PhD from the School of Computing at the Queen's University. He received his MMath and BMath degrees in Computer Science from the University of Waterloo.

Andreas Brunnert leads the Performance & Virtualization team [5] at fortiss GmbH, Germany. The team focuses on all aspects required to ensure that given performance goals (i.e., response time, throughput and resource utilization) for application systems are met. One of the focus areas of the team is the integration of software performance engineering (SPE) and application performance management (APM) activities throughout the whole life cycle of an application system [7]. Prior to joining fortiss, he worked as Software Engineer and Advisory IT Specialst in the WebSphere Application Server and Portal Server development and lab services teams at IBM Germany Research & Development GmbH. He received his M.Sc. degree in Information Systems from the University of Bamberg and a diploma in Computer Science from the University of Applied Sciences Brandenburg.

Acknowledgement

We would like to thank all the authors who submitted their works to LT 2015. In addition, we would also like to thank the program committee members for their detailed and constructive feedbacks. Finally, we are also very grateful for the invited keynote speakers for their interesting and thought-provoking talks.

7. REFERENCES

[1] ACM SIG proceedings template. http://www.acm.org/sigs/publications/proceedings-templates.

[2] Apache JMeter. http://jakarta.apache.org/jmeter/.

[3] Homepage at the York University. http://www.cse.yorku.ca/~zmjiang/.

[4] Homepage of the Fourth International Workshop on Large-Scale Testing (LT 2015). http://lt2015.eecs.yorku.ca/.

[5] Homepage of the Performance & Virtualization Team. http://pmw.fortiss.org/.

[6] HP LoadRunner software. http://www8.hp.com/us/en/software/software-product.html?compURI=tcm:245-935779&pageTitle=loadrunner-software.

[7] A. Brunnert, C. Vögele, A. Danciu, M. Pfaff, M. Mayer, and H. Krcmar. Performance management work. *Business & Information Systems Engineering*, 6(3):177–179, 2014.

[8] W. Visser. Who really cares if the program crashes? In *Proceedings of the 16th International SPIN Workshop on Model Checking Software*, pages 5–5, Berlin, Heidelberg, 2009. Springer-Verlag.

PABS 2015: 1st Workshop on Performance Analysis of Big Data Systems

Rekha Singhal
Tata Innovation Lab
Mumbai, India
rekha.singhal@tcs.com

Dheeraj Chahal
Tata Innovation Lab
Mumbai, India
d.chahal@tcs.com

ABSTRACT

The first ACM international workshop on performance analysis of big data system is held in Austin, Texas, USA on February 1, 2015 and co-located with the ACM fifth International Conference on Performance Engineering (ICPE). The main objective of the workshop is to discuss the performance challenges imposed by big data systems and the different state-of-the-art solutions proposed to overcome these challenges. The workshop aims at providing a platform for scientific researchers, academicians and practitioners to discuss techniques, models, benchmarks, tools and experiences while dealing with performance issues in big data systems. We have constructed an exciting program of one big data expert keynote talk, one invited talk and two refereed papers that will give participants a full dose of emerging research.

Categories and Subject Descriptors

A. General Literature

General Terms

Algorithms, Performance, Architectures

Keywords

Big Data; Performance; Analysis; Prediction; Case study

1. INTRODUCTION

Big data systems deal with velocity, variety, volume and veracity of the application data. We witness an explosive growth in the complexity, diversity, number of deployments and capabilities of big data processing systems such as Map-Reduce, Cassandra, Big Table, HPCC, Hyracks, Dryad, Pregel and Mongo DB. The big data system may use new operating system designs, advanced data processing algorithms, parallelization of application, high performance architectures and clusters to improve the performance. Looking at the volume of data to mine, and complex architectures, one may need to analyze, identify or predict bottlenecks to optimize the system and improve its performance.

The workshop on performance analysis of big data systems (PABS) aims at providing a platform for scientific researchers, academicians and practitioners to discuss techniques, models, benchmarks, tools and experiences while dealing with performance issues in big data systems. The primary objective is to discuss performance bottlenecks and improvements during big

ICPE'15, Jan. 31 – Feb. 4, 2015, Austin, Texas, USA.
ACM 978-1-4503-3248-4/15/01.
http://dx.doi.org/10.1145/2668930.2688199

data analysis using different paradigms, architectures and technologies such as Map-Reduce, MPP, Big Table, NOSQL, graph based models (e.g. Pregel, giraph) and any other new upcoming paradigms. We propose to use this platform as an opportunity to discuss systems, architectures, tools, and optimization algorithms that are parallel in nature and hence make use of advancements to improve the system performance. This workshop shall focus on the performance challenges imposed by big data systems and on the different state-of-the-art solutions proposed to overcome these challenges.

2. TOPICS OF INTEREST

All novel performance analysis or prediction techniques, benchmarks, architectures, models and tools for data-intensive computing system for optimizing application performance on cutting-edge high performance solutions are of interest to the workshop. Examples of topics include but not limited to:

- Performance analysis and optimization of Big data systems and technologies.

- Case studies/ Benchmarks to optimize/evaluate performance of Big data applications/systems and Big data workload characterizations.

- Tools or models to identify performance bottlenecks and /or predict performance metrics in Big data

- Performance analysis while querying, visualization and processing of large network datasets on clusters of multicore, many core processors, and accelerators.

- Performance issues in heterogeneous computing for Big data architectures.

- Analysis of Big data applications in science, engineering, finance, business, healthcare and telecommunication etc.

- Data structure and algorithms for performance optimizations in big data systems.

3. WORKSHOP FORMAT

The workshop is scheduled for half a day. We have domain expert key note speaker Prof. D.K. Panda from Ohio State University, USA. He is well known for his contribution in the field of "Big data Performance Accelerators". Key note lecture shall be of 45 minute duration with 15 min for Q/A. The key note will be followed by an invited talk by Prof. Amy W. Apon from Clemson University, USA. Two refereed papers will be presented for 40 minutes duration each including 30 minutes for presentation and 10 minutes for Q/A. Finally, the workshop will be concluded by the chairs.

4. KEYNOTE TALK

The keynote talk will be given by Prof. Dhabaleswar (DK) Panda from Ohio State University, USA. The title of the talk is "Accelerating Big Data Processing on Modern Clusters".

Abstract:

Modern clusters are having multi-/many-core architectures, high-performance rdma-enabled interconnects and SSD-based storage devices. Hadoop framework is extensively being used these days for Big Data processing. Spark framework is emerging for real-time analytics. Similarly, Memcached is being used in data centers with Web 2.0 environment. This talk will provide an overview of challenges in accelerating Hadoop, Spark and Memcached on modern clusters. An overview of RDMA-based designs for multiple components of Hadoop (HDFS, MapReduce, RPC and HBase), Spark and Memcached will be presented. Performance benefits of these designs on various cluster configurations will be shown. The talk will also address the need for designing benchmarks using a multi-layered and systematic approach, which can be used to evaluate the performance of these middleware.

Bio:

Dhabaleswar K. (DK) Panda is a Professor of Computer Science and Engineering at the Ohio State University. He has published over 350 papers in major journals and international conferences. Prof. Panda and his research group members have been doing extensive research on modern networking technologies including InfiniBand, High-Speed Ethernet and RDMA over Converged Enhanced Ethernet (RoCE). The MVAPICH2 (High Performance MPI over InfiniBand, iWARP and RoCE) and MVAPICH2-X software libraries, developed by his research group (http://mvapich.cse.ohio-state.edu), are currently being used by more than 2,250 organizations worldwide (in 74 countries). This software has enabled several InfiniBand clusters to get into the latest TOP500 ranking during the last decade. More than 226,000 downloads of this software have taken place from the project's website alone. The new RDMA-enabled Apache Hadoop package, RDMA-enabled Memcached package, and OSU HiBD benchmarks (OHB) are publicly available from the High-Performance Big Data project site (http://hibd.cse.ohio-state.edu). Prof. Panda's research has been supported by funding from US National Science Foundation, US Department of Energy, and several industry including Intel, Cisco, Cray, SUN, Mellanox, QLogic, NVIDIA and NetApp. He is an IEEE Fellow and a member of ACM. More details about Prof. Panda are available at http://www.cse.ohio-state.edu/~panda

5. WORKSHOP ORGANIZERS

Dr. Rekha Singhal has 20 years of research and teaching experience. Currently she is working as Senior Scientist with TCS Innovation Lab and leading Big Data Performance Modelling and Analysis initiatives. She has numerous international publications and patents to her credit. One of the products, Revival 2000, developed under her guidance had received NASSCOM Technology award. Her research interests are Big Data System Performance, Query Performance Prediction, Database Performance Modelling, IP Storage Area Networks, Distributed Systems and Health IT. She is Ph.D and M.tech from IIT Delhi

Dr. Dheeraj Chahal is a Consultant and research team lead with Performance Engineering group at TCS innovations lab, Mumbai. Prior to joining TCS, he worked as Staff Software Engineer with HPC team at IBM, Bangalore and successfully conducted workshop on performance engineering at HiPC 2012 and 2013 (http://www.hipc.org/hipc2013/workshops.php). Dheeraj holds a PhD degree in Computer Science from Clemson University, SC, USA.

6. PROGRAM COMMITTEE

- Amitabha Bagchi , IITD, India
- Amy. W. Apon, Clemson University, USA
- Arno Jacobsen, University of Toronto, Canada
- Bojan Cukic, UNC, USA
- Dhableshwar Panda, Ohio State University, USA
- Gautam Shroff, TCS Innovation Lab, India
- Henrique Madeira, University of Coimbra, Portugal
- Kishor Trivedi, Duke University, USA
- Jeff Ullman, Stanford University and Gradiance, USA
- Narendra Bhandari, Intel, India
- Rajesh Mansharamani, CMG India
- Saumil Merchant, Shell, India
- Sebastien Goasguen, Citrix, Switzerland
- Steven J Stuart, Clemson University, USA
- Veena Mendiratta, Alcatel-Lucent, USA
- Vikram Narayana, George Washington University, USA
- Zia Saquib, CDAC, India

7. ACKNOWLEDGEMENTS

We thank Tata Consultancy Services for supporting our initiatives.

WOSP-C '15: Workshop on Challenges in Performance Methods for Software Development

Murray Woodside
Carleton University
Ottawa, Canada
1-613-520-5721
cmw@sce.carleton.ca

ABSTRACT

The first ACM Workshop on Challenges in Performance Methods for Software Development is held in Austin, Texas, on Jan. 31 2015, and is co-located with the 2015 ACM/SPEC International Conference on Performance Engineering (ICPE). Its purpose is to open up new avenues of research on methods for software developers to address performance problems. The software world is changing, and there are new challenges. As its name implies, the workshop includes the description of problems as well as solutions. The acronym WOSP-C also recalls the original discussion-heavy format of WOSP, the ACM International Workshop on Software and Performance, which has been a co-organizer of ICPE since 2010.

Categories and Subject Descriptors

D.2 Software Engineering

General Terms

Software performance, Performance engineering.

Keywords

Software Performance Engineering.

1. CHALLENGES

The workshop papers and discussions will explore the new challenges to product performance that have arisen due to changes in software and in the development process, such as:

- faster development means less time for performance-related planning and analysis,

- the need for scalability and adaptability increases the pressure while introducing new sources of delay,

- model-driven engineering, component engineering and software development tools offer opportunities but their exploitation requires effort and carries risks,

- use of third-party services and components reduces the developer's control over the end-to-end performance

- mobile applications require fast response in a difficult environment

These software-related challenges have led to important performance failures, such as the roll-out of the healthcare.gov web site in the US. It is probably fair to say that

(1) performance is a major problem in system development today,

(2) no one is satisfied with the methods available to address it,

(3) there is no agreement on how to improve the situation.

This workshop is intended to describe the challenges and to explore ways in which software performance engineering methods can be developed to provide solutions.

New challenges imply new opportunities for progress, and there are new tools that we may be able to incorporate (for example, methods for big-data analysis). So suggestions for new lines of attack are as important for the workshop, as the characterization of the challenges.

2. SOFTWARE PERFORMANCE ENGINEERING METHODS

Three books that provide the background on methods for dealing with performance of software are those of Smith and Williams [1] (including making performance models from UML design models), Cortellessa et al [2] (using various kinds of models to analyze performance) and Bondi [3] (a book on useful processes, not model-based, and going beyond software).

Software performance engineering methods as understood for this workshop seek to structure and unify the understanding of performance effects and their causes, and to support extrapolation of existing knowledge to provide predictions of performance for new developments and configurations of a system. This generally requires some kind of model.

All kinds of models may be considered, ranging from regression models of data, through mathematical and simulation models of flows, contention, executions and timing in the system, to dynamic control models and semantic models of data gathered from execution. To be effective the models must relate seamlessly to existing or future system execution data. While purely data-driven performance tuning is not our main concern in this workshop, closely allied concerns such as measurement and monitoring methods are important.

3. DISCUSSION TOPICS

Roughly half of the workshop will be devoted to sessions for focused discussion. The issues for discussion will arise out of the paper presentations, and out of the concerns of those present.

Some topics which are expected to be prominent are:

- **DevOps and Software Performance Engineering (SPE)**: is this a new opportunity? DevOps [4] integrates quality assurance (which includes performance concerns) with development and operations. QA usually means just testing: can SPE provide greater insights?

- **Model-driven SPE: is it a success?** Since the first WOSP there has been substantial research on S PE based on software models (e.g. UML models) (e.g. [5], [6], [7]). Is it ready for widespread use?

- **Clouds, scale, complexity and unpredictability**: large systems, rapid evolution, unpredictable workloads, complexity introduced by the combination of components that are not engineered to work together, make analysis unwieldy. New solutions may include big-data methods for analysis. A survey of current ideas is given in [8].

- **Adaptive systems: how can SPE contribute?** Model-based adaptation has the potential to be faster and to provide better and cheaper performance. A survey is given in [9].

The papers in this proceedings address these and other issues, and other topics of discussion will undoubtedly arise.

REFERENCES

[1] Connie U. Smith, Lloyd Williams, "Performance Solutions: A Practical Guide to Creating Responsive, Scalable Software", Addison-Wesley, 2002.

[2] Vittorio Cortellessa, Antinisca di Marco, Paola Inverardi, "Model-Based Software Performance Analysis", Springer, 2011.

[3] Andre Bondi, "Foundations of Software and System Performance Engineering", Addison-Wesley, 2014.

[4] DevOps description at http://en.wikipedia.org/wiki/DevOps

[5] Fabian Brosig, Philipp Meier, Steffen Becker, Anne Koziolek, Heiko Koziolek, and Samuel Kounev. "Quantitative evaluation of model-driven performance analysis and simulation of component-based architectures", IEEE Trans on Software Engineering, IEEE Transactions, Oct 2014.

[6] Murray Woodside, Dorina C. Petriu, Jose Merseguer, Dorin B. Petriu, Mohammad Alhaj, Transformation challenges: from software models to performance models, Software and Systems Modeling, v. 13 n 4 pp 1529-1552 Oct 2014.

[7] Murray Woodside, Greg Franks, Dorina C. Petriu, "The Future of Software Performance Engineering", Proc Future of Software Engineering 2007, eds L. Briand, and A. Wolf, IEEE Computer Society Order Number P2829, May 2007, pp 171-187.

[8] Yasir Shoaib and Olivia Das, "Performance-oriented Cloud Provisioning: Taxonomy and Survey", Nov 2014, submitted for publication, available on http://arxiv.org/abs/1411.5077

[9] Matthias Becker, Markus Luckey, Steffen Becker, "Model-Driven Performance Engineering of Self-Adaptive Systems: A Survey", Proc. QoSA'12, June 25–28, 2012, Bertinoro, Italy.

Author Index